2022 EDI

BEST COLLEGES

HOW TO ORDER: Additional copies of U.S. News & World Report's Best Colleges 2022
guidebook are available for purchase at usnews.com/collegeguide or by calling (800) 836-6397.
For permission to republish articles, data or other content from this book, email permissions@usnews.com.

Copyright © 2021 by U.S. News & World Report L.P., 1050 Thomas Jefferson Street, N.W., Washington, D.C. 20007-3837, ISBN 978-1-931469-98-2
All rights reserved. Published by U.S. News & World Report L.P., Washington, D.C.

**The Howard University Showtime Marching Band
leads the homecoming parade.**
HOWARD UNIVERSITY

CONTENTS

34

26

STUDY THE SCHOOLS

FROM TOP: COURTESY OF THE GEORGE WASHINGTON UNIVERSITY; STEFAN SMITH

THE CHALLENGE
OF THE WORLD
IS CALLING.

A CALL TO BRING REAL CHANGE, SOLVE REAL PROBLEMS AND HAVE REAL IMPACT

... and we say,
CHALLENGE ACCEPTED.

Through The Furman Advantage, you will engage in hands-on, real-world experiences, participate in unique research and forge deep connections. Led by a team of mentors, you'll create a personalized learning pathway filled with opportunities designed to give you the tools and the knowledge to land a dream-fulfilling career.

The Furman Advantage will draw you in with powerful experiences and launch you with confidence to answer the call.

MOST INNOVATIVE SCHOOL

FIVE YEARS IN A ROW

– U.S. News & World Report

3x

MORE LIKELY FOR ALUMNI TO BE THRIVING IN LIFE

– Furman-Gallup Study

#9

BEST SCHOOLS FOR MAKING AN IMPACT

– The Princeton Review

FURMAN
UNIVERSITY
FURMAN.EDU ✦ GREENVILLE, S.C.

② The U.S. News Rankings

GETTY IMAGES

Build *your* future at Queens College.

- Named a "Best Value College" by *The Princeton Review* for four years in a row

- Ranked fourth on *Business Insider's* list of colleges offering the best return on investment

- Offers over 100 areas of study on a beautiful 80-acre campus with a world-class faculty of top researchers and master teachers

- Generous financial aid, over 100 student organizations and clubs, and affordable on-campus housing in The Summit Apartments

www.qc.cuny.edu

QUEENS COLLEGE | CUNY

CONTENTS

GETTING IN

FIND THE MONEY

112

118

132

FROM TOP: JIM LO SCALZO FOR USN&WR; ILLUSTRATION BY YAO XIAO FOR USN&WR; MARIANO AGUILERA

Are You Ready for the Future of Work?

Built for a future that has yet to be defined, Thomas Jefferson University is crossing disciplines to bring unrivaled innovation and discovery to higher education. Through boundary-breaking collaboration, research and hands-on experiential learning, we equip graduates with leadership and analytical skills shaped for an accelerated job market.

Ten colleges and four schools comprise our National Doctoral Research University that offers everything from traditional undergraduate programs to programs for professionals who want to advance their careers.

At Jefferson, we are reshaping education for the 21st century.

College of Architecture and the Built Environment

College of Health Professions

College of Humanities and Sciences

College of Life Sciences
— Graduate School of Biomedical Sciences

College of Nursing

College of Pharmacy

College of Population Health

College of Rehabilitation Sciences

Kanbar College of Design, Engineering and Commerce
— School of Business
— School of Design and Engineering

School of Continuing and Professional Studies

Sidney Kimmel Medical College

Jefferson
Thomas Jefferson University
HOME OF SIDNEY KIMMEL MEDICAL COLLEGE

Jefferson.edu
Follow us

REDEFINING HUMANLY POSSIBLE

What's @usnews.com

You'll find a wealth of advice and data to guide your college search

YOUR COLLEGE GAME PLAN
Insider Advice

If you're looking for college advice, you've come to the right place. We provide expert tips to help families research, apply to and pay for college. Our articles and slideshows feature college admissions and financial aid officers, counselors, current students, graduates, parents and more, who all share their insights to help demystify the process. **usnews.com/collegeadvice**

IN-DEPTH DATA
College Compass

Gain access to the U.S. News College Compass, which offers comprehensive searchable data and tools for high school students starting down the path to campus. To get a 25% discount, subscribe at **usnews.com/compassoffer**

RANKINGS INSIGHT
Morse Code Blog

Get the inside scoop on the rankings – and the commentary and controversy surrounding them – from U.S. News' Bob Morse, the mastermind behind our education rankings projects. **usnews.com/morsecode**

GETTING IN
College Admissions Playbook

Get tips from Varsity Tutors, an academic tutoring and test-prep provider (and advertiser with U.S. News). This blog offers advice on mastering the SAT and ACT as well as the college application process. **usnews.com/collegeplaybook**

COLLEGE VISITS
Take a Road Trip

We've gone on numerous trips to visit campuses in case you can't. Check out our compendium of more than 30 different trips to 100-plus schools. **usnews.com/roadtrips**

PAYING FOR COLLEGE
Researching Aid

Visit our guide to all your possible sources of college funds. Learn about your savings options and financial aid, including which schools meet students' full need. **usnews.com/payforcollege**

The Student Loan Ranger

If you're borrowing to finance your degree, don't fall into the trap of taking on too much debt. Experts provide guidance on this blog for those who must turn to student loans to pay for college. **usnews.com/studentloanranger**

DISTANCE LEARNING
Online Education

Are you grappling with how to balance school with work or other obligations? Consult our rankings of the best online degree programs for leads on how to get your diploma without having to leave your home. **usnews.com/online**

FOR SCHOOLS ONLY
Academic Insights

U.S. News Academic Insights is a peer benchmarking and performance assessment tool designed for colleges and universities. Gain exclusive access to 20-plus years of previously unpublished historical rankings data for undergraduate, graduate, online and high school programs. **ai.usnews.com**

GETTY IMAGES

BIG ON PURPOSE

Our purpose is to help you find yours.

With a reset tuition rate of $33,510 beginning in the Fall of 2022, Roanoke College is now making it easier for students to build lives with meaning and purpose and launch high-value careers.

Find out how at **roanoke.edu/purpose**

ROANOKE COLLEGE®

LOOK DEEPER

and the beautiful campus

we call home, and you'll

see a whole other world.

One equally stunning.

Because here, world-renowned

professors, Nobel laureates and

students reimagine what's

possible. Their collaboration

has transformed oil rigs into reefs

and reshaped international law.

Over half a century of invention — and

reinvention — has allowed our students

to achieve the unimaginable.

Picture what you might discover at

the No. 1 public university in the nation.

UC San Diego

lookdeeper.ucsd.edu

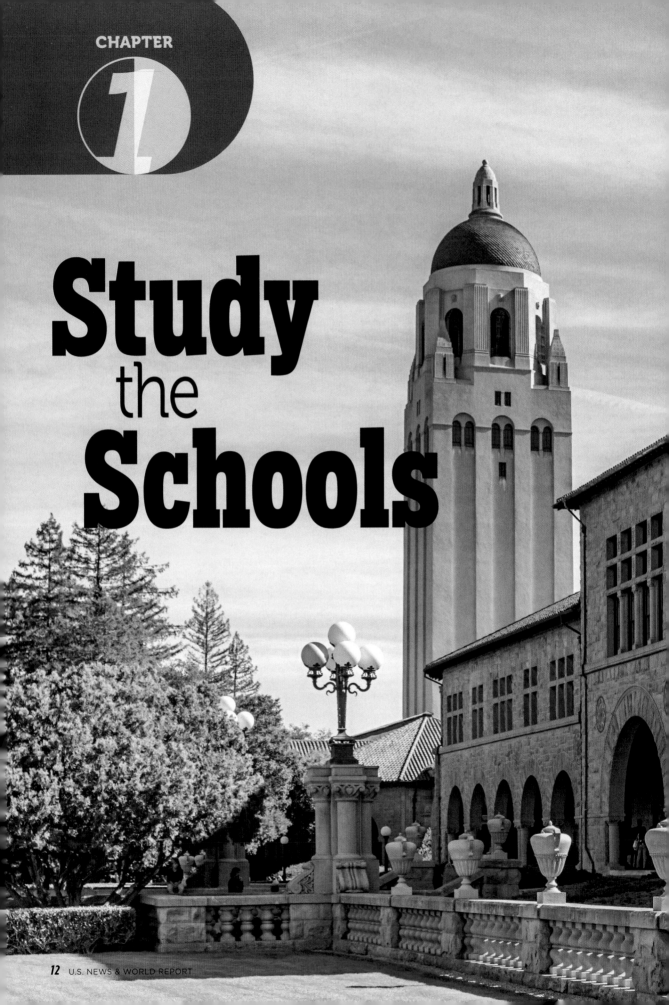

Study the Schools

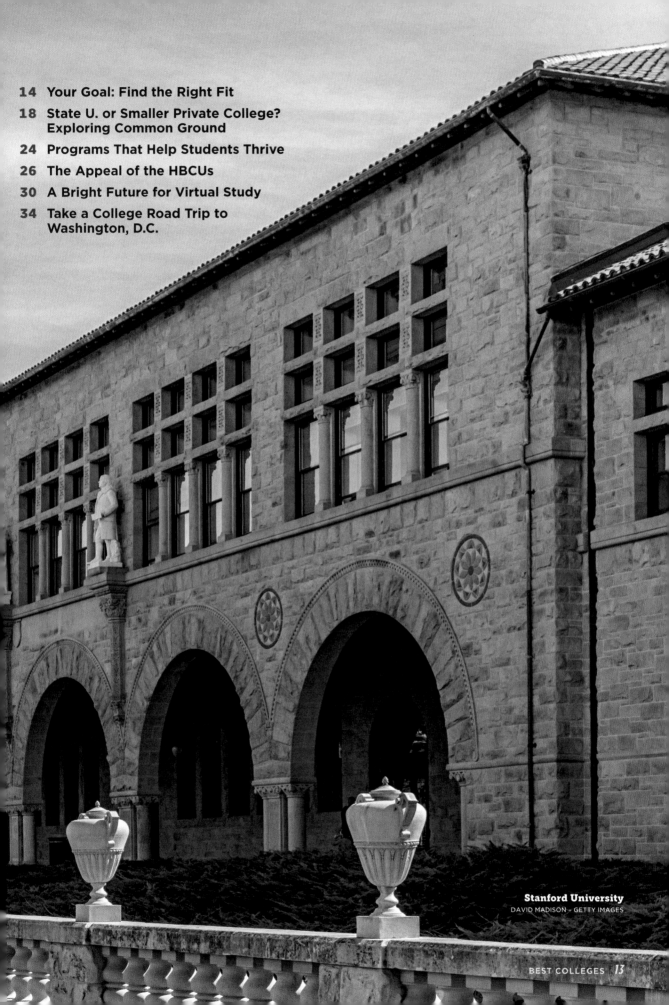

Stanford University
DAVID MADISON – GETTY IMAGES

Finding the Right Fit

Remember, as you start your journey to college, that your goal is a place where you will thrive

by **Katherine Hobson**

CHASE DUSEK TOOK HIS college search seriously. He started his research the summer after his sopho-more year, turned to an outside counselor for help, went on a whopping 26 college tours and – most importantly – took time to soul-search about ex-actly what he wanted in a school. He really enjoyed the small humanities program in his public high school, and realized he wanted to find that kind of experience in college. "I learned I loved interaction and engage-ment with the teacher and classmates," he says. That impetus – as well as prioritizing an academically challenging environment and the opportunity to participate in Greek life – ultimately led him to Ohio Wesleyan University; he'll graduate this fall.

While the coronavirus has certainly complicated the pro-cess of researching colleges for the last couple of application cycles, by making it difficult if not impossible to visit campus or sit in on a class, getting a genuine feel for the schools you're considering is a vital step in the process. Whether your college search is mainly in person or online, there are

FRANK MILLER

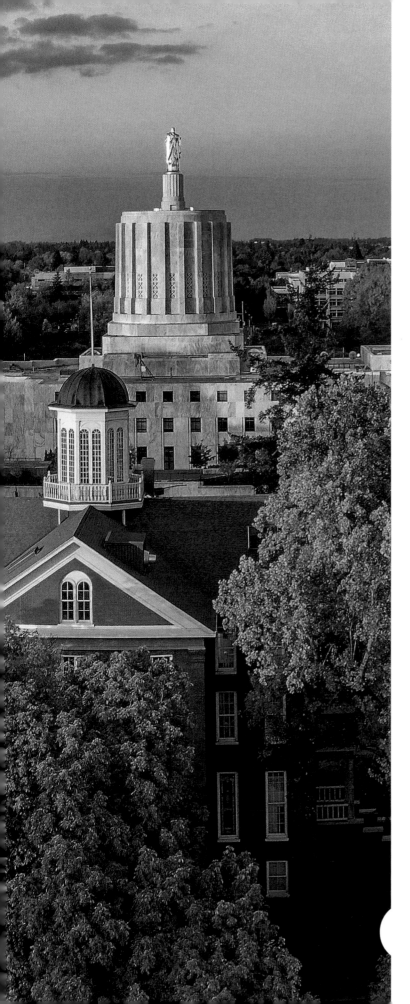

plenty of obvious factors to weigh as you narrow your list: large or small, urban or rural, public or private. But at the end of the day, a school needs to be a fit academically, socially and financially, says Maria Furtado, director emerita of the nonprofit Colleges That Change Lives.

A good academic fit includes strength in the major that you are considering, interesting classes and programs within that major, and an appropriate level of challenge, she says. Jayne Caflin Fonash, an independent education consultant in Potomac Falls, Virginia, and former president of the National Association for College Admission Counseling, agrees that it's important to find a place where you have a good chance of thriving academically: "You want to be challenged and to grow, but you don't want to be overwhelmed." She advises making sure there are appealing avenues beyond your chosen major in case you end up changing focus.

LEARNING APPROACHES. Consider what kind of learning environment you want, and not only in terms of class size or format. Experiential education, in the form of outside internships or co-ops (work experience integrated into the curriculum), study abroad or research with professors, can be just as key.

"Ask yourself: Why am I doing this? What do I expect?" suggests Tamara Byland, executive director of recruitment and admissions at Kansas State University. When a campus visit is possible, ask if you can sit in on a class in your areas of interest; seeing how faculty members engage students and how students interact with each other can tell you a lot, says Stefanie Niles, vice president for enrollment and communications at Ohio Wesleyan. And dig deep into what especially matters to you. To see how seriously schools took research opportunities, Dusek looked up academic publications by professors, then checked to see if any undergrads were co-authors.

Social and personal fit are also crucial, Furtado says. "Will you find your people? Will you find your next set of really good friends?" Again, campus visits can be extremely helpful, but don't stop with the tour, suggests Shannon Carr, until recently associate vice president of admission at the University of Puget Sound. She advises prospective students to ideally eat in the dining hall, go to an event, read bulletin boards for information on student activities

A view of Willamette University in Salem, Oregon, with the State Capitol in the background

and check out the residence halls.

You can also explore the town by walking around and by checking the local chamber of commerce or visitors' website to see if it's a place you want to live. Other virtual sources of information: the school's community events calendar and alumni magazine, which can give you a peek into what people do after they graduate, Carr says.

Financial fit is the third key component. "I think, in light of global events of the last year-plus, that financial fit for students and families is going to be even more critical of a factor than it's ever been," says Emmi Harward, executive director of the Association of College Counselors in Independent Schools. "Families need to spend more time talking candidly together about cost." That means using online calculators to figure out exactly what your financing options are and considering how much debt your family is willing to take on, she says. Fonash suggests

> ## "Will you find your people? Will you find your next set of really good friends?"

checking out data for average salaries in your possible post-collegiate career field to get a reality check about what you can afford to borrow. Find out if merit-based aid – grant money keyed to academic achievements or special talents – is an option.

Experts advise figuring out the factors that are most important to you, and then keeping an open mind. If your priorities point you toward schools that you didn't expect or whose names you don't recognize, investigate them anyway, suggests Harward. And don't rely entirely on your first impression. Dusek's first visit to Ohio Wesleyan didn't wow him, but he was sold by his second visit, when he sat in on a macroeconomics class and was "blown away" by the professor. Now Dusek works as an Ohio Wesleyan lobby host, checking in prospective students and hoping they, too, will find a great fit. ●

With Alison Murtagh

Visiting Campus From Your Couch

WITH CLASSES HELD REMOTELY and schools limiting visitors, it's been a difficult 18 months for prospective students to experience campus: stepping onto the quad for the first time, visiting a class, watching students interact in the dining hall. But the college tour has been evolving, and even as normalcy returns you may want to check out the possibilities at schools you're considering. Many are finding new ways to help students get a feel for the college.

Take Hamilton College's "Tour From Your Sofa." Student guides walk around the Clinton, New York, campus with selfie sticks, connecting individually with prospective applicants through video chat. Joe Largo, who will graduate in 2023, says the tours he gives are more personal than the in-person version and allow students to see spaces they might not typically experience.

TAILORED TOURS. "I try to give a different tour every single time, and especially catered to their interests," Largo says. Without a group tagging along, he feels more able to take visitors inside certain buildings, such as dorms. And since the tours are usually one-on-one, students seem more confident about asking questions.

Want to see what's happening on Lehigh University's campus in Bethlehem, Pennsylvania? Try scrolling through TikTok, where the university showcases as-

pects of campus life and community in quick videos, often following trending topics. A look last spring at Lehigh Admission's profile on TikTok revealed clips of students having fun on a snow day and dancing in the dorm, as well as tips about the application process. "Unexpected experiences [are what make] college recruiting and visits so fun," and the pandemic has unfortunately interfered with that, says recent graduate Samantha Margolis, formerly an intern with the school's TikTok team. She says the platform has helped the school put some of the fun back into college searches.

VIRTUAL REALITY. Would-be visitors to Bucknell University in Lewisburg, Pennsylvania, can put on an Oculus headset and wander through the university's iconic gates via virtual reality, choosing spots they want to explore – a lab, classroom, a theater, the residence halls. You can even "walk around" downtown.

"The entire time that you are immersed in the experience, it feels very much all about Bucknell," says Lisa Keegan, vice president for enrollment management. Prospective students can also check out the virtual reality experience online, using a mobile device or computer.

Nothing beats the real thing for getting a sense of place, of course. But even when traveling to campus is easy, the tech can offer enjoyable new ways to do your research. *–Alison Murtagh*

The quality of a private campus
with the affordability of a public university.

Academic Excellence
Offering 63 distinct programs, SU is one of those rare universities that celebrates individual talents and encourages big ideas.

National Recognition
SU consistently ranks among the nation's best in *U.S. News & World Report*, *The Princeton Review* and *Forbes*. On the field, the Sea Gulls have won 12 NCAA Division III national team championships.

Accomplished Alumni
Over 58,000 graduates are taking the lead in the boardroom, the lab, the legislature and even on Broadway. SU helps put students' education to work, supporting job searches and graduate school applications.

Beautiful Campus
Home to 8,100 students from 31 states and 52 countries, the University, a national arboretum, is situated between the Atlantic Ocean and Chesapeake Bay.

Find out how
Salisbury University is the right – and affordable – fit
for you.

Salisbury
UNIVERSITY

www.salisbury.edu

SU is an Equal Opportunity/AA/Title IX university and provides reasonable accommodation given sufficient notice to the University office or staff sponsoring the event or program.

Exploring
Common
Ground

Many of the key perks of smaller private schools and of large public universities can be found in both settings.

by **Margaret Loftus**

THE DAUGHTER OF CLEMSON ALUMNI, Cate Tedford initially resisted following in her parents' footsteps to the big state school. She had her sights set instead on a handful of smaller private universities and liberal arts programs. But once she compared aid packages, the Fort Mill, South Carolina, native had a change of heart: First picks Boston College and Georgetown University would have cost her roughly $50,000 a year. Clemson? Between in-state tuition and scholarships, her annual tally came to less than $4,000.

The clincher was that, as a student in Clemson's honors college, she felt she would have the kind of access to faculty, special courses and guidance not unlike that found at the schools she'd had her heart set on. "At the end of the day, the value for how much I'd be paying and all the resources – I couldn't pass it up," she says.

As competition for a shrinking pool of college-aged students heats up, many applicants are surprised and intrigued to see more and more overlap in the types of campus experience available to talent-

ed students at large public universities and at smaller private institutions. Like Tedford, those who are looking for the academic rigor, tight-knit communities and intimate class settings characteristic of smaller schools are finding more of those options in honors and other programs at public universities for a fraction of the cost. At the same time, even liberal arts colleges have been ramping up the sort of hands-on offerings more traditionally found at big universities, including undergraduate research, entrepreneurial opportunities and career prep. (And while tuition and fees at in-state publics are considerably less than at private colleges, the latter

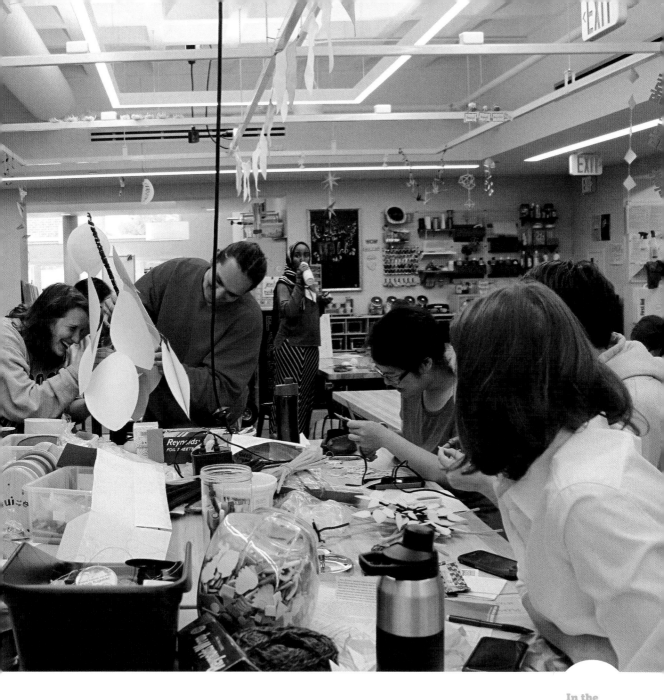

can often offset the sticker price substantially – especially for students they really want.)

The bottom line: If you crave the culture and social life of, say, a football powerhouse, you may not have to sacrifice smaller-school amenities after all. And the inverse is also true: If an intimate, seminar-heavy liberal arts community is where you think you'll feel most comfortable, you don't necessarily have to give up the practical experiences that may ease the way to a job after graduation.

HONORS ADVANTAGE. Now a junior majoring in philosophy and Spanish with an eye toward a career in immigration law, Tedford couldn't be more

pleased with her choice. As an honors student, she's required to take at least one honors class per semester and maintain a GPA of 3.4. While Clemson doesn't offer scholarships specific to the honors program, students in the college enjoy perks such as priority status for course registration, free tickets to cultural events and dinners with faculty. The university also supports undergrad research, internships and conference travel through grants, which Tedford was able to leverage to attend a women's conference in Washington, D.C., during her freshman year. That experience alone was life-altering, she says. "I felt very empowered. It set a flame in me to pursue the things I'm interested in."

Often, there's help with tuition as well. The University of Arkansas Honors College offers numerous freshman fellowships covering four years, as well as grants for study abroad and research, for example. First-year students get access to honors-only housing. There's a "Futures Hub" to guide honors students' academic trajectory, and seminars and courses on cutting-edge topics such as blockchain.

When weighing offers from the University of Arkansas and other

In the Idea Lab, Macalester students tackle real-world problems.

Arkansas honors students studying in Peru meet for a history discussion.

schools, in-stater Mary Jia of Stuttgart was won over by the honors college's pledge of free tuition and a stipend to boot. Today, the biomedical engineering junior is conducting her own research on gene-editing solutions to rare genetic diseases. And as someone who aspires to a life in academia, Jia especially appreciates the access to top faculty. When her plans to study abroad in China senior year hit a brick wall – the university isn't affiliated with a program there – an engineering dean worked with his contacts in Hong Kong to arrange for her to study there. "It's very easy to get access to higher-up people and communicate with them," she says.

PASSION FOR STEM. It's not just honors programs that roll out the red carpet for high-achievers. The Meyerhoff Scholars Program at the University of Maryland–Baltimore County recruits a diverse population of applicants, particularly Black and other underrepresented students, who plan to pursue a Ph.D. in STEM and offers them financial, academic and community support. "We often say we are looking for students who have a fire in the belly and a passion for STEM," says Director Keith Harmon. Students participate in a summer program before freshman year and must conduct undergraduate research. The Meyerhoff program has been lauded for its success – it's the No. 1 producer of Black graduates who go on to get an M.D.-Ph.D., as well as of those who earn Ph.D. degrees in the natural sciences and engineering – and has been replicated on campuses across the country, including the University of North Carolina–Chapel Hill and the University of California–Berkeley.

Key to its mission is collaboration over competition, and fostering a tight bond among students and faculty. That struck a chord for Talmesha Richards-Smith, who chose the program over full rides to Johns Hopkins University and Princeton. "Science and engineering are difficult, and I knew I was going to have the support. It was important to me that there were

people on campus who cared about me," she says. For instance, students are highly encouraged to form study groups, which Richards-Smith believes made her a better scientist. "It definitely set me up for success," she says. After graduating with two degrees, one in chemical engineering and one in math, she went on to earn a Ph.D. in cellular and

A Sharp New Focus on Career Prep

S **TUDENTS WHO HAD A GOOD** experience with career services at college were more likely to say their school prepared them well for life and more likely to think their university was worth the cost, according to a 2016 Gallup survey. And grads who took advantage were more likely to be employed full time than those who hadn't.

Sounds good, right? But barely half of students actually make it through the doors of their college career center, a record many schools are scrambling to improve. Indeed, there's a movement afoot to make career prep much more integral to the student experience. What should you look for in a college's efforts to help launch you on the right path?

A FACULTY ROLE. "We're not asking faculty to teach something different or saying we should become a vocational school,"

says Brandi Fuhrman, head of Oregon State University's Caree Development Center. Instead, in a pilot program, the school is asking profs to tweak course learning outcomes to include résumé-enhancing competencies from the National Association of Colleges and Employers. For example, a media course included competencies such as "teamwork" (because working pairs is required) and "information technology application" (fo publishing on a content management system.)

Something similar is happening at the University of Central Florida, where the goal is to align course content with the NAC competencies and make the links clear so that students, emplo ers, and faculty "are all speaking the same language," says Lyn Hansen, executive director of career services. Where appropri ate, faculty are also adding assignments that encourage career

dispel the perception that a broad education doesn't prepare students for the job world, are emphasizing more hands-on experiences like research and entrepreneurship. "People assume that if I go to a small school I'm not going to have research opportunities, but in some cases, you're going to have more because there's no layer of graduate students," says Hannah Serota, founder and CEO of Creative College Connections in Leesburg, Virginia. "And students are not just getting to assist, they're getting to present at conferences."

HELP WITH COSTS. Increasingly, many such schools are underwriting these experiential learning opportunities as well. At Furman University, a liberal arts college in South Carolina, 8 in 10 students participate in off-campus internships, study "away" programs and undergrad research made possible by cash grants through the Furman Advantage program.

Colgate University in New York also funds undergrad research and

molecular medicine at the Johns Hopkins School of Medicine, all while traveling the world as an NFL cheerleader. Meyerhoff encourages student pursuits beyond academia, too, she says. "I was supported not just from a financial perspective but a whole-being perspective."

Meanwhile, small liberal arts colleges, keen to

unpaid or low-paying internships. As a freshman, recent grad Jacob Watts was surprised at the extent to which research opportunities were available to students. A casual conversation with a professor about his interest in plants led him to become a research assistant for most of his college career and eventually publish a paper on plant physiology with faculty. His research earned him a number of grants and scholarships

ploration. One associate professor of geographic information stems asked students to look through listings for their dream b, then write a cover letter applying. One student was so emldened by how well she did on the assignment that she sent r letter to the Smithsonian – and got the internship.

A BETTER CAREER SERVICES EXPERIENCE. The University of Denver wanted to end the dentist-office vibe of a typil career center: a sterile place students visited only for an pointment. In September 2020, the school opened the new ree-story Burwell Center for Career Achievement, where stunts are encouraged to hang out, since you never know what twork-expanding person you might meet. There's an executive unge for meeting with employers, rooms to mix with alumni, d even a "Career Closet" of professional clothing students n borrow for interviews. The school's new 4D program makes reer development a core dimension along with intellectual owth, character development and well-being. Someone from reer services takes part in the first-year seminars.

EMPHASIS ON REAL WORK. Many schools, including liberal arts colleges, emphasize internships; Arizona State University's College of Liberal Arts and Sciences, for example, makes internship credit available in most departments. At the University of Illinois, a program called Life + Career Design encourages students to develop professional goals and find internships to help fulfill them.

CAREER-PREP COURSES. Illinois State University, as one model, offers a three-credit course for first-years that includes an interest inventory, asking students to start to consider their skills and personalities and what career might be a fit. There's a follow-up course for sophomores and juniors. Pamela Cooper, the director of ISU's career services, says the classes are an attempt to help students develop a growth mindset. "Most students come to college either not knowing what they want to do, or they get to their major and start taking courses and say, 'Oh heck no, I don't want to do that anymore,'" she says. "So there's a huge demand for this kind of support." *–Courtney Rubin*

RUSSELL COTHREN, COURTESY OF UNIVERSITY OF ARKANSAS

as an undergrad and will launch his career as an academic: He's currently working on his master's at the University of Cambridge in the U.K. as the recipient of the Churchill Scholarship, after which he heads to the University of Minnesota for his Ph.D. That will be fully underwritten by the National Science Foundation's Graduate Research Fellowship Program. "My ultimate goal is to be a professor at a liberal arts school just like Colgate," he says. "All of that wouldn't be possible without my undergraduate experience."

ENTREPRENEURIAL EDGE. At Macalester College in Minnesota, students are able to choose from a host of ways to engage with real-world problems in the classroom and outside it, including by taking advantage of a collaborative workspace called the Idea Lab and stipends for students to realize their own entrepreneurial ideas. In 2015, the school named alum Kate Ryan Reiling as its inaugural entrepreneur-in-residence; until her recent departure, she was responsible for helping to set the strategic direction of entrepreneurial programs. In her Introduction to Entrepreneurship course, Reiling asked her students

Colgate students have the opportunity to conduct undergraduate research.

to present solutions to sticky problems like St. Paul's struggle to plow the streets satisfactorily in winter. That's the sort of issue that on the surface seems like it should be simple, she says, but has been complicated by factors such as wetter storms that have more sleet in the mix, privilege (those who have driveways vs. those who park on city streets), a lack of real-time communication and the fact that some residents don't speak English.

There's also the newly created Innovation Partners extracurricular program – a model pioneered with the Mayo Clinic – in which multidisciplinary teams of students team up with MBA students at other colleges in Minnesota to work on the development of early stage medical companies. Think business school entrepreneurship course but with a broader lens. Issues explored "include cultural context, competition, the nature of technology and things like bioethics," says Liz Jansen, academic program director for Innovation Partners and one of the teams' faculty mentors. "You are bringing fresh and – frankly – naive eyes to harness the power of liberal arts." That, she says, is how ideas are generated. ●

ANDREW M. DADDIO – COLGATE UNIVERSITY

HOKIE

I SERVE
I EXPLORE
I IMAGINE
I DISCOVER

Virginia Tech will inspire you to act as a force for positive change–to serve, explore, imagine, and discover your potential through interdisciplinary education that goes beyond boundaries. With a strong work ethic and a can-do attitude, You Will Thrive Here.

vt.edu

Do you have what it takes to be a Hokie?
Claim your role at Virginia Tech.

150 VIRGINIA TECH.

Programs That Promote Student Success

SOME COLLEGES AND UNIVERSITIES are much more determined than others to provide undergrads with the best possible educational experience, recognizing that certain enriched offerings, from learning communities and internships to senior capstone projects, are linked to success. Here, U.S. News highlights schools with outstanding examples of eight programs that education experts, including staff members of the Association of American Colleges and Universities, agree are key. Excellence in such programs isn't directly measured in the Best Colleges overall rankings.

U.S. News surveyed college presidents, chief academic officers and deans of admissions in the spring and early summer of 2021, asking them to nominate up to 15 institutions with stellar examples of each program. The colleges ranked here received the most nominations for having especially strong programs.

(*Public)

▶ First-Year Experience

Orientation can go only so far in making freshmen feel connected. Many schools now build into the curriculum first-year seminars or other academic programs that bring small groups of students together with faculty or staff on a regular basis.

1 **Agnes Scott College** (GA)
2 **Elon University** (NC)
3 **Univ. of South Carolina***
4 **Amherst College** (MA)
4 **Berea College** (KY)
6 **Georgia State University***
7 **Abilene Christian University** (TX)
8 **Yale University** (CT)
9 **Carleton College** (MN)
10 **Arizona State University***
10 **Bard College** (NY)
10 **Colorado College**
13 **Brown University** (RI)
13 **Princeton University** (NJ)
15 **Baylor University** (TX)
16 **Bates College** (ME)
16 **Boston College**
16 **Butler University** (IN)
19 **Alverno College** (WI)
19 **Bryn Mawr College** (PA)

▶ Learning Communities

In these communities, students typically take two or more linked courses as a group and get to know one another and their professors well. Some learning communities are also residential.

1 **Elon University** (NC)
2 **Agnes Scott College** (GA)

3 **Yale University** (CT)
4 **Michigan State University***
5 **Georgia State University***
6 **Princeton University** (NJ)
7 **University of Michigan-Ann Arbor***
7 **Vanderbilt University** (TN)
9 **Abilene Christian University** (TX)
9 **Spelman College** (GA)
11 **Amherst College** (MA)
12 **Boston College**
13 **Appalachian State University** (NC)*
13 **Belmont University** (TN)
13 **Dartmouth College** (NH)
13 **Univ. of Maryland-College Park***
13 **Virginia Tech***
18 **Bucknell University** (PA)
18 **Duke University** (NC)
18 **Rice University** (TX)
18 **Syracuse University** (NY)
18 **University of South Carolina***

▶ Co-ops/Internships

Schools nominated in this category require or encourage students to apply what they're learning in the classroom to work in the real world through closely supervised internships or practicums, or through cooperative education, in which one period of study typically alternates with one of work.

1 **Northeastern University** (MA)
2 **Drexel University** (PA)
3 **Berea College** (KY)
4 **Georgia Institute of Technology***
4 **University of Cincinnati***

6 **Elon University** (NC)
7 **Massachusetts Institute of Technology**
8 **Stanford University** (CA)
9 **Agnes Scott College** (GA)
9 **Duke University** (NC)
9 **Endicott College** (MA)
12 **Rochester Inst. of Technology** (NY)
13 **Purdue University-West Lafayette** (IN)*
14 **Cornell University** (NY)
15 **Carnegie Mellon University** (PA)
15 **Clemson University** (SC)*
15 **Worcester Polytechnic Inst.** (MA)
18 **Bentley University** (MA)
18 **George Washington University** (DC)
20 **Bucknell University** (PA)

▶ Service Learning

Required (or for-credit) volunteer work in the community is an instructional strategy in these programs. What's learned in the field bolsters what happens in class, and vice versa.

1 **Berea College** (KY)
2 **Elon University** (NC)
3 **University of Notre Dame** (IN)
4 **Tulane University** (LA)
5 **Boston College**
6 **Duke University** (NC)
7 **Portland State University** (OR)*
7 **Stanford University** (CA)
9 **Abilene Christian University** (TX)
10 **Georgetown University** (DC)
11 **Vanderbilt University** (TN)
11 **Warren Wilson College** (NC)

Stanford University

▶ Writing in the Disciplines

These colleges typically make writing a priority at all levels of instruction and across the curriculum. Students are encouraged to produce and refine various forms of writing for a range of audiences in different disciplines.

1 **Brown University** (RI)
2 **Duke University** (NC)
3 **Carleton College** (MN)
3 **Yale University** (CT)
5 **Amherst College** (MA)
6 **Cornell University** (NY)
6 **Swarthmore College** (PA)
8 **Harvard University** (MA)
9 **Stanford University** (CA)
10 **Columbia University** (NY)
10 **Hamilton College** (NY)
10 **University of Iowa**∗
13 **Princeton University** (NJ)
14 **Bowdoin College** (ME)
14 **Wellesley College** (MA)
16 **Elon University** (NC)
16 **Oberlin College and Conservatory** (OH)
18 **Dartmouth College** (NH)
18 **Dickinson College** (PA)
18 **Williams College** (MA)

13 **Michigan State University**∗
14 **Agnes Scott College** (GA)
14 **Berry College** (GA)
14 **Brown University** (RI)
14 **Loyola University Chicago**
14 **Loyola University Maryland**
14 **Northeastern University** (MA)
20 **Belmont University** (TN)

▶ Study Abroad

Programs at these schools involve substantial academic work abroad for credit – a year, a semester or an intensive experience equal to a course – and considerable interaction with the local culture.

1 **Elon University** (NC)
1 **New York University**
3 **Middlebury College** (VT)
4 **Agnes Scott College** (GA)
5 **Goucher College** (MD)
6 **Kalamazoo College** (MI)
7 **American University** (DC)
8 **Arcadia University** (PA)
9 **Georgetown University** (DC)
10 **Syracuse University** (NY)
11 **Michigan State University**∗
12 **Pepperdine University** (CA)
13 **Duke University** (NC)
13 **Macalester College** (MN)
15 **Carleton College** (MN)
16 **Dartmouth College** (NH)
16 **Dickinson College** (PA)
18 **Northeastern University** (MA)

19 **University of Notre Dame** (IN)
20 **Boston University**
20 **Earlham College** (IN)
20 **Yale University** (CT)

▶ Undergraduate Research/Creative Projects

Independently or in small teams, and mentored by a faculty member, students do intensive and self-directed research or creative work that results in an original scholarly paper or product that can be formally presented on or off campus.

1 **Massachusetts Institute of Technology**
2 **Carnegie Mellon University** (PA)
2 **Yale University** (CT)
4 **Harvard University** (MA)
5 **California Institute of Technology**
5 **Princeton University** (NJ)
7 **Stanford University** (CA)
8 **Amherst College** (MA)
8 **College of Wooster** (OH)
10 **Davidson College** (NC)
11 **Carleton College** (MN)
12 **Duke University** (NC)
13 **Elon University** (NC)
14 **Georgia Institute of Technology**∗
14 **Harvey Mudd College** (CA)
16 **University of Michigan-Ann Arbor**∗
17 **Baylor University** (TX)
17 **Johns Hopkins University** (MD)
17 **Rice University** (TX)
20 **Allegheny College** (PA)
20 **Grinnell College** (IA)

▶ Senior Capstone

Whether they're called a senior capstone or go by some other name, these culminating experiences ask students nearing the end of their college years to create a project that integrates and synthesizes what they've learned. The project might be a thesis, a performance or an exhibit of artwork.

1 **Princeton University** (NJ)
2 **College of Wooster** (OH)
3 **Elon University** (NC)
3 **Yale University** (CT)
5 **Brown University** (RI)
6 **Duke University** (NC)
7 **Massachusetts Institute of Technology**
8 **Carleton College** (MN)
9 **Swarthmore College** (PA)
10 **Agnes Scott College** (GA)
10 **Carnegie Mellon University** (PA)
12 **Allegheny College** (PA)
12 **Stanford University** (CA)
14 **Amherst College** (MA)
14 **Harvard University** (MA)
14 **Northeastern University** (MA)
17 **Bard College** (NY)
17 **Harvey Mudd College** (CA)
17 **Haverford College** (PA)
17 **University of Michigan-Ann Arbor**∗

DAVID MADISON – GETTY IMAGES

The Appeal of the
HBCUs

You might want to weigh the unique qualities of historically Black colleges and universities

by **Josh Moody**

I**N A NATION WHERE BLACK STUDENTS** integrating schools were met with riots in the 1960s, historically Black colleges and universities have been instrumental in the education of African Americans. These schools, known as HBCUs, served a student population that other institutions overwhelmingly refused.

Indeed, it was nearly 100 years after the Civil War ended before white colleges began to open their doors to African American students. While some colleges did accept Black students before emancipation, they were a rarity. Schools serving freed slaves cropped up as a response, typically with a focus on vocational skills.

In the mid- to late-1800s, "African Americans took their educational aspirations in their own hands," explains Joseph Montgomery, vice president for enrollment management and student success at Tuskegee University, an HBCU in Alabama.

There are around 100 HBCUs across the U.S., including two-

Tuskegee's "mask on" campaign educated returning students about taking key precautions.

STEFAN SMITH

year institutions (see Best HBCUs, Page 92). While their mission and values may be largely shared, these schools can vary greatly. "We are not monolithic, whatsoever. We all have our individual histories, we all have our strengths and our weaknesses," says Anthony E. Jones, vice president of enrollment management and student experience at Bethune-Cookman University in Daytona Beach, Florida.

While Black students have many more choices today, the role of the HBCU remains a vital one, experts say. Writing in 2015, Michael Lomax, president and CEO of the United Negro College Fund, argued that HBCUs are "more relevant than ever, and essential to advancing our country's future."

Morehouse College, an HBCU in Atlanta, is a men's liberal arts school.

Lomax cited six points to make his case: the lower average tuition cost of HBCUs; their success in meeting the needs of low-income and first-generation students; the potential of lighter burdens of student debt to lessen wealth disparity along racial lines; a supportive campus climate; the HBCU track record for postgraduate employment; and how the values of these institutions align with those of their students.

"Any student or family today that is thinking about a four-year degree has to at the same time be thinking about cost and investment," says Jones, noting that HBCUs, on average, cost less than many comparable primarily white institutions.

At Tuskegee, Montgomery sees the impact on students daily. "We still serve a large number of students who are financially dependent on government assistance to educate themselves: first-generation students, low-income students," he says.

That's also true on the graduate level, says Dr. Hugh E. Mighty, dean of the College of Medicine at Howard University in Washington, D.C. (story, Page 41), and vice president, clinical affairs. "A significant

JIM LO SCLAZO FOR USN&WR

number of our students are financially challenged," Mighty says. He adds that Howard is willing to take chances on applicants with lower test scores for medical school and has a history of steering students to success. "We may take students who begin with lower test scores, but we are graduating them and placing them into residency programs at the same rate as the rest of the nation."

By the numbers, UNCF research suggests that HBCUs have an outsized effect on the education of Black students. A 2019 UNCF report, titled HBCUs Punching Above Their Weight, looked at 21 states and territories with HBCUs. Those schools enrolled 24% of all Black undergraduates in four-year programs, and awarded 26% of bachelor's

One major appeal of HBCUs is that they are welcoming academic homes for Black students, a place to be – often for the first time – part of a majority. "Socially or culturally, they may have had to make some compromises or adjustments" before, Jones says. "When that student is looking for a four-year experience, it could be attractive to them to be on a campus where there doesn't have to be compromises, where there's an ease of adjustment."

OPEN TO ALL. Despite the historic mission of these schools, HBCUs don't limit enrollment to Black students. "Our universities have always been very open, to allow others to come," Montgomery says.

Alijah Steele, a 2020 graduate of Tuskegee who majored in aerospace engineering,

"An HBCU offers a place to be part of a majority."

degrees and 32% of science, technology, engineering and math degrees at the bachelor's level to Black students though they represented only 9% of the four-year undergraduate institutions.

Despite these successes, many of the schools face challenges. A 2018 Government Accountability Office report highlighted issues of deferred maintenance and infrastructure needs at HBCUs. Other issues include significantly lower endowments than those of primarily white institutions and lagging financial resources. As a result, some HBCUs, particularly smaller regional schools, find themselves struggling to maintain accreditation. Nonetheless, advocates see reasons to be optimistic, such as recent upticks in applications and enrollment, the government's decision to renew annual federal funding for HBCUs and the billions steered to HBCUs this past year by coronavirus relief programs.

Campus culture varies by institution, but students can expect HBCUs to be rooted in the African American experience and to pride themselves on providing a rich cultural and academic life and a highly supportive community. HBCU graduates have played important roles in the Civil Rights movement and in literature and the arts, and include Martin Luther King Jr., Thurgood Marshall, Oprah Winfrey, Toni Morrison and Samuel L. Jackson, among scores of renowned alumni.

A WELCOMING HOME. "HBCUs do, in a great way, mirror the cultural value system of the African American community," says Jones, noting the significance of elders on campus, the communal environment and a commitment to social justice. Some HBCUs were founded by missionaries or religious institutions both white and Black, and "there is still a heavy presence of religious life on campus," Montgomery says.

was initially interested in attending Auburn University in his home state of Alabama or Mississippi State University. But a visit to Tuskegee won him over, and he became one of the university's student ambassadors leading prospective students on their own visits. "They know of HBCUs, but they don't know the opportunities that HBCUs offer," Steele says. He points to the campus culture and opportunities for internships and job placement after graduation as selling points for him.

Students considering an HBCU should go through the same checklist they would in weighing other colleges, experts say. "I don't think it's largely different than how a student might determine if any school is a fit," Jones says. Experts encourage prospective students to look at the academic programs offered, make a campus visit virtually or in person when possible, and meet with faculty. They should also consider what support systems are in place, the faculty-to-student ratio and extracurricular activities. And they should ask the questions on their minds, Steele advises. "No question is a wrong question, no question is a dumb question," he says.

Montgomery believes prospective applicants will find HBCUs to be a valuable launching pad for anyone who wants to blaze his or her own path. "Tuskegee is a historic place," he says, "but we still have opportunities for you to make history now." ●

A Bright Future for Virtual Study

Experts expect these trends to shape
online learning as the pandemic ends

by **Jordan Friedman** and **Josh Moody**

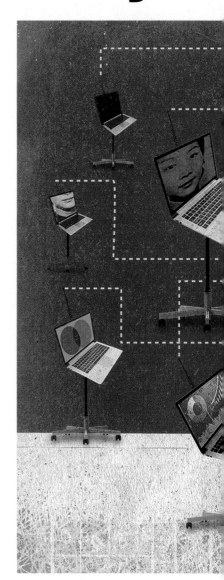

IN A WORLD SHAPED BY the coronavirus pandemic, online education has shined bright over the past 18 months. While hastily planned remote delivery differs from fully planned online programs (Best Online Degree Programs, Page 102), education experts say the sudden shift will accelerate the growth of online learning and tap its true potential. Here's a look at what the future is expected to bring:

Colleges will add new online programs.

After what has been a test run for many schools, colleges will be emboldened to offer more degree programs virtually, experts say. Shifting programs online allows schools to cast a broader net for students, says Ray Schroeder, senior fellow for online learning at the University of Illinois–Springfield. Phil Regier, university dean for educational initiatives and CEO of EdPlus at Arizona State University, expects "more STEM offerings in physical sciences and data science, focus areas in social justice, and study areas that focus on the ethics and rules surrounding media and data consumption."

Blended learning is here to stay.

Even as students have streamed back to campus, classes have often been taught both in person and online in a blended learning model, which is likely to stick. "The need for accessible, affordable, blended, relevant and high-quality online learning will extend far beyond the pandemic," predicts Chip Paucek, co-founder and CEO of the online higher education company 2U. "Higher education is never going back to the world in which it existed" before.

More colleges will turn to open educational resources.

Open educational resources, commonly referred to as OER, are education tools in the public domain or licensed for free use. Textbooks, online learning materials and streaming videos are examples of OER. Long hailed for their affordability, such resources are expected to become more widely accepted along with online education. Jenna Sheffield, assistant provost for curriculum innovation at the University of New Haven in Connecticut, notes that there's research showing that engaging students with OER can improve their performance, particularly when the students are helping produce those resources.

Technology will enhance the ability to offer hands-on programs online.

The demands of an English course can more easily be fulfilled online than those of a biology lab. But Schroeder predicts that virtual reality will make such hands-on courses more accessible online,

and others point to experience with interactive videos, online skill demonstrations and similar practices. Many nursing and science programs have already been relying on interactive video tools and recorded skill demonstrations to engage students outside the classroom, according to Ryan Lufkin, senior director of product marketing for Canvas in Higher Education at Instructure, an educational software company. COVID-19 has led to a broader view of where such tools can be useful, Lufkin points out.

Online learning will be increasingly data-driven.

Tracking how students are – or aren't – engaging with course materials can help pinpoint why some of them struggle and suggest how to improve

learning outcomes. "What videos are they watching? Are they participating in discussions? Are their responses showing they're mastering the concepts? Technology enhanced learning provides a level of insights never before seen, and the ability to support students in ways we've only started to explore," Lufkin believes.

Virtual student spaces and programming will expand.
John Watret, chancellor of Florida-based Embry-Riddle Aeronautical University–Worldwide, expects colleges to offer more ways to help remote students "get the whole student experience." Distance learners can expect virtual student unions, group activities and more virtual programming, he says.

Competency-based education will see slow but steady growth.
A 2019 survey of colleges conducted by the American Institutes for Research found "slow but steady" growth in competency-based education, which allows students to progress by taking assessments and demonstrating mastery. The top three areas of study primed for competency-based undergraduate education, according to the survey, are nursing and health professions, computer and information science, and business administration.

Public-private partnerships will bolster boot camps.
So-called "boot camps" have been around for years, offering students crash courses in areas such as cod-

"Quality programs abound, but be on the lookout for warning signs."

Certificates, badges and microcredentials will continue to grow.
Universities and companies for years have offered alternative credentials to older students, such as graduate certificates, digital badges and nanodegrees. Often these credentials are focused on industry-specific skills. Sheffield believes that such programs may also hold appeal for students coming straight out of high school, given the high cost of college. Schools have also launched programs in recent years that allow students to earn several "stackable" microcredentials as they progress toward a full degree.

MOOCs are on the rise.
Online learners can take these typically free "massive open online courses" offered by top universities and other institutions to master a variety of skills and subjects. In recent years, colleges have partnered with MOOC platforms to offer various credentials, including bachelor's degrees, much more cheaply than via the traditional route. Schroeder expects these low-cost options to grow.

ing. While online boot camps aren't new, Paucek expects such programs to expand. He points to partnerships such as those between 2U and Norfolk State University in Virginia that make online boot camps available to current students and recent alumni wanting to add skills. "We'll see an increase in the number of public-private partnerships created to broaden access to higher education," he predicts.

More online options will require more due diligence.
With more online options emerging, "the big challenge for students has been and will continue to be quality discernment," Regier says. "There are horrible programs in the space, focusing primarily on getting students in and accessing their financial aid to pay for tuition, with little thought or concern about the quality of the learning outcomes or learning experience." While quality programs abound, students should be on the lookout for warning signs such as a lack of program accreditation, an absence of student services and degree paths that seem too fast and easy. ●

ILLUSTRATION BY DAVID VOGIN FOR USN&WR; GETTY IMAGES

What if all college degrees came with a financial education?

Leading universities give students access to the OneEleven money app so they can build real life skills.

- ✓ **Bite-size educational video lessons**
- ✓ **Real time budgeting tools**
- ✓ **Financial aid + student loan management**
- ✓ **1-on-1 private coaching**

⑪ one·eleven

Students should leave college knowing how to manage their money.

Learn more about partnering with us at

oneeleven.co/for-universities

GW's mascot, George, is a fixture at many athletic and other campus events.

George Washington University

by **Mariya Greeley**

DURING THE SECOND semester of her sophomore year, Nia Lartey split her days between The George Washington University campus and CNN's Washington bureau, interning at the program then called "State of the Union with Jake Tapper."

"One morning I'm in class, the next I'm at CNN watching the entire Iowa Caucus debacle," says Lartey, a senior now from Philadelphia who is

Take a
Road Trip to
Washington, D.C.

Join U.S. News on a college "road trip" to the D.C. area, where we visit six universities with varied personalities; all provide rich opportunities to take advantage of the city's offerings. While many of the images are necessarily pre-COVID, you'll get a close look at — and a feel for — life on campus.

majoring in political communication and minoring in journalism and mass communication.

For the roughly 12,000 undergrads at GW, hands-on learning opportunities like these abound. The majority of GW's classes and residence halls are located in the city's Foggy Bottom neighborhood, within a mile of the White House, State Department and the National Mall. A metro stop on campus makes the rest of the nation's

capital easily accessible, too. About 70% of students complete one to three internships by the time they graduate.

Given the urban five-by-six square block campus setting, "you're walking through the city streets with professionals walking beside you," says Karen Mani, a recent computer science grad from Staten Island, New York. Mani now works as a business tech analyst at Deloitte after interning at the company virtually during the pandemic. GW's

other Mount Vernon campus, affectionately known as "the Vern," is home to about a third of first-year students and offers a more traditional campus feel. There, students find their fix of brick buildings and green spaces where they can chat, study or lounge in a hammock available from the Eckles Library second-floor porch.

IN EASY REACH. Foggy Bottom and the Vern are a 15-minute ride from each other on the school's buses, which run

COURTESY OF THE GEORGE WASHINGTON UNIVERSITY

every five minutes when classes are in session and feature Wi-Fi, charging outlets and views of the Potomac River.

GW's seven undergraduate schools offer over 75 majors. About half of students are part of the Columbian College of Arts and Sciences; other schools include the Elliott School of International Affairs, the School of Media & Public Affairs and the Milken Institute School of Public Health.

Asher Price, a recent graduate from Houston, came to GW wanting to major in political science, but after taking a public health class his first year opted to join the Milken School as a nutrition science major. "It literally took one piece of paper to fill out to transfer," he says. "The fluidity with academics and what you want to study here is great."

PRACTICE. GW emphasizes a balance of theory and real-world preparation, which is evident in everything from its faculty to its open dining plan. "You get to work with really cool professors who have worked in the field," says Mani. A former Secret Service agent taught her Psychology of Crime and Violence class. One of Lartey's professors was a former president of the White House Correspondents' Association, and a former senior economist at the U.S. Department of Agriculture worked with Price on his nutrition science capstone. As for the

Chemistry is one of many STEM fields that GW students can choose as a major.

dining plan, undergrads are given a lump sum of "GWorld funds" per semester to spend at any of more than 100 restaurant and grocery partners, including one traditional all-you-can-eat dining hall at the Vern (students recommend the Sunday brunch) and a wide range of retailers from Whole Foods to a Foggy Bottom farmers market.

With a student-faculty ratio of 13:1 and an average class size of 29, students can expect individual attention from professors, especially if they make the effort to go to office hours. "Even when you have a larger class of maybe 100 people, the professor actually does get to know you," notes Price. "They'll call on the students by name."

Students hail from all 50 states, D.C., and about 130 countries; international students make up over 10% of the population. And with more than 450 student organizations, 20 NCAA sports teams and an active Greek Life (which about a third of students join), "there's a place for everybody," says Lartey.

Although GW doesn't "have the big football team," says Price, sports-oriented Colonials wholeheartedly cheer on their D1 athletes and their mascot – a George Washington-costumed character – while wearing their blue and buff, the colors he wore into battle.

The university was founded by an act of Congress about 200 years ago to abide by George Washington's will, and D.C. and politics remain at the heart of the student experience. Every four years the school hosts a black-tie inaugural ball. College Democrats and College Republicans are two of the largest student organizations. They share office space in the Marvin Center, and host pundits and politicians from across the spectrum. Students log many thousands of hours of community service every year. And GW is the only university whose commencement takes place on the National Mall. Students cross their tassels under the shadow of the Washington monument. ●

COURTESY OF THE GEORGE WASHINGTON UNIVERSITY

Georgetown University

by **Mariya Greeley**

THE SUMMER AFTER her freshman year at Georgetown, Bayley Wivell spent 10 weeks interning in the Philippines. A marketing major and global business fellow from Rochester, New York, Wivell helped an eco-tourism resort promote its sustainability efforts. "Whether you're a freshman or senior, these opportunities are for every Georgetown student," says Wivell, who will graduate in 2022.

The campus overlooks the Potomac River in Washington's Georgetown neighborhood. Inside the front gates, students might be reading on Healy Lawn, singing with their a capella group in front of the Lauinger Library, or strolling through the student-run farmers market. "We're a very active community," says Lea Frawley, a junior

Georgetown's Healy Hall, and a statue of the university's founder, John Carroll

studying psychology from New York City. "There's a feeling that everyone's always doing something, and it really just makes you motivated to want to do something, too." Unless they have a reason to be exempted, students are required to live on campus, known as "The Hilltop," for their first three years, in housing ranging from dorms to apartments and townhouses.

Georgetown's roughly 7,500 undergraduates can enroll in four of the university's nine schools: Georgetown College (where about half of undergrads study the arts and sciences), the Walsh School of Foreign Services, the McDonough School of Business and the School of Nursing & Health Studies (which will become two schools by the fall of 2022).

For their first two years, students typically focus on a university-wide and school-specific core curriculums. The university core consists of courses in writing, humanities, theology, philosophy, science and engaging diversity. With many options available to fulfill most requirements, students can tailor their core experience to their interests. Abby Donnelly, a junior majoring in global health from Wilmington, Delaware, took a medical anthropology course as one of her humanities requirements, for instance.

SUPPORT. An 11:1 student-to-faculty ratio and average class size of about 25 allow for individualized attention and support. When Frawley didn't do well on a cognitive neuroscience test freshman year, her professor suggested she come to office hours each week. She "ended up doing really well in the class," Frawley says.

Hoyas often pursue internships in the D.C. area and beyond. "Georgetown doesn't just want students to learn, they want them to do," says Janice Negvesky, a senior double majoring in government and history from Mount Pocono, Pennsylvania. Negvesky has interned for Pennsylvania senator Mario Scavello, a lobbying and public policy firm and Biden's 2020 presidential campaign.

Research is another common experience. Donnelly has worked on child development research with a professor and research with the U.S.-Afghan Women's Council. Her supervisor from that first experience "has become one of my biggest advocates," she says.

The school's D.C. location draws high-caliber speakers to campus, from alums like Bradley Cooper and Maria Shriver to numerous U.S. presidents. Students are a short walk or bike ride from downtown, and free university shuttle buses run to nearby metro stops.

More than 350 student clubs are central to the social life, students say. "The clubs that you're in really do, to a large extent, make up your friend groups," says Jean-Claude Kradin, a senior finance and international business double major from Dallas. Kradin is a member of the Hilltop Microfinance Initiative, which manages real small business loans. "It's really great to speak to clients and to really build relationships with small businesses," he says.

Club and intramural sports are a popular option, with more than

A class in session at Georgetown University

2,500 students participating. And there's plenty of interest in Georgetown's D1 games (especially basketball), where fans in their blue and gray chant "Hoya Saxa" and cheer on their mascot, Jack the Bulldog.

Georgetown is the country's oldest Catholic and Jesuit university, and original Jesuit values remain ingrained today, like a commitment to "people for others" through community engagement and social justice. There are classes like the one on prison reform through which students helped exonerate a man in 2018 who'd been wrongfully convicted and imprisoned for 27 years. Half of students do service or community work during all four years. "You're really getting more than just a degree," says Negvesky. "You leave the school shaped as an individual." ●

American University

by **Lindsay Cates**

SYEDAH ASGHAR, a junior journalism major with a passion for social justice and service, jumped at the chance to get involved in American University's Community-Based Scholars Program as a freshman. The first-year living-learning community is focused on community-based research opportunities. "It has provided me with a family," Asghar says – one that lasted when her freshman campus experience was cut short by the pandemic. The Douglasville, Georgia, native worked with local high school students hoping to create a more inclusive environment. The project turned into a virtual summer internship during which Asghar planned a curriculum to help other universities implement similar service programs.

This kind of experiential learning is common in almost every area of study at AU, where the curriculum is centered on connecting what students learn in the classroom to life in the real world, says Jessica Waters, dean of undergraduate education and vice provost for academic student services. More than 90% of AU's 8,000 students participate in at least one internship, and at least 65% study abroad in over 130 countries. "AU Abroad Centers" in Brussels, Madrid and Nairobi are popular options.

"Being in D.C. offers so many opportunities," says Victoria Kent, a 2021 biology and pre-med graduate from Phoenixville, Pennsylvania. Kent was able to complement her undergraduate research on the cellular biology of skin cancer with volunteer work she arranged at Children's

The capstone performance of AU's graduating dance majors

FROM LEFT: GEORGETOWN UNIVERSITY; JEFF WATTS – COURTESY OF AMERICAN UNIVERSITY

National Hospital under the guidance of a physician in the bone health clinic.

AU's picturesque campus – a designated arboretum with more than 4,000 trees – appeals to students looking for the perks of a city without the hustle and bustle of downtown. The enclosed3 84-acre campus nestled in a residential district in Northwest D.C. fosters a tight-knit community, but students have access to resources and research options more typical of a much larger institution.

Six undergraduate schools and colleges offer more than 70 majors and programs. A big draw is the School of Public Affairs, which offers degrees in legal studies, political science and data sciences. The School of International Service, Kogod School of Business, School of Communication, School of Education, and College of Arts & Sciences round out the possibilites.

Students wanting to combine different interests can choose from several unique interdisciplinary programs. The three-year Public Health; Global Scholars; and Politics, Policy and Law degrees are popular options to save time and potentially tack on a master's degree. Adit Roy, a senior from Basking Ridge, New Jersey, chose the Communications, Legal Institutions, Economics and Government major to gain a holistic view of public affairs, law and communications before pursuing law school. He's taken classes in policy, education, writing and public health, and has completed three internships – one with a political action committee; one with South Asians for Biden, a grassroots organization; and one with a political consulting firm.

Small classes (AU boasts an average class size of 22 and an 11:1 student-to-faculty ratio) encourage connections between students and professors, and AU's first-year experience program is designed to ensure that incoming students develop close relationships fast. All first-years take a two-semester

Performing arts students attend a class in the university's Katzen Arts Center.

class covering the transition to college and the topics of race, social identity and structures of power. All also take a first-year Complex Problems seminar, which teaches interdisciplinary approaches to solving societal problems. Over 130 options include "Juvenile Injustice," "Plagues, Plots, and People" and "Asteroid Apocalypse."

GETTING INVOLVED. Outside of class, "there are a lot of ways for a student to be involved," says Asghar. The Eagles field 16 Division I teams; arts groups, club and intramural sports teams, advocacy organizations, Greek life and political organizations are popular. During the 2020-2021 school year, the Kennedy Political Union's roster of high-profile speakers featured Andrew Yang, Stacey Abrams and Dr. Anthony Fauci.

AU provides all students with a discounted public transit card so they have unlimited access to the city's attractions, and a free shuttle connects campus to the nearby Tenleytown neighborhood's metro station and shopping and dining. ●

JEFF WATTS – COURTESY OF AMERICAN UNIVERSITY

Howard University

by **Lindsay Cates**

KENNEDY GERARD visited several historically Black universities on a bus tour up the East Coast her senior year of high school. But it wasn't until she was on Howard's campus, the last stop, that she found exactly the vibrant culture and diverse community she was looking for. "The atmosphere was just different," says Gerard, a political science major who hails from LaPlace, Louisiana, and graduated one year early this past July.

At Howard, it's common (in non-pandemic times) to see impromptu step shows and students playing musical instruments, jumping rope and gathering with friends on "the Yard," a green space in the center of campus. The more than 6,500 undergraduates come from 48 states and 71 countries, yet students say they feel a strong sense of unity.

"There's always music and concerts going on," says Amorr Nelson, a fourth-year student in Howard's accelerated six-year BS/MD program who is from New York City. "The community alone gives me the confidence boost that I need to succeed."

Nelson was drawn to Howard University Medical Center's focus on serving the underserved, and while the accelerated program is challenging (students overload on undergraduate credits the first two years), it brings major cost savings to those set on entering the medical field, along with opportunities in clinical and research work across Howard's Colleges of

Howard students walk across "the Yard," a popular gathering space on campus.

Medicine, Nursing & Allied Health Sciences, Dentistry and Pharmacy.

Here, "you see the physical manifestations of what people have told you that you cannot be," Nelson says. "There's constant encouragement to push yourself and do more." An inspiring list of alumni includes Vice President Kamala Harris, author Toni Morrison, actor Chadwick Boseman and actress Taraji P. Henson.

NO BARRIERS. Howard's determination to eliminate barriers to education (just under half of students are Pell Grant recipients) and its expansive offerings are what set the university apart from its HBCU peers, says President Wayne A. I. Frederick. The 256-acre campus atop a hill in Northwest Washington is home to 13 schools and colleges offering more than 140 majors and programs in the arts and sciences, business, education, engineering and architecture – and the university is the top producer of minority students in medicine, journalism, law and business. If Howard doesn't offer a course, students can enroll in classes at schools nearby, including Georgetown, George Washington and George Mason universities.

To explore academic opportunities further off campus, students can participate in dozens of study abroad programs. Despite her rigorous medical curriculum, Nelson traveled to Mexico to work in a pediatric clinic in her second year.

With a student-faculty ratio of 10:1, and more than 50% of classes having fewer than 20 students, Howard feels small, Gerard says, and "you can really get a personal connection with professors." Within her political science major, Gerard formed close bonds with her professors in classes on Black politics and policing, and during her last (virtual) year at Howard, she snagged a campaign internship, working mostly in person, for a judge back home in Louisiana.

CHANCE TO NETWORK. Hands-on academic opportunities such as Howard West (an immersive computer science program at Google's headquarters) and Howard Entertainment (a partnership between the university and Amazon Studios) provide ample ways for participants to learn from, and network with, industry professionals.

Beyond academics, Howard offers more than 200 clubs and activities. The "Bleed Blue Crew" cheers on 21 NCAA Division I teams, and many students join geographic clubs (like California Club or Texas Club). Some 8% of undergrads opt to join a historically Black Greek organization; Howard is home to all of the Divine Nine organizations in the National Pan-Hellenic Council, and five were founded at the school.

Just steps away from campus are U Street's restaurants and bars, where some entrepreneurial students set up pop-up shops in the retail spaces. Two metro stops provide easy access to other D.C. neighborhoods, where students say they enjoy joining demonstrations for causes they are passionate about and visiting city attractions like the Smithsonian museums and D.C.'s monuments and memorials. •

The Catholic University of America

by **Mariya Greeley**

THE CATHOLIC UNIVERSITY of America is the only college founded by U.S. bishops and the only one that three popes have visited. In 2015, Pope Francis celebrated Mass at the neighboring Basilica of the National Shrine of the Immaculate Conception (the largest Roman Catholic church in North America) in front of tens of thousands gathered on the Catholic University Mall, a green space where students can usually be found studying, lounging, playing lawn games with friends and – in recent months – interning remotely.

Also the second-oldest research

university in the U.S. after Johns Hopkins University, CatholicU aims to marry faith and reason for more than 3,500 undergraduate and over 3,000 graduate students. Of 12 schools, 10 offer undergraduate programs, including professional options in architecture and nursing. All-told, undergrads can choose from upwards of 70 majors.

TRADITIONAL FEEL. About 3 miles north of Capitol Hill, CatholicU's manicured green spaces and gothic and romanesque-revival-style buildings offer a traditional campus feel inside the District. "You don't really feel like you're in the city," says Sydney Hartman, a recent marketing grad from Eldersburg, Maryland.

Cardinal Fest, celebrating CatholicU and the red and black, kicks off homecoming weekend.

Students are required to live in one of the single-sex residence halls until senior year, which tends to build relationships. "I can't walk 3 feet without having a 15-minute conversation," says Gemma Del Carmen, a senior studying political science and psychology from the Dallas-Fort Worth area. "It's really what makes this place feel like home."

But with a metro stop next to campus, the entire city is only minutes away. Del Carmen recommends studying at the Library of Congress and strolling the National Mall's monu-

ments at night with friends.

From jobs to internships, "D.C. is full of opportunities," says Kelly Woodson, a senior studying psychology and brain science from Hollywood, Florida. "I've interned at Capitol Hill and I've worked at a gym at the same time." With the help of the Center for Academic and Career Success, 80% of CatholicU students complete an internship by graduation; some 60% complete two or more.

In the first year, students are grouped into learning communities of about 18 that take four core classes together in philosophy, theology and English. This cohort experience kicks off the larger core curriculum, which requires up to 15 courses across disciplines. The liberal arts framework allows for an opportunity to "round out your education" and "sample classes from different schools," says Huey Bodger, a junior philosophy major from Woodbridge, Virginia.

SMALL CLASSES. CatholicU has a student-to-faculty ratio of 10:1, and the average class size is under 20. This encourages close working relationships, Woodson says. "Some of the professors that I have had really have gotten to know me as a person."

In addition to required theology courses, there are "tons of opportunities to grow your faith," says Hartman. About 80% of students are Catholic, and about half say they go to Mass on campus weekly. Campus Ministry hosts frequent events, some professors pray before class, and students can even request to have their rooms blessed by a priest during the first month of every academic year. "It's a very welcoming community that meets you where you are on your faith journey, whatever that faith

is," says Del Carmen. "We all just respect each other."

There are more than 100 clubs, and events take place pretty much every night, students say. "You're always going to find things that you would like to do," says Woodson, a member of the Black Student Alliance, Red Line A Capella and March For Our Lives, an anti-gun violence group. The Cardinals have 25 Division III teams that count about one-fifth of students on their rosters.

Students flock to community service experiences, collectively logging over 28,000 hours each year. Two initiatives are particularly popular: Mother Teresa Day of Service in the fall and Martin Luther King Jr. Day of Service in the spring, when students, faculty and staff spread out across D.C. to serve people experiencing homelessness, harvest vegetables from the nearby Franciscan Monastery's garden, and teach children to read, among other possibilities. The days "are just really rewarding," Hartman says. •

CatholicU's engineering program boasts a healthy enrollment of women.

University of Maryland
College Park

by **Lindsay Cates**

THE **UNIVERSITY** of Maryland's 1,340-acre campus sits outside D.C., of course, but is just 9 miles from downtown. Students say the school simply has everything – a huge selection of academic offerings and research opportunities, Division 1 athletics,

Maryland students explore the many ways to get involved on campus at the 2019 First Look Fair.

proximity to a major city without giving up a traditional campus feel. The school is enormous, diverse and extraordinarily lively, says Ruda Nighot, a 2021 economics grad from Hershey, Pennsylvania. "There's something going on at all times." Although about 76% of UMD's 30,875 undergraduates are from Maryland, the student body represents all 50 states and 123 countries, and 46% are students of color.

Despite UMD's size, "it's really easy to find a community of people," says Andrew Nash, a senior electrical engineering major from Mount Airy, Maryland. Many first-year students find friends through one of more than 30 academic-themed living-learning communities, as they live and take some classes as a group during their first few semesters. Many communities are connected to UMD's honors programs or the College Park Scholars Program; students choose a focus from among themes like "Justice and Legal Thought" or "Environment, Technology and Economy." Others are connected to programs like Hinman CEOs (for entrepreneurship), the Jiménez-Porter Writers' House (for creative writing), and CIVICUS (for community service learning, leadership development and political engagement).

Alicia Perkovich, a junior from Syracuse, New York, says the Honors Humanities community allowed her to form close connections with faculty; her art history advisor alerted her to an on-campus internship at the Michelle Smith Collaboratory for Visual Culture. There, she gained technical experience working with metadata and photogrammetry (obtaining information about objects and the environment by analyzing photographs) useful for her history and art history majors.

GROUP RESEARCH. Nash connected with other freshmen through the First-Year Innovation & Research Experience program, a faculty-mentored opportunity for more than 600 students to participate in group investigation of topics like molecular diagnostics, addiction science, sustainability and cloud computing. For his project on

Celebrating the close of four years at Maryland at the 2018 graduation ceremony

unmanned autonomous systems, Nash worked with his group to design a robot that could draw lines and shapes.

Research is ingrained in academic life across all departments and majors, says Associate Provost and Dean for Undergraduate Studies William A. Cohen. And proximity to research centers for the National Institutes of Health and other federal agencies creates pathways to internships and jobs. Over half of undergrads complete at least one internship.

UMD's 12 schools and colleges offer more than 90 majors, including strong programs in science, technology, engineering, and math. A unique degree in the College of Information Studies blends classes on web development, data analytics and cybersecurity with social sciences, leadership and humanities. Other schools include those of journalism, business, arts and humanities, education, agriculture, and behavioral and social sciences.

A new public policy degree and UMD's Do Good Institute appeal to students who are passionate about social issues and are aiming to make a difference, with programs in social entrepreneurship, internships, volunteer opportunities and research grants.

In addition to courses in writing, math and diversity, students across all schools must complete two "I-Series" courses focused on such questions as how to solve poverty or the origins of life, and two "Scholarship in Practice" courses, which teach the real-world work of a discipline. For example, an art course had students design a public art installation for UMD's campus.

QUESTION OF ACCESS. With an 18:1 student-faculty ratio, there are some larger classes, but fewer than 10% of classes have more than 100 students. Large classes are broken into smaller discussion groups led by a teaching assistant, and professors make themselves available during office hours.

Alongside academics, showing "Maryland pride" and cheering on the Terps is a big part of student life. "I think the atmosphere is probably one of the best," says Nash. Students also get involved in UMD's more than 800 student organizations and activities, which include club and intramural sports, TERP THON (which raises funds to support pediatric patients) and other service groups, Greek organizations and more.

A highlight of the campus is the beloved statue of Testudo, UMD's diamondback terrapin mascot, whose nose students rub for luck before finals. (They also leave creative "offerings," which have included traffic cones, couches and microwave ovens). Just off campus in College Park, casual restaurants and coffee shops line Route One, popular spots for doing schoolwork or gathering with friends. A metro stop on campus provides easy access to D.C., and Baltimore, Annapolis and the Chesapeake Bay are each just over 30 minutes away by car. ●

"The independence
AP Seminar gives
students helped me
prepare for college."
— *Nelly, Fashion Institute of Technology*

"It made me feel good that I created
such a beautiful app because
now I could show people what I
did thanks to this class"
— *Mariama, Former AP CSP Student*

Explore The Latest Advanced Placement Courses

AP Seminar and **AP Computer Science Principles** let students think creatively and develop key skills for college and career. These AP courses empower students to drive their learning by designing projects that address real-world issues that matter to them and to their communities.

Learn more at:
collegeboard.org/apseminar
collegeboard.org/csp

© 2021 College Board 2021-010

The U.S. News

Rankings

George Washington University's graduation on the National Mall
COURTESY OF THE GEORGE WASHINGTON UNIVERSITY

How We Rank Colleges

You can make use of our statistics as you search for a good fit

by **Robert J. Morse** and **Eric M. Brooks**

DECIDING WHERE TO APPLY CAN BE TOUGH. But the U.S. News Best Colleges rankings, now in their 37th year, are an excellent resource to tap as you begin your search. They can help you compare the academic quality of institutions you're considering based on such widely accepted indicators of excellence as graduation rates and the strength of the faculty. As you learn about colleges already on your shortlist, you may narrow your choices even further or discover unfamiliar new options. Yes, many factors other than those spotlighted here will figure in your decision, including location and the feel of campus life, the range of academic offerings and activities and the cost. But combined with attention to such factors and to your own intuition, our rankings can be a powerful tool in your quest for the best fit.

How does the methodology work? The U.S. News ranking system rests on two pillars. The formula uses quantitative and qualitative statistical measures that education experts have proposed as reliable indicators of academic quality, and it is based on our researched view of what matters in education.

First, we categorize regionally accredited institutions by their mission, to establish valid comparisons: National Universities, National Liberal Arts Colleges, Regional Universities and Regional Colleges. The national universities offer a full range of undergraduate majors, plus master's and Ph.D. programs or professional practice doctorates, and emphasize faculty research (Page 54). The national liberal arts colleges focus almost exclusively on undergraduate education (Page 64). They award at least 50% of their degrees in the arts and sciences.

The regional universities (Page 70) offer a broad scope of undergraduate degrees and some master's degree programs but few, if any, doctoral programs. The regional colleges (Page 86) focus on undergraduate education but grant fewer than 50% of their degrees in liberal arts disciplines; this category also includes schools that have small bachelor's programs but primarily grant two-year associate degrees. The regional universities and regional colleges are further divided and ranked in four geographical groups: North, South, Midwest and West.

The framework used to group schools is derived from the 2018 update of the Carnegie Classification of Institutions of Higher Education's Basic Classification. The Carnegie classification is used extensively by higher education researchers; the U.S. Department of Education and many higher education associations use the system to organize their data and to determine colleges' eligibility for grant money, for example.

Next, we gather data from each college on 17 indicators of academic excellence. Each ranking factor is assigned a weight that reflects our research about how much a measure matters. Finally, the schools in each category are ranked against their peers using their overall scores,

GETTY IMAGES

which are calculated from the sum of their indicators. The data used in these rankings pertain to fall 2020 or the 2020-2021 academic year and earlier periods.

Some colleges and universities are not ranked. The most common reasons were because the institutions lacked regional accreditation, did not have campus-based offerings, did not enroll first-year (freshmen) students, or because U.S. News could not obtain a six-year graduation rate of bachelor's degree-seeking students. As a result of these standards, many for-profit and upper division institutions are not included. We also did not calculate overall college rankings of highly specialized schools such as those in arts, business, engineering and nursing, although many are included in our rankings of programs in business and nursing, for example. A change from previous editions: Schools are no longer removed from the rankings for receiving too few ratings on the peer assessment survey, described below.

Colleges report most of the data themselves, via the annual U.S. News statistical survey. This year, 83% of the 1,466 ranked colleges and universities returned their statistical information. To ensure the highest possible quality of data, U.S. News compared schools' survey responses to their earlier cohorts' statistics, third-party data, and data reported by other schools. Schools were instructed to review, revise and verify the accuracy of their data, particularly any flagged by U.S. News as requiring a second look. They were also instructed to have a top academic official sign off on the accuracy of the data. Schools that declined to do so could still submit data and be ranked but are footnoted.

For eligible colleges that declined to complete our survey (identified as nonresponders), we made extensive use of data they reported to the National Center for Education Statistics and College Scorecard. Estimates were used in the calculations when schools failed to report data not available from other sources, although the estimates are not published. Missing data are reported in the tables as N/A.

The indicators we use to capture academic quality, described below, include input measures that reflect schools' student bodies, faculties and resources as well as outcome measures that signal how well institutions are engaging and educating their students. A more detailed explanation of the methodology can be found at usnews.com/collegemeth.

OUTCOMES (weighted at 40%): The higher the proportion of first-year students who return to campus for sophomore year and eventually graduate, the better a school most likely is at offering the classes and services needed to succeed. More than one-third of a school's rank reflects its success at retaining students and graduating them within six years.

This measure has several components: six-year graduation

and first-year retention rates (together accounting for 22% of the score); graduation rate performance, or how well a school performs at graduating students compared to a predicted graduation rate based on student and school characteristics (8%); a school's record on promoting social mobility by graduating students from low-income backgrounds (5%); and two measures of the indebtedness of bachelor's degree graduates (5% total).

The average six-year graduation rate (of students entering in fall 2011 through fall 2014) was weighted at 17.6% of the score. Average first-year retention rate (of fall 2016 through fall 2019 entrants) was weighted at 4.4%.

A school's graduation rate performance shows the effect of programs and policies on the graduation rate when controlling for other factors that might influence it. These include spending per student, admissions selectivity, the proportion of undergraduates receiving Pell Grants, the proportion of federal financial aid recipients who were first-generation students, and – for national universities only – the proportion of undergrad degrees awarded in science, technology, engineering and mathematics disciplines. We compare a school's six-year graduation rate to the graduation rate we predicted for that class. If the actual graduation rate is higher than the predicted rate, then the college is enhancing achievement. This is based on the average of the cohorts entering in fall 2013 and fall 2014.

The social mobility measure assesses a school's performance at supporting students from underserved backgrounds relative to all students. It considers both a school's six-year graduation rate among students who received Pell Grants and how that performance compares with the graduation rate of all other students. Scores were then adjusted by the proportion of the entering class that was awarded Pell Grants, because achieving a higher graduation rate among students from low-income backgrounds is more challenging when a school has a larger proportion of such students. This is based on the average of the cohorts entering in fall 2013 and fall 2014.

The two graduate indebtedness indicators are average accumulated federal loan debt of students who borrowed (including co-signed loans but excluding parent loans) among 2019 and 2020 grads earning bachelor's degrees (3%), and the average percentage among the classes of 2019 and 2020 that took out federal loans (2%).

FACULTY RESOURCES (20%): Research shows that the greater access students have to quality instructors, the more engaged they will be in class, the more they will learn, and the more likely they are to graduate. U.S. News uses five factors to assess commitment to instruction: class size, faculty salary,

Weighing What's Important

The U.S. News rankings are based on several categories of quality indicators, listed below. Scores for each group are weighted as shown to arrive at a final overall score.

The Scoring Breakdown

Outcomes*	40%
Faculty Resources	20%
Expert Opinion	20%
Financial Resources	10%
Student Excellence	7%
Alumni Giving	3%

*Graduation, retention, graduation rate performance, graduate indebtedness, social mobility

faculty with the highest degree in their field, student-faculty ratio, and proportion of faculty who are full time.

Class size is the most heavily weighted, at 8% of the score. The larger the proportion of fall 2019 and fall 2020 classes a school reported as being of a smaller size, the more credit the school receives.

Faculty salary (7%) reflects the average pay of assistant, associate and full professors during the 2019-2020 and 2020-2021 academic years. The faculty salary figures were adjusted for regional price differences. The other factors were specific to the 2020-2021 academic year and were weighted as follows: proportion of full-time professors with the highest degree in their field (3%), student-faculty ratio (1%), and proportion of faculty who are full time (1%).

EXPERT OPINION (20%): We survey presidents, provosts and deans of admissions, asking them to rate the academic quality of peer institutions with which they are familiar on a scale of 1 (marginal) to 5 (distinguished). An institution known for having innovative approaches to teaching may perform especially well on this indicator, for example, whereas a school struggling to keep its accreditation will likely perform poorly. The peer assessment score is derived from averaging survey results from 2020 and 2021. Of the 4,741 academics who were sent questionnaires in 2021, 34.1% responded.

FINANCIAL RESOURCES (10%): Generous per-student spending indicates that a college can offer a variety of programs and services. U.S. News measures financial resources using average spending per student on instruction, research, student services and related educational expenditures in the 2019 and 2020 fiscal years, based on full-time and part-time undergraduate and graduate enrollments in fall 2018 and fall 2019.

STUDENT EXCELLENCE (7%): Selective admissions enables talented, hard-working students to share a learning environment with their academic peers and enables instructors to design classes that have great rigor. Excellence is based on two ranking indicators: standardized tests and high school class standing. The test scores for the fall 2020 entering class used in this year's rankings were weighted at 5%. High school class standing for the fall 2020 entering class was weighted at 2%. Schools sometimes fail to report SAT and ACT scores for athletes, international students, minority students, legacies, those admitted by special arrangement and those

Footnotes
to the
Rankings Tables

1. This school declined to fill out the U.S. News & World Report main statistical survey. Data that appear are from either what the school reported in previous years or from another source, such as the National Center for Education Statistics.

2. SAT and/or ACT not required by school for some or all applicants.

3. In reporting SAT/ACT scores, the school did not include all students for whom it had scores or refused to tell U.S. News whether all students with scores had been included.

4. Data reported to U.S. News in previous years.

5. Data based on fewer than 20% of enrolled freshmen.

6. Some or all data reported to the National Center for Education Statistics.

7. School declined to have a school official verify the accuracy of the information contained in the U.S. News main statistical survey.

8. This rate, normally based on four years of data, is given here for fewer than four years because school didn't report rate for the most recent year or years to U.S. News.

9. SAT and/or ACT may not be required by school for some or all applicants, and in reporting SAT/ACT scores, the school did not include all students for whom it had scores or refused to tell U.S. News whether all students with scores had been included.

N/A means not available.

who started in the summer. For any school that did not report all scores (or declined to say whether all scores were reported), U.S. News discounted its test-score value by 15%. Additionally, if test scores reported represented less than 50% of students entering – down from 75% in most recent editions – the value was discounted by 15%. The adjustment was made to reflect the recent growth of test-optional admissions policies and the impact of the COVID-19 pandemic on the fall 2020 admissions process.

As for high school class standing, U.S. News incorporates the proportion of first-year students at national universities and national liberal arts colleges who graduated in the top 10% of their high school classes. For regional universities and regional colleges, we used the proportion of those who graduated in the top quarter of their high school classes.

ALUMNI GIVING (3%): This measure is the average percentage of living alumni with bachelor's degrees who gave to their college or university during 2018-2019 and 2019-2020. Giving indicates student satisfaction and postgraduate engagement.

TO ARRIVE AT A SCHOOL'S RANK, we calculated the weighted sum of its standardized scores. The scores were rescaled so the top college or university in each category received a value of 100 and the other schools' weighted scores were calculated as a proportion of the top score. Final scores were rounded to the nearest whole number and ranked in descending order. Tied schools appear in alphabetical order. Colleges and universities that fall in the bottom 25% of each ranking are presented alphabetically rather than in rank order.

As you mine the tables that follow for insights (a sense of which schools might be impressed enough by your ACT or SAT scores to offer some merit aid, for example, or where you will be likely to get the most attention from professors), keep in mind that the rankings provide a launching pad for more research, not an easy answer. ●

USNEWS.COM/BESTCOLLEGES

▶ Visit **usnews.com** regularly while conducting your research, as U.S. News frequently adds content aimed at helping collegebound students find the best fit and get in. We also occasionally make updates when new data become available or new information changes the data.

GETTY IMAGES

YOU WERE CHOSEN
to belong

PBA is a place where you are more than a number—you were chosen for a purpose. You have incredible gifts, unique passions, and a calling to use them for the good of all. From student clubs to focused worship and learning during Christival to Workship experiences that will open the door for you to serve others, we do all we can to create a life of meaning as part of our intentional community.

Palm Beach
Atlantic
UNIVERSITY

FIND OUT MORE AT **PBA.EDU** OR CALL **561-803-2100**

Best National Unive

Rank	School (State) (*Public)	Overall score	Peer assessment score (5.0=highest)	Graduation and retention rank	Average first-year student retention rate	2020 graduation rate Predicted	2020 graduation rate Actual	Over-performance (+) Under-performance (-)	Pell recipient grad rate	Soci mobi ran
1.	Princeton University (NJ)	100	4.8	1	94%	93%	98%	+5	98%	19:
2.	Columbia University (NY)	97	4.7	1	98%	93%	97%	+4	95%	19:
2.	Harvard University (MA)	97	4.9	4	92%	94%	98%	+4	97%	21:
2.	Massachusetts Institute of Technology	97	4.9	4	99%	93%	96%	+3	94%	17!
5.	Yale University (CT)	96	4.8	11	91%	96%	96%	None	94%	26!
6.	Stanford University (CA)	95	4.9	17	96%	93%	95%	+2	95%	24!
6.	University of Chicago	95	4.6	4	99%	97%	96%	-1	94%	32:
8.	University of Pennsylvania	94	4.6	4	97%	96%	96%	None	92%	27!
9.	California Institute of Technology	93	4.6	22	97%	97%	92%	-5	92%	26!
9.	Duke University (NC)	93	4.5	4	97%	96%	95%	-1	94%	31:
9.	Johns Hopkins University (MD)	93	4.7	17	98%	96%	94%	-2	93%	29:
9.	Northwestern University (IL)	93	4.4	11	98%	95%	95%	None	93%	25(
13.	Dartmouth College (NH)	91	4.4	4	97%	96%	95%	-1	91%	26!
14.	Brown University (RI)	88	4.5	4	97%	94%	95%	+1	92%	16!
14.	Vanderbilt University (TN)	88	4.3	17	97%	96%	93%	-3	90%	28!
14.	Washington University in St. Louis	88	4.2	11	96%	98%	94%	-4	92%	37!
17.	Cornell University (NY)	87	4.6	11	97%	94%	95%	+1	94%	24:
17.	Rice University (TX)	87	4.1	17	97%	94%	94%	None	90%	26!
19.	University of Notre Dame (IN)	85	4.2	1	98%	97%	97%	None	94%	33!
20.	University of California–Los Angeles*	84	4.4	25	97%	88%	91%	+3	88%	2
21.	Emory University (GA)	83	4.2	33	94%	92%	90%	-2	87%	15:
22.	University of California–Berkeley*	82	4.7	22	97%	91%	92%	+1	89%	8:
23.	Georgetown University (DC)	81	4.2	11	96%	96%	94%	-2	93%	29:
23.	University of Michigan–Ann Arbor*	81	4.5	22	97%	89%	93%	+4	89%	29:
25.	Carnegie Mellon University (PA)	80	4.3	28	97%	93%	93%	None	90%	28!
25.	University of Virginia*	80	4.3	11	97%	95%	94%	-1	90%	29:
27.	University of Southern California	79	3.9	25	95%	92%	92%	None	91%	16:
28.	New York University	78	4.0	48	93%	82%	88%	+6	86%	13:
28.	Tufts University (MA)	78	3.8	17	95%	96%	94%	-2	93%	27!
28.	University of California–Santa Barbara*	78	3.7	61	93%	83%	89%	+6	86%	1!
28.	University of Florida*	78	3.8	33	97%	84%	89%	+5	86%	5:
28.	U. of North Carolina–Chapel Hill*	78	4.2	28	96%	90%	91%	+1	89%	12:
28.	Wake Forest University (NC)	78	3.7	36	94%	95%	89%	-6	82%	35:
34.	University of California–San Diego*	77	3.9	43	94%	86%	87%	+1	84%	2:
34.	University of Rochester (NY)	77	3.5	43	95%	89%	86%	-3	84%	17:
36.	Boston College	76	3.8	25	95%	94%	92%	-2	91%	27:
36.	University of California–Irvine*	76	3.8	54	94%	80%	85%	+5	83%	:
38.	Georgia Institute of Technology*	74	4.3	36	97%	91%	90%	-1	86%	32:
38.	University of California–Davis*	74	3.9	48	93%	84%	86%	+2	83%	1:
38.	University of Texas at Austin*	74	4.1	48	96%	83%	88%	+5	81%	14:
38.	William & Mary (VA)*	74	3.9	28	95%	94%	91%	-3	88%	35:
42.	Boston University	73	3.8	39	93%	86%	89%	+3	89%	23:
42.	Brandeis University (MA)	73	3.7	39	92%	89%	89%	None	90%	14:
42.	Case Western Reserve Univ. (OH)	73	3.7	61	93%	90%	85%	-5	83%	20:
42.	Tulane University (LA)	73	3.6	54	93%	88%	86%	-2	78%	38:
42.	Univ. of Wisconsin–Madison*	73	4.1	39	95%	84%	89%	+5	83%	34:
47.	University of Illinois–Urbana-Champaign*	72	4.0	54	93%	81%	86%	+5	80%	16:
48.	University of Georgia*	71	3.7	43	95%	81%	87%	+6	81%	20:
49.	Lehigh University (PA)	70	3.3	39	94%	86%	88%	+2	88%	27:
49.	Northeastern University (MA)	70	3.5	33	97%	88%	90%	+2	90%	29:
49.	Ohio State University–Columbus*	70	3.9	48	94%	84%	87%	+3	80%	25(
49.	Pepperdine University (CA)	70	3.5	61	89%	81%	89%	+8	89%	16:
49.	Purdue University–West Lafayette (IN)*	70	3.8	75	93%	78%	83%	+5	77%	27:
49.	Villanova University (PA)	70	3.4	28	96%	87%	92%	+5	87%	31:

Note: Key to footnotes, Page 52.

Faculty resources rank	% of classes under 20 ('20)	% of classes of 50 or more ('20)	Student/faculty ratio ('20)	Selectivity rank	SAT/ACT 25th-75th percentile ('20)	Freshmen in top 10% of HS class ('20)	Acceptance rate ('20)	Financial resources rank	Average alumni giving rate
3	78%	9%	4/1	15	1450-1570	89%	6%	13	50%
2	83%	9%	6/1	5	1470-1570	96%	6%	9	28%
6	76%	10%	5/1	8	1460-1580	94%	5%	7	27%
11	70%	11%	3/1	1	1510-1580	100%	7%	2	29%
6	77%	8%	4/1	8	1460-1580[2]	94%	7%	1	24%
12	69%	12%	5/1	8	1420-1570[2]	96%	5%	5	23%
1	79%	6%	5/1	1	1500-1570[2]	99%	7%	9	32%
6	70%	9%	6/1	5	1460-1570[2]	96%	9%	14	38%
10	67%	9%	3/1	3	1530-1580[2]	96%	7%	3	25%
3	75%	7%	6/1	5	34-35	95%	8%	15	30%
15	74%	9%	6/1	3	1480-1570[2]	99%	9%	4	30%
5	78%	6%	6/1	8	1430-1550[2]	95%	9%	7	29%
9	63%	6%	7/1	15	1440-1560[2]	93%	9%	16	42%
16	70%	11%	6/1	8	1440-1560[2]	95%	8%	22	27%
17	57%	13%	8/1	8	33-35[2]	90%	12%	12	28%
12	67%	8%	7/1	15	33-35[2]	86%	16%	5	22%
25	63%	14%	9/1	20	1400-1540[2]	84%	11%	18	21%
14	69%	7%	6/1	8	1460-1570[2]	92%	11%	22	30%
18	59%	11%	8/1	18	32-35[2]	90%	19%	25	38%
34	48%	23%	18/1	20	1290-1520[2]	97%[4]	14%	18	6%
22	57%	13%	9/1	24	1380-1530[2]	83%	19%	18	17%
52	55%	21%	19/1	24	1290-1530[2]	96%	18%	49	8%
28	60%	6%	11/1	24	1380-1550	83%	17%	32	25%
37	57%	17%	14/1	31	1340-1560[2]	77%	26%	41	15%
20	67%	12%	6/1	18	1460-1560[2]	89%	17%	39	15%
37	52%	14%	14/1	24	1320-1510[2]	90%	23%	41	17%
48	63%	12%	9/1	78	1340-1530[2]	N/A	16%	22	35%
23	63%	9%	8/1	28	1370-1540[2]	82%	21%	29	9%
37	66%	7%	9/1	20	1380-1530[2]	84%	16%	32	20%
21	54%	20%	17/1	29	1230-1480[2]	100%	37%	58	17%
48	53%	9%	17/1	36	1290-1460	82%	31%	44	18%
37	46%	12%	15/1	41	27-33	74%	24%	32	15%
23	50%	1%	11/1	37	1290-1470[2]	73%	32%	9	21%
48	46%	24%	19/1	29	1260-1480[2]	100%	38%	25	3%
18	79%	8%	9/1	37	1310-1500[2]	71%	35%	21	20%
28	65%	1%	11/1	31	1330-1500[2]	79%	26%	59	21%
52	51%	23%	18/1	34	1215-1450[2]	99%	30%	64	7%[4]
76	33%	28%	18/1	20	1370-1530	88%	21%	59	15%
39	32%	31%	20/1	48	1140-1400[2]	100%	46%	32	6%
59	48%	14%	18/1	41	1210-1470[2]	87%	32%	70	9%
56	49%	8%	12/1	34	1300-1490[2]	77%	42%	109	23%
34	56%	15%	10/1	41	1310-1500[2]	66%	20%	49	9%
56	55%	10%	10/1	46	1320-1510[2]	59%	34%	52	17%
32	63%	13%	11/1	31	1340-1520[2]	70%	30%	39	16%
25	57%	8%	8/1	37	30-33[2]	63%	11%	25	16%
07	47%	24%	17/1	59	27-32[2]	51%	57%	52	14%
97	38%[4]	21%[4]	20/1	63	1210-1470	52%	63%	64	6%
72	46%	11%	17/1	56	1220-1400	56%	48%	116	13%
34	47%	8%	9/1	49	1260-1433[2]	66%	50%	52	13%
45	62%	6%	14/1	41	1410-1540[2]	76%[5]	20%	70	12%
39	30%	24%	19/1	59	26-32[2]	55%	68%	81	14%
48	65%	3%	13/1	81	1200-1410[2]	49%[5]	42%	52	8%
33	44%	19%	13/1	70	1190-1430	48%	67%	103	16%
97	43%	3%	11/1	37	1320-1460[2]	72%	31%	81	24%

What Is a National University?

TO ASSESS MORE than 1,800 of the country's four-year colleges and universities, U.S. News first assigns each to a group of its peers, based on the categories of higher education institutions developed by the Carnegie Foundation for the Advancement of Teaching. The National Universities category consists of 392 institutions (209 public, 179 private and 4 for-profit) that offer a wide range of undergraduate majors as well as master's and doctoral degrees or professional practice doctorates; some institutions emphasize research. A list of the top 30 public national universities appears on Page 63.

Data on 17 indicators of academic quality are gathered from each institution. Schools are ranked by total weighted score; those tied are listed alphabetically. For a description of the methodology, see Page 50. For more on a college, turn to the directory at the back of the book.

Rank	School (State) (*Public)	Overall score	Peer assessment score (5.0=highest)	Average first-year student retention rate	2020 graduation rate Predicted	2020 graduation rate Actual	Pell recipient grad rate	% of classes under 20 ('20)	% of classes of 50 or more ('20)	SAT/ACT 25th-75th percentile ('20)	Freshmen in top 10% of HS class ('20)	Accept-ance rate ('20)	Average alumni giving rate
55.	Florida State University*	69	3.3	94%	73%	84%	80%	61%	11%	1220-1350	46%	32%	17%
55.	Rensselaer Polytechnic Inst. (NY)	69	3.6	92%	88%	87%	82%	45%	12%	1300-1500[2]	55%	57%	10%
55.	Santa Clara University (CA)	69	3.2	94%	86%	92%	91%	38%	1%	1270-1450[2]	40%[5]	51%	17%
55.	University of Miami (FL)	69	3.4	92%	89%	83%	78%	53%	8%	1250-1420	51%	33%	10%
59.	Syracuse University (NY)	68	3.5	91%	76%	83%	80%	54%	10%	1160-1370[2]	33%	69%	10%
59.	Univ. of Maryland–College Park*	68	3.8	95%	88%	87%	82%	45%	18%	1270-1480[2]	73%	49%	6%
59.	University of Pittsburgh*	68	3.6	93%	83%	83%	76%	43%	17%	1243-1420	54%	64%	8%
59.	University of Washington*	68	3.9	94%	89%	84%	80%	28%	26%	1200-1457[2]	56%	56%	9%
63.	George Washington University (DC)	67	3.6	91%	85%	85%	83%	43%	12%	1270-1450[2]	50%	43%	6%
63.	Pennsylvania State U.–Univ. Park*	67	3.7	93%	77%	86%	79%	34%	18%	1150-1340[2]	N/A	54%	10%
63.	Rutgers University–New Brunswick (NJ)*	67	3.4	93%	70%	84%	83%	39%	21%	1180-1410[2]	30%[5]	67%	6%
63.	University of Connecticut*	67	3.4	94%	79%	83%	76%	54%	15%	1170-1390[2]	51%	56%	7%
63.	Worcester Polytechnic Inst. (MA)	67	3.1	95%	88%	89%	85%	64%	9%	1310-1470[4]	56%	59%	8%
68.	Fordham University (NY)	66	3.3	90%	81%	83%	81%	51%	1%	1230-1410[2]	44%	53%	14%
68.	Indiana University–Bloomington*	66	3.7	91%	74%	80%	67%	47%	12%	1120-1350[2]	32%	80%	11%
68.	Southern Methodist University (TX)	66	3.2	91%	85%	81%	76%	55%	11%	29-33	47%	53%	11%
68.	Texas A&M University*	66	3.7	93%	80%	83%	73%	26%	28%	1160-1380[2]	66%	63%	16%
68.	Univ. of Massachusetts–Amherst*	66	3.5	91%	74%	83%	81%	47%	19%	1200-1390[2]	34%	65%	7%
68.	University of Minnesota–Twin Cities*	66	3.6	93%	81%	84%	78%	36%	20%	25-31[2]	49%	70%	7%
68.	Yeshiva University (NY)	66	2.9	92%	79%	78%	69%	64%	1%	24-31[2]	59%	67%	16%
75.	Baylor University (TX)	65	3.3	90%	78%	79%	71%	52%	9%	26-31[2]	50%	68%	14%
75.	Clemson University (SC)*	65	3.4	93%	83%	85%	74%	38%	17%	1210-1390	53%	62%	20%
75.	Loyola Marymount University (CA)	65	3.1	88%	77%	83%	80%	50%	1%	1210-1390[2]	37%[5]	50%	9%
75.	Virginia Tech*	65	3.7	93%	78%	86%	80%	28%	24%	1170-1370[2]	N/A	67%	14%
79.	American University (DC)	64	3.3	88%	88%	79%	75%	59%	1%	1220-1390[2]	35%	39%	5%
79.	Brigham Young Univ.–Provo (UT)	64	3.2	90%	85%	75%	68%	50%	13%	26-32[2]	59%	69%	10%
79.	Gonzaga University (WA)	64	3.2	94%	80%	88%	85%	37%	2%	1160-1350[2]	39%	73%	10%
79.	North Carolina State U.*	64	3.2	94%	80%	85%	81%	37%	18%	27-32[2]	47%	46%	11%
83.	Binghamton University–SUNY*	63	3.0	91%	76%	82%	79%	46%	15%	1290-1450	54%	43%	5%
83.	Colorado School of Mines*	63	3.5	92%	84%	84%	79%	31%	26%	1270-1440[2]	55%	55%	7%
83.	Elon University (NC)	63	3.0	90%	79%	83%	77%	51%	0%	1140-1320[2]	25%	72%	24%
83.	Howard University (DC)	63	3.4	89%	62%	64%	59%	47%	7%	1130-1260[2]	27%	39%	12%
83.	Marquette University (WI)	63	3.2	89%	75%	84%	74%	48%	8%	25-30[2]	39%	82%	17%
83.	Michigan State University*	63	3.5	92%	73%	82%	70%	24%	26%	1100-1300	27%	76%	6%
83.	Stevens Institute of Technology (NJ)	63	3.0	94%	87%	88%	81%	35%	14%	1320-1480[2]	67%	53%	14%
83.	Texas Christian University	63	3.0	92%	80%	82%	74%	43%	4%	25-31[2]	39%	48%	14%
83.	University of California–Riverside*	63	3.2	90%	73%	77%	77%	18%	34%	1060-1290[2]	94%	66%	2%
83.	University of Iowa*	63	3.6	87%	73%	72%	62%	52%	14%	22-29	34%	84%	6%
93.	Stony Brook–SUNY*	62	3.3	90%	71%	76%	78%	38%	25%	1230-1440	44%	49%	4%
93.	University at Buffalo–SUNY*	62	3.2	87%	66%	75%	71%	37%	20%	1140-1310	29%	67%	10%
93.	University of California–Merced*	62	2.9	83%	47%	69%	68%	32%	28%	940-1140	N/A	85%	6%
93.	University of Delaware*	62	3.3	91%	78%	84%	73%	29%	18%	1170-1340[2]	24%	63%	7%
93.	University of Denver	62	3.1	86%	79%	75%	73%	55%	6%	1170-1360[2]	39%	61%	8%
93.	University of San Diego	62	3.1	89%	79%	80%	76%	42%	0.1%	1160-1340[2]	37%	59%	9%
99.	Auburn University (AL)*	61	3.3	91%	76%	78%	66%	35%	16%	25-31	34%	85%	14%
99.	University of Colorado Boulder*	61	3.7	87%	74%	72%	66%	50%	13%	1130-1350[2]	26%	84%	5%
99.	University of Oregon*	61	3.5	85%	67%	74%	64%	37%	21%	1090-1290[2]	26%[4]	83%	6%
99.	University of Utah*	61	3.3	90%	68%	67%	58%	46%	16%	22-29[2]	N/A	79%	12%
103.	Clark University (MA)	60	2.8	87%	77%	75%	75%	59%	3%	1150-1350[2]	36%	47%	13%
103.	Creighton University (NE)	60	3.1	90%	79%	79%	66%	40%	5%	24-30[2]	43%	77%	12%
103.	Drexel University (PA)	60	3.0	89%	69%	71%	65%	51%	9%	1180-1380[2]	40%	77%	5%
103.	Loyola University Chicago	60	3.3	85%	72%	76%	70%	32%	6%	1130-1330[2]	39%	71%	5%
103.	Miami University–Oxford (OH)*	60	3.2	91%	77%	82%	76%	34%	10%	24-30	33%	92%	15%
103.	New Jersey Inst. of Technology*	60	2.9	88%	62%	70%	64%	35%	2%	1200-1390[2]	36%	66%	9%
103.	Saint Louis University	60	3.1	90%	79%	80%	67%	42%	9%	25-31[2]	39%	56%	9%
103.	Temple University (PA)*	60	3.1	89%	64%	75%	69%	40%	8%	1090-1280[2]	36%[4]	71%	5%

Note: Key to footnotes, Page 52.

Cornell University,
...ied at No. 17

...ETTY IMAGES

Rank School (State) (*Public)	Overall score	Peer assessment score (5.0=highest)	Average first-year student retention rate	2020 graduation rate Predicted	Actual	Pell recipient grad rate	% of classes under 20 ('20)	% of classes of 50 or more ('20)	SAT/ACT 25th-75th percentile ('20)	Freshmen in top 10% of HS class ('20)	Accept- ance rate ('20)	Average alumni giving rate
103. University of Arizona*	60	3.6	83%	68%	65%	59%	36%	17%	21-29[2]	35%	85%	8%
103. University of California–Santa Cruz*	60	3.3	88%	83%	76%	74%	21%	30%	1150-1370[2]	94%	65%	2%
103. University of Illinois–Chicago*	60	3.1	80%	53%	63%	62%	29%	21%	1030-1250	32%	73%	2%
103. University of San Francisco	60	3.1	82%	67%	71%	67%	46%	1%	1140-1330[2]	35%	70%	5%
103. University of South Florida*	60	2.8	92%[8]	64%	74%	72%	46%	13%	1160-1320	32%	49%	10%
103. University of Tennessee*	60	3.3	87%	76%	71%	61%	38%	14%	25-31[2]	41%	78%	11%
117. Arizona State University*	59	3.3	86%[8]	65%	67%	59%	41%	17%	21-28[2]	30%	88%	7%
117. Rochester Inst. of Technology (NY)	59	3.4	89%	70%	73%	67%	48%	5%	1220-1420[2]	39%	74%	5%
117. SUNY Col. of Envir. Sci. and Forestry*	59	2.6	78%	71%	77%	81%	58%	8%	1130-1300[2]	31%[4]	60%	14%
117. Univ. of South Carolina*	59	3.2	89%	74%	78%	68%	44%	13%	1140-1340[2]	28%	68%	6%
117. University of Vermont*	59	3.1	86%	76%	76%	71%	45%	16%	1160-1350[2]	33%	71%	7%
122. Chapman University (CA)	58	2.7	89%	80%	80%	75%	46%	2%	1170-1350[2]	30%	58%	6%
122. Illinois Institute of Technology	58	2.9	90%	71%	72%	70%	43%	10%	1200-1390[2]	41%	61%	5%
122. Iowa State University of Sci. and Tech.*	58	3.2	88%	71%	75%	63%	35%	19%	22-28[2]	14%	88%	11%
122. University of Kansas*	58	3.4	85%	71%	63%	46%	61%	10%	22-29[2]	31%	91%	11%
122. Univ. of Missouri*	58	3.3	88%	73%	73%	62%	41%[4]	15%[4]	23-30	35%	82%	11%
127. Clarkson University (NY)	57	2.7	89%	75%	77%	66%	59%	11%	1150-1350[2]	37%	78%	12%
127. DePaul University (IL)	57	3.0	85%	65%	71%	67%	37%	2%	1060-1280[2]	N/A	70%	5%
127. Gallaudet University (DC)	57	3.0	71%	50%	44%	43%	99%	0%	14-18	N/A	63%	12%
127. Rutgers University–Newark (NJ)*	57	2.8	86%	53%	65%	64%	25%	21%	1010-1170[2]	15%	74%	4%
127. Seattle University	57	2.7	85%	73%	73%	72%	60%	0.3%	1130-1330[2]	24%	83%	5%
127. Seton Hall University (NJ)	57	3.0	84%	71%	72%	62%	46%	2%	1150-1310[2]	33%	78%	10%
127. University of Dayton (OH)	57	2.8	90%	76%	81%	74%	38%	3%	23-29[9]	27%	81%	N/A
127. University of Kentucky*	57	3.2	85%	71%	66%	53%	40%	14%	22-29[2]	33%	96%	9%
127. University of Oklahoma*	57	3.2	89%	72%	72%	59%	48%	10%	23-29[2]	31%	83%	7%
136. The Catholic University of America (DC)	56	2.9	87%	73%	74%	68%	64%	5%	1130-1325[2]	28%	82%	9%
136. Drake University (IA)	56	2.8	87%	80%	77%	68%	48%	6%	23-30[2]	37%	68%	9%
136. The New School (NY)	56	2.9	79%	66%	68%	62%	78%	1%	1140-1360[9]	17%[5]	68%	1%
136. Samford University (AL)	56	2.6	89%	77%	77%	70%	51%	4%	23-29	29%	84%	5%
136. Simmons University (MA)	56	2.4	83%	70%	79%	74%	56%	0.2%	1060-1250[2]	29%	83%	11%
136. University of La Verne (CA)	56	2.1	81%	50%	66%	65%	61%	0.3%	960-1150[2]	18%	76%	3%
136. Univ. of Nebraska–Lincoln*	56	3.2	84%	69%	67%	57%	35%	18%	22-28[2]	30%	78%	16%
136. University of New Hampshire*	56	3.0	86%	67%	77%	70%	37%	16%	1090-1280[2]	23%	85%	7%
136. University of St. Thomas (MN)	56	2.6	87%	76%	80%	76%	34%	1%	23-29[2]	22%	89%	9%
136. University of Texas at Dallas*	56	3.0	89%	70%	72%	69%	23%	28%	1220-1450[2]	42%	79%	3%
136. University of the Pacific (CA)	56	2.6	84%	67%	66%	65%	44%	7%	1080-1340[2]	40%	71%	5%
136. University of Tulsa (OK)	56	2.7	87%	88%	73%	61%	56%	3%	23-31[2]	48%	69%	12%
148. Colorado State University*	55	3.1	85%	68%	70%	60%	31%	24%	1070-1280[2]	21%	84%	9%
148. CUNY–City College*	55	2.9	84%	51%	60%	59%	30%	10%	1050-1260[9]	N/A	51%	N/A
148. Duquesne University (PA)	55	2.7	85%	73%	77%	73%	40%	7%	1120-1270[2]	17%	77%	5%
148. George Mason University (VA)*	55	3.2	87%	66%	72%	72%	34%	14%	1100-1300[2]	16%	89%	2%
148. Michigan Technological University*	55	2.8	84%	72%	72%	66%	50%	13%	1160-1350[2]	32%	70%	7%
148. Quinnipiac University (CT)	55	2.7	86%	72%	76%	71%	45%	2%	1080-1260[2]	18%	82%	3%
148. Rutgers University–Camden (NJ)*	55	2.7	86%	53%	65%	57%	36%	11%	980-1170[2]	18%	76%	3%
148. San Diego State University*	55	3.0	89%	64%	78%	74%	26%	25%	1090-1300[2]	33%	37%	4%
148. Thomas Jefferson University (PA)	55	2.5	83%	73%	70%	64%	63%	0%	1090-1270[2]	27%	70%	2%
148. University of Alabama*	55	3.1	87%	77%	72%	56%	36%	22%	23-31	45%	80%	21%
148. University of Alabama at Birmingham*	55	2.9	84%	64%	61%	52%	44%	16%	22-30	29%	67%	5%
148. University of Central Florida*	55	2.9	91%	66%	74%	72%	28%	25%	1160-1340	35%	45%	5%
148. University of Cincinnati*	55	2.9	87%	67%	72%	61%	39%	20%	23-29[2]	25%	76%	8%
148. University of Mississippi*	55	3.0	86%	68%	67%	52%	57%	11%	22-30[2]	23%	88%	8%
162. Belmont University (TN)	54	2.7	83%	76%	71%	63%	53%	0.2%	23-30[2]	29%	83%	9%
162. Florida International University*	54	2.7	90%	53%	66%	68%	35%	16%	1110-1260	28%	58%	5%
162. Hofstra University (NY)	54	2.9	82%	71%	65%	54%	44%	2%	1160-1330[2]	32%	69%	11%
162. Kansas State University*	54	3.0	86%	69%	68%	55%	49%	10%	20-27[2]	25%	95%	16%

Note: Key to footnotes, Page 52

Rank	School (State) (*Public)	Overall score	Peer assessment score (5.0=highest)	Average first-year student retention rate	2020 graduation rate Predicted	2020 graduation rate Actual	Pell recipient grad rate	% of classes under 20 ('20)	% of classes of 50 or more ('20)	SAT/ACT 25th-75th percentile ('20)	Freshmen in top 10% of HS class ('20)	Acceptance rate ('20)	Average alumni giving rate
162.	Mercer University (GA)	54	2.5	87%	72%	73%	71%	54%	6%	1180-1340[2]	39%	78%	10%
162.	Oregon State University*	54	3.1	85%	65%	69%	59%	33%	22%	1080-1310[2]	28%	84%	4%
162.	University of Arkansas*	54	3.0	84%	71%	68%	54%	47%	17%	23-29[2]	29%	78%	16%
162.	University of Hawaii–Manoa*	54	2.8	80%	65%	62%	58%	47%	12%	1060-1260[2]	30%	62%	4%
162.	Univ. of Maryland–Baltimore County*	54	3.0	87%	68%	70%	65%	36%	14%	1150-1350	22%	69%	3%
162.	University of Rhode Island*	54	3.0	85%	64%	69%	62%	42%	10%	1090-1260[9]	19%	76%	4%
172.	Adelphi University (NY)	53	2.4	81%	64%	72%	67%	47%	1%	1060-1250[9]	30%	75%	5%
172.	Chatham University (PA)	53	2.3	80%	59%	62%	58%	69%	0.3%	1050-1250[2]	29%	66%	14%
172.	Louisiana State University–Baton Rouge*	53	2.9	84%	69%	70%	57%	37%	22%	23-28	24%	73%	11%
172.	St. John's University (NY)	53	2.9	83%	59%	64%	61%	37%	2%	1080-1300[2]	20%	75%	4%
172.	University at Albany–SUNY*	53	2.9	82%	59%	65%	64%	28%	19%	1080-1240[2]	18%	57%	6%
172.	Valparaiso University (IN)	53	2.7	83%	68%	65%	55%	62%	6%	1070-1280[2]	36%	87%	11%
172.	Virginia Commonwealth University*	53	3.0	84%	63%	66%	62%	42%	15%	1060-1250[2]	18%	91%	4%
179.	Missouri U. of Science and Technology*	52	2.8	83%	73%	67%	55%	47%	10%	25-31[2]	42%	81%	10%
179.	Montclair State University (NJ)*	52	2.4	81%	49%	68%	65%	26%	3%	980-1160[2]	11%	83%	3%
179.	Ohio University*	52	3.0	81%	62%	66%	55%	33%	11%	21-26[2]	20%	87%	3%
179.	Rowan University (NJ)*	52	2.5	84%	65%	68%	57%	45%	0.3%	1020-1240[2]	N/A	79%	3%
179.	University of Houston*	52	2.9	85%	61%	62%	61%	24%	27%	1120-1310[2]	33%	63%	8%
179.	University of Idaho*	52	2.7	79%	59%	59%	54%	65%	7%	990-1220	18%	74%	8%
179.	Univ. of Massachusetts–Lowell*	52	2.6	85%	64%	69%	67%	31%	11%	1150-1320[2]	25%	75%	9%
179.	Washington State University*	52	3.2	80%	65%	59%	51%	34%	19%	1020-1210[2]	N/A	80%	10%
187.	Oklahoma State University*	51	2.9	83%	66%	64%	51%	37%	20%	21-27[2]	29%	67%	9%
187.	Pacific University (OR)	51	2.5	81%	63%	64%	57%	57%	3%	1050-1230[2]	N/A	89%	5%

One application. 10+ Lenders. Real offers.
Automate Your Private Student Loan Search.

www.sparrowfi.usnews.com

Sparrow

Rank School (State) (*Public)	Overall score	Peer assessment score (5.0=highest)	Average first-year student retention rate	2020 graduation rate		Pell recipient grad rate	% of classes under 20 ('20)	% of classes of 50 or more ('20)	SAT/ACT 25th-75th percentile ('20)	Freshmen in top 10% of HS class ('20)	Accept-ance rate ('20)	Average alumni giving rate
				Predicted	Actual							
187. Robert Morris University (PA)	51	2.2	82%	61%	69%	59%	58%	0%	1040-1230[2]	24%	86%	5%
187. St. John Fisher College (NY)	51	2.2	88%	64%	72%	69%	28%	3%	1060-1240[2]	22%	68%	5%
187. Union University (TN)	51	2.0	85%	69%	66%	56%	76%	0.2%	22-30	36%	58%	3%
187. University of Detroit Mercy	51	2.1	85%	66%	73%	62%	53%	2%	1050-1260[2]	26%	79%	5%
187. University of Louisville (KY)*	51	2.9	81%	67%	60%	50%	42%	9%	21-29[9]	31%	66%	9%
187. University of North Carolina–Wilmington*	51	2.6	85%	69%	74%	66%	46%	7%	23-27	22%	68%	4%
187. University of Saint Joseph (CT)	51	2.2	80%	48%	56%	49%	71%	0%	970-1166[2]	21%	78%	8%
196. Biola University (CA)	50	2.1	84%	68%	71%	65%	59%	4%	1070-1290	28%	64%	6%
196. Indiana University-Purdue U.–Indianapolis*	50	3.0	74%	55%	53%	46%	46%	10%	1000-1190[2]	17%	79%	6%
196. Mississippi State University*	50	2.7	81%	66%	64%	47%	50%	13%	22-30	29%	80%	19%
196. Towson University (MD)*	50	2.6	85%	63%	73%	73%	30%	3%	1040-1200[2]	14%	79%	3%
196. University of New Mexico*	50	2.9	77%	61%	53%	49%	49%	10%	17-25	N/A	54%	N/A
196. University of Wyoming*	50	2.8	78%	68%	59%	52%	46%	11%	21-28[2]	23%	94%	8%
202. Ball State University (IN)*	49	2.7	78%	61%	67%	58%	38%	7%	1020-1200[2]	N/A	69%	9%
202. Bellarmine University (KY)	49	2.2	79%	64%	64%	50%	59%	2%	21-28[2]	N/A	82%	10%
202. Bethel University (MN)	49	2.1	85%	72%	74%	67%	60%	1%	21-28[2]	26%	87%	5%
202. Florida A&M University*	49	2.5	82%	44%	56%	55%	40%	7%	1030-1150	18%	33%	5%
202. Florida Institute of Technology	49	2.6	81%	64%	60%	55%	57%	6%	1130-1330	26%	70%	7%
202. Hampton University (VA)	49	2.4	74%	59%	60%	54%	58%	5%	980-1160[2]	13%	36%	26%
202. Illinois State University*	49	2.6	81%	66%	68%	56%	38%	10%	1020-1220	N/A	81%	5%
202. Loyola University New Orleans	49	2.8	82%	66%	59%	52%	38%	2%	21-26[2]	N/A[5]	72%	4%
202. Maryville Univ. of St. Louis	49	2.0	84%	68%	75%	85%	66%	1%	19-26[2]	26%	95%	5%
202. Misericordia University (PA)	49	2.0	83%	68%	74%	72%	55%	0%	1040-1215[2]	19%	83%	10%
202. Sacred Heart University (CT)	49	2.3	84%	66%	73%	65%	36%	3%	1140-1260[2]	9%	66%	10%
213. California State University–Fresno*	48	2.6	83%	40%	58%	55%	14%	9%	890-1100[2]	15%	90%	3%
213. East Carolina University (NC)*	48	2.5	82%	59%	66%	63%	33%	14%	19-24	13%	88%	2%
213. George Fox University (OR)	48	2.1	83%	65%	68%	66%	48%	3%	1020-1240[2]	32%	91%	6%
213. Kent State University (OH)*	48	2.7	81%	59%	63%	53%	52%	8%	20-26[2]	17%	84%	3%
213. Lipscomb University (TN)	48	2.2	82%	70%	69%	54%	58%	7%	22-29[2]	29%	62%	12%
213. Nova Southeastern University (FL)	48	2.1	80%	64%	62%	63%	63%	5%	1030-1240	28%	76%	3%
213. Pace University (NY)	48	2.6	78%	60%	59%	52%	52%	3%	1060-1240[2]	14%	83%	4%
213. Texas Tech University*	48	3.0	86%	64%	63%	57%	27%	28%	1070-1240[2]	18%	70%	9%
213. Touro College (NY)	48	1.8	84%	46%	63%	47%	87%	0%	1120-1360[2]	N/A	76%	9%
213. University of Hartford (CT)	48	2.5	76%	56%	62%	49%	72%	0.1%	1020-1210[2]	N/A	77%	3%
213. University of Maine*	48	2.9	76%	62%	56%	48%	41%	16%	1050-1250[2]	22%	92%	6%
213. Western New England University (MA)	48	2.1	78%	63%	64%	58%	57%	0.4%	1070-1270[2]	16%	89%	4%
213. Widener University (PA)	48	2.3	80%	60%	65%	56%	64%	2%	1035-1210[2]	N/A	75%	3%
213. Wilkes University (PA)	48	1.9	77%	59%	64%	57%	66%	4%	1040-1230	18%	92%	13%
227. Gannon University (PA)	47	2.0	83%	61%	68%	60%	55%	1%	990-1210[2]	31%[4]	79%	6%
227. Immaculata University (PA)	47	1.9	81%	57%	70%	67%	77%	0%	993-1170[2]	14%	83%	7%
227. New Mexico State University*	47	2.6	75%	52%	51%	45%	62%	8%	17-23	22%	63%	5%
227. Regis University (CO)	47	2.2	79%	63%	67%	57%	59%	0.4%	1000-1220[2]	51%	78%	3%
227. Russell Sage College (NY)	47	2.1	77%	48%	62%	57%	51%	0%	910-1160[2]	1%	74%	6%
227. Seattle Pacific University	47	2.4	79%	68%	65%	50%	59%	2%	1010-1160	N/A	91%	4%
227. St. Catherine University (MN)	47	2.1	80%	58%	69%	64%	64%	2%	19-25[2]	25%	77%	8%
227. University of Colorado Denver*	47	2.9	71%	58%	44%	47%	44%	9%	995-1210[2]	25%	66%	2%
227. Univ. of Massachusetts–Boston*	47	2.8	76%	52%	49%	49%	34%	8%	1010-1210[2]	15%	80%	4%
227. Univ. of Massachusetts–Dartmouth*	47	2.7	72%	53%	52%	47%	47%	9%	990-1190[2]	12%	76%	2%
227. University of Nevada–Reno*	47	2.5	81%	62%	61%	53%	48%	16%	20-26	25%	87%	5%
227. U. of North Carolina–Charlotte*	47	2.9	83%	62%	65%	63%	25%	25%	1100-1280[2]	17%	80%	3%
239. Central Michigan University*	46	2.4	77%	60%	64%	54%	34%	6%	1000-1210	18%[4]	69%	6%
239. Clarke University (IA)	46	2.2	73%	59%	65%	59%	75%	0%	19-25[2]	16%	57%	11%
239. The College of St. Scholastica (MN)	46	1.9	81%	64%	69%	60%	64%	1%	22-27[9]	21%	73%	4%
239. Edgewood College[1] (WI)	46	1.8	78%[8]	62%	63%[8]	N/A	82%[4]	0.3%[4]	20-25[4]	16%[4]	72%[4]	5%[4]
239. Georgia State University*	46	2.9	80%	53%	53%	54%	21%	23%	950-1160[3]	N/A	67%	2%

Note: Key to footnotes, Page 52

Rank	School (State) (*Public)	Overall score	Peer assessment score (5.0=highest)	Average first-year student retention rate	2020 graduation rate		Pell recipient grad rate	% of classes under 20 ('20)	% of classes of 50 or more ('20)	SAT/ACT 25th-75th percentile ('20)	Freshmen in top 10% of HS class ('20)	Accept-ance rate ('20)	Average alumni giving rate
					Predicted	Actual							
239.	Oklahoma City University[7]	46	2.1	81%	75%	64%[6]	N/A	77%	1%	22-29[3]	N/A	72%	3%[4]
239.	UNC Greensboro*	46	2.7	77%	53%	59%	56%	39%	13%	980-1160	15%	88%	4%
239.	University of Indianapolis	46	2.4	74%	59%	62%	48%	55%	1%	960-1170[2]	15%	73%	10%
239.	Univ. of Missouri–St. Louis*	46	2.5	77%	59%	56%	46%	55%[4]	7%[4]	21-27[2]	38%	58%	5%
239.	University of South Dakota*	46	2.7	77%	64%	60%	47%	52%	6%	20-25[2]	15%	91%	4%
249.	Bowling Green State University (OH)*	45	2.7	78%	58%	61%	50%	39%	12%	20-26	19%	75%	4%
249.	Harding University (AR)	45	1.9	85%	70%	72%	62%	60%	4%	21-29	32%	55%	9%
249.	Lesley University[1] (MA)	45	2.2	80%[8]	62%	60%[6]	N/A	70%[4]	0%[4]	1000-1210[4]	5%[4]	75%[4]	N/A
249.	Lincoln Memorial University (TN)	45	1.9	75%	55%	53%	43%	69%	3%	19-25[9]	23%	69%	4%
249.	Sam Houston State University (TX)*	45	2.4	77%	50%	59%	57%	30%	11%	970-1120[2]	33%	92%	6%
249.	University of Memphis*	45	2.6	77%	52%	51%	43%	48%	8%	19-26	19%	85%	4%
249.	Univ. of Missouri–Kansas City*	45	2.6	75%	63%	54%	43%	68%	5%	20-28[2]	33%	63%	4%
249.	University of Nevada–Las Vegas*	45	2.8	77%	54%	44%	41%	38%	13%	19-25	22%	81%	3%
249.	University of New England (ME)	45	2.2	78%	63%	62%	57%	53%	7%	1040-1210[2]	N/A	87%	5%
249.	University of North Dakota*	45	2.7	80%	69%	61%	49%	39%	14%	21-26[2]	23%	87%	6%
249.	University of St. Francis (IL)	45	2.0	80%	55%	60%	51%	73%	0%	970-1170[2]	N/A	60%	5%
249.	Utah State University*	45	2.7	72%	63%	48%	48%	51%	11%	21-29	22%	91%	4%
249.	Wayne State University (MI)*	45	2.6	80%	56%	52%	45%	27%	14%	1000-1200[2]	N/A	68%	4%
249.	West Virginia University[1]*	45	2.9	78%[8]	63%	59%[6]	N/A	N/A	N/A	1030-1230[4]	N/A	84%[4]	N/A
263.	Azusa Pacific University (CA)	44	2.1	79%[8]	61%	66%	54%	68%	2%	1040-1290[2]	N/A	94%	N/A
263.	Baker University (KS)	44	1.9	76%	59%	62%	54%	76%	0%	19-24	11%	93%	7%
263.	Delaware State University*	44	2.3	72%	44%	48%	45%	52%	2%	810-1010	10%	39%	14%
263.	Inter American U. of Puerto Rico–San German	44	1.9	79%[8]	25%	44%[8]	44%[4]	47%	2%	N/A[2]	N/A	45%	N/A
263.	Montana State University*	44	2.6	77%	67%	56%	43%	47%	12%	21-28[2]	20%	81%	7%
263.	Old Dominion University (VA)*	44	2.7	79%	53%	53%	46%	34%	9%	960-1170[2]	10%	95%	4%
263.	Shenandoah University (VA)	44	2.0	82%	60%	61%	58%	62%	8%	990-1220[2]	15%	74%	4%
263.	Southern Illinois University–Carbondale*	44	2.4	74%	54%	47%	35%	67%	3%	970-1345[2]	15%	92%	4%
263.	University of Alabama–Huntsville*	44	2.5	83%	68%	57%	48%	31%	9%	24-31	33%	77%	1%
263.	University of Findlay (OH)	44	1.9	80%	69%	63%[6]	N/A	65%	2%	20-26	22%[4]	79%	9%
263.	University of Nebraska–Omaha*	44	2.7	76%	57%	56%	44%	39%	6%	18-26	20%	82%	4%
263.	University of North Florida*	44	2.4	82%	61%	61%	58%	27%	13%	1040-1230	14%	80%	2%
263.	University of the Incarnate Word (TX)	44	2.0	75%	49%	58%	53%	62%	2%	950-1140[2]	18%	97%	4%
263.	Western Michigan University*	44	2.5	79%	58%	57%	49%	44%	10%	1010-1220[2]	14%	85%	4%
277.	Campbell University (NC)	43	2.2	75%	59%	54%	42%	57%	4%	1010-1210[2]	24%	81%	5%
277.	Concordia University Wisconsin	43	2.1	80%	65%	62%	53%	57%	2%	20-26[2]	32%	71%	3%
277.	Florida Atlantic University*	43	2.5	82%	54%	55%	56%	17%	22%	1060-1220	15%	75%	4%
277.	Gardner-Webb University[1] (NC)	43	2.0	74%[8]	59%	54%[6]	N/A	73%[4]	0%[4]	970-1180[4]	13%[4]	67%[4]	1%[4]
277.	Louisiana Tech University*	43	2.6	80%	62%	62%	49%	48%	8%	22-28	25%	64%	9%
277.	North Carolina A&T State Univ.*	43	2.4	79%	45%	52%	48%	28%	5%	960-1130	14%	57%	10%
277.	North Dakota State University*	43	2.6	80%	68%	62%	50%	34%	24%	20-26[9]	16%	94%	5%
277.	Regent University (VA)	43	1.8	78%	52%	61%	53%	69%	0%	940-1220	15%	50%	1%
277.	Tennessee Tech Univ.*	43	2.3	77%	61%	57%	48%	52%	9%	21-28[2]	31%	80%	6%
277.	University of Montana*	43	2.8	71%	60%	48%	37%	59%	8%	20-27	16%	96%	8%
277.	University of North Texas*	43	2.6	79%	58%	58%	57%	31%	19%	1050-1240[2]	20%	84%	4%
288.	Dallas Baptist University	42	2.1	74%	63%	56%	41%	66%	3%	980-1200	18%	99%	1%
288.	East Tennessee State University*	42	2.2	75%[8]	55%	50%	40%	56%	6%	20-27[2]	34%	78%	N/A
288.	Long Island University (NY)	42	2.2	76%[8]	53%	45%	42%	64%	1%	1080-1290	19%	85%	3%
288.	Marshall University (WV)*	42	2.5	74%	53%	51%	42%	50%	4%	940-1150	N/A	89%	3%
288.	Middle Tennessee State Univ.*	42	2.3	77%	54%	51%	44%	60%	5%	20-26	N/A	94%	3%
288.	Northern Arizona University*	42	2.6	76%	58%	57%	50%	22%	19%	19-25[2]	22%	82%	2%
288.	Portland State University (OR)*	42	2.6	73%	52%	48%	44%	39%	11%	1000-1190[2]	16%	95%	1%
288.	South Dakota State University*	42	2.6	78%	65%	59%	47%	30%	19%	20-26[2]	18%	89%	7%
288.	University of Hawaii at Hilo*	42	2.6	70%	53%	38%	45%	50%	3%	16-22	16%	45%	N/A
288.	University of Puerto Rico–Río Piedras[1]*	42	2.4	81%[8]	54%	57%[6]	N/A	N/A	N/A	N/A[2]	N/A	49%[4]	N/A
288.	University of Texas at Arlington*	42	2.7	74%	56%	52%	51%	29%	30%	1050-1250[2]	28%	88%	1%

School (State) (*Public)	Peer assessment score (5.0=highest)	Average first-year student retention rate	2020 graduation rate Predicted	2020 graduation rate Actual	Pell recipient grad rate	% of classes under 20 ('20)	% of classes of 50 or more ('20)	SAT/ACT 25th-75th percentile ('20)	Freshmen in top 10% of HS class ('20)	Accept- ance rate ('20)	Average alumni giving rate
SCHOOLS RANKED 299 THROUGH 391 ARE LISTED HERE ALPHABETICALLY											
Alliant International University (CA)	1.4	67%[8]	46%	21%[8]	N/A	N/A	N/A	N/A[2]	N/A	67%[4]	N/A
Andrews University[1] (MI)	1.8	85%[8]	66%	57%[6]	N/A	68%[4]	3%[4]	21-29[4]	17%[4]	67%[4]	4%[4]
Arkansas State University*	2.2	76%	58%	51%	41%	66%	3%	20-26[2]	25%	67%	9%
Augusta University (GA)*	2.2	73%	59%	33%[6]	N/A	N/A	N/A	1020-1210[3]	N/A	83%	3%
Aurora University[1] (IL)	1.9	74%[8]	52%	54%[6]	N/A	N/A	N/A	965-1130[4]	N/A	87%[4]	N/A
Barry University (FL)	2.1	64%	44%	36%	34%	65%	0.1%	900-1070	N/A	66%	N/A
Benedictine University (IL)	2.1	70%	55%	46%	42%	65%	0.3%	980-1160[2]	13%[4]	61%	3%
Boise State University (ID)*	2.7	80%	58%	54%	45%	44%	9%	1030-1210[2]	12%[5]	77%	5%
Cardinal Stritch University (WI)	1.8	70%	51%	50%	42%	83%	0%	17-23[2]	21%	77%	1%
Carson-Newman University (TN)	2.0	68%	57%	52%	46%	62%	0.2%	19-25	N/A	79%	9%
Clark Atlanta University	2.4	69%	39%	42%	39%	42%	7%	880-1040	10%	59%	11%
Cleveland State University*	2.3	73%	52%	48%	41%	36%	9%	18-24[4]	14%[4]	100%	3%
Colorado Technical University[1]	2.2	42%[8]	31%	23%[6]	N/A	N/A	N/A	N/A[2]	N/A	N/A	N/A
Daemen College (NY)	1.7	78%	57%	59%	49%	82%	0%	1060-1250[2]	24%	62%	5%
D'Youville College (NY)	1.8	78%	60%	60%	52%	53%	1%	960-1150	10%	84%	10%
Eastern Michigan University*	2.4	71%	53%	47%	39%	49%	2%	980-1200	16%	75%	1%
Ferris State University (MI)*	2.1	78%	53%	59%	47%	50%	2%	940-1160[2]	N/A	82%	1%
Georgia Southern University*	2.5	79%	62%	54%	52%	35%	7%	993-1170	20%[5]	91%	N/A
Grand Canyon University[1] (AZ)	1.8	65%[8]	50%	40%[6]	N/A	N/A	N/A	N/A[2]	N/A	77%[4]	N/A
Husson University (ME)	1.8	75%	53%	58%	48%	62%	0%	960-1140[2]	14%	85%	3%
Idaho State University[1]*	2.4	64%[8]	56%	32%[6]	N/A	N/A	N/A	N/A[2]	N/A	N/A	N/A
Indiana State University*	2.5	66%	46%	41%	32%	44%	6%	910-1130[2]	11%	92%	5%
Indiana Univ. of Pennsylvania*	2.1	72%	51%	54%	43%	37%	13%	930-1130[9]	11%	93%	4%
Inter Amer. U. of Puerto Rico–Metrop. Campus[1]	2.0	72%[8]	34%	34%[6]	35%[4]	56%[4]	2%[4]	N/A[2]	N/A	26%[4]	N/A
Jackson State University (MS)*	2.1	66%	43%	44%	39%	N/A	N/A	17-20	N/A	90%	N/A
Keiser University[1] (FL)	1.7	81%[8]	39%	57%[6]	N/A	45%[4]	30%[4]	N/A[2]	N/A	85%[4]	N/A
Kennesaw State University (GA)*	2.5	79%	63%	47%	42%	25%	16%	1030-1200	13%	83%	1%
Lamar University (TX)*	2.1	66%	49%	37%	29%	48%	8%	940-1120	12%	84%	1%
Liberty University (VA)	1.7	83%	55%	58%	45%	39%	4%	1040-1250	N/A[5]	50%	1%
Lindenwood University (MO)	1.9	72%	58%	47%	33%	49%	0%	19-25[2]	N/A	92%	1%
Mary Baldwin University (VA)	2.0	67%	45%	42%	41%	62%	1%	940-1120[2]	10%[4]	87%	6%
Metropolitan State University[1] (MN)*	1.9	72%[8]	34%	33%[6]	N/A	N/A	N/A	N/A[2]	N/A	56%[4]	N/A
Mississippi College	2.0	78%	68%	66%	49%	63%	2%	21-29[3]	35%	29%	2%
Missouri State University[1]*	2.4	78%[8]	63%	55%[6]	N/A	N/A	N/A	21-27[4]	N/A	88%[4]	N/A
Morgan State University (MD)*	2.4	73%	43%	46%	42%	38%	3%	920-1070	8%	73%	14%
National Louis University (IL)	2.0	62%	35%	31%[6]	N/A	63%	0%	N/A[2]	N/A	97%	N/A
Northern Illinois University*	2.5	74%	51%	48%	38%	46%	10%	900-1140[2]	14%	59%	3%
Northern Kentucky University*	2.2	72%	55%	48%	36%	41%[4]	3%[4]	20-26[2]	16%	87%	3%
Oakland University (MI)*	2.3	77%	60%	56%	48%	37%	10%	980-1210[2]	20%	81%	2%
Our Lady of the Lake University (TX)	1.9	64%	41%	38%	35%	68%	0%	890-1060[2]	13%	98%	7%
Palm Beach Atlantic University (FL)	1.8	75%	60%	58%	47%	64%	1%	1000-1210[2]	N/A	92%	2%
Pontifical Catholic U. of Puerto Rico–Ponce[1]	2.3	81%[8]	25%	42%[6]	N/A	N/A	N/A	N/A[2]	N/A	93%[4]	N/A
Roosevelt University (IL)	2.1	70%	50%	44%	38%	56%	0.4%	890-1130[9]	N/A	77%	3%
Southern Illinois University Edwardsville*	2.2	76%	61%	52%	36%	51%	7%	21-27[9]	21%	85%	3%
Spalding University[1] (KY)	1.8	70%[8]	49%	41%[6]	N/A	N/A	N/A	17-22[4]	N/A	79%[4]	N/A
Stephen F. Austin State University[1] (TX)*	2.4	71%[8]	53%	48%[6]	N/A	N/A	N/A	990-1180[4]	N/A	68%[4]	N/A
Tennessee State University*	2.3	63%	39%	31%	29%	N/A	N/A	16-20	N/A	57%	N/A
Texas A&M University–Commerce*	2.3	65%	45%	43%	34%	38%	7%	955-1150[2]	19%	32%	2%
Texas A&M University–Corpus Christi*	2.3	58%	49%	37%	33%	37%	12%	1000-1180	16%	90%	2%
Texas A&M Univ.–Kingsville*	2.2	68%	42%	45%	40%	36%	4%	920-1090[2]	16%	88%	2%
Texas Southern University*	2.1	54%	33%	19%	17%	45%	6%	890-1030	9%	66%	5%
Texas State University*	2.3	77%	54%	55%	49%	33%	15%	1010-1180	11%	85%	2%
Texas Wesleyan University	2.2	56%	51%	34%	45%	70%	0.2%	1008-1160	N/A	19%[4]	5%
Texas Woman's University*	2.4	75%	47%	48%	43%	44%	11%	940-1140[2]	18%	94%	1%

Note: Key to footnotes, Page 52.

School (State) (*Public)	Peer assessment score (5.0=highest)	Average first-year student retention rate	2020 graduation rate Predicted	2020 graduation rate Actual	Pell recipient grad rate	% of classes under 20 ('20)	% of classes of 50 or more ('20)	SAT/ACT 25th-75th percentile ('20)	Freshmen in top 10% of HS class ('20)	Acceptance rate ('20)	Average alumni giving rate
CONTINUED (SCHOOLS RANKED 299 THROUGH 391 ARE LISTED HERE ALPHABETICALLY)											
Trevecca Nazarene University (TN)	1.8	75%[8]	59%	55%	51%	76%	4%	20-25	18%	63%	4%
Trinity International University[1] (IL)	1.9	63%[8]	55%	52%[6]	N/A	N/A	N/A	930-1160[4]	N/A	60%[4]	N/A
Union Institute and University[1] (OH)	1.9	55%[8]	24%	35%[8]	N/A	N/A	N/A	N/A[2]	N/A	N/A	N/A
U. Ana G. Mendez–Gurabo Campus[1] (PR)	2.0	77%[8]	19%	29%[6]	N/A	N/A	N/A	N/A[2]	N/A	N/A	N/A
University of Akron (OH)*	2.3	73%	56%	53%	39%	29%	8%	19-26	19%	77%	2%
University of Alaska–Fairbanks[1]*	2.6	74%[8]	61%	40%[6]	N/A	N/A	N/A	1030-1280[4]	N/A	76%[4]	N/A
University of Arkansas at Little Rock*	2.4	69%	52%	40%	34%	N/A	N/A	18-25	N/A	62%	N/A
University of Bridgeport[1] (CT)	1.9	69%[8]	41%	43%[6]	N/A	N/A	N/A	910-1100[4]	N/A	55%[4]	N/A
University of Central Arkansas*	2.1	75%	55%	46%	34%	48%	1%	20-27[2]	23%	94%	7%
University of Charleston (WV)	2.3	65%	50%	46%	38%	63%	0%	19-23[2]	N/A	61%	4%
University of Colorado–Colorado Springs*	2.7	69%	60%	45%	38%	40%	6%	1010-1200	13%	90%	3%
University of Louisiana at Lafayette*	2.3	75%	58%	51%	41%	34%[4]	9%[4]	20-26	19%	67%	4%
University of Louisiana–Monroe*	2.1	73%	57%	58%	50%	45%	11%	20-24	23%	77%	3%
University of Mary (ND)	1.9	80%[8]	64%	59%	41%	66%	3%	20-26	N/A	97%	N/A
Univ. of Maryland Eastern Shore*	2.2	66%	44%	41%	38%	77%	2%	840-1010[2]	N/A	62%	4%
University of Michigan–Flint*	2.3	74%	52%	38%	30%	43%	3%	970-1210	19%	77%	3%
University of New Orleans*	2.4	68%	52%	42%	40%	32%	12%	18-24[2]	13%	83%	3%
University of Northern Colorado*	2.4	71%	57%	52%	40%	48%	6%	980-1200	15%	88%	2%
University of Phoenix[1] (AZ)	1.4	33%[8]	29%	11%[6]	N/A	N/A	N/A	N/A[2]	N/A	N/A	N/A
University of South Alabama*	2.1	76%	57%	45%	38%	54%	5%	20-27[2]	N/A	73%	5%
Univ. of Southern Mississippi*	2.3	72%	55%	50%	40%	32%	17%	19-26	N/A	96%	6%
University of Tennessee–Chattanooga*	2.6	74%	62%	50%	46%	36%	11%	21-26	N/A	83%	4%
University of Texas at San Antonio*	2.7	75%	53%	46%	47%	15%	39%	1020-1210	18%	84%	4%
University of Texas at Tyler*	2.2	65%	57%	43%	40%	48%	14%	1030-1220	14%	92%	2%
University of Texas–El Paso*	2.6	75%	44%	44%	41%	32%	16%	900-1100[2]	18%	100%	3%
University of Texas–Rio Grande Valley*	2.2	77%	41%	46%[6]	N/A	18%	20%	17-22	22%	80%	0.3%
University of the Cumberlands[1] (KY)	1.9	64%[8]	51%	39%[6]	N/A	N/A	N/A	18-24[4]	N/A	80%[4]	N/A
University of Toledo (OH)*	2.4	76%	58%	53%	38%	42%	12%	20-26[2]	23%	95%	5%
University of West Georgia*	2.2	71%	46%	44%	41%	43%	7%	900-1040	N/A	78%	1%
Univ. of Wisconsin–Milwaukee*	2.9	74%	55%	46%	38%	46%[4]	10%[4]	19-24[2]	12%	97%	3%
Valdosta State University (GA)*	2.2	69%	50%	40%	35%	55%[4]	3%[4]	930-1100	N/A	78%	2%
Washburn University (KS)*	2.2	69%	55%	51%	38%	56%	3%	18-24[2]	15%	93%	8%
Western Kentucky University*	2.3	73%	59%	55%	42%	45%	5%	19-26[2]	20%	98%	5%
Wichita State University (KS)*	2.5	73%	60%	48%	38%	46%	8%	20-27[2]	23%	55%	6%
William Carey University (MS)	1.8	80%	49%	51%	48%	79%	1%	20-28	27%	55%	3%
William Woods University[1] (MO)	1.9	73%[8]	60%	59%[6]	N/A	N/A	N/A	20-26[4]	N/A	64%[4]	N/A
Wilmington University (DE)	2.2	58%	47%	23%	12%	96%	0%	N/A[2]	N/A	99%	N/A
Wingate University (NC)	2.1	68%	58%	49%	43%	39%	0.4%	930-1140	11%	88%	8%[4]
Wright State University (OH)*	2.4	64%	56%	43%	32%	N/A	N/A	18-25[2]	21%	96%	N/A

► The Top 30 Public National Universities

Rank School (State)	Rank School (State)	Rank School (State)	Rank School (State)
1. University of California–Los Angeles	9. University of California–Irvine	17. Ohio State University–Columbus	23. Rutgers U.–New Brunswick (NJ)
2. University of California–Berkeley	10. Georgia Institute of Technology	17. Purdue University– West Lafayette (IN)	23. University of Connecticut
3. University of Michigan–Ann Arbor	10. University of California–Davis	19. Florida State University	26. Indiana University–Bloomington
4. University of Virginia	10. University of Texas at Austin	20. U. of Maryland–College Park	26. Texas A&M University
5. University of California– Santa Barbara	10. William & Mary (VA)	20. University of Pittsburgh	26. University of Massachusetts– Amherst
5. University of Florida	14. University of Wisconsin–Madison	20. University of Washington	26. University of Minnesota–Twin Cities
5. U. of North Carolina–Chapel Hill	15. University of Illinois– Urbana-Champaign	23. Pennsylvania State U.– University Park	30. Clemson University (SC)
8. University of California–San Diego	16. University of Georgia		30. Virginia Tech

Best
National Liberal

						2020 graduation rate				
Rank	School (State) (*Public)	Overall score	Peer assessment score (5.0=highest)	Graduation and retention rank	Average first-year student retention rate	Predicted	Actual	Over-performance (+) Under-performance (-)	Pell recipient grad rate	Soc mob ra
1.	Williams College (MA)	100	4.7	1	96%	95%	96%	+1	96%	98
2.	Amherst College (MA)	98	4.6	2	95%	92%	95%	+3	93%	38
3.	Swarthmore College (PA)	94	4.6	2	95%	92%	97%	+5	98%	13
4.	Pomona College (CA)	93	4.5	6	95%	92%	94%	+2	91%	8
5.	Wellesley College (MA)	92	4.5	14	95%	92%	94%	+2	95%	9
6.	Bowdoin College (ME)	91	4.5	2	95%	93%	95%	+2	96%	14
6.	United States Naval Academy (MD)*	91	4.3	10	97%	91%	90%	-1	N/A	N/A
8.	Claremont McKenna College (CA)	90	4.3	14	94%	92%	92%	None	91%	18
9.	Carleton College (MN)	89	4.3	6	96%	90%	93%	+3	84%	18
9.	Middlebury College (VT)	89	4.3	6	94%	93%	94%	+1	88%	14
11.	United States Military Academy (NY)*	88	4.3	32	97%	88%	85%	-3	N/A	N/A
11.	Washington and Lee University (VA)	88	4.0	2	97%	93%	93%	None	96%	19
13.	Davidson College (NC)	87	4.3	14	95%	90%	93%	+3	94%	13
13.	Grinnell College (IA)	87	4.3	32	91%	89%	87%	-2	88%	4
13.	Hamilton College (NY)	87	4.0	10	94%	91%	91%	None	90%	12
16.	Haverford College (PA)	86	4.2	10	95%	94%	93%	-1	92%	12
17.	Barnard College (NY)	84	4.1	10	95%	90%	90%	None	89%	6
17.	Colby College (ME)	84	4.1	23	93%	91%	90%	-1	98%	19
17.	Colgate University (NY)	84	4.1	18	94%	90%	91%	+1	91%	19
17.	Smith College (MA)	84	4.3	32	89%	88%	87%	-1	85%	12
17.	Wesleyan University (CT)	84	4.1	18	94%	85%	91%	+6	89%	12
22.	United States Air Force Academy (CO)*	83	4.2	40	95%	91%	87%	-4	N/A	N/A
22.	University of Richmond (VA)	83	4.0	25	94%	88%	88%	None	91%	12
22.	Vassar College (NY)	83	4.2	18	95%	90%	88%	-2	86%	3
25.	Bates College (ME)	82	4.1	18	93%	90%	92%	+2	98%	18
26.	Colorado College	81	4.0	29	93%	91%	88%	-3	91%	18
27.	Macalester College (MN)	80	4.0	18	93%	87%	93%	+6	96%	10
28.	Harvey Mudd College (CA)	79	4.4	6	96%	94%	93%	-1	84%	6
29.	Soka University of America (CA)	78	2.8	23	93%	85%	87%	+2	79%	6
30.	Berea College (KY)	77	3.5	121	84%	52%	67%	+15	66%	
30.	Bryn Mawr College (PA)	77	4.1	42	90%	90%	85%	-5	88%	15
30.	Kenyon College (OH)	77	3.9	25	91%	90%	89%	-1	87%	20
30.	Mount Holyoke College (MA)	77	3.9	47	89%	84%	84%	None	92%	12
30.	Scripps College (CA)	77	3.9	29	89%	93%	88%	-5	92%	20
35.	College of the Holy Cross (MA)	76	3.7	14	93%	85%	93%	+8	90%	13
35.	Pitzer College (CA)	76	3.8	42	90%	86%	84%	-2	91%	14
37.	Oberlin College and Conservatory (OH)	75	3.9	40	89%	91%	86%	-5	86%	20
38.	Bucknell University (PA)	74	3.9	25	93%	91%	88%	-3	87%	20
38.	Lafayette College (PA)	74	3.6	25	92%	89%	90%	+1	85%	20
38.	Skidmore College (NY)	74	3.7	32	91%	83%	86%	+3	94%	15
38.	Whitman College (WA)	74	3.4	37	87%	87%	86%	-1	80%	20
42.	Denison University (OH)	72	3.6	47	89%	78%	80%	+2	78%	11
42.	Franklin & Marshall College (PA)	72	3.6	42	90%	85%	85%	None	83%	9
42.	Occidental College (CA)	72	3.7	42	89%	83%	84%	+1	81%	8
42.	Thomas Aquinas College (CA)	72	2.9	42	92%	73%	84%	+11	83%	
46.	DePauw University (IN)	71	3.4	47	89%	81%	87%	+6	87%	
46.	Furman University (SC)	71	3.6	61	89%	82%	81%	-1	77%	20
46.	Hillsdale College (MI)	71	2.6	32	94%	85%	88%	+3	N/A	N/A
46.	Trinity College (CT)	71	3.6	54	90%	84%	82%	-2	86%	19
50.	Connecticut College	70	3.6	47	90%	85%	82%	-3	87%	14
50.	Dickinson College (PA)	70	3.5	54	88%	84%	84%	None	83%	19
50.	Union College (NY)	70	3.4	37	92%	90%	86%	-4	90%	15
50.	The University of the South (TN)	70	3.6	63	88%	81%	80%	-1	79%	11

Note: Key to footnotes, Page 52

Arts Colleges

Faculty resources rank	% of classes under 20 ('20)	% of classes of 50 or more ('20)	Student/faculty ratio ('20)	Selectivity rank	SAT/ACT 25th-75th percentile ('20)	Freshmen in top 10% of HS class ('20)	Acceptance rate ('20)	Financial resources rank	Average alumni giving rate
2	84%	1%	6/1	1	1410-1560[2]	95%	15%	2	47%
8	80%	2%	7/1	5	1410-1550[2]	85%	12%	5	42%
3	76%	1%	7/1	3	1395-1540[2]	93%	9%	6	31%
3	78%	0.2%	7/1	3	1390-1540[2]	90%	9%	8	23%
0	71%	0.2%	7/1	8	1350-1520[2]	85%	20%	8	40%
3	78%	1%	8/1	10	1330-1510[2]	84%	9%	14	42%
3	80%	1%	8/1	27	1230-1450	55%	9%	3	16%
3	82%	0%	8/1	22	1330-1500[2]	73%[5]	13%	14	33%
7	66%	0%	8/1	16	30-34[2]	70%	21%	33	41%
1	64%	3%	8/1	10	1340-1520[2]	80%	22%	7	33%
2	96%	0%	7/1	44	1210-1440	43%	9%	12	38%
1	78%	0%	8/1	9	1350-1500[2]	80%	24%	30	38%
7	72%	0.2%	9/1	14	1300-1460[2]	76%	20%	30	39%
9	65%	0%	8/1	14	30-34	72%	19%	19	27%
5	76%	0.4%	9/1	5	1380-1510[2]	86%	18%	29	37%
2	77%	1%	9/1	2	1360-1520[2]	94%	18%	26	32%
7	74%	8%	9/1	5	1350-1518[2]	90%	14%	36	21%
1	68%	2%	10/1	12	1380-1520[2]	74%	10%	25	34%
3	67%	2%	9/1	31	1300-1470[2]	65%[5]	27%	30	32%
1	68%	3%	7/1	16	1325-1510[2]	72%	37%	19	26%
3	74%	3%	8/1	18	1340-1520[2]	67%	21%	42	24%
3	79%	0.3%	6/1	31	29-33	55%	13%	3	14%
5	73%	0%	8/1	31	1280-1460	50%	31%	19	22%
1	68%	0.3%	8/1	12	1360-1520[2]	73%	25%	17	22%
2	65%	0.4%	10/1	31	1210-1420[2]	60%	14%	48	34%
1	75%	0%	9/1	19	1240-1460[2]	73%	14%	19	18%
4	69%	0.4%	10/1	20	1280-1450[2]	66%	39%	48	29%
6	63%	6%	8/1	48	1490-1570	N/A	18%	24	17%
4	96%	0%	7/1	51	1180-1410[2]	60%[5]	52%	1	17%
4	83%	0.1%	9/1	109	22-26[2]	25%	33%	17	14%
9	75%	3%	8/1	22	1240-1500[2]	66%	38%	33	29%
5	79%	0%	9/1	38	1280-1460[2]	55%[5]	37%	37	29%
3	76%	1%	9/1	35	1270-1500[2]	49%	52%	37	30%
7	78%	0%	9/1	22	1320-1480[2]	75%[5]	35%	33	17%
6	52%	1%	10/1	38	1290-1430[2]	61%[5]	38%	56	41%
5	81%	0%	9/1	25	1325-1510[2]	51%	17%	37	19%
3	82%	1%	9/1	35	1270-1450[2]	51%	35%	42	22%
6	49%	2%	9/1	41	1220-1400[2]	54%	38%	37	23%
9	68%	1%	10/1	27	1250-1440[2]	61%	36%	42	26%
9	72%	1%	8/1	51	1220-1403[2]	33%	32%	50	19%
0	76%	0%	8/1	41	1230-1430[2]	49%	54%	50	27%
9	72%	0%	9/1	20	1220-1430[2]	71%	28%	62	16%
9	63%	1%	9/1	35	1210-1440[2]	61%	37%	50	18%
1	69%	0.2%	8/1	25	1270-1460	59%	41%	50	17%
3	100%	0%	11/1	74	1200-1380	20%[5]	86%	67	37%
8	81%	0%	8/1	66	1110-1360	43%	68%	64	19%
7	81%	0%	9/1	41	28-32[2]	44%	65%	50	21%
1	77%	1%	9/1	56	29-33[2]	N/A	36%	16	14%
7	71%	0.4%	9/1	71	1290-1450[2]	51%[5]	36%	26	25%
9	74%	2%	9/1	59	1310-1450[2]	54%	38%	56	26%[4]
0	79%	0%	9/1	46	1220-1380[2]	49%	52%	67	23%
3	69%	0%	9/1	27	1210-1400[2]	58%	41%	60	21%
1	59%	0%	10/1	69	25-30[2]	31%	56%	56	30%

What Is a National Liberal Arts College?

THE COUNTRY'S 223 liberal arts colleges emphasize undergraduate education and award at least half of their degrees in the arts and sciences, which include such disciplines as English, the biological and physical sciences, history, foreign languages, and the visual and performing arts but exclude professional disciplines such as business, education and nursing. There are 199 private and 24 public liberal arts colleges; none are for-profit. The top public colleges appear below.

The Top 10 Public Colleges

Rank School (State)

1. United States Naval Academy (MD)
2. United States Military Academy (NY)
3. United States Air Force Academy (CO)
4. Virginia Military Institute
5. New College of Florida
6. St. Mary's College of Maryland
7. Massachusetts Col. of Liberal Arts
8. University of Minnesota Morris
9. U. of North Carolina Asheville
10. Purchase College–SUNY

Rank, School (State) (*Public)	Overall score	Peer assessment score (5.0=highest)	Average first-year student retention rate	2020 graduation rate Predicted	2020 graduation rate Actual	Pell recipient grad rate	% of classes under 20 ('20)	% of classes of 50 or more ('20)	SAT/ACT 25th-75th percentile ('20)	Freshmen in top 10% of HS class ('20)	Accept-ance rate ('20)	Average alumni giving rate
54. Gettysburg College (PA)	68	3.5	91%	88%	85%	87%	70%	1%	1270-1410[2]	60%	48%	20%
54. Rhodes College (TN)	68	3.6	90%	81%	82%	84%	76%	0%	27-32[2]	53%	51%	24%
54. Spelman College (GA)	68	3.8	89%	63%	75%	68%	52%	1%	1050-1200	30%	53%	30%
57. St. Lawrence University (NY)	67	3.3	90%	78%	80%	72%	67%	1%	1180-1360[2]	40%	47%	19%
57. Wabash College (IN)	67	3.3	87%	74%	75%	60%	74%	1%	1120-1320[2]	30%	63%	39%
59. Centre College (KY)	66	3.4	90%	80%	83%	76%	59%	0.3%	26-32[2]	46%	72%	37%
59. Principia College (IL)	66	2.2	89%	73%	75%	N/A	100%	0%	1018-1206[2]	17%[5]	93%	21%[4]
59. Wheaton College (IL)	66	3.2	92%	80%	88%	89%	68%	1%	1210-1450[2]	49%	87%	17%
62. Bard College (NY)	65	3.5	83%	88%	74%	73%	87%	1%	1220-1418[2]	34%	59%	15%
62. Lawrence University (WI)	65	3.2	87%	77%	79%	71%	80%	1%	26-32[2]	40%	69%	28%
62. Reed College[1] (OR)	65	3.7	89%[8]	89%	79%[6]	N/A	N/A	N/A	1325-1520[4]	N/A	39%[4]	N/A
62. St. Olaf College (MN)	65	3.6	91%	81%	85%	84%	50%	3%	25-32[2]	39%	51%	17%
66. Agnes Scott College (GA)	64	3.4	84%	73%	72%	69%	58%	0%	1080-1290[2]	33%	68%	25%
67. Muhlenberg College (PA)	63	3.1	89%	79%	82%	99%	83%	0.3%	1170-1350[2]	40%	62%	16%
67. St. John's College (MD)	63	3.4	84%	80%	66%	64%	98%	0%	1130-1440[2]	25%	61%	21%
67. Virginia Military Institute*	63	3.1	85%	73%	85%	81%	83%	0%	1070-1260[3]	12%	60%	25%
67. Wofford College (SC)	63	3.2	90%	77%	80%	79%	58%	0%	1160-1328[2]	34%	53%	19%
71. College of Wooster (OH)	62	3.3	87%	79%	74%	66%	74%	1%	24-31[2]	46%	65%	16%
71. Kalamazoo College (MI)	62	3.3	88%	75%	79%	75%	54%	0.4%	1150-1360[2]	42%	74%	23%
71. Sarah Lawrence College (NY)	62	3.4	79%	82%	73%	78%	88%	0.3%	1220-1410[2]	29%	55%	17%
71. Willamette University (OR)	62	3.2	84%	75%	74%	70%	77%	0%	1130-1360[2]	46%	80%	11%
75. Beloit College (WI)	61	3.2	83%	74%	78%	76%	76%	0.4%	21-29[2]	28%	58%	12%
75. Hobart & William Smith Colleges (NY)	61	3.3	85%	78%	77%	80%	64%	0%	1180-1360[2]	36%	62%	19%
75. Juniata College[1] (PA)	61	2.9	84%[8]	70%	80%[6]	N/A	73%[4]	1%[4]	1118-1320[4]	30%[4]	71%[4]	23%[4]
75. St. John's College (NM)	61	3.3	72%	75%	67%	80%	100%	0%	1180-1430[2]	47%	69%	18%
79. Bennington College (VT)	60	2.9	79%	80%	71%	63%	89%	0.4%	1240-1400[2]	39%	60%	17%
79. Gustavus Adolphus College (MN)	60	3.3	88%	72%	78%	82%	68%	0.2%	24-30[2]	29%	71%	18%
79. Knox College (IL)	60	3.1	83%	67%	71%	60%	75%	1%	1080-1320[2]	24%	71%	27%
82. Lake Forest College (IL)	59	3.0	86%	65%	75%	75%	56%	0.3%	1085-1290[2]	41%	58%	19%
82. Lewis & Clark College (OR)	59	3.4	83%	76%	74%	66%	61%	1%	1198-1380[2]	29%	81%	14%
82. New College of Florida*	59	3.0	80%	74%	63%	60%	88%	0%	1160-1375	25%	70%	12%
85. Allegheny College (PA)	58	3.1	83%	72%	73%	63%	81%	0.2%	1140-1350[2]	31%	73%	19%
85. University of Puget Sound (WA)	58	3.3	81%	78%	77%	75%	70%	0.2%	1130-1342[2]	28%	86%	10%
85. Ursinus College (PA)	58	3.0	87%	72%	74%	70%	68%	0.3%	1150-1330[2]	24%	80%	15%
85. Wheaton College (MA)	58	3.4	86%	77%	78%	75%	58%	2%	1160-1350[2]	31%	77%	16%
89. Cornell College (IA)	57	3.2	78%	68%	67%	57%	77%	0%	23-29[2]	20%	82%	14%
89. Illinois Wesleyan University	57	3.0	88%	76%	82%	76%	64%	1%	1100-1300[2]	26%	57%	14%
89. St. Mary's College of Maryland*	57	3.0	84%	72%	72%	62%	67%	0.3%	1070-1280[2]	22%	79%	9%
92. Augustana College (IL)	56	3.0	86%	68%	77%	69%	66%	0%	1090-1280[2]	29%	57%	21%
92. College of St. Benedict (MN)	56	3.1	88%	71%	85%	80%	45%	0%	21-28[2]	30%	84%	14%
92. College of the Atlantic (ME)	56	2.8	81%	73%	66%	61%	97%	0%	1210-1400[2]	33%[5]	76%	26%
92. Earlham College (IN)	56	3.1	81%	76%	65%	57%	82%	2%	1110-1340[2]	31%	59%	25%
92. Transylvania University (KY)	56	2.9	82%	77%	74%	71%	77%	0%	24-30[2]	30%	92%	26%
92. Washington and Jefferson Col. (PA)	56	3.0	84%	69%	68%	61%	81%	0%	1040-1270[2]	25%	90%	13%
98. Hampden-Sydney College (VA)	55	3.0	81%	70%	71%	57%	81%	0%	1040-1220[2]	15%	47%	21%
98. Hanover College (IN)	55	2.8	79%	66%	72%	60%	74%	0.4%	1060-1230[2]	25%	69%	18%
98. Hendrix College (AR)	55	3.2	85%	74%	61%	41%	71%	0%	25-32[2]	37%	71%	18%
98. Ohio Wesleyan University	55	3.1	79%	69%	67%	54%	70%	1%	23-29[2]	28%	68%	18%
98. Southwestern University (TX)	55	3.1	85%	71%	73%	75%	52%	0.3%	1110-1300[2]	27%	49%	23%
98. Stonehill College (MA)	55	2.8	85%	73%	82%	79%	64%	0.4%	1120-1290[2]	20%	69%	12%
98. Washington College (MD)	55	2.8	83%	76%	71%	67%	79%	0%	1070-1280	29%	80%	15%
105. Grove City College[1] (PA)	54	2.5	89%[8]	71%	83%[6]	N/A	N/A	N/A	1130-1384[4]	N/A	79%[4]	N/A
105. Hollins University (VA)	54	2.8	78%	63%	62%	55%	91%	0%	1050-1260[3]	20%	81%	23%
105. Luther College (IA)	54	2.9	82%	74%	77%	69%	63%	1%	23-29	30%	64%	23%
105. Saint Anselm College[1] (NH)	54	2.7	90%[8]	75%	78%[8]	N/A	75%[4]	2%[4]	1140-1300[4]	28%[4]	75%[4]	17%[4]
105. Saint Mary's College (IN)	54	2.9	84%	72%	81%	76%	40%	7%	1060-1260[2]	26%	82%	29%
105. St. John's University (MN)	54	3.1	86%	70%	74%	68%	45%	0%	22-27[2]	14%	81%	21%

Note: Key to footnotes, Page 52

Hamilton College,
ied at No. 13

ANCY L. FORD

Rank	School (State) (*Public)	Overall score	Peer assessment score (5.0=highest)	Average first-year student retention rate	2020 graduation rate Predicted	2020 graduation rate Actual	Pell recipient grad rate	% of classes under 20 ('20)	% of classes of 50 or more ('20)	SAT/ACT 25th-75th percentile ('20)	Freshmen in top 10% of HS class ('20)	Accept-ance rate ('20)	Average alumni giving rate
111.	Austin College (TX)	53	3.0	81%	66%	71%	69%	58%	0.4%	1110-1310[2]	26%	49%	12%
111.	Hope College (MI)	53	3.0	90%	72%	76%	63%	57%	2%	1090-1310[2]	35%	78%	15%
111.	Randolph-Macon College (VA)	53	3.0	85%	67%	66%	60%	63%	0%	1030-1218[2]	21%	71%	29%
114.	Millsaps College (MS)	52	3.0	75%	75%	68%	54%	90%	0.3%	21-26[3]	N/A	70%	14%
114.	Westmont College (CA)	52	2.7	80%	75%	72%	72%	68%	1%	1110-1370	36%	70%	10%
114.	Whittier College (CA)	52	3.1	77%	63%	63%	64%	51%	1%	1050-1220[2]	20%[4]	72%	16%
117.	Drew University (NJ)	51	2.9	86%	70%	69%	65%	68%	0.3%	1100-1300[2]	26%	73%	12%
117.	Elizabethtown College (PA)	51	2.6	88%	69%	72%	65%	66%	1%	1080-1280[2]	28%	86%	13%
117.	Goucher College (MD)	51	3.1	75%	71%	66%	63%	76%	0%	990-1230[2]	21%	79%	12%
117.	Linfield University (OR)	51	2.6	81%	67%	75%	71%	78%	0.3%	1050-1210[2]	N/A	80%	11%
117.	St. Norbert College (WI)	51	2.8	83%	70%	72%	70%	50%	0%	22-28[2]	27%	84%	15%
117.	Susquehanna University (PA)	51	2.9	87%	68%	74%	70%	57%	0.2%	1070-1240[2]	23%	87%	13%
117.	Westminster College (PA)	51	2.6	78%	62%	71%	67%	68%	0%	990-1200[2]	22%	95%	14%
124.	Houghton College (NY)	50	2.6	82%	63%	68%	57%	82%	0.3%	1060-1300[2]	18%	93%	16%
124.	Lycoming College (PA)	50	2.6	76%	56%	62%	58%	78%	0.4%	1010-1210[2]	23%	65%	17%
126.	Monmouth College (IL)	49	2.7	74%	57%	58%	54%	84%	0%	1050-1360[2]	8%	69%	16%[4]
126.	Saint Michael's College (VT)	49	2.6	84%	73%	75%	68%	57%	1%	1130-1280[2]	26%	88%	18%
128.	Albion College (MI)	48	2.8	77%	63%	68%	59%	71%	0%	930-1160[2]	17%	75%	10%
128.	Birmingham-Southern College (AL)	48	2.7	79%	70%	71%	53%	75%	0%	22-28[2]	18%	60%	14%
128.	Eckerd College (FL)	48	2.9	81%	71%	64%	69%	59%	0%	1090-1285[2]	N/A	69%	N/A
128.	Massachusetts Col. of Liberal Arts*	48	2.6	72%	53%	53%	50%	93%	0%	960-1180[2]	22%	88%	5%
128.	Morehouse College (GA)	48	3.6	82%	60%	56%	48%	52%	2%	995-1180[4]	N/A	74%	14%
128.	Presbyterian College (SC)	48	2.7	78%	67%	61%	55%	65%	0.3%	1030-1200[2]	25%	71%	18%
128.	Ripon College (WI)	48	2.7	76%	64%	67%	56%	58%	3%	18-25[2]	12%	74%	28%
128.	Roanoke College (VA)	48	2.9	80%	66%	70%	65%	55%	0%	1040-1240[2]	16%	78%	15%
136.	Central College (IA)	47	2.6	79%	67%	68%	63%	66%	0%	19-25[2]	23%	64%	9%
136.	Coe College (IA)	47	2.9	79%	65%	61%	49%	71%	0%	20-26[2]	21%	81%	14%
136.	College of Idaho	47	2.7	80%	63%	64%	61%	57%	2%	1050-1240[2]	N/A	48%	18%
136.	Meredith College (NC)	47	2.6	82%	62%	64%	56%	71%	0.3%	1008-1200[3]	17%	72%	19%
136.	Salem College (NC)	47	2.2	65%[8]	60%	67%	69%	94%	0%	17-23	12%	85%	16%
141.	Concordia College at Moorhead (MN)	46	2.7	83%	72%	68%	58%	53%	0.4%	20-27[2]	20%	58%	13%
141.	Hampshire College (MA)	46	2.7	73%[8]	76%	66%	59%	87%	0%	N/A[2]	N/A	59%	15%
141.	Moravian College (PA)	46	2.6	82%	59%	69%	58%	57%	2%	1030-1190[9]	19%	79%	15%
141.	Randolph College (VA)	46	2.6	68%	63%	56%	40%	92%	0%	950-1160[2]	23%	90%	18%
141.	University of Minnesota Morris*	46	2.6	79%	63%	60%	54%	74%	1%	21-28	26%	65%	9%
146.	Covenant College (GA)	45	2.3	86%	66%	68%	65%	64%	0%	22-29[2]	36%	98%	8%
146.	Fisk University (TN)	45	3.0	80%	49%	50%	50%	75%	0%	990-1210	32%	66%	34%
146.	Franklin College (IN)	45	2.6	76%	58%	63%	53%	69%	0%	970-1150[2]	12%	76%	17%
146.	Hartwick College (NY)	45	2.7	72%	59%	58%	61%	76%	0.3%	1020-1180[2]	N/A	93%	7%
146.	Illinois College	45	2.5	77%	59%	68%	55%	54%	0%	960-1160[2]	18%	76%	17%
146.	Saint Vincent College (PA)	45	2.2	83%	62%	73%	67%	56%	0.2%	960-1190[2]	20%	72%	12%
146.	Simpson College (IA)	45	2.5	78%	64%	71%	60%	66%	1%	20-26[2]	18%	87%	9%
146.	U. of North Carolina Asheville*	45	3.1	74%	62%	62%	60%	55%	1%	1060-1270[2]	15%	79%	4%
146.	Wells College[1] (NY)	45	2.6	71%[8]	61%	54%[6]	N/A	84%[4]	0%[4]	950-1240[4]	19%[4]	83%[4]	N/A
155.	Purchase College–SUNY*	44	2.8	81%	61%	61%	58%	67%	4%	1100-1280[2]	N/A	74%	2%
155.	Wittenberg University (OH)	44	2.7	72%	62%	63%	51%	64%	1%	18-26[2]	17%	97%	16%
157.	Wesleyan College (GA)	43	2.9	72%	51%	51%	42%	74%	0%	946-1113[2]	N/A	60%	19%
158.	Aquinas College (MI)	42	2.4	76%	60%	65%	59%	78%	1%	1010-1220[2]	N/A	71%	8%
158.	Emory and Henry College (VA)	42	2.6	76%	53%	54%	42%	68%	0%	960-1150[2]	16%	80%	17%
158.	Gordon College (MA)	42	2.5	83%	71%	72%	67%	66%	4%	1020-1280[2]	24%	68%	8%
158.	University of Puerto Rico–Ponce[1]*	42	2.4	80%[8]	27%	50%[6]	N/A	N/A	N/A	N/A	N/A	73%[4]	N/A
158.	University of Virginia–Wise*	42	2.5	68%	49%	46%[6]	N/A	75%	0%	980-1170	20%	82%	5%
158.	Westminster College[7] (MO)	42	2.4	75%	63%	60%	44%	78%	0%	19-26[2]	19%	97%	N/A
164.	Centenary College[1]	41	2.4	75%[8]	69%	56%[8]	N/A	72%[4]	1%[4]	19-26[4]	25%[4]	60%[4]	9%
165.	Oglethorpe University (GA)	40	2.9	79%	61%	50%	42%	73%	0%	1100-1280[2]	23%[4]	67%	6%
165.	Sweet Briar College (VA)	40	2.4	72%	71%	32%	33%	87%	0%	1010-1210[2]	N/A	76%	33%
165.	Wartburg College (IA)	40	2.6	80%	69%	68%	61%	49%	1%	19-25[9]	21%[4]	72%	19%

Note: Key to footnotes, Page 52

School (State) (*Public)	Peer assessment score (5.0=highest)	Average first-year student retention rate	2020 graduation rate Predicted	Actual	Pell recipient grad rate	% of classes under 20 ('20)	% of classes of 50 or more ('20)	SAT/ACT 25th-75th percentile ('20)	Freshmen in top 10% of HS class ('20)	Accept-ance rate ('20)	Average alumni giving rate
SCHOOLS RANKED 168 THROUGH 222 ARE LISTED HERE ALPHABETICALLY											
Albright College (PA)	2.5	70%	52%	60%	55%	75%	0%	1000-1190[2]	15%	82%	N/A
Allen University (SC)	2.0	40%	24%	14%	17%	N/A	N/A	699-821[2]	1%	61%	7%
Ave Maria University[1] (FL)	2.2	70%[8]	65%	56%[8]	N/A	55%[4]	0.4%[4]	1040-1230[4]	N/A	85%[4]	2%[4]
Bennett College[1] (NC)	2.3	49%[8]	38%	44%[6]	N/A	N/A	N/A	N/A	N/A	59%[4]	N/A
Bethany College (WV)	2.3	67%	51%	43%	32%	80%	0%	850-1090[3]	7%	92%	14%
Bethany Lutheran College (MN)	2.2	80%	61%	62%	58%	67%	0%	20-26[2]	15%	65%	15%
Bethune-Cookman University (FL)	2.4	65%	32%	33%	32%	65%	2%	870-980	12%	98%	4%[4]
Blackburn College (IL)	2.1	63%	43%	45%	36%	80%	0%	890-1078	10%	55%	15%
Bloomfield College (NJ)	2.2	63%	30%	34%	33%	82%	0%	800-970[2]	N/A	85%	4%
Brewton-Parker College (GA)	1.8	46%[8]	34%	15%	15%	69%	0%	860-1030	6%	98%	3%
Bridgewater College (VA)	2.3	72%	57%	63%	55%	61%	0%	980-1170[2]	15%	76%	12%
Bryn Athyn Col. of New Church[7] (PA)	1.8	76%[8]	52%	29%	31%	81%	0%	930-1198[3]	N/A	78%	N/A
Cheyney U. of Pennsylvania[1]*	2.1	53%[8]	39%	22%[6]	N/A	N/A	N/A	N/A	N/A	N/A	N/A
Chowan University (NC)	2.0	54%	29%	31%	30%	48%	1%	800-1020[2]	5%	67%	6%
Dillard University (LA)	2.6	69%	42%	49%	44%	63%	1%	18-22	N/A	65%	14%
Doane University (NE)	2.3	74%	61%	60%	46%	83%	1%	20-25[9]	14%	69%	13%
East-West University[1] (IL)	1.8	35%[8]	21%	11%[6]	N/A	N/A	N/A	N/A	N/A	N/A	N/A
Emmanuel College (MA)	2.4	77%	64%	62%	55%	50%	0%	1110-1280[2]	28%	76%	15%
Fort Lewis College (CO)*	2.5	63%	53%	42%	36%	49%	1%	16-22	11%	92%	2%
Georgetown College (KY)	2.5	68%	58%	56%	49%	73%	0%	20-26	15%	72%	11%
Guilford College (NC)	2.9	68%	55%	49%	46%	58%	0%	930-1170[2]	12%	78%	7%
Johnson C. Smith University (NC)	2.3	68%[8]	38%	43%[6]	N/A	92%	0%	800-980	N/A	49%	10%
Judson College[1] (AL)	2.0	59%[8]	50%	35%[6]	N/A	97%[4]	0%[4]	17-21[4]	N/A	37%[4]	N/A
The King's College[1] (NY)	2.4	77%[8]	63%	52%[6]	N/A	54%[4]	4%[4]	1100-1310[4]	N/A	42%[4]	N/A
Lane College[7] (TN)	2.2	54%	18%	23%	21%	48%	1%	14-16[2]	N/A	61%	N/A
Louisiana State University–Alexandria[1]*	2.1	56%[8]	36%	21%[6]	N/A	59%[4]	2%[4]	17-21[4]	15%[4]	67%[4]	3%[4]
Lyon College (AR)	2.4	68%	60%	43%	35%	69%	1%	22-28	21%	50%	7%
Mansfield University of Pennsylvania*	2.0	73%	49%	57%	48%	40%	5%	960-1130[2]	11%	96%	N/A
Marlboro College[1] (VT)	2.1	63%[8]	66%	54%[6]	N/A	N/A	N/A	N/A[2]	N/A	83%[4]	N/A
Marymount California University	3.0	61%	50%	32%	52%	68%	0%	950-1100[2]	N/A	95%	N/A
Marymount Manhattan College (NY)	2.5	70%	60%	58%	56%	87%	0%	960-1200[2]	N/A	88%	3%
Providence Christian College[1] (CA)	2.2	64%[8]	60%	37%[8]	N/A	N/A	N/A	19-25[4]	N/A	42%[4]	N/A
Rust College[1] (MS)	2.1	65%[8]	23%	32%[6]	N/A	N/A	N/A	N/A	N/A	50%[4]	N/A
Shepherd University (WV)*	2.3	70%	44%	46%	38%	69%	1%	940-1150	N/A	98%	7%
Southern Virginia University[1]	1.9	81%[8]	57%	30%[6]	N/A	N/A	N/A	19-26[4]	N/A	98%[4]	N/A
Spring Hill College (AL)	2.3	76%	64%	57%	48%	67%	0%	20-25[2]	24%	54%	11%
Sterling College[1] (VT)	2.2	57%[8]	56%	54%[6]	N/A	N/A	N/A	N/A[2]	N/A	86%[4]	N/A
Stillman College (AL)	2.5	65%[8]	32%	22%	21%	N/A	N/A	N/A	N/A	56%	8%
Talladega College[1] (AL)	2.0	66%[8]	30%	36%[6]	N/A	48%[4]	6%[4]	20-24[4]	N/A	63%[4]	7%[4]
Thomas More Col. of Lib. Arts[1] (NH)	2.4	87%[8]	54%	53%[6]	N/A	N/A	N/A	1290-1590[4]	N/A	94%[4]	N/A
Tougaloo College[1] (MS)	2.3	72%[8]	46%	45%[6]	N/A	N/A	N/A	15-22[4]	N/A	71%[4]	N/A
University of Maine–Machias*	2.2	54%[8]	34%	27%	25%	91%	0%	900-1090[2]	7%	94%	N/A
University of Pikeville (KY)	2.2	60%	42%	33%	25%	59%	2%	17-24	21%	100%	3%
Univ. of Pittsburgh–Greensburg[1]*	2.1	60%[8]	47%	33%[6]	N/A	N/A	N/A	1010-1190[4]	N/A	84%[4]	N/A
University of Puerto Rico–Cayey[1]*	2.3	85%[8]	44%	48%[6]	N/A	N/A	N/A	984-1185[4]	N/A	88%[4]	N/A
Univ. of Science and Arts of Okla.*	2.3	64%[8]	49%	40%	50%	75%	3%	19-24[4]	N/A	13%	N/A
University of South Carolina–Beaufort*	2.3	61%[8]	45%	34%	33%	62%	1%	940-1110	7%	67%	N/A
University of the West[1] (CA)	2.1	56%[8]	44%	33%[6]	N/A	N/A	N/A	N/A[2]	N/A	N/A	N/A
Univ. of Wisconsin–Parkside[7]*	2.1	72%	46%	39%	39%	55%	17%	17-23[2]	15%	66%	1%
University of Wisconsin–Superior[1]*	2.2	69%[8]	56%	42%[6]	N/A	60%[4]	2%[4]	18-23[4]	8%[4]	78%[4]	3%[4]
Virginia Union University	2.1	62%	30%	36%	34%	65%	1%	780-920[2]	3%	75%	8%
Virginia Wesleyan University	2.4	62%	54%	50%	43%	66%	1%	960-1190[2]	14%	74%	5%
Warren Wilson College (NC)	2.6	62%	68%	42%	38%	85%	0%	21-29[2]	10%	85%	14%
Williams Baptist University (AR)	1.7	57%	46%	37%	35%	52%	3%	18-24	16%	69%	3%
Young Harris College (GA)	2.2	66%	52%	46%	42%	68%	0%	930-1160[2]	13%	65%	6%

Best
Regional Universities

What Is a Regional University?

LIKE THE NATIONAL UNIVERSITIES, the institutions that appear here provide a full range of undergraduate majors and master's programs; the difference is that they offer few, if any, doctoral programs. The 596 universities in this category are not ranked nationally but rather against their peer group in one of four regions – North, South, Midwest and West – because in general they tend to draw students most heavily from surrounding states.

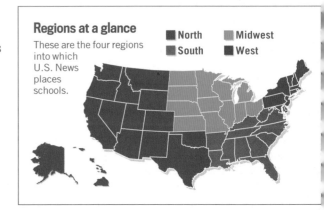

Regions at a glance
These are the four regions into which U.S. News places schools.

■ North ▨ Midwest
■ South ■ West

NORTH ▶

Rank	School (State) (*Public)	Overall score	Peer assessment score (5.0=highest)	Average first-year student retention rate	2020 graduation rate Predicted	2020 graduation rate Actual	% of classes under 20 ('20)	% of classes of 50 or more ('20)	Student/faculty ratio ('20)	SAT/ACT 25th-75th percentile ('20)	Freshmen in top 25% of HS class ('20)	Acceptance rate ('20)	Average alumni giving rate
1.	Providence College (RI)	100	3.8	92%	82%	85%	50%	2%	11/1	1135-1310[2]	73%	54%	11%
2.	Bentley University (MA)	99	3.6	92%	86%	90%	19%	0%	11/1	1180-1360	75%	58%	6%
3.	Fairfield University (CT)	96	3.7	91%	82%	82%	41%	2%	12/1	1190-1340[2]	70%[5]	56%	17%
4.	Loyola University Maryland	94	3.8	87%	83%	81%	44%	2%	12/1	1140-1328[2]	57%	80%	8%
5.	University of Scranton (PA)	93	3.5	88%	74%	82%	67%	0.2%	12/1	1100-1280	63%	80%	11%
6.	The College of New Jersey*	91	3.5	94%	84%	86%	35%	0.3%	13/1	1140-1320[2]	67%	51%	5%
7.	Bryant University (RI)	90	3.2	89%	78%	82%	24%	0%	13/1	1120-1280[2]	52%	76%	7%
8.	Emerson College (MA)	87	3.4	86%	84%	79%	80%	0%	13/1	1190-1380[2]	60%	41%	3%
8.	Saint Joseph's University (PA)	87	3.4	89%	75%	81%	44%	1%	11/1	1100-1290[2]	51%	80%	9%
10.	Ithaca College (NY)	86	3.5	83%	79%	78%	63%	3%	9/1	1160-1320[2]	59%	76%	6%
10.	Marist College (NY)	86	3.5	88%	76%	85%	44%	0%	16/1	1130-1300[2]	53%	55%	8%
12.	SUNY Polytechnic Inst. – Utica/Albany*	85	2.7	79%	75%	54%	57%	0.2%	14/1	1000-1350[2]	73%	73%	1%
13.	Le Moyne College (NY)	79	3.0	85%	65%	78%	45%	2%	13/1	1060-1250[2]	55%	75%	14%
13.	Manhattan College (NY)	79	3.1	83%	65%	70%	55%	0.1%	12/1	1030-1220[2]	52%[4]	78%	12%
13.	Siena College (NY)	79	3.0	88%	70%	81%	36%	0%	13/1	1060-1240[2]	47%	81%	13%
16.	CUNY–Baruch College*	78	3.1	89%	59%	73%	16%	17%	20/1	1150-1350	77%	41%	3%
16.	SUNY–Geneseo*	78	3.4	85%	76%	78%	35%	8%	18/1	1140-1310	72%	61%	6%
18.	CUNY–Hunter College*	74	3.2	85%	53%	56%	30%	8%	13/1	1150-1350[4]	N/A	40%	12%
18.	Monmouth University (NJ)	74	3.1	80%	64%	74%	48%	0%	12/1	1040-1210[2]	44%	79%	3%
18.	St. Bonaventure University (NY)	74	3.0	85%	66%	74%	46%	0%	12/1	1030-1220[2]	44%	76%	17%
21.	Canisius College (NY)	73	2.8	84%	64%	69%	53%	0%	11/1	1040-1240[2]	48%	76%	10%
21.	Niagara University (NY)	73	2.8	84%	61%	77%	59%	0.4%	11/1	1015-1200[2]	43%	92%	9%
23.	Endicott College (MA)	72	2.9	84%	68%	78%	68%	0%	13/1	1100-1240[2]	48%	70%	12%
23.	Messiah University (PA)	72	2.7	88%	76%	79%	51%	2%	13/1	1080-1310[2]	62%	78%	7%
23.	Salve Regina University (RI)	72	2.9	84%	68%	76%	47%	0%	13/1	1100-1240[2]	43%	75%	12%
23.	St. Francis University (PA)	72	2.6	87%	68%	76%	68%	2%	14/1	1010-1220[2]	58%	75%	13%
27.	Molloy College (NY)	71	2.5	87%	65%	73%	66%	2%	10/1	1040-1230[2]	66%	74%	6%
27.	Rider University (NJ)	71	2.8	79%	64%	65%	63%	1%	10/1	1020-1220[2]	46%	76%	5%
27.	Roger Williams University (RI)	71	2.9	82%	72%	69%	49%	0.2%	15/1	1070-1240[2]	40%	86%	3%
27.	Springfield College (MA)	71	2.9	85%	62%	73%	49%	3%	12/1	1080-1270[2]	42%	63%	11%
31.	McDaniel College (MD)	69	2.9	78%	65%	62%	62%	0%	13/1	980-1210[2]	47%	81%	13%
31.	SUNY–New Paltz*	69	3.0	86%	70%	76%	37%	3%	15/1	1070-1260	N/A	62%	2%
31.	Wentworth Inst. of Technology (MA)	69	3.1	83%	64%	69%	54%	1%	16/1	1090-1280[9]	41%[4]	94%	5%
34.	Assumption University (MA)	68	2.8	83%	68%	73%	40%	0.2%	13/1	1070-1220[2]	41%	81%	11%
34.	Merrimack College (MA)	68	3.0	83%	65%	74%	28%	1%	17/1	960-1276[2]	24%	82%	7%
34.	Nazareth College (NY)	68	2.7	83%	70%	71%	69%	0%	9/1	1110-1280[2]	62%	76%	8%
34.	New York Inst. of Technology	68	3.0	76%	62%	50%	64%	1%	11/1	1060-1290[2]	N/A	75%	2%
34.	Ramapo College of New Jersey*	68	2.8	86%	58%	72%	40%	0%	16/1	1030-1220	43%[5]	67%	2%

Note: Key to footnotes, Page 52

Rank School (State) (*Public)	Overall score	Peer assessment score (5.0=highest)	Average first-year student retention rate	2020 graduation rate		% of classes under 20 ('20)	% of classes of 50 or more ('20)	Student/faculty ratio ('20)	SAT/ACT 25th-75th percentile ('20)	Freshmen in top 25% of HS class ('20)	Acceptance rate ('20)	Average alumni giving rate
				Predicted	Actual							
34. Seton Hill University (PA)	68	2.7	81%	65%	68%	68%	0.3%	14/1	1000-1200[2]	50%	79%	14%[4]
34. Stockton University (NJ)*	68	2.7	85%	60%	74%	27%	2%	18/1	1013-1190[2]	36%	77%	1%
34. Suffolk University (MA)	68	2.9	76%	64%	59%	45%	1%	14/1	1010-1210[2]	42%	86%	5%
34. Wagner College (NY)	68	2.8	80%	75%	71%	67%	2%	10/1	1050-1250[2]	48%	70%	6%
43. La Salle University (PA)	67	2.8	75%	54%	66%	56%	0.1%	13/1	980-1180[2]	34%[4]	76%	7%
44. Alfred University (NY)	65	2.8	70%	60%	61%	67%	2%	11/1	970-1200[2]	42%	64%	7%
44. Arcadia University (PA)	65	2.6	78%	65%	65%	74%	1%	11/1	1030-1230[2]	48%	74%	6%
44. CUNY–John Jay Col. of Crim. Justice*	65	3.1	80%	44%	48%[6]	19%	1%	19/1	1000-1150	N/A	37%	13%
44. Fairleigh Dickinson University (NJ)	65	3.1	80%	51%	59%	68%	1%	12/1	933-1140[2]	36%	87%	2%[4]
44. Marywood University (PA)	65	2.6	85%	63%	71%	57%	0.2%	12/1	1000-1200[2]	49%	82%	10%
44. Mount St. Mary's University (MD)	65	3.1	76%	66%	63%	54%	0%	14/1	961-1185[2]	35%[4]	80%	13%
50. CUNY–Queens College*	64	3.0	83%	54%	53%	26%	9%	17/1	1040-1190[2]	N/A	53%	12%
50. Hood College (MD)	64	2.8	75%	55%	61%	69%	0.3%	11/1	1000-1220[2]	37%	71%	11%
50. Mercyhurst University (PA)	64	2.7	79%	57%	70%	60%	1%	16/1	1030-1220[2]	N/A	88%	9%
50. SUNY–Oswego*	64	2.9	78%	59%	65%	48%	5%	16/1	1020-1190	42%	69%	5%
50. West Chester Univ. of Pennsylvania*	64	3.0	85%	61%	75%	22%	6%	20/1	1010-1180[2]	36%	86%	3%
55. Iona College (NY)	63	2.9	75%	56%	60%	32%	0.3%	15/1	1000-1190[2]	32%	86%	6%
55. Norwich University (VT)	63	2.7	80%	63%	57%	56%	1%	13/1	1040-1230[2]	34%[4]	74%	16%
55. University of New Haven (CT)	63	2.7	78%	65%	64%	55%	1%	18/1	1050-1220[2]	41%	91%	5%
58. Manhattanville College (NY)	62	2.5	74%	58%	64%	76%	0%	10/1	1010-1160[2]	18%	90%	8%
58. Saint Peter's University (NJ)	62	2.7	80%	42%	55%	58%	0%	12/1	910-1090[2]	40%	85%	9%
58. SUNY Maritime College*	62	2.9	82%	72%	72%	36%	3%	15/1	1070-1230[3]	N/A[5]	73%	4%
58. Waynesburg University (PA)	62	2.3	77%	61%	65%	72%	0.2%	11/1	980-1170[2]	49%	90%	8%
62. Champlain College (VT)	61	2.5	80%	65%	66%	83%	0%	12/1	1110-1300[2]	32%	85%	2%
62. CUNY–Lehman College*	61	2.7	82%	38%	53%	37%	3%	18/1[4]	960-1080	N/A	42%	11%
62. King's College (PA)	61	2.6	74%	61%	59%	62%	0%	11/1	1010-1210[2]	38%	81%	11%
62. Monroe College (NY)	61	1.9	79%	34%	77%	63%	0%	16/1	1098-1113[2]	N/A	49%	1%
62. Notre Dame of Maryland University	61	2.8	73%	56%	49%	88%	0%	7/1	870-1060[2]	52%	62%	10%
62. Salisbury University (MD)*	61	2.8	81%	65%	69%	48%	2%	15/1	1093-1268[2]	40%	78%	6%
62. SUNY–Fredonia*	61	2.6	75%	58%	62%	57%	3%	14/1	1000-1210	40%	72%	3%
62. SUNY–Plattsburgh*	61	2.7	79%	57%	67%	39%	5%	15/1	910-1130[2]	38%	59%	6%
70. Carlow University (PA)	60	2.3	80%	49%	58%	76%	1%	10/1	980-1140	32%	94%	8%[4]
70. CUNY–Brooklyn College*	60	2.8	82%	47%	54%	22%	5%	19/1	1020-1180[3]	N/A	50%	5%
70. SUNY College–Cortland*	60	2.8	81%	64%	67%	39%	5%	15/1	1100-1220[9]	44%	52%	6%
73. DeSales University (PA)	59	2.5	82%	64%	65%	54%	2%	12/1	1010-1240[9]	N/A	82%	7%
73. Geneva College (PA)	59	2.3	77%	62%	72%	72%	2%	12/1	980-1240[2]	43%	73%	8%
73. Lebanon Valley College[1] (PA)	59	2.6	79%[8]	71%	75%[6]	N/A	N/A	11/1[4]	1050-1270[4]	N/A	80%[4]	N/A
73. SUNY Brockport*	59	2.7	76%	57%	66%	39%	3%	16/1	1000-1160[2]	33%	58%	2%
73. SUNY College–Oneonta[1]*	59	2.8	83%[8]	65%	74%[6]	N/A	N/A	17/1[4]	980-1180[4]	N/A	56%[4]	N/A
78. Roberts Wesleyan College (NY)	58	2.4	81%	59%	59%	85%	0%	11/1	1020-1250[2]	54%	76%	7%
78. Slippery Rock U. of Pennsylvania*	58	2.8	82%	56%	69%	17%	9%	23/1	980-1150	39%	74%	4%
78. St. Joseph's College (NY)	58	2.5	83%[8]	54%	70%	65%	0.1%	12/1	1020-1200[2]	N/A	71%	3%
78. SUNY College–Potsdam*	58	2.6	76%	50%	50%	63%	2%	11/1	1068-1240[9]	N/A	72%	5%
82. Caldwell University (NJ)	57	2.3	81%	50%	64%	53%	2%	14/1	920-1110[2]	40%[5]	92%	9%
82. Point Park University (PA)	57	2.4	76%	54%	55%	89%	0.1%	11/1	953-1180	31%	70%	1%
82. Stevenson University (MD)	57	2.6	81%	61%	62%	66%	0%	15/1	980-1160[2]	38%	89%	2%
85. Cedar Crest College (PA)	56	2.2	79%	52%	62%	76%	3%	10/1	970-1170	48%	70%	9%
85. Eastern Connecticut State University*	56	2.5	78%	57%	56%	45%	0%	14/1	990-1180[2]	39%	70%	5%
85. Elms College (MA)	56	2.2	81%	49%	64%	76%	0%	12/1	1000-1170[2]	38%[4]	70%	10%
85. Westfield State University (MA)*	56	2.5	75%	53%	63%	42%	1%	15/1	960-1140[2]	22%	92%	2%
85. York College of Pennsylvania	56	2.5	79%	61%	65%	46%	0.2%	14/1	990-1180	35%	71%	7%
90. Bay Path University (MA)	55	2.2	72%	45%		88%	0%	10/1[4]	940-1170[2]	50%	78%	N/A
90. College of Mount St. Vincent (NY)	55	2.3	76%	39%	63%	63%	0%	14/1	940-1060[2]	24%	93%	10%[4]
90. Utica College (NY)	55	2.5	74%	50%	54%	62%	0.2%	12/1	1015-1210[2]	38%	86%	6%
90. William Paterson Univ. of N.J.*	55	2.6	72%	49%	55%	51%	0.4%	13/1	N/A[2]	N/A	91%	3%
94. Johnson & Wales University (RI)	54	2.8	73%	57%	60%	47%	0%	15/1	980-1170[2]	29%	87%	1%[4]
94. Mount St. Mary College (NY)	54	2.4	80%	56%	60%	65%	0.3%	12/1	1000-1150[2]	26%[5]	90%	4%
94. Shippensburg U. of Pennsylvania*	54	2.7	74%	53%	51%	38%	3%	17/1	940-1150	28%	94%	7%
97. Albertus Magnus College (CT)	53	2.3	69%	37%	46%	85%	0%	14/1	820-1040[2]	15%	81%	5%

NORTH ▶

Rank	School (State) (*Public)	Overall score	Peer assessment score (5.0=highest)	Average first-year student retention rate	2020 graduation rate		% of classes under 20 ('20)	% of classes of 50 or more ('20)	Student/faculty ratio ('20)	SAT/ACT 25th-75th percentile ('20)	Freshmen in top 25% of HS class ('20)	Accept-ance rate ('20)	Average alumni giving rate
					Predicted	Actual							
97.	Alvernia University (PA)	53	2.4	74%	52%	61%	58%	3%	14/1	940-1130[2]	N/A	70%	6%
97.	Bridgewater State University (MA)*	53	2.6	77%	52%	59%	38%	0.2%	19/1	950-1140[2]	N/A	82%	3%
97.	Central Connecticut State University*	53	2.5	75%	51%	52%	39%	3%	14/1	970-1150[2]	27%	65%	2%
97.	Fitchburg State University (MA)*	53	2.4	76%	51%	58%	55%	0%	14/1	970-1140[2]	N/A	88%	3%
97.	Millersville U. of Pennsylvania*	53	2.6	76%	58%	56%	25%	5%	19/1	980-1170[2]	37%	85%	3%
103.	The College of Saint Rose (NY)	52	2.2	73%	53%	59%	70%	0.3%	14/1	1020-1190[9]	35%	82%	7%
103.	Eastern University (PA)	52	2.3	78%	58%	58%	81%	3%	12/1	1010-1190[2]	58%[4]	64%	5%
103.	Framingham State University (MA)*	52	2.6	70%	52%	61%	53%	0%	13/1	950-1130[2]	N/A	79%	3%
103.	Southern Connecticut State U.*	52	2.5	75%	47%	51%	56%	1%	12/1	910-1110[2]	30%	80%	3%
103.	SUNY Buffalo State[7]*	52	2.9	63%	45%	40%	43%	3%	15/1	860-1060	N/A	80%	2%
103.	Worcester State University (MA)*	52	2.5	80%	55%	59%	54%	0%	16/1	1000-1190[2]	N/A	81%	5%
109.	Centenary University[1] (NJ)	51	2.1	70%[8]	52%	59%[6]	78%[4]	0%[4]	12/1[4]	938-1148[4]	N/A	75%[4]	3%[4]
109.	Frostburg State University (MD)*	51	2.6	75%	50%	52%	51%	3%	14/1	910-1130[3]	34%	74%	4%
109.	Georgian Court University (NJ)	51	2.2	77%	49%	57%	87%	0.2%	12/1	940-1138[2]	36%	81%	6%
109.	Lock Haven U. of Pennsylvania*	51	2.3	69%	51%	51%	52%	9%	14/1	930-1130[2]	34%	93%	3%
109.	University of Baltimore*	51	2.6	78%	48%	34%	48%	0%	13/1	930-1070	N/A	80%	3%
114.	Clarion U. of Pennsylvania*	50	2.2	75%	50%	57%	29%	6%	17/1	950-1120[2]	32%	94%	4%
114.	Lasell University (MA)	50	2.3	74%	57%	62%	50%	0%	15/1	980-1180[2]	32%	84%	4%
114.	Saint Elizabeth University (NJ)	50	2.2	69%	34%	51%	78%	0%	10/1	803-1048[2]	N/A	75%	9%
114.	St. Thomas Aquinas College (NY)	50	2.5	75%	53%	61%	70%	0%	17/1	900-1150[3]	N/A[5]	87%	1%
114.	Western Connecticut State U.*	50	2.5	74%	54%	51%	41%	1%	13/1	1020-1200[2]	28%[4]	81%	1%
119.	Bloomsburg U. of Pennsylvania*	49	2.5	74%	53%	58%	25%	7%	19/1	960-1150[2]	32%	89%	3%
119.	Chestnut Hill College (PA)	49	2.3	72%	49%	53%	87%	0%	12/1	900-1090	24%	97%	11%
119.	Gwynedd Mercy University (PA)	49	2.4	81%	48%	61%	71%	3%	12/1	950-1140[2]	30%	98%	4%
119.	Rhode Island College*	49	2.5	75%	46%	46%	47%	2%	14/1	870-1100	36%	81%	3%
123.	Kutztown Univ. of Pennsylvania*	48	2.6	75%	51%	52%	31%	6%	18/1	950-1120	26%	93%	4%
123.	Plymouth State University (NH)*	48	2.5	69%	53%	59%	48%	1%	17/1	980-1130[2]	16%	89%	3%
123.	Salem State University (MA)*	48	2.4	75%	51%	59%	48%	0.3%	14/1	1000-1150[2]	N/A	87%	2%
126.	Curry College[7] (MA)	47	2.2	65%	56%	55%	71%	0%	12/1	943-1108[4]	23%[4]	82%	2%[4]
126.	Delaware Valley University (PA)	47	2.3	72%	55%	55%	64%	2%	13/1	940-1155[2]	29%	92%	4%
126.	Kean University (NJ)*	47	2.6	74%	44%	50%	39%	1%	18/1	920-1100[2]	N/A	78%	1%
126.	Keuka College (NY)	47	2.3	71%	47%	50%	66%	2%	12/1	980-1150[2]	N/A	91%	9%
126.	Wilson College[1] (PA)	47	2.0	71%[8]	54%	52%[8]	79%[4]	0.3%[4]	12/1[4]	910-1190[4]	41%[4]	93%[4]	13%[4]

School (State) (*Public)	Peer assessment score (5.0=highest)	Average first-year student retention rate	2020 graduation rate		% of classes under 20 ('20)	% of classes of 50 or more ('20)	Student/faculty ratio ('20)	SAT/ACT 25th-75th percentile ('20)	Freshmen in top 25% of HS class ('20)	Accept-ance rate ('20)	Average alumni giving rate
			Predicted	Actual							
SCHOOLS RANKED 131 THROUGH 171 ARE LISTED HERE ALPHABETICALLY											
American International College (MA)	2.0	66%[8]	46%	48%	29%	1%	18/1	890-1100[9]	N/A	69%	N/A
Anna Maria College[1] (MA)	1.9	67%[8]	47%	44%[6]	N/A	N/A	12/1[4]	N/A[2]	N/A	74%[4]	5%[4]
Bowie State University (MD)*	2.4	72%	42%	43%	45%	3%	18/1	850-1010	N/A	81%	4%
Cabrini University[1] (PA)	2.3	72%[8]	48%	57%[6]	N/A	N/A	15/1[4]	1000-1180[4]	N/A	76%[4]	N/A
Cairn University[1] (PA)	2.1	80%[8]	53%	59%[6]	N/A	N/A	11/1[4]	1000-1247[4]	N/A	83%[4]	N/A
California U. of Pennsylvania*	2.3	72%	48%	50%	38%	8%	18/1	920-1120[2]	26%	94%	2%
Cambridge College[1] (MA)	1.9	33%[8]	53%	8%[6]	N/A	N/A	N/A	N/A[2]	N/A	N/A	N/A
Coppin State University (MD)*	2.3	66%	41%	30%	64%	2%	12/1	820-970	N/A	40%	5%
CUNY–College of Staten Island*	2.4	78%	43%	50%	19%	10%	21/1	990-1160[2]	N/A	91%	1%
Dominican College (NY)	2.1	73%	46%	48%	67%	0%	13/1	880-1080[2]	N/A	75%	2%
East Stroudsburg University (PA)*	2.5	69%	44%	50%	33%	13%	20/1	900-1110[2]	12%	80%	N/A
Edinboro Univ. of Pennsylvania*	2.2	71%	49%	50%	45%	3%	15/1	960-1160	34%	85%	3%
Felician University (NJ)	2.2	78%	41%	53%	63%	0.2%	14/1	890-1050[2]	38%	94%	1%
Franklin Pierce University[1] (NH)	2.3	66%[8]	56%	49%[6]	N/A	N/A	12/1[4]	N/A[2]	N/A	66%[4]	N/A
Granite State College[1] (NH)*	1.9	52%[8]	35%	19%[6]	88%[4]	0%[4]	11/1[4]	N/A[2]	N/A	100%[4]	5%[4]
Harrisburg Univ. of Science and Tech.[1] (PA)	2.1	69%[8]	30%	33%[6]	56%[4]	0%[4]	29/1[4]	N/A[2]	39%[4]	84%[4]	1%[4]
Holy Family University[1] (PA)	2.2	77%[8]	46%	57%[6]	N/A	N/A	12/1[4]	930-1110[4]	N/A	73%[4]	N/A
Lancaster Bible College (PA)	2.0	78%	54%	60%	80%	0%	15/1	980-1210[9]	N/A	97%	2%
La Roche University[1] (PA)	2.1	71%[8]	56%	53%[6]	69%[4]	1%[4]	12/1[4]	870-1140[4]	26%[4]	99%[4]	6%[4]
Lincoln University (PA)*	2.0	72%	41%	45%	63%	0%	14/1	860-1028[2]	20%	90%	3%
Medaille College[1] (NY)	2.0	62%[8]	40%	38%[6]	N/A	N/A	12/1[4]	N/A	N/A	62%[4]	N/A

Note: Key to footnotes, Page 52.

SMALL CAMPUS & GLOBAL REACH

When the bright lights of the big city are in the backyard of a close-knit campus community, the opportunities are limitless.

Manhattan College
1853

EXPERIENCE THE UNCOMMON
MANHATTAN.EDU

BEST REGIONAL UNIVERSITIES

NORTH ▶

School (State) (*Public)	Peer assessment score (5.0=highest)	Average first-year student retention rate	2020 graduation rate Predicted	2020 graduation rate Actual	% of classes under 20 ('20)	% of classes of 50 or more ('20)	Student/faculty ratio ('20)	SAT/ACT 25th-75th percentile ('20)	Freshmen in top 25% of HS class ('20)	Acceptance rate ('20)	Average alumni giving rate
CONTINUED (SCHOOLS RANKED 131 THROUGH 171 ARE LISTED HERE ALPHABETICALLY)											
Mercy College (NY)	2.2	75%	38%	48%	56%	0.1%	16/1	930-1110[2]	N/A	82%	1%
Metropolitan College of New York[1]	1.9	53%[8]	35%	19%[6]	N/A	N/A	10/1[4]	N/A[2]	N/A	32%[4]	N/A
Neumann University (PA)	2.3	75%	49%	51%	66%	1%	14/1	900-1080[2]	N/A	80%	5%
New England College (NH)	2.2	57%	36%	30%	94%	0%	12/1	920-940[4]	N/A	99%	5%
New Jersey City University*	2.2	75%	36%	36%	35%	1%	14/1	880-1090[2]	44%	96%	2%[4]
Northern Vermont University[1] (VT)*	2.0	64%[8]	47%	39%[6]	N/A	N/A	13/1[4]	N/A[2]	N/A	78%[4]	N/A
Nyack College (NY)	2.0	63%	44%	43%	81%[4]	0.4%[4]	16/1	845-1075[2]	21%[5]	97%	2%
Post University (CT)	2.1	51%	37%	27%	45%	0%	20/1	900-900[4]	N/A	61%	0%[4]
Rivier University[1] (NH)	2.1	69%[8]	53%	50%[6]	N/A	N/A	15/1[4]	N/A[2]	N/A	75%[4]	N/A
Rosemont College[1] (PA)	2.2	65%[8]	46%	54%[6]	85%[4]	0%[4]	12/1[4]	920-1130[4]	N/A	66%[4]	N/A
Southern New Hampshire University	2.8	72%	39%	48%[6]	57%	0%	13/1	N/A[2]	26%	87%	N/A
St. Joseph's College[1] (ME)	2.4	82%[8]	58%	64%[6]	N/A	N/A	10/1[4]	988-1153[4]	N/A	87%[4]	N/A
SUNY College–Old Westbury[1]*	2.4	77%[8]	47%	48%[6]	N/A	N/A	24/1[4]	910-1090[4]	N/A	78%[4]	N/A
SUNY Empire State College*	2.3	52%[8]	34%	22%[6]	N/A	N/A	18/1	N/A[2]	N/A	59%	N/A
Thomas College[1] (ME)	2.0	67%[8]	48%	49%[6]	N/A	N/A	24/1[4]	N/A[2]	N/A	84%[4]	N/A
Trinity Washington University[1] (DC)	2.7	65%[8]	31%	34%[6]	N/A	N/A	12/1[4]	N/A[2]	N/A	97%[4]	N/A
University of Maryland Global Campus*	3.0	53%[8]	46%	12%[6]	91%	0%	19/1	N/A[2]	N/A	100%	N/A
University of Southern Maine*	2.6	69%	52%	36%	55%	2%	12/1	958-1160[2]	38%	88%	2%
Univ. of the District of Columbia*	2.0	68%	46%	42%	72%	0.1%	8/1	N/A	N/A	66%	N/A
Washington Adventist University (MD)	1.8	71%	51%	41%	N/A	N/A	11/1	760-930[2]	N/A	N/A	1%

SOUTH ▶

Rank	School (State) (*Public)	Overall score	Peer assessment score (5.0=highest)	Average first-year student retention rate	2020 graduation rate Predicted	2020 graduation rate Actual	% of classes under 20 ('20)	% of classes of 50 or more ('20)	Student/faculty ratio ('20)	SAT/ACT 25th-75th percentile ('20)	Freshmen in top 25% of HS class ('20)	Acceptance rate ('20)	Average alumni giving rate
1.	**Rollins College** (FL)	100	4.0	86%	78%	81%	60%	0.2%	12/1	1120-1330[2]	60%	61%	6%
2.	**The Citadel, Military Coll. of SC***	93	4.0	86%	66%	72%	46%	0.1%	12/1	1030-1210[2]	32%	80%	26%
3.	**James Madison University** (VA)*	90	4.1	90%	68%	82%	35%	13%	17/1	1120-1280[2]	48%	80%	6%
4.	**Berry College** (GA)	88	3.5	82%	80%	70%	58%	0%	12/1	23-29[2]	63%	77%	20%
5.	**Stetson University** (FL)	86	3.6	77%	68%	64%	61%	0.3%	13/1	1100-1285[2]	53%	81%	6%
6.	**Appalachian State University** (NC)*	82	3.8	87%	65%	73%	35%	7%	16/1	22-27[2]	50%	80%	6%
6.	**Christopher Newport Univ.** (VA)*	82	3.4	87%	72%	80%	53%	4%	14/1	1090-1270[2]	47%	76%	15%
8.	**Florida Southern College**	77	3.2	81%	68%	68%	62%	1%	14/1	1110-1285[2]	55%	50%	9%
9.	**College of Charleston** (SC)*	76	3.8	80%	69%	66%	38%	4%	15/1	1070-1240[2]	51%	74%	4%
10.	**Embry-Riddle Aero. U.–Daytona Beach** (FL)	73	3.7	80%	67%	61%	23%	4%	18/1	1120-1330[2]	54%	61%	2%
10.	**John Brown University** (AR)	73	3.0	83%	67%	64%	53%	0%	14/1	22-29[2]	70%[4]	60%	8%
10.	**Milligan University** (TN)	73	2.9	76%	68%	61%	78%	1%	9/1	21-26	52%	99%	15%
13.	**Asbury University** (KY)	72	3.1	82%	65%	63%	72%	0%	12/1	21-28[2]	57%	98%	16%
13.	**University of Tampa**[1] (FL)	72	3.6	77%[8]	65%	59%[8]	37%[4]	3%[4]	17/1[4]	1100-1250[4]	47%[4]	45%[4]	19%[4]
15.	**Queens University of Charlotte** (NC)	71	3.3	79%	68%	57%	70%	1%	10/1	1040-1230[2]	39%	68%	19%
15.	**Xavier University of Louisiana**	71	3.4	74%	58%	47%	61%	4%	12/1	20-25	55%	81%	17%
17.	**Tuskegee University** (AL)	70	3.1	73%	59%	58%	69%	0%	11/1	19-27	43%	61%	22%
17.	**Winthrop University** (SC)*	70	3.5	73%	58%	61%	58%	1%	12/1	940-1150[2]	41%	64%	5%
19.	**Longwood University** (VA)*	67	3.0	78%	59%	67%	60%	1%	15/1	960-1140[2]	32%	87%	7%
19.	**Univ. of Mary Washington** (VA)*	67	3.2	81%	67%	65%	55%	4%	13/1	1090-1270[2]	50%	74%	8%
21.	**Georgia College & State University***	66	3.3	84%	68%	62%	56%	2%	17/1	1100-1245	N/A	86%	3%
21.	**University of Lynchburg** (VA)	66	3.0	77%	59%	57%	61%	0%	10/1	960-1160[2]	25%	97%	7%
21.	**Western Carolina University** (NC)*	66	3.2	80%	52%	64%	29%	4%	17/1	20-25	41%	48%	3%
24.	**Christian Brothers University** (TN)	65	2.7	79%	60%	58%	72%	0%	11/1	22-27[2]	57%	50%	5%
25.	**Murray State University** (KY)*	63	3.2	78%	57%	53%	65%	3%	16/1	21-27[2]	51%	77%	5%
26.	**University of Montevallo** (AL)*	62	3.0	76%	60%	54%	N/A	N/A	12/1	19-26[2]	N/A	62%	7%
27.	**Lee University** (TN)	61	3.0	80%	57%	62%	60%	7%	15/1	21-27	53%	83%	5%
27.	**University of North Alabama***	61	3.1	76%	51%	50%	62%	2%	18/1	20-26[2]	51%	64%	5%
29.	**Radford University** (VA)*	60	3.1	73%	50%	56%	55%	3%	14/1	920-1110[2]	23%	79%	3%
29.	**Saint Leo University**[1] (FL)	60	2.9	71%[8]	41%	47%[8]	42%[4]	0%[4]	18/1[4]	1040-1190[4]	27%[4]	72%[4]	4%[4]
31.	**Bob Jones University** (SC)	59	2.2	82%	52%	63%	69%	5%	12/1	21-28	14%	84%	8%
31.	**Freed-Hardeman University** (TN)	59	2.4	82%	66%	66%	55%	3%	13/1	21-27	63%	81%	10%
31.	**Jacksonville University** (FL)	59	3.0	73%	59%	51%	71%	1%	11/1	18-26[2]	42%	78%	4%
31.	**University of Tennessee–Martin***	59	2.9	75%	55%	54%	63%	3%	15/1	21-26	44%	65%	6%

Note: Key to footnotes, Page 52

**Tuskegee University,
tied at No. 17 in the South**

STEFAN SMITH

SOUTH ▷

Rank School (State) (*Public)	Overall score	Peer assessment score (5.0=highest)	Average first-year student retention rate	2020 graduation rate		% of classes under 20 ('20)	% of classes of 50 or more ('20)	Student/faculty ratio ('20)	SAT/ACT 25th-75th percentile ('20)	Freshmen in top 25% of HS class ('20)	Accept-ance rate ('20)	Average alumni giving rate
				Predicted	Actual							
35. Eastern Mennonite University (VA)	57	2.4	78%	59%	61%	72%	1%	10/1	980-1230[2]	N/A	72%	19%
35. University of North Georgia*	57	3.1	79%	58%	52%	40%	2%	19/1	1060-1210	46%	77%	6%
35. University of West Florida*	57	3.0	82%	56%	48%	35%	7%	20/1	22-27	44%	58%	4%
38. Columbia International Univ. (SC)	56	2.3	74%	54%	65%	65%	5%	10/1	940-1150	31%	51%	5%
38. Marymount University (VA)	56	3.0	73%	55%	54%	41%	0.2%	14/1	983-1188[2]	14%	85%	1%
40. Brenau University (GA)	55	2.6	57%	46%	45%	89%	1%	9/1	940-1170[2]	34%	67%	4%
40. Columbia College (SC)	55	2.5	67%	54%	66%	75%	0%	12/1	820-1050[2]	23%	97%	6%
40. Converse College[1] (SC)	55	2.8	72%[8]	57%	57%[6]	N/A	N/A	13/1[4]	1000-1230[4]	N/A	89%[4]	N/A
40. Lenoir-Rhyne University (NC)	55	2.8	72%	52%	45%	53%	0%	13/1	18-23[2]	N/A	77%	11%
44. Anderson University (SC)	54	3.0	80%	66%	57%	44%	5%	16/1	1040-1230[2]	64%	59%	5%
44. Austin Peay State University (TN)*	54	3.2	66%	44%	45%	63%	2%	16/1	19-24[2]	36%	91%	3%
44. Mississippi Univ. for Women*	54	2.9	69%	53%	47%	67%	4%	12/1	19-24	63%	99%	9%
44. Troy University (AL)*	54	3.1	74%	55%	51%	60%	4%	19/1	18-25	N/A	92%	5%
48. Coastal Carolina University (SC)*	53	3.1	69%	55%	46%	37%	1%	17/1	1020-1180[2]	37%	70%	8%
48. Morehead State University (KY)*	53	2.9	74%	48%	43%	65%	2%	15/1	20-26[2]	61%	77%	9%
48. North Carolina Central Univ.*	53	2.6	78%	38%	52%	42%	4%	16/1	850-1010	21%	87%	7%
48. Winston-Salem State Univ.[1] (NC)*	53	2.7	77%[8]	35%	49%[6]	N/A	N/A	15/1[4]	890-1030[4]	N/A	68%[4]	N/A
52. Eastern Kentucky University*	52	2.9	75%	49%	52%	50%	4%	15/1	19-25	39%	98%	5%
52. King University (TN)	52	2.5	68%	51%	50%	82%	0%	11/1	19-25[2]	39%	60%	5%
54. Belhaven University[7] (MS)	51	2.8	66%	45%	47%	90%	0.4%	12/1	19-23[9]	N/A	53%	3%
54. Lynn University (FL)	51	2.9	71%	60%	58%	43%	0.4%	17/1	810-1280[2]	N/A	79%	2%
56. Florida Gulf Coast University*	50	2.9	80%	55%	56%	34%	7%	21/1	1060-1210	28%	77%	1%[4]
57. Charleston Southern University (SC)	49	3.0	67%	54%	44%	65%	0.1%	13/1	990-1170	54%	79%	5%
57. Piedmont University (GA)	49	2.4	68%	53%	43%	79%	0%	10/1	980-1140[3]	33%	70%	4%
59. West Liberty University (WV)*	48	2.4	72%	44%	53%	72%	1%	11/1	17-23	43%	68%	N/A
60. Francis Marion University (SC)*	47	2.8	67%	47%	44%	52%	4%	14/1	15-21	39%	75%	10%
60. West Virginia Wesleyan College	47	2.5	73%	61%	55%	60%	0.4%	12/1	880-1100[2]	30%	66%	13%
62. University of Holy Cross (LA)	46	2.5	74%[8]	46%	38%	88%	1%	10/1	18-22[2]	N/A	53%	3%
62. University of Mount Olive (NC)	46	2.3	64%[8]	45%	46%	60%	0%	14/1	16-22[2]	25%	62%	N/A
62. U. of Puerto Rico-Mayaguez[1]*	46	2.5	89%[8]	45%	48%[6]	N/A	N/A	21/1[4]	N/A[2]	N/A	80%[4]	N/A
65. Bryan College (TN)	45	2.4	69%	53%	49%	67%	4%	13/1	18-25[2]	41%	55%	6%
65. Southern Adventist University (TN)	45	2.3	77%	62%	59%	63%	6%	13/1	19-27[3]	N/A	74%	7%
65. Thomas More University (KY)	45	2.5	64%	48%	39%	75%	0%	14/1	19-24[2]	34%	92%	7%
65. U. of North Carolina-Pembroke*	45	2.7	72%	43%	42%	57%	1%	18/1	17-21[2]	34%	91%	1%
69. Arkansas Tech University*	44	2.6	70%	38%	46%	54%	2%	16/1	18-25	39%	98%	3%
70. Alabama State University*	43	2.4	60%	34%	32%	63%	0.3%	15/1	14-20	N/A[5]	99%	6%[4]
70. Auburn U. at Montgomery (AL)*	43	3.1	68%	50%	35%	53%	3%	16/1	18-23	44%	96%	4%
70. Norfolk State University (VA)*	43	2.6	71%	39%	40%	52%	2%	16/1	840-1020	15%	91%	N/A
70. North Greenville University (SC)	43	2.6	71%	54%	56%	61%	1%	14/1	950-1170	33%	68%	N/A
74. Alcorn State University (MS)*	42	2.6	76%	34%	45%	N/A	N/A	16/1	16-25	24%	38%	7%
74. Columbus State University (GA)*	42	2.6	75%	48%	39%	61%	4%	17/1	860-1080	31%	78%	3%
74. Delta State University (MS)*	42	2.5	68%	51%	39%	69%	0%	11/1	18-23	41%	100%	3%
77. Fayetteville State University (NC)*	41	2.4	72%	35%	36%	56%	1%	17/1	840-1000[2]	23%	79%	2%
77. Jacksonville State University[1] (AL)*	41	2.8	75%[8]	52%	40%[6]	N/A	N/A	18/1[4]	18-24[4]	N/A	55%[4]	N/A
77. Southeastern Baptist Theol. Sem.[1] (NC)	41	2.4	79%[8]	42%	50%[6]	N/A	N/A	27/1[4]	N/A[2]	N/A	92%[4]	N/A
80. EDP U. of Puerto Rico Inc-San Juan[1] (PR)	40	1.8	54%[8]	25%	50%[6]	N/A	N/A	14/1[4]	N/A[2]	N/A	70%[4]	N/A
80. Shorter University (GA)	40	2.3	61%[8]	48%	40%[6]	68%	0.3%	15/1	18-24[2]	N/A	71%	1%[4]
80. St. Thomas University (FL)	40	2.4	65%	45%	35%	57%	0%	11/1	890-1070[2]	N/A	60%	9%
80. Wheeling University (WV)	40	2.1	69%	58%	49%	N/A	N/A	12/1	890-1090[2]	N/A	79%	4%
84. Lindsey Wilson College (KY)	39	2.4	62%	38%	40%	85%	0%	15/1	18-24[2]	38%	N/A	N/A
84. Northwestern State U. of Louisiana*	39	2.4	73%	45%	48%	72%	2%	19/1	19-24	38%	85%	N/A
84. Southern Wesleyan University[1] (SC)	39	2.3	71%[8]	45%	50%[6]	N/A	N/A	14/1[4]	948-1153[4]	N/A	35%[4]	N/A
84. Virginia State University[1]*	39	2.5	67%[8]	40%	40%[6]	N/A	N/A	13/1[4]	830-1010[4]	N/A	95%[4]	N/A
88. Nicholls State University (LA)*	38	2.6	73%	48%	44%	41%	9%	18/1	19-24	42%	93%	6%
88. South Carolina State University[7]*	38	2.4	68%	39%	30%	61%	0.3%	14/1	14-18	30%	94%	5%
88. Tusculum University (TN)	38	2.5	65%[8]	43%	35%[6]	58%	0%	18/1	18-24[2]	N/A	67%	2%
91. Concord University (WV)*	37	2.3	62%	44%	38%	69%	0.3%	16/1	880-1090	42%	92%	3%
91. Fairmont State University (WV)*	37	2.5	65%	45%	37%	67%	3%	15/1	890-1110	39%	94%	1%
93. Cumberland University (TN)	36	2.5	65%	47%	54%	50%	0.2%	17/1	18-23[2]	N/A	54%	2%
93. Southeastern Louisiana University*	36	2.5	68%	44%	40%	37%	6%	19/1	20-25	37%	97%	3%
93. Southern Arkansas University*	36	2.2	68%	40%	41%	61%	2%	18/1	19-25	42%	67%	3%

Note: Key to footnotes, Page 52

INTERNSHIPS

JUNIOR JOURNEY

4-YEAR GRADUATION

OUR GUARANTEES

Florida Southern College goes beyond the conventional college experience, guaranteeing each student an internship, a travel-study experience, and graduation in four years. These signature opportunities, combined with our devoted faculty and stunning historic campus, create a college experience unlike any other.

flsouthern.edu/**guarantees**

SOUTH ▶

Rank School (State) (*Public)	Overall score	Peer assessment score (5.0=highest)	Average first-year student retention rate	2020 graduation rate		% of classes under 20 ('20)	% of classes of 50 or more ('20)	Student/faculty ratio ('20)	SAT/ACT 25th-75th percentile ('20)	Freshmen in top 25% of HS class ('20)	Acceptance rate ('20)	Average alumni giving rate
				Predicted	Actual							
93. Southern U. and A&M College (LA)*	36	2.4	63%	29%	28%	56%	2%	17/1	18-20[2]	38%	41%	17%
93. University of West Alabama*	36	2.6	65%	43%	40%	76%	0%	14/1	17-22[2]	N/A	93%	3%[4]
98. Campbellsville University (KY)	35	2.5	65%	42%	36%	73%	0.2%	14/1	17-23[2]	12%	78%	8%
98. McNeese State University[1] (LA)*	35	2.5	69%[8]	49%	43%[8]	41%[4]	7%[4]	20/1[4]	20-24[4]	46%[4]	81%[4]	5%[4]
98. Midway University (KY)	35	2.1	73%	50%	53%	55%	1%	15/1	18-24	26%	73%	1%
98. Southeastern University (FL)	35	2.5	66%	44%	44%	55%	3%	30/1	970-1190[3]	32%	43%	N/A
102. Louisiana State U.–Shreveport[1]*	34	2.5	65%[8]	46%	31%[6]	55%[4]	3%[4]	27/1[4]	20-24[4]	N/A	96%[4]	N/A
102. Methodist University[1] (NC)	34	2.4	60%[8]	51%	41%[6]	N/A	N/A	9/1[4]	950-1140[4]	N/A	63%[4]	N/A

School (State) (*Public)	Peer assessment score (5.0=highest)	Average first-year student retention rate	2020 graduation rate		% of classes under 20 ('20)	% of classes of 50 or more ('20)	Student/faculty ratio ('20)	SAT/ACT 25th-75th percentile ('20)	Freshmen in top 25% of HS class ('20)	Acceptance rate ('20)	Average alumni giving rate
			Predicted	Actual							
SCHOOLS RANKED 104 THROUGH 137 ARE LISTED HERE ALPHABETICALLY											
Alabama A&M University[7]*	2.5	59%[8]	37%	27%[8]	36%[4]	5%[4]	20/1[4]	15-19	N/A	90%	14%[4]
Albany State University[1] (GA)*	2.3	60%[8]	36%	35%[6]	N/A	N/A	19/1[4]	740-890[4]	N/A	66%[4]	N/A
Bayamon Central University[1] (PR)	1.9	58%[8]	18%	19%[6]	N/A	N/A	18/1[4]	N/A[2]	N/A	77%[4]	N/A
Bethel University[1] (TN)	2.2	56%[8]	36%	29%[6]	66%[4]	3%[4]	15/1[4]	16-20[4]	18%[4]	90%[4]	N/A
Caribbean University[1] (PR)	1.8	70%[8]	21%	22%[6]	N/A	N/A	13/1[4]	N/A[2]	N/A	N/A	N/A
Clayton State University (GA)*	2.4	70%	35%	31%	33%	3%	19/1	880-1060[2]	N/A	68%	2%
Coker College[1] (SC)	2.6	58%[8]	44%	40%[6]	N/A	N/A	12/1[4]	900-1230[4]	N/A	63%[4]	N/A
ECPI University (VA)	1.6	50%	36%	39%	96%	0.3%	16/1	N/A[2]	N/A	80%	N/A
Everglades University[1] (FL)	1.8	63%[8]	38%	54%[6]	N/A	N/A	18/1[4]	N/A[2]	N/A	75%[4]	N/A
Faulkner University[1] (AL)	2.5	58%[8]	39%	29%[6]	N/A	N/A	13/1[4]	18-23[4]	N/A	78%[4]	N/A
Fort Valley State University (GA)*	2.2	74%	37%	43%	48%	3%	27/1	16-19	16%	78%	10%
Georgia Southwestern State University*	2.3	66%	49%	36%	57%	0.2%	18/1	940-1110	38%	73%	2%
Grambling State University[1] (LA)*	2.6	71%[8]	28%	34%[6]	N/A	N/A	24/1[4]	16-20[4]	N/A	97%[4]	N/A
Henderson State University[1] (AR)*	2.3	64%[8]	52%	35%[6]	N/A	N/A	14/1[4]	19-24[4]	N/A	76%[4]	N/A
Hodges University[1] (FL)	1.8	48%[8]	32%	14%[6]	N/A	N/A	15/1[4]	N/A[2]	N/A	61%[4]	N/A
Inter American U. of Puerto Rico–Aguadilla	1.8	72%[8]	26%	37%	66%	1%	27/1[4]	N/A	N/A	43%	N/A
Inter American U. of Puerto Rico–Arecibo[1]	1.9	71%[8]	29%	36%	52%	0%	28/1[4]	N/A[2]	N/A	39%	N/A
Inter American U. of Puerto Rico–Fajardo[1]	1.8	75%[8]	31%	33%[6]	N/A	N/A	24/1[4]	N/A[2]	N/A	53%[4]	N/A
Inter American University of Puerto Rico–Ponce[1]	2.1	75%[8]	30%	35%	42%	1%	25/1[4]	N/A[2]	N/A	35%	N/A
Louisiana College	2.1	60%	48%	33%	76%	0.3%	11/1	18-24	23%	71%	N/A
Mississippi Valley State U.*	2.2	61%[8]	33%	27%	57%	0%	13/1	14-18	35%	83%	N/A
Montreat College[1] (NC)	2.2	62%[8]	55%	36%[6]	N/A	N/A	7/1[4]	922-1150[4]	N/A	56%[4]	N/A
Pfeiffer University[1] (NC)	2.3	61%[8]	51%	43%[6]	N/A	N/A	13/1[4]	915-1140[4]	N/A	64%[4]	N/A
Pontifical Catholic U. of Puerto Rico–Arecibo[1]	2.2	78%[8]	32%	35%[6]	N/A	N/A	15/1[4]	N/A[2]	N/A	99%[4]	N/A
Reinhardt University (GA)	2.3	61%	49%	35%	77%	0%	11/1	940-1160[2]	35%	99%	2%
Salem University[1] (WV)	2.1	47%[8]	31%	13%[6]	N/A	N/A	18/1[4]	N/A[2]	N/A	N/A	N/A
Savannah State University[7] (GA)*	2.3	60%[8]	31%	28%[6]	44%[4]	1%[4]	17/1	900-1030[4]	N/A	69%	N/A
Southern University at New Orleans[7]*	2.1	49%[8]	27%	19%	47%[4]	0.3%[4]	21/1[4]	15-18[4]	27%[4]	60%[4]	1%
Thomas University[1] (GA)	1.9	67%[8]	37%	31%[6]	N/A	N/A	10/1[4]	N/A[2]	N/A	38%[4]	N/A
Union College[1] (KY)	2.3	62%[8]	41%	33%[6]	N/A	N/A	12/1[4]	17-22[4]	N/A	55%[4]	N/A
Universidad Ana G. Mendez–Carolina Campus[1] (PR)	1.8	74%[8]	19%	27%[6]	N/A	N/A	22/1[4]	N/A[2]	N/A	N/A	N/A
Universidad Ana G. Mendez–Cupey Campus[1] (PR)	1.9	70%[8]	18%	30%[6]	N/A	N/A	21/1[4]	N/A[2]	N/A	N/A	N/A
Universidad del Sagrado Corazon (PR)	2.5	77%[8]	29%	42%	50%	0.2%	23/1	N/A[2]	N/A	43%	0.3%
University of Arkansas–Monticello[1]*	2.3	64%[8]	34%	21%[6]	N/A	N/A	13/1[4]	N/A[2]	N/A	N/A	N/A

MIDWEST ▶

Rank School (State) (*Public)	Overall score	Peer assessment score (5.0=highest)	Average first-year student retention rate	2020 graduation rate		% of classes under 20 ('20)	% of classes of 50 or more ('20)	Student/faculty ratio ('20)	SAT/ACT 25th-75th percentile ('20)	Freshmen in top 25% of HS class ('20)	Acceptance rate ('20)	Average alumni giving rate
				Predicted	Actual							
1. Butler University (IN)	100	4.1	88%	86%	82%	45%	4%	12/1	1150-1320[2]	81%	76%	20%
2. Bradley University (IL)	88	3.7	85%	71%	75%	57%	3%	14/1	1080-1280[2]	65%	73%	7%
2. John Carroll University (OH)	88	3.6	86%	70%	75%	41%	0%	13/1	22-28[2]	50%	88%	14%
4. Calvin University (MI)	87	3.5	87%	76%	76%	39%	1%	12/1	1100-1320[2]	62%	76%	17%
5. Xavier University (OH)	86	3.9	84%	72%	69%	40%	1%	12/1	22-28[9]	55%	81%	14%
6. Truman State University (MO)*	85	3.8	85%	74%	75%	58%	3%	14/1	24-30	82%	72%	6%
7. University of Evansville (IN)	84	3.4	85%	71%	67%	72%	0%	10/1	1070-1278[2]	65%	64%	12%

Note: Key to footnotes, Page 52.

MIDWEST ▶

Rank	School (State) (*Public)	Overall score	Peer assessment score (5.0=highest)	Average first-year student retention rate	2020 graduation rate		% of classes under 20 ('20)	% of classes of 50 or more ('20)	Student/faculty ratio ('20)	SAT/ACT 25th-75th percentile ('20)	Freshmen in top 25% of HS class ('20)	Acceptance rate ('20)	Average alumni giving rate
					Predicted	Actual							
8.	Milwaukee School of Engineering	82	3.6	84%	78%	70%	43%	0%	14/1	25-30[2]	N/A	60%	6%
9.	Baldwin Wallace University (OH)	79	3.4	82%	61%	70%	59%	1%	11/1	21-27[2]	46%	70%	6%
10.	Augustana University (SD)	77	3.4	84%	77%	72%	53%	1%	12/1	22-28[2]	65%	71%	10%
10.	Dominican University (IL)	77	3.1	81%	48%	63%	60%	0%	10/1	960-1160[2]	47%	76%	10%
12.	Drury University (MO)	76	3.0	82%	61%	60%	62%	0.3%	13/1	21-28[2]	64%	71%	10%
12.	Hamline University (MN)	76	3.4	77%	61%	65%	55%	1%	13/1	20-26[2]	43%	69%	8%
12.	Kettering University (MI)	76	3.1	92%	79%	67%	46%	1%	13/1	1180-1360[2]	71%	74%	6%
12.	Otterbein University (OH)	76	3.5	81%	68%	66%	64%	2%	12/1	20-27	54%	76%	7%
16.	Webster University (MO)	75	3.0	78%	60%	55%	88%	0.3%	8/1	20-27	54%	67%	2%
17.	Cedarville University (OH)	74	2.9	86%	75%	74%	55%	9%	17/1	23-30[2]	62%	59%	7%
17.	Elmhurst University (IL)	74	3.2	79%	58%	68%	49%	0.1%	13/1	980-1170[2]	46%	66%	5%
19.	Franciscan Univ. of Steubenville (OH)	73	2.8	87%	74%	77%	47%	2%	13/1	1070-1290	74%[4]	73%	8%
19.	Indiana Wesleyan University	73	2.9	79%	60%	71%	68%	1%	13/1	1010-1200[2]	54%	91%	6%
19.	Lewis University (IL)	73	2.9	82%	58%	70%	61%	0%	14/1	1010-1220[2]	45%	66%	4%
19.	North Central College (IL)	73	3.2	79%	67%	66%	46%	0%	13/1	1050-1230[2]	30%	53%	15%
19.	University of Northern Iowa*	73	3.4	84%	66%	63%	44%	4%	17/1	19-25[2]	52%	79%	7%
24.	Augsburg University (MN)	72	3.3	74%	55%	59%	63%	1%	12/1	17-23[2]	N/A	73%	9%
24.	Nebraska Wesleyan University	72	3.2	79%	66%	63%	68%	0.4%	13/1	22-29[2]	51%	70%	13%
24.	Rockhurst University (MO)	72	3.2	86%	71%	73%	30%	2%	14/1	21-27[4]	50%	73%	11%
27.	Grand Valley State University[1] (MI)*	70	3.2	84%[8]	62%	66%[6]	24%[4]	6%[4]	16/1[4]	1040-1250[4]	46%[4]	83%[4]	4%[4]
27.	Marian University (IN)	70	3.2	81%	60%	60%	58%	0.4%	13/1	980-1180[2]	48%	64%	8%
27.	St. Ambrose University (IA)	70	3.1	79%	60%	64%	63%	0.3%	12/1	20-25[3]	56%[4]	74%	6%
30.	Univ. of Illinois–Springfield*	69	3.0	77%	57%	55%	54%	1%	12/1	980-1190[2]	46%	77%	4%
31.	Carroll University (WI)	68	3.1	81%	67%	70%	57%	4%	14/1	21-26[2]	54%	N/A	7%
31.	Huntington University (IN)	68	2.6	83%	60%	65%	74%	1%	11/1	970-1198[2]	47%	78%	16%

Doing an internship, co-op, or apprenticeship?

Tell your employer to get on **Symba**, the leading all-in-one program management and data analytics platform.

Join our mission to **#OpenUpTheWorkforce**.

Learn more at symba.io

MIDWEST ▶

Rank	School (State) (*Public)	Overall score	Peer assessment score (5.0=highest)	Average first-year student retention rate	2020 graduation rate Predicted	2020 graduation rate Actual	% of classes under 20 ('20)	% of classes of 50 or more ('20)	Student/faculty ratio ('20)	SAT/ACT 25th-75th percentile ('20)	Freshmen in top 25% of HS class ('20)	Acceptance rate ('20)	Average alumni giving rate
31.	University of Michigan–Dearborn*	68	2.9	81%	58%	55%	41%	6%	16/1	1090-1320	N/A	68%	6%
34.	St. Mary's Univ. of Minnesota	67	3.0	81%	57%	62%	65%	0%	18/1	20-26[2]	N/A	93%	7%
34.	Univ. of Nebraska–Kearney*	67	2.9	79%	54%	59%	55%	2%	13/1	19-26	46%	88%	7%
36.	Muskingum University (OH)	66	3.0	74%	49%	56%	74%	0%	13/1	18-23[2]	39%	80%	10%
37.	Capital University (OH)	65	2.8	77%	61%	60%	62%	0.4%	12/1	21-26[9]	50%	74%	7%
37.	Concordia University (NE)	65	2.8	78%	62%	63%	63%	0%	14/1	20-26[2]	39%	76%	18%
37.	Lawrence Technological Univ. (MI)	65	2.9	78%[8]	70%	59%	72%	2%	11/1	1020-1280[2]	N/A[5]	82%	5%
37.	Univ. of Wisconsin–La Crosse*	65	3.2	85%	70%	71%	27%	12%	19/1	22-26[2]	60%	82%	3%
41.	North Park University (IL)	64	2.9	74%	55%	59%	63%	0.4%	10/1	940-1120[2]	N/A	44%	N/A
41.	Saint Mary-of-the-Woods College (IN)	64	2.7	68%	46%	52%	90%	0%	7/1	940-1119[2]	N/A	71%	20%
41.	University of Minnesota–Duluth*	64	3.1	79%	66%	61%	37%	13%	17/1	21-26[2]	47%	79%	4%
41.	Univ. of Wisconsin–Eau Claire*	64	3.2	82%	64%	67%	27%	11%	21/1	21-26[2]	48%	90%	5%
41.	Winona State University (MN)*	64	3.0	76%	59%	61%	47%	7%	18/1	19-25[2]	33%	75%	3%
46.	Anderson University (IN)	63	2.9	71%[8]	64%	64%	83%	1%	9/1	950-1160[2]	42%	68%	9%
46.	Bethel University (IN)	63	2.7	72%	55%	62%	64%	4%	11/1	930-1160[2]	40%	93%	7%
46.	Univ. of Northwestern–St. Paul (MN)	63	2.8	83%	64%	71%	55%	5%	17/1	21-27[2]	50%	92%	N/A
49.	Buena Vista University (IA)	62	2.6	70%	59%	62%	74%	0.4%	11/1	19-24[2]	41%	56%	4%
49.	Univ. of Wisconsin–Whitewater*	62	3.0	80%	54%	62%	31%	4%	20/1	19-24[2]	27%	94%	4%
51.	Fontbonne University (MO)	61	2.7	75%	63%	66%	87%	0%	10/1	17-23[2]	N/A	85%	5%
51.	Mount Mary University (WI)	61	2.5	72%	44%	51%	88%	0%	10/1	16-20[2]	41%	53%	5%
51.	Mount Mercy University[1] (IA)	61	2.5	72%[8]	56%	64%[8]	65%[4]	1%[4]	14/1[4]	18-24[4]	41%[4]	66%[4]	9%[4]
54.	Ashland University (OH)	60	2.6	77%	54%	62%	55%	1%	16/1	19-24	38%	74%	5%
54.	Eastern Illinois University*	60	2.8	73%	52%	51%	55%	0.2%	14/1	18-23	43%	56%	3%
54.	McKendree University (IL)	60	2.7	76%	55%	54%	67%	0%	14/1	871-1277[2]	33%	70%	5%
54.	Saint Xavier University (IL)	60	2.9	75%	48%	55%	43%	0.3%	16/1	950-1120[2]	50%	79%	4%
54.	Spring Arbor University (MI)	60	2.6	79%	54%	65%	78%	0.4%	12/1	983-1190	48%	63%	4%
54.	Walsh University (OH)	60	2.6	74%	58%	60%	71%	1%	15/1	19-26[2]	N/A	77%	8%[4]
54.	Western Illinois University*	60	2.7	70%	48%	46%	68%	1%	13/1	880-1090[2]	40%	67%	3%
61.	Concordia University Chicago	59	2.8	68%	43%	50%	79%	0%	12/1	990-1180[2]	N/A	79%	6%
61.	Morningside University (IA)	59	2.7	70%	60%	59%	59%	0%	13/1	19-25[4]	32%	66%	18%
61.	Viterbo University (WI)	59	2.8	79%[8]	64%	65%	61%[4]	4%[4]	12/1	20-25[2]	43%	79%	6%
64.	College of Saint Mary (NE)	58	2.6	79%	64%	59%	72%	0%	9/1	19-23	44%	51%	9%
64.	Ohio Dominican University	58	2.7	63%	53%	54%	56%[4]	0%[4]	16/1	19-26[2]	40%	49%	3%
64.	Olivet Nazarene University (IL)	58	2.6	77%	62%	65%	49%	7%	17/1	950-1180[2]	43%	67%	10%
64.	Univ. of Wisconsin–Stevens Point*	58	3.0	75%	57%	59%	31%	10%	19/1	19-24[9]	30%	86%	4%
64.	Ursuline College (OH)	58	2.7	73%	52%	36%	79%	0%	8/1	18-24[2]	39%	71%	10%
69.	Alverno College (WI)	57	3.0	71%	44%	43%	90%	0.2%	9/1	17-20	N/A	78%	7%
69.	Trine University[1] (IN)	57	2.7	77%[8]	61%	61%[6]	N/A	N/A	15/1[4]	1040-1260[4]	N/A	82%[4]	N/A
69.	University of Dubuque (IA)	57	2.8	63%	45%	46%	81%	1%	15/1	17-23[9]	22%	79%	7%
69.	University of Saint Francis (IN)	57	2.9	72%	50%	50%	61%	0.3%	12/1	960-1160[2]	44%	99%	7%
69.	University of Wisconsin–Stout*	57	2.8	71%	56%	60%	33%	1%	18/1	20-25	32%	89%	1%
74.	Cornerstone University (MI)	56	2.5	80%	56%	66%	63%	2%	15/1	930-1170[2]	10%	87%	4%
74.	Madonna University (MI)	56	2.6	75%	53%	57%	71%	0%	13/1	920-1110[2]	28%	68%	1%
74.	Mount Vernon Nazarene U. (OH)	56	2.4	79%	53%	62%	64%	2%	19/1	20-25[4]	48%[4]	72%	N/A
74.	Southeast Missouri State Univ.*	56	2.9	76%	52%	51%	52%	2%	19/1	19-25[2]	46%	93%	3%
74.	University of Central Missouri*	56	2.9	73%	51%	51%	61%	2%	16/1	19-25[2]	37%	64%	2%[4]
79.	Minnesota State Univ.–Mankato*	55	2.9	76%	54%	51%	37%	9%	22/1	19-24[2]	29%	67%	3%
79.	Mount St. Joseph University (OH)	55	2.6	73%[8]	52%	50%	61%	8%	11/1	20-24	39%	60%	6%
79.	Northern State University (SD)*	55	2.6	75%	50%	48%	63%	3%	18/1	19-25	34%	79%	8%
82.	Dakota State University (SD)*	54	2.7	69%	50%	47%	54%	1%	18/1	19-26[2]	30%	83%	5%
82.	Emporia State University (KS)*	54	2.8	76%	51%	46%	58%	4%	17/1	19-24[2]	40%	86%	6%
82.	Malone University (OH)	54	2.5	71%	56%	54%	61%	1%	13/1	19-25[2]	N/A	74%	6%
82.	Northern Michigan University*	54	3.1	76%	54%	50%	38%	8%	20/1	950-1180[9]	N/A	67%	2%
82.	University of Sioux Falls (SD)	54	2.8	76%	60%	56%	57%	3%	17/1	20-25[2]	39%	92%	3%
82.	Univ. of Wisconsin–Platteville[1]*	54	2.9	78%[8]	58%	54%[6]	N/A	N/A	20/1[4]	20-26[4]	N/A	85%[4]	N/A
88.	Bemidji State University (MN)*	53	2.8	71%	52%	46%	50%	4%	18/1	19-24[4]	36%	69%	6%[4]
88.	Columbia College Chicago	53	2.7	69%	61%	50%	64%	2%	14/1	950-1170[2]	34%	90%	0.4%
88.	Concordia University–St. Paul (MN)	53	2.9	69%	48%	47%	66%	0%	20/1	17-24[9]	N/A	69%	3%
88.	Minnesota State Univ.–Moorhead*	53	2.7	73%	58%	54%	46%	6%	18/1	19-24[2]	35%	66%	3%
88.	Pittsburg State University[1] (KS)*	53	2.7	74%[8]	51%	50%[8]	56%[4]	5%[4]	16/1[4]	19-24[4]	39%[4]	96%[4]	5%[4]
88.	University of Southern Indiana*	53	2.8	71%	52%	52%	45%[4]	3%[4]	17/1	980-1170[2]	44%	94%	3%

Note: Key to footnotes, Page 52

Rank	School (State) (*Public)	Overall score	Peer assessment score (5.0=highest)	Average first-year student retention rate	2020 graduation rate		% of classes under 20 ('20)	% of classes of 50 or more ('20)	Student/ faculty ratio ('20)	SAT/ACT 25th-75th percentile ('20)	Freshmen in top 25% of HS class ('20)	Accept-ance rate ('20)	Average alumni giving rate
					Predicted	Actual							
88.	Wayne State College (NE)*	53	2.6	72%	50%	53%	43%	0.3%	20/1	18-25[2]	35%	100%	9%
95.	Davenport University (MI)	52	2.5	75%	54%	54%	66%	0%	14/1	940-1170[2]	N/A	93%	1%
95.	Friends University[1] (KS)	52	2.6	73%[8]	52%	42%[6]	73%[4]	2%[4]	11/1[4]	19-25[4]	43%[4]	46%[4]	5%[4]
95.	Greenville University[1] (IL)	52	2.4	68%[8]	54%	52%[6]	59%[4]	6%[4]	13/1[4]	960-1180[4]	N/A	57%[4]	N/A
95.	Judson University (IL)	52	2.4	68%	58%	61%	77%	1%	10/1	860-1120[2]	25%	92%	2%
95.	St. Cloud State University (MN)*	52	2.7	68%	51%	44%	53%	2%	17/1	18-24[2]	20%	93%	2%
95.	Univ. of Wisconsin–River Falls*	52	2.8	75%	57%	58%	36%	8%	21/1	19-25[3]	24%	77%	N/A
101.	Northwest Missouri State Univ.*	51	2.9	76%	55%	53%	51%	6%	20/1	19-24	42%	71%	5%[4]
101.	University of Saint Mary (KS)	51	2.6	64%	45%	56%	61%	0%	13/1	17-23[2]	26%	60%	6%
101.	Univ. of Wisconsin–Oshkosh[1]*	51	2.9	76%[8]	56%	55%[6]	N/A	N/A	23/1[4]	19-24[4]	N/A	76%[4]	N/A
104.	Minot State University (ND)*	50	2.7	71%	58%	55%	73%	1%	11/1	18-24	34%	77%	3%
104.	Univ. of Wisconsin–Green Bay[1]*	50	3.0	72%[8]	58%	52%[6]	N/A	N/A	22/1[4]	18-24[4]	N/A	85%[4]	N/A
106.	Grace College and Seminary[1] (IN)	49	2.2	82%[8]	59%	63%[6]	N/A	N/A	20/1[4]	N/A	N/A	80%[4]	N/A
106.	Purdue University–Fort Wayne*	49	2.9	60%	51%	38%	56%	3%	13/1	980-1180	39%	83%	3%[4]
108.	Fort Hays State University (KS)*	48	2.8	75%[8]	45%	46%	57%	2%	19/1	17-24[2]	39%	91%	N/A
108.	Indiana Tech	48	2.4	66%	30%	38%	53%	0%	15/1	920-1130[2]	N/A	63%	3%
108.	Mount Marty University (SD)	48	2.5	73%	54%	53%	67%	2%	14/1	17-22	N/A	78%	5%
108.	Stephens College[1] (MO)	48	2.7	63%[8]	52%	52%[6]	N/A	N/A	9/1[4]	20-25[4]	N/A	56%[4]	N/A
112.	Indiana University East*	47	2.4	65%	44%	45%	79%	2%	14/1	920-1120[2]	34%	67%	5%
112.	Marian University (WI)	47	2.5	69%[8]	48%	47%	64%	0.3%	13/1	17-22[3]	30%	68%	2%
112.	Newman University (KS)	47	2.6	76%	54%	53%	80%	1%	9/1	19-26[2]	41%	83%	3%[4]
112.	Purdue University–Northwest (IN)*	47	2.8	69%	55%	42%	43%	5%	16/1	960-1150[2]	39%	30%	N/A
112.	Saginaw Valley State Univ. (MI)*	47	2.7	76%	55%	48%	34%	3%	17/1	970-1190[2]	45%	89%	N/A
117.	MidAmerica Nazarene U. (KS)	46	2.4	66%	52%	48%	77%	6%	10/1	16-24[2]	N/A	100%	N/A
117.	Southwest Baptist University (MO)	46	2.3	67%	50%	48%	80%	1%	13/1	19-25	47%	74%	2%

CRIMSON

If you could attend any university in the world, where would you go?

Get into your dream university!

Crimson Education empowers students to unlock their potential through personalized 1:1 college counseling! Programs can include:

+ Strategic guidance & planning,
+ Extracurricular and leadership mentoring,
+ Essay mentoring,
+ Internship & research placement,
+ and Standardized test tutoring.

Crimson students are **4x more likely** to receive admissions to their dream university.

Mention code "USN guidebook" for **$200** off your curated Crimson program.

I'm in!

Learn more at **pages.crimsoneducation.org/usnews** or scan the QR code:

MIDWEST ▶

School (State) (*Public)	Peer assessment score (5.0=highest)	Average first-year student retention rate	2020 graduation rate Predicted	2020 graduation rate Actual	% of classes under 20 ('20)	% of classes of 50 or more ('20)	Student/ faculty ratio ('20)	SAT/ACT 25th-75th percentile ('20)	Freshmen in top 25% of HS class ('20)	Accept- ance rate ('20)	Average alumni giving rate
SCHOOLS RANKED 119 THROUGH 157 ARE LISTED HERE ALPHABETICALLY											
Avila University[1] (MO)	2.6	70%[8]	52%	49%[6]	N/A	N/A	12/1[4]	19-23[4]	N/A	41%[4]	N/A
Baker College of Flint[1] (MI)	1.8	49%[8]	38%	15%[6]	N/A	N/A	7/1[4]	N/A[2]	N/A	73%[4]	N/A
Bellevue University[1] (NE)	2.4	78%[8]	46%	24%[6]	N/A	N/A	27/1[4]	N/A[2]	N/A	N/A	N/A
Black Hills State University (SD)*	2.6	65%	51%	34%[6]	64%	1%	16/1[4]	18-24[2]	N/A	83%	N/A
Calumet College of St. Joseph (IN)	2.3	55%	40%	32%	85%	2%	10/1	790-1005[2]	14%[4]	26%	1%
Chadron State College[1] (NE)*	2.4	64%[8]	51%	43%[6]	N/A	N/A	17/1[4]	N/A[2]	N/A	N/A	N/A
Chicago State University*	2.0	57%	42%	17%	73%	0%	9/1	750-963[2]	N/A	46%	1%
Columbia College[1] (MO)	2.6	67%[8]	37%	23%[6]	N/A	N/A	23/1[4]	N/A[2]	N/A	N/A	N/A
Crown College[1] (MN)	2.1	70%[8]	46%	55%[6]	N/A	N/A	15/1[4]	18-23[4]	N/A	50%[4]	N/A
DeVry University[1] (IL)	1.6	48%[8]	27%	25%[6]	N/A	N/A	23/1[4]	N/A[2]	N/A	96%[4]	N/A
Evangel University[7] (MO)	2.4	80%	54%	48%	N/A	N/A	15/1	20-26[2]	N/A	74%[4]	5%
Governors State University (IL)*	2.3	54%	41%	23%	64%	0.4%	11/1	830-1050	34%	48%	N/A
Graceland University (IA)	2.2	64%	44%	41%	66%	1%	14/1	15-26[2]	17%	68%	14%
Herzing University[1] (WI)	1.8	38%[8]	30%	19%[6]	56%	0%	17/1[4]	N/A[2]	N/A	91%[4]	N/A
Holy Family College[1] (WI)	2.0	57%[8]	41%	46%[6]	N/A	N/A	9/1[4]	15-22[4]	N/A	51%[4]	N/A
Indiana University Northwest*	2.4	67%	44%	32%	60%	4%	14/1	890-1090[2]	37%	82%	5%
Indiana University–South Bend*	2.6	66%	43%	38%	58%	0.4%	13/1	930-1140[2]	32%	87%	5%
Indiana University Southeast*	2.4	61%	45%	36%	73%	0.2%	13/1	17-23[2]	34%	85%	5%
Lake Erie College (OH)	2.4	64%	50%	48%	69%	0%	14/1	N/A[2]	N/A	96%	N/A
Lakeland University[1] (WI)	2.2	66%[8]	49%	51%[6]	N/A	N/A	13/1[4]	17-22[4]	N/A	78%[4]	N/A
Lourdes University[1] (OH)	2.5	67%[8]	52%	34%[6]	N/A	N/A	11/1[4]	17-23[4]	N/A	69%[4]	N/A
Maharishi University of Management[1] (IA)	1.7	55%[8]	44%	67%[6]	N/A	N/A	11/1[4]	N/A[2]	N/A	81%[4]	N/A
Midland University[1] (NE)	2.4	61%[8]	53%	44%[6]	N/A	N/A	14/1[4]	18-24[4]	N/A	49%[4]	N/A
Missouri Baptist University[1]	2.3	65%[8]	48%	40%[6]	N/A	N/A	19/1[4]	19-23[4]	N/A	61%[4]	N/A
Missouri Western State University[1]*	2.2	64%[8]	42%	33%[6]	N/A	N/A	16/1[4]	N/A[2]	N/A	N/A	N/A
Northeastern Illinois University*	2.7	51%[8]	44%	22%[8]	65%	0.1%	12/1	830-1020	22%	61%	2%[4]
Notre Dame College of Ohio[1]	2.4	62%[8]	48%	38%[6]	N/A	N/A	13/1[4]	16-21[4]	N/A	98%[4]	N/A
Ohio Christian University	2.1	64%[8]	31%	46%	N/A	N/A	8/1	N/A[2]	N/A	N/A	N/A
Park University (MO)	2.7	57%	40%	27%	73%	0%	15/1	17-23[4]	N/A	N/A	1%
Peru State College[1] (NE)*	2.3	65%[8]	43%	35%[6]	N/A	N/A	20/1[4]	N/A[2]	N/A	N/A	N/A
Rockford University (IL)	2.6	66%	51%	46%	70%	0%	10/1	900-1100	33%	51%	6%
Shawnee State University (OH)*	2.2	73%	43%	42%	65%	2%	15/1	18-24[4]	44%	72%	2%
Siena Heights University[1] (MI)	2.7	69%[8]	50%	44%[6]	N/A	N/A	12/1[4]	N/A[2]	N/A	73%[4]	N/A
Southwestern College (KS)	2.1	58%	55%	38%	68%	4%	10/1	17-22	26%	56%	5%
Southwest Minnesota State University[1]*	2.5	64%[8]	48%	46%[6]	N/A	N/A	16/1[4]	18-24[4]	N/A	64%[4]	N/A
Tiffin University[7] (OH)	2.6	66%	47%	41%	58%	0%	15/1	17-22[2]	N/A	62%	4%[4]
Upper Iowa University[1]	2.2	64%[8]	49%	44%[6]	N/A	N/A	12/1[4]	19-23[4]	N/A	51%[4]	N/A
Waldorf University[1] (IA)	1.9	53%[8]	38%	29%[6]	N/A	N/A	21/1[4]	17-22[4]	N/A	66%[4]	N/A
Youngstown State University (OH)*	2.7	76%	46%	48%	43%	6%	19/1	18-24[2]	40%	70%	4%

WEST ▶

Rank School (State) (*Public)	Overall score	Peer assessment score (5.0=highest)	Average first-year student retention rate	2020 graduation rate Predicted	2020 graduation rate Actual	% of classes under 20 ('20)	% of classes of 50 or more ('20)	Student/ faculty ratio ('20)	SAT/ACT 25th-75th percentile ('20)	Freshmen in top 25% of HS class ('20)	Accept- ance rate ('20)	Average alumni giving rate
1. Trinity University (TX)	100	4.1	90%	86%	79%	64%	1%	9/1	1260-1430[2]	84%	34%	16%
2. Calif. Poly. State U.–San Luis Obispo*	83	4.3	94%	81%	85%	14%	14%	19/1	1220-1410[9]	86%	38%	3%
3. University of Portland (OR)	81	3.8	89%	80%	84%	48%	2%	11/1	1130-1320[2]	N/A	77%	8%
4. Whitworth University (WA)	78	3.8	83%	66%	77%	55%	2%	12/1	1050-1270[2]	64%	91%	11%
5. St. Mary's College of California	73	3.4	84%	76%	73%	54%	0%	9/1	1070-1253[2]	N/A	77%	5%
6. University of Dallas	72	3.5	83%	74%	69%	61%	2%	12/1	1130-1350[2]	76%[5]	54%	17%
6. University of Redlands (CA)	72	3.2	82%	67%	71%	68%	0.3%	12/1	1070-1250[2]	72%	77%	10%
8. California Lutheran University	70	3.3	83%	67%	71%	62%	0.3%	14/1	1070-1240[2]	69%	74%	10%
9. St. Edward's University (TX)	69	3.5	78%	63%	67%	46%	0.1%	14/1	1030-1225[2]	49%	91%	6%
10. Mills College (CA)	68	3.2	72%	67%	64%	94%	0%	8/1	1005-1290[4]	54%	84%	14%
10. St. Mary's Univ. of San Antonio	68	3.3	74%	57%	59%	58%	0%	10/1	1020-1220[2]	53%	85%	9%
12. California State U.–Long Beach*	67	3.5	87%	46%	73%	24%	8%	27/1	1020-1240	N/A	42%	2%
12. Point Loma Nazarene University (CA)	67	3.2	87%	73%	72%	42%	2%	15/1	1100-1290[2]	77%	84%	5%
14. Calif. State Polytechnic U.–Pomona*	66	4.0	87%	49%	67%	12%	18%	28/1	1010-1250[9]	N/A	65%	3%
14. Pacific Lutheran University (WA)	66	3.4	82%	68%	71%	49%	4%	13/1	1100-1300[2]	69%	86%	8%

Note: Key to footnotes, Page 52

Rank	School (State) (*Public)	Overall score	Peer assessment score (5.0=highest)	Average first-year student retention rate	2020 graduation rate		% of classes under 20 ('20)	% of classes of 50 or more ('20)	Student/ faculty ratio ('20)	SAT/ACT 25th-75th percentile ('20)	Freshmen in top 25% of HS class ('20)	Accept- ance rate ('20)	Average alumni giving rate
					Predicted	Actual							
16.	Abilene Christian University (TX)	65	3.5	78%	72%	66%	47%	6%	13/1	1010-1220[2]	54%	63%	10%
16.	Western Washington University*	65	3.6	81%	64%	68%	45%	12%	18/1	1080-1270[2]	51%[4]	94%	4%
18.	Westminster College (UT)	64	3.2	78%	70%	69%	87%	0.3%	9/1	21-28[2]	54%	87%	6%
19.	California State University–Fullerton*	63	3.4	88%	51%	69%	16%	9%	26/1	1000-1180	62%	68%	3%
20.	New Mexico Tech*	60	2.9	76%	75%	54%	73%	2%	10/1	23-30	57%	97%	N/A
20.	University of St. Thomas (TX)	60	3.1	84%	59%	66%	47%	1%	14/1	1005-1170[2]	50%	96%	8%
22.	San Jose State University (CA)*	59	3.5	86%	49%	66%	24%	8%	26/1	1030-1260[9]	N/A	67%	1%
23.	California State U.–Los Angeles*	57	3.3	82%	22%	52%	18%	7%	23/1	870-1060[2]	N/A	76%	2%
23.	Dominican University of California	57	2.7	87%	71%	74%	52%	0%	10/1	1070-1250[2]	52%	86%	6%
25.	California State U.–Monterey Bay*	56	3.1	81%	48%	60%	16%	4%	24/1	960-1160	43%	86%	1%
25.	Chaminade University of Honolulu	56	2.9	81%	44%	58%	64%	0%	11/1	970-1155[2]	41%[4]	88%	3%
27.	Mount Saint Mary's University (CA)	55	3.0	75%	44%	62%	68%[4]	1%[4]	10/1	900-1110[2]	52%	89%	7%
27.	University of Washington–Bothell[1]*	55	3.2	85%[8]	55%	65%[6]	N/A	N/A	23/1[4]	1020-1260[4]	N/A	74%[4]	N/A
29.	San Francisco State University*	53	3.3	80%	46%	55%	22%	12%	22/1	930-1130[2]	N/A	84%	1%
30.	California State U.–Stanislaus*	51	2.9	83%	38%	57%	17%	4%	22/1	890-1070[2]	N/A	89%	1%
30.	Humboldt State University (CA)*	51	3.1	72%	48%	50%	40%	6%	18/1	970-1190[2]	31%	83%	3%[4]
30.	LeTourneau University (TX)	51	2.8	79%	65%	56%	65%	1%	15/1	1110-1330[9]	54%	56%	3%
30.	University of Washington–Tacoma[1]*	51	3.2	81%[8]	49%	57%[6]	N/A	N/A	17/1[4]	980-1190[4]	N/A	87%[4]	N/A
34.	California Baptist University	50	2.8	77%	51%	61%	54%	5%	19/1	950-1150[2]	43%	80%	1%
35.	Montana Technological University*	49	2.8	77%	68%	56%	60%	4%	13/1	21-27[2]	58%	96%	13%
35.	Saint Martin's University (WA)	49	2.7	77%	64%	61%	76%	0%	11/1	950-1145[2]	57%[4]	94%	4%
37.	California State U.–San Bernardino*	48	2.9	85%	34%	59%	20%	16%	26/1	910-1080[2]	N/A	78%	N/A
37.	Sonoma State University (CA)*	48	3.2	79%	54%	60%	23%	15%	21/1	970-1170[4]	N/A	89%	N/A
39.	California State University–Chico*	47	3.1	85%	56%	65%	26%	11%	23/1	970-1170[3]	N/A[5]	90%	4%
39.	California State U.–Northridge*	47	3.3	81%	37%	55%	8%	17%	28/1	900-1110[2]	N/A	65%	3%

ACADEMIC INSIGHTS®
YOUR SCHOOL BY THE NUMBERS

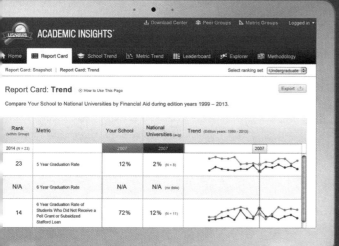

Why Academic Insights?

- Get access to robust Higher Ed data sets
- Benchmark against peer institutions
- Highlight interesting trends quickly
- Validate strategic decision making
- Making data driven decisions

ai.usnews.com

WEST ▶

Rank School (State) (*Public)	Overall score	Peer assessment score (5.0=highest)	Average first-year student retention rate	2020 graduation rate Predicted	2020 graduation rate Actual	% of classes under 20 ('20)	% of classes of 50 or more ('20)	Student/faculty ratio ('20)	SAT/ACT 25th-75th percentile ('20)	Freshmen in top 25% of HS class ('20)	Acceptance rate ('20)	Average alumni giving rate
41. California State U.–Channel Islands[1]*	46	3.0	78%[8]	44%	56%[6]	N/A	N/A	21/1[4]	N/A[2]	N/A	86%[4]	N/A
41. California State Univ.–San Marcos*	46	3.0	82%[8]	46%	57%	16%	7%	26/1	950-1130[2]	N/A	79%	N/A
41. Fresno Pacific University[1] (CA)	46	2.5	75%[8]	54%	66%[6]	72%[4]	1%[4]	13/1[4]	870-980[4]	55%[4]	65%[4]	N/A
41. Hardin-Simmons University (TX)	46	2.9	69%	59%	55%	66%	2%	15/1	960-1150[2]	48%	91%	13%
41. Univ. of Mary Hardin-Baylor (TX)	46	3.2	70%	57%	51%	50%	3%	17/1	1010-1190[3]	45%	90%	4%
46. California State U.–Sacramento*	45	3.2	83%	40%	54%	14%	17%	25/1	930-1130[2]	N/A	83%	1%
46. Central Washington University*	45	2.9	71%	52%	60%	38%	3%	24/1	910-1110[9]	N/A	85%	2%
46. Oklahoma Christian U.	45	2.9	76%	66%	57%	59%	6%	15/1	20-27	51%[4]	61%	11%
46. Vanguard U. of Southern California	45	2.3	75%	47%	63%	53%	3%	16/1	960-1150[2]	47%	50%	4%
50. The Evergreen State College[1] (WA)*	44	3.1	64%[8]	49%	54%[8]	43%[4]	9%[4]	21/1[4]	960-1210[4]	N/A	98%[4]	2%
51. California State Univ.–Bakersfield*	42	2.9	78%	32%	47%	35%[4]	9%[4]	22/1	900-1080[2]	N/A	78%	N/A
51. Northwest Nazarene University (ID)	42	2.6	78%	57%	62%	59%	3%	17/1	990-1210[2]	51%	77%	N/A
53. The Master's U. and Seminary (CA)	41	2.3	84%	67%	64%	72%	7%	11/1	1040-1340	70%	60%	6%
53. Woodbury University (CA)	41	2.2	77%	55%	60%	83%	0%	10/1	970-1225[2]	N/A	70%	1%
55. Concordia University – Irvine (CA)	40	2.5	74%	59%	59%	57%	0.3%	20/1	1020-1210[2]	47%	78%	4%
55. Northwest University (WA)	40	2.3	81%	56%	64%	51%	5%	10/1	1010-1205[2]	N/A	93%	1%
55. Rocky Mountain College (MT)	40	2.6	67%	61%	53%	74%	1%	11/1	18-24	43%	71%	5%
55. Western Oregon University*	40	2.9	71%	49%	45%	58%	1%	13/1	950-1200[2]	42%	79%	2%
59. California State U.–Dominguez Hills*	39	3.0	78%	33%	48%	14%	7%	27/1	15-19[2]	N/A	87%	1%
60. Eastern Washington University*	38	2.8	73%	49%	51%	42%[4]	8%[4]	22/1	880-1100[9]	N/A	80%	N/A
61. Colorado Christian University	37	2.6	80%	57%	60%	57%	1%	15/1	21-27[2]	N/A	63%[4]	2%
61. Houston Baptist University	37	2.8	71%	54%	47%	44%	9%	16/1	1000-1180[2]	58%	72%	2%
61. Western Colorado University*	37	2.6	66%	57%	51%	67%	0%	18/1	1000-1190[2]	31%	88%	N/A
64. Southern Nazarene University (OK)	36	2.6	76%[8]	55%	47%	82%	1%	14/1	18-23	34%	40%	3%
64. Texas A&M International University*	36	2.6	76%	43%	47%	30%	19%	24/1	920-1100	52%	59%	6%
64. U. of Texas of the Permian Basin*	36	2.7	60%	55%	40%	48%	5%	17/1	940-1130	40%	88%	1%
67. La Sierra University (CA)	35	2.3	81%	47%	50%	76%	2%	11/1	940-1170	33%	57%	2%
67. Southern Oregon University*	35	2.8	69%	53%	46%	53%	3%	19/1	980-1200	N/A	90%	1%
67. Southern Utah University*	35	2.8	73%	58%	39%	37%	10%	23/1	21-27[2]	47%	76%	3%
70. Hawaii Pacific University	34	2.9	62%	63%	46%	75%	0%	16/1	970-1170[2]	N/A	80%	1%
71. California State University–East Bay*	33	2.9	76%	42%	47%	8%	22%	26/1	890-1090[9]	N/A	73%	N/A
71. Lubbock Christian University (TX)	33	2.6	69%	57%	48%	70%	2%	14/1	19-25[3]	46%	97%	5%
71. Texas A&M University–Texarkana[1]*	33	2.6	58%[8]	50%	31%[6]	67%[4]	0.4%[4]	12/1[4]	19-23[4]	36%[4]	94%[4]	N/A
71. University of Alaska–Anchorage*	33	3.0	68%	58%	31%	64%	2%	13/1	990-1200[2]	35%	77%	2%
71. University of Central Oklahoma*	33	2.9	66%	45%	35%	54%	1%	17/1	19-24	41%	81%	1%
71. West Texas A&M University*	33	2.9	67%	52%	46%	45%	7%	15/1	18-23	44%	82%	2%
77. Hope International University (CA)	32	2.3	70%	43%	47%	68%	0%	13/1	930-1100	40%	38%	5%
77. Midwestern State University (TX)*	32	2.4	67%	50%	44%	38%	8%	16/1	910-1100[2]	37%	90%	3%
77. Tarleton State University (TX)*	32	2.7	68%	45%	46%	37%	7%	21/1	950-1130	27%	58%	2%
77. Walla Walla University (WA)	32	2.9	82%	63%	59%	70%	3%	14/1	N/A[2]	N/A	71%	N/A
77. Weber State University (UT)*	32	3.2	66%	44%	36%	46%	7%	21/1	18-24[2]	32%	100%	2%
82. Southwestern Oklahoma State U.*	31	2.7	68%	50%	43%	57%	3%	17/1	18-23[2]	43%	93%	N/A
82. University of North Texas at Dallas[1]*	31	3.3	73%[8]	33%	24%[6]	N/A	N/A	17/1[4]	740-940[4]	N/A	47%[4]	N/A
84. Alaska Pacific University	30	2.4	69%[8]	58%	56%	N/A	N/A	8/1	N/A[2]	N/A	91%	1%
84. Bushnell University (OR)	30	2.2	68%	54%	49%	82%	1%	15/1	1023-1186[2]	N/A	68%	4%
84. Holy Names University (CA)	30	2.2	70%	50%	38%	69%	0%	7/1	695-855	19%[4]	89%	N/A
87. Colorado State University–Pueblo*	29	2.9	66%	41%	36%	64%	4%	13/1	910-1110[2]	37%	94%	2%
88. Simpson University[1] (CA)	28	2.3	66%[8]	52%	54%[6]	N/A	N/A	12/1[4]	930-1140[4]	N/A	52%[4]	N/A
88. University of Houston–Downtown*	28	3.1	71%	38%	30%	23%	1%	20/1	900-1080[2]	26%	93%	1%
90. Colorado Mesa University*	27	2.6	74%	42%	44%	51%	7%	19/1	940-1170	26%	75%	2%
90. University of Guam*	27	2.2	75%[8]	48%	38%	60%	2%	17/1	N/A[2]	46%	100%	N/A
92. Angelo State University (TX)*	26	2.6	69%	45%	42%	35%	6%	20/1	950-1130[2]	41%	76%	2%
92. Eastern Oregon University*	26	2.6	70%	48%	28%	73%	2%	15/1	930-1145[4]	40%	94%	N/A

Note: Key to footnotes, Page 52

School (State) (*Public)	Peer assessment score (5.0=highest)	Average first-year student retention rate	2020 graduation rate		% of classes under 20 ('20)	% of classes of 50 or more ('20)	Student/faculty ratio ('20)	SAT/ACT 25th-75th percentile ('20)	Freshmen in top 25% of HS class ('20)	Acceptance rate ('20)	Average alumni giving rate
			Predicted	Actual							
SCHOOLS RANKED 94 THROUGH 122 ARE LISTED HERE ALPHABETICALLY											
Academy of Art University (CA)	2.2	74%	60%	40%[6]	93%	0%	14/1	N/A[2]	N/A	100%	N/A
Adams State University[1] (CO)*	2.5	58%[8]	47%	32%[6]	N/A	N/A	15/1[4]	890-1090[4]	N/A	99%[4]	N/A
Cameron University (OK)*	2.4	65%	36%	34%	53%	1%	18/1	16-21[2]	13%	100%	0.5%
Concordia University Texas[1]	2.4	62%[8]	54%	40%[6]	N/A	N/A	14/1[4]	960-1130[4]	N/A	90%[4]	N/A
East Central University (OK)*	2.3	57%	47%	39%	90%	0.3%	18/1	17-23	N/A	96%	N/A
Eastern New Mexico University[1]*	2.6	63%[8]	42%	32%[6]	N/A	N/A	17/1[4]	17-22[4]	N/A	58%[4]	N/A
Heritage University[1] (WA)	2.1	69%[8]	31%	32%[6]	N/A	N/A	6/1[4]	N/A[2]	N/A	N/A	N/A
Langston University[1] (OK)*	2.2	56%[8]	43%	25%[6]	N/A	N/A	15/1[4]	N/A	N/A	N/A	N/A
Metropolitan State University of Denver*	3.0	64%	42%	32%	38%	2%	22/1	870-1090[3]	17%	83%	N/A
Mid-America Christian University[1] (OK)	2.2	62%[8]	39%	31%[6]	N/A	N/A	11/1[4]	N/A[2]	N/A	N/A	N/A
Montana State Univ.–Billings*	2.9	58%	48%	26%	47%	0%	14/1	17-24[2]	21%	100%	4%
Naropa University[1] (CO)	2.2	64%[8]	59%	36%[6]	89%[4]	1%[4]	8/1[4]	N/A[2]	N/A	100%	N/A
National University (CA)	2.0	44%[8]	55%	43%	67%	0.4%	16/1	750-1170[4]	N/A	37%	N/A
New Mexico Highlands University[1]*	2.3	54%[8]	36%	22%[6]	N/A	N/A	13/1[4]	15-20[4]	30%[4]	65%[4]	N/A
Northeastern State University (OK)*	2.4	63%	46%	36%	63%	1%	19/1	17-23	52%	100%	1%
Northwestern Oklahoma State U.*	2.5	58%	46%	26%	N/A	N/A	14/1	17-22	32%	70%	4%
Oklahoma Wesleyan University[1]	2.5	51%[8]	53%	38%[6]	N/A	N/A	10/1[4]	18-23[4]	N/A	58%[4]	N/A
Prairie View A&M University[1] (TX)*	2.6	70%[8]	37%	35%[8]	18%[4]	8%[4]	17/1[4]	870-1040[4]	25%[4]	80%[4]	N/A
Prescott College[1] (AZ)	2.6	68%[8]	55%	39%[6]	N/A	N/A	9/1[4]	N/A[2]	N/A	97%[4]	N/A
Sierra Nevada University[1] (NV)	2.3	60%[8]	52%	45%[6]	N/A	N/A	9/1[4]	930-1150[4]	N/A	64%[4]	N/A
Southeastern Oklahoma State U.[1]*	2.5	63%[8]	41%	32%[6]	N/A	N/A	24/1[4]	18-23[4]	N/A	74%[4]	N/A
Southwestern Assemblies of God University[1] (TX)	1.9	70%[8]	45%	48%[6]	N/A	N/A	10/1[4]	918-1103[4]	N/A	88%[4]	N/A
Sul Ross State University (TX)*	2.2	54%[8]	36%	30%	74%	0%	11/1	848-1040[2]	15%	100%	N/A
University of Alaska–Southeast*	2.5	64%[8]	61%	19%	90%	0%	10/1	N/A[2]	N/A	64%	N/A
University of Houston–Victoria[1]*	2.6	58%[8]	37%	19%[6]	N/A	N/A	18/1[4]	930-1088[4]	N/A	56%[4]	N/A
University of the Southwest[1] (NM)	2.2	55%[8]	40%	24%[6]	N/A	N/A	17/1[4]	N/A	N/A	45%[4]	N/A
Utah Valley University[1]*	2.4	65%[8]	49%	29%[8]	40%[4]	6%[4]	24/1[4]	18-25[4]	27%[4]	100%[4]	N/A
Wayland Baptist University (TX)	2.2	43%	45%	25%	83%	2%	9/1	900-1090[2]	23%	84%	1%
Western New Mexico University*	2.3	62%[8]	36%	25%	87%	0.2%	12/1	N/A[2]	N/A	N/A	N/A

The Top Public Regional Universities ▶

NORTH
Rank School (State)

1. The College of New Jersey
2. SUNY Polytechnic Institute – Utica/Albany
3. CUNY–Baruch College
3. SUNY–Geneseo
5. CUNY–Hunter College
6. SUNY–New Paltz
7. Ramapo College of New Jersey
7. Stockton University (NJ)
9. CUNY–John Jay College of Criminal Justice
10. CUNY–Queens College
10. SUNY–Oswego
10. West Chester University of Pennsylvania
13. SUNY Maritime College
14. CUNY–Lehman College
14. Salisbury University (MD)
14. SUNY–Fredonia
14. SUNY–Plattsburgh

SOUTH
Rank School (State)

1. The Citadel, Military College of South Carolina
2. James Madison University (VA)
3. Appalachian State University (NC)
3. Christopher Newport University (VA)
5. College of Charleston (SC)
6. Winthrop University (SC)
7. Longwood University (VA)
7. University of Mary Washington (VA)
9. Georgia College & State University
9. Western Carolina University (NC)
11. Murray State University (KY)
12. University of Montevallo (AL)
13. University of North Alabama
14. Radford University (VA)
15. University of Tennessee–Martin

MIDWEST
Rank School (State)

1. Truman State University (MO)
2. University of Northern Iowa
3. Grand Valley State University (MI)
4. University of Illinois–Springfield
5. University of Michigan–Dearborn
6. University of Nebraska–Kearney
7. University of Wisconsin–La Crosse
8. University of Minnesota–Duluth
8. University of Wisconsin–Eau Claire
8. Winona State University (MN)
11. University of Wisconsin–Whitewater
12. Eastern Illinois University
12. Western Illinois University
14. University of Wisconsin–Stevens Point
15. University of Wisconsin–Stout

WEST
Rank School (State)

1. California Polytechnic State University–San Luis Obispo
2. California State University–Long Beach
3. California State Polytechnic University–Pomona
4. Western Washington University
5. California State University–Fullerton
6. New Mexico Tech
7. San Jose State University (CA)
8. California State University–Los Angeles
9. California State U.–Monterey Bay
10. University of Washington–Bothell
11. San Francisco State University
12. California State University–Stanislaus
12. Humboldt State University (CA)
12. University of Washington–Tacoma
15. Montana Technological University

Best
Regional Colleges

What Is a Regional College?

THESE SCHOOLS FOCUS almost entirely on the undergraduate experience and offer a broad range of programs in the liberal arts (which account for fewer than half of bachelor's degrees granted) and in fields such as business, nursing and education. They grant few graduate degrees. Because most of the 371 colleges in the category draw heavily from nearby states, they are ranked by region: North, South, Midwest, West.

Regions at a glance

These are the four regions into which U.S. News places schools.

■ North ■ Midwest ■ South ■ West

NORTH ▶

Rank School (State) (*Public)	Overall score	Peer assessment score (5.0=highest)	Average first-year student retention rate	2020 graduation rate Predicted	2020 graduation rate Actual	% of classes under 20 ('20)	% of classes of 50 or more ('20)	Student/faculty ratio ('20)	SAT/ACT 25th-75th percentile ('20)	Freshmen in top 25% of HS class ('20)	Acceptance rate ('20)	Average alumni giving rate
1. U.S. Coast Guard Academy (CT)*	100	4.3	96%	82%	86%	54%	0%	7/1	1220-1400[3]	88%	13%	N/A
2. Cooper Union for Adv. of Sci. & Art (NY)	99	4.0	91%	85%	79%	71%	1%	8/1	1330-1500[2]	73%	18%	18%
3. U.S. Merchant Marine Acad. (NY)*	66	3.9	94%[8]	86%	82%[6]	N/A	N/A	13/1[4]	1190-1330[4]	N/A	16%	N/A
4. Maine Maritime Academy*	65	4.0	80%	65%	73%	58%	0%	9/1	1000-1160	57%	50%	23%
5. Massachusetts Maritime Academy*	63	3.9	87%	64%	85%	37%	1%	14/1	1030-1185	N/A	92%	7%
6. SUNY College of Technology at Alfred*	49	3.5	73%	39%	66%	61%	1%	17/1	940-1170[2]	N/A	72%	2%
6. University of Maine at Farmington*	49	3.4	72%	47%	60%	75%	1%	11/1	940-1150[2]	39%	95%	3%
8. Colby-Sawyer College (NH)	47	3.3	73%	59%	64%	70%	1%	15/1	1010-1190[2]	N/A	89%	10%
9. Elmira College (NY)	42	3.1	73%	64%	67%	80%	1%	10/1	1020-1220[4]	N/A	98%	N/A
9. Keene State College (NH)*	42	3.1	73%	54%	60%	56%	0.3%	13/1	980-1170[2]	25%	91%	3%
9. Pennsylvania College of Technology*	42	3.1	78%	45%	55%	75%	0%	12/1	980-1160[2]	21%	73%	1%
12. SUNY College of Technology at Canton*	39	3.4	73%	33%	52%	41%	2%	18/1	920-1130[2]	22%	83%	2%
13. Cazenovia College (NY)	37	3.0	69%	47%	58%	92%	0%	10/1	893-1116[2]	11%[4]	72%	5%
13. SUNY College of Technology–Delhi*	37	3.5	73%	34%	51%	59%	2%	16/1	920-1110[2]	20%	71%	3%
15. Farmingdale State College–SUNY*	35	3.4	83%	43%	51%	27%	0.4%	19/1	990-1150	34%[5]	60%	0.2%
15. St. Francis College (NY)	35	3.0	76%	40%	54%	51%	2%	15/1	890-1030[2]	N/A	85%	6%
17. SUNY Cobleskill*	34	3.1	73%	42%	56%	44%	4%	16/1	900-1110[2]	10%	93%	1%
18. Thiel College (PA)	29	3.2	65%[8]	50%	49%[6]	N/A	N/A	10/1[4]	890-1150[4]	30%	84%	N/A
18. Univ. of Pittsburgh at Bradford[1]*	29	3.2	68%[8]	50%	43%[6]	66%[4]	2%[4]	15/1[4]	970-1160[4]	39%[4]	58%[4]	4%[4]
20. The College of Westchester[1] (NY)	28	3.2	61%[8]	25%	46%[6]	N/A	N/A	19/1[4]	N/A[2]	N/A	94%[4]	N/A
20. Vaughn Col. of Aeron. and Tech.[1] (NY)	28	3.0	76%[8]	38%	43%[8]	60%[4]	0%[4]	16/1[4]	963-1165[4]	N/A	82%[4]	N/A
22. Paul Smith's College (NY)	26	3.0	71%	51%	57%	63%	3%	12/1	N/A[2]	22%	70%	8%
22. SUNY Morrisville (NY)*	26	3.1	67%	39%	48%	51%	0.2%	14/1	860-1060[2]	14%	77%	3%
22. Unity College[7] (ME)	26	2.8	62%	47%	46%	85%	0%	15/1	N/A[2]	N/A	100%	N/A
25. University of Valley Forge (PA)	25	3.0	71%	42%	45%	82%	1%	11/1	900-1088[2]	27%	63%	2%
26. Castleton University[1] (VT)*	23	3.0	68%[8]	48%	53%[6]	N/A	N/A	16/1[4]	920-1118[4]	N/A	84%[4]	N/A
26. Vermont Technical College*	23	2.9	74%	47%	37%	84%	0%	8/1	988-1170[2]	N/A	60%	1%
28. Dean College (MA)	22	3.0	70%	45%	52%	58%	0%	16/1	930-1128[2]	N/A	71%	4%
28. Keystone College (PA)	22	2.8	64%	31%	44%	71%	0%	14/1	880-1090[9]	N/A	79%	3%
28. Univ. of Pittsburgh–Johnstown[1]*	22	3.2	73%[8]	49%	51%[6]	N/A	N/A	17/1[4]	1020-1220[4]	N/A	79%[4]	N/A
31. University of Maine–Presque Isle*	21	3.1	63%	37%	34%	89%	0%	16/1	860-1080[9]	27%	99%	0.4%[4]
32. Berkeley College (NJ)	19	3.1	62%	23%	36%	59%	0%	16/1	N/A[2]	N/A	92%	N/A
33. CUNY–York College*	18	3.0	65%	27%	32%	24%	9%	19/1	870-1050[2]	N/A	53%	0.4%
33. University of Maine–Fort Kent*	18	3.0	64%	34%	45%	72%	1%	16/1	870-1040[9]	28%	100%	4%[4]
35. CUNY–New York City Col. of Tech.*	16	3.2	69%	20%	24%	27%	0%	18/1[4]	N/A[2]	N/A	79%	N/A
35. Mount Aloysius College (PA)	16	2.9	70%[8]	38%	40%[6]	76%	0.3%	11/1	N/A[2]	N/A	95%	N/A
37. Five Towns College[1] (NY)	15	2.8	70%[8]	45%	42%[6]	79%[4]	0%[4]	11/1[4]	N/A[2]	N/A	34%[4]	N/A

Note: Key to footnotes, Page 52

School (State) (*Public)	Peer assessment score (5.0=highest)	Average first-year student retention rate	2020 graduation rate		% of classes under 20 ('20)	% of classes of 50 or more ('20)	Student/ faculty ratio ('20)	SAT/ACT 25th-75th percentile ('20)	Freshmen in top 25% of HS class ('20)	Accept- ance rate ('20)	Average alumni giving rate
			Predicted	Actual							
SCHOOLS RANKED 38 THROUGH 49 ARE LISTED HERE ALPHABETICALLY											
Bay State College[1] (MA)	2.6	53%[8]	37%	34%[6]	N/A	N/A	11/1[4]	N/A[2]	N/A	67%[4]	N/A
Becker College[1] (MA)	2.3	75%[8]	47%	43%[6]	N/A	N/A	12/1[4]	950-1170[4]	N/A	70%[4]	N/A
Boricua College[1] (NY)	2.6	50%[8]	19%	28%[6]	N/A	N/A	20/1[4]	N/A[2]	N/A	N/A	N/A
Central Penn College[1]	2.8	54%[8]	35%	33%[6]	N/A	N/A	10/1[4]	N/A[2]	N/A	84%[4]	N/A
CUNY–Medgar Evers College*	3.0	64%	21%	20%	20%	0.1%	23/1	710-900[9]	N/A	79%	N/A
Eastern Nazarene College[1] (MA)	2.5	65%[8]	47%	45%[6]	N/A	N/A	10/1[4]	880-1110[4]	N/A	59%[4]	N/A
Fisher College (MA)	2.6	62%	32%	30%	73%	0%	11/1	830-1060[2]	N/A	78%	N/A
Hilbert College[1] (NY)	2.7	73%[8]	41%	52%[6]	N/A	N/A	11/1[4]	N/A[2]	N/A	93%[4]	N/A
Mitchell College[1] (CT)	2.3	63%[8]	47%	41%[6]	N/A	N/A	13/1[4]	N/A[2]	N/A	78%[4]	N/A
University of Maine–Augusta[1]*	3.3	58%[8]	24%	14%[6]	N/A	N/A	14/1[4]	N/A[2]	N/A	N/A	N/A
Villa Maria College[1] (NY)	2.6	57%[8]	33%	33%[6]	N/A	N/A	9/1[4]	N/A[2]	N/A	74%[4]	N/A
Wesley College[1] (DE)	2.9	57%[8]	33%	26%[6]	N/A	N/A	10/1[4]	820-1060[4]	N/A	61%[4]	N/A

SOUTH ▶

Rank School (State) (*Public)	Overall score	Peer assessment score (5.0=highest)	Average first-year student retention rate	2020 graduation rate		% of classes under 20 ('20)	% of classes of 50 or more ('20)	Student/ faculty ratio ('20)	SAT/ACT 25th-75th percentile ('20)	Freshmen in top 25% of HS class ('20)	Accept- ance rate ('20)	Average alumni giving rate
				Predicted	Actual							
1. High Point University (NC)	100	3.9	81%	71%	69%	43%	1%	17/1	1070-1240[2]	49%	77%	12%
2. Ouachita Baptist University (AR)	90	3.5	81%	62%	60%	59%	2%	12/1	22-29	66%	62%	15%
3. Florida Polytechnic University*	85	3.2	76%	62%	50%	30%	1%	16/1	1210-1370	61%	58%	29%
4. Flagler College (FL)	82	3.7	71%	54%	55%[8]	79%	0%	16/1	1040-1220[2]	N/A	56%	7%
5. Maryville College (TN)	73	3.3	72%	49%	45%	64%	1%	12/1	20-28	45%	62%	N/A
5. University of the Ozarks (AR)	73	3.3	68%	51%	47%	59%	0%	16/1	18-23[2]	11%	100%	9%
7. Claflin University (SC)	71	2.7	75%	35%	50%	61%	1%	13/1	840-1040	36%	65%	38%
8. Catawba College (NC)	70	3.1	75%	51%	52%	60%	0%	12/1	940-1130[9]	38%	52%	9%
8. Welch College (TN)	70	2.7	76%	52%	62%	86%	0%	9/1	20-26	0%[4]	79%	14%
10. LaGrange College (GA)	66	3.0	63%	59%	44%	81%	1%	10/1	980-1123[2]	46%	59%	10%
11. Erskine College (SC)	65	2.7	65%	51%	52%	70%	1%	14/1	919-1137[2]	29%	67%	17%
11. Newberry College (SC)	65	2.8	65%	44%	53%	70%	2%	14/1	890-1100[2]	20%	57%	14%
13. Huntingdon College (AL)	64	3.0	66%	46%	42%	60%	6%	14/1	19-24[2]	38%	54%	26%
14. Barton College (NC)	63	2.7	68%	48%	52%	59%	1%	13/1	930-1120[2]	36%	42%	5%
15. University of Mobile (AL)	61	2.9	75%	49%	49%	73%	1%	14/1	19-26[2]	52%	67%	1%
15. U. of South Carolina–Upstate*	61	2.9	68%	41%	48%	73%	2%	17/1	900-1090	36%	53%	0.4%
17. Blue Mountain College (MS)	59	2.8	69%	45%	51%	64%	1%	17/1	18-23	27%	99%	6%
17. Univ. of South Carolina–Aiken*	59	3.0	66%	47%	41%	66%	1%	15/1	970-1150	44%	56%	5%
19. Belmont Abbey College (NC)	58	3.0	65%	47%	46%	60%	0.2%	15/1	970-1180[2]	24%	80%	8%
19. Tennessee Wesleyan University	58	3.0	71%	41%	49%	75%	3%	11/1	19-25[2]	N/A	61%	2%
21. Averett University (VA)	57	2.7	63%	44%	50%	85%	0%	11/1	880-1090	21%	100%	3%
21. Brevard College (NC)	57	3.1	66%[8]	45%	35%[6]	77%	0%	11/1	18-22[2]	19%	49%	N/A
21. Florida National U.–Main Campus	57	1.8	88%	13%	57%	44%	1%	22/1	N/A[2]	N/A	81%	N/A
21. Kentucky Wesleyan College	57	3.0	68%	44%	38%	99%	0%	14/1	18-25[9]	N/A	60%	8%
25. Greensboro College (NC)	56	2.6	64%	37%	34%	91%	0%	11/1	16-21[2]	25%[4]	40%	13%
25. Toccoa Falls College (GA)	56	2.8	62%	41%	48%	72%	0%	16/1	930-1130[2]	34%	58%	2%
27. Davis and Elkins College (WV)	55	2.7	70%[8]	39%	53%	74%	0.4%	12/1	860-1060	N/A	69%	7%
28. Lees-McRae College (NC)	54	2.8	65%	38%	44%	84%	0%	11/1	963-1140[2]	N/A	73%	4%
29. Mars Hill University (NC)	53	2.9	63%	39%	35%	74%	0%	10/1	17-21[2]	27%	67%	7%
30. William Peace University (NC)	52	2.9	67%	40%	38%	70%	0%	12/1	18-23[2]	N/A	61%	2%
31. Alice Lloyd College (KY)	50	2.9	58%[8]	38%	35%	54%	2%	17/1	17-22[2]	18%	7%	44%
31. Brescia University (KY)	50	2.8	66%	39%	39%	84%	0%	13/1	19-25	N/A	48%	7%
33. Elizabeth City State University (NC)*	48	2.4	73%	32%	40%[6]	59%	0.2%	16/1	875-1059	5%	75%	N/A
33. University of Arkansas–Pine Bluff*	48	2.7	72%	36%	39%	63%	2%	14/1	14-18	27%	60%	5%
35. Beacon College[1] (FL)	47	2.3	72%[8]	63%	65%[6]	N/A	N/A	10/1[4]	N/A[2]	N/A	51%[4]	N/A
35. Kentucky State University*	47	2.8	67%	38%	30%	65%	1%	14/1	15-20	12%	84%	5%
35. The U. of Tennessee Southern (TN)	47	2.7	55%	37%	31%	75%	0%	13/1	17-23	N/A	98%	18%
35. University of the Virgin Islands*	47	2.5	68%	33%	29%	87%	0.2%	12/1	813-1020[2]	49%	100%	2%
39. Lander University (SC)*	46	2.7	68%	43%	49%	48%	1%	17/1	920-1110[2]	34%	57%	4%
40. Emmanuel College (GA)	45	2.7	62%	41%	39%	67%	0%	16/1	920-1100	N/A	53%	4%

SOUTH ▶

Rank School (State) (*Public)	Overall score	Peer assessment score (5.0=highest)	Average first-year student retention rate	2020 graduation rate		% of classes under 20 ('20)	% of classes of 50 or more ('20)	Student/ faculty ratio ('20)	SAT/ACT 25th-75th percentile ('20)	Freshmen in top 25% of HS class ('20)	Accept- ance rate ('20)	Average alumni giving rate
				Predicted	Actual							
41. Oakwood University[1] (AL)	44	2.5	71%[1]	49%	49%[6]	N/A	N/A	11/1[4]	16-23[4]	N/A	65%[4]	N/A
42. Philander Smith College (AR)	43	2.5	63%	30%	34%	77%	0%	12/1	16-22[2]	25%	21%	10%
43. Glenville State College (WV)*	42	2.3	62%	27%	43%	73%	0.2%	17/1	840-1040[4]	24%[4]	98%	3%
44. Middle Georgia State University*	40	3.0	59%	37%	28%	62%	2%	19/1	880-1100[2]	N/A	99%	1%
44. North Carolina Wesleyan College	40	2.6	64%	29%	31%	74%	0%	13/1	15-20[9]	9%	48%	2%
44. Truett McConnell University (GA)	40	2.7	68%	42%	35%	70%	2%	17/1	920-1140	32%	97%	1%
47. University of Puerto Rico–Humacao[1]*	39	2.2	86%[8]	37%	53%[6]	N/A	N/A	16/1[4]	N/A[2]	N/A	48%[4]	N/A
48. Bluefield State College (WV)*	38	2.4	63%	33%	35%	98%	0%	14/1	850-1070	46%	90%	1%
48. University of Arkansas–Fort Smith[7]*	38	2.7	65%[8]	34%	33%[6]	N/A	N/A	17/1[4]	N/A	N/A	N/A	N/A
48. Voorhees College (SC)	38	2.3	57%[8]	32%	38%[6]	86%	1%	12/1	12-17[2]	N/A	64%[4]	N/A
51. Alderson Broaddus University (WV)	37	2.6	52%	42%	32%	67%	2%	14/1	850-1050	22%	53%	5%
52. University of Puerto Rico–Arecibo*	36	2.2	80%	33%	47%[6]	42%	1%	22/1	N/A[2]	N/A	70%	N/A
53. American U. of Puerto Rico–Bayamon[1]	35	2.4	63%[8]	29%	37%[6]	N/A	N/A	17/1[4]	N/A[2]	N/A	N/A	N/A
53. Limestone University (SC)	35	2.5	57%	32%	33%	74%	1%	13/1	930-1140[2]	26%	68%	3%
55. Ferrum College (VA)	34	2.6	52%	32%	29%	72%	0.3%	13/1	910-1060[2]	N/A	76%	N/A
55. Warner University (FL)	34	2.4	57%	30%	43%	61%	0%	14/1	870-1040[2]	20%	54%	3%
57. University of Puerto Rico–Aguadilla[1]*	33	2.1	77%[8]	31%	44%[6]	N/A	N/A	21/1[4]	932-1126[4]	N/A	87%[4]	N/A
58. Florida College[1]	32	2.7	67%[8]	57%	23%[6]	N/A	N/A	13/1[4]	20-27[4]	N/A	75%[4]	N/A
58. Florida Memorial University[1]	32	2.4	64%[8]	29%	37%[6]	N/A	N/A	13/1[4]	N/A[2]	N/A	40%[4]	N/A
58. Georgia Gwinnett College*	32	3.0	66%	30%	18%	32%	0.1%	18/1	920-1110[2]	30%[5]	95%	4%
61. Seminole State College of Florida[1]*	30	2.5	72%[8]	34%	41%[6]	31%[4]	0.4%[4]	23/1[4]	N/A[2]	N/A	75%	N/A
62. Inter American U. of PR–Barranquitas	29	1.9	72%	19%	46%	60%	4%	20/1	N/A[2]	N/A	41%	N/A
62. University of Puerto Rico–Bayamon[1]*	29	2.3	83%[8]	39%	36%[6]	N/A	N/A	21/1[4]	N/A[2]	N/A	78%[4]	N/A
62. West Virginia State University[1]*	29	2.7	58%[8]	36%	29%[6]	N/A	N/A	11/1[4]	17-22[4]	N/A	95%[4]	N/A
65. Kentucky Christian University[1]	28	2.7	59%[8]	43%	34%[6]	N/A	N/A	11/1[4]	17-21[4]	N/A	40%[4]	N/A
66. Central Baptist College (AR)	27	2.4	59%	40%	17%	92%	0%	11/1[4]	18-22	N/A	50%	6%
66. U. Adventista de las Antillas[1] (PR)	27	2.2	72%[8]	22%	43%[6]	N/A	N/A	16/1[4]	N/A[2]	N/A	99%[4]	N/A
66. Webber International University (FL)	27	2.4	52%[8]	38%	39%	34%	0%	18/1	900-1050[4]	52%[4]	62%	2%
66. West Virginia U. Inst. of Technology[1]*	27	2.5	59%[8]	46%	26%[6]	N/A	N/A	14/1[4]	930-1130[4]	N/A	51%[4]	N/A
70. West Virginia U.–Parkersburg[1]*	26	2.5	N/A	28%	30%[6]	N/A	N/A	N/A	N/A[2]	N/A	N/A	N/A

School (State) (*Public)	Peer assessment score (5.0=highest)	Average first-year student retention rate	2020 graduation rate		% of classes under 20 ('20)	% of classes of 50 or more ('20)	Student/ faculty ratio ('20)	SAT/ACT 25th-75th percentile ('20)	Freshmen in top 25% of HS class ('20)	Accept- ance rate ('20)	Average alumni giving rate
			Predicted	Actual							
SCHOOLS RANKED 71 THROUGH 93 ARE LISTED HERE ALPHABETICALLY											
Abraham Baldwin Agricultural College[1] (GA)*	2.4	64%[8]	41%	24%[6]	N/A	N/A	17/1[4]	930-1120[4]	N/A	73%[4]	N/A
American University of Puerto Rico–Manati[1]	2.0	69%[8]	28%	39%[6]	N/A	N/A	22/1[4]	N/A[2]	N/A	N/A	N/A
Arkansas Baptist College[1]	2.4	38%[8]	26%	5%[6]	68%[4]	0%[4]	24/1[4]	N/A	N/A	26%[4]	N/A
Benedict College (SC)	2.5	55%[8]	24%	24%	32%	4%	15/1	800-1010[2]	31%	73%	7%
Bluefield College[1] (VA)	2.7	52%[8]	32%	28%[6]	N/A	N/A	14/1[4]	900-1070[4]	N/A	99%[4]	N/A
Colegio Universitario de San Juan[1] (PR)*	2.1	49%[8]	11%	24%[6]	N/A	N/A	15/1[4]	N/A[2]	N/A	95%[4]	N/A
College of Coastal Georgia*	2.5	59%	32%	23%	49%	1%	21/1	900-1100[2]	N/A	96%	1%
Crowley's Ridge College[1] (AR)	2.1	54%[8]	35%	35%[6]	N/A	N/A	13/1[4]	N/A[2]	N/A	N/A	N/A
Dalton State College[1] (GA)*	2.5	67%[8]	22%	26%[6]	N/A	N/A	18/1[4]	N/A[2]	N/A	N/A	N/A
Edward Waters College[1] (FL)	2.2	56%[8]	17%	26%[6]	N/A	N/A	23/1[4]	757-1092[4]	N/A	61%[4]	N/A
Gordon State College (GA)*	2.4	49%[8]	25%	21%	N/A	N/A	22/1	890-1070	N/A	79%	1%
Inter American U. of Puerto Rico–Bayamon	2.4	74%	36%	31%	28%	2%	28/1	N/A[2]	N/A	48%	5%
Inter American U. of Puerto Rico–Guayama[7]	2.1	78%[8]	28%	34%	52%	5%	22/1[4]	N/A[2]	N/A	42%	N/A
LeMoyne-Owen College[1] (TN)	2.2	56%[8]	18%	13%[6]	78%[4]	0%[4]	13/1[4]	15-17[4]	N/A	41%[4]	N/A
Livingstone College (NC)	2.2	49%	25%	28%	77%	2%	13/1	765-930	11%	69%	9%
Miles College[1] (AL)	2.7	59%[8]	26%	23%[6]	N/A	N/A	16/1[4]	N/A[2]	N/A	N/A	N/A
Morris College[1] (SC)	1.9	46%[8]	29%	26%[6]	N/A	N/A	13/1[4]	N/A	N/A	N/A	N/A
Ohio Valley University (WV)	2.0	54%[8]	41%	37%[6]	79%[4]	0%[4]	9/1	18-23[3]	N/A	95%	7%[4]
Paine College[1] (GA)	2.0	58%[8]	32%	19%[6]	N/A	N/A	10/1[4]	798-943[4]	N/A	65%[4]	N/A
Point University[1] (GA)	2.6	55%[8]	34%	28%[6]	N/A	N/A	17/1[4]	16-20[4]	N/A	29%[4]	N/A
Saint Augustine's University (NC)	2.1	54%[8]	29%	19%	76%	0.2%	12/1	780-940	N/A	67%	N/A
Shaw University[1] (NC)	2.2	49%[8]	29%	17%[8]	58%[4]	0%[4]	15/1[4]	737-902[4]	6%[4]	63%[4]	N/A
University of Puerto Rico–Utuado[1]*	1.9	66%[8]	33%	19%[6]	N/A	N/A	14/1[4]	N/A[2]	N/A	63%[4]	N/A

Note: Key to footnotes, Page 52

Rank School (State) (*Public)	Overall score	Peer assessment score (5.0=highest)	Average first-year student retention rate	2020 graduation rate		% of classes under 20 ('20)	% of classes of 50 or more ('20)	Student/faculty ratio ('20)	SAT/ACT 25th-75th percentile ('20)	Freshmen in top 25% of HS class ('20)	Acceptance rate ('20)	Average alumni giving rate
				Predicted	Actual							
1. College of the Ozarks (MO)	100	3.7	78%	48%	60%	52%	1%	13/1	21-25	67%	14%	20%
1. Taylor University (IN)	100	3.7	88%	74%	78%	65%	4%	13/1	1090-1290[2]	71%	70%	16%
3. Ohio Northern University	97	3.6	84%	65%	71%	67%	0.4%	11/1	22-28[2]	57%[4]	65%	9%
4. Cottey College (MO)	94	3.1	69%	58%	65%	96%	0%	6/1	19-24[2]	36%	99%	6%
5. Dordt University (IA)	92	3.5	81%	65%	65%	67%	2%	10/1	22-28[2]	48%	71%	18%
6. Marietta College (OH)	88	3.3	74%	63%	55%	83%	0%	8/1	20-25[2]	N/A	74%	17%
6. Northwestern College (IA)	88	3.4	77%	69%	68%	66%	0.4%	11/1	20-26[2]	42%	70%	16%
8. Goshen College (IN)	86	3.4	76%	58%	63%	62%	1%	10/1	940-1180[2]	71%[5]	92%	20%
8. William Jewell College (MO)	86	3.2	77%	69%	67%	76%	0%	9/1	20-27[2]	56%	36%	6%
10. University of Mount Union (OH)	85	3.2	75%	58%	66%	64%	1%	12/1	19-25	53%[5]	77%	14%
11. Alma College[1] (MI)	82	3.2	78%[8]	63%	66%[8]	59%[4]	1%[4]	14/1[4]	1030-1230[4]	29%[4]	61%[4]	14%[4]
12. Millikin University (IL)	81	3.3	75%	51%	53%	79%	0.2%	10/1	940-1160[2]	43%	71%	7%
13. Loras College (IA)	80	3.4	78%	62%	66%	47%	0%	12/1	19-25[2]	N/A	58%	16%
14. Carthage College (WI)	79	3.3	78%	60%	62%	53%	0%	13/1	20-26[2]	45%	77%	10%
15. Hiram College (OH)	77	3.2	72%	45%	50%	75%	0.4%	11/1	16-24[2]	40%	93%	9%
16. Benedictine College (KS)	76	3.2	81%	63%	66%	60%	2%	13/1	21-29[2]	43%[5]	97%	20%
17. Hastings College (NE)	75	3.2	68%	57%	66%	66%	0%	14/1	19-26[2]	N/A	66%	17%
18. Adrian College (MI)	73	3.3	66%	58%	54%	71%	1%	14/1	930-1120[3]	28%	61%	14%
19. Northland College (WI)	72	2.7	69%	62%	57%	75%	0%	10/1	22-23[2]	51%	64%	9%
19. Trinity Christian College (IL)	72	2.8	81%	53%	64%	71%	0.4%	10/1	980-1180	23%	64%	9%
19. Wisconsin Lutheran College	72	2.9	78%	56%	64%	59%	1%	13/1	21-27[2]	47%	96%	16%
22. Dakota Wesleyan University (SD)	71	3.3	67%	50%	46%	76%	2%	12/1	18-23[2]	36%	64%	4%
23. Heidelberg University (OH)	69	3.2	71%	52%	52%	N/A	N/A	14/1	19-24	N/A	81%	10%
23. Holy Cross College (IN)	69	3.1	47%	52%	40%	93%	0%	12/1	1070-1370[2]	57%	77%	23%
25. Eureka College (IL)	64	2.7	63%	44%	60%	75%	0%	11/1	940-1130[2]	33%	61%	12%
25. Maranatha Baptist University (WI)	64	2.6	74%	51%	57%	79%	2%	10/1	20-28	52%	80%	N/A
25. University of Minnesota–Crookston*	64	2.8	68%	48%	51%	73%	1%	18/1	18-22[2]	43%	72%	N/A
28. Oakland City University (IN)	63	2.4	70%	40%	64%	88%	0%	12/1	912-1136[2]	32%	63%	4%
29. Briar Cliff University (IA)	62	2.8	63%	46%	50%	83%	1%	11/1	18-23	37%	77%	7%
29. Quincy University (IL)	62	2.6	67%	45%	50%	77%	0%	15/1	19-25[2]	39%	67%	11%
31. Bethel College (KS)	61	2.8	64%	50%	44%	77%	2%	10/1	17-22	36%	61%	11%
31. Bluffton University (OH)	61	2.7	65%	49%	55%	70%	1%	12/1	16-23[2]	26%	61%	7%
31. Union College (NE)	61	2.7	78%	53%	56%	76%	0.4%	9/1	18-24[9]	N/A	74%	N/A

ETTY IMAGES

MIDWEST ▶

Rank	School (State) (*Public)	Overall score	Peer assessment score (5.0=highest)	Average first-year student retention rate	2020 graduation rate		% of classes under 20 ('20)	% of classes of 50 or more ('20)	Student/ faculty ratio ('20)	SAT/ACT 25th-75th percentile ('20)	Freshmen in top 25% of HS class ('20)	Accept-ance rate ('20)	Average alumni giving rate
					Predicted	Actual							
34.	Culver-Stockton College (MO)	60	2.7	65%	43%	46%	72%	0%	14/1	18-22	25%	98%	19%
35.	Grand View University[1] (IA)	59	2.7	68%[8]	45%	52%[8]	66%[4]	1%[4]	12/1[4]	17-22[4]	38%[4]	96%[4]	3%[4]
35.	Manchester University[1] (IN)	59	3.1	63%[8]	52%	54%[6]	N/A	N/A	15/1[4]	N/A[2]	N/A	56%[4]	N/A
35.	McPherson College (KS)	59	2.9	64%	47%	38%	69%	0%	15/1	19-23[2]	21%[4]	36%	10%
35.	University of Jamestown (ND)	59	2.9	69%	57%	55%	66%	1%	12/1	19-24[9]	35%	72%	12%
35.	Wilmington College (OH)	59	2.7	67%	46%	52%	62%	0%	14/1	18-24	42%[4]	73%	10%
40.	Central Methodist University (MO)	57	2.6	70%	47%	44%	78%	1%	13/1	18-23[2]	23%	95%	10%
41.	Kansas Wesleyan University	56	2.8	61%	49%	47%	69%	0%	11/1	18-24[2]	31%	62%	9%
41.	York College (NE)	56	2.7	61%	43%	51%	71%[4]	1%[4]	12/1	17-21	43%	57%[4]	18%
43.	Sterling College (KS)	55	2.6	57%[8]	40%	47%	79%	0%	10/1	18-25[2]	24%	37%	9%
44.	Valley City State University (ND)*	53	2.8	71%	52%	45%	70%	1%	13/1	17-22[2]	N/A	81%	9%
45.	Lake Superior State University (MI)*	52	2.6	70%	46%	50%	59%	5%	17/1	950-1180[2]	31%	69%	1%
45.	Olivet College[7] (MI)	52	2.9	62%	38%	48%[6]	63%	3%	15/1	N/A	N/A	N/A	N/A
45.	St. Augustine College[1] (IL)	52	2.8	N/A	12%	24%[6]	N/A	N/A	8/1[4]	N/A	N/A	N/A	N/A
48.	Dickinson State University (ND)*	50	2.7	67%	53%	36%	71%	1%	13/1	17-22[2]	N/A	99%	2%
49.	North Central University[1] (MN)	49	3.0	78%[8]	54%	47%[6]	57%[4]	8%[4]	16/1[4]	18-24[4]	27%[4]	90%[4]	2%
50.	Defiance College (OH)	48	2.6	55%	46%	45%	73%	1%	12/1	16-22[2]	17%	96%	7%
50.	Ottawa University (KS)	48	2.8	60%	51%	37%	63%	1%	10/1	18-22[2]	13%	24%	14%
50.	Tabor College (KS)	48	3.0	58%	44%	37%	56%	2%	15/1	18-23	29%	46%	9%
53.	Purdue University Global[1] (IN)*	45	2.5	100%[8]	29%	10%[6]	N/A	N/A	24/1[4]	N/A[2]	N/A	N/A	N/A
53.	Rochester University (MI)	45	2.7	63%	41%	42%	62%	0%	12/1	840-1060[3]	N/A	99%	N/A
55.	Hannibal-LaGrange University[1] (MO)	43	2.5	58%[8]	40%	45%[6]	N/A	N/A	9/1[4]	18-25[4]	N/A	61%[4]	N/A
55.	Indiana University–Kokomo*	43	2.3	64%	37%	43%	56%	4%	16/1	940-1130[2]	31%	83%	5%
55.	Kuyper College[1] (MI)	43	2.4	70%[8]	56%	45%[6]	N/A	N/A	11/1[4]	850-1080[4]	N/A	62%[4]	N/A

School (State) (*Public)	Peer assessment score (5.0=highest)	Average first-year student retention rate	2020 graduation rate		% of classes under 20 ('20)	% of classes of 50 or more ('20)	Student/ faculty ratio ('20)	SAT/ACT 25th-75th percentile ('20)	Freshmen in top 25% of HS class ('20)	Accept-ance rate ('20)	Average alumni giving rate
			Predicted	Actual							
SCHOOLS RANKED 58 THROUGH 76 ARE LISTED HERE ALPHABETICALLY											
Bethany College[1] (KS)	2.5	57%	41%	37%[6]	N/A	N/A	14/1[4]	18-23[4]	N/A	68%[4]	N/A
Central Christian College of Kansas (KS)	2.3	60%	30%	20%	77%	2%	10/1	15-21[2]	23%	100%	6%
Central State University (OH)*	2.3	51%	29%	28%	60%	0%	19/1	14-17[2]	N/A	58%	9%
Concordia University[1] (MI)	2.7	64%[8]	50%	33%[6]	N/A	N/A	11/1[4]	18-23[4]	N/A	49%[4]	N/A
Finlandia University[1] (MI)	2.3	50%[8]	44%	30%[6]	N/A	N/A	10/1[4]	920-1090[4]	N/A	72%[4]	N/A
Harris-Stowe State University[1] (MO)*	2.1	58%[8]	20%	11%[8]	N/A	N/A	18/1[4]	15-19[4]	N/A	52%[4]	N/A
Iowa Wesleyan University	2.4	61%	36%	30%	70%	0%	11/1	16-21	29%	71%	5%
Lincoln College (IL)	2.3	53%	28%	14%	76%	0%	10/1	N/A[2]	N/A	70%	N/A
Lincoln University (MO)*	2.3	52%	31%	26%	75%	0%	14/1	14-19	12%	61%	3%
Martin University[1] (IN)	2.1	46%[8]	18%	6%[6]	N/A	N/A	22/1[4]	N/A[2]	N/A	N/A	N/A
Mayville State University[1] (ND)*	2.5	61%[8]	51%	32%[6]	75%[4]	1%[4]	12/1[4]	18-23[4]	N/A	70%[4]	N/A
Missouri Southern State University[1]*	2.5	64%[8]	32%	33%[8]	49%[4]	1%[4]	17/1[4]	18-24[4]	40%[4]	94%[4]	3%
Missouri Valley College	2.1	46%[8]	33%	23%	66%	0.3%	16/1	15-20[9]	47%[4]	62%	N/A
Ranken Technical College[1] (MO)	2.3	59%[8]	41%	36%[6]	N/A	N/A	N/A	N/A[2]	N/A	N/A	N/A
University of Northwestern Ohio[1]	2.4	50%[8]	35%	37%[6]	N/A	N/A	23/1[4]	N/A[2]	N/A	N/A	N/A
University of Rio Grande[1] (OH)	2.4	53%[8]	25%	23%[6]	N/A	N/A	16/1[4]	N/A[2]	N/A	N/A	N/A
Vincennes University (IN)*	2.7	47%[8]	32%	21%[6]	88%	0%	21/1	N/A[2]	N/A	84%	N/A
Wilberforce University[1] (OH)	2.5	41%[8]	25%	21%[6]	N/A	N/A	15/1[4]	15-19[4]	N/A	39%[4]	N/A
William Penn University[1] (IA)	2.4	54%[8]	37%	32%[6]	N/A	N/A	13/1[4]	16-21[4]	N/A	58%[4]	N/A

WEST ▶

Rank	School (State) (*Public)	Overall score	Peer assessment score (5.0=highest)	Average first-year student retention rate	2020 graduation rate		% of classes under 20 ('20)	% of classes of 50 or more ('20)	Student/ faculty ratio ('20)	SAT/ACT 25th-75th percentile ('20)	Freshmen in top 25% of HS class ('20)	Accept-ance rate ('20)	Average alumni giving rate
					Predicted	Actual							
1.	Carroll College (MT)	100	3.4	82%	70%	67%	66%	1%	11/1	22-27[2]	68%	73%	10%
2.	Embry-Riddle Aeronautical U.–Prescott (AZ)	99	3.8	83%	51%	59%	36%	1%	18/1	1140-1320[2]	59%	67%	2%
3.	California State U.–Maritime Academy[1]*	90	3.5	78%[8]	70%	64%[8]	39%[4]	1%[4]	13/1[4]	1068-1263[4]	N/A	76%[4]	N/A
3.	William Jessup University (CA)	90	3.4	76%	47%	52%	72%	1%	12/1	948-1213[2]	36%	65%	4%
5.	Texas Lutheran University	88	3.5	71%	55%	55%	55%	0%	14/1	1020-1170[2]	46%	59%	10%
6.	Oklahoma Baptist University	81	3.1	72%	54%	55%	71%	2%	14/1	20-26	58%	58%	4%
7.	Oral Roberts University (OK)	79	3.3	82%	53%	55%	52%	7%	17/1	18-27	43%	78%	4%

Note: Key to footnotes, Page 52

WEST ▶

Rank School (State) (*Public)	Overall score	Peer assessment score (5.0=highest)	Average first-year student retention rate	2020 graduation rate Predicted	2020 graduation rate Actual	% of classes under 20 ('20)	% of classes of 50 or more ('20)	Student/faculty ratio ('20)	SAT/ACT 25th-75th percentile ('20)	Freshmen in top 25% of HS class ('20)	Acceptance rate ('20)	Average alumni giving rate
8. Schreiner University (TX)	77	3.2	65%	47%	51%	69%	0%	14/1	920-1160[2]	29%	96%	8%
9. Warner Pacific University[1] (OR)	76	2.8	68%[8]	40%	43%[6]	86%[4]	0%[4]	11/1[4]	15-20[4]	45%[4]	97%[4]	2%[4]
10. Oregon Tech[1]*	75	3.3	79%[8]	50%	47%[8]	57%[4]	2%[4]	15/1[4]	1000-1200[4]	50%[4]	97%[4]	3%[4]
11. McMurry University (TX)	68	3.1	65%	39%	35%	75%	0.3%	11/1	940-1130[2]	32%	47%	7%
12. Corban University (OR)	66	2.9	79%	63%	60%[6]	49%	1%	13/1	975-1185[2]	35%	48%	N/A
13. Arizona Christian University (AZ)	65	3.2	52%[8]	45%	50%	61%	7%	18/1	935-1120	N/A	74%	N/A
14. Brigham Young University–Hawaii[1]	61	3.1	62%[8]	68%	46%[6]	N/A	N/A	16/1[4]	22-27[4]	N/A	97%[4]	N/A
15. East Texas Baptist University	59	2.9	60%	48%	35%	57%	2%	14/1	17-22[2]	33%	72%	4%
16. Brigham Young University–Idaho[1]	57	3.2	72%[8]	49%	51%[6]	N/A	N/A	19/1[4]	19-25[4]	N/A	96%[4]	N/A
17. Life Pacific University (CA)	56	2.8	65%	36%	31%	66%	0%	9/1	930-1090	N/A	93%	2%
17. San Diego Christian College[1]	56	2.8	63%[8]	46%	48%[6]	N/A	N/A	8/1[4]	930-1170[4]	N/A	55%[4]	N/A
19. John Paul the Great Catholic U. (CA)	53	N/A	78%	55%	61%	53%	1%	19/1	1006-1173	N/A	77%	3%[4]
20. Howard Payne University (TX)	51	2.6	48%	45%	40%	N/A	N/A	10/1	920-1090[2]	35%	49%	3%
21. Lewis-Clark State College[1] (ID)*	50	2.8	60%[8]	35%	29%[6]	77%[4]	1%[4]	12/1[4]	890-1110[4]	24%[4]	100%[4]	N/A
22. University of Montana Western[1]*	49	N/A	76%[8]	39%	45%[8]	72%[4]	0%[4]	17/1[4]	17-22[4]	22%[4]	56%[4]	3%[4]
23. University of Providence[7] (MT)	48	N/A	62%[8]	44%	42%	80%	0%	12/1	16-23[2]	N/A	99%	N/A
24. Oklahoma Panhandle State Univ.*	47	2.7	48%[8]	34%	42%	72%	4%	18/1	14-23[2]	28%	93%	4%
25. Pacific Union College (CA)	46	N/A	75%	53%	47%	70%	4%	10/1	900-1140	N/A	59%	2%
25. Rogers State University (OK)*	46	3.0	66%	29%	38%	70%	0.2%	19/1	17-20	19%	86%	N/A
27. University of Silicon Valley (CA)	39	N/A	66%	49%	46%	79%	0%	16/1	830-1330[9]	N/A	42%	0%[4]
28. Snow College[1] (UT)*	38	N/A	63%[8]	48%	71%[6]	N/A	N/A	19/1[4]	N/A[2]	N/A	N/A	N/A
29. Humphreys University[1] (CA)	36	N/A	100%[8]	23%	39%[6]	N/A	N/A	12/1[4]	N/A[2]	N/A	N/A	N/A
29. University of Hawaii–West Oahu*	36	N/A	72%	43%	39%	41%	0%	19/1	16-21[2]	37%	95%	2%
31. Okla. State U. Inst. of Tech.–Okmulgee*	33	3.3	61%	30%	4%[6]	69%	0%	17/1	15-20[9]	25%	44%	1%
32. Southwestern Adventist Univ.[1] (TX)	32	N/A	71%[8]	42%	42%[6]	N/A	N/A	15/1[4]	880-1090[4]	N/A	58%[4]	N/A
33. Southwestern Christian U. (OK)	31	2.5	47%	37%	30%	73%	0%	12/1	16-20	N/A	32%	6%
34. Huston-Tillotson University[1] (TX)	28	2.2	60%[8]	26%	25%[6]	76%[4]	0%[4]	18/1[4]	800-980[4]	N/A	63%[4]	N/A
34. Northern New Mexico College[1]*	28	2.5	51%[8]	20%	14%[6]	N/A	N/A	12/1[4]	N/A[2]	N/A	N/A	N/A
36. Wiley College (TX)	26	N/A	54%	23%	28%	78%	2%	17/1	13-15[2]	N/A	15%	4%

School (State) (*Public)	Peer assessment score (5.0=highest)	Average first-year student retention rate	2020 graduation rate Predicted	2020 graduation rate Actual	% of classes under 20 ('20)	% of classes of 50 or more ('20)	Student/faculty ratio ('20)	SAT/ACT 25th-75th percentile ('20)	Freshmen in top 25% of HS class ('20)	Acceptance rate ('20)	Average alumni giving rate
SCHOOLS RANKED 37 THROUGH 48 ARE LISTED HERE ALPHABETICALLY											
Bacone College[1] (OK)	1.5	39%[8]	26%	15%[6]	N/A	N/A	11/1[4]	13-18[4]	N/A	72%[4]	N/A
Colorado Mountain College[7]*	N/A	42%[8]	47%	14%[6]	84%	1%	N/A	N/A[2]	N/A	100%	N/A
Dixie State University[1] (UT)*	N/A	56%[8]	37%	21%[6]	N/A	N/A	25/1[4]	N/A[2]	N/A	N/A	N/A
Great Basin College[1] (NV)*	N/A	60%[8]	35%	6%[6]	N/A	N/A	17/1[4]	N/A[2]	N/A	N/A	N/A
Jarvis Christian College[1] (TX)	2.1	49%[8]	18%	17%[6]	N/A	N/A	18/1[4]	N/A	N/A	N/A	N/A
Montana State Univ.–Northern[1]*	N/A	60%[8]	44%	29%[6]	N/A	N/A	13/1[4]	N/A[2]	N/A	N/A	N/A
Nevada State College[1]*	N/A	73%[8]	34%	19%[6]	N/A	N/A	17/1[4]	N/A[2]	N/A	85%[4]	N/A
Northern Marianas College[1] (MP)*	N/A	73%[8]	23%	17%[6]	N/A	N/A	26/1[4]	N/A[2]	N/A	N/A	N/A
Paul Quinn College[1] (TX)	2.0	62%[8]	30%	20%[6]	N/A	N/A	23/1[4]	800-910[4]	N/A	79%[4]	N/A
South Texas College[1]*	N/A	68%[8]	17%	15%[6]	N/A	N/A	23/1[4]	N/A[2]	N/A	N/A	N/A
Texas College[1]	1.8	56%[8]	25%	11%[6]	N/A	N/A	25/1[4]	N/A[2]	N/A	N/A	N/A
University of Antelope Valley[1] (CA)	N/A	74%[8]	29%	41%[6]	N/A	N/A	15/1[4]	N/A[2]	N/A	N/A	N/A

The Top Public Regional Colleges ▶

NORTH
Rank School (State)

1. U.S. Coast Guard Academy (CT)
2. U.S. Merchant Marine Acad. (NY)
3. Maine Maritime Academy
4. Massachusetts Maritime Academy
5. SUNY College of Tech. at Alfred
5. University of Maine at Farmington

SOUTH
Rank School (State)

1. Florida Polytechnic University
2. University of South Carolina–Upstate
3. University of South Carolina–Aiken
4. Elizabeth City State University (NC)
4. University of Arkansas–Pine Bluff

MIDWEST
Rank School (State)

1. University of Minnesota–Crookston
2. Valley City State University (ND)
3. Lake Superior State University (MI)
4. Dickinson State University (ND)
5. Purdue University Global (IN)

WEST
Rank School (State)

1. California State University–Maritime Academy
2. Oregon Tech
3. Lewis-Clark State College (ID)
4. University of Montana Western
5. Oklahoma Panhandle State U.

Best
Historically Black Colleges

INCREASINGLY, THE NATION'S TOP historically Black colleges and universities are an appealing option for applicants of all races; many HBCUs, in fact, actively recruit Hispanic, international and white students in addition to African American high school grads. Which offer the best undergraduate education? U.S. News each year surveys administrators at the HBCUs, asking the president, provost and admissions dean to rate the academic quality of all other HBCUs with which they are familiar.

In addition to the two most recent years of survey results reflected in the peer assessment score, the rankings are based on nearly all the indicators (although weighted slightly differently) used in ranking the regional universities: graduation and retention rates, social mobility, high school class standing, graduate indebtedness, admission test scores, and the strength of the faculty, among others. Outcomes measures such as graduation and retention rates are together given the most weight, at 40%, as in the overall Best Colleges rankings.

To be part of the universe, a school must be designated by the Department of Education as an HBCU, be a baccalaureate-granting institution that enrolls primarily first-year, first-time students, and have been part of this year's Best Colleges ranking process. If an HBCU is unranked in the 2022 Best Colleges rankings, it is unranked here; reasons that schools are not ranked vary.

Of 79 HBCUs, 78 were ranked. HBCUs in the top three-quarters are numerically ranked; those in the bottom quarter appear alphabetically. For more detail on the methodology and changes made for this ranking, visit **usnews.com/hbcu**.

Key Measures

Measure	%
Outcomes	40%
Peer Assessment	20%
Faculty Resources	20%
Financial Resources	10%
Student Excellence	7%
Alumni Giving	3%

Rank School (State) (*Public)	Overall score	Peer assessment score (5.0=highest)	Average first-year student retention rate	Average graduation rate	% of classes under 20 ('20)	% of classes of 50 or more ('20)	Student/ faculty ratio ('20)	% of faculty who are full time ('20)	SAT/ACT 25th-75th percentile ('20)	Freshmen in top 25% of HS class ('20)	Accept- ance rate ('20)	Average alumni giving rate
1. Spelman College (GA)	100	4.7	89%	75%	52%	1%	11/1	89%	1050-1200	59%	53%	30%
2. Howard University (DC)	95	4.3	89%	64%	47%	7%	12/1	92%	1130-1260[2]	59%	39%	12%
3. Xavier University of Louisiana	75	4.2	74%	48%	61%	4%	12/1	94%	20-25	55%	81%	17%
4. Hampton University (VA)	73	4.1	74%	59%[6]	58%	5%	15/1	93%	980-1160[2]	20%	36%	26%
4. Morehouse College (GA)	73	4.2	82%	55%	52%	2%	12/1	84%	995-1180[4]	N/A	74%	14%
4. Tuskegee University (AL)	73	3.8	73%	51%[6]	69%	0%	11/1	94%	19-27	43%	61%	22%
7. Florida A&M University	71	4.0	82%	52%	40%	7%	14/1	93%	1030-1150	31%	33%	5%
8. North Carolina A&T State Univ.	67	4.3	79%	50%[6]	28%	5%	18/1	80%	960-1130	40%	57%	10%
9. Fisk University (TN)	64	3.4	80%	48%[6]	75%	0%	12/1	88%	990-1210	50%	66%	34%
10. Claflin University (SC)	59	3.6	75%	51%	61%	1%	13/1	81%	840-1040	36%	65%	38%
10. Delaware State University	59	3.6	72%	42%	52%	2%	16/1	83%	810-1010	32%	39%	14%
12. Morgan State University (MD)	56	3.7	73%	42%	38%	3%	15/1	90%	920-1070	24%	73%	14%
13. North Carolina Central Univ.	54	3.6	78%	48%	42%	4%	16/1	84%	850-1010	21%	87%	7%
14. Dillard University (LA)	52	3.5	69%	46%[6]	63%	1%	14/1	81%	18-22	N/A	65%	14%
15. Tougaloo College[1] (MS)	51	3.1	72%[8]	45%[6]	N/A	N/A	9/1[4]	90%[4]	15-22[4]	N/A	71%[4]	N/A
16. Winston-Salem State Univ.[1] (NC)	50	3.3	77%[8]	49%[6]	N/A	N/A	15/1[4]	85%[4]	890-1030[4]	N/A	68%[4]	N/A
17. Univ. of Maryland Eastern Shore	48	3.1	66%	40%	77%	2%	10/1	88%	840-1010[2]	N/A	62%	4%
18. Clark Atlanta University	47	3.4	69%	43%	42%	7%	19/1	84%	880-1040	30%	59%	11%
18. Jackson State University (MS)	47	3.4	66%	40%[6]	N/A	N/A	14/1	82%	17-20	N/A	90%	N/A
20. Norfolk State University (VA)	44	3.4	71%	38%	52%	2%	16/1	86%	840-1020	15%	91%	N/A
20. Southern U. and A&M College (LA)	44	3.2	63%	30%[6]	56%	2%	17/1	87%	18-20[2]	38%	41%	17%
22. Alabama State University	43	3.0	60%	31%	63%	0.3%	15/1	85%	14-20	N/A[5]	99%	6%[4]
22. Elizabeth City State University (NC)	43	2.9	73%	40%[6]	59%	0.2%	16/1	93%	875-1059	5%	75%	N/A
24. Alcorn State University (MS)	42	3.1	76%	39%[6]	N/A	N/A	16/1	85%	16-25	24%	38%	7%
24. Bowie State University (MD)	42	3.2	72%	42%	45%	3%	18/1	75%	850-1010	N/A	81%	4%
24. Fayetteville State University (NC)	42	3.0	72%	35%[6]	56%	1%	17/1	89%	840-1000[2]	23%	79%	2%
24. Lincoln University (PA)	42	2.8	72%	46%	63%	0%	14/1	75%	860-1028[2]	20%	90%	9%
24. Prairie View A&M University[1] (TX)	42	3.8	70%[8]	35%[8]	18%[4]	8%[4]	17/1[4]	94%[4]	870-1040[4]	25%[4]	80%[4]	N/A
29. Virginia State University[1]	41	3.4	67%[8]	40%[6]	N/A	N/A	13/1[4]	82%[4]	830-1010[4]	N/A	95%[4]	N/A
30. Johnson C. Smith University (NC)	40	3.0	68%[8]	43%[6]	92%	0%	13/1	74%	800-980	N/A	49%	10%
30. Oakwood University[1] (AL)	40	2.8	71%[8]	49%[6]	N/A	N/A	11/1[4]	86%[4]	16-23[4]	N/A	65%[4]	N/A

Note: Key to footnotes, Page 52

Rank	School (State) (*Public)	Overall score	Peer assessment score (5.0=highest)	Average first-year student retention rate	Average graduation rate	% of classes under 20 ('20)	% of classes of 50 or more ('20)	Student/ faculty ratio ('20)	% of faculty who are full time ('20)	SAT/ACT 25th-75th percentile ('20)	Freshmen in top 25% of HS class ('20)	Accept- ance rate ('20)	Average alumni giving rate
30.	University of Arkansas–Pine Bluff	40	2.9	72%	33%	63%	2%	14/1	92%	14-18	27%	60%	5%
30.	Univ. of the District of Columbia	40	2.9	68%	39%	72%	0.1%	8/1	60%	N/A	N/A	66%	N/A
34.	Kentucky State University	39	3.0	67%	24%	65%	1%	14/1	91%	15-20	12%	84%	5%
35.	Tennessee State University	38	3.4	63%	32%[6]	N/A	N/A	15/1	90%	16-20	N/A	57%	N/A
36.	Coppin State University (MD)	35	2.8	66%	26%[6]	64%	2%	12/1	76%	820-970	N/A	40%	5%
36.	South Carolina State University[7]	35	2.8	68%	34%	61%	0.3%	14/1	87%	14-18	30%	94%	5%
38.	Bennett College[1] (NC)	34	2.6	49%[8]	44%[6]	N/A	N/A	10/1[4]	81%[4]	N/A	N/A	59%[4]	N/A
38.	Fort Valley State University (GA)	34	2.8	74%	33%[6]	48%	3%	27/1	90%	16-19	16%	78%	10%
40.	Alabama A&M University[7]	33	3.3	59%[8]	27%[8]	36%[4]	5%[4]	20/1[4]	87%[4]	15-19	N/A	90%	14%[4]
40.	Philander Smith College (AR)	33	2.7	63%	37%	77%	0%	12/1	75%	16-22[2]	25%	21%	10%
42.	Talladega College[1] (AL)	32	2.8	66%[8]	36%[6]	48%[4]	6%[4]	20/1[4]	75%[4]	20-24[4]	N/A	63%[4]	7%[4]
43.	Cheyney U. of Pennsylvania[1]	31	2.2	53%[8]	22%[6]	N/A	N/A	14/1[4]	84%[4]	N/A	N/A	N/A	N/A
43.	Texas Southern University	31	3.2	54%	22%	45%	6%	14/1	82%	890-1030	27%	66%	5%
45.	Bethune-Cookman University (FL)	30	2.8	65%	34%	65%	2%	15/1	87%	870-980	30%	98%	4%[4]
46.	Voorhees College (SC)	28	2.5	57%[8]	38%[6]	86%	1%	12/1	94%	12-17[2]	N/A	64%[4]	N/A
47.	Mississippi Valley State Univ.	27	2.7	61%[8]	30%[6]	57%	0%	13/1	89%	14-18	35%	83%	N/A
48.	Bluefield State College (WV)	26	2.5	63%	28%[6]	98%	0%	14/1	83%	850-1070	46%	90%	1%
48.	Florida Memorial University[1]	26	2.6	64%[8]	37%[6]	N/A	N/A	13/1[4]	89%[4]	N/A[2]	N/A	40%[4]	N/A
48.	Virginia Union University	26	2.8	62%	31%	65%	1%	16/1	68%	780-920[2]	22%	75%	8%
51.	Central State University (OH)	25	2.8	51%	25%	60%	0%	19/1	70%	14-17[2]	N/A	58%	9%
51.	Savannah State University[7] (GA)	25	2.8	60%[8]	28%[6]	44%[4]	1%[4]	17/1	91%	900-1030[4]	N/A	69%	N/A
53.	Benedict College (SC)	24	2.7	55%[8]	26%[6]	32%	4%	15/1	89%	800-1010[2]	31%	73%	7%
53.	Grambling State University[1] (LA)	24	3.2	71%[8]	34%[6]	N/A	N/A	24/1[4]	100%[4]	16-20[4]	N/A	97%[4]	N/A
53.	West Virginia State University[1]	24	2.6	58%[8]	29%[6]	N/A	N/A	11/1[4]	81%[4]	17-22[4]	N/A	95%[4]	N/A
56.	Langston University[1] (OK)	23	2.7	56%[8]	25%[6]	N/A	N/A	15/1	92%[4]	N/A	N/A	N/A	N/A
56.	Stillman College (AL)	23	2.6	65%[8]	27%[6]	N/A	N/A	17/1	72%	N/A	N/A	56%	8%
58.	Albany State University[1] (GA)	22	2.8	60%[8]	35%[6]	N/A	N/A	19/1[4]	88%[4]	740-890[4]	N/A	66%[4]	N/A
59.	Rust College[1] (MS)	20	2.4	65%[8]	32%[6]	N/A	N/A	12/1[4]	97%[4]	N/A	N/A	50%[4]	N/A

School (State) (*Public)	Peer assessment score (5.0=highest)	Average first-year student retention rate	Average graduation rate	% of classes under 20 ('20)	% of classes of 50 or more ('20)	Student/ faculty ratio ('20)	% of faculty who are full time ('20)	SAT/ACT 25th-75th percentile ('20)	Freshmen in top 25% of HS class ('20)	Accept- ance rate ('20)	Average alumni giving rate
SCHOOLS RANKED 60 THROUGH 78 ARE LISTED HERE ALPHABETICALLY											
Allen University (SC)	2.3	40%	23%[6]	N/A	N/A	15/1	84%	699-821[2]	7%	61%	7%
Arkansas Baptist College[1]	2.1	38%[8]	5%[6]	68%[4]	0%[4]	24/1[4]	48%[4]	N/A[2]	N/A	26%[4]	N/A
Edward Waters College[1] (FL)	2.4	56%[8]	26%[6]	N/A	N/A	23/1[4]	100%[4]	757-1092[4]	N/A	61%[4]	N/A
Harris-Stowe State University[1] (MO)	2.5	58%[8]	11%[8]	N/A	N/A	18/1[4]	43%[4]	15-19[4]	N/A	52%[4]	N/A
Huston-Tillotson University[1] (TX)	2.6	60%[8]	25%[6]	76%[4]	0%[4]	18/1[4]	74%[4]	800-980[4]	N/A	63%[4]	N/A
Jarvis Christian College[1] (TX)	2.4	49%[8]	17%[6]	N/A	N/A	18/1[4]	100%[4]	N/A	N/A	N/A	N/A
Lane College[7] (TN)	2.7	54%	23%[6]	48%	1%	20/1[4]	97%[4]	14-16[2]	N/A	61%	N/A
LeMoyne-Owen College[1] (TN)	2.4	56%	13%[6]	78%[4]	0%[4]	13/1[4]	72%[4]	15-17[4]	N/A	41%[4]	N/A
Lincoln University (MO)	2.6	52%	22%	75%	0%	14/1	87%	14-19	12%	61%	3%
Livingstone College (NC)	2.5	49%	26%[6]	77%	2%	13/1	95%	765-930	11%	69%	9%
Miles College[1] (AL)	2.5	59%[8]	23%[6]	N/A	N/A	16/1[4]	85%[4]	N/A[2]	N/A	N/A	N/A
Morris College[1] (SC)	2.3	46%[8]	26%[6]	N/A	N/A	13/1[4]	86%[4]	N/A	N/A	N/A	N/A
Paine College[1] (GA)	2.3	58%[8]	19%[6]	N/A	N/A	10/1[4]	87%[4]	798-943[4]	N/A	65%[4]	N/A
Saint Augustine's University (NC)	2.4	54%[8]	24%[6]	76%	0.2%	12/1	78%	780-940	N/A	67%	N/A
Shaw University[1] (NC)	2.6	49%[8]	17%[8]	58%[4]	0%[4]	15/1[4]	78%[4]	737-902[4]	6%[4]	63%[4]	N/A
Southern University at New Orleans[7]	2.7	49%[8]	22%[6]	47%[4]	0.3%[4]	21/1[4]	81%[4]	15-18[4]	27%[4]	60%[4]	1%
Texas College[1]	2.5	56%[8]	11%[6]	N/A	N/A	25/1[4]	86%[4]	N/A[2]	N/A	N/A	N/A
Wilberforce University[1] (OH)	2.5	41%[8]	21%[6]	N/A	N/A	15/1[4]	64%[4]	15-19[4]	N/A	39%[4]	N/A
Wiley College (TX)	2.6	54%	27%[6]	78%	2%	17/1	84%	13-15[2]	N/A	15%	4%

Sources: Statistical data from the schools. The 2021 peer assessment data were collected by U.S. News.

Best
Business Programs

EACH YEAR, U.S. NEWS RANKS undergraduate business programs accredited by AACSB International; the results are based solely on surveys of B-school deans and senior faculty. Participants were asked to rate the quality of business programs with which they're familiar on a scale of 1 (marginal) to 5 (distinguished); 49.5% of those canvassed responded to the most recent survey conducted in the spring and early summer of 2021. In a change from previous years, only data from the 2021 surveys were used to calculate the peer assessment score. Deans and faculty members also were asked to nominate up to 15 programs they consider best in a number of specialty areas; the five schools receiving the most mentions in the 2021 survey appear here.

▶ Top Programs

Rank	School (B-school) (State) (*Public)	Peer assessment score (5.0=highest)
1.	University of Pennsylvania (Wharton)	4.8
2.	Massachusetts Institute of Technology (Sloan)	4.7
3.	University of California–Berkeley (Haas)*	4.6
4.	University of Michigan–Ann Arbor (Ross)*	4.5
5.	New York University (Stern)	4.4
5.	University of Texas at Austin (McCombs)*	4.4
7.	Carnegie Mellon University (Tepper) (PA)	4.3
8.	Cornell University (Dyson) (NY)	4.2
8.	Indiana University–Bloomington (Kelley)*	4.2
8.	U. of N. Carolina–Chapel Hill (Kenan-Flagler)*	4.2
8.	University of Virginia (McIntire)*	4.2
12.	University of Notre Dame (Mendoza) (IN)	4.1
12.	University of Southern California (Marshall)	4.1
14.	Emory University (Goizueta) (GA)	4.0
14.	Georgetown University (McDonough) (DC)	4.0
14.	Ohio State University–Columbus (Fisher)*	4.0
14.	U. of Illinois–Urbana-Champaign (Gies)*	4.0
14.	Washington University in St. Louis (Olin)	4.0
19.	Georgia Institute of Technology (Scheller)*	3.9
19.	University of Wisconsin–Madison*	3.9
19.	U. of Minnesota–Twin Cities (Carlson)*	3.9
19.	University of Washington (Foster)*	3.9
23.	Arizona State University (Carey)*	3.8
23.	Michigan State University (Broad)*	3.8
23.	Pennsylvania State U.–Univ. Park (Smeal)*	3.8
23.	Texas A&M University (Mays)*	3.8
23.	Univ. of Maryland–College Park (Smith)*	3.8
23.	University of Florida (Warrington)*	3.8
23.	University of Georgia (Terry)*	3.8
30.	Boston College (Carroll)	3.7
30.	Johns Hopkins University (MD)	3.7
30.	Purdue U.–West Lafayette (Krannert) (IN)*	3.7
30.	University of Arizona (Eller)*	3.7
30.	University of California–Irvine (Merage)*	3.7
30.	University of Colorado Boulder (Leeds)*	3.7
36.	Babson College (Olin) (MA)	3.6
36.	Case Western Reserve U. (Weatherhead) (OH)	3.6
36.	University of Arkansas (Walton)*	3.6
36.	University of Iowa (Tippie)*	3.6
36.	University of Rochester (NY)	3.6
41.	Brigham Young Univ.–Provo (Marriott) (UT)	3.5
41.	Southern Methodist University (Cox) (TX)	3.5
41.	Tulane University (Freeman) (LA)	3.5
41.	University of Oregon (Lundquist)*	3.5
41.	University of Texas at Dallas (Jindal)*	3.5
41.	University of Utah (Eccles)*	3.5
41.	Virginia Tech (Pamplin)*	3.5
41.	Wake Forest University (NC)	3.5
49.	Auburn University (Harbert) (AL)*	3.4
49.	Boston University (Questrom)	3.4
49.	George Washington University (DC)	3.4
49.	Georgia State University (Robinson)*	3.4
49.	Santa Clara University (Leavey) (CA)	3.4
49.	U. of Massachusetts–Amherst (Isenberg)*	3.4
49.	Univ. of Nebraska–Lincoln*	3.4
49.	Univ. of South Carolina (Moore)*	3.4
49.	University of Alabama (Culverhouse)*	3.4
49.	University of California–San Diego (Rady)*	3.4
49.	University of Connecticut*	3.4
49.	University of Pittsburgh*	3.4
49.	University of Tennessee (Haslam)*	3.4
49.	Villanova University (PA)	3.4
49.	William & Mary (Mason) (VA)*	3.4
64.	Clemson University (SC)*	3.3
64.	Florida State University*	3.3
64.	Northeastern U. (D'Amore-McKim) (MA)	3.3
64.	Pepperdine University (CA)	3.3
64.	Rutgers University–New Brunswick (NJ)*	3.3
64.	Syracuse University (Whitman) (NY)	3.3
64.	Texas Christian University (Neeley)	3.3
64.	University of Kansas*	3.3
64.	University of Kentucky (Gatton)*	3.3
64.	University of Miami (FL)	3.3
74.	Baylor University (Hankamer) (TX)	3.2
74.	Bentley University (MA)	3.2
74.	Fordham University (Gabelli) (NY)	3.2
74.	Iowa State University (Ivy)*	3.2
74.	Rensselaer Polytechnic Inst. (Lally) (NY)	3.2
74.	Rochester Inst. of Tech. (Saunders) (NY)	3.2
74.	San Diego State University (Fowler)*	3.2
74.	United States Air Force Academy (CO)*	3.2
74.	University of Oklahoma (Price)*	3.2
74.	Washington State University (Carson)*	3.2
84.	American University (Kogod) (DC)	3.1
84.	Brandeis University (MA)	3.1
84.	CUNY–Baruch College (Zicklin)*	3.1
84.	DePaul University (Driehaus) (IL)	3.1
84.	George Mason University (VA)*	3.1
84.	Gonzaga University (WA)	3.1
84.	Howard University (DC)	3.1
84.	Lehigh University (PA)	3.1
84.	Louisiana State U.–Baton Rouge (Ourso)*	3.1
84.	Loyola University Chicago (Quinlan)	3.1
84.	Miami University–Oxford (Farmer) (OH)*	3.1
84.	North Carolina State U. (Poole)*	3.1
84.	Oklahoma State University (Spears)*	3.1
84.	Univ. of Missouri (Trulaske)*	3.1
84.	University at Buffalo–SUNY*	3.1
84.	University of Cincinnati (Lindner)*	3.1
84.	University of Delaware (Lerner)*	3.1
84.	University of Denver (Daniels)	3.1
84.	University of Houston (Bauer)*	3.1
84.	University of Illinois–Chicago*	3.1
84.	University of Richmond (Robins) (VA)	3.1
84.	University of San Diego	3.1
106.	Colorado State University*	3.0
106.	Creighton University (Heider) (NE)	3.0
106.	Drexel University (LeBow) (PA)	3.0
106.	James Madison University (VA)*	3.0
106.	Kansas State University*	3.0
106.	Loyola Marymount University (CA)	3.0
106.	Marquette University (WI)	3.0
106.	Oregon State University*	3.0
106.	Saint Joseph's University (Haub) (PA)	3.0
106.	Saint Louis University (Cook)	3.0
106.	Seton Hall University (Stillman) (NJ)	3.0
106.	Texas Tech University (Rawls)*	3.0
106.	U. of North Carolina–Charlotte (Belk)*	3.0
106.	Univ. of Wisconsin–Milwaukee (Lubar)*	3.0
106.	University of California–Riverside*	3.0
106.	University of Central Florida*	3.0
106.	University of Hawaii–Manoa (Shidler)*	3.0
106.	University of Louisville (KY)*	3.0
106.	Virginia Commonwealth University*	3.0
125.	Binghamton University–SUNY*	2.9
125.	Bucknell University (PA)	2.9
125.	Calif. Poly. State U.–San Luis Obispo (Orfalea)*	2.9
125.	Elon University (Love) (NC)	2.9
125.	Florida International University*	2.9
125.	Hofstra University (Zarb) (NY)	2.9
125.	Loyola University Maryland (Sellinger)	2.9
125.	Rutgers University–Camden (NJ)*	2.9
125.	Rutgers University–Newark (NJ)*	2.9
125.	Stevens Institute of Technology (NJ)	2.9
125.	Temple University (Fox) (PA)*	2.9
125.	UNC Greensboro (Bryan)*	2.9
125.	U. of Alabama at Birmingham (Collat)*	2.9
125.	University of Mississippi*	2.9
125.	University of San Francisco	2.9
125.	University of South Florida (Muma)*	2.9
125.	University of Texas at Arlington*	2.9
125.	West Virginia University*	2.9
143.	Boise State University (ID)*	2.8
143.	Butler University (IN)	2.8

►Top Programs

Rank	School (B-school) (State) (*Public)	Peer assessment score (5.0=highest)
143.	California State University–Los Angeles*	2.8
143.	Kennesaw State University (Coles) (GA)*	2.8
143.	Mississippi State University*	2.8
143.	Ohio University*	2.8
143.	Providence College (RI)	2.8
143.	Quinnipiac University (CT)	2.8
143.	San Jose State University (Lucas) (CA)*	2.8
143.	Seattle University (Albers)	2.8
143.	St. John's University (Tobin) (NY)	2.8
143.	United States Coast Guard Academy (CT)*	2.8
143.	Univ. of Massachusetts–Boston*	2.8
143.	University at Albany–SUNY*	2.8
143.	University of Colorado Denver*	2.8
143.	University of Memphis (Fogelman)*	2.8
143.	University of Nevada–Las Vegas (Lee)*	2.8
143.	University of New Hampshire (Paul)*	2.8
143.	University of New Mexico (Anderson)*	2.8
143.	University of Vermont*	2.8
143.	Utah State University (Huntsman)*	2.8
143.	Washington and Lee U. (Williams) (VA)	2.8
143.	Xavier University (Williams) (OH)	2.8
166.	Ball State University (Miller) (IN)*	2.7
166.	Bowling Green State University (OH)*	2.7

Rank	School (B-school) (State) (*Public)	Peer assessment score (5.0=highest)
166.	Chapman University (Argyros) (CA)	2.7
166.	Fairfield University (Dolan) (CT)	2.7
166.	John Carroll University (Boler) (OH)	2.7
166.	Loyola University New Orleans	2.7
166.	Old Dominion University (Strome) (VA)*	2.7
166.	Samford University (Brock) (AL)	2.7
166.	San Francisco State University*	2.7
166.	U. of Massachusetts–Dartmouth (Charlton)*	2.7
166.	University of Missouri–Kansas City (Bloch)*	2.7
166.	University of Alabama–Huntsville*	2.7
166.	University of Dallas (Gupta)	2.7
166.	University of Dayton (OH)	2.7
166.	University of Idaho*	2.7
166.	University of Maine*	2.7
166.	University of Montana*	2.7
166.	University of Nebraska–Omaha*	2.7
166.	University of North Texas (Ryan)*	2.7
166.	University of Rhode Island*	2.7
166.	University of Scranton (Kania) (PA)	2.7
166.	University of St. Thomas (Opus) (MN)	2.7
166.	University of Tampa (Sykes) (FL)	2.7
166.	University of Tennessee–Chattanooga*	2.7
190.	Appalachian State U. (Walker) (NC)*	2.6

Rank	School (B-school) (State) (*Public)	Peer assessment score (5.0=highest)
190.	California State Polytechnic U.–Pomona*	2.6
190.	California State U.–Fullerton (Mihaylo)*	2.6
190.	Clarkson University (Reh) (NY)	2.6
190.	Duquesne University (Palumbo) (PA)	2.6
190.	Florida Atlantic University*	2.6
190.	Kent State University (OH)*	2.6
190.	Marshall University (Lewis) (WV)*	2.6
190.	Morehouse College (GA)	2.6
190.	New Jersey Inst. of Technology*	2.6
190.	Northern Illinois University*	2.6
190.	Rollins College (FL)	2.6
190.	Southern Illinois University–Carbondale*	2.6
190.	The Citadel, Military Coll. of SC*	2.6
190.	Univ. of Massachusetts–Lowell (Manning)*	2.6
190.	Univ. of Missouri–St. Louis*	2.6
190.	University of Colorado–Colorado Springs*	2.6
190.	University of Nevada–Reno*	2.6
190.	University of Portland (Pamplin) (OR)	2.6
190.	University of Wyoming*	2.6
190.	Wayne State University (MI)*	2.6
190.	Worcester Polytechnic Inst. (MA)	2.6

Note: Peer assessment surveys in 2021 conducted by U.S. News. To be ranked in a specialty, an undergraduate business school may have either a program or course offerings in that subject area. Extended undergraduate business rankings can be found at usnews.com/bestcolleges. U.S. News surveyed 514 business programs.

► Best in the Specialties (*Public)

ACCOUNTING
1. University of Texas at Austin (McCombs)*
2. Brigham Young University–Provo (Marriott) (UT)
3. University of Illinois–Urbana-Champaign (Gies)*
4. Indiana University–Bloomington (Kelley)*
5. University of Michigan–Ann Arbor (Ross)*

BUSINESS ANALYTICS
1. Massachusetts Institute of Technology (Sloan)
2. Carnegie Mellon University (Tepper) (PA)
3. Georgia Institute of Technology (Scheller)*
4. University of Pennsylvania (Wharton)
5. Arizona State University (Carey)*
5. University of Texas at Austin (McCombs)*

ENTREPRENEURSHIP
1. Babson College (Olin) (MA)
2. Massachusetts Institute of Technology (Sloan)
2. University of California–Berkeley (Haas)*
4. Indiana University–Bloomington (Kelley)*
5. University of Michigan–Ann Arbor (Ross)*
5. University of Pennsylvania (Wharton)

FINANCE
1. University of Pennsylvania (Wharton)
2. New York University (Stern)
3. University of Michigan–Ann Arbor (Ross)*
4. Massachusetts Institute of Technology (Sloan)
5. University of Texas at Austin (McCombs)*

INSURANCE/RISK MANAGEMENT
1. Florida State University*
1. University of Georgia (Terry)*
3. University of Wisconsin–Madison*
4. Georgia State University (Robinson)*
5. Temple University (Fox) (PA)*

INTERNATIONAL BUSINESS
1. University of South Carolina (Moore)*
2. Florida International University*
3. Georgetown University (McDonough) (DC)
4. New York University (Stern)
5. University of California–Berkeley (Haas)*

MANAGEMENT
1. University of Pennsylvania (Wharton)
2. University of Michigan–Ann Arbor (Ross)*
3. University of California–Berkeley (Haas)*
4. University of Texas at Austin (McCombs)*
5. New York University (Stern)

MANAGEMENT INFORMATION SYSTEMS
1. Carnegie Mellon University (Tepper) (PA)
2. Massachusetts Institute of Technology (Sloan)
3. University of Texas at Austin (McCombs)*
4. University of Arizona (Eller)*
5. Georgia Institute of Technology (Scheller)*

MARKETING
1. University of Michigan–Ann Arbor (Ross)*
2. University of Pennsylvania (Wharton)

3. Indiana University–Bloomington (Kelley)*
4. New York University (Stern)
4. University of Texas at Austin (McCombs)*

PRODUCTION/OPERATIONS MANAGEMENT
1. Massachusetts Institute of Technology (Sloan)
2. Ohio State University–Columbus (Fisher)*
3. University of Michigan–Ann Arbor (Ross)*
4. Carnegie Mellon University (Tepper) (PA)
5. Michigan State University (Broad)*
5. University of Pennsylvania (Wharton)

QUANTITATIVE ANALYSIS/METHODS
1. Massachusetts Institute of Technology (Sloan)
2. Carnegie Mellon University (Tepper) (PA)
3. University of Pennsylvania (Wharton)
3. University of Texas at Austin (McCombs)*
5. Georgia Institute of Technology (Scheller)*

REAL ESTATE
1. University of Pennsylvania (Wharton)
2. Univ. of Wisconsin–Madison*
3. University of California–Berkeley (Haas)*
4. New York University (Stern)
4. University of Texas at Austin (McCombs)*

SUPPLY CHAIN MANAGEMENT/LOGISTICS
1. Michigan State University (Broad)*
2. Arizona State University (Carey)*
3. University of Tennessee (Haslam)*
4. Pennsylvania State U.–Univ. Park (Smeal)*
5. Massachusetts Institute of Technology (Sloan)

Best

Engineering Programs

O**N THESE PAGES,** U.S. News ranks undergraduate engineering programs accredited by ABET. Rankings are based solely on surveys of engineering deans and senior faculty at accredited programs. Participants were asked to rate programs with which they're familiar on a scale from 1 (marginal) to 5 (distinguished). Whereas previously the two most recent years' survey results were used to calculate the peer assessment score, this year the current results alone were used.

Students who prefer a program focused on its undergrads can use the list of institutions whose terminal degree is a bachelor's or master's; universities that grant doctorates in engineering, whose programs are ranked separately, may boast more offerings at the undergraduate level. For the 2021 surveys, 42.0% of those canvassed returned ratings; 56.9% did so for the doctorate group. Respondents were also asked to name up to 15 top programs in specialty areas; those mentioned most often in 2021 appear here.

Top Programs ▶ AT ENGINEERING SCHOOLS WHOSE HIGHEST DEGREE IS A BACHELOR'S OR MASTER'S

Rank	School (State) (*Public)	Peer assessment score (5.0=highest)
1.	Rose-Hulman Institute of Technology (IN)	4.6
2.	Harvey Mudd College (CA)	4.5
3.	Franklin W. Olin College of Engineering (MA)	4.4
4.	United States Military Academy (NY)*	4.3
5.	United States Naval Academy (MD)*	4.2
6.	United States Air Force Academy (CO)*	4.1
7.	Bucknell University (PA)	4.0
7.	Calif. Polytechnic State U.–San Luis Obispo*	4.0
9.	Cooper Union for Adv. of Sci. and Art (NY)	3.8
9.	Milwaukee School of Engineering	3.8
11.	California State Polytechnic U.–Pomona*	3.7
11.	Embry-Riddle Aeronautical U.–Prescott (AZ)	3.7
13.	Kettering University (MI)	3.6
13.	United States Coast Guard Academy (CT)*	3.6
13.	University of San Diego	3.6
16.	Smith College (MA)	3.5
16.	The Citadel, Military Coll. of SC*	3.5
16.	Valparaiso University (IN)	3.5
19.	Lafayette College (PA)	3.4
19.	Rowan University (NJ)*	3.4
19.	San Jose State University (CA)*	3.4
22.	California State University–Los Angeles*	3.3
22.	Gonzaga University (WA)	3.3
22.	James Madison University (VA)*	3.3
22.	Loyola Marymount University (CA)	3.3

Rank	School (State) (*Public)	Peer assessment score (5.0=highest)
22.	Swarthmore College (PA)	3.3
22.	U.S. Merchant Marine Acad. (NY)*	3.3
22.	Union College (NY)	3.3
29.	California State University–Fullerton*	3.2
29.	Ohio Northern University	3.2
29.	Seattle University	3.2
29.	Virginia Military Institute*	3.2
33.	Bradley University (IL)	3.1
33.	Massachusetts Maritime Academy*	3.1
33.	New York Inst. of Technology	3.1
33.	Purdue University–Fort Wayne*	3.1
33.	University of Portland (OR)	3.1
33.	University of Puerto Rico–Mayaguez*	3.1
39.	California State U.–Maritime Academy*	3.0
39.	California State University–Northridge*	3.0
39.	Calvin University (MI)	3.0
39.	Hofstra University (NY)	3.0
39.	LeTourneau University (TX)	3.0
39.	Loyola University Chicago	3.0
39.	Manhattan College (NY)	3.0
39.	Penn State Univ.–Erie, Behrend Col.*	3.0
39.	SUNY Maritime College*	3.0
39.	Texas Christian University	3.0
39.	Univ. of Wisconsin–Platteville*	3.0
39.	University of Minnesota–Duluth*	3.0

Rank	School (State) (*Public)	Peer assessment score (5.0=highest)
39.	University of St. Thomas (MN)	3.0
39.	Wentworth Inst. of Technology (MA)	3.0
53.	California State University–Fresno*	2.9
53.	California State University–Sacramento*	2.9
53.	Cedarville University (OH)	2.9
53.	Florida Polytechnic University*	2.9
53.	Mercer University (GA)	2.9
53.	Miami University–Oxford (OH)*	2.9
53.	Purdue University–Northwest (IN)*	2.9
53.	Southern Illinois University Edwardsville*	2.9
53.	University of Hartford (CT)	2.9
62.	George Fox University (OR)	2.8
62.	Grand Valley State University (MI)*	2.8
62.	Loyola University Maryland	2.8
62.	Maine Maritime Academy*	2.8
62.	Minnesota State Univ.–Mankato*	2.8
62.	Northern Illinois University*	2.8
62.	Oregon Tech*	2.8
62.	San Francisco State University*	2.8
62.	Seattle Pacific University	2.8
62.	Trinity University (TX)	2.8
62.	Univ. of Massachusetts–Boston*	2.8
62.	University of New Haven (CT)	2.8
62.	University of the Pacific (CA)	2.8

Best in the Specialties ▶

(*Public)

CIVIL
1. Rose-Hulman Institute of Technology (IN)
2. California Polytechnic State University–San Luis Obispo*
3. Bucknell University (PA)
4. California State Polytechnic University–Pomona*
5. United States Military Academy (NY)*

COMPUTER ENGINEERING
1. Rose-Hulman Institute of Technology (IN)
2. California Polytechnic State University–San Luis Obispo*

3. California State Polytechnic University–Pomona*
4. Harvey Mudd College (CA)
5. United States Air Force Academy (CO)*
5. United States Naval Academy (MD)*

ELECTRICAL/ELECTRONIC/COMMUNICATIONS
1. Rose-Hulman Institute of Technology (IN)
2. California Polytechnic State University–San Luis Obispo*
3. Harvey Mudd College (CA)
4. Bucknell University (PA)
4. California State Polytechnic University–Pomona*

MECHANICAL
1. Rose-Hulman Institute of Technology (IN)
2. California Polytechnic State University–San Luis Obispo*
3. Franklin W. Olin College of Engineering (MA)
4. Harvey Mudd College (CA)
5. United States Naval Academy (MD)*

Top Programs ▶ AT ENGINEERING SCHOOLS WHOSE HIGHEST DEGREE IS A DOCTORATE

Rank	School (State) (*Public)	Peer assessment score (5.0=highest)
1.	Massachusetts Institute of Technology	4.8
2.	Stanford University (CA)	4.7
2.	University of California–Berkeley*	4.7
4.	California Institute of Technology	4.6
4.	Georgia Institute of Technology*	4.6
6.	Carnegie Mellon University (PA)	4.4
6.	University of Illinois–Urbana-Champaign*	4.4
6.	University of Michigan–Ann Arbor*	4.4
9.	Cornell University (NY)	4.3
10.	Purdue University–West Lafayette (IN)*	4.2
10.	University of Texas at Austin*	4.2
12.	Princeton University (NJ)	4.1
13.	Johns Hopkins University (MD)	4.0
13.	Virginia Tech*	4.0
15.	Northwestern University (IL)	3.9
15.	Texas A&M University*	3.9
15.	Univ. of Wisconsin–Madison*	3.9
15.	University of California–Los Angeles*	3.9
19.	Rice University (TX)	3.8
19.	University of California–San Diego*	3.8
21.	Columbia University (NY)	3.7
21.	Pennsylvania State U.–Univ. Park*	3.7
21.	Univ. of Maryland–College Park*	3.7
21.	University of Minnesota–Twin Cities*	3.7
21.	University of Pennsylvania	3.7
21.	University of Washington*	3.7
27.	Duke University (NC)	3.6
27.	Harvard University (MA)	3.6
27.	Ohio State University–Columbus*	3.6
27.	University of California–Davis*	3.6
31.	Rensselaer Polytechnic Inst. (NY)	3.5
31.	University of California–Santa Barbara*	3.5
31.	University of Colorado Boulder*	3.5
31.	University of Florida*	3.5
31.	University of Southern California	3.5
36.	Arizona State University*	3.4
36.	Brown University (RI)	3.4
36.	North Carolina State U.*	3.4
36.	University of Notre Dame (IN)	3.4
36.	University of Virginia*	3.4
36.	Vanderbilt University (TN)	3.4
42.	Colorado School of Mines*	3.3
42.	University of California–Irvine*	3.3
42.	Yale University (CT)	3.3
45.	Case Western Reserve Univ. (OH)	3.2
45.	Iowa State University*	3.2
45.	Lehigh University (PA)	3.2
45.	Michigan State University*	3.2
45.	Northeastern University (MA)	3.2
45.	Rutgers University–New Brunswick (NJ)*	3.2
45.	Washington University in St. Louis	3.2
52.	Boston University	3.1
52.	Dartmouth College (NH)	3.1
52.	Drexel University (PA)	3.1
52.	University of Arizona*	3.1
56.	Auburn University (AL)*	3.0
56.	Clemson University (SC)*	3.0
56.	Rochester Inst. of Technology (NY)	3.0
56.	Tufts University (MA)	3.0
56.	Univ. of Massachusetts–Amherst*	3.0
56.	University of Delaware*	3.0
56.	University of Pittsburgh*	3.0

Best in the Specialties ▶

(*Public)

AEROSPACE/AERONAUTICAL/ASTRONAUTICAL
1. Massachusetts Institute of Technology
2. Georgia Institute of Technology*
3. California Institute of Technology
4. Purdue University–West Lafayette (IN)*
5. Embry-Riddle Aeronautical University (FL)

BIOLOGICAL/AGRICULTURAL
1. Purdue University–West Lafayette (IN)*
2. Iowa State University*
2. University of California–Davis*
4. Texas A&M University*
5. University of Illinois–Urbana-Champaign*

BIOMEDICAL/BIOMEDICAL ENGINEERING
1. Johns Hopkins University (MD)
2. Massachusetts Institute of Technology
3. Georgia Institute of Technology*
4. Duke University (NC)
5. Stanford University (CA)

CHEMICAL
1. Massachusetts Institute of Technology
2. Georgia Institute of Technology*
3. University of California–Berkeley*
4. California Institute of Technology
5. Stanford University (CA)
5. University of Texas at Austin*

CIVIL
1. University of California–Berkeley*
2. Georgia Institute of Technology*
3. University of Illinois–Urbana-Champaign*
4. Massachusetts Institute of Technology
5. University of Texas at Austin*

COMPUTER ENGINEERING
1. Massachusetts Institute of Technology
2. Carnegie Mellon University (PA)
3. University of California–Berkeley*
4. Stanford University (CA)
5. Georgia Institute of Technology*

ELECTRICAL/ELECTRONIC/COMMUNICATIONS
1. Massachusetts Institute of Technology
2. University of California–Berkeley*
3. California Institute of Technology
4. Georgia Institute of Technology*
5. University of Michigan–Ann Arbor*

ENVIRONMENTAL/ENVIRONMENTAL HEALTH
1. University of California–Berkeley*
2. University of Michigan–Ann Arbor*
3. Georgia Institute of Technology*
4. Massachusetts Institute of Technology
5. Stanford University (CA)

INDUSTRIAL/MANUFACTURING
1. Georgia Institute of Technology*
2. Purdue University–West Lafayette (IN)*
3. University of Michigan–Ann Arbor*
3. Virginia Tech*
5. Cornell University (NY)

MATERIALS
1. Massachusetts Institute of Technology
2. University of Illinois–Urbana-Champaign*
3. University of California–Berkeley*
4. Georgia Institute of Technology*
5. University of Michigan–Ann Arbor*

MECHANICAL
1. Massachusetts Institute of Technology
2. Georgia Institute of Technology*
3. Stanford University (CA)
4. University of California–Berkeley*
5. California Institute of Technology

PETROLEUM
1. Texas A&M University*
1. University of Texas at Austin*
3. Colorado School of Mines*
3. University of Oklahoma*
5. Pennsylvania State U.–Univ. Park*
5. University of Tulsa (OK)

Note: Peer assessment survey in 2021 conducted by U.S. News. To be ranked in a specialty, a school may have either a program or course offerings in that subject area; ABET accreditation of that program is not needed. Extended rankings can be found at usnews.com/bestcolleges. U.S. News surveyed 210 undergraduate engineering programs at colleges that offer doctoral degrees in engineering and 239 engineering programs at colleges where the terminal degree in engineering is a bachelor's or master's.

Best
Computer Science Programs

TO BE ELIGIBLE FOR the U.S. News ranking of undergraduate computer science programs, a program must be accredited by ABET or be at a regionally accredited institution and have recently granted at least 20 computer science bachelor's degrees, according to U.S. Department of Education data. Results are based solely on surveys conducted in 2021 of computer science deans and senior faculty, who were asked to rate the quality of programs with which they're familiar on a scale of 1 (marginal) to 5 (distinguished); 23.4% responded. Those surveyed also were asked to nominate up to 15 programs they consider to be best in various specialty areas; the five receiving the most mentions appear.

▶ Top Programs

Rank School (State) (*Public)	Peer assessment score (5.0=highest)
1. Carnegie Mellon University (PA)	4.9
1. Massachusetts Institute of Technology	4.9
1. Stanford University (CA)	4.9
1. University of California–Berkeley*	4.9
5. Cornell University (NY)	4.6
5. Georgia Institute of Technology*	4.6
5. University of Illinois–Urbana-Champaign*	4.6
8. California Institute of Technology	4.5
8. Princeton University (NJ)	4.5
10. University of California–Los Angeles*	4.4
10. University of Texas at Austin*	4.4
10. University of Washington*	4.4
13. Columbia University (NY)	4.3
13. Harvard University (MA)	4.3
13. University of Michigan–Ann Arbor*	4.3
16. University of California–San Diego*	4.2
16. University of Pennsylvania	4.2
18. Johns Hopkins University (MD)	4.1
18. Purdue University–West Lafayette (IN)*	4.1
18. Univ. of Maryland–College Park*	4.1
18. Univ. of Wisconsin–Madison*	4.1
18. Yale University (CT)	4.1
23. Brown University (RI)	4.0
23. Duke University (NC)	4.0
23. Harvey Mudd College (CA)	4.0
23. Northwestern University (IL)	4.0
23. University of Southern California	4.0
28. Rice University (TX)	3.9
28. University of California–Irvine*	3.9
28. University of Chicago	3.9
31. New York University	3.8
31. U. of North Carolina–Chapel Hill*	3.8
31. Univ. of Massachusetts–Amherst*	3.8
31. University of California–Davis*	3.8
31. University of Virginia*	3.8
31. Virginia Tech*	3.8
37. Dartmouth College (NH)	3.7
37. Ohio State University–Columbus*	3.7
37. Pennsylvania State U.–Univ. Park*	3.7
37. Rutgers University–New Brunswick (NJ)*	3.7
37. University of California–Santa Barbara*	3.7
37. University of Colorado Boulder*	3.7
37. University of Florida*	3.7
37. University of Minnesota–Twin Cities*	3.7
37. Washington University in St. Louis	3.7
46. Northeastern University (MA)	3.6
46. Rensselaer Polytechnic Inst. (NY)	3.6
46. Stony Brook–SUNY*	3.6
46. Texas A&M University*	3.6
46. Vanderbilt University (TN)	3.6
51. North Carolina State U.*	3.5
51. Rose-Hulman Institute of Technology (IN)	3.5
51. University of Arizona*	3.5
54. Arizona State University*	3.4
54. Boston University	3.4
54. Rochester Inst. of Technology (NY)	3.4
54. University of California–Riverside*	3.4
54. University of Notre Dame (IN)	3.4
54. University of Utah*	3.4
60. Case Western Reserve Univ. (OH)	3.3
60. Colorado School of Mines*	3.3
60. Indiana University–Bloomington*	3.3
60. Iowa State University*	3.3
60. Michigan State University*	3.3
60. Stevens Institute of Technology (NJ)	3.3
60. Tufts University (MA)	3.3
60. United States Naval Academy (MD)*	3.3
60. University of California–Santa Cruz*	3.3
60. University of Pittsburgh*	3.3
60. Worcester Polytechnic Inst. (MA)	3.3
71. Clemson University (SC)*	3.2
71. Emory University (GA)	3.2
71. George Washington University (DC)	3.2
71. Georgetown University (DC)	3.2
71. Syracuse University (NY)	3.2
71. University of Connecticut*	3.2
71. University of Illinois–Chicago*	3.2
71. University of Iowa*	3.2
71. University of Rochester (NY)	3.2
71. University of Texas at Dallas*	3.2
71. William & Mary (VA)*	3.2
82. Amherst College (MA)	3.1
82. Auburn University (AL)*	3.1
82. Boston College	3.1
82. Calif. Polytechnic State U.–San Luis Obispo*	3.1
82. Drexel University (PA)	3.1
82. George Mason University (VA)*	3.1
82. Illinois Institute of Technology	3.1
82. Oregon State University*	3.1
82. Pomona College (CA)	3.1
82. United States Air Force Academy (CO)*	3.1
82. United States Military Academy (NY)*	3.1
82. Univ. of Maryland–Baltimore County*	3.1
82. University at Buffalo–SUNY*	3.1
82. University of Central Florida*	3.1
82. University of Oregon*	3.1
82. Washington State University*	3.1
98. California State University–Los Angeles*	3.0
98. Colorado State University*	3.0
98. Florida State University*	3.0
98. Lehigh University (PA)	3.0
98. Michigan Technological University*	3.0
98. Univ. of Nebraska–Lincoln*	3.0
98. University of Alabama*	3.0
98. University of Delaware*	3.0
98. University of Georgia*	3.0
98. University of San Diego	3.0
98. University of Tennessee*	3.0
98. Williams College (MA)	3.0
110. Brigham Young Univ.–Provo (UT)	2.9
110. Grinnell College (IA)	2.9
110. Howard University (DC)	2.9
110. Kansas State University*	2.9
110. New Jersey Inst. of Technology*	2.9
110. San Diego State University*	2.9
110. San Jose State University (CA)*	2.9
110. Temple University (PA)*	2.9
110. U. of North Carolina–Charlotte*	2.9
110. University of Kansas*	2.9
110. University of Kentucky*	2.9
110. University of Texas at Arlington*	2.9
122. Binghamton University–SUNY*	2.8
122. Brandeis University (MA)	2.8
122. Bucknell University (PA)	2.8
122. California State Polytechnic U.–Pomona*	2.8
122. Indiana University-Purdue U.–Indianapolis*	2.8
122. Louisiana State University–Baton Rouge*	2.8
122. Missouri U. of Science and Technology*	2.8
122. Smith College (MA)	2.8
122. Univ. of Missouri*	2.8
122. Univ. of South Carolina*	2.8
122. University of New Mexico*	2.8
122. University of Oklahoma*	2.8
122. Villanova University (PA)	2.8
135. Baylor University (TX)	2.7
135. Carleton College (MN)	2.7
135. Georgia State University*	2.7
135. Mount Holyoke College (MA)	2.7
135. Santa Clara University (CA)	2.7
135. Texas Tech University*	2.7
135. Tulane University (LA)	2.7
135. University of Alabama at Birmingham*	2.7
135. University of Cincinnati*	2.7
135. University of Colorado Denver*	2.7
135. University of Colorado–Colorado Springs*	2.7
135. University of Hawaii–Manoa*	2.7
135. University of Houston*	2.7
135. University of Miami (FL)	2.7
135. University of South Florida*	2.7
135. University of Texas at San Antonio*	2.7
135. University of Vermont*	2.7
135. Utah State University*	2.7
135. Wake Forest University (NC)	2.7

► Top Programs

Rank	School (State) (*Public)	Peer assessment score (5.0=highest)
154.	Bowdoin College (ME)	2.6
154.	CUNY–City College*	2.6
154.	DePaul University (IL)	2.6
154.	Embry-Riddle Aeronautical University (FL)	2.6
154.	Florida International University*	2.6
154.	Mississippi State University*	2.6
154.	New Mexico State University*	2.6
154.	Ohio University*	2.6
154.	Oklahoma State University*	2.6
154.	San Francisco State University*	2.6
154.	Southern Methodist University (TX)	2.6
154.	Univ. of Massachusetts–Dartmouth*	2.6
154.	Univ. of Massachusetts–Lowell*	2.6
154.	University at Albany–SUNY*	2.6
154.	University of Alabama–Huntsville*	2.6
154.	University of Arkansas*	2.6
154.	University of Idaho*	2.6
154.	University of Maine*	2.6
154.	University of Nebraska–Omaha*	2.6
154.	University of Rhode Island*	2.6
154.	University of San Francisco	2.6
154.	Virginia Commonwealth University*	2.6
154.	Wayne State University (MI)*	2.6
154.	Wesleyan University (CT)	2.6
178.	Boise State University (ID)*	2.5
178.	Florida Institute of Technology	2.5
178.	Loyola University Maryland	2.5
178.	Montana State University*	2.5
178.	Portland State University (OR)*	2.5
178.	Univ. of Massachusetts–Boston*	2.5
178.	Univ. of Wisconsin–Milwaukee*	2.5
178.	University of Louisiana at Lafayette*	2.5
178.	University of Mississippi*	2.5
178.	University of New Hampshire*	2.5
178.	University of North Texas*	2.5
178.	University of Tulsa (OK)	2.5
178.	Wichita State University (KS)*	2.5
191.	CUNY–Brooklyn College*	2.4
191.	California State University–Fullerton*	2.4
191.	California State University–Long Beach*	2.4
191.	California State University–Northridge*	2.4
191.	Colby College (ME)	2.4
191.	Florida A&M University*	2.4
191.	Florida Atlantic University*	2.4
191.	Gonzaga University (WA)	2.4
191.	Indiana State University*	2.4
191.	Kennesaw State University (GA)*	2.4
191.	Louisiana Tech University*	2.4
191.	Marquette University (WI)	2.4
191.	Miami University–Oxford (OH)*	2.4
191.	Middlebury College (VT)	2.4
191.	New York Inst. of Technology	2.4
191.	Old Dominion University (VA)*	2.4
191.	Purdue University–Fort Wayne*	2.4
191.	Saint Louis University	2.4
191.	Seattle University	2.4
191.	Towson University (MD)*	2.4
191.	Univ. of Missouri–Kansas City*	2.4
191.	University of Dayton (OH)	2.4
191.	University of Denver	2.4
191.	University of Michigan–Dearborn*	2.4
191.	University of Montana*	2.4
191.	University of Nevada–Reno*	2.4
191.	University of Northern Iowa*	2.4
191.	University of Portland (OR)	2.4
191.	University of Wyoming*	2.4
191.	Valparaiso University (IN)	2.4
191.	Virginia Military Institute*	2.4
191.	West Virginia University*	2.4
191.	Wright State University (OH)*	2.4
224.	Brigham Young University–Idaho	2.3
224.	CUNY–Queens College*	2.3
224.	California State U.–Monterey Bay*	2.3
224.	California State University–Fresno*	2.3
224.	Clarkson University (NY)	2.3
224.	Colgate University (NY)	2.3
224.	Elon University (NC)	2.3
224.	Hofstra University (NY)	2.3
224.	Kent State University (OH)*	2.3
224.	N.M. Inst. of Mining and Tech.*	2.3
224.	North Dakota State University*	2.3
224.	Rowan University (NJ)*	2.3
224.	S.D. School of Mines and Tech.*	2.3
224.	Southern Illinois University–Carbondale*	2.3
224.	Tennessee Technological Univ.*	2.3
224.	The Citadel, Military Coll. of SC*	2.3
224.	UNC Greensboro*	2.3
224.	Univ. of Illinois–Springfield*	2.3
224.	Univ. of Missouri–St. Louis*	2.3
224.	University of Alaska–Anchorage*	2.3
224.	University of Memphis*	2.3
224.	University of Minnesota–Duluth*	2.3
224.	University of Nevada–Las Vegas*	2.3
224.	University of Puerto Rico–Mayaguez*	2.3
224.	University of Tennessee–Chattanooga*	2.3
224.	University of Texas–El Paso*	2.3
224.	University of Washington–Bothell*	2.3
224.	University of Washington–Tacoma*	2.3

Note: Peer assessment surveys in 2021 conducted by U.S. News. To be ranked in a specialty, a school may have either a program or course offerings in that subject area. Extended undergraduate computer science rankings can be found at usnews.com/bestcolleges. U.S. News surveyed and ranked 538 computer science programs.

► Best in the Specialties (*Public)

ARTIFICIAL INTELLIGENCE
1. Carnegie Mellon University (PA)
2. Massachusetts Institute of Technology
3. Stanford University (CA)
3. University of California–Berkeley*
5. Cornell University (NY)

BIOCOMPUTING/BIOINFORMATICS/BIOTECHNOLOGY
1. Massachusetts Institute of Technology
1. University of California–San Diego*
3. Carnegie Mellon University (PA)
4. University of Illinois–Urbana-Champaign*
5. Stanford University (CA)

COMPUTER SYSTEMS
1. Massachusetts Institute of Technology
2. University of California–Berkeley*
3. Carnegie Mellon University (PA)
4. Georgia Institute of Technology*
4. University of Illinois–Urbana-Champaign*

CYBERSECURITY
1. Carnegie Mellon University (PA)

2. Georgia Institute of Technology*
2. Massachusetts Institute of Technology
4. University of California–Berkeley*
5. Stanford University (CA)
5. University of Illinois–Urbana-Champaign*

DATA ANALYTICS/SCIENCE
1. University of California–Berkeley*
2. Carnegie Mellon University (PA)
3. Massachusetts Institute of Technology
4. Stanford University (CA)
5. University of Washington*

GAME/SIMULATION DEVELOPMENT
1. Carnegie Mellon University (PA)
1. University of Southern California
3. Massachusetts Institute of Technology
3. New York University
3. University of Utah*

MOBILE/WEB APPLICATIONS
1. Massachusetts Institute of Technology
2. Carnegie Mellon University (PA)
3. University of Illinois–Urbana-Champaign*

4. University of Washington*
5. Stanford University (CA)
5. University of California–Berkeley*

PROGRAMMING LANGUAGES
1. Carnegie Mellon University (PA)
2. Massachusetts Institute of Technology
3. Cornell University (NY)
3. Stanford University (CA)
5. University of California–Berkeley*

SOFTWARE ENGINEERING
1. Carnegie Mellon University (PA)
2. Massachusetts Institute of Technology
2. University of California–Berkeley*
4. Georgia Institute of Technology*
5. University of Illinois–Urbana-Champaign*

THEORY
1. Massachusetts Institute of Technology
2. Carnegie Mellon University (PA)
3. University of California–Berkeley*
4. Princeton University (NJ)
5. Stanford University (CA)

Best Nursing Programs

THE U.S. NEWS ranking of nursing programs consolidates schools with four-year BSN programs and schools with RN to BSN programs. To be eligible, an institution must house a baccalaureate-level program accredited by the Commission on Collegiate Nursing Education or the Accreditation Commission for Education in Nursing and have recently awarded at least 35 Bachelor of Science in Nursing degrees, according to the U.S. Department of Education. Results are based solely on peer assessent score, derived from ratings by nursing school deans, department heads and senior faculty in 2021. Officials were asked to rate the quality of programs with which they're familiar on a scale of 1 (marginal) to 5 (distinguished); 28.3% responded.

▶ Top Programs

Rank School (State) (*Public)	Peer assessment score (5.0=highest)
1. University Rutgers of Pennsylvania	4.6
2. Duke University (NC)	4.5
2. University of Washington*	4.5
4. Emory University (GA)	4.4
4. U. of North Carolina–Chapel Hill*	4.4
4. University of Michigan–Ann Arbor*	4.4
7. New York University	4.3
7. Oregon Health and Science University*	4.3
7. University of Pittsburgh*	4.3
10. Case Western Reserve Univ. (OH)	4.2
10. Ohio State University–Columbus*	4.2
10. University of Alabama at Birmingham*	4.2
10. University of California–Los Angeles*	4.2
10. University of Iowa*	4.2
10. University of Maryland–Baltimore*	4.2
10. University of Minnesota–Twin Cities*	4.2
10. University of Nebraska Medical Center*	4.2
10. University of Virginia*	4.2
19. Boston College	4.1
19. Univ. of Wisconsin–Madison*	4.1
19. University of Illinois–Chicago*	4.1
19. University of Rochester (NY)	4.1
23. Medical University of South Carolina*	4.0
23. University of Arizona*	4.0
23. University of Florida*	4.0
23. University of Kentucky*	4.0
23. University of San Francisco	4.0
23. University of Texas at Austin*	4.0
23. Villanova University (PA)	4.0
23. Virginia Commonwealth University*	4.0
31. George Washington University (DC)	3.9
31. Indiana University-Purdue U.–Indianapolis*	3.9
31. Loyola University Chicago	3.9
31. Pennsylvania State U.–University Park*	3.9
31. Rutgers School of Nursing (NJ)	3.9
31. University of Alabama*	3.9
31. University of California–Irvine*	3.9
31. University of Colorado Denver*	3.9
31. University of Kansas*	3.9
31. University of Miami (FL)	3.9
31. U. of Texas Health Science Center–Houston*	3.9
31. University of Utah*	3.9
43. Creighton University (NE)	3.8
43. Louisiana State U. Health Sciences Center*	3.8

Rank School (State) (*Public)	Peer assessment score (5.0=highest)
43. Marquette University (WI)	3.8
43. Michigan State University*	3.8
43. Saint Louis University	3.8
43. The Catholic University of America (DC)	3.8
43. Univ. of Massachusetts–Boston*	3.8
43. Univ. of South Carolina*	3.8
43. U. of Arkansas for Medical Sciences*	3.8
43. University of Cincinnati*	3.8
43. University of Nevada–Las Vegas*	3.8
43. University of New Mexico*	3.8
43. U. of Tennessee Health Sciences Center*	3.8
43. U. of Texas Health Science Ctr.–San Antonio*	3.8
43. Wayne State University (MI)*	3.8
58. Auburn University (AL)*	3.7
58. Baylor University (TX)	3.7
58. Clemson University (SC)*	3.7
58. Duquesne University (PA)	3.7
58. MGH Institute of Health Professions (MA)	3.7
58. Texas Woman's University*	3.7
58. Thomas Jefferson University (PA)	3.7
58. U. of North Carolina–Charlotte*	3.7
58. UNC Greensboro*	3.7
58. Univ. of Massachusetts–Amherst*	3.7
58. Univ. of Missouri*	3.7
58. Univ. of Missouri–Kansas City*	3.7
58. University of Connecticut*	3.7
58. University of Louisville (KY)*	3.7
58. U. of Oklahoma Health Sciences Center*	3.7
58. University of South Florida*	3.7
58. University of Tennessee*	3.7
58. Washington State University*	3.7
76. Arizona State U.–Immersion Campus*	3.6
76. East Carolina University (NC)*	3.6
76. Fairfield University (CT)	3.6
76. Gonzaga University (WA)	3.6
76. Indiana State University*	3.6
76. Loma Linda University (CA)	3.6
76. San Diego State University*	3.6
76. Seton Hall University (NJ)	3.6
76. Stony Brook–SUNY*	3.6
76. Texas Tech U. Health Sciences Ctr.-Lubbock*	3.6
76. University of Wisconsin–Milwaukee*	3.6
76. University at Buffalo–SUNY*	3.6
76. University of Alabama–Huntsville*	3.6

Rank School (State) (*Public)	Peer assessment score (5.0=highest)
76. University of Colorado–Colorado Springs*	3.6
76. University of Delaware*	3.6
76. University of Maine*	3.6
76. University of Michigan–Flint*	3.6
76. University of Northern Colorado*	3.6
76. University of Portland (OR)	3.6
76. U. of Texas Medical Branch–Galveston (TX)*	3.6
96. Binghamton University–SUNY*	3.5
96. Boise State University (ID)*	3.5
96. Brigham Young Univ.–Provo (UT)	3.5
96. Drexel University (PA)	3.5
96. Florida International University*	3.5
96. Florida State University*	3.5
96. George Mason University (VA)*	3.5
96. Georgia State University*	3.5
96. Howard University (DC)	3.5
96. Mercer University (GA)	3.5
96. Minnesota State Univ.–Mankato*	3.5
96. Montana State University*	3.5
96. Samford University (AL)	3.5
96. San Jose State University (CA)*	3.5
96. Seattle University	3.5
96. South Dakota State University*	3.5
96. Texas Christian University	3.5
96. Univ. of Massachusetts–Dartmouth*	3.5
96. University of Central Florida*	3.5
96. University of Hawaii–Manoa*	3.5
96. University of Memphis*	3.5
96. University of Mississippi*	3.5
96. University of North Dakota*	3.5
96. University of Rhode Island*	3.5
120. CUNY–Hunter College*	3.4
120. California State University–Long Beach*	3.4
120. Florida Atlantic University*	3.4
120. Georgia College & State University*	3.4
120. Illinois State University*	3.4
120. Illinois Wesleyan University	3.4
120. Indiana University–South Bend*	3.4
120. James Madison University (VA)*	3.4
120. Mount Saint Mary's University (CA)	3.4
120. New Mexico State University*	3.4
120. Northeastern University (MA)	3.4
120. Pace University (NY)	3.4
120. Purdue University–West Lafayette (IN)*	3.4

▶Top Programs

Rank	School (State) (*Public)	Peer assessment score (5.0=highest)
120.	SUNY Downstate Medical Center*	3.4
120.	San Francisco State University*	3.4
120.	Simmons University (MA)	3.4
120.	Temple University (PA)*	3.4
120.	University of Massachusetts–Lowell*	3.4
120.	University of Missouri–St. Louis*	3.4
120.	University of Wisconsin–Eau Claire*	3.4
120.	University of Wisconsin–Oshkosh*	3.4
120.	University of Arkansas*	3.4
120.	University of Nevada–Reno*	3.4
120.	University of New Hampshire*	3.4
120.	University of North Carolina–Wilmington*	3.4
120.	University of Vermont*	3.4
120.	Valparaiso University (IN)	3.4
120.	West Virginia University*	3.4
148.	Augusta University (GA)*	3.3
148.	Augustana University (SD)	3.3
148.	Azusa Pacific University (CA)	3.3
148.	Ball State University (IN)*	3.3
148.	Belmont University (TN)	3.3
148.	California State University–Fullerton*	3.3
148.	California State University–Los Angeles*	3.3
148.	College of New Jersey*	3.3
148.	East Tennessee State University*	3.3
148.	Georgia Southern University*	3.3
148.	Goldfarb Sch. of Nursing, Barnes-Jewish Col. (MO)	3.3
148.	Kennesaw State University (GA)*	3.3
148.	Kent State University (OH)*	3.3
148.	Middle Tennessee State University.*	3.3
148.	Minnesota State University.–Moorhead*	3.3
148.	North Dakota State University*	3.3
148.	Oklahoma City University	3.3
148.	Purdue University–Northwest (IN)*	3.3
148.	Quinnipiac University (CT)	3.3
148.	Rutgers University–Camden (NJ)*	3.3
148.	Texas A&M University–Corpus Christi*	3.3
148.	Texas State University*	3.3
148.	Univ. of Southern Mississippi*	3.3
148.	University of Alaska–Anchorage*	3.3
148.	University of Arkansas at Little Rock*	3.3
148.	University of Detroit Mercy	3.3
148.	University of Hawaii–Hilo*	3.3
148.	University of Scranton (PA)	3.3
148.	University of South Dakota*	3.3
148.	University of Southern Maine*	3.3
148.	University of Tennessee–Chattanooga*	3.3
148.	University of Texas at Arlington*	3.3
148.	Western Carolina University (NC)*	3.3
148.	Western Kentucky University*	3.3
148.	Xavier University (OH)	3.3
183.	Auburn University at Montgomery (AL)*	3.2
183.	Brigham Young University–Idaho	3.2

Rank	School (State) (*Public)	Peer assessment score (5.0=highest)
183.	Bryan College of Health Sciences (NE)	3.2
183.	Eastern Kentucky University*	3.2
183.	Eastern Michigan University*	3.2
183.	Farmingdale State College–SUNY*	3.2
183.	Grand Valley State University (MI)*	3.2
183.	Hawaii Pacific University	3.2
183.	Idaho State University*	3.2
183.	Molloy College (NY)	3.2
183.	Northern Arizona University*	3.2
183.	Northern Kentucky University*	3.2
183.	Northern Michigan University*	3.2
183.	Oakland University (MI)*	3.2
183.	Ohio University*	3.2
183.	Old Dominion University (VA)*	3.2
183.	Pacific Lutheran University (WA)	3.2
183.	Queens University of Charlotte (NC)	3.2
183.	Sacred Heart University (CT)	3.2
183.	Saint Mary's College (IN)	3.2
183.	Samuel Merritt University (CA)	3.2
183.	Seattle Pacific University	3.2
183.	Texas A&M International University*	3.2
183.	Texas A&M University–Commerce*	3.2
183.	Towson University (MD)*	3.2
183.	Truman State University (MO)*	3.2
183.	University of Mary Hardin-Baylor (TX)	3.2
183.	University of Central Arkansas*	3.2
183.	University of Houston*	3.2
183.	University of Maryland Global Campus*	3.2
183.	University of South Alabama*	3.2
183.	University of Texas at Tyler*	3.2
183.	University of Wyoming*	3.2
183.	University of the Incarnate Word (TX)	3.2
183.	Western Michigan University*	3.2
183.	Wichita State University (KS)*	3.2
183.	Widener University (PA)	3.2
183.	Winona State University (MN)*	3.2
221.	Alverno College (WI)	3.1
221.	Bellarmine University (KY)	3.1
221.	California State Univ.–Bakersfield*	3.1
221.	California State U.–Dominguez Hills*	3.1
221.	California State University–East Bay*	3.1
221.	California State University–Northridge*	3.1
221.	California State University–Sacramento*	3.1
221.	Indiana University Southeast*	3.1
221.	Indiana University–Kokomo*	3.1
221.	Marymount University (VA)	3.1
221.	Millikin University (IL)	3.1
221.	Mississippi Univ. for Women*	3.1
221.	Morehead State University (KY)*	3.1
221.	Murray State University (KY)*	3.1
221.	Point Loma Nazarene University (CA)	3.1
221.	Radford University (VA)*	3.1

Rank	School (State) (*Public)	Peer assessment score (5.0=highest)
221.	Research College of Nursing (MO)	3.1
221.	Southern Illinois University Edwardsville*	3.1
221.	Texas Tech U. Health Sciences Center-El Paso*	3.1
221.	U. of North Carolina–Pembroke*	3.1
221.	University of South Carolina–Aiken*	3.1
221.	University of Indianapolis	3.1
221.	University of Louisiana at Lafayette*	3.1
221.	University of Louisiana–Monroe*	3.1
221.	University of North Florida*	3.1
221.	University of Tampa (FL)	3.1
221.	University of West Georgia*	3.1
221.	Valdosta State University (GA)*	3.1
221.	Weber State University (UT)*	3.1
221.	Wright State University (OH)*	3.1
251.	Adelphi University (NY)	3.0
251.	Appalachian State University (NC)*	3.0
251.	Barry University (FL)	3.0
251.	Benedictine University (IL)	3.0
251.	Bethel University (MN)	3.0
251.	Biola University (CA)	3.0
251.	California Baptist University	3.0
251.	California State U.–Monterey Bay*	3.0
251.	California State University–Channel Islands*	3.0
251.	California State University–Chico*	3.0
251.	California State University–Fresno*	3.0
251.	California State University–San Bernardino*	3.0
251.	Clayton State University (GA)*	3.0
251.	Curry College (MA)	3.0
251.	Fairleigh Dickinson University (NJ)	3.0
251.	Hope College (MI)	3.0
251.	Indiana University Northwest*	3.0
251.	Indiana Wesleyan University	3.0
251.	Le Moyne College (NY)	3.0
251.	Marian University (IN)	3.0
251.	Marshall University (WV)*	3.0
251.	Nebraska Methodist College	3.0
251.	Northwestern State University of Louisiana*	3.0
251.	Russell Sage College (NY)	3.0
251.	SUNY Brockport*	3.0
251.	Shenandoah University (VA)	3.0
251.	Sonoma State University (CA)*	3.0
251.	St. John Fisher College (NY)	3.0
251.	Union University (TN)	3.0
251.	University of Wisconsin–Green Bay*	3.0
251.	University of Central Oklahoma*	3.0
251.	University of Sioux Falls (SD)	3.0
251.	University of Southern Indiana*	3.0
251.	University of Texas–El Paso*	3.0
251.	University of Toledo (OH)*	3.0
251.	West Chester Univ. of Pennsylvania*	3.0
251.	Winston-Salem State Univ. (NC)*	3.0

Note: Peer assessment surveys in 2021 conducted by U.S. News. Extended undergraduate nursing degree rankings can be found at usnews.com/bestcolleges.
U.S. News surveyed and ranked 694 undergraduatrc nursing degree programs.

Best
Online Bachelor's Programs

WHEN WE SURVEYED COLLEGES IN 2020 about their online options, more than 350 schools reported having bachelor's programs that can be completed mostly without showing up in person for class (attendance may sporadically be required for things like testing, orientations and support services). These offerings, typically degree-completion programs aimed at working adults and community college grads, were evaluated on their success at engaging students, the credentials of their faculty, and the services and technologies made available remotely. The table below features some of the most significant ranking factors, such as the prevalence of faculty holding a Ph.D. or other terminal degree, class size, the percentages of new entrants who stayed enrolled and later graduated, and the debt loads of recent graduates. The top half of programs are listed here. Ranks are determined by the institutions' overall program scores, displayed below. To see the rest of the ranked online bachelor's programs and to read the full details about the methodology, visit usnews.com/online. There you'll also find detail-rich profile pages for each of the schools and (in case you want to plan ahead) rankings of online MBA programs and graduate programs in engineering, nursing, education and more.

(*Public, **For profit)

Rank	School	Overall program score	Average peer assessment score (5.0=highest)	'20 total program enrollment	'20 - '21 tuition[1]	'20 full-time faculty with Ph.D.	'20 average class size	'20 retention rate	'20 graduation rate[2]	% graduates with debt ('20)	Average debt of graduates ('20)
1.	Embry-Riddle Aeronautical U.–Worldwide (FL)	100	3.6	15,321	$413	64%	21	79%	29%	11%	$7,815
2.	University of Illinois–Chicago*	98	3.6	385	$462	39%	24	88%	82%	55%	$19,643
3.	University of Florida*	96	3.8	3,340	$500	81%	27	87%	55%	44%	$17,696
4.	Ohio State University–Columbus*	95	3.6	542	$642	66%	40	87%	94%	43%	$13,713
4.	Oregon State University*	95	3.8	6,948	$318	69%	35	86%	41%	56%	$23,711
6.	Arizona State University*	94	3.9	52,819	$541	75%	51	86%	44%	64%	$22,043
7.	University of Arizona*	93	3.7	3,362	$525	74%	12	85%	0%	65%	$26,187
8.	CUNY School of Professional Studies*	92	3.4	2,666	$305	81%	18	59%	41%	26%	$17,408
8.	University at Buffalo–SUNY*	92	3.5	110	$353	89%	32	85%	100%	N/A	N/A
10.	Colorado State University–Global Campus*	91	3.5	11,945	$350	N/A	13	68%	47%	65%	$28,209
10.	Medical University of South Carolina*	91	N/A	28	$658	71%	34	95%	N/A	48%	$12,962
10.	Pennsylvania State University–World Campus*	91	4.1	9,449	$576	65%	29	80%	37%	67%	$38,796
10.	University of Georgia*	91	3.7	29	$326	100%	17	85%	85%	63%	$20,771
14.	Illinois State University*	90	3.2	119	$768	45%	17	94%	N/A	42%	$12,174
14.	North Carolina State University*	90	3.4	68	$900	100%	17	72%	77%	46%	$20,864
14.	University of Central Florida*	90	3.9	12,553	$616	74%	69	84%	79%	53%	$20,783
14.	University of Missouri*	90	3.5	662	$391	80%	23	71%	69%	45%	$13,285
14.	University of Oklahoma*	90	3.6	918	$672	75%	16	81%	43%	61%	$24,736
19.	George Washington University (DC)	89	3.6	375	$615	75%	16	67%	42%	15%	$15,298
19.	University of North Carolina–Wilmington*	89	3.2	2,692	$644	63%	25	92%	82%	34%	$16,485
21.	Charleston Southern University (SC)	88	2.7	264	$490	80%	12	62%	62%	62%	$34,312
21.	Indiana University–Online*	88	3.6	3,291	$341	64%	24	78%	45%	71%	$23,751
21.	Loyola University Chicago (IL)	88	3.6	318	$715	73%	16	77%	47%	53%	$27,093
21.	University of Arkansas*	88	3.4	1,091	$253	58%	28	73%	63%	53%	$24,506
21.	University of Massachusetts–Amherst*	88	3.7	1,415	$450	73%	26	67%	62%	67%	$26,124
21.	Utah State University*	88	3.4	1,771	$422	60%	49	60%	68%	57%	$17,354
21.	West Texas A&M University*	88	3.1	1,525	$355	70%	39	84%	74%	56%	$16,700
28.	Pace University (NY)	87	3.0	169	$555	94%	12	78%	60%	28%	$41,468
28.	University of Alabama–Birmingham*	87	3.4	1,752	$441	79%	41	83%	41%	57%	$26,972
28.	Washington State University*	87	3.6	2,437	$591	71%	26	73%	50%	68%	$24,707
31.	Colorado State University*	86	3.5	962	$476	63%	11	78%	41%	63%	$34,410
31.	Concordia University Chicago (IL)	86	2.6	389	$506	73%	12	100%	100%	81%	$21,335
31.	University of Massachusetts–Lowell*	86	3.4	2,186	$380	82%	23	80%	48%	56%	$24,751
34.	Siena Heights University (MI)	85	2.5	1,077	$535	67%	14	79%	56%	62%	$20,687
34.	University of Illinois–Springfield*	85	3.6	942	$362	87%	19	75%	46%	45%	$26,167
34.	University of North Carolina–Charlotte*	85	3.4	388	$258	63%	22	90%	93%	30%	$14,915
37.	Daytona State College* (FL)	84	2.5	1,822	$550	67%	31	71%	53%	41%	$24,365
37.	University of Wisconsin–Milwaukee*	84	3.3	3,989	$337	50%	29	76%	35%	65%	$26,861
39.	Ball State University* (IN)	83	3.3	1,199	$551	64%	27	81%	28%	69%	$28,537
39.	Boise State University* (ID)	83	3.4	2,461	$300	54%	18	75%	75%	56%	$4,072
39.	Cambridge College (MA)	83	N/A	470	$400	67%	14	85%	37%	31%	$21,256
42.	Clarion University of Pennsylvania*	82	2.7	675	$347	93%	25	72%	55%	67%	$27,710

N/A=Data were not provided by the school.
1. Tuition is reported on a per-credit-hour basis. Out-of-state tuition is listed for public institutions. **2.** Displayed here for standardization are six-year graduation rates.

(*Public, **For profit)

Rank	School	Overall program score	Average peer assessment score (5.0=highest)	'20 total program enrollment	'20 - '21 tuition[1]	'20 full-time faculty with Ph.D.	'20 average class size	'20 retention rate	'20 graduation rate[2]	% graduates with debt ('20)	Average debt of graduates ('20)
42.	Concordia University Wisconsin & Ann Arbor	82	2.8	361	$526	100%	12	71%	73%	N/A	N/A
42.	Duquesne University (PA)	82	3.3	64	$1,011	75%	9	58%	N/A	58%	$27,426
42.	Texas A&M University–Commerce*	82	3.1	2,223	$569	67%	22	84%	N/A	51%	$20,717
42.	The Citadel* (SC)	82	3.0	222	$665	88%	17	72%	N/A	58%	$24,049
42.	University of Missouri–St. Louis*	82	3.3	34	$452	100%	23	60%	90%	39%	$22,964
48.	Kansas State University*	81	3.5	502	$512	92%	22	78%	N/A	66%	$34,673
48.	Purdue University–Northwest* (IN)	81	3.0	1,415	$373	60%	26	85%	76%	32%	$6,883
48.	Sacred Heart University (CT)	81	2.7	170	$590	100%	13	70%	56%	57%	$16,968
48.	University of Louisville* (KY)	81	3.4	876	$499	68%	18	72%	48%	65%	$22,407
48.	University of North Florida*	81	3.1	183	$285	88%	36	90%	N/A	47%	$11,829
53.	Bowling Green State University* (OH)	80	3.1	585	$405	72%	18	85%	55%	42%	$19,398
53.	Florida Atlantic University*	80	3.3	607	$752	64%	8	90%	69%	42%	$14,867
53.	Florida International University*	80	3.3	6,549	$264	80%	47	86%	42%	56%	$22,450
53.	Marist College (NY)	80	3.0	110	$730	63%	13	87%	55%	69%	$27,761
53.	Maryville University of St. Louis (MO)	80	2.8	2,484	$500	76%	15	N/A	N/A	50%	$10,700
53.	Pensacola State College* (FL)	80	2.4	171	$486	100%	24	86%	51%	17%	$579
53.	Regent University (VA)	80	2.7	4,849	$395	74%	19	73%	38%	71%	$28,904
53.	University of Memphis* (TN)	80	3.1	2,823	$463	69%	33	81%	41%	74%	$28,279
53.	University of Nebraska–Omaha*	80	3.4	870	$495	71%	23	90%	82%	63%	$20,273
53.	University of North Texas*	80	3.4	3,358	$871	73%	60	79%	61%	61%	$21,759
53.	University of South Alabama*	80	2.9	50	$328	63%	11	92%	97%	100%	$4,000
53.	University of St. Francis (IL)	80	2.7	285	$399	69%	13	90%	73%	44%	$23,140
53.	University of West Florida*	80	3.0	1,920	$342	64%	16	78%	52%	39%	$14,783
53.	University of the Incarnate Word (TX)	80	2.7	1,249	$540	100%	20	48%	54%	78%	$24,267
67.	California Baptist University	79	2.8	2,618	$613	85%	21	84%	52%	84%	$29,660
67.	Eastern Kentucky University*	79	3.1	2,540	$409	75%	18	77%	44%	69%	$31,869
67.	Northern Arizona University*	79	3.2	4,199	$455	63%	29	86%	64%	66%	$20,105
67.	Palm Beach Atlantic University (FL)	79	2.7	116	$460	78%	10	51%	59%	86%	$22,299
67.	University of Colorado–Colorado Springs*	79	3.2	3,752	$514	78%	23	75%	57%	56%	$16,254
67.	University of Denver	79	3.3	234	$685	100%	11	86%	41%	57%	$40,907
67.	University of Massachusetts–Dartmouth*	79	3.3	682	$332	77%	15	69%	56%	68%	$37,442
67.	University of North Carolina–Greensboro*	79	3.4	2,233	$662	79%	39	70%	42%	88%	$23,374
75.	Cornerstone University (MI)	78	2.4	229	$450	63%	8	51%	74%	77%	$19,650
75.	Lee University (TN)	78	2.8	806	$262	74%	7	78%	30%	67%	$27,718
75.	Maranatha Baptist University (WI)	78	2.4	129	$450	48%	10	83%	N/A	24%	$7,685
75.	McKendree University (IL)	78	2.4	382	$390	89%	12	81%	61%	60%	$23,461
75.	Sam Houston State University* (TX)	78	3.0	1,279	$244	84%	34	N/A	N/A	65%	$26,888
75.	Savannah College of Art and Design (GA)	78	3.1	625	$835	24%	20	72%	25%	64%	$54,748
75.	St. Petersburg College* (FL)	78	2.7	5,525	$426	83%	25	87%	57%	55%	$25,687
75.	Troy University* (AL)	78	2.9	4,612	$338	77%	26	59%	24%	55%	$26,981
75.	University of Cincinnati*	78	3.4	N/A	$450	65%	33	91%	54%	61%	$24,276
75.	University of Louisiana–Lafayette*	78	3.0	1,451	$380	53%	31	55%	73%	N/A	N/A
75.	University of Southern Mississippi*	78	3.1	3,343	$371	62%	30	78%	N/A	86%	$27,652
86.	Berkeley College** (NY)	77	2.8	1,413	$870	68%	20	62%	43%	85%	$31,048
86.	Linfield University (OR)	77	2.6	279	$495	73%	9	83%	71%	58%	$21,509
86.	Old Dominion University* (VA)	77	3.2	8,336	$407	69%	34	83%	62%	N/A	N/A
86.	Rutgers University–Camden* (NJ)	77	3.5	385	$550	100%	34	75%	N/A	72%	$27,012
86.	University of Houston–Downtown*	77	3.1	294	$649	100%	33	58%	73%	64%	$19,950
86.	University of Northern Colorado*	77	2.9	503	$424	58%	23	81%	69%	50%	$14,125
86.	Westfield State University* (MA)	77	2.5	266	$330	86%	16	77%	31%	60%	$18,088
93.	Arkansas State University*	76	2.9	2,950	$218	N/A	9	83%	66%	65%	$18,336
93.	California State University–Dominguez Hills*	76	2.9	387	$809	86%	19	81%	62%	29%	$14,162
93.	Drexel University (PA)	76	3.5	1,417	$530	80%	20	80%	36%	64%	$32,228
93.	Saint Joseph's University (PA)	76	3.1	70	$584	77%	13	81%	59%	100%	$29,158
93.	Saint Leo University (FL)	76	2.8	5,213	$380	84%	10	57%	25%	62%	$37,758
93.	University of Maine–Augusta*	76	3.0	2,803	$306	72%	27	77%	23%	66%	$25,534
93.	University of Massachusetts–Boston*	76	3.4	247	$410	N/A	24	75%	69%	63%	$20,770
93.	University of North Dakota*	76	3.3	1,650	$356	62%	19	60%	N/A	60%	N/A
93.	Utica College (NY)	76	3.0	861	$475	59%	15	79%	50%	50%	$13,926
102.	Auburn University–Montgomery* (AL)	75	3.0	125	$353	N/A	13	88%	N/A	49%	$14,921
102.	Friends University (KS)	75	N/A	461	$445	56%	15	79%	49%	69%	$17,387
102.	Northwestern College (IA)	75	2.8	99	$340	82%	14	80%	N/A	55%	$11,052
102.	Syracuse University (NY)	75	3.7	83	$695	67%	19	100%	N/A	N/A	N/A
102.	University of South Carolina–Aiken*	75	2.8	445	$869	61%	18	77%	63%	71%	$19,150
107.	Appalachian State University* (NC)	74	3.1	431	$643	68%	21	83%	77%	39%	$10,486

(*Public, **For profit)

Rank	School	Overall program score	Average peer assessment score (5.0=highest)	'20 total program enrollment	'20 - '21 tuition[1]	'20 full-time faculty with Ph.D.	'20 average class size	'20 retention rate	'20 graduation rate[2]	% graduates with debt ('20)	Average debt of graduates ('20)
107.	Brandman University (CA)	74	2.7	3,316	$500	91%	27	74%	52%	67%	$31,751
107.	Central Michigan University*	74	3.1	1,375	$427	72%	25	59%	38%	62%	$23,315
107.	DePaul University (IL)	74	N/A	1,092	$655	74%	26	69%	75%	68%	$32,109
107.	Fort Hays State University* (KS)	74	3.0	4,605	$227	65%	19	90%	39%	60%	$23,779
107.	Granite State College* (NH)	74	2.5	2,005	$365	45%	12	82%	45%	59%	$19,112
107.	Johnson & Wales University (RI)	74	2.8	1,675	$495	46%	18	60%	50%	90%	N/A
107.	Marian University (IN)	74	2.6	951	$850	37%	19	83%	81%	88%	$52,767
107.	Ohio University*	74	3.4	7,400	$243	66%	50	84%	70%	48%	$17,814
116.	Ferris State University* (MI)	73	2.9	639	$470	69%	17	81%	55%	51%	$18,750
116.	Florida Institute of Technology	73	2.9	1,646	$510	56%	16	74%	12%	73%	$40,611
116.	Lynn University (FL)	73	2.7	319	$300	61%	12	57%	66%	60%	$21,873
116.	SUNY College of Technology–Canton*	73	2.9	1,319	$353	63%	23	83%	50%	74%	$26,996
116.	SUNY College of Technology–Delhi*	73	2.9	821	$353	45%	16	73%	51%	54%	$20,933
116.	University of West Georgia*	73	3.0	235	$191	69%	11	40%	N/A	49%	$17,349
122.	Anderson University (SC)	72	2.6	349	$390	63%	N/A	84%	49%	87%	$21,420
122.	Central Washington University*	72	3.0	1,747	$752	24%	20	60%	N/A	45%	$4,920
122.	Herzing University (WI)	72	2.1	1,200	$585	56%	18	86%	33%	82%	$20,245
122.	Kentucky Wesleyan College	72	2.5	61	$455	58%	9	67%	60%	N/A	N/A
122.	Neumann University (PA)	72	2.3	179	$550	N/A	12	81%	67%	39%	$23,187
122.	Oakland University* (MI)	72	2.8	415	$312	90%	31	84%	41%	50%	$14,887
122.	SUNY Polytechnic Institute*	72	3.0	64	$353	67%	14	75%	N/A	N/A	N/A
122.	Southwestern College (KS)	72	2.4	1,153	$550	88%	8	83%	41%	17%	$23,419
122.	Valdosta State University* (GA)	72	3.0	1,136	$183	80%	13	75%	N/A	68%	$21,863
122.	Western Michigan University*	72	2.9	1,829	$504	65%	26	84%	N/A	54%	$10,568
132.	Asbury University (KY)	71	2.5	525	$399	50%	13	79%	N/A	33%	$2,665
132.	Campbellsville University (KY)	71	2.5	571	$399	55%	21	62%	48%	51%	$7,481
132.	Lindenwood University (MO)	71	2.4	529	$450	63%	18	66%	N/A	87%	$23,037
132.	Loyola University New Orleans (LA)	71	3.1	321	$450	90%	13	76%	N/A	N/A	N/A
132.	New England Institute of Technology (RI)	71	2.9	143	$200	89%	10	60%	N/A	73%	N/A
137.	Campbell University (NC)	70	2.5	700	$450	75%	12	75%	20%	51%	$23,660
137.	Southeast Missouri State University*	70	2.7	884	$325	N/A	23	71%	45%	70%	$24,473
137.	University of Alaska–Fairbanks*	70	3.0	2,127	$258	54%	24	N/A	N/A	44%	$32,805
137.	University of La Verne (CA)	70	2.3	363	$645	70%	17	82%	58%	70%	$33,120

URGITA VAICIKEVICIENE – GETTY IMAGES

(*Public, **For profit)

Rank	School	Overall program score	Average peer assessment score (5.0=highest)	'20 total program enrollment	'20 - '21 tuition[1]	'20 full-time faculty with Ph.D.	'20 average class size	'20 retention rate	'20 graduation rate[2]	% graduates with debt ('20)	Average debt of graduates ('20)
137.	University of Tennessee*	70	N/A	112	$588	100%	38	73%	N/A	41%	$21,034
137.	University of Toledo* (OH)	70	2.9	2,706	$388	66%	32	71%	58%	66%	$19,913
137.	Western Illinois University*	70	2.9	2,006	$296	79%	22	88%	63%	71%	$28,057
144.	Dominican University (IL)	69	2.9	53	$475	N/A	7	70%	N/A	N/A	N/A
144.	Eastern Oregon University*	69	2.6	2,533	$265	59%	17	87%	41%	60%	$23,428
144.	Mount Carmel College of Nursing (OH)	69	N/A	239	$430	33%	120	61%	N/A	11%	$9,770
144.	SUNY College of Technology–Alfred*	69	3.1	216	$353	27%	16	81%	N/A	77%	$21,632
144.	Simpson College (IA)	69	2.7	57	$435	8%	13	91%	N/A	N/A	N/A
144.	Slippery Rock University of Pennsylvania*	69	2.8	218	$328	86%	33	64%	60%	45%	$15,697
144.	Texas A&M – Central Texas*	69	3.0	1,108	$834	79%	20	N/A	N/A	68%	$20,274
144.	University of Tennessee–Martin*	69	2.8	481	$399	72%	21	81%	N/A	62%	$20,154
152.	Ashland University (OH)	68	2.3	287	$540	71%	17	81%	N/A	53%	$21,877
152.	Champlain College (VT)	68	2.6	2,087	$318	67%	15	83%	45%	50%	$29,374
152.	Graceland University (IA)	68	2.1	87	$430	50%	8	62%	51%	74%	$17,433
152.	Millersville University of Pennsylvania*	68	2.5	534	$398	96%	19	89%	N/A	44%	$13,584
152.	Moody Bible Institute (IL)	68	2.5	679	$360	57%	14	67%	41%	41%	$21,312
152.	Oregon Health and Science University*	68	2.8	118	$293	40%	44	82%	N/A	53%	$12,010
152.	Peirce College (PA)	68	2.4	1,044	$600	78%	12	72%	30%	83%	$32,000
152.	Purdue University–Fort Wayne*	68	2.9	56	$699	74%	21	51%	26%	42%	$32,025
152.	Rochester Institute of Technology (NY)	68	3.6	297	$1,094	N/A	23	N/A	N/A	N/A	N/A
152.	Southwestern Oklahoma State University*	68	2.5	457	$577	17%	16	83%	68%	55%	$15,785
152.	University of Alabama*	68	N/A	2,544	$375	65%	33	77%	12%	60%	$29,476
152.	University of North Alabama*	68	N/A	359	$300	76%	N/A	67%	N/A	75%	$20,576
164.	Colorado Technical University**	67	2.5	30,680	$340	77%	32	82%	18%	71%	$19,370
164.	Columbia College (MO)	67	2.5	7,000	$375	68%	16	68%	8%	56%	$28,050
164.	La Salle University (PA)	67	3.0	193	$400	N/A	16	N/A	N/A	N/A	N/A
164.	National University (CA)	67	2.2	7,895	$370	85%	16	68%	32%	54%	$26,496
164.	Northeastern State University* (OK)	67	2.6	1,379	$477	64%	23	76%	N/A	N/A	N/A
164.	Texas Tech University*	67	3.5	1,083	$268	84%	33	N/A	N/A	57%	$20,379
164.	Western Carolina University* (NC)	67	2.9	1,774	$189	81%	24	79%	71%	N/A	N/A

▶ Best Online Bachelor's Programs For Veterans

WHICH PROGRAMS OFFER MILITARY VETERANS and active-duty service members the best distance education? To ensure academic quality, all schools included in this ranking had to first qualify for a spot by being in the top half of the Best Online Bachelor's Programs ranking, above. Secondly, because veterans and active-duty members wish to take full advantage of federal financial benefits, programs also had to be certified for the GI Bill and participate in the Yellow Ribbon Program or charge in-state tuition that can be fully covered by the GI Bill to veterans from out of state. A third criterion is that a program must have enrolled a total of at least 25 veterans and active-duty service members. Qualifying programs were ranked in descending order based on their spot in the overall ranking, with additional credit awarded based on whether Yellow Ribbon Program benefits were made available to all eligible students and whether the program consistently made available maximum Yellow Ribbon funding – defined as all tuition that is left after Post-9/11 GI Bill funds are applied.

Rank School (State)

1. Embry-Riddle Aeronautical University–Worldwide (FL)
2. University of Florida*
3. Oregon State University*
4. Arizona State University*
5. University of Arizona*
6. CUNY School of Professional Studies*
7. Colorado State University–Global Campus*
7. Pennsylvania State University–World Campus*
9. University of Missouri*
10. University of Oklahoma*
11. George Washington University (DC)
12. Utah State University*

13. Charleston Southern University (SC)
13. University of Arkansas*
13. University of Massachusetts–Amherst*
13. West Texas A&M University*
17. Indiana University–Online*
17. Washington State University*
19. University of Alabama–Birmingham*
20. University of Central Florida*
21. Colorado State University*
22. University of Massachusetts–Lowell*
23. University of Illinois–Springfield*
24. Daytona State College* (FL)

24. University of Wisconsin–Milwaukee*
26. Boise State University* (ID)
26. Concordia University Chicago (IL)
28. Cambridge College (MA)
29. Clarion University of Pennsylvania*
29. The Citadel* (SC)
31. Siena Heights University (MI)
32. Kansas State University*
33. University of Louisville* (KY)
34. Regent University (VA)
34. University of Memphis* (TN)
34. University of the Incarnate Word (TX)
37. Ball State University* (IN)

37. Bowling Green State University* (OH)
37. Florida International University*
37. Pensacola State College* (FL)
37. University of Nebraska–Omaha*
37. University of West Florida*
43. University of North Carolina–Greensboro*
44. Eastern Kentucky University*
44. University of Colorado–Colorado Springs*
44. University of Massachusetts–Dartmouth*
47. Northern Arizona University*
48. Sam Houston State University* (TX)
48. St. Petersburg College* (FL)

Colleges for Social Mobility

ECONOMICALLY DISADVANTAGED STUDENTS are less likely than others to finish college. This ranking reveals which schools stand out among their peers at serving recipients of Pell Grants, federal awards that go to students with exceptional financial need – what U.S. News defines as advancing social mobility. The ranking is based on an average of the six-year graduation rates of students entering in fall 2013 and 2014 (though we show actual data for those entering in 2014 below) and how that performance compares with the rates of all other students. Scores were adjusted by the proportion of the classes awarded Pell Grants, because achieving great results among low-income students is more challenging with a larger proportion of such students enrolled. Find additional schools doing a good job at usnews.com, and see page 50 for more on the methodology.

▶ National Universities

Rank	School (State) (*Public)	% of Pell recipients (entering 2014)	Pell graduation rate
1.	University of California–Riverside*	52%	77%
2.	University of California–Irvine*	43%	83%
3.	Rutgers University–Newark (NJ)*	52%	64%
4.	University of California–Merced*	62%	68%
5.	Keiser University (FL)	N/A	N/A
6.	Florida International University*	44%	68%
7.	University of La Verne (CA)	47%	65%
8.	University of Illinois–Chicago*	55%	62%
9.	Russell Sage College (NY)	58%	57%
10.	CUNY–City College*	63%	59%
11.	Georgia State University*	66%	54%
12.	University of California–Santa Cruz*	40%	74%
13.	Florida A&M University*	70%	55%
13.	UNC Greensboro*	50%	56%
15.	Howard University (DC)	48%	59%
16.	University of California–Davis*	37%	83%
16.	University of California–Santa Barbara*	38%	86%
18.	Rutgers University–Camden (NJ)*	45%	57%
19.	Chatham University (PA)	47%	58%
19.	Montclair State University (NJ)*	42%	65%
21.	California State University–Fresno*	69%	55%
21.	Gallaudet University (DC)	49%	43%
21.	University of California–Los Angeles*	35%	88%
24.	Sam Houston State University (TX)*	47%	57%
24.	University of South Florida*	36%	72%
26.	Trinity International University (IL)	N/A	N/A
26.	University of California–San Diego*	33%	84%
26.	University of Texas at Arlington*	45%	51%
26.	University of Texas at San Antonio*	47%	47%
30.	Delaware State University*	59%	45%
30.	Stony Brook–SUNY*	32%	78%
30.	University of Hawaii at Hilo*	50%	45%
33.	Inter Amer. U. of Puerto Rico–Metropolitan Campus	N/A	N/A
33.	University at Albany–SUNY*	37%	64%
33.	University of Texas–Rio Grande Valley*	N/A	N/A
36.	Florida Atlantic University*	38%	56%
36.	Univ. of Maryland Eastern Shore*	63%	38%
36.	Univ. of Massachusetts–Boston*	45%	49%
39.	North Carolina A&T State Univ.*	65%	48%
39.	University of Houston*	39%	61%
41.	St. Catherine University (MN)	44%	64%
41.	St. John's University (NY)	41%	61%
41.	University of the Incarnate Word (TX)	47%	53%
41.	University of West Georgia*	52%	41%
45.	Inter American U. of Puerto Rico–San German	N/A	N/A
45.	University of the Pacific (CA)	31%	65%
47.	Lincoln Memorial University (TN)	43%	43%
47.	Our Lady of the Lake University (TX)	64%	35%
47.	University of New Orleans*	47%	40%
47.	U. of North Carolina–Charlotte*	35%	63%
51.	Husson University (ME)	49%	48%
51.	Portland State University (OR)*	44%	44%
51.	Rutgers University–New Brunswick (NJ)*	30%	83%
51.	University of Central Florida*	33%	72%
55.	East Carolina University (NC)*	41%	63%
55.	University at Buffalo–SUNY*	33%	71%
55.	University of Colorado Denver*	40%	47%
55.	University of Florida*	27%	86%
59.	Nova Southeastern University (FL)	35%	63%
59.	University of Idaho*	39%	54%
59.	Univ. of Massachusetts–Dartmouth*	45%	47%
62.	Clarke University (IA)	39%	59%
62.	Gardner-Webb University (NC)	N/A	N/A
62.	Long Island University (NY)	57%	42%
62.	University of the Cumberlands (KY)	N/A	N/A
66.	Aurora University (IL)	N/A	N/A
66.	George Fox University (OR)	31%	66%
66.	Maryville Univ. of St. Louis	26%	85%
66.	New Jersey Inst. of Technology*	33%	64%
66.	San Diego State University*	28%	74%
66.	Wayne State University (MI)*	49%	45%
72.	Clark Atlanta University	74%	39%
72.	Middle Tennessee State Univ.*	47%	44%
72.	Morgan State University (MD)*	59%	42%
72.	Roosevelt University (IL)	48%	38%
72.	St. John Fisher College (NY)	30%	69%
72.	University of Texas–El Paso*	65%	41%
78.	Barry University (FL)	55%	34%
78.	DePaul University (IL)	33%	67%
78.	Grand Canyon University (AZ)	N/A	N/A
78.	University of Memphis*	51%	43%
82.	Eastern Michigan University*	47%	39%
82.	Hampton University (VA)	43%	54%
82.	Illinois Institute of Technology	29%	70%
82.	Simmons University (MA)	25%	74%
82.	Texas Woman's University*	53%	43%
82.	University of California–Berkeley*	26%	89%
82.	University of Texas at Dallas*	32%	69%
82.	Wilkes University (PA)	43%	57%
90.	Alliant International University (CA)	N/A	N/A
90.	Benedictine University (IL)	43%	42%
90.	Binghamton University–SUNY*	24%	79%
90.	Carson-Newman University (TN)	44%	46%
90.	Florida State University*	25%	80%

N/A=Data for 2014 were not provided by the school. Rank is based on 2013 data from the school or the federal government.

Rank	School (State) (*Public)	% of Pell recipients (entering 2014)	Pell graduation rate
95.	Adelphi University (NY)	30%	67%
95.	Edgewood College (WI)	N/A	N/A
95.	University of Findlay (OH)	N/A	N/A
95.	University of Saint Joseph (CT)	46%	49%
95.	Wingate University (NC)	43%	43%
100.	The College of St. Scholastica (MN)	32%	60%
100.	Mary Baldwin University (VA)	64%	41%
100.	New Mexico State University*	45%	45%
100.	Regent University (VA)	35%	53%
100.	Rochester Inst. of Technology (NY)	30%	67%
100.	Texas A&M University–Commerce*	56%	34%
100.	Texas A&M Univ.–Kingsville*	57%	40%
100.	Texas Wesleyan University	35%	45%
100.	University of Louisiana–Monroe*	42%	50%
100.	Univ. of Missouri–St. Louis*	44%	46%
100.	University of Nevada–Las Vegas*	41%	41%
100.	University of North Florida*	31%	58%
100.	University of St. Francis (IL)	42%	51%

▶ National Liberal Arts Colleges

Rank	School (State) (*Public)	% of Pell recipients (entering 2014)	Pell graduation rate
1.	Bennett College (NC)	N/A	N/A
2.	Tougaloo College (MS)	N/A	N/A
3.	Lake Forest College (IL)	44%	75%
4.	Salem College (NC)	54%	69%
4.	Spelman College (GA)	55%	68%
6.	Agnes Scott College (GA)	42%	69%
6.	Berea College (KY)	89%	66%
8.	Thomas Aquinas College (CA)	27%	83%
8.	University of Virginia–Wise*	N/A	N/A
10.	Westminster College (PA)	42%	67%
11.	Talladega College (AL)	N/A	N/A
12.	Wells College (NY)	N/A	N/A
13.	Fisk University (TN)	59%	50%
13.	Johnson C. Smith University (NC)	N/A	N/A
15.	College of Idaho	45%	61%
16.	Hollins University (VA)	57%	55%
17.	Monmouth College (IL)	49%	54%
18.	Louisiana State University–Alexandria*	N/A	N/A
18.	Morehouse College (GA)	53%	48%
18.	Whittier College (CA)	29%	64%
21.	Massachusetts Col. of Liberal Arts*	46%	50%
22.	East-West University (IL)	N/A	N/A
22.	Hartwick College (NY)	43%	61%
22.	Illinois College	47%	55%
22.	Knox College (IL)	38%	60%
22.	Williams Baptist University (AR)	45%	35%
27.	Bethune-Cookman University (FL)	82%	32%
27.	Bloomfield College (NJ)	84%	33%
27.	Juniata College (PA)	N/A	N/A
27.	Sterling College (VT)	N/A	N/A
27.	Virginia Union University	75%	34%
32.	Albright College (PA)	49%	55%
32.	Drew University (NJ)	30%	65%
32.	Lycoming College (PA)	39%	58%
32.	Stillman College (AL)	79%	21%
32.	Vassar College (NY)	30%	86%
37.	Houghton College (NY)	42%	57%
38.	Amherst College (MA)	24%	93%
38.	Bryn Athyn Col. of New Church (PA)	66%	31%
40.	Aquinas College (MI)	38%	59%

Rank	School (State) (*Public)	% of Pell recipients (entering 2014)	Pell graduation rate
40.	Bethany Lutheran College (MN)	44%	58%
40.	Blackburn College (IL)	61%	36%
40.	Lyon College (AR)	46%	35%
40.	Purchase College–SUNY*	32%	58%
40.	St. Norbert College (WI)	24%	70%
40.	Warren Wilson College (NC)	43%	38%
47.	Dillard University (LA)	83%	44%
47.	Grinnell College (IA)	20%	88%
47.	Gustavus Adolphus College (MN)	26%	82%
47.	University of Maine–Machias*	75%	25%
51.	Guilford College (NC)	38%	46%
51.	Marymount California University	34%	52%
51.	Univ. of Wisconsin–Parkside*	42%	39%
54.	U. of North Carolina Asheville*	34%	60%
54.	University of Wisconsin–Superior*	N/A	N/A
54.	Wabash College (IN)	36%	60%
57.	Beloit College (WI)	21%	76%
57.	Franklin College (IN)	35%	53%
57.	Georgetown College (KY)	38%	49%
57.	Ripon College (WI)	38%	56%
61.	Covenant College (GA)	25%	65%
61.	Presbyterian College (SC)	28%	55%
61.	Soka University of America (CA)	24%	79%
61.	U. of Pittsburgh–Greensburg*	N/A	N/A
65.	Austin College (TX)	26%	69%
65.	College of the Atlantic (ME)	29%	61%

▶ Regional Universities

Rank	School (State) (*Public)	% of Pell recipients (entering 2014)	Pell graduation rate
NORTH			
1.	Monroe College (NY)	79%	74%
2.	CUNY–Baruch College*	44%	82%
3.	CUNY–Hunter College*	52%	57%
4.	CUNY–Lehman College*	73%	54%
5.	CUNY–John Jay Col. of Crim. Justice*	N/A	N/A
6.	Manhattanville College (NY)	43%	64%
7.	Rosemont College (PA)	N/A	N/A
8.	Saint Elizabeth University (NJ)	75%	50%
9.	CUNY–Queens College*	49%	52%
10.	Thomas College (ME)	N/A	N/A
11.	Cedar Crest College (PA)	53%	61%
11.	CUNY–Brooklyn College*	59%	52%
11.	Elms College (MA)	49%	52%
11.	Saint Peter's University (NJ)	71%	53%
11.	SUNY College–Old Westbury*	N/A	N/A
16.	Caldwell University (NJ)	49%	59%
17.	College of Mount St. Vincent (NY)	50%	58%
17.	Washington Adventist University (MD)	59%	41%
19.	SUNY Polytechnic Institute – Utica/Albany*	42%	59%
20.	SUNY Buffalo State*	61%	39%
21.	Dominican College (NY)	51%	53%
21.	Notre Dame of Maryland University	57%	39%
23.	Carlow University (PA)	54%	51%
23.	Kean University (NJ)*	50%	47%
23.	St. Joseph's College (NY)	41%	65%
26.	Bay Path University (MA)	47%	70%
26.	Canisius College (NY)	40%	59%
26.	Mercy College (NY)	63%	45%
26.	William Paterson Univ. of N.J.*	47%	50%
30.	Utica College (NY)	50%	47%
31.	Cabrini University (PA)	N/A	N/A

▶ Regional Universities (continued)

Rank	School (State) (*Public)	% of Pell recipients (entering 2014)	Pell graduation rate
32.	Felician University (NJ)	62%	49%
33.	La Roche University (PA)	N/A	N/A
33.	New Jersey City University*	74%	34%
35.	La Salle University (PA)	41%	61%
35.	SUNY Brockport*	40%	58%
35.	SUNY–New Paltz*	36%	72%
35.	SUNY–Oswego*	41%	62%
39.	Chestnut Hill College (PA)	35%	49%
39.	Roberts Wesleyan College (NY)	41%	53%
39.	SUNY–Fredonia*	37%	58%

SOUTH

Rank	School (State) (*Public)	% of Pell recipients (entering 2014)	Pell graduation rate
1.	Converse College (SC)	N/A	N/A
2.	Bob Jones University (SC)	58%	60%
3.	Winston-Salem State Univ. (NC)*	N/A	N/A
4.	Columbia College (SC)	38%	69%
5.	Christian Brothers University (TN)	49%	54%
6.	Hodges University (FL)	N/A	N/A
6.	North Greenville University (SC)	39%	68%
8.	Norfolk State University (VA)*	62%	42%
9.	Fort Valley State University (GA)*	82%	44%
10.	Columbia International Univ. (SC)	47%	65%
10.	Everglades University (FL)	N/A	N/A
10.	Mississippi Univ. for Women*	61%	44%
10.	North Carolina Central Univ.*	74%	49%
14.	Milligan University (TN)	33%	62%
15.	King University (TN)	44%	46%
16.	Western Carolina University (NC)*	41%	60%
16.	Winthrop University (SC)*	46%	55%
18.	Fayetteville State University (NC)*	80%	36%
18.	U. of North Carolina–Pembroke*	60%	41%
20.	Clayton State University (GA)*	67%	32%
20.	Piedmont University (GA)	43%	42%
22.	Bethel University (TN)	N/A	N/A
22.	Inter American U. of Puerto Rico–Ponce	96%	35%
24.	Stetson University (FL)	36%	63%
25.	Brenau University (GA)	57%	40%
25.	Midway University (KY)	41%	46%
27.	Bryan College (TN)	47%	42%
27.	Lenoir-Rhyne University (NC)	51%	40%
27.	Tuskegee University (AL)	77%	52%
30.	West Liberty University (WV)*	51%	39%
31.	Alabama A&M University*	N/A	N/A
31.	Albany State University (GA)*	N/A	N/A
31.	Alcorn State University (MS)*	84%	42%
31.	Southern Adventist University (TN)	35%	58%
31.	Southern Wesleyan University (SC)	N/A	N/A
31.	Universidad del Sagrado Corazon (PR)	77%	39%
37.	Charleston Southern University (SC)	49%	40%
37.	University of Mount Olive (NC)	51%	37%
39.	Mississippi Valley State Univ.*	86%	27%
39.	Saint Leo University (FL)	N/A	N/A

MIDWEST

Rank	School (State) (*Public)	% of Pell recipients (entering 2014)	Pell graduation rate
1.	Mount Mary University (WI)	64%	52%
2.	Greenville University (IL)	N/A	N/A
3.	Dominican University (IL)	59%	58%
4.	Friends University (KS)	N/A	N/A
5.	Augsburg University (MN)	44%	56%
6.	North Park University (IL)	45%	52%

Rank	School (State) (*Public)	% of Pell recipients (entering 2014)	Pell graduation rate
7.	Mount Mercy University (IA)	N/A	N/A
7.	Saint Mary-of-the-Woods College (IN)	63%	47%
7.	Saint Xavier University (IL)	64%	50%
10.	Bethel University (IN)	45%	52%
10.	Holy Family College (WI)	N/A	N/A
12.	Baker College of Flint (MI)	N/A	N/A
12.	Crown College (MN)	N/A	N/A
14.	Mount Vernon Nazarene U. (OH)	43%	56%
14.	University of Michigan–Dearborn*	43%	53%
16.	Concordia University Chicago	48%	46%
17.	Grace College and Seminary (IN)	N/A	N/A
17.	Spring Arbor University (MI)	43%	55%
19.	Elmhurst University (IL)	36%	63%
19.	Lewis University (IL)	34%	66%
21.	Hamline University (MN)	41%	57%
21.	Muskingum University (OH)	49%	50%
21.	Siena Heights University (MI)	N/A	N/A
21.	Univ. of Northwestern–St. Paul (MN)	35%	68%
25.	Governors State University (IL)*	72%	24%
25.	Indiana University–South Bend*	51%	34%
25.	University of Saint Mary (KS)	39%	57%
28.	Northeastern Illinois University*	N/A	N/A
29.	Alverno College (WI)	69%	44%
29.	Huntington University (IN)	38%	53%
29.	Indiana University East*	52%	39%
32.	Ashland University (OH)	35%	57%
32.	Baldwin Wallace University (OH)	37%	64%
32.	Buena Vista University (IA)	34%	58%
32.	Cornerstone University (MI)	41%	56%
32.	Trine University (IN)	N/A	N/A
37.	Univ. of Nebraska–Kearney*	36%	52%
38.	McKendree University (IL)	40%	47%
38.	Southwest Baptist University (MO)	47%	41%
38.	University of Sioux Falls (SD)	28%	51%

WEST

Rank	School (State) (*Public)	% of Pell recipients (entering 2014)	Pell graduation rate
1.	California State University–Long Beach*	53%	73%
2.	Mount Saint Mary's University (CA)	67%	66%
3.	California State University–Fullerton*	48%	67%
4.	California State U.–Monterey Bay*	51%	58%
4.	Mills College (CA)	55%	70%
6.	California State University–Stanislaus*	63%	57%
7.	California State Polytechnic U.–Pomona*	46%	63%
7.	University of Washington–Tacoma*	N/A	N/A
9.	California State Univ.–San Marcos*	50%	57%
9.	San Jose State University (CA)*	50%	63%
11.	La Sierra University (CA)	54%	50%
11.	San Francisco State University*	48%	55%
13.	California State University–San Bernardino*	67%	58%
13.	Fresno Pacific University (CA)	N/A	N/A
15.	California State University–Los Angeles*	73%	52%
15.	Texas A&M International University*	73%	47%
17.	California State University–Channel Islands*	N/A	N/A
18.	St. Edward's University (TX)	41%	67%
19.	California State University–Northridge*	62%	53%
19.	St. Mary's Univ. of San Antonio	52%	53%
21.	California State University–Sacramento*	58%	51%
22.	University of Washington–Bothell*	N/A	N/A
23.	California State University–Dominguez Hills*	73%	46%
24.	California State University–Chico*	46%	59%

Rank	School (State) (*Public)	% of Pell recipients (entering 2014)	Pell graduation rate
24.	Midwestern State University (TX)*	51%	43%
24.	University of St. Thomas (TX)	38%	68%
27.	Vanguard University of Southern California	43%	60%
28.	California State Univ.–Bakersfield*	68%	45%
29.	California Baptist University	48%	55%
29.	Hope International University (CA)	44%	38%
29.	Humboldt State University (CA)*	55%	46%
32.	University of Houston–Downtown*	64%	31%
33.	Western Oregon University*	43%	44%
34.	California State University–East Bay*	57%	42%
34.	Prescott College (AZ)	N/A	N/A
34.	Southwestern Assemblies of God U. (TX)	N/A	N/A
34.	Woodbury University (CA)	41%	55%
38.	Chaminade University of Honolulu	39%	53%
38.	Sul Ross State University (TX)*	65%	30%
40.	Colorado State University–Pueblo*	50%	36%

▶ # Regional Colleges

Rank	School (State) (*Public)	% of Pell recipients (entering 2014)	Pell graduation rate
NORTH			
1.	The College of Westchester (NY)	N/A	N/A
2.	Cazenovia College (NY)	59%	52%
2.	University of Maine at Farmington*	51%	52%
4.	St. Francis College (NY)	50%	51%
5.	Thiel College (PA)	N/A	N/A
6.	Bay State College (MA)	N/A	N/A
6.	Keystone College (PA)	52%	43%
8.	Univ. of Pittsburgh at Bradford*	N/A	N/A
8.	Villa Maria College (NY)	N/A	N/A
10.	Unity College (ME)	45%	46%
11.	CUNY–York College*	75%	31%
12.	Five Towns College (NY)	N/A	N/A
13.	SUNY College of Technology at Alfred*	37%	71%
13.	Vaughn Col. of Aeron. and Tech. (NY)	N/A	N/A
15.	SUNY College of Technology at Canton*	52%	41%
16.	Mitchell College (CT)	N/A	N/A
16.	SUNY Cobleskill*	46%	41%
16.	SUNY Morrisville (NY)*	56%	39%
19.	Colby-Sawyer College (NH)	31%	56%
20.	Elmira College (NY)	34%	59%
20.	Wesley College (DE)	N/A	N/A
SOUTH			
1.	Welch College (TN)	38%	53%
2.	Florida National University–Main Campus	82%	69%
3.	Claflin University (SC)	78%	50%
4.	Voorhees College (SC)	N/A	N/A
5.	University of Arkansas–Fort Smith*	N/A	N/A
6.	Barton College (NC)	49%	51%
7.	Newberry College (SC)	51%	44%
8.	Toccoa Falls College (GA)	54%	45%
9.	U. of South Carolina–Upstate*	53%	43%
10.	Elizabeth City State University (NC)*	N/A	N/A
11.	Oakwood University (AL)	N/A	N/A
12.	Alice Lloyd College (KY)	63%	31%
12.	Catawba College (NC)	50%	45%
14.	Averett University (VA)	55%	44%
14.	Brevard College (NC)	N/A	N/A

Rank	School (State) (*Public)	% of Pell recipients (entering 2014)	Pell graduation rate
16.	Glenville State College (WV)*	56%	40%
17.	Tennessee Wesleyan University	56%	43%
18.	University of the Ozarks (AR)	52%	39%
19.	Morris College (SC)	N/A	N/A
19.	Warner University (FL)	66%	40%
MIDWEST			
1.	College of the Ozarks (MO)	64%	60%
2.	Bluffton University (OH)	43%	60%
3.	Maranatha Baptist University (WI)	45%	58%
4.	Sterling College (KS)	58%	40%
4.	University of Rio Grande (OH)	N/A	N/A
6.	Bethany College (KS)	N/A	N/A
7.	Wilmington College (OH)	49%	48%
8.	Union College (NE)	32%	73%
9.	McPherson College (KS)	50%	37%
10.	Alma College (MI)	N/A	N/A
11.	Marietta College (OH)	41%	45%
12.	Hiram College (OH)	55%	42%
13.	Holy Cross College (IN)	34%	47%
14.	Cottey College (MO)	49%	43%
15.	North Central University (MN)	N/A	N/A
15.	Trinity Christian College (IL)	37%	63%
17.	Culver-Stockton College (MO)	43%	45%
17.	Kansas Wesleyan University	46%	38%
17.	Olivet College (MI)	N/A	N/A
17.	Ottawa University (KS)	47%	30%
WEST			
1.	William Jessup University (CA)	47%	51%
2.	San Diego Christian College	N/A	N/A
2.	Southwestern Adventist Univ. (TX)	N/A	N/A
4.	Warner Pacific University (OR)	N/A	N/A
5.	Texas College	N/A	N/A
6.	Schreiner University (TX)	41%	52%
7.	Life Pacific University (CA)	48%	26%
8.	John Paul the Great Catholic University (CA)	37%	61%
9.	Corban University (OR)	N/A	N/A
10.	East Texas Baptist University	51%	30%
10.	Oklahoma Panhandle State Univ.*	55%	37%
10.	Oral Roberts University (OK)	38%	44%
13.	Pacific Union College (CA)	41%	43%
14.	Oklahoma Baptist University	39%	47%
15.	Bacone College (OK)	N/A	N/A
15.	Montana State Univ.–Northern*	N/A	N/A
17.	Colorado Mountain College*	N/A	N/A
17.	McMurry University (TX)	53%	25%
19.	University of Silicon Valley (CA)	50%	36%
20.	Texas Lutheran University	34%	40%
20.	University of Montana Western*	N/A	N/A

Getting In

The Catholic University Cardinals
PATRICK RYAN – CATHOLIC UNIVERSITY

6 Key Ways to Wow Admissions

Get a feel for how much grades, tests and your résumé
really matter from those who review the applications

by **Stacey Colino** *and* **Margaret Loftus**

WHEN APPLYING TO COLLEGE, many students think they know which strategies will help them attract the attention (in a good way) of admissions officers. But there's often a gap between perception and reality about what actually matters – and what matters most – when it comes to grades, test scores, extracurricular activities and other factors. And what holds true in this unprecedented time will differ in some ways from the norm.

Many colleges report that, while academic performance is key, they take a multifaceted approach to reviewing applicants, looking well beyond what can be seen on a transcript, says Joe Shields, an admissions counselor at Goucher College in Baltimore. "A holistic admissions review process allows a student to demonstrate their best qualities and discuss how they would be a good fit for that college," he says.

Another often misunderstood fact: It's not as difficult as many students think to get admitted to a college, beyond the most selective schools. A 2019 report from the National Association for College Admission Counseling revealed that, on average, two-thirds of first-time freshman applicants were offered admission to a four-year school in the U.S. Some 80% of places accepted 50% or more of applicants. "There are many good colleges you may not have heard of," says Hannah Serota, founder and CEO of Creative College Connections, a consulting practice dedicated to helping applicants find the right fit. Read on for several key strategies that will ease your way in:

Colorado State University

1 Getting A's is important, but maybe not the way you think.

Of course your grades matter. But what that means depends on a college's selectivity as well as the classes you took, based on the offerings at your high school. Some places offer more honors, Advanced Placement or International Baccalaureate courses than others, and a B in one of these more challenging courses can signify a higher level of mastery than an A in a grade-level class at a school with both. College admissions officers are often well aware of how different high school curricula are from one school to another because they work with many of the same ones every year and receive detailed profiles of the course offerings, along with context about the student body. "GPAs can present very differently from each institution to the next," says Janine Bissic, an education consultant and former director of admission at Whittier College in California.

For the next few years, admissions officers will be evaluating transcripts that may have one or two terms that appear quite different from applicants' overall records, thanks to the varied experiences students have had studying from home during the pandemic. They plan to be forgiving to those who, say, didn't receive letter grades for a semester or two. Everyone evaluating applicants is in the same boat, says Todd Rinehart, vice chancellor for enrollment at the University of Denver. He expects counselors to "remain empathetic and flexible" as they weigh candidates. "We are trying to find reasons to admit students," he says.

That said, they will – as usual – be looking for evidence that applicants can succeed in college. At Vanderbilt University in Tennessee, "we would expect the most rigorous schedule that's appropriate for the student and the highest grades. We would be looking for both," says Douglas Christiansen, vice provost for university enrollment affairs and dean of admissions and financial aid. Being able to handle a challenging course load while maintaining strong marks is a signal that you have the academic grit and discipline to handle college-level work.

Balance is also key. Taking a handful of AP classes can help you look good, but more isn't always better; the idea is to take the most rigorous set of courses that makes sense given your abilities. While a B in an AP English lit class may be more impressive than an A in a grade-level class, a C or D isn't likely to wow anyone. "Challenge yourself where you are strong, and then work hard and do well in all of your courses," advises Clark Brigger, executive director of admissions at the University of Colorado–Boulder. Now that the College Board has eliminated the SAT Subject Tests, doing well on AP exams may be an increasingly important data point for highly selective colleges, Serota says.

"When a student takes a challenging course and does well, it is predictive of how they will perform in college," Brigger says. "However, there are always some students who stretch too far and then struggle with their performance and subsequently their health." If your grades dropped during a semester when you had personal hardships (such as a parent's job loss or a serious illness or death in the family), it's wise to explain the reason somewhere in your application. If the issue is coronavirus-related, the Common App and Coalition Application have provided optional ways for applicants to elaborate.

Don't be discouraged if your grades weren't where you'd have liked them to be early in high school. Many admissions officers look for an upward trend, improvements over time that enable a student to finish strong. "At the end of the day, we want to feel confident that if we admit a student, they can handle the rigor of the courses," says Yvonne Romero da Silva, vice president for enrollment at Rice University in Houston.

2 Your test scores are unlikely to make or break your chances.

"There are many students we've denied with perfect test scores because they didn't have anything else to set them apart," Christiansen says. Even in normal times, different institutions place varying levels of importance on standardized tests. This year, some two-thirds of colleges and universities, including the eight Ivy League schools, are (or are expected to be) test-optional or test-blind for fall 2022 admissions; in many cases, schools are extending this beyond next fall. The University of Maryland–College Park is one of many state flagships temporarily suspending their test requirements. The University of California system settled a lawsuit in May that claimed the tests discriminate against disadvantaged students; it won't consider scores at all in admissions decisions, although the agreement left open the possibility of using a new test in the future.

Even before the pandemic, many schools were shifting their test policies to optional, including Ohio Wesleyan University, the University of Denver and the University of Chicago. Bowdoin College in Maine has been test-optional for more than half a century. This trend is partly because admissions officers recognize that many applicants have intellectual abilities and academic strengths that aren't reflected in exam scores.

But before you decide to skip the tests, consider whether you'll be applying for scholarships, some of which may depend on the scores to qualify applicants, and whether having good results might be beneficial to your chances even at a test-optional school. Colleges and universities publish the data related to incoming classes online, so officials suggest that students can benchmark their own exam results and weigh whether it might enhance their application to submit scores.

Among colleges that do require the SAT or ACT, many will "superscore," which means they use your best section-level scores even if they're from different test dates. In other words, if your SAT reading score was 70 points higher the second time you took the test but your math score was 50 points higher on the first, the better of both attempts is what the admissions office looks at.

3 Quality means more than quantity when it comes to extracurriculars.

"Being passionate about key interests is more important than joining a lot of clubs," says Christiansen. "We're looking for depth and progression of leadership, not just participation." David Senter, a 2020 graduate of Rice University,

**Middlebury College
in Vermont**

Even in normal times, some students simply don't have time for clubs and sports because of family obligations. Rather, they might need to take care of younger siblings after school or hold a job. Admissions staffers get it. If that's the case, students would do well to be honest about their situation and to focus on the qualities that emerge from those experiences and what they get out of them, says Stacey Kostell, chief executive officer for the Coalition for College, a group of more than 150 colleges and universities dedicated to increasing students' access to higher education.

4 The best person to ask for a recommendation isn't necessarily a teacher who gave you an A.

It's better to consider whether a teacher can help admissions officers get to know a different side of you and better understand who you are. You might choose the teacher who taught your most difficult class, for example, or a class you thought you wouldn't like but did. Students "should really be looking for recommendations from teachers and mentors who know them especially well and can give rich context to their work ethic, character, persistence and growth," Bissic says.

Shields agrees: "If you struggled with a subject and had a good rapport with the teacher, you can get a helpful recommendation if the teacher can talk about how you came for extra help or you were able to advocate for yourself."

5 The key job of your essay is to reveal something about who you are.

If you're not funny, don't try to be. If you're not impassioned about a controversial subject, don't pretend to be. "You need to make the case for why you care about something and what you're doing about it," Serota advises. But do think carefully about choosing to share a mental health issue or a drug problem, for instance. "Be careful about revealing things that would make the reader feel a sense of caution about you," Serota says.

And while you may be tempted to write about how the pandemic affected you and your family, consider that admissions officers will likely be inundated with essays on the topic. "It's likely to blend in, and it becomes that much more difficult to stand out," says Ethan Sawyer, founder of CollegeEssayGuy.com and author of "College Admission Essentials." He encourages students to instead use the extra space provided by the Common and Coalition applications to describe the effects of the pandemic on their families.

An essay's most important quality is that it should feel authentic, Serota and others say. Make sure that it addresses the prompt, but also think of your essay as an opportunity to reveal your true voice and to highlight who you really are. Admissions folks are experts at distinguishing between viewpoints that feel genuine and those that don't. The most compelling essays reveal something about an applicant's personality, Kostell says. (For more on writing a great essay, see page 118.)

When it comes to large universities in particular, it may be

thinks his experience swimming competitively and working his way up to varsity team captain helped demonstrate his dedication and added something important to his strong academic record, along with his participation on the academic quiz bowl team. "You have to show you care," says Senter. "I was never the fastest, and I never went to the state championships, but I showed up every day and bonded with the team."

When reviewing your contributions outside of the classroom, admissions officers really want to know things like: What did you do in high school that made an organization better or furthered its cause and helped you grow? or What are you doing with your time that would contribute to our campus in a meaningful way if you were to come here? "Colleges are looking for a well-rounded student body, not necessarily a well-rounded student," says Serota.

These days, of course, they will have to be sensitive to the fact that some students weren't able to participate in extracurricular activities for an extended period because of the pandemic. "Admissions officers won't red flag a gap in, say, debate participation," says Mimi Doe, co-founder of the counseling firm Top Tier Admissions. "But for very top schools, they want to see what a student did instead. How they reached out beyond their own school and became engaged, even online, in some sort of initiative."

Haverford College
in Pennsylvania

hard to believe that there are human beings who are actually reading and giving careful consideration to your app, but it's true. During the review process, "multiple sets of eyes read every piece of the application, essay and letters of recommendation," says Brigger, whose university reviewed more than 54,000 first-year applications this past cycle. "Admissions officers and university faculty and staff are the ones making admissions decisions, not a computer or automated process." The essay is your opportunity to connect and make an impression.

6 A campus visit, real or virtual, can be helpful in more ways than one.

Since the coronavirus brought visits to a screeching halt, schools have introduced a wide range of virtual options, from informal chats to "tours" that are meant to offer students a taste of campus life. Many competitive colleges are using these new approaches as one tool to gauge an applicant's "demonstrated interest." This can be shown in various ways: by calling or emailing with questions, requesting a virtual interview, contacting alumni or interacting with a representative on social media or, when possible, at a college fair. Some 40% of colleges indicate that demonstrated interest is a moderately or considerably important factor in decisions, according to the most recent NACAC data.

Admissions officers can track how many contacts you've had with their institution, and they can even see if you've opened and engaged with emails. "The artificial intelligence and the way they use data has become super sophisticated," Doe says.

As colleges begin fully welcoming in-person visitors again, spending a day on campus sitting in on a class and talking with students, or perhaps attending a summer program for high schoolers at a college that appeals to you, can both signal your interest and help you (and the admissions office) establish whether you'll be a good fit. That's key. "Fit continues to be the most important factor to us – we want students to succeed here," says Marc Harding, vice provost for enrollment at the University of Pittsburgh. Participating in such a program shows that you're passionate and curious enough about a subject to take it to the next level, too. And that says a lot about your college readiness. ●

BRETT ZIEGLER FOR USN&WR

This Spider is
a biologist.

AT THE UNIVERSITY OF RICHMOND, you won't have to choose between your passions. We'll work closely with you to combine, expand, and ignite your interests through our rigorous curriculum: the hallmark of a Richmond education. When your ambition meets our journey-defining opportunities for real-world experience, you'll join a web of fellow Spiders who bring all they've got to all there is.

It starts within you. See how we help you bring it together.
ADMISSION.RICHMOND.EDU

UNIVERSITY OF
RICHMOND

Making
Your Voice
Heard

Ready to tackle your college essay? U.S. News invited
several experts to share their tips for success

by **Kelly Mae Ross, Devon Haynie** and **Josh Moody**

NOT ONLY IS THE COLLEGE ESSAY a place to showcase your writing skills, it's also one of the only parts of a college application where your unique voice and personality can shine through. "The essays are important in part because this is a student's chance to really speak directly to the admissions office," says Adam Sapp, assistant vice president and director of admissions at Pomona College in California.

Needing to make a memorable impression in only several hundred words can feel like a lot of pressure. "I think this is the part of the application process that students are sometimes most challenged by," says Niki Barron, associate dean of admission at Hamilton College in New York. "They're looking at a blank piece of paper and they don't know where to get started."

Experts emphasize the importance of being concise, coherent, congenial, honest and accurate. You should also flex some intellectual muscle and include vivid details or anecdotes (see sample essays, Page 120).

When should you get started? A good time to begin working on your essay is the summer before senior year, experts say, when homework and extracurricular activities aren't taking up time and mental energy. Starting early will allow for plenty of time to work through multiple drafts before application deadlines, which can be as early as November for students applying for early decision or early action.

Students can go online to review the requirements of colleges they want to apply to, such as essay topics and word limits. Many students may start with the Common App, an application platform accepted by some 900 schools.

Along with the main essay, some colleges ask applicants to submit one or more additional writing samples. Students are often asked to explain why they are interested in a particular school or academic field in these supplemental essays. You'll want to budget more time for the writing process if the schools you're applying to ask for supplemental essays.

The Common App – which students can submit to multiple colleges – asks for a main essay cap of 650 words. The word count is much shorter for institution-specific supplemental essays, typically around 250 words.

The first and sometimes most daunting step in the writing process is figuring out what to write about. There are usually sev-

eral essay prompts to choose from, and they tend to be broad, open-ended questions, giving students the freedom to take their response in many directions, Barron says.

NARROWED FOCUS. The essay shouldn't be an autobiography, notes Mimi Doe, co-founder of the counseling firm Top Tier Admissions. Rather, students should narrow their focus and write about a specific experience, hobby or quirk that reveals something about how they think, what they value, or what their strengths are.

Students can also write about something that illustrates an aspect of their background. It doesn't have to be a major achievement, which is a common misconception. Even an essay on a seemingly mundane topic can be compelling when handled well. Admissions officers who spoke with U.S. News cited memorable essays that focused on fly-fishing, a student's commute to and from school, and a family's dining room table.

What's most important, experts say, is that a college essay be thoughtful and tell a story that offers insight into who a student is as a person. No matter what topic students choose, they'll ultimately be writing about themselves, says Ethan Sawyer, founder of the College Essay Guy website, which offers essay-writing resources. "What we think of as the topic is just the frame or the lens that we're using to get into other parts of you," he notes.

If students are having trouble brainstorming potential topics, they can ask friends or family members for help, suggests Stephanie Klein Wassink, founder of Winning Applications and AdmissionsCheckup, Connecticut-based college admissions advising companies. Wassink says students can ask peers or family members questions such as, "What do you think differentiates me?" Or, "What are my quirks?"

Finally, the essay should tell college admissions officers something they don't already know. Make sure you're writing about something that isn't mentioned elsewhere in your application, or expand greatly on the topic if it is noted elsewhere.

Some experts encourage students to outline their essay before jumping into the actual writing. But there isn't one correct way of doing things, says Sara Newhouse, senior consultant at Enrollment Research Associates and formerly vice president of enrollment management at Birmingham-Southern College in Alabama. "Your writing process is your own," she says. Newhouse suggests using whatever process worked for you when completing writing assignments for English and other high school classes.

The first draft of an essay doesn't need to be perfect. "Just do a brain dump," Doe advises. "Don't edit yourself, just lay it all out on the page." If you're having a hard time getting started, focus on the opening sentence, Doe suggests. An essay's opening sentence, or hook, should grab the reader's attention, she says. Doe offers an example of a strong hook from the essay

of a student she worked with: "I first got into politics the day the cafeteria outlawed creamed corn."

"I want to know about this kid," she says. "I'm interested."

Admissions officers are also gauging writing skills. So you'll want to make sure to submit your best work. "The best writing is rewriting," Sapp says. "You should never be giving me your first draft."

It's a good idea to make sure your writing is showing, not

Two Essays That Worked

What makes a college admissions essay successful? Below are two submissions that helped students get into **Johns Hopkins University** in Baltimore, plus commentary from **Ellen Kim,** dean of undergraduate admissions, about what these applicants did right. Remember, Kim advises, that "what works in these essays works because of who the student is" and how it fits into the rest of the application. In other words, you'll want to apply these principles to a topic that reveals something intriguing about you.

"This title is interesting," Kim says. "But it's up to students to decide whether they want to title an essay." If nothing brilliant comes to mind, then you can skip.

More Than Thick Eyebrows

By Caroline

Rarely have I studied a topic that flows from my ears to my brain to my tongue as easily as the Italian language. The Italian blood that runs through me is more than the genetics that gave me my dark hair and thick eyebrows. It is the work of the generation that traveled from Istria in the north and Sicilia in the south, meeting through friends in Chicago, and encouraging their children to study hard and make a living for their future families. In time, that influence would be passed on to me; finding my grandfather's meticulously-written electricity notes circa 1935 – filled with drawings and words I did not yet understand – inspired me to take Italian at my own high school.

The moment I realized that my Italian heritage was wholly a part of me was a rather insignificant one, yet to me is one of the most remarkable realizations of my life. The summer after my second year of Italian study, I was driving in my car, listening to a young trio of Italian teenagers, *Il Volo*, meaning "The Flight." As one of the tenors sang a solo, *Ti voglio tanto bene*, I realized that I could understand every word he was singing. Though it was a simple declaration of love and devotion in a beautiful tune, what mattered was that I was not just listening to three cute teenagers sing a song. I was fully engaged with the words and could finally sing along.

After that moment, I sought out all the Italian I could get my hands on: watching *Cinema Paradiso* and *La Dolce Vita*, absorbing phrases of the language I felt I could now call my own. Even better, I could use it with my closest living Italian relative, that I felt confident enough in my skill that I could use it with my closest living Italian relative, my father's mother, *la mia nonna*. More than speaking the language, I discovered my family's past. In conversing with her and my father, I discovered that I will be only the third person in my paternal grandparents' family to attend college, that my grandmother had only a sixth-grade education, that my grandfather, despite never holding a degree in mathematics or physics, worked for three decades on CTA train cars as an electrician. The marriage of my grandparents in 195_ represented a synthesis of the culture of northern and southern Italy and America.

Having now studied three full years of this language, I only want to consume more of it. I want to read Dante's *Divina Commedia* in its original vernacular, to watch my favorite Italian films without the subtitles, to sing every Italian refrain with fluid understanding of what the melody means, and to finally – finally! – visit my grandparents' childhood homes: the town of Trapa_ in Sicilia and the Istrian peninsula on the Adriatic coast. To me, the Italian language holds an essential connection to my past, but also a constant goal for the future. It is likely that I will never fully master the vernacular and colloquialisms, yet learning this language will stimulate me intellectually and culturally for life. I believe I can claim Italian as mine now, but there is still so much more to learn. Italian is a gift that I will hold dear forever, and I am glad that I received it so early in life.

The author takes a straightforward approach to starting, Kim says. "But you can tell you are going to get to know her."

Many personal statements include short scenes, Kim notes. But the strongest essays are the ones that put those anecdotes toward a larger purpose, as the author does here. "She is helping us understand where she is in her journey with Italian," Kim says. "It's not just being descriptive for the sake of being descriptive."

The author chose to write about something very accessible and approachable, Kim notes. "Everyone can relate to family heritage," she says. "It would have been very easy to talk about the members of the family, but she does a good job of making it say something about herself," which is the goal.

In this paragraph, Kim says, "We learn not just about her intellectual appetite for something, but also about what she does when she is passionate."

"This is a good way to close the essay, by describing why this matters to who she is as a person," Kim says.

telling, Doe says. This means giving readers examples that prove you embody certain traits or beliefs, as opposed to just stating that you do.

After editing your essay, seek outside editing help, experts recommend. While there are individuals and companies that offer assistance for a fee – from editing services to essay-writing boot camps – someone from among your peers, teachers, school counselors and family members may be willing to help you polish your essay. Newhouse says it works well to have other people proofread an essay in two stages, looking first for information gaps – anything they are confused about. Once the content is nailed down, the second proofing stage focuses on style, grammar, punctuation and spelling. But "don't let anyone edit out your voice," Doe cautions.

And while proofreading is fair game, having someone else rewrite your essay is not. •

String Theory
By Joanna

If string theory is really true, then the entire world is made up of strings, and I cannot tie a single one. This past summer, I applied for my very first job at a small, busy bakery and café in my neighborhood. I knew that if I were hired there, I would learn how to use a cash register, prepare sandwiches, and take cake orders. I imagined that my biggest struggle would be catering to demanding New Yorkers, but I never thought that it would be the benign act of tying a box that would become both my biggest obstacle and greatest teacher.

On my first day of work in late August, one of the bakery's employees hastily explained the procedure. It seemed simple: wrap the string around your hand, then wrap it three times around the box both ways, and knot it. I recited the anthem in my head, "three times, turn it, three times, knot" until it became my mantra. After observing multiple employees, it was clear that anyone tying the box could complete it in a matter of seconds. For weeks, I labored endlessly, only to watch the strong and small pieces of my pride unravel each time I tried.

As I rushed to discreetly shove half-tied cake boxes into plastic bags, I could not help but wonder what was wrong with me. I have learned Mozart arias, memorized the functional groups in organic chemistry, and calculated the anti-derivatives of functions that I will probably never use in real life – all with a modest amount of energy. For some reason though, after a month's effort, tying string around a cake box still left me in a quandary.

As the weeks progressed, my skills slowly began to improve. Of course there were days when I just wanted to throw all of the string in the trash and use Scotch tape; this sense of defeat was neither welcome nor wanted, but remarks like "Oh, you must be new" from snarky customers catapulted my determination to greater heights.

It should be more difficult to develop an internal pulse and sense of legato in a piece of music than it is to find the necessary rhythm required to tie a box, but this seemingly trivial task has clearly proven not to be trivial at all. The difficulties that I encountered trying to keep a single knot intact are proof of this. The lack of cooperation between my coordination and my understanding left me frazzled, but the satisfaction I felt when I successfully tied my first box was almost as great as any I had felt before.

Scientists developing string theory say that string can exist in a straight line, but it can also bend, oscillate, or break apart. I am thankful that the string I work with is not quite as temperamental, but still cringe when someone asks for a chocolate mandel bread. Supposedly, the string suggested in string theory is responsible for unifying general relativity with quantum physics. The only thing I am responsible for when I use string is delivering someone's pie to them without the box falling apart. Tying a cake box may not be quantum physics, but it is just as crucial to holding together what matters.

I'm beginning to realize that I should not be ashamed if it takes me longer to learn. I persist, continue to tie boxes every weekend at work. Even though I occasionally backslide into feelings of desperation, I always rewrap the string around my hand and start over because I have learned the most gratifying victories come from tenacity. If the universe really is comprised of strings, I am confident that I will be able to tie them together, even if I do have to keep my fingers crossed that it's hold up.

Students should try to grab the reader's attention at the first sentence. "Her opening paragraph is interesting," says Kim. "You read it, and you aren't sure what the essay is going to be about. It makes you curious about what she is going to tell you."

"A lot of times students feel like they need to write an essay about a life accomplishment or a life-changing event or something really extraordinary," Kim says. "But it's also possible to write a very effective personal statement about an ordinary thing. It's not the topic that has to be unique. It's what you say that has to be unique."

The author does a good job of providing a window into her thought process, Kim notes. "You also see how she responds to a challenge in a very approachable way."

In this instance, dropping in some academic references works with the theme of the essay, but students shouldn't think they have to follow suit, Kim cautions. It only works if it reinforces your central point.

This essay, like all strong essays, was well-written, clear and error-free, Kim notes. The writing felt natural - not as though the author was reaching for a thesaurus. "This should sound like you," she says.

Personal statements are called "personal" for a reason, Kim observes. They should tell the admissions committee something about the student. This essay does a good job of wrapping up the piece on a personal note.

What We Look For

An admissions dean on what really counts, especially when tests are optional

by **Robert Alexander**

MANY COLLEGES MADE standardized tests optional for this fall's entering freshmen after students' access to SAT or ACT administrations was severely limited by the pandemic. Another influence was a 2020 report by the National Association for College Admission Counseling urging colleges to consider how the tests can undermine college access and equity in the admissions process. Now, many institutions are announcing that they'll be test-optional for the foreseeable future.

Data show that high school students are applying to more colleges – and more selective ones – at least partially because they feel less limited by their scores. How can students best prepare for this new reality? They can:

1. Understand that high school academic performance is paramount.

In 2019, the University of Rochester became test-optional, like many institutions, in favor of a holistic process that empowers students to showcase their academic achievements and potential mainly through their work in high school. We evaluate much more than the digits of their GPA, including the menu of courses offered at their schools, those they elected to take, and grades they earned. A student's comprehensive academic record provides a broad view of achievement over four years, as opposed to a snapshot over four hours on one test.

2. Maximize opportunities and resources available to them.

Admission committees work hard to consider each individual's background and family resources, which can impact our assessment of their transcript (since private schools and publics in wealthier zip codes tend to have more advanced course options) and standardized test scores (because affluent students are much more likely to benefit from test prep or private tutoring—an industry worth $17.5 billion in 2020). Some schools partner with nearby colleges to offer high-schoolers dual-enrollment credits. We are aware of the wide range of advantages that privileged students have, and we do our best to account for relative inequities.

Our most important consideration is how students have taken advantage of the chances they do have to explore their interests and passions, perhaps by conducting independent research; by leveraging teachers, counselors, or coaches for mentorship; by shadowing someone on the job or taking on part-time employment. We also value the lessons learned by working to supplement family income, the perspectives gained from caring for family members, and leadership demonstrated through activism in the resurgent movement for racial justice and social equality, for example. Ultimately, descriptions of activities should focus beyond what students have done and highlight what they've learned and how they'll use that knowledge in the future.

3. Develop character strengths.

As colleges craft classes, they aren't only looking for academic superstars but also are attempting to cultivate a community and prepare civic leaders to improve society. If test scores are a waning indicator, character strength assessments are waxing. A cadre of admissions and education leaders are collaborating to elevate character attributes in the admission equation, which we believe will lead to the deepening of these characteristics throughout school and in life. Members of the Character Collaborative are incorporating the work of researchers including Angela Duckworth to create frameworks to measure strengths like resilience, determination, follow-through, intellectual curiosity, compassion for other people and care for the common good. By developing clear prompts to elicit information from applicants, we're also communicating what we value.

Standardized testing likely won't disappear, but it may lose its traditional status as prima facie evidence of college readiness. As we collectively navigate what comes next, let's remember that college admission is about making great matches. ●

Robert Alexander is the dean of admissions, financial aid, and enrollment management at the University of Rochester.

J. ADAM FENSTER – UNIVERSITY OF ROCHESTER

Shop the U.S. News Store

Find Your Perfect School
U.S. News
College Compass

- See complete U.S. News rankings
- Premium data on more than 1,800 schools
- Compare schools side by side
- Detailed financial aid and alumni salary information
- See entering student SAT scores and GPAs
- Match schools to your preferences with the MyFit Engine
- See how you stack up with the Admissions Calculator

visit usnews.com/store

For discounted bulk orders, or to order by phone, call 1-800-836-6397.

Your College Search:
A To-Do List

PREPARE FOR A GREAT HIGH SCHOOL EXPERIENCE. *You'll be able to grow inside and outside the classroom, while making sure you're ready to apply to college in a few years. Although the pandemic has disrupted opportunities for standardized tests and shifted many college visits from campus to online, you can remain curious, investigate virtually, and continue to work toward your future goals. Careful planning and good choices over time make for strong options later. Ready, set, go!* **–by Ned Johnson**

Freshman Year

LISTEN AND OBSERVE. Faced with more challenging high school class work, you'll need to pay attention to what your new teachers expect from you and look for ways to work harder and smarter. Grades are important in ninth grade, but seek balance so that you are challenged without being overwhelmed. Don't be afraid to ask for help if you need it.

☐ **Get involved.** High school is not a four-year audition for college but rather a time in which to develop yourself. Beyond grades, social connections and extracurriculars are important. Use part-time jobs, community service, arts and music, robotics clubs and other activities to engage with others.

☐ **Read voraciously.** Dive into books, newspapers, magazines and blogs. Explore subjects that engage you. Additionally, check out TED Talks, YouTube videos and free online courses.

☐ **Find mentors.** Look for knowledgeable people who can offer helpful advice: teachers, coaches, counselors and friends. These relationships can pay off in other ways, too. People like to help students they know.

☐ **Schedule downtime.** That means turning off electronic devices. No phones. No screens. We all need time to daydream and think about ourselves and our place in the world.

☐ **Identify ways to relieve stress.** For school and college, you'll need a model for success that is sustainable and that includes finding healthy ways to manage stress and getting enough rest.

Sophomore Year

KEEP EVOLVING AS A LEARNER. Focus on better understanding your strengths and interests – and how to develop them.

☐ **Challenge yourself (wisely).** Strive for strong grades and take on new challenges inside the classroom and out. Ask for help if needed; avoid overtaxing yourself. Balance is the goal.

☐ **Speak up in class.** Learning at the college level is about an exchange of ideas between professors and peers. Critical thinking and the ability to articulate your thoughts and ideas are skills that contribute to college success.

☐ **Sleep.** The typical 15-year-old brain needs eight to 10 hours of sleep to function at 100%.

☐ **Refine your route.** Look ahead to 11th- and 12th-grade courses of interest and plan on any prerequisites. Take advantage of rigorous courses that are in line with your academic path.

☐ **Learn from the masters.** As you take inventory of your own interests, find people who work in related areas. Listen to their stories. A 20-minute conversation with a professional could even turn into a fruitful internship opportunity.

☐ **Create an activities list.** Keep track of your hobbies, jobs, extracurriculars and accomplishments.

ILLUSTRATION BY KIRSTEN ULVE FOR USN&WR

This will form the basis of your résumé and will be essential in preparing for college interviews and applications as well as for possible jobs, internships and summer programs.

☐ **Make your summer matter.** Work, volunteer, play sports, travel or take a class. Research summer programs and internships to move beyond the scope of your high school courses. Plunge into an activity that excites you.

☐ **Settle on a testing strategy and test-prep plan.** Use your PSAT scores and other practice tests to help you identify the right test for you (i.e., SAT vs. ACT). Not a great test-taker? With so many colleges now test-optional, the tests are something you may want – but not need – to take.

☐ **Consult your parents.** Talk with them about expectations for college, including how much your family can pay. It's much better to discuss costs at the start of the process.

Junior Year

ESSAYS, TESTS AND AP EXAMS, OH MY! Your grades, test scores and activities this year form a large part of what colleges consider for admission. Prepare for your exams, do your best in class, and stay active and involved.

☐ **Plot out your calendar.** Talk with your parents and guidance counselor about which exams to take and when. If your 10th-grade PSAT scores put you in reach of a National Merit Scholarship, concentrated prep time might be worth it. Then take the SAT or ACT. As most colleges that are test-optional will likely remain so, good scores can help but aren't a must-have. You may be able to use AP exams to show rigor instead of, or in addition to, the ACT or SAT.

☐ **Immerse yourself in activities.** It's your turn: Junior year is the time to fully engage in and become a leader in extracurriculars you enjoy both in and out of school. These are opportunities to grow intellectually and socially and to show you are dedicated and play well with others.

☐ **Build your college list in the spring.** Once you have a sense of your grades and get your test scores, if any, talk to a counselor and assemble a list of target, reach and likely schools. Use tools to aid your research. Explore college websites and other resources such as ed.gov/finaid and usnews.com/

bestcolleges. And clean up social media (e.g., Instagram, Facebook, Twitter) since admissions folks may check it out.

☐ **Visit, and connect digitally.** Ideally you can check out a few campuses in person; if not, make use of COVID-improved college websites

and webinars. Attend college fairs and information sessions if possible. Grab the admissions rep's card and follow up via email with a thank-you note or with questions whose answers aren't already available on the college website.

☐ **Get recommendations.** Right after spring break, ask two teachers with different perspectives on your performance if they will write letters for you. Choose teachers who will effectively communicate your academic and personal qualities.

☐ **Write.** Reflect on your experiences and strengths as you prepare to write your college essay. Procrastination causes stress, so aim to have first drafts done by Labor Day of senior year. Share them with an English teacher, parent or counselor.

Senior Year

DON'T SLACK OFF. Colleges look at senior-year transcripts, so keep working hard in your classes.

☐ **Finish testing.** If necessary, you can retake the SAT or ACT in the early fall. Check the admissions testing policies of your schools. Are they test-optional or do they require you to submit SAT or ACT scores? It may be strategic to share scores with some schools but not others.

☐ **Know your deadlines.** Many colleges have multiple deadline options. Consider the implications of early action and early,

rolling or regular decision – and confirm the rules and deadlines for aid – so you can plan accordingly.

☐ **Apply.** Craft your essays with a well-thought-out narrative. Fill out applications carefully. Review a copy of your transcript. Have you displayed an upward trend that should be discussed? Does an anomaly need context? Discuss any issues with your counselor. Leave yourself time to reread essays and clean up any errors.

☐ **Follow up.** Check that your colleges have received records and recs from your high school and your SAT or ACT scores from the testing organization. A month after you submit your application, call the college and confirm that your file is complete.

☐ **Confirm aid rules.** Check with each college for specific financial aid application requirements. Dates and forms may vary.

☐ **Make a choice.** Try to visit or even revisit the colleges where you've been accepted before committing. Talk with alumni; attend an accepted-student reception. Then make your college choice official by sending in your deposit. Congrats! ●

Ned Johnson is founder of and tutor-geek at PrepMatters (prepmatters.com) where, along with colleagues, he torments teens with test prep, educational counseling and general attempts to help them thrive. He is also co-author with Dr. William Stixrud of "The Self-Driven Child: The Science and Sense of Giving Your Kids More Control Over Their Lives."

A+ Schools for B Students

SO YOU'RE A SCHOLAR WITH LOTS to offer and the GPA of a B student, and your heart is set on going to a great college. No problem. U.S. News has screened the universe of colleges and universities to identify those where nonsuperstars have a decent shot at being accepted and thriving – where spirit and hard work could make all the difference to the admissions office.

To make this list, which is presented alphabetically, schools had to admit a meaningful proportion of applicants whose test scores and class standing put them in non-A territory (methodology, Page 129). Since many truly seek a broad and engaged student body, be sure to display your individuality and seriousness of purpose as you apply.

▶ National Universities

School (State) (*Public)	SAT/ACT 25th-75th percentile ('20)	Average high school GPA ('20)	Freshmen in top 25% of class ('20)
Adelphi University (NY)	1060-1250[9]	3.4	59%
Arizona State University*	21-28[2]	3.5	60%
Belmont University (TN)	23-30[2]	3.8	61%
Bethel University (MN) (MN)	21-28[2]	3.6	53%
Biola University (CA)	1070-1290	3.6	63%
Bowling Green State University (OH)*	20-26	3.6	43%
The Catholic University of America (DC)	1130-1325[2]	3.5	55%
Chapman University (CA)	1170-1350[2]	N/A	71%
Chatham University (PA)	1050-1250[2]	3.7	55%
Clarkson University (NY)	1150-1350[2]	3.8	71%
Clark University (MA)	1150-1350[2]	3.7	70%
The College of St. Scholastica (MN)	22-27[9]	3.5	54%
Colorado State University*	1070-1280[2]	3.7	48%
Concordia University Wisconsin	20-26[2]	N/A	58%
Creighton University (NE)	24-30[2]	3.9	73%
Drake University (IA)	23-30[2]	3.7	69%
Duquesne University (PA)	1120-1270[2]	3.8	48%
East Tennessee State University*	20-27[2]	N/A	42%
Elon University (NC)	1140-1320[2]	3.9	52%
Florida Atlantic University*	1060-1220	3.7	41%
Florida Institute of Technology	1130-1330	3.7	52%
Florida International University*	1110-1260	3.9	51%
George Fox University (OR)	1020-1240[2]	3.3	61%
George Mason University (VA)*	1100-1300[2]	3.7	41%
Gonzaga University (WA)	1160-1350[2]	3.7	75%
Harding University (AR)	21-29	3.7	56%
Hofstra University (NY)	1160-1330[2]	3.7	61%
Howard University (DC)	1130-1260[2]	3.6	59%
Indiana University–Bloomington*	1120-1350[2]	3.8	66%
Kansas State University*	20-27[2]	3.6	52%
Kent State University (OH)*	20-26[2]	3.6	45%
Lipscomb University (TN)	22-29[2]	3.7	63%
Louisiana State University–Baton Rouge*	23-28	3.5	49%
Louisiana Tech University*	22-28	3.6	51%
Loyola University Chicago	1130-1330[2]	3.8	72%
Loyola University New Orleans	21-26[2]	3.5	49%[5]
Marquette University (WI)	25-30[2]	N/A	75%
Mercer University (GA)	1180-1340[2]	3.9	66%
Miami University–Oxford (OH)*	24-30	3.8	61%
Michigan State University*	1100-1300	3.7	59%
Michigan Technological University*	1160-1350[2]	3.8	64%
Misericordia University (PA)	1040-1215[2]	3.4	51%
Mississippi State University*	22-30	3.6	55%
Montana State University*	21-28[2]	3.6	47%
North Dakota State University*	20-26[9]	3.5	42%
Nova Southeastern University (FL)	1030-1240	3.9	56%
Ohio University*	21-26[2]	3.6	49%
Oklahoma State University*	21-27[2]	3.6	57%
Oregon State University*	1080-1310[2]	3.6	55%
Pace University (NY)	1060-1240[2]	3.2	43%
Quinnipiac University (CT)	1080-1260[2]	3.5	52%
Robert Morris University (PA)	1040-1230[2]	3.6	48%
Rutgers University–Newark (NJ)*	1010-1170[2]	N/A	40%
Samford University (AL)	23-29	3.8	57%
San Diego State University*	1090-1300[2]	3.8	72%
Seattle University	1130-1330[2]	3.6	55%
Seton Hall University (NJ)	1150-1310[2]	3.6	60%
Shenandoah University (VA)	990-1220[2]	3.5	41%
Simmons University (MA)	1060-1250[2]	3.7	55%
South Dakota State University*	20-26[2]	3.5	43%
St. John Fisher College (NY)	1060-1240[2]	3.7	58%
St. John's University (NY) (NY)	1080-1300[2]	3.5	46%
Tennessee Techn University*	21-28[2]	3.6	59%
Texas Tech University*	1070-1240[2]	3.6	51%
Thomas Jefferson University (PA)	1090-1270[2]	3.7	56%
UNC Greensboro*	980-1160	3.7	42%
Union University (TN)	22-30	3.8	61%
University at Albany–SUNY*	1080-1240[2]	3.4	49%
University at Buffalo–SUNY*	1140-1310	3.7	61%
University of Alabama at Birmingham*	22-30	3.8	56%
University of Arizona*	21-29[2]	3.4	63%
University of Arkansas*	23-29[2]	3.8	57%
University of Central Florida*	1160-1340	3.9	72%
University of Cincinnati*	23-29[2]	3.7	52%
University of Colorado Boulder*	1130-1350[2]	3.6	53%
University of Dayton (OH)	23-29[9]	3.7	55%
University of Delaware*	1170-1340[2]	3.9	53%
University of Detroit Mercy	1050-1260[2]	3.7	56%
University of Hawaii–Manoa*	1060-1260[2]	3.6	60%
University of Houston*	1120-1310[2]	3.8	67%
University of Illinois–Chicago*	1030-1250	3.4	62%
University of Iowa*	22-29	3.8	67%
University of Kansas*	22-29[2]	3.6	56%
University of Kentucky*	22-29[2]	3.6	62%
University of Louisville (KY)*	21-29[9]	3.6	55%
University of Maine*	1050-1250[2]	3.4	50%
University of Maryland–Baltimore County*	1150-1350	3.9	50%
University of Massachusetts–Boston*	1010-1210[2]	3.3	41%
University of Massachusetts–Lowell*	1150-1320[2]	3.7	54%
University of Mississippi*	22-30[2]	3.6	46%
University of Missouri*	23-30	N/A	65%
University of Missouri–St. Louis*	21-27[2]	3.5	64%

Note: Key to footnotes, Page 52

School (State) (*Public)	SAT/ACT 25th-75th percentile ('20)	Average high school GPA ('20)	Freshmen in top 25% of class ('20)
University of Nebraska–Lincoln*	22-28[2]	3.6	59%
University of Nevada–Reno*	20-26	3.5	56%
University of New Hampshire*	1090-1280[2]	3.6	51%
University of North Carolina–Charlotte*	1100-1280[2]	3.5	46%
University of North Carolina–Wilmington*	23-27	3.9	46%
University of North Dakota*	21-26[2]	3.6	48%
University of North Texas*	1050-1240[2]	N/A	53%
University of Oklahoma*	23-29[2]	3.6	62%
University of Rhode Island*	1090-1260[9]	3.5	51%
University of San Diego	1160-1340[2]	3.9	70%
University of San Francisco	1140-1330[2]	3.5	73%
University of South Carolina*	1140-1340[2]	3.5	58%
University of South Dakota*	20-25[2]	N/A	40%
University of South Florida*	1160-1320	3.9	66%
University of St. Thomas (MN) (MN)	23-29[2]	3.7	56%
University of the Pacific (CA)	1080-1340[2]	3.6	72%
University of Vermont*	1160-1350[2]	3.7	74%
University of Wyoming*	21-28[2]	3.5	52%
Valparaiso University (IN)	1070-1280[2]	3.8	68%
Virginia Commonwealth University*	1060-1250[2]	3.7	47%
Western New England University (MA)	1070-1270[2]	3.5	47%
Wilkes University (PA)	1040-1230	3.6	46%

▶ National Liberal Arts Colleges

School (State) (*Public)	SAT/ACT 25th-75th percentile ('20)	Average high school GPA ('20)	Freshmen in top 25% of class ('20)
Agnes Scott College (GA)	1080-1290[2]	3.7	60%
Allegheny College (PA)	1140-1350[2]	3.5	62%
Augustana College (IL)	1090-1280[2]	3.5	55%
Austin College (TX)	1110-1310[2]	3.5	57%
Beloit College (WI)	21-29[2]	3.3	59%
Berea College (KY)	22-26[2]	3.6	69%
Birmingham-Southern College (AL)	22-28[2]	2.6	47%
College of St. Benedict (MN)	21-28[2]	3.7	61%
Concordia College at Moorhead (MN)	20-27[2]	3.6	49%
Cornell College (IA)	23-29[2]	3.5	46%
Covenant College (GA)	22-29[2]	3.7	52%
Drew University (NJ)	1100-1300[2]	3.6	57%
Earlham College (IN)	1110-1340[2]	3.6	69%
Elizabethtown College (PA)	1080-1280[2]	N/A	58%
Fisk University (TN)	990-1210	N/A	50%
Gordon College (MA)	1020-1280[2]	3.6	51%
Goucher College (MD)	990-1230[2]	3.1	42%
Gustavus Adolphus College (MN)	24-30[2]	3.6	63%
Hanover College (IN)	1060-1230[2]	3.7	59%
Hollins University (VA)	1050-1260[3]	3.7	54%
Hope College (MI)	1090-1310[2]	3.8	64%
Houghton College (NY)	1060-1300[2]	3.5	50%
Illinois Wesleyan University	1100-1300[2]	3.8	58%
Knox College (IL)	1080-1320[2]	N/A	62%
Lake Forest College (IL)	1085-1290[2]	3.7	74%
Luther College (IA)	23-29	3.6	55%
Lycoming College (PA)	1010-1210[2]	3.5	52%
Moravian University (PA)	1030-1190[9]	3.6	48%
Muhlenberg College (PA)	1170-1350[2]	3.4	72%
Ohio Wesleyan University	23-29[2]	3.6	56%
Presbyterian College (SC)	1030-1200[2]	3.4	55%

School (State) (*Public)	SAT/ACT 25th-75th percentile ('20)	Average high school GPA ('20)	Freshmen in top 25% of class ('20)
Randolph-Macon College (VA)	1030-1218[2]	3.7	48%
Saint Mary's College (IN)	1060-1260[2]	3.8	63%
Saint Michael's College (VT)	1130-1280[2]	3.3	55%
Simpson College (IA)	20-26[2]	3.7	41%
Southwestern University (TX)	1110-1300[2]	3.4	63%
Spelman College (GA)	1050-1200	3.6	59%
St. Mary's College of Maryland*	1070-1280[2]	3.4	57%
St. Norbert College (WI)	22-28[2]	3.6	60%
Stonehill College (MA)	1120-1290[2]	3.3	48%
Susquehanna University (PA)	1070-1240[2]	3.5	53%
Transylvania University (KY)	24-30[2]	3.7	61%
University of Minnesota Morris*	21-28	3.6	52%
University of Puget Sound (WA)	1130-1342[2]	3.6	62%
The University of the South (TN)	25-30[2]	N/A	66%
Ursinus College (PA)	1150-1330[2]	3.5	54%
Virginia Military Institute*	1070-1260[3]	3.6	40%
Wabash College (IN)	1120-1320[2]	3.8	61%
Washington and Jefferson College (PA)	1040-1270[2]	3.4	49%
Washington College (MD)	1070-1280	3.7	57%
Wheaton College (MA) (MA)	1160-1350[2]	3.4	63%
Wofford College (SC)	1160-1328[2]	3.7	66%

▶ Regional Universities

School (State) (*Public)	SAT/ACT 25th-75th percentile ('20)	Average high school GPA ('20)	Freshmen in top 25% of class ('20)
NORTH			
Arcadia University (PA)	1030-1230[2]	3.4	48%
Assumption University (MA)	1070-1220[2]	3.4	41%
Bryant University (RI)	1120-1280[2]	3.4	52%
Canisius College (NY)	1040-1240[2]	3.6	48%
The College of New Jersey*	1140-1320[2]	N/A	67%
CUNY–Baruch College*	1150-1350	3.3	77%
Endicott College (MA)	1100-1240[2]	3.4	48%
Fairfield University (CT)	1190-1340[2]	3.6	70%[5]
Geneva College (PA)	980-1240[2]	3.6	43%
Ithaca College (NY)	1160-1320[2]	N/A	59%
Le Moyne College (NY)	1060-1250[2]	3.5	55%
Loyola University Maryland	1140-1328[2]	3.6	57%
Marist College (NY)	1130-1300[2]	3.6	53%
Marywood University (PA)	1000-1180[2]	3.5	49%
McDaniel College (MD)	980-1210[2]	3.6	47%
Messiah University (PA)	1080-1310[2]	3.8	62%
Molloy College (NY)	1040-1230[2]	3.1	66%
Monmouth University (NJ)	1040-1210[2]	3.5	44%
Nazareth College (NY)	1110-1280[2]	3.6	62%
Niagara University (NY)	1015-1200[2]	3.5	43%
Providence College (RI)	1135-1310[2]	3.5	73%
Ramapo College of New Jersey*	1030-1220	3.5	43%[5]
Rider University (NJ)	1020-1220[2]	3.4	46%
Roberts Wesleyan College (NY)	1020-1250[2]	3.6	54%
Roger Williams University (RI)	1070-1240[2]	3.4	40%
Saint Joseph's University (PA)	1100-1290[2]	3.6	51%
Salisbury University (MD)*	1093-1268[2]	3.7	40%
Salve Regina University (RI)	1100-1240[2]	3.4	43%
Seton Hill University (PA)	1000-1200[2]	3.6	50%
Siena College (NY)	1060-1240[2]	3.5	47%
Springfield College (MA)	1080-1270[2]	3.5	42%

▶ Regional Universities (continued)

School (State) (*Public)	SAT/ACT 25th-75th percentile ('20)	Average high school GPA ('20)	Freshmen in top 25% of class ('20)
St. Bonaventure University (NY)	1030-1220[2]	3.4	44%
St. Francis University (PA)	1010-1220[2]	3.7	58%
Suffolk University (MA)	1010-1210[2]	3.4	42%
SUNY College–Cortland*	1100-1220[9]	3.6	44%
SUNY–Geneseo*	1140-1310	3.7	72%
SUNY Maritime College*	1070-1230[3]	3.4	50%[5]
SUNY–Oswego*	1020-1190	3.3	42%
SUNY Polytechnic Inst. – Utica/Albany*	1000-1350[2]	3.7	73%

School (State) (*Public)	SAT/ACT 25th-75th percentile ('20)	Average high school GPA ('20)	Freshmen in top 25% of class ('20)
University of New Haven (CT)	1050-1220[2]	3.5	41%
University of Scranton (PA)	1100-1280	3.6	63%
Wagner College (NY)	1050-1250[2]	3.5	48%
Waynesburg University (PA)	980-1170[2]	3.7	49%
SOUTH			
Anderson University (SC)	1040-1230[2]	3.7	64%
Appalachian State University (NC)*	22-27[2]	3.6	50%

Gonzaga students gather at a watch party as their Bulldogs play the NCAA basketball championship game.

DAVID RYDER – GETTY IMAGES

School (State) (*Public)	SAT/ACT 25th-75th percentile ('20)	Average high school GPA ('20)	Freshmen in top 25% of class ('20)
Asbury University (KY)	21-28[2]	3.7	57%
Berry College (GA)	23-29[2]	3.7	63%
Christian Brothers University (TN)	22-27[2]	3.8	57%
Christopher Newport University (VA)*	1090-1270[2]	3.8	47%
College of Charleston (SC)*	1070-1240[2]	3.9	51%
Embry-Riddle Aero. U.–Daytona Beach (FL)	1120-1330[2]	N/A	54%
Florida Southern College	1110-1285[2]	3.7	55%
Freed-Hardeman University (TN)	21-27	3.7	63%
James Madison University (VA)*	1120-1280[2]	N/A	48%
Lee University (TN)	21-27	3.6	53%
Milligan University (TN)	21-26	3.7	52%
Murray State University (KY)*	21-27[2]	3.6	51%
Rollins College (FL)	1120-1330[2]	3.4	60%
Stetson University (FL)	1100-1285[2]	3.8	53%
University of Mary Washington (VA)*	1090-1270[2]	0.0	50%
University of North Alabama*	20-26[2]	3.5	51%
University of North Georgia*	1060-1210	3.6	46%
University of West Florida*	22-27	3.8	44%
Western Carolina University (NC)*	20-25	3.5	41%

MIDWEST

School (State) (*Public)	SAT/ACT 25th-75th percentile ('20)	Average high school GPA ('20)	Freshmen in top 25% of class ('20)
Augustana University (SD)	22-28[2]	3.7	65%
Baldwin Wallace University (OH)	21-27[2]	N/A	46%
Bradley University (IL)	1080-1280[2]	3.8	65%
Calvin University (MI)	1100-1320[2]	3.8	62%
Capital University (OH)	21-26[9]	3.6	50%
Carroll University (WI)	21-26[2]	N/A	54%
Cedarville University (OH)	23-30[2]	N/A	62%
Drury University (MO)	21-28[2]	3.8	64%
Elmhurst University (IL)	980-1170[2]	3.6	46%
Hamline University (MN)	20-26[2]	3.5	43%
Indiana Wesleyan University	1010-1200[2]	3.6	54%
John Carroll University (OH)	22-28[2]	3.7	50%
Lewis University (IL)	1010-1220[2]	3.6	45%
Marian University (IN) (IN)	980-1180[2]	N/A	48%
Nebraska Wesleyan University	22-29[2]	3.7	51%
Otterbein University (OH)	20-27	3.6	54%
Spring Arbor University (MI)	983-1190	3.6	48%
University of Evansville (IN)	1070-1278[2]	3.8	65%
University of Illinois–Springfield*	980-1190[2]	N/A	46%
University of Minnesota–Duluth*	21-26[2]	3.5	47%
U. of Northwestern–St. Paul (MN)	21-27[2]	3.6	50%
University of Wisconsin–Eau Claire*	21-26[2]	3.5	48%
University of Wisconsin–La Crosse*	22-26[2]	3.6	60%
Viterbo University (WI)	20-25[2]	3.5	43%
Webster University (MO)	20-27	N/A	54%
Xavier University (OH)	22-28[9]	3.7	55%

WEST

School (State) (*Public)	SAT/ACT 25th-75th percentile ('20)	Average high school GPA ('20)	Freshmen in top 25% of class ('20)
Abilene Christian University (TX)	1010-1220[2]	3.7	54%
California Lutheran University	1070-1240[2]	3.7	69%
California State University–Fullerton*	1000-1180	3.7	62%
Dominican University of California	1070-1250[2]	3.6	52%
LeTourneau University (TX)	1110-1330[9]	3.6	54%
The Master's U. and Seminary (CA)	1040-1340	3.8	70%
Montana Technological University*	21-27[2]	3.6	58%
New Mexico Tech*	23-30	3.7	57%
Northwest Nazarene University (ID)	990-1210[2]	3.6	51%

School (State) (*Public)	SAT/ACT 25th-75th percentile ('20)	Average high school GPA ('20)	Freshmen in top 25% of class ('20)
Pacific Lutheran University (WA)	1100-1300[2]	3.7	69%
Point Loma Nazarene University (CA)	1100-1290[2]	3.6	77%
St. Edward's University (TX)	1030-1225[2]	N/A	49%
University of Dallas	1130-1350[2]	3.9	76%[5]
University of Redlands (CA)	1070-1250[2]	3.8	72%
University of St. Thomas (TX)	1005-1170[2]	3.5	50%
Westminster College (UT) (UT)	21-28[2]	3.6	54%
Whitworth University (WA)	1050-1270[2]	3.6	64%

▶ Regional Colleges

School (State) (*Public)	SAT/ACT 25th-75th percentile ('20)	Average high school GPA ('20)	Freshmen in top 25% of class ('20)
NORTH			
Maine Maritime Academy*	1000-1160	3.4	57%
SOUTH			
High Point University (NC)	1070-1240[2]	3.4	49%
Ouachita Baptist University (AR)	22-29	3.7	66%
MIDWEST			
Benedictine College (KS)	21-29[2]	N/A	43%[5]
Carthage College (WI)	20-26[2]	3.3	45%
College of the Ozarks (MO)	21-25	3.7	67%
Dordt University (IA)	22-28[2]	3.6	48%
Northwestern College (IA)	20-26[2]	3.6	42%
Taylor University (IN)	1090-1290[2]	3.8	71%
William Jewell College (MO)	20-27[2]	3.6	56%
Wisconsin Lutheran College	21-27[2]	3.5	47%
WEST			
Carroll College (MT)	22-27[2]	3.7	68%
Embry-Riddle Aero. U.–Prescott (AZ)	1140-1320[2]	N/A	59%

Methodology: To be eligible, national universities, liberal arts colleges, regional universities and regional colleges all had to be numerically ranked among the top three-quarters of their peer groups in the 2022 Best Colleges rankings. They had to admit a meaningful proportion of non-A students, as indicated by fall 2020 admissions data on SAT Evidence-based Reading and Writing and Math scores or Composite ACT scores and high school class standing. The cutoffs were: The 75th percentile for the SAT had to be less than or equal to 1,350; the 25th percentile, greater than or equal to 980. The ACT composite range: less than or equal to 30 and greater than or equal to 20. The proportion of freshmen from the top 10% of their high school class had to be less than or equal to 50% (for national universities and liberal arts colleges only); for all schools, the proportion of freshmen from the top 25% of their high school class had to be less than or equal to 80%, and greater than or equal to 40%. Average freshman retention rates for all schools had to be greater than or equal to 75%. Average high school GPA itself was not used in the calculations identifying the A-plus schools. N/A means not available.

Colgate University
MARK DIORIO – COLGATE UNIVERSITY

Find the Money

How to Get a Great Aid Package

Understanding how financial aid is doled out can help you maximize your chances – and your award

by **Farran Powell** *and* **Emma Kerr**

NEWS YOU CAN USE

WHILE THE STICKER price of a year in college can certainly be shocking, financial aid can go a long way in making that degree more affordable. In fact, income and savings are quite generously supplemented by other resources to cover college expenses, according to the 2021 Sallie Mae/Ipsos survey How America Pays for College. The survey found that for a typical family, scholarships and grants covered 25% of college costs in 2020-2021. Here are some answers to common questions about how to end up with the best possible package:

How does the process of applying work?

There are several categories of financial aid: Grants, scholarships, federal and private loans and work-study and other programs. Your first step in going after such funds is to file the Free Application for Federal Student Aid, or FAFSA. This application is used to determine your eligibility for federal aid and your "expected family contribution," or EFC, the amount your family will be expected to pay. Many state agencies and colleges and universities use the FAFSA to determine how much they'll offer as well.

The form is available for free through the Department of Education's website. Families can begin filling it out as of Oct. 1 for the following academic year. The deadline for filing the FAFSA is

June 30, though that dead-line is only for federal financial aid. Many schools that use the FAFSA to determine aid set earlier deadlines.

Some schools – mostly private colleges – rely on a supplemental form called the College Scholarship Service Profile to determine how to give out their own funds. The form is more detailed than the FAFSA, and can be time-consuming to complete. The initial submission fee for the CSS Profile is $25; each additional report costs $16. A list of schools that require the CSS Profile can be found on the website of the College Board, the organization that administers and maintains the application.

"Generally, it's more elite colleges that require the CSS Pro-

file," says Joseph Orsolini, president of College Aid Planners Inc. "Bear in mind, the CSS Profile will dig much deeper into your family's finances than the FAFSA." For instance, it takes into account assets that are excluded on the FAFSA such as the value of a family's home, small business or a grandparent-funded 529 plan.

What are the main categories of aid?

There are two types of aid: need-based and merit-based. Federal need-based aid, for instance, is determined by a family's demonstrated ability to pay for college as calculated by the FAFSA. Merit aid, on the other hand, can be awarded by an institution or private organization for a specific talent or athletic or academic ability. These awards aren't based on financial need. According to the Department of Education, most students qualify for some type of federal student aid, such as:

● **FEDERAL STUDENT LOANS.** These are fixed-interest-rate loans from the government. The interest rate for each academic year is set on July 1, and that rate is secured for the life of the loan. Currently, the interest rate is 3.73% for undergrads.

Under the direct loan program, undergraduate students can borrow subsidized or unsubsidized loans up to $31,000 in total if they're a dependent. An undergrad classified as independent can borrow up to $57,500 in total. Subsidized loans – meaning the government pays accumulating interest while you're in school – are available to students with demonstrated need. Unsubsidized loans – you're responsible for the accrued interest when repayment begins – are available to those who don't qualify for need-based aid. (For more on the benefits of federal student loans, see page 138.)

● **FEDERAL GRANTS.** This money doesn't need to be repaid. Eligibility for the most well-known grant, the Pell Grant, is based on a family's expected family contribution. Most Pell Grant recipients have an adjusted family income of $40,000 or less. The maximum Pell for the 2021-2022 school year is $6,495. A family with an EFC of zero, for example, will qualify for the full Pell.

● **WORK-STUDY.** This program provides part-time work, typically on campus, to help students cover college-related expenses. Students need to qualify through the FAFSA by showing financial need. The average amount of federal work-study funding used in 2020 was $1,847, according to the How America Pays for College report.

When it comes to state aid, "by and large, the student would have to be a resident of the state and stay within the state to attend higher ed to be able to receive grants," says Marty Somero, director of the office of financial aid at the University of Northern Colorado.

Not all schools award merit aid, but these scholarships based on academic excellence or special talent can be one way to close the gap between the cost of attendance and need-based aid. (For other possible sources of scholarship funds, see page 139.)

What should I know about financial aid deadlines?

It's important to meet colleges' aid application deadlines, which can vary considerably. The University of Florida, for example, sets its deadline as Dec. 15, which is early compared with many schools. And the university's site encourages students to apply "well before December 15 to ensure that the federal processor has time to analyze and send the results of your FAFSA to UF Student Financial Affairs." The University of Northern Colorado, by contrast, sets its deadline as March 1. Missing the deadline by one day "can cost a student $5,000 to $6,000 in free aid," Somero says.

Beyond institutional deadlines, "some states have early deadlines for state grant eligibility, and some schools may not be able to provide as generous a financial aid offer if

Denice Aguilera (in cap and gown) at home with (from left) her sister, her mother and her brother.

DENICE AGUILERA

CSU–Bakersfield
Bakersfield, California

ONE STUDENT'S STRATEGY:
Choose Community College

● **DENICE AGUILERA,** a self-described introvert, was nervous when applying to college, especially since many of her friends were heading off to California State University–Bakersfield and she wasn't. Aguilera, who lives in Bakersfield, was looking for a path

MARIANO AGUILERA

BAKERSFIELD COLLEGE
We Are
BC
CONGRATULATIONS

she is a Finish in 4 student, the Kern Promise also awarded a few hundred dollars per year for the two years she attended Bakersfield College. The program provides for priority registration at both schools, helping students get into all classes needed to graduate on time. Aguilera qualified for a Cal Grant B, and received about $1,600 a year, as well as a Student Success Completion grant of $649 a semester from the state of California for finishing her requirements at BC. She also received a Pell Grant of about $6,000 per year for those with significant need. Since her tuition was covered by the California Promise grant, she was able to use this money for additional expenses. Last spring, Aguilera graduated from Bakersfield College with an associate degree in business administration; she now is majoring in business administration with a concentration in accounting.

LOOKING AHEAD. A Pell Grant and Cal Grant B will help Aguilera pay her CSUB tuition as well, which for in-state students runs just under $11,000 annually. She is also benefiting from the MDRC SUCCESS (for Scaling Up College Completion Efforts for Student Success) Program, which provides $150 every semester if she meets monthly with her academic coach.

Aguilera lives at home, saving on living expenses, and works as a peer mentor for other students taking advantage of the Kern Promise. The introvert now acts as a leader, offering advice and answering questions as students adjust to college. While at Bakersfield College, she also tutored students and volunteered at the computer commons. She expects to graduate debt-free.

Aguilera encourages high-school students not to overlook community colleges. "It's a smaller community," she notes, and "staff, faculty and students can know you." Her plan now is to graduate with honors, become a certified public accountant, and "come back to work for Bakersfield College. I fell in love with BC. It's my home." –*Alison Murtagh*

to her degree that would be as affordable as possible — even if it meant striking out on her own. "I just tell myself, 'this is to help my family, and I'm going to do anything to take care of them,'" says Aguilera, who spent her first two years at Bakersfield College, a local community college. This fall, with the help of a program known as the Kern Promise, she, too, is a junior at the university, and she hasn't paid a cent for her education so far.

Through the Kern Promise, high school students in Kern County who attend community colleges in California are guaranteed admission to one of the California

State University system schools, as long as they meet all program requirements. Since Aguilera knew that she wanted to end up at CSUB, she took advantage of a direct partnership between Bakersfield College and the university called "Finish in 4," laying out a clear course pathway. She would be guaranteed admission at CSUB as a junior as long as she had a GPA of at least 2.0 (she had a 3.5) and had completed her associate degree following that pathway.

The California College Promise Grant covered all of her community college tuition (now about $1,325 annually). Since

Graham Webb

Washington University in St. Louis

ONE STUDENT'S STRATEGY:
Join the Army

● **JOINING THE MILITARY** hadn't occurred to Graham Webb until he happened upon the Army ROTC booth at the activity fair freshman year at WashU. "I thought it was very cool," says Webb, a second lieutenant in the Army's CyberCorps, which defends military networks and conducts electronic warfare. The Darien, Connecticut, native graduated from WashU in 2020 with a major in systems engineering.

The scholarship, which fully funds a cadet's college education in exchange for a four-year commitment in the Army (some serve in the reserves for a longer period), appealed to Webb. Mainly, it would lift a burden from his parents, who had taken out loans and remortgaged their house to cover the school's sticker price, which was about $50,000 plus over $10,000 in room and board. And there would be a "cool job" waiting when he graduated, he says.

Getting accepted proved more difficult than Webb had anticipated. He struggled in his original course of study, biomedical engineering, earning a 2.2 grade point average freshman year. (The Army requires a minimum GPA of 2.5, but in Webb's case, recruiters were looking for a 3.3 or 3.4

thanks to stiff competition for the scholarship.) Passing the physical fitness test was also a challenge. Over the course of the next year, he switched his major to systems engineering and embarked on a self-improvement program, buckling down on academics and working out regularly to get fit. His grades improved steadily, reaching a 3.79 senior year. By junior year, he was able to hike 24 miles in the mountains of New Mexico with a 45-pound backpack.

THE PAYOFF. The effort bore results when he reapplied to ROTC sophomore year. In addition to covering tuition, room and board and books, Webb received a stipend of $420 month, plus $250 per credit hour in "critical language incentive pay" for taking Mandarin, amounting to

An ROTC scholarship helped put Graham Webb through WashU.

about $1,250 a semester. He also received a $5,000 grant from a Chicago law firm for those studying engineering and Mandarin.

Now stationed in the Washington, D.C., area as a cyber operations officer for the 780th Military Intelligence Brigade, Webb feels fortunate for the way things turned out. Having to juggle his ROTC duties, including 5 a.m. workouts, military science classes and weekly labs, a summer internship at the Army Cyber Institute at the U.S. Military Academy, and informal mentoring of younger cadets, taught him time-management, organizational and leadership skills. His only regret is that he didn't apply earlier. "It's much easier to get the scholarship while you're still in high school," he says. "Otherwise you're fighting for leftover funds." **–Margaret Loftus**

ALYSSA HILKO

the application is late," says Brad Lindberg, associate vice president for enrollment and administrative services at Grinnell College in Iowa.

How do schools award aid?

Financial aid officers say that while there are many similarities between how schools award aid, each has its own unique process for arriving at awards. Two equal amounts of aid from different colleges can vary widely in how generous they actually are, for example, because one is more heavily weighted toward grants while the other emphasizes loans. Sometimes this kind of decision is influenced by how much a school wants a certain applicant to enroll.

Rob Durkle, who recently retired after serving as chief recruitment and admissions officer at Wright State University in Ohio, encourages families to ask about each school's award methodology. For example, when a school claims to meet a family's full financial need with aid, will the package include loans? A handful of institutions, including Brown University and Princeton University, package awards with no loans regardless of a family's household income.

At the University of Dayton, where Durkle previously worked, the school raises a student's financial aid each year to match any tuition increases, he says. In essence, the net price of tuition for students' freshman year will be the same as for their senior year.

It's important to compare your aid offers carefully so you have a full understanding of how much you'll have to pay out of pocket – or via loans – at each school you're considering.

How do I appeal a financial aid award?

The process of appealing an award is known as a professional judgment review, and many students are unaware that such a review is a possibility. According to a 2020 College Ave Student Loans survey conducted by Barnes & Noble College Insights, 30% of students said that, in hindsight, they would have reached out to the financial aid office to ask for more aid.

But, notes Orsolini, simply saying "I need more money" isn't the way to make your case. Families need to offer a legitimate reason for schools to re-examine their financial situation, he says.

To be successful, you'll have to demonstrate that there's been a significant change in your circumstances since you submitted the application, says Dan Blednick, senior director of college guidance at The TEAK Fellowship, a nonprofit organization that serves students from low-income families in New York City. Experts say a family will usually be asked to submit a letter summarizing the circumstance affecting their ability to pay. A qualifying circumstance might be a recent job loss, divorce or death in the family or sudden medical expenses, to name a few examples. The coronavirus pandemic has caused many students to appeal for additional aid because of illness or sudden unemployment in the family. "I would recommend trying to connect with a specific person in the college's financial aid office who is assigned to your case," Blednick says, and providing documents that reflect your a need for additional help. ●

10 Perks of Federal Student Loans

Need to borrow? Here are a few reasons to reach out to the government first

by **Farran Powell** *and* **Emma Kerr**

MOST COLLEGE STUDENTS these days take out student loans to pay for the cost of higher education. But not all terms and conditions are the same. Consider 10 benefits of taking out a federal vs. a private loan.

1. No credit history is needed. Most loans from financial institutions require a credit history, but federal student loans don't.

2. No co-signer is required. The fact that a federal student loan isn't based on a credit history means the borrower can take on the responsibility for repayment without asking a family member or friend to co-sign.

3. The loans have fixed interest rates. Federal student loan interest rates do not change over the life of the loan. Private loans can have either fixed or variable rates, which can mean higher payments should rates rise.

4. They typically have lower interest rates than private loans. For undergraduates whose new federal student loan was disbursed on or after July 1, 2021, and before July 1, 2022, the interest rate is 3.73%. Experts say private higher education loans tend to have higher interest rates because they are considered risky to the lender.

5. You may not owe interest until after college. Students with demonstrated financial need who receive a subsidized federal student loan do not pay interest as long as they are enrolled at least half-time. Rather, the government covers the interest. (Those with unsubsidized loans will owe the accrued interest when repayment begins after graduation.) Private lenders often do not offer subsidized loans, meaning students are responsible for interest from the time the loan is disbursed.

6. You have more favorable forbearance and deferment options. Applying for forbearance or deferment postpones payments. "Usually you get up to three years on federal student loans and typically with private lenders it will be around a year" unless the terms are different, says Andrew Josuweit, formerly a consultant at LendingTree, an online marketplace where borrowers can connect to lenders. The government pays the interest on subsidized federal loans during deferment.

7. You get a grace period before repayment starts. Once a student leaves college, he or she has a six-month grace period before repayment must begin. This grace period is available to students who borrowed direct subsidized loans and direct unsubsidized loans. For subsidized loans, the government pays the interest that is accruing during the grace period.

8. There are income-driven repayment options. Four income-driven repayment plans are offered under the federal student loan program. The Pay As You Earn Repayment Plan and the Revised Pay As You Earn Repayment Plan, for example, generally cap payments at 10% of the borrower's discretionary income.

9. Loans can be discharged. According to the Department of Education, if the borrower dies, the loan is canceled and the debt is discharged by the government. Experts say more private lenders are starting to offer this protection on private student loans. Federal loans can also be discharged if the borrower can prove total and permanent disability.

10. There are loan forgiveness options. The Public Service Loan Forgiveness program allows borrowers to have loans forgiven after 10 years of public service and 120 qualifying monthly payments. Loan forgiveness is also available to borrowers after they have been enrolled in an income-driven repayment plan for 20 or 25 years, depending on the plan. One caution: The forgiven debt under an income-driven plan is currently considered taxable income by the IRS. ●

GETTY IMAGES

Scholarship Strategies

There's lots of grant funding out there for those willing to search – and apply

by **Farran Powell** *and* **Emma Kerr**

WHILE UNIVERSITIES PROVIDE the bulk of scholarship awards to college students, there is also plenty of money up for grabs each year from states, employers and other institutions and private sources. To win some of that money, follow these tips.

Use a free scholarship search site. Students can take advantage of scholarship databases such as Chegg, FastWeb.com or the U.S. News Scholarship Finder to explore awards for which they are eligible. The more information a student enters, the better the odds of landing one or more scholarships, experts say. Answer all the optional questions to increase the chances of a match, especially for the lesser-known awards, advises Mark Kantrowitz, a financial aid expert and author of "How to Appeal for More College Financial Aid."

Check out what local groups are offering. Organizations, nonprofits and faith communities in a student's hometown may offer scholarships to member families or area students. Local awards are typically less competitive than national ones.

Contact colleges about institutional scholarships. It's important that prospective students not underestimate the power of institutional aid, says James W. Lewis, president of the National Society of High School Scholars. "A lot of people don't realize there are great institutions that have very generous scholarship offerings." Applying early may improve your odds.

Earn a merit scholarship. Merit scholarships are linked to academic performance and other accomplishments and are not based on need. Academic scholarships are often awarded by a school or private organization, sometimes based on GPA or performance on a standardized test such as the ACT or SAT.

Apply for scholarships based on majors. There are scholarships available for students pursuing a specific major, from education and biology to engineering. Students pursuing a career in STEM – the fields of science, technology, engineering and math – can apply for a range of awards, such as the Generation Google Scholarship, which provides undergrads and grad students studying computer science, computer engineering or a closely related technical field in the U.S. the opportunity to win $10,000.

Take advantage of employer awards. Many companies – from Taco Bell to ExxonMobil – offer scholarships to employees or their children. If a parent works for the federal government, the child may be eligible for the Federal Employee Education and Assistance Fund, a national scholarship competition.

Try for an athletic scholarship. Not all athletic scholarships are provided directly by NCAA Division I or II schools. High school athletes can also find money to support their studies through private scholarships. One example, the Foot Locker Scholar Athletes Program, offers a $20,000 scholarship to 20 student-athletes for their academic abilities and strong leadership skills in sports, school and within their communities.

Tap into your talents and passions. For students who enjoy the spotlight, there are specialized scholarships for acting, dancing and music. Musicians, for example, may send samples of their vocal or instrumental performances to competitions. Similarly, there are scholarships associated with many other types of extracurricular activities.

Students should ask themselves, "Who am I? What am I passionate about? What do I want to study? What do I want to do with my life?" Lewis suggests. "Scholarship providers are looking for highly motivated individuals with a passion for something."

Write an award-winning essay. Essay competitions with small prizes are less competitive because most students don't like applying for these scholarships, Kantrowitz says. "Consider the odds of only 10 applications for a $500 prize."

Enter a scholarship sweepstakes. One of the easiest ways to go after a scholarship is through a sweepstakes competition. Simply fill in the requested information, answer a few short questions and the application is complete. But the numbers are not in your favor. Thousands – if not millions – enter these contests, experts say. ●

GETTY IMAGES

Great Schools, Great Prices

WHICH SCHOOLS offer students the best value? The calculation used here takes into account a school's academic quality based on its Best Colleges ranking, the 2020-21 net cost of attendance for a student who received the average level of need-based financial aid, and the proportion of aid recipients who also received a scholarship or grant. The higher the quality of the program and the lower the cost, the better the deal. Only schools in the top half of their U.S. News ranking categories are included because U.S. News considers the most significant values to be among colleges that perform well academically.

▶ National Universities

Rank School (State) (*Public)	% students receiving grants based on need ('20)	% aid recipients receiving grants ('20)	Average cost after grants ('20)
1. Yale University (CT)	57%	100%	$18,826
2. Massachusetts Institute of Technology	60%	99%	$19,422
3. Harvard University (MA)	62%	100%	$20,023
4. Princeton University (NJ)	62%	100%	$23,572
5. Rice University (TX)	44%	98%	$20,513
6. Brigham Young Univ.–Provo (UT)	38%	83%	$13,790
7. Columbia University (NY)	50%	99%	$25,614
8. Vanderbilt University (TN)	48%	98%	$23,036
9. Stanford University (CA)	51%	97%	$25,218
10. U. of North Carolina–Chapel Hill*	35%	97%	$19,738
11. University of Chicago	39%	100%	$26,094
12. Gallaudet University (DC)	83%	96%	$18,443
13. Duke University (NC)	41%	99%	$26,059
14. University of Pennsylvania	44%	99%	$26,857
15. California Institute of Technology	51%	100%	$27,912
16. Johns Hopkins University (MD)	54%	100%	$28,689
17. Washington University in St. Louis	41%	98%	$26,033
18. Northwestern University (IL)	45%	98%	$28,608
19. Brown University (RI)	44%	99%	$27,850
20. Dartmouth College (NH)	50%	96%	$30,221
21. Emory University (GA)	46%	95%	$28,434
22. Cornell University (NY)	47%	97%	$31,185
23. Villanova University (PA)	41%	91%	$24,346
24. Wake Forest University (NC)	26%	97%	$26,211
25. University of Notre Dame (IN)	47%	98%	$31,318
26. University of Rochester (NY)	52%	100%	$30,792
27. Tufts University (MA)	35%	95%	$30,085
28. University of Idaho*	85%	98%	$26,509
29. Lehigh University (PA)	42%	100%	$29,364
30. Carnegie Mellon University (PA)	39%	98%	$32,309
31. University of Virginia*	37%	97%	$33,031
32. University of Michigan–Ann Arbor*	30%	83%	$30,302
33. Yeshiva University (NY)	48%	97%	$29,849
34. Mercer University (GA)	68%	99%	$27,820
35. University of Detroit Mercy	60%	98%	$24,355
36. Clark University (MA)	62%	100%	$30,310
37. University of Dayton (OH)	58%	100%	$28,549
38. Boston University	43%	99%	$33,183
39. Boston College	36%	89%	$31,900
40. Brandeis University (MA)	42%	97%	$32,934
41. Howard University (DC)	71%	83%	$29,680
42. Illinois Institute of Technology	68%	100%	$33,444
43. Valparaiso University (IN)	77%	100%	$31,851
44. Florida State University*	40%	91%	$28,177
45. Quinnipiac University (CT)	61%	98%	$30,630
46. St. John Fisher College (NY)	76%	100%	$30,411
47. Pepperdine University (CA)	54%	100%	$37,161
48. Robert Morris University (PA)	78%	98%	$30,705
49. Clarkson University (NY)	79%	100%	$37,754
50. Case Western Reserve Univ. (OH)	46%	97%	$35,903

▶ National Liberal Arts Colleges

Rank School (State) (*Public)	% students receiving grants based on need ('20)	% aid recipients receiving grants ('20)	Average cost after grants ('20)
1. Williams College (MA)	54%	100%	$15,019
2. Swarthmore College (PA)	56%	100%	$22,589
3. Pomona College (CA)	58%	100%	$22,597
4. Wellesley College (MA)	58%	99%	$23,494
5. Colby College (ME)	42%	100%	$20,715
6. Principia College (IL)	64%	100%	$18,366
7. Bowdoin College (ME)	50%	100%	$24,158
8. Davidson College (NC)	50%	100%	$23,551
9. Washington and Lee University (VA)	45%	100%	$24,486
10. Grinnell College (IA)	66%	100%	$27,978
11. College of the Atlantic (ME)	79%	97%	$19,282
12. Middlebury College (VT)	47%	97%	$24,919
13. Soka University of America (CA)	91%	100%	$28,244
14. Wesleyan University (CT)	41%	98%	$23,359
15. Hamilton College (NY)	53%	100%	$27,046
16. Earlham College (IN)	87%	100%	$22,980
17. Macalester College (MN)	66%	99%	$27,237
18. Colgate University (NY)	32%	100%	$23,647
19. Claremont McKenna College (CA)	43%	98%	$26,394
20. Wabash College (IN)	76%	99%	$24,840
21. Lake Forest College (IL)	81%	100%	$24,005
22. Carleton College (MN)	60%	100%	$30,474
23. Haverford College (PA)	45%	99%	$26,746
24. Colorado College	37%	100%	$24,504
25. University of Richmond (VA)	39%	99%	$24,715
26. Centre College (KY)	60%	100%	$22,894
27. Bard College (NY)	74%	97%	$24,969
28. Knox College (IL)	82%	100%	$25,378
29. St. Olaf College (MN)	72%	100%	$25,980
30. Vassar College (NY)	56%	100%	$29,332
31. Franklin & Marshall College (PA)	57%	100%	$26,570
32. Hollins University (VA)	75%	100%	$22,949
33. Beloit College (WI)	66%	99%	$24,176
34. Bates College (ME)	39%	100%	$26,972
35. Hanover College (IN)	75%	100%	$23,486
36. Lawrence University (WI)	64%	100%	$25,982
37. Bryn Mawr College (PA)	49%	100%	$28,309
38. Barnard College (NY)	32%	94%	$25,337
39. Kalamazoo College (MI)	70%	99%	$26,592
40. Agnes Scott College (GA)	75%	100%	$28,912

Methodology: The rankings were based on four variables: **1.** Ratio of quality to price: a school's overall score in the Best Colleges rankings divided by the net cost to a student receiving the average need-based scholarship or grant. The higher the ratio of rank to the discounted cost (tuition, fees, room and board, and other expenses less average need-based scholarship or grant), the better the value. **2.** Percentage of undergrads receiving need-based scholarships or grants during the 2020-2021 school year. **3.** Proportion of need-based aid recipients receiving a need-based scholarship or grant. **4.** Average discount: percentage of a school's total costs for 2020-2021 school year covered by the average need-based scholarship or grant to undergrads. For public institutions, 2020-2021 out-of-state tuition and percentage of out-of-state students receiving scholarships or grants were used. Only schools in the top half of their U.S. News ranking categories were considered. Ratio of quality to price accounted for 50% of the overall score; percentage of undergrads receiving need-based grants, for 20%; proportion of aid recipients receiving scholarships or grants, for 20%; and average discount, for 10%. The school with the most total weighted points became No. 1 in its category.

MAKE IT HAPPEN. Scan the QR code to apply online, download a brochure about NJIT or schedule a campus tour.

THE FUTURE IN THE MAKING.

At NJIT, we are hands-on in shaping the minds that will pursue the nation's most future-forward careers. As a top-tier public research university and national leader in STEM education, we prepare our students to drive industry transformations and make significant contributions to the world at large. From engineers to biologists, computer programmers to fighter pilots, entrepreneurs in FinTech to architects, the momentum built at NJIT is **the future in the making.**

njit.edu • Newark, NJ 07102

▶ Regional Universities

Rank School (State) (*Public)	% students receiving grants based on need ('20)	% aid recipients receiving grants ('20)	Average cost after grants ('20)
NORTH			
1. McDaniel College (MD)	81%	100%	$22,236
2. Niagara University (NY)	68%	98%	$24,724
3. Le Moyne College (NY)	79%	100%	$28,538
4. Canisius College (NY)	69%	99%	$26,421
5. St. Bonaventure University (NY)	73%	100%	$27,925
6. Geneva College (PA)	83%	100%	$23,356
7. Saint Peter's University (NJ)	87%	99%	$25,615
8. Waynesburg University (PA)	66%	84%	$22,685
9. Alfred University (NY)	83%	98%	$26,754
10. Ithaca College (NY)	68%	99%	$34,687
11. Messiah University (PA)	71%	99%	$29,781
12. Providence College (RI)	48%	99%	$39,097
13. Bentley University (MA)	44%	98%	$38,981
14. Caldwell University (NJ)	81%	100%	$26,134
15. Siena College (NY)	74%	100%	$34,402
SOUTH			
1. Berry College (GA)	71%	100%	$26,069
2. Milligan University (TN)	75%	100%	$24,140
3. Bob Jones University (SC)	73%	100%	$19,634
4. Freed-Hardeman University (TN)	71%	99%	$19,870
5. Coastal Carolina University (SC)*	19%	41%	$13,754
6. University of Montevallo (AL)*	45%	96%	$19,832
7. King University (TN)	70%	87%	$17,327
8. Western Carolina University (NC)*	40%	95%	$19,259
9. Christian Brothers University (TN)	64%	99%	$22,980
10. Rollins College (FL)	52%	100%	$34,405
11. Columbia International Univ. (SC)	80%	100%	$20,779
12. Lee University (TN)	65%	93%	$20,752
13. Stetson University (FL)	68%	99%	$31,758
14. Florida Southern College	68%	100%	$28,950
15. Mississippi Univ. for Women*	41%	77%	$16,216
MIDWEST			
1. Truman State University (MO)*	37%	95%	$21,332
2. Drury University (MO)	67%	100%	$23,228
3. St. Mary's Univ. of Minnesota	73%	99%	$22,446
4. Dominican University (IL)	79%	97%	$25,797
5. Bradley University (IL)	69%	99%	$28,824
6. Buena Vista University (IA)	87%	100%	$22,041
7. Milwaukee School of Engineering	80%	100%	$29,079
8. Univ. of Nebraska–Kearney*	40%	98%	$20,698
9. Franciscan Univ. of Steubenville (OH)	61%	99%	$24,477
10. Olivet Nazarene University (IL)	82%	100%	$21,517
11. Augustana University (SD)	61%	98%	$26,485
12. University of Evansville (IN)	65%	96%	$29,207
13. College of Saint Mary (NE)	74%	98%	$20,621
14. Hamline University (MN)	85%	100%	$28,919
15. Carroll University (WI)	76%	100%	$25,211
WEST			
1. Mills College (CA)	72%	99%	$1,699
2. Whitworth University (WA)	73%	99%	$28,672
3. Pacific Lutheran University (WA)	74%	100%	$28,037
4. University of Redlands (CA)	78%	97%	$34,479
5. St. Mary's Univ. of San Antonio	73%	99%	$25,632
6. California State U.–Los Angeles*	96%	97%	$30,111
7. St. Edward's University (TX)	72%	99%	$32,707
8. Saint Martin's University (WA)	77%	100%	$29,379

Rank School (State) (*Public)	% students receiving grants based on need ('20)	% aid recipients receiving grants ('20)	Average cost after grants ('20)
9. University of Dallas	64%	98%	$28,560
10. Houston Baptist University	76%	100%	$25,256
11. Northwest University (WA)	75%	100%	$25,318
12. Trinity University (TX)	46%	100%	$26,875
13. University of St. Thomas (TX)	67%	96%	$23,805
14. California Lutheran University	69%	99%	$34,126
15. U. of Mary Hardin-Baylor (TX)	82%	100%	$29,649

▶ Regional Colleges

Rank School (State) (*Public)	% students receiving grants based on need ('20)	% aid recipients receiving grants ('20)	Average cost after grants ('20)
NORTH			
1. Cooper Union for Adv. of Sci. & Art (NY)	60%	100%	$26,216
2. Cazenovia College (NY)	73%	100%	$16,447
3. Colby-Sawyer College (NH)	83%	100%	$28,422
4. University of Maine at Farmington*	68%	76%	$22,702
5. Elmira College (NY)	80%	100%	$26,283
6. University of Valley Forge (PA)	86%	99%	$25,573
7. SUNY College of Technology at Alfred*	39%	42%	$25,262
8. Maine Maritime Academy*	42%	68%	$38,087
9. Farmingdale State College–SUNY*	68%	92%	$30,454
10. Keene State College (NH)*	54%	86%	$33,208
SOUTH			
1. University of the Ozarks (AR)	79%	100%	$15,828
2. Blue Mountain College (MS)	78%	99%	$16,981
3. Ouachita Baptist University (AR)	62%	97%	$25,341
4. Newberry College (SC)	84%	100%	$22,275
5. Maryville College (TN)	81%	100%	$25,256
6. Alice Lloyd College (KY)	89%	100%	$17,442
7. Kentucky State University*	82%	99%	$15,802
8. Barton College (NC)	85%	100%	$23,883
9. Flagler College (FL)	54%	98%	$26,401
10. Huntingdon College (AL)	77%	100%	$24,694
MIDWEST			
1. College of the Ozarks (MO)	65%	72%	$6,742
2. Marietta College (OH)	81%	98%	$19,915
3. Hiram College (OH)	87%	100%	$20,074
4. Ohio Northern University	79%	100%	$24,284
5. Heidelberg University (OH)	86%	99%	$22,733
6. Goshen College (IN)	77%	100%	$24,111
7. Loras College (IA)	79%	100%	$23,416
8. Northland College (WI)	79%	99%	$23,096
9. Bluffton University (OH)	85%	99%	$23,360
10. Hastings College (NE)	79%	100%	$23,927
WEST			
1. Texas Lutheran University	79%	97%	$23,335
2. Carroll College (MT)	62%	99%	$27,815
3. Oral Roberts University (OK)	68%	99%	$23,833
4. McMurry University (TX)	84%	99%	$24,622
5. Warner Pacific University (OR)	67%	79%	$22,743
6. William Jessup University (CA)	70%	94%	$31,005
7. Howard Payne University (TX)	92%	100%	$23,652
8. Lewis-Clark State College (ID)*	79%	93%	$23,305
9. University of Montana Western*	78%	100%	$24,601
10. Oklahoma Baptist University	62%	82%	$35,617

FIND THE
Money

The Payback Picture

RISING TUITION and limited financial aid mean borrowing may be necessary to earn a degree. U.S. News has compiled lists of schools whose students have graduated carrying the heaviest and lightest debt loads. Because of the availabilty of federal data, comparisons pertain only to loans from the federal government – a significant majority of student borrowing. Private loans, state and local government loans and loans to parents (like Parent PLUS loans) were not included. The first data column is the percentage of first-time, full-time undergrads who received federal loans during the 2018-2019 academic year. The second column shows the 50th percentile amount of cumulative borrowing across 2018 and 2019 graduates who incurred debt.

MOST DEBT

▶ National Universities

School (State) (*Public)	% undergrads with loans	Median debt of graduates
Colorado Technical University	76%	$31,250
Jackson State University (MS)*	67%	$30,488
Texas Southern University*	77%	$29,531
Cardinal Stritch University (WI)	70%	$29,500
Morgan State University (MD)*	76%	$29,473
Barry University (FL)	71%	$28,500
North Carolina A&T State Univ.*	82%	$27,706
Central Michigan University*	77%	$27,000
Clark Atlanta University	87%	$27,000
Duquesne University (PA)	70%	$27,000
Gannon University (PA)	71%	$27,000
Husson University (ME)	84%	$27,000
Immaculata University (PA)	81%	$27,000
Lindenwood University (MO)	62%	$27,000
Mary Baldwin University (VA)	80%	$27,000
Misericordia University (PA)	80%	$27,000
Robert Morris University (PA)	73%	$27,000
Rochester Inst. of Technology (NY)	68%	$27,000
Syracuse University (NY)	43%	$27,000
Tennessee State University*	79%	$27,000
University of Hartford (CT)	76%	$27,000
Univ. of Maryland Eastern Shore*	68%	$27,000
University of New Hampshire*	68%	$27,000
University of Saint Joseph (CT)	81%	$27,000
University of the Incarnate Word (TX)	74%	$27,000
Valparaiso University (IN)	56%	$27,000
Widener University (PA)	78%	$27,000
Worcester Polytechnic Inst. (MA)	56%	$27,000

▶ National Liberal Arts Colleges

School (State) (*Public)	% undergrads with loans	Median debt of graduates
Lane College (TN)	90%	$35,063
Tougaloo College (MS)	67%	$34,037
Bethune-Cookman University (FL)	86%	$32,750
Allen University (SC)	91%	$32,530
Stillman College (AL)	85%	$32,500
Chowan University (NC)	91%	$32,414
Dillard University (LA)	88%	$32,000
Talladega College (AL)	65%	$31,990
Bennett College (NC)	93%	$31,000
Johnson C. Smith University (NC)	83%	$31,000
Virginia Union University	78%	$30,500
Bloomfield College (NJ)	84%	$27,499

▶ Regional Universities

School (State) (*Public)	% undergrads with loans	Median debt of graduates
NORTH		
Lincoln University (PA)*	80%	$30,855
Trinity Washington University (DC)	58%	$29,545
Albertus Magnus College (CT)	85%	$29,250
Post University (CT)	76%	$28,757
Cedar Crest College (PA)	85%	$28,750
SOUTH		
Everglades University (FL)	61%	$40,659
Grambling State University (LA)*	92%	$37,192
Fort Valley State University (GA)*	87%	$33,560
Alabama A&M University*	71%	$33,375
Alabama State University*	78%	$32,000
MIDWEST		
Chicago State University*	93%	$32,000
DeVry University (IL)	92%	$30,500
Alverno College (WI)	77%	$29,313
Ohio Christian University	76%	$29,037
Kettering University (MI)	62%	$28,000
WEST		
Academy of Art University (CA)	44%	$31,000
Prairie View A&M University (TX)*	74%	$29,000
Woodbury University (CA)	64%	$28,750
Mid-America Christian University (OK)	65%	$28,109
Colorado Christian University	52%	$28,001

▶ Regional Colleges

School (State) (*Public)	% undergrads with loans	Median debt of graduates
NORTH		
Wesley College (DE)	86%	$31,000
The College of Westchester (NY)	88%	$27,875
SOUTH		
Benedict College (SC)	75%	$36,000
Livingstone College (NC)	88%	$35,000
Saint Augustine's University (NC)	86%	$35,000
Paine College (GA)	91%	$34,949
Shaw University (NC)	89%	$34,315
MIDWEST		
Martin University (IN)	95%	$45,222
Harris-Stowe State University (MO)*	78%	$31,688
Central State University (OH)*	80%	$31,000
Lincoln University (MO)*	84%	$29,750
WEST		
Humphreys University (CA)	40%	$31,334
Bacone College (OK)	66%	$31,000
Texas College	79%	$31,000
University of Silicon Valley (CA)	72%	$31,000
Jarvis Christian College (TX)	78%	$29,406

Note: Student debt data are from the U.S. Department of Education College Scorecard.

▶ **More** @ usnews.com/bestcolleges

BEST COLLEGES **143**

LEAST DEBT

▶ National Universities

School (State) (*Public)	% undergrads with loans	Median debt of graduates
Princeton University (NJ)	4%	$10,750
California Institute of Technology	5%	$11,242
CUNY–City College*	7%	$11,500
Stanford University (CA)	7%	$11,750
Rice University (TX)	14%	$11,989
Brigham Young Univ.–Provo (UT)	12%	$12,000
Massachusetts Institute of Technology	9%	$12,500
Alliant International University (CA)	52%	$12,563
Duke University (NC)	20%	$12,582
University of Texas–Rio Grande Valley*	21%	$12,750
University of California–Davis*	31%	$13,000
Yale University (CT)	7%	$13,060
University of California–Berkeley*	21%	$13,478
Harvard University (MA)	2%	$13,750
Utah State University*	27%	$14,500
Cornell University (NY)	35%	$14,661
Vanderbilt University (TN)	11%	$14,962
California State University–Fresno*	25%	$14,974
Brown University (RI)	19%	$15,000
Dartmouth College (NH)	23%	$15,000
Touro College (NY)	19%	$15,000
University of California–Los Angeles*	29%	$15,000
University of California–Santa Barbara*	35%	$15,000
University of Washington*	25%	$15,000
University of North Carolina–Chapel Hill*	26%	$15,400

▶ National Liberal Arts Colleges

School (State) (*Public)	% undergrads with loans	Median debt of graduates
Berea College (KY)	10%	$4,833
Pomona College (CA)	13%	$9,990
Wellesley College (MA)	21%	$11,000
Haverford College (PA)	18%	$12,106
Amherst College (MA)	15%	$13,500
Williams College (MA)	19%	$13,500
Bates College (ME)	18%	$13,625
Scripps College (CA)	32%	$14,000
Middlebury College (VT)	24%	$14,016
Claremont McKenna College (CA)	22%	$15,000
Whitman College (WA)	47%	$15,500
Carleton College (MN)	41%	$15,538
New College of Florida*	32%	$15,719
Colgate University (NY)	21%	$15,750
Bowdoin College (ME)	16%	$15,831
Wesleyan University (CT)	23%	$16,103
Hamilton College (NY)	39%	$16,500
Pitzer College (CA)	34%	$16,750
Grinnell College (IA)	39%	$17,500
University of Minnesota Morris*	55%	$17,866
University of Maine–Machias*	46%	$17,920
Thomas Aquinas College (CA)	69%	$18,000
Sterling College (VT)	62%	$18,133
Barnard College (NY)	30%	$18,150
University of Virginia–Wise*	41%	$18,350

▶ Regional Universities

School (State) (*Public)	% undergrads with loans	Median debt of graduates
NORTH		
CUNY–Lehman College*	5%	$10,830
CUNY–John Jay Col. of Crim. Justice*	6%	$11,000
CUNY–Baruch College*	6%	$11,500
CUNY–Brooklyn College*	5%	$11,500
CUNY–Queens College*	5%	$12,254
SOUTH		
Mississippi Univ. for Women*	64%	$15,000
University of West Florida*	33%	$17,250
University of Arkansas–Monticello*	57%	$17,500
Lynn University (FL)	35%	$17,556
Lindsey Wilson College (KY)	64%	$17,624
MIDWEST		
Northeastern Illinois University*	26%	$14,662
MidAmerica Nazarene University (KS)	71%	$15,625
Siena Heights University (MI)	74%	$18,463
Indiana University East*	44%	$18,519
Waldorf University (IA)	77%	$18,810
WEST		
Southern Utah University*	57%	$12,700
California State U.–Monterey Bay*	45%	$13,500
California State University–Los Angeles*	17%	$13,750
New Mexico Highlands University*	25%	$13,896
California State University–Dominguez Hills*	20%	$14,000

▶ Regional Colleges

School (State) (*Public)	% undergrads with loans	Median debt of graduates
NORTH		
Boricua College (NY)	6%	$5,500
CUNY–Medgar Evers College*	7%	$10,124
CUNY–York College*	3%	$10,315
CUNY–New York City Col. of Tech.*	4%	$10,354
U.S. Merchant Marine Acad. (NY)*	10%	$12,000
SOUTH		
Florida Polytechnic University*	32%	$7,500
Seminole State College of Florida*	16%	$11,000
Florida College	64%	$12,000
Dalton State College (GA)*	19%	$13,750
West Virginia University–Parkersburg*	34%	$14,787
MIDWEST		
Ranken Technical College (MO)	69%	$12,000
Vincennes University (IN)*	55%	$13,000
Cottey College (MO)	58%	$16,317
Maranatha Baptist University (WI)	41%	$16,375
Lincoln College (IL)	79%	$17,500
WEST		
Snow College (UT)*	63%	$6,687
Brigham Young University–Hawaii	17%	$9,453
Northern New Mexico College*	3%	$9,520
Colorado Mountain College*	35%	$11,000
University of Antelope Valley (CA)	37%	$11,212

2022 EDITION

DIRECTORY

OF

COLLEGES

AND

UNIVERSITIES

INSIDE

The latest facts and figures on over
1,600 American colleges and universities,
including schools' U.S. News rankings

New data on tuition, admissions, the
makeup of the undergraduate student body,
popular majors and financial aid

Statistical profiles of freshman classes, including entrance
exam scores and high school class standing

Using the Directory

How to interpret the statistics in the following entries on more than 1,600 American colleges and universities – and how to get the most out of them

THE SNAPSHOTS OF colleges and universities presented here, alphabetized by state, contain a wealth of information on everything from the most popular majors offered to the stats on the freshman class that arrived in the fall of 2020. The statistics were collected in 2021 and are as of Aug. 16, 2021; they are explained in detail below. A school whose name has been footnoted with a 1 did not return the U.S. News statistical questionnaire, so limited data appear; a 7 means the school declined to have an official verify the data's accuracy. If a college did not reply to a particular question, you'll see N/A, for "not available." Our online directory allows you to search our database for schools based on major, location and other criteria (go to usnews.com/collegesearch). To find a school of interest in the rankings tables, consult the index at the back of the book.

EXAMPLE

Fairfield University

Fairfield CT

1 — (203) 254-4100

2 — **U.S. News ranking:**
Reg. U. (N), No. 3

3 — **Website:** www.fairfield.edu

4 — **Admissions email:**
admis@fairfield.edu

5 — **Private;** founded 1942
Affiliation: Roman Catholic

6 — **Freshman admissions:** more selective; 2020-2021: 12,586 applied, 7,065 accepted. Neither SAT nor ACT required. SAT 25/75 percentile: 1190-1340. High school rank: 40% in top tenth, 70% in top quarter, 95% in top half

7 — **Early decision deadline:** 11/15, notification date: 12/15
Early action deadline: 11/1, notification date: 12/20

8 — **Application deadline (fall):** 1/15

9 — **Undergraduate student body:** 4,231 full time, 123 part time; 42% male, 58% female; 0% American Indian, 3% Asian, 2% black, 7% Hispanic, 2% multiracial, 0% Pacific Islander, 78% white, 3% international; 24% from in state; 72% live on campus; N/A of students in fraternities, N/A in sororities

10 — **Most popular majors:** 41% Business, Management, Marketing, and Related Support Services, 16% Health Professions and Related Programs, 9% Communication, Journalism, and Related Programs, 9% Social Sciences, 6% Psychology

11 — **Expenses:** 2021-2022: $52,870; room/board: $16,110

12 — **Financial aid:** (203) 254-4000; 37% of undergrads determined to have financial need; average aid package $31,290

1. TELEPHONE NUMBER

This number reaches the admissions office.

2. U.S. NEWS RANKING

The abbreviation indicates which category of institution the school falls into: National Universities (Nat. U.), National Liberal Arts Colleges (Nat. Lib. Arts), Regional Universities (Reg. U.), or Regional Colleges (Reg. Coll.). The regional universities and regional colleges are further divided by region: North (N), South (S), Midwest (Mid. W.), and West (W). "Business" refers to business specialty schools, and "Engineering" refers to engineering specialty schools. "Arts" refers to schools devoted to the fine and performing arts.

Next, you'll find the school's 2022 rank within its category. Schools falling in the top three-fourths of their categories are ranked numerically. (Those ranked in the bottom 25% of their category are listed alphabetically in the ranking tables.) You cannot compare ranks of schools in different categories; U.S. News ranks schools only against their peers. Specialty schools that focus on business, engineering and the arts aren't ranked. Also unranked are schools with fewer than 200 students, those with a high percentage of older or part-time students, those that don't admit freshmen and those that didn't have a six-year bachelor's degree graduation rate.

3. WEBSITE

Visit the school's website to research programs, take a virtual tour, or submit an application.

4. ADMISSIONS EMAIL

You can use this email address to request information or to submit an application.

5. TYPE/AFFILIATION

Is the school public, private or for-profit? Affiliated with a religious denomination?

6. FRESHMAN ADMISSIONS

How competitive is the admissions process at this institution? Schools are designated "most selective," "more selective," "selective," "less selective" or "least selective." The more selective a school, the harder it will probably be to get in. All of the admissions statistics reported are for the class that entered in the fall of 2020. The 25/75 percentiles for the SAT Evidence-Based Reading and Writing and Math or ACT Composite scores show the range in which half the students scored: 25% of students scored at or below the lower end, and 75% scored at or below the upper end. If a school reported the averages and not the 25/75 percentiles, the average score is listed. The test score that is published represents the test that the greatest percentage of entering students took.

7. EARLY DECISION/ EARLY ACTION DEADLINES

Applicants who plan to take the early decision route to fall 2022 enrollment will have to meet the deadline listed for the school. If the school offers an early action option, the application deadline and notification date are also shown.

8. APPLICATION DEADLINE

The date shown is the regular admission deadline for the academic year starting in the fall of 2022. "Rolling" means the school makes admissions decisions as applications come in until the class is filled.

9. UNDERGRADUATE STUDENT BODY

This section gives the breakdown of full-time vs. part-time students and male and female enrollment, the ethnic makeup of the student body, proportions of in-state and out-of-state students, percentage living on campus, and percentage in fraternities and sororities. Figures are for 2020-2021.

10. MOST POPULAR MAJORS

The five most popular majors appear, along with the percentage majoring in each among 2020 graduates with a bachelor's degree.

11. EXPENSES

The first figure represents tuition (including required fees); next is total room and board. Figures are for the 2021-2022 academic year; if data are not available, we use figures for the 2020-2021 academic year. For public schools, we list both in-state and out-of-state tuition.

12. FINANCIAL AID

The percentage of undergrads determined to have financial need and the amount of the average package (grants, loans and jobs) in 2020-2021. We also provide the phone number of the financial aid office.

ALABAMA

Alabama A&M University[7]
Normal AL
(256) 372-5245
U.S. News ranking: Reg. U. (S), second tier
Website: www.aamu.edu/admissions/undergraduateadmissions/pages/default.aspx
Admissions email: admissions@aamu.edu
Public; founded 1875
Freshman admissions: less selective; 2020-2021: 9,850 applied, 8,831 accepted. Either SAT or ACT required. ACT 25/75 percentile: 15-19. High school rank: N/A
Early decision deadline: N/A, notification date: N/A
Early action deadline: N/A, notification date: N/A
Application deadline (fall): 7/15
Undergraduate student body: 4,663 full time, 430 part time
Most popular majors: 13% Biology/Biological Sciences, General, 7% Business Administration and Management, General, 7% Mechanical Engineering, 6% Criminal Justice/Law Enforcement Administration, 6% Social Work
Expenses: 2020-2021: $10,024 in state, $18,634 out of state; room/board: N/A
Financial aid: (256) 372-5400

Alabama State University
Montgomery AL
(334) 229-4291
U.S. News ranking: Reg. U. (S), No. 70
Website: www.alasu.edu
Admissions email: admissions@alasu.edu
Public; founded 1867
Freshman admissions: less selective; 2020-2021: 6,989 applied, 6,912 accepted. Either SAT or ACT required. ACT 25/75 percentile: 14-20. High school rank: 8% in top tenth, 32% in top quarter, 40% in top half
Early decision deadline: N/A, notification date: N/A
Early action deadline: N/A, notification date: N/A
Application deadline (fall): 7/30
Undergraduate student body: 3,289 full time, 325 part time; 36% male, 64% female; 0% American Indian, 0% Asian, 93% black, 1% Hispanic, 1% multiracial, 0% Pacific Islander, 2% white, 2% international; 64% from in state; N/A live on campus; 3% of students in fraternities, 5% in sororities
Most popular majors: Information not available
Expenses: 2021-2022: $11,068 in state, $19,396 out of state; room/board: $6,050
Financial aid: (334) 229-4712; 95% of undergrads determined to have financial need; average aid package $23,039

Auburn University
Auburn AL
(334) 844-6425
U.S. News ranking: Nat. U., No. 99
Website: www.auburn.edu
Admissions email: admissions@auburn.edu
Public; founded 1856
Freshman admissions: more selective; 2020-2021: 17,946 applied, 15,266 accepted. Either SAT or ACT required. ACT 25/75 percentile: 25-31. High school rank: 34% in top tenth, 64% in top quarter, 91% in top half
Early decision deadline: N/A, notification date: N/A
Early action deadline: 11/1, notification date: 12/1
Application deadline (fall): 2/3
Undergraduate student body: 22,458 full time, 2,047 part time; 51% male, 49% female; 0% American Indian, 2% Asian, 5% black, 4% Hispanic, 3% multiracial, 0% Pacific Islander, 81% white, 5% international; 61% from in state; 19% live on campus; 24% of students in fraternities, 45% in sororities
Most popular majors: 25% Business, Management, Marketing, and Related Support Services, 20% Engineering, 11% Biological and Biomedical Sciences, 5% Communication, Journalism, and Related Programs, 4% Health Professions and Related Programs
Expenses: 2021-2022: $11,796 in state, $31,956 out of state; room/board: $13,778
Financial aid: (334) 844-4634; 33% of undergrads determined to have financial need; average aid package $11,987

Auburn University at Montgomery
Montgomery AL
(334) 244-3615
U.S. News ranking: Reg. U. (S), No. 70
Website: www.aum.edu
Admissions email: admissions@aum.edu
Public; founded 1967
Freshman admissions: selective; 2020-2021: 4,606 applied, 4,401 accepted. Either SAT or ACT required. ACT 25/75 percentile: 18-23. High school rank: 15% in top tenth, 44% in top quarter, 82% in top half
Early decision deadline: N/A, notification date: N/A
Early action deadline: N/A, notification date: N/A
Application deadline (fall): 8/1
Undergraduate student body: 3,374 full time, 1,001 part time; 34% male, 66% female; 0% American Indian, 2% Asian, 45% black, 1% Hispanic, 4% multiracial, 0% Pacific Islander, 42% white, 4% international; 95% from in state; 23% live on campus; N/A of students in fraternities, N/A in sororities
Most popular majors: 27% Health Professions and Related Programs, 17% Business, Management, Marketing, and Related Support Services, 8% Education, 7%

Computer and Information Sciences and Support Services, 7% Multi/Interdisciplinary Studies
Expenses: 2021-2022: $8,860 in state, $18,820 out of state; room/board: $6,980
Financial aid: (334) 244-3571; 71% of undergrads determined to have financial need; average aid package $3,352

Birmingham-Southern College
Birmingham AL
(205) 226-4696
U.S. News ranking: Nat. Lib. Arts, No. 128
Website: www.bsc.edu
Admissions email: admiss@bsc.edu
Private; founded 1856
Affiliation: United Methodist
Freshman admissions: more selective; 2020-2021: 2,460 applied, 1,487 accepted. Neither SAT nor ACT required. ACT 25/75 percentile: 22-28. High school rank: 18% in top tenth, 47% in top quarter, 73% in top half
Early decision deadline: 11/1, notification date: 12/1
Early action deadline: 11/15, notification date: 12/15
Application deadline (fall): rolling
Undergraduate student body: 1,126 full time, 3 part time; 46% male, 54% female; 0% American Indian, 2% Asian, 14% black, 5% Hispanic, 1% multiracial, 0% Pacific Islander, 77% white, 1% international; 63% from in state; 73% live on campus; 40% of students in fraternities, 50% in sororities
Most popular majors: 20% Business Administration and Management, General, 10% Biology/Biological Sciences, General, 7% Chiropractic, 7% Psychology, General, 7% Social Sciences, General
Expenses: 2021-2022: $20,100; room/board: $13,550
Financial aid: (205) 226-4688; 51% of undergrads determined to have financial need; average aid package $17,722

Faulkner University[1]
Montgomery AL
(334) 386-7200
U.S. News ranking: Reg. U. (S), second tier
Website: www.faulkner.edu
Admissions email: admissions@faulkner.edu
Private; founded 1942
Affiliation: Churches of Christ
Application deadline (fall): 8/1
Undergraduate student body: 3,374 full time, 1,001 part time; 34% male, 66% female; 0% American Indian, 2% Asian, 45% black, 1% Hispanic, 4% multiracial, 0% Pacific Islander, 42% white, 4% international; 95% from in state; 23% live on campus; N/A of students in fraternities, N/A in sororities
Most popular majors: 27% Health Professions and Related Programs, 17% Business, Management, Marketing, and Related Support Services, 8% Education, 7%

Huntingdon College
Montgomery AL
(334) 833-4497
U.S. News ranking: Reg. Coll. (S), No. 13
Website: www.huntingdon.edu
Admissions email: admission@hawks.huntingdon.edu

Private; founded 1854
Affiliation: United Methodist
Freshman admissions: selective; 2020-2021: 2,129 applied, 1,158 accepted. Neither SAT nor ACT required. ACT 25/75 percentile: 19-24. High school rank: 14% in top tenth, 38% in top quarter, 75% in top half
Early decision deadline: N/A, notification date: N/A
Early action deadline: N/A, notification date: N/A
Application deadline (fall): rolling
Undergraduate student body: 789 full time, 131 part time; 50% male, 50% female; N/A American Indian, N/A Asian, N/A black, N/A Hispanic, N/A multiracial, N/A Pacific Islander, N/A white, N/A international
Most popular majors: Information not available
Expenses: 2021-2022: $27,900; room/board: $10,460
Financial aid: (334) 833-4428; 77% of undergrads determined to have financial need; average aid package $19,076

Jacksonville State University[1]
Jacksonville AL
(256) 782-5268
U.S. News ranking: Reg. U. (S), No. 77
Website: www.jsu.edu
Admissions email: info@jsu.edu
Public; founded 1883
Application deadline (fall): rolling
Undergraduate student body: N/A full time, N/A part time
Expenses: 2020-2021: $11,120 in state, $20,840 out of state; room/board: $8,110
Financial aid: (256) 782-5006

Judson College[1]
Marion AL
(800) 447-9472
U.S. News ranking: Nat. Lib. Arts, second tier
Website: www.judson.edu/
Admissions email: admissions@judson.edu
Private; founded 1838
Affiliation: Southern Baptist
Application deadline (fall): rolling
Undergraduate student body: N/A full time, N/A part time
Expenses: 2020-2021: $18,640; room/board: $11,380
Financial aid: N/A

Miles College[1]
Birmingham AL
(205) 929-1000
U.S. News ranking: Reg. Coll. (S), second tier
Website: www.miles.edu
Admissions email: admissions@mail.miles.edu
Private
Application deadline (fall): N/A
Undergraduate student body: N/A full time, N/A part time
Expenses: 2020-2021: $12,714; room/board: $7,348
Financial aid: N/A

Oakwood University[1]
Huntsville AL
(256) 726-7356
U.S. News ranking: Reg. Coll. (S), No. 41
Website: www.oakwood.edu
Admissions email: admissions@oakwood.edu
Private; founded 1896
Affiliation: Seventh Day Adventist
Application deadline (fall): N/A
Undergraduate student body: N/A full time, N/A part time
Expenses: 2020-2021: $19,990; room/board: $9,374
Financial aid: N/A

Samford University
Birmingham AL
(205) 726-2011
U.S. News ranking: Nat. U., No. 136
Website: www.samford.edu
Admissions email: admission@samford.edu
Private; founded 1841
Affiliation: Baptist
Freshman admissions: more selective; 2020-2021: 3,867 applied, 3,248 accepted. Either SAT or ACT required. ACT 25/75 percentile: 23-29. High school rank: 29% in top tenth, 57% in top quarter, 85% in top half
Early decision deadline: N/A, notification date: N/A
Early action deadline: N/A, notification date: N/A
Application deadline (fall): 5/1
Undergraduate student body: 3,501 full time, 75 part time; 32% male, 68% female; 0% American Indian, 1% Asian, 6% black, 4% Hispanic, 2% multiracial, 0% Pacific Islander, 86% white, 1% international; 30% from in state; 61% live on campus; 35% of students in fraternities, 61% in sororities
Most popular majors: 31% Health Professions and Related Programs, 21% Business, Management, Marketing, and Related Support Services, 9% Communication, Journalism, and Related Programs, 5% Family and Consumer Sciences/Human Sciences, 5% Visual and Performing Arts
Expenses: 2021-2022: $35,360; room/board: $11,260
Financial aid: (205) 726-2905; 40% of undergrads determined to have financial need; average aid package $23,186

Spring Hill College
Mobile AL
(251) 380-3030
U.S. News ranking: Nat. Lib. Arts, second tier
Website: www.shc.edu
Admissions email: admit@shc.edu
Private; founded 1830
Affiliation: Roman Catholic
Freshman admissions: selective; 2020-2021: 2,736 applied, 1,479 accepted. Neither SAT nor ACT required. ACT 25/75 percentile: 20-25. High school rank: 24% in top tenth, 51% in top quarter, 80% in top half
Early decision deadline: N/A, notification date: N/A

Early action deadline: N/A, notification date: N/A
Application deadline (fall): 7/15
Undergraduate student body: 1,034 full time, 27 part time; 39% male, 61% female; 1% American Indian, 2% Asian, 14% black, 6% Hispanic, 2% multiracial, 0% Pacific Islander, 65% white, 5% international; N/A from in state; 66% live on campus; N/A of students in fraternities, N/A in sororities
Most popular majors: 28% Business, Management, Marketing, and Related Support Services, 17% Health Professions and Related Programs, 12% Foreign Languages, Literatures, and Linguistics
Expenses: 2021-2022: $21,100; room/board: $10,800
Financial aid: (800) 548-7886; 77% of undergrads determined to have financial need; average aid package $41,472

Stillman College
Tuscaloosa AL
(205) 366-8817
U.S. News ranking: Nat. Lib. Arts, second tier
Website: www.stillman.edu
Admissions email: admissions@stillman.edu
Private; founded 1876
Affiliation: Presbyterian Church (USA)
Freshman admissions: less selective; 2020-2021: 1,230 applied, 683 accepted. Either SAT or ACT required. SAT 25/75 percentile: N/A. High school rank: N/A
Early decision deadline: N/A, notification date: N/A
Early action deadline: N/A, notification date: N/A
Application deadline (fall): rolling
Undergraduate student body: 650 full time, 62 part time; 46% male, 54% female; N/A American Indian, N/A Asian, N/A black, N/A Hispanic, N/A multiracial, N/A Pacific Islander, N/A white, N/A international
Most popular majors: 21% Business/Commerce, General, 13% Physical Education Teaching and Coaching, 10% Psychology, General, 9% Biology/Biological Sciences, General, 8% Corrections and Criminal Justice, Other
Expenses: 2021-2022: $11,025; room/board: $8,840
Financial aid: (205) 366-8817

Talladega College[1]
Talladega AL
(256) 761-6235
U.S. News ranking: Nat. Lib. Arts, second tier
Website: www.talladega.edu
Admissions email: admissions@talladega.edu
Private; founded 1867
Affiliation: United Church of Christ
Application deadline (fall): N/A
Undergraduate student body: N/A full time, N/A part time
Expenses: 2020-2021: $13,571; room/board: $6,704
Financial aid: (256) 761-6237

Troy University
Troy AL
(334) 670-3179
U.S. News ranking: Reg. U. (S), No. 44
Website: www.troy.edu
Admissions email: admit@troy.edu
Public; founded 1887
Freshman admissions: selective; 2020-2021: 7,018 applied, 6,487 accepted. Either SAT or ACT required. ACT 25/75 percentile: 18-25. High school rank: N/A
Early decision deadline: N/A, notification date: N/A
Early action deadline: N/A, notification date: N/A
Application deadline (fall): rolling
Undergraduate student body: 8,208 full time, 4,504 part time; 37% male, 63% female; 0% American Indian, 1% Asian, 32% black, 4% Hispanic, 4% multiracial, 0% Pacific Islander, 52% white, 2% international; 68% from in state; 14% live on campus; 10% of students in fraternities, 11% in sororities
Most popular majors: 12% Business Administration and Management, General, 12% Psychology, General, 8% Criminal Justice/Safety Studies, 6% Computer and Information Sciences, General, 5% Social Work
Expenses: 2021-2022: $11,640 in state, $23,280 out of state; room/board: $7,599
Financial aid: (334) 808-6332; 64% of undergrads determined to have financial need; average aid package $3,090

Tuskegee University
Tuskegee AL
(334) 727-8500
U.S. News ranking: Reg. U. (S), No. 17
Website: www.tuskegee.edu
Admissions email: admissions@tuskegee.edu
Private; founded 1881
Freshman admissions: selective; 2020-2021: 11,435 applied, 6,933 accepted. Either SAT or ACT required. ACT 25/75 percentile: 19-27. High school rank: 16% in top tenth, 43% in top quarter, 77% in top half
Early decision deadline: N/A, notification date: N/A
Early action deadline: N/A, notification date: N/A
Application deadline (fall): rolling
Undergraduate student body: 2,170 full time, 110 part time; 36% male, 64% female; 0% American Indian, 1% Asian, 91% black, 2% Hispanic, 0% multiracial, 1% Pacific Islander, 0% white, 0% international
Most popular majors: 7% Animal Sciences, General, 7% Mechanical Engineering, 6% Biology/Biological Sciences, General, 4% Aerospace, Aeronautical and Astronautical/Space Engineering, 4% Electrical and Electronics Engineering
Expenses: 2021-2022: $22,679; room/board: $9,844
Financial aid: (334) 727-8088; 97% of undergrads determined to have financial need; average aid package $24,500

University of Alabama
Tuscaloosa AL
(205) 348-5666
U.S. News ranking: Nat. U., No. 148
Website: www.ua.edu
Admissions email: admissions@ua.edu
Public; founded 1831
Freshman admissions: more selective; 2020-2021: 39,560 applied, 31,804 accepted. Either SAT or ACT required. ACT 25/75 percentile: 23-31. High school rank: 45% in top tenth, 65% in top quarter, 86% in top half
Early decision deadline: N/A, notification date: N/A
Early action deadline: N/A, notification date: N/A
Application deadline (fall): rolling
Undergraduate student body: 27,750 full time, 3,920 part time; 44% male, 56% female; 0% American Indian, 1% Asian, 10% black, 5% Hispanic, 4% multiracial, 0% Pacific Islander, 77% white, 2% international; 41% from in state; 25% live on campus; 27% of students in fraternities, 40% in sororities
Most popular majors: 30% Business, Management, Marketing, and Related Support Services, 12% Engineering, 9% Communication, Journalism, and Related Programs, 8% Health Professions and Related Programs, 7% Family and Consumer Sciences/Human Sciences
Expenses: 2021-2022: $11,620 in state, $31,090 out of state; room/board: $11,012
Financial aid: (205) 348-6756; 42% of undergrads determined to have financial need; average aid package $15,008

University of Alabama at Birmingham
Birmingham AL
(205) 934-8221
U.S. News ranking: Nat. U., No. 148
Website: www.uab.edu
Admissions email: chooseuab@uab.edu
Public; founded 1969
Freshman admissions: more selective; 2020-2021: 9,817 applied, 6,547 accepted. Either SAT or ACT required. ACT 25/75 percentile: 22-30. High school rank: 29% in top tenth, 56% in top quarter, 85% in top half
Early decision deadline: N/A, notification date: N/A
Early action deadline: N/A, notification date: N/A
Application deadline (fall): rolling
Undergraduate student body: 10,402 full time, 3,476 part time; 38% male, 62% female; 0% American Indian, 7% Asian, 24% black, 6% Hispanic, 5% multiracial, 0% Pacific Islander, 55% white, 2% international; N/A from in state; 19% live on campus; 3% of students in fraternities, 5% in sororities
Most popular majors: 24% Health Professions and Related Programs, 18% Business, Management, Marketing, and Related Support

Services, 10% Biological and Biomedical Sciences, 7% Psychology, 6% Education
Expenses: 2021-2022: $10,710 in state, $25,380 out of state; room/board: N/A
Financial aid: (205) 934-8223; 56% of undergrads determined to have financial need; average aid package $7,007

University of Alabama–Huntsville
Huntsville AL
(256) 824-6070
U.S. News ranking: Nat. U., No. 263
Website: www.uah.edu/
Admissions email: admissions@uah.edu
Public; founded 1969
Freshman admissions: more selective; 2020-2021: 5,793 applied, 4,467 accepted. Either SAT or ACT required. ACT 25/75 percentile: 24-31. High school rank: 33% in top tenth, 63% in top quarter, 87% in top half
Early decision deadline: N/A, notification date: N/A
Early action deadline: N/A, notification date: N/A
Application deadline (fall): 8/17
Undergraduate student body: 6,730 full time, 1,297 part time; 59% male, 41% female; 1% American Indian, 4% Asian, 9% black, 6% Hispanic, 4% multiracial, 0% Pacific Islander, 72% white, 2% international; 74% from in state; 21% live on campus; 5% of students in fraternities, 7% in sororities
Most popular majors: 28% Engineering, 18% Business, Management, Marketing, and Related Support Services, 16% Health Professions and Related Programs, 6% Biological and Biomedical Sciences, 6% Computer and Information Sciences and Support Services
Expenses: 2021-2022: $11,338 in state, $23,734 out of state; room/board: $10,652
Financial aid: (256) 824-6650; 48% of undergrads determined to have financial need; average aid package $15,342

University of Mobile
Mobile AL
(251) 442-2222
U.S. News ranking: Reg. Coll. (S), No. 15
Website: www.umobile.edu
Admissions email: umenrollment@umobile.edu
Private; founded 1961
Affiliation: Baptist
Freshman admissions: selective; 2020-2021: 2,037 applied, 1,356 accepted. Neither SAT nor ACT required. ACT 25/75 percentile: 19-26. High school rank: 22% in top tenth, 52% in top quarter, 89% in top half
Early decision deadline: N/A, notification date: N/A
Early action deadline: N/A, notification date: N/A
Application deadline (fall): rolling
Undergraduate student body: 1,106 full time, 644 part time; 35%

male, 65% female; 2% American Indian, 2% Asian, 17% black, 1% Hispanic, 3% multiracial, 1% Pacific Islander, 64% white, 4% international; N/A from in state; 58% live on campus; N/A of students in fraternities, N/A in sororities
Most popular majors: 20% Registered Nursing/Registered Nurse, 15% Business Administration and Management, General, 11% Music, General
Expenses: 2021-2022: $24,540; room/board: $10,160
Financial aid: (251) 442-2222; 75% of undergrads determined to have financial need; average aid package $22,316

University of Montevallo
Montevallo AL
(205) 665-6030
U.S. News ranking: Reg. U. (S), No. 26
Website: www.montevallo.edu
Admissions email: admissions@montevallo.edu
Public; founded 1896
Freshman admissions: selective; 2020-2021: 5,315 applied, 3,274 accepted. Neither SAT nor ACT required. ACT 25/75 percentile: 19-26. High school rank: N/A
Early decision deadline: N/A, notification date: N/A
Early action deadline: N/A, notification date: N/A
Application deadline (fall): 8/15
Undergraduate student body: 1,998 full time, 230 part time; 35% male, 65% female; 0% American Indian, 1% Asian, 17% black, 6% Hispanic, 4% multiracial, 0% Pacific Islander, 67% white, 3% international
Most popular majors: Information not available
Expenses: 2021-2022: $13,710 in state, $26,730 out of state; room/board: $9,810
Financial aid: (205) 665-6050; 68% of undergrads determined to have financial need; average aid package $13,623

University of North Alabama
Florence AL
(256) 765-4608
U.S. News ranking: Reg. U. (S), No. 27
Website: www.una.edu
Admissions email: admissions@una.edu
Public; founded 1830
Freshman admissions: selective; 2020-2021: 3,523 applied, 2,268 accepted. Neither SAT nor ACT required. ACT 25/75 percentile: 20-26. High school rank: 20% in top tenth, 51% in top quarter, 83% in top half
Early decision deadline: N/A, notification date: N/A
Early action deadline: N/A, notification date: N/A
Application deadline (fall): rolling
Undergraduate student body: 4,707 full time, 1,398 part time; 38% male, 62% female; 1% American Indian, 2% Asian, 13% black,

4% Hispanic, 3% multiracial, 0% Pacific Islander, 74% white, 3% international; 79% from in state; 26% live on campus; 16% of students in fraternities, 20% in sororities
Most popular majors: 24% Business, Management, Marketing, and Related Support Services, 12% Health Professions and Related Programs, 10% Education, 8% Parks, Recreation, Leisure, and Fitness Studies, 6% Visual and Performing Arts
Expenses: 2021-2022: $10,800 in state, $20,400 out of state; room/board: $7,966
Financial aid: (256) 765-4278; 61% of undergrads determined to have financial need; average aid package $11,071

University of South Alabama

Mobile AL
(251) 460-6141
U.S. News ranking: Nat. U., second tier
Website: www.southalabama.edu
Admissions email: recruitment@southalabama.edu
Public; founded 1963
Freshman admissions: selective; 2020-2021: 8,084 applied, 5,904 accepted. Neither SAT nor ACT required. ACT 25/75 percentile: 20-27. High school rank: N/A
Early decision deadline: 8/1, notification date: 10/1
Early action deadline: N/A, notification date: N/A
Application deadline (fall): 7/15
Undergraduate student body: 7,611 full time, 1,439 part time; 39% male, 61% female; 1% American Indian, 3% Asian, 22% black, 4% Hispanic, 4% multiracial, 0% Pacific Islander, 60% white, 2% international; N/A from in state; 20% live on campus; N/A of students in fraternities, N/A in sororities
Most popular majors: 25% Health Professions and Related Programs, 13% Business, Management, Marketing, and Related Support Services, 11% Engineering, 10% Education, 8% Biological and Biomedical Sciences
Expenses: 2021-2022: $10,520 in state, $20,840 out of state; room/board: $8,170
Financial aid: (251) 460-6231; 65% of undergrads determined to have financial need; average aid package $10,884

University of West Alabama

Livingston AL
(205) 652-3578
U.S. News ranking: Reg. U. (S), No. 93
Website: www.uwa.edu
Admissions email: admissions@uwa.edu
Public; founded 1835
Freshman admissions: selective; 2020-2021: 1,834 applied, 1,708 accepted. Either SAT or ACT required. ACT 25/75 percentile: 17-22. High school rank: N/A

Early decision deadline: N/A, notification date: N/A
Early action deadline: N/A, notification date: N/A
Application deadline (fall): rolling
Undergraduate student body: 1,776 full time, 472 part time; 34% male, 66% female; 1% American Indian, 0% Asian, 41% black, 2% Hispanic, 2% multiracial, 0% Pacific Islander, 44% white, 3% international; 81% from in state; 47% live on campus; 12% of students in fraternities, 12% in sororities
Most popular majors: 20% Multi-/Interdisciplinary Studies, Other, 9% Biology/Biological Sciences, General, 9% Engineering Technologies and Engineering-Related Fields, Other, 7% Business Administration and Management, General, 6% Psychology, General
Expenses: 2021-2022: $10,990 in state, $20,090 out of state; room/board: $8,434
Financial aid: (205) 652-3576; 78% of undergrads determined to have financial need; average aid package $11,756

Alaska Pacific University

Anchorage AK
(800) 252-7528
U.S. News ranking: Reg. U. (W), No. 84
Website: www.alaskapacific.edu
Admissions email: admissions@alaskapacific.edu
Private; founded 1959
Freshman admissions: least selective; 2020-2021: 428 applied, 388 accepted. Neither SAT nor ACT required. SAT 25/75 percentile: N/A. High school rank: N/A
Early decision deadline: N/A, notification date: N/A
Early action deadline: N/A, notification date: N/A
Application deadline (fall): rolling
Undergraduate student body: 247 full time, 65 part time; 23% male, 77% female; 27% American Indian, 2% Asian, 2% black, 10% Hispanic, 15% multiracial, 1% Pacific Islander, 31% white, 0% international
Most popular majors: Information not available
Expenses: 2021-2022: $20,760; room/board: $8,400
Financial aid: (907) 564-8342

University of Alaska–Anchorage

Anchorage AK
(907) 786-1480
U.S. News ranking: Reg. U. (W), No. 71
Website: www.uaa.alaska.edu
Admissions email: futureseawolf@alaska.edu
Public; founded 1954
Freshman admissions: selective; 2020-2021: 3,081 applied, 2,367 accepted. Neither SAT nor ACT required. SAT 25/75 percentile: 990-1200. High school rank: N/A

rank: 15% in top tenth, 35% in top quarter, 65% in top half
Early decision deadline: N/A, notification date: N/A
Early action deadline: N/A, notification date: N/A
Application deadline (fall): 7/15
Undergraduate student body: 4,724 full time, 6,674 part time; 39% male, 6% female; 5% American Indian, 9% Asian, 4% black, 9% Hispanic, 13% multiracial, 4% Pacific Islander, 51% white, 2% international
Most popular majors: 24% Health Professions and Related Programs, 19% Business, Management, Marketing, and Related Support Services, 9% Engineering, 6% Psychology, 5% Social Sciences
Expenses: 2021-2022: $8,418 in state, $25,398 out of state; room/board: $12,662
Financial aid: (907) 786-6170; 53% of undergrads determined to have financial need; average aid package $11,836

University of Alaska–Fairbanks[1]

Fairbanks AK
(800) 478-1823
U.S. News ranking: Nat. U., second tier
Website: www.uaf.edu
Admissions email: admissions@uaf.edu
Public; founded 1917
Application deadline (fall): 6/15
Undergraduate student body: N/A full time, N/A part time
Expenses: N/A
Financial aid: (907) 474-7256

University of Alaska–Southeast

Juneau AK
(907) 796-6100
U.S. News ranking: Reg. U. (W), second tier
Website: www.uas.alaska.edu
Admissions email: admissions@uas.alaska.edu
Public; founded 1983
Freshman admissions: less selective; 2020-2021: 488 applied, 310 accepted. Neither SAT nor ACT required. SAT 25/75 percentile: N/A. High school rank: N/A
Early decision deadline: N/A, notification date: N/A
Early action deadline: N/A, notification date: N/A
Application deadline (fall): 8/15
Undergraduate student body: 534 full time, 1,271 part time; 34% male, 66% female; 12% American Indian, 3% Asian, 0% black, 9% Hispanic, 12% multiracial, 3% Pacific Islander, 55% white, 0% international; 11% from in state; 10% live on campus; N/A of students in fraternities, N/A in sororities
Most popular majors: Information not available
Expenses: N/A
Financial aid: N/A

American Samoa Community College[1]

Pago Pago AS
(684) 699-9155
U.S. News ranking: Reg. Coll. (W), unranked
Website: www.amsamoa.edu
Admissions email: admissions@amsamoa.edu
Public; founded 1970
Undergraduate student body: N/A full time, N/A part time
Expenses: 2020-2021: $3,950 in state, $4,250 out of state; room/board: N/A
Financial aid: N/A

Arizona Christian University

Glendale AZ
(602) 489-5300
U.S. News ranking: Reg. Coll. (W), No. 13
Website: arizonachristian.edu/
Admissions email: admissions@arizonachristian.edu
Private; founded 1960
Affiliation: Undenominational
Freshman admissions: selective; 2020-2021: 749 applied, 557 accepted. Either SAT or ACT required. SAT 25/75 percentile: 935-1120. High school rank: N/A
Early decision deadline: N/A, notification date: N/A
Early action deadline: N/A, notification date: N/A
Application deadline (fall): 8/24
Undergraduate student body: 779 full time, 155 part time; 61% male, 39% female; 1% American Indian, 1% Asian, 13% black, 27% Hispanic, 7% multiracial, 0% Pacific Islander, 45% white, 3% international; 57% live on campus; N/A of students in fraternities, N/A in sororities
Most popular majors: 38% Business, Management, Marketing, and Related Support Services, 14% Psychology, 11% Biological and Biomedical Sciences, 11% Education, 7% Theology and Religious Vocations
Expenses: 2021-2022: $29,250; room/board: $12,000
Financial aid: (602) 386-4115; 65% of undergrads determined to have financial need; average aid package $28,171

Arizona State University

Tempe AZ
(480) 965-7788
U.S. News ranking: Nat. U., No. 117
Website: www.asu.edu
Admissions email: admissions@asu.edu
Public; founded 1885
Freshman admissions: more selective; 2020-2021: 53,516 applied, 47,290 accepted. Neither SAT nor ACT required. ACT 25/75 percentile: 21-28. High school rank: 30% in top tenth, 60% in

top quarter, 87% in top half
Early decision deadline: N/A, notification date: N/A
Early action deadline: N/A, notification date: N/A
Application deadline (fall): rolling
Undergraduate student body: 57,485 full time, 5,639 part time; 50% male, 50% female; 1% American Indian, 8% Asian, 4% black, 26% Hispanic, 5% multiracial, 0% Pacific Islander, 47% white, 7% international; 75% from in state; 19% live on campus; 8% of students in fraternities, 10% in sororities
Most popular majors: 20% Business, Management, Marketing, and Related Support Services, 11% Engineering, 8% Biological and Biomedical Sciences, 6% Social Sciences, 5% Health Professions and Related Programs
Expenses: 2021-2022: $11,348 in state, $29,438 out of state; room/board: $8,176
Financial aid: (855) 278-5080; 56% of undergrads determined to have financial need; average aid package $15,655

Embry-Riddle Aeronautical University–Prescott

Prescott AZ
(928) 777-6600
U.S. News ranking: Reg. Coll. (W), No. 2
Website: prescott.erau.edu/
Admissions email: Prescott@erau.edu
Private; founded 1926
Freshman admissions: more selective; 2020-2021: 4,250 applied, 2,841 accepted. Neither SAT nor ACT required. SAT 25/75 percentile: 1140-1320. High school rank: 25% in top tenth, 59% in top quarter, 88% in top half
Early decision deadline: N/A, notification date: N/A
Early action deadline: N/A, notification date: N/A
Application deadline (fall): rolling
Undergraduate student body: 2,853 full time, 108 part time; 73% male, 27% female; 0% American Indian, 6% Asian, 2% black, 14% Hispanic, 6% multiracial, 0% Pacific Islander, 62% white, 7% international; N/A from in state; 44% live on campus; N/A of students in fraternities, N/A in sororities
Most popular majors: 36% Engineering, 23% Transportation and Materials Moving, 16% Social Sciences, 9% Homeland Security, Law Enforcement, Firefighting and Related Protective Services, 8% Business, Management, Marketing, and Related Support Services
Expenses: 2021-2022: $38,966; room/board: $12,736
Financial aid: (800) 888-3728; 89% of undergrads determined to have financial need; average aid package $17,948

Grand Canyon University[1]

Phoenix AZ
(800) 800-9776
U.S. News ranking: Nat. U., second tier
Website: apply.gcu.edu
Admissions email: golopes@gcu.edu
For-profit; founded 1949
Application deadline (fall): rolling
Undergraduate student body: N/A full time, N/A part time
Expenses: 2020-2021: $17,800; room/board: $7,800
Financial aid: (602) 639-6600

Northern Arizona University

Flagstaff AZ
(928) 523-5511
U.S. News ranking: Nat. U., No. 288
Website: www.nau.edu
Admissions email: admissions@nau.edu
Public; founded 1899
Freshman admissions: selective; 2020-2021: 37,386 applied, 30,523 accepted. Neither SAT nor ACT required. ACT 25/75 percentile: 19-25. High school rank: 22% in top tenth, 55% in top quarter, 86% in top half
Early decision deadline: N/A, notification date: N/A
Early action deadline: N/A, notification date: N/A
Application deadline (fall): 8/1
Undergraduate student body: 20,642 full time, 4,588 part time; 37% male, 63% female; 3% American Indian, 2% Asian, 3% black, 26% Hispanic, 6% multiracial, 0% Pacific Islander, 55% white, 2% international; 68% from in state; 32% live on campus; 8% of students in fraternities, 11% in sororities
Most popular majors: 17% Business, Management, Marketing, and Related Support Services, 14% Health Professions and Related Programs, 9% Education, 8% Liberal Arts and Sciences, General Studies and Humanities, 8% Social Sciences
Expenses: 2021-2022: $11,896 in state, $26,642 out of state; room/board: $11,338
Financial aid: (928) 523-4951; 61% of undergrads determined to have financial need; average aid package $13,825

Prescott College[1]

Prescott AZ
(877) 350-2100
U.S. News ranking: Reg. U. (W), second tier
Website: www.prescott.edu/
Admissions email: admissions@prescott.edu
Private; founded 1966
Application deadline (fall): 8/15
Undergraduate student body: N/A full time, N/A part time
Expenses: 2020-2021: $33,669; room/board: $9,520
Financial aid: (928) 350-1104

Southwest University of Visual Arts[1]

Tucson AZ
(520) 325-0123
U.S. News ranking: Arts, unranked
Website: www.suva.edu/
Admissions email: N/A
Private
Application deadline (fall): N/A
Undergraduate student body: N/A full time, N/A part time
Expenses: 2020-2021: $23,069; room/board: N/A
Financial aid: N/A

University of Arizona

Tucson AZ
(520) 621-3237
U.S. News ranking: Nat. U., No. 103
Website: www.arizona.edu
Admissions email: admissions@arizona.edu
Public; founded 1885
Freshman admissions: more selective; 2020-2021: 43,540 applied, 37,064 accepted. Neither SAT nor ACT required. ACT 25/75 percentile: 21-29. High school rank: 35% in top tenth, 63% in top quarter, 87% in top half
Early decision deadline: N/A, notification date: N/A
Early action deadline: N/A, notification date: N/A
Application deadline (fall): 5/1
Undergraduate student body: 28,877 full time, 7,626 part time; 45% male, 55% female; 1% American Indian, 5% Asian, 4% black, 29% Hispanic, 5% multiracial, 0% Pacific Islander, 48% white, 5% international; 65% from in state; 16% live on campus; 9% of students in fraternities, 17% in sororities
Most popular majors: 15% Business, Management, Marketing, and Related Support Services, 10% Biological and Biomedical Sciences, 8% Engineering, 8% Social Sciences, 7% Health Professions and Related Programs
Expenses: 2021-2022: $12,384 in state, $34,667 out of state; room/board: $13,350
Financial aid: (520) 621-1858; 52% of undergrads determined to have financial need; average aid package $15,603

University of Phoenix[1]

Phoenix AZ
(866) 766-0766
U.S. News ranking: Nat. U., second tier
Website: www.phoenix.edu
Admissions email: N/A
For-profit
Application deadline (fall): N/A
Undergraduate student body: N/A full time, N/A part time
Expenses: 2020-2021: $9,552; room/board: N/A
Financial aid: N/A

ARKANSAS

Arkansas Baptist College[1]

Little Rock AR
(501) 420-1234
U.S. News ranking: Reg. Coll. (S), second tier
Website: www.arkansasbaptist.edu
Admissions email: admissions@arkansasbaptist.edu
Private; founded 1884
Affiliation: Baptist
Application deadline (fall): 8/3
Undergraduate student body: N/A full time, N/A part time
Expenses: 2020-2021: $20,882; room/board: $8,826
Financial aid: (501) 420-1222

Arkansas State University

State University AR
(870) 972-2782
U.S. News ranking: Nat. U., second tier
Website: www.astate.edu
Admissions email: admissions@astate.edu
Public; founded 1909
Freshman admissions: selective; 2020-2021: 5,836 applied, 3,921 accepted. Neither SAT nor ACT required. ACT 25/75 percentile: 20-26. High school rank: 25% in top tenth, 55% in top quarter, 81% in top half
Early decision deadline: N/A, notification date: N/A
Early action deadline: N/A, notification date: N/A
Application deadline (fall): 8/22
Undergraduate student body: 5,835 full time, 2,642 part time; 39% male, 61% female; 0% American Indian, 1% Asian, 14% black, 4% Hispanic, 2% multiracial, 0% Pacific Islander, 73% white, 4% international
Most popular majors: 12% Registered Nursing/Registered Nurse, 10% General Studies, 6% Business Administration and Management, General, 5% Early Childhood Education and Teaching, 4% Criminology
Expenses: 2020-2021: $8,900 in state, $16,070 out of state; room/board: $10,022
Financial aid: (870) 972-2310

Arkansas Tech University

Russellville AR
(479) 968-0343
U.S. News ranking: Reg. U. (S), No. 69
Website: www.atu.edu
Admissions email: tech.enroll@atu.edu
Public; founded 1909
Freshman admissions: selective; 2020-2021: 7,139 applied, 6,972 accepted. Either SAT or ACT required. ACT 25/75 percentile: 18-25. High school rank: 16% in top tenth, 39% in top quarter, 70% in top half
Early decision deadline: N/A, notification date: N/A
Early action deadline: N/A, notification date: N/A
Application deadline (fall): rolling

Undergraduate student body: 6,227 full time, 3,883 part time; 44% male, 56% female; 1% American Indian, 2% Asian, 7% black, 9% Hispanic, 5% multiracial, 0% Pacific Islander, 74% white, 3% international
Most popular majors: 15% Health Professions and Related Programs, 14% Business, Management, Marketing, and Related Support Services, 14% Education, 11% Multi/Interdisciplinary Studies, 8% Engineering
Expenses: 2021-2022: $9,875 in state, $17,045 out of state; room/board: $8,996
Financial aid: (479) 968-0399; 68% of undergrads determined to have financial need; average aid package $10,870

Central Baptist College

Conway AR
(501) 329-6873
U.S. News ranking: Reg. Coll. (S), No. 66
Website: www.cbc.edu
Admissions email: admissions@cbc.edu
Private; founded 1952
Affiliation: Baptist
Freshman admissions: selective; 2020-2021: 530 applied, 264 accepted. Either SAT or ACT required. ACT 25/75 percentile: 18-22. High school rank: N/A
Early decision deadline: N/A, notification date: N/A
Early action deadline: N/A, notification date: N/A
Application deadline (fall): 8/15
Undergraduate student body: 521 full time, 33 part time; 55% male, 45% female; 1% American Indian, 6% Asian, 13% black, 11% Hispanic, 3% multiracial, 0% Pacific Islander, 61% white, 3% international; 51% from in state; 24% live on campus; N/A of students in fraternities, N/A in sororities
Most popular majors: 17% Business, Management, Marketing, and Related Support Services, Other, 13% Bible/Biblical Studies, 9% Psychology, General, 8% Kinesiology and Exercise Science, 7% Sport and Fitness Administration/Management
Expenses: 2021-2022: $17,400; room/board: $7,500
Financial aid: (501) 205-8809; 70% of undergrads determined to have financial need; average aid package $14,026

Crowley's Ridge College[1]

Paragould AR
(870) 236-6901
U.S. News ranking: Reg. Coll. (S), second tier
Admissions email: N/A
Private
Application deadline (fall): N/A
Undergraduate student body: N/A full time, N/A part time
Expenses: 2020-2021: $15,100; room/board: $6,400
Financial aid: N/A

Harding University

Searcy AR
(800) 477-4407
U.S. News ranking: Nat. U., No. 249
Website: www.harding.edu
Admissions email: admissions@harding.edu
Private; founded 1924
Affiliation: Churches of Christ
Freshman admissions: more selective; 2020-2021: 2,200 applied, 1,211 accepted. Either SAT or ACT required. ACT 25/75 percentile: 21-29. High school rank: 32% in top tenth, 56% in top quarter, 85% in top half
Early decision deadline: N/A, notification date: N/A
Early action deadline: N/A, notification date: N/A
Application deadline (fall): rolling
Undergraduate student body: 3,296 full time, 278 part time; 44% male, 56% female; 0% American Indian, 1% Asian, 5% black, 4% Hispanic, 4% multiracial, 0% Pacific Islander, 80% white, 6% international; 31% from in state; 0% live on campus; 0% of students in fraternities, 0% in sororities
Most popular majors: Information not available
Expenses: 2021-2022: $22,470; room/board: $7,674
Financial aid: (501) 279-4257; 55% of undergrads determined to have financial need; average aid package $14,664

Henderson State University[1]

Arkadelphia AR
(870) 230-5028
U.S. News ranking: Reg. U. (S), second tier
Website: www.hsu.edu/pages/future-students/admissions/
Admissions email: admissions@hsu.edu
Public; founded 1890
Application deadline (fall): rolling
Undergraduate student body: N/A full time, N/A part time
Expenses: 2020-2021: $7,392 in state, $9,312 out of state; room/board: $9,200
Financial aid: (870) 230-5148

Hendrix College

Conway AR
(800) 277-9017
U.S. News ranking: Nat. Lib. Arts, No. 98
Website: www.hendrix.edu
Admissions email: adm@hendrix.edu
Private; founded 1876
Affiliation: United Methodist
Freshman admissions: more selective; 2020-2021: 1,775 applied, 1,252 accepted. Neither SAT nor ACT required. ACT 25/75 percentile: 25-32. High school rank: 37% in top tenth, 67% in top quarter, 92% in top half
Early decision deadline: N/A, notification date: N/A
Early action deadline: 11/15, notification date: 12/15
Application deadline (fall): 6/1
Undergraduate student body:

1,060 full time, 6 part time; 49% male, 51% female; 0% American Indian, 3% Asian, 6% black, 8% Hispanic, 22% multiracial, 0% Pacific Islander, 47% white, 0% international

Most popular majors: 15% Psychology, General, 9% Biochemistry and Molecular Biology, 9% Biology/Biological Sciences, General, 8% Health Professions and Related Programs, 7% Economics, General
Expenses: 2020-2021: $49,490; room/board: $12,820
Financial aid: (501) 450-1368

John Brown University
Siloam Springs AR
(479) 524-9500
U.S. News ranking: Reg. U. (S), No. 10
Website: www.jbu.edu
Admissions email: jbuinfo@jbu.edu
Private; founded 1919
Affiliation: Interdenominational
Freshman admissions: more selective; 2020-2021: 1,373 applied, 829 accepted. Neither SAT nor ACT required. ACT 25/75 percentile: 22-29. High school rank: N/A
Early decision deadline: N/A, notification date: N/A
Early action deadline: N/A, notification date: N/A
Application deadline (fall): rolling
Undergraduate student body: 1,226 full time, 401 part time; 41% male, 59% female; 1% American Indian, 1% Asian, 1% black, 8% Hispanic, 5% multiracial, 0% Pacific Islander, 72% white, 8% international; N/A from in state; 70% live on campus; 0% of students in fraternities, 0% in sororities
Most popular majors: 22% Business, Management, Marketing, and Related Support Services, 15% Visual and Performing Arts, 10% Psychology, 7% Engineering, 7% Parks, Recreation, Leisure, and Fitness Studies
Expenses: 2021-2022: $28,288; room/board: $9,554
Financial aid: (479) 524-7427; 70% of undergrads determined to have financial need; average aid package $21,857

Lyon College
Batesville AR
(800) 423-2542
U.S. News ranking: Nat. Lib. Arts, second tier
Website: www.lyon.edu
Admissions email: admissions@lyon.edu
Private; founded 1872
Affiliation: Presbyterian Church (USA)
Freshman admissions: more selective; 2020-2021: 2,062 applied, 1,034 accepted. Either SAT or ACT required. ACT 25/75 percentile: 22-28. High school rank: 21% in top tenth, 50% in top quarter, 80% in top half
Early decision deadline: N/A, notification date: N/A
Early action deadline: 1/15,

notification date: 3/15
Application deadline (fall): 8/10
Undergraduate student body: 650 full time, 15 part time; 55% male, 45% female; 1% American Indian, 2% Asian, 8% black, 9% Hispanic, 2% multiracial, 0% Pacific Islander, 56% white, 5% international
Most popular majors: Information not available
Expenses: 2021-2022: $30,414; room/board: $10,730
Financial aid: (870) 307-7250; 73% of undergrads determined to have financial need; average aid package $23,217

Ouachita Baptist University
Arkadelphia AR
(870) 245-5110
U.S. News ranking: Reg. Coll. (S), No. 2
Website: www.obu.edu
Admissions email: admissions@obu.edu
Private; founded 1886
Affiliation: Southern Baptist
Freshman admissions: more selective; 2020-2021: 2,521 applied, 1,557 accepted. Either SAT or ACT required. ACT 25/75 percentile: 22-29. High school rank: 36% in top tenth, 66% in top quarter, 89% in top half
Early decision deadline: N/A, notification date: N/A
Early action deadline: N/A, notification date: N/A
Application deadline (fall): rolling
Undergraduate student body: 1,502 full time, 162 part time; 42% male, 58% female; 0% American Indian, 1% Asian, 7% black, 6% Hispanic, 3% multiracial, 0% Pacific Islander, 81% white, 2% international; N/A from in state; 96% live on campus; 14% of students in fraternities, 34% in sororities
Most popular majors: 19% Business, Management, Marketing, and Related Support Services, 10% Visual and Performing Arts, 9% Biological and Biomedical Sciences
Expenses: 2021-2022: $30,140; room/board: $8,510
Financial aid: (870) 245-5570; 64% of undergrads determined to have financial need; average aid package $29,316

Philander Smith College
Little Rock AR
(501) 370-5221
U.S. News ranking: Reg. Coll. (S), No. 42
Website: www.philander.edu
Admissions email: admissions@philander.edu
Private; founded 1877
Affiliation: United Methodist
Freshman admissions: selective; 2020-2021: 3,985 applied, 853 accepted. Neither SAT nor ACT required. ACT 25/75 percentile: 16-22. High school rank: 5% in top tenth, 25% in top quarter, 70% in top half
Early decision deadline: N/A, notification date: N/A

Early action deadline: N/A, notification date: N/A
Application deadline (fall): rolling
Undergraduate student body: 699 full time, 100 part time; 35% male, 65% female; 0% American Indian, 0% Asian, 91% black, 3% Hispanic, 2% multiracial, 0% Pacific Islander, 0% white, 4% international; 48% from in state; 25% live on campus; 12% of students in fraternities, 15% in sororities
Most popular majors: 30% Business Administration and Management, General, 12% Biological and Physical Sciences, 12% Psychology, General, 10% Social Work, 9% Health and Physical Education/Fitness, General
Expenses: 2021-2022: $13,014; room/board: $8,250
Financial aid: (501) 370-5350; 93% of undergrads determined to have financial need; average aid package $13,514

Southern Arkansas University
Magnolia AR
(870) 235-4040
U.S. News ranking: Reg. U. (S), No. 93
Website: www.saumag.edu
Admissions email: muleriders@saumag.edu
Public; founded 1909
Freshman admissions: selective; 2020-2021: 3,532 applied, 2,356 accepted. Either SAT or ACT required. ACT 25/75 percentile: 19-25. High school rank: 20% in top tenth, 42% in top quarter, 75% in top half
Early decision deadline: N/A, notification date: N/A
Early action deadline: N/A, notification date: N/A
Application deadline (fall): 8/27
Undergraduate student body: 2,950 full time, 497 part time; 44% male, 56% female; 1% American Indian, 1% Asian, 25% black, 5% Hispanic, 0% multiracial, 0% Pacific Islander, 67% white, 2% international; 74% from in state; 51% live on campus; 1% of students in fraternities, 1% in sororities
Most popular majors: 15% Business, Management, Marketing, and Related Support Services, 14% Education, 9% Health Professions and Related Programs, 8% Liberal Arts and Sciences, General Studies and Humanities, 7% Visual and Performing Arts
Expenses: 2021-2022: $8,067 in state, $10,677 out of state; room/board: $6,824
Financial aid: (870) 235-4023; 79% of undergrads determined to have financial need; average aid package $13,341

University of Arkansas
Fayetteville AR
(800) 377-8632
U.S. News ranking: Nat. U., No. 162
Website: www.uark.edu
Admissions email: uofa@uark.edu

Public; founded 1871
Freshman admissions: more selective; 2020-2021: 19,777 applied, 15,361 accepted. Neither SAT nor ACT required. ACT 25/75 percentile: 23-29. High school rank: 29% in top tenth, 57% in top quarter, 86% in top half
Early decision deadline: N/A, notification date: N/A
Early action deadline: 11/1, notification date: 12/15
Application deadline (fall): 8/1
Undergraduate student body: 20,252 full time, 2,573 part time; 45% male, 55% female; 1% American Indian, 3% Asian, 4% black, 10% Hispanic, 4% multiracial, 0% Pacific Islander, 75% white, 2% international; 54% from in state; 21% live on campus; 25% of students in fraternities, 38% in sororities
Most popular majors: 28% Business, Management, Marketing, and Related Support Services, 10% Engineering, 8% Health Professions and Related Programs, 6% Communication, Journalism, and Related Programs, 6% Social Sciences
Expenses: 2021-2022: $9,574 in state, $26,390 out of state; room/board: $11,942
Financial aid: (479) 575-3806; 40% of undergrads determined to have financial need; average aid package $10,385

University of Arkansas at Little Rock
Little Rock AR
(501) 916-3127
U.S. News ranking: Nat. U., second tier
Website: www.ualr.edu/
Admissions email: admissions@ualr.edu
Public; founded 1927
Freshman admissions: selective; 2020-2021: 2,980 applied, 1,843 accepted. Either SAT or ACT required. ACT 25/75 percentile: 18-25. High school rank: N/A
Early decision deadline: N/A, notification date: N/A
Early action deadline: N/A, notification date: N/A
Application deadline (fall): 8/17
Undergraduate student body: 3,599 full time, 3,407 part time; 36% male, 64% female; 1% American Indian, 2% Asian, 27% black, 4% Hispanic, 14% multiracial, 0% Pacific Islander, 49% white, 3% international
Most popular majors: Information not available
Expenses: 2020-2021: $8,366 in state, $18,957 out of state; room/board: $9,162
Financial aid: (501) 569-3035

University of Arkansas–Fort Smith[7]
Fort Smith AR
(479) 788-7120
U.S. News ranking: Reg. Coll. (S), No. 48
Website: www.uafs.edu

Admissions email: admissions@uafs.edu
Public; founded 1928
Freshman admissions: less selective; 2020-2021: N/A applied, N/A accepted. Either SAT or ACT required. SAT 25/75 percentile: N/A. High school rank: N/A
Early decision deadline: N/A, notification date: N/A
Early action deadline: N/A, notification date: N/A
Application deadline (fall): rolling
Undergraduate student body: 5,830 full time, 0 part time
Most popular majors: 8% Business Administration and Management, General, 7% Registered Nursing/Registered Nurse, 5% Biology/Biological Sciences, General, 4% Criminal Justice/Law Enforcement Administration, 4% Organizational Leadership
Expenses: 2021-2022: $7,338 in state, $16,428 out of state; room/board: N/A
Financial aid: N/A

University of Arkansas–Monticello[1]
Monticello AR
(870) 367-6811
U.S. News ranking: Reg. U. (S), second tier
Website: www.uamont.edu
Admissions email: admissions@uamont.edu
Public
Application deadline (fall): N/A
Undergraduate student body: N/A full time, N/A part time
Expenses: 2020-2021: $7,909 in state, $13,759 out of state; room/board: $7,058
Financial aid: N/A

University of Arkansas–Pine Bluff
Pine Bluff AR
(870) 575-8492
U.S. News ranking: Reg. Coll. (S), No. 33
Website: www.uapb.edu/
Admissions email: greenet@uapb.edu
Public; founded 1873
Freshman admissions: less selective; 2020-2021: 5,464 applied, 3,260 accepted. Either SAT or ACT required. ACT 25/75 percentile: 14-18. High school rank: 10% in top tenth, 27% in top quarter, 53% in top half
Early decision deadline: N/A, notification date: N/A
Early action deadline: N/A, notification date: N/A
Application deadline (fall): rolling
Undergraduate student body: 2,158 full time, 349 part time; 41% male, 59% female; 0% American Indian, 0% Asian, 90% black, 2% Hispanic, 2% multiracial, 0% Pacific Islander, 3% white, 1% international; 64% from in state; 44% live on campus; 1% of students in fraternities, 3% in sororities
Most popular majors: 12% Biology/Biological Sciences, General, 9% Business Administration and Management, General, 8% General Studies, 6% Industrial Technology/Technician, 6%

Physical Education Teaching and Coaching
Expenses: 2021-2022: $8,326 in state, $15,196 out of state; room/board: $8,472
Financial aid: (870) 575-8302; 90% of undergrads determined to have financial need; average aid package $13,760

University of Central Arkansas
Conway AR
(501) 450-3128
U.S. News ranking: Nat. U., second tier
Website: www.uca.edu
Admissions email: admissions@uca.edu
Public; founded 1907
Freshman admissions: selective; 2020-2021: 5,642 applied, 5,291 accepted. Neither SAT nor ACT required. ACT 25/75 percentile: 20-27. High school rank: 23% in top tenth, 48% in top quarter, 80% in top half
Early decision deadline: N/A, notification date: N/A
Early action deadline: N/A, notification date: N/A
Application deadline (fall): rolling
Undergraduate student body: 7,301 full time, 1,314 part time; 39% male, 61% female; 0% American Indian, 2% Asian, 16% black, 6% Hispanic, 4% multiracial, 0% Pacific Islander, 67% white, 4% international; N/A from in state; 34% live on campus; 14% of students in fraternities, 16% in sororities
Most popular majors: 20% Health Professions and Related Programs, 19% Business, Management, Marketing, and Related Support Services, 9% Education, 7% Psychology, 7% Visual and Performing Arts
Expenses: 2021-2022: $9,563 in state, $16,433 out of state; room/board: $7,896
Financial aid: (501) 450-3140

University of the Ozarks
Clarksville AR
(479) 979-1227
U.S. News ranking: Reg. Coll. (S), No. 5
Website: www.ozarks.edu
Admissions email: admiss@ozarks.edu
Private; founded 1834
Affiliation: Presbyterian Church (USA)
Freshman admissions: selective; 2020-2021: 959 applied, 959 accepted. Neither SAT nor ACT required. ACT 25/75 percentile: 18-23. High school rank: 3% in top tenth, 11% in top quarter, 36% in top half
Early decision deadline: N/A, notification date: N/A
Early action deadline: N/A, notification date: N/A
Application deadline (fall): rolling
Undergraduate student body: 826 full time, 10 part time; 50% male, 50% female; 0% American Indian, 1% Asian, 7% black, 13% Hispanic, 3% multiracial, 0% Pacific Islander, 41% white,

28% international; 57% from in state; 54% live on campus; N/A of students in fraternities, N/A in sororities
Most popular majors: 24% Business Administration and Management, General, 15% Public Health Education and Promotion, 11% Biology/Biological Sciences, General, 7% Psychology, General, 4% Environmental Studies
Expenses: 2021-2022: $25,950; room/board: $8,000
Financial aid: (479) 979-1201; 79% of undergrads determined to have financial need; average aid package $25,737

Williams Baptist University
Walnut Ridge AR
(800) 722-4434
U.S. News ranking: Nat. Lib. Arts, second tier
Website: williamsbu.edu/
Admissions email: admissions@williamsbu.edu
Private; founded 1941
Affiliation: Southern Baptist
Freshman admissions: selective; 2020-2021: 1,226 applied, 850 accepted. Either SAT or ACT required. ACT 25/75 percentile: 18-24. High school rank: 16% in top tenth, 44% in top quarter, 73% in top half
Early decision deadline: N/A, notification date: N/A
Early action deadline: N/A, notification date: N/A
Application deadline (fall): rolling
Undergraduate student body: 577 full time, 12 part time; 48% male, 52% female; 2% American Indian, 0% Asian, 11% black, 4% Hispanic, 2% multiracial, 0% Pacific Islander, 76% white, 5% international; N/A from in state; 75% live on campus; N/A of students in fraternities, N/A in sororities
Most popular majors: 20% Business Administration and Management, General, 14% Liberal Arts and Sciences, General Studies and Humanities, 8% Elementary Education and Teaching, 5% Biology, General, 5% History
Expenses: 2021-2022: $18,570; room/board: $8,550
Financial aid: (870) 759-4112; 83% of undergrads determined to have financial need; average aid package $19,248

CALIFORNIA

Academy of Art University
San Francisco CA
(800) 544-2787
U.S. News ranking: Reg. U. (W), second tier
Website: www.academyart.edu/
Admissions email: admissions@academyart.edu
For-profit; founded 1929
Freshman admissions: least selective; 2020-2021: 2,246 applied, 2,246 accepted. Neither SAT nor ACT required. SAT 25/75

percentile: N/A. High school rank: N/A
Early decision deadline: N/A, notification date: N/A
Early action deadline: N/A, notification date: N/A
Application deadline (fall): rolling
Undergraduate student body: 2,882 full time, 3,242 part time; 43% male, 57% female; 0% American Indian, 5% Asian, 7% black, 12% Hispanic, 3% multiracial, 0% Pacific Islander, 16% white, 20% international; N/A from in state; 4% live on campus; N/A of students in fraternities, N/A in sororities
Most popular majors: 37% Visual and Performing Arts, 22% Computer and Information Sciences and Support Services, 13% Communications Technologies/Technicians and Support Services, 12% Engineering Technologies and Engineering-Related Fields, 8% Family and Consumer Sciences/Human Sciences
Expenses: 2021-2022: $31,170; room/board: $19,486
Financial aid: (415) 618-6190; 50% of undergrads determined to have financial need; average aid package $9,592

Alliant International University
San Diego CA
(866) 679-3032
U.S. News ranking: Nat. U., second tier
Website: www.alliant.edu
Admissions email: admissions@alliant.edu
For-profit; founded 1969
Freshman admissions: less selective; 2020-2021: N/A applied, N/A accepted. Neither SAT nor ACT required. SAT 25/75 percentile: N/A. High school rank: N/A
Early decision deadline: N/A, notification date: N/A
Early action deadline: N/A, notification date: N/A
Application deadline (fall): rolling
Undergraduate student body: 38 full time, 211 part time; 46% male, 54% female; N/A American Indian, N/A Asian, N/A black, N/A Hispanic, N/A multiracial, N/A Pacific Islander, N/A white, N/A international
Most popular majors: Business Administration and Management, General
Expenses: 2020-2021: $17,190; room/board: N/A
Financial aid: (858) 635-4700

ArtCenter College of Design[1]
Pasadena CA
(626) 396-2373
U.S. News ranking: Arts, unranked
Website: www.artcenter.edu
Admissions email: admissions@artcenter.edu
Private; founded 1930
Application deadline (fall): rolling
Undergraduate student body: N/A full time, N/A part time
Expenses: 2020-2021: $44,932; room/board: N/A
Financial aid: (626) 396-2215

Azusa Pacific University
Azusa CA
(800) 825-5278
U.S. News ranking: Nat. U., No. 263
Website: www.apu.edu
Admissions email: admissions@apu.edu
Private; founded 1899
Affiliation: Evangelical Christian
Freshman admissions: selective; 2020-2021: 4,534 applied, 4,244 accepted. Neither SAT nor ACT required. SAT 25/75 percentile: 1040-1290. High school rank: N/A
Early decision deadline: N/A, notification date: N/A
Early action deadline: 11/15, notification date: 1/15
Application deadline (fall): 6/1
Undergraduate student body: 3,798 full time, 687 part time; 34% male, 66% female; 0% American Indian, 12% Asian, 6% black, 36% Hispanic, 6% multiracial, 1% Pacific Islander, 32% white, 3% international
Most popular majors: 39% Health Professions and Related Programs, 11% Business, Management, Marketing, and Related Support Services, 8% Psychology
Expenses: 2021-2022: $41,410; room/board: $9,302
Financial aid: (626) 815-2020; 73% of undergrads determined to have financial need; average aid package $36,107

Bakersfield College[1]
Bakersfield CA
(661) 395-4011
U.S. News ranking: Reg. Coll. (W), unranked
Website: www.bakersfieldcollege.edu/
Admissions email: N/A
Public
Application deadline (fall): N/A
Undergraduate student body: N/A full time, N/A part time
Expenses: 2020-2021: $1,418 in state, $9,908 out of state; room/board: N/A
Financial aid: N/A

Biola University
La Mirada CA
(562) 903-4752
U.S. News ranking: Nat. U., No. 196
Website: www.biola.edu
Admissions email: admissions@biola.edu
Private; founded 1908
Affiliation: Multiple Protestant Denomination
Freshman admissions: more selective; 2020-2021: 4,324 applied, 2,784 accepted. Either SAT or ACT required. SAT 25/75 percentile: 1070-1290. High school rank: 28% in top tenth, 63% in top quarter, 90% in top half
Early decision deadline: N/A, notification date: N/A
Early action deadline: 3/1, notification date: 2/15
Application deadline (fall): rolling

Undergraduate student body: 3,391 full time, 291 part time; 37% male, 63% female; 0% American Indian, 15% Asian, 3% black, 21% Hispanic, 7% multiracial, 1% Pacific Islander, 44% white, 5% international; N/A from in state; 5% live on campus; N/A of students in fraternities, N/A in sororities
Most popular majors: 11% Communication, Journalism, and Related Programs, 8% Theology and Religious Vocations, 6% Education, 5% Biological and Biomedical Sciences, 3% English Language and Literature/Letters
Expenses: 2021-2022: $44,382; room/board: $11,712
Financial aid: (562) 903-4742; 64% of undergrads determined to have financial need; average aid package $27,285

Brandman University
Irvine CA
(800) 746-0082
U.S. News ranking: Nat. U., unranked
Website: www.brandman.edu
Admissions email: apply@brandman.edu
Private; founded 1958
Freshman admissions: least selective; 2020-2021: 219 applied, 208 accepted. Neither SAT nor ACT required. SAT 25/75 percentile: N/A. High school rank: N/A
Early decision deadline: N/A, notification date: N/A
Early action deadline: N/A, notification date: N/A
Application deadline (fall): rolling
Undergraduate student body: 2,090 full time, 4,024 part time; 35% male, 65% female; 1% American Indian, 5% Asian, 10% black, 16% Hispanic, 4% multiracial, 1% Pacific Islander, 58% white, 0% international; 56% from in state; N/A live on campus; N/A of students in fraternities, N/A in sororities
Most popular majors: 17% Psychology, General, 15% Organizational Leadership, 14% Liberal Arts and Sciences/Liberal Studies, 13% Business Administration and Management, General, 10% Social Work
Expenses: 2021-2022: $15,480; room/board: N/A
Financial aid: (800) 746-0082; 61% of undergrads determined to have financial need; average aid package $5,057

California Baptist University
Riverside CA
(877) 228-8866
U.S. News ranking: Reg. U. (W), No. 34
Website: www.calbaptist.edu
Admissions email: admissions@calbaptist.edu
Private; founded 1950
Affiliation: Southern Baptist
Freshman admissions: selective; 2020-2021: 6,961 applied, 5,581 accepted. Neither SAT nor ACT required. SAT 25/75 percentile: 950-1150. High school

rank: 15% in top tenth, 43% in top quarter, 78% in top half
Early decision deadline: N/A, notification date: N/A
Early action deadline: 12/15, notification date: 1/31
Application deadline (fall): rolling
Undergraduate student body: 7,243 full time, 866 part time; 37% male, 63% female; 1% American Indian, 6% Asian, 6% black, 38% Hispanic, 6% multiracial, 1% Pacific Islander, 37% white, 2% international; 92% from in state; 23% live on campus; 0% of students in fraternities, 0% in sororities
Most popular majors: 20% Health Professions and Related Programs, 17% Business, Management, Marketing, and Related Support Services, 10% Psychology, 7% Parks, Recreation, Leisure, and Fitness Studies, 6% Engineering
Expenses: 2021-2022: $37,328; room/board: $11,980
Financial aid: (951) 343-4235; 82% of undergrads determined to have financial need; average aid package $24,463

California College of the Arts
San Francisco CA
(800) 447-1278
U.S. News ranking: Arts, unranked
Website: www.cca.edu
Admissions email: enroll@cca.edu
Private; founded 1907
Freshman admissions: least selective; 2020-2021: 2,625 applied, 2,243 accepted. Neither SAT nor ACT required. SAT 25/75 percentile: N/A. High school rank: N/A
Early decision deadline: N/A, notification date: N/A
Early action deadline: N/A, notification date: N/A
Application deadline (fall): rolling
Undergraduate student body: 1,162 full time, 77 part time; 38% male, 62% female; 1% American Indian, 18% Asian, 5% black, 15% Hispanic, 1% multiracial, 0% Pacific Islander, 17% white, 39% international
Most popular majors: Information not available
Expenses: 2021-2022: $52,312; room/board: $19,117
Financial aid: (415) 338-9538; 44% of undergrads determined to have financial need; average aid package $39,639

California Institute of Technology
Pasadena CA
(626) 395-6341
U.S. News ranking: Nat. U., No. 9
Website: www.caltech.edu
Admissions email: ugadmissions@caltech.edu
Private; founded 1891
Freshman admissions: most selective; 2020-2021: 8,007 applied, 536 accepted. Neither SAT nor ACT required. SAT 25/75 percentile: 1530-1580. High school rank: 96% in top tenth, 100% in top quarter, 100% in top half

Early decision deadline: N/A, notification date: N/A
Early action deadline: 11/1, notification date: 12/15
Application deadline (fall): 1/3
Undergraduate student body: 901 full time, 0 part time; 54% male, 46% female; 0% American Indian, 40% Asian, 2% black, 18% Hispanic, 9% multiracial, 0% Pacific Islander, 23% white, 8% international; 35% from in state; 1% live on campus; 0% of students in fraternities, 0% in sororities
Most popular majors: 35% Computer and Information Sciences and Support Services, 26% Engineering, 24% Physical Sciences, 8% Mathematics and Statistics, 7% Biological and Biomedical Sciences
Expenses: 2021-2022: $58,680; room/board: $17,748
Financial aid: (626) 395-6280; 51% of undergrads determined to have financial need; average aid package $52,493

California Institute of the Arts[1]
Valencia CA
(661) 255-1050
U.S. News ranking: Arts, unranked
Website: www.calarts.edu
Admissions email: admissions@calarts.edu
Private; founded 1961
Application deadline (fall): N/A
Undergraduate student body: N/A full time, N/A part time
Expenses: 2020-2021: $53,466; room/board: $12,809
Financial aid: (661) 253-7869

California Lutheran University
Thousand Oaks CA
(877) 258-3678
U.S. News ranking: Reg. U. (W), No. 8
Website: www.callutheran.edu
Admissions email: admissions@callutheran.edu
Private; founded 1959
Affiliation: Evangelical Lutheran Church
Freshman admissions: selective; 2020-2021: 5,568 applied, 4,142 accepted. Neither SAT nor ACT required. SAT 25/75 percentile: 1070-1240. High school rank: 21% in top tenth, 69% in top quarter, 93% in top half
Early decision deadline: N/A, notification date: N/A
Early action deadline: 11/1, notification date: 1/15
Application deadline (fall): 8/15
Undergraduate student body: 2,716 full time, 88 part time; 43% male, 57% female; 0% American Indian, 5% Asian, 4% black, 39% Hispanic, 7% multiracial, 1% Pacific Islander, 39% white, 2% international; 89% from in state; 53% live on campus; 0% of students in fraternities, 0% in sororities
Most popular majors: 25% Business, Management, Marketing, and Related Support Services, 12% Psychology, 11%

Communication, Journalism, and Related Programs, 10% Biological and Biomedical Sciences, 6% Social Sciences
Expenses: 2021-2022: $46,012; room/board: $14,970
Financial aid: (805) 493-3139; 70% of undergrads determined to have financial need; average aid package $34,046

California Polytechnic State University–San Luis Obispo
San Luis Obispo CA
(805) 756-2311
U.S. News ranking: Reg. U. (W), No. 2
Website: www.calpoly.edu/
Admissions email: admissions@calpoly.edu
Public; founded 1901
Freshman admissions: more selective; 2020-2021: 52,371 applied, 20,127 accepted. Neither SAT nor ACT required. SAT 25/75 percentile: 1220-1410. High school rank: 55% in top tenth, 86% in top quarter, 99% in top half
Early decision deadline: N/A, notification date: N/A
Early action deadline: N/A, notification date: N/A
Application deadline (fall): 11/30
Undergraduate student body: 20,186 full time, 1,261 part time; 51% male, 49% female; 0% American Indian, 13% Asian, 1% black, 18% Hispanic, 8% multiracial, 0% Pacific Islander, 54% white, 2% international; N/A from in state; 20% live on campus; 6% of students in fraternities, 9% in sororities
Most popular majors: 27% Engineering, 13% Business, Management, Marketing, and Related Support Services, 11% Agriculture, Agriculture Operations, and Related Sciences
Expenses: 2021-2022: $8,658 in state, $22,116 out of state; room/board: $16,377
Financial aid: (805) 756-2927; 36% of undergrads determined to have financial need; average aid package $12,059

California State Polytechnic University–Pomona
Pomona CA
(909) 869-5299
U.S. News ranking: Reg. U. (W), No. 14
Website: www.cpp.edu
Admissions email: admissions@cpp.edu
Public; founded 1938
Freshman admissions: selective; 2020-2021: 38,026 applied, 24,646 accepted. Neither SAT nor ACT required. SAT 25/75 percentile: 1010-1250. High school rank: N/A
Early decision deadline: N/A, notification date: N/A
Early action deadline: N/A, notification date: N/A
Application deadline (fall): 11/30
Undergraduate student body: 24,380 full time, 3,522 part time; 53% male, 47% female;

0% American Indian, 22% Asian, 3% black, 49% Hispanic, 3% multiracial, 0% Pacific Islander, 14% white, 5% international; 3% from in state; N/A live on campus; 2% of students in fraternities, 1% in sororities
Most popular majors: 24% Business Administration and Management, General, 5% Hospitality Administration/Management, General, 5% Psychology, General, 4% Civil Engineering, General, 4% Computer Science
Expenses: 2021-2022: $7,438 in state, $19,318 out of state; room/board: $16,570
Financial aid: (909) 869-3700; 70% of undergrads determined to have financial need; average aid package $11,260

California State University–Bakersfield
Bakersfield CA
(661) 654-3036
U.S. News ranking: Reg. U. (W), No. 51
Website: www.csub.edu
Admissions email: admissions@csub.edu
Public
Freshman admissions: less selective; 2020-2021: 12,235 applied, 9,590 accepted. Neither SAT nor ACT required. SAT 25/75 percentile: 900-1080. High school rank: N/A
Early decision deadline: N/A, notification date: N/A
Early action deadline: N/A, notification date: N/A
Application deadline (fall): 11/30
Undergraduate student body: 8,432 full time, 1,547 part time; 36% male, 64% female; 0% American Indian, 6% Asian, 4% black, 62% Hispanic, 2% multiracial, 0% Pacific Islander, 14% white, 4% international; N/A from in state; 4% live on campus; 3% of students in fraternities, 3% in sororities
Most popular majors: Information not available
Expenses: 2021-2022: $7,582 in state, $17,086 out of state; room/board: $13,200
Financial aid: (661) 654-3016; 86% of undergrads determined to have financial need; average aid package $11,111

California State University–Channel Islands[1]
Camarillo CA
(805) 437-8500
U.S. News ranking: Reg. U. (W), No. 41
Website: www.csuci.edu
Admissions email: N/A
Public
Application deadline (fall): N/A
Undergraduate student body: N/A full time, N/A part time
Expenses: 2020-2021: $6,802 in state, $18,682 out of state; room/board: $16,300
Financial aid: N/A

California State University–Chico
Chico CA
(530) 898-6322
U.S. News ranking: Reg. U. (W), No. 39
Website: www.csuchico.edu
Admissions email: info@csuchico.edu
Public; founded 1887
Freshman admissions: less selective; 2020-2021: 19,999 applied, 18,034 accepted. Either SAT or ACT required. SAT 25/75 percentile: 970-1170. High school rank: 35% in top tenth, 76% in top quarter, 100% in top half
Early decision deadline: N/A, notification date: N/A
Early action deadline: N/A, notification date: N/A
Application deadline (fall): 1/15
Undergraduate student body: 14,218 full time, 1,458 part time; 46% male, 54% female; 0% American Indian, 5% Asian, 3% black, 36% Hispanic, 7% multiracial, 0% Pacific Islander, 44% white, 2% international; 0% from in state; 2% live on campus; 7% of students in fraternities, 7% in sororities
Most popular majors: 15% Business, Management, Marketing, and Related Support Services, 10% Social Sciences, 8% Psychology, 7% Health Professions and Related Programs, 7% Parks, Recreation, Leisure, and Fitness Studies
Expenses: 2021-2022: $7,776 in state, $19,686 out of state; room/board: $11,927
Financial aid: (530) 898-6451; 65% of undergrads determined to have financial need; average aid package $12,476

California State University–Dominguez Hills
Carson CA
(310) 243-3300
U.S. News ranking: Reg. U. (W), No. 59
Website: www.csudh.edu
Admissions email: info@csudh.edu
Public; founded 1960
Freshman admissions: less selective; 2020-2021: 18,101 applied, 15,752 accepted. Neither SAT nor ACT required. ACT 25/75 percentile: 15-19. High school rank: N/A
Early decision deadline: N/A, notification date: N/A
Early action deadline: N/A, notification date: N/A
Application deadline (fall): 1/15
Undergraduate student body: 12,448 full time, 3,510 part time; 37% male, 63% female; 0% American Indian, 7% Asian, 11% black, 67% Hispanic, 2% multiracial, 0% Pacific Islander, 5% white, 5% international; N/A from in state; 1% live on campus; 1% of students in fraternities, 1% in sororities
Most popular majors: 18% Business, Management, Marketing, and Related Support Services, 15% Psychology, 10% Health Professions and Related

Programs, 9% Social Sciences, 6% Homeland Security, Law Enforcement, Firefighting and Related Protective Services
Expenses: 2021-2022: $8,140 in state, $17,644 out of state; room/board: $15,120
Financial aid: (310) 243-3189; 77% of undergrads determined to have financial need; average aid package $11,666

California State University–East Bay
Hayward CA
(510) 885-3500
U.S. News ranking: Reg. U. (W), No. 71
Website: www.csueastbay.edu
Admissions email: admissions@csueastbay.edu
Public; founded 1957
Freshman admissions: less selective; 2020-2021: 13,858 applied, 10,155 accepted. Neither SAT nor ACT required. SAT 25/75 percentile: 890-1090. High school rank: N/A
Early decision deadline: N/A, notification date: N/A
Early action deadline: N/A, notification date: N/A
Application deadline (fall): 11/30
Undergraduate student body: 10,191 full time, 2,261 part time; 40% male, 60% female; 0% American Indian, 23% Asian, 10% black, 38% Hispanic, 5% multiracial, 1% Pacific Islander, 14% white, 5% international; 99% from in state; 2% live on campus; N/A of students in fraternities, N/A in sororities
Most popular majors: 19% Business Administration and Management, General, 13% Health Professions and Related Programs, 10% Psychology, General, 10% Sociology, 6% Family and Consumer Economics and Related Studies
Expenses: 2020-2021: $6,890 in state, $18,770 out of state; room/board: $15,140
Financial aid: (510) 885-2784

California State University–Fresno
Fresno CA
(559) 278-2191
U.S. News ranking: Nat. U., No. 213
Website: www.csufresno.edu
Admissions email: lyager@csufresno.edu
Public; founded 1911
Freshman admissions: selective; 2020-2021: 15,447 applied, 13,920 accepted. Neither SAT nor ACT required. SAT 25/75 percentile: 890-1100. High school rank: 15% in top tenth, 80% in top quarter, 100% in top half
Early decision deadline: N/A, notification date: N/A
Early action deadline: N/A, notification date: N/A
Application deadline (fall): 11/30
Undergraduate student body: 19,216 full time, 3,395 part time; 41% male, 59% female; 0% American Indian, 12% Asian, 3% black, 57% Hispanic, 3% multiracial, 0% Pacific Islander,

17% white, 5% international; 99% from in state; 1% live on campus; 4% of students in fraternities, 4% in sororities
Most popular majors: 14% Business, Management, Marketing, and Related Support Services, 10% Health Professions and Related Programs, 9% Liberal Arts and Sciences, General Studies and Humanities, 8% Psychology, 7% Homeland Security, Law Enforcement, Firefighting and Related Protective Services
Expenses: 2021-2022: $6,651 in state, $12,789 out of state; room/board: $10,758
Financial aid: (559) 278-2182; 77% of undergrads determined to have financial need; average aid package $13,149

California State University–Fullerton
Fullerton CA
(657) 278-7788
U.S. News ranking: Reg. U. (W), No. 19
Website: www.fullerton.edu
Admissions email: admissions@fullerton.edu
Public; founded 1957
Freshman admissions: selective; 2020-2021: 45,449 applied, 30,733 accepted. Either SAT or ACT required. SAT 25/75 percentile: 1000-1180. High school rank: 21% in top tenth, 62% in top quarter, 94% in top half
Early decision deadline: N/A, notification date: N/A
Early action deadline: N/A, notification date: N/A
Application deadline (fall): 11/30
Undergraduate student body: 29,671 full time, 7,099 part time; 42% male, 58% female; 0% American Indian, 21% Asian, 2% black, 48% Hispanic, 4% multiracial, 0% Pacific Islander, 17% white, 5% international; N/A from in state; 0% live on campus; 1% of students in fraternities, 2% in sororities
Most popular majors: 25% Business, Management, Marketing, and Related Support Services, 10% Communication, Journalism, and Related Programs, 10% Health Professions and Related Programs, 8% Psychology, 6% Social Sciences
Expenses: 2021-2022: $6,975 in state, $17,632 out of state; room/board: $16,703
Financial aid: (657) 278-5256; 69% of undergrads determined to have financial need; average aid package $10,484

California State University–Long Beach
Long Beach CA
(562) 985-5471
U.S. News ranking: Reg. U. (W), No. 12
Website: www.csulb.edu
Admissions email: eslb@csulb.edu
Public; founded 1949

Freshman admissions: selective; 2020-2021: 67,402 applied, 28,400 accepted. Either SAT or ACT required. SAT 25/75 percentile: 1020-1240. High school rank: N/A
Early decision deadline: N/A, notification date: N/A
Early action deadline: N/A, notification date: N/A
Application deadline (fall): rolling
Undergraduate student body: 28,954 full time, 4,965 part time; 43% male, 57% female; 0% American Indian, 21% Asian, 4% black, 46% Hispanic, 5% multiracial, 0% Pacific Islander, 16% white, 6% international; N/A from in state; 1% live on campus; N/A of students in fraternities, N/A in sororities
Most popular majors: 17% Business, Management, Marketing, and Related Support Services, 10% Visual and Performing Arts, 9% Engineering, 9% Health Professions and Related Programs, 8% Social Sciences
Expenses: 2021-2022: $6,846 in state, $17,142 out of state; room/board: $14,270
Financial aid: (562) 985-8403; 74% of undergrads determined to have financial need; average aid package $14,683

California State University–Los Angeles
Los Angeles CA
(323) 343-3901
U.S. News ranking: Reg. U. (W), No. 23
Website: www.calstatela.edu
Admissions email: admission@calstatela.edu
Public; founded 1947
Freshman admissions: less selective; 2020-2021: 31,442 applied, 24,046 accepted. Neither SAT nor ACT required. SAT 25/75 percentile: 870-1060. High school rank: N/A
Early decision deadline: N/A, notification date: N/A
Early action deadline: N/A, notification date: N/A
Application deadline (fall): 1/19
Undergraduate student body: 19,251 full time, 3,315 part time; 41% male, 59% female; 0% American Indian, 11% Asian, 3% black, 72% Hispanic, 1% multiracial, 0% Pacific Islander, 4% white, 6% international; 100% from in state; 0% live on campus; 0% of students in fraternities, 0% in sororities
Most popular majors: 19% Business, Management, Marketing, and Related Support Services, 10% Health Professions and Related Programs, 10% Social Sciences, 6% Education, 6% Homeland Security, Law Enforcement, Firefighting and Related Protective Services
Expenses: 2021-2022: $6,782 in state, $18,662 out of state; room/board: $16,860
Financial aid: (323) 343-6260; 89% of undergrads determined to have financial need; average aid package $12,197

California State University–Maritime Academy[1]
Vallejo CA
(707) 654-1330
U.S. News ranking: Reg. Coll. (W), No. 3
Website: www.csum.edu
Admissions email: admission@csum.edu
Public; founded 1929
Application deadline (fall): 11/30
Undergraduate student body: N/A full time, N/A part time
Expenses: 2020-2021: $18,643 in state, $18,643 out of state; room/board: $12,828
Financial aid: N/A

California State University–Monterey Bay
Seaside CA
(831) 582-3783
U.S. News ranking: Reg. U. (W), No. 25
Website: www.csumb.edu
Admissions email: admissions@csumb.edu
Public; founded 1994
Freshman admissions: selective; 2020-2021: 11,461 applied, 9,813 accepted. Either SAT or ACT required. SAT 25/75 percentile: 960-1160. High school rank: 14% in top tenth, 43% in top quarter, 84% in top half
Early decision deadline: N/A, notification date: N/A
Early action deadline: N/A, notification date: N/A
Application deadline (fall): 11/30
Undergraduate student body: 5,698 full time, 814 part time; 38% male, 62% female; 1% American Indian, 7% Asian, 4% black, 44% Hispanic, 9% multiracial, 1% Pacific Islander, 27% white, 4% international; N/A from in state; N/A live on campus; 3% of students in fraternities, 2% in sororities
Most popular majors: 14% Business, Management, Marketing, and Related Support Services, 14% Liberal Arts and Sciences, General Studies and Humanities, 12% Psychology, 9% Computer and Information Sciences and Support Services, 9% Parks, Recreation, Leisure, and Fitness Studies
Expenses: 2021-2022: $7,143 in state, $19,023 out of state; room/board: $10,895
Financial aid: N/A; 68% of undergrads determined to have financial need; average aid package $11,181

California State University–Northridge
Northridge CA
(818) 677-3700
U.S. News ranking: Reg. U. (W), No. 39
Website: www.csun.edu
Admissions email: admissions.records@csun.edu
Public; founded 1958
Freshman admissions: less selective; 2020-2021: 55,768

applied, 36,070 accepted. Neither SAT nor ACT required. SAT 25/75 percentile: 900-1110. High school rank: N/A
Early decision deadline: N/A, notification date: N/A
Early action deadline: N/A, notification date: N/A
Application deadline (fall): 11/30
Undergraduate student body: 29,077 full time, 5,626 part time; 45% male, 55% female; 0% American Indian, 9% Asian, 5% black, 53% Hispanic, 3% multiracial, 0% Pacific Islander, 21% white, 6% international; 97% from in state; 1% live on campus; N/A of students in fraternities, N/A in sororities
Most popular majors: 18% Business, Management, Marketing, and Related Support Services, 10% Education, 9% Social Sciences, 8% Communication, Journalism, and Related Programs, 8% Health Professions and Related Programs
Expenses: 2021-2022: $6,747 in state, $18,897 out of state; room/board: $17,322
Financial aid: (818) 677-4085; 82% of undergrads determined to have financial need; average aid package $19,015

California State University–Sacramento
Sacramento CA
(916) 278-1000
U.S. News ranking: Reg. U. (W), No. 46
Website: www.csus.edu
Admissions email: admissions@csus.edu
Public; founded 1947
Freshman admissions: selective; 2020-2021: 25,734 applied, 21,368 accepted. Neither SAT nor ACT required. SAT 25/75 percentile: 930-1130. High school rank: N/A
Early decision deadline: N/A, notification date: N/A
Early action deadline: N/A, notification date: 12/1
Application deadline (fall): 11/30
Undergraduate student body: 23,850 full time, 4,839 part time; 44% male, 56% female; 0% American Indian, 20% Asian, 6% black, 36% Hispanic, 6% multiracial, 1% Pacific Islander, 24% white, 4% international; 98% from in state; N/A live on campus; N/A of students in fraternities, N/A in sororities
Most popular majors: 13% Business, Management, Marketing, and Related Support Services, 10% Social Sciences, 8% Communication, Journalism, and Related Programs, 8% Engineering, 8% Family and Consumer Sciences/Human Sciences
Expenses: 2021-2022: $9,068 in state, $16,988 out of state; room/board: $16,134
Financial aid: (916) 278-1000; 74% of undergrads determined to have financial need; average aid package $11,291

California State University–San Bernardino
San Bernardino CA
(909) 537-5188
U.S. News ranking: Reg. U. (W), No. 37
Website: www.csusb.edu
Admissions email: moreinfo@csusb.edu
Public; founded 1962
Freshman admissions: less selective; 2020-2021: 14,435 applied, 11,277 accepted. Neither SAT nor ACT required. SAT 25/75 percentile: 910-1080. High school rank: N/A
Early decision deadline: N/A, notification date: N/A
Early action deadline: N/A, notification date: 5/1
Application deadline (fall): rolling
Undergraduate student body: 14,506 full time, 2,617 part time; 38% male, 62% female; 0% American Indian, 5% Asian, 5% black, 68% Hispanic, 2% multiracial, 0% Pacific Islander, 11% white, 5% international; N/A from in state; 1% live on campus; 2% of students in fraternities, 2% in sororities
Most popular majors: 24% Business, Management, Marketing, and Related Support Services, 14% Psychology, 9% Social Sciences
Expenses: 2021-2022: $7,046 in state, $13,629 out of state; room/board: $12,822
Financial aid: (909) 537-5227; 91% of undergrads determined to have financial need; average aid package $11,187

California State University–San Marcos
San Marcos CA
(760) 750-4848
U.S. News ranking: Reg. U. (W), No. 41
Website: www.csusm.edu
Admissions email: apply@csusm.edu
Public; founded 1989
Freshman admissions: selective; 2020-2021: 15,398 applied, 12,230 accepted. Neither SAT nor ACT required. SAT 25/75 percentile: 950-1130. High school rank: N/A
Early decision deadline: N/A, notification date: N/A
Early action deadline: N/A, notification date: N/A
Application deadline (fall): 11/30
Undergraduate student body: 11,607 full time, 2,355 part time; 40% male, 60% female; 0% American Indian, 9% Asian, 3% black, 49% Hispanic, 5% multiracial, 0% Pacific Islander, 26% white, 4% international
Most popular majors: 18% Social Sciences, 16% Business, Management, Marketing, and Related Support Services, 10% Health Professions and Related Programs, 8% Family and Consumer Sciences/Human Sciences, 8% Psychology
Expenses: 2021-2022: $7,712 in state, $17,216 out of state; room/

board: $13,150
Financial aid: (760) 750-4881; 72% of undergrads determined to have financial need; average aid package $10,921

California State University–Stanislaus
Turlock CA
(209) 667-3070
U.S. News ranking: Reg. U. (W), No. 30
Website: www.csustan.edu
Admissions email: Outreach_Help_Desk@csustan.edu
Public; founded 1957
Freshman admissions: less selective; 2020-2021: 7,136 applied, 6,374 accepted. Neither SAT nor ACT required. SAT 25/75 percentile: 890-1070. High school rank: N/A
Early decision deadline: N/A, notification date: N/A
Early action deadline: N/A, notification date: N/A
Application deadline (fall): 11/30
Undergraduate student body: 8,309 full time, 1,594 part time; 34% male, 66% female; 0% American Indian, 9% Asian, 2% black, 58% Hispanic, 3% multiracial, 1% Pacific Islander, 19% white, 4% international; 100% from in state; 1% live on campus; 2% of students in fraternities, 3% in sororities
Most popular majors: 17% Business, Management, Marketing, and Related Support Services, 16% Psychology, 12% Social Sciences, 10% Liberal Arts and Sciences, General Studies and Humanities, 9% Homeland Security, Law Enforcement, Firefighting and Related Protective Services
Expenses: 2021-2022: $7,644 in state, $19,524 out of state; room/board: $10,950
Financial aid: (209) 667-3336; 79% of undergrads determined to have financial need; average aid package $17,447

Chapman University
Orange CA
(888) 282-7759
U.S. News ranking: Nat. U., No. 122
Website: www.chapman.edu
Admissions email: admit@chapman.edu
Private; founded 1861
Affiliation: Christian Church (Disciples of Christ)
Freshman admissions: more selective; 2020-2021: 14,252 applied, 8,303 accepted. Neither SAT nor ACT required. SAT 25/75 percentile: 1170-1350. High school rank: 30% in top tenth, 71% in top quarter, 92% in top half
Early decision deadline: 11/1, notification date: 12/20
Early action deadline: 11/1, notification date: 12/20
Application deadline (fall): 1/15
Undergraduate student body: 6,843 full time, 561 part time; 40% male, 60% female; 0% American Indian, 15% Asian, 2% black, 17% Hispanic, 8% multiracial,

0% Pacific Islander, 52% white, 3% international; 70% from in state; 11% live on campus; 20% of students in fraternities, 27% in sororities
Most popular majors: 24% Business Administration and Management, General, 8% Cinematography and Film/Video Production, 6% Business/Corporate Communications, 6% Psychology, General, 5% Speech Communication and Rhetoric
Expenses: 2020-2021: $57,214; room/board: $16,138
Financial aid: (714) 997-6741

Claremont McKenna College
Claremont CA
(909) 621-8088
U.S. News ranking: Nat. Lib. Arts, No. 8
Website: www.claremontmckenna.edu
Admissions email: admission@cmc.edu
Private; founded 1946
Freshman admissions: most selective; 2020-2021: 5,306 applied, 708 accepted. Neither SAT nor ACT required. SAT 25/75 percentile: 1330-1500. High school rank: 73% in top tenth, 94% in top quarter, 100% in top half
Early decision deadline: 11/1, notification date: 12/15
Early action deadline: N/A, notification date: N/A
Application deadline (fall): 1/5
Undergraduate student body: 1,240 full time, 22 part time; 49% male, 51% female; 0% American Indian, 13% Asian, 5% black, 17% Hispanic, 7% multiracial, 0% Pacific Islander, 38% white, 14% international; N/A from in state; 4% live on campus; N/A of students in fraternities, N/A in sororities
Most popular majors: 23% Econometrics and Quantitative Economics, 10% Political Science and Government, General, 8% Experimental Psychology, 6% Computer Science, 5% Multi-/Interdisciplinary Studies, Other
Expenses: 2021-2022: $58,111; room/board: $17,906
Financial aid: (909) 621-8356; 45% of undergrads determined to have financial need; average aid package $54,560

Columbia College Hollywood[1]
Tarzana CA
(818) 345-8414
U.S. News ranking: Arts, unranked
Website: flashpoint.columbiacollege.edu/
Admissions email: admissions@columbiacollege.edu
Private; founded 1953
Application deadline (fall): rolling
Undergraduate student body: N/A full time, N/A part time
Expenses: 2020-2021: $26,175; room/board: N/A
Financial aid: (818) 345-8414

Concordia University – Irvine
Irvine CA
(949) 214-3010
U.S. News ranking: Reg. U. (W), No. 55
Website: www.cui.edu
Admissions email: admissions@cui.edu
Private; founded 1972
Affiliation: Lutheran Church - Missouri Synod
Freshman admissions: selective; 2020-2021: 3,327 applied, 2,601 accepted. Neither SAT nor ACT required. SAT 25/75 percentile: 1020-1210. High school rank: 16% in top tenth, 47% in top quarter, 84% in top half
Early decision deadline: N/A, notification date: N/A
Early action deadline: 12/1, notification date: 12/15
Application deadline (fall): 8/1
Undergraduate student body: 1,538 full time, 166 part time; 38% male, 62% female; 0% American Indian, 11% Asian, 4% black, 26% Hispanic, 8% multiracial, 1% Pacific Islander, 47% white, 4% international; 76% from in state; 38% live on campus; N/A of students in fraternities, N/A in sororities
Most popular majors: 24% Health Professions and Related Programs, 18% Business, Management, Marketing, and Related Support Services, 10% Parks, Recreation, Leisure, and Fitness Studies, 9% Liberal Arts and Sciences, General Studies and Humanities, 7% Visual and Performing Arts
Expenses: 2021-2022: $38,740; room/board: $12,560
Financial aid: (949) 214-3066; 72% of undergrads determined to have financial need; average aid package $26,282

Cypress College[1]
Cypress CA
(714) 484-7000
U.S. News ranking: Reg. Coll. (W), unranked
Website: www.cypresscollege.edu
Admissions email: N/A
Public
Application deadline (fall): N/A
Undergraduate student body: N/A full time, N/A part time
Expenses: 2020-2021: $1,146 in state, $8,898 out of state; room/board: N/A
Financial aid: N/A

Design Institute of San Diego[1]
San Diego CA
(858) 566-1200
U.S. News ranking: Arts, unranked
Website: www.disd.edu
Admissions email: admissions@disd.edu
For-profit; founded 1977
Application deadline (fall): N/A
Undergraduate student body: N/A full time, N/A part time
Expenses: 2020-2021: $25,649; room/board: N/A
Financial aid: (858) 566-1200

Dominican University of California
San Rafael CA
(415) 485-3204
U.S. News ranking: Reg. U. (W), No. 23
Website: www.dominican.edu
Admissions email: enroll@dominican.edu
Private; founded 1890
Freshman admissions: selective; 2020-2021: 1,944 applied, 1,665 accepted. Neither SAT nor ACT required. SAT 25/75 percentile: 1070-1250. High school rank: 22% in top tenth, 52% in top quarter, 86% in top half
Early decision deadline: N/A, notification date: N/A
Early action deadline: N/A, notification date: N/A
Application deadline (fall): rolling
Undergraduate student body: 1,229 full time, 153 part time; 34% male, 66% female; 0% American Indian, 30% Asian, 5% black, 28% Hispanic, 5% multiracial, 1% Pacific Islander, 27% white, 2% international; 86% from in state; 15% live on campus; 0% of students in fraternities, 0% in sororities
Most popular majors: 42% Health Professions and Related Programs, 14% Business, Management, Marketing, and Related Support Services, 11% Psychology, 9% Biological and Biomedical Sciences, 6% Visual and Performing Arts
Expenses: 2021-2022: $47,910; room/board: $15,772
Financial aid: (415) 257-1350; 77% of undergrads determined to have financial need; average aid package $31,063

Fashion Institute of Design & Merchandising
Los Angeles CA
(800) 624-1200
U.S. News ranking: Arts, unranked
Website: fidm.edu/
Admissions email: admissions@fidm.edu
For-profit; founded 1969
Freshman admissions: least selective; 2020-2021: 1,733 applied, 662 accepted. Neither SAT nor ACT required. SAT 25/75 percentile: N/A. High school rank: N/A
Early decision deadline: N/A, notification date: N/A
Early action deadline: N/A, notification date: N/A
Application deadline (fall): rolling
Undergraduate student body: 1,678 full time, 282 part time; 17% male, 83% female; 1% American Indian, 12% Asian, 8% black, 23% Hispanic, 1% multiracial, 1% Pacific Islander, 32% white, 16% international; 50% from in state; 0% live on campus; 0% of students in fraternities, 0% in sororities
Most popular majors: 36% Fashion Merchandising, 27% Fashion/Apparel Design, 12% Business,

Management, Marketing, and
Related Support Services, Other
Expenses: 2020-2021: $31,870;
room/board: N/A
Financial aid: (213) 624-1200

Feather River Community College District[1]
Quincy CA
(530) 283-0202
U.S. News ranking: Reg. Coll. (W),
unranked
Website: www.frc.edu
Admissions email:
N/A
Public
Application deadline (fall): N/A
Undergraduate student body: N/A
full time, N/A part time
Expenses: 2020-2021: $1,465 in
state, $9,865 out of state; room/
board: $10,766
Financial aid: N/A

Foothill College[1]
Los Altos Hills CA
(650) 949-7777
U.S. News ranking: Reg. Coll. (W),
unranked
Website: www.foothill.edu
Admissions email:
N/A
Public
Application deadline (fall): N/A
Undergraduate student body: N/A
full time, N/A part time
Expenses: 2020-2021: $1,563 in
state, $10,248 out of state; room/
board: N/A
Financial aid: N/A

Fresno Pacific University[1]
Fresno CA
(559) 453-2039
U.S. News ranking: Reg. U. (W),
No. 41
Website: www.fresno.edu
Admissions email:
ugadmis@fresno.edu
Private; founded 1944
Affiliation: Mennonite Brethren
Church
Application deadline (fall): 7/31
Undergraduate student body: N/A
full time, N/A part time
Expenses: 2020-2021: $32,977;
room/board: $8,954
Financial aid: (559) 453-7195

Harvey Mudd College
Claremont CA
(909) 621-8011
U.S. News ranking: Nat. Lib. Arts,
No. 28
Website: www.hmc.edu
Admissions email:
admission@hmc.edu
Private; founded 1955
Freshman admissions: more
selective; 2020-2021: 3,397
applied, 610 accepted. Either
SAT or ACT required. SAT 25/75
percentile: 1490-1570. High
school rank: N/A
Early decision deadline: 11/5,
notification date: 12/15
Early action deadline: N/A,
notification date: N/A
Application deadline (fall): 1/5

Undergraduate student body: 821
full time, 33 part time; 51%
male, 49% female; 0% American
Indian, 23% Asian, 4% black,
20% Hispanic, 10% multiracial,
0% Pacific Islander, 28% white,
7% international; 42% from in
state; 2% live on campus; 0%
of students in fraternities, 0% in
sororities
Most popular majors: 31%
Engineering, 24% Multi/
Interdisciplinary Studies, 22%
Computer and Information
Sciences and Support Services,
8% Physical Sciences, 7%
Biological and Biomedical
Sciences
Expenses: 2021-2022: $60,703;
room/board: $19,333
Financial aid: (909) 621-8055;
49% of undergrads determined to
have financial need; average aid
package $50,494

Holy Names University
Oakland CA
(510) 436-1351
U.S. News ranking: Reg. U. (W),
No. 84
Website: www.hnu.edu
Admissions email:
admissions@hnu.edu
Private; founded 1868
Affiliation: Roman Catholic
Freshman admissions: least
selective; 2020-2021: 1,884
applied, 1,679 accepted. Either
SAT or ACT required. SAT 25/75
percentile: 695-855. High school
rank: N/A
Early decision deadline: N/A,
notification date: N/A
Early action deadline: N/A,
notification date: N/A
Application deadline (fall): rolling
Undergraduate student body: 587
full time, 43 part time; 34%
male, 66% female; 0% American
Indian, 10% Asian, 17% black,
40% Hispanic, 6% multiracial,
1% Pacific Islander, 12% white,
3% international
Most popular majors: Information
not available
Expenses: 2021-2022: $40,904;
room/board: $13,994
Financial aid: (510) 436-1327;
89% of undergrads determined to
have financial need; average aid
package $37,657

Hope International University
Fullerton CA
(888) 352-4673
U.S. News ranking: Reg. U. (W),
No. 77
Website: www.hiu.edu
Admissions email:
admissions@hiu.edu
Private; founded 1928
Affiliation: Christian Churches and
Churches of Christ
Freshman admissions: selective;
2020-2021: 794 applied, 304
accepted. Either SAT or ACT
required. SAT 25/75 percentile:
930-1100. High school rank: 2%
in top tenth, 40% in top quarter,
73% in top half
Early decision deadline: N/A,
notification date: N/A

Early action deadline: N/A,
notification date: N/A
Application deadline (fall): rolling
Undergraduate student body: 530
full time, 126 part time; 44%
male, 56% female; 1% American
Indian, 5% Asian, 8% black,
27% Hispanic, 11% multiracial,
2% Pacific Islander, 36% white,
1% international; 78% from in
state; N/A live on campus; N/A
of students in fraternities, N/A in
sororities
Most popular majors: 34%
Business Administration and
Management, General, 15%
Theological and Ministerial
Studies, Other, 12% Education,
General, 11% Human
Development and Family Studies,
General, 10% Social Sciences,
General
Expenses: 2021-2022: $35,450;
room/board: $11,350
Financial aid: (714) 879-3901;
85% of undergrads determined to
have financial need; average aid
package $20,976

Humboldt State University
Arcata CA
(707) 826-4402
U.S. News ranking: Reg. U. (W),
No. 30
Website: www.humboldt.edu
Admissions email:
hsuinfo@humboldt.edu
Public; founded 1913
Freshman admissions: selective;
2020-2021: 17,115 applied,
14,242 accepted. Neither SAT
nor ACT required. SAT 25/75
percentile: 970-1190. High
school rank: 5% in top tenth, 31%
in top quarter, 71% in top half
Early decision deadline: N/A,
notification date: N/A
Early action deadline: N/A,
notification date: N/A
Application deadline (fall): 11/30
Undergraduate student body: 5,187
full time, 682 part time; 42%
male, 58% female; 3% American
Indian, 3% Asian, 5% black,
26% Hispanic, 10% multiracial,
1% Pacific Islander, 48% white,
1% international; 94% from in
state; 13% live on campus; 1%
of students in fraternities, 1% in
sororities
Most popular majors: 18% Natural
Resources and Conservation,
10% Biological and Biomedical
Sciences, 10% Psychology, 9%
Social Sciences, 8% Business,
Management, Marketing, and
Related Support Services
Expenses: 2021-2022: $7,870 in
state, $16,124 out of state; room/
board: $12,238
Financial aid: (707) 826-4321;
78% of undergrads determined to
have financial need; average aid
package $16,018

Humphreys University[1]
Stockton CA
(209) 478-0800
U.S. News ranking: Reg. Coll. (W),
No. 29
Website: www.humphreys.edu
Admissions email:
ugadmission@humphreys.edu

Private
Application deadline (fall): N/A
Undergraduate student body: N/A
full time, N/A part time
Expenses: 2020-2021: $14,580;
room/board: N/A
Financial aid: N/A

John Paul the Great Catholic University
Escondido CA
(858) 653-6740
U.S. News ranking: Reg. Coll. (W),
No. 19
Website: jpcatholic.edu/
Admissions email:
N/A
Private; founded 2006
Affiliation: Roman Catholic
Freshman admissions: selective;
2020-2021: 310 applied, 238
accepted. Either SAT or ACT
required. SAT 25/75 percentile:
1006-1173. High school rank:
N/A
Early decision deadline: N/A,
notification date: N/A
Early action deadline: N/A,
notification date: N/A
Application deadline (fall): rolling
Undergraduate student body: 256
full time, 18 part time; 47%
male, 53% female; 0% American
Indian, 3% Asian, 1% black,
29% Hispanic, 6% multiracial,
1% Pacific Islander, 46% white,
4% international; 54% from in
state; 69% live on campus; N/A
of students in fraternities, N/A in
sororities
Most popular majors: 72%
Communication and Media
Studies, 15% Entrepreneurship/
Entrepreneurial Studies, 12%
Humanities/Humanistic Studies
Expenses: 2021-2022: $28,000;
room/board: $7,950
Financial aid: (858) 653-6740

Laguna College of Art and Design[1]
Laguna Beach CA
(949) 376-6000
U.S. News ranking: Arts, unranked
Website: www.lcad.edu/
Admissions email:
admissions@lcad.edu
Private; founded 1961
Application deadline (fall): 8/1
Undergraduate student body: N/A
full time, N/A part time
Expenses: 2020-2021: $32,600;
room/board: $16,016
Financial aid: (949) 376-6000

La Sierra University
Riverside CA
(951) 785-2176
U.S. News ranking: Reg. U. (W),
No. 67
Website: lasierra.edu/about/
Admissions email:
admissions@lasierra.edu
Private; founded 1922
Affiliation: Seventh Day Adventist
Freshman admissions: selective;
2020-2021: 4,200 applied,
2,410 accepted. Either SAT
or ACT required. SAT 25/75
percentile: 940-1170. High school
rank: 13% in top tenth, 33% in
top quarter, 77% in top half
Early decision deadline: N/A,

notification date: N/A
Early action deadline: N/A,
notification date: N/A
Application deadline (fall): 7/15
Undergraduate student body: 1,476
full time, 267 part time; 42%
male, 58% female; 0% American
Indian, 16% Asian, 7% black,
50% Hispanic, 4% multiracial,
1% Pacific Islander, 12% white,
9% international; 88% from in
state; 29% live on campus; N/A
of students in fraternities, N/A in
sororities
Most popular majors: 16% Criminal
Justice/Safety Studies, 7%
Kinesiology and Exercise Science,
6% Social Work, 5% Biomedical
Sciences, General, 3% Accounting
Expenses: 2021-2022: $34,218;
room/board: $8,790
Financial aid: (951) 785-2175;
76% of undergrads determined to
have financial need; average aid
package $19,962

Life Pacific University
San Dimas CA
(877) 886-5433
U.S. News ranking: Reg. Coll. (W),
No. 17
Website: www.lifepacific.edu
Admissions email:
adm@lifepacific.edu
Private; founded 1923
Affiliation: Other Protestant
Freshman admissions: less
selective; 2020-2021: 116
applied, 108 accepted. Either
SAT or ACT required. SAT 25/75
percentile: 930-1090. High
school rank: N/A
Early decision deadline: N/A,
notification date: N/A
Early action deadline: N/A,
notification date: N/A
Application deadline (fall): rolling
Undergraduate student body: 411
full time, 79 part time; 43%
male, 57% female; 1% American
Indian, 3% Asian, 4% black,
42% Hispanic, 6% multiracial,
1% Pacific Islander, 37% white,
1% international; 84% from in
state; 34% live on campus; N/A
of students in fraternities, N/A in
sororities
Most popular majors: 32%
Pastoral Studies/Counseling,
29% Behavioral Sciences, 16%
Business Administration and
Management, General, 13%
Bible/Biblical Studies, 8% Mass
Communication/Media Studies
Expenses: 2021-2022: $18,300;
room/board: $9,800
Financial aid: (909) 706-3026;
76% of undergrads determined to
have financial need; average aid
package $11,934

Lincoln University[1]
Oakland CA
510-628-8010
U.S. News ranking: Business,
unranked
Admissions email:
N/A
Private
Application deadline (fall): N/A
Undergraduate student body: N/A
full time, N/A part time
Expenses: 2020-2021: $11,390;
room/board: N/A
Financial aid: N/A

Loyola Marymount University

Los Angeles CA
(310) 338-2750
U.S. News ranking: Nat. U., No. 75
Website: www.lmu.edu
Admissions email:
admission@lmu.edu
Private; founded 1911
Affiliation: Roman Catholic
Freshman admissions: more selective; 2020-2021: 18,576 applied, 9,314 accepted. Neither SAT nor ACT required. SAT 25/75 percentile: 1210-1390. High school rank: 37% in top tenth, 72% in top quarter, 96% in top half
Early decision deadline: 11/1, notification date: 12/15
Early action deadline: 11/1, notification date: 12/20
Application deadline (fall): 1/15
Undergraduate student body: 6,383 full time, 290 part time; 46% male, 54% female; 0% American Indian, 10% Asian, 7% black, 23% Hispanic, 7% multiracial, 0% Pacific Islander, 43% white, 10% international; N/A from in state; 3% live on campus; 18% of students in fraternities, 24% in sororities
Most popular majors: 25% Business, Management, Marketing, and Related Support Services, 17% Visual and Performing Arts, 15% Social Sciences
Expenses: 2021-2022: $53,051; room/board: $17,154
Financial aid: (310) 338-2753; 46% of undergrads determined to have financial need; average aid package $32,245

Marymount California University

Rancho Palos Verdes CA
(310) 303-7311
U.S. News ranking: Nat. Lib. Arts, second tier
Website:
www.marymountcalifornia.edu
Admissions email:
admissions@marymountcalifornia.edu
Private; founded 1933
Affiliation: Roman Catholic
Freshman admissions: less selective; 2020-2021: 1,054 applied, 1,002 accepted. Neither SAT nor ACT required. SAT 25/75 percentile: 950-1100. High school rank: N/A
Early decision deadline: N/A, notification date: N/A
Early action deadline: N/A, notification date: N/A
Application deadline (fall): rolling
Undergraduate student body: 504 full time, 11 part time; 47% male, 53% female; 0% American Indian, 6% Asian, 8% black, 46% Hispanic, 8% multiracial, 1% Pacific Islander, 21% white, 8% international
Most popular majors: 38% Business, Management, Marketing, and Related Support Services, 17% Liberal Arts and Sciences, General Studies and Humanities, 17% Psychology, 15% Homeland Security, Law Enforcement, Firefighting and

Related Protective Services, 13% Biological and Biomedical Sciences
Expenses: 2020-2021: $36,908; room/board: $15,999
Financial aid: (310) 303-7217

The Master's University and Seminary

Santa Clarita CA
(800) 568-6248
U.S. News ranking: Reg. U. (W), No. 53
Website: www.masters.edu
Admissions email:
admissions@masters.edu
Private; founded 1927
Affiliation: Other
Freshman admissions: more selective; 2020-2021: 1,924 applied, 1,152 accepted. Either SAT or ACT required. SAT 25/75 percentile: 1040-1340. High school rank: 40% in top tenth, 70% in top quarter, 95% in top half
Early decision deadline: N/A, notification date: N/A
Early action deadline: 11/15, notification date: 12/22
Application deadline (fall): rolling
Undergraduate student body: 917 full time, 732 part time; 53% male, 47% female; 0% American Indian, 4% Asian, 3% black, 7% Hispanic, 9% multiracial, 0% Pacific Islander, 67% white, 1% international; 67% from in state; 75% live on campus; N/A of students in fraternities, N/A in sororities
Most popular majors: 25% Business Administration and Management, General, 21% Bible/Biblical Studies, 13% Communication and Media Studies, 7% Biology/Biological Sciences, General, 7% Music, General
Expenses: 2021-2022: $28,740; room/board: $11,500
Financial aid: (661) 362-2290; 51% of undergrads determined to have financial need; average aid package $8,478

Menlo College[1]

Atherton CA
(800) 556-3656
U.S. News ranking: Business, unranked
Website: www.menlo.edu
Admissions email:
admissions@menlo.edu
Private; founded 1927
Application deadline (fall): 4/1
Undergraduate student body: N/A full time, N/A part time
Expenses: 2020-2021: $45,860; room/board: $15,400
Financial aid: N/A

Mills College

Oakland CA
(510) 430-2135
U.S. News ranking: Reg. U. (W), No. 10
Website: www.mills.edu
Admissions email:
admission@mills.edu
Private; founded 1852
Freshman admissions: selective;

2020-2021: 848 applied, 711 accepted. Neither SAT nor ACT required. SAT 25/75 percentile: 1005-1290. High school rank: 27% in top tenth, 54% in top quarter, 84% in top half
Early decision deadline: N/A, notification date: N/A
Early action deadline: 11/15, notification date: 12/1
Application deadline (fall): rolling
Undergraduate student body: 565 full time, 44 part time; 0% male, 100% female; 1% American Indian, 8% Asian, 12% black, 33% Hispanic, 11% multiracial, 0% Pacific Islander, 34% white, 1% international; N/A from in state; 58% live on campus; N/A of students in fraternities, N/A in sororities
Most popular majors: 17% Social Sciences, 15% Psychology, 15% Visual and Performing Arts
Expenses: 2021-2022: $30,950; room/board: $13,470
Financial aid: (510) 430-2039; 72% of undergrads determined to have financial need; average aid package $49,120

MiraCosta College[1]

Oceanside CA
(760) 757-2121
U.S. News ranking: Reg. Coll. (W), unranked
Website: www.miracosta.edu
Admissions email:
N/A
Public
Application deadline (fall): N/A
Undergraduate student body: N/A full time, N/A part time
Expenses: 2020-2021: $1,152 in state, $8,112 out of state; room/board: N/A
Financial aid: N/A

Modesto Junior College[1]

Modesto CA
(209) 575-6550
U.S. News ranking: Reg. Coll. (W), unranked
Website: www.mjc.edu
Admissions email:
N/A
Public
Application deadline (fall): N/A
Undergraduate student body: N/A full time, N/A part time
Expenses: 2020-2021: $1,270 in state, $7,538 out of state; room/board: N/A
Financial aid: N/A

Mount Saint Mary's University

Los Angeles CA
(310) 954-4250
U.S. News ranking: Reg. U. (W), No. 27
Website: www.msmu.edu
Admissions email:
admissions@msmu.edu
Private; founded 1925
Affiliation: Roman Catholic
Freshman admissions: selective; 2020-2021: 1,986 applied, 1,774 accepted. Neither SAT nor ACT required. SAT 25/75 percentile: 900-1110. High school rank: 18% in top tenth, 52% in

top quarter, 82% in top half
Early decision deadline: N/A, notification date: N/A
Early action deadline: 12/1, notification date: 1/30
Application deadline (fall): 8/1
Undergraduate student body: 1,607 full time, 407 part time; 6% male, 94% female; 0% American Indian, 15% Asian, 6% black, 59% Hispanic, 1% multiracial, 0% Pacific Islander, 9% white, 0% international; N/A from in state; 2% live on campus; N/A of students in fraternities, 1% in sororities
Most popular majors: 38% Health Professions and Related Programs, 14% Health Professions and Related Programs, 11% Psychology
Expenses: 2021-2022: $45,388; room/board: $12,959
Financial aid: (310) 954-4190; 90% of undergrads determined to have financial need; average aid package $37,518

National University

La Jolla CA
(844) 873-1037
U.S. News ranking: Reg. U. (W), second tier
Website: www.nu.edu/
Admissions email:
advisor@nu.edu
Private; founded 1971
Freshman admissions: less selective; 2020-2021: 59 applied, 22 accepted. Neither SAT nor ACT required. SAT 25/75 percentile: 750-1170. High school rank: N/A
Early decision deadline: N/A, notification date: N/A
Early action deadline: N/A, notification date: N/A
Application deadline (fall): rolling
Undergraduate student body: 3,290 full time, 5,147 part time; 47% male, 53% female; 1% American Indian, 0% Asian, 10% black, 29% Hispanic, 3% multiracial, 2% Pacific Islander, 35% white, 0% international
Most popular majors: 18% Registered Nursing/Registered Nurse, 13% Business Administration and Management, General, 9% Psychology, General, 8% Early Childhood Education and Teaching, 6% Criminal Justice/ Law Enforcement Administration
Expenses: 2021-2022: $13,320; room/board: $0
Financial aid: (858) 642-8500; 61% of undergrads determined to have financial need; average aid package $8,687

NewSchool of Architecture and Design[1]

San Diego CA
(619) 684-8828
U.S. News ranking: Arts, unranked
Website: newschoolarch.edu/
Admissions email:
fguidali@newschoolarch.edu
For-profit; founded 1980
Application deadline (fall): rolling
Undergraduate student body: N/A full time, N/A part time
Expenses: 2020-2021: $29,427; room/board: N/A
Financial aid: (619) 684-8803

Occidental College

Los Angeles CA
(323) 259-2700
U.S. News ranking: Nat. Lib. Arts, No. 42
Website: www.oxy.edu
Admissions email:
admission@oxy.edu
Private; founded 1887
Freshman admissions: more selective; 2020-2021: 6,939 applied, 2,838 accepted. Either SAT or ACT required. SAT 25/75 percentile: 1270-1460. High school rank: 59% in top tenth, 89% in top quarter, 98% in top half
Early decision deadline: 11/15, notification date: 12/15
Early action deadline: N/A, notification date: N/A
Application deadline (fall): 1/10
Undergraduate student body: 1,791 full time, 48 part time; 41% male, 59% female; 0% American Indian, 15% Asian, 4% black, 16% Hispanic, 10% multiracial, 0% Pacific Islander, 46% white, 6% international; 45% from in state; N/A live on campus; N/A of students in fraternities, N/A in sororities
Most popular majors: 16% Econometrics and Quantitative Economics, 8% International Relations and Affairs, 7% Biology/ Biological Sciences, General, 6% Political Science and Government, General, 5% Psychology, General
Expenses: 2021-2022: $58,426; room/board: $16,712
Financial aid: (323) 259-2548; 56% of undergrads determined to have financial need; average aid package $48,609

Otis College of Art and Design

Los Angeles CA
(310) 665-6820
U.S. News ranking: Arts, unranked
Website: www.otis.edu
Admissions email:
admissions@otis.edu
Private; founded 1918
Freshman admissions: selective; 2020-2021: 2,342 applied, 1,881 accepted. Neither SAT nor ACT required. SAT 25/75 percentile: 1080-1310. High school rank: 12% in top tenth, 35% in top quarter, 68% in top half
Early decision deadline: N/A, notification date: N/A
Early action deadline: 12/1, notification date: 12/18
Application deadline (fall): N/A
Undergraduate student body: 1,005 full time, 25 part time; 33% male, 67% female; 0% American Indian, 25% Asian, 5% black, 21% Hispanic, 6% multiracial, 0% Pacific Islander, 23% white, 16% international; 7% from in state; 24% live on campus; N/A of students in fraternities, N/A in sororities
Most popular majors: 28% Digital Arts, 21% Design and Visual Communications, General, 14% Fine/Studio Arts, General, 12% Fashion/Apparel Design, 9% Industrial and Product Design

Expenses: 2021-2022: $48,600; room/board: $15,744
Financial aid: (310) 665-6999; 92% of undergrads determined to have financial need; average aid package $7,629

Pacific Union College
Angwin CA
(707) 965-6336
U.S. News ranking: Reg. Coll. (W), No. 25
Website: www.puc.edu
Admissions email: admissions@puc.edu
Private; founded 1882
Affiliation: Seventh Day Adventist
Freshman admissions: selective; 2020-2021: 1,543 applied, 913 accepted. Either SAT or ACT required. SAT 25/75 percentile: 900-1140. High school rank: N/A
Early decision deadline: N/A, notification date: N/A
Early action deadline: 12/15, notification date: 11/15
Application deadline (fall): rolling
Undergraduate student body: 832 full time, 123 part time; 38% male, 62% female; 0% American Indian, 22% Asian, 7% black, 29% Hispanic, 7% multiracial, 1% Pacific Islander, 22% white, 3% international; 87% from in state; N/A live on campus; 0% of students in fraternities, 0% in sororities
Most popular majors: 26% Registered Nursing/Registered Nurse, 15% Business/Commerce, General, 12% Biology/Biological Sciences, General, 5% Health Communication, 5% Social Work
Expenses: 2021-2022: $32,103; room/board: $8,916
Financial aid: (707) 965-7200; 77% of undergrads determined to have financial need; average aid package $24,921

Pepperdine University
Malibu CA
(310) 506-4392
U.S. News ranking: Nat. U., No. 49
Website: www.pepperdine.edu
Admissions email: admission-seaver@pepperdine.edu
Private; founded 1937
Affiliation: Churches of Christ
Freshman admissions: more selective; 2020-2021: 11,768 applied, 4,925 accepted. Neither SAT nor ACT required. SAT 25/75 percentile: 1200-1410. High school rank: 49% in top tenth, 88% in top quarter, 99% in top half
Early decision deadline: N/A, notification date: N/A
Early action deadline: 11/1, notification date: 1/10
Application deadline (fall): 1/15
Undergraduate student body: 3,132 full time, 327 part time; 42% male, 58% female; 0% American Indian, 12% Asian, 5% black, 16% Hispanic, 7% multiracial, 0% Pacific Islander, 48% white, 10% international; N/A from in state; N/A live on campus; 14% of students in fraternities, 28% in sororities
Most popular majors: 26% Business, Management, Marketing, and Related Support Services, 17% Communication, Journalism, and Related Programs, 11% Social Sciences, 8% Multi/Interdisciplinary Studies, 8% Psychology
Expenses: 2021-2022: $59,702; room/board: $16,700
Financial aid: (310) 506-4301; 54% of undergrads determined to have financial need; average aid package $43,668

Pitzer College
Claremont CA
(909) 621-8129
U.S. News ranking: Nat. Lib. Arts, No. 35
Website: www.pitzer.edu
Admissions email: admission@pitzer.edu
Private; founded 1963
Freshman admissions: most selective; 2020-2021: 4,260 applied, 706 accepted. Neither SAT nor ACT required. SAT 25/75 percentile: 1325-1510. High school rank: 51% in top tenth, 80% in top quarter, 98% in top half
Early decision deadline: 11/15, notification date: 12/18
Early action deadline: N/A, notification date: N/A
Application deadline (fall): 1/1
Undergraduate student body: 802 full time, 120 part time; 42% male, 58% female; 1% American Indian, 12% Asian, 6% black, 16% Hispanic, 8% multiracial, 0% Pacific Islander, 45% white, 8% international; 42% from in state; 0% live on campus; 0% of students in fraternities, 0% in sororities
Most popular majors: 22% Social Sciences, 11% Natural Resources and Conservation, 9% Psychology, 8% Multi/Interdisciplinary Studies, 7% Biological and Biomedical Sciences
Expenses: 2021-2022: $57,978; room/board: $19,180
Financial aid: (909) 621-8208; 42% of undergrads determined to have financial need; average aid package $44,830

Point Loma Nazarene University
San Diego CA
(619) 849-2273
U.S. News ranking: Reg. U. (W), No. 12
Website: www.pointloma.edu
Admissions email: admissions@pointloma.edu
Private; founded 1902
Affiliation: Church of the Nazarene
Freshman admissions: more selective; 2020-2021: 2,949 applied, 2,464 accepted. Neither SAT nor ACT required. SAT 25/75 percentile: 1100-1290. High school rank: 46% in top tenth, 77% in top quarter, 94% in top half
Early decision deadline: N/A, notification date: N/A
Early action deadline: 11/15, notification date: 12/21
Application deadline (fall): 2/15
Undergraduate student body: 2,543 full time, 673 part time; 34% male, 66% female; 0% American Indian, 7% Asian, 2% black, 27% Hispanic, 8% multiracial, 0% Pacific Islander, 53% white, 1% international; 82% from in state; N/A live on campus; N/A of students in fraternities, N/A in sororities
Most popular majors: 23% Health Professions and Related Programs, 19% Business, Management, Marketing, and Related Support Services, 7% Biological and Biomedical Sciences, 7% Family and Consumer Sciences/Human Sciences, 6% Education
Expenses: 2021-2022: $39,500; room/board: $11,300
Financial aid: (619) 849-2538; 64% of undergrads determined to have financial need; average aid package $25,374

Pomona College
Claremont CA
(909) 621-8134
U.S. News ranking: Nat. Lib. Arts, No. 4
Website: www.pomona.edu
Admissions email: admissions@pomona.edu
Private; founded 1887
Freshman admissions: most selective; 2020-2021: 10,388 applied, 895 accepted. Neither SAT nor ACT required. SAT 25/75 percentile: 1390-1540. High school rank: 90% in top tenth, 98% in top quarter, 100% in top half
Early decision deadline: 11/15, notification date: 12/15
Early action deadline: N/A, notification date: N/A
Application deadline (fall): 1/8
Undergraduate student body: 1,467 full time, 10 part time; 46% male, 54% female; 0% American Indian, 18% Asian, 11% black, 19% Hispanic, 7% multiracial, 0% Pacific Islander, 30% white, 11% international
Most popular majors: 23% Social Sciences, 10% Biological and Biomedical Sciences, 9% Mathematics and Statistics, 7% Computer and Information Sciences and Support Services, 7% Physical Sciences
Expenses: 2021-2022: $56,686; room/board: $18,524
Financial aid: (909) 621-8205; 58% of undergrads determined to have financial need; average aid package $54,114

Providence Christian College[1]
Pasadena CA
(866) 323-0233
U.S. News ranking: Nat. Lib. Arts, second tier
Website: www.providencecc.net/
Admissions email: N/A
Private; founded 2003
Application deadline (fall): rolling
Undergraduate student body: N/A full time, N/A part time
Expenses: 2020-2021: $33,396; room/board: $10,838
Financial aid: N/A

Rio Hondo College[1]
Whittier CA
(562) 692-0921
U.S. News ranking: Reg. Coll. (W), unranked
Website: www.riohondo.edu
Admissions email: N/A
Public
Application deadline (fall): N/A
Undergraduate student body: N/A full time, N/A part time
Expenses: 2020-2021: $1,360 in state, $8,779 out of state; room/board: N/A
Financial aid: N/A

San Diego Christian College[1]
Santee CA
(800) 676-2242
U.S. News ranking: Reg. Coll. (W), No. 17
Website: www.sdcc.edu/
Admissions email: admissions@sdcc.edu
Private; founded 1970
Affiliation: Undenominational
Application deadline (fall): rolling
Undergraduate student body: N/A full time, N/A part time
Expenses: 2020-2021: $33,312; room/board: $12,588
Financial aid: N/A

San Diego Mesa College[1]
San Diego CA
(619) 388-2604
U.S. News ranking: Reg. Coll. (W), unranked
Website: www.sdmesa.edu/
Admissions email: N/A
Public
Application deadline (fall): N/A
Undergraduate student body: N/A full time, N/A part time
Expenses: 2020-2021: $1,144 in state, $8,104 out of state; room/board: N/A
Financial aid: N/A

San Diego State University
San Diego CA
(619) 594-6336
U.S. News ranking: Nat. U., No. 148
Website: www.sdsu.edu
Admissions email: admissions@sdsu.edu
Public; founded 1897
Freshman admissions: more selective; 2020-2021: 64,784 applied, 23,778 accepted. Neither SAT nor ACT required. SAT 25/75 percentile: 1090-1300. High school rank: 33% in top tenth, 72% in top quarter, 95% in top half
Early decision deadline: N/A, notification date: N/A
Early action deadline: N/A, notification date: N/A
Application deadline (fall): 11/30
Undergraduate student body: 27,922 full time, 3,144 part time; 44% male, 56% female; 0% American Indian, 13% Asian, 4% black, 34% Hispanic, 7% multiracial, 0% Pacific Islander, 34% white, 5% international; 86% from in state; 8% live on campus; 8% of students in fraternities, 12% in sororities
Most popular majors: 21% Business Administration and Management, General, 5% Health and Physical Education/Fitness, General, 5% Psychology, General, 4% Mechanical Engineering, 4% Multi-/Interdisciplinary Studies, Other
Expenses: 2021-2022: $8,136 in state, $20,016 out of state; room/board: $19,330
Financial aid: (619) 594-6323; 56% of undergrads determined to have financial need; average aid package $8,690

San Francisco Conservatory of Music[1]
San Francisco CA
(800) 899-7326
U.S. News ranking: Arts, unranked
Website: www.sfcm.edu
Admissions email: admit@sfcm.edu
Private; founded 1917
Affiliation: Other
Application deadline (fall): 12/1
Undergraduate student body: N/A full time, N/A part time
Expenses: 2020-2021: $49,050; room/board: $18,400
Financial aid: (415) 503-6214

San Francisco State University
San Francisco CA
(415) 338-6486
U.S. News ranking: Reg. U. (W), No. 29
Website: www.sfsu.edu
Admissions email: ugadmit@sfsu.edu
Public; founded 1899
Freshman admissions: selective; 2020-2021: 31,430 applied, 26,431 accepted. Neither SAT nor ACT required. SAT 25/75 percentile: 930-1130. High school rank: N/A
Early decision deadline: N/A, notification date: N/A
Early action deadline: N/A, notification date: N/A
Application deadline (fall): 11/30
Undergraduate student body: 19,824 full time, 4,172 part time; 45% male, 55% female; 0% American Indian, 26% Asian, 6% black, 36% Hispanic, 6% multiracial, 1% Pacific Islander, 16% white, 7% international; N/A from in state; 2% live on campus; 1% of students in fraternities, 2% in sororities
Most popular majors: 25% Business, Management, Marketing, and Related Support Services, 10% Communication, Journalism, and Related Programs, 9% Visual and Performing Arts, 8% Social Sciences, 6% Psychology
Expenses: 2021-2022: $7,484 in state, $19,364 out of state; room/board: $20,469
Financial aid: (415) 338-7000; 71% of undergrads determined to have financial need; average aid package $14,314

San Joaquin Valley College–Visalia[1]
Visalia CA
(559) 734-9000
U.S. News ranking: Reg. Coll. (W), unranked
Website: www.sjvc.edu
Admissions email: N/A
For-profit
Application deadline (fall): N/A
Undergraduate student body: N/A full time, N/A part time
Expenses: N/A
Financial aid: N/A

San Jose State University
San Jose CA
(408) 283-7500
U.S. News ranking: Reg. U. (W), No. 22
Website: www.sjsu.edu/Admissions/
Admissions email: admissions@sjsu.edu
Public; founded 1857
Freshman admissions: selective; 2020-2021: 32,375 applied, 21,810 accepted. Neither SAT nor ACT required. SAT 25/75 percentile: 1030-1260. High school rank: N/A
Early decision deadline: N/A, notification date: N/A
Early action deadline: N/A, notification date: N/A
Application deadline (fall): 1/8
Undergraduate student body: 23,300 full time, 4,380 part time; 50% male, 50% female; 0% American Indian, 37% Asian, 4% black, 30% Hispanic, 5% multiracial, 1% Pacific Islander, 14% white, 7% international; N/A from in state; 3% live on campus; N/A of students in fraternities, N/A in sororities
Most popular majors: 24% Business, Management, Marketing, and Related Support Services, 15% Engineering, 7% Communication, Journalism, and Related Programs, 7% Social Sciences, 7% Visual and Performing Arts
Expenses: 2021-2022: $7,852 in state, $19,466 out of state; room/board: $16,946
Financial aid: (408) 924-6086; 63% of undergrads determined to have financial need; average aid package $19,836

Santa Ana College[1]
Santa Ana CA
(714) 564-6000
U.S. News ranking: Reg. Coll. (W), unranked
Website: www.sac.edu
Admissions email: N/A
Public
Application deadline (fall): N/A
Undergraduate student body: N/A full time, N/A part time
Expenses: 2020-2021: $1,160 in state, $8,960 out of state; room/board: N/A
Financial aid: N/A

Santa Clara University
Santa Clara CA
(408) 554-4700
U.S. News ranking: Nat. U., No. 55
Website: www.scu.edu
Admissions email: Admission@scu.edu
Private; founded 1851
Affiliation: Roman Catholic
Freshman admissions: more selective; 2020-2021: 16,488 applied, 8,362 accepted. Neither SAT nor ACT required. SAT 25/75 percentile: 1270-1450. High school rank: 40% in top tenth, 73% in top quarter, 95% in top half
Early decision deadline: 11/1, notification date: 12/31
Early action deadline: 11/1, notification date: 12/31
Application deadline (fall): 1/7
Undergraduate student body: 5,478 full time, 130 part time; 52% male, 48% female; 0% American Indian, 19% Asian, 3% black, 18% Hispanic, 8% multiracial, 0% Pacific Islander, 44% white, 5% international; 59% from in state; N/A live on campus; 0% of students in fraternities, 0% in sororities
Most popular majors: 25% Business, Management, Marketing, and Related Support Services, 14% Social Sciences, 13% Engineering, 8% Communication, Journalism, and Related Programs, 7% Biological and Biomedical Sciences
Expenses: 2021-2022: $55,860; room/board: $16,533
Financial aid: (408) 551-1000; 42% of undergrads determined to have financial need; average aid package $39,298

Santa Monica College[1]
Santa Monica CA
(310) 434-4000
U.S. News ranking: Reg. Coll. (W), unranked
Website: www.smc.edu
Admissions email: N/A
Public
Application deadline (fall): N/A
Undergraduate student body: N/A full time, N/A part time
Expenses: 2020-2021: $1,148 in state, $9,044 out of state; room/board: N/A
Financial aid: N/A

Scripps College
Claremont CA
(909) 621-8149
U.S. News ranking: Nat. Lib. Arts, No. 30
Website: www.scrippscollege.edu/
Admissions email: admission@scrippscollege.edu
Private; founded 1926
Freshman admissions: more selective; 2020-2021: 2,938 applied, 1,032 accepted. Neither SAT nor ACT required. SAT 25/75 percentile: 1320-1480. High school rank: 75% in top tenth, 93% in top quarter, 96% in top half

Early decision deadline: 12/1, notification date: 12/15
Early action deadline: N/A, notification date: N/A
Application deadline (fall): 1/5
Undergraduate student body: 861 full time, 75 part time; 0% male, 100% female; 0% American Indian, 17% Asian, 4% black, 15% Hispanic, 8% multiracial, 0% Pacific Islander, 50% white, 4% international; N/A from in state; 0% live on campus; N/A of students in fraternities, N/A in sororities
Most popular majors: 14% Social Sciences, 12% Biological and Biomedical Sciences, 9% Area, Ethnic, Cultural, Gender, and Group Studies, 8% Psychology, 8% Visual and Performing Arts
Expenses: 2021-2022: $58,442; room/board: $18,998
Financial aid: (909) 621-8275; 39% of undergrads determined to have financial need; average aid package $43,700

Shasta College[1]
Redding CA
(530) 242-7500
U.S. News ranking: Reg. Coll. (W), unranked
Website: www.shastacollege.edu
Admissions email: N/A
Public
Application deadline (fall): N/A
Undergraduate student body: N/A full time, N/A part time
Expenses: 2020-2021: $1,187 in state, $7,907 out of state; room/board: $5,125
Financial aid: N/A

Simpson University[1]
Redding CA
(530) 226-4606
U.S. News ranking: Reg. U. (W), No. 88
Website: www.simpsonu.edu
Admissions email: admissions@simpsonu.edu
Private; founded 1921
Affiliation: Christ and Missionary Alliance Church
Application deadline (fall): 8/1
Undergraduate student body: N/A full time, N/A part time
Expenses: 2020-2021: $33,630; room/board: $10,452
Financial aid: (530) 226-4621

Skyline College[1]
San Bruno CA
(650) 738-4100
U.S. News ranking: Reg. Coll. (W), unranked
Website: skylinecollege.edu
Admissions email: N/A
Public
Application deadline (fall): N/A
Undergraduate student body: N/A full time, N/A part time
Expenses: 2020-2021: $1,464 in state, $10,164 out of state; room/board: N/A
Financial aid: N/A

Soka University of America
Aliso Viejo CA
(888) 600-7652
U.S. News ranking: Nat. Lib. Arts, No. 29
Website: www.soka.edu
Admissions email: admission@soka.edu
Private; founded 1987
Freshman admissions: more selective; 2020-2021: 430 applied, 222 accepted. Neither SAT nor ACT required. SAT 25/75 percentile: 1180-1410. High school rank: 60% in top tenth, 80% in top quarter, 100% in top half
Early decision deadline: N/A, notification date: N/A
Early action deadline: 11/1, notification date: 12/1
Application deadline (fall): 1/15
Undergraduate student body: 392 full time, 0 part time; 34% male, 66% female; 0% American Indian, 13% Asian, 3% black, 14% Hispanic, 5% multiracial, 1% Pacific Islander, 17% white, 47% international; 44% from in state; 100% live on campus; 0% of students in fraternities, 0% in sororities
Most popular majors: 100% Liberal Arts and Sciences/Liberal Studies
Expenses: 2021-2022: $34,166; room/board: $13,032
Financial aid: (949) 480-4000; 91% of undergrads determined to have financial need; average aid package $38,399

Solano Community College[1]
Fairfield CA
(707) 864-7000
U.S. News ranking: Reg. Coll. (W), unranked
Website: www.solano.edu
Admissions email: N/A
Public
Application deadline (fall): N/A
Undergraduate student body: N/A full time, N/A part time
Expenses: N/A
Financial aid: N/A

Sonoma State University
Rohnert Park CA
(707) 664-2778
U.S. News ranking: Reg. U. (W), No. 37
Website: sonoma.edu/
Admissions email: student.outreach@sonoma.edu
Public; founded 1960
Freshman admissions: less selective; 2020-2021: 13,353 applied, 11,900 accepted. Neither SAT nor ACT required. SAT 25/75 percentile: 970-1170. High school rank: N/A
Early decision deadline: N/A, notification date: N/A
Early action deadline: N/A, notification date: N/A
Application deadline (fall): 11/30
Undergraduate student body: 6,419 full time, 836 part time; 37% male, 63% female; 0% American Indian, 5% Asian, 2% black,

37% Hispanic, 6% multiracial, 0% Pacific Islander, 42% white, 3% international; 98% from in state; N/A live on campus; N/A of students in fraternities, N/A in sororities
Most popular majors: Information not available
Expenses: 2021-2022: $7,988 in state, $22,114 out of state; room/board: $14,526
Financial aid: (707) 664-2389; 53% of undergrads determined to have financial need; average aid package $10,134

Southern California Institute of Architecture[1]
Los Angeles CA
(213) 613-2200
U.S. News ranking: Arts, unranked
Website: www.sciarc.edu
Admissions email: admissions@sciarc.edu
Private
Application deadline (fall): N/A
Undergraduate student body: N/A full time, N/A part time
Expenses: 2020-2021: $49,278; room/board: N/A
Financial aid: N/A

Stanford University
Stanford CA
(650) 723-2091
U.S. News ranking: Nat. U., No. 6
Website: www.stanford.edu
Admissions email: admission@stanford.edu
Private; founded 1885
Freshman admissions: most selective; 2020-2021: 45,227 applied, 2,349 accepted. Neither SAT nor ACT required. SAT 25/75 percentile: 1420-1570. High school rank: 96% in top tenth, 100% in top quarter, 100% in top half
Early decision deadline: N/A, notification date: N/A
Early action deadline: 11/1, notification date: 12/15
Application deadline (fall): 1/2
Undergraduate student body: 5,752 full time, 614 part time; 49% male, 51% female; 1% American Indian, 25% Asian, 7% black, 17% Hispanic, 10% multiracial, 0% Pacific Islander, 29% white, 11% international; N/A from in state; 11% live on campus; N/A of students in fraternities, N/A in sororities
Most popular majors: 17% Computer and Information Sciences and Support Services, 17% Multi/Interdisciplinary Studies, 16% Engineering
Expenses: 2021-2022: $56,169; room/board: $17,860
Financial aid: (650) 723-3058; 55% of undergrads determined to have financial need; average aid package $55,000

St. Mary's College of California

Moraga CA
(925) 631-4224
U.S. News ranking: Reg. U. (W),
No. 5
Website: www.stmarys-ca.edu
Admissions email:
smcadmit@stmarys-ca.edu
Private; founded 1863
Affiliation: Roman Catholic
Freshman admissions: selective;
2020-2021: 5,364 applied,
4,147 accepted. Neither SAT
nor ACT required. SAT 25/75
percentile: 1070-1253. High
school rank: N/A
Early decision deadline: N/A,
notification date: N/A
Early action deadline: 11/15,
notification date: 1/1
Application deadline (fall): 1/15
Undergraduate student body: 2,308
full time, 160 part time; 42%
male, 58% female; 0% American
Indian, 11% Asian, 4% black,
30% Hispanic, 9% multiracial,
2% Pacific Islander, 39% white,
3% international; 88% from in
state; 60% live on campus; 0%
of students in fraternities, 0% in
sororities
Most popular majors: 28%
Business, Management,
Marketing, and Related Support
Services, 10% Social Sciences,
8% Liberal Arts and Sciences,
General Studies and Humanities,
8% Psychology, 7% Parks,
Recreation, Leisure, and Fitness
Studies
Expenses: 2021-2022: $51,568;
room/board: $16,300
Financial aid: (925) 631-4370;
62% of undergrads determined to
have financial need; average aid
package $37,615

Thomas Aquinas College

Santa Paula CA
(805) 525-4417
U.S. News ranking: Nat. Lib. Arts,
No. 42
Website: www.thomasaquinas.edu
Admissions email:
admissions@thomasaquinas.edu
Private; founded 1971
Affiliation: Roman Catholic
Freshman admissions: more
selective; 2020-2021: 235
applied, 201 accepted. Either
SAT or ACT required. SAT 25/75
percentile: 1200-1380. High
school rank: 20% in top tenth,
40% in top quarter, 100% in
top half
Early decision deadline: N/A,
notification date: N/A
Early action deadline: N/A,
notification date: N/A
Application deadline (fall): rolling
Undergraduate student body:
462 full time, 0 part time; 51%
male, 49% female; 0% American
Indian, 2% Asian, 0% black,
16% Hispanic, 6% multiracial,
0% Pacific Islander, 69% white,
4% international; 65% from in
state; 100% live on campus; N/A
of students in fraternities, N/A in
sororities
Most popular majors: 100% Liberal
Arts and Sciences/Liberal Studies

Expenses: 2021-2022: $26,000;
room/board: $9,400
Financial aid: (805) 421-5936;
72% of undergrads determined to
have financial need; average aid
package $22,697

United States University[1]

Chula Vista CA
(800) 316-6314
U.S. News ranking: Reg. U. (W),
unranked
Admissions email:
N/A
For-profit
Application deadline (fall): N/A
Undergraduate student body: N/A
full time, N/A part time
Expenses: 2020-2021: $6,480;
room/board: N/A
Financial aid: N/A

University of Antelope Valley[1]

Lancaster CA
(661) 722-6300
U.S. News ranking: Reg. Coll. (W),
second tier
Website: www.uav.edu
Admissions email:
N/A
For-profit
Application deadline (fall): N/A
Undergraduate student body: N/A
full time, N/A part time
Expenses: N/A
Financial aid: N/A

University of California–Berkeley

Berkeley CA
(510) 642-3175
U.S. News ranking: Nat. U., No. 22
Website: www.berkeley.edu
Admissions email:
N/A
Public; founded 1868
Freshman admissions: most
selective; 2020-2021: 88,076
applied, 15,448 accepted. Neither
SAT nor ACT required. SAT 25/75
percentile: 1290-1530. High
school rank: 96% in top tenth,
100% in top quarter, 100% in
top half
Early decision deadline: N/A,
notification date: N/A
Early action deadline: N/A,
notification date: N/A
Application deadline (fall): 11/30
Undergraduate student body:
29,100 full time, 1,611 part
time; 46% male, 54% female;
0% American Indian, 35% Asian,
2% black, 19% Hispanic, 6%
multiracial, 0% Pacific Islander,
22% white, 13% international;
84% from in state; 8% live
on campus; 1% of students in
fraternities, 7% in sororities
Most popular majors: 19% Social
Sciences, 12% Computer and
Information Sciences and Support
Services, 10% Biological and
Biomedical Sciences, 10%
Engineering, 6% Mathematics and
Statistics
Expenses: 2021-2022: $14,361
in state, $44,115 out of state;
room/board: $21,304

Financial aid: (510) 642-7117;
46% of undergrads determined to
have financial need; average aid
package $25,413

University of California–Davis

Davis CA
(530) 752-2971
U.S. News ranking: Nat. U., No. 38
Website: www.ucdavis.edu
Admissions email:
undergraduateadmissions@
ucdavis.edu
Public; founded 1905
Freshman admissions: more
selective; 2020-2021: 76,225
applied, 35,304 accepted. Neither
SAT nor ACT required. SAT 25/75
percentile: 1140-1400. High
school rank: 100% in top tenth,
100% in top quarter, 100% in
top half
Early decision deadline: N/A,
notification date: N/A
Early action deadline: N/A,
notification date: N/A
Application deadline (fall): 11/30
Undergraduate student body:
30,186 full time, 976 part time;
39% male, 61% female; 0%
American Indian, 28% Asian,
2% black, 24% Hispanic, 6%
multiracial, 0% Pacific Islander,
21% white, 16% international
Most popular majors: Information
not available
Expenses: 2021-2022: $14,654
in state, $44,408 out of state;
room/board: $16,480
Financial aid: (530) 752-2396;
56% of undergrads determined to
have financial need; average aid
package $21,653

University of California–Irvine

Irvine CA
(949) 824-6703
U.S. News ranking: Nat. U., No. 36
Website: www.uci.edu
Admissions email:
admissions@uci.edu
Public; founded 1965
Freshman admissions: most
selective; 2020-2021: 97,942
applied, 29,301 accepted. Neither
SAT nor ACT required. SAT 25/75
percentile: 1215-1450. High
school rank: 99% in top tenth,
100% in top quarter, 100% in
top half
Early decision deadline: N/A,
notification date: N/A
Early action deadline: N/A,
notification date: N/A
Application deadline (fall): 11/30
Undergraduate student body:
28,987 full time, 651 part time;
47% male, 53% female; 0%
American Indian, 37% Asian,
2% black, 25% Hispanic, 5%
multiracial, 0% Pacific Islander,
13% white, 16% international;
N/A from in state; 5% live on
campus; N/A of students in
fraternities, N/A in sororities
Most popular majors: 10%
Business/Managerial Economics,
10% Public Health, Other, 9%
Biology/Biological Sciences,
General, 8% Economics, General,
6% Social Psychology

Expenses: 2021-2022: $13,955
in state, $43,709 out of state;
room/board: $16,561
Financial aid: (949) 824-5337;
59% of undergrads determined to
have financial need; average aid
package $24,042

University of California–Los Angeles

Los Angeles CA
(310) 825-3101
U.S. News ranking: Nat. U., No. 20
Website: www.ucla.edu/
Admissions email:
ugadm@saonet.ucla.edu
Public; founded 1919
Freshman admissions: most
selective; 2020-2021: 108,877
applied, 15,602 accepted. Neither
SAT nor ACT required. SAT 25/75
percentile: 1290-1520. High
school rank: N/A
Early decision deadline: N/A,
notification date: N/A
Early action deadline: N/A,
notification date: N/A
Application deadline (fall): 11/30
Undergraduate student body:
30,980 full time, 566 part time;
41% male, 59% female; 0%
American Indian, 29% Asian,
3% black, 22% Hispanic, 6%
multiracial, 0% Pacific Islander,
26% white, 11% international;
78% from in state; 48% live
on campus; 11% of students in
fraternities, 13% in sororities
Most popular majors: 27% Social
Sciences, 16% Biological and
Biomedical Sciences, 10%
Psychology, 7% Engineering, 7%
Mathematics and Statistics
Expenses: 2021-2022: $13,268
in state, $43,022 out of state;
room/board: $16,667
Financial aid: (310) 206-0401;
46% of undergrads determined to
have financial need; average aid
package $21,245

University of California–Merced

Merced CA
(866) 270-7301
U.S. News ranking: Nat. U., No. 93
Website: www.ucmerced.edu
Admissions email:
admissions@ucmerced.edu
Public; founded 2005
Freshman admissions: selective;
2020-2021: 25,924 applied,
21,982 accepted. Either SAT
or ACT required. SAT 25/75
percentile: 940-1140. High
school rank: N/A
Early decision deadline: N/A,
notification date: N/A
Early action deadline: N/A,
notification date: N/A
Application deadline (fall): 11/30
Undergraduate student body: 8,194
full time, 82 part time; 47%
male, 53% female; 0% American
Indian, 18% Asian, 4% black,
58% Hispanic, 3% multiracial,
0% Pacific Islander, 8% white,
8% international
Most popular majors: 23%
Biological and Biomedical
Sciences, 21% Engineering, 15%
Psychology, 12% Social Sciences,

11% Business, Management,
Marketing, and Related Support
Services
Expenses: 2021-2022: $13,565
in state, $43,319 out of state;
room/board: $18,887
Financial aid: (209) 228-7178;
89% of undergrads determined to
have financial need; average aid
package $23,399

University of California–Riverside

Riverside CA
(951) 827-3411
U.S. News ranking: Nat. U., No. 83
Website: www.ucr.edu
Admissions email:
admissions@ucr.edu
Public; founded 1954
Freshman admissions: more
selective; 2020-2021: 49,434
applied, 32,786 accepted. Neither
SAT nor ACT required. SAT 25/75
percentile: 1060-1290. High
school rank: 94% in top tenth,
100% in top quarter, 100% in
top half
Early decision deadline: N/A,
notification date: N/A
Early action deadline: N/A,
notification date: 11/30
Application deadline (fall): 11/30
Undergraduate student body:
21,729 full time, 618 part time;
46% male, 54% female; 0%
American Indian, 34% Asian,
3% black, 42% Hispanic, 6%
multiracial, 0% Pacific Islander,
11% white, 3% international; N/A
from in state; 9% live on campus;
4% of students in fraternities, 6%
in sororities
Most popular majors: 18%
Social Sciences, 15% Biological
and Biomedical Sciences,
15% Business, Management,
Marketing, and Related Support
Services, 10% Psychology, 8%
Engineering
Expenses: 2021-2022: $13,742
in state, $43,496 out of state;
room/board: $16,864
Financial aid: (951) 827-3878;
75% of undergrads determined to
have financial need; average aid
package $21,430

University of California–San Diego

La Jolla CA
(858) 534-4831
U.S. News ranking: Nat. U., No. 34
Website: www.ucsd.edu/
Admissions email:
admissionsreply@ucsd.edu
Public; founded 1960
Freshman admissions: most
selective; 2020-2021: 100,073
applied, 38,325 accepted. Neither
SAT nor ACT required. SAT 25/75
percentile: 1260-1480. High
school rank: 100% in top tenth,
100% in top quarter, 100% in
top half
Early decision deadline: N/A,
notification date: N/A
Early action deadline: N/A,
notification date: N/A
Application deadline (fall): 11/30
Undergraduate student body:
31,102 full time, 505 part time;
50% male, 50% female; 0%
American Indian, 37% Asian,

3% black, 21% Hispanic, 0% multiracial, 0% Pacific Islander, 19% white, 17% international; 76% from in state; 9% live on campus; 8% of students in fraternities, 8% in sororities
Most popular majors: 9% Biology/Biological Sciences, General, 6% Computer Science, 6% International/Global Studies, 4% Biochemistry, 4% Econometrics and Quantitative Economics
Expenses: 2021-2022: $14,733 in state, $44,487 out of state; room/board: $16,026
Financial aid: (858) 534-3800; 52% of undergrads determined to have financial need; average aid package $23,197

University of California–Santa Barbara
Santa Barbara CA
(805) 893-2881
U.S. News ranking: Nat. U., No. 28
Website: www.ucsb.edu/
Admissions email: admissions@sa.ucsb.edu
Public; founded 1909
Freshman admissions: most selective; 2020-2021: 90,963 applied, 33,385 accepted. Neither SAT nor ACT required. SAT 25/75 percentile: 1230-1480. High school rank: 100% in top tenth, 100% in top quarter, 100% in top half
Early decision deadline: N/A, notification date: N/A
Early action deadline: N/A, notification date: N/A
Application deadline (fall): 11/30
Undergraduate student body: 22,366 full time, 713 part time; 45% male, 55% female; 0% American Indian, 21% Asian, 2% black, 26% Hispanic, 7% multiracial, 0% Pacific Islander, 31% white, 12% international; 94% from in state; N/A live on campus; N/A of students in fraternities, N/A in sororities
Most popular majors: 28% Social Sciences, 9% Biological and Biomedical Sciences, 8% Mathematics and Statistics, 8% Multi/Interdisciplinary Studies, 7% Communication, Journalism, and Related Programs
Expenses: 2021-2022: $14,442 in state, $44,196 out of state; room/board: $16,061
Financial aid: (805) 893-2432; 53% of undergrads determined to have financial need; average aid package $22,669

University of California–Santa Cruz
Santa Cruz CA
(831) 459-4008
U.S. News ranking: Nat. U., No. 103
Website: www.ucsc.edu
Admissions email: admissions@ucsc.edu
Public; founded 1965
Freshman admissions: more selective; 2020-2021: 55,073 applied, 35,935 accepted. Neither SAT nor ACT required. SAT 25/75 percentile: 1150-1370. High school rank: 94% in top tenth,

100% in top quarter, 100% in top half
Early decision deadline: N/A, notification date: N/A
Early action deadline: N/A, notification date: N/A
Application deadline (fall): 11/30
Undergraduate student body: 16,521 full time, 686 part time; 53% male, 47% female; 0% American Indian, 23% Asian, 2% black, 27% Hispanic, 8% multiracial, 0% Pacific Islander, 30% white, 8% international; 91% from in state; 5% live on campus; 3% of students in fraternities, 3% in sororities
Most popular majors: 10% Computer and Information Sciences, General, 9% Psychology, General, 6% Business/Managerial Economics, 6% Cell/Cellular and Molecular Biology, 5% Sociology
Expenses: 2021-2022: $14,066 in state, $43,820 out of state; room/board: $16,069
Financial aid: (831) 459-2963; 55% of undergrads determined to have financial need; average aid package $23,529

University of La Verne
La Verne CA
(800) 876-4858
U.S. News ranking: Nat. U., No. 136
Website: www.laverne.edu
Admissions email: admission@laverne.edu
Private; founded 1891
Freshman admissions: selective; 2020-2021: 8,212 applied, 6,262 accepted. Neither SAT nor ACT required. SAT 25/75 percentile: 960-1150. High school rank: 18% in top tenth, 45% in top quarter, 81% in top half
Early decision deadline: N/A, notification date: N/A
Early action deadline: N/A, notification date: N/A
Application deadline (fall): rolling
Undergraduate student body: 2,425 full time, 59 part time; 40% male, 60% female; 0% American Indian, 6% Asian, 6% black, 61% Hispanic, 4% multiracial, 0% Pacific Islander, 15% white, 5% international; 89% from in state; 6% live on campus; 4% of students in fraternities, 10% in sororities
Most popular majors: 27% Business, Management, Marketing, and Related Support Services, 13% Social Sciences, 11% Education, 11% Psychology, 8% Communication, Journalism, and Related Programs
Expenses: 2021-2022: $45,850; room/board: $14,740
Financial aid: (800) 649-0160; 85% of undergrads determined to have financial need; average aid package $47,338

University of Redlands
Redlands CA
(800) 455-5064
U.S. News ranking: Reg. U. (W), No. 6
Website: www.redlands.edu

Admissions email: admissions@redlands.edu
Private; founded 1907
Freshman admissions: more selective; 2020-2021: 4,345 applied, 3,367 accepted. Neither SAT nor ACT required. SAT 25/75 percentile: 1070-1250. High school rank: 43% in top tenth, 72% in top quarter, 95% in top half
Early decision deadline: 11/15, notification date: 1/15
Early action deadline: 11/15, notification date: 1/15
Application deadline (fall): 1/15
Undergraduate student body: 2,446 full time, 442 part time; 40% male, 60% female; 0% American Indian, 6% Asian, 4% black, 42% Hispanic, 5% multiracial, 0% Pacific Islander, 35% white, 2% international
Most popular majors: 38% Business, Management, Marketing, and Related Support Services, 11% Social Sciences, 8% Health Professions and Related Programs, 8% Visual and Performing Arts, 7% Psychology
Expenses: 2021-2022: $54,066; room/board: $15,562
Financial aid: (909) 748-8047; 80% of undergrads determined to have financial need; average aid package $43,050

University of San Diego
San Diego CA
(619) 260-4506
U.S. News ranking: Nat. U., No. 93
Website: www.SanDiego.edu
Admissions email: admissions@SanDiego.edu
Private; founded 1949
Affiliation: Roman Catholic
Freshman admissions: more selective; 2020-2021: 13,171 applied, 7,731 accepted. Neither SAT nor ACT required. SAT 25/75 percentile: 1160-1340. High school rank: 37% in top tenth, 70% in top quarter, 97% in top half
Early decision deadline: N/A, notification date: N/A
Early action deadline: N/A, notification date: N/A
Application deadline (fall): 12/15
Undergraduate student body: 5,294 full time, 235 part time; 43% male, 57% female; 0% American Indian, 7% Asian, 3% black, 22% Hispanic, 7% multiracial, 0% Pacific Islander, 49% white, 7% international; 62% from in state; 16% live on campus; 21% of students in fraternities, 31% in sororities
Most popular majors: 39% Business, Management, Marketing, and Related Support Services, 12% Biological and Biomedical Sciences, 11% Social Sciences, 10% Engineering, 7% Communication, Journalism, and Related Programs
Expenses: 2021-2022: $52,864; room/board: $16,246
Financial aid: (619) 260-2700; 55% of undergrads determined to have financial need; average aid package $42,291

University of San Francisco
San Francisco CA
(415) 422-6563
U.S. News ranking: Nat. U., No. 103
Website: www.usfca.edu
Admissions email: admission@usfca.edu
Private; founded 1855
Affiliation: Roman Catholic
Freshman admissions: more selective; 2020-2021: 21,477 applied, 15,099 accepted. Neither SAT nor ACT required. SAT 25/75 percentile: 1140-1330. High school rank: 35% in top tenth, 73% in top quarter, 95% in top half
Early decision deadline: 11/1, notification date: 12/1
Early action deadline: 11/1, notification date: 12/14
Application deadline (fall): 1/15
Undergraduate student body: 5,572 full time, 280 part time; 37% male, 63% female; 0% American Indian, 26% Asian, 6% black, 21% Hispanic, 10% multiracial, 0% Pacific Islander, 24% white, 12% international; 63% from in state; 3% live on campus; N/A of students in fraternities, N/A in sororities
Most popular majors: 30% Business, Management, Marketing, and Related Support Services, 15% Health Professions and Related Programs, 12% Social Sciences, 8% Psychology, 7% Communication, Journalism, and Related Programs
Expenses: 2021-2022: $53,472; room/board: $16,140
Financial aid: (415) 422-3387; 61% of undergrads determined to have financial need; average aid package $36,470

University of Silicon Valley
San Jose CA
(408) 498-5160
U.S. News ranking: Reg. Coll. (W), No. 27
Website: www. usv.edu
Admissions email: admissions@usv.edu
For-profit; founded 1887
Freshman admissions: less selective; 2020-2021: 155 applied, 65 accepted. Neither SAT nor ACT required. SAT 25/75 percentile: 830-1330. High school rank: N/A
Early decision deadline: N/A, notification date: N/A
Early action deadline: 12/1, notification date: 12/1
Application deadline (fall): rolling
Undergraduate student body: 421 full time, 93 part time; 70% male, 30% female; 1% American Indian, 20% Asian, 7% black, 24% Hispanic, 8% multiracial, 1% Pacific Islander, 28% white, 2% international; 91% from in state; N/A live on campus; 0% of students in fraternities, 0% in sororities
Most popular majors: 48% Animation, Interactive Technology, Video Graphics and Special Effects, 18% Game and

Interactive Media Design, 14% Modeling, Virtual Environments and Simulation, 6% Computer Programming/Programmer, General, 6% Music Technology
Expenses: 2021-2022: $26,980; room/board: $12,790
Financial aid: (408) 498-5145; 72% of undergrads determined to have financial need; average aid package $11,820

University of Southern California
Los Angeles CA
(213) 740-1111
U.S. News ranking: Nat. U., No. 27
Website: www.usc.edu/
Admissions email: admitusc@usc.edu
Private; founded 1880
Freshman admissions: more selective; 2020-2021: 59,712 applied, 9,618 accepted. Neither SAT nor ACT required. SAT 25/75 percentile: 1340-1530. High school rank: N/A
Early decision deadline: N/A, notification date: N/A
Early action deadline: N/A, notification date: N/A
Application deadline (fall): 1/15
Undergraduate student body: 18,560 full time, 1,046 part time; 48% male, 52% female; 0% American Indian, 23% Asian, 5% black, 17% Hispanic, 6% multiracial, 0% Pacific Islander, 35% white, 12% international; 53% from in state; 98% live on campus; 11% of students in fraternities, 14% in sororities
Most popular majors: 24% Business, Management, Marketing, and Related Support Services, 12% Social Sciences, 12% Visual and Performing Arts, 9% Communication, Journalism, and Related Programs, 8% Engineering
Expenses: 2021-2022: $60,275; room/board: $15,437
Financial aid: (213) 740-4444; 38% of undergrads determined to have financial need; average aid package $56,626

University of the Pacific
Stockton CA
(209) 946-2011
U.S. News ranking: Nat. U., No. 136
Website: www.pacific.edu
Admissions email: admissions@pacific.edu
Private; founded 1851
Freshman admissions: more selective; 2020-2021: 14,063 applied, 9,949 accepted. Neither SAT nor ACT required. SAT 25/75 percentile: 1080-1340. High school rank: 40% in top tenth, 72% in top quarter, 94% in top half
Early decision deadline: N/A, notification date: N/A
Early action deadline: 11/15, notification date: 1/15
Application deadline (fall): 1/15
Undergraduate student body: 3,412 full time, 112 part time; 48% male, 52% female; 0% American Indian, 37% Asian, 4% black,

23% Hispanic, 5% multiracial, 0% Pacific Islander, 21% white, 7% international; N/A from in state; 4% live on campus; 7% of students in fraternities, 5% in sororities
Most popular majors: 16% Business, Management, Marketing, and Related Support Services, 15% Biological and Biomedical Sciences, 11% Multi/Interdisciplinary Studies, 8% Engineering, 8% Social Sciences
Expenses: 2021-2022: $52,352; room/board: $14,070
Financial aid: (209) 946-2421; 72% of undergrads determined to have financial need; average aid package $41,427

University of the West[1]
Rosemead CA
(855) 468-9378
U.S. News ranking: Nat. Lib. Arts, second tier
Website: www.uwest.edu
Admissions email: admission@uwest.edu
Private; founded 1991
Application deadline (fall): 5/1
Undergraduate student body: N/A full time, N/A part time
Expenses: 2020-2021: $13,556; room/board: $8,396
Financial aid: (626) 571-8811

Vanguard University of Southern California
Costa Mesa CA
(800) 722-6279
U.S. News ranking: Reg. U. (W), No. 46
Website: www.vanguard.edu
Admissions email: admissions@vanguard.edu
Private; founded 1920
Affiliation: Assemblies of God Church
Freshman admissions: selective; 2020-2021: 4,055 applied, 2,027 accepted. Neither SAT nor ACT required. SAT 25/75 percentile: 960-1150. High school rank: 16% in top tenth, 47% in top quarter, 79% in top half
Early decision deadline: N/A, notification date: N/A
Early action deadline: 12/1, notification date: 1/15
Application deadline (fall): 8/1
Undergraduate student body: 1,750 full time, 175 part time; 33% male, 67% female; 0% American Indian, 5% Asian, 5% black, 46% Hispanic, 2% multiracial, 1% Pacific Islander, 34% white, 0% international; 90% from in state; 27% live on campus; 0% of students in fraternities, 2% in sororities
Most popular majors: 18% Health Professions and Related Programs, 16% Business, Management, Marketing, and Related Support Services, 16% Psychology, 9% Communication, Journalism, and Related Programs, 7% Social Sciences
Expenses: 2021-2022: $37,700; room/board: $9,980

Financial aid: (714) 619-6691; 90% of undergrads determined to have financial need; average aid package $17,388

Westcliff University[1]
Irvine CA
(888) 491-8686
U.S. News ranking: Business, unranked
Admissions email: N/A
For-profit
Application deadline (fall): N/A
Undergraduate student body: N/A full time, N/A part time
Expenses: 2020-2021: $13,560; room/board: $11,976
Financial aid: N/A

West Los Angeles College[1]
Culver City CA
(310) 287-4501
U.S. News ranking: Reg. Coll. (W), unranked
Website: www.wlac.edu
Admissions email: N/A
Public; founded 1969
Application deadline (fall): N/A
Undergraduate student body: N/A full time, N/A part time
Expenses: 2020-2021: $1,238 in state, $8,570 out of state; room/board: N/A
Financial aid: N/A

Westmont College
Santa Barbara CA
(805) 565-6000
U.S. News ranking: Nat. Lib. Arts, No. 114
Website: www.westmont.edu
Admissions email: admissions@westmont.edu
Private; founded 1937
Affiliation: Undenominational
Freshman admissions: more selective; 2020-2021: 2,494 applied, 1,749 accepted. Either SAT or ACT required. SAT 25/75 percentile: 1110-1370. High school rank: 36% in top tenth, 60% in top quarter, 92% in top half
Early decision deadline: N/A, notification date: N/A
Early action deadline: 12/1, notification date: 12/1
Application deadline (fall): rolling
Undergraduate student body: 1,215 full time, 3 part time; 40% male, 60% female; 0% American Indian, 7% Asian, 2% black, 20% Hispanic, 6% multiracial, 1% Pacific Islander, 54% white, 2% international; 69% from in state; 81% live on campus; 0% of students in fraternities, 0% in sororities
Most popular majors: 18% Business, Management, Marketing, and Related Support Services, 10% Parks, Recreation, Leisure, and Fitness Studies, 10% Psychology, 9% Biological and Biomedical Sciences, 7% Communication, Journalism, and Related Programs
Expenses: 2021-2022: $48,660; room/board: $15,370

Financial aid: (805) 565-6063; 65% of undergrads determined to have financial need; average aid package $34,711

Whittier College
Whittier CA
(562) 907-4200
U.S. News ranking: Nat. Lib. Arts, No. 114
Admissions email: N/A
Private; founded 1887
Freshman admissions: selective; 2020-2021: 5,038 applied, 3,644 accepted. Neither SAT nor ACT required. SAT 25/75 percentile: 1050-1220. High school rank: N/A
Early decision deadline: N/A, notification date: N/A
Early action deadline: 11/15, notification date: 12/20
Application deadline (fall): rolling
Undergraduate student body: 1,455 full time, 35 part time; 43% male, 57% female; 0% American Indian, 7% Asian, 5% black, 53% Hispanic, 7% multiracial, 0% Pacific Islander, 23% white, 4% international
Most popular majors: 14% Business, Management, Marketing, and Related Support Services, 12% Biological and Biomedical Sciences, 10% Social Sciences, 8% Psychology, 8% Visual and Performing Arts
Expenses: 2021-2022: $49,514; room/board: $15,176
Financial aid: (562) 907-4285; 74% of undergrads determined to have financial need; average aid package $39,603

William Jessup University
Rocklin CA
(916) 577-2222
U.S. News ranking: Reg. Coll. (W), No. 3
Website: www.jessup.edu
Admissions email: admissions@jessup.edu
Private; founded 1939
Affiliation: Protestant, not specified
Freshman admissions: selective; 2020-2021: 710 applied, 463 accepted. Neither SAT nor ACT required. SAT 25/75 percentile: 948-1213. High school rank: 13% in top tenth, 36% in top quarter, 60% in top half
Early decision deadline: N/A, notification date: N/A
Early action deadline: N/A, notification date: N/A
Application deadline (fall): rolling
Undergraduate student body: 1,100 full time, 189 part time; 40% male, 60% female; 2% American Indian, 5% Asian, 4% black, 21% Hispanic, 2% multiracial, 1% Pacific Islander, 49% white, 6% international; 94% from in state; 49% live on campus; 0% of students in fraternities, 0% in sororities
Most popular majors: 21% Psychology, General, 20% Business Administration and Management, General, 13% Elementary Education and Teaching, 7% Kinesiology and

Exercise Science, 6% Theology/Theological Studies
Expenses: 2021-2022: $36,750; room/board: $12,368
Financial aid: (916) 577-2232; 75% of undergrads determined to have financial need; average aid package $23,876

Woodbury University
Burbank CA
(818) 252-5221
U.S. News ranking: Reg. U. (W), No. 53
Website: woodbury.edu/
Admissions email: info@woodbury.edu
Private; founded 1884
Freshman admissions: selective; 2020-2021: 1,554 applied, 1,094 accepted. Neither SAT nor ACT required. SAT 25/75 percentile: 970-1225. High school rank: N/A
Early decision deadline: N/A, notification date: N/A
Early action deadline: N/A, notification date: N/A
Application deadline (fall): rolling
Undergraduate student body: 966 full time, 54 part time; 47% male, 53% female; 0% American Indian, 10% Asian, 5% black, 40% Hispanic, 3% multiracial, 0% Pacific Islander, 34% white, 7% international; 88% from in state; 8% live on campus; N/A of students in fraternities, N/A in sororities
Most popular majors: 28% Architectural and Building Sciences/Technology, 9% Business Administration and Management, General, 8% Marketing/Marketing Management, General, 6% Accounting, 6% Cinematography and Film/Video Production
Expenses: 2021-2022: $43,418; room/board: $13,896
Financial aid: (818) 252-5273; 80% of undergrads determined to have financial need; average aid package $32,276

COLORADO

Adams State University[1]
Alamosa CO
(800) 824-6494
U.S. News ranking: Reg. U. (W), second tier
Website: www.adams.edu
Admissions email: ascadmit@adams.edu
Public
Application deadline (fall): N/A
Undergraduate student body: N/A full time, N/A part time
Expenses: 2020-2021: $9,560 in state, $21,296 out of state; room/board: $8,916
Financial aid: N/A

Colorado Christian University
Lakewood CO
(303) 963-3200
U.S. News ranking: Reg. U. (W), No. 61
Website: www.ccu.edu

Admissions email: admission@ccu.edu
Private; founded 1914
Affiliation: Interdenominational
Freshman admissions: selective; 2020-2021: N/A applied, N/A accepted. Neither SAT nor ACT required. ACT 25/75 percentile: 21-27. High school rank: N/A
Early decision deadline: N/A, notification date: N/A
Early action deadline: N/A, notification date: N/A
Application deadline (fall): N/A
Undergraduate student body: 1,704 full time, 4,957 part time; 33% male, 67% female; 1% American Indian, 2% Asian, 13% black, 17% Hispanic, 4% multiracial, 0% Pacific Islander, 61% white, 0% international
Most popular majors: Information not available
Expenses: 2021-2022: $35,436; room/board: $12,200
Financial aid: N/A

Colorado College
Colorado Springs CO
(719) 389-6344
U.S. News ranking: Nat. Lib. Arts, No. 26
Website: www.ColoradoCollege.edu
Admissions email: admission@ColoradoCollege.edu
Private; founded 1874
Freshman admissions: most selective; 2020-2021: 10,257 applied, 1,395 accepted. Neither SAT nor ACT required. SAT 25/75 percentile: 1240-1460. High school rank: 73% in top tenth, 91% in top quarter, 100% in top half
Early decision deadline: 11/1, notification date: 12/15
Early action deadline: 11/1, notification date: 12/20
Application deadline (fall): 1/15
Undergraduate student body: 1,886 full time, 139 part time; 44% male, 56% female; 0% American Indian, 5% Asian, 3% black, 11% Hispanic, 7% multiracial, 0% Pacific Islander, 64% white, 7% international
Most popular majors: 30% Social Sciences, 18% Biological and Biomedical Sciences, 6% Computer and Information Sciences and Support Services, 6% Natural Resources and Conservation, 6% Physical Sciences
Expenses: 2021-2022: $62,070; room/board: $13,668
Financial aid: (719) 389-6651; 37% of undergrads determined to have financial need; average aid package $59,315

Colorado Mesa University
Grand Junction CO
(970) 248-1875
U.S. News ranking: Reg. U. (W), No. 90
Website: www.coloradomesa.edu/
Admissions email: admissions@coloradomesa.edu
Public; founded 1925
Freshman admissions: selective; 2020-2021: 8,796 applied, 6,636 accepted. Either SAT

or ACT required. SAT 25/75 percentile: 940-1170. High school rank: 11% in top tenth, 26% in top quarter, 50% in top half
Early decision deadline: N/A, notification date: N/A
Early action deadline: N/A, notification date: N/A
Application deadline (fall): rolling
Undergraduate student body: 6,857 full time, 2,088 part time; 46% male, 54% female; 1% American Indian, 2% Asian, 2% black, 21% Hispanic, 4% multiracial, 1% Pacific Islander, 66% white, 1% international; 85% from in state; 26% live on campus; 1% of students in fraternities, 1% in sororities
Most popular majors: Information not available
Expenses: 2021-2022: $9,306 in state, $23,163 out of state; room/board: $11,168
Financial aid: (970) 248-1851; 60% of undergrads determined to have financial need; average aid package $10,871

Colorado Mountain College[7]
Glenwood Springs CO
(970) 945-8691
U.S. News ranking: Reg. Coll. (W), second tier
Admissions email: joinus@coloradomtn.edu
Public; founded 1967
Freshman admissions: least selective; 2020-2021: 1,771 applied, 1,767 accepted. Neither SAT nor ACT required. SAT 25/75 percentile: N/A. High school rank: N/A
Early decision deadline: N/A, notification date: N/A
Early action deadline: N/A, notification date: N/A
Application deadline (fall): rolling
Undergraduate student body: 1,561 full time, 3,343 part time
Most popular majors: 7% Business, Management, Marketing, and Related Support Services, 3% Multi/Interdisciplinary Studies, 1% Health Professions and Related Programs
Expenses: 2021-2022: $5,700 in state, $13,890 out of state; room/board: $9,658
Financial aid: N/A

Colorado School of Mines
Golden CO
(303) 273-3220
U.S. News ranking: Nat. U., No. 83
Website: www.mines.edu
Admissions email: admissions@mines.edu
Public; founded 1874
Freshman admissions: more selective; 2020-2021: 12,044 applied, 6,620 accepted. Neither SAT nor ACT required. SAT 25/75 percentile:. 1270-1440. High school rank: 55% in top tenth, 87% in top quarter, 99% in top half
Early decision deadline: N/A, notification date: N/A
Early action deadline: N/A, notification date: N/A
Application deadline (fall): 5/1

Undergraduate student body: 4,931 full time, 285 part time; 69% male, 31% female; 0% American Indian, 5% Asian, 1% black, 12% Hispanic, 5% multiracial, 0% Pacific Islander, 70% white, 4% international; 55% from in state; 35% live on campus; 13% of students in fraternities, 20% in sororities
Most popular majors: 30% Mechanical Engineering, 12% Computer Science, 10% Chemical Engineering, 8% Petroleum Engineering, 7% Electrical and Electronics Engineering
Expenses: 2021-2022: $19,100 in state, $39,800 out of state; room/board: $14,720
Financial aid: (303) 273-3301; 46% of undergrads determined to have financial need; average aid package $16,918

Colorado State University
Fort Collins CO
(970) 491-6909
U.S. News ranking: Nat. U., No. 148
Website: www.colostate.edu
Admissions email: admissions@colostate.edu
Public; founded 1870
Freshman admissions: selective; 2020-2021: 28,906 applied, 24,154 accepted. Neither SAT nor ACT required. SAT 25/75 percentile: 1070-1280. High school rank: 21% in top tenth, 48% in top quarter, 83% in top half
Early decision deadline: N/A, notification date: N/A
Early action deadline: 12/1, notification date: 1/1
Application deadline (fall): 7/1
Undergraduate student body: 20,727 full time, 4,459 part time; 46% male, 54% female; 1% American Indian, 3% Asian, 2% black, 16% Hispanic, 5% multiracial, 0% Pacific Islander, 70% white, 3% international; 68% from in state; 20% live on campus; 5% of students in fraternities, 6% in sororities
Most popular majors: 14% Business, Management, Marketing, and Related Support Services, 13% Biological and Biomedical Sciences, 11% Engineering, 9% Social Sciences, 7% Family and Consumer Sciences/Human Sciences
Expenses: 2021-2022: $12,260 in state, $31,540 out of state; room/board: $13,038
Financial aid: (970) 491-6321; 47% of undergrads determined to have financial need; average aid package $11,987

Colorado State University–Pueblo
Pueblo CO
(719) 549-2462
U.S. News ranking: Reg. U. (W), No. 87
Website: www.csupueblo.edu
Admissions email: info@csupueblo.edu
Public; founded 1933

Freshman admissions: selective; 2020-2021: 2,161 applied, 2,037 accepted. Neither SAT nor ACT required. SAT 25/75 percentile: 910-1110. High school rank: 13% in top tenth, 37% in top quarter, 70% in top half
Early decision deadline: N/A, notification date: N/A
Early action deadline: N/A, notification date: N/A
Application deadline (fall): 8/1
Undergraduate student body: 2,798 full time, 1,311 part time; 45% male, 55% female; 0% American Indian, 1% Asian, 6% black, 36% Hispanic, 6% multiracial, 0% Pacific Islander, 45% white, 2% international; 82% from in state; 18% live on campus; 1% of students in fraternities, 1% in sororities
Most popular majors: 16% Registered Nursing/Registered Nurse, 12% Business/Commerce, General, 9% Sociology, 6% Kinesiology and Exercise Science, 6% Psychology, General
Expenses: 2021-2022: $10,984 in state, $19,428 out of state; room/board: $11,256
Financial aid: (719) 549-2753; 75% of undergrads determined to have financial need; average aid package $12,208

Colorado Technical University[1]
Colorado Springs CO
(888) 404-7555
U.S. News ranking: Nat. U., second tier
Website: www.coloradotech.edu
Admissions email: info@ctuonline.edu
For-profit
Application deadline (fall): N/A
Undergraduate student body: N/A full time, N/A part time
Expenses: 2020-2021: $12,573; room/board: N/A
Financial aid: N/A

Community College of Denver[1]
Denver CO
(303) 556-2600
U.S. News ranking: Reg. Coll. (W), unranked
Website: www.ccd.edu
Admissions email: N/A
Public
Application deadline (fall): N/A
Undergraduate student body: N/A full time, N/A part time
Expenses: 2020-2021: $4,788 in state, $16,210 out of state; room/board: N/A
Financial aid: N/A

Fort Lewis College
Durango CO
(877) 352-2656
U.S. News ranking: Nat. Lib. Arts, second tier
Website: www.fortlewis.edu
Admissions email: admission@fortlewis.edu
Public; founded 1911
Freshman admissions: selective; 2020-2021: 3,497 applied, 3,230 accepted. Either SAT

or ACT required. ACT 25/75 percentile: 16-22. High school rank: 11% in top tenth, 30% in top quarter, 67% in top half
Early decision deadline: N/A, notification date: N/A
Early action deadline: 11/15, notification date: 12/24
Application deadline (fall): 8/1
Undergraduate student body: 2,894 full time, 455 part time; 46% male, 54% female; 34% American Indian, 0% Asian, 1% black, 13% Hispanic, 10% multiracial, 0% Pacific Islander, 39% white, 1% international; N/A from in state; 42% live on campus; 0% of students in fraternities, 0% in sororities
Most popular majors: 20% Business, Management, Marketing, and Related Support Services, 12% Parks, Recreation, Leisure, and Fitness Studies, 12% Social Sciences
Expenses: 2021-2022: $9,005 in state, $19,661 out of state; room/board: $10,384
Financial aid: (970) 247-7142; 59% of undergrads determined to have financial need; average aid package $18,622

Metropolitan State University of Denver
Denver CO
(303) 556-3058
U.S. News ranking: Reg. U. (W), second tier
Website: www.msudenver.edu
Admissions email: askmetro@msudenver.edu
Public; founded 1963
Freshman admissions: less selective; 2020-2021: 12,003 applied, 10,003 accepted. Either SAT or ACT required. SAT 25/75 percentile: 870-1090. High school rank: 3% in top tenth, 17% in top quarter, 55% in top half
Early decision deadline: N/A, notification date: N/A
Early action deadline: N/A, notification date: N/A
Application deadline (fall): 7/1
Undergraduate student body: 11,135 full time, 6,853 part time; 45% male, 55% female; 1% American Indian, 4% Asian, 7% black, 32% Hispanic, 5% multiracial, 0% Pacific Islander, 49% white, 1% international
Most popular majors: Information not available
Expenses: 2021-2022: $10,021 in state, $27,502 out of state; room/board: N/A
Financial aid: (303) 605-5504; 70% of undergrads determined to have financial need; average aid package $10,279

Naropa University[1]
Boulder CO
(303) 546-3572
U.S. News ranking: Reg. U. (W), second tier
Website: www.naropa.edu
Admissions email: admissions@naropa.edu
Private; founded 1974
Application deadline (fall): rolling

Undergraduate student body: 287 full time, 23 part time
Expenses: 2020-2021: $34,600; room/board: $11,137
Financial aid: (303) 546-3509

Pueblo Community College[1]
Pueblo CO
(719) 549-3200
U.S. News ranking: Reg. Coll. (W), unranked
Website: www.pueblocc.edu
Admissions email: N/A
Public
Application deadline (fall): N/A
Undergraduate student body: N/A full time, N/A part time
Expenses: 2020-2021: $4,520 in state, $15,942 out of state; room/board: N/A
Financial aid: N/A

Red Rocks Community College[1]
Lakewood CO
(303) 914-6600
U.S. News ranking: Reg. Coll. (W), unranked
Website: www.rrcc.edu
Admissions email: N/A
Public
Application deadline (fall): N/A
Undergraduate student body: N/A full time, N/A part time
Expenses: 2020-2021: $4,379 in state, $15,801 out of state; room/board: N/A
Financial aid: N/A

Regis University
Denver CO
(303) 458-4900
U.S. News ranking: Nat. U., No. 227
Website: www.regis.edu
Admissions email: ruadmissions@regis.edu
Private; founded 1877
Affiliation: Roman Catholic
Freshman admissions: selective; 2020-2021: 5,912 applied, 4,623 accepted. Neither SAT nor ACT required. SAT 25/75 percentile: 1000-1220. High school rank: 51% in top tenth, 59% in top quarter, 85% in top half
Early decision deadline: N/A, notification date: N/A
Early action deadline: N/A, notification date: N/A
Application deadline (fall): 8/1
Undergraduate student body: 2,090 full time, 1,107 part time; 38% male, 62% female; 0% American Indian, 5% Asian, 5% black, 26% Hispanic, 4% multiracial, 0% Pacific Islander, 53% white, 1% international; 64% from in state; 15% live on campus; 0% of students in fraternities, 0% in sororities
Most popular majors: 31% Health Professions and Related Programs, 21% Business, Management, Marketing, and Related Support Services, 6% Biological and Biomedical Sciences, 6% Computer and Information Sciences and Support Services

Expenses: 2021-2022: $39,610; room/board: $12,962
Financial aid: (303) 458-4126; 72% of undergrads determined to have financial need; average aid package $32,934

Rocky Mountain College of Art and Design[1]

Lakewood CO
(303) 753-6046
U.S. News ranking: Arts, unranked
Website: www.rmcad.edu/
Admissions email: admissions@rmcad.edu
For-profit; founded 1963
Application deadline (fall): N/A
Undergraduate student body: N/A full time, N/A part time
Expenses: 2020-2021: $20,725; room/board: N/A
Financial aid: (303) 225-8551

United States Air Force Academy

USAF Academy CO
(800) 443-9266
U.S. News ranking: Nat. Lib. Arts, No. 22
Website: academyadmissions.com
Admissions email: rr_webmail@usafa.edu
Public; founded 1954
Freshman admissions: most selective; 2020-2021: 10,747 applied, 1,443 accepted. Either SAT or ACT required. ACT 25/75 percentile: 29-33. High school rank: 55% in top tenth, 82% in top quarter, 98% in top half
Early decision deadline: N/A, notification date: N/A
Early action deadline: N/A, notification date: N/A
Application deadline (fall): 12/31
Undergraduate student body: 4,307 full time, 0 part time; 72% male, 28% female; 0% American Indian, 7% Asian, 7% black, 11% Hispanic, 7% multiracial, 0% Pacific Islander, 64% white, 1% international; 7% from in state; 100% live on campus; 0% of students in fraternities, 0% in sororities
Most popular majors: 28% Engineering, 21% Business, Management, Marketing, and Related Support Services, 14% Social Sciences, 13% Multi/Interdisciplinary Studies, 6% Biological and Biomedical Sciences
Expenses: N/A
Financial aid: N/A

University of Colorado Boulder

Boulder CO
(303) 492-6301
U.S. News ranking: Nat. U., No. 99
Website: www.colorado.edu
Admissions email: apply@colorado.edu
Public; founded 1876
Freshman admissions: more selective; 2020-2021: 44,171 applied, 37,189 accepted. Neither SAT nor ACT required. SAT 25/75 percentile: 1130-1350. High school rank: 26% in top

tenth, 53% in top quarter, 85% in top half
Early decision deadline: N/A, notification date: N/A
Early action deadline: 11/15, notification date: 2/1
Application deadline (fall): 1/15
Undergraduate student body: 27,687 full time, 2,613 part time; 54% male, 46% female; 0% American Indian, 6% Asian, 2% black, 13% Hispanic, 6% multiracial, 0% Pacific Islander, 68% white, 4% international; 59% from in state; 22% live on campus; 10% of students in fraternities, N/A in sororities
Most popular majors: 15% Business, Management, Marketing, and Related Support Services, 14% Engineering, 12% Biological and Biomedical Sciences, 12% Social Sciences, 9% Communication, Journalism, and Related Programs
Expenses: 2021-2022: $12,494 in state, $38,312 out of state; room/board: $15,676
Financial aid: (303) 492-5091; 34% of undergrads determined to have financial need; average aid package $17,482

University of Colorado–Colorado Springs

Colorado Springs CO
(719) 255-3084
U.S. News ranking: Nat. U., second tier
Website: www.uccs.edu
Admissions email: go@uccs.edu
Public; founded 1965
Freshman admissions: selective; 2020-2021: 8,956 applied, 8,025 accepted. Either SAT or ACT required. SAT 25/75 percentile: 1010-1200. High school rank: 13% in top tenth, 35% in top quarter, 69% in top half
Early decision deadline: N/A, notification date: N/A
Early action deadline: N/A, notification date: N/A
Application deadline (fall): rolling
Undergraduate student body: 7,815 full time, 2,304 part time; 46% male, 54% female; 0% American Indian, 4% Asian, 4% black, 20% Hispanic, 8% multiracial, 0% Pacific Islander, 62% white, 1% international; 88% from in state; 13% live on campus; 3% of students in fraternities, 2% in sororities
Most popular majors: 18% Business, Management, Marketing, and Related Support Services, 12% Health Professions and Related Programs, 10% Biological and Biomedical Sciences, 10% Social Sciences, 8% Engineering
Expenses: 2021-2022: $10,480 in state, $25,600 out of state; room/board: $11,158
Financial aid: (719) 255-3460; 59% of undergrads determined to have financial need; average aid package $9,398

University of Colorado Denver

Denver CO
(303) 315-2601
U.S. News ranking: Nat. U., No. 227
Website: www.ucdenver.edu
Admissions email: admissions@ucdenver.edu
Public; founded 1912
Freshman admissions: selective; 2020-2021: 9,458 applied, 6,271 accepted. Neither SAT nor ACT required. SAT 25/75 percentile: 995-1210. High school rank: 25% in top tenth, 53% in top quarter, 83% in top half
Early decision deadline: N/A, notification date: N/A
Early action deadline: N/A, notification date: N/A
Application deadline (fall): rolling
Undergraduate student body: 8,622 full time, 6,373 part time; 42% male, 58% female; 0% American Indian, 11% Asian, 6% black, 25% Hispanic, 6% multiracial, 0% Pacific Islander, 43% white, 9% international; 9% from in state; N/A live on campus; N/A of students in fraternities, N/A in sororities
Most popular majors: 17% Business, Management, Marketing, and Related Support Services, 14% Health Professions and Related Programs, 10% Social Sciences, 9% Biological and Biomedical Sciences, 8% Psychology
Expenses: 2021-2022: $11,580 in state, $32,820 out of state; room/board: $13,466
Financial aid: (303) 315-1850; 59% of undergrads determined to have financial need; average aid package $10,652

University of Denver

Denver CO
(303) 871-2036
U.S. News ranking: Nat. U., No. 93
Website: www.du.edu
Admissions email: admission@du.edu
Private; founded 1864
Freshman admissions: more selective; 2020-2021: 22,723 applied, 13,785 accepted. Neither SAT nor ACT required. SAT 25/75 percentile: 1170-1360. High school rank: 39% in top tenth, 74% in top quarter, 94% in top half
Early decision deadline: 11/1, notification date: 12/15
Early action deadline: 11/1, notification date: 1/15
Application deadline (fall): 1/15
Undergraduate student body: 5,362 full time, 337 part time; 46% male, 54% female; 0% American Indian, 4% Asian, 2% black, 13% Hispanic, 6% multiracial, 0% Pacific Islander, 68% white, 5% international; 35% from in state; 48% live on campus; 25% of students in fraternities, 28% in sororities
Most popular majors: 36% Business, Management, Marketing, and Related Support Services, 17% Social Sciences, 8% Biological and Biomedical

Sciences, 8% Psychology, 6% Communication, Journalism, and Related Programs
Expenses: 2021-2022: $54,819; room/board: $14,674
Financial aid: (303) 871-4020; 42% of undergrads determined to have financial need; average aid package $44,062

University of Northern Colorado

Greeley CO
(970) 351-2881
U.S. News ranking: Nat. U., second tier
Website: www.unco.edu
Admissions email: admissions@unco.edu
Public; founded 1890
Freshman admissions: selective; 2020-2021: 9,160 applied, 8,033 accepted. Either SAT or ACT required. SAT 25/75 percentile: 980-1200. High school rank: 15% in top tenth, 40% in top quarter, 74% in top half
Early decision deadline: N/A, notification date: N/A
Early action deadline: N/A, notification date: N/A
Application deadline (fall): 8/1
Undergraduate student body: 6,726 full time, 1,768 part time; 33% male, 67% female; 0% American Indian, 2% Asian, 5% black, 23% Hispanic, 5% multiracial, 0% Pacific Islander, 63% white, 1% international; 86% from in state; 29% live on campus; 7% of students in fraternities, 8% in sororities
Most popular majors: 18% Health Professions and Related Programs, 12% Education, 10% Business, Management, Marketing, and Related Support Services, 9% Psychology, 8% Visual and Performing Arts
Expenses: 2021-2022: $10,424 in state, $22,496 out of state; room/board: $11,684
Financial aid: (970) 351-2502; 61% of undergrads determined to have financial need; average aid package $15,359

Western Colorado University

Gunnison CO
(970) 943-2119
U.S. News ranking: Reg. U. (W), No. 61
Website: www.western.edu
Admissions email: admissions@western.edu
Public; founded 1901
Freshman admissions: selective; 2020-2021: 2,625 applied, 2,323 accepted. Neither SAT nor ACT required. SAT 25/75 percentile: 1000-1190. High school rank: 10% in top tenth, 31% in top quarter, 67% in top half
Early decision deadline: N/A, notification date: N/A
Early action deadline: N/A, notification date: N/A
Application deadline (fall): rolling
Undergraduate student body: 1,616 full time, 1,112 part time; 50% male, 50% female; 0% American Indian, 1% Asian, 3% black,

9% Hispanic, 5% multiracial, 0% Pacific Islander, 69% white, 0% international; N/A from in state; 56% live on campus; N/A of students in fraternities, N/A in sororities
Most popular majors: 20% Business, Management, Marketing, and Related Support Services, 12% Parks, Recreation, Leisure, and Fitness Studies, 11% Psychology
Expenses: 2021-2022: $10,663 in state, $22,447 out of state; room/board: $9,990
Financial aid: (970) 943-7015; 57% of undergrads determined to have financial need; average aid package $13,660

CONNECTICUT

Albertus Magnus College

New Haven CT
(203) 773-8501
U.S. News ranking: Reg. U. (N), No. 97
Website: www.albertus.edu
Admissions email: admissions@albertus.edu
Private; founded 1925
Affiliation: Roman Catholic
Freshman admissions: less selective; 2020-2021: 1,697 applied, 1,379 accepted. Neither SAT nor ACT required. SAT 25/75 percentile: 820-1040. High school rank: 4% in top tenth, 15% in top quarter, 51% in top half
Early decision deadline: N/A, notification date: N/A
Early action deadline: N/A, notification date: N/A
Application deadline (fall): 8/20
Undergraduate student body: 943 full time, 145 part time; 37% male, 63% female; 1% American Indian, 1% Asian, 29% black, 21% Hispanic, 2% multiracial, 0% Pacific Islander, 32% white, 3% international; 92% from in state; 21% live on campus; 0% of students in fraternities, 0% in sororities
Most popular majors: 36% Business, Management, Marketing, and Related Support Services, 11% Psychology, 10% Social Sciences, 9% Homeland Security, Law Enforcement, Firefighting and Related Protective Services, 8% Health Professions and Related Programs
Expenses: 2021-2022: $36,442; room/board: $14,898
Financial aid: (203) 773-8508; 87% of undergrads determined to have financial need; average aid package $19,971

Central Connecticut State University

New Britain CT
(860) 832-2278
U.S. News ranking: Reg. U. (N), No. 97
Website: www.ccsu.edu
Admissions email: admissions@ccsu.edu
Public; founded 1849
Freshman admissions: selective; 2020-2021: 7,724 applied,

5,009 accepted. Neither SAT nor ACT required. SAT 25/75 percentile: 970-1150. High school rank: 9% in top tenth, 27% in top quarter, 67% in top half
Early decision deadline: N/A, notification date: N/A
Early action deadline: N/A, notification date: N/A
Application deadline (fall): 5/1
Undergraduate student body: 6,811 full time, 1,782 part time; 53% male, 47% female; 0% American Indian, 5% Asian, 13% black, 17% Hispanic, 3% multiracial, 0% Pacific Islander, 58% white, 1% international; 96% from in state; 12% live on campus; N/A of students in fraternities, N/A in sororities
Most popular majors: 8% Criminology, 8% Psychology, General, 6% Accounting, 6% Business Administration and Management, General, 5% Finance, General
Expenses: 2021-2022: $11,542 in state, $23,816 out of state; room/board: $12,174
Financial aid: (860) 832-2200; 68% of undergrads determined to have financial need; average aid package $9,673

Connecticut College

New London CT
(860) 439-2200
U.S. News ranking: Nat. Lib. Arts, No. 50
Website: www.conncoll.edu
Admissions email: admission@conncoll.edu
Private; founded 1911
Freshman admissions: more selective; 2020-2021: 6,882 applied, 2,596 accepted. Neither SAT nor ACT required. SAT 25/75 percentile: 1310-1450. High school rank: 54% in top tenth, 78% in top quarter, 98% in top half
Early decision deadline: 11/15, notification date: 12/15
Early action deadline: N/A, notification date: N/A
Application deadline (fall): 1/1
Undergraduate student body: 1,689 full time, 48 part time; 38% male, 62% female; 0% American Indian, 4% Asian, 5% black, 10% Hispanic, 4% multiracial, 0% Pacific Islander, 67% white, 8% international; 17% from in state; N/A live on campus; 0% of students in fraternities, 0% in sororities
Most popular majors: 20% Economics, 13% Political Science and Government, 11% Psychology, General, 7% International Relations and Affairs, 7% Sociology
Expenses: 2021-2022: $60,795; room/board: $16,780
Financial aid: (860) 439-2058; 55% of undergrads determined to have financial need; average aid package $46,927

Eastern Connecticut State University

Willimantic CT
(860) 465-5286
U.S. News ranking: Reg. U. (N), No. 85
Website: www.easternct.edu
Admissions email: admissions@easternct.edu
Public; founded 1889
Freshman admissions: selective; 2020-2021: 5,182 applied, 3,612 accepted. Neither SAT nor ACT required. SAT 25/75 percentile: 990-1180. High school rank: 12% in top tenth, 39% in top quarter, 77% in top half
Early decision deadline: N/A, notification date: N/A
Early action deadline: N/A, notification date: N/A
Application deadline (fall): rolling
Undergraduate student body: 3,713 full time, 762 part time; 42% male, 58% female; 0% American Indian, 3% Asian, 9% black, 13% Hispanic, 4% multiracial, 0% Pacific Islander, 64% white, 1% international; 90% from in state; 44% live on campus; N/A of students in fraternities, N/A in sororities
Most popular majors: 14% Business, Management, Marketing, and Related Support Services, 11% Social Sciences, 10% Liberal Arts and Sciences, General Studies and Humanities, 8% Communication, Journalism, and Related Programs, 8% Psychology
Expenses: 2021-2022: $12,304 in state, $24,578 out of state; room/board: $14,434
Financial aid: (860) 465-5205; 62% of undergrads determined to have financial need; average aid package $10,865

Fairfield University

Fairfield CT
(203) 254-4100
U.S. News ranking: Reg. U. (N), No. 3
Website: www.fairfield.edu
Admissions email: admis@fairfield.edu
Private; founded 1942
Affiliation: Roman Catholic
Freshman admissions: more selective; 2020-2021: 12,586 applied, 7,065 accepted. Neither SAT nor ACT required. SAT 25/75 percentile: 1190-1340. High school rank: 40% in top tenth, 70% in top quarter, 95% in top half
Early decision deadline: 11/15, notification date: 12/15
Early action deadline: 11/1, notification date: 12/20
Application deadline (fall): 1/15
Undergraduate student body: 4,231 full time, 123 part time; 42% male, 58% female; 0% American Indian, 3% Asian, 2% black, 7% Hispanic, 2% multiracial, 0% Pacific Islander, 78% white, 3% international; 24% from in state; 72% live on campus; N/A of students in fraternities, N/A in sororities
Most popular majors: 41% Business, Management,

Marketing, and Related Support Services, 16% Health Professions and Related Programs, 9% Communication, Journalism, and Related Programs, 9% Social Sciences, 6% Psychology
Expenses: 2021-2022: $52,870; room/board: $16,110
Financial aid: (203) 254-4000; 37% of undergrads determined to have financial need; average aid package $31,290

Mitchell College[1]

New London CT
(860) 701-5000
U.S. News ranking: Reg. Coll. (N), second tier
Website: www.mitchell.edu
Admissions email: admissions@mitchell.edu
Private
Application deadline (fall): N/A
Undergraduate student body: N/A full time, N/A part time
Expenses: 2020-2021: $35,072; room/board: $13,906
Financial aid: N/A

Post University

Waterbury CT
(800) 660-6615
U.S. News ranking: Reg. U. (N), second tier
Website: www.post.edu
Admissions email: admissions@post.edu
For-profit; founded 1890
Freshman admissions: least selective; 2020-2021: 16,401 applied, 9,978 accepted. Neither SAT nor ACT required. SAT 25/75 percentile: 900-900. High school rank: N/A
Early decision deadline: N/A, notification date: N/A
Early action deadline: N/A, notification date: N/A
Application deadline (fall): rolling
Undergraduate student body: 3,609 full time, 9,239 part time; 26% male, 74% female; 1% American Indian, 1% Asian, 28% black, 8% Hispanic, 14% multiracial, 0% Pacific Islander, 39% white, 0% international; 17% from in state; 5% live on campus; 0% of students in fraternities, 0% in sororities
Most popular majors: 57% Business, Management, Marketing, and Related Support Services, 16% Homeland Security, Law Enforcement, Firefighting and Related Protective Services, 8% Public Administration and Social Service Professions, 5% Family and Consumer Sciences/Human Sciences, 4% Legal Professions and Studies
Expenses: 2020-2021: $17,810; room/board: $11,600
Financial aid: (800) 345-2562; 85% of undergrads determined to have financial need; average aid package $8,763

Quinnipiac University

Hamden CT
(203) 582-8600
U.S. News ranking: Nat. U., No. 148
Website: www.qu.edu

Admissions email: admissions@qu.edu
Private; founded 1929
Affiliation: Undenominational
Freshman admissions: selective; 2020-2021: 19,787 applied, 16,311 accepted. Neither SAT nor ACT required. SAT 25/75 percentile: 1080-1260. High school rank: 18% in top tenth, 52% in top quarter, 83% in top half
Early decision deadline: 11/1, notification date: 12/15
Early action deadline: N/A, notification date: N/A
Application deadline (fall): 2/1
Undergraduate student body: 6,480 full time, 361 part time; 38% male, 62% female; 0% American Indian, 4% Asian, 4% black, 10% Hispanic, 3% multiracial, 0% Pacific Islander, 75% white, 2% international; N/A from in state; 55% live on campus; 15% of students in fraternities, 18% in sororities
Most popular majors: 35% Health Professions and Related Programs, 25% Business, Management, Marketing, and Related Support Services, 9% Communication, Journalism, and Related Programs, 6% Psychology, 5% Visual and Performing Arts
Expenses: 2021-2022: $51,270; room/board: $16,160
Financial aid: (203) 582-8750; 63% of undergrads determined to have financial need; average aid package $30,977

Sacred Heart University

Fairfield CT
(203) 371-7880
U.S. News ranking: Nat. U., No. 202
Website: www.sacredheart.edu
Admissions email: enroll@sacredheart.edu
Private; founded 1963
Affiliation: Roman Catholic
Freshman admissions: selective; 2020-2021: 12,189 applied, 7,988 accepted. Neither SAT nor ACT required. SAT 25/75 percentile: 1140-1260. High school rank: 9% in top tenth, 38% in top quarter, 77% in top half
Early decision deadline: 12/1, notification date: 12/15
Early action deadline: 12/15, notification date: 1/31
Application deadline (fall): 7/28
Undergraduate student body: 5,671 full time, 746 part time; 32% male, 68% female; 0% American Indian, 2% Asian, 4% black, 13% Hispanic, 2% multiracial, 0% Pacific Islander, 74% white, 1% international; N/A from in state; 48% live on campus; 21% of students in fraternities, 44% in sororities
Most popular majors: 28% Health Professions and Related Programs, 26% Business, Management, Marketing, and Related Support Services, 8% Psychology, 5% Biological and Biomedical Sciences, 5% Communication, Journalism, and Related Programs
Expenses: 2021-2022: $45,230; room/board: $16,868

Financial aid: (203) 371-7980; 63% of undergrads determined to have financial need; average aid package $23,579

Southern Connecticut State University

New Haven CT
(203) 392-5644
U.S. News ranking: Reg. U. (N), No. 103
Website: www.southernct.edu/
Admissions email: admissions@southernct.edu
Public; founded 1893
Freshman admissions: less selective; 2020-2021: 8,504 applied, 6,776 accepted. Neither SAT nor ACT required. SAT 25/75 percentile: 910-1110. High school rank: 12% in top tenth, 30% in top quarter, 66% in top half
Early decision deadline: N/A, notification date: N/A
Early action deadline: N/A, notification date: N/A
Application deadline (fall): 8/16
Undergraduate student body: 6,268 full time, 1,172 part time; 37% male, 63% female; 0% American Indian, 3% Asian, 19% black, 14% Hispanic, 5% multiracial, 0% Pacific Islander, 51% white, 1% international; 97% from in state; 20% live on campus; 1% of students in fraternities, 3% in sororities
Most popular majors: 16% Health Professions and Related Programs, 15% Business, Management, Marketing, and Related Support Services, 11% Multi/Interdisciplinary Studies, 9% Psychology, 8% Parks, Recreation, Leisure, and Fitness Studies
Expenses: 2021-2022: $11,882 in state, $24,156 out of state; room/board: $13,666
Financial aid: (203) 392-5222; 78% of undergrads determined to have financial need; average aid package $8,652

Trinity College

Hartford CT
(860) 297-2180
U.S. News ranking: Nat. Lib. Arts, No. 46
Website: www.trincoll.edu
Admissions email: admissions.office@trincoll.edu
Private; founded 1823
Affiliation: Undenominational
Freshman admissions: more selective; 2020-2021: 5,952 applied, 2,145 accepted. Neither SAT nor ACT required. SAT 25/75 percentile: 1290-1450. High school rank: 51% in top tenth, 82% in top quarter, 100% in top half
Early decision deadline: 11/15, notification date: 12/15
Early action deadline: N/A, notification date: N/A
Application deadline (fall): 1/15
Undergraduate student body: 2,167 full time, 33 part time; 50% male, 51% female; 0% American Indian, 4% Asian, 7% black, 9% Hispanic, 3% multiracial, 0% Pacific Islander, 62% white, 13% international; N/A from in state; 74% live on campus; 29% of

students in fraternities, 17% in sororities

Most popular majors: 31% Social Sciences, 12% Biological and Biomedical Sciences, 7% Psychology, 6% Area, Ethnic, Cultural, Gender, and Group Studies

Expenses: 2021-2022: $61,370; room/board: $15,900

Financial aid: (860) 297-2046; 37% of undergrads determined to have financial need; average aid package $52,765

United States Coast Guard Academy

New London CT

(800) 883-8724

U.S. News ranking: Reg. Coll. (N), No. 1

Website: www.uscga.edu

Admissions email: admissions@uscga.edu

Public; founded 1876

Freshman admissions: more selective; 2020-2021: 2,017 applied, 271 accepted. Either SAT or ACT required. SAT 25/75 percentile: 1220-1400. High school rank: 49% in top tenth, 88% in top quarter, 100% in top half

Early decision deadline: N/A, notification date: N/A

Early action deadline: 10/15, notification date: 12/24

Application deadline (fall): 1/15

Undergraduate student body: 1,056 full time, 0 part time; 62% male, 38% female; 0% American Indian, 7% Asian, 5% black, 12% Hispanic, 10% multiracial, 0% Pacific Islander, 62% white, 3% international

Most popular majors: 19% Business Administration, Management and Operations, 18% Applied Mathematics, 14% Physical Sciences, 14% Political Science and Government, 12% Civil Engineering

Expenses: 2020-2021: $0 in state, $0 out of state; room/board: $0

Financial aid: N/A

University of Bridgeport[1]

Bridgeport CT

(203) 576-4552

U.S. News ranking: Nat. U., second tier

Website: www.bridgeport.edu

Admissions email: admit@bridgeport.edu

Private; founded 1927

Application deadline (fall): rolling

Undergraduate student body: N/A full time, N/A part time

Expenses: N/A

Financial aid: (203) 576-4568

University of Connecticut

Storrs CT

(860) 486-3137

U.S. News ranking: Nat. U., No. 63

Website: www.uconn.edu

Admissions email: beahusky@uconn.edu

Public; founded 1881

Freshman admissions: more selective; 2020-2021: 34,437 applied, 19,316 accepted. Neither SAT nor ACT required. SAT 25/75 percentile: 1170-1390. High school rank: 51% in top tenth, 84% in top quarter, 96% in top half

Early decision deadline: N/A, notification date: N/A

Early action deadline: N/A, notification date: N/A

Application deadline (fall): 1/15

Undergraduate student body: 18,090 full time, 827 part time; 48% male, 52% female; 0% American Indian, 12% Asian, 7% black, 13% Hispanic, 4% multiracial, 0% Pacific Islander, 53% white, 10% international; 72% from in state; 25% live on campus; 10% of students in fraternities, 12% in sororities

Most popular majors: 7% Economics, General, 7% Psychology, General, 6% Speech Communication and Rhetoric, 5% Registered Nursing/Registered Nurse, 4% Biology/Biological Sciences, General

Expenses: 2021-2022: $18,524 in state, $41,192 out of state; room/board: $13,258

Financial aid: (860) 486-2819; 53% of undergrads determined to have financial need; average aid package $16,828

University of Hartford

West Hartford CT

(860) 768-4296

U.S. News ranking: Nat. U., No. 213

Website: www.hartford.edu

Admissions email: admission@hartford.edu

Private; founded 1877

Freshman admissions: selective; 2020-2021: 12,660 applied, 9,800 accepted. Neither SAT nor ACT required. SAT 25/75 percentile: 1020-1210. High school rank: N/A

Early decision deadline: N/A, notification date: N/A

Early action deadline: 11/15, notification date: 12/1

Application deadline (fall): rolling

Undergraduate student body: 4,073 full time, 448 part time; 46% male, 54% female; 0% American Indian, 4% Asian, 16% black, 14% Hispanic, 3% multiracial, 0% Pacific Islander, 52% white, 5% international; 48% from in state; 54% live on campus; N/A of students in fraternities, N/A in sororities

Most popular majors: 16% Business, Management, Marketing, and Related Support Services, 16% Visual and Performing Arts, 15% Engineering, 10% Health Professions and Related Programs, 7% Engineering Technologies and Engineering-Related Fields

Expenses: 2021-2022: $44,885; room/board: $13,353

Financial aid: (860) 768-4296; 73% of undergrads determined to have financial need; average aid package $33,177

University of New Haven

West Haven CT

(203) 932-7319

U.S. News ranking: Reg. U. (N), No. 55

Website: www.newhaven.edu

Admissions email: admissions@newhaven.edu

Private; founded 1920

Freshman admissions: selective; 2020-2021: 10,671 applied, 9,721 accepted. Neither SAT nor ACT required. SAT 25/75 percentile: 1050-1220. High school rank: 17% in top tenth, 41% in top quarter, 76% in top half

Early decision deadline: 12/1, notification date: 12/15

Early action deadline: 12/15, notification date: 1/15

Application deadline (fall): rolling

Undergraduate student body: 4,837 full time, 260 part time; 44% male, 56% female; 0% American Indian, 4% Asian, 11% black, 16% Hispanic, 1% multiracial, 0% Pacific Islander, 63% white, 2% international; 43% from in state; 52% live on campus; N/A of students in fraternities, N/A in sororities

Most popular majors: 41% Homeland Security, Law Enforcement, Firefighting and Related Protective Services, 11% Business, Management, Marketing, and Related Support Services, 10% Visual and Performing Arts, 8% Engineering, 6% Psychology

Expenses: 2021-2022: $42,898; room/board: $17,360

Financial aid: (203) 932-7220

University of Saint Joseph

West Hartford CT

(860) 231-5216

U.S. News ranking: Nat. U., No. 187

Website: www.usj.edu

Admissions email: admissions@usj.edu

Private; founded 1932

Affiliation: Roman Catholic

Freshman admissions: selective; 2020-2021: 1,579 applied, 1,232 accepted. Neither SAT nor ACT required. SAT 25/75 percentile: 970-1166. High school rank: 21% in top tenth, 43% in top quarter, 76% in top half

Early decision deadline: N/A, notification date: N/A

Early action deadline: N/A, notification date: N/A

Application deadline (fall): rolling

Undergraduate student body: 820 full time, 78 part time; 22% male, 78% female; 0% American Indian, 5% Asian, 12% black, 16% Hispanic, 4% multiracial, 0% Pacific Islander, 61% white, 1% international

Most popular majors: 41% Registered Nursing/Registered Nurse, 10% Social Work, 8% Psychology, General, 7% Business Administration and Management, General, 7% Foods, Nutrition, and Wellness Studies, General

Expenses: 2021-2022: $42,934; room/board: $12,732

Financial aid: (860) 231-5223; 93% of undergrads determined to have financial need; average aid package $26,925

Wesleyan University

Middletown CT

(860) 685-3000

U.S. News ranking: Nat. Lib. Arts, No. 17

Website: www.wesleyan.edu

Admissions email: admission@wesleyan.edu

Private; founded 1831

Freshman admissions: most selective; 2020-2021: 12,632 applied, 2,640 accepted. Neither SAT nor ACT required. SAT 25/75 percentile: 1340-1520. High school rank: 67% in top tenth, 94% in top quarter, 98% in top half

Early decision deadline: 11/15, notification date: 12/15

Early action deadline: N/A, notification date: N/A

Application deadline (fall): 1/1

Undergraduate student body: 2,836 full time, 16 part time; 42% male, 58% female; 0% American Indian, 8% Asian, 6% black, 12% Hispanic, 7% multiracial, 0% Pacific Islander, 55% white, 11% international; 7% from in state; 97% live on campus; 4% of students in fraternities, 1% in sororities

Most popular majors: 25% Social Sciences, 14% Psychology, 12% Area, Ethnic, Cultural, Gender, and Group Studies, 11% Visual and Performing Arts, 7% English Language and Literature/Letters

Expenses: 2021-2022: $61,749; room/board: $17,531

Financial aid: (860) 685-2800; 41% of undergrads determined to have financial need; average aid package $61,316

Western Connecticut State University

Danbury CT

(203) 837-9000

U.S. News ranking: Reg. U. (N), No. 114

Website: www.wcsu.edu

Admissions email: admissions@wcsu.edu

Public; founded 1903

Freshman admissions: selective; 2020-2021: 5,194 applied, 4,192 accepted. Neither SAT nor ACT required. SAT 25/75 percentile: 1020-1200. High school rank: N/A

Early decision deadline: N/A, notification date: N/A

Early action deadline: N/A, notification date: N/A

Application deadline (fall): rolling

Undergraduate student body: 3,794 full time, 847 part time; 48% male, 52% female; 0% American Indian, 5% Asian, 9% black, 23% Hispanic, 4% multiracial, 0% Pacific Islander, 57% white, 0% international; 22% from in state; 27% live on campus; 3% of students in fraternities, 5% in sororities

Most popular majors: 22% Business, Management, Marketing, and Related Support Services, 13% Health Professions and Related Programs, 9% Homeland Security, Law Enforcement, Firefighting and Related Protective Services, 9% Psychology, 9% Visual and Performing Arts

Expenses: 2021-2022: $11,781 in state, $24,055 out of state; room/board: $13,921

Financial aid: (203) 837-8580; 53% of undergrads determined to have financial need; average aid package $9,492

Yale University

New Haven CT

(203) 432-9316

U.S. News ranking: Nat. U., No. 5

Website: www.yale.edu/

Admissions email: student.questions@yale.edu

Private; founded 1701

Freshman admissions: most selective; 2020-2021: 35,220 applied, 2,299 accepted. Neither SAT nor ACT required. SAT 25/75 percentile: 1460-1580. High school rank: 94% in top tenth, 99% in top quarter, 100% in top half

Early decision deadline: N/A, notification date: N/A

Early action deadline: 11/1, notification date: 12/15

Application deadline (fall): 1/2

Undergraduate student body: 4,696 full time, 7 part time; 50% male, 50% female; 0% American Indian, 24% Asian, 9% black, 15% Hispanic, 6% multiracial, 0% Pacific Islander, 35% white, 10% international; N/A from in state; 58% live on campus; N/A of students in fraternities, N/A in sororities

Most popular majors: 27% Social Sciences, 11% Biological and Biomedical Sciences, 8% Mathematics and Statistics, 7% Computer and Information Sciences and Support Services, 7% History

Expenses: 2021-2022: $59,950; room/board: $17,800

Financial aid: (203) 432-2700; 57% of undergrads determined to have financial need; average aid package $61,920

DELAWARE

Delaware State University

Dover DE

(302) 857-6353

U.S. News ranking: Nat. U., No. 263

Website: www.desu.edu

Admissions email: admissions@desu.edu

Public; founded 1891

Freshman admissions: less selective; 2020-2021: 11,317 applied, 4,452 accepted. Either SAT or ACT required. SAT 25/75 percentile: 810-1010. High school rank: 10% in top tenth, 32% in top quarter, 69% in top half

Early decision deadline: N/A,

notification date: N/A
Early action deadline: N/A, notification date: N/A
Application deadline (fall): rolling
Undergraduate student body: 3,617 full time, 514 part time; 32% male, 68% female; 0% American Indian, 1% Asian, 73% black, 7% Hispanic, 6% multiracial, 0% Pacific Islander, 8% white, 4% international
Most popular majors: 12% Business, Management, Marketing, and Related Support Services, 11% Biological and Biomedical Sciences, 10% Communication, Journalism, and Related Programs, 10% Parks, Recreation, Leisure, and Fitness Studies, 10% Social Sciences
Expenses: 2020-2021: $8,258 in state, $17,294 out of state; room/board: $11,984
Financial aid: (302) 857-6250; 79% of undergrads determined to have financial need; average aid package $19,275

Delaware Technical Community College–Terry[1]
Dover DE
(302) 857-1000
U.S. News ranking: Reg. Coll. (N), unranked
Website: www.dtcc.edu/our-campuses/dover
Admissions email: N/A
Public
Application deadline (fall): N/A
Undergraduate student body: N/A full time, N/A part time
Expenses: 2020-2021: $4,945 in state, $11,808 out of state; room/board: N/A
Financial aid: N/A

Goldey-Beacom College[1]
Wilmington DE
(302) 998-8814
U.S. News ranking: Business, unranked
Website: www.gbc.edu
Admissions email: admissions@gbc.edu
Private; founded 1886
Application deadline (fall): N/A
Undergraduate student body: N/A full time, N/A part time
Expenses: 2020-2021: $25,500; room/board: $10,040
Financial aid: (302) 225-6265

University of Delaware
Newark DE
(302) 831-8123
U.S. News ranking: Nat. U., No. 93
Website: www.udel.edu/
Admissions email: admissions@udel.edu
Public; founded 1743
Freshman admissions: more selective; 2020-2021: 33,505 applied, 21,125 accepted. Neither SAT nor ACT required. SAT 25/75 percentile: 1170-1340. High school rank: 24% in top tenth, 53% in top quarter, 83% in top half

Early decision deadline: N/A, notification date: N/A
Early action deadline: N/A, notification date: N/A
Application deadline (fall): 1/15
Undergraduate student body: 17,047 full time, 1,366 part time; 42% male, 58% female; 0% American Indian, 5% Asian, 6% black, 9% Hispanic, 4% multiracial, 0% Pacific Islander, 68% white, 5% international; 37% from in state; 7% live on campus; 18% of students in fraternities, 23% in sororities
Most popular majors: 22% Business, Management, Marketing, and Related Support Services, 11% Social Sciences, 10% Health Professions and Related Programs, 8% Engineering, 6% Biological and Biomedical Sciences
Expenses: 2021-2022: $15,020 in state, $36,880 out of state; room/board: $13,742
Financial aid: (302) 831-2126; 51% of undergrads determined to have financial need; average aid package $14,775

Wesley College[1]
Dover DE
(302) 736-2400
U.S. News ranking: Reg. Coll. (N), second tier
Website: www.wesley.edu
Admissions email: admissions@wesley.edu
Private; founded 1873
Affiliation: United Methodist
Application deadline (fall): 4/30
Undergraduate student body: N/A full time, N/A part time
Expenses: 2020-2021: $27,284; room/board: $11,864
Financial aid: (302) 736-2483

Wilmington University
New Castle DE
(302) 328-9407
U.S. News ranking: Nat. U., second tier
Website: www.wilmu.edu
Admissions email: undergradadmissions@wilmu.edu
Private; founded 1968
Freshman admissions: least selective; 2020-2021: 1,745 applied, 1,728 accepted. Neither SAT nor ACT required. SAT 25/75 percentile: N/A. High school rank: N/A
Early decision deadline: N/A, notification date: N/A
Early action deadline: N/A, notification date: N/A
Application deadline (fall): rolling
Undergraduate student body: 3,041 full time, 6,167 part time; 37% male, 63% female; 1% American Indian, 3% Asian, 21% black, 12% Hispanic, 4% multiracial, 0% Pacific Islander, 52% white, 5% international
Most popular majors: 26% Registered Nursing/Registered Nurse, 9% Social Sciences, General, 8% Business Administration and Management, General, 7% Computer and Information Systems Security/Information Assurance, 6% Criminal Justice/Law Enforcement

Administration
Expenses: 2021-2022: $11,750; room/board: N/A
Financial aid: (302) 356-4636; 51% of undergrads determined to have financial need

DISTRICT OF COLUMBIA

American University
Washington DC
(202) 885-6000
U.S. News ranking: Nat. U., No. 79
Website: www.american.edu
Admissions email: admissions@american.edu
Private; founded 1893
Affiliation: United Methodist
Freshman admissions: more selective; 2020-2021: 20,036 applied, 7,744 accepted. Neither SAT nor ACT required. SAT 25/75 percentile: 1220-1390. High school rank: 35% in top tenth, 68% in top quarter, 95% in top half
Early decision deadline: 11/15, notification date: 12/31
Early action deadline: N/A, notification date: N/A
Application deadline (fall): 1/15
Undergraduate student body: 7,453 full time, 500 part time; 38% male, 62% female; 0% American Indian, 7% Asian, 8% black, 12% Hispanic, 5% multiracial, 0% Pacific Islander, 53% white, 12% international; N/A from in state; N/A live on campus; 9% of students in fraternities, 9% in sororities
Most popular majors: 37% Social Sciences, 16% Business, Management, Marketing, and Related Support Services, 10% Communication, Journalism, and Related Programs
Expenses: 2021-2022: $51,334; room/board: $15,150
Financial aid: (202) 885-6500; 44% of undergrads determined to have financial need; average aid package $35,942

The Catholic University of America
Washington DC
(800) 673-2772
U.S. News ranking: Nat. U., No. 136
Website: www.catholic.edu/
Admissions email: cua-admissions@cua.edu
Private; founded 1887
Affiliation: Roman Catholic
Freshman admissions: more selective; 2020-2021: 6,258 applied, 5,146 accepted. Neither SAT nor ACT required. SAT 25/75 percentile: 1130-1325. High school rank: 28% in top tenth, 55% in top quarter, 88% in top half
Early decision deadline: 11/1, notification date: 12/15
Early action deadline: 11/1, notification date: 1/15
Application deadline (fall): 1/15
Undergraduate student body: 2,926 full time, 120 part time; 44% male, 56% female; 0% American Indian, 3% Asian, 4% black,

15% Hispanic, 4% multiracial, 0% Pacific Islander, 68% white, 4% international; 4% from in state; 23% live on campus; 0% of students in fraternities, 0% in sororities
Most popular majors: 11% Political Science and Government, General, 8% Registered Nursing/Registered Nurse, 6% Architecture, 5% Mechanical Engineering, 5% Psychology, General
Expenses: 2021-2022: $52,156; room/board: $16,020
Financial aid: (202) 319-5307; 53% of undergrads determined to have financial need; average aid package $35,325

Gallaudet University
Washington DC
(202) 651-5750
U.S. News ranking: Nat. U., No. 127
Website: www.gallaudet.edu
Admissions email: admissions.office@gallaudet.edu
Private; founded 1864
Freshman admissions: less selective; 2020-2021: 412 applied, 258 accepted. Either SAT or ACT required. ACT 25/75 percentile: 14-18. High school rank: N/A
Early decision deadline: N/A, notification date: N/A
Early action deadline: N/A, notification date: N/A
Application deadline (fall): rolling
Undergraduate student body: 905 full time, 114 part time; 45% male, 55% female; 1% American Indian, 5% Asian, 16% black, 18% Hispanic, 3% multiracial, 1% Pacific Islander, 45% white, 5% international; N/A from in state; 6% live on campus; N/A of students in fraternities, N/A in sororities
Most popular majors: Information not available
Expenses: 2021-2022: $17,112; room/board: $14,500
Financial aid: (202) 651-5290; 87% of undergrads determined to have financial need; average aid package $23,560

Georgetown University
Washington DC
(202) 687-3600
U.S. News ranking: Nat. U., No. 23
Website: www.georgetown.edu
Admissions email: guadmiss@georgetown.edu
Private; founded 1789
Affiliation: Roman Catholic
Freshman admissions: more selective; 2020-2021: 21,190 applied, 3,561 accepted. Either SAT or ACT required. SAT 25/75 percentile: 1380-1550. High school rank: 83% in top tenth, 96% in top quarter, 99% in top half
Early decision deadline: N/A, notification date: N/A
Early action deadline: 11/1, notification date: 12/15
Application deadline (fall): 1/10
Undergraduate student body: 6,610 full time, 747 part time; 44% male, 56% female; 0% American

Indian, 12% Asian, 7% black, 10% Hispanic, 5% multiracial, 0% Pacific Islander, 49% white, 14% international
Most popular majors: Information not available
Expenses: 2021-2022: $59,957; room/board: $18,748
Financial aid: (202) 687-4547; 37% of undergrads determined to have financial need; average aid package $42,100

George Washington University
Washington DC
(202) 994-6040
U.S. News ranking: Nat. U., No. 63
Website: www.gwu.edu
Admissions email: gwadm@gwu.edu
Private; founded 1821
Freshman admissions: more selective; 2020-2021: 26,405 applied, 11,366 accepted. Neither SAT nor ACT required. SAT 25/75 percentile: 1270-1450. High school rank: 50% in top tenth, 83% in top quarter, 98% in top half
Early decision deadline: 11/1, notification date: 12/15
Early action deadline: N/A, notification date: N/A
Application deadline (fall): 1/1
Undergraduate student body: 10,140 full time, 1,622 part time; 36% male, 64% female; 0% American Indian, 12% Asian, 8% black, 12% Hispanic, 5% multiracial, 0% Pacific Islander, 50% white, 10% international; 3% from in state; 4% live on campus; 0% of students in fraternities, 0% in sororities
Most popular majors: 32% Social Sciences, 16% Business, Management, Marketing, and Related Support Services, 16% Health Professions and Related Programs, 6% Computer and Information Sciences and Support Services, 6% Engineering
Expenses: 2021-2022: $59,870; room/board: $15,440
Financial aid: (202) 994-6620; 46% of undergrads determined to have financial need; average aid package $43,575

Howard University
Washington DC
(202) 806-2755
U.S. News ranking: Nat. U., No. 83
Website: www.howard.edu
Admissions email: admission@howard.edu
Private; founded 1867
Freshman admissions: more selective; 2020-2021: 24,325 applied, 9,398 accepted. Neither SAT nor ACT required. SAT 25/75 percentile: 1130-1260. High school rank: 27% in top tenth, 59% in top quarter, 89% in top half
Early decision deadline: 11/1, notification date: 12/18
Early action deadline: 11/1, notification date: 12/18
Application deadline (fall): 2/15
Undergraduate student body: 7,497 full time, 360 part time; 28% male, 72% female; 2% American

Indian, 3% Asian, 67% black, 7% Hispanic, 4% multiracial, 0% Pacific Islander, 1% white, 4% international; 2% from in state; N/A live on campus; 5% of students in fraternities, 3% in sororities
Most popular majors: 12% Biology/Biological Sciences, General, 9% Political Science and Government, General, 7% Public Relations, Advertising, and Applied Communication, 6% Communication, Journalism, and Related Programs, Other, 6% Health and Physical Education/Fitness, General
Expenses: 2021-2022: $28,916; room/board: $14,678
Financial aid: (202) 806-2747; 85% of undergrads determined to have financial need; average aid package $23,224

Strayer University[1]
Washington DC
(202) 408-2400
U.S. News ranking: Reg. U. (N), unranked
Website: www.strayer.edu
Admissions email: mzm@strayer.edu
For-profit; founded 1892
Application deadline (fall): N/A
Undergraduate student body: N/A full time, N/A part time
Expenses: 2020-2021: $13,515; room/board: N/A
Financial aid: N/A

Trinity Washington University[1]
Washington DC
(202) 884-9400
U.S. News ranking: Reg. U. (N), second tier
Website: www.trinitydc.edu
Admissions email: admissions@trinitydc.edu
Private
Application deadline (fall): N/A
Undergraduate student body: N/A full time, N/A part time
Expenses: 2020-2021: $25,110; room/board: $10,925
Financial aid: N/A

University of the District of Columbia
Washington DC
(202) 274-5010
U.S. News ranking: Reg. U. (N), second tier
Website: www.udc.edu/
Admissions email: N/A
Public; founded 1976
Freshman admissions: less selective; 2020-2021: 2,852 applied, 1,880 accepted. Either SAT or ACT required. SAT 25/75 percentile: N/A. High school rank: N/A
Early decision deadline: N/A, notification date: N/A
Early action deadline: N/A, notification date: N/A
Application deadline (fall): rolling
Undergraduate student body: 1,563 full time, 1,702 part time; 37% male, 63% female; 0% American Indian, 2% Asian, 64% black, 11% Hispanic, 0% multiracial,

0% Pacific Islander, 6% white, 6% international
Most popular majors: Information not available
Expenses: 2020-2021: $6,152 in state, $13,004 out of state; room/board: N/A
Financial aid: (202) 274-6053

University of the Potomac[1]
Washington DC
(202) 274-2303
U.S. News ranking: Business, unranked
Website: www.potomac.edu
Admissions email: admissions@potomac.edu
For-profit; founded 1991
Application deadline (fall): rolling
Undergraduate student body: N/A full time, N/A part time
Expenses: 2020-2021: $6,660; room/board: N/A
Financial aid: N/A

FLORIDA

Ave Maria University[1]
Ave Maria FL
(877) 283-8648
U.S. News ranking: Nat. Lib. Arts, second tier
Website: www.avemaria.edu
Admissions email: admissions@avemaria.edu
Private; founded 2003
Affiliation: Roman Catholic
Application deadline (fall): rolling
Undergraduate student body: N/A full time, N/A part time
Expenses: 2020-2021: $23,188; room/board: $12,580
Financial aid: (239) 280-2423

Barry University
Miami Shores FL
(305) 899-3100
U.S. News ranking: Nat. U., second tier
Website: www.barry.edu
Admissions email: admissions@barry.edu
Private; founded 1940
Affiliation: Roman Catholic
Freshman admissions: less selective; 2020-2021: 10,584 applied, 6,950 accepted. Either SAT or ACT required. SAT 25/75 percentile: 900-1070. High school rank: N/A
Early decision deadline: N/A, notification date: N/A
Early action deadline: N/A, notification date: N/A
Application deadline (fall): rolling
Undergraduate student body: 2,857 full time, 666 part time; 33% male, 67% female; 0% American Indian, 1% Asian, 38% black, 38% Hispanic, 2% multiracial, 0% Pacific Islander, 14% white, 6% international
Most popular majors: 26% Business Administration and Management, General, 14% Registered Nursing/Registered Nurse, 8% Biology/Biological Sciences, General, 7% Public Administration, 4% Psychology, General

Expenses: 2021-2022: $30,014; room/board: $11,474
Financial aid: (305) 899-3673; 82% of undergrads determined to have financial need; average aid package $25,159

Beacon College[1]
Leesburg FL
(352) 787-7660
U.S. News ranking: Reg. Coll. (S), No. 35
Website: www.beaconcollege.edu/
Admissions email: admissions@beaconcollege.edu
Private
Application deadline (fall): N/A
Undergraduate student body: N/A full time, N/A part time
Expenses: 2020-2021: $42,900; room/board: $12,816
Financial aid: N/A

Bethune-Cookman University
Daytona Beach FL
(800) 448-0228
U.S. News ranking: Nat. Lib. Arts, second tier
Website: www.bethune.cookman.edu
Admissions email: admissions@cookman.edu
Private; founded 1904
Affiliation: United Methodist
Freshman admissions: less selective; 2020-2021: 5,938 applied, 5,804 accepted. Either SAT or ACT required. SAT 25/75 percentile: 870-980. High school rank: 12% in top tenth, 30% in top quarter, 67% in top half
Early decision deadline: N/A, notification date: N/A
Early action deadline: N/A, notification date: N/A
Application deadline (fall): rolling
Undergraduate student body: 2,614 full time, 132 part time; 36% male, 64% female; 0% American Indian, 0% Asian, 81% black, 5% Hispanic, 3% multiracial, 0% Pacific Islander, 1% white, 2% international; 74% from in state; 57% live on campus; 38% of students in fraternities, 62% in sororities
Most popular majors: 15% Business, Management, Marketing, and Related Support Services, 14% Homeland Security, Law Enforcement, Firefighting and Related Protective Services, 14% Psychology, 10% Liberal Arts and Sciences, General Studies and Humanities
Expenses: 2021-2022: $14,794; room/board: $10,396
Financial aid: (386) 481-2620; 95% of undergrads determined to have financial need; average aid package $14,909

Broward College
Fort Lauderdale FL
(954) 201-7350
U.S. News ranking: Reg. Coll. (S), unranked
Website: www.broward.edu
Admissions email: N/A
Public; founded 1960
Freshman admissions: least

selective; 2020-2021: 20,618 applied, 20,618 accepted. Neither SAT nor ACT required. SAT 25/75 percentile: N/A. High school rank: N/A
Early decision deadline: N/A, notification date: N/A
Early action deadline: N/A, notification date: N/A
Application deadline (fall): rolling
Undergraduate student body: 10,715 full time, 22,528 part time; 38% male, 62% female; 0% American Indian, 3% Asian, 28% black, 38% Hispanic, 7% multiracial, 0% Pacific Islander, 15% white, 5% international; 98% from in state; 0% live on campus; 0% of students in fraternities, 0% in sororities
Most popular majors: 42% Business Administration, Management and Operations, Other, 17% Information Technology, 16% Registered Nursing/Registered Nurse, 8% Logistics, Materials, and Supply Chain Management, 7% Special Education and Teaching, General
Expenses: N/A
Financial aid: (954) 201-2330; average aid package $0

Chipola College[1]
Marianna FL
(850) 718-2211
U.S. News ranking: Reg. Coll. (S), unranked
Website: www.chipola.edu
Admissions email: N/A
Public
Application deadline (fall): N/A
Undergraduate student body: N/A full time, N/A part time
Expenses: 2020-2021: $3,120 in state, $8,950 out of state; room/board: $4,560
Financial aid: N/A

College of Central Florida[1]
Ocala FL
(352) 854-2322
U.S. News ranking: Reg. Coll. (S), unranked
Website: www.cf.edu
Admissions email: admissions@cf.edu
Public; founded 1957
Application deadline (fall): 8/12
Undergraduate student body: N/A full time, N/A part time
Expenses: N/A
Financial aid: (352) 854-2322

Daytona State College[1]
Daytona Beach FL
(386) 506-3000
U.S. News ranking: Reg. Coll. (S), unranked
Website: www.daytonastate.edu
Admissions email: N/A
Public; founded 1957
Application deadline (fall): N/A
Undergraduate student body: N/A full time, N/A part time
Expenses: 2020-2021: $3,106 in state, $11,994 out of state; room/board: N/A
Financial aid: N/A

Eastern Florida State College
Cocoa FL
(321) 433-7300
U.S. News ranking: Reg. Coll. (S), unranked
Website: www.easternflorida.edu
Admissions email: cocoaadmissions@easternflorida.edu
Public; founded 1960
Freshman admissions: least selective; 2020-2021: N/A applied, N/A accepted. Neither SAT nor ACT required. SAT 25/75 percentile: N/A. High school rank: N/A
Early decision deadline: N/A, notification date: N/A
Early action deadline: N/A, notification date: N/A
Application deadline (fall): rolling
Undergraduate student body: 4,508 full time, 9,429 part time; 38% male, 62% female; 0% American Indian, 2% Asian, 11% black, 16% Hispanic, 5% multiracial, 0% Pacific Islander, 62% white, 1% international
Most popular majors: 10% Business Administration, Management and Operations, Other, 2% Information Science/Studies, 1% Health Services Administration, 0% Registered Nursing/Registered Nurse
Expenses: N/A
Financial aid: N/A

Eckerd College
St. Petersburg FL
(727) 864-8331
U.S. News ranking: Nat. Lib. Arts, No. 128
Website: www.eckerd.edu
Admissions email: admissions@eckerd.edu
Private; founded 1958
Affiliation: Presbyterian Church (USA)
Freshman admissions: selective; 2020-2021: 4,815 applied, 3,302 accepted. Neither SAT nor ACT required. SAT 25/75 percentile: 1090-1285. High school rank: N/A
Early decision deadline: N/A, notification date: N/A
Early action deadline: 11/15, notification date: 12/15
Application deadline (fall): rolling
Undergraduate student body: 1,764 full time, 58 part time; 32% male, 68% female; 0% American Indian, 2% Asian, 3% black, 10% Hispanic, 5% multiracial, 0% Pacific Islander, 77% white, 3% international; 77% from in state; 74% live on campus; N/A of students in fraternities, N/A in sororities
Most popular majors: 16% Environmental Studies, 13% Marine Biology and Biological Oceanography, 10% Biology/Biological Sciences, General, 8% Psychology, General, 5% Developmental and Child Psychology
Expenses: 2021-2022: $47,704; room/board: $13,482
Financial aid: (727) 864-8334; 62% of undergrads determined to have financial need; average aid package $33,159

Edward Waters College[1]
Jacksonville FL
(904) 470-8200
U.S. News ranking: Reg. Coll. (S), second tier
Website: www.ewc.edu
Admissions email: admissions@ewc.edu
Private
Application deadline (fall): N/A
Undergraduate student body: N/A full time, N/A part time
Expenses: 2020-2021: $14,878; room/board: $8,010
Financial aid: N/A

Embry-Riddle Aeronautical University – Daytona Beach
Daytona Beach FL
(800) 862-2416
U.S. News ranking: Reg. U. (S), No. 10
Website: www.embryriddle.edu
Admissions email: dbadmit@erau.edu
Private; founded 1926
Freshman admissions: more selective; 2020-2021: 9,581 applied, 5,806 accepted. Neither SAT nor ACT required. SAT 25/75 percentile: 1120-1330. High school rank: 24% in top tenth, 54% in top quarter, 83% in top half
Early decision deadline: N/A, notification date: N/A
Early action deadline: N/A, notification date: N/A
Application deadline (fall): rolling
Undergraduate student body: 6,035 full time, 364 part time; 76% male, 24% female; 0% American Indian, 5% Asian, 5% black, 14% Hispanic, 4% multiracial, 0% Pacific Islander, 58% white, 11% international; 35% from in state; 40% live on campus; N/A of students in fraternities, N/A in sororities
Most popular majors: 37% Aeronautics/Aviation/Aerospace Science and Technology, General, 18% Aerospace, Aeronautical and Astronautical/Space Engineering, 7% Business Administration, Management and Operations, Other, 7% Mechanical Engineering, 6% Homeland Security
Expenses: 2021-2022: $39,066; room/board: $12,774
Financial aid: (386) 226-6300; 92% of undergrads determined to have financial need; average aid package $18,043

Everglades University[1]
Boca Raton FL
(888) 772-6077
U.S. News ranking: Reg. U. (S), second tier
Website: www.evergladesuniversity.edu
Admissions email: rheintz@evergladesuniversity.edu
Private; founded 2002
Application deadline (fall): rolling
Undergraduate student body: N/A full time, N/A part time
Expenses: 2020-2021: $18,320; room/board: N/A
Financial aid: (561) 912-1211

Flagler College
St. Augustine FL
(800) 304-4208
U.S. News ranking: Reg. Coll. (S), No. 4
Website: www.flagler.edu
Admissions email: admissions@flagler.edu
Private; founded 1968
Freshman admissions: selective; 2020-2021: 5,431 applied, 3,068 accepted. Neither SAT nor ACT required. SAT 25/75 percentile: 1040-1220. High school rank: N/A
Early decision deadline: 11/1, notification date: 12/15
Early action deadline: N/A, notification date: N/A
Application deadline (fall): 3/1
Undergraduate student body: 2,591 full time, 80 part time; 32% male, 68% female; 0% American Indian, 1% Asian, 5% black, 12% Hispanic, 3% multiracial, 0% Pacific Islander, 72% white, 3% international; 77% from in state; 41% live on campus; N/A of students in fraternities, N/A in sororities
Most popular majors: Information not available
Expenses: 2021-2022: $21,140; room/board: $13,070
Financial aid: (904) 819-6225; 55% of undergrads determined to have financial need; average aid package $13,864

Florida A&M University
Tallahassee FL
(850) 599-3796
U.S. News ranking: Nat. U., No. 202
Website: www.famu.edu
Admissions email: ugrdadmissions@famu.edu
Public; founded 1887
Freshman admissions: selective; 2020-2021: 9,472 applied, 3,124 accepted. Either SAT or ACT required. SAT 25/75 percentile: 1030-1150. High school rank: 18% in top tenth, 31% in top quarter, 83% in top half
Early decision deadline: 11/1, notification date: N/A
Early action deadline: N/A, notification date: N/A
Application deadline (fall): 5/1
Undergraduate student body: 6,244 full time, 1,158 part time; 35% male, 65% female; 0% American Indian, 0% Asian, 89% black, 5% Hispanic, 3% multiracial, 0% Pacific Islander, 3% white, 0% international; 84% from in state; 18% live on campus; 62% of students in fraternities, 0% in sororities
Most popular majors: 23% Health Professions and Related Programs, 11% Multi/Interdisciplinary Studies, 10% Business, Management, Marketing, and Related Support Services, 8% Homeland Security, Law Enforcement, Firefighting and Related Protective Services, 7% Psychology
Expenses: 2021-2022: $5,785 in state, $17,725 out of state; room/board: $10,986
Financial aid: (850) 599-3730; 87% of undergrads determined to have financial need; average aid package $13,083

Florida Atlantic University
Boca Raton FL
(561) 297-3040
U.S. News ranking: Nat. U., No. 277
Website: www.fau.edu
Admissions email: admissions@fau.edu
Public; founded 1961
Freshman admissions: selective; 2020-2021: 25,300 applied, 18,919 accepted. Either SAT or ACT required. SAT 25/75 percentile: 1060-1220. High school rank: 15% in top tenth, 41% in top quarter, 79% in top half
Early decision deadline: N/A, notification date: N/A
Early action deadline: N/A, notification date: N/A
Application deadline (fall): 5/1
Undergraduate student body: 16,617 full time, 8,945 part time; 41% male, 59% female; 0% American Indian, 4% Asian, 20% black, 29% Hispanic, 4% multiracial, 0% Pacific Islander, 39% white, 2% international; 93% from in state; 13% live on campus; N/A of students in fraternities, N/A in sororities
Most popular majors: 20% Business, Management, Marketing, and Related Support Services, 10% Health Professions and Related Programs, 9% Multi/Interdisciplinary Studies, 8% Psychology, 7% Biological and Biomedical Sciences
Expenses: 2021-2022: $6,099 in state, $21,655 out of state; room/board: $12,336
Financial aid: (561) 297-3531; 62% of undergrads determined to have financial need; average aid package $14,875

Florida College[1]
Temple Terrace FL
(800) 326-7655
U.S. News ranking: Reg. Coll. (S), No. 58
Website: www.floridacollege.edu/
Admissions email: admissions@floridacollege.edu
Private; founded 1946
Application deadline (fall): 8/25
Undergraduate student body: N/A full time, N/A part time
Expenses: 2020-2021: $18,060; room/board: $8,690
Financial aid: (813) 988-5131

Florida Gateway College[1]
Lake City FL
(386) 754-4280
U.S. News ranking: Reg. Coll. (S), unranked
Website: www.fgc.edu

Florida Gulf Coast University
Fort Myers FL
(239) 590-7878
U.S. News ranking: Reg. U. (S), No. 56
Website: www.fgcu.edu
Admissions email: admissions@fgcu.edu
Public; founded 1991
Freshman admissions: selective; 2020-2021: 15,430 applied, 11,956 accepted. Either SAT or ACT required. SAT 25/75 percentile: 1060-1210. High school rank: 19% in top tenth, 28% in top quarter, 60% in top half
Early decision deadline: N/A, notification date: N/A
Early action deadline: N/A, notification date: N/A
Application deadline (fall): 4/1
Undergraduate student body: 11,077 full time, 2,749 part time; 44% male, 56% female; 0% American Indian, 2% Asian, 7% black, 24% Hispanic, 4% multiracial, 0% Pacific Islander, 60% white, 2% international; 91% from in state; 30% live on campus; 7% of students in fraternities, 5% in sororities
Most popular majors: 25% Business, Management, Marketing, and Related Support Services, 19% Health Professions and Related Programs, 11% Multi/Interdisciplinary Studies, 7% Communication, Journalism, and Related Programs, 6% Psychology
Expenses: 2021-2022: $6,118 in state, $25,161 out of state; room/board: $9,672
Financial aid: (239) 590-1210; 47% of undergrads determined to have financial need; average aid package $8,642

Florida Institute of Technology
Melbourne FL
(321) 674-8000
U.S. News ranking: Nat. U., No. 202
Website: www.fit.edu
Admissions email: admission@fit.edu
Private; founded 1958
Freshman admissions: more selective; 2020-2021: 9,803 applied, 6,898 accepted. Either SAT or ACT required. SAT 25/75 percentile: 1130-1330. High school rank: 26% in top tenth, 52% in top quarter, 84% in top half
Early decision deadline: N/A, notification date: N/A
Early action deadline: N/A, notification date: N/A
Application deadline (fall): rolling
Undergraduate student body: 3,013 full time, 462 part time; 69% male, 31% female; 0% American Indian, 2% Asian, 5% black, 11% Hispanic, 3% multiracial, 0% Pacific Islander, 54% white, 22% international; 37% from in state; 46% live on campus; 2% of students in fraternities, 1% in sororities
Most popular majors: 15% Mechanical Engineering, 10% Aerospace, Aeronautical and Astronautical/Space Engineering, 8% Aeronautics/Aviation/Aerospace Science and Technology, General, 6% Bioengineering and Biomedical Engineering, 5% Electrical and Electronics Engineering
Expenses: 2021-2022: $43,246; room/board: $13,396
Financial aid: (321) 674-8070; 58% of undergrads determined to have financial need; average aid package $37,766

Florida International University
Miami FL
(305) 348-2363
U.S. News ranking: Nat. U., No. 162
Website: www.fiu.edu
Admissions email: admiss@fiu.edu
Public; founded 1972
Freshman admissions: more selective; 2020-2021: 16,911 applied, 9,784 accepted. Either SAT or ACT required. SAT 25/75 percentile: 1110-1260. High school rank: 28% in top tenth, 51% in top quarter, 58% in top half
Early decision deadline: N/A, notification date: N/A
Early action deadline: N/A, notification date: N/A
Undergraduate student body: 27,545 full time, 21,119 part time; 43% male, 57% female; 0% American Indian, 2% Asian, 11% black, 68% Hispanic, 2% multiracial, 0% Pacific Islander, 9% white, 7% international; N/A from in state; 5% live on campus; N/A of students in fraternities, N/A in sororities
Most popular majors: 26% Business, Management, Marketing, and Related Support Services, 10% Psychology, 9% Multi/Interdisciplinary Studies, 7% Biological and Biomedical Sciences, 6% Communication, Journalism, and Related Programs
Expenses: 2021-2022: $6,566 in state, $18,964 out of state; room/board: $10,528
Financial aid: (305) 348-2333; 73% of undergrads determined to have financial need; average aid package $9,986

Florida Keys Community College[1]
Key West FL
(305) 296-9081
U.S. News ranking: Reg. Coll. (S), unranked
Website: www.fkcc.edu
Admissions email: N/A
Public
Application deadline (fall): N/A

Undergraduate student body: N/A full time, N/A part time
Expenses: N/A
Financial aid: N/A

Florida Memorial University[1]
Miami FL
(305) 626-3750
U.S. News ranking: Reg. Coll. (S), No. 58
Website: www.fmuniv.edu/
Admissions email: admit@fmuniv.edu
Private; founded 1879
Affiliation: Baptist
Application deadline (fall): rolling
Undergraduate student body: N/A full time, N/A part time
Expenses: 2020-2021: $16,176; room/board: $7,776
Financial aid: (305) 626-3745

Florida National University–Main Campus
Hialeah FL
(305) 821-3333
U.S. News ranking: Reg. Coll. (S), No. 21
Website: www.fnu.edu/
Admissions email: rlopez@fnu.edu
For-profit; founded 1988
Freshman admissions: less selective; 2020-2021: 2,831 applied, 2,303 accepted. Neither SAT nor ACT required. SAT 25/75 percentile: N/A. High school rank: N/A
Early decision deadline: N/A, notification date: N/A
Early action deadline: N/A, notification date: N/A
Application deadline (fall): N/A
Undergraduate student body: 2,013 full time, 1,254 part time; 27% male, 73% female; 0% American Indian, 0% Asian, 5% black, 84% Hispanic, 0% multiracial, 0% Pacific Islander, 2% white, 9% international; 97% from in state; N/A live on campus; N/A of students in fraternities, N/A in sororities
Most popular majors: 45% Registered Nursing/Registered Nurse, 14% Health Services Administration, 12% Accounting, 12% Business Administration and Management, General, 7% Psychology, General
Expenses: 2021-2022: $13,688; room/board: N/A
Financial aid: (305) 821-3333; 90% of undergrads determined to have financial need; average aid package $7,325

Florida Polytechnic University
Lakeland FL
(863) 874-4774
U.S. News ranking: Reg. Coll. (S), No. 3
Website: floridapoly.edu/
Admissions email: admissions@floridapoly.edu
Public; founded 2012
Freshman admissions: more selective; 2020-2021: 1,665 applied, 973 accepted. Either SAT or ACT required. SAT 25/75

percentile: 1210-1370. High school rank: 32% in top tenth, 61% in top quarter, 88% in top half
Early decision deadline: N/A, notification date: N/A
Early action deadline: N/A, notification date: N/A
Application deadline (fall): 4/1
Undergraduate student body: 1,145 full time, 204 part time; 84% male, 16% female; 0% American Indian, 5% Asian, 6% black, 21% Hispanic, 4% multiracial, 0% Pacific Islander, 61% white, 2% international
Most popular majors: 50% Computer Software and Media Applications, Other, 21% Mechanical Engineering, 14% Computer Engineering, General, 6% Electrical and Electronics Engineering, 5% Data Modeling/Warehousing and Database Administration
Expenses: 2021-2022: $4,940 in state, $21,005 out of state; room/board: $10,580
Financial aid: (863) 874-4774; 52% of undergrads determined to have financial need; average aid package $12,958

Florida Southern College
Lakeland FL
(863) 680-4131
U.S. News ranking: Reg. U. (S), No. 8
Website: www.flsouthern.edu
Admissions email: fscadm@flsouthern.edu
Private; founded 1883
Affiliation: United Methodist
Freshman admissions: more selective; 2020-2021: 9,117 applied, 4,591 accepted. Neither SAT nor ACT required. SAT 25/75 percentile: 1110-1285. High school rank: 25% in top tenth, 55% in top quarter, 87% in top half
Early decision deadline: 11/1, notification date: 12/1
Early action deadline: 11/1, notification date: 12/15
Application deadline (fall): rolling
Undergraduate student body: 2,579 full time, 255 part time; 36% male, 64% female; 1% American Indian, 3% Asian, 7% black, 14% Hispanic, 1% multiracial, 0% Pacific Islander, 71% white, 3% international; 66% from in state; 46% live on campus; 24% of students in fraternities, 26% in sororities
Most popular majors: 21% Business, Management, Marketing, and Related Support Services, 16% Health Professions and Related Programs, 13% Biological and Biomedical Sciences, 12% Education, 8% Communication, Journalism, and Related Programs
Expenses: 2021-2022: $38,980; room/board: $12,006
Financial aid: (863) 680-4140; 69% of undergrads determined to have financial need; average aid package $32,283

Florida SouthWestern State College[1]
Fort Myers FL
(239) 489-9054
U.S. News ranking: Reg. Coll. (S), unranked
Website: www.fsw.edu
Admissions email: admissions@fsw.edu
Public; founded 1962
Application deadline (fall): 7/31
Undergraduate student body: N/A full time, N/A part time
Expenses: N/A
Financial aid: (239) 489-9336

Florida State College–Jacksonville[1]
Jacksonville FL
(904) 359-5433
U.S. News ranking: Reg. Coll. (S), unranked
Website: www.fscj.edu
Admissions email: N/A
Public
Application deadline (fall): N/A
Undergraduate student body: N/A full time, N/A part time
Expenses: 2020-2021: $2,878 in state, $9,992 out of state; room/board: $8,496
Financial aid: N/A

Florida State University
Tallahassee FL
(850) 644-6200
U.S. News ranking: Nat. U., No. 55
Website: www.fsu.edu
Admissions email: admissions@admin.fsu.edu
Public; founded 1851
Freshman admissions: more selective; 2020-2021: 63,691 applied, 20,668 accepted. Either SAT or ACT required. SAT 25/75 percentile: 1220-1350. High school rank: 46% in top tenth, 81% in top quarter, 98% in top half
Early decision deadline: N/A, notification date: N/A
Early action deadline: N/A, notification date: N/A
Application deadline (fall): 3/1
Undergraduate student body: 29,072 full time, 3,471 part time; 43% male, 57% female; 0% American Indian, 3% Asian, 9% black, 22% Hispanic, 4% multiracial, 0% Pacific Islander, 59% white, 1% international; 89% from in state; 14% live on campus; 13% of students in fraternities, 22% in sororities
Most popular majors: 8% Psychology, General, 6% Finance, General, 5% Criminal Justice/Safety Studies, 4% Biology/Biological Sciences, General, 4% Marketing/Marketing Management, General
Expenses: 2021-2022: $6,517 in state, $21,683 out of state; room/board: $11,472
Financial aid: (850) 644-5716; 55% of undergrads determined to have financial need; average aid package $12,476

Gulf Coast State College[1]
Panama City FL
(850) 769-1551
U.S. News ranking: Reg. Coll. (S), unranked
Admissions email: N/A
Public
Application deadline (fall): N/A
Undergraduate student body: N/A full time, N/A part time
Expenses: 2020-2021: $2,370 in state, $7,685 out of state; room/board: N/A
Financial aid: (850) 873-3543

Hodges University[1]
Naples FL
(239) 513-1122
U.S. News ranking: Reg. U. (S), second tier
Website: www.hodges.edu
Admissions email: admit@hodges.edu
Private; founded 1990
Application deadline (fall): rolling
Undergraduate student body: N/A full time, N/A part time
Expenses: 2020-2021: $14,660; room/board: N/A
Financial aid: (239) 938-7765

Indian River State College[1]
Fort Pierce FL
(772) 462-7460
U.S. News ranking: Reg. Coll. (S), unranked
Website: www.irsc.edu
Admissions email: records@irsc.edu
Public; founded 1960
Application deadline (fall): rolling
Undergraduate student body: N/A full time, N/A part time
Expenses: N/A
Financial aid: (772) 462-7450

Jacksonville University
Jacksonville FL
(800) 225-2027
U.S. News ranking: Reg. U. (S), No. 31
Website: www.ju.edu/index.php
Admissions email: admiss@ju.edu
Private; founded 1934
Freshman admissions: selective; 2020-2021: 7,354 applied, 5,717 accepted. Neither SAT nor ACT required. ACT 25/75 percentile: 18-26. High school rank: 16% in top tenth, 42% in top quarter, 77% in top half
Early decision deadline: N/A, notification date: N/A
Early action deadline: N/A, notification date: N/A
Application deadline (fall): rolling
Undergraduate student body: 2,354 full time, 417 part time; 39% male, 61% female; 0% American Indian, 2% Asian, 20% black, 14% Hispanic, 4% multiracial, 0% Pacific Islander, 49% white, 7% international; 65% from in state; 52% live on campus; 13% of students in fraternities, 10% in sororities
Most popular majors: 47% Health Professions and Related Programs,

14% Business, Management, Marketing, and Related Support Services, 7% Visual and Performing Arts, 6% Social Sciences, 4% Transportation and Materials Moving
Expenses: 2021-2022: $43,150; room/board: $15,320
Financial aid: (904) 256-7062; 71% of undergrads determined to have financial need; average aid package $31,016

Keiser University[1]
Ft. Lauderdale FL
(954) 776-4456
U.S. News ranking: Nat. U., second tier
Website: www.keiseruniversity.edu/admissions/
Admissions email: N/A
Private; founded 1977
Application deadline (fall): rolling
Undergraduate student body: N/A full time, N/A part time
Expenses: 2021-2022: $34,968; room/board: $13,486
Financial aid: (954) 776-4476; 88% of undergrads determined to have financial need; average aid package $7,420

Lake-Sumter State College[1]
Leesburg FL
(352) 323-3665
U.S. News ranking: Reg. Coll. (S), unranked
Website: www.lssc.edu/future-students/admissions/
Admissions email: AdmissionsOffice@lssc.edu
Public; founded 1962
Application deadline (fall): 8/5
Undergraduate student body: N/A full time, N/A part time
Expenses: 2020-2021: $3,292 in state, $13,276 out of state; room/board: N/A
Financial aid: (352) 365-3567

Lynn University
Boca Raton FL
(561) 237-7900
U.S. News ranking: Reg. U. (S), No. 54
Website: www.lynn.edu
Admissions email: admission@lynn.edu
Private; founded 1962
Freshman admissions: selective; 2020-2021: 8,050 applied, 6,336 accepted. Neither SAT nor ACT required. SAT 25/75 percentile: 810-1280. High school rank: N/A
Early decision deadline: N/A, notification date: N/A
Early action deadline: 11/15, notification date: 12/15
Application deadline (fall): 3/1
Undergraduate student body: 2,247 full time, 212 part time; 50% male, 50% female; 0% American Indian, 1% Asian, 11% black, 18% Hispanic, 3% multiracial, 0% Pacific Islander, 47% white, 16% international; 47% from in state; 59% live on campus; 2% of students in fraternities, 4% in sororities

Most popular majors: Information not available
Expenses: 2021-2022: $40,900; room/board: $12,720
Financial aid: (561) 237-7973; 48% of undergrads determined to have financial need; average aid package $24,799

Miami Dade College[1]
Miami FL
(305) 237-8888
U.S. News ranking: Reg. Coll. (S), unranked
Website: www.mdc.edu/
Admissions email: mdcinfo@mdc.edu
Public
Application deadline (fall): N/A
Undergraduate student body: N/A full time, N/A part time
Expenses: N/A
Financial aid: N/A

Miami International University of Art & Design[1]
Miami FL
(305) 428-5700
U.S. News ranking: Arts, unranked
Website: www.aimiu.aii.edu/
Admissions email: N/A
For-profit
Application deadline (fall): 9/14
Undergraduate student body: N/A full time, N/A part time
Expenses: 2020-2021: $19,354; room/board: N/A
Financial aid: N/A

New College of Florida
Sarasota FL
(941) 487-5000
U.S. News ranking: Nat. Lib. Arts, No. 82
Website: www.ncf.edu
Admissions email: admissions@ncf.edu
Public; founded 1960
Freshman admissions: more selective; 2020-2021: 1,382 applied, 967 accepted. Either SAT or ACT required. SAT 25/75 percentile: 1160-1375. High school rank: 25% in top tenth, 58% in top quarter, 86% in top half
Early decision deadline: 11/1, notification date: 12/15
Early action deadline: 11/1, notification date: 12/15
Application deadline (fall): 4/15
Undergraduate student body: 546 full time, 0 part time; 35% male, 65% female; 0% American Indian, 4% Asian, 4% black, 18% Hispanic, 4% multiracial, 0% Pacific Islander, 67% white, 3% international; 82% from in state; 85% live on campus; 0% of students in fraternities, 0% in sororities
Most popular majors: 42% Liberal Arts and Sciences, General Studies and Humanities, Other, 11% Biological and Physical Sciences, 8% Foreign Languages and Literatures, General, 6% Environmental Studies, 4% International/Global Studies

Expenses: 2021-2022: $6,916 in state, $29,944 out of state; room/board: $10,542
Financial aid: (941) 487-5000; 53% of undergrads determined to have financial need; average aid package $15,334

North Florida Community College[1]
Madison FL
(850) 973-2288
U.S. News ranking: Reg. Coll. (S), unranked
Admissions email: N/A
Public
Application deadline (fall): rolling
Undergraduate student body: N/A full time, N/A part time
Expenses: N/A
Financial aid: N/A

Northwest Florida State College[1]
Niceville FL
(850) 678-5111
U.S. News ranking: Reg. Coll. (S), unranked
Website: www.nwfsc.edu/
Admissions email: N/A
Public
Application deadline (fall): rolling
Undergraduate student body: N/A full time, N/A part time
Expenses: N/A
Financial aid: (850) 729-5370

Nova Southeastern University
Ft. Lauderdale FL
(954) 262-8000
U.S. News ranking: Nat. U., No. 213
Website: www.nova.edu
Admissions email: admissions@nova.edu
Private; founded 1964
Freshman admissions: selective; 2020-2021: 13,727 applied, 10,466 accepted. Either SAT or ACT required. SAT 25/75 percentile: 1030-1240. High school rank: 28% in top tenth, 56% in top quarter, 81% in top half
Early decision deadline: 11/1, notification date: N/A
Early action deadline: 11/1, notification date: N/A
Application deadline (fall): 2/1
Undergraduate student body: 5,366 full time, 948 part time; 29% male, 71% female; 0% American Indian, 11% Asian, 14% black, 36% Hispanic, 4% multiracial, 0% Pacific Islander, 27% white, 5% international; N/A from in state; 26% live on campus; 10% of students in fraternities, 9% in sororities
Most popular majors: 43% Health Professions and Related Programs, 22% Biological and Biomedical Sciences, 10% Business, Management, Marketing, and Related Support Services, 6% Psychology, 3% Liberal Arts and Sciences, General Studies and Humanities

Palm Beach Atlantic University
West Palm Beach FL
(888) 468-6722
U.S. News ranking: Nat. U., second tier
Website: www.pba.edu
Admissions email: admit@pba.edu
Private; founded 1968
Affiliation: Interdenominational
Freshman admissions: selective; 2020-2021: 1,581 applied, 1,450 accepted. Neither SAT nor ACT required. SAT 25/75 percentile: 1000-1210. High school rank: N/A
Early decision deadline: N/A, notification date: N/A
Early action deadline: N/A, notification date: N/A
Application deadline (fall): rolling
Undergraduate student body: 2,240 full time, 676 part time; 36% male, 64% female; 0% American Indian, 2% Asian, 11% black, 16% Hispanic, 3% multiracial, 0% Pacific Islander, 60% white, 4% international; N/A from in state; 47% live on campus; N/A of students in fraternities, N/A in sororities
Most popular majors: 23% Business, Management, Marketing, and Related Support Services, 18% Health Professions and Related Programs, 11% Psychology, 8% Theology and Religious Vocations, 7% Biological and Biomedical Sciences
Expenses: 2021-2022: $34,136; room/board: $11,026
Financial aid: (561) 803-2629; 73% of undergrads determined to have financial need; average aid package $24,282

Palm Beach State College[1]
Lake Worth FL
866-576-7222
U.S. News ranking: Reg. Coll. (S), unranked
Admissions email: N/A
Public
Application deadline (fall): N/A
Undergraduate student body: N/A full time, N/A part time
Expenses: 2020-2021: $2,444 in state, $8,732 out of state; room/board: N/A
Financial aid: N/A

Pasco-Hernando State College[1]
New Port Richey FL
(727) 847-2727
U.S. News ranking: Reg. Coll. (S), unranked
Website: www.phsc.edu
Admissions email: N/A
Public
Application deadline (fall): N/A

Undergraduate student body: N/A full time, N/A part time
Expenses: N/A
Financial aid: N/A

Pensacola State College
Pensacola FL
(850) 484-2544
U.S. News ranking: Reg. Coll. (S), unranked
Website: www.pensacolastate.edu
Admissions email: askus@pensacolastate.edu
Public; founded 1948
Freshman admissions: less selective; 2020-2021: 2,659 applied, 2,659 accepted. Neither SAT nor ACT required. ACT 25/75 percentile: 15-26. High school rank: N/A
Early decision deadline: N/A, notification date: N/A
Early action deadline: N/A, notification date: N/A
Application deadline (fall): rolling
Undergraduate student body: 3,913 full time, 7,252 part time; 35% male, 65% female; 1% American Indian, 3% Asian, 19% black, 9% Hispanic, 2% multiracial, 1% Pacific Islander, 61% white, 0% international; 75% from in state; 1% live on campus; N/A of students in fraternities, N/A in sororities
Most popular majors: 45% Business, Management, Marketing, and Related Support Services, 31% Health Professions and Related Programs, 13% Computer and Information Sciences and Support Services, 6% Homeland Security, Law Enforcement, Firefighting and Related Protective Services, 5% Visual and Performing Arts
Expenses: 2021-2022: $3,467 in state, $17,225 out of state; room/board: $0
Financial aid: (850) 484-1708; 44% of undergrads determined to have financial need; average aid package $1,697

Polk State College[1]
Winter Haven FL
(863) 297-1000
U.S. News ranking: Reg. Coll. (S), unranked
Admissions email: N/A
Public
Application deadline (fall): N/A
Undergraduate student body: N/A full time, N/A part time
Expenses: N/A
Financial aid: N/A

Ringling College of Art and Design
Sarasota FL
(800) 255-7695
U.S. News ranking: Arts, unranked
Website: www.ringling.edu
Admissions email: admissions@ringling.edu
Private; founded 1931
Freshman admissions: least selective; 2020-2021: 2,420 applied, 1,658 accepted. Neither SAT nor ACT required. SAT 25/75 percentile: N/A. High school rank: N/A

Undergraduate student body: (continued)
Early decision deadline: N/A, notification date: N/A
Early action deadline: 11/1, notification date: 12/15
Application deadline (fall): rolling
Undergraduate student body: 1,588 full time, 36 part time; 28% male, 72% female; 0% American Indian, 9% Asian, 3% black, 15% Hispanic, 5% multiracial, 0% Pacific Islander, 46% white, 18% international; 34% from in state; 49% live on campus; 0% of students in fraternities, 0% in sororities
Most popular majors: 33% Animation, Interactive Technology, Video Graphics and Special Effects, 32% Illustration, 11% Art/Art Studies, General, 11% Cinematography and Film/Video Production, 5% Graphic Design
Expenses: 2021-2022: $51,170; room/board: $16,000
Financial aid: (941) 359-7532; 57% of undergrads determined to have financial need; average aid package $28,843

Rollins College
Winter Park FL
(407) 646-2161
U.S. News ranking: Reg. U. (S), No. 1
Website: www.rollins.edu
Admissions email: admission@rollins.edu
Private; founded 1885
Affiliation: Undenominational
Freshman admissions: more selective; 2020-2021: 6,086 applied, 3,696 accepted. Neither SAT nor ACT required. SAT 25/75 percentile: 1120-1330. High school rank: 28% in top tenth, 60% in top quarter, 83% in top half
Early decision deadline: 11/15, notification date: 12/15
Early action deadline: N/A, notification date: N/A
Application deadline (fall): 2/1
Undergraduate student body: 2,120 full time, 7 part time; 40% male, 60% female; 0% American Indian, 3% Asian, 4% black, 18% Hispanic, 5% multiracial, 0% Pacific Islander, 59% white, 9% international; N/A from in state; 42% live on campus; 30% of students in fraternities, 34% in sororities
Most popular majors: 31% Business, Management, Marketing, and Related Support Services, 14% Social Sciences, 12% Communication, Journalism, and Related Programs, 8% Visual and Performing Arts, 7% Biological and Biomedical Sciences
Expenses: 2021-2022: $54,740; room/board: $15,000
Financial aid: (407) 646-2395; 52% of undergrads determined to have financial need; average aid package $41,323

Saint Johns River State College[1]

Palatka FL
(904) 276-6800
U.S. News ranking: Reg. Coll. (S), unranked
Admissions email: N/A
Public
Application deadline (fall): N/A
Undergraduate student body: N/A full time, N/A part time
Expenses: N/A
Financial aid: N/A

Saint Leo University[1]

Saint Leo FL
(800) 334-5532
U.S. News ranking: Reg. U. (S), No. 29
Website: www.saintleo.edu
Admissions email: admission@saintleo.edu
Private; founded 1889
Affiliation: Roman Catholic
Application deadline (fall): rolling
Undergraduate student body: N/A full time, N/A part time
Expenses: 2020-2021: $23,750; room/board: $11,250
Financial aid: (800) 240-7658

Santa Fe College[1]

Gainesville FL
(352) 395-5000
U.S. News ranking: Reg. Coll. (S), unranked
Admissions email: N/A
Public
Application deadline (fall): N/A
Undergraduate student body: N/A full time, N/A part time
Expenses: N/A
Financial aid: N/A

Seminole State College of Florida[1]

Sanford FL
(407) 708-2380
U.S. News ranking: Reg. Coll. (S), No. 61
Website: www.seminolestate.edu
Admissions email: admissions@seminolestate.edu
Public; founded 1965
Application deadline (fall): N/A
Undergraduate student body: N/A full time, N/A part time
Expenses: 2021-2022: $3,131 in state, $11,456 out of state; room/board: N/A
Financial aid: N/A

Southeastern University

Lakeland FL
(800) 500-8760
U.S. News ranking: Reg. U. (S), No. 98
Website: www.seu.edu
Admissions email: admission@seu.edu
Private; founded 1935
Affiliation: Assemblies of God Church
Freshman admissions: selective; 2020-2021: 5,710 applied, 2,447 accepted. Either SAT or ACT required. SAT 25/75 percentile: 970-1190. High school

rank: 14% in top tenth, 32% in top quarter, 60% in top half
Early decision deadline: N/A, notification date: N/A
Early action deadline: N/A, notification date: N/A
Application deadline (fall): 5/1
Undergraduate student body: 4,804 full time, 3,508 part time; 41% male, 59% female; 1% American Indian, 2% Asian, 12% black, 22% Hispanic, 3% multiracial, 0% Pacific Islander, 57% white, 2% international; 50% from in state; 28% live on campus; N/A of students in fraternities, N/A in sororities
Most popular majors: 22% Theology and Religious Vocations, 15% Business, Management, Marketing, and Related Support Services, 7% Psychology, 6% Communication, Journalism, and Related Programs, 5% Parks, Recreation, Leisure, and Fitness Studies
Expenses: 2021-2022: $28,320; room/board: $10,380
Financial aid: (863) 667-5306; 76% of undergrads determined to have financial need; average aid package $16,434

South Florida State College

Avon Park FL
(863) 453-6661
U.S. News ranking: Reg. Coll. (S), unranked
Website: www.southflorida.edu
Admissions email: jonathan.stern@southflorida.edu
Public; founded 1966
Freshman admissions: least selective; 2020-2021: 563 applied, 563 accepted. Neither SAT nor ACT required. ACT 25/75 percentile: 17-18. High school rank: 17% in top tenth, 19% in top quarter, 39% in top half
Early decision deadline: N/A, notification date: N/A
Early action deadline: N/A, notification date: N/A
Application deadline (fall): rolling
Undergraduate student body: 1,114 full time, 1,871 part time; 35% male, 65% female; 0% American Indian, 2% Asian, 11% black, 38% Hispanic, 2% multiracial, 0% Pacific Islander, 44% white, 1% international
Most popular majors: Registered Nursing, Nursing Administration, Nursing Research and Clinical Nursing, Other
Expenses: 2020-2021: $3,165 in state, $11,859 out of state; room/board: N/A
Financial aid: (863) 784-7108

State College of Florida–Manatee-Sarasota[1]

Bradenton FL
941-752-5000
U.S. News ranking: Reg. Coll. (S), unranked
Admissions email: N/A
Public
Application deadline (fall): N/A

Undergraduate student body: N/A full time, N/A part time
Expenses: N/A
Financial aid: N/A

Stetson University

DeLand FL
(800) 688-0101
U.S. News ranking: Reg. U. (S), No. 5
Website: www.stetson.edu
Admissions email: admissions@stetson.edu
Private; founded 1883
Freshman admissions: more selective; 2020-2021: 11,957 applied, 9,744 accepted. Neither SAT nor ACT required. SAT 25/75 percentile: 1100-1285. High school rank: 20% in top tenth, 53% in top quarter, 87% in top half
Early decision deadline: 11/1, notification date: N/A
Early action deadline: 11/1, notification date: N/A
Application deadline (fall): rolling
Undergraduate student body: 3,082 full time, 43 part time; 43% male, 57% female; 0% American Indian, 2% Asian, 9% black, 19% Hispanic, 6% multiracial, 0% Pacific Islander, 56% white, 6% international; N/A from in state; 43% live on campus; 20% of students in fraternities, 23% in sororities
Most popular majors: 31% Business, Management, Marketing, and Related Support Services, 11% Psychology, 10% Visual and Performing Arts, 8% Biological and Biomedical Sciences, 7% Health Professions and Related Programs
Expenses: 2021-2022: $50,800; room/board: $14,810
Financial aid: (386) 822-7120; 68% of undergrads determined to have financial need; average aid package $43,736

St. Petersburg College

St. Petersburg FL
(727) 341-3400
U.S. News ranking: Reg. Coll. (S), unranked
Website: www.spcollege.edu/
Admissions email: admissions@SPC.edu
Public; founded 1927
Freshman admissions: less selective; 2020-2021: 3,250 applied, 3,250 accepted. Neither SAT nor ACT required. SAT 25/75 percentile: 920-1110. High school rank: N/A
Early decision deadline: N/A, notification date: N/A
Early action deadline: N/A, notification date: N/A
Application deadline (fall): rolling
Undergraduate student body: 8,152 full time, 18,278 part time; 37% male, 63% female; 0% American Indian, 4% Asian, 14% black, 17% Hispanic, 4% multiracial, 0% Pacific Islander, 59% white, 1% international; N/A from in state; 0% live on campus; 0% of students in fraternities, 0% in sororities
Most popular majors: 32% Health

Professions and Related Programs, 28% Business, Management, Marketing, and Related Support Services, 12% Education, 9% Computer and Information Sciences and Support Services, 5% Biological and Biomedical Sciences
Expenses: 2021-2022: $2,682 in state, $8,513 out of state; room/board: N/A
Financial aid: (727) 791-2485; 85% of undergrads determined to have financial need; average aid package $7,537

St. Thomas University

Miami Gardens FL
(305) 628-6546
U.S. News ranking: Reg. U. (S), No. 80
Website: www.stu.edu
Admissions email: signup@stu.edu
Private; founded 1961
Affiliation: Roman Catholic
Freshman admissions: less selective; 2020-2021: 5,649 applied, 3,368 accepted. Neither SAT nor ACT required. SAT 25/75 percentile: 890-1070. High school rank: N/A
Early decision deadline: N/A, notification date: N/A
Early action deadline: N/A, notification date: N/A
Application deadline (fall): rolling
Undergraduate student body: 1,434 full time, 2,113 part time; 47% male, 53% female; 0% American Indian, 1% Asian, 35% black, 37% Hispanic, 3% multiracial, 0% Pacific Islander, 9% white, 10% international; 89% from in state; 17% live on campus; 0% of students in fraternities, 0% in sororities
Most popular majors: 35% Registered Nursing/Registered Nurse, 8% Business Administration, Management and Operations, Other, 8% Criminal Justice/Safety Studies, 7% Business Administration and Management, General, 6% Organizational Leadership
Expenses: 2021-2022: $32,940; room/board: $12,130
Financial aid: (305) 474-6960; 56% of undergrads determined to have financial need; average aid package $11,886

Tallahassee Community College[1]

Tallahassee FL
(850) 201-6200
U.S. News ranking: Reg. Coll. (S), unranked
Website: www.tcc.fl.edu
Admissions email: N/A
Public
Application deadline (fall): N/A
Undergraduate student body: N/A full time, N/A part time
Expenses: N/A
Financial aid: N/A

University of Central Florida

Orlando FL
(407) 823-3000
U.S. News ranking: Nat. U., No. 148
Website: www.ucf.edu
Admissions email: admission@ucf.edu
Public; founded 1963
Freshman admissions: more selective; 2020-2021: 47,957 applied, 21,661 accepted. Either SAT or ACT required. SAT 25/75 percentile: 1160-1340. High school rank: 35% in top tenth, 72% in top quarter, 96% in top half
Early decision deadline: N/A, notification date: N/A
Early action deadline: N/A, notification date: N/A
Application deadline (fall): 5/1
Undergraduate student body: 43,513 full time, 17,938 part time; 45% male, 55% female; 0% American Indian, 7% Asian, 10% black, 29% Hispanic, 4% multiracial, 0% Pacific Islander, 46% white, 3% international; 93% from in state; 15% live on campus; 3% of students in fraternities, 6% in sororities
Most popular majors: 17% Health Professions and Related Programs, 16% Business, Management, Marketing, and Related Support Services, 8% Engineering, 8% Psychology, 7% Education
Expenses: 2021-2022: $6,368 in state, $22,467 out of state; room/board: $9,760
Financial aid: (407) 823-2827; 58% of undergrads determined to have financial need; average aid package $11,036

University of Florida

Gainesville FL
(352) 392-1365
U.S. News ranking: Nat. U., No. 28
Website: www.ufl.edu
Admissions email: webrequests@admissions.ufl.edu
Public; founded 1853
Freshman admissions: most selective; 2020-2021: 48,193 applied, 15,002 accepted. Either SAT or ACT required. SAT 25/75 percentile: 1290-1460. High school rank: 82% in top tenth, 98% in top quarter, 100% in top half
Early decision deadline: N/A, notification date: N/A
Early action deadline: N/A, notification date: N/A
Application deadline (fall): 3/1
Undergraduate student body: 31,476 full time, 3,455 part time; 43% male, 57% female; 0% American Indian, 10% Asian, 6% black, 23% Hispanic, 4% multiracial, 0% Pacific Islander, 51% white, 2% international; 92% from in state; 16% live on campus; 14% of students in fraternities, 22% in sororities
Most popular majors: 15% Engineering, 13% Business, Management, Marketing, and Related Support Services, 11% Social Sciences, 10% Biological and Biomedical Sciences, 8%

Communication, Journalism, and Related Programs
Expenses: 2021-2022: $6,380 in state, $28,658 out of state; room/board: $10,400
Financial aid: (352) 294-3226; 43% of undergrads determined to have financial need; average aid package $16,231

University of Miami
Coral Gables FL
(305) 284-4323
U.S. News ranking: Nat. U., No. 55
Website: www.miami.edu
Admissions email: admission@miami.edu
Private; founded 1925
Freshman admissions: more selective; 2020-2021: 40,131 applied, 13,280 accepted. Either SAT or ACT required. SAT 25/75 percentile: 1250-1420. High school rank: 51% in top tenth, 78% in top quarter, 95% in top half
Early decision deadline: 11/1, notification date: 12/15
Early action deadline: 11/1, notification date: 1/31
Application deadline (fall): 1/1
Undergraduate student body: 10,737 full time, 597 part time; 47% male, 53% female; 0% American Indian, 5% Asian, 9% black, 23% Hispanic, 3% multiracial, 0% Pacific Islander, 42% white, 13% international; 16% from in state; 33% live on campus; 16% of students in fraternities, 17% in sororities
Most popular majors: 8% Finance, General, 8% Registered Nursing/Registered Nurse, 5% Psychology, General, 4% Biology/Biological Sciences, General, 4% Economics, General
Expenses: 2021-2022: $54,760; room/board: $15,880
Financial aid: (305) 284-2270; 46% of undergrads determined to have financial need; average aid package $43,805

University of North Florida
Jacksonville FL
(904) 620-2624
U.S. News ranking: Nat. U., No. 263
Website: www.unf.edu
Admissions email: admissions@unf.edu
Public; founded 1965
Freshman admissions: selective; 2020-2021: 16,551 applied, 13,228 accepted. Either SAT or ACT required. SAT 25/75 percentile: 1040-1230. High school rank: 14% in top tenth, 38% in top quarter, 73% in top half
Early decision deadline: N/A, notification date: N/A
Early action deadline: N/A, notification date: N/A
Application deadline (fall): 6/1
Undergraduate student body: 10,817 full time, 3,733 part time; 43% male, 57% female; 1% American Indian, 6% Asian, 10% black, 15% Hispanic, 5% multiracial, 0% Pacific Islander, 62% white, 2% international;

4% from in state; 13% live on campus; N/A of students in fraternities, N/A in sororities
Most popular majors: 20% Business, Management, Marketing, and Related Support Services, 17% Health Professions and Related Programs, 9% Psychology, 7% Communication, Journalism, and Related Programs, 5% Social Sciences
Expenses: 2021-2022: $7,075 in state, $20,793 out of state; room/board: $10,045
Financial aid: (904) 620-5555; 47% of undergrads determined to have financial need; average aid package $9,379

University of South Florida
Tampa FL
(813) 974-3350
U.S. News ranking: Nat. U., No. 103
Website: www.usf.edu
Admissions email: admission@admin.usf.edu
Public; founded 1956
Freshman admissions: more selective; 2020-2021: 38,696 applied, 19,054 accepted. Either SAT or ACT required. SAT 25/75 percentile: 1160-1320. High school rank: 32% in top tenth, 66% in top quarter, 91% in top half
Early decision deadline: N/A, notification date: N/A
Early action deadline: N/A, notification date: N/A
Application deadline (fall): 5/1
Undergraduate student body: 29,653 full time, 8,926 part time; 43% male, 57% female; 0% American Indian, 7% Asian, 9% black, 22% Hispanic, 4% multiracial, 0% Pacific Islander, 48% white, 6% international; N/A from in state; 10% live on campus; 4% of students in fraternities, 6% in sororities
Most popular majors: 18% Business, Management, Marketing, and Related Support Services, 18% Health Professions and Related Programs, 12% Biological and Biomedical Sciences, 12% Social Sciences, 7% Engineering
Expenses: 2021-2022: $6,410 in state, $17,324 out of state; room/board: $12,256
Financial aid: (813) 974-4700; 56% of undergrads determined to have financial need; average aid package $10,580

University of Tampa[1]
Tampa FL
(888) 646-2738
U.S. News ranking: Reg. U. (S), No. 13
Website: www.ut.edu
Admissions email: admissions@ut.edu
Private; founded 1931
Application deadline (fall): rolling
Undergraduate student body: N/A full time, N/A part time
Expenses: 2020-2021: $30,884; room/board: $11,526
Financial aid: (813) 253-6219

University of West Florida
Pensacola FL
(850) 474-2230
U.S. News ranking: Reg. U. (S), No. 35
Website: uwf.edu
Admissions email: admissions@uwf.edu
Public; founded 1963
Affiliation: Undenominational
Freshman admissions: selective; 2020-2021: 7,232 applied, 4,163 accepted. Either SAT or ACT required. ACT 25/75 percentile: 22-27. High school rank: 15% in top tenth, 44% in top quarter, 80% in top half
Early decision deadline: N/A, notification date: N/A
Early action deadline: N/A, notification date: N/A
Application deadline (fall): 6/30
Undergraduate student body: 6,537 full time, 3,098 part time; 42% male, 58% female; 0% American Indian, 4% Asian, 11% black, 10% Hispanic, 6% multiracial, 0% Pacific Islander, 65% white, 2% international; 89% from in state; 13% live on campus; N/A of students in fraternities, N/A in sororities
Most popular majors: 19% Registered Nursing/Registered Nurse, 6% Health Professions and Related Programs, 5% Psychology, General, 4% Mass Communication/Media Studies, 3% Criminal Justice/Safety Studies
Expenses: 2021-2022: $6,360 in state, $18,628 out of state; room/board: $11,268
Financial aid: (850) 474-2398; 28% of undergrads determined to have financial need; average aid package $10,981

Valencia College[1]
Orlando FL
(407) 299-5000
U.S. News ranking: Reg. Coll. (S), unranked
Admissions email: N/A
Public
Application deadline (fall): N/A
Undergraduate student body: N/A full time, N/A part time
Expenses: N/A
Financial aid: N/A

Warner University
Lake Wales FL
(800) 309-9563
U.S. News ranking: Reg. Coll. (S), No. 55
Website: www.warner.edu
Admissions email: admissions@warner.edu
Private; founded 1964
Affiliation: Church of God
Freshman admissions: less selective; 2020-2021: 1,172 applied, 637 accepted. Neither SAT nor ACT required. SAT 25/75 percentile: 870-1040. High school rank: 7% in top tenth, 20% in top quarter, 44% in top half
Early decision deadline: N/A, notification date: N/A
Early action deadline: N/A,

notification date: N/A
Application deadline (fall): rolling
Undergraduate student body: 747 full time, 73 part time; 53% male, 47% female; 0% American Indian, 0% Asian, 33% black, 15% Hispanic, 1% multiracial, 0% Pacific Islander, 46% white, 3% international
Most popular majors: 20% Elementary Education and Teaching, 12% Business Administration and Management, General, 11% Criminal Justice/Police Science, 9% Business Administration, Management and Operations, Other, 8% Agriculture, Agriculture Operations, and Related Sciences
Expenses: 2021-2022: $25,050; room/board: $9,540
Financial aid: (863) 638-7202; 79% of undergrads determined to have financial need; average aid package $8,263

Webber International University
Babson Park FL
(800) 741-1844
U.S. News ranking: Reg. Coll. (S), No. 66
Website: www.webber.edu
Admissions email: admissions@webber.edu
Private; founded 1927
Freshman admissions: selective; 2020-2021: 4,133 applied, 2,569 accepted. Either SAT or ACT required. SAT 25/75 percentile: 900-1050. High school rank: N/A
Early decision deadline: N/A, notification date: N/A
Early action deadline: N/A, notification date: N/A
Application deadline (fall): 8/1
Undergraduate student body: 696 full time, 52 part time; 68% male, 32% female; 1% American Indian, 1% Asian, 29% black, 7% Hispanic, 4% multiracial, 1% Pacific Islander, 41% white, 9% international
Most popular majors: 22% Criminal Justice/Law Enforcement Administration, 15% Sport and Fitness Administration/Management, 14% Business Administration, Management and Operations, Other
Expenses: 2021-2022: $29,314; room/board: $13,250
Financial aid: (863) 638-2929; 75% of undergrads determined to have financial need; average aid package $21,206

GEORGIA

Abraham Baldwin Agricultural College[1]
Tifton GA
(800) 733-3653
U.S. News ranking: Reg. Coll. (S), second tier
Website: www.abac.edu/
Admissions email: N/A
Public; founded 1908
Application deadline (fall): 8/1
Undergraduate student body: N/A full time, N/A part time

Expenses: 2020-2021: $3,565 in state, $10,471 out of state; room/board: $7,910
Financial aid: (229) 391-4985

Agnes Scott College
Decatur GA
(800) 868-8602
U.S. News ranking: Nat. Lib. Arts, No. 66
Website: www.agnesscott.edu
Admissions email: admission@agnesscott.edu
Private; founded 1889
Affiliation: Presbyterian Church (USA)
Freshman admissions: more selective; 2020-2021: 1,838 applied, 1,241 accepted. Neither SAT nor ACT required. SAT 25/75 percentile: 1080-1290. High school rank: 33% in top tenth, 60% in top quarter, 88% in top half
Early decision deadline: 11/1, notification date: 12/1
Early action deadline: 11/15, notification date: 12/15
Application deadline (fall): 5/1
Undergraduate student body: 1,003 full time, 11 part time; 1% male, 99% female; 0% American Indian, 6% Asian, 35% black, 15% Hispanic, 7% multiracial, 0% Pacific Islander, 31% white, 3% international; 63% from in state; N/A live on campus; 0% of students in fraternities, 0% in sororities
Most popular majors: 12% Psychology, General, 8% Biology/Biological Sciences, General, 7% Neuroscience, 7% Public Health, General, 6% Creative Writing
Expenses: 2021-2022: $44,250; room/board: $13,050
Financial aid: (404) 471-6395; 75% of undergrads determined to have financial need; average aid package $37,091

Albany State University[1]
Albany GA
(229) 500-4358
U.S. News ranking: Reg. U. (S), second tier
Website: www.asurams.edu/
Admissions email: admissions@asurams.edu
Public; founded 1903
Application deadline (fall): 7/1
Undergraduate student body: N/A full time, N/A part time
Expenses: 2020-2021: $5,934 in state, $16,656 out of state; room/board: $10,076
Financial aid: (229) 500-4358

Andrew College[1]
Cuthbert GA
(229) 732-5938
U.S. News ranking: Reg. Coll. (S), unranked
Website: www.andrewcollege.edu/
Admissions email: admissions@andrewcollege.edu
Private; founded 1854
Affiliation: United Methodist
Application deadline (fall): N/A
Undergraduate student body: N/A full time, N/A part time

Expenses: 2021-2022: $18,214; room/board: $11,728
Financial aid: (229) 732-5923; 89% of undergrads determined to have financial need; average aid package $19,082

Art Institute of Atlanta[1]
Atlanta GA
(770) 394-8300
U.S. News ranking: Arts, unranked
Website: www.artinstitutes.edu/atlanta/
Admissions email: aiaadm@aii.edu
For-profit
Application deadline (fall): N/A
Undergraduate student body: N/A full time, N/A part time
Expenses: 2020-2021: $19,354; room/board: N/A
Financial aid: N/A

Atlanta Metropolitan State College[1]
Atlanta GA
(404) 756-4004
U.S. News ranking: Reg. Coll. (S), unranked
Website: www.Atlm.edu
Admissions email: admissions@atlm.edu
Public; founded 1974
Application deadline (fall): rolling
Undergraduate student body: N/A full time, N/A part time
Expenses: 2020-2021: $3,505 in state, $10,131 out of state; room/board: N/A
Financial aid: N/A

Augusta University
Augusta GA
(706) 737-1632
U.S. News ranking: Nat. U., second tier
Website: www.augusta.edu/
Admissions email: admissions@augusta.edu
Public; founded 1828
Freshman admissions: selective; 2020-2021: 3,698 applied, 3,063 accepted. Either SAT or ACT required. SAT 25/75 percentile: 1020-1210. High school rank: N/A
Early decision deadline: N/A, notification date: N/A
Early action deadline: N/A, notification date: N/A
Application deadline (fall): N/A
Undergraduate student body: 4,522 full time, 1,153 part time; 34% male, 66% female; N/A American Indian, N/A Asian, N/A black, N/A Hispanic, N/A multiracial, N/A Pacific Islander, N/A white, N/A international; 90% from in state; N/A live on campus; 5% of students in fraternities, 7% in sororities
Most popular majors: 18% Registered Nursing/Registered Nurse, 7% Kinesiology and Exercise Science, 7% Psychology, General, 5% Cell/Cellular and Molecular Biology, 4% Biology/Biological Sciences, General
Expenses: 2020-2021: $8,832 in state, $24,210 out of state; room/board: $10,666
Financial aid: (706) 737-1524

Berry College
Mount Berry GA
(706) 236-2215
U.S. News ranking: Reg. U. (S), No. 4
Website: www.berry.edu/
Admissions email: admissions@berry.edu
Private; founded 1902
Freshman admissions: more selective; 2020-2021: 4,166 applied, 3,217 accepted. Neither SAT nor ACT required. ACT 25/75 percentile: 23-29. High school rank: 34% in top tenth, 63% in top quarter, 91% in top half
Early decision deadline: N/A, notification date: N/A
Early action deadline: 11/1, notification date: 12/15
Application deadline (fall): 5/1
Undergraduate student body: 1,982 full time, 24 part time; 38% male, 62% female; 0% American Indian, 3% Asian, 7% black, 8% Hispanic, 5% multiracial, 0% Pacific Islander, 75% white, 1% international; 72% from in state; 88% live on campus; 0% of students in fraternities, 0% in sororities
Most popular majors: 19% Biological and Biomedical Sciences, 17% Business, Management, Marketing, and Related Support Services, 9% Psychology, 8% Education, 8% Health Professions and Related Programs
Expenses: 2021-2022: $38,656; room/board: $13,620
Financial aid: (706) 236-1714; 71% of undergrads determined to have financial need; average aid package $31,609

Brenau University
Gainesville GA
(770) 534-6100
U.S. News ranking: Reg. U. (S), No. 40
Website: www.brenau.edu
Admissions email: admissions@brenau.edu
Private; founded 1878
Freshman admissions: selective; 2020-2021: 1,304 applied, 871 accepted. Neither SAT nor ACT required. SAT 25/75 percentile: 940-1170. High school rank: 9% in top tenth, 34% in top quarter, 71% in top half
Early decision deadline: N/A, notification date: N/A
Early action deadline: N/A, notification date: N/A
Application deadline (fall): rolling
Undergraduate student body: 1,095 full time, 615 part time; 10% male, 90% female; 1% American Indian, 2% Asian, 30% black, 11% Hispanic, 2% multiracial, 0% Pacific Islander, 46% white, 6% international; 94% from in state; 20% live on campus; N/A of students in fraternities, 8% in sororities
Most popular majors: 31% Health Professions and Related Programs, 20% Education, 16% Business, Management, Marketing, and Related Support Services, 11% Visual and Performing Arts, 8% English Language and Literature/Letters

Expenses: 2021-2022: $32,530; room/board: $12,200
Financial aid: (770) 534-6176; 80% of undergrads determined to have financial need; average aid package $19,145

Brewton-Parker College
Mount Vernon GA
(912) 583-3265
U.S. News ranking: Nat. Lib. Arts, second tier
Website: www.bpc.edu
Admissions email: admissions@bpc.edu
Private; founded 1904
Affiliation: Baptist
Freshman admissions: least selective; 2020-2021: 483 applied, 474 accepted. Either SAT or ACT required. SAT 25/75 percentile: 860-1030. High school rank: 6% in top tenth, 15% in top quarter, 47% in top half
Early decision deadline: N/A, notification date: N/A
Early action deadline: N/A, notification date: N/A
Application deadline (fall): rolling
Undergraduate student body: 535 full time, 300 part time; 57% male, 43% female; 1% American Indian, 1% Asian, 39% black, 13% Hispanic, 0% multiracial, 1% Pacific Islander, 40% white, 3% international; 84% from in state; N/A live on campus; N/A of students in fraternities, N/A in sororities
Most popular majors: 25% Business Administration and Management, General, 17% Psychology, General, 12% General Studies, 8% Christian Studies, 7% Criminal Justice and Corrections
Expenses: 2021-2022: $19,100; room/board: $8,380
Financial aid: (912) 583-3221; 86% of undergrads determined to have financial need; average aid package $17,387

Clark Atlanta University
Atlanta GA
(800) 688-3228
U.S. News ranking: Nat. U., second tier
Website: www.cau.edu
Admissions email: cauadmissions@cau.edu
Private; founded 1988
Affiliation: United Methodist
Freshman admissions: less selective; 2020-2021: 15,613 applied, 9,219 accepted. Either SAT or ACT required. SAT 25/75 percentile: 880-1040. High school rank: 10% in top tenth, 30% in top quarter, 62% in top half
Early decision deadline: N/A, notification date: N/A
Early action deadline: N/A, notification date: N/A
Application deadline (fall): 4/1
Undergraduate student body: 2,951 full time, 145 part time; 24% male, 76% female; 0% American Indian, 0% Asian, 87% black, 0% Hispanic, 0% multiracial, 0% Pacific Islander, 0% white, 1% international
Most popular majors: 25%

Business, Management, Marketing, and Related Support Services, 18% Communication, Journalism, and Related Programs, 11% Psychology, 11% Visual and Performing Arts, 9% Homeland Security, Law Enforcement, Firefighting and Related Protective Services
Expenses: 2021-2022: $24,430; room/board: $11,636
Financial aid: (404) 880-8992; 92% of undergrads determined to have financial need; average aid package $6,172

Clayton State University
Morrow GA
(678) 466-4115
U.S. News ranking: Reg. U. (S), second tier
Website: www.clayton.edu
Admissions email: csuinfo@clayton.edu
Public; founded 1969
Freshman admissions: less selective; 2020-2021: 2,356 applied, 1,592 accepted. Neither SAT nor ACT required. SAT 25/75 percentile: 880-1060. High school rank: N/A
Early decision deadline: N/A, notification date: N/A
Early action deadline: N/A, notification date: N/A
Application deadline (fall): 7/1
Undergraduate student body: 3,680 full time, 2,696 part time; 29% male, 71% female; 0% American Indian, 6% Asian, 67% black, 8% Hispanic, 3% multiracial, 0% Pacific Islander, 12% white, 2% international; 94% from in state; 14% live on campus; N/A of students in fraternities, N/A in sororities
Most popular majors: 10% Health Professions and Related Programs, 10% Liberal Arts and Sciences/Liberal Studies, 10% Registered Nursing/Registered Nurse, 9% Community Psychology, 7% Business Administration and Management, General
Expenses: 2021-2022: $6,584 in state, $19,986 out of state; room/board: $10,397
Financial aid: (678) 466-4181; 83% of undergrads determined to have financial need; average aid package $4,949

College of Coastal Georgia
Brunswick GA
(912) 279-5730
U.S. News ranking: Reg. Coll. (S), second tier
Website: www.ccga.edu
Admissions email: admiss@ccga.edu
Public; founded 1961
Freshman admissions: less selective; 2020-2021: 2,267 applied, 2,175 accepted. Neither SAT nor ACT required. SAT 25/75 percentile: 900-1100. High school rank: N/A
Early decision deadline: N/A, notification date: N/A
Early action deadline: N/A, notification date: N/A
Application deadline (fall): 8/5

Undergraduate student body: 1,844 full time, 1,613 part time; 30% male, 70% female; 0% American Indian, 2% Asian, 21% black, 8% Hispanic, 4% multiracial, 0% Pacific Islander, 62% white, 1% international; 92% from in state; 15% live on campus; 0% of students in fraternities, 0% in sororities
Most popular majors: 24% Business/Commerce, General, 13% Psychology, General, 13% Registered Nursing/Registered Nurse, 10% Biology/Biological Sciences, General, 7% Multi-Interdisciplinary Studies
Expenses: 2021-2022: $4,574 in state, $13,206 out of state; room/board: $10,784
Financial aid: (912) 279-5726; 62% of undergrads determined to have financial need; average aid package $10,680

Columbus State University
Columbus GA
(706) 507-8800
U.S. News ranking: Reg. U. (S), No. 74
Website: www.columbusstate.edu
Admissions email: admissions@columbusstate.edu
Public; founded 1958
Freshman admissions: less selective; 2020-2021: 5,275 applied, 4,123 accepted. Either SAT or ACT required. SAT 25/75 percentile: 860-1080. High school rank: 10% in top tenth, 31% in top quarter, 61% in top half
Early decision deadline: N/A, notification date: N/A
Early action deadline: N/A, notification date: N/A
Application deadline (fall): 6/30
Undergraduate student body: 4,760 full time, 2,117 part time; 39% male, 61% female; 0% American Indian, 3% Asian, 41% black, 7% Hispanic, 3% multiracial, 0% Pacific Islander, 44% white, 1% international; N/A from in state; 1% live on campus; 5% of students in fraternities, 5% in sororities
Most popular majors: 25% Health Professions and Related Programs, 17% Business, Management, Marketing, and Related Support Services, 8% Visual and Performing Arts, 6% Education, 6% Social Sciences
Expenses: 2021-2022: $7,334 in state, $21,152 out of state; room/board: $10,628
Financial aid: (706) 507-8800; 76% of undergrads determined to have financial need; average aid package $10,264

Covenant College
Lookout Mountain GA
(706) 820-2398
U.S. News ranking: Nat. Lib. Arts, No. 146
Website: www.covenant.edu
Admissions email: admissions@covenant.edu
Private; founded 1955
Affiliation: The Presbyterian Church in America
Freshman admissions: more

selective; 2020-2021: 612 applied, 597 accepted. Neither SAT nor ACT required. ACT 25/75 percentile: 22-29. High school rank: 36% in top tenth, 52% in top quarter, 74% in top half **Early decision deadline:** N/A, notification date: N/A **Early action deadline:** 11/15, notification date: 12/1 **Application deadline (fall):** 3/1 **Undergraduate student body:** 801 full time, 64 part time; 46% male, 54% female; 1% American Indian, 1% Asian, 3% black, 1% Hispanic, 5% multiracial, 0% Pacific Islander, 88% white, 2% international; 31% from in state; 78% live on campus; 0% of students in fraternities, 0% in sororities **Most popular majors:** 10% Business/Commerce, General, 10% English Language and Literature, General, 8% Elementary Education and Teaching, 7% Art/Art Studies, General, 7% Psychology, General **Expenses:** 2021-2022: $37,770; room/board $11,300 **Financial aid:** (706) 419-1447; 65% of undergrads determined to have financial need; average aid package $30,791

Dalton State College[1]

Dalton GA
(706) 272-4436
U.S. News ranking: Reg. Coll. (S), second tier
Website: www.daltonstate.edu/
Admissions email: N/A
Public
Application deadline (fall): N/A
Undergraduate student body: N/A full time, N/A part time
Expenses: 2020-2021: $3,683 in state, $10,589 out of state; room/board: $8,588
Financial aid: N/A

East Georgia State College[1]

Swainsboro GA
(478) 289-2017
U.S. News ranking: Reg. Coll. (S), unranked
Website: www.ega.edu/admissions
Admissions email: Ask_EGSC@ega.edu
Public; founded 1973
Application deadline (fall): 8/15
Undergraduate student body: N/A full time, N/A part time
Expenses: 2020-2021: $3,136 in state, $9,488 out of state; room/board: $9,664
Financial aid: N/A

Emmanuel College

Franklin Springs GA
(800) 860-8800
U.S. News ranking: Reg. Coll. (S), No. 40
Website: www.ec.edu
Admissions email: admissions@ec.edu
Private; founded 1919
Affiliation: Pentecostal Holiness Church
Freshman admissions: selective; 2020-2021: 946 applied, 499

accepted. Either SAT or ACT required. SAT 25/75 percentile: 920-1100. High school rank: N/A **Early decision deadline:** N/A, notification date: N/A **Early action deadline:** N/A, notification date: N/A **Application deadline (fall):** 8/1 **Undergraduate student body:** 773 full time, 110 part time; 55% male, 45% female; 1% American Indian, 0% Asian, 14% black, 7% Hispanic, 4% multiracial, 1% Pacific Islander, 63% white, 10% international **Most popular majors:** 24% Business Administration and Management, General, 9% Criminal Justice and Corrections, 9% Sport and Fitness Administration/Management **Expenses:** 2020-2021: $21,220; room/board: $8,234 **Financial aid:** (706) 245-2844

Emory University

Atlanta GA
(404) 727-6036
U.S. News ranking: Nat. U., No. 21
Website: www.emory.edu
Admissions email: admission@emory.edu
Private; founded 1836
Affiliation: United Methodist
Freshman admissions: most selective; 2020-2021: 28,211 applied, 5,407 accepted. Neither SAT nor ACT required. SAT 25/75 percentile: 1380-1530. High school rank: 83% in top tenth, 98% in top quarter, 100% in top half **Early decision deadline:** 11/1, notification date: 12/9 **Early action deadline:** N/A, notification date: N/A **Application deadline (fall):** 1/1 **Undergraduate student body:** 6,814 full time, 196 part time; 41% male, 59% female; 0% American Indian, 23% Asian, 9% black, 11% Hispanic, 4% multiracial, 0% Pacific Islander, 37% white, 15% international; 80% from in state; 22% live on campus; 14% of students in fraternities, 13% in sororities **Most popular majors:** 14% Registered Nursing/Registered Nurse, 13% Business Administration and Management, General, 8% Biology/Biological Sciences, General, 6% Neuroscience, 5% Psychology, General **Expenses:** 2021-2022: $55,468; room/board: $16,302 **Financial aid:** (404) 727-6039; 49% of undergrads determined to have financial need; average aid package $47,542

Fort Valley State University

Fort Valley GA
(478) 825-6307
U.S. News ranking: Reg. U. (S), second tier
Website: www.fvsu.edu
Admissions email: admissap@mail.fvsu.edu
Public; founded 1895
Freshman admissions: least selective; 2020-2021: 5,180

applied, 4,039 accepted. Either SAT or ACT required. ACT 25/75 percentile: 16-19. High school rank: 7% in top tenth, 16% in top quarter, 49% in top half **Early decision deadline:** N/A, notification date: N/A **Early action deadline:** N/A, notification date: N/A **Application deadline (fall):** 7/19 **Undergraduate student body:** 2,244 full time, 298 part time; 38% male, 62% female; 0% American Indian, 0% Asian, 93% black, 2% Hispanic, 2% multiracial, 0% Pacific Islander, 1% white, 0% international **Most popular majors:** 15% Homeland Security, Law Enforcement, Firefighting and Related Protective Services, 12% Biological and Biomedical Sciences, 10% Psychology, 8% Communication, Journalism, and Related Programs, 7% Business, Management, Marketing, and Related Support Services **Expenses:** 2021-2022: $6,848 in state, $20,250 out of state; room/board: $9,632 **Financial aid:** (478) 825-6363; 94% of undergrads determined to have financial need; average aid package $7,860

Georgia College & State University

Milledgeville GA
(478) 445-1283
U.S. News ranking: Reg. U. (S), No. 21
Website: www.gcsu.edu
Admissions email: admissions@gcsu.edu
Public; founded 1889
Freshman admissions: selective; 2020-2021: 4,514 applied, 3,879 accepted. Either SAT or ACT required. SAT 25/75 percentile: 1100-1245. High school rank: N/A **Early decision deadline:** N/A, notification date: N/A **Early action deadline:** 10/15, notification date: 11/30 **Application deadline (fall):** 4/1 **Undergraduate student body:** 5,167 full time, 438 part time; 35% male, 65% female; 0% American Indian, 1% Asian, 5% black, 6% Hispanic, 4% multiracial, 0% Pacific Islander, 83% white, 0% international; 99% from in state; 36% live on campus; 8% of students in fraternities, 11% in sororities **Most popular majors:** 10% Kinesiology and Exercise Science, 8% Business Administration and Management, General, 8% Marketing/Marketing Management, General, 8% Registered Nursing/Registered Nurse, 6% Research and Experimental Psychology, Other **Expenses:** 2021-2022: $9,524 in state, $28,704 out of state; room/board: $10,948 **Financial aid:** (478) 445-5149; 43% of undergrads determined to have financial need; average aid package $11,567

Georgia Gwinnett College

Lawrenceville GA
(678) 407-5313
U.S. News ranking: Reg. Coll. (S), No. 58
Website: www.ggc.edu
Admissions email: ggcadmissions@ggc.edu
Public; founded 2005
Freshman admissions: less selective; 2020-2021: 5,903 applied, 5,579 accepted. Neither SAT nor ACT required. SAT 25/75 percentile: 920-1110. High school rank: 9% in top tenth, 30% in top quarter, 66% in top half **Early decision deadline:** N/A, notification date: N/A **Early action deadline:** N/A, notification date: N/A **Application deadline (fall):** 5/1 **Undergraduate student body:** 7,620 full time, 4,007 part time; 41% male, 59% female; 0% American Indian, 10% Asian, 33% black, 24% Hispanic, 4% multiracial, 0% Pacific Islander, 26% white, 3% international; N/A from in state; 5% live on campus; N/A of students in fraternities, N/A in sororities **Most popular majors:** 32% Business, Management, Marketing, and Related Support Services, 12% Biological and Biomedical Sciences, 12% Computer and Information Sciences and Support Services **Expenses:** 2021-2022: $5,762 in state, $16,744 out of state; room/board: $13,930 **Financial aid:** (678) 407-5701; 77% of undergrads determined to have financial need

Georgia Highlands College[1]

Rome GA
706-802-5000
U.S. News ranking: Reg. Coll. (S), unranked
Admissions email: N/A
Public
Application deadline (fall): N/A
Undergraduate student body: N/A full time, N/A part time
Expenses: 2020-2021: $3,344 in state, $9,696 out of state; room/board: N/A
Financial aid: N/A

Georgia Institute of Technology

Atlanta GA
(404) 894-4154
U.S. News ranking: Nat. U., No. 38
Website: admission.gatech.edu
Admissions email: admission@gatech.edu
Public; founded 1885
Freshman admissions: most selective; 2020-2021: 40,852 applied, 8,719 accepted. Either SAT or ACT required. SAT 25/75 percentile: 1370-1530. High school rank: 88% in top tenth, 98% in top quarter, 99% in top half **Early decision deadline:** N/A, notification date: N/A **Early action deadline:** 10/15,

notification date: 12/4 **Application deadline (fall):** 1/4 **Undergraduate student body:** 14,493 full time, 2,068 part time; 61% male, 39% female; 0% American Indian, 25% Asian, 7% black, 7% Hispanic, 4% multiracial, 0% Pacific Islander, 45% white, 9% international; 64% from in state; 50% live on campus; 22% of students in fraternities, 26% in sororities **Most popular majors:** 18% Computer and Information Sciences, General, 14% Mechanical Engineering, 10% Industrial Engineering, 9% Business Administration and Management, General, 6% Bioengineering and Biomedical Engineering **Expenses:** 2021-2022: $12,682 in state, $33,794 out of state; room/board: $14,986 **Financial aid:** (404) 894-4160; 38% of undergrads determined to have financial need; average aid package $14,026

Georgia Military College[1]

Milledgeville GA
(478) 387-4900
U.S. News ranking: Reg. Coll. (S), unranked
Website: www.hfcc.edu
Admissions email: N/A
Public
Application deadline (fall): N/A
Undergraduate student body: N/A full time, N/A part time
Expenses: 2020-2021: $6,615 in state, $6,615 out of state; room/board: $7,500
Financial aid: N/A

Georgia Southern University

Statesboro GA
(912) 478-5391
U.S. News ranking: Nat. U., second tier
Website: www.georgiasouthern.edu/
Admissions email: admissions@georgiasouthern.edu
Public; founded 1906
Freshman admissions: selective; 2020-2021: 17,250 applied, 15,727 accepted. Either SAT or ACT required. SAT 25/75 percentile: 993-1170. High school rank: 20% in top tenth, 50% in top quarter, 82% in top half **Early decision deadline:** N/A, notification date: N/A **Early action deadline:** N/A, notification date: N/A **Application deadline (fall):** 5/1 **Undergraduate student body:** 19,435 full time, 4,034 part time; 43% male, 57% female; 0% American Indian, 2% Asian, 27% black, 7% Hispanic, 4% multiracial, 0% Pacific Islander, 58% white, 1% international; 93% from in state; 23% live on campus; 10% of students in fraternities, 14% in sororities **Most popular majors:** 18% Business, Management, Marketing, and Related Support Services, 14% Health Professions

and Related Programs, 8% Engineering, 8% Parks, Recreation, Leisure, and Fitness Studies, 7% Biological and Biomedical Sciences
Expenses: 2021-2022: $7,578 in state, $21,396 out of state; room/board: $10,510
Financial aid: (912) 478-5413

Georgia Southwestern State University

Americus GA
(229) 928-1273
U.S. News ranking: Reg. U. (S), second tier
Website: www.gsw.edu
Admissions email: admissions@gsw.edu
Public; founded 1906
Freshman admissions: selective; 2020-2021: 2,597 applied, 1,907 accepted. Either SAT or ACT required. SAT 25/75 percentile: 940-1110. High school rank: 14% in top tenth, 38% in top quarter, 68% in top half
Early decision deadline: N/A, notification date: N/A
Early action deadline: N/A, notification date: N/A
Application deadline (fall): 7/21
Undergraduate student body: 1,683 full time, 951 part time; 36% male, 64% female; 0% American Indian, 2% Asian, 30% black, 6% Hispanic, 3% multiracial, 0% Pacific Islander, 57% white, 2% international; 89% from in state; 27% live on campus; 7% of students in fraternities, 9% in sororities
Most popular majors: 13% Accounting, 13% Business Administration and Management, General, 13% Registered Nursing/Registered Nurse, 12% Elementary Education and Teaching, 8% Psychology, General
Expenses: 2021-2022: $6,516 in state, $19,918 out of state; room/board: $8,600
Financial aid: (229) 928-1378; 73% of undergrads determined to have financial need; average aid package $10,574

Georgia State University

Atlanta GA
(404) 413-2500
U.S. News ranking: Nat. U., No. 239
Website: www.gsu.edu
Admissions email: admissions@gsu.edu
Public; founded 1913
Freshman admissions: selective; 2020-2021: 24,457 applied, 16,300 accepted. Either SAT or ACT required. SAT 25/75 percentile: 950-1160. High school rank: N/A
Early decision deadline: N/A, notification date: N/A
Early action deadline: 12/8, notification date: 1/15
Application deadline (fall): 4/1
Undergraduate student body: 22,342 full time, 6,430 part time; 40% male, 60% female; 0% American Indian, 15% Asian, 41% black, 13% Hispanic, 6% multiracial, 0% Pacific Islander,

21% white, 3% international; N/A from in state; 15% live on campus; N/A of students in fraternities, N/A in sororities
Most popular majors: 10% Computer and Information Sciences and Support Services, 10% Social Sciences, 9% Psychology, 8% Biological and Biomedical Sciences, 8% Visual and Performing Arts
Expenses: 2021-2022: $11,076 in state, $30,114 out of state; room/board: $13,088
Financial aid: (404) 413-2600; 76% of undergrads determined to have financial need; average aid package $11,704

Gordon State College

Barnesville GA
(678) 359-5021
U.S. News ranking: Reg. Coll. (S), second tier
Website: www.gordonstate.edu/
Admissions email: admissions@gordonstate.edu
Public; founded 1852
Freshman admissions: less selective; 2020-2021: 2,231 applied, 1,763 accepted. Either SAT or ACT required. SAT 25/75 percentile: 890-1070. High school rank: N/A
Early decision deadline: N/A, notification date: N/A
Early action deadline: N/A, notification date: N/A
Application deadline (fall): rolling
Undergraduate student body: 1,856 full time, 1,375 part time; 33% male, 67% female; 0% American Indian, 1% Asian, 41% black, 5% Hispanic, 3% multiracial, 0% Pacific Islander, 48% white, 0% international
Most popular majors: 22% Business Administration and Management, General, 22% Public Administration and Social Service Professions, 20% Registered Nursing/Registered Nurse, 12% Biology/Biological Sciences, General, 12% Elementary Education and Teaching
Expenses: 2020-2021: $4,084 in state, $11,946 out of state; room/board: $8,666
Financial aid: (678) 359-5990

Kennesaw State University

Kennesaw GA
(770) 423-6300
U.S. News ranking: Nat. U., second tier
Website: www.kennesaw.edu
Admissions email: KSUAdmit@kennesaw.edu
Public; founded 1963
Freshman admissions: selective; 2020-2021: 18,601 applied, 15,460 accepted. Either SAT or ACT required. SAT 25/75 percentile: 1030-1200. High school rank: 13% in top tenth, 37% in top quarter, 72% in top half
Early decision deadline: N/A, notification date: N/A
Early action deadline: N/A, notification date: N/A
Application deadline (fall): 6/1

Undergraduate student body: 27,688 full time, 9,702 part time; 51% male, 49% female; 0% American Indian, 5% Asian, 24% black, 13% Hispanic, 5% multiracial, 0% Pacific Islander, 50% white, 1% international; 89% from in state; 12% live on campus; 3% of students in fraternities, 6% in sororities
Most popular majors: Information not available
Expenses: 2021-2022: $7,548 in state, $21,616 out of state; room/board: $12,947
Financial aid: (770) 423-6074; 65% of undergrads determined to have financial need; average aid package $9,601

LaGrange College

LaGrange GA
(706) 880-8005
U.S. News ranking: Reg. Coll. (S), No. 10
Website: www.lagrange.edu
Admissions email: admissions@lagrange.edu
Private; founded 1831
Affiliation: United Methodist
Freshman admissions: selective; 2020-2021: 1,633 applied, 969 accepted. Neither SAT nor ACT required. SAT 25/75 percentile: 980-1123. High school rank: 21% in top tenth, 46% in top quarter, 74% in top half
Early decision deadline: N/A, notification date: N/A
Early action deadline: N/A, notification date: N/A
Application deadline (fall): 8/31
Undergraduate student body: 720 full time, 30 part time; 51% male, 49% female; 1% American Indian, 1% Asian, 22% black, 3% Hispanic, 2% multiracial, 0% Pacific Islander, 69% white, 1% international; 81% from in state; 63% live on campus; 10% of students in fraternities, 26% in sororities
Most popular majors: 21% Registered Nursing/Registered Nurse, 14% Business Administration and Management, General, 9% Psychology, General, 8% Kinesiology and Exercise Science, 7% Visual and Performing Arts, General
Expenses: 2021-2022: $32,880; room/board: $12,060
Financial aid: (706) 880-8249; 88% of undergrads determined to have financial need; average aid package $28,713

Mercer University

Macon GA
(478) 301-2650
U.S. News ranking: Nat. U., No. 162
Website: www.mercer.edu
Admissions email: admissions@mercer.edu
Private; founded 1833
Freshman admissions: more selective; 2020-2021: 5,651 applied, 4,417 accepted. Neither SAT nor ACT required. SAT 25/75 percentile: 1180-1340. High school rank: 39% in top tenth, 66% in top quarter, 91% in top half

Early decision deadline: N/A, notification date: N/A
Early action deadline: 11/15, notification date: 12/8
Application deadline (fall): 7/1
Undergraduate student body: 4,219 full time, 692 part time; 36% male, 64% female; 0% American Indian, 8% Asian, 30% black, 7% Hispanic, 4% multiracial, 0% Pacific Islander, 46% white, 1% international; 85% from in state; 77% live on campus; 20% of students in fraternities, 25% in sororities
Most popular majors: 18% Health Professions and Related Programs, 16% Business, Management, Marketing, and Related Support Services, 12% Engineering, 10% Biological and Biomedical Sciences, 8% Social Sciences
Expenses: 2021-2022: $38,746; room/board: $13,438
Financial aid: (478) 301-2670; 68% of undergrads determined to have financial need; average aid package $34,869

Middle Georgia State University

Macon GA
(478) 471-2725
U.S. News ranking: Reg. Coll. (S), No. 44
Website: www.mga.edu/
Admissions email: admissions@mga.edu
Public; founded 2013
Freshman admissions: less selective; 2020-2021: 3,237 applied, 3,215 accepted. Neither SAT nor ACT required. SAT 25/75 percentile: 880-1100. High school rank: N/A
Early decision deadline: N/A, notification date: N/A
Early action deadline: N/A, notification date: N/A
Application deadline (fall): rolling
Undergraduate student body: 4,802 full time, 3,213 part time; 43% male, 57% female; 0% American Indian, 2% Asian, 36% black, 6% Hispanic, 4% multiracial, 0% Pacific Islander, 49% white, 2% international
Most popular majors: 20% Registered Nursing/Registered Nurse, 14% Business Administration and Management, General, 12% Computer and Information Sciences, General, 11% Psychology, General, 7% Aviation/Airway Management and Operations
Expenses: 2021-2022: $4,742 in state, $13,926 out of state; room/board: $9,010
Financial aid: (478) 387-0580; 77% of undergrads determined to have financial need; average aid package $9,415

Morehouse College

Atlanta GA
(404) 215-2618
U.S. News ranking: Nat. Lib. Arts, No. 128
Website: www.morehouse.edu
Admissions email: admissions@morehouse.edu
Private; founded 1867
Freshman admissions: selective;

2020-2021: 3,291 applied, 2,451 accepted. Neither SAT nor ACT required. SAT 25/75 percentile: 995-1180. High school rank: N/A
Early decision deadline: 11/1, notification date: 12/15
Early action deadline: 11/1, notification date: 12/5
Application deadline (fall): 2/15
Undergraduate student body: 2,008 full time, 144 part time; 100% male, 0% female; 0% American Indian, 0% Asian, 74% black, 0% Hispanic, 2% multiracial, 0% Pacific Islander, 0% white, 1% international; 30% from in state; 0% live on campus; 20% of students in fraternities, 0% in sororities
Most popular majors: 27% Business Administration and Management, General, 9% Sociology, 8% Biology/Biological Sciences, General, 7% English Language and Literature, General, 7% Psychology, General
Expenses: 2021-2022: $29,468; room/board: $14,040
Financial aid: (844) 512-6672

Oglethorpe University

Atlanta GA
(404) 364-8307
U.S. News ranking: Nat. Lib. Arts, No. 165
Website: oglethorpe.edu
Admissions email: admission@oglethorpe.edu
Private; founded 1835
Freshman admissions: more selective; 2020-2021: 2,375 applied, 1,586 accepted. Neither SAT nor ACT required. SAT 25/75 percentile: 1100-1280. High school rank: N/A
Early decision deadline: N/A, notification date: N/A
Early action deadline: 11/1, notification date: N/A
Application deadline (fall): 11/1
Undergraduate student body: 1,371 full time, 80 part time; 39% male, 61% female; 1% American Indian, 5% Asian, 24% black, 15% Hispanic, 1% multiracial, 0% Pacific Islander, 41% white, 11% international; 22% from in state; 16% live on campus; 5% of students in fraternities, 10% in sororities
Most popular majors: 23% Business Administration and Management, General, 12% Biology/Biological Sciences, General, 8% Accounting, 8% Psychology, General, 4% Rhetoric and Composition
Expenses: 2021-2022: $42,754; room/board: $14,200
Financial aid: (404) 504-1500; 69% of undergrads determined to have financial need; average aid package $36,421

Paine College[1]

Augusta GA
(706) 821-8320
U.S. News ranking: Reg. Coll. (S), second tier
Website: www.paine.edu
Admissions email: admissions@paine.edu
Private; founded 1882

Application deadline (fall): 7/15
Undergraduate student body: N/A
full time, N/A part time
Expenses: 2020-2021: $14,595;
room/board: $6,662
Financial aid: N/A

Piedmont University

Demorest GA
(800) 277-7020
U.S. News ranking: Reg. U. (S),
No. 57
Website: www.piedmont.edu
Admissions email:
ugrad@piedmont.edu
Private; founded 1897
Affiliation: United Church of Christ
Freshman admissions: selective;
2020-2021: 1,457 applied,
1,021 accepted. Either SAT
or ACT required. SAT 25/75
percentile: 980-1140. High school
rank: 14% in top tenth, 33% in
top quarter, 68% in top half
Early decision deadline: N/A,
notification date: N/A
Early action deadline: N/A,
notification date: N/A
Application deadline (fall): 7/15
Undergraduate student body: 1,153
full time, 130 part time; 34%
male, 66% female; 0% American
Indian, 2% Asian, 12% black,
7% Hispanic, 1% multiracial,
0% Pacific Islander, 69% white,
0% international; 89% from in
state; 73% live on campus; N/A
of students in fraternities, N/A in
sororities
Most popular majors: 27% Health
Professions and Related Programs,
23% Education, 13% Business,
Management, Marketing, and
Related Support Services, 5%
Homeland Security, Law
Enforcement, Firefighting and
Related Protective Services, 6%
Psychology
Expenses: 2021-2022: $28,340;
room/board: $11,200
Financial aid: (706) 776-0114;
83% of undergrads determined to
have financial need; average aid
package $23,910

Point University[1]

West Point GA
706) 385-1202
U.S. News ranking: Reg. Coll. (S),
second tier
Website: www.point.edu
Admissions email:
admissions@point.edu
Private; founded 1937
Affiliation: Christian Churches and
Churches of Christ
Application deadline (fall): 8/1
Undergraduate student body: N/A
full time, N/A part time
Expenses: 2020-2021: $21,850;
room/board: $8,000
Financial aid: (706) 385-1462

Reinhardt University

Waleska GA
770) 720-5526
U.S. News ranking: Reg. U. (S),
second tier
Website: www.reinhardt.edu/
Admissions email:
admissions@reinhardt.edu
Private; founded 1883
Affiliation: United Methodist

Freshman admissions: selective;
2020-2021: 1,142 applied,
1,127 accepted. Neither SAT
nor ACT required. SAT 25/75
percentile: 940-1160. High
school rank: 9% in top tenth, 35%
in top quarter, 67% in top half
Early decision deadline: N/A,
notification date: N/A
Early action deadline: N/A,
notification date: N/A
Application deadline (fall): 8/20
Undergraduate student body: 1,157
full time, 135 part time; 50%
male, 50% female; 0% American
Indian, 1% Asian, 18% black,
11% Hispanic, 3% multiracial,
0% Pacific Islander, 61% white,
2% international; 90% from in
state; 49% live on campus; 1%
of students in fraternities, 5% in
sororities
Most popular majors: 27%
Business, Management,
Marketing, and Related Support
Services, 19% Health Professions
and Related Programs, 12%
Parks, Recreation, Leisure, and
Fitness Studies, 7% Biological
and Biomedical Sciences,
7% Homeland Security, Law
Enforcement, Firefighting and
Related Protective Services
Expenses: 2021-2022: $26,180;
room/board: $11,340
Financial aid: (770) 720-5667;
79% of undergrads determined to
have financial need; average aid
package $19,638

Savannah College of Art and Design

Savannah GA
(912) 525-5100
U.S. News ranking: Arts, unranked
Website: www.scad.edu
Admissions email:
admission@scad.edu
Private; founded 1978
Freshman admissions: selective;
2020-2021: 14,254 applied,
11,155 accepted. Neither SAT
nor ACT required. SAT 25/75
percentile: 1040-1240. High
school rank: N/A
Early decision deadline: N/A,
notification date: N/A
Early action deadline: N/A,
notification date: N/A
Application deadline (fall): rolling
Undergraduate student body: 9,224
full time, 2,565 part time; 31%
male, 69% female; 1% American
Indian, 5% Asian, 12% black,
7% Hispanic, 0% multiracial,
0% Pacific Islander, 51% white,
19% international; 15% from in
state; 13% live on campus; N/A
of students in fraternities, N/A in
sororities
Most popular majors: 58% Visual
and Performing Arts, 16%
Communications Technologies/
Technicians and Support Services,
14% Communication, Journalism,
and Related Programs, 5% Family
and Consumer Sciences/Human
Sciences, 3% Architecture and
Related Services
Expenses: 2021-2022: $38,340;
room/board: $15,348
Financial aid: (912) 525-5100;
47% of undergrads determined to
have financial need; average aid
package $16,252

Savannah State University[7]

Savannah GA
(912) 358-4338
U.S. News ranking: Reg. U. (S),
second tier
Website: www. savannahstate.edu
Admissions email:
admissions@savannahstate.edu
Public; founded 1890
Freshman admissions: less
selective; 2020-2021: 6,083
applied, 4,179 accepted. Either
SAT or ACT required. SAT 25/75
percentile: 900-1030. High
school rank: N/A
Early decision deadline: N/A,
notification date: N/A
Early action deadline: N/A,
notification date: N/A
Application deadline (fall): 7/15
Undergraduate student body: 2,634
full time, 616 part time
Most popular majors: 10% Biology/
Biological Sciences, General, 10%
Business/Commerce, General,
10% Journalism, 9% Corrections
and Criminal Justice, Other, 5%
Social Work
Expenses: 2020-2021: $5,902 in
state, $16,624 out of state; room/
board: $7,762
Financial aid: (912) 358-4162

Shorter University

Rome GA
(800) 868-6980
U.S. News ranking: Reg. U. (S),
No. 80
Website: www.shorter.edu/
Admissions email:
admissions@shorter.edu
Private; founded 1873
Affiliation: Baptist
Freshman admissions: selective;
2020-2021: 1,548 applied,
1,098 accepted. Neither SAT
nor ACT required. ACT 25/75
percentile: 18-24. High school
rank: N/A
Early decision deadline: N/A,
notification date: N/A
Early action deadline: N/A,
notification date: N/A
Application deadline (fall): rolling
Undergraduate student body: 1,077
full time, 229 part time; 43%
male, 57% female; N/A American
Indian, N/A Asian, N/A black, N/A
Hispanic, N/A multiracial, N/A
Pacific Islander, N/A white, N/A
international
Most popular majors: Business
Administration and Management,
General, Criminal Justice/Safety
Studies, Registered Nursing/
Registered Nurse, Religion/
Religious Studies, Sport
and Fitness Administration/
Management
Expenses: 2021-2022: $22,810;
room/board: $5,050
Financial aid: (706) 233-7227

South Georgia State College[1]

Douglas GA
(912) 260-4206
U.S. News ranking: Reg. Coll. (S),
unranked
Website: www.sgsc.edu
Admissions email:
admissions@sgsc.edu

Public
Application deadline (fall): rolling
Undergraduate student body: N/A
full time, N/A part time
Expenses: 2020-2021: $3,310 in
state, $9,662 out of state; room/
board: $8,750
Financial aid: N/A

Spelman College

Atlanta GA
(800) 982-2411
U.S. News ranking: Nat. Lib. Arts,
No. 54
Website: www.spelman.edu
Admissions email:
admiss@spelman.edu
Private; founded 1881
Freshman admissions: selective;
2020-2021: 9,118 applied,
4,794 accepted. Either SAT
or ACT required. SAT 25/75
percentile: 1050-1200. High
school rank: 30% in top tenth,
59% in top quarter, 88% in
top half
Early decision deadline: 11/1,
notification date: 12/15
Early action deadline: 11/15,
notification date: 12/31
Application deadline (fall): 2/1
Undergraduate student body: 2,132
full time, 75 part time; 0% male,
100% female; 1% American
Indian, 0% Asian, 98% black,
0% Hispanic, 0% multiracial,
0% Pacific Islander, 0% white,
0% international; 27% from in
state; N/A live on campus; N/A
of students in fraternities, N/A in
sororities
Most popular majors: 14%
Psychology, General, 12% Political
Science and Government, General,
11% Biology/Biological Sciences,
General, 10% Economics,
General, 8% Health and Wellness,
General
Expenses: 2021-2022: $28,181;
room/board: $15,063
Financial aid: (404) 270-5209;
74% of undergrads determined to
have financial need; average aid
package $17,798

Thomas University[1]

Thomasville GA
(229) 227-6934
U.S. News ranking: Reg. U. (S),
second tier
Website: www.thomasu.edu
Admissions email:
rgagliano@thomasu.edu
Private; founded 1950
Application deadline (fall): rolling
Undergraduate student body: N/A
full time, N/A part time
Expenses: 2020-2021: $16,970;
room/board: $7,040
Financial aid: (229) 226-1621

Toccoa Falls College

Toccoa Falls GA
(888) 785-5624
U.S. News ranking: Reg. Coll. (S),
No. 25
Website: tfc.edu
Admissions email:
admissions@tfc.edu
Private; founded 1907
Affiliation: Christ and Missionary
Alliance Church
Freshman admissions: selective;

2020-2021: 1,119 applied, 646
accepted. Neither SAT nor ACT
required. SAT 25/75 percentile:
930-1130. High school rank:
10% in top tenth, 34% in top
quarter, 64% in top half
Early decision deadline: N/A,
notification date: N/A
Early action deadline: N/A,
notification date: N/A
Application deadline (fall): rolling
Undergraduate student body: 880
full time, 797 part time; 36%
male, 64% female; 0% American
Indian, 4% Asian, 9% black,
6% Hispanic, 3% multiracial,
0% Pacific Islander, 76% white,
1% international; 72% from in
state; 50% live on campus; 0%
of students in fraternities, 0% in
sororities
Most popular majors: 12%
Registered Nursing/Registered
Nurse, 10% Counseling
Psychology, 7% Biology/Biological
Sciences, General, 6% Business
Administration and Management,
General, 6% Youth Ministry
Expenses: 2021-2022: $21,490;
room/board: $8,500
Financial aid: (706) 886-7299;
85% of undergrads determined to
have financial need; average aid
package $15,356

Truett McConnell University

Cleveland GA
(706) 865-2134
U.S. News ranking: Reg. Coll. (S),
No. 44
Website: truett.edu/
Admissions email:
admissions@truett.edu
Private; founded 1946
Affiliation: Southern Baptist
Freshman admissions: selective;
2020-2021: 702 applied, 683
accepted. Either SAT or ACT
required. SAT 25/75 percentile:
920-1140. High school rank:
13% in top tenth, 32% in top
quarter, 55% in top half
Early decision deadline: N/A,
notification date: N/A
Early action deadline: N/A,
notification date: N/A
Application deadline (fall): 8/1
Undergraduate student body: 856
full time, 1,970 part time; 45%
male, 55% female; 0% American
Indian, 0% Asian, 9% black, 5%
Hispanic, 0% multiracial, 0%
Pacific Islander, 73% white, 3%
international
Most popular majors: 24%
Business/Commerce, General,
12% Psychology, General, 12%
Registered Nursing/Registered
Nurse, 10% Bible/Biblical
Studies, 10% Elementary
Education and Teaching
Expenses: 2021-2022: $22,852;
room/board: $8,412
Financial aid: (706) 865-2134;
74% of undergrads determined to
have financial need; average aid
package $16,637

University of Georgia

Athens GA
(706) 542-8776
U.S. News ranking: Nat. U., No. 48
Website: www.admissions.uga.edu
Admissions email:
adm-info@uga.edu
Public; founded 1785
Freshman admissions: more selective; 2020-2021: 28,024 applied, 13,549 accepted. Either SAT or ACT required. SAT 25/75 percentile: 1220-1400. High school rank: 56% in top tenth, 89% in top quarter, 99% in top half
Early decision deadline: N/A, notification date: N/A
Early action deadline: 10/15, notification date: 12/1
Application deadline (fall): 1/1
Undergraduate student body: 27,860 full time, 1,872 part time; 42% male, 58% female; 0% American Indian, 11% Asian, 7% black, 7% Hispanic, 4% multiracial, 0% Pacific Islander, 69% white, 1% international; 88% from in state; 32% live on campus; 22% of students in fraternities, 33% in sororities
Most popular majors: 7% Finance, General, 6% Biology/Biological Sciences, General, 6% Psychology, General, 4% Management Information Systems, General, 4% Marketing/Marketing Management, General
Expenses: 2021-2022: $12,080 in state, $31,120 out of state; room/board: $10,452
Financial aid: (706) 542-6147; 40% of undergrads determined to have financial need; average aid package $12,980

University of North Georgia

Dahlonega GA
(706) 864-1800
U.S. News ranking: Reg. U. (S), No. 35
Website: ung.edu/
Admissions email:
admissions-dah@ung.edu
Public; founded 1873
Freshman admissions: selective; 2020-2021: 7,033 applied, 5,429 accepted. Either SAT or ACT required. SAT 25/75 percentile: 1060-1210. High school rank: 15% in top tenth, 46% in top quarter, 82% in top half
Early decision deadline: N/A, notification date: N/A
Early action deadline: 11/15, notification date: 12/15
Application deadline (fall): 2/15
Undergraduate student body: 12,967 full time, 6,052 part time; 43% male, 57% female; 0% American Indian, 3% Asian, 4% black, 15% Hispanic, 4% multiracial, 0% Pacific Islander, 72% white, 1% international; 98% from in state; 15% live on campus; 4% of students in fraternities, 5% in sororities
Most popular majors: 23% Business, Management, Marketing, and Related Support Services, 9% Health Professions and Related Programs, 8%

Education, 7% Biological and Biomedical Sciences, 6% Parks, Recreation, Leisure, and Fitness Studies
Expenses: 2021-2022: $7,462 in state, $21,620 out of state; room/board: $11,510
Financial aid: (706) 864-1412; 56% of undergrads determined to have financial need; average aid package $8,395

University of West Georgia

Carrollton GA
(678) 839-5600
U.S. News ranking: Nat. U., second tier
Website: www.westga.edu
Admissions email:
admiss@westga.edu
Public; founded 1906
Freshman admissions: selective; 2020-2021: 6,634 applied, 5,149 accepted. Either SAT or ACT required. SAT 25/75 percentile: 900-1040. High school rank: N/A
Early decision deadline: N/A, notification date: N/A
Early action deadline: N/A, notification date: N/A
Application deadline (fall): 6/1
Undergraduate student body: 7,528 full time, 2,803 part time; 35% male, 65% female; 0% American Indian, 1% Asian, 36% black, 8% Hispanic, 4% multiracial, 0% Pacific Islander, 48% white, 1% international; 94% from in state; 20% live on campus; N/A of students in fraternities, N/A in sororities
Most popular majors: 23% Business, Management, Marketing, and Related Support Services, 16% Social Sciences, 15% Health Professions and Related Programs, 9% Psychology, 7% Education
Expenses: 2021-2022: $7,614 in state, $21,432 out of state; room/board: $10,584
Financial aid: (678) 839-6421; 72% of undergrads determined to have financial need; average aid package $8,724

Valdosta State University

Valdosta GA
(229) 333-5791
U.S. News ranking: Nat. U., second tier
Website: www.valdosta.edu
Admissions email:
admissions@valdosta.edu
Public; founded 1906
Freshman admissions: less selective; 2020-2021: 9,910 applied, 7,694 accepted. Either SAT or ACT required. SAT 25/75 percentile: 930-1100. High school rank: N/A
Early decision deadline: N/A, notification date: N/A
Early action deadline: N/A, notification date: N/A
Application deadline (fall): 6/15
Undergraduate student body: 7,253 full time, 2,317 part time; 34% male, 66% female; 0% American Indian, 1% Asian, 42% black, 9% Hispanic, 4% multiracial,

0% Pacific Islander, 41% white, 1% international; 81% from in state; 28% live on campus; 1% of students in fraternities, 2% in sororities
Most popular majors: 26% Business, Management, Marketing, and Related Support Services, 13% Health Professions and Related Programs, 8% Communication, Journalism, and Related Programs, 7% Education, 7% Psychology
Expenses: 2021-2022: $6,583 in state, $17,638 out of state; room/board: $8,536
Financial aid: (229) 333-5935; 79% of undergrads determined to have financial need; average aid package $15,898

Wesleyan College

Macon GA
(800) 447-6610
U.S. News ranking: Nat. Lib. Arts, No. 157
Website: www.wesleyancollege.edu
Admissions email:
admissions@wesleyancollege.edu
Private; founded 1836
Affiliation: United Methodist
Freshman admissions: selective; 2020-2021: 1,142 applied, 683 accepted. Neither SAT nor ACT required. SAT 25/75 percentile: 946-1113. High school rank: N/A
Early decision deadline: N/A, notification date: N/A
Early action deadline: N/A, notification date: N/A
Application deadline (fall): rolling
Undergraduate student body: 500 full time, 245 part time; 6% male, 94% female; 0% American Indian, 1% Asian, 40% black, 8% Hispanic, 3% multiracial, 0% Pacific Islander, 41% white, 6% international; 93% from in state; 53% live on campus; 0% of students in fraternities, 0% in sororities
Most popular majors: 26% Registered Nursing/Registered Nurse, 18% Business, Management, Marketing, and Related Support Services, 15% Psychology, General, 12% Social Sciences, 8% Visual and Performing Arts
Expenses: 2021-2022: $26,390; room/board: $10,676
Financial aid: (478) 757-5146; 82% of undergrads determined to have financial need; average aid package $24,274

Young Harris College

Young Harris GA
(706) 379-3111
U.S. News ranking: Nat. Lib. Arts, second tier
Website: www.yhc.edu
Admissions email:
admissions@yhc.edu
Private; founded 1886
Affiliation: United Methodist
Freshman admissions: selective; 2020-2021: 2,216 applied, 1,441 accepted. Neither SAT nor ACT required. SAT 25/75 percentile: 930-1160. High school rank: 13% in top tenth, 62% in top quarter, 75% in top half

Early decision deadline: N/A, notification date: N/A
Early action deadline: N/A, notification date: N/A
Application deadline (fall): rolling
Undergraduate student body: 922 full time, 474 part time; 42% male, 58% female; 1% American Indian, 0% Asian, 11% black, 7% Hispanic, 3% multiracial, 0% Pacific Islander, 68% white, 6% international; 84% from in state; 86% live on campus; 2% of students in fraternities, 5% in sororities
Most popular majors: 23% Business, Management, Marketing, and Related Support Services, 13% Visual and Performing Arts, 12% Psychology, 7% Biological and Biomedical Sciences, 7% Communication, Journalism, and Related Programs
Expenses: 2021-2022: $29,667; room/board: N/A
Financial aid: N/A; 75% of undergrads determined to have financial need; average aid package $26,871

University of Guam

Mangilao GU
(671) 735-2201
U.S. News ranking: Reg. U. (W), No. 90
Website: www.uog.edu
Admissions email:
admitme@triton.uog.edu
Public; founded 1952
Freshman admissions: less selective; 2020-2021: 554 applied, 553 accepted. Neither SAT nor ACT required. SAT 25/75 percentile: N/A. High school rank: 24% in top tenth, 46% in top quarter, 73% in top half
Early decision deadline: N/A, notification date: N/A
Early action deadline: N/A, notification date: N/A
Application deadline (fall): 6/1
Undergraduate student body: 2,403 full time, 715 part time; 41% male, 59% female; 0% American Indian, 48% Asian, 0% black, 1% Hispanic, 0% multiracial, 45% Pacific Islander, 2% white, 1% international; 99% from in state; 3% live on campus; 0% of students in fraternities, 0% in sororities
Most popular majors: 17% Business Administration and Management, General, 7% Public Administration, 6% Biology/Biological Sciences, General, 6% Criminal Justice/Safety Studies, 5% Health Professions and Related Programs
Expenses: 2021-2022: $6,242 in state, $11,138 out of state; room/board: $3,888
Financial aid: (671) 735-2288; 66% of undergrads determined to have financial need; average aid package $3,653

Brigham Young University–Hawaii[1]

Laie Oahu HI
(808) 293-3738
U.S. News ranking: Reg. Coll. (W), No. 14
Website: www.byuh.edu
Admissions email:
admissions@byuh.edu
Private
Application deadline (fall): N/A
Undergraduate student body: N/A full time, N/A part time
Expenses: 2020-2021: $5,890; room/board: $7,064
Financial aid: N/A

Chaminade University of Honolulu

Honolulu HI
(808) 735-8340
U.S. News ranking: Reg. U. (W), No. 25
Website: chaminade.edu/
Admissions email:
admissions@chaminade.edu
Private; founded 1955
Affiliation: Roman Catholic
Freshman admissions: selective; 2020-2021: 1,593 applied, 1,404 accepted. Neither SAT nor ACT required. SAT 25/75 percentile: 970-1155. High school rank: N/A
Early decision deadline: N/A, notification date: N/A
Early action deadline: N/A, notification date: N/A
Application deadline (fall): rolling
Undergraduate student body: 1,032 full time, 32 part time; 24% male, 76% female; 1% American Indian, 34% Asian, 2% black, 8% Hispanic, 11% multiracial, 24% Pacific Islander, 12% white, 1% international; 73% from in state; 15% live on campus; N/A of students in fraternities, N/A in sororities
Most popular majors: 25% Registered Nursing/Registered Nurse, 13% Criminal Justice/Safety Studies, 11% Business Administration and Management, General, 9% Biology/Biological Sciences, General, 9% Psychology, General
Expenses: 2021-2022: $27,454; room/board: $15,050
Financial aid: (808) 735-4780; 71% of undergrads determined to have financial need; average aid package $23,655

Hawaii Pacific University

Honolulu HI
(808) 544-0238
U.S. News ranking: Reg. U. (W), No. 70
Website: www.hpu.edu/
Admissions email:
admissions@hpu.edu
Private; founded 1965
Freshman admissions: selective; 2020-2021: 8,296 applied, 6,602 accepted. Neither SAT nor ACT required. SAT 25/75 percentile: 970-1170. High school rank: N/A

Early decision deadline: N/A, notification date: N/A
Early action deadline: 11/14, notification date: 12/31
Application deadline (fall): 8/15
Undergraduate student body: 2,152 full time, 1,648 part time; 38% male, 63% female; 0% American Indian, 18% Asian, 7% black, 18% Hispanic, 18% multiracial, 3% Pacific Islander, 27% white, 6% international; N/A from in state; 17% live on campus; N/A of students in fraternities, N/A in sororities
Most popular majors: 28% Business, Management, Marketing, and Related Support Services, 23% Health Professions and Related Programs, 12% Biological and Biomedical Sciences, 6% Homeland Security, Law Enforcement, Firefighting and Related Protective Services, 6% Psychology
Expenses: 2021-2022: $30,020; room/board: $16,764
Financial aid: (808) 544-0253; 64% of undergrads determined to have financial need; average aid package $21,197

University of Hawaii at Hilo
Hilo HI
(800) 897-4456
U.S. News ranking: Nat. U., No. 288
Website: hilo.hawaii.edu
Admissions email: uhhadm@hawaii.edu
Public; founded 1947
Freshman admissions: selective; 2020-2021: 5,135 applied, 2,327 accepted. Either SAT or ACT required. ACT 25/75 percentile: 16-22. High school rank: 16% in top tenth, 43% in top quarter, 79% in top half
Early decision deadline: N/A, notification date: N/A
Early action deadline: N/A, notification date: N/A
Application deadline (fall): 7/1
Undergraduate student body: 2,112 full time, 559 part time; 36% male, 64% female; 0% American Indian, 16% Asian, 1% black, 15% Hispanic, 37% multiracial, 8% Pacific Islander, 19% white, 3% international; N/A from in state; 26% live on campus; N/A of students in fraternities, N/A in sororities
Most popular majors: 17% Health Professions and Related Programs, 10% Social Sciences, 9% Biological and Biomedical Sciences, 9% Business, Management, Marketing, and Related Support Services, 8% Psychology
Expenses: 2021-2022: $7,838 in state, $20,798 out of state; room/board: $12,206
Financial aid: (808) 932-7449; 48% of undergrads determined to have financial need; average aid package $11,964

University of Hawaii– Manoa
Honolulu HI
(808) 956-8975
U.S. News ranking: Nat. U., No. 162
Website: www.manoa.hawaii.edu/
Admissions email: manoa.admissions@hawaii.edu
Public; founded 1907
Freshman admissions: more selective; 2020-2021: 17,747 applied, 11,081 accepted. Neither SAT nor ACT required. SAT 25/75 percentile: 1060-1260. High school rank: 30% in top tenth, 60% in top quarter, 89% in top half
Early decision deadline: N/A, notification date: N/A
Early action deadline: N/A, notification date: N/A
Application deadline (fall): 3/1
Undergraduate student body: 10,688 full time, 2,515 part time; 42% male, 58% female; 0% American Indian, 37% Asian, 2% black, 2% Hispanic, 17% multiracial, 18% Pacific Islander, 21% white, 3% international; 66% from in state; 9% live on campus; 1% of students in fraternities, 1% in sororities
Most popular majors: 21% Business, Management, Marketing, and Related Support Services, 8% Biological and Biomedical Sciences, 8% Social Sciences
Expenses: 2021-2022: $12,186 in state, $34,218 out of state; room/board: $11,180
Financial aid: (808) 956-7251; 53% of undergrads determined to have financial need; average aid package $15,172

University of Hawaii– Maui College[1]
Kahului HI
(808) 984-3267
U.S. News ranking: Reg. Coll. (W), unranked
Website: www.maui.hawaii.edu/
Admissions email: N/A
Public
Application deadline (fall): N/A
Undergraduate student body: N/A full time, N/A part time
Expenses: 2020-2021: $3,278 in state, $8,414 out of state; room/board: N/A
Financial aid: N/A

University of Hawaii– West Oahu
Kapolei HI
(808) 689-2900
U.S. News ranking: Reg. Coll. (W), No. 29
Website: westoahu.hawaii.edu/
Admissions email: uhwo.admissions@hawaii.edu
Public; founded 1976
Freshman admissions: selective; 2020-2021: 713 applied, 679 accepted. Neither SAT nor ACT required. ACT 25/75 percentile: 16-21. High school rank: 14% in top tenth, 37% in top quarter, 76% in top half

Early decision deadline: N/A, notification date: N/A
Early action deadline: N/A, notification date: N/A
Application deadline (fall): 7/1
Undergraduate student body: 1,734 full time, 1,372 part time; 33% male, 67% female; 1% American Indian, 38% Asian, 2% black, 1% Hispanic, 16% multiracial, 31% Pacific Islander, 12% white, 0% international; 97% from in state; N/A live on campus; N/A of students in fraternities, N/A in sororities
Most popular majors: 41% Business Administration and Management, General, 18% Public Administration, 17% Social Sciences, General, 12% Multi-/Interdisciplinary Studies, Other, 5% Education, General
Expenses: 2021-2022: $7,584 in state, $20,544 out of state; room/board: N/A
Financial aid: (808) 689-2900; 39% of undergrads determined to have financial need; average aid package $8,912

Boise State University
Boise ID
(208) 426-1156
U.S. News ranking: Nat. U., second tier
Website: www.boisestate.edu
Admissions email: admissions@boisestate.edu
Public; founded 1932
Freshman admissions: selective; 2020-2021: 15,510 applied, 12,020 accepted. Neither SAT nor ACT required. SAT 25/75 percentile: 1030-1210. High school rank: 12% in top tenth, 39% in top quarter, 73% in top half
Early decision deadline: N/A, notification date: N/A
Early action deadline: N/A, notification date: N/A
Application deadline (fall): 8/1
Undergraduate student body: 12,973 full time, 7,815 part time; 43% male, 57% female; 0% American Indian, 3% Asian, 2% black, 14% Hispanic, 5% multiracial, 0% Pacific Islander, 74% white, 1% international
Most popular majors: 11% Registered Nursing/Registered Nurse, 7% Business Administration and Management, General, 6% Health Professions and Related Clinical Sciences, Other, 5% Business/Commerce, General, 4% Multi-/Interdisciplinary Studies
Expenses: 2021-2022: $8,068 in state, $24,988 out of state; room/board: $13,460
Financial aid: (208) 426-1664; 56% of undergrads determined to have financial need; average aid package $10,964

Brigham Young University–Idaho[1]
Rexburg ID
(208) 496-1036
U.S. News ranking: Reg. Coll. (W), No. 16
Website: www.byui.edu
Admissions email: admissions@byui.edu
Private
Application deadline (fall): N/A
Undergraduate student body: N/A full time, N/A part time
Expenses: 2020-2021: $4,300; room/board: $4,368
Financial aid: N/A

College of Idaho
Caldwell ID
(208) 459-5011
U.S. News ranking: Nat. Lib. Arts, No. 136
Website: www.collegeofidaho.edu
Admissions email: admissions@collegeofidaho.edu
Private; founded 1891
Freshman admissions: selective; 2020-2021: 3,677 applied, 1,778 accepted. Neither SAT nor ACT required. SAT 25/75 percentile: 1050-1240. High school rank: N/A
Early decision deadline: N/A, notification date: N/A
Early action deadline: 11/16, notification date: 12/21
Application deadline (fall): 2/16
Undergraduate student body: 1,085 full time, 15 part time; 49% male, 51% female; 1% American Indian, 2% Asian, 2% black, 13% Hispanic, 6% multiracial, 1% Pacific Islander, 57% white, 18% international; 71% from in state; N/A live on campus; N/A of students in fraternities, N/A in sororities
Most popular majors: 27% Business, Management, Marketing, and Related Support Services, 17% Health Professions and Related Programs, 11% Biological and Biomedical Sciences, 10% Psychology, 8% Social Sciences
Expenses: 2021-2022: $33,805; room/board: $10,820
Financial aid: (208) 459-5307; 67% of undergrads determined to have financial need; average aid package $31,866

Idaho State University[1]
Pocatello ID
(208) 282-0211
U.S. News ranking: Nat. U., second tier
Website: www.isu.edu
Admissions email: info@isu.edu
Public
Application deadline (fall): N/A
Undergraduate student body: N/A full time, N/A part time
Expenses: 2020-2021: $7,872 in state, $24,494 out of state; room/board: $7,214
Financial aid: N/A

Lewis-Clark State College[1]
Lewiston ID
(208) 792-2210
U.S. News ranking: Reg. Coll. (W), No. 21
Website: www.lcsc.edu
Admissions email: admissions@lcsc.edu
Public; founded 1893
Application deadline (fall): 8/8
Undergraduate student body: N/A full time, N/A part time
Expenses: 2021-2022: $6,982 in state, $20,238 out of state; room/board: $7,860
Financial aid: (208) 792-2224; 68% of undergrads determined to have financial need; average aid package $8,903

Northwest Nazarene University
Nampa ID
(208) 467-8000
U.S. News ranking: Reg. U. (W), No. 51
Website: www.nnu.edu
Admissions email: admissions@nnu.edu
Private; founded 1913
Affiliation: Church of the Nazarene
Freshman admissions: selective; 2020-2021: 2,793 applied, 2,146 accepted. Neither SAT nor ACT required. SAT 25/75 percentile: 990-1210. High school rank: 25% in top tenth, 51% in top quarter, 77% in top half
Early decision deadline: N/A, notification date: N/A
Early action deadline: 1/15, notification date: 9/15
Application deadline (fall): 8/15
Undergraduate student body: 1,086 full time, 155 part time; 41% male, 59% female; 1% American Indian, 1% Asian, 2% black, 13% Hispanic, 5% multiracial, 0% Pacific Islander, 76% white, 1% international; N/A from in state; 74% live on campus; N/A of students in fraternities, N/A in sororities
Most popular majors: 28% Business, Management, Marketing, and Related Support Services, 14% Health Professions and Related Programs, 10% Education, 7% Engineering, 6% Visual and Performing Arts
Expenses: 2021-2022: $34,390; room/board: $9,600
Financial aid: (208) 467-8347

University of Idaho
Moscow ID
(888) 884-3246
U.S. News ranking: Nat. U., No. 179
Website: www.uidaho.edu/admissions
Admissions email: admissions@uidaho.edu
Public; founded 1889
Freshman admissions: selective; 2020-2021: 9,938 applied, 7,398 accepted. Either SAT or ACT required. SAT 25/75 percentile: 990-1220. High school rank: 18% in top tenth, 39% in top quarter, 71% in top half
Early decision deadline: N/A,

notification date: N/A
Early action deadline: N/A,
notification date: N/A
Application deadline (fall): rolling
Undergraduate student body: 6,323
full time, 2,043 part time; 48%
male, 52% female; 1% American
Indian, 2% Asian, 1% black,
11% Hispanic, 4% multiracial,
0% Pacific Islander, 76% white,
3% international; 75% from in
state; 36% live on campus; 22%
of students in fraternities, 25%
in sororities
Most popular majors: 6%
Psychology, General, 4%
Marketing/Marketing Management,
General, 4% Mechanical
Engineering, 3% Animal Sciences,
General, 3% Sociology
Expenses: 2021-2022: $8,340 in
state, $27,576 out of state; room/
board: $9,308
Financial aid: (208) 885-6312;
61% of undergrads determined to
have financial need; average aid
package $13,779

ILLINOIS

American Academy of Art[1]
Chicago IL
(312) 461-0600
U.S. News ranking: Arts, unranked
Website: www.aaart.edu
Admissions email:
N/A
Private
Application deadline (fall): N/A
Undergraduate student body: N/A
full time, N/A part time
Expenses: 2020-2021: $35,270;
room/board: N/A
Financial aid: N/A

Augustana College
Rock Island IL
(800) 798-8100
U.S. News ranking: Nat. Lib. Arts,
No. 92
Website: www.augustana.edu
Admissions email:
admissions@augustana.edu
Private; founded 1860
Affiliation: Evangelical Lutheran
Church
Freshman admissions: more
selective; 2020-2021: 6,894
applied, 3,954 accepted. Neither
SAT nor ACT required. SAT
25/75 percentile: 1090-1280.
High school rank: 29% in top
tenth, 55% in top quarter, 89%
in top half
Early decision deadline: 11/1,
notification date: 11/15
Early action deadline: 11/1,
notification date: 12/20
Application deadline (fall): 8/1
Undergraduate student body: 2,358
full time, 19 part time; 45%
male, 55% female; 0% American
Indian, 3% Asian, 4% black,
12% Hispanic, 4% multiracial,
0% Pacific Islander, 66% white,
11% international; 83% from in
state; 59% live on campus; 12%
of students in fraternities, 24%
in sororities
Most popular majors: 22%
Business Administration and
Management, General, 21%

Biology/Biological Sciences,
General, 9% Pre-Medicine/
Pre-Medical Studies, 8% Social
Sciences, Other, 7% Psychology,
General
Expenses: 2021-2022: $46,189;
room/board: $11,496
Financial aid: (309) 794-7207;
73% of undergrads determined to
have financial need; average aid
package $35,153

Aurora University[1]
Aurora IL
(800) 742-5281
U.S. News ranking: Nat. U.,
second tier
Website: www.aurora.edu
Admissions email:
admission@aurora.edu
Private
Application deadline (fall): N/A
Undergraduate student body: N/A
full time, N/A part time
Expenses: 2020-2021: $25,600;
room/board: $10,474
Financial aid: N/A

Benedictine University
Lisle IL
(630) 829-6300
U.S. News ranking: Nat. U.,
second tier
Website: www.ben.edu
Admissions email:
admissions@ben.edu
Private; founded 1887
Affiliation: Roman Catholic
Freshman admissions: selective;
2020-2021: 3,017 applied,
1,840 accepted. Neither SAT
nor ACT required. SAT 25/75
percentile: 980-1160. High
school rank: N/A
Early decision deadline: N/A,
notification date: N/A
Early action deadline: N/A,
notification date: N/A
Application deadline (fall): rolling
Undergraduate student body: 1,939
full time, 360 part time; 49%
male, 51% female; 1% American
Indian, 16% Asian, 9% black,
18% Hispanic, 2% multiracial,
1% Pacific Islander, 42% white,
1% international; N/A from in
state; 17% live on campus; 3%
of students in fraternities, 3% in
sororities
Most popular majors: 30%
Business, Management,
Marketing, and Related Support
Services, 27% Health Professions
and Related Programs, 10%
Psychology
Expenses: 2021-2022: $34,290;
room/board: $10,100
Financial aid: (630) 829-6100;
74% of undergrads determined to
have financial need; average aid
package $29,189

Blackburn College
Carlinville IL
(800) 233-3550
U.S. News ranking: Nat. Lib. Arts,
second tier
Website: www.blackburn.edu
Admissions email:
admissions@blackburn.edu
Private; founded 1837

Affiliation: Presbyterian Church
(USA)
Freshman admissions: selective;
2020-2021: 734 applied, 405
accepted. Either SAT or ACT
required. SAT 25/75 percentile:
890-1078. High school rank:
10% in top tenth, 26% in top
quarter, 72% in top half
Early decision deadline: N/A,
notification date: N/A
Early action deadline: N/A,
notification date: N/A
Application deadline (fall): rolling
Undergraduate student body: 504
full time, 12 part time; 43%
male, 57% female; 1% American
Indian, 1% Asian, 10% black,
7% Hispanic, 4% multiracial,
0% Pacific Islander, 77% white,
1% international; 84% from in
state; 58% live on campus; 0%
of students in fraternities, 0% in
sororities
Most popular majors: 15%
Business, Management,
Marketing, and Related Support
Services, 14% Education,
14% Homeland Security, Law
Enforcement, Firefighting and
Related Protective Services,
12% Biological and Biomedical
Sciences, 12% Visual and
Performing Arts
Expenses: 2021-2022: $25,570;
room/board: $8,820
Financial aid: (217) 854-5774;
91% of undergrads determined to
have financial need; average aid
package $22,830

Bradley University
Peoria IL
(309) 677-1000
U.S. News ranking: Reg. U. (Mid.
W), No. 2
Website: www.bradley.edu
Admissions email:
admissions@bradley.edu
Private; founded 1897
Freshman admissions: more
selective; 2020-2021: 10,202
applied, 7,476 accepted. Neither
SAT nor ACT required. SAT
25/75 percentile: 1080-1280.
High school rank: 29% in top
tenth, 65% in top quarter, 94%
in top half
Early decision deadline: N/A,
notification date: N/A
Early action deadline: 10/15,
notification date: N/A
Application deadline (fall): rolling
Undergraduate student body: 4,450
full time, 124 part time; 49%
male, 51% female; 0% American
Indian, 4% Asian, 7% black,
12% Hispanic, 4% multiracial,
0% Pacific Islander, 70% white,
2% international; 83% from in
state; 54% live on campus; 4%
of students in fraternities, 6% in
sororities
Most popular majors: 19%
Business, Management,
Marketing, and Related Support
Services, 14% Engineering, 13%
Health Professions and Related
Programs, 9% Communication,
Journalism, and Related Programs,
8% Visual and Performing Arts
Expenses: 2021-2022: $36,360;
room/board: $11,628

Financial aid: (309) 677-3089;
70% of undergrads determined to
have financial need; average aid
package $25,648

Chicago State University
Chicago IL
(773) 995-2513
U.S. News ranking: Reg. U. (Mid.
W), second tier
Website: www.csu.edu
Admissions email:
ug-admissions@csu.edu
Public; founded 1867
Freshman admissions: less
selective; 2020-2021: 4,151
applied, 1,927 accepted. Neither
SAT nor ACT required. SAT 25/75
percentile: 750-963. High school
rank: N/A
Early decision deadline: N/A,
notification date: N/A
Early action deadline: N/A,
notification date: N/A
Application deadline (fall): N/A
Undergraduate student body: 1,086
full time, 599 part time; 28%
male, 72% female; 0% American
Indian, 1% Asian, 73% black,
8% Hispanic, 3% multiracial,
0% Pacific Islander, 2% white,
3% international; 91% from in
state; N/A live on campus; N/A
of students in fraternities, N/A in
sororities
Most popular majors: 17%
Psychology, General, 12%
Business Administration and
Management, General, 10%
Registered Nursing/Registered
Nurse, 7% Criminal Justice/Safety
Studies, 6% Sociology
Expenses: 2021-2022: $11,299
in state, $11,299 out of state;
room/board: $8,724
Financial aid: (773) 995-2304;
92% of undergrads determined to
have financial need; average aid
package $15,261

Columbia College Chicago
Chicago IL
(312) 369-7130
U.S. News ranking: Reg. U. (Mid.
W), No. 88
Website: www.colum.edu/
Admissions email:
admissions@colum.edu
Private; founded 1890
Freshman admissions: selective;
2020-2021: 8,061 applied,
7,217 accepted. Neither SAT
nor ACT required. SAT 25/75
percentile: 950-1170. High school
rank: 11% in top tenth, 34% in
top quarter, 72% in top half
Early decision deadline: N/A,
notification date: N/A
Early action deadline: N/A,
notification date: N/A
Application deadline (fall): 8/15
Undergraduate student body: 6,117
full time, 425 part time; 41%
male, 59% female; 0% American
Indian, 4% Asian, 15% black,
23% Hispanic, 5% multiracial,
0% Pacific Islander, 48% white,
3% international; N/A from in
state; 26% live on campus; N/A
of students in fraternities, N/A in
sororities

Most popular majors: 19%
Cinematography and Film/Video
Production, 6% Animation,
Interactive Technology, Video
Graphics and Special Effects, 5%
Fashion/Apparel Design, 5% Game
and Interactive Media Design, 5%
Graphic Design
Expenses: 2021-2022: $27,786;
room/board: $16,456
Financial aid: (312) 369-7140;
67% of undergrads determined to
have financial need; average aid
package $16,464

Concordia University Chicago
River Forest IL
(877) 282-4422
U.S. News ranking: Reg. U. (Mid.
W), No. 61
Website: www.cuchicago.edu/
Admissions email:
admission@cuchicago.edu
Private; founded 1864
Affiliation: Lutheran Church -
Missouri Synod
Freshman admissions: selective;
2020-2021: 4,786 applied,
3,759 accepted. Neither SAT
nor ACT required. SAT 25/75
percentile: 990-1180. High
school rank: N/A
Early decision deadline: N/A,
notification date: N/A
Early action deadline: N/A,
notification date: N/A
Application deadline (fall): rolling
Undergraduate student body: 1,288
full time, 194 part time; 43%
male, 57% female; 0% American
Indian, 2% Asian, 13% black,
34% Hispanic, 4% multiracial,
0% Pacific Islander, 46% white,
1% international; 68% from in
state; 24% live on campus; 0%
of students in fraternities, 0% in
sororities
Most popular majors: 25%
Business, Management,
Marketing, and Related Support
Services, 16% Education, 14%
Parks, Recreation, Leisure, and
Fitness Studies, 10% Health
Professions and Related Programs,
6% Psychology
Expenses: 2021-2022: $33,636;
room/board: $10,226
Financial aid: (708) 209-3113;
86% of undergrads determined to
have financial need; average aid
package $23,769

DePaul University
Chicago IL
(312) 362-8300
U.S. News ranking: Nat. U.,
No. 127
Website: www.depaul.edu/
Admissions email:
admission@depaul.edu
Private; founded 1898
Affiliation: Roman Catholic
Freshman admissions: selective;
2020-2021: 27,869 applied,
19,575 accepted. Neither SAT
nor ACT required. SAT 25/75
percentile: 1060-1280. High
school rank: N/A
Early decision deadline: N/A,
notification date: N/A
Early action deadline: 11/15,
notification date: 12/15
Application deadline (fall): 2/1

Undergraduate student body: 12,776 full time, 1,369 part time; 47% male, 53% female; 0% American Indian, 11% Asian, 8% black, 21% Hispanic, 5% multiracial, 0% Pacific Islander, 51% white, 2% international; 76% from in state; 1% live on campus; 5% of students in fraternities, 8% in sororities
Most popular majors: 32% Business, Management, Marketing, and Related Support Services, 12% Communication, Journalism, and Related Programs, 11% Visual and Performing Arts, 9% Computer and Information Sciences and Support Services, 7% Social Sciences
Expenses: 2021-2022: $42,012; room/board: $15,225
Financial aid: (312) 362-8520; 71% of undergrads determined to have financial need; average aid package $26,872

DeVry University[1]
Downers Grove IL
(630) 515-3000
U.S. News ranking: Reg. U. (Mid. W), second tier
Website: www.devry.edu
Admissions email: N/A
For-profit; founded 1931
Application deadline (fall): rolling
Undergraduate student body: N/A full time, N/A part time
Expenses: 2020-2021: $17,680; room/board: N/A
Financial aid: N/A

Dominican University
River Forest IL
(708) 524-6800
U.S. News ranking: Reg. U. (Mid. W), No. 10
Website: www.dom.edu/
Admissions email: domadmis@dom.edu
Private; founded 1901
Affiliation: Roman Catholic
Freshman admissions: selective; 2020-2021: 4,342 applied, 3,320 accepted. Neither SAT nor ACT required. SAT 25/75 percentile: 960-1160. High school rank: 20% in top tenth, 47% in top quarter, 81% in top half
Early decision deadline: N/A, notification date: N/A
Early action deadline: N/A, notification date: N/A
Application deadline (fall): 8/31
Undergraduate student body: 2,001 full time, 165 part time; 31% male, 69% female; 0% American Indian, 3% Asian, 5% black, 61% Hispanic, 1% multiracial, 0% Pacific Islander, 24% white, 1% international; 92% from in state; 17% live on campus; 0% of students in fraternities, 0% in sororities
Most popular majors: 12% Business Administration and Management, General, 9% Registered Nursing/Registered Nurse, 7% Psychology, General, 6% Criminology, 6% Sociology
Expenses: 2021-2022: $35,420; room/board: $10,865
F

inancial aid: (708) 524-6950; 81% of undergrads determined to have financial need; average aid package $25,943

Eastern Illinois University
Charleston IL
(877) 581-2348
U.S. News ranking: Reg. U. (Mid. W), No. 54
Website: www.eiu.edu
Admissions email: admissions@eiu.edu
Public; founded 1895
Freshman admissions: selective; 2020-2021: 8,923 applied, 4,992 accepted. Either SAT or ACT required. ACT 25/75 percentile: 18-23. High school rank: 17% in top tenth, 43% in top quarter, 76% in top half
Early decision deadline: N/A, notification date: N/A
Early action deadline: N/A, notification date: N/A
Application deadline (fall): 8/15
Undergraduate student body: 4,082 full time, 2,887 part time; 41% male, 59% female; 0% American Indian, 1% Asian, 22% black, 9% Hispanic, 3% multiracial, 0% Pacific Islander, 58% white, 2% international; 91% from in state; 28% live on campus; 6% of students in fraternities, 6% in sororities
Most popular majors: 15% Business, Management, Marketing, and Related Support Services, 11% Liberal Arts and Sciences, General Studies and Humanities, 10% Education, 9% Parks, Recreation, Leisure, and Fitness Studies, 9% Psychology
Expenses: 2021-2022: $12,562 in state, $14,930 out of state; room/board: $10,548
Financial aid: (217) 581-3713; 72% of undergrads determined to have financial need; average aid package $13,767

East-West University[1]
Chicago IL
(312) 939-0111
U.S. News ranking: Nat. Lib. Arts, second tier
Website: www.eastwest.edu
Admissions email: seeyou@eastwest.edu
Private; founded 1980
Application deadline (fall): rolling
Undergraduate student body: N/A full time, N/A part time
Expenses: 2020-2021: $22,650; room/board: N/A
Financial aid: N/A

Elmhurst University
Elmhurst IL
(630) 617-3400
U.S. News ranking: Reg. U. (Mid. W), No. 17
Website: www.elmhurst.edu/
Admissions email: admit@elmhurst.edu
Private; founded 1871
Affiliation: United Church of Christ
Freshman admissions: selective; 2020-2021: 4,299 applied, 2,817 accepted. Neither SAT nor ACT required. SAT 25/75

percentile: 980-1170. High school rank: 20% in top tenth, 46% in top quarter, 82% in top half
Early decision deadline: N/A, notification date: N/A
Early action deadline: 11/1, notification date: 12/1
Application deadline (fall): rolling
Undergraduate student body: 2,687 full time, 151 part time; 38% male, 62% female; 0% American Indian, 7% Asian, 6% black, 27% Hispanic, 3% multiracial, 0% Pacific Islander, 55% white, 1% international; 91% from in state; 26% live on campus; 7% of students in fraternities, 11% in sororities
Most popular majors: 24% Business, Management, Marketing, and Related Support Services, 14% Psychology, 13% Health Professions and Related Programs, 10% Education, 6% Visual and Performing Arts
Expenses: 2021-2022: $39,400; room/board: $11,172
Financial aid: (630) 617-3015; 79% of undergrads determined to have financial need; average aid package $31,545

Eureka College
Eureka IL
(309) 467-6350
U.S. News ranking: Reg. Coll. (Mid. W), No. 25
Website: www.eureka.edu
Admissions email: admissions@eureka.edu
Private; founded 1855
Affiliation: Christian Church (Disciples of Christ)
Freshman admissions: selective; 2020-2021: 1,098 applied, 675 accepted. Neither SAT nor ACT required. SAT 25/75 percentile: 940-1130. High school rank: 12% in top tenth, 33% in top quarter, 62% in top half
Early decision deadline: N/A, notification date: N/A
Early action deadline: N/A, notification date: N/A
Application deadline (fall): 8/15
Undergraduate student body: 485 full time, 26 part time; 51% male, 49% female; 1% American Indian, 1% Asian, 11% black, 2% Hispanic, 2% multiracial, 0% Pacific Islander, 79% white, 1% international; 94% from in state; N/A live on campus; N/A of students in fraternities, N/A in sororities
Most popular majors: 28% Business Administration and Management, General, 12% Homeland Security, Law Enforcement, Firefighting and Related Protective Services, 10% Psychology, General, 7% Elementary Education and Teaching, 6% Accounting
Expenses: 2021-2022: $28,110; room/board: $10,229
Financial aid: (309) 467-6310; 82% of undergrads determined to have financial need; average aid package $19,638

Governors State University
University Park IL
(708) 534-4490
U.S. News ranking: Reg. U. (Mid. W), second tier
Website: www.govst.edu/
Admissions email: admissions@govst.edu
Public; founded 1969
Freshman admissions: less selective; 2020-2021: 1,459 applied, 698 accepted. Either SAT or ACT required. SAT 25/75 percentile: 830-1050. High school rank: 11% in top tenth, 34% in top quarter, 67% in top half
Early decision deadline: 11/15, notification date: 12/15
Early action deadline: N/A, notification date: N/A
Application deadline (fall): 4/1
Undergraduate student body: 1,829 full time, 1,192 part time; 36% male, 64% female; 0% American Indian, 2% Asian, 38% black, 17% Hispanic, 3% multiracial, 0% Pacific Islander, 30% white, 1% international; 0% from in state; 3% live on campus; 0% of students in fraternities, 0% in sororities
Most popular majors: 19% Health Professions and Related Programs, 17% Business, Management, Marketing, and Related Support Services, 13% Liberal Arts and Sciences, General Studies and Humanities
Expenses: 2021-2022: $12,616 in state, $22,006 out of state; room/board: $10,729
Financial aid: (708) 534-4480

Greenville University[1]
Greenville IL
(618) 664-7100
U.S. News ranking: Reg. U. (Mid. W), No. 95
Website: www.greenville.edu
Admissions email: admissions@greenville.edu
Private; founded 1892
Affiliation: Free Methodist
Application deadline (fall): rolling
Undergraduate student body: N/A full time, N/A part time
Expenses: 2021-2022: $29,810; room/board: $9,348
Financial aid: (618) 664-7108; 79% of undergrads determined to have financial need; average aid package $23,300

Illinois College
Jacksonville IL
(217) 245-3030
U.S. News ranking: Nat. Lib. Arts, No. 146
Website: www.ic.edu
Admissions email: admissions@mail.ic.edu
Private; founded 1829
Affiliation: Presbyterian Church (USA)
Freshman admissions: selective; 2020-2021: 3,760 applied, 2,846 accepted. Neither SAT nor ACT required. SAT 25/75 percentile: 960-1160. High school rank: 18% in top tenth, 47% in top quarter, 83% in top half
Early decision deadline: N/A,

notification date: N/A
Early action deadline: 12/1, notification date: 12/23
Application deadline (fall): rolling
Undergraduate student body: 1,129 full time, 25 part time; 47% male, 53% female; 0% American Indian, 1% Asian, 10% black, 7% Hispanic, 3% multiracial, 0% Pacific Islander, 72% white, 3% international; N/A from in state; 86% live on campus; 0% of students in fraternities, 0% in sororities
Most popular majors: 29% Business, Management, Marketing, and Related Support Services, 10% Psychology, 9% Biological and Biomedical Sciences, 8% Social Sciences, 6% English Language and Literature/Letters
Expenses: 2021-2022: $35,302; room/board: $9,674
Financial aid: (217) 245-3035; 83% of undergrads determined to have financial need; average aid package $30,285

Illinois Institute of Technology
Chicago IL
(800) 448-2329
U.S. News ranking: Nat. U., No. 122
Website: www.iit.edu
Admissions email: admission@iit.edu
Private; founded 1890
Freshman admissions: more selective; 2020-2021: 5,033 applied, 3,053 accepted. Neither SAT nor ACT required. SAT 25/75 percentile: 1200-1390. High school rank: 41% in top tenth, 72% in top quarter, 91% in top half
Early decision deadline: N/A, notification date: N/A
Early action deadline: N/A, notification date: N/A
Application deadline (fall): 8/1
Undergraduate student body: 2,817 full time, 306 part time; 68% male, 32% female; 0% American Indian, 16% Asian, 5% black, 19% Hispanic, 4% multiracial, 0% Pacific Islander, 39% white, 15% international; 70% from in state; 9% live on campus; 5% of students in fraternities, 3% in sororities
Most popular majors: 51% Engineering, 21% Computer and Information Sciences and Support Services, 10% Architecture and Related Services, 4% Business, Management, Marketing, and Related Support Services, 3% Physical Sciences
Expenses: 2021-2022: $50,640; room/board: $15,570
Financial aid: (312) 567-7219; 68% of undergrads determined to have financial need; average aid package $42,793

Illinois State University
Normal IL
(309) 438-2181
U.S. News ranking: Nat. U., No. 202
Website: illinoisstate.edu/

Admissions email: admissions@ilstu.edu
Public; founded 1857
Freshman admissions: selective; 2020-2021: 15,487 applied, 12,593 accepted. Either SAT or ACT required. SAT 25/75 percentile: 1020-1220. High school rank: N/A
Early decision deadline: N/A, notification date: N/A
Early action deadline: N/A, notification date: N/A
Application deadline (fall): 4/1
Undergraduate student body: 16,666 full time, 1,321 part time; 43% male, 57% female; 0% American Indian, 2% Asian, 10% black, 12% Hispanic, 3% multiracial, 0% Pacific Islander, 71% white, 1% international; 97% from in state; 18% live on campus; 13% of students in fraternities, 14% in sororities
Most popular majors: 23% Business, Management, Marketing, and Related Support Services, 15% Education, 9% Health Professions and Related Programs, 6% Communication, Journalism, and Related Programs, 6% Visual and Performing Arts
Expenses: 2021-2022: $14,757 in state, $26,281 out of state; room/board: $9,850
Financial aid: (309) 438-2231; 63% of undergrads determined to have financial need; average aid package $12,415

Illinois Wesleyan University
Bloomington IL
(800) 332-2498
U.S. News ranking: Nat. Lib. Arts, No. 89
Website: www.iwu.edu
Admissions email: iwuadmit@iwu.edu
Private; founded 1850
Freshman admissions: more selective; 2020-2021: 3,896 applied, 2,218 accepted. Neither SAT nor ACT required. SAT 25/75 percentile: 1100-1300. High school rank: 26% in top tenth, 58% in top quarter, 94% in top half
Early decision deadline: N/A, notification date: N/A
Early action deadline: 11/15, notification date: 12/15
Application deadline (fall): rolling
Undergraduate student body: 1,622 full time, 14 part time; 48% male, 52% female; 0% American Indian, 7% Asian, 7% black, 9% Hispanic, 4% multiracial, 0% Pacific Islander, 70% white, 3% international; 70% from in state; 73% live on campus; 30% of students in fraternities, 32% in sororities
Most popular majors: 14% Accounting, 13% Business Administration and Management, General, 11% Registered Nursing/Registered Nurse, 6% Sociology, 6% Teacher Education and Professional Development, Specific Levels and Methods
Expenses: 2021-2022: $52,512; room/board: $12,112

Financial aid: (309) 556-3096; 72% of undergrads determined to have financial need; average aid package $38,765

Judson University
Elgin IL
(847) 628-2510
U.S. News ranking: Reg. U. (Mid. W), No. 95
Website: www.judsonu.edu
Admissions email: admissions@judsonu.edu
Private; founded 1963
Affiliation: American Baptist
Freshman admissions: selective; 2020-2021: 551 applied, 506 accepted. Neither SAT nor ACT required. SAT 25/75 percentile: 860-1120. High school rank: 8% in top tenth, 25% in top quarter, 60% in top half
Early decision deadline: N/A, notification date: N/A
Early action deadline: N/A, notification date: N/A
Application deadline (fall): rolling
Undergraduate student body: 856 full time, 99 part time; 44% male, 56% female; 0% American Indian, 2% Asian, 13% black, 30% Hispanic, 2% multiracial, 0% Pacific Islander, 40% white, 5% international; 82% from in state; 37% live on campus; 0% of students in fraternities, 0% in sororities
Most popular majors: 14% Business Administration and Management, General, 13% Architecture, 13% Public Administration and Social Service Professions, 11% Psychology, General, 6% Business Administration and Management, General
Expenses: 2021-2022: $29,870; room/board: $10,990
Financial aid: (847) 628-2531; 77% of undergrads determined to have financial need; average aid package $13,264

Knox College
Galesburg IL
(800) 678-5669
U.S. News ranking: Nat. Lib. Arts, No. 79
Website: www.knox.edu
Admissions email: admission@knox.edu
Private; founded 1837
Freshman admissions: more selective; 2020-2021: 3,111 applied, 2,205 accepted. Neither SAT nor ACT required. SAT 25/75 percentile: 1080-1320. High school rank: 24% in top tenth, 62% in top quarter, 94% in top half
Early decision deadline: 11/1, notification date: 12/15
Early action deadline: 11/1, notification date: 12/15
Application deadline (fall): 1/15
Undergraduate student body: 1,119 full time, 35 part time; 43% male, 57% female; 0% American Indian, 4% Asian, 8% black, 13% Hispanic, 6% multiracial, 0% Pacific Islander, 50% white, 16% international; 50% from in state; 73% live on campus; 21% of students in fraternities, 16%

in sororities
Most popular majors: 12% Creative Writing, 9% Biology/Biological Sciences, General, 9% Business/Commerce, General, 7% Research and Experimental Psychology, Other, 6% Computer Science
Expenses: 2021-2022: $51,576; room/board: $10,221
Financial aid: (309) 341-7149; 82% of undergrads determined to have financial need; average aid package $41,908

Lake Forest College
Lake Forest IL
(847) 735-5000
U.S. News ranking: Nat. Lib. Arts, No. 82
Website: www.lakeforest.edu
Admissions email: admissions@lakeforest.edu
Private; founded 1857
Freshman admissions: more selective; 2020-2021: 4,482 applied, 2,582 accepted. Neither SAT nor ACT required. SAT 25/75 percentile: 1085-1290. High school rank: 41% in top tenth, 74% in top quarter, 96% in top half
Early decision deadline: 11/1, notification date: 12/15
Early action deadline: 11/1, notification date: 12/15
Application deadline (fall): 2/15
Undergraduate student body: 1,526 full time, 32 part time; 41% male, 59% female; 0% American Indian, 5% Asian, 4% black, 18% Hispanic, 4% multiracial, 0% Pacific Islander, 49% white, 13% international; 65% from in state; 82% live on campus; 10% of students in fraternities, 11% in sororities
Most popular majors: 19% Business, Management, Marketing, and Related Support Services, 16% Social Sciences, 10% Biological and Biomedical Sciences, 8% Psychology, 7% Communication, Journalism, and Related Programs
Expenses: 2021-2022: $51,002; room/board: $11,498
Financial aid: (847) 735-5104; 81% of undergrads determined to have financial need; average aid package $44,575

Lewis University
Romeoville IL
(800) 897-9000
U.S. News ranking: Reg. U. (Mid. W), No. 19
Website: www.lewisu.edu
Admissions email: admissions@lewisu.edu
Private; founded 1932
Affiliation: Roman Catholic
Freshman admissions: selective; 2020-2021: 6,458 applied, 4,266 accepted. Neither SAT nor ACT required. SAT 25/75 percentile: 1010-1220. High school rank: 16% in top tenth, 45% in top quarter, 83% in top half
Early decision deadline: N/A, notification date: N/A
Early action deadline: 12/1, notification date: 12/22
Application deadline (fall): rolling

Undergraduate student body: 3,484 full time, 822 part time; 50% male, 50% female; 0% American Indian, 6% Asian, 6% black, 23% Hispanic, 3% multiracial, 0% Pacific Islander, 59% white, 2% international; 92% from in state; 22% live on campus; 2% of students in fraternities, 2% in sororities
Most popular majors: 11% Registered Nursing/Registered Nurse, 10% Criminal Justice/Safety Studies, 9% Computer Science, 7% Aviation/Airway Management and Operations, 7% Business Administration and Management, General
Expenses: 2021-2022: $35,462; room/board: $11,222
Financial aid: (815) 836-5263; 74% of undergrads determined to have financial need; average aid package $29,459

Lincoln College
Lincoln IL
(800) 569-0556
U.S. News ranking: Reg. Coll. (Mid. W), second tier
Website: www.lincolncollege.edu
Admissions email: admission@lincolncollege.edu
Private; founded 1865
Freshman admissions: less selective; 2020-2021: 1,403 applied, 980 accepted. Neither SAT nor ACT required. SAT 25/75 percentile: N/A. High school rank: N/A
Early decision deadline: N/A, notification date: N/A
Early action deadline: N/A, notification date: N/A
Application deadline (fall): rolling
Undergraduate student body: 688 full time, 279 part time; 43% male, 57% female; 0% American Indian, 1% Asian, 45% black, 7% Hispanic, 4% multiracial, 0% Pacific Islander, 38% white, 3% international; 91% from in state; 60% live on campus; 0% of students in fraternities, 0% in sororities
Most popular majors: 34% General Studies, 16% Business Administration and Management, General, 16% Organizational Leadership, 12% Criminal Justice/Law Enforcement Administration, 6% Sport and Fitness Administration/Management
Expenses: 2021-2022: $19,800; room/board: $8,400
Financial aid: (217) 735-7231; 99% of undergrads determined to have financial need

Loyola University Chicago
Chicago IL
(800) 262-2373
U.S. News ranking: Nat. U., No. 103
Website: www.luc.edu
Admissions email: admission@luc.edu
Private; founded 1870
Affiliation: Roman Catholic
Freshman admissions: more selective; 2020-2021: 25,453 applied, 17,954 accepted. Neither SAT nor ACT required. SAT

25/75 percentile: 1130-1330. High school rank: 39% in top tenth, 72% in top quarter, 93% in top half
Early decision deadline: N/A, notification date: N/A
Early action deadline: N/A, notification date: N/A
Application deadline (fall): rolling
Undergraduate student body: 10,924 full time, 688 part time; 33% male, 67% female; 0% American Indian, 13% Asian, 5% black, 18% Hispanic, 5% multiracial, 0% Pacific Islander, 54% white, 4% international; 61% from in state; 1% live on campus; 8% of students in fraternities, 15% in sororities
Most popular majors: 17% Registered Nursing/Registered Nurse, 11% Biology/Biological Sciences, General, 8% Psychology, General, 4% Finance, General, 4% Marketing/Marketing Management, General
Expenses: 2021-2022: $47,498; room/board: $15,180
Financial aid: (773) 508-7704; 61% of undergrads determined to have financial need; average aid package $35,050

McKendree University
Lebanon IL
(618) 537-6831
U.S. News ranking: Reg. U. (Mid. W), No. 54
Website: www.mckendree.edu
Admissions email: inquiry@mckendree.edu
Private; founded 1828
Affiliation: United Methodist
Freshman admissions: selective; 2020-2021: 1,965 applied, 1,377 accepted. Neither SAT nor ACT required. SAT 25/75 percentile: 871-1277. High school rank: 12% in top tenth, 33% in top quarter, 66% in top half
Early decision deadline: N/A, notification date: N/A
Early action deadline: N/A, notification date: N/A
Application deadline (fall): rolling
Undergraduate student body: 1,431 full time, 271 part time; 51% male, 49% female; 0% American Indian, 1% Asian, 12% black, 6% Hispanic, 5% multiracial, 0% Pacific Islander, 60% white, 5% international; N/A from in state; 68% live on campus; N/A of students in fraternities, N/A in sororities
Most popular majors: 12% Registered Nursing/Registered Nurse, 10% Business Administration and Management, General, 9% Psychology, General, 6% Accounting, 6% Management Science
Expenses: 2021-2022: $33,050; room/board: $10,970
Financial aid: (618) 537-6828; 71% of undergrads determined to have financial need; average aid package $24,971

Millikin University

Decatur IL
(217) 424-6210
U.S. News ranking: Reg. Coll. (Mid. W), No. 12
Website: millikin.edu
Admissions email: admis@millikin.edu
Private; founded 1901
Freshman admissions: selective; 2020-2021: 3,071 applied, 2,185 accepted. Neither SAT nor ACT required. SAT 25/75 percentile: 940-1160. High school rank: 14% in top tenth, 43% in top quarter, 72% in top half
Early decision deadline: N/A, notification date: N/A
Early action deadline: N/A, notification date: N/A
Application deadline (fall): rolling
Undergraduate student body: 1,784 full time, 91 part time; 43% male, 57% female; 0% American Indian, 2% Asian, 13% black, 4% Hispanic, 3% multiracial, 0% Pacific Islander, 69% white, 4% international; 77% from in state; 58% live on campus; 14% of students in fraternities, 22% in sororities
Most popular majors: 22% Visual and Performing Arts, 17% Business, Management, Marketing, and Related Support Services, 14% Education, 12% Health Professions and Related Programs, 6% Parks, Recreation, Leisure, and Fitness Studies
Expenses: 2021-2022: $39,592; room/board: $11,542
Financial aid: (217) 424-6317; 80% of undergrads determined to have financial need; average aid package $31,499

Monmouth College

Monmouth IL
(800) 747-2687
U.S. News ranking: Nat. Lib. Arts, No. 126
Website: www.monmouthcollege.edu/admissions
Admissions email: admissions@monmouthcollege.edu
Private; founded 1853
Affiliation: Presbyterian
Freshman admissions: selective; 2020-2021: 2,663 applied, 1,849 accepted. Neither SAT nor ACT required. SAT 25/75 percentile: 1050-1360. High school rank: 8% in top tenth, 38% in top quarter, 73% in top half
Early decision deadline: N/A, notification date: N/A
Early action deadline: N/A, notification date: N/A
Application deadline (fall): rolling
Undergraduate student body: 858 full time, 15 part time; 48% male, 52% female; 0% American Indian, 1% Asian, 9% black, 12% Hispanic, 4% multiracial, 0% Pacific Islander, 66% white, 2% international; 78% from in state; 93% live on campus; 18% of students in fraternities, 24% in sororities
Most popular majors: 18% Business/Commerce, General, 8% Kinesiology and Exercise Science, 5% Economics, General, 6% Psychology, General, 6% Speech Communication and Rhetoric

and Fitness Studies
Expenses: 2021-2022: $42,206; room/board: $13,680
Financial aid: (630) 637-5600; 75% of undergrads determined to have financial need; average aid package $30,885

National Louis University

Chicago IL
(888) 658-8632
U.S. News ranking: Nat. U., second tier
Website: www.nl.edu
Admissions email: nluinfo@nl.edu
Private
Freshman admissions: least selective; 2020-2021: 2,984 applied, 2,893 accepted. Neither SAT nor ACT required. SAT 25/75 percentile: N/A. High school rank: N/A
Early decision deadline: N/A, notification date: N/A
Early action deadline: N/A, notification date: N/A
Application deadline (fall): N/A
Undergraduate student body: 2,564 full time, 1,040 part time; 27% male, 73% female; 0% American Indian, 2% Asian, 20% black, 53% Hispanic, 2% multiracial, 0% Pacific Islander, 15% white, 2% international; N/A from in state; N/A live on campus; 0% of students in fraternities, 0% in sororities
Most popular majors: Information not available
Expenses: 2021-2022: $11,325; room/board: N/A
Financial aid: N/A

North Central College

Naperville IL
(630) 637-5800
U.S. News ranking: Reg. U. (Mid. W), No. 19
Website: www.northcentralcollege.edu
Admissions email: admissions@noctrl.edu
Private; founded 1861
Affiliation: United Methodist
Freshman admissions: selective; 2020-2021: 6,919 applied, 3,687 accepted. Neither SAT nor ACT required. SAT 25/75 percentile: 1050-1230. High school rank: 27% in top tenth, 30% in top quarter, 90% in top half
Early decision deadline: N/A, notification date: N/A
Early action deadline: N/A, notification date: N/A
Application deadline (fall): rolling
Undergraduate student body: 2,414 full time, 61 part time; 46% male, 54% female; 0% American Indian, 3% Asian, 4% black, 16% Hispanic, 3% multiracial, 0% Pacific Islander, 66% white, 3% international; N/A from in state; 59% live on campus; N/A of students in fraternities, N/A in sororities
Most popular majors: 24% Business, Management, Marketing, and Related Support Services, 11% Science Technologies/Technicians, 10% Social Sciences, 9% Education, 7% Parks, Recreation, Leisure,

Northeastern Illinois University

Chicago IL
(773) 442-4000
U.S. News ranking: Reg. U. (Mid. W), second tier
Website: www.neiu.edu
Admissions email: admrec@neiu.edu
Public; founded 1867
Freshman admissions: less selective; 2020-2021: 4,885 applied, 2,965 accepted. Either SAT or ACT required. SAT 25/75 percentile: 830-1020. High school rank: 7% in top tenth, 22% in top quarter, 52% in top half
Early decision deadline: N/A, notification date: N/A
Early action deadline: N/A, notification date: N/A
Application deadline (fall): 7/15
Undergraduate student body: 3,019 full time, 2,201 part time; 41% male, 59% female; 0% American Indian, 9% Asian, 11% black, 42% Hispanic, 2% multiracial, 0% Pacific Islander, 24% white, 1% international; N/A from in state; 3% live on campus; 1% of students in fraternities, 1% in sororities
Most popular majors: 23% Business, Management, Marketing, and Related Support Services, 11% Liberal Arts and Sciences, General Studies and Humanities, 10% Public Administration and Social Service Professions
Expenses: 2021-2022: $12,062 in state, $22,153 out of state; room/board: $9,742
Financial aid: (773) 442-5016; 70% of undergrads determined to have financial need; average aid package $11,276

Northern Illinois University

DeKalb IL
(815) 753-0446
U.S. News ranking: Nat. U., second tier
Website: www.niu.edu/
Admissions email: admissions@niu.edu
Public; founded 1895
Freshman admissions: selective; 2020-2021: 16,690 applied, 9,888 accepted. Neither SAT nor ACT required. SAT 25/75 percentile: 900-1140. High school rank: 14% in top tenth, 37% in top quarter, 73% in top half
Early decision deadline: N/A, notification date: N/A
Early action deadline: N/A, notification date: N/A
Application deadline (fall): 8/1
Undergraduate student body: 10,472 full time, 1,805 part time; 47% male, 53% female; 0% American Indian, 6% Asian, 19% black, 21% Hispanic, 4% multiracial, 0% Pacific Islander,

48% white, 1% international; 96% from in state; 20% live on campus; 3% of students in fraternities, 3% in sororities
Most popular majors: 6% Psychology, General, 5% Accounting, 5% Health/Medical Preparatory Programs, Other, 5% Registered Nursing/Registered Nurse, 5% Speech Communication and Rhetoric
Expenses: 2021-2022: $12,478 in state, $12,478 out of state; room/board: $11,000
Financial aid: (815) 753-1300; 71% of undergrads determined to have financial need; average aid package $13,425

North Park University

Chicago IL
(773) 244-5500
U.S. News ranking: Reg. U. (Mid. W), No. 41
Website: www.northpark.edu
Admissions email: admissions@northpark.edu
Private; founded 1891
Affiliation: Evangelical Covenant Church of America
Freshman admissions: selective; 2020-2021: 4,783 applied, 2,103 accepted. Neither SAT nor ACT required. SAT 25/75 percentile: 940-1120. High school rank: N/A
Early decision deadline: N/A, notification date: N/A
Early action deadline: N/A, notification date: N/A
Application deadline (fall): 7/1
Undergraduate student body: 1,684 full time, 169 part time; 41% male, 59% female; 0% American Indian, 10% Asian, 10% black, 32% Hispanic, 3% multiracial, 0% Pacific Islander, 35% white, 6% international; 84% from in state; 32% live on campus; 0% of students in fraternities, 0% in sororities
Most popular majors: 23% Business Administration and Management, General, 16% Registered Nursing/Registered Nurse, 7% Biology/Biological Sciences, General, 6% Health/Health Care Administration/Management, 5% Psychology, General
Expenses: 2020-2021: $32,100; room/board: $9,810
Financial aid: N/A

Northwestern University

Evanston IL
(847) 491-7271
U.S. News ranking: Nat. U., No. 9
Website: www.northwestern.edu
Admissions email: ug-admission@northwestern.edu
Private; founded 1851
Freshman admissions: most selective; 2020-2021: 39,263 applied, 3,654 accepted. Neither SAT nor ACT required. SAT 25/75 percentile: 1430-1550. High school rank: 95% in top tenth, 99% in top quarter, 100% in top half
Early decision deadline: 11/1, notification date: 12/15
Early action deadline: N/A,

notification date: N/A
Application deadline (fall): 1/3
Undergraduate student body: 7,975 full time, 219 part time; 48% male, 52% female; 0% American Indian, 20% Asian, 6% black, 13% Hispanic, 6% multiracial, 0% Pacific Islander, 41% white, 10% international; 30% from in state; 60% live on campus; 23% of students in fraternities, 16% in sororities
Most popular majors: Information not available
Expenses: 2021-2022: $60,984; room/board: $18,213
Financial aid: (847) 491-7400; 46% of undergrads determined to have financial need; average aid package $54,794

Olivet Nazarene University

Bourbonnais IL
(815) 939-5011
U.S. News ranking: Reg. U. (Mid. W), No. 64
Website: www.olivet.edu
Admissions email: admissions@olivet.edu
Private; founded 1907
Affiliation: Church of the Nazarene
Freshman admissions: selective; 2020-2021: 4,711 applied, 3,136 accepted. Neither SAT nor ACT required. SAT 25/75 percentile: 950-1180. High school rank: 18% in top tenth, 43% in top quarter, 70% in top half
Early decision deadline: N/A, notification date: N/A
Early action deadline: N/A, notification date: N/A
Application deadline (fall): rolling
Undergraduate student body: 2,562 full time, 240 part time; 41% male, 59% female; 0% American Indian, 2% Asian, 8% black, 11% Hispanic, 4% multiracial, 0% Pacific Islander, 71% white, 1% international
Most popular majors: 19% Registered Nursing/Registered Nurse, 10% Engineering, General, 7% Business Administration and Management, General, 4% Criminal Justice/Safety Studies, 4% Economics, General
Expenses: 2021-2022: $37,440; room/board: $9,490
Financial aid: (815) 939-5249; 82% of undergrads determined to have financial need; average aid package $32,537

Principia College

Elsah IL
(618) 374-5181
U.S. News ranking: Nat. Lib. Arts, No. 59
Website: www.principiacollege.edu
Admissions email: collegeadmissions@principia.edu
Private; founded 1910
Affiliation: Other
Freshman admissions: selective; 2020-2021: 74 applied, 69 accepted. Neither SAT nor ACT required. SAT 25/75 percentile: 1018-1206. High school rank: 17% in top tenth, 33% in top quarter, 50% in top half
Early decision deadline: N/A, notification date: N/A

Early action deadline: N/A, notification date: N/A
Application deadline (fall): 6/1
Undergraduate student body: 316 full time, 24 part time; 53% male, 47% female; 0% American Indian, 3% Asian, 2% black, 6% Hispanic, 2% multiracial, 1% Pacific Islander, 64% white, 20% international; 17% from in state; 72% live on campus; 0% of students in fraternities, 0% in sororities
Most popular majors: 17% Visual and Performing Arts, General, 14% Education, General, 13% Sociology and Anthropology, 9% Business Administration and Management, General, 9% Multi/Interdisciplinary Studies
Expenses: 2021-2022: $30,800; room/board: $12,270
Financial aid: (618) 374-5187; 64% of undergrads determined to have financial need; average aid package $30,938

Quincy University
Quincy IL
(217) 228-5210
U.S. News ranking: Reg. Coll. (Mid. W), No. 29
Website: www.quincy.edu
Admissions email: admissions@quincy.edu
Private; founded 1860
Affiliation: Roman Catholic
Freshman admissions: selective; 2020-2021: 1,223 applied, 821 accepted. Neither SAT nor ACT required. ACT 25/75 percentile: 19-25. High school rank: 18% in top tenth, 39% in top quarter, 77% in top half
Early decision deadline: N/A, notification date: N/A
Early action deadline: 11/15, notification date: 12/15
Application deadline (fall): rolling
Undergraduate student body: 931 full time, 161 part time; 48% male, 52% female; 0% American Indian, 1% Asian, 12% black, 4% Hispanic, 0% multiracial, 0% Pacific Islander, 74% white, 3% international
Most popular majors: 15% Registered Nursing/Registered Nurse, 9% Biology/Biological Sciences, General, 6% Finance, General
Expenses: 2021-2022: $31,160; room/board: $11,050
Financial aid: (217) 228-5260; 72% of undergrads determined to have financial need; average aid package $25,536

Rockford University
Rockford IL
(815) 226-4050
U.S. News ranking: Reg. U. (Mid. W), second tier
Website: www.rockford.edu
Admissions email: Admissions@Rockford.edu
Private; founded 1847
Freshman admissions: selective; 2020-2021: 2,021 applied, 1,027 accepted. Either SAT or ACT required. SAT 25/75 percentile: 900-1100. High school rank: 16% in top tenth, 33% in top quarter, 66% in top half

Early decision deadline: N/A, notification date: N/A
Early action deadline: N/A, notification date: N/A
Application deadline (fall): 8/15
Undergraduate student body: 948 full time, 71 part time; 43% male, 57% female; 0% American Indian, 2% Asian, 13% black, 18% Hispanic, 3% multiracial, 0% Pacific Islander, 52% white, 10% international
Most popular majors: 25% Registered Nursing/Registered Nurse, 21% Business Administration and Management, General, 8% Psychology, General, 6% Computer Science, 6% Health and Physical Education/Fitness, General
Expenses: 2021-2022: $34,000; room/board: $10,040
Financial aid: (815) 226-3385; 86% of undergrads determined to have financial need; average aid package $23,168

Roosevelt University
Chicago IL
(877) 277-5978
U.S. News ranking: Nat. U., second tier
Website: www.roosevelt.edu
Admissions email: admission@roosevelt.edu
Private; founded 1945
Freshman admissions: less selective; 2020-2021: 5,379 applied, 4,116 accepted. Neither SAT nor ACT required. SAT 25/75 percentile: 890-1130. High school rank: N/A
Early decision deadline: N/A, notification date: N/A
Early action deadline: N/A, notification date: N/A
Application deadline (fall): rolling
Undergraduate student body: 2,612 full time, 385 part time; 40% male, 60% female; 0% American Indian, 4% Asian, 20% black, 30% Hispanic, 2% multiracial, 0% Pacific Islander, 36% white, 3% international; 82% from in state; 18% live on campus; 0% of students in fraternities, 2% in sororities
Most popular majors: 15% Business/Commerce, General, 10% Psychology, General, 7% Accounting, 6% Hospitality Administration/Management, General, 5% Biology/Biological Sciences, General
Expenses: 2021-2022: $31,493; room/board: $12,000
Financial aid: (312) 341-3868; 87% of undergrads determined to have financial need; average aid package $30,000

Saint Xavier University
Chicago IL
(773) 298-3050
U.S. News ranking: Reg. U. (Mid. W), No. 54
Website: www.sxu.edu/admissions/
Admissions email: admission@sxu.edu
Private; founded 1846
Affiliation: Roman Catholic

Freshman admissions: selective; 2020-2021: 8,306 applied, 6,562 accepted. Neither SAT nor ACT required. SAT 25/75 percentile: 950-1120. High school rank: 20% in top tenth, 50% in top quarter, 84% in top half
Early decision deadline: N/A, notification date: N/A
Early action deadline: N/A, notification date: N/A
Application deadline (fall): rolling
Undergraduate student body: 2,878 full time, 202 part time; 36% male, 64% female; 0% American Indian, 3% Asian, 12% black, 44% Hispanic, 2% multiracial, 0% Pacific Islander, 37% white, 0% international; 96% from in state; 11% live on campus; 0% of students in fraternities, 0% in sororities
Most popular majors: 25% Business, Management, Marketing, and Related Support Services, 23% Health Professions and Related Programs, 10% Psychology, 6% Homeland Security, Law Enforcement, Firefighting and Related Protective Services, 5% Biological and Biomedical Sciences
Expenses: 2021-2022: $35,070; room/board: $11,640
Financial aid: (773) 298-3073; 88% of undergrads determined to have financial need; average aid package $29,976

School of the Art Institute of Chicago[1]
Chicago IL
(312) 629-6100
U.S. News ranking: Arts, unranked
Website: www.saic.edu
Admissions email: admiss@saic.edu
Private; founded 1866
Application deadline (fall): 4/15
Undergraduate student body: N/A full time, N/A part time
Expenses: 2020-2021: $52,200; room/board: $16,700
Financial aid: (312) 629-6600

Southern Illinois University–Carbondale
Carbondale IL
(618) 536-4405
U.S. News ranking: Nat. U., No. 263
Website: www.siu.edu
Admissions email: admissions@siu.edu
Public; founded 1869
Freshman admissions: selective; 2020-2021: 6,165 applied, 5,658 accepted. Neither SAT nor ACT required. SAT 25/75 percentile: 970-1345. High school rank: 15% in top tenth, 39% in top quarter, 68% in top half
Early decision deadline: N/A, notification date: N/A
Early action deadline: N/A, notification date: N/A
Application deadline (fall): rolling
Undergraduate student body: 6,765 full time, 1,486 part time; 52% male, 48% female; 0% American Indian, 2% Asian, 15% black, 10% Hispanic, 3% multiracial,

0% Pacific Islander, 67% white, 3% international; 80% from in state; 35% live on campus; 9% of students in fraternities, 6% in sororities
Most popular majors: 12% Business, Management, Marketing, and Related Support Services, 10% Education, 9% Engineering Technologies and Engineering-Related Fields, 9% Health Professions and Related Programs, 5% Transportation and Materials Moving
Expenses: 2021-2022: $15,240 in state, $15,240 out of state; room/board: $10,622
Financial aid: (618) 453-4613; 71% of undergrads determined to have financial need; average aid package $16,175

Southern Illinois University Edwardsville
Edwardsville IL
(618) 650-3705
U.S. News ranking: Nat. U., second tier
Website: www.siue.edu
Admissions email: admissions@siue.edu
Public; founded 1957
Affiliation: Undenominational
Freshman admissions: selective; 2020-2021: 8,773 applied, 7,461 accepted. Neither SAT nor ACT required. ACT 25/75 percentile: 21-27. High school rank: 21% in top tenth, 46% in top quarter, 78% in top half
Early decision deadline: N/A, notification date: N/A
Early action deadline: N/A, notification date: N/A
Application deadline (fall): 5/1
Undergraduate student body: 8,071 full time, 1,871 part time; 44% male, 56% female; 0% American Indian, 3% Asian, 13% black, 5% Hispanic, 4% multiracial, 0% Pacific Islander, 72% white, 2% international; 84% from in state; 19% live on campus; 7% of students in fraternities, 10% in sororities
Most popular majors: 19% Registered Nursing/Registered Nurse, 10% Business Administration and Management, General, 7% Psychology, General, 5% Biology/Biological Sciences, General, 5% Criminal Justice/Safety Studies
Expenses: 2021-2022: $12,300 in state, $12,300 out of state; room/board: $10,140
Financial aid: (618) 650-3834; 62% of undergrads determined to have financial need; average aid package $13,236

St. Augustine College[1]
Chicago IL
(773) 878-8756
U.S. News ranking: Reg. Coll. (Mid. W), No. 45
Website: www.staugustinecollege.edu/index.asp
Admissions email: info@staugustine.edu
Private
Application deadline (fall): N/A

Trinity Christian College
Palos Heights IL
(800) 748-0085
U.S. News ranking: Reg. Coll. (Mid. W), No. 19
Website: www.trnty.edu
Admissions email: admissions@trnty.edu
Private; founded 1959
Affiliation: Other
Freshman admissions: selective; 2020-2021: 1,208 applied, 769 accepted. Either SAT or ACT required. SAT 25/75 percentile: 980-1180. High school rank: 18% in top tenth, 23% in top quarter, 71% in top half
Early decision deadline: N/A, notification date: N/A
Early action deadline: N/A, notification date: N/A
Application deadline (fall): rolling
Undergraduate student body: 846 full time, 169 part time; 35% male, 65% female; 1% American Indian, 2% Asian, 12% black, 18% Hispanic, 0% multiracial, 0% Pacific Islander, 62% white, 4% international; N/A from in state; 58% live on campus; N/A of students in fraternities, N/A in sororities
Most popular majors: 23% Education, 22% Business, Management, Marketing, and Related Support Services, 15% Psychology, 11% Health Professions and Related Programs
Expenses: 2020-2021: $32,000; room/board: $10,100
Financial aid: (708) 239-4872

Trinity International University[1]
Deerfield IL
(800) 822-3225
U.S. News ranking: Nat. U., second tier
Website: www.tiu.edu
Admissions email: admissions@tiu.edu
Private; founded 1897
Affiliation: Evangelical Free Church of America
Application deadline (fall): rolling
Undergraduate student body: N/A full time, N/A part time
Expenses: 2020-2021: $33,298; room/board: $10,800
Financial aid: (847) 317-8060

University of Chicago
Chicago IL
(773) 702-8650
U.S. News ranking: Nat. U., No. 6
Website: www.uchicago.edu
Admissions email: collegeadmissions@uchicago.edu
Private; founded 1890
Freshman admissions: most selective; 2020-2021: 34,350 applied, 2,510 accepted. Neither SAT nor ACT required. SAT 25/75 percentile: 1500-1570. High school rank: 99% in top tenth, 100% in top quarter, 100% in

top half
Early decision deadline: 11/1, notification date: N/A
Early action deadline: 11/1, notification date: N/A
Application deadline (fall): 11/1
Undergraduate student body: 6,983 full time, 6 part time; 52% male, 48% female; 0% American Indian, 20% Asian, 5% black, 15% Hispanic, 7% multiracial, 0% Pacific Islander, 36% white, 15% international
Most popular majors: 21% Econometrics and Quantitative Economics, 8% Mathematics, General, 7% Biology/Biological Sciences, General, 6% Public Policy Analysis, General, 5% Political Science and Government, General
Expenses: 2021-2022: $60,963; room/board: $17,685
Financial aid: (773) 702-8666; 39% of undergrads determined to have financial need; average aid package $59,328

University of Illinois–Chicago

Chicago IL
(312) 996-4350
U.S. News ranking: Nat. U., No. 103
Website: www.uic.edu
Admissions email: admissions@uic.edu
Public; founded 1965
Freshman admissions: selective; 2020-2021: 22,798 applied, 16,558 accepted. Either SAT or ACT required. SAT 25/75 percentile: 1030-1250. High school rank: 32% in top tenth, 62% in top quarter, 91% in top half
Early decision deadline: N/A, notification date: N/A
Early action deadline: 11/1, notification date: 12/1
Application deadline (fall): 1/15
Undergraduate student body: 20,023 full time, 1,898 part time; 48% male, 52% female; 0% American Indian, 21% Asian, 8% black, 35% Hispanic, 3% multiracial, 0% Pacific Islander, 26% white, 6% international; 90% from in state; 6% live on campus; 5% of students in fraternities, 5% in sororities
Most popular majors: 16% Health Professions and Related Programs, 12% Education, 12% Library Science, 11% Visual and Performing Arts
Expenses: 2021-2022: $17,437 in state, $31,787 out of state; room/board: $12,000
Financial aid: (312) 996-5563; 74% of undergrads determined to have financial need; average aid package $15,982

University of Illinois–Springfield

Springfield IL
(217) 206-4847
U.S. News ranking: Reg. U. (Mid. W), No. 30
Website: www.uis.edu
Admissions email: admissions@uis.edu
Public; founded 1969

Freshman admissions: selective; 2020-2021: 3,634 applied, 2,810 accepted. Neither SAT nor ACT required. SAT 25/75 percentile: 980-1190. High school rank: 23% in top tenth, 46% in top quarter, 82% in top half
Early decision deadline: N/A, notification date: N/A
Early action deadline: N/A, notification date: N/A
Application deadline (fall): 8/23
Undergraduate student body: 1,840 full time, 814 part time; 47% male, 53% female; 0% American Indian, 4% Asian, 14% black, 11% Hispanic, 4% multiracial, 0% Pacific Islander, 62% white, 2% international; 87% from in state; 29% live on campus; 4% of students in fraternities, 3% in sororities
Most popular majors: 20% Business Administration and Management, General, 15% Computer Science, 10% Psychology, General, 7% Accounting, 5% Communication and Media Studies
Expenses: 2021-2022: $11,921 in state, $21,536 out of state; room/board: $9,760
Financial aid: (217) 206-6724; 67% of undergrads determined to have financial need; average aid package $14,429

University of Illinois–Urbana-Champaign

Champaign IL
(217) 333-0302
U.S. News ranking: Nat. U., No. 47
Website: illinois.edu
Admissions email: ugradadmissions@illinois.edu
Public; founded 1867
Freshman admissions: more selective; 2020-2021: 43,473 applied, 27,520 accepted. Either SAT or ACT required. SAT 25/75 percentile: 1210-1470. High school rank: 52% in top tenth, 86% in top quarter, 99% in top half
Early decision deadline: N/A, notification date: N/A
Early action deadline: 11/1, notification date: 12/14
Application deadline (fall): 1/5
Undergraduate student body: 32,107 full time, 1,576 part time; 54% male, 46% female; 0% American Indian, 20% Asian, 6% black, 14% Hispanic, 4% multiracial, 0% Pacific Islander, 42% white, 13% international; 11% from in state; 50% live on campus; 21% of students in fraternities, 27% in sororities
Most popular majors: 18% Engineering, 13% Business, Management, Marketing, and Related Support Services, 10% Social Sciences, 7% Communication, Journalism, and Related Programs, 5% Biological and Biomedical Sciences
Expenses: 2021-2022: $16,866 in state, $34,316 out of state; room/board: $12,494
Financial aid: (217) 333-0100; 47% of undergrads determined to have financial need; average aid package $19,452

Western Illinois University

Macomb IL
(309) 298-3157
U.S. News ranking: Reg. U. (Mid. W), No. 54
Website: www.wiu.edu
Admissions email: admissions@wiu.edu
Public; founded 1899
Freshman admissions: selective; 2020-2021: 7,603 applied, 5,091 accepted. Neither SAT nor ACT required. SAT 25/75 percentile: 880-1090. High school rank: 15% in top tenth, 40% in top quarter, 77% in top half
Early decision deadline: N/A, notification date: N/A
Early action deadline: N/A, notification date: N/A
Application deadline (fall): rolling
Undergraduate student body: 4,999 full time, 855 part time; 45% male, 55% female; 0% American Indian, 1% Asian, 22% black, 13% Hispanic, 3% multiracial, 0% Pacific Islander, 58% white, 1% international; 87% from in state; 72% live on campus; 16% of students in fraternities, 14% in sororities
Most popular majors: 20% Homeland Security, Law Enforcement, Firefighting and Related Protective Services, 14% Business, Management, Marketing, and Related Support

University of St. Francis

Joliet IL
(800) 735-7500
U.S. News ranking: Nat. U., No. 249
Website: www.stfrancis.edu
Admissions email: admissions@stfrancis.edu
Private; founded 1920
Affiliation: Roman Catholic
Freshman admissions: selective; 2020-2021: 1,914 applied, 1,145 accepted. Neither SAT nor ACT required. SAT 25/75 percentile: 970-1170. High school rank: N/A
Early decision deadline: N/A, notification date: N/A
Early action deadline: N/A, notification date: N/A
Application deadline (fall): 8/1
Undergraduate student body: 1,365 full time, 262 part time; 31% male, 69% female; 0% American Indian, 4% Asian, 9% black, 24% Hispanic, 3% multiracial, 0% Pacific Islander, 56% white, 3% international; 92% from in state; 18% live on campus; 1% of students in fraternities, 3% in sororities
Most popular majors: 26% Registered Nursing/Registered Nurse, 15% Health/Health Care Administration/Management, 5% Management Science, 5% Psychology, General, 4% Accounting
Expenses: 2021-2022: $35,000; room/board: $10,210
Financial aid: (815) 740-3403; 81% of undergrads determined to have financial need; average aid package $26,223

Wheaton College

Wheaton IL
(800) 222-2419
U.S. News ranking: Nat. Lib. Arts, No. 59
Website: www.wheaton.edu
Admissions email: admissions@wheaton.edu
Private; founded 1860
Affiliation: Protestant, not specified
Freshman admissions: more selective; 2020-2021: 1,800 applied, 1,566 accepted. Neither SAT nor ACT required. SAT 25/75 percentile: 1210-1450. High school rank: 49% in top tenth, 74% in top quarter, 91% in top half
Early decision deadline: N/A, notification date: N/A
Early action deadline: 11/1, notification date: 12/31
Application deadline (fall): 1/10
Undergraduate student body: 2,195 full time, 70 part time; 44% male, 56% female; 0% American Indian, 10% Asian, 3% black, 7% Hispanic, 6% multiracial, 0% Pacific Islander, 69% white, 4% international; N/A from in state; 81% live on campus; 0% of students in fraternities, 0% in sororities
Most popular majors: 19% Social Sciences, 10% Business, Management, Marketing, and Related Support Services, 7% Education
Expenses: 2021-2022: $40,570; room/board: $11,100
Financial aid: (630) 752-5021; 60% of undergrads determined to have financial need; average aid package $29,630

INDIANA

Anderson University

Anderson IN
(765) 641-4080
U.S. News ranking: Reg. U. (Mid. W), No. 46
Website: anderson.edu
Admissions email: info@anderson.edu
Private; founded 1917
Affiliation: Church of God
Freshman admissions: selective; 2020-2021: 3,836 applied, 2,597 accepted. Neither SAT nor ACT required. SAT 25/75 percentile: 950-1160. High school rank: 14% in top tenth, 42% in top quarter, 71% in top half
Early decision deadline: N/A, notification date: N/A
Early action deadline: N/A, notification date: N/A
Application deadline (fall): rolling

Services, 10% Liberal Arts and Sciences, General Studies and Humanities, 6% Agriculture, Agriculture Operations, and Related Sciences, 6% Communication, Journalism, and Related Programs
Expenses: 2021-2022: $12,079 in state, $12,079 out of state; room/board: $10,412
Financial aid: (309) 298-2446; 75% of undergrads determined to have financial need; average aid package $14,004

Undergraduate student body: 1,125 full time, 80 part time; 42% male, 58% female; 0% American Indian, 1% Asian, 7% black, 8% Hispanic, 5% multiracial, 0% Pacific Islander, 77% white, 1% international; 20% from in state; 61% live on campus; N/A of students in fraternities, N/A in sororities
Most popular majors: 17% Health Professions and Related Programs, 14% Education, 13% Business, Management, Marketing, and Related Support Services, 12% Visual and Performing Arts, 6% Psychology
Expenses: 2021-2022: $32,950; room/board: $11,710
Financial aid: (765) 641-4180; 86% of undergrads determined to have financial need; average aid package $30,543

Ball State University

Muncie IN
(765) 285-8300
U.S. News ranking: Nat. U., No. 202
Website: www.bsu.edu
Admissions email: askus@bsu.edu
Public; founded 1918
Freshman admissions: selective; 2020-2021: 24,475 applied, 16,859 accepted. Neither SAT nor ACT required. SAT 25/75 percentile: 1020-1200. High school rank: N/A
Early decision deadline: N/A, notification date: N/A
Early action deadline: N/A, notification date: N/A
Application deadline (fall): 8/10
Undergraduate student body: 14,334 full time, 1,446 part time; 39% male, 61% female; 0% American Indian, 2% Asian, 10% black, 7% Hispanic, 4% multiracial, 0% Pacific Islander, 76% white, 1% international; 87% from in state; 38% live on campus; 11% of students in fraternities, 10% in sororities
Most popular majors: 20% Business, Management, Marketing, and Related Support Services, 11% Communication, Journalism, and Related Programs, 10% Education, 8% Health Professions and Related Programs, 7% Liberal Arts and Sciences, General Studies and Humanities
Expenses: 2021-2022: $10,248 in state, $27,406 out of state; room/board: $10,904
Financial aid: (765) 285-5600; 67% of undergrads determined to have financial need; average aid package $14,630

Bethel University

Mishawaka IN
(800) 422-4101
U.S. News ranking: Reg. U. (Mid. W), No. 46
Website: www.betheluniversity.edu
Admissions email: admissions@betheluniversity.edu
Private; founded 1947
Affiliation: Missionary Church Inc
Freshman admissions: selective; 2020-2021: 1,235 applied, 1,146 accepted. Neither SAT nor ACT required. SAT 25/75

percentile: 930-1160. High school rank: 15% in top tenth, 40% in top quarter, 68% in top half
Early decision deadline: N/A, notification date: N/A
Early action deadline: N/A, notification date: N/A
Application deadline (fall): rolling
Undergraduate student body: 1,002 full time, 159 part time; 36% male, 64% female; 0% American Indian, 2% Asian, 9% black, 10% Hispanic, 6% multiracial, 0% Pacific Islander, 69% white, 4% international; 77% from in state; 67% live on campus; 0% of students in fraternities, 0% in sororities
Most popular majors: 20% Business, Management, Marketing, and Related Support Services, 18% Health Professions and Related Programs, 8% Education, 6% Biological and Biomedical Sciences, 6% Liberal Arts and Sciences, General Studies and Humanities
Expenses: 2021-2022: $30,830; room/board: $9,620
Financial aid: (574) 807-7239; 77% of undergrads determined to have financial need; average aid package $22,390

Butler University
Indianapolis IN
(317) 940-8100
U.S. News ranking: Reg. U. (Mid. W), No. 1
Website: www.butler.edu
Admissions email: admission@butler.edu
Private; founded 1855
Freshman admissions: more selective; 2020-2021: 14,592 applied, 11,045 accepted. Neither SAT nor ACT required. SAT 25/75 percentile: 1150-1320. High school rank: 50% in top tenth, 81% in top quarter, 96% in top half
Early decision deadline: N/A, notification date: N/A
Early action deadline: 11/1, notification date: 12/15
Application deadline (fall): rolling
Undergraduate student body: 4,339 full time, 145 part time; 40% male, 60% female; 0% American Indian, 3% Asian, 4% black, 6% Hispanic, 3% multiracial, 0% Pacific Islander, 83% white, 1% international; 45% from in state; 66% live on campus; 23% of students in fraternities, 36% in sororities
Most popular majors: 30% Business, Management, Marketing, and Related Support Services, 10% Communication, Journalism, and Related Programs, 9% Education, 9% Health Professions and Related Programs, 8% Social Sciences
Expenses: 2021-2022: $43,400; room/board: $14,380
Financial aid: (317) 940-8200; 53% of undergrads determined to have financial need; average aid package $27,253

Calumet College of St. Joseph
Whiting IN
(219) 473-4295
U.S. News ranking: Reg. U. (Mid. W), second tier
Website: www.ccsj.edu
Admissions email: admissions@ccsj.edu
Private; founded 1951
Affiliation: Roman Catholic
Freshman admissions: less selective; 2020-2021: 1,421 applied, 375 accepted. Neither SAT nor ACT required. SAT 25/75 percentile: 790-1005. High school rank: N/A
Early decision deadline: N/A, notification date: N/A
Early action deadline: N/A, notification date: N/A
Application deadline (fall): rolling
Undergraduate student body: 395 full time, 161 part time; 54% male, 46% female; 0% American Indian, 1% Asian, 23% black, 31% Hispanic, 4% multiracial, 0% Pacific Islander, 29% white, 0% international; 50% from in state; 8% live on campus; N/A of students in fraternities, N/A in sororities
Most popular majors: 49% Criminal Justice/Safety Studies, 17% Business Administration and Management, General, 6% English Language and Literature, General, 5% Elementary Education and Teaching
Expenses: 2021-2022: $21,010; room/board: $6,000
Financial aid: (219) 473-4296; 87% of undergrads determined to have financial need; average aid package $15,895

DePauw University
Greencastle IN
(800) 447-2495
U.S. News ranking: Nat. Lib. Arts, No. 46
Website: www.depauw.edu
Admissions email: admission@depauw.edu
Private; founded 1837
Freshman admissions: more selective; 2020-2021: 5,481 applied, 3,754 accepted. Either SAT or ACT required. SAT 25/75 percentile: 1110-1360. High school rank: 43% in top tenth, 69% in top quarter, 94% in top half
Early decision deadline: 11/1, notification date: 12/1
Early action deadline: 12/1, notification date: 1/15
Application deadline (fall): 2/1
Undergraduate student body: 1,718 full time, 34 part time; 48% male, 52% female; 0% American Indian, 3% Asian, 6% black, 9% Hispanic, 2% multiracial, 0% Pacific Islander, 63% white, 15% international; 45% from in state; 95% live on campus; 66% of students in fraternities, 57% in sororities
Most popular majors: 18% Social Sciences, 12% Biological and Biomedical Sciences, 11% Communication, Journalism, and Related Programs, 9% Visual and Performing Arts, 8% Computer and Information Sciences and Support Services
Expenses: 2021-2022: $53,896; room/board: $14,098
Financial aid: (765) 658-4030; 57% of undergrads determined to have financial need; average aid package $43,733

Earlham College
Richmond IN
(765) 983-1600
U.S. News ranking: Nat. Lib. Arts, No. 92
Website: earlham.edu
Admissions email: admission@earlham.edu
Private; founded 1847
Affiliation: Friends
Freshman admissions: more selective; 2020-2021: 2,201 applied, 1,300 accepted. Neither SAT nor ACT required. SAT 25/75 percentile: 1110-1340. High school rank: 31% in top tenth, 69% in top quarter, 90% in top half
Early decision deadline: N/A, notification date: N/A
Early action deadline: 12/1, notification date: 1/15
Application deadline (fall): 3/1
Undergraduate student body: 910 full time, 5 part time; 43% male, 57% female; 0% American Indian, 4% Asian, 8% black, 2% Hispanic, 6% multiracial, 0% Pacific Islander, 54% white, 23% international
Most popular majors: 12% Business Administration and Management, General, 5% Biology/Biological Sciences, General, 5% Research and Experimental Psychology, Other, 4% Computer Science, 4% English Language and Literature/ Letters, Other
Expenses: 2021-2022: $49,053; room/board: $11,854
Financial aid: (765) 983-1217; 87% of undergrads determined to have financial need; average aid package $45,953

Franklin College
Franklin IN
(317) 738-8062
U.S. News ranking: Nat. Lib. Arts, No. 146
Website: www.franklincollege.edu
Admissions email: admissions@franklincollege.edu
Private; founded 1834
Affiliation: American Baptist
Freshman admissions: selective; 2020-2021: 2,073 applied, 1,577 accepted. Neither SAT nor ACT required. SAT 25/75 percentile: 970-1150. High school rank: 12% in top tenth, 35% in top quarter, 76% in top half
Early decision deadline: N/A, notification date: N/A
Early action deadline: N/A, notification date: N/A
Application deadline (fall): rolling
Undergraduate student body: 896 full time, 42 part time; 48% male, 52% female; 0% American Indian, 1% Asian, 4% black, 4% Hispanic, 3% multiracial, 0% Pacific Islander, 86% white, 0% international; 93% from in state;

71% live on campus; 30% of students in fraternities, 30% in sororities
Most popular majors: 12% Kinesiology and Exercise Science, 10% Biology/Biological Sciences, General, 8% Public Relations/ Image Management, 7% Applied Mathematics, General, 6% Psychology, General
Expenses: 2021-2022: $34,966; room/board: $10,860
Financial aid: (317) 738-8075; 83% of undergrads determined to have financial need; average aid package $26,874

Goshen College
Goshen IN
(574) 535-7535
U.S. News ranking: Reg. Coll. (Mid. W), No. 8
Website: www.goshen.edu
Admissions email: admissions@goshen.edu
Private; founded 1894
Affiliation: Mennonite Church
Freshman admissions: selective; 2020-2021: 984 applied, 909 accepted. Neither SAT nor ACT required. SAT 25/75 percentile: 940-1180. High school rank: 25% in top tenth, 71% in top quarter, 88% in top half
Early decision deadline: N/A, notification date: N/A
Early action deadline: N/A, notification date: N/A
Application deadline (fall): 7/1
Undergraduate student body: 753 full time, 74 part time; 38% male, 62% female; 1% American Indian, 2% Asian, 4% black, 27% Hispanic, 3% multiracial, 0% Pacific Islander, 52% white, 8% international; 63% from in state; 54% live on campus; 0% of students in fraternities, 0% in sororities
Most popular majors: 22% Registered Nursing/Registered Nurse, 8% Molecular Biology, 6% Multi-/Interdisciplinary Studies, Other, 6% Sign Language Interpretation and Translation, 5% Accounting
Expenses: 2021-2022: $35,940; room/board: $10,980
Financial aid: (574) 535-7525; 77% of undergrads determined to have financial need; average aid package $29,503

Grace College and Seminary[1]
Winona Lake IN
(574) 372-5100
U.S. News ranking: Reg. U. (Mid. W), No. 106
Website: www.grace.edu
Admissions email: enroll@grace.edu
Private; founded 1948
Affiliation: Other
Application deadline (fall): 3/1
Undergraduate student body: N/A full time, N/A part time
Expenses: 2020-2021: $27,432; room/board: $9,828
Financial aid: (574) 372-5100

Hanover College
Hanover IN
(812) 866-7021
U.S. News ranking: Nat. Lib. Arts, No. 98
Website: www.hanover.edu
Admissions email: admission@hanover.edu
Private; founded 1827
Affiliation: Presbyterian Church (USA)
Freshman admissions: more selective; 2020-2021: 2,565 applied, 1,778 accepted. Neither SAT nor ACT required. SAT 25/75 percentile: 1060-1230. High school rank: 25% in top tenth, 59% in top quarter, 87% in top half
Early decision deadline: N/A, notification date: N/A
Early action deadline: 12/1, notification date: 12/1
Application deadline (fall): rolling
Undergraduate student body: 1,018 full time, 10 part time; 46% male, 54% female; 0% American Indian, 1% Asian, 4% black, 4% Hispanic, 3% multiracial, 0% Pacific Islander, 76% white, 3% international; 67% from in state; 88% live on campus; 37% of students in fraternities, 36% in sororities
Most popular majors: 17% Parks, Recreation, Leisure, and Fitness Studies, 16% Homeland Security, Law Enforcement, Firefighting and Related Protective Services, 12% Biological and Biomedical Sciences, 10% Communication, Journalism, and Related Programs, 7% Psychology
Expenses: 2021-2022: $40,250; room/board: $12,540
Financial aid: (812) 866-7091; 75% of undergrads determined to have financial need; average aid package $35,067

Holy Cross College at Notre Dame, Indiana
Notre Dame IN
(574) 239-8400
U.S. News ranking: Reg. Coll. (Mid. W), No. 23
Website: www.hcc-nd.edu
Admissions email: admissions@hcc-nd.edu
Private; founded 1966
Affiliation: Roman Catholic
Freshman admissions: more selective; 2020-2021: 644 applied, 496 accepted. Neither SAT nor ACT required. SAT 25/75 percentile: 1070-1370. High school rank: 28% in top tenth, 57% in top quarter, 91% in top half
Early decision deadline: N/A, notification date: N/A
Early action deadline: 11/1, notification date: 11/20
Application deadline (fall): 7/28
Undergraduate student body: 415 full time, 40 part time; 56% male, 44% female; 0% American Indian, 2% Asian, 6% black, 22% Hispanic, 5% multiracial, 0% Pacific Islander, 55% white, 5% international; 48% from in state; 72% live on campus; 0% of students in fraternities, 0% in sororities

More @ usnews.com/bestcolleges

Most popular majors: 43% Business/Commerce, General, 21% Psychology, General, 14% Communication and Media Studies, 8% Liberal Arts and Sciences/Liberal Studies, 4% Fine/Studio Arts, General
Expenses: 2021-2022: $34,050; room/board: $11,650
Financial aid: (574) 239-8400; 63% of undergrads determined to have financial need; average aid package $32,630

Huntington University
Huntington IN
(800) 642-6493
U.S. News ranking: Reg. U. (Mid. W), No. 31
Website: www.huntington.edu
Admissions email: admissions@huntington.edu
Private; founded 1897
Affiliation: Other
Freshman admissions: selective; 2020-2021: 1,070 applied, 831 accepted. Neither SAT nor ACT required. SAT 25/75 percentile: 970-1198. High school rank: 18% in top tenth, 47% in top quarter, 77% in top half
Early decision deadline: N/A, notification date: N/A
Early action deadline: N/A, notification date: N/A
Application deadline (fall): 8/1
Undergraduate student body: 903 full time, 247 part time; 40% male, 60% female; 0% American Indian, 1% Asian, 3% black, 6% Hispanic, 5% multiracial, 0% Pacific Islander, 80% white, 3% international
Most popular majors: 19% Visual and Performing Arts, 12% Education, 11% Business, Management, Marketing, and Related Support Services, 10% Health Professions and Related Programs, 6% Communication, Journalism, and Related Programs
Expenses: 2021-2022: $28,192; room/board: $9,154
Financial aid: (260) 359-4326; 76% of undergrads determined to have financial need; average aid package $19,589

Indiana State University
Terre Haute IN
(812) 237-2121
U.S. News ranking: Nat. U., second tier
Website: www.indstate.edu/
Admissions email: admissions@indstate.edu
Public; founded 1865
Freshman admissions: selective; 2020-2021: 13,477 applied, 12,438 accepted. Neither SAT nor ACT required. SAT 25/75 percentile: 910-1130. High school rank: 11% in top tenth, 32% in top quarter, 70% in top half
Early decision deadline: N/A, notification date: N/A
Early action deadline: N/A, notification date: N/A
Application deadline (fall): 8/15
Undergraduate student body: 7,420 full time, 1,519 part time; 43% male, 57% female; 0% American Indian, 2% Asian, 17% black,

6% Hispanic, 4% multiracial, 0% Pacific Islander, 69% white, 2% international; 70% from in state; 31% live on campus; 11% of students in fraternities, 11% in sororities
Most popular majors: 18% Business, Management, Marketing, and Related Support Services, 16% Health Professions and Related Programs, 9% Social Sciences, 8% Education, 8% Engineering Technologies and Engineering-Related Fields
Expenses: 2020-2021: $9,466 in state, $20,570 out of state; room/board: $11,016
Financial aid: (800) 841-4744; 71% of undergrads determined to have financial need; average aid package $10,478

Indiana Tech
Fort Wayne IN
(800) 937-2448
U.S. News ranking: Reg. U. (Mid. W), No. 108
Website: www.indianatech.edu
Admissions email: admissions@indianatech.edu
Private; founded 1930
Freshman admissions: selective; 2020-2021: 3,396 applied, 2,142 accepted. Neither SAT nor ACT required. SAT 25/75 percentile: 920-1130. High school rank: N/A
Early decision deadline: N/A, notification date: N/A
Early action deadline: N/A, notification date: N/A
Application deadline (fall): 8/1
Undergraduate student body: 1,435 full time, 64 part time; 62% male, 38% female; 0% American Indian, 2% Asian, 18% black, 7% Hispanic, 6% multiracial, 0% Pacific Islander, 51% white, 11% international; 57% from in state; 44% live on campus; 2% of students in fraternities, N/A in sororities
Most popular majors: 17% Business Administration and Management, General, 11% Criminal Justice/Safety Studies, 8% Electrical and Electronics Engineering, 6% Computer and Information Systems Security/Information Assurance, 6% Environmental/Environmental Health Engineering
Expenses: 2021-2022: $28,840; room/board: $12,614
Financial aid: (260) 422-5561; 79% of undergrads determined to have financial need; average aid package $30,026

Indiana University–Bloomington
Bloomington IN
(812) 855-0661
U.S. News ranking: Nat. U., No. 68
Website: www.indiana.edu
Admissions email: admissions@indiana.edu
Public; founded 1820
Freshman admissions: more selective; 2020-2021: 44,129 applied, 35,469 accepted. Neither SAT nor ACT required. SAT 25/75 percentile: 1120-1350. High school rank: 32% in top

tenth, 66% in top quarter, 94% in top half
Early decision deadline: N/A, notification date: N/A
Early action deadline: 11/1, notification date: 1/15
Application deadline (fall): rolling
Undergraduate student body: 31,632 full time, 1,354 part time; 50% male, 50% female; 0% American Indian, 7% Asian, 5% black, 8% Hispanic, 5% multiracial, 0% Pacific Islander, 69% white, 6% international; 64% from in state; 27% live on campus; 21% of students in fraternities, 21% in sororities
Most popular majors: 26% Business, Management, Marketing, and Related Support Services, 8% Biological and Biomedical Sciences, 8% Communication, Journalism, and Related Programs, 8% Computer and Information Sciences and Support Services, 8% Public Administration and Social Service Professions
Expenses: 2021-2022: $11,334 in state, $38,354 out of state; room/board: $11,598
Financial aid: (812) 855-6500; 40% of undergrads determined to have financial need; average aid package $14,643

Indiana University East
Richmond IN
(765) 973-8208
U.S. News ranking: Reg. U. (Mid. W), No. 112
Website: www.iue.edu
Admissions email: applynow@iue.edu
Public; founded 1971
Freshman admissions: selective; 2020-2021: 1,980 applied, 1,333 accepted. Neither SAT nor ACT required. SAT 25/75 percentile: 920-1120. High school rank: 10% in top tenth, 34% in top quarter, 70% in top half
Early decision deadline: N/A, notification date: N/A
Early action deadline: N/A, notification date: N/A
Application deadline (fall): rolling
Undergraduate student body: 1,916 full time, 1,284 part time; 35% male, 65% female; 0% American Indian, 1% Asian, 6% black, 6% Hispanic, 4% multiracial, 0% Pacific Islander, 76% white, 2% international; 69% from in state; 0% live on campus; 0% of students in fraternities, 0% in sororities
Most popular majors: 29% Business, Management, Marketing, and Related Support Services, 14% Psychology, 10% Health Professions and Related Programs, 7% Liberal Arts and Sciences, General Studies and Humanities, 6% Homeland Security, Law Enforcement, Firefighting and Related Protective Services
Expenses: 2021-2022: $7,828 in state, $20,936 out of state; room/board: N/A

Financial aid: (765) 973-8206; 69% of undergrads determined to have financial need; average aid package $9,369

Indiana University–Kokomo
Kokomo IN
(765) 455-9217
U.S. News ranking: Reg. Coll. (Mid. W), No. 55
Website: www.iuk.edu
Admissions email: iuadmis@iuk.edu
Public; founded 1945
Freshman admissions: selective; 2020-2021: 2,319 applied, 1,918 accepted. Neither SAT nor ACT required. SAT 25/75 percentile: 940-1130. High school rank: 10% in top tenth, 31% in top quarter, 69% in top half
Early decision deadline: N/A, notification date: N/A
Early action deadline: N/A, notification date: N/A
Application deadline (fall): rolling
Undergraduate student body: 2,417 full time, 599 part time; 35% male, 65% female; 0% American Indian, 1% Asian, 5% black, 8% Hispanic, 4% multiracial, 0% Pacific Islander, 80% white, 1% international; 97% from in state; 0% live on campus; 0% of students in fraternities, 0% in sororities
Most popular majors: 39% Health Professions and Related Programs, 14% Business, Management, Marketing, and Related Support Services, 12% Liberal Arts and Sciences, General Studies and Humanities, 6% Education, 4% Homeland Security, Law Enforcement, Firefighting and Related Protective Services
Expenses: 2021-2022: $7,828 in state, $20,936 out of state; room/board: N/A
Financial aid: (765) 455-9216; 59% of undergrads determined to have financial need; average aid package $9,063

Indiana University Northwest
Gary IN
(219) 980-6991
U.S. News ranking: Reg. U. (Mid. W), second tier
Website: www.iun.edu
Admissions email: admit@iun.edu
Public; founded 1948
Freshman admissions: less selective; 2020-2021: 2,506 applied, 2,047 accepted. Neither SAT nor ACT required. SAT 25/75 percentile: 890-1090. High school rank: 13% in top tenth, 37% in top quarter, 70% in top half
Early decision deadline: N/A, notification date: N/A
Early action deadline: N/A, notification date: N/A
Application deadline (fall): rolling
Undergraduate student body: 2,476 full time, 938 part time; 28% male, 72% female; 0% American Indian, 3% Asian, 15% black, 26% Hispanic, 4% multiracial, 0% Pacific Islander, 50% white, 1% international; 96% from in state; 0% live on campus; 0%

of students in fraternities, 0% in sororities
Most popular majors: 30% Health Professions and Related Programs, 11% Business, Management, Marketing, and Related Support Services, 10% Liberal Arts and Sciences, General Studies and Humanities, 8% Psychology, 7% Public Administration and Social Service Professions
Expenses: 2021-2022: $7,828 in state, $20,936 out of state; room/board: N/A
Financial aid: (219) 980-6778; 68% of undergrads determined to have financial need; average aid package $9,221

Indiana University-Purdue University–Indianapolis
Indianapolis IN
(317) 274-4591
U.S. News ranking: Nat. U., No. 196
Website: www.iupui.edu
Admissions email: apply@iupui.edu
Public; founded 1969
Freshman admissions: selective; 2020-2021: 16,220 applied, 12,739 accepted. Neither SAT nor ACT required. SAT 25/75 percentile: 1000-1190. High school rank: 17% in top tenth, 45% in top quarter, 85% in top half
Early decision deadline: N/A, notification date: N/A
Early action deadline: N/A, notification date: N/A
Application deadline (fall): 5/15
Undergraduate student body: 17,311 full time, 3,655 part time; 40% male, 60% female; 0% American Indian, 6% Asian, 10% black, 10% Hispanic, 5% multiracial, 0% Pacific Islander, 65% white, 3% international; 94% from in state; 8% live on campus; 1% of students in fraternities, 2% in sororities
Most popular majors: 20% Health Professions and Related Programs, 16% Business, Management, Marketing, and Related Support Services, 7% Engineering, 6% Computer and Information Sciences and Support Services, 6% Liberal Arts and Sciences, General Studies and Humanities
Expenses: 2021-2022: $10,044 in state, $32,101 out of state; room/board: $10,617
Financial aid: (317) 274-4162; 65% of undergrads determined to have financial need; average aid package $12,379

Indiana University–South Bend
South Bend IN
(574) 520-4839
U.S. News ranking: Reg. U. (Mid. W), second tier
Website: www.iusb.edu
Admissions email: admissions@iusb.edu
Public; founded 1961
Freshman admissions: selective; 2020-2021: 2,712 applied, 2,356 accepted. Neither SAT nor ACT required. SAT 25/75

percentile: 930-1140. High school rank: 10% in top tenth, 32% in top quarter, 65% in top half
Early decision deadline: N/A, notification date: N/A
Early action deadline: N/A, notification date: N/A
Application deadline (fall): rolling
Undergraduate student body: 3,350 full time, 1,025 part time; 35% male, 65% female; 0% American Indian, 2% Asian, 8% black, 15% Hispanic, 6% multiracial, 0% Pacific Islander, 66% white, 3% international; 94% from in state; 6% live on campus; 0% of students in fraternities, 0% in sororities
Most popular majors: 24% Health Professions and Related Programs, 23% Business, Management, Marketing, and Related Support Services, 10% Liberal Arts and Sciences, General Studies and Humanities, 8% Education, 5% Public Administration and Social Service Professions
Expenses: 2021-2022: $7,828 in state, $20,936 out of state; room/board: $7,457
Financial aid: (574) 520-4357; 65% of undergrads determined to have financial need; average aid package $9,572

Indiana University Southeast
New Albany IN
(812) 941-2212
U.S. News ranking: Reg. U. (Mid. W), second tier
Website: www.ius.edu
Admissions email: admissions@ius.edu
Public; founded 1941
Freshman admissions: selective; 2020-2021: 2,549 applied, 2,177 accepted. Neither SAT nor ACT required. ACT 25/75 percentile: 17-23. High school rank: 12% in top tenth, 34% in top quarter, 69% in top half
Early decision deadline: N/A, notification date: N/A
Early action deadline: N/A, notification date: N/A
Application deadline (fall): 8/9
Undergraduate student body: 2,901 full time, 1,189 part time; 38% male, 62% female; 0% American Indian, 2% Asian, 7% black, 6% Hispanic, 4% multiracial, 0% Pacific Islander, 81% white, 1% international; 70% from in state; 5% live on campus; 1% of students in fraternities, 3% in sororities
Most popular majors: 21% Business, Management, Marketing, and Related Support Services, 12% Liberal Arts and Sciences, General Studies and Humanities, 11% Health Professions and Related Programs, 10% Psychology, 8% Education
Expenses: 2021-2022: $7,828 in state, $20,936 out of state; room/board: $7,200
Financial aid: (812) 941-2100; 57% of undergrads determined to have financial need; average aid package $8,737

Indiana Wesleyan University
Marion IN
(866) 468-6498
U.S. News ranking: Reg. U. (Mid. W), No. 19
Website: www.indwes.edu
Admissions email: admissions@indwes.edu
Private; founded 1920
Affiliation: Wesleyan
Freshman admissions: selective; 2020-2021: 2,942 applied, 2,691 accepted. Neither SAT nor ACT required. SAT 25/75 percentile: 1010-1200. High school rank: 27% in top tenth, 54% in top quarter, 84% in top half
Early decision deadline: N/A, notification date: N/A
Early action deadline: N/A, notification date: N/A
Application deadline (fall): rolling
Undergraduate student body: 2,415 full time, 262 part time; 35% male, 65% female; 0% American Indian, 2% Asian, 4% black, 4% Hispanic, 3% multiracial, 0% Pacific Islander, 83% white, 2% international
Most popular majors: 22% Registered Nursing/Registered Nurse, 6% Psychology, General, 5% Elementary Education and Teaching, 4% Exercise Physiology, 4% Social Work
Expenses: 2021-2022: $28,960; room/board: $9,574
Financial aid: (765) 677-2116; 75% of undergrads determined to have financial need; average aid package $31,512

Manchester University[1]
North Manchester IN
(800) 852-3648
U.S. News ranking: Reg. Coll. (Mid. W), No. 35
Website: www.manchester.edu
Admissions email: admitinfo@manchester.edu
Private; founded 1889
Affiliation: Church of Brethren
Application deadline (fall): rolling
Undergraduate student body: N/A full time, N/A part time
Expenses: 2020-2021: $34,436; room/board: $10,122
Financial aid: (260) 982-5237

Marian University
Indianapolis IN
(317) 955-6300
U.S. News ranking: Reg. U. (Mid. W), No. 27
Website: www.marian.edu
Admissions email: admissions@marian.edu
Private; founded 1851
Affiliation: Roman Catholic
Freshman admissions: selective; 2020-2021: 2,816 applied, 1,809 accepted. Neither SAT nor ACT required. SAT 25/75 percentile: 980-1180. High school rank: 21% in top tenth, 48% in top quarter, 80% in top half
Early decision deadline: N/A, notification date: N/A
Early action deadline: N/A, notification date: N/A

Application deadline (fall): 8/1
Undergraduate student body: 2,218 full time, 348 part time; 35% male, 65% female; 0% American Indian, 3% Asian, 13% black, 8% Hispanic, 5% multiracial, 0% Pacific Islander, 66% white, 2% international; 77% from in state; 42% live on campus; 0% of students in fraternities, 0% in sororities
Most popular majors: 55% Registered Nursing/Registered Nurse, 7% Business Administration and Management, General, 4% Biology/Biological Sciences, General, 3% Kinesiology and Exercise Science, 2% Marketing/Marketing Management, General
Expenses: 2021-2022: $36,600; room/board: $11,660
Financial aid: (317) 955-6040; 76% of undergrads determined to have financial need; average aid package $29,907

Martin University[1]
Indianapolis IN
(317) 543-3235
U.S. News ranking: Reg. Coll. (Mid. W), second tier
Website: www.martin.edu
Admissions email: admissions@martin.edu
Private
Application deadline (fall): N/A
Undergraduate student body: N/A full time, N/A part time
Expenses: 2020-2021: $13,200; room/board: N/A
Financial aid: N/A

Oakland City University
Oakland City IN
(800) 737-5125
U.S. News ranking: Reg. Coll. (Mid. W), No. 28
Website: www.oak.edu
Admissions email: admission@oak.edu
Private; founded 1885
Affiliation: General Baptist
Freshman admissions: less selective; 2020-2021: 913 applied, 577 accepted. Neither SAT nor ACT required. SAT 25/75 percentile: 912-1136. High school rank: 7% in top tenth, 32% in top quarter, 56% in top half
Early decision deadline: N/A, notification date: N/A
Early action deadline: N/A, notification date: N/A
Application deadline (fall): rolling
Undergraduate student body: 611 full time, 489 part time; 45% male, 55% female; 0% American Indian, 2% Asian, 9% black, 3% Hispanic, 6% multiracial, 0% Pacific Islander, 71% white, 5% international; 80% from in state; 58% live on campus; 0% of students in fraternities, 0% in sororities
Most popular majors: 42% Business, Management, Marketing, and Related Support Services, 12% Education, 11% Homeland Security, Law Enforcement, Firefighting and Related Protective Services, 8% Psychology, 7% Biological and

Biomedical Sciences
Expenses: 2021-2022: $25,740; room/board: $10,400
Financial aid: (812) 749-1225; 81% of undergrads determined to have financial need; average aid package $15,000

Purdue University–Fort Wayne
Fort Wayne IN
(260) 481-6812
U.S. News ranking: Reg. U. (Mid. W), No. 106
Website: www.pfw.edu
Admissions email: ask@pfw.edu
Public; founded 1964
Freshman admissions: selective; 2020-2021: 5,540 applied, 4,586 accepted. Either SAT or ACT required. SAT 25/75 percentile: 980-1180. High school rank: 13% in top tenth, 39% in top quarter, 72% in top half
Early decision deadline: N/A, notification date: N/A
Early action deadline: N/A, notification date: N/A
Application deadline (fall): 8/1
Undergraduate student body: 5,161 full time, 2,423 part time; 47% male, 53% female; 0% American Indian, 4% Asian, 7% black, 9% Hispanic, 5% multiracial, 0% Pacific Islander, 72% white, 2% international; 93% from in state; 16% live on campus; 0% of students in fraternities, 1% in sororities
Most popular majors: 19% Business, Management, Marketing, and Related Support Services, 13% Health Professions and Related Programs, 10% Education, 7% Liberal Arts and Sciences, General Studies and Humanities, 7% Public Administration and Social Service Professions
Expenses: 2021-2022: $24,919 in state, $25,689 out of state; room/board: $1,332
Financial aid: (260) 481-6820; 67% of undergrads determined to have financial need; average aid package $10,758

Purdue University Global[1]
IN
(765) 494-1776
U.S. News ranking: Reg. Coll. (Mid. W), No. 53
Admissions email: admissions@purdue.edu
Public; founded 1869
Application deadline (fall): N/A
Undergraduate student body: N/A full time, N/A part time
Expenses: N/A
Financial aid: N/A

Purdue University–Northwest
Hammond IN
(219) 989-2213
U.S. News ranking: Reg. U. (Mid. W), No. 112
Website: www.pnw.edu/
Admissions email: admissons@pnw.edu
Public; founded 2016

Freshman admissions: selective; 2020-2021: 5,300 applied, 1,605 accepted. Neither SAT nor ACT required. SAT 25/75 percentile: 960-1150. High school rank: 14% in top tenth, 39% in top quarter, 76% in top half
Early decision deadline: N/A, notification date: N/A
Early action deadline: N/A, notification date: N/A
Application deadline (fall): 8/1
Undergraduate student body: 5,196 full time, 2,050 part time; 44% male, 56% female; 0% American Indian, 3% Asian, 10% black, 23% Hispanic, 3% multiracial, 0% Pacific Islander, 58% white, 2% international; N/A from in state; 7% live on campus; N/A of students in fraternities, N/A in sororities
Most popular majors: 30% Registered Nursing/Registered Nurse, 5% Business Administration and Management, General, 4% Accounting, 4% Engineering/Industrial Management, 4% Mechanical Engineering
Expenses: 2021-2022: $8,057 in state, $11,688 out of state; room/board: N/A
Financial aid: (855) 608-4600; 64% of undergrads determined to have financial need; average aid package $2,685

Purdue University–West Lafayette
West Lafayette IN
(765) 494-1776
U.S. News ranking: Nat. U., No. 49
Website: www.purdue.edu
Admissions email: admissions@purdue.edu
Public; founded 1869
Freshman admissions: more selective; 2020-2021: 57,279 applied, 38,457 accepted. Either SAT or ACT required. SAT 25/75 percentile: 1190-1430. High school rank: 48% in top tenth, 79% in top quarter, 97% in top half
Early decision deadline: N/A, notification date: N/A
Early action deadline: 11/1, notification date: 12/12
Application deadline (fall): rolling
Undergraduate student body: 33,069 full time, 1,851 part time; 57% male, 43% female; 0% American Indian, 11% Asian, 3% black, 6% Hispanic, 4% multiracial, 0% Pacific Islander, 63% white, 12% international; 54% from in state; 36% live on campus; 14% of students in fraternities, 18% in sororities
Most popular majors: 27% Engineering, 12% Business, Management, Marketing, and Related Support Services, 10% Computer and Information Sciences and Support Services, 7% Engineering Technologies and Engineering-Related Fields, 7% Health Professions and Related Programs
Expenses: 2021-2022: $9,992 in state, $28,794 out of state; room/board: $10,030

Financial aid: (765) 494-5050; 38% of undergrads determined to have financial need; average aid package $13,586

Rose-Hulman Institute of Technology

Terre Haute IN
(812) 877-8213
U.S. News ranking: Engineering, unranked
Website: www.rose-hulman.edu
Admissions email: admissions@rose-hulman.edu
Private; founded 1874
Freshman admissions: more selective; 2020-2021: 4,376 applied, 3,353 accepted. Neither SAT nor ACT required. SAT 25/75: 1260-1460. High school rank: 66% in top tenth, 91% in top quarter, 99% in top half
Early decision deadline: N/A, notification date: N/A
Early action deadline: 11/1, notification date: 12/15
Application deadline (fall): 2/1
Undergraduate student body: 1,952 full time, 20 part time; 76% male, 24% female; 0% American Indian, 6% Asian, 5% black, 5% Hispanic, 5% multiracial, 0% Pacific Islander, 66% white, 11% international; 31% from in state; 58% live on campus; 33% of students in fraternities, 36% in sororities
Most popular majors: 31% Mechanical Engineering, 15% Computer Science, 10% Chemical Engineering, 9% Bioengineering and Biomedical Engineering, 7% Computer Engineering, General
Expenses: 2021-2022: $50,619; room/board: $16,161
Financial aid: (812) 877-8672; 59% of undergrads determined to have financial need; average aid package $35,451

Saint Mary-of-the-Woods College

St. Mary-of-the-Woods IN
(800) 926-7692
U.S. News ranking: Reg. U. (Mid. W), No. 41
Website: www.smwc.edu
Admissions email: admission@smwc.edu
Private; founded 1840
Affiliation: Roman Catholic
Freshman admissions: selective; 2020-2021: 657 applied, 468 accepted. Neither SAT nor ACT required. SAT 25/75 percentile: 940-1119. High school rank: N/A
Early decision deadline: N/A, notification date: N/A
Early action deadline: N/A, notification date: N/A
Application deadline (fall): rolling
Undergraduate student body: 606 full time, 155 part time; 17% male, 83% female; 0% American Indian, 1% Asian, 6% black, 4% Hispanic, 5% multiracial, 0% Pacific Islander, 81% white, 0% international; 74% from in state; 50% live on campus; 0% of students in fraternities, 0% in sororities
Most popular majors: 25% Registered Nursing/Registered

Nurse, 11% Business Administration and Management, General, 10% Education/Teaching of Individuals Who are Developmentally Delayed, 10% Psychology, General, 8% Public Administration and Social Service Professions
Expenses: 2021-2022: $30,550; room/board: $11,240
Financial aid: (812) 535-5110; 100% of undergrads determined to have financial need; average aid package $25,891

Saint Mary's College

Notre Dame IN
(574) 284-4587
U.S. News ranking: Nat. Lib. Arts, No. 105
Website: www.saintmarys.edu
Admissions email: admission@saintmarys.edu
Private; founded 1844
Affiliation: Roman Catholic
Freshman admissions: more selective; 2020-2021: 2,411 applied, 1,965 accepted. Neither SAT nor ACT required. SAT 25/75 percentile: 1060-1260. High school rank: 26% in top tenth, 63% in top quarter, 92% in top half
Early decision deadline: 11/15, notification date: 12/15
Early action deadline: N/A, notification date: N/A
Application deadline (fall): rolling
Undergraduate student body: 1,403 full time, 35 part time; 1% male, 99% female; 0% American Indian, 1% Asian, 2% black, 15% Hispanic, 3% multiracial, 0% Pacific Islander, 76% white, 0% international; 34% from in state; 84% live on campus; 0% of students in fraternities, 0% in sororities
Most popular majors: 12% Business Administration and Management, General, 12% Registered Nursing/Registered Nurse, 8% Psychology, General, 7% Communication and Media Studies, 5% Social Work
Expenses: 2021-2022: $48,010; room/board: $13,470
Financial aid: (574) 284-4557; 74% of undergrads determined to have financial need; average aid package $40,335

Taylor University

Upland IN
(765) 998-5134
U.S. News ranking: Reg. Coll. (Mid. W), No. 1
Website: www.taylor.edu
Admissions email: admissions@taylor.edu
Private; founded 1846
Affiliation: Interdenominational
Freshman admissions: more selective; 2020-2021: 2,177 applied, 1,526 accepted. Neither SAT nor ACT required. SAT 25/75 percentile: 1090-1290. High school rank: 30% in top tenth, 71% in top quarter, 92% in top half
Early decision deadline: N/A, notification date: N/A
Early action deadline: N/A, notification date: N/A

Application deadline (fall): 8/1
Undergraduate student body: 1,724 full time, 352 part time; 44% male, 56% female; 0% American Indian, 2% Asian, 3% black, 5% Hispanic, 2% multiracial, 0% Pacific Islander, 83% white, 4% international; 43% from in state; 91% live on campus; N/A of students in fraternities, N/A in sororities
Most popular majors: 18% Business, Management, Marketing, and Related Support Services, 11% Biological and Biomedical Sciences, 11% Education, 9% Visual and Performing Arts, 8% Computer and Information Sciences and Support Services
Expenses: 2021-2022: $36,570; room/board: $10,659
Financial aid: (765) 998-5358; 63% of undergrads determined to have financial need; average aid package $26,575

Trine University[1]

Angola IN
(260) 665-4100
U.S. News ranking: Reg. U. (Mid. W), No. 69
Website: www.trine.edu
Admissions email: admit@trine.edu
Private; founded 1884
Application deadline (fall): 8/1
Undergraduate student body: N/A full time, N/A part time
Expenses: 2021-2022: $34,200; room/board: $11,380
Financial aid: (260) 665-4438; 51% of undergrads determined to have financial need; average aid package $25,490

University of Evansville

Evansville IN
(812) 488-2468
U.S. News ranking: Reg. U. (Mid. W), No. 7
Website: www.evansville.edu
Admissions email: admission@evansville.edu
Private; founded 1854
Affiliation: United Methodist
Freshman admissions: more selective; 2020-2021: 4,709 applied, 3,028 accepted. Neither SAT nor ACT required. SAT 25/75 percentile: 1070-1278. High school rank: 35% in top tenth, 65% in top quarter, 93% in top half
Early decision deadline: N/A, notification date: N/A
Early action deadline: 12/1, notification date: 12/15
Application deadline (fall): rolling
Undergraduate student body: 1,716 full time, 325 part time; 42% male, 58% female; 0% American Indian, 3% Asian, 4% black, 4% Hispanic, 3% multiracial, 0% Pacific Islander, 77% white, 8% international; 64% from in state; 54% live on campus; N/A of students in fraternities, N/A in sororities
Most popular majors: 8% Kinesiology and Exercise Science, 6% Registered Nursing/Registered Nurse, 4% Finance, General, 4% Health/Health Care Administration/

Management, 4% Neuroscience
Expenses: 2021-2022: $39,806; room/board: $13,420
Financial aid: (800) 424-8634; 68% of undergrads determined to have financial need; average aid package $33,719

University of Indianapolis

Indianapolis IN
(317) 788-3216
U.S. News ranking: Nat. U., No. 239
Website: www.uindy.edu
Admissions email: admissions@uindy.edu
Private; founded 1902
Affiliation: United Methodist
Freshman admissions: selective; 2020-2021: 9,492 applied, 6,968 accepted. Neither SAT nor ACT required. SAT 25/75 percentile: 960-1170. High school rank: 15% in top tenth, 44% in top quarter, 84% in top half
Early decision deadline: N/A, notification date: N/A
Early action deadline: N/A, notification date: N/A
Application deadline (fall): rolling
Undergraduate student body: 3,863 full time, 305 part time; 37% male, 63% female; 0% American Indian, 3% Asian, 13% black, 8% Hispanic, 4% multiracial, 0% Pacific Islander, 63% white, 6% international; 88% from in state; 49% live on campus; 0% of students in fraternities, 0% in sororities
Most popular majors: 16% Registered Nursing/Registered Nurse, 7% Kinesiology and Exercise Science, 7% Psychology, General, 4% Banking and Financial Support Services, 4% Speech Communication and Rhetoric
Expenses: 2021-2022: $33,520; room/board: $12,444
Financial aid: (317) 788-3217; 78% of undergrads determined to have financial need; average aid package $28,661

University of Notre Dame

Notre Dame IN
(574) 631-7505
U.S. News ranking: Nat. U., No. 19
Website: www.nd.edu
Admissions email: admissions@nd.edu
Private; founded 1842
Affiliation: Roman Catholic
Freshman admissions: most selective; 2020-2021: 21,253 applied, 4,035 accepted. Neither SAT nor ACT required. ACT 25/75 percentile: 32-35. High school rank: 90% in top tenth, 98% in top quarter, 100% in top half
Early decision deadline: N/A, notification date: N/A
Early action deadline: 11/1, notification date: 12/15
Application deadline (fall): 1/1
Undergraduate student body: 8,833 full time, 41 part time; 52% male, 48% female; 0% American Indian, 5% Asian, 3% black, 11% Hispanic, 6% multiracial, 0% Pacific Islander, 68% white,

5% international; 8% from in state; 73% live on campus; N/A of students in fraternities, N/A in sororities
Most popular majors: 8% Econometrics and Quantitative Economics, 8% Finance, General, 6% Political Science and Government, General, 4% Computer and Information Sciences, General, 4% Mechanical Engineering
Expenses: 2021-2022: $58,843; room/board: $16,304
Financial aid: (574) 631-6436; 48% of undergrads determined to have financial need; average aid package $55,556

University of Saint Francis

Fort Wayne IN
(260) 399-8000
U.S. News ranking: Reg. U. (Mid. W), No. 69
Website: www.sf.edu
Admissions email: admis@sf.edu
Private; founded 1890
Affiliation: Roman Catholic
Freshman admissions: selective; 2020-2021: 1,676 applied, 1,660 accepted. Neither SAT nor ACT required. SAT 25/75 percentile: 960-1160. High school rank: 17% in top tenth, 44% in top quarter, 74% in top half
Early decision deadline: N/A, notification date: N/A
Early action deadline: N/A, notification date: N/A
Application deadline (fall): 8/18
Undergraduate student body: 1,475 full time, 278 part time; 31% male, 69% female; 0% American Indian, 2% Asian, 10% black, 9% Hispanic, 3% multiracial, 0% Pacific Islander, 72% white, 1% international; 89% from in state; 21% live on campus; N/A of students in fraternities, N/A in sororities
Most popular majors: 35% Registered Nursing/Registered Nurse, 8% Health and Wellness, General, 4% Biology/Biological Sciences, General, 4% Music Technology, 4% Psychology, General
Expenses: 2021-2022: $33,390; room/board: $10,700
Financial aid: (260) 399-8003; 83% of undergrads determined to have financial need; average aid package $23,849

University of Southern Indiana

Evansville IN
(812) 464-1765
U.S. News ranking: Reg. U. (Mid. W), No. 88
Website: www.usi.edu
Admissions email: enroll@usi.edu
Public; founded 1965
Freshman admissions: selective; 2020-2021: 4,158 applied, 3,903 accepted. Neither SAT nor ACT required. SAT 25/75 percentile: 980-1170. High school rank: 18% in top tenth, 44% in top quarter, 77% in top half
Early decision deadline: N/A, notification date: N/A
Early action deadline: N/A,

notification date: N/A
Application deadline (fall): 8/15
Undergraduate student body: 5,754 full time, 985 part time; 36% male, 64% female; 0% American Indian, 2% Asian, 4% black, 4% Hispanic, 3% multiracial, 0% Pacific Islander, 85% white, 2% international; 82% from in state; 29% live on campus; 8% of students in fraternities, 8% in sororities
Most popular majors: 24% Health Professions and Related Programs, 17% Business, Management, Marketing, and Related Support Services, 7% Education, 7% Psychology, 5% Communication, Journalism, and Related Programs
Expenses: 2020-2021: $8,716 in state, $20,252 out of state; room/board: $9,514
Financial aid: (812) 464-1767; 55% of undergrads determined to have financial need; average aid package $9,078

Valparaiso University
Valparaiso IN
(888) 468-2576
U.S. News ranking: Nat. U., No. 172
Website: www.valpo.edu
Admissions email: undergrad.admission@valpo.edu
Private; founded 1859
Freshman admissions: more selective; 2020-2021: 5,991 applied, 5,190 accepted. Neither SAT nor ACT required. SAT 25/75 percentile: 1070-1280. High school rank: 36% in top tenth, 68% in top quarter, 92% in top half
Early decision deadline: N/A, notification date: N/A
Early action deadline: N/A, notification date: N/A
Application deadline (fall): rolling
Undergraduate student body: 2,678 full time, 45 part time; 44% male, 56% female; 0% American Indian, 2% Asian, 6% black, 11% Hispanic, 3% multiracial, 0% Pacific Islander, 72% white, 3% international; 46% from in state; 56% live on campus; 29% of students in fraternities, 32% in sororities
Most popular majors: 21% Health Professions and Related Programs, 15% Business, Management, Marketing, and Related Support Services, 14% Engineering, 7% Social Sciences, 5% Education
Expenses: 2021-2022: $44,796; room/board: $12,872
Financial aid: (219) 464-5015; 77% of undergrads determined to have financial need; average aid package $34,595

Vincennes University
Vincennes IN
(800) 742-9198
U.S. News ranking: Reg. Coll. (Mid. W), second tier
Website: www.vinu.edu
Admissions email: N/A
Public; founded 1801
Freshman admissions: less selective; 2020-2021: 4,185 applied, 3,501 accepted. Neither

SAT nor ACT required. SAT 25/75 percentile: N/A. High school rank: N/A
Early decision deadline: N/A, notification date: N/A
Early action deadline: N/A, notification date: N/A
Application deadline (fall): rolling
Undergraduate student body: 4,405 full time, 11,643 part time; 51% male, 49% female; 0% American Indian, 1% Asian, 7% black, 15% Hispanic, 2% multiracial, 0% Pacific Islander, 72% white, 1% international; N/A from in state; 33% live on campus; N/A of students in fraternities, N/A in sororities
Most popular majors: 36% Homeland Security, Law Enforcement, Firefighting and Related Protective Services, 28% Engineering Technologies and Engineering-Related Fields, 25% Health Professions and Related Programs, 11% Education
Expenses: 2020-2021: $6,251 in state, $14,781 out of state; room/board: $10,590
Financial aid: (812) 888-4361

Wabash College
Crawfordsville IN
(765) 361-6225
U.S. News ranking: Nat. Lib. Arts, No. 57
Website: www.wabash.edu
Admissions email: admissions@wabash.edu
Private; founded 1832
Freshman admissions: more selective; 2020-2021: 1,522 applied, 962 accepted. Neither SAT nor ACT required. SAT 25/75 percentile: 1120-1320. High school rank: 30% in top tenth, 61% in top quarter, 95% in top half
Early decision deadline: 11/1, notification date: 12/5
Early action deadline: 12/1, notification date: 12/31
Application deadline (fall): 7/1
Undergraduate student body: 868 full time, 0 part time; 100% male, 0% female; 0% American Indian, 1% Asian, 4% black, 9% Hispanic, 4% multiracial, 0% Pacific Islander, 76% white, 4% international; 77% from in state; 96% live on campus; 61% of students in fraternities, N/A in sororities
Most popular majors: 14% Political Science and Government, General, 12% Economics, General, 8% Religion/Religious Studies, 7% Biology/Biological Sciences, General, 7% History, General
Expenses: 2021-2022: $45,850; room/board: $11,600
Financial aid: (765) 361-6370; 77% of undergrads determined to have financial need; average aid package $43,756

IOWA

Briar Cliff University
Sioux City IA
(712) 279-5200
U.S. News ranking: Reg. Coll. (Mid. W), No. 29
Website: www.briarcliff.edu

Admissions email: admissions@briarcliff.edu
Private; founded 1930
Affiliation: Roman Catholic
Freshman admissions: selective; 2020-2021: 1,088 applied, 842 accepted. Either SAT or ACT required. ACT 25/75 percentile: 18-23. High school rank: 15% in top tenth, 37% in top quarter, 63% in top half
Early decision deadline: N/A, notification date: N/A
Early action deadline: N/A, notification date: N/A
Application deadline (fall): rolling
Undergraduate student body: 587 full time, 230 part time; 45% male, 55% female; 1% American Indian, 1% Asian, 10% black, 21% Hispanic, 4% multiracial, 1% Pacific Islander, 56% white, 6% international; 50% from in state; 50% live on campus; 0% of students in fraternities, 0% in sororities
Most popular majors: 22% Registered Nursing/Registered Nurse, 19% Social Work, 11% Business Administration and Management, General, 10% Kinesiology and Exercise Science, 5% Psychology, General
Expenses: 2020-2021: $33,128; room/board: $9,390
Financial aid: (712) 279-1614

Buena Vista University
Storm Lake IA
(800) 383-9600
U.S. News ranking: Reg. U. (Mid. W), No. 49
Website: www.bvu.edu
Admissions email: admissions@bvu.edu
Private; founded 1891
Affiliation: Presbyterian Church (USA)
Freshman admissions: selective; 2020-2021: 1,787 applied, 995 accepted. Neither SAT nor ACT required. ACT 25/75 percentile: 19-24. High school rank: 13% in top tenth, 41% in top quarter, 76% in top half
Early decision deadline: N/A, notification date: N/A
Early action deadline: N/A, notification date: N/A
Application deadline (fall): rolling
Undergraduate student body: 1,228 full time, 223 part time; 36% male, 64% female; 1% American Indian, 1% Asian, 3% black, 10% Hispanic, 4% multiracial, 0% Pacific Islander, 74% white, 0% international; 68% from in state; 88% live on campus; 0% of students in fraternities, 0% in sororities
Most popular majors: 23% Business, Management, Marketing, and Related Support Services, 11% Education, 10% Parks, Recreation, Leisure, and Fitness Studies, 9% Biological and Biomedical Sciences, 7% Communication, Journalism, and Related Programs
Expenses: 2021-2022: $37,518; room/board: $10,370

Financial aid: (712) 749-2164; 87% of undergrads determined to have financial need; average aid package $32,556

Central College
Pella IA
(641) 628-5286
U.S. News ranking: Nat. Lib. Arts, No. 136
Website: www.central.edu
Admissions email: admission@central.edu
Private; founded 1853
Affiliation: Reformed Church in America
Freshman admissions: selective; 2020-2021: 2,340 applied, 1,490 accepted. Neither SAT nor ACT required. ACT 25/75 percentile: 19-25. High school rank: 23% in top tenth, 44% in top quarter, 79% in top half
Early decision deadline: N/A, notification date: N/A
Early action deadline: N/A, notification date: N/A
Application deadline (fall): 8/15
Undergraduate student body: 1,079 full time, 41 part time; 52% male, 48% female; 0% American Indian, 2% Asian, 3% black, 5% Hispanic, 3% multiracial, 0% Pacific Islander, 85% white, 0% international; 70% from in state; N/A live on campus; N/A of students in fraternities, N/A in sororities
Most popular majors: 36% Biological and Physical Sciences, 11% Business Administration and Management, General, 9% Exercise Physiology, 7% Elementary Education and Teaching, 5% Sociology
Expenses: 2021-2022: $19,250; room/board: $10,552
Financial aid: (641) 628-5336; 69% of undergrads determined to have financial need; average aid package $16,333

Clarke University
Dubuque IA
(563) 588-6316
U.S. News ranking: Nat. U., No. 239
Website: www.clarke.edu
Admissions email: admissions@clarke.edu
Private; founded 1843
Affiliation: Roman Catholic
Freshman admissions: selective; 2020-2021: 1,725 applied, 983 accepted. Neither SAT nor ACT required. ACT 25/75 percentile: 19-25. High school rank: 16% in top tenth, 33% in top quarter, 62% in top half
Early decision deadline: N/A, notification date: N/A
Early action deadline: N/A, notification date: N/A
Application deadline (fall): rolling
Undergraduate student body: 634 full time, 25 part time; 49% male, 51% female; 1% American Indian, 1% Asian, 10% black, 11% Hispanic, 4% multiracial, 0% Pacific Islander, 65% white, 2% international; N/A from in state; 57% live on campus; 0% of students in fraternities, 0% in sororities

Most popular majors: 23% Health Professions and Related Programs, 16% Business, Management, Marketing, and Related Support Services, 12% Psychology, 10% Education
Expenses: 2021-2022: $36,870; room/board: $10,400
Financial aid: (563) 588-6327

Coe College
Cedar Rapids IA
(319) 399-8500
U.S. News ranking: Nat. Lib. Arts, No. 136
Website: www.coe.edu
Admissions email: admission@coe.edu
Private; founded 1851
Freshman admissions: selective; 2020-2021: 6,839 applied, 5,539 accepted. Neither SAT nor ACT required. ACT 25/75 percentile: 20-26. High school rank: 21% in top tenth, 39% in top quarter, 85% in top half
Early decision deadline: N/A, notification date: N/A
Early action deadline: 12/10, notification date: 1/20
Application deadline (fall): 3/1
Undergraduate student body: 1,355 full time, 38 part time; 44% male, 56% female; 0% American Indian, 3% Asian, 9% black, 12% Hispanic, 3% multiracial, 0% Pacific Islander, 65% white, 2% international; 41% from in state; 92% live on campus; 21% of students in fraternities, 21% in sororities
Most popular majors: 18% Biological and Biomedical Sciences, 18% Business, Management, Marketing, and Related Support Services, 9% Social Sciences, 8% Psychology, 6% Visual and Performing Arts
Expenses: 2021-2022: $48,822; room/board: $10,520
Financial aid: (319) 399-8540; 84% of undergrads determined to have financial need; average aid package $41,183

Cornell College
Mount Vernon IA
(800) 747-1112
U.S. News ranking: Nat. Lib. Arts, No. 89
Website: www.cornellcollege.edu
Admissions email: admission@cornellcollege.edu
Private; founded 1853
Affiliation: United Methodist
Freshman admissions: more selective; 2020-2021: 2,615 applied, 2,155 accepted. Neither SAT nor ACT required. ACT 25/75 percentile: 23-29. High school rank: 20% in top tenth, 46% in top quarter, 81% in top half
Early decision deadline: N/A, notification date: N/A
Early action deadline: 11/1, notification date: N/A
Application deadline (fall): rolling
Undergraduate student body: 992 full time, 5 part time; 52% male, 48% female; 1% American Indian, 2% Asian, 6% black, 7% Hispanic, 2% multiracial, 0% Pacific Islander, 74% white, 5% international; 27% from in state;

79% live on campus; 13% of students in fraternities, 35% in sororities
Most popular majors: 8% Biochemistry and Molecular Biology, 8% Psychology, General, 7% Kinesiology and Exercise Science, 4% Creative Writing, 4% Secondary Education and Teaching
Expenses: 2021-2022: $47,726; room/board: $10,556
Financial aid: (319) 895-4216; 74% of undergrads determined to have financial need; average aid package $35,006

Dordt University
Sioux Center IA
(800) 343-6738
U.S. News ranking: Reg. Coll. (Mid. W), No. 5
Website: www.dordt.edu
Admissions email: admissions@dordt.edu
Private; founded 1955
Affiliation: Christian Reformed Church
Freshman admissions: more selective; 2020-2021: 1,500 applied, 1,071 accepted. Neither SAT nor ACT required. ACT 25/75 percentile: 22-28. High school rank: 21% in top tenth, 48% in top quarter, 78% in top half
Early decision deadline: N/A, notification date: N/A
Early action deadline: N/A, notification date: N/A
Application deadline (fall): 8/16
Undergraduate student body: 1,340 full time, 102 part time; 52% male, 48% female; 0% American Indian, 1% Asian, 1% black, 3% Hispanic, 1% multiracial, 0% Pacific Islander, 82% white, 9% international; 40% from in state; 91% live on campus; 0% of students in fraternities, 0% in sororities
Most popular majors: 23% Education, 16% Business, Management, Marketing, and Related Support Services, 9% Agriculture, Agriculture Operations, and Related Sciences, 7% Engineering, 6% Health Professions and Related Programs
Expenses: 2021-2022: $33,590; room/board: $10,780
Financial aid: (712) 722-6082; 67% of undergrads determined to have financial need; average aid package $27,040

Drake University
Des Moines IA
(800) 443-7253
U.S. News ranking: Nat. U., No. 136
Website: www.drake.edu
Admissions email: admission@drake.edu
Private; founded 1881
Freshman admissions: more selective; 2020-2021: 6,624 applied, 4,499 accepted. Neither SAT nor ACT required. ACT 25/75 percentile: 23-30. High school rank: 37% in top tenth, 69% in top quarter, 92% in top half
Early decision deadline: N/A, notification date: N/A
Early action deadline: N/A,

notification date: N/A
Application deadline (fall): rolling
Undergraduate student body: 2,731 full time, 117 part time; 41% male, 59% female; 0% American Indian, 5% Asian, 6% black, 8% Hispanic, 4% multiracial, 2% Pacific Islander, 74% white, 3% international; N/A from in state; 41% live on campus; 24% of students in fraternities, 28% in sororities
Most popular majors: 29% Business, Management, Marketing, and Related Support Services, 10% Communication, Journalism, and Related Programs, 8% Biological and Biomedical Sciences, 7% Social Sciences, 6% Visual and Performing Arts
Expenses: 2021-2022: $45,962; room/board: $11,288
Financial aid: (515) 271-2905; 63% of undergrads determined to have financial need; average aid package $32,198

Graceland University
Lamoni IA
(866) 472-2352
U.S. News ranking: Reg. U. (Mid. W), second tier
Website: www.graceland.edu
Admissions email: admissions@graceland.edu
Private; founded 1895
Affiliation: Other
Freshman admissions: selective; 2020-2021: 2,528 applied, 1,723 accepted. Neither SAT nor ACT required. ACT 25/75 percentile: 15-26. High school rank: 7% in top tenth, 17% in top quarter, 57% in top half
Early decision deadline: N/A, notification date: N/A
Early action deadline: N/A, notification date: N/A
Application deadline (fall): rolling
Undergraduate student body: 868 full time, 94 part time; 44% male, 56% female; 0% American Indian, 1% Asian, 11% black, 12% Hispanic, 4% multiracial, 2% Pacific Islander, 60% white, 5% international; N/A from in state; 87% live on campus; N/A of students in fraternities, N/A in sororities
Most popular majors: 31% Health Professions and Related Programs, 14% Business, Management, Marketing, and Related Support Services, 11% Education, 7% Parks, Recreation, Leisure, and Fitness Studies, 4% Biological and Biomedical Sciences
Expenses: 2021-2022: $31,920; room/board: $9,810
Financial aid: (641) 784-5051; 83% of undergrads determined to have financial need; average aid package $22,005

Grand View University[1]
Des Moines IA
(515) 263-2810
U.S. News ranking: Reg. Coll. (Mid. W), No. 35
Website: www.grandview.edu
Admissions email: admissions@grandview.edu
Private; founded 1896

Affiliation: Evangelical Lutheran Church
Application deadline (fall): 8/15
Undergraduate student body: N/A full time, N/A part time
Expenses: 2020-2021: $29,960; room/board: $9,614
Financial aid: (515) 263-2853

Grinnell College
Grinnell IA
(800) 247-0113
U.S. News ranking: Nat. Lib. Arts, No. 13
Website: www.grinnell.edu
Admissions email: admission@grinnell.edu
Private; founded 1846
Freshman admissions: most selective; 2020-2021: 8,137 applied, 1,566 accepted. Either SAT or ACT required. ACT 25/75 percentile: 30-34. High school rank: 72% in top tenth, 94% in top quarter, 98% in top half
Early decision deadline: 11/15, notification date: 12/15
Early action deadline: N/A, notification date: N/A
Application deadline (fall): 1/15
Undergraduate student body: 1,459 full time, 34 part time; 47% male, 53% female; 0% American Indian, 8% Asian, 5% black, 9% Hispanic, 5% multiracial, 0% Pacific Islander, 51% white, 19% international; 7% from in state; 88% live on campus; 0% of students in fraternities, 0% in sororities
Most popular majors: 25% Social Sciences, 15% Biological and Biomedical Sciences, 12% Computer and Information Sciences and Support Services, 8% Foreign Languages, Literatures, and Linguistics, 7% Mathematics and Statistics
Expenses: 2021-2022: $58,648; room/board: $14,350
Financial aid: (641) 269-3250; 66% of undergrads determined to have financial need; average aid package $48,649

Iowa State University of Science and Technology
Ames IA
(515) 294-5836
U.S. News ranking: Nat. U., No. 122
Website: www.iastate.edu
Admissions email: admissions@iastate.edu
Public; founded 1858
Freshman admissions: selective; 2020-2021: 20,223 applied, 17,882 accepted. Neither SAT nor ACT required. ACT 25/75 percentile: 22-28. High school rank: 14% in top tenth, 28% in top quarter, 95% in top half
Early decision deadline: N/A, notification date: N/A
Early action deadline: N/A, notification date: N/A
Application deadline (fall): rolling
Undergraduate student body: 25,274 full time, 1,572 part time; 57% male, 43% female; 0% American Indian, 4% Asian, 3% black, 7% Hispanic, 3% multiracial, 0% Pacific Islander,

77% white, 4% international; 64% from in state; 20% live on campus; 13% of students in fraternities, 18% in sororities
Most popular majors: 22% Engineering, 18% Business, Management, Marketing, and Related Support Services, 11% Agriculture, Agriculture Operations, and Related Sciences, 6% Biological and Biomedical Sciences, 5% Computer and Information Sciences and Support Services
Expenses: 2021-2022: $9,316 in state, $24,504 out of state; room/board: $9,193
Financial aid: (515) 294-2223; 51% of undergrads determined to have financial need; average aid package $13,805

Iowa Wesleyan University
Mount Pleasant IA
(319) 385-6231
U.S. News ranking: Reg. Coll. (Mid. W), second tier
Website: www.iw.edu
Admissions email: admit@iw.edu
Private; founded 1842
Affiliation: United Methodist
Freshman admissions: selective; 2020-2021: 4,153 applied, 2,956 accepted. Either SAT or ACT required. ACT 25/75 percentile: 16-21. High school rank: 15% in top tenth, 29% in top quarter, 47% in top half
Early decision deadline: N/A, notification date: N/A
Early action deadline: N/A, notification date: N/A
Application deadline (fall): rolling
Undergraduate student body: 624 full time, 26 part time; 54% male, 46% female; 1% American Indian, 0% Asian, 22% black, 7% Hispanic, 9% multiracial, 0% Pacific Islander, 44% white, 12% international
Most popular majors: 29% Business Administration and Management, General, 14% Criminal Justice/Law Enforcement Administration, 9% Biology/Biological Sciences, General, 9% Registered Nursing/Registered Nurse, 8% Elementary Education and Teaching
Expenses: 2021-2022: $33,650; room/board: $11,340
Financial aid: (319) 385-6242; 80% of undergrads determined to have financial need; average aid package $29,166

Loras College
Dubuque IA
(800) 245-6727
U.S. News ranking: Reg. Coll. (Mid. W), No. 13
Website: www.loras.edu
Admissions email: admission@loras.edu
Private; founded 1839
Affiliation: Roman Catholic
Freshman admissions: selective; 2020-2021: 2,482 applied, 1,449 accepted. Neither SAT nor ACT required. ACT 25/75 percentile: 19-25. High school rank: N/A
Early decision deadline: N/A,

notification date: N/A
Early action deadline: N/A, notification date: N/A
Application deadline (fall): rolling
Undergraduate student body: 1,214 full time, 97 part time; 56% male, 44% female; 0% American Indian, 1% Asian, 4% black, 10% Hispanic, 3% multiracial, 0% Pacific Islander, 76% white, 2% international; 40% from in state; 60% live on campus; N/A of students in fraternities, N/A in sororities
Most popular majors: 10% Kinesiology and Exercise Science, 9% Business Administration and Management, General, 7% Elementary Education and Teaching, 7% Finance, General, 7% Psychology, General
Expenses: 2021-2022: $35,268; room/board: $8,760
Financial aid: (563) 588-7136; 80% of undergrads determined to have financial need; average aid package $29,424

Luther College
Decorah IA
(563) 387-1287
U.S. News ranking: Nat. Lib. Arts, No. 105
Website: www.luther.edu
Admissions email: admissions@luther.edu
Private; founded 1861
Affiliation: Evangelical Lutheran Church
Freshman admissions: more selective; 2020-2021: 3,640 applied, 2,340 accepted. Either SAT or ACT required. ACT 25/75 percentile: 23-29. High school rank: 30% in top tenth, 55% in top quarter, 87% in top half
Early decision deadline: N/A, notification date: N/A
Early action deadline: N/A, notification date: N/A
Application deadline (fall): rolling
Undergraduate student body: 1,775 full time, 27 part time; 42% male, 58% female; 0% American Indian, 2% Asian, 2% black, 7% Hispanic, 3% multiracial, 0% Pacific Islander, 78% white, 8% international
Most popular majors: 12% Music, General, 10% Registered Nursing/Registered Nurse, 9% Biology/Biological Sciences, General, 8% Business Administration and Management, General, 4% Speech Communication and Rhetoric
Expenses: 2021-2022: $46,760; room/board: $10,360
Financial aid: (563) 387-1018

Maharishi International University[1]
Fairfield IA
(641) 472-7000
U.S. News ranking: Reg. U. (Mid. W), second tier
Website: www.mum.edu
Admissions email: admissions@mum.edu
Private
Application deadline (fall): N/A

Undergraduate student body: N/A full time, N/A part time
Expenses: 2020-2021: $16,530; room/board: $7,400
Financial aid: N/A

Morningside University
Sioux City IA
(712) 274-5111
U.S. News ranking: Reg. U. (Mid. W), No. 61
Website: www.morningside.edu
Admissions email: admissions@morningside.edu
Private; founded 1894
Affiliation: United Methodist
Freshman admissions: selective; 2020-2021: 3,621 applied, 2,400 accepted. Neither SAT nor ACT required. ACT 25/75 percentile: 19-25. High school rank: 12% in top tenth, 32% in top quarter, 70% in top half
Early decision deadline: N/A, notification date: N/A
Early action deadline: N/A, notification date: N/A
Application deadline (fall): rolling
Undergraduate student body: 1,157 full time, 124 part time; 49% male, 51% female; 0% American Indian, 1% Asian, 4% black, 8% Hispanic, 4% multiracial, 1% Pacific Islander, 69% white, 5% international
Most popular majors: 18% Business Administration and Management, General, 13% Biology/Biological Sciences, General, 10% Registered Nursing/Registered Nurse, 9% Elementary Education and Teaching, 6% Counseling Psychology
Expenses: 2021-2022: $35,270; room/board: $10,410
Financial aid: (712) 274-5159; 80% of undergrads determined to have financial need

Mount Mercy University[1]
Cedar Rapids IA
(319) 368-6460
U.S. News ranking: Reg. U. (Mid. W), No. 51
Website: www.mtmercy.edu
Admissions email: admission@mtmercy.edu
Private; founded 1928
Affiliation: Roman Catholic
Application deadline (fall): rolling
Undergraduate student body: N/A full time, N/A part time
Expenses: 2020-2021: $35,574; room/board: $10,112
Financial aid: (319) 368-6467

Northwestern College
Orange City IA
(800) 747-4757
U.S. News ranking: Reg. Coll. (Mid. W), No. 6
Website: www.nwciowa.edu
Admissions email: admissions@nwciowa.edu
Private; founded 1882
Affiliation: Reformed Church in America
Freshman admissions: selective; 2020-2021: 1,188 applied, 836 accepted. Neither SAT nor ACT required. ACT 25/75 percentile:

20-26. High school rank: 21% in top tenth, 42% in top quarter, 76% in top half
Early decision deadline: N/A, notification date: N/A
Early action deadline: N/A, notification date: N/A
Application deadline (fall): rolling
Undergraduate student body: 974 full time, 106 part time; 48% male, 52% female; 0% American Indian, 1% Asian, 2% black, 5% Hispanic, 2% multiracial, 0% Pacific Islander, 84% white, 3% international; 57% from in state; 88% live on campus; 0% of students in fraternities, 0% in sororities
Most popular majors: 14% Business Administration and Management, General, 10% Elementary Education and Teaching, 9% Registered Nursing/Registered Nurse, 7% Biology/Biological Sciences, General, 5% Kinesiology and Exercise Science
Expenses: 2021-2022: $33,590; room/board: $10,000
Financial aid: (712) 707-7131; 75% of undergrads determined to have financial need; average aid package $27,278

Simpson College
Indianola IA
(515) 961-1624
U.S. News ranking: Nat. Lib. Arts, No. 146
Website: www.simpson.edu
Admissions email: admiss@simpson.edu
Private; founded 1860
Affiliation: United Methodist
Freshman admissions: selective; 2020-2021: 1,300 applied, 1,126 accepted. Neither SAT nor ACT required. ACT 25/75 percentile: 20-26. High school rank: 18% in top tenth, 41% in top quarter, 82% in top half
Early decision deadline: N/A, notification date: N/A
Early action deadline: N/A, notification date: N/A
Application deadline (fall): rolling
Undergraduate student body: 1,108 full time, 117 part time; 48% male, 52% female; 0% American Indian, 2% Asian, 4% black, 7% Hispanic, 5% multiracial, 0% Pacific Islander, 79% white, 1% international; 79% from in state; 79% live on campus; 18% of students in fraternities, 20% in sororities
Most popular majors: 15% Business Administration and Management, General, 8% Biology/Biological Sciences, General, 7% Accounting, 6% Psychology, General, 5% Computer Science
Expenses: 2021-2022: $44,030; room/board: $9,654
Financial aid: (515) 961-1596; 87% of undergrads determined to have financial need; average aid package $35,455

St. Ambrose University
Davenport IA
(563) 333-6300
U.S. News ranking: Reg. U. (Mid. W), No. 27
Website: www.sau.edu
Admissions email: admit@sau.edu
Private; founded 1882
Affiliation: Roman Catholic
Freshman admissions: selective; 2020-2021: 4,601 applied, 3,400 accepted. Either SAT or ACT required. ACT 25/75 percentile: 20-25. High school rank: N/A
Early decision deadline: N/A, notification date: N/A
Early action deadline: N/A, notification date: N/A
Application deadline (fall): rolling
Undergraduate student body: 2,180 full time, 125 part time; 44% male, 56% female; 0% American Indian, 2% Asian, 5% black, 9% Hispanic, 3% multiracial, 0% Pacific Islander, 74% white, 2% international; 34% from in state; 67% live on campus; 0% of students in fraternities, 0% in sororities
Most popular majors: 23% Business, Management, Marketing, and Related Support Services, 13% Health Professions and Related Programs, 11% Parks, Recreation, Leisure, and Fitness Studies, 9% Engineering, 9% Psychology
Expenses: 2021-2022: $34,200; room/board: $11,638
Financial aid: (563) 333-6318; 74% of undergrads determined to have financial need; average aid package $25,311

University of Dubuque
Dubuque IA
(563) 589-3200
U.S. News ranking: Reg. U. (Mid. W), No. 69
Website: www.dbq.edu
Admissions email: admssns@dbq.edu
Private; founded 1852
Affiliation: Presbyterian Church (USA)
Freshman admissions: less selective; 2020-2021: 1,844 applied, 1,450 accepted. Neither SAT nor ACT required. ACT 25/75 percentile: 17-23. High school rank: 8% in top tenth, 22% in top quarter, 48% in top half
Early decision deadline: N/A, notification date: N/A
Early action deadline: N/A, notification date: N/A
Application deadline (fall): rolling
Undergraduate student body: 1,490 full time, 325 part time; 58% male, 42% female; 0% American Indian, 1% Asian, 15% black, 9% Hispanic, 3% multiracial, 0% Pacific Islander, 63% white, 5% international; 43% from in state; 48% live on campus; N/A of students in fraternities, N/A in sororities
Most popular majors: 26% Business, Management, Marketing, and Related Support Services, 12% Communications Technologies/Technicians

and Support Services, 9% Transportation and Materials Moving, 8% Health Professions and Related Programs, 8% Homeland Security, Law Enforcement, Firefighting and Related Protective Services
Expenses: 2021-2022: $36,010; room/board: $10,300
Financial aid: (563) 589-3125; 81% of undergrads determined to have financial need; average aid package $31,458

University of Iowa
Iowa City IA
(319) 335-3847
U.S. News ranking: Nat. U., No. 83
Website: www.uiowa.edu
Admissions email: admissions@uiowa.edu
Public; founded 1847
Freshman admissions: more selective; 2020-2021: 24,132 applied, 20,338 accepted. Either SAT or ACT required. ACT 25/75 percentile: 22-29. High school rank: 34% in top tenth, 67% in top quarter, 92% in top half
Early decision deadline: N/A, notification date: N/A
Early action deadline: N/A, notification date: N/A
Application deadline (fall): 5/1
Undergraduate student body: 20,172 full time, 2,064 part time; 45% male, 55% female; 0% American Indian, 5% Asian, 3% black, 8% Hispanic, 4% multiracial, 0% Pacific Islander, 74% white, 4% international; 62% from in state; 23% live on campus; 13% of students in fraternities, 17% in sororities
Most popular majors: 7% Finance, General, 7% Kinesiology and Exercise Science, 4% Marketing/Marketing Management, General, 4% Organizational Leadership, 4% Psychology, General
Expenses: 2021-2022: $9,606 in state, $31,569 out of state; room/board: $11,590
Financial aid: (319) 335-1450; 46% of undergrads determined to have financial need; average aid package $12,868

University of Northern Iowa
Cedar Falls IA
(800) 772-2037
U.S. News ranking: Reg. U. (Mid. W), No. 19
Website: uni.edu/
Admissions email: admissions@uni.edu
Public; founded 1876
Affiliation: Undenominational
Freshman admissions: selective; 2020-2021: 5,085 applied, 4,011 accepted. Neither SAT nor ACT required. ACT 25/75 percentile: 19-25. High school rank: 21% in top tenth, 52% in top quarter, 84% in top half
Early decision deadline: N/A, notification date: N/A
Early action deadline: N/A, notification date: N/A
Application deadline (fall): 8/15
Undergraduate student body: 7,632 full time, 672 part time; 40% male, 60% female; 0% American

Indian, 1% Asian, 3% black, 5% Hispanic, 3% multiracial, 0% Pacific Islander, 83% white, 2% international; 91% from in state; 34% live on campus; 5% of students in fraternities, 7% in sororities
Most popular majors: 22% Education, 21% Business, Management, Marketing, and Related Support Services, 6% Communication, Journalism, and Related Programs, 5% Parks, Recreation, Leisure, and Fitness Studies, 5% Social Sciences
Expenses: 2021-2022: $9,053 in state, $19,753 out of state; room/board: $9,160
Financial aid: (319) 273-2722; 59% of undergrads determined to have financial need; average aid package $8,510

Upper Iowa University[1]
Fayette IA
(800) 553-4150
U.S. News ranking: Reg. U. (Mid. W), second tier
Website: uiu.edu/
Admissions email: admissionsoffice@uiu.edu
Private; founded 1857
Application deadline (fall): rolling
Undergraduate student body: N/A full time, N/A part time
Expenses: 2020-2021: $32,945; room/board: $9,105
Financial aid: (563) 425-5299

Waldorf University[1]
Forest City IA
(641) 585-8112
U.S. News ranking: Reg. U. (Mid. W), second tier
Website: www.waldorf.edu
Admissions email: admissions@waldorf.edu
For-profit
Application deadline (fall): N/A
Undergraduate student body: N/A full time, N/A part time
Expenses: 2020-2021: $23,088; room/board: $7,866
Financial aid: N/A

Wartburg College
Waverly IA
(319) 352-8264
U.S. News ranking: Nat. Lib. Arts, No. 165
Website: www.wartburg.edu/
Admissions email: admissions@wartburg.edu
Private; founded 1852
Affiliation: Evangelical Lutheran Church
Freshman admissions: selective; 2020-2021: 4,796 applied, 3,440 accepted. Neither SAT nor ACT required. ACT 25/75 percentile: 19-25. High school rank: N/A
Early decision deadline: N/A, notification date: N/A
Early action deadline: 12/1, notification date: N/A
Application deadline (fall): rolling
Undergraduate student body: 1,524 full time, 32 part time; 46% male, 54% female; 0% American Indian, 1% Asian, 5% black, 5% Hispanic, 3% multiracial,

0% Pacific Islander, 79% white, 7% international; 69% from in state; 81% live on campus; N/A of students in fraternities, N/A in sororities
Most popular majors: 21% Business/Commerce, General, 13% Biology/Biological Sciences, General, 7% Music Teacher Education, 7% Neuroscience, 6% Elementary Education and Teaching
Expenses: 2021-2022: $47,500; room/board: $9,990
Financial aid: (319) 352-8262; 77% of undergrads determined to have financial need; average aid package $35,348

William Penn University[1]
Oskaloosa IA
(641) 673-1012
U.S. News ranking: Reg. Coll. (Mid. W), second tier
Website: www.wmpenn.edu
Admissions email: admissions@wmpenn.edu
Private
Application deadline (fall): N/A
Undergraduate student body: N/A full time, N/A part time
Expenses: 2020-2021: $26,600; room/board: $7,176
Financial aid: N/A

KANSAS

Baker University
Baldwin City KS
(800) 873-4282
U.S. News ranking: Nat. U., No. 263
Website: www.bakeru.edu
Admissions email: admission@bakeru.edu
Private; founded 1858
Affiliation: United Methodist
Freshman admissions: selective; 2020-2021: 814 applied, 761 accepted. Either SAT or ACT required. ACT 25/75 percentile: 19-24. High school rank: 11% in top tenth, 30% in top quarter, 70% in top half
Early decision deadline: N/A, notification date: N/A
Early action deadline: N/A, notification date: N/A
Application deadline (fall): rolling
Undergraduate student body: 873 full time, 274 part time; 51% male, 49% female; 1% American Indian, 1% Asian, 8% black, 10% Hispanic, 6% multiracial, 0% Pacific Islander, 67% white, 3% international; 71% from in state; 81% live on campus; 35% of students in fraternities, 36% in sororities
Most popular majors: 19% Business/Commerce, General, 8% Biology/Biological Sciences, General, 8% Kinesiology and Exercise Science, 8% Psychology, General, 7% Mass Communication/Media Studies
Expenses: 2021-2022: $31,600; room/board: $8,522
Financial aid: (785) 594-4595; 76% of undergrads determined to have financial need; average aid package $25,673

Benedictine College
Atchison KS
(800) 467-5340
U.S. News ranking: Reg. Coll. (Mid. W), No. 16
Website: www.benedictine.edu
Admissions email: bcadmiss@benedictine.edu
Private; founded 1858
Affiliation: Roman Catholic
Freshman admissions: selective; 2020-2021: 2,504 applied, 2,424 accepted. Neither SAT nor ACT required. ACT 25/75 percentile: 21-29. High school rank: 4% in top tenth, 43% in top quarter, 73% in top half
Early decision deadline: N/A, notification date: N/A
Early action deadline: N/A, notification date: N/A
Application deadline (fall): rolling
Undergraduate student body: 1,970 full time, 154 part time; 48% male, 52% female; 0% American Indian, 1% Asian, 3% black, 10% Hispanic, 4% multiracial, 0% Pacific Islander, 77% white, 1% international; N/A from in state; N/A live on campus; 0% of students in fraternities, 0% in sororities
Most popular majors: 12% Finance, General, 10% Theology/Theological Studies, 8% Elementary Education and Teaching, 8% Marketing/Marketing Management, General, 7% Registered Nursing/Registered Nurse
Expenses: 2021-2022: $33,030; room/board: $11,140
Financial aid: (913) 360-7484; 63% of undergrads determined to have financial need; average aid package $24,076

Bethany College[1]
Lindsborg KS
(800) 826-2281
U.S. News ranking: Reg. Coll. (Mid. W), second tier
Website: www.bethanylb.edu
Admissions email: admissions@bethanylb.edu
Private; founded 1881
Affiliation: Evangelical Lutheran Church
Application deadline (fall): rolling
Undergraduate student body: 767 full time, 59 part time
Expenses: 2020-2021: $30,580; room/board: $12,360
Financial aid: (785) 227-3380

Bethel College
North Newton KS
(800) 522-1887
U.S. News ranking: Reg. Coll. (Mid. W), No. 31
Website: www.bethelks.edu
Admissions email: admissions@bethelks.edu
Private; founded 1887
Affiliation: Mennonite Church
Freshman admissions: selective; 2020-2021: 1,034 applied, 634 accepted. Either SAT or ACT required. ACT 25/75 percentile: 17-22. High school rank: 21% in top tenth, 36% in top quarter, 71% in top half
Early decision deadline: N/A, notification date: N/A

Early action deadline: N/A, notification date: N/A
Application deadline (fall): N/A
Undergraduate student body: 454 full time, 15 part time; 51% male, 49% female; 3% American Indian, 3% Asian, 14% black, 14% Hispanic, 1% multiracial, 0% Pacific Islander, 59% white, 6% international; 54% from in state; 68% live on campus; 0% of students in fraternities, 0% in sororities
Most popular majors: 28% Health Professions and Related Programs, 13% Visual and Performing Arts, 12% Public Administration and Social Service Professions, 11% Business, Management, Marketing, and Related Support Services, 6% Education
Expenses: 2021-2022: $31,164; room/board: $9,810
Financial aid: (316) 284-5232; 90% of undergrads determined to have financial need; average aid package $28,934

Central Christian College of Kansas
McPherson KS
(620) 241-0723
U.S. News ranking: Reg. Coll. (Mid. W), second tier
Website: www.centralchristian.edu
Admissions email: admissions@centralchristian.edu
Private; founded 1884
Affiliation: Free Methodist
Freshman admissions: less selective; 2020-2021: 350 applied, 350 accepted. Neither SAT nor ACT required. ACT 25/75 percentile: 15-21. High school rank: 7% in top tenth, 23% in top quarter, 51% in top half
Early decision deadline: N/A, notification date: N/A
Early action deadline: N/A, notification date: N/A
Application deadline (fall): rolling
Undergraduate student body: 536 full time, 93 part time; 46% male, 54% female; 1% American Indian, 1% Asian, 16% black, 20% Hispanic, 3% multiracial, 1% Pacific Islander, 55% white, 2% international; 23% from in state; 81% live on campus; 0% of students in fraternities, 0% in sororities
Most popular majors: 20% Homeland Security, Law Enforcement, Firefighting and Related Protective Services, 18% Business, Management, Marketing, and Related Support Services, 15% Liberal Arts and Sciences, General Studies and Humanities, 15% Parks, Recreation, Leisure, and Fitness Studies, 11% Psychology
Expenses: 2021-2022: $29,500; room/board: $8,000
Financial aid: (620) 241-0723; 75% of undergrads determined to have financial need; average aid package $26,341

Donnelly College
Kansas City KS
(913) 621-8700
U.S. News ranking: Reg. Coll. (Mid. W), unranked
Website: donnelly.edu
Admissions email: admissions@donnelly.edu
Private; founded 1949
Affiliation: Roman Catholic
Freshman admissions: least selective; 2020-2021: N/A applied, N/A accepted. Neither SAT nor ACT required. SAT 25/75 percentile: N/A. High school rank: N/A
Early decision deadline: N/A, notification date: N/A
Early action deadline: N/A, notification date: N/A
Application deadline (fall): rolling
Undergraduate student body: 201 full time, 116 part time; 21% male, 79% female; 0% American Indian, 9% Asian, 35% black, 44% Hispanic, 1% multiracial, 0% Pacific Islander, 9% white, 1% international
Most popular majors: 49% Licensed Practical/Vocational Nurse Training, 33% Liberal Arts and Sciences/Liberal Studies, 11% Registered Nursing/Registered Nurse, 4% Non-Profit/Public/Organizational Management, 1% Computer and Information Sciences, General
Expenses: 2020-2021: $8,100; room/board: N/A
Financial aid: N/A

Emporia State University
Emporia KS
(620) 341-5465
U.S. News ranking: Reg. U. (Mid. W), No. 82
Website: www.emporia.edu
Admissions email: go2esu@emporia.edu
Public; founded 1863
Freshman admissions: selective; 2020-2021: 1,544 applied, 1,329 accepted. Neither SAT nor ACT required. ACT 25/75 percentile: 19-24. High school rank: 14% in top tenth, 40% in top quarter, 72% in top half
Early decision deadline: N/A, notification date: N/A
Early action deadline: N/A, notification date: N/A
Application deadline (fall): rolling
Undergraduate student body: 2,909 full time, 272 part time; 36% male, 64% female; 0% American Indian, 1% Asian, 5% black, 8% Hispanic, 11% multiracial, 0% Pacific Islander, 69% white, 5% international; 87% from in state; 20% live on campus; 11% of students in fraternities, 10% in sororities
Most popular majors: 29% Education, 19% Business, Management, Marketing, and Related Support Services, 11% Health Professions and Related Programs, 5% Liberal Arts and Sciences, General Studies and Humanities, 5% Psychology
Expenses: 2021-2022: $5,278 in state, $13,195 out of state; room/board: N/A

Financial aid: (620) 341-5457; 59% of undergrads determined to have financial need; average aid package $9,624

Fort Hays State University
Hays KS
(800) 628-3478
U.S. News ranking: Reg. U. (Mid. W), No. 108
Website: www.fhsu.edu
Admissions email: tigers@fhsu.edu
Public; founded 1902
Freshman admissions: selective; 2020-2021: 1,920 applied, 1,754 accepted. Neither SAT nor ACT required. ACT 25/75 percentile: 17-24. High school rank: 17% in top tenth, 39% in top quarter, 74% in top half
Early decision deadline: N/A, notification date: N/A
Early action deadline: N/A, notification date: N/A
Application deadline (fall): rolling
Undergraduate student body: 5,580 full time, 6,631 part time; 40% male, 60% female; 0% American Indian, 1% Asian, 3% black, 8% Hispanic, 2% multiracial, 0% Pacific Islander, 50% white, 35% international; 71% from in state; 10% live on campus; N/A of students in fraternities, N/A in sororities
Most popular majors: Information not available
Expenses: 2020-2021: $5,430 in state, $15,870 out of state; room/board: $8,414
Financial aid: (785) 628-4408

Friends University[1]
Wichita KS
(316) 295-5100
U.S. News ranking: Reg. U. (Mid. W), No. 95
Website: www.friends.edu
Admissions email: admission@friends.edu
Private; founded 1898
Application deadline (fall): rolling
Undergraduate student body: N/A full time, N/A part time
Expenses: 2020-2021: $30,120; room/board: $8,350
Financial aid: (316) 295-5200

Hesston College
Hesston KS
(620) 327-4221
U.S. News ranking: Reg. Coll. (Mid. W), unranked
Website: www.hesston.edu/admissions
Admissions email: admissions@hesston.edu
Private; founded 1909
Affiliation: Mennonite Church
Freshman admissions: selective; 2020-2021: 604 applied, 303 accepted. Either SAT or ACT required. ACT 25/75 percentile: 17-23. High school rank: 0% in top tenth, 9% in top quarter, 40% in top half
Early decision deadline: N/A, notification date: N/A
Early action deadline: N/A, notification date: N/A
Application deadline (fall): rolling
Undergraduate student body: 330

full time, 29 part time; 42% male, 58% female; 1% American Indian, 3% Asian, 6% black, 15% Hispanic, 4% multiracial, 0% Pacific Islander, 58% white, 13% international; N/A from in state; N/A live on campus; 0% of students in fraternities, 0% in sororities
Most popular majors: 100% Registered Nursing/Registered Nurse
Expenses: 2021-2022: $28,992; room/board: $9,768
Financial aid: (620) 327-8220; 76% of undergrads determined to have financial need; average aid package $22,613

Kansas State University
Manhattan KS
(785) 532-6250
U.S. News ranking: Nat. U., No. 162
Website: www.k-state.edu
Admissions email: apply@k-state.edu
Public; founded 1863
Freshman admissions: more selective; 2020-2021: 8,937 applied, 8,459 accepted. Neither SAT nor ACT required. ACT 25/75 percentile: 20-27. High school rank: 25% in top tenth, 52% in top quarter, 84% in top half
Early decision deadline: N/A, notification date: N/A
Early action deadline: N/A, notification date: N/A
Application deadline (fall): rolling
Undergraduate student body: 14,497 full time, 1,760 part time; 51% male, 49% female; 0% American Indian, 2% Asian, 3% black, 8% Hispanic, 4% multiracial, 0% Pacific Islander, 79% white, 3% international; N/A from in state; 21% live on campus; N/A of students in fraternities, N/A in sororities
Most popular majors: 19% Business, Management, Marketing, and Related Support Services, 14% Engineering, 12% Agriculture, Agriculture Operations, and Related Sciences, 7% Biological and Biomedical Sciences, 7% Education
Expenses: 2021-2022: $10,466 in state, $26,342 out of state; room/board: $10,100
Financial aid: (785) 532-7626; 49% of undergrads determined to have financial need; average aid package $14,278

Kansas Wesleyan University
Salina KS
(785) 833-4305
U.S. News ranking: Reg. Coll. (Mid. W), No. 41
Website: www.kwu.edu
Admissions email: admissions@kwu.edu
Private; founded 1886
Affiliation: United Methodist
Freshman admissions: selective; 2020-2021: 1,293 applied, 799 accepted. Neither SAT nor ACT required. ACT 25/75 percentile: 18-24. High school rank: 12% in top tenth, 31% in top quarter,

67% in top half
Early decision deadline: N/A, notification date: N/A
Early action deadline: N/A, notification date: N/A
Application deadline (fall): rolling
Undergraduate student body: 698 full time, 51 part time; 58% male, 42% female; 1% American Indian, 0% Asian, 11% black, 22% Hispanic, 5% multiracial, 0% Pacific Islander, 60% white, 1% international; 43% from in state; 58% live on campus; N/A of students in fraternities, N/A in sororities
Most popular majors: 22% Business, Management, Marketing, and Related Support Services, 16% Homeland Security, Law Enforcement, Firefighting and Related Protective Services, 12% Education, 12% Health Professions and Related Programs, 9% Visual and Performing Arts
Expenses: 2021-2022: $31,340; room/board: $10,300
Financial aid: (785) 833-4317; 85% of undergrads determined to have financial need; average aid package $24,314

McPherson College
McPherson KS
(800) 365-7402
U.S. News ranking: Reg. Coll. (Mid. W), No. 35
Website: www.mcpherson.edu
Admissions email: admissions@mcpherson.edu
Private; founded 1887
Affiliation: Church of Brethren
Freshman admissions: selective; 2020-2021: 2,127 applied, 766 accepted. Neither SAT nor ACT required. ACT 25/75 percentile: 19-23. High school rank: N/A
Early decision deadline: N/A, notification date: N/A
Early action deadline: N/A, notification date: N/A
Application deadline (fall): 8/1
Undergraduate student body: 790 full time, 48 part time; 69% male, 31% female; 3% American Indian, 1% Asian, 16% black, 18% Hispanic, 4% multiracial, 0% Pacific Islander, 53% white, 0% international; 30% from in state; 68% live on campus; 0% of students in fraternities, 0% in sororities
Most popular majors: 21% Mechanical Engineering Related Technologies/Technicians, Other, 9% Business Administration and Management, General, 7% Health Professions and Related Programs, 6% Elementary Education and Teaching, 5% Health and Physical Education/Fitness, General
Expenses: 2021-2022: $32,408; room/board: $8,932
Financial aid: (620) 242-0400; 87% of undergrads determined to have financial need; average aid package $27,899

MidAmerica Nazarene University
Olathe KS
(913) 971-3380
U.S. News ranking: Reg. U. (Mid. W), No. 117
Website: www.mnu.edu
Admissions email: admissions@mnu.edu
Private; founded 1966
Affiliation: Church of the Nazarene
Freshman admissions: selective; 2020-2021: 734 applied, 734 accepted. Neither SAT nor ACT required. ACT 25/75 percentile: 16-24. High school rank: N/A
Early decision deadline: N/A, notification date: N/A
Early action deadline: N/A, notification date: N/A
Application deadline (fall): N/A
Undergraduate student body: 745 full time, 132 part time; 49% male, 51% female; 1% American Indian, 1% Asian, 15% black, 0% Hispanic, 4% multiracial, 1% Pacific Islander, 63% white, 5% international
Most popular majors: 47% Health Professions and Related Programs, 24% Business, Management, Marketing, and Related Support Services, 8% Education, 6% Parks, Recreation, Leisure, and Fitness Studies, 3% Psychology
Expenses: 2021-2022: $17,295; room/board: $9,562
Financial aid: (913) 971-3298

Newman University
Wichita KS
(877) 639-6268
U.S. News ranking: Reg. U. (Mid. W), No. 112
Website: www.newmanu.edu
Admissions email: admissions@newmanu.edu
Private; founded 1933
Affiliation: Roman Catholic
Freshman admissions: selective; 2020-2021: 597 applied, 496 accepted. Neither SAT nor ACT required. ACT 25/75 percentile: 19-26. High school rank: 21% in top tenth, 41% in top quarter, 58% in top half
Early decision deadline: N/A, notification date: N/A
Early action deadline: N/A, notification date: N/A
Application deadline (fall): 8/15
Undergraduate student body: 915 full time, 662 part time; 36% male, 64% female; 2% American Indian, 6% Asian, 5% black, 11% Hispanic, 1% multiracial, 0% Pacific Islander, 66% white, 5% international; 82% from in state; 16% live on campus; N/A of students in fraternities, N/A in sororities
Most popular majors: 21% Elementary Education and Teaching, 19% Registered Nursing/Registered Nurse, 11% Biology/Biological Sciences, General, 5% Business Administration and Management, General, 5% Criminal Justice/Safety Studies
Expenses: 2021-2022: $34,220; room/board: $9,094

Financial aid: (316) 942-4291; 77% of undergrads determined to have financial need; average aid package $24,088

Ottawa University
Ottawa KS
(785) 242-5200
U.S. News ranking: Reg. Coll. (Mid. W), No. 50
Website: www.ottawa.edu
Admissions email: admiss@ottawa.edu
Private; founded 1865
Affiliation: American Baptist
Freshman admissions: selective; 2020-2021: 1,840 applied, 450 accepted. Neither SAT nor ACT required. ACT 25/75 percentile: 18-22. High school rank: 6% in top tenth, 13% in top quarter, 48% in top half
Early decision deadline: N/A, notification date: N/A
Early action deadline: N/A, notification date: N/A
Application deadline (fall): 8/15
Undergraduate student body: 677 full time, 43 part time; 61% male, 39% female; 1% American Indian, 1% Asian, 12% black, 15% Hispanic, 1% multiracial, 0% Pacific Islander, 55% white, 0% international
Most popular majors: 27% Business Administration and Management, General, 13% Sports Studies, 11% Kinesiology and Exercise Science, 6% Management Information Systems, General, 4% Public Administration and Social Service Professions
Expenses: 2021-2022: $33,380; room/board: $12,184
Financial aid: (602) 749-5120; 86% of undergrads determined to have financial need; average aid package $26,966

Pittsburg State University[1]
Pittsburg KS
(800) 854-7488
U.S. News ranking: Reg. U. (Mid. W), No. 88
Website: www.pittstate.edu
Admissions email: psuadmit@pittstate.edu
Public; founded 1903
Application deadline (fall): 2/1
Undergraduate student body: N/A full time, N/A part time
Expenses: 2020-2021: $7,504 in state, $18,848 out of state; room/board: $8,196
Financial aid: (620) 235-4240

Southwestern College
Winfield KS
(620) 229-6236
U.S. News ranking: Reg. U. (Mid. W), second tier
Website: www.sckans.edu
Admissions email: scadmit@sckans.edu
Private; founded 1885
Affiliation: United Methodist
Freshman admissions: selective; 2020-2021: 1,404 applied, 787 accepted. Either SAT or ACT required. ACT 25/75 percentile: 17-22. High school rank: 5% in top tenth, 26% in top quarter,

64% in top half
Early decision deadline: N/A, notification date: N/A
Early action deadline: N/A, notification date: N/A
Application deadline (fall): 8/26
Undergraduate student body: 707 full time, 565 part time; 66% male, 34% female; 1% American Indian, 2% Asian, 10% black, 12% Hispanic, 3% multiracial, 1% Pacific Islander, 36% white, 3% international; 30% from in state; 71% live on campus; N/A of students in fraternities, N/A in sororities
Most popular majors: 11% Business Administration and Management, General, 10% Computer Programming/Programmer, General, 7% Business, Management, Marketing, and Related Support Services, Other, 6% Operations Management and Supervision, 6% Organizational Leadership
Expenses: 2021-2022: $34,900; room/board: $8,930
Financial aid: (620) 229-6215; 84% of undergrads determined to have financial need; average aid package $25,462

Sterling College
Sterling KS
(800) 346-1017
U.S. News ranking: Reg. Coll. (Mid. W), No. 43
Website: www.sterling.edu
Admissions email: admissions@sterling.edu
Private; founded 1887
Affiliation: Presbyterian
Freshman admissions: selective; 2020-2021: 1,898 applied, 700 accepted. Neither SAT nor ACT required. ACT 25/75 percentile: 18-25. High school rank: 12% in top tenth, 24% in top quarter, 51% in top half
Early decision deadline: N/A, notification date: N/A
Early action deadline: N/A, notification date: N/A
Application deadline (fall): rolling
Undergraduate student body: 529 full time, 136 part time; 58% male, 42% female; 2% American Indian, 1% Asian, 16% black, 12% Hispanic, 6% multiracial, 0% Pacific Islander, 55% white, 4% international; 38% from in state; 75% live on campus; 0% of students in fraternities, 0% in sororities
Most popular majors: 19% Health Professions and Related Programs, 15% Parks, Recreation, Leisure, and Fitness Studies, 14% Visual and Performing Arts, 13% Business, Management, and Related Support Services, 10% Psychology
Expenses: 2020-2021: $27,000; room/board: $8,610
Financial aid: (620) 278-4226

Tabor College

Hillsboro KS
(620) 947-3121
U.S. News ranking: Reg. Coll. (Mid. W), No. 50
Website: www.tabor.edu
Admissions email: admissions@tabor.edu
Private; founded 1908
Affiliation: Mennonite Brethren Church
Freshman admissions: selective; 2020-2021: 1,052 applied, 488 accepted. Either SAT or ACT required. ACT 25/75 percentile: 18-23. High school rank: 9% in top tenth, 29% in top quarter, 54% in top half
Early decision deadline: N/A, notification date: N/A
Early action deadline: N/A, notification date: N/A
Application deadline (fall): rolling
Undergraduate student body: 496 full time, 90 part time; 60% male, 40% female; 1% American Indian, 0% Asian, 16% black, 18% Hispanic, 9% multiracial, 0% Pacific Islander, 52% white, 4% international; 38% from in state; 97% live on campus; 0% of students in fraternities, 0% in sororities
Most popular majors: 14% Registered Nursing, Nursing Administration, Nursing Research and Clinical Nursing, Other, 8% Elementary Education and Teaching, 7% Sport and Fitness Administration/Management, 6% Biology/Biological Sciences, General, 6% Kinesiology and Exercise Science
Expenses: 2020-2021: $32,100; room/board: $9,100
Financial aid: (620) 947-3121

University of Kansas

Lawrence KS
(785) 864-3911
U.S. News ranking: Nat. U., No. 122
Website: www.ku.edu
Admissions email: adm@ku.edu
Public; founded 1865
Freshman admissions: more selective; 2020-2021: 15,042 applied, 13,678 accepted. Neither SAT nor ACT required. ACT 25/75 percentile: 22-29. High school rank: 31% in top tenth, 56% in top quarter, 83% in top half
Early decision deadline: N/A, notification date: N/A
Early action deadline: 11/1, notification date: 11/8
Application deadline (fall): 8/16
Undergraduate student body: 16,439 full time, 2,696 part time; 47% male, 53% female; 0% American Indian, 5% Asian, 4% black, 9% Hispanic, 5% multiracial, 0% Pacific Islander, 70% white, 5% international; 66% from in state; 21% live on campus; 17% of students in fraternities, 24% in sororities
Most popular majors: 6% Journalism, 6% Psychology, General, 5% Finance, General, 4% Marketing/Marketing Management, General, 4% Registered Nursing/Registered Nurse
Expenses: 2021-2022: $11,166 in state, $28,034 out of state;

room/board: $9,900
Financial aid: (785) 864-4700; 44% of undergrads determined to have financial need; average aid package $16,223

University of Saint Mary

Leavenworth KS
(913) 758-5151
U.S. News ranking: Reg. U. (Mid. W), No. 101
Website: www.stmary.edu
Admissions email: admiss@stmary.edu
Private; founded 1923
Affiliation: Roman Catholic
Freshman admissions: selective; 2020-2021: 1,375 applied, 819 accepted. Neither SAT nor ACT required. ACT 25/75 percentile: 17-23. High school rank: 9% in top tenth, 26% in top quarter, 61% in top half
Early decision deadline: N/A, notification date: N/A
Early action deadline: N/A, notification date: N/A
Application deadline (fall): rolling
Undergraduate student body: 732 full time, 78 part time; 49% male, 51% female; 1% American Indian, 2% Asian, 15% black, 16% Hispanic, 5% multiracial, 1% Pacific Islander, 50% white, 1% international; 47% from in state; 41% live on campus; N/A of students in fraternities, N/A in sororities
Most popular majors: 27% Registered Nursing/Registered Nurse, 11% Biology/Biological Sciences, General, 11% Psychology, General, 10% Business Administration and Management, General, 7% Criminology
Expenses: 2021-2022: $31,630; room/board: $8,310
Financial aid: (913) 758-6172; 84% of undergrads determined to have financial need; average aid package $22,993

Washburn University

Topeka KS
(785) 670-1030
U.S. News ranking: Nat. U., second tier
Website: www.washburn.edu
Admissions email: admissions@washburn.edu
Public; founded 1865
Freshman admissions: selective; 2020-2021: 2,107 applied, 1,962 accepted. Neither SAT nor ACT required. ACT 25/75 percentile: 18-24. High school rank: 15% in top tenth, 35% in top quarter, 68% in top half
Early decision deadline: N/A, notification date: N/A
Early action deadline: N/A, notification date: N/A
Application deadline (fall): rolling
Undergraduate student body: 3,325 full time, 1,739 part time; 38% male, 62% female; 1% American Indian, 1% Asian, 7% black, 13% Hispanic, 5% multiracial, 0% Pacific Islander, 66% white, 3% international
Most popular majors: 30% Health Professions and Related Programs,

19% Business, Management, Marketing, and Related Support Services, 6% Communication, Journalism, and Related Programs, 5% Homeland Security, Law Enforcement, Firefighting and Related Protective Services, 4% Public Administration and Social Service Professions
Expenses: 2021-2022: $8,872 in state, $19,876 out of state; room/board: $9,715
Financial aid: (785) 670-2770; 62% of undergrads determined to have financial need; average aid package $9,553

Wichita State University

Wichita KS
(316) 978-3085
U.S. News ranking: Nat. U., second tier
Website: www.wichita.edu
Admissions email: admissions@wichita.edu
Public; founded 1895
Freshman admissions: selective; 2020-2021: 6,311 applied, 3,456 accepted. Neither SAT nor ACT required. ACT 25/75 percentile: 20-27. High school rank: 23% in top tenth, 48% in top quarter, 82% in top half
Early decision deadline: N/A, notification date: N/A
Early action deadline: N/A, notification date: N/A
Application deadline (fall): rolling
Undergraduate student body: 8,586 full time, 3,820 part time; 44% male, 56% female; 1% American Indian, 7% Asian, 6% black, 14% Hispanic, 5% multiracial, 0% Pacific Islander, 60% white, 5% international; 14% from in state; 11% live on campus; 8% of students in fraternities, 8% in sororities
Most popular majors: 18% Business, Management, Marketing, and Related Support Services, 17% Health Professions and Related Programs, 13% Engineering, 11% Education, 6% Biological and Biomedical Sciences
Expenses: 2021-2022: $8,800 in state, $18,166 out of state; room/board: N/A
Financial aid: (316) 978-3430; 59% of undergrads determined to have financial need; average aid package $7,914

Alice Lloyd College

Pippa Passes KY
(888) 280-4252
U.S. News ranking: Reg. Coll. (S), No. 31
Website: www.alc.edu
Admissions email: admissions@alc.edu
Private; founded 1923
Freshman admissions: selective; 2020-2021: 4,024 applied, 294 accepted. Neither SAT nor ACT required. ACT 25/75 percentile: 17-22. High school rank: 8% in top tenth, 18% in top quarter, 38% in top half

Early decision deadline: N/A, notification date: N/A
Early action deadline: N/A, notification date: N/A
Application deadline (fall): 7/1
Undergraduate student body: 565 full time, 19 part time; 51% male, 49% female; 0% American Indian, 0% Asian, 4% black, 1% Hispanic, 0% multiracial, 0% Pacific Islander, 93% white, 1% international
Most popular majors: 20% Biology, General, 14% Education, General, 12% Kinesiology and Exercise Science, 10% Accounting and Business/Management, 8% Sociology
Expenses: 2021-2022: $14,230; room/board: $7,510
Financial aid: (606) 368-6058; 90% of undergrads determined to have financial need; average aid package $15,683

Asbury University

Wilmore KY
(800) 888-1818
U.S. News ranking: Reg. U. (S), No. 13
Website: asbury.edu
Admissions email: admissions@asbury.edu
Private; founded 1890
Affiliation: Wesleyan
Freshman admissions: more selective; 2020-2021: 1,018 applied, 999 accepted. Neither SAT nor ACT required. ACT 25/75 percentile: 21-28. High school rank: 28% in top tenth, 57% in top quarter, 80% in top half
Early decision deadline: N/A, notification date: N/A
Early action deadline: N/A, notification date: N/A
Application deadline (fall): rolling
Undergraduate student body: 1,240 full time, 252 part time; 40% male, 60% female; 0% American Indian, 2% Asian, 5% black, 7% Hispanic, 1% multiracial, 0% Pacific Islander, 78% white, 5% international
Most popular majors: 22% Business, Management, Marketing, and Related Support Services, 15% Communication, Journalism, and Related Programs, 13% Education, 9% Parks, Recreation, Leisure, and Fitness Studies, 7% Theology and Religious Vocations
Expenses: 2021-2022: $32,652; room/board: $8,340
Financial aid: (859) 858-3511; 77% of undergrads determined to have financial need; average aid package $22,994

Bellarmine University

Louisville KY
(502) 272-7100
U.S. News ranking: Nat. U., No. 202
Website: www.bellarmine.edu
Admissions email: admissions@bellarmine.edu
Private; founded 1950
Affiliation: Roman Catholic
Freshman admissions: selective; 2020-2021: 4,190 applied, 3,454 accepted. Neither SAT nor ACT required. ACT 25/75

percentile: 21-28. High school rank: N/A
Early decision deadline: N/A, notification date: N/A
Early action deadline: 11/1, notification date: 11/15
Application deadline (fall): 8/15
Undergraduate student body: 2,369 full time, 115 part time; 37% male, 63% female; 0% American Indian, 2% Asian, 6% black, 6% Hispanic, 5% multiracial, 0% Pacific Islander, 77% white, 1% international; 72% from in state; 35% live on campus; 1% of students in fraternities, 1% in sororities
Most popular majors: 28% Registered Nursing/Registered Nurse, 8% Psychology, General, 7% Business Administration and Management, General, 7% Speech Communication and Rhetoric, 6% Kinesiology and Exercise Science
Expenses: 2021-2022: $44,520; room/board: $9,030
Financial aid: (502) 272-7300; 78% of undergrads determined to have financial need; average aid package $35,816

Berea College

Berea KY
(859) 985-3500
U.S. News ranking: Nat. Lib. Arts, No. 30
Website: www.berea.edu
Admissions email: admissions@berea.edu
Private; founded 1855
Freshman admissions: more selective; 2020-2021: 1,857 applied, 612 accepted. Neither SAT nor ACT required. ACT 25/75 percentile: 22-26. High school rank: 25% in top tenth, 69% in top quarter, 98% in top half
Early decision deadline: N/A, notification date: N/A
Early action deadline: N/A, notification date: N/A
Application deadline (fall): 3/31
Undergraduate student body: 1,423 full time, 9 part time; 40% male, 60% female; 0% American Indian, 3% Asian, 18% black, 14% Hispanic, 9% multiracial, 0% Pacific Islander, 50% white, 6% international; 46% from in state; 56% live on campus; 0% of students in fraternities, 0% in sororities
Most popular majors: 7% Biology/Biological Sciences, General, 7% Computer and Information Sciences, General, 6% Mass Communication/Media Studies
Expenses: 2021-2022: $712; room/board: $7,484
Financial aid: (859) 985-3313; 100% of undergrads determined to have financial need; average aid package $49,395

Brescia University

Owensboro KY
(270) 686-4241
U.S. News ranking: Reg. Coll. (S), No. 31
Website: www.brescia.edu
Admissions email: admissions@brescia.edu
Private; founded 1925
Affiliation: Roman Catholic

Freshman admissions: selective; 2020-2021: 2,490 applied, 1,191 accepted. Either SAT or ACT required. ACT 25/75 percentile: 19-25. High school rank: N/A
Early decision deadline: N/A, notification date: N/A
Early action deadline: N/A, notification date: N/A
Application deadline (fall): rolling
Undergraduate student body: 715 full time, 190 part time; 37% male, 63% female; 1% American Indian, 3% Asian, 11% black, 7% Hispanic, 0% multiracial, 0% Pacific Islander, 62% white, 1% international
Most popular majors: 41% Social Work, 13% Psychology, General, 7% Business/Commerce, General, 6% Accounting, 5% Liberal Arts and Sciences/Liberal Studies
Expenses: 2021-2022: $26,950; room/board: $10,204
Financial aid: (270) 686-4253; 85% of undergrads determined to have financial need; average aid package $19,894

Campbellsville University
Campbellsville KY
(270) 789-5220
U.S. News ranking: Reg. U. (S), No. 98
Website: www.campbellsville.edu
Admissions email: admissions@campbellsville.edu
Private; founded 1906
Freshman admissions: selective; 2020-2021: 5,130 applied, 3,983 accepted. Neither SAT nor ACT required. ACT 25/75 percentile: 17-23. High school rank: 3% in top tenth, 12% in top quarter, 38% in top half
Early decision deadline: N/A, notification date: N/A
Early action deadline: N/A, notification date: N/A
Application deadline (fall): rolling
Undergraduate student body: 2,495 full time, 3,299 part time; 40% male, 60% female; 0% American Indian, 1% Asian, 16% black, 5% Hispanic, 1% multiracial, 0% Pacific Islander, 67% white, 7% international; 93% from in state; 20% live on campus; 0% of students in fraternities, 0% in sororities
Most popular majors: 17% Business/Commerce, General, 14% Social Work, 8% Criminal Justice/Law Enforcement Administration, 8% Registered Nursing/Registered Nurse, 6% Psychology, General
Expenses: 2021-2022: $25,400; room/board: $8,800
Financial aid: (270) 789-5013; 82% of undergrads determined to have financial need; average aid package $20,190

Centre College
Danville KY
(859) 238-5350
U.S. News ranking: Nat. Lib. Arts, No. 59
Website: www.centre.edu
Admissions email: admission@centre.edu

Private; founded 1819
Affiliation: Presbyterian
Freshman admissions: more selective; 2020-2021: 2,142 applied, 1,541 accepted. Neither SAT nor ACT required. ACT 25/75 percentile: 26-32. High school rank: 46% in top tenth, 75% in top quarter, 93% in top half
Early decision deadline: 12/15, notification date: 12/15
Early action deadline: 12/1, notification date: 1/15
Application deadline (fall): 1/15
Undergraduate student body: 1,333 full time, 0 part time; 49% male, 51% female; 0% American Indian, 5% Asian, 5% black, 7% Hispanic, 4% multiracial, 0% Pacific Islander, 72% white, 5% international; 60% from in state; 99% live on campus; 51% of students in fraternities, 50% in sororities
Most popular majors: 19% Economics, Other, 9% Biology/Biological Sciences, General, 8% International/Global Studies, 7% History, General, 7% Physiological Psychology/Psychobiology
Expenses: 2021-2022: $46,000; room/board: $11,600
Financial aid: (859) 238-5365; 60% of undergrads determined to have financial need; average aid package $38,674

Eastern Kentucky University
Richmond KY
(859) 622-2106
U.S. News ranking: Reg. U. (S), No. 52
Website: www.eku.edu
Admissions email: admissions@eku.edu
Public; founded 1906
Freshman admissions: selective; 2020-2021: 9,206 applied, 9,017 accepted. Either SAT or ACT required. ACT 25/75 percentile: 19-25. High school rank: 16% in top tenth, 39% in top quarter, 69% in top half
Early decision deadline: N/A, notification date: N/A
Early action deadline: N/A, notification date: N/A
Application deadline (fall): 8/1
Undergraduate student body: 9,572 full time, 2,982 part time; 44% male, 56% female; 0% American Indian, 1% Asian, 6% black, 4% Hispanic, 4% multiracial, 0% Pacific Islander, 82% white, 1% international; N/A from in state; 0% live on campus; 1% of students in fraternities, 1% in sororities
Most popular majors: 15% Health Professions and Related Programs, 13% Business, Management, Marketing, and Related Support Services, 11% Homeland Security, Law Enforcement, Firefighting and Related Protective Services
Expenses: 2021-2022: $9,806 in state, $10,713 out of state; room/board: $10,173
Financial aid: (859) 622-2361; 69% of undergrads determined to have financial need; average aid package $12,633

Georgetown College
Georgetown KY
(800) 788-9985
U.S. News ranking: Nat. Lib. Arts, second tier
Website: www.georgetowncollege.edu
Admissions email: admissions@georgetowncollege.edu
Private; founded 1829
Affiliation: Baptist
Freshman admissions: selective; 2020-2021: 2,712 applied, 1,957 accepted. Either SAT or ACT required. ACT 25/75 percentile: 20-26. High school rank: 15% in top tenth, 39% in top quarter, 70% in top half
Early decision deadline: N/A, notification date: N/A
Early action deadline: N/A, notification date: N/A
Application deadline (fall): rolling
Undergraduate student body: 1,067 full time, 42 part time; 45% male, 55% female; 0% American Indian, 0% Asian, 8% black, 5% Hispanic, 5% multiracial, 0% Pacific Islander, 77% white, 2% international; 78% from in state; 95% live on campus; N/A of students in fraternities, N/A in sororities
Most popular majors: 20% Psychology, General, 8% Communication and Media Studies, 7% Biology/Biological Sciences, General, 7% Health and Physical Education/Fitness, General, 6% Business/Commerce, General
Expenses: 2021-2022: $41,200; room/board: $10,990
Financial aid: (502) 863-8027; 84% of undergrads determined to have financial need; average aid package $41,264

Kentucky Christian University[1]
Grayson KY
(800) 522-3181
U.S. News ranking: Reg. Coll. (S), No. 65
Website: www.kcu.edu
Admissions email: knights@kcu.edu
Private; founded 1919
Application deadline (fall): 8/1
Undergraduate student body: N/A full time, N/A part time
Expenses: 2020-2021: $21,200; room/board: $8,700
Financial aid: (606) 474-3226

Kentucky State University
Frankfort KY
(800) 633-9415
U.S. News ranking: Reg. Coll. (S), No. 35
Website: www.kysu.edu
Admissions email: admissions@kysu.edu
Public; founded 1886
Freshman admissions: less selective; 2020-2021: 3,377 applied, 2,836 accepted. Either SAT or ACT required. ACT 25/75 percentile: 15-20. High school rank: 2% in top tenth, 12% in top quarter, 43% in top half

Early decision deadline: N/A, notification date: N/A
Early action deadline: N/A, notification date: N/A
Application deadline (fall): rolling
Undergraduate student body: 1,393 full time, 755 part time; 41% male, 59% female; 0% American Indian, 1% Asian, 78% black, 4% Hispanic, 4% multiracial, 0% Pacific Islander, 10% white, 1% international; 47% from in state; 42% live on campus; 7% of students in fraternities, 5% in sororities
Most popular majors: 12% Liberal Arts and Sciences/Liberal Studies, 10% Business Administration and Management, General, 10% Physical Education Teaching and Coaching, 7% Computer and Information Sciences, General, 7% Psychology, General
Expenses: 2021-2022: $9,190 in state, $13,040 out of state; room/board: $6,690
Financial aid: (502) 597-5759; 90% of undergrads determined to have financial need; average aid package $12,875

Kentucky Wesleyan College
Owensboro KY
(800) 999-0592
U.S. News ranking: Reg. Coll. (S), No. 21
Website: kwc.edu/
Admissions email: admissions@kwc.edu
Private; founded 1858
Affiliation: United Methodist
Freshman admissions: selective; 2020-2021: 1,761 applied, 1,061 accepted. Neither SAT nor ACT required. ACT 25/75 percentile: 18-25. High school rank: N/A
Early decision deadline: N/A, notification date: N/A
Early action deadline: N/A, notification date: N/A
Application deadline (fall): 9/1
Undergraduate student body: 817 full time, 64 part time; 50% male, 50% female; 1% American Indian, 1% Asian, 14% black, 3% Hispanic, 1% multiracial, 0% Pacific Islander, 69% white, 0% international
Most popular majors: 13% Business/Commerce, General, 9% Accounting, 9% Zoology/Animal Biology, 8% Biology/Biological Sciences, General, 7% Sport and Fitness Administration/Management
Expenses: 2020-2021: $28,540; room/board: $10,000
Financial aid: (270) 852-3130

Lindsey Wilson College
Columbia KY
(800) 264-0138
U.S. News ranking: Reg. U. (S), No. 84
Website: www.lindsey.edu
Admissions email: admissions@lindsey.edu
Private; founded 1903
Affiliation: United Methodist
Freshman admissions: selective; 2020-2021: N/A applied, N/A

accepted. Neither SAT nor ACT required. ACT 25/75 percentile: 18-24. High school rank: 15% in top tenth, 38% in top quarter, 68% in top half
Early decision deadline: N/A, notification date: N/A
Early action deadline: N/A, notification date: N/A
Application deadline (fall): rolling
Undergraduate student body: 1,762 full time, 163 part time; 39% male, 61% female; 0% American Indian, 0% Asian, 10% black, 0% Hispanic, 2% multiracial, 0% Pacific Islander, 68% white, 1% international
Most popular majors: 39% Public Administration and Social Service Professions, 10% Business/Commerce, General, 8% Speech Communication and Rhetoric, 6% Health Professions and Related Programs, 4% General Studies
Expenses: 2021-2022: $25,718; room/board: $9,495
Financial aid: (270) 384-8022; 92% of undergrads determined to have financial need; average aid package $23,428

Midway University
Midway KY
(800) 952-4122
U.S. News ranking: Reg. U. (S), No. 98
Website: www.midway.edu
Admissions email: admissions@midway.edu
Private; founded 1847
Affiliation: Christian Church (Disciples of Christ)
Freshman admissions: selective; 2020-2021: 1,043 applied, 762 accepted. Either SAT or ACT required. ACT 25/75 percentile: 18-24. High school rank: 6% in top tenth, 26% in top quarter, 68% in top half
Early decision deadline: N/A, notification date: N/A
Early action deadline: N/A, notification date: N/A
Application deadline (fall): rolling
Undergraduate student body: 933 full time, 660 part time; 35% male, 65% female; 0% American Indian, 1% Asian, 9% black, 7% Hispanic, 4% multiracial, 0% Pacific Islander, 73% white, 2% international; 80% from in state; 50% live on campus; N/A of students in fraternities, N/A in sororities
Most popular majors: 22% Business, Management, Marketing, and Related Support Services, 15% Psychology, 14% Agriculture, Agriculture Operations, and Related Sciences, 11% Parks, Recreation, Leisure, and Fitness Studies, 10% Health Professions and Related Programs
Expenses: 2021-2022: $24,850; room/board: $8,600
Financial aid: (859) 846-5494; 84% of undergrads determined to have financial need; average aid package $19,499

Morehead State University

Morehead KY
(800) 585-6781
U.S. News ranking: Reg. U. (S), No. 48
Website: www.moreheadstate.edu
Admissions email: admissions@moreheadstate.edu
Public; founded 1887
Freshman admissions: selective; 2020-2021: 8,684 applied, 6,661 accepted. Neither SAT nor ACT required. ACT 25/75 percentile: 20-26. High school rank: 28% in top tenth, 61% in top quarter, 93% in top half
Early decision deadline: N/A, notification date: N/A
Early action deadline: N/A, notification date: N/A
Application deadline (fall): rolling
Undergraduate student body: 5,299 full time, 3,322 part time; 39% male, 61% female; 0% American Indian, 0% Asian, 4% black, 2% Hispanic, 3% multiracial, 0% Pacific Islander, 89% white, 1% international; 90% from in state; 37% live on campus; 11% of students in fraternities, 10% in sororities
Most popular majors: 12% General Studies, 6% Registered Nursing/Registered Nurse, 5% Social Work, 4% Biomedical Sciences, General, 4% Engineering Technologies and Engineering-Related Fields
Expenses: 2021-2022: $9,462 in state, $14,142 out of state; room/board: $10,040
Financial aid: (606) 783-2011; 76% of undergrads determined to have financial need; average aid package $12,166

Murray State University

Murray KY
(270) 809-3741
U.S. News ranking: Reg. U. (S), No. 25
Website: www.murraystate.edu
Admissions email: msu.admissions@murraystate.edu
Public; founded 1922
Freshman admissions: selective; 2020-2021: 9,549 applied, 7,358 accepted. Neither SAT nor ACT required. ACT 25/75 percentile: 21-27. High school rank: 26% in top tenth, 51% in top quarter, 82% in top half
Early decision deadline: N/A, notification date: N/A
Early action deadline: N/A, notification date: N/A
Application deadline (fall): rolling
Undergraduate student body: 6,185 full time, 1,754 part time; 38% male, 62% female; 0% American Indian, 1% Asian, 6% black, 3% Hispanic, 3% multiracial, 0% Pacific Islander, 79% white, 5% international; N/A from in state; 30% live on campus; N/A of students in fraternities, N/A in sororities
Most popular majors: 16% Health Professions and Related Programs, 12% Business, Management, Marketing, and Related Support Services, 10% Education, 8%

Engineering Technologies and Engineering-Related Fields, 6% Liberal Arts and Sciences, General Studies and Humanities
Expenses: 2021-2022: $9,252 in state, $14,058 out of state; room/board: $10,394
Financial aid: (270) 809-2546; 66% of undergrads determined to have financial need; average aid package $12,750

Northern Kentucky University

Highland Heights KY
(859) 572-5220
U.S. News ranking: Nat. U., second tier
Website: www.nku.edu/
Admissions email: beanorse@nku.edu
Public; founded 1968
Freshman admissions: selective; 2020-2021: 6,686 applied, 5,819 accepted. Neither SAT nor ACT required. ACT 25/75 percentile: 20-26. High school rank: 16% in top tenth, 41% in top quarter, 74% in top half
Early decision deadline: N/A, notification date: N/A
Early action deadline: N/A, notification date: N/A
Application deadline (fall): 8/21
Undergraduate student body: 8,024 full time, 3,483 part time; 40% male, 60% female; 0% American Indian, 2% Asian, 7% black, 4% Hispanic, 3% multiracial, 0% Pacific Islander, 80% white, 3% international; 68% from in state; 10% live on campus; 7% of students in fraternities, 10% in sororities
Most popular majors: 13% Business Administration and Management, General, 10% Registered Nursing/Registered Nurse, 5% Organizational Behavior Studies, 4% Liberal Arts and Sciences/Liberal Studies, 4% Psychology, General
Expenses: 2021-2022: $10,392 in state, $20,448 out of state; room/board: $9,920
Financial aid: (859) 572-5143; 61% of undergrads determined to have financial need; average aid package $13,932

Spalding University[1]

Louisville KY
(502) 585-7111
U.S. News ranking: Nat. U., second tier
Website: www.spalding.edu
Admissions email: admissions@spalding.edu
Private; founded 1814
Application deadline (fall): rolling
Undergraduate student body: N/A full time, N/A part time
Expenses: 2020-2021: $25,975; room/board: $7,600
Financial aid: N/A

Sullivan University[1]

Louisville KY
(502) 456-6504
U.S. News ranking: Reg. U. (S), unranked
Website: www.sullivan.edu

Admissions email: admissions@sullivan.edu
For-profit
Application deadline (fall): N/A
Undergraduate student body: N/A full time, N/A part time
Expenses: 2020-2021: $13,860; room/board: $10,485
Financial aid: N/A

Thomas More University

Crestview Hills KY
(800) 825-4557
U.S. News ranking: Reg. U. (S), No. 65
Website: www.thomasmore.edu
Admissions email: admissions@thomasmore.edu
Private; founded 1921
Affiliation: Roman Catholic
Freshman admissions: selective; 2020-2021: 2,646 applied, 2,432 accepted. Neither SAT nor ACT required. ACT 25/75 percentile: 19-24. High school rank: 13% in top tenth, 34% in top quarter, 65% in top half
Early decision deadline: N/A, notification date: N/A
Early action deadline: N/A, notification date: N/A
Application deadline (fall): rolling
Undergraduate student body: 1,323 full time, 569 part time; 48% male, 52% female; 0% American Indian, 1% Asian, 9% black, 3% Hispanic, 5% multiracial, 0% Pacific Islander, 76% white, 2% international; 59% from in state; 26% live on campus; N/A of students in fraternities, N/A in sororities
Most popular majors: 25% Business Administration and Management, General, 14% Registered Nursing/Registered Nurse, 13% Liberal Arts and Sciences/Liberal Studies, 6% Accounting, 6% Psychology, General
Expenses: 2021-2022: $34,760; room/board: $9,320
Financial aid: (859) 344-3319; 81% of undergrads determined to have financial need; average aid package $27,844

Transylvania University

Lexington KY
(859) 233-8242
U.S. News ranking: Nat. Lib. Arts, No. 92
Website: www.transy.edu
Admissions email: admissions@transy.edu
Private; founded 1780
Affiliation: Christian Church (Disciples of Christ)
Freshman admissions: more selective; 2020-2021: 1,663 applied, 1,532 accepted. Neither SAT nor ACT required. ACT 25/75 percentile: 24-30. High school rank: 30% in top tenth, 61% in top quarter, 89% in top half
Early decision deadline: N/A, notification date: N/A
Early action deadline: 10/15, notification date: 11/1
Application deadline (fall): rolling
Undergraduate student body: 953 full time, 5 part time; 41%

male, 59% female; 1% American Indian, 3% Asian, 5% black, 4% Hispanic, 5% multiracial, 0% Pacific Islander, 78% white, 0% international; 20% from in state; 53% live on campus; 45% of students in fraternities, 41% in sororities
Most popular majors: 20% Business/Commerce, General, 14% Biology/Biological Sciences, General, 11% Social Sciences, General, 9% Psychology, General
Expenses: 2021-2022: $42,520; room/board: $12,200
Financial aid: (859) 233-8239; 71% of undergrads determined to have financial need; average aid package $31,169

Union College[1]

Barbourville KY
(606) 546-4151
U.S. News ranking: Reg. U. (S), second tier
Website: www.unionky.edu
Admissions email: enroll@unionky.edu
Private
Application deadline (fall): N/A
Undergraduate student body: N/A full time, N/A part time
Expenses: 2020-2021: $28,000; room/board: $6,700
Financial aid: (606) 546-1224

University of Kentucky

Lexington KY
(859) 257-2000
U.S. News ranking: Nat. U., No. 127
Website: www.uky.edu
Admissions email: admissions@uky.edu
Public; founded 1865
Freshman admissions: more selective; 2020-2021: 19,648 applied, 18,932 accepted. Neither SAT nor ACT required. ACT 25/75 percentile: 22-29. High school rank: 33% in top tenth, 62% in top quarter, 87% in top half
Early decision deadline: N/A, notification date: N/A
Early action deadline: 12/1, notification date: 1/15
Application deadline (fall): 2/15
Undergraduate student body: 20,239 full time, 1,988 part time; 43% male, 57% female; 0% American Indian, 3% Asian, 7% black, 6% Hispanic, 4% multiracial, 0% Pacific Islander, 75% white, 2% international; 69% from in state; 29% live on campus; 21% of students in fraternities, 33% in sororities
Most popular majors: 22% Business, Management, Marketing, and Related Support Services, 11% Health Professions and Related Programs, 9% Engineering, 8% Communication, Journalism, and Related Programs, 8% Education
Expenses: 2021-2022: $12,610 in state, $31,608 out of state; room/board: $14,186
Financial aid: (859) 257-3172; 51% of undergrads determined to have financial need; average aid package $14,893

University of Louisville

Louisville KY
(502) 852-6531
U.S. News ranking: Nat. U., No. 187
Website: www.louisville.edu
Admissions email: admitme@louisville.edu
Public; founded 1798
Affiliation: Undenominational
Freshman admissions: selective; 2020-2021: 16,598 applied, 10,910 accepted. Neither SAT nor ACT required. ACT 25/75 percentile: 21-29. High school rank: 31% in top tenth, 55% in top quarter, 83% in top half
Early decision deadline: N/A, notification date: N/A
Early action deadline: N/A, notification date: N/A
Application deadline (fall): 8/1
Undergraduate student body: 11,598 full time, 4,329 part time; 45% male, 55% female; 0% American Indian, 5% Asian, 13% black, 6% Hispanic, 6% multiracial, 0% Pacific Islander, 68% white, 1% international; 80% from in state; 32% live on campus; 18% of students in fraternities, 14% in sororities
Most popular majors: 18% Business, Management, Marketing, and Related Support Services, 13% Engineering, 11% Health Professions and Related Programs, 8% Education, 8% Parks, Recreation, Leisure, and Fitness Studies
Expenses: 2021-2022: $12,370 in state, $196 out of state; room/board: $9,564
Financial aid: (502) 852-5511; 63% of undergrads determined to have financial need; average aid package $12,765

University of Pikeville

Pikeville KY
(606) 218-5251
U.S. News ranking: Nat. Lib. Arts, second tier
Website: www.upike.edu/
Admissions email: wewantyou@upike.edu
Private; founded 1889
Affiliation: Presbyterian Church (USA)
Freshman admissions: selective; 2020-2021: 1,737 applied, 1,737 accepted. Either SAT or ACT required. ACT 25/75 percentile: 17-24. High school rank: 21% in top tenth, 42% in top quarter, 74% in top half
Early decision deadline: N/A, notification date: N/A
Early action deadline: N/A, notification date: N/A
Application deadline (fall): rolling
Undergraduate student body: 1,048 full time, 303 part time; 46% male, 54% female; 1% American Indian, 1% Asian, 12% black, 1% Hispanic, 1% multiracial, 0% Pacific Islander, 82% white, 2% international; 79% from in state; 53% live on campus; N/A of students in fraternities, N/A in sororities
Most popular majors: Information not available

Expenses: 2021-2022: $22,650; room/board: $8,200
Financial aid: (606) 218-5254; 95% of undergrads determined to have financial need; average aid package $21,759

University of the Cumberlands[1]
Williamsburg KY
(800) 343-1609
U.S. News ranking: Nat. U., second tier
Website: www.ucumberlands.edu
Admissions email: admiss@ucumberlands.edu
Private; founded 1888
Affiliation: Baptist
Application deadline (fall): 8/31
Undergraduate student body: N/A full time, N/A part time
Expenses: 2020-2021: $9,875; room/board: $9,300
Financial aid: (606) 539-4239

Western Kentucky University
Bowling Green KY
(270) 745-2551
U.S. News ranking: Nat. U., second tier
Website: www.wku.edu
Admissions email: admission@wku.edu
Public; founded 1906
Freshman admissions: selective; 2020-2021: 8,578 applied, 8,385 accepted. Neither SAT nor ACT required. ACT 25/75 percentile: 19-26. High school rank: 20% in top tenth, 46% in top quarter, 76% in top half
Early decision deadline: N/A, notification date: N/A
Early action deadline: N/A, notification date: N/A
Application deadline (fall): 8/1
Undergraduate student body: 11,749 full time, 3,537 part time; 39% male, 61% female; 0% American Indian, 2% Asian, 10% black, 4% Hispanic, 4% multiracial, 0% Pacific Islander, 78% white, 2% international; 75% from in state; 33% live on campus; 16% of students in fraternities, 18% in sororities
Most popular majors: 8% Registered Nursing/Registered Nurse, 7% General Studies, 4% Business Administration and Management, General, 4% Management Science, 4% Organizational Leadership
Expenses: 2021-2022: $10,992 in state, N/A out of state; room/board: N/A
Financial aid: (270) 745-2051; 63% of undergrads determined to have financial need; average aid package $14,948

LOUISIANA

Centenary College[1]
Shreveport LA
(318) 869-5011
U.S. News ranking: Nat. Lib. Arts, No. 164
Website: www.centenary.edu/
Admissions email: admission@centenary.edu

Private; founded 1825
Affiliation: United Methodist
Application deadline (fall): rolling
Undergraduate student body: N/A full time, N/A part time
Expenses: 2021-2022: $38,060; room/board: $13,940
Financial aid: (318) 869-5137

Dillard University
New Orleans LA
(800) 216-6637
U.S. News ranking: Nat. Lib. Arts, second tier
Website: www.dillard.edu
Admissions email: admissions@dillard.edu
Private; founded 1869
Affiliation: Interdenominational
Freshman admissions: selective; 2020-2021: 5,783 applied, 3,777 accepted. Either SAT or ACT required. ACT 25/75 percentile: 18-22. High school rank: N/A
Early decision deadline: N/A, notification date: N/A
Early action deadline: N/A, notification date: N/A
Application deadline (fall): rolling
Undergraduate student body: 1,152 full time, 63 part time; 23% male, 77% female; 0% American Indian, 0% Asian, 84% black, 3% Hispanic, 2% multiracial, 0% Pacific Islander, 0% white, 0% international; 54% from in state; 53% live on campus; 9% of students in fraternities, 4% in sororities
Most popular majors: 15% Biological and Biomedical Sciences, 9% Psychology, 7% Communication, Journalism, and Related Programs, 6% Physical Sciences, 5% Computer and Information Sciences and Support Services
Expenses: 2021-2022: $18,112; room/board: $10,466
Financial aid: (504) 816-4864; 94% of undergrads determined to have financial need; average aid package $17,840

Grambling State University[1]
Grambling LA
(318) 274-6183
U.S. News ranking: Reg. U. (S), second tier
Website: www.gram.edu/
Admissions email: admissions@gram.edu
Public; founded 1901
Application deadline (fall): rolling
Undergraduate student body: N/A full time, N/A part time
Expenses: N/A
Financial aid: (318) 274-6328

Louisiana College
Pineville LA
(318) 487-7259
U.S. News ranking: Reg. U. (S), second tier
Website: www.lacollege.edu
Admissions email: admissions@lacollege.edu
Private; founded 1906
Affiliation: Southern Baptist
Freshman admissions: selective; 2020-2021: 808 applied, 575

accepted. Either SAT or ACT required. ACT 25/75 percentile: 18-24. High school rank: 6% in top tenth, 23% in top quarter, 58% in top half
Early decision deadline: N/A, notification date: N/A
Early action deadline: N/A, notification date: N/A
Application deadline (fall): rolling
Undergraduate student body: 835 full time, 107 part time; 52% male, 48% female; 1% American Indian, 1% Asian, 28% black, 2% Hispanic, 3% multiracial, 0% Pacific Islander, 64% white, 1% international
Most popular majors: 17% Health Professions and Related Programs, 14% Business, Management, Marketing, and Related Support Services, 11% Liberal Arts and Sciences, General Studies and Humanities, 10% Education, 8% Communication, Journalism, and Related Programs
Expenses: 2020-2021: $17,500; room/board: $5,854
Financial aid: (318) 487-7387

Louisiana State University–Alexandria[1]
Alexandria LA
(318) 473-6417
U.S. News ranking: Nat. Lib. Arts, second tier
Website: www.lsua.edu
Admissions email: admissions@lsua.edu
Public; founded 1960
Application deadline (fall): 8/1
Undergraduate student body: N/A full time, N/A part time
Expenses: N/A
Financial aid: (318) 473-6477

Louisiana State University–Baton Rouge
Baton Rouge LA
(225) 578-1175
U.S. News ranking: Nat. U., No. 172
Website: www.lsu.edu
Admissions email: admissions@lsu.edu
Public; founded 1860
Freshman admissions: more selective; 2020-2021: 28,960 applied, 21,252 accepted. Either SAT or ACT required. ACT 25/75 percentile: 23-28. High school rank: 24% in top tenth, 49% in top quarter, 78% in top half
Early decision deadline: N/A, notification date: N/A
Early action deadline: N/A, notification date: N/A
Application deadline (fall): 4/15
Undergraduate student body: 24,097 full time, 3,728 part time; 46% male, 54% female; 1% American Indian, 5% Asian, 15% black, 8% Hispanic, 3% multiracial, 0% Pacific Islander, 67% white, 2% international; N/A from in state; 28% live on campus; 15% of students in fraternities, 25% in sororities
Most popular majors: 24% Business, Management, Marketing, and Related Support

Services, 14% Engineering, 9% Education, 7% Biological and Biomedical Sciences, 7% Social Sciences
Expenses: 2021-2022: $11,328 in state, $28,005 out of state; room/board: $13,154
Financial aid: (225) 578-3103; 55% of undergrads determined to have financial need; average aid package $14,955

Louisiana State University–Shreveport[1]
Shreveport LA
(318) 797-5061
U.S. News ranking: Reg. U. (S), No. 102
Website: www.lsus.edu
Admissions email: admissions@lsus.edu
Public; founded 1967
Application deadline (fall): rolling
Undergraduate student body: N/A full time, N/A part time
Expenses: N/A
Financial aid: (318) 797-5363

Louisiana Tech University
Ruston LA
(318) 257-3036
U.S. News ranking: Nat. U., No. 277
Website: www.latech.edu/
Admissions email: bulldog@latech.edu
Public; founded 1894
Freshman admissions: more selective; 2020-2021: 7,087 applied, 4,505 accepted. Either SAT or ACT required. ACT 25/75 percentile: 22-28. High school rank: 25% in top tenth, 51% in top quarter, 80% in top half
Early decision deadline: N/A, notification date: N/A
Early action deadline: N/A, notification date: N/A
Application deadline (fall): rolling
Undergraduate student body: 7,854 full time, 2,159 part time; 52% male, 48% female; 0% American Indian, 1% Asian, 12% black, 4% Hispanic, 3% multiracial, 0% Pacific Islander, 73% white, 2% international; 14% from in state; 20% live on campus; N/A of students in fraternities, N/A in sororities
Most popular majors: 7% Biology/Biological Sciences, General, 5% Mechanical Engineering, 4% Accounting, 4% Business Administration and Management, General, 4% Computer Science
Expenses: 2021-2022: $10,635 in state, $19,548 out of state; room/board: $9,210
Financial aid: (318) 257-2641; 59% of undergrads determined to have financial need; average aid package $11,447

Loyola University New Orleans
New Orleans LA
(800) 456-9652
U.S. News ranking: Nat. U., No. 202
Website: www.loyno.edu

Admissions email: admit@loyno.edu
Private; founded 1912
Affiliation: Roman Catholic
Freshman admissions: selective; 2020-2021: 6,259 applied, 4,531 accepted. Neither SAT nor ACT required. ACT 25/75 percentile: 21-26. High school rank: 35% in top tenth, 49% in top quarter, 76% in top half
Early decision deadline: N/A, notification date: N/A
Early action deadline: 11/15, notification date: 12/1
Application deadline (fall): rolling
Undergraduate student body: 2,955 full time, 264 part time; 34% male, 66% female; 0% American Indian, 3% Asian, 19% black, 20% Hispanic, 5% multiracial, 0% Pacific Islander, 45% white, 3% international; 55% from in state; 32% live on campus; 12% of students in fraternities, 13% in sororities
Most popular majors: 10% Psychology, General, 8% Music Management, 5% Criminology, 4% Creative Writing, 4% Journalism
Expenses: 2021-2022: $43,498; room/board: $13,992
Financial aid: (504) 865-3231; 72% of undergrads determined to have financial need; average aid package $34,870

McNeese State University[1]
Lake Charles LA
(337) 475-5504
U.S. News ranking: Reg. U. (S), No. 98
Website: www.mcneese.edu
Admissions email: admissions@mcneese.edu
Public; founded 1939
Application deadline (fall): 8/1
Undergraduate student body: N/A full time, N/A part time
Expenses: 2020-2021: $8,382 in state, $16,420 out of state; room/board: $9,062
Financial aid: (337) 475-5065

Nicholls State University
Thibodaux LA
(985) 448-4507
U.S. News ranking: Reg. U. (S), No. 88
Website: www.nicholls.edu
Admissions email: nicholls@nicholls.edu
Public; founded 1948
Freshman admissions: selective; 2020-2021: 3,189 applied, 2,975 accepted. Either SAT or ACT required. ACT 25/75 percentile: 19-24. High school rank: 17% in top tenth, 42% in top quarter, 72% in top half
Early decision deadline: N/A, notification date: N/A
Early action deadline: N/A, notification date: N/A
Application deadline (fall): 8/1
Undergraduate student body: 4,966 full time, 708 part time; 36% male, 64% female; 2% American Indian, 1% Asian, 20% black, 4% Hispanic, 3% multiracial, 0% Pacific Islander, 67% white, 1% international; 0% from in state;

22% live on campus; 10% of students in fraternities, 12% in sororities
Most popular majors: 24% Business, Management, Marketing, and Related Support Services, 23% Health Professions and Related Programs, 11% Multi/Interdisciplinary Studies, 5% Education, 5% Engineering Technologies and Engineering-Related Fields
Expenses: 2021-2022: $7,946 in state, $9,039 out of state; room/board: $10,038
Financial aid: (985) 448-4047; 67% of undergrads determined to have financial need; average aid package $10,500

Northwestern State University of Louisiana

Natchitoches LA
(800) 767-8115
U.S. News ranking: Reg. U. (S), No. 84
Website: www.nsula.edu
Admissions email: applications@nsula.edu
Public; founded 1884
Freshman admissions: selective; 2020-2021: 4,780 applied, 4,057 accepted. Either SAT or ACT required. ACT 25/75 percentile: 19-24. High school rank: 14% in top tenth, 38% in top quarter, 71% in top half
Early decision deadline: N/A, notification date: N/A
Early action deadline: N/A, notification date: N/A
Application deadline (fall): 10/15
Undergraduate student body: 6,163 full time, 4,134 part time; 29% male, 71% female; 1% American Indian, 1% Asian, 31% black, 7% Hispanic, 5% multiracial, 0% Pacific Islander, 52% white, 1% international; 84% from in state; 18% live on campus; 15% of students in fraternities, 15% in sororities
Most popular majors: 26% Health Professions and Related Programs, 14% Business, Management, Marketing, and Related Support Services, 11% Liberal Arts and Sciences, General Studies and Humanities
Expenses: 2020-2021: $8,670 in state, $19,458 out of state; room/board: $9,374
Financial aid: (318) 357-5961; 78% of undergrads determined to have financial need; average aid package $15,595

Southeastern Louisiana University

Hammond LA
(985) 549-2066
U.S. News ranking: Reg. U. (S), No. 93
Website: www.southeastern.edu
Admissions email: admissions@southeastern.edu
Public; founded 1925
Freshman admissions: selective; 2020-2021: 6,035 applied, 5,853 accepted. Either SAT or ACT required. ACT 25/75 percentile: 20-25. High school

rank: 14% in top tenth, 37% in top quarter, 70% in top half
Early decision deadline: N/A, notification date: N/A
Early action deadline: N/A, notification date: N/A
Application deadline (fall): 8/1
Undergraduate student body: 9,383 full time, 4,107 part time; 37% male, 63% female; 0% American Indian, 1% Asian, 22% black, 7% Hispanic, 4% multiracial, 0% Pacific Islander, 64% white, 1% international; 96% from in state; 21% live on campus; 6% of students in fraternities, 6% in sororities
Most popular majors: 20% Business, Management, Marketing, and Related Support Services, 14% Health Professions and Related Programs, 13% Liberal Arts and Sciences, General Studies and Humanities, 7% Parks, Recreation, Leisure, and Fitness Studies, 6% Education
Expenses: 2020-2021: $8,289 in state, $20,767 out of state; room/board: $8,710
Financial aid: (985) 549-2244; 63% of undergrads determined to have financial need; average aid package $10,454

Southern University and A&M College

Baton Rouge LA
(225) 771-2430
U.S. News ranking: Reg. U. (S), No. 93
Website: www.subr.edu/
Admissions email: admit@subr.edu
Public; founded 1880
Freshman admissions: selective; 2020-2021: 10,795 applied, 4,429 accepted. Neither SAT nor ACT required. ACT 25/75 percentile: 18-20. High school rank: 5% in top tenth, 38% in top quarter, 57% in top half
Early decision deadline: N/A, notification date: N/A
Early action deadline: N/A, notification date: N/A
Application deadline (fall): 8/1
Undergraduate student body: 4,547 full time, 1,598 part time; 34% male, 66% female; 0% American Indian, 0% Asian, 93% black, 1% Hispanic, 2% multiracial, 0% Pacific Islander, 2% white, 1% international; 15% from in state; N/A live on campus; 0% of students in fraternities, 24% in sororities
Most popular majors: 27% Health Professions and Related Programs, 13% Business, Management, Marketing, and Related Support Services, 9% Homeland Security, Law Enforcement, Firefighting and Related Protective Services, 7% Psychology, 5% Engineering
Expenses: 2021-2022: $9,290 in state, $10,479 out of state; room/board: $2,926
Financial aid: (225) 771-4530; 88% of undergrads determined to have financial need; average aid package $9,845

Southern University at New Orleans[7]

New Orleans LA
(504) 286-5314
U.S. News ranking: Reg. U. (S), second tier
Website: www.suno.edu
Admissions email: N/A
Public; founded 1956
Freshman admissions: less selective; 2020-2021: N/A applied, N/A accepted. Either SAT or ACT required. ACT 25/75 percentile: 15-18. High school rank: N/A
Early decision deadline: N/A, notification date: N/A
Early action deadline: N/A, notification date: N/A
Application deadline (fall): N/A
Undergraduate student body: 1,087 full time, 854 part time
Most popular majors: Information not available
Expenses: 2020-2021: $7,059 in state, $15,960 out of state; room/board: $9,040
Financial aid: (504) 286-5263

Tulane University

New Orleans LA
(504) 865-5731
U.S. News ranking: Nat. U., No. 42
Website: tulane.edu
Admissions email: undergrad.admission@tulane.edu
Private; founded 1834
Freshman admissions: most selective; 2020-2021: 43,892 applied, 4,877 accepted. Neither SAT nor ACT required. ACT 25/75 percentile: 30-33. High school rank: 63% in top tenth, 88% in top quarter, 97% in top half
Early decision deadline: 11/1, notification date: 12/15
Early action deadline: 11/15, notification date: 1/15
Application deadline (fall): 11/15
Undergraduate student body: 7,650 full time, 50 part time; 39% male, 61% female; 0% American Indian, 5% Asian, 5% black, 8% Hispanic, 4% multiracial, 0% Pacific Islander, 72% white, 5% international
Most popular majors: 25% Business, Management, Marketing, and Related Support Services, 18% Social Sciences, 10% Biological and Biomedical Sciences, 10% Health Professions and Related Programs, 7% Psychology
Expenses: 2021-2022: $60,814; room/board: $16,818
Financial aid: (504) 865-5723; 29% of undergrads determined to have financial need; average aid package $50,930

University of Holy Cross

New Orleans LA
(504) 398-2175
U.S. News ranking: Reg. U. (S), No. 62
Website: www.uhcno.edu/
Admissions email: admissions@UHCNO.edu
Private; founded 1916
Affiliation: Roman Catholic

Freshman admissions: selective; 2020-2021: 1,335 applied, 704 accepted. Neither SAT nor ACT required. ACT 25/75 percentile: 18-22. High school rank: N/A
Early decision deadline: N/A, notification date: N/A
Early action deadline: N/A, notification date: N/A
Application deadline (fall): rolling
Undergraduate student body: 382 full time, 393 part time; 19% male, 81% female; 1% American Indian, 3% Asian, 30% black, 12% Hispanic, 4% multiracial, 0% Pacific Islander, 46% white, 0% international
Most popular majors: 42% Registered Nursing/Registered Nurse, 12% Biology/Biological Sciences, General, 6% Accounting, 6% Counselor Education/School Counseling and Guidance Services, 5% Elementary Education and Teaching
Expenses: 2021-2022: $14,720; room/board: N/A
Financial aid: (504) 398-2133; 82% of undergrads determined to have financial need; average aid package $9,663

University of Louisiana at Lafayette

Lafayette LA
(337) 482-6553
U.S. News ranking: Nat. U., second tier
Website: www.louisiana.edu
Admissions email: admissions@louisiana.edu
Public; founded 1898
Freshman admissions: selective; 2020-2021: 10,195 applied, 6,854 accepted. Either SAT or ACT required. ACT 25/75 percentile: 20-26. High school rank: 19% in top tenth, 42% in top quarter, 72% in top half
Early decision deadline: N/A, notification date: N/A
Early action deadline: N/A, notification date: N/A
Application deadline (fall): rolling
Undergraduate student body: 11,318 full time, 2,702 part time; 42% male, 58% female; 0% American Indian, 2% Asian, 22% black, 6% Hispanic, 3% multiracial, 0% Pacific Islander, 62% white, 1% international; 94% from in state; 23% live on campus; 9% of students in fraternities, 12% in sororities
Most popular majors: 20% Health Professions and Related Programs, 14% Business, Management, Marketing, and Related Support Services, 11% Engineering, 11% Liberal Arts and Sciences, General Studies and Humanities, 9% Education
Expenses: 2020-2021: $10,382 in state, $24,110 out of state; room/board: $10,708
Financial aid: (337) 482-6506; 65% of undergrads determined to have financial need; average aid package $11,092

University of Louisiana–Monroe

Monroe LA
(318) 342-7777
U.S. News ranking: Nat. U., second tier
Website: www.ulm.edu
Admissions email: admissions@ulm.edu
Public; founded 1931
Freshman admissions: selective; 2020-2021: 4,960 applied, 3,828 accepted. Either SAT or ACT required. ACT 25/75 percentile: 20-24. High school rank: 23% in top tenth, 48% in top quarter, 78% in top half
Early decision deadline: N/A, notification date: N/A
Early action deadline: N/A, notification date: N/A
Application deadline (fall): 8/15
Undergraduate student body: 4,563 full time, 2,296 part time; 35% male, 65% female; 0% American Indian, 2% Asian, 24% black, 3% Hispanic, 3% multiracial, 0% Pacific Islander, 61% white, 4% international; 88% from in state; 28% live on campus; N/A of students in fraternities, N/A in sororities
Most popular majors: 27% Health Professions and Related Programs, 16% History, 12% Psychology
Expenses: 2021-2022: $9,551 in state, $21,651 out of state; room/board: $9,390
Financial aid: (318) 342-5325; 67% of undergrads determined to have financial need; average aid package $12,673

University of New Orleans

New Orleans LA
(504) 280-6595
U.S. News ranking: Nat. U., second tier
Website: www.uno.edu
Admissions email: admissions@uno.edu
Public; founded 1958
Freshman admissions: selective; 2020-2021: 5,382 applied, 4,462 accepted. Neither SAT nor ACT required. ACT 25/75 percentile: 18-24. High school rank: 13% in top tenth, 31% in top quarter, 61% in top half
Early decision deadline: N/A, notification date: N/A
Early action deadline: N/A, notification date: N/A
Application deadline (fall): 8/15
Undergraduate student body: 5,060 full time, 1,835 part time; 48% male, 52% female; 0% American Indian, 8% Asian, 23% black, 13% Hispanic, 4% multiracial, 0% Pacific Islander, 46% white, 2% international; N/A from in state; 8% live on campus; 2% of students in fraternities, 4% in sororities
Most popular majors: 27% Business, Management, Marketing, and Related Support Services, 12% Engineering, 11% Biological and Biomedical Sciences, 10% Multi/Interdisciplinary Studies, 7% Psychology

Expenses: 2020-2021: $16,762 in state, $16,762 out of state; room/board: $11,200
Financial aid: (504) 280-6603

Xavier University of Louisiana
New Orleans LA
(504) 520-7388
U.S. News ranking: Reg. U. (S), No. 15
Website: www.xula.edu
Admissions email: apply@xula.edu
Private; founded 1915
Affiliation: Roman Catholic
Freshman admissions: selective; 2020-2021: 9,517 applied, 7,673 accepted. Either SAT or ACT required. ACT 25/75 percentile: 20-25. High school rank: 29% in top tenth, 55% in top quarter, 81% in top half
Early decision deadline: N/A, notification date: N/A
Early action deadline: N/A, notification date: N/A
Application deadline (fall): 7/1
Undergraduate student body: 2,406 full time, 111 part time; 23% male, 77% female; 0% American Indian, 3% Asian, 83% black, 5% Hispanic, 4% multiracial, 0% Pacific Islander, 2% white, 2% international; 64% from in state; 54% live on campus; 1% of students in fraternities, 5% in sororities
Most popular majors: 36% Biology, General, 14% Psychology, General, 10% Business Administration, Management and Operations, 9% Biochemistry, Biophysics and Molecular Biology, 6% Public Health
Expenses: 2021-2022: $26,398; room/board: $10,302
Financial aid: (504) 520-7835; 72% of undergrads determined to have financial need; average aid package $11,389

MAINE

Bates College
Lewiston ME
(855) 228-3755
U.S. News ranking: Nat. Lib. Arts, No. 25
Website: www.bates.edu
Admissions email: admission@bates.edu
Private; founded 1855
Freshman admissions: most selective; 2020-2021: 7,696 applied, 1,085 accepted. Neither SAT nor ACT required. SAT 25/75 percentile: 1210-1420. High school rank: 60% in top tenth, 82% in top quarter, 97% in top half
Early decision deadline: 11/15, notification date: 12/20
Early action deadline: N/A, notification date: N/A
Application deadline (fall): 1/1
Undergraduate student body: 1,876 full time, 0 part time; 49% male, 51% female; 0% American Indian, 5% Asian, 6% black, 7% Hispanic, 6% multiracial, 0% Pacific Islander, 67% white, 8% international; 91% from in

state; 92% live on campus; 0% of students in fraternities, 0% in sororities
Most popular majors: 33% Social Sciences, 10% Psychology, 9% Biological and Biomedical Sciences, 7% English Language and Literature/Letters, 6% Mathematics and Statistics
Expenses: 2021-2022: $59,062; room/board: $16,658
Financial aid: (207) 786-6096; 39% of undergrads determined to have financial need; average aid package $52,508

Bowdoin College
Brunswick ME
(207) 725-3100
U.S. News ranking: Nat. Lib. Arts, No. 6
Website: www.bowdoin.edu
Admissions email: admissions@bowdoin.edu
Private; founded 1794
Freshman admissions: most selective; 2020-2021: 9,402 applied, 861 accepted. Neither SAT nor ACT required. SAT 25/75 percentile: 1330-1510. High school rank: 84% in top tenth, 97% in top quarter, 100% in top half
Early decision deadline: 11/15, notification date: 12/15
Early action deadline: N/A, notification date: N/A
Application deadline (fall): 1/5
Undergraduate student body: 1,776 full time, 1 part time; 49% male, 51% female; 0% American Indian, 9% Asian, 8% black, 11% Hispanic, 8% multiracial, 0% Pacific Islander, 56% white, 7% international; 11% from in state; 90% live on campus; N/A of students in fraternities, N/A in sororities
Most popular majors: 18% Political Science and Government, General, 13% Econometrics and Quantitative Economics, 10% Mathematics, General, 8% Environmental Studies, 8% Neuroscience
Expenses: 2021-2022: $58,322; room/board: $15,898
Financial aid: (207) 725-3144; 50% of undergrads determined to have financial need; average aid package $49,642

Colby College
Waterville ME
(800) 723-3032
U.S. News ranking: Nat. Lib. Arts, No. 17
Website: www.colby.edu
Admissions email: admissions@colby.edu
Private; founded 1813
Freshman admissions: most selective; 2020-2021: 13,922 applied, 1,430 accepted. Neither SAT nor ACT required. SAT 25/75 percentile: 1380-1520. High school rank: 74% in top tenth, 89% in top quarter, 95% in top half
Early decision deadline: 11/15, notification date: 12/15
Early action deadline: N/A, notification date: N/A
Application deadline (fall): 1/1

Undergraduate student body: 2,155 full time, 0 part time; 47% male, 53% female; 0% American Indian, 9% Asian, 5% black, 8% Hispanic, 6% multiracial, 0% Pacific Islander, 61% white, 9% international
Most popular majors: Information not available
Expenses: 2021-2022: $61,220; room/board: $15,745
Financial aid: (800) 723-4033; 42% of undergrads determined to have financial need; average aid package $55,590

College of the Atlantic
Bar Harbor ME
(800) 528-0025
U.S. News ranking: Nat. Lib. Arts, No. 92
Website: www.coa.edu/
Admissions email: inquiry@coa.edu
Private; founded 1969
Freshman admissions: more selective; 2020-2021: 405 applied, 307 accepted. Neither SAT nor ACT required. SAT 25/75 percentile: 1210-1400. High school rank: 33% in top tenth, 73% in top quarter, 100% in top half
Early decision deadline: 12/1, notification date: 12/15
Early action deadline: N/A, notification date: N/A
Application deadline (fall): 2/1
Undergraduate student body: 350 full time, 16 part time; 31% male, 69% female; 0% American Indian, 2% Asian, 1% black, 5% Hispanic, 2% multiracial, 0% Pacific Islander, 64% white, 23% international; 22% from in state; 41% live on campus; 0% of students in fraternities, 0% in sororities
Most popular majors: Information not available
Expenses: 2021-2022: $43,542; room/board: $9,747
Financial aid: (207) 801-5645; 82% of undergrads determined to have financial need; average aid package $40,304

Husson University
Bangor ME
(207) 941-7100
U.S. News ranking: Nat. U., second tier
Website: www.husson.edu
Admissions email: admit@husson.edu
Private; founded 1898
Freshman admissions: selective; 2020-2021: 2,298 applied, 1,945 accepted. Neither SAT nor ACT required. SAT 25/75 percentile: 960-1140. High school rank: 14% in top tenth, 41% in top quarter, 74% in top half
Early decision deadline: N/A, notification date: N/A
Early action deadline: N/A, notification date: N/A
Application deadline (fall): rolling
Undergraduate student body: 2,267 full time, 410 part time; 40% male, 60% female; 1% American Indian, 1% Asian, 5% black, 1% Hispanic, 3% multiracial, 0% Pacific Islander, 83% white, 2% international; 75% from in

state; 35% live on campus; 5% of students in fraternities, 5% in sororities
Most popular majors: 28% Health Professions and Related Programs, 26% Business, Management, Marketing, and Related Support Services, 10% Homeland Security, Law Enforcement, Firefighting and Related Protective Services
Expenses: 2021-2022: $20,430; room/board: $11,006
Financial aid: (207) 941-7156; 80% of undergrads determined to have financial need; average aid package $18,258

Maine College of Art[1]
Portland ME
(800) 699-1509
U.S. News ranking: Arts, unranked
Website: www.meca.edu
Admissions email: admissions@meca.edu
Private; founded 1882
Application deadline (fall): rolling
Undergraduate student body: N/A full time, N/A part time
Expenses: 2020-2021: $38,310; room/board: $12,770
Financial aid: (207) 699-5073

Maine Maritime Academy
Castine ME
(207) 326-2206
U.S. News ranking: Reg. Coll. (N), No. 4
Website: www.mainemaritime.edu
Admissions email: admissions@mma.edu
Public; founded 1941
Freshman admissions: selective; 2020-2021: 1,204 applied, 596 accepted. Either SAT or ACT required. SAT 25/75 percentile: 1000-1160. High school rank: 23% in top tenth, 57% in top quarter, 87% in top half
Early decision deadline: N/A, notification date: N/A
Early action deadline: 11/30, notification date: 2/1
Application deadline (fall): 3/1
Undergraduate student body: 901 full time, 27 part time; 83% male, 17% female; 1% American Indian, 2% Asian, 2% black, 4% Hispanic, 1% multiracial, 0% Pacific Islander, 82% white, 1% international; 64% from in state; 61% live on campus; 0% of students in fraternities, 0% in sororities
Most popular majors: 39% Naval Architecture and Marine Engineering, 20% International Business/Trade/Commerce, 16% Marine Science/Merchant Marine Officer, 13% Engineering Technologies and Engineering-Related Fields, Other, 4% Systems Engineering
Expenses: 2021-2022: $14,338 in state, $29,258 out of state; room/board: $10,910
Financial aid: (207) 326-2339; 78% of undergrads determined to have financial need; average aid package $11,936

St. Joseph's College[1]
Standish ME
(207) 893-7746
U.S. News ranking: Reg. U. (N), second tier
Website: www.sjcme.edu
Admissions email: admission@sjcme.edu
Private
Application deadline (fall): N/A
Undergraduate student body: N/A full time, N/A part time
Expenses: 2020-2021: $38,820; room/board: $14,500
Financial aid: N/A

Thomas College[1]
Waterville ME
(800) 339-7001
U.S. News ranking: Reg. U. (N), second tier
Website: www.thomas.edu
Admissions email: admiss@thomas.edu
Private; founded 1894
Application deadline (fall): rolling
Undergraduate student body: N/A full time, N/A part time
Expenses: 2021-2022: $29,152; room/board: $11,736
Financial aid: (207) 859-1105; 88% of undergrads determined to have financial need; average aid package $23,083

Unity College[7]
Unity ME
(800) 624-1024
U.S. News ranking: Reg. Coll. (N), No. 22
Website: www.unity.edu
Admissions email: admissions@unity.edu
Private; founded 1965
Freshman admissions: least selective; 2020-2021: 885 applied, 883 accepted. Neither SAT nor ACT required. SAT 25/75 percentile: N/A. High school rank: N/A
Early decision deadline: N/A, notification date: N/A
Early action deadline: N/A, notification date: N/A
Application deadline (fall): rolling
Undergraduate student body: 1,193 full time, 0 part time
Most popular majors: Information not available
Expenses: 2020-2021: $12,640; room/board: $10,900
Financial aid: (207) 509-7235

University of Maine
Orono ME
(877) 486-2364
U.S. News ranking: Nat. U., No. 213
Website: www.umaine.edu
Admissions email: umaineadmissions@maine.edu
Public; founded 1865
Freshman admissions: selective; 2020-2021: 14,785 applied, 13,633 accepted. Neither SAT nor ACT required. SAT 25/75 percentile: 1050-1250. High school rank: 22% in top tenth, 50% in top quarter, 79% in top half
Early decision deadline: N/A, notification date: N/A
Early action deadline: 12/1,

notification date: 1/15
Application deadline (fall): rolling
Undergraduate student body: 7,847 full time, 1,618 part time; 53% male, 47% female; 1% American Indian, 2% Asian, 2% black, 5% Hispanic, 4% multiracial, 0% Pacific Islander, 83% white, 2% international; 74% from in state; 29% live on campus; N/A of students in fraternities, N/A in sororities
Most popular majors: 18% Business, Management, Marketing, and Related Support Services, 13% Engineering, 8% Education, 7% Social Sciences, 6% Health Professions and Related Programs
Expenses: 2021-2022: $11,986 in state, $33,586 out of state; room/board: $11,574
Financial aid: (207) 581-1324; 62% of undergrads determined to have financial need; average aid package $14,801

University of Maine at Farmington
Farmington ME
(207) 778-7050
U.S. News ranking: Reg. Coll. (N), No. 6
Website: www.farmington.edu
Admissions email: umfadmit@maine.edu
Public; founded 1864
Freshman admissions: selective; 2020-2021: 1,595 applied, 1,509 accepted. Neither SAT nor ACT required. SAT 25/75 percentile: 940-1150. High school rank: 10% in top tenth, 39% in top quarter, 73% in top half
Early decision deadline: N/A, notification date: N/A
Early action deadline: 11/15, notification date: 12/15
Application deadline (fall): rolling
Undergraduate student body: 1,414 full time, 168 part time; 32% male, 68% female; 1% American Indian, 0% Asian, 2% black, 3% Hispanic, 4% multiracial, 0% Pacific Islander, 88% white, 0% international; 83% from in state; 46% live on campus; 0% of students in fraternities, 0% in sororities
Most popular majors: 34% Education, 14% Business, Management, Marketing, and Related Support Services, 10% Health Professions and Related Programs, 10% Psychology, 8% English Language and Literature/Letters
Expenses: 2021-2022: $9,590 in state, $20,780 out of state; room/board: $10,336
Financial aid: (207) 778-7100; 75% of undergrads determined to have financial need; average aid package $14,741

University of Maine–Augusta[1]
Augusta ME
(207) 621-3465
U.S. News ranking: Reg. Coll. (N), second tier
Website: www.uma.edu
Admissions email: umaadm@maine.edu

Public; founded 1965
Application deadline (fall): 9/1
Undergraduate student body: N/A full time, N/A part time
Expenses: 2020-2021: $8,378 in state, $18,788 out of state; room/board: $8,200
Financial aid: (207) 621-3141

University of Maine–Fort Kent
Fort Kent ME
(207) 834-7600
U.S. News ranking: Reg. Coll. (N), No. 33
Website: www.umfk.edu
Admissions email: umfkadm@maine.edu
Public; founded 1878
Freshman admissions: least selective; 2020-2021: 599 applied, 598 accepted. Neither SAT nor ACT required. SAT 25/75 percentile: 870-1040. High school rank: 9% in top tenth, 28% in top quarter, 61% in top half
Early decision deadline: 12/1, notification date: 12/1
Early action deadline: 12/1, notification date: 12/1
Application deadline (fall): rolling
Undergraduate student body: 531 full time, 1,094 part time; 28% male, 72% female; 0% American Indian, 1% Asian, 6% black, 3% Hispanic, 4% multiracial, 0% Pacific Islander, 73% white, 9% international; 17% from in state; 20% live on campus; 0% of students in fraternities, 0% in sororities
Most popular majors: 76% Health Professions and Related Programs, 6% Business, Management, Marketing, and Related Support Services, 5% Multi/Interdisciplinary Studies, 3% Biological and Biomedical Sciences, 3% Liberal Arts and Sciences, General Studies and Humanities
Expenses: 2021-2022: $8,504 in state, $12,914 out of state; room/board: $8,750
Financial aid: (207) 834-7607; 62% of undergrads determined to have financial need; average aid package $11,517

University of Maine–Machias
Machias ME
(888) 468-6866
U.S. News ranking: Nat. Lib. Arts, second tier
Website: machias.edu/
Admissions email: ummadmissions@maine.edu
Public; founded 1909
Freshman admissions: least selective; 2020-2021: 1,004 applied, 940 accepted. Neither SAT nor ACT required. SAT 25/75 percentile: 900-1090. High school rank: 7% in top tenth, 31% in top quarter, 60% in top half
Early decision deadline: N/A, notification date: N/A
Early action deadline: 12/15, notification date: N/A
Application deadline (fall): 8/15
Undergraduate student body: 274 full time, 488 part time; 32% male, 68% female; 4% American

Indian, 0% Asian, 3% black, 5% Hispanic, 4% multiracial, 0% Pacific Islander, 76% white, 4% international; 92% from in state; 13% live on campus; N/A of students in fraternities, N/A in sororities
Most popular majors: 25% Psychology, 18% Liberal Arts and Sciences, General Studies and Humanities, 12% Business, Management, Marketing, and Related Support Services, 12% Education, 9% English Language and Literature/Letters
Expenses: 2021-2022: $8,930 in state, $16,670 out of state; room/board: $10,070
Financial aid: (207) 255-1203; 77% of undergrads determined to have financial need; average aid package $13,224

University of Maine–Presque Isle
Presque Isle ME
(207) 768-9532
U.S. News ranking: Reg. Coll. (N), No. 31
Website: www.umpi.edu/admissions/
Admissions email: umpi-admissions@maine.edu
Public; founded 1903
Freshman admissions: least selective; 2020-2021: 700 applied, 693 accepted. Neither SAT nor ACT required. SAT 25/75 percentile: 860-1080. High school rank: 3% in top tenth, 27% in top quarter, 62% in top half
Early decision deadline: N/A, notification date: N/A
Early action deadline: N/A, notification date: N/A
Application deadline (fall): rolling
Undergraduate student body: 721 full time, 748 part time; 36% male, 64% female; 1% American Indian, 1% Asian, 3% black, 5% Hispanic, 3% multiracial, 0% Pacific Islander, 80% white, 4% international; 83% from in state; 25% live on campus; 0% of students in fraternities, 0% in sororities
Most popular majors: 31% Business Administration and Management, General, 13% Psychology, General, 11% Education, General, 10% Liberal Arts and Sciences/Liberal Studies
Expenses: 2021-2022: $8,574 in state, $12,984 out of state; room/board: $8,737
Financial aid: (207) 768-9510; 66% of undergrads determined to have financial need; average aid package $10,463

University of New England
Biddeford ME
(800) 477-4863
U.S. News ranking: Nat. U., No. 249
Website: www.une.edu
Admissions email: admissions@une.edu
Private; founded 1831
Freshman admissions: selective; 2020-2021: 4,843 applied, 4,229 accepted. Neither SAT nor ACT required. SAT 25/75

percentile: 1040-1210. High school rank: N/A
Early decision deadline: N/A, notification date: N/A
Early action deadline: 11/15, notification date: 12/31
Application deadline (fall): 2/15
Undergraduate student body: 2,292 full time, 1,773 part time; 32% male, 68% female; 0% American Indian, 3% Asian, 1% black, 1% Hispanic, 3% multiracial, 0% Pacific Islander, 88% white, 0% international; 27% from in state; 60% live on campus; N/A of students in fraternities, N/A in sororities
Most popular majors: 17% Registered Nursing/Registered Nurse, 11% Biomedical Sciences, General, 8% Dental Hygiene/Hygienist, 8% Health and Wellness, General, 6% Kinesiology and Exercise Science
Expenses: 2021-2022: $39,820; room/board: $14,810
Financial aid: (207) 602-2342; 74% of undergrads determined to have financial need; average aid package $24,986

University of Southern Maine
Portland ME
(207) 780-5670
U.S. News ranking: Reg. U. (N), second tier
Website: www.usm.maine.edu
Admissions email: admitusm@maine.edu
Public; founded 1878
Freshman admissions: selective; 2020-2021: 4,774 applied, 4,198 accepted. Neither SAT nor ACT required. SAT 25/75 percentile: 958-1160. High school rank: 13% in top tenth, 38% in top quarter, 73% in top half
Early decision deadline: N/A, notification date: N/A
Early action deadline: N/A, notification date: N/A
Application deadline (fall): rolling
Undergraduate student body: 3,773 full time, 2,325 part time; 40% male, 60% female; 1% American Indian, 3% Asian, 8% black, 4% Hispanic, 3% multiracial, 0% Pacific Islander, 78% white, 1% international; N/A from in state; 14% live on campus; N/A of students in fraternities, N/A in sororities
Most popular majors: Information not available
Expenses: 2020-2021: $9,900 in state, $23,640 out of state; room/board: $10,124
Financial aid: (207) 780-5118; 70% of undergrads determined to have financial need; average aid package $14,551

MARYLAND

Bowie State University
Bowie MD
(301) 860-3415
U.S. News ranking: Reg. U. (N), second tier
Website: www.bowiestate.edu
Admissions email: ugradadmissions@bowiestate.edu

Public; founded 1865
Freshman admissions: less selective; 2020-2021: 5,167 applied, 4,197 accepted. Either SAT or ACT required. SAT 25/75 percentile: 850-1010. High school rank: N/A
Early decision deadline: N/A, notification date: N/A
Early action deadline: N/A, notification date: N/A
Application deadline (fall): 5/15
Undergraduate student body: 4,429 full time, 925 part time; 38% male, 62% female; 0% American Indian, 2% Asian, 82% black, 4% Hispanic, 4% multiracial, 0% Pacific Islander, 2% white, 2% international; 18% from in state; 27% live on campus; 0% of students in fraternities, 0% in sororities
Most popular majors: 18% Business, Management, Marketing, and Related Support Services, 13% Computer and Information Sciences and Support Services, 11% Homeland Security, Law Enforcement, Firefighting and Related Protective Services, 10% Communications Technologies/Technicians and Support Services, 10% Psychology
Expenses: 2021-2022: $8,558 in state, $19,298 out of state; room/board: $11,444
Financial aid: (301) 860-3540; 82% of undergrads determined to have financial need; average aid package $8,561

Coppin State University
Baltimore MD
(410) 951-3600
U.S. News ranking: Reg. U. (N), second tier
Website: www.coppin.edu
Admissions email: admissions@coppin.edu
Public; founded 1900
Freshman admissions: less selective; 2020-2021: 5,873 applied, 2,361 accepted. Either SAT or ACT required. SAT 25/75 percentile: 820-970. High school rank: N/A
Early decision deadline: N/A, notification date: N/A
Early action deadline: N/A, notification date: N/A
Application deadline (fall): rolling
Undergraduate student body: 1,606 full time, 502 part time; 23% male, 77% female; 0% American Indian, 0% Asian, 82% black, 4% Hispanic, 3% multiracial, 0% Pacific Islander, 2% white, 7% international
Most popular majors: 20% Registered Nursing/Registered Nurse, 14% Psychology, General, 10% Criminal Justice/Safety Studies, 10% Social Work, 6% Early Childhood Education and Teaching
Expenses: 2021-2022: $6,809 in state, $13,334 out of state; room/board: $11,012
Financial aid: (410) 951-3636

Frostburg State University

Frostburg MD
(301) 687-4201
U.S. News ranking: Reg. U. (N), No. 109
Website: www.frostburg.edu
Admissions email: fsuadmissions@frostburg.edu
Public; founded 1898
Freshman admissions: less selective; 2020-2021: 4,335 applied, 3,191 accepted. Either SAT or ACT required. SAT 25/75 percentile: 910-1130. High school rank: 10% in top tenth, 34% in top quarter, 69% in top half
Early decision deadline: 12/15, notification date: N/A
Early action deadline: N/A, notification date: N/A
Application deadline (fall): rolling
Undergraduate student body: 3,221 full time, 898 part time; 46% male, 54% female; 0% American Indian, 2% Asian, 32% black, 5% Hispanic, 5% multiracial, 0% Pacific Islander, 54% white, 2% international
Most popular majors: Information not available
Expenses: 2021-2022: $9,594 in state, $24,080 out of state; room/board: $10,678
Financial aid: (301) 687-4301; 52% of undergrads determined to have financial need; average aid package $11,191

Goucher College

Baltimore MD
(410) 337-6100
U.S. News ranking: Nat. Lib. Arts, No. 117
Website: www.goucher.edu
Admissions email: admissions@goucher.edu
Private; founded 1885
Freshman admissions: selective; 2020-2021: 2,598 applied, 2,063 accepted. Neither SAT nor ACT required. SAT 25/75 percentile: 990-1230. High school rank: 21% in top tenth, 42% in top quarter, 77% in top half
Early decision deadline: N/A, notification date: N/A
Early action deadline: 12/1, notification date: 2/1
Application deadline (fall): 1/15
Undergraduate student body: 1,086 full time, 28 part time; 32% male, 68% female; 0% American Indian, 4% Asian, 21% black, 13% Hispanic, 5% multiracial, 0% Pacific Islander, 48% white, 2% international; N/A from in state; N/A live on campus; 0% of students in fraternities, 0% in sororities
Most popular majors: 15% Psychology, 14% Social Sciences, 11% Business, Management, Marketing, and Related Support Services
Expenses: 2021-2022: $48,200; room/board: $15,500
Financial aid: (410) 337-6141; 73% of undergrads determined to have financial need; average aid package $35,983

Hood College

Frederick MD
(800) 922-1599
U.S. News ranking: Reg. U. (N), No. 50
Website: www.hood.edu
Admissions email: admission@hood.edu
Private; founded 1893
Freshman admissions: selective; 2020-2021: 3,425 applied, 2,443 accepted. Neither SAT nor ACT required. SAT 25/75 percentile: 1000-1220. High school rank: 14% in top tenth, 37% in top quarter, 77% in top half
Early decision deadline: N/A, notification date: N/A
Early action deadline: N/A, notification date: N/A
Application deadline (fall): 8/17
Undergraduate student body: 1,131 full time, 51 part time; 36% male, 64% female; 0% American Indian, 3% Asian, 19% black, 12% Hispanic, 6% multiracial, 0% Pacific Islander, 57% white, 1% international; 74% from in state; 52% live on campus; N/A of students in fraternities, N/A in sororities
Most popular majors: 20% Business, Management, Marketing, and Related Support Services, 10% Communication, Journalism, and Related Programs, 9% Social Sciences, 8% Health Professions and Related Programs, 7% Biological and Biomedical Sciences
Expenses: 2021-2022: $43,140; room/board: $13,200
Financial aid: (301) 696-3411; 81% of undergrads determined to have financial need; average aid package $33,012

Johns Hopkins University

Baltimore MD
(410) 516-8171
U.S. News ranking: Nat. U., No. 9
Website: www.jhu.edu
Admissions email: gotojhu@jhu.edu
Private; founded 1876
Freshman admissions: most selective; 2020-2021: 29,612 applied, 2,735 accepted. Neither SAT nor ACT required. SAT 25/75 percentile: 1480-1570. High school rank: 99% in top tenth, 100% in top quarter, 100% in top half
Early decision deadline: 11/1, notification date: 12/15
Early action deadline: N/A, notification date: N/A
Application deadline (fall): 1/2
Undergraduate student body: 5,739 full time, 592 part time; 45% male, 55% female; 0% American Indian, 27% Asian, 8% black, 17% Hispanic, 7% multiracial, 0% Pacific Islander, 26% white, 12% international; 11% from in state; 1% live on campus; 13% of students in fraternities, 26% in sororities
Most popular majors: 11% Public Health, General, 10% Bioengineering and Biomedical Engineering, 10% Neuroscience, 9% Cell/Cellular and Molecular Biology, 8% Computer and Information Sciences, General
Expenses: 2021-2022: $58,720; room/board: $16,800
Financial aid: (410) 516-8028; 55% of undergrads determined to have financial need; average aid package $49,492

Loyola University Maryland

Baltimore MD
(410) 617-5012
U.S. News ranking: Reg. U. (N), No. 4
Website: www.loyola.edu
Admissions email: admission@loyola.edu
Private; founded 1852
Affiliation: Roman Catholic
Freshman admissions: more selective; 2020-2021: 10,489 applied, 8,416 accepted. Neither SAT nor ACT required. SAT 25/75 percentile: 1140-1328. High school rank: 31% in top tenth, 57% in top quarter, 90% in top half
Early decision deadline: N/A, notification date: N/A
Early action deadline: 11/15, notification date: 1/15
Application deadline (fall): 1/15
Undergraduate student body: 3,736 full time, 86 part time; 42% male, 58% female; 0% American Indian, 3% Asian, 7% black, 12% Hispanic, 3% multiracial, 0% Pacific Islander, 73% white, 1% international; 24% from in state; 1% live on campus; 0% of students in fraternities, 0% in sororities
Most popular majors: 38% Business, Management, Marketing, and Related Support Services, 13% Communication, Journalism, and Related Programs, 9% Social Sciences, 6% Biological and Biomedical Sciences, 6% Psychology
Expenses: 2021-2022: $52,130; room/board: $16,100
Financial aid: (410) 617-2576; 55% of undergrads determined to have financial need; average aid package $37,198

Maryland Institute College of Art

Baltimore MD
(410) 225-2222
U.S. News ranking: Arts, unranked
Website: www.mica.edu
Admissions email: admissions@mica.edu
Private; founded 1826
Freshman admissions: selective; 2020-2021: 2,990 applied, 2,686 accepted. Neither SAT nor ACT required. SAT 25/75 percentile: 1020-1300. High school rank: N/A
Early decision deadline: 11/15, notification date: 12/15
Early action deadline: 11/15, notification date: 1/13
Application deadline (fall): 2/1
Undergraduate student body: 1,252 full time, 57 part time; 28% male, 72% female; 0% American Indian, 12% Asian, 10% black, 11% Hispanic, 7% multiracial, 0% Pacific Islander, 30% white, 28% international; 36% from in state; 0% live on campus; 0% of students in fraternities, 0% in sororities
Most popular majors: 23% Illustration, 20% Graphic Design, 12% Intermedia/Multimedia, 8% Digital Arts, 8% Painting
Expenses: 2021-2022: $52,040; room/board: $14,770
Financial aid: (410) 225-2285

McDaniel College

Westminster MD
(800) 638-5005
U.S. News ranking: Reg. U. (N), No. 31
Website: www.mcdaniel.edu
Admissions email: admissions@mcdaniel.edu
Private; founded 1867
Freshman admissions: selective; 2020-2021: 4,207 applied, 3,413 accepted. Neither SAT nor ACT required. SAT 25/75 percentile: 980-1210. High school rank: 19% in top tenth, 47% in top quarter, 77% in top half
Early decision deadline: 11/1, notification date: 12/1
Early action deadline: 12/15, notification date: 1/15
Application deadline (fall): rolling
Undergraduate student body: 1,789 full time, 29 part time; 45% male, 55% female; 0% American Indian, 2% Asian, 24% black, 8% Hispanic, 3% multiracial, 0% Pacific Islander, 55% white, 3% international
Most popular majors: 13% Business Administration and Management, General, 8% Health and Physical Education/Fitness, General, 8% Political Science and Government, Other, 7% Psychology, General, 7% Speech Communication and Rhetoric
Expenses: 2021-2022: $46,336; room/board: $12,302
Financial aid: (410) 857-2233; 81% of undergrads determined to have financial need; average aid package $41,532

Morgan State University

Baltimore MD
(800) 332-6674
U.S. News ranking: Nat. U., second tier
Website: morgan.edu
Admissions email: admissions@morgan.edu
Public; founded 1867
Freshman admissions: less selective; 2020-2021: 9,623 applied, 7,020 accepted. Either SAT or ACT required. SAT 25/75 percentile: 920-1070. High school rank: 8% in top tenth, 24% in top quarter, 54% in top half
Early decision deadline: N/A, notification date: N/A
Early action deadline: 11/15, notification date: 2/15
Application deadline (fall): 2/15
Undergraduate student body: 5,575 full time, 689 part time; 39% male, 61% female; 0% American Indian, 1% Asian, 83% black, 4% Hispanic, 3% multiracial, 0% Pacific Islander, 2% white, 4% international; 67% from in state; 54% live on campus; N/A of students in fraternities, N/A in sororities
Most popular majors: 9% Civil Engineering, 8% Electrical, Electronics and Communications Engineering, 8% Liberal Arts and Sciences, General Studies and Humanities, 7% Business Administration and Management, General, 6% Social Work
Expenses: 2021-2022: $8,008 in state, $18,480 out of state; room/board: $10,994
Financial aid: (443) 885-3170; 78% of undergrads determined to have financial need; average aid package $10,273

Mount St. Mary's University

Emmitsburg MD
(800) 448-4347
U.S. News ranking: Reg. U. (N), No. 44
Website: msmary.edu
Admissions email: admissions@msmary.edu
Private; founded 1808
Affiliation: Roman Catholic
Freshman admissions: selective; 2020-2021: 6,542 applied, 5,263 accepted. Neither SAT nor ACT required. SAT 25/75 percentile: 961-1185. High school rank: N/A
Early decision deadline: N/A, notification date: N/A
Early action deadline: 12/1, notification date: 12/25
Application deadline (fall): 3/1
Undergraduate student body: 1,931 full time, 140 part time; 47% male, 53% female; 0% American Indian, 3% Asian, 20% black, 14% Hispanic, 5% multiracial, 0% Pacific Islander, 54% white, 2% international; 54% from in state; 63% live on campus; 0% of students in fraternities, 0% in sororities
Most popular majors: 27% Business, Management, Marketing, and Related Support Services, 12% Social Sciences, 10% Biological and Biomedical Sciences, 8% Education, 6% Psychology
Expenses: 2021-2022: $44,750; room/board: $13,960
Financial aid: (301) 447-8364; 73% of undergrads determined to have financial need; average aid package $33,021

Notre Dame of Maryland University

Baltimore MD
(410) 532-5330
U.S. News ranking: Reg. U. (N), No. 62
Website: www.ndm.edu
Admissions email: admiss@ndm.edu
Private; founded 1895
Affiliation: Roman Catholic
Freshman admissions: less selective; 2020-2021: 1,558 applied, 968 accepted. Neither SAT nor ACT required. SAT 25/75 percentile: 870-1060. High school rank: 24% in top tenth, 52% in top quarter, 76% in top half
Early decision deadline: N/A,

notification date: N/A
Early action deadline: 12/1,
notification date: 12/15
Application deadline (fall): rolling
Undergraduate student body: 563
full time, 192 part time; 3%
male, 97% female; 0% American
Indian, 5% Asian, 21% black,
13% Hispanic, 4% multiracial,
0% Pacific Islander, 40% white,
1% international; 94% from in
state; 9% live on campus; N/A
of students in fraternities, N/A in
sororities
Most popular majors: 42%
Registered Nursing/Registered
Nurse, 14% Liberal Arts and
Sciences, General Studies and
Humanities, Other, 10% Liberal
Arts and Sciences/Liberal Studies,
7% Biology/Biological Sciences,
General, 4% Psychology, General
Expenses: 2021-2022: $39,745;
room/board: $12,565
Financial aid: (410) 532-5369;
87% of undergrads determined to
have financial need; average aid
package $32,878

Salisbury University
Salisbury MD
(410) 543-6161
U.S. News ranking: Reg. U. (N),
No. 62
Website: www.salisbury.edu/
Admissions email:
admissions@salisbury.edu
Public; founded 1925
Freshman admissions: selective;
2020-2021: 8,701 applied,
6,754 accepted. Neither SAT
nor ACT required. SAT 25/75
percentile: 1093-1268. High
school rank: 16% in top tenth,
40% in top quarter, 80% in
top half
Early decision deadline: 11/15,
notification date: 12/15
Early action deadline: 12/1,
notification date: 1/15
Application deadline (fall): 1/15
Undergraduate student body: 6,599
full time, 523 part time; 45%
male, 55% female; 1% American
Indian, 4% Asian, 14% black,
5% Hispanic, 2% multiracial,
0% Pacific Islander, 71% white,
1% international; 87% from in
state; 25% live on campus; 11%
of students in fraternities, 7% in
sororities
Most popular majors: 16%
Business, Management,
Marketing, and Related Support
Services, 11% Education, 9%
Communication, Journalism, and
Related Programs, 7% Parks,
Recreation, Leisure, and Fitness
Studies, 7% Public Administration
and Social Service Professions
Expenses: 2021-2022: $10,188
in state, $20,458 out of state;
room/board: $12,500
Financial aid: (410) 543-6165;
54% of undergrads determined to
have financial need; average aid
package $9,471

Stevenson University
Stevenson MD
(877) 468-6852
U.S. News ranking: Reg. U. (N),
No. 82
Website: www.stevenson.edu/

Admissions email:
admissions@stevenson.edu
Private; founded 1947
Freshman admissions: selective;
2020-2021: 4,177 applied,
3,725 accepted. Neither SAT
nor ACT required. SAT 25/75
percentile: 980-1160. High school
rank: 12% in top tenth, 38% in
top quarter, 72% in top half
Early decision deadline: N/A,
notification date: N/A
Early action deadline: N/A,
notification date: N/A
Application deadline (fall): rolling
Undergraduate student body: 2,680
full time, 347 part time; 36%
male, 64% female; 0% American
Indian, 4% Asian, 26% black,
9% Hispanic, 5% multiracial,
0% Pacific Islander, 53% white,
1% international; 78% from in
state; 17% live on campus; 0%
of students in fraternities, 1% in
sororities
Most popular majors: 26%
Health Professions and Related
Programs, 21% Business,
Management, Marketing, and
Related Support Services, 9%
Visual and Performing Arts,
8% Biological and Biomedical
Sciences, 7% Homeland Security,
Law Enforcement, Firefighting and
Related Protective Services
Expenses: 2021-2022: $38,168;
room/board: $14,170
Financial aid: (443) 334-3200;
73% of undergrads determined to
have financial need; average aid
package $29,639

St. John's College
Annapolis MD
(410) 626-2522
U.S. News ranking: Nat. Lib. Arts,
No. 67
Website: www.sjc.edu
Admissions email:
annapolis.admissions@sjc.edu
Private; founded 1696
Freshman admissions: more
selective; 2020-2021: 777
applied, 477 accepted. Neither
SAT nor ACT required. SAT
25/75 percentile: 1130-1440.
High school rank: 25% in top
tenth, 43% in top quarter, 86%
in top half
Early decision deadline: 11/1,
notification date: 12/1
Early action deadline: 11/15,
notification date: 12/15
Application deadline (fall): rolling
Undergraduate student body:
382 full time, 1 part time; 48%
male, 52% female; 0% American
Indian, 5% Asian, 3% black, 5%
Hispanic, 7% multiracial, 0%
Pacific Islander, 63% white, 17%
international
Most popular majors: 100%
Liberal Arts and Sciences, General
Studies and Humanities
Expenses: 2021-2022: $36,170;
room/board: $13,858
Financial aid: (410) 626-2502;
68% of undergrads determined to
have financial need; average aid
package $27,953

St. Mary's College of Maryland
St. Marys City MD
(800) 492-7181
U.S. News ranking: Nat. Lib. Arts,
No. 89
Website: www.smcm.edu
Admissions email:
admissions@smcm.edu
Public; founded 1840
Freshman admissions: more
selective; 2020-2021: 2,604
applied, 2,058 accepted. Neither
SAT nor ACT required. SAT
25/75 percentile: 1070-1280.
High school rank: 22% in top
tenth, 57% in top quarter, 85%
in top half
Early decision deadline: 11/1,
notification date: 12/1
Early action deadline: 11/1,
notification date: 1/1
Application deadline (fall): 1/15
Undergraduate student body: 1,420
full time, 68 part time; 40%
male, 60% female; 0% American
Indian, 3% Asian, 10% black,
8% Hispanic, 6% multiracial,
0% Pacific Islander, 70% white,
1% international; 93% from in
state; 61% live on campus; 0%
of students in fraternities, 0% in
sororities
Most popular majors: 21% Social
Sciences, 13% Biological and
Biomedical Sciences, 11%
Psychology, 9% English Language
and Literature/Letters, 8% Natural
Resources and Conservation
Expenses: 2021-2022: $15,124
in state, $31,200 out of state;
room/board: $13,869
Financial aid: (240) 895-3000;
50% of undergrads determined to
have financial need; average aid
package $15,942

Towson University
Towson MD
(410) 704-2113
U.S. News ranking: Nat. U.,
No. 196
Website: www.towson.edu
Admissions email:
admissions@towson.edu
Public; founded 1866
Freshman admissions: selective;
2020-2021: 12,295 applied,
9,689 accepted. Neither SAT
nor ACT required. SAT 25/75
percentile: 1040-1200. High
school rank: 14% in top tenth,
39% in top quarter, 79% in
top half
Early decision deadline: N/A,
notification date: N/A
Early action deadline: 12/1,
notification date: 12/31
Application deadline (fall): 1/15
Undergraduate student body:
16,238 full time, 2,492 part
time; 40% male, 60% female;
0% American Indian, 7% Asian,
26% black, 9% Hispanic, 6%
multiracial, 0% Pacific Islander,
49% white, 1% international; N/A
from in state; 6% live on campus;
8% of students in fraternities, 9%
in sororities
Most popular majors: 14%
Business, Management,
Marketing, and Related Support
Services, 14% Health Professions
and Related Programs, 10%

Communication, Journalism, and
Related Programs, 10% Social
Sciences, 8% Education
Expenses: 2021-2022: $9,354 in
state, $22,532 out of state; room/
board: $13,232
Financial aid: (410) 704-4236;
57% of undergrads determined to
have financial need; average aid
package $10,918

United States Naval Academy
Annapolis MD
(410) 293-1858
U.S. News ranking: Nat. Lib. Arts,
No. 6
Website: www.usna.edu
Admissions email:
inquire@usna.edu
Public; founded 1845
Freshman admissions: most
selective; 2020-2021: 15,701
applied, 1,421 accepted. Either
SAT or ACT required. SAT 25/75
percentile: 1230-1450. High
school rank: 55% in top tenth,
81% in top quarter, 94% in
top half
Early decision deadline: N/A,
notification date: N/A
Early action deadline: N/A,
notification date: N/A
Application deadline (fall): 1/31
Undergraduate student body:
4,594 full time, 0 part time; 72%
male, 28% female; 0% American
Indian, 8% Asian, 7% black, 12%
Hispanic, 10% multiracial, 0%
Pacific Islander, 61% white, 1%
international
Most popular majors: 36%
Engineering, 24% Social
Sciences, 12% Physical
Sciences, 6% English Language
and Literature/Letters, 6%
Military Science, Leadership and
Operational Art
Expenses: 2021-2022: $0 in
state, $0 out of state; room/
board: N/A
Financial aid: N/A

University of Baltimore
Baltimore MD
(410) 837-6565
U.S. News ranking: Reg. U. (N),
No. 109
Website: www.ubalt.edu
Admissions email:
admissions@ubalt.edu
Public; founded 1925
Freshman admissions: less
selective; 2020-2021: 274
applied, 219 accepted. Either
SAT or ACT required. SAT 25/75
percentile: 930-1070. High
school rank: N/A
Early decision deadline: N/A,
notification date: N/A
Early action deadline: N/A,
notification date: N/A
Application deadline (fall): rolling
Undergraduate student body: 1,042
full time, 838 part time; 41%
male, 59% female; 0% American
Indian, 5% Asian, 48% black,
8% Hispanic, 5% multiracial, 0%
Pacific Islander, 28% white, 3%
international
Most popular majors: Information
not available

Expenses: 2021-2022: $9,364 in
state, $22,550 out of state; room/
board: N/A
Financial aid: (410) 837-4772;
73% of undergrads determined to
have financial need; average aid
package $9,067

University of Maryland–Baltimore County
Baltimore MD
(410) 455-2292
U.S. News ranking: Nat. U.,
No. 162
Website: www.umbc.edu
Admissions email:
admissions@umbc.edu
Public; founded 1966
Freshman admissions: more
selective; 2020-2021: 11,459
applied, 7,962 accepted. Either
SAT or ACT required. SAT 25/75
percentile: 1150-1350. High
school rank: 22% in top tenth,
50% in top quarter, 81% in
top half
Early decision deadline: N/A,
notification date: N/A
Early action deadline: 11/1,
notification date: 12/15
Application deadline (fall): 2/1
Undergraduate student body: 9,220
full time, 1,712 part time; 54%
male, 46% female; 0% American
Indian, 22% Asian, 20% black,
9% Hispanic, 5% multiracial,
0% Pacific Islander, 37% white,
4% international; 91% from in
state; N/A live on campus; 3%
of students in fraternities, 5% in
sororities
Most popular majors: 22%
Computer and Information
Sciences and Support Services,
15% Biological and Biomedical
Sciences, 12% Psychology, 9%
Engineering, 9% Social Sciences
Expenses: 2021-2022: $12,280
in state, $28,470 out of state;
room/board: $12,600
Financial aid: (410) 455-2387;
50% of undergrads determined to
have financial need; average aid
package $11,411

University of Maryland–College Park
College Park MD
(301) 314-8385
U.S. News ranking: Nat. U., No. 59
Website: www.umd.edu/
Admissions email:
ApplyMaryland@umd.edu
Public; founded 1856
Freshman admissions: most
selective; 2020-2021: 32,211
applied, 15,737 accepted. Neither
SAT nor ACT required. SAT
25/75 percentile: 1270-1480.
High school rank: 73% in top
tenth, 89% in top quarter, 98%
in top half
Early decision deadline: N/A,
notification date: N/A
Early action deadline: 11/1,
notification date: 1/31
Application deadline (fall): 1/20
Undergraduate student body:
28,160 full time, 2,715 part
time; 52% male, 48% female;
0% American Indian, 19% Asian,

12% black, 10% Hispanic, 5% multiracial, 0% Pacific Islander, 47% white, 4% international
Most popular majors: 9% Computer Science, 6% Biology/Biological Sciences, General, 4% Finance, General, 4% Information Science/Studies, 4% Mechanical Engineering
Expenses: 2021-2022: $10,954 in state, $38,636 out of state; room/board: $13,258
Financial aid: (301) 314-9000; 38% of undergrads determined to have financial need; average aid package $12,715

University of Maryland Eastern Shore
Princess Anne MD
(410) 651-6410
U.S. News ranking: Nat. U., second tier
Website: www.umes.edu
Admissions email: umesadmissions@umes.edu
Public; founded 1886
Freshman admissions: less selective; 2020-2021: 8,511 applied, 5,279 accepted. Neither SAT nor ACT required. SAT 25/75 percentile: 840-1010. High school rank: N/A
Early decision deadline: N/A, notification date: N/A
Early action deadline: N/A, notification date: N/A
Application deadline (fall): 6/30
Undergraduate student body: 1,860 full time, 210 part time; 45% male, 55% female; 0% American Indian, 1% Asian, 52% black, 5% Hispanic, 2% multiracial, 0% Pacific Islander, 11% white, 2% international; 79% from in state; N/A live on campus; N/A of students in fraternities, N/A in sororities
Most popular majors: Information not available
Expenses: 2020-2021: $8,558 in state, $18,968 out of state; room/board: $10,085
Financial aid: (410) 651-6172

University of Maryland Global Campus
Adelphi MD
(800) 888-8682
U.S. News ranking: Reg. U. (N), second tier
Website: www.umgc.edu/
Admissions email: studentsfirst@umgc.edu
Public; founded 1947
Freshman admissions: least selective; 2020-2021: 3,500 applied, 3,500 accepted. Neither SAT nor ACT required. SAT 25/75 percentile: N/A. High school rank: N/A
Early decision deadline: N/A, notification date: N/A
Early action deadline: N/A, notification date: N/A
Application deadline (fall): rolling
Undergraduate student body: 10,425 full time, 36,655 part time; 55% male, 45% female; 0% American Indian, 5% Asian, 26% black, 15% Hispanic, 5%

multiracial, 1% Pacific Islander, 37% white, 1% international
Most popular majors: 34% Computer and Information Sciences and Support Services, 29% Business, Management, Marketing, and Related Support Services, 7% Health Professions and Related Programs, 7% Psychology, 6% Homeland Security, Law Enforcement, Firefighting and Related Protective Services
Expenses: 2021-2022: $7,560 in state, $12,336 out of state; room/board: N/A
Financial aid: (240) 684-5680; 58% of undergrads determined to have financial need; average aid package $8,028

Washington Adventist University
Takoma Park MD
(301) 891-4000
U.S. News ranking: Reg. U. (N), second tier
Website: www.wau.edu
Admissions email: enroll@wau.edu
Private; founded 1904
Affiliation: Seventh Day Adventist
Freshman admissions: least selective; 2020-2021: N/A applied, N/A accepted. Neither SAT nor ACT required. SAT 25/75 percentile: 760-930. High school rank: N/A
Early decision deadline: N/A, notification date: N/A
Early action deadline: N/A, notification date: N/A
Application deadline (fall): 8/1
Undergraduate student body: 624 full time, 221 part time; 32% male, 68% female; 0% American Indian, 3% Asian, 52% black, 21% Hispanic, 2% multiracial, 0% Pacific Islander, 5% white, 9% international
Most popular majors: Information not available
Expenses: 2020-2021: $24,300; room/board: $9,830
Financial aid: (301) 891-4005

Washington College
Chestertown MD
(410) 778-7700
U.S. News ranking: Nat. Lib. Arts, No. 98
Website: www.washcoll.edu
Admissions email: wc_admissions@washcoll.edu
Private; founded 1782
Freshman admissions: more selective; 2020-2021: 2,901 applied, 2,329 accepted. Either SAT or ACT required. SAT 25/75 percentile: 1070-1280. High school rank: 29% in top tenth, 57% in top quarter, 84% in top half
Early decision deadline: 11/15, notification date: 12/15
Early action deadline: 12/1, notification date: 1/15
Application deadline (fall): 2/15
Undergraduate student body: 1,075 full time, 14 part time; 39% male, 61% female; 0% American Indian, 4% Asian, 11% black, 7% Hispanic, 0% multiracial, 0% Pacific Islander, 67% white, 3% international; 366% from in

state; 3% live on campus; 22% of students in fraternities, 31% in sororities
Most popular majors: 22% Social Sciences, 14% Biological and Biomedical Sciences, 14% Business, Management, Marketing, and Related Support Services, 10% Psychology, 6% Physical Sciences
Expenses: 2021-2022: $50,842; room/board: $13,363
Financial aid: (410) 778-7214; 67% of undergrads determined to have financial need; average aid package $26,182

MASSACHUSETTS

American International College
Springfield MA
(413) 205-3201
U.S. News ranking: Reg. U. (N), second tier
Website: www.aic.edu
Admissions email: admissions@aic.edu
Private; founded 1885
Freshman admissions: less selective; 2020-2021: 1,956 applied, 1,357 accepted. Neither SAT nor ACT required. SAT 25/75 percentile: 890-1100. High school rank: N/A
Early decision deadline: N/A, notification date: N/A
Early action deadline: N/A, notification date: N/A
Application deadline (fall): 9/16
Undergraduate student body: 1,274 full time, 99 part time; 40% male, 60% female; 1% American Indian, 2% Asian, 24% black, 23% Hispanic, 7% multiracial, 1% Pacific Islander, 34% white, 4% international
Most popular majors: 31% Registered Nursing/Registered Nurse, 8% Criminal Justice/Safety Studies, 7% Business Administration and Management, General, 7% Psychology, General, 7% Public Health, General
Expenses: 2020-2021: $38,220; room/board: $14,660
Financial aid: (413) 205-3521

Amherst College
Amherst MA
(413) 542-2328
U.S. News ranking: Nat. Lib. Arts, No. 2
Website: www.amherst.edu
Admissions email: admission@amherst.edu
Private; founded 1821
Freshman admissions: most selective; 2020-2021: 10,603 applied, 1,254 accepted. Neither SAT nor ACT required. SAT 25/75 percentile: 1410-1550. High school rank: 85% in top tenth, 96% in top quarter, 100% in top half
Early decision deadline: 11/15, notification date: 12/15
Early action deadline: N/A, notification date: N/A
Application deadline (fall): 1/3
Undergraduate student body: 1,745 full time, 0 part time; 48% male, 52% female; 1% American

Indian, 15% Asian, 10% black, 14% Hispanic, 7% multiracial, 0% Pacific Islander, 40% white, 10% international; 14% from in state; 54% live on campus; 0% of students in fraternities, 0% in sororities
Most popular majors: 12% Econometrics and Quantitative Economics, 11% Mathematics, General, 9% Research and Experimental Psychology, Other, 7% Computer Science, 6% Political Science and Government, General
Expenses: 2020-2021: $60,890; room/board: $15,910
Financial aid: (413) 542-2296

Anna Maria College[1]
Paxton MA
(508) 849-3360
U.S. News ranking: Reg. U. (N), second tier
Website: www.annamaria.edu
Admissions email: admissions@annamaria.edu
Private; founded 1946
Affiliation: Roman Catholic
Application deadline (fall): rolling
Undergraduate student body: N/A full time, N/A part time
Expenses: 2020-2021: $39,470; room/board: $14,950
Financial aid: (508) 849-3363

Assumption University
Worcester MA
(866) 477-7776
U.S. News ranking: Reg. U. (N), No. 34
Website: www.assumption.edu
Admissions email: admiss@assumption.edu
Private; founded 1904
Affiliation: Roman Catholic
Freshman admissions: selective; 2020-2021: 4,970 applied, 4,019 accepted. Neither SAT nor ACT required. SAT 25/75 percentile: 1070-1220. High school rank: 15% in top tenth, 41% in top quarter, 83% in top half
Early decision deadline: 11/1, notification date: 12/1
Early action deadline: 11/1, notification date: 12/15
Application deadline (fall): 2/15
Undergraduate student body: 1,970 full time, 29 part time; 44% male, 56% female; 0% American Indian, 3% Asian, 5% black, 9% Hispanic, 3% multiracial, 0% Pacific Islander, 75% white, 1% international; N/A from in state; 35% live on campus; N/A of students in fraternities, N/A in sororities
Most popular majors: 26% Business, Management, Marketing, and Related Support Services, 16% Health Professions and Related Programs, 14% Social Sciences
Expenses: 2021-2022: $45,900; room/board: $14,068
Financial aid: (508) 767-7158; 74% of undergrads determined to have financial need; average aid package $31,913

Babson College
Babson Park MA
(781) 239-4006
U.S. News ranking: Business, unranked
Website: www.babson.edu
Admissions email: ugradadmission@babson.edu
Private; founded 1919
Freshman admissions: more selective; 2020-2021: 6,501 applied, 1,753 accepted. Either SAT or ACT required. SAT 25/75 percentile: 1270-1450. High school rank: N/A
Early decision deadline: 11/1, notification date: 12/15
Early action deadline: 11/1, notification date: 1/1
Application deadline (fall): 1/2
Undergraduate student body: 2,441 full time, 16 part time; 55% male, 45% female; 0% American Indian, 12% Asian, 4% black, 14% Hispanic, 3% multiracial, 0% Pacific Islander, 35% white, 27% international; 18% from in state; 52% live on campus; N/A of students in fraternities, N/A in sororities
Most popular majors: 100% Business Administration and Management, General
Expenses: 2021-2022: $54,944; room/board: $18,234
Financial aid: (781) 239-4015; 42% of undergrads determined to have financial need; average aid package $46,000

Bard College at Simon's Rock[1]
Great Barrington MA
(800) 235-7186
U.S. News ranking: Reg. Coll. (N), unranked
Website: www.simons-rock.edu
Admissions email: admit@simons-rock.edu
Private; founded 1966
Application deadline (fall): rolling
Undergraduate student body: N/A full time, N/A part time
Expenses: 2020-2021: $60,098; room/board: $15,902
Financial aid: (413) 528-7297

Bay Path University
Longmeadow MA
(413) 565-1331
U.S. News ranking: Reg. U. (N), No. 90
Website: www.baypath.edu
Admissions email: admiss@baypath.edu
Private; founded 1897
Freshman admissions: selective; 2020-2021: 1,148 applied, 899 accepted. Neither SAT nor ACT required. SAT 25/75 percentile: 940-1170. High school rank: 15% in top tenth, 50% in top quarter, 80% in top half
Early decision deadline: N/A, notification date: N/A
Early action deadline: 12/15, notification date: 1/2
Application deadline (fall): 8/1
Undergraduate student body: 1,014 full time, 775 part time; 0% male, 100% female; 1% American Indian, 2% Asian, 14% black, 23% Hispanic, 2% multiracial,

More @ usnews.com/bestcolleges

0% Pacific Islander, 52% white, 1% international
Most popular majors: Information not available
Expenses: 2021-2022: $35,781; room/board: $12,799
Financial aid: (413) 565-1256; 91% of undergrads determined to have financial need; average aid package $27,643

Bay State College[1]
Boston MA
(617) 217-9000
U.S. News ranking: Reg. Coll. (N), second tier
Website: www.baystate.edu/
Admissions email: admissions@baystate.edu
For-profit; founded 1946
Affiliation: Undenominational
Application deadline (fall): rolling
Undergraduate student body: N/A full time, N/A part time
Expenses: 2020-2021: $29,200; room/board: $13,300
Financial aid: (617) 217-9003

Becker College[1]
Worcester MA
(877) 523-2537
U.S. News ranking: Reg. Coll. (N), second tier
Website: www.beckercollege.edu
Admissions email: admissions@beckercollege.edu
Private; founded 1784
Application deadline (fall): rolling
Undergraduate student body: N/A full time, N/A part time
Expenses: 2020-2021: $40,150; room/board: $13,800
Financial aid: (508) 373-9430

Bentley University
Waltham MA
(781) 891-2244
U.S. News ranking: Reg. U. (N), No. 2
Website: www.bentley.edu
Admissions email: ugadmission@bentley.edu
Private; founded 1917
Freshman admissions: more selective; 2020-2021: 8,298 applied, 4,798 accepted. Either SAT or ACT required. SAT 25/75 percentile: 1180-1360. High school rank: 42% in top tenth, 75% in top quarter, 95% in top half
Early decision deadline: 11/15, notification date: 12/31
Early action deadline: N/A, notification date: N/A
Application deadline (fall): 1/7
Undergraduate student body: 4,008 full time, 53 part time; 60% male, 40% female; 0% American Indian, 9% Asian, 4% black, 9% Hispanic, 3% multiracial, 0% Pacific Islander, 58% white, 15% international; 43% from in state; 78% live on campus; 4% of students in fraternities, 8% in sororities
Most popular majors: 23% Finance, General, 14% Marketing/Marketing Management, General, 11% Accounting, 11% Business Administration and Management, General, 11% Business, Management, Marketing, and

Related Support Services, Other
Expenses: 2021-2022: $54,910; room/board: $18,130
Financial aid: (781) 891-3441; 46% of undergrads determined to have financial need; average aid package $38,635

Berklee College of Music
Boston MA
(800) 237-5533
U.S. News ranking: Arts, unranked
Website: www.berklee.edu
Admissions email: admissions@berklee.edu
Private; founded 1945
Freshman admissions: least selective; 2020-2021: 7,860 applied, 4,056 accepted. Neither SAT nor ACT required. SAT 25/75 percentile: N/A. High school rank: N/A
Early decision deadline: N/A, notification date: N/A
Early action deadline: 11/1, notification date: 1/31
Application deadline (fall): 1/15
Undergraduate student body: 4,224 full time, 1,780 part time; 57% male, 43% female; 0% American Indian, 5% Asian, 7% black, 13% Hispanic, 5% multiracial, 0% Pacific Islander, 43% white, 24% international; 11% from in state; N/A live on campus; 0% of students in fraternities, 0% in sororities
Most popular majors: 64% Visual and Performing Arts, 22% Computer and Information Sciences and Support Services, 10% Engineering Technologies and Engineering-Related Fields, 2% Health Professions and Related Programs, 1% Education
Expenses: 2021-2022: $46,800; room/board: $18,828
Financial aid: (617) 747-2274; 43% of undergrads determined to have financial need; average aid package $25,776

Boston Architectural College[1]
Boston MA
(617) 585-0123
U.S. News ranking: Arts, unranked
Website: www.the-bac.edu
Admissions email: admissions@the-bac.edu
Private; founded 1889
Application deadline (fall): rolling
Undergraduate student body: N/A full time, N/A part time
Expenses: 2020-2021: $21,844; room/board: N/A
Financial aid: (617) 585-0183

Boston College
Chestnut Hill MA
(617) 552-3100
U.S. News ranking: Nat. U., No. 36
Website: www.bc.edu
Admissions email: admission@bc.edu
Private; founded 1863
Affiliation: Roman Catholic
Freshman admissions: most selective; 2020-2021: 29,382 applied, 7,752 accepted. SAT nor ACT required. SAT 25/75 percentile: 1330-1500.

High school rank: 79% in top tenth, 94% in top quarter, 99% in top half
Early decision deadline: 11/1, notification date: 12/15
Early action deadline: N/A, notification date: N/A
Application deadline (fall): 1/1
Undergraduate student body: 9,445 full time, 0 part time; 47% male, 53% female; 0% American Indian, 11% Asian, 4% black, 11% Hispanic, 4% multiracial, 0% Pacific Islander, 58% white, 8% international; N/A from in state; 76% live on campus; 0% of students in fraternities, 0% in sororities
Most popular majors: 14% Finance, General, 11% Economics, General, 9% Biology/Biological Sciences, General, 8% Speech Communication and Rhetoric, 6% Political Science and Government, General
Expenses: 2021-2022: $61,706; room/board: $15,602
Financial aid: (617) 552-3300; 41% of undergrads determined to have financial need; average aid package $49,589

Boston University
Boston MA
(617) 353-2300
U.S. News ranking: Nat. U., No. 42
Website: www.bu.edu
Admissions email: admissions@bu.edu
Private; founded 1839
Freshman admissions: most selective; 2020-2021: 61,007 applied, 12,254 accepted. Neither SAT nor ACT required. SAT 25/75 percentile: 1310-1500. High school rank: 66% in top tenth, 93% in top quarter, 100% in top half
Early decision deadline: 11/1, notification date: 12/15
Early action deadline: N/A, notification date: N/A
Application deadline (fall): 1/4
Undergraduate student body: 16,026 full time, 846 part time; 42% male, 58% female; 0% American Indian, 19% Asian, 4% black, 12% Hispanic, 5% multiracial, 0% Pacific Islander, 35% white, 21% international; N/A from in state; 70% live on campus; N/A of students in fraternities, 1% in sororities
Most popular majors: 16% Business, Management, Marketing, and Related Support Services, 15% Communication, Journalism, and Related Programs, 15% Social Sciences, 10% Biological and Biomedical Sciences, 9% Engineering
Expenses: 2021-2022: $59,816; room/board: $16,840
Financial aid: (617) 353-2965; 44% of undergrads determined to have financial need; average aid package $49,407

Brandeis University
Waltham MA
(781) 736-3500
U.S. News ranking: Nat. U., No. 42
Website: www.brandeis.edu
Admissions email: admissions@brandeis.edu

Private; founded 1948
Freshman admissions: most selective; 2020-2021: 10,223 applied, 3,445 accepted. Neither SAT nor ACT required. SAT 25/75 percentile: 1320-1510. High school rank: 59% in top tenth, 85% in top quarter, 97% in top half
Early decision deadline: 11/1, notification date: 12/15
Early action deadline: N/A, notification date: N/A
Application deadline (fall): 1/1
Undergraduate student body: 3,465 full time, 28 part time; 40% male, 60% female; 0% American Indian, 15% Asian, 6% black, 8% Hispanic, 4% multiracial, 0% Pacific Islander, 44% white, 20% international; 30% from in state; 52% live on campus; 0% of students in fraternities, 0% in sororities
Most popular majors: 11% Biology/Biological Sciences, General, 11% Economics, General, 9% Business/Commerce, General, 7% Computer Science, 7% Experimental Psychology
Expenses: 2021-2022: $60,391; room/board: $16,650
Financial aid: (781) 736-3700; 44% of undergrads determined to have financial need; average aid package $47,230

Bridgewater State University
Bridgewater MA
(508) 531-1237
U.S. News ranking: Reg. U. (N), No. 97
Website: www.bridgew.edu/
Admissions email: admission@bridgew.edu
Public; founded 1840
Freshman admissions: selective; 2020-2021: 9,549 applied, 7,865 accepted. Neither SAT nor ACT required. SAT 25/75 percentile: 950-1140. High school rank: N/A
Early decision deadline: N/A, notification date: N/A
Early action deadline: 11/15, notification date: 12/15
Application deadline (fall): rolling
Undergraduate student body: 7,133 full time, 1,895 part time; 40% male, 60% female; 0% American Indian, 2% Asian, 12% black, 8% Hispanic, 5% multiracial, 0% Pacific Islander, 71% white, 0% international; 96% from in state; 17% live on campus; 1% of students in fraternities, 1% in sororities
Most popular majors: 17% Business, Management, Marketing, and Related Support Services, 17% Education, 15% Psychology, 9% Homeland Security, Law Enforcement, Firefighting and Related Protective Services, 7% Communication, Journalism, and Related Programs
Expenses: 2021-2022: $10,732 in state, $16,872 out of state; room/board: $13,832
Financial aid: (508) 531-1341; 68% of undergrads determined to have financial need; average aid package $9,040

Cambridge College[1]
Cambridge MA
(617) 868-1000
U.S. News ranking: Reg. U. (N), second tier
Website: www.cambridgecollege.edu
Admissions email: N/A
Private; founded 1971
Application deadline (fall): N/A
Undergraduate student body: N/A full time, N/A part time
Expenses: 2020-2021: $16,266; room/board: N/A
Financial aid: (617) 873-0440

Clark University
Worcester MA
(508) 793-7431
U.S. News ranking: Nat. U., No. 103
Website: www.clarku.edu
Admissions email: admissions@clarku.edu
Private; founded 1887
Freshman admissions: more selective; 2020-2021: 7,153 applied, 3,371 accepted. Neither SAT nor ACT required. SAT 25/75 percentile: 1150-1350. High school rank: 36% in top tenth, 70% in top quarter, 88% in top half
Early decision deadline: 11/1, notification date: 12/15
Early action deadline: 11/1, notification date: 12/15
Application deadline (fall): 1/15
Undergraduate student body: 2,191 full time, 50 part time; 38% male, 62% female; 0% American Indian, 7% Asian, 5% black, 10% Hispanic, 3% multiracial, 0% Pacific Islander, 62% white, 9% international; N/A from in state; 53% live on campus; 0% of students in fraternities, 0% in sororities
Most popular majors: 26% Social Sciences, 15% Psychology, 12% Biological and Biomedical Sciences
Expenses: 2021-2022: $50,302; room/board: $10,150
Financial aid: (508) 793-7478; 64% of undergrads determined to have financial need; average aid package $35,867

College of the Holy Cross
Worcester MA
(508) 793-2443
U.S. News ranking: Nat. Lib. Arts, No. 35
Website: www.holycross.edu
Admissions email: admissions@holycross.edu
Private; founded 1843
Affiliation: Roman Catholic
Freshman admissions: more selective; 2020-2021: 7,087 applied, 2,689 accepted. Neither SAT nor ACT required. SAT 25/75 percentile: 1290-1430. High school rank: 61% in top tenth, 86% in top quarter, 97% in top half
Early decision deadline: 11/15, notification date: 12/15
Early action deadline: N/A, notification date: N/A

sororities
Most popular majors: 22%
Business Administration and
Management, General, 19%
Dance, General, 13% Psychology,
General, 12% Sport and Fitness
Administration/Management, 8%
Drama and Dramatics/Theatre
Arts, General
Expenses: 2021-2022: $42,346;
room/board: $18,090
Financial aid: (508) 541-1518;
74% of undergrads determined to
have financial need; average aid
package $28,091

Eastern Nazarene College[1]
Quincy MA
(617) 745-3711
U.S. News ranking: Reg. Coll. (N),
second tier
Website: www.enc.edu
Admissions email:
admissions@enc.edu
Private; founded 1918
Affiliation: Church of the Nazarene
Application deadline (fall): rolling
Undergraduate student body: N/A
full time, N/A part time
Expenses: 2020-2021: $26,952;
room/board: $9,985
Financial aid: (617) 745-3865

Elms College
Chicopee MA
(413) 592-3189
U.S. News ranking: Reg. U. (N),
No. 85
Website: www.elms.edu
Admissions email:
admissions@elms.edu
Private; founded 1928
Affiliation: Roman Catholic
Freshman admissions: selective;
2020-2021: 1,479 applied,
1,032 accepted. Neither SAT
nor ACT required. SAT 25/75
percentile: 1000-1170. High
school rank: N/A
Early decision deadline: N/A,
notification date: N/A
Early action deadline: N/A,
notification date: N/A
Application deadline (fall): rolling
Undergraduate student body: 881
full time, 149 part time; 23%
male, 77% female; 0% American
Indian, 2% Asian, 9% black,
15% Hispanic, 2% multiracial,
0% Pacific Islander, 50% white,
0% international; 72% from in
state; 19% live on campus; 0%
of students in fraternities, 0% in
sororities
Most popular majors: 33%
Registered Nursing/Registered
Nurse, 13% Social Work,
6% Business Administration
and Management, General,
5% Psychology, General, 4%
Education, General
Expenses: 2021-2022: $39,449;
room/board: $14,395
Financial aid: (413) 265-2303;
89% of undergrads determined to
have financial need; average aid
package $21,964

Emerson College
Boston MA
(617) 824-8600
U.S. News ranking: Reg. U. (N),
No. 8
Website: www.emerson.edu
Admissions email:
admission@emerson.edu
Private; founded 1880
Freshman admissions: more
selective; 2020-2021: 13,326
applied, 5,470 accepted. Neither
SAT nor ACT required. SAT
25/75 percentile: 1190-1380.
High school rank: 27% in top
tenth, 60% in top quarter, 92%
in top half
Early decision deadline: 11/1,
notification date: 12/15
Early action deadline: 11/1,
notification date: 12/15
Application deadline (fall): 1/15
Undergraduate student body: 3,626
full time, 82 part time; 37%
male, 63% female; 0% American
Indian, 5% Asian, 4% black,
13% Hispanic, 4% multiracial,
0% Pacific Islander, 59% white,
13% international; 20% from in
state; 49% live on campus; 2%
of students in fraternities, 3% in
sororities
Most popular majors: Information
not available
Expenses: 2021-2022: $52,190;
room/board: $19,144
Financial aid: (617) 824-8655;
54% of undergrads determined to
have financial need; average aid
package $27,625

Emmanuel College
Boston MA
(617) 735-9715
U.S. News ranking: Nat. Lib. Arts,
second tier
Website: www.emmanuel.edu
Admissions email:
admissions@emmanuel.edu
Private; founded 1919
Affiliation: Roman Catholic
Freshman admissions: more
selective; 2020-2021: 5,450
applied, 4,116 accepted. Neither
SAT nor ACT required. SAT
25/75 percentile: 1110-1280.
High school rank: 28% in top
tenth, 52% in top quarter, 85%
in top half
Early decision deadline: N/A,
notification date: N/A
Early action deadline: 11/15,
notification date: 12/15
Application deadline (fall): 2/15
Undergraduate student body: 1,735
full time, 103 part time; 22%
male, 78% female; 0% American
Indian, 5% Asian, 7% black,
11% Hispanic, 3% multiracial,
0% Pacific Islander, 68% white,
1% international; 63% from in
state; N/A live on campus; N/A
of students in fraternities, N/A in
sororities
Most popular majors: 17%
Biological and Biomedical
Sciences, 12% Business,
Management, Marketing, and
Related Support Services, 12%
Psychology, 12% Social Sciences,
8% Education
Expenses: 2021-2022: $43,572;
room/board: $16,242

Financial aid: (617) 735-9938;
79% of undergrads determined to
have financial need; average aid
package $30,609

Endicott College
Beverly MA
(978) 921-1000
U.S. News ranking: Reg. U. (N),
No. 23
Website: www.endicott.edu
Admissions email:
admission@endicott.edu
Private; founded 1939
Freshman admissions: selective;
2020-2021: 5,355 applied,
3,770 accepted. Neither SAT
nor ACT required. SAT 25/75
percentile: 1100-1240. High
school rank: 18% in top tenth,
48% in top quarter, 84% in
top half
Early decision deadline: 11/1,
notification date: 12/15
Early action deadline: 11/1,
notification date: 12/23
Application deadline (fall): 2/15
Undergraduate student body: 3,029
full time, 240 part time; 38%
male, 62% female; 0% American
Indian, 1% Asian, 1% black,
7% Hispanic, 2% multiracial,
0% Pacific Islander, 82% white,
1% international; 53% from in
state; 89% live on campus; 0%
of students in fraternities, 0% in
sororities
Most popular majors: 13%
Registered Nursing/Registered
Nurse, 12% Business
Administration and Management,
General, 8% Early Childhood
Education and Teaching, 7%
Sport and Fitness Administration/
Management, 6% Liberal Arts and
Sciences/Liberal Studies
Expenses: 2021-2022: $36,614;
room/board: $16,534
Financial aid: (978) 232-2060;
60% of undergrads determined to
have financial need; average aid
package $22,926

Fisher College
Boston MA
(617) 236-8818
U.S. News ranking: Reg. Coll. (N),
second tier
Website: www.fisher.edu
Admissions email:
admissions@fisher.edu
Private; founded 1903
Freshman admissions: less
selective; 2020-2021: 2,612
applied, 2,030 accepted. Neither
SAT nor ACT required. SAT 25/75
percentile: 830-1060. High
school rank: N/A
Early decision deadline: N/A,
notification date: N/A
Early action deadline: N/A,
notification date: N/A
Application deadline (fall): rolling
Undergraduate student body: 594
full time, 717 part time; 31%
male, 69% female; 0% American
Indian, 1% Asian, 13% black,
16% Hispanic, 2% multiracial,
0% Pacific Islander, 24% white,
9% international; N/A from in
state; 35% live on campus; N/A
of students in fraternities, N/A in
sororities

Most popular majors: 45%
Business, Management,
Marketing, and Related
Support Services, 19% Public
Administration and Social Service
Professions, 13% Homeland
Security, Law Enforcement,
Firefighting and Related Protective
Services
Expenses: 2021-2022: $33,600;
room/board: $17,000
Financial aid: (617) 236-8821;
82% of undergrads determined to
have financial need; average aid
package $26,862

Fitchburg State University
Fitchburg MA
(978) 665-3144
U.S. News ranking: Reg. U. (N),
No. 97
Website: www.fitchburgstate.edu
Admissions email:
admissions@fitchburgstate.edu
Public; founded 1894
Freshman admissions: less
selective; 2020-2021: 2,998
applied, 2,638 accepted. Neither
SAT nor ACT required. SAT 25/75
percentile: 970-1140. High
school rank: N/A
Early decision deadline: N/A,
notification date: N/A
Early action deadline: N/A,
notification date: N/A
Application deadline (fall): rolling
Undergraduate student body: 2,831
full time, 984 part time; 46%
male, 54% female; 0% American
Indian, 3% Asian, 12% black,
14% Hispanic, 3% multiracial,
0% Pacific Islander, 67% white,
1% international; N/A from in
state; 29% live on campus; N/A
of students in fraternities, N/A in
sororities
Most popular majors: 14%
Visual and Performing Arts,
12% Business, Management,
Marketing, and Related Support
Services, 11% Health Professions
and Related Programs, 11%
Multi/Interdisciplinary Studies,
10% Biological and Biomedical
Sciences
Expenses: 2021-2022: $10,655
in state, $16,735 out of state;
room/board: $11,160
Financial aid: (978) 665-3302;
63% of undergrads determined to
have financial need; average aid
package $10,181

Framingham State University
Framingham MA
(508) 626-4500
U.S. News ranking: Reg. U. (N),
No. 103
Website: www.framingham.edu
Admissions email:
admissions@framingham.edu
Public; founded 1839
Freshman admissions: selective;
2020-2021: 5,695 applied,
4,472 accepted. Neither SAT
nor ACT required. SAT 25/75
percentile: 950-1130. High
school rank: N/A
Early decision deadline: N/A,
notification date: N/A
Early action deadline: 11/15,
notification date: 12/15

Application deadline (fall): 1/15
Undergraduate student body:
2,996 full time, 1 part time; 45%
male, 55% female; 0% American
Indian, 4% Asian, 4% black,
11% Hispanic, 3% multiracial,
0% Pacific Islander, 72% white,
3% international; 40% from in
state; 90% live on campus; 0%
of students in fraternities, 0% in
sororities
Most popular majors: 13%
Economics, General, 13% Political
Science and Government, General,
13% Psychology, General, 8%
English Language and Literature,
General, 6% Biology/Biological
Sciences, General
Expenses: 2021-2022: $56,540;
room/board: $16,080
Financial aid: (508) 793-2265;
51% of undergrads determined to
have financial need; average aid
package $39,926

Curry College[7]
Milton MA
(800) 669-0686
U.S. News ranking: Reg. U. (N),
No. 126
Website: www.curry.edu
Admissions email: adm@curry.edu
Private; founded 1879
Freshman admissions: less
selective; 2020-2021: 6,183
applied, 5,057 accepted. Neither
SAT nor ACT required. SAT 25/75
percentile: 943-1108. High
school rank: N/A
Early decision deadline: N/A,
notification date: N/A
Early action deadline: 12/1,
notification date: 12/15
Application deadline (fall): rolling
Undergraduate student body: 1,895
full time, 311 part time
Most popular majors: Information
not available
Expenses: 2021-2022: $43,270;
room/board: $16,555
Financial aid: (617) 333-2354;
75% of undergrads determined to
have financial need; average aid
package $31,482

Dean College
Franklin MA
(508) 541-1508
U.S. News ranking: Reg. Coll. (N),
No. 28
Website: www.dean.edu
Admissions email:
admissions@dean.edu
Private; founded 1865
Freshman admissions: selective;
2020-2021: 5,919 applied,
4,174 accepted. Neither SAT
nor ACT required. SAT 25/75
percentile: 930-1128. High
school rank: N/A
Early decision deadline: N/A,
notification date: N/A
Early action deadline: 12/1,
notification date: 1/15
Application deadline (fall): 9/7
Undergraduate student body: 1,035
full time, 145 part time; 49%
male, 51% female; 0% American
Indian, 1% Asian, 12% black,
9% Hispanic, 4% multiracial,
0% Pacific Islander, 62% white,
4% international; 49% from in
state; 88% live on campus; 0%
of students in fraternities, 0% in

Application deadline (fall): rolling
Undergraduate student body: 3,056 full time, 464 part time; 42% male, 58% female; 0% American Indian, 3% Asian, 15% black, 17% Hispanic, 4% multiracial, 0% Pacific Islander, 59% white, 1% international; 7% from in state; 21% live on campus; 0% of students in fraternities, 0% in sororities
Most popular majors: 22% Business, Management, Marketing, and Related Support Services, 15% Social Sciences, 13% Psychology, 10% Family and Consumer Sciences/Human Sciences, 6% Biological and Biomedical Sciences
Expenses: 2020-2021: $11,380 in state, $17,460 out of state; room/board: $12,920
Financial aid: N/A

Franklin W. Olin College of Engineering
Needham MA
(781) 292-2222
U.S. News ranking: Engineering, unranked
Website: www.olin.edu/
Admissions email: info@olin.edu
Private; founded 1997
Freshman admissions: more selective; 2020-2021: 900 applied, 148 accepted. Neither SAT nor ACT required. SAT 25/75 percentile: 1450-1570. High school rank: N/A
Early decision deadline: N/A, notification date: N/A
Early action deadline: N/A, notification date: N/A
Application deadline (fall): 1/1
Undergraduate student body: 290 full time, 20 part time; 48% male, 52% female; 0% American Indian, 18% Asian, 4% black, 12% Hispanic, 10% multiracial, 0% Pacific Islander, 41% white, 8% international; 12% from in state; 39% live on campus; 0% of students in fraternities, 0% in sororities
Most popular majors: 40% Mechanical Engineering, 39% Engineering, General, 21% Electrical and Electronics Engineering
Expenses: 2021-2022: $56,342; room/board: $17,984
Financial aid: (781) 292-2215; 47% of undergrads determined to have financial need; average aid package $48,839

Gordon College
Wenham MA
(866) 464-6736
U.S. News ranking: Nat. Lib. Arts, No. 158
Website: www.gordon.edu
Admissions email: admissions@gordon.edu
Private; founded 1889
Affiliation: Other
Freshman admissions: selective; 2020-2021: 2,884 applied, 1,969 accepted. Neither SAT nor ACT required. SAT 25/75 percentile: 1020-1280. High school rank: 24% in top tenth, 51% in top quarter, 77% in

top half
Early decision deadline: N/A, notification date: N/A
Early action deadline: 11/1, notification date: 11/15
Application deadline (fall): 8/1
Undergraduate student body: 1,390 full time, 61 part time; 39% male, 61% female; 0% American Indian, 5% Asian, 5% black, 11% Hispanic, 2% multiracial, 0% Pacific Islander, 67% white, 8% international; 36% from in state; 87% live on campus; 0% of students in fraternities, 0% in sororities
Most popular majors: 9% Psychology, General, 8% Business Administration and Management, General, 8% Speech Communication and Rhetoric, 6% Biology/Biological Sciences, General, 5% Political Science and Government, General
Expenses: 2021-2022: $26,250; room/board: $11,700
Financial aid: (800) 343-1379; 69% of undergrads determined to have financial need; average aid package $29,505

Hampshire College
Amherst MA
(413) 559-5471
U.S. News ranking: Nat. Lib. Arts, No. 141
Website: www.hampshire.edu
Admissions email: admissions@hampshire.edu
Private; founded 1965
Freshman admissions: less selective; 2020-2021: 1,202 applied, 707 accepted. Neither SAT nor ACT required. SAT 25/75 percentile: N/A. High school rank: N/A
Early decision deadline: 11/15, notification date: 12/15
Early action deadline: 12/1, notification date: 2/15
Application deadline (fall): 1/15
Undergraduate student body: 522 full time, 0 part time; 38% male, 62% female; 0% American Indian, 3% Asian, 8% black, 12% Hispanic, 6% multiracial, 0% Pacific Islander, 61% white, 4% international; N/A from in state; 80% live on campus; N/A of students in fraternities, N/A in sororities
Most popular majors: 32% Visual and Performing Arts, 9% Social Sciences, 8% Area, Ethnic, Cultural, Gender, and Group Studies, 6% English Language and Literature/Letters, 6% Psychology
Expenses: 2021-2022: $53,098; room/board: $14,432
Financial aid: (413) 559-5484; 73% of undergrads determined to have financial need; average aid package $42,614

Harvard University
Cambridge MA
(617) 495-1551
U.S. News ranking: Nat. U., No. 2
Website: www.harvard.edu/
Admissions email: college@fas.harvard.edu
Private; founded 1636
Freshman admissions: most

selective; 2020-2021: 40,248 applied, 2,015 accepted. Either SAT or ACT required. SAT 25/75 percentile: 1460-1580. High school rank: 94% in top tenth, 98% in top quarter, 100% in top half
Early decision deadline: N/A, notification date: N/A
Early action deadline: 11/1, notification date: 12/16
Application deadline (fall): 1/1
Undergraduate student body: 5,198 full time, 24 part time; 49% male, 51% female; 0% American Indian, 23% Asian, 11% black, 12% Hispanic, 7% multiracial, 0% Pacific Islander, 33% white, 11% international
Most popular majors: 27% Social Sciences, General, 12% Biology/ Biological Sciences, General, 12% Mathematics, General, 11% Computer and Information Sciences, General, 9% History, General
Expenses: 2021-2022: $55,587; room/board: $18,941
Financial aid: (617) 495-1581; 62% of undergrads determined to have financial need; average aid package $56,469

Hult International Business School
Cambridge MA
(617) 746-1990
U.S. News ranking: Business, unranked
Website: www.hult.edu
Admissions email: undergraduate.info@hult.edu
Private; founded 1964
Freshman admissions: least selective; 2020-2021: 3,718 applied, 1,410 accepted. Neither SAT nor ACT required. SAT 25/75 percentile: N/A. High school rank: N/A
Early decision deadline: 11/1, notification date: 12/15
Early action deadline: N/A, notification date: N/A
Application deadline (fall): rolling
Undergraduate student body: 1,599 full time, 0 part time; 62% male, 38% female; N/A American Indian, N/A Asian, N/A black, N/A Hispanic, N/A multiracial, N/A Pacific Islander, N/A white, N/A international
Most popular majors: Information not available
Expenses: 2021-2022: $49,950; room/board: $18,200
Financial aid: N/A; 68% of undergrads determined to have financial need; average aid package $15,391

Lasell University
Newton MA
(617) 243-2225
U.S. News ranking: Reg. U. (N), No. 114
Website: www.lasell.edu
Admissions email: info@lasell.edu
Private; founded 1851
Freshman admissions: selective; 2020-2021: 2,496 applied, 2,108 accepted. Neither SAT nor ACT required. SAT 25/75 percentile: 980-1180. High school rank: 6% in top tenth, 32%

in top quarter, 75% in top half
Early decision deadline: N/A, notification date: N/A
Early action deadline: 11/15, notification date: 12/1
Application deadline (fall): rolling
Undergraduate student body: 1,450 full time, 42 part time; 38% male, 62% female; 0% American Indian, 4% Asian, 11% black, 11% Hispanic, 3% multiracial, 0% Pacific Islander, 63% white, 3% international; 60% from in state; 50% live on campus; 0% of students in fraternities, 0% in sororities
Most popular majors: 34% Business, Management, Marketing, and Related Support Services, 16% Communication, Journalism, and Related Programs, 10% Parks, Recreation, Leisure, and Fitness Studies, 9% Visual and Performing Arts, 6% Psychology
Expenses: 2021-2022: $42,000; room/board: $16,500
Financial aid: (617) 243-2227; 78% of undergrads determined to have financial need; average aid package $37,444

Lesley University[1]
Cambridge MA
(617) 349-8800
U.S. News ranking: Nat. U., No. 249
Website: www.lesley.edu
Admissions email: admissions@lesley.edu
Private; founded 1909
Application deadline (fall): 7/15
Undergraduate student body: N/A full time, N/A part time
Expenses: 2020-2021: $29,450; room/board: $16,630
Financial aid: (617) 349-8760

Massachusetts College of Art and Design
Boston MA
(617) 879-7222
U.S. News ranking: Arts, unranked
Website: www.massart.edu
Admissions email: admissions@massart.edu
Public; founded 1873
Freshman admissions: least selective; 2020-2021: 2,677 applied, 1,881 accepted. Neither SAT nor ACT required. SAT 25/75 percentile: N/A. High school rank: N/A
Early decision deadline: N/A, notification date: N/A
Early action deadline: 12/1, notification date: 1/5
Application deadline (fall): 5/1
Undergraduate student body: 1,505 full time, 265 part time; 27% male, 73% female; 0% American Indian, 8% Asian, 4% black, 12% Hispanic, 4% multiracial, 0% Pacific Islander, 56% white, 4% international; 77% from in state; 25% live on campus; 0% of students in fraternities, 0% in sororities
Most popular majors: 17% Illustration, 11% Design and Visual Communications, General, 11% Film/Video and Photographic Arts, Other, 10% Painting

Expenses: 2021-2022: $14,200 in state, $39,800 out of state; room/board: $14,800
Financial aid: (617) 879-7849; 64% of undergrads determined to have financial need; average aid package $12,192

Massachusetts College of Liberal Arts
North Adams MA
(413) 662-5410
U.S. News ranking: Nat. Lib. Arts, No. 128
Website: www.mcla.edu
Admissions email: admissions@mcla.edu
Public; founded 1894
Freshman admissions: selective; 2020-2021: 1,355 applied, 1,188 accepted. Neither SAT nor ACT required. SAT 25/75 percentile: 960-1180. High school rank: 22% in top tenth, 45% in top quarter, 78% in top half
Early decision deadline: N/A, notification date: N/A
Early action deadline: 12/1, notification date: 12/15
Application deadline (fall): rolling
Undergraduate student body: 931 full time, 145 part time; 37% male, 63% female; 0% American Indian, 1% Asian, 9% black, 11% Hispanic, 3% multiracial, 0% Pacific Islander, 72% white, 0% international; 69% from in state; 51% live on campus; N/A of students in fraternities, N/A in sororities
Most popular majors: 15% English Language and Literature/Letters, 15% Multi/Interdisciplinary Studies, 14% Business, Management, Marketing, and Related Support Services, 10% Psychology, 9% Social Sciences
Expenses: 2020-2021: $11,105 in state, $20,050 out of state; room/board: $11,430
Financial aid: (413) 662-5219; 77% of undergrads determined to have financial need; average aid package $16,105

Massachusetts Institute of Technology
Cambridge MA
(617) 253-3400
U.S. News ranking: Nat. U., No. 2
Website: web.mit.edu/
Admissions email: admissions@mit.edu
Private; founded 1861
Freshman admissions: most selective; 2020-2021: 20,075 applied, 1,457 accepted. Either SAT or ACT required. SAT 25/75 percentile: 1510-1580. High school rank: 100% in top tenth, 100% in top quarter, 100% in top half
Early decision deadline: N/A, notification date: N/A
Early action deadline: 11/1, notification date: 12/20
Application deadline (fall): 1/1
Undergraduate student body: 4,234 full time, 127 part time; 52% male, 48% female; 0% American Indian, 32% Asian, 7% black, 16% Hispanic, 8% multiracial,

0% Pacific Islander, 26% white, 10% international; N/A from in state; 20% live on campus; 39% of students in fraternities, 26% in sororities
Most popular majors: 32% Computer Science, 11% Mechanical Engineering, 9% Mathematics, General, 6% Physics, General, 4% Aerospace, Aeronautical and Astronautical/ Space Engineering
Expenses: 2021-2022: $55,878; room/board: $18,100
Financial aid: (617) 258-8600; 60% of undergrads determined to have financial need; average aid package $51,076

Massachusetts Maritime Academy
Buzzards Bay MA
(800) 544-3411
U.S. News ranking: Reg. Coll. (N), No. 5
Website: www.maritime.edu
Admissions email: admissions@maritime.edu
Public; founded 1891
Freshman admissions: selective; 2020-2021: 785 applied, 726 accepted. Either SAT or ACT required. SAT 25/75 percentile: 1030-1185. High school rank: N/A
Early decision deadline: N/A, notification date: N/A
Early action deadline: 11/15, notification date: 12/7
Application deadline (fall): 4/15
Undergraduate student body: 1,494 full time, 44 part time; 87% male, 13% female; 0% American Indian, 1% Asian, 1% black, 4% Hispanic, 3% multiracial, 0% Pacific Islander, 83% white, 0% international; 78% from in state; 44% live on campus; 0% of students in fraternities, 0% in sororities
Most popular majors: 44% Engineering
Expenses: 2021-2022: $10,516 in state, $25,104 out of state; room/board: $13,578
Financial aid: (508) 830-5400; 56% of undergrads determined to have financial need; average aid package $15,479

Merrimack College
North Andover MA
(978) 837-5100
U.S. News ranking: Reg. U. (N), No. 34
Website: www.merrimack.edu
Admissions email: Admission@Merrimack.edu
Private; founded 1947
Affiliation: Roman Catholic
Freshman admissions: selective; 2020-2021: 10,934 applied, 8,927 accepted. Neither SAT nor ACT required. SAT 25/75 percentile: 960-1276. High school rank: 8% in top tenth, 24% in top quarter, 64% in top half
Early decision deadline: 11/15, notification date: 12/15
Early action deadline: 1/15, notification date: 2/15
Application deadline (fall): 9/1
Undergraduate student body: 3,932 full time, 270 part time; 46%

male, 54% female; 0% American Indian, 2% Asian, 4% black, 8% Hispanic, 2% multiracial, 0% Pacific Islander, 78% white, 2% international; 69% from in state; 74% live on campus; N/A of students in fraternities, N/A in sororities
Most popular majors: 34% Business Administration and Management, General, 10% Human Development and Family Studies, General, 5% Criminal Justice/Law Enforcement Administration, 4% Human Development, Family Studies, and Related Services, Other, 4% Psychology, General
Expenses: 2021-2022: $46,916; room/board: $16,816
Financial aid: (978) 837-5112; 69% of undergrads determined to have financial need; average aid package $26,491

Montserrat College of Art[1]
Beverly MA
(978) 922-8222
U.S. News ranking: Arts, unranked
Website: www.montserrat.edu
Admissions email: admissions@montserrat.edu
Private; founded 1970
Application deadline (fall): N/A
Undergraduate student body: N/A full time, N/A part time
Expenses: 2020-2021: $35,300; room/board: $13,800
Financial aid: (978) 921-4242

Mount Holyoke College
South Hadley MA
(413) 538-2023
U.S. News ranking: Nat. Lib. Arts, No. 30
Website: www.mtholyoke.edu
Admissions email: admission@mtholyoke.edu
Private; founded 1837
Freshman admissions: more selective; 2020-2021: 3,480 applied, 1,826 accepted. Neither SAT nor ACT required. SAT 25/75 percentile: 1270-1500. High school rank: 49% in top tenth, 82% in top quarter, 97% in top half
Early decision deadline: 11/15, notification date: N/A
Early action deadline: N/A, notification date: N/A
Application deadline (fall): 1/15
Undergraduate student body: 1,892 full time, 23 part time; 0% male, 100% female; 0% American Indian, 7% Asian, 6% black, 9% Hispanic, 4% multiracial, 0% Pacific Islander, 44% white, 28% international; 18% from in state; 8% live on campus; N/A of students in fraternities, N/A in sororities
Most popular majors: 12% Experimental Psychology, 8% Biology/Biological Sciences, General, 8% Computer Science, 8% English Language and Literature, General, 7% Econometrics and Quantitative Economics
Expenses: 2021-2022: $56,518; room/board: $16,580

Financial aid: (413) 538-2291; 54% of undergrads determined to have financial need; average aid package $39,435

New England Conservatory of Music[1]
Boston MA
(617) 585-1101
U.S. News ranking: Arts, unranked
Website: www.newenglandconservatory.edu
Admissions email: admission@newenglandconservatory.edu
Private; founded 1867
Application deadline (fall): 12/1
Undergraduate student body: N/A full time, N/A part time
Expenses: 2021-2022: $53,730; room/board: $18,060
Financial aid: (617) 585-1110; 35% of undergrads determined to have financial need; average aid package $29,700

Nichols College
Dudley MA
(800) 470-3379
U.S. News ranking: Business, unranked
Website: www.nichols.edu/
Admissions email: admissions@nichols.edu
Private; founded 1815
Freshman admissions: selective; 2020-2021: 2,507 applied, 2,015 accepted. Neither SAT nor ACT required. SAT 25/75 percentile: 950-1150. High school rank: N/A
Early decision deadline: N/A, notification date: N/A
Early action deadline: 12/1, notification date: N/A
Application deadline (fall): rolling
Undergraduate student body: 1,152 full time, 127 part time; 65% male, 35% female; 0% American Indian, 1% Asian, 7% black, 10% Hispanic, 3% multiracial, 0% Pacific Islander, 75% white, 2% international
Most popular majors: 19% Sport and Fitness Administration/ Management, 14% Business/ Commerce, General, 11% Accounting, 11% Criminal Justice/ Safety Studies, 8% Marketing/ Marketing Management, General
Expenses: 2021-2022: $37,300; room/board: $13,950
Financial aid: (508) 213-2288; 77% of undergrads determined to have financial need; average aid package $28,632

Northeastern University
Boston MA
(617) 373-2200
U.S. News ranking: Nat. U., No. 49
Website: www.northeastern.edu/
Admissions email: admissions@northeastern.edu
Private; founded 1898
Freshman admissions: most selective; 2020-2021: 64,459 applied, 13,199 accepted. Neither SAT nor ACT required. SAT 25/75 percentile: 1410-1540. High

school rank: 76% in top tenth, 95% in top quarter, 100% in top half
Early decision deadline: 11/1, notification date: 12/15
Early action deadline: 11/1, notification date: 2/1
Application deadline (fall): 1/1
Undergraduate student body: 15,131 full time, 25 part time; 49% male, 51% female; 0% American Indian, 17% Asian, 4% black, 9% Hispanic, 5% multiracial, 0% Pacific Islander, 45% white, 16% international; 29% from in state; 33% live on campus; 10% of students in fraternities, 18% in sororities
Most popular majors: 26% Business, Management, Marketing, and Related Support Services, 19% Engineering, 10% Social Sciences, 9% Health Professions and Related Programs, 8% Computer and Information Sciences and Support Services
Expenses: 2021-2022: $57,592; room/board: $17,810
Financial aid: (617) 373-3190; 32% of undergrads determined to have financial need; average aid package $36,838

Salem State University
Salem MA
(978) 542-6200
U.S. News ranking: Reg. U. (N), No. 123
Website: www.salemstate.edu
Admissions email: admissions@salemstate.edu
Public; founded 1854
Freshman admissions: selective; 2020-2021: 6,557 applied, 5,688 accepted. Neither SAT nor ACT required. SAT 25/75 percentile: 1000-1150. High school rank: N/A
Early decision deadline: N/A, notification date: N/A
Early action deadline: 11/15, notification date: 1/1
Application deadline (fall): rolling
Undergraduate student body: 4,444 full time, 1,272 part time; 35% male, 65% female; 0% American Indian, 3% Asian, 9% black, 20% Hispanic, 3% multiracial, 0% Pacific Islander, 58% white, 3% international; N/A from in state; 17% live on campus; N/A of students in fraternities, N/A in sororities
Most popular majors: 22% Business, Management, Marketing, and Related Support Services, 16% Health Professions and Related Programs, 9% Psychology, 8% Homeland Security, Law Enforcement, Firefighting and Related Protective Services, 7% Education
Expenses: N/A
Financial aid: N/A

Simmons University
Boston MA
(617) 521-2051
U.S. News ranking: Nat. U., No. 136
Website: www.simmons.edu
Admissions email: ugadm@simmons.edu

Private; founded 1899
Freshman admissions: selective; 2020-2021: 2,905 applied, 2,398 accepted. Neither SAT nor ACT required. SAT 25/75 percentile: 1060-1250. High school rank: 29% in top tenth, 55% in top quarter, 72% in top half
Early decision deadline: N/A, notification date: N/A
Early action deadline: 11/1, notification date: 12/15
Application deadline (fall): 2/1
Undergraduate student body: 1,609 full time, 135 part time; 0% male, 100% female; 0% American Indian, 12% Asian, 8% black, 12% Hispanic, 4% multiracial, 0% Pacific Islander, 57% white, 5% international; 63% from in state; 5% live on campus; 0% of students in fraternities, 0% in sororities
Most popular majors: 42% Health Professions and Related Programs, 8% Parks, Recreation, Leisure, and Fitness Studies, 7% Biological and Biomedical Sciences, 7% Multi/Interdisciplinary Studies, 6% Communication, Journalism, and Related Programs
Expenses: 2021-2022: $43,112; room/board: $15,892
Financial aid: (617) 521-2001; 72% of undergrads determined to have financial need; average aid package $30,076

Smith College
Northampton MA
(413) 585-2500
U.S. News ranking: Nat. Lib. Arts, No. 17
Website: www.smith.edu
Admissions email: admission@smith.edu
Private; founded 1871
Freshman admissions: most selective; 2020-2021: 5,249 applied, 1,917 accepted. Neither SAT nor ACT required. SAT 25/75 percentile: 1325-1510. High school rank: 72% in top tenth, 96% in top quarter, 99% in top half
Early decision deadline: 11/15, notification date: 12/15
Early action deadline: N/A, notification date: N/A
Application deadline (fall): 1/15
Undergraduate student body: 2,160 full time, 23 part time; 0% male, 100% female; 0% American Indian, 10% Asian, 7% black, 14% Hispanic, 5% multiracial, 0% Pacific Islander, 47% white, 15% international; 80% from in state; 5% live on campus; 0% of students in fraternities, 0% in sororities
Most popular majors: 7% Research and Experimental Psychology, Other, 6% Biology/Biological Sciences, General, 6% Computer Science, 5% English Language and Literature, General, 5% Political Science and Government, General
Expenses: 2021-2022: $56,114; room/board: $19,420
Financial aid: (413) 585-2530; 61% of undergrads determined to have financial need; average aid package $45,834

Springfield College

Springfield MA
(413) 748-3136
U.S. News ranking: Reg. U. (N),
No. 27
Website: springfield.edu/
Admissions email:
admissions@springfieldcollege.edu
Private; founded 1885
Freshman admissions: selective;
2020-2021: 3,441 applied,
2,182 accepted. Neither SAT
nor ACT required. SAT 25/75
percentile: 1080-1270. High
school rank: 16% in top tenth,
42% in top quarter, 76% in
top half
Early decision deadline: 12/1,
notification date: 2/1
Early action deadline: N/A,
notification date: N/A
Application deadline (fall): 8/1
Undergraduate student body: 2,156
full time, 32 part time; 49%
male, 51% female; 0% American
Indian, 2% Asian, 6% black,
8% Hispanic, 2% multiracial,
0% Pacific Islander, 74% white,
3% international; 39% from in
state; 77% live on campus; N/A
of students in fraternities, N/A in
sororities
Most popular majors: 11%
Health Professions and Related
Programs, 8% Kinesiology and
Exercise Science, 8% Physician
Assistant, 7% Physical Therapy/
Therapist, 6% Sport and Fitness
Administration/Management
Expenses: 2021-2022: $39,720;
room/board: $13,320
Financial aid: (413) 748-3108;
80% of undergrads determined to
have financial need; average aid
package $28,642

Stonehill College

Easton MA
(508) 565-1373
U.S. News ranking: Nat. Lib. Arts,
No. 98
Website: www.stonehill.edu
Admissions email:
admission@stonehill.edu
Private; founded 1948
Affiliation: Roman Catholic
Freshman admissions: more
selective; 2020-2021: 7,096
applied, 4,891 accepted. Neither
SAT nor ACT required. SAT
25/75 percentile: 1120-1290.
High school rank: 20% in top
tenth, 48% in top quarter, 87%
in top half
Early decision deadline: 12/1,
notification date: 12/31
Early action deadline: 11/1,
notification date: 12/31
Application deadline (fall): 2/15
Undergraduate student body: 2,391
full time, 26 part time; 42%
male, 58% female; 0% American
Indian, 2% Asian, 4% black, 6%
Hispanic, 3% multiracial, 0%
Pacific Islander, 82% white, 1%
international
Most popular majors: Information
not available
Expenses: 2021-2022: $47,808;
room/board: $17,034
Financial aid: (508) 565-1088;
79% of undergrads determined to
have financial need; average aid
package $33,815

Suffolk University

Boston MA
(617) 573-8460
U.S. News ranking: Reg. U. (N),
No. 34
Website: www.suffolk.edu
Admissions email:
admission@suffolk.edu
Private; founded 1906
Freshman admissions: selective;
2020-2021: 7,831 applied,
6,714 accepted. Neither SAT
nor ACT required. SAT 25/75
percentile: 1010-1210. High
school rank: 14% in top tenth,
42% in top quarter, 79% in
top half
Early decision deadline: N/A,
notification date: N/A
Early action deadline: 11/15,
notification date: 12/15
Application deadline (fall): rolling
Undergraduate student body: 4,180
full time, 218 part time; 42%
male, 58% female; 0% American
Indian, 8% Asian, 6% black,
14% Hispanic, 3% multiracial,
0% Pacific Islander, 49% white,
17% international; 68% from in
state; 20% live on campus; 0%
of students in fraternities, 1% in
sororities
Most popular majors: 12%
Finance, General, 10% Marketing/
Marketing Management, General,
9% Business Administration
and Management, General,
6% Psychology, General, 5%
Entrepreneurship/Entrepreneurial
Studies
Expenses: 2021-2022: $41,648;
room/board: $17,766
Financial aid: (617) 573-8470;
63% of undergrads determined to
have financial need; average aid
package $29,877

Tufts University

Medford MA
(617) 627-3170
U.S. News ranking: Nat. U., No. 28
Website: www.tufts.edu
Admissions email:
undergraduate.admissions@tufts.edu
Private; founded 1852
Freshman admissions: most
selective; 2020-2021: 23,127
applied, 3,770 accepted. Neither
SAT nor ACT required. SAT 25/75
percentile: 1380-1530. High
school rank: 84% in top tenth,
97% in top quarter, 100% in
top half
Early decision deadline: 11/1,
notification date: 12/15
Early action deadline: N/A,
notification date: N/A
Application deadline (fall): 1/1
Undergraduate student body: 5,938
full time, 176 part time; 46%
male, 54% female; 0% American
Indian, 15% Asian, 5% black,
8% Hispanic, 6% multiracial, 0%
Pacific Islander, 51% white, 11%
international
Most popular majors: 26% Social
Sciences, 11% Biological and
Biomedical Sciences, 10%
Computer and Information
Sciences and Support Services,
9% Multi/Interdisciplinary Studies,
8% Engineering
Expenses: 2021-2022: $63,000;
room/board: $16,210

Financial aid: (617) 627-2000;
37% of undergrads determined to
have financial need; average aid
package $50,466

University of Massachusetts–Amherst

Amherst MA
(413) 545-0222
U.S. News ranking: Nat. U., No. 68
Website: www.umass.edu
Admissions email:
mail@admissions.umass.edu
Public; founded 1863
Freshman admissions: more
selective; 2020-2021: 40,315
applied, 26,335 accepted. Neither
SAT nor ACT required. SAT
25/75 percentile: 1200-1390.
High school rank: 34% in top
tenth, 75% in top quarter, 97%
in top half
Early decision deadline: N/A,
notification date: N/A
Early action deadline: 11/5,
notification date: 1/15
Application deadline (fall): 1/15
Undergraduate student body:
22,212 full time, 2,021 part
time; 49% male, 51% female;
0% American Indian, 11% Asian,
5% black, 8% Hispanic, 3%
multiracial, 0% Pacific Islander,
61% white, 7% international;
78% from in state; 63% live
on campus; 8% of students in
fraternities, 8% in sororities
Most popular majors: 15%
Business, Management,
Marketing, and Related Support
Services, 10% Biological and
Biomedical Sciences, 10% Social
Sciences, 8% Health Professions
and Related Programs, 7%
Engineering
Expenses: 2021-2022: $16,439
in state, $36,964 out of state;
room/board: $14,217
Financial aid: (413) 545-0801;
49% of undergrads determined to
have financial need; average aid
package $17,357

University of Massachusetts–Boston

Boston MA
(617) 287-6100
U.S. News ranking: Nat. U.,
No. 227
Website: www.umb.edu
Admissions email:
undergrad.admissions@umb.edu
Public; founded 1964
Freshman admissions: selective;
2020-2021: 14,029 applied,
11,178 accepted. Neither SAT
nor ACT required. SAT 25/75
percentile: 1010-1210. High
school rank: 15% in top tenth,
41% in top quarter, 77% in
top half
Early decision deadline: N/A,
notification date: N/A
Early action deadline: 11/1,
notification date: 12/31
Application deadline (fall): 3/1
Undergraduate student body:
10,279 full time, 2,592 part
time; 43% male, 57% female;
0% American Indian, 15% Asian,
18% black, 18% Hispanic, 4%

multiracial, 0% Pacific Islander,
34% white, 7% international;
94% from in state; 2% live on
campus; N/A of students in
fraternities, N/A in sororities
Most popular majors: 19%
Business, Management,
Marketing, and Related Support
Services, 11% Health Professions
and Related Programs, 11%
Social Sciences, 10% Psychology,
9% Computer and Information
Sciences and Support Services
Expenses: 2021-2022: $14,677
in state, $35,139 out of state;
room/board: N/A
Financial aid: (617) 297-6300;
69% of undergrads determined to
have financial need; average aid
package $18,003

University of Massachusetts–Dartmouth

North Dartmouth MA
(508) 999-8605
U.S. News ranking: Nat. U.,
No. 227
Website: https://www.umassd.edu
Admissions email:
admissions@umassd.edu
Public; founded 1895
Freshman admissions: selective;
2020-2021: 8,738 applied,
6,657 accepted. Neither SAT
nor ACT required. SAT 25/75
percentile: 990-1190. High school
rank: 12% in top tenth, 35% in
top quarter, 68% in top half
Early decision deadline: N/A,
notification date: N/A
Early action deadline: 11/18,
notification date: 12/15
Application deadline (fall): rolling
Undergraduate student body: 5,122
full time, 905 part time; 49%
male, 51% female; 0% American
Indian, 3% Asian, 16% black,
11% Hispanic, 5% multiracial,
0% Pacific Islander, 60% white,
1% international; 89% from in
state; 11% live on campus; N/A
of students in fraternities, N/A in
sororities
Most popular majors: 28%
Business, Management,
Marketing, and Related Support
Services, 15% Health Professions
and Related Programs, 10%
Engineering, 10% Psychology,
10% Social Sciences
Expenses: 2021-2022: $14,408
in state, $30,153 out of state;
room/board: $15,885
Financial aid: (508) 999-8643;
73% of undergrads determined to
have financial need; average aid
package $17,378

University of Massachusetts–Lowell

Lowell MA
(978) 934-3931
U.S. News ranking: Nat. U.,
No. 179
Website: www.uml.edu
Admissions email:
admissions@uml.edu
Public; founded 1894
Freshman admissions: more
selective; 2020-2021: 12,858
applied, 9,657 accepted. Neither

SAT nor ACT required. SAT
25/75 percentile: 1150-1320.
High school rank: 25% in top
tenth, 54% in top quarter, 88%
in top half
Early decision deadline: N/A,
notification date: N/A
Early action deadline: 11/1,
notification date: 12/10
Application deadline (fall): 2/1
Undergraduate student body:
10,637 full time, 3,178 part
time; 59% male, 41% female;
0% American Indian, 12% Asian,
7% black, 13% Hispanic, 3%
multiracial, 0% Pacific Islander,
57% white, 3% international
Most popular majors: 21%
Business, Management,
Marketing, and Related Support
Services, 21% Engineering,
11% Computer and Information
Sciences and Support Services,
10% Health Professions and
Related Programs, 7% Psychology
Expenses: 2021-2022: $15,698
in state, $33,624 out of state;
room/board: $13,570
Financial aid: (978) 934-2000;
56% of undergrads determined to
have financial need; average aid
package $14,952

Wellesley College

Wellesley MA
(781) 283-2270
U.S. News ranking: Nat. Lib. Arts,
No. 5
Website: www.wellesley.edu
Admissions email:
admission@wellesley.edu
Private; founded 1870
Freshman admissions: most
selective; 2020-2021: 6,581
applied, 1,343 accepted. Neither
SAT nor ACT required. SAT 25/75
percentile: 1350-1520. High
school rank: 85% in top tenth,
100% in top quarter, 100% in
top half
Early decision deadline: 11/1,
notification date: 12/15
Early action deadline: N/A,
notification date: N/A
Application deadline (fall): 1/8
Undergraduate student body: 2,238
full time, 42 part time; 0% male,
100% female; 0% American
Indian, 23% Asian, 7% black,
14% Hispanic, 6% multiracial,
0% Pacific Islander, 35% white,
14% international; N/A from in
state; 55% live on campus; N/A
of students in fraternities, N/A in
sororities
Most popular majors: 24% Social
Sciences, 11% Biological and
Biomedical Sciences, 11%
Computer and Information
Sciences and Support Services,
8% Area, Ethnic, Cultural,
Gender, and Group Studies, 8%
Psychology
Expenses: 2021-2022: $60,752;
room/board: $18,288
Financial aid: (781) 283-2360;
59% of undergrads determined to
have financial need; average aid
package $57,044

Wentworth Institute of Technology
Boston MA
(617) 989-4000
U.S. News ranking: Reg. U. (N),
No. 31
Website: www.wit.edu
Admissions email:
admissions@wit.edu
Private; founded 1904
Freshman admissions: selective;
2020-2021: 5,601 applied,
5,239 accepted. Neither SAT
nor ACT required. SAT 25/75
percentile: 1090-1280. High
school rank: N/A
Early decision deadline: N/A,
notification date: N/A
Early action deadline: N/A,
notification date: N/A
Application deadline (fall): rolling
Undergraduate student body: 3,847
full time, 383 part time; 78%
male, 22% female; 0% American
Indian, 9% Asian, 7% black,
10% Hispanic, 3% multiracial,
0% Pacific Islander, 60% white,
6% international; 66% from in
state; 26% live on campus; 0%
of students in fraternities, 0% in
sororities
Most popular majors: 14%
Construction Management, 12%
Mechanical Engineering, 10%
Computer Science, 9% Business,
Management, Marketing, and
Related Support Services, Other,
8% Architectural and Building
Sciences/Technology
Expenses: 2021-2022: $37,050;
room/board: $14,846
Financial aid: (617) 989-4020;
69% of undergrads determined to
have financial need; average aid
package $8,368

Western New England University
Springfield MA
(413) 782-1321
U.S. News ranking: Nat. U.,
No. 213
Website: www.wne.edu
Admissions email: learn@wne.edu
Private; founded 1919
Freshman admissions: selective;
2020-2021: 6,235 applied,
5,576 accepted. Neither SAT
nor ACT required. SAT 25/75
percentile: 1070-1270. High
school rank: 16% in top tenth,
47% in top quarter, 83% in
top half
Early decision deadline: N/A,
notification date: N/A
Early action deadline: N/A,
notification date: 11/1
Application deadline (fall): rolling
Undergraduate student body: 2,486
full time, 66 part time; 59%
male, 41% female; 0% American
Indian, 3% Asian, 5% black,
10% Hispanic, 3% multiracial,
0% Pacific Islander, 75% white,
2% international; 53% from in
state; 55% live on campus; 0%
of students in fraternities, 0% in
sororities
Most popular majors: 8%
Mechanical Engineering, 8%
Psychology, General, 7% Criminal
Justice/Safety Studies, 5%
Accounting, 4% Pharmaceutical
Sciences

Expenses: 2021-2022: $40,380;
room/board: $14,430
Financial aid: (413) 796-2080;
78% of undergrads determined to
have financial need; average aid
package $28,322

Westfield State University
Westfield MA
(413) 579-3040
U.S. News ranking: Reg. U. (N),
No. 85
Website: www.westfield.ma.edu
Admissions email:
admissions@westfield.ma.edu
Public; founded 1839
Freshman admissions: selective;
2020-2021: 4,055 applied,
3,749 accepted. Neither SAT
nor ACT required. SAT 25/75
percentile: 960-1140. High
school rank: 7% in top tenth, 22%
in top quarter, 56% in top half
Early decision deadline: N/A,
notification date: N/A
Early action deadline: N/A,
notification date: N/A
Application deadline (fall): 3/1
Undergraduate student body: 3,799
full time, 802 part time; 44%
male, 56% female; 0% American
Indian, 2% Asian, 6% black,
12% Hispanic, 3% multiracial,
0% Pacific Islander, 74% white,
0% international; 91% from in
state; 31% live on campus; 0%
of students in fraternities, 0% in
sororities
Most popular majors: 15%
Business/Commerce, General,
15% Criminal Justice/Safety
Studies, 11% Liberal Arts and
Sciences/Liberal Studies, 8%
Psychology, General, 5% Speech
Communication and Rhetoric
Expenses: 2021-2022: $11,139
in state, $17,219 out of state;
room/board: $12,197
Financial aid: (413) 572-5218;
65% of undergrads determined to
have financial need; average aid
package $9,436

Wheaton College
Norton MA
(508) 286-8251
U.S. News ranking: Nat. Lib. Arts,
No. 85
Website: www.wheatoncollege.edu
Admissions email:
admission@wheatoncollege.edu
Private; founded 1834
Freshman admissions: more
selective; 2020-2021: 3,580
applied, 2,760 accepted. Neither
SAT nor ACT required. SAT
25/75 percentile: 1160-1350.
High school rank: 31% in top
tenth, 63% in top quarter, 86%
in top half
Early decision deadline: 11/20,
notification date: 12/15
Early action deadline: 12/1,
notification date: 1/15
Application deadline (fall): 2/15
Undergraduate student body: 1,658
full time, 11 part time; 40%
male, 60% female; 0% American
Indian, 5% Asian, 6% black,
9% Hispanic, 4% multiracial,
0% Pacific Islander, 68% white,
5% international; N/A from in
state; 67% live on campus; N/A

of students in fraternities, N/A in
sororities
Most popular majors: 13%
Business Administration and
Management, General, 9%
Psychology, General, 8% Biology/
Biological Sciences, General, 6%
Film/Cinema/Video Studies, 5%
Neuroscience
Expenses: 2021-2022: $58,180;
room/board: $14,670
Financial aid: (508) 286-8232;
71% of undergrads determined to
have financial need; average aid
package $47,307

Williams College
Williamstown MA
(413) 597-2211
U.S. News ranking: Nat. Lib. Arts,
No. 1
Website: www.williams.edu
Admissions email:
admission@williams.edu
Private; founded 1793
Freshman admissions: most
selective; 2020-2021: 8,745
applied, 1,322 accepted. Neither
SAT nor ACT required. SAT
25/75 percentile: 1410-1560.
High school rank: 95% in top
tenth, 99% in top quarter, 99%
in top half
Early decision deadline: 11/16,
notification date: 12/11
Early action deadline: N/A,
notification date: N/A
Application deadline (fall): 1/8
Undergraduate student body: 1,917
full time, 45 part time; 50%
male, 50% female; 0% American
Indian, 14% Asian, 7% black,
13% Hispanic, 6% multiracial,
0% Pacific Islander, 46% white,
9% international; 16% from in
state; 69% live on campus; N/A
of students in fraternities, N/A in
sororities
Most popular majors: 14%
Econometrics and Quantitative
Economics, 8% Biology/Biological
Sciences, General, 8% Computer
Science, 8% Political Science
and Government, General, 7%
Psychology, General
Expenses: 2021-2022: $59,660;
room/board: $15,000
Financial aid: (413) 597-4181;
54% of undergrads determined to
have financial need; average aid
package $52,289

Worcester Polytechnic Institute
Worcester MA
(508) 831-5286
U.S. News ranking: Nat. U., No. 63
Website: www.wpi.edu/
Admissions email:
admissions@wpi.edu
Private; founded 1865
Freshman admissions: more
selective; 2020-2021: 11,269
applied, 6,654 accepted. Neither
SAT nor ACT required. SAT 25/75
percentile: 1310-1470. High
school rank: 56% in top tenth,
87% in top quarter, 100% in
top half
Early decision deadline: 11/1,
notification date: 12/15
Early action deadline: 11/1,
notification date: 1/15

Application deadline (fall): 2/15
Undergraduate student body: 4,709
full time, 183 part time; 60%
male, 40% female; 0% American
Indian, 8% Asian, 3% black, 9%
Hispanic, 3% multiracial, 0%
Pacific Islander, 64% white, 7%
international; 42% from in state;
47% live on campus; 28% of
students in fraternities, 36% in
sororities
Most popular majors: 23%
Mechanical Engineering,
16% Computer Science, 9%
Bioengineering and Biomedical
Engineering, 8% Electrical and
Electronics Engineering, 8%
Mechatronics, Robotics, and
Automation Engineering
Expenses: 2021-2022: $55,531;
room/board: $16,140
Financial aid: (508) 831-5469;
56% of undergrads determined to
have financial need; average aid
package $31,203

Worcester State University
Worcester MA
(508) 929-8040
U.S. News ranking: Reg. U. (N),
No. 103
Website: www.worcester.edu
Admissions email:
admissions@worcester.edu
Public; founded 1874
Freshman admissions: selective;
2020-2021: 4,047 applied,
3,279 accepted. Neither SAT
nor ACT required. SAT 25/75
percentile: 1000-1190. High
school rank: N/A
Early decision deadline: N/A,
notification date: N/A
Early action deadline: 11/15,
notification date: 12/15
Application deadline (fall): 5/1
Undergraduate student body: 3,871
full time, 1,087 part time; 39%
male, 61% female; 0% American
Indian, 5% Asian, 8% black,
14% Hispanic, 3% multiracial,
0% Pacific Islander, 65% white,
1% international; N/A from in
state; 24% live on campus; N/A
of students in fraternities, N/A in
sororities
Most popular majors: 21% Health
Professions and Related Programs,
17% Business, Management,
Marketing, and Related Support
Services, 10% Homeland Security,
Law Enforcement, Firefighting and
Related Protective Services, 10%
Psychology, 9% Biological and
Biomedical Sciences
Expenses: 2021-2022: $10,586
in state, $16,666 out of state;
room/board: $12,568
Financial aid: (508) 929-8056;
63% of undergrads determined to
have financial need; average aid
package $20,492

MICHIGAN

Adrian College
Adrian MI
(800) 877-2246
U.S. News ranking: Reg. Coll. (Mid.
W), No. 18
Website: www.adrian.edu

Admissions email:
admissions@adrian.edu
Private; founded 1859
Affiliation: United Methodist
Freshman admissions: less
selective; 2020-2021: 4,439
applied, 2,717 accepted. Either
SAT or ACT required. SAT 25/75
percentile: 930-1120. High school
rank: 12% in top tenth, 28% in
top quarter, 60% in top half
Early decision deadline: N/A,
notification date: N/A
Early action deadline: N/A,
notification date: N/A
Application deadline (fall): rolling
Undergraduate student body: 1,738
full time, 50 part time; 50%
male, 50% female; 0% American
Indian, 0% Asian, 8% black,
6% Hispanic, 4% multiracial,
0% Pacific Islander, 67% white,
0% international; 70% from in
state; 90% live on campus; 5%
of students in fraternities, 5% in
sororities
Most popular majors: 29%
Business, Management,
Marketing, and Related Support
Services, 11% Health Professions
and Related Programs, 10%
Education, 10% Homeland
Security, Law Enforcement,
Firefighting and Related Protective
Services, 10% Parks, Recreation,
Leisure, and Fitness Studies
Expenses: 2021-2022: $39,107;
room/board: $12,490
Financial aid: (888) 876-0194;
82% of undergrads determined to
have financial need; average aid
package $32,868

Albion College
Albion MI
(800) 858-6770
U.S. News ranking: Nat. Lib. Arts,
No. 128
Website: www.albion.edu/
Admissions email:
admission@albion.edu
Private; founded 1835
Freshman admissions: selective;
2020-2021: 4,685 applied,
3,491 accepted. Neither SAT
nor ACT required. SAT 25/75
percentile: 930-1160. High school
rank: 17% in top tenth, 39% in
top quarter, 78% in top half
Early decision deadline: N/A,
notification date: N/A
Early action deadline: 12/1,
notification date: N/A
Application deadline (fall): rolling
Undergraduate student body: 1,492
full time, 14 part time; 48%
male, 52% female; 0% American
Indian, 2% Asian, 18% black,
14% Hispanic, 4% multiracial,
0% Pacific Islander, 55% white,
1% international; 72% from in
state; 92% live on campus; 35%
of students in fraternities, 31%
in sororities
Most popular majors: 12% Biology
Biological Sciences, General,
12% Research and Experimental
Psychology, Other, 9%
Communication, Journalism, and
Related Programs, 9% Economics
General, 6% Kinesiology and
Exercise Science
Expenses: 2021-2022: $53,090;
room/board: $12,380

Financial aid: (517) 629-0440; 83% of undergrads determined to have financial need; average aid package $48,445

Alma College[1]

Alma MI
(800) 321-2562
U.S. News ranking: Reg. Coll. (Mid. W), No. 11
Website: www.alma.edu
Admissions email: admissions@alma.edu
Private; founded 1886
Affiliation: Presbyterian Church (USA)
Application deadline (fall): rolling
Undergraduate student body: N/A full time, N/A part time
Expenses: 2021-2022: $43,872; room/board: $12,138
Financial aid: (989) 463-7347; 83% of undergrads determined to have financial need; average aid package $32,733

Alpena Community College[1]

Alpena MI
(989) 356-9021
U.S. News ranking: Reg. Coll. (Mid. W), unranked
Website: www. lakemichigancollege.edu
Admissions email: N/A
Public
Application deadline (fall): N/A
Undergraduate student body: N/A full time, N/A part time
Expenses: 2020-2021: $7,110 in state, $7,110 out of state; room/board: $7,150
Financial aid: N/A

Andrews University[1]

Berrien Springs MI
(800) 253-2874
U.S. News ranking: Nat. U., second tier
Website: www.andrews.edu
Admissions email: enroll@andrews.edu
Private; founded 1874
Affiliation: Seventh Day Adventist
Application deadline (fall): rolling
Undergraduate student body: N/A full time, N/A part time
Expenses: 2020-2021: $31,008; room/board: $9,540
Financial aid: (269) 471-3334

Aquinas College

Grand Rapids MI
(616) 632-2900
U.S. News ranking: Nat. Lib. Arts, No. 158
Website: www.aquinas.edu
Admissions email: admissions@aquinas.edu
Private; founded 1886
Affiliation: Roman Catholic
Freshman admissions: selective; 2020-2021: 1,853 applied, 1,314 accepted. Neither SAT nor ACT required. SAT 25/75 percentile: 1010-1220. High school rank: N/A
Early decision deadline: N/A, notification date: N/A
Early action deadline: N/A, notification date: N/A

Application deadline (fall): rolling
Undergraduate student body: 1,129 full time, 243 part time; 42% male, 58% female; 0% American Indian, 1% Asian, 4% black, 8% Hispanic, 3% multiracial, 0% Pacific Islander, 67% white, 4% international; N/A from in state; 46% live on campus; N/A of students in fraternities, N/A in sororities
Most popular majors: 22% Business, Management, Marketing, and Related Support Services, 12% Education, 7% Liberal Arts and Sciences, General Studies and Humanities, 6% Foreign Languages, Literatures, and Linguistics, 6% Parks, Recreation, Leisure, and Fitness Studies
Expenses: 2021-2022: $36,084; room/board: $10,264
Financial aid: (616) 632-2893; 73% of undergrads determined to have financial need; average aid package $27,213

Baker College of Flint[1]

Flint MI
(810) 767-7600
U.S. News ranking: Reg. U. (Mid. W), second tier
Website: www.baker.edu
Admissions email: troy.crowe@baker.edu
Private
Application deadline (fall): N/A
Undergraduate student body: N/A full time, N/A part time
Expenses: 2020-2021: $10,160; room/board: $6,300
Financial aid: N/A

Calvin University

Grand Rapids MI
(800) 688-0122
U.S. News ranking: Reg. U. (Mid. W), No. 4
Website: calvin.edu
Admissions email: admissions@calvin.edu
Private; founded 1876
Affiliation: Christian Reformed Church
Freshman admissions: more selective; 2020-2021: 3,198 applied, 2,428 accepted. Neither SAT nor ACT required. SAT 25/75 percentile: 1100-1320. High school rank: 34% in top tenth, 62% in top quarter, 91% in top half
Early decision deadline: N/A, notification date: N/A
Early action deadline: N/A, notification date: N/A
Application deadline (fall): 8/15
Undergraduate student body: 2,914 full time, 267 part time; 47% male, 53% female; 0% American Indian, 5% Asian, 4% black, 5% Hispanic, 3% multiracial, 0% Pacific Islander, 70% white, 13% international; 55% from in state; 52% live on campus; 0% of students in fraternities, 0% in sororities
Most popular majors: 9% Engineering, General, 7% Registered Nursing/Registered Nurse, 6% Accounting, 5% Psychology, General, 4%

Biochemistry
Expenses: 2020-2021: $37,806; room/board: $10,800
Financial aid: (616) 526-6134

Central Michigan University

Mount Pleasant MI
(989) 774-3076
U.S. News ranking: Nat. U., No. 239
Website: www.cmich.edu
Admissions email: cmuadmit@cmich.edu
Public; founded 1892
Freshman admissions: selective; 2020-2021: 19,396 applied, 13,320 accepted. Either SAT or ACT required. SAT 25/75 percentile: 1000-1210. High school rank: N/A
Early decision deadline: N/A, notification date: N/A
Early action deadline: N/A, notification date: N/A
Application deadline (fall): rolling
Undergraduate student body: 11,272 full time, 1,776 part time; 40% male, 60% female; 1% American Indian, 1% Asian, 11% black, 5% Hispanic, 4% multiracial, 0% Pacific Islander, 75% white, 1% international; 90% from in state; 33% live on campus; 8% of students in fraternities, 9% in sororities
Most popular majors: Information not available
Expenses: 2021-2022: $13,538 in state, $13,538 out of state; room/board: $10,792
Financial aid: (989) 774-3674; 69% of undergrads determined to have financial need; average aid package $15,197

Cleary University[1]

Howell MI
(800) 686-1883
U.S. News ranking: Business, unranked
Website: www.cleary.edu
Admissions email: admissions@cleary.edu
Private; founded 1883
Application deadline (fall): 8/24
Undergraduate student body: N/A full time, N/A part time
Expenses: 2020-2021: $22,230; room/board: $12,600
Financial aid: (517) 338-3015

College for Creative Studies[1]

Detroit MI
(313) 664-7425
U.S. News ranking: Arts, unranked
Website: www.collegeforcreativestudies.edu
Admissions email: admissions@ collegeforcreativestudies.edu
Private; founded 1906
Application deadline (fall): N/A
Undergraduate student body: N/A full time, N/A part time
Expenses: 2020-2021: $47,585; room/board: $7,750
Financial aid: (313) 664-7495

Concordia University– Ann Arbor[1]

Ann Arbor MI
(734) 995-7300
U.S. News ranking: Reg. Coll. (Mid. W), second tier
Admissions email: N/A
Private
Application deadline (fall): N/A
Undergraduate student body: N/A full time, N/A part time
Expenses: 2020-2021: $31,060; room/board: $11,130
Financial aid: N/A

Cornerstone University

Grand Rapids MI
(616) 222-1426
U.S. News ranking: Reg. U. (Mid. W), No. 74
Website: www.cornerstone.edu
Admissions email: admissions@cornerstone.edu
Private; founded 1941
Affiliation: Interdenominational
Freshman admissions: selective; 2020-2021: 1,964 applied, 1,708 accepted. Neither SAT nor ACT required. SAT 25/75 percentile: 930-1170. High school rank: 5% in top tenth, 10% in top quarter, 41% in top half
Early decision deadline: N/A, notification date: N/A
Early action deadline: N/A, notification date: N/A
Application deadline (fall): rolling
Undergraduate student body: 1,024 full time, 437 part time; 39% male, 61% female; 1% American Indian, 2% Asian, 9% black, 7% Hispanic, 3% multiracial, 0% Pacific Islander, 75% white, 5% international; N/A from in state; 52% live on campus; N/A of students in fraternities, N/A in sororities
Most popular majors: 43% Business, Management, Marketing, and Related Support Services, 17% Psychology, 7% Education, 7% Theology and Religious Vocations, 5% Communication, Journalism, and Related Programs
Expenses: 2021-2022: $27,040; room/board: $10,310
Financial aid: (616) 222-1424; 74% of undergrads determined to have financial need; average aid package $19,509

Davenport University

Grand Rapids MI
(866) 925-3884
U.S. News ranking: Reg. U. (Mid. W), No. 95
Website: www.davenport.edu
Admissions email: Davenport.Admissions@davenport. edu
Private; founded 1866
Freshman admissions: selective; 2020-2021: 3,036 applied, 2,810 accepted. Neither SAT nor ACT required. SAT 25/75 percentile: 940-1170. High school rank: N/A
Early decision deadline: N/A, notification date: N/A
Early action deadline: N/A,

notification date: N/A
Application deadline (fall): rolling
Undergraduate student body: 2,408 full time, 2,591 part time; 44% male, 56% female; 1% American Indian, 2% Asian, 13% black, 7% Hispanic, 3% multiracial, 0% Pacific Islander, 66% white, 3% international; 93% from in state; 28% live on campus; 0% of students in fraternities, 0% in sororities
Most popular majors: 24% Business Administration and Management, General, 12% Registered Nursing/Registered Nurse, 9% Business/Commerce, General, 8% Accounting, 6% Health/Health Care Administration/ Management
Expenses: 2020-2021: $20,260; room/board: $10,268
Financial aid: (616) 732-1132

Eastern Michigan University

Ypsilanti MI
(734) 487-3060
U.S. News ranking: Nat. U., second tier
Website: www.emich.edu
Admissions email: admissions@emich.edu
Public; founded 1849
Freshman admissions: selective; 2020-2021: 15,957 applied, 11,997 accepted. Either SAT or ACT required. SAT 25/75 percentile: 980-1200. High school rank: 16% in top tenth, 39% in top quarter, 73% in top half
Early decision deadline: N/A, notification date: N/A
Early action deadline: N/A, notification date: N/A
Application deadline (fall): rolling
Undergraduate student body: 9,630 full time, 3,942 part time; 39% male, 61% female; 0% American Indian, 3% Asian, 17% black, 7% Hispanic, 4% multiracial, 0% Pacific Islander, 61% white, 2% international
Most popular majors: 19% Business, Management, Marketing, and Related Support Services, 19% Health Professions and Related Programs, 8% Education, 7% Social Sciences, 6% Psychology
Expenses: 2021-2022: N/A in state, N/A out of state; room/board: N/A
Financial aid: (734) 487-1048

Ferris State University

Big Rapids MI
(231) 591-2100
U.S. News ranking: Nat. U., second tier
Website: www.ferris.edu
Admissions email: Admissions@Ferris.edu
Public; founded 1884
Freshman admissions: selective; 2020-2021: 8,581 applied, 7,076 accepted. Neither SAT nor ACT required. SAT 25/75 percentile: 940-1160. High school rank: N/A
Early decision deadline: N/A, notification date: N/A
Early action deadline: N/A, notification date: N/A

Application deadline (fall): rolling
Undergraduate student body: 7,127 full time, 2,802 part time; 47% male, 53% female; 0% American Indian, 1% Asian, 9% black, 6% Hispanic, 4% multiracial, 0% Pacific Islander, 77% white, 1% international; 92% from in state; 25% live on campus; 2% of students in fraternities, 2% in sororities
Most popular majors: 23% Business, Management, Marketing, and Related Support Services, 14% Health Professions and Related Programs, 13% Engineering Technologies and Engineering-Related Fields, 13% Homeland Security, Law Enforcement, Firefighting and Related Protective Services, 7% Visual and Performing Arts
Expenses: 2021-2022: $13,290 in state, $13,290 out of state; room/board: $10,340
Financial aid: (231) 591-2113; 68% of undergrads determined to have financial need; average aid package $12,420

Finlandia University[1]
Hancock MI
(906) 487-7274
U.S. News ranking: Reg. Coll. (Mid. W), second tier
Website: www.finlandia.edu
Admissions email: admissions@finlandia.edu
Private; founded 1896
Affiliation: Evangelical Lutheran Church
Application deadline (fall): N/A
Undergraduate student body: N/A full time, N/A part time
Expenses: 2020-2021: $23,990; room/board: $9,156
Financial aid: N/A

Grand Valley State University[1]
Allendale MI
(800) 748-0246
U.S. News ranking: Reg. U. (Mid. W), No. 27
Website: www.gvsu.edu
Admissions email: admissions@gvsu.edu
Public; founded 1960
Application deadline (fall): 5/1
Undergraduate student body: N/A full time, N/A part time
Expenses: 2020-2021: $13,244 in state, $18,844 out of state; room/board: $9,000
Financial aid: (616) 331-3234

Henry Ford College[1]
Dearborn MI
(313) 845-9600
U.S. News ranking: Reg. Coll. (Mid. W), unranked
Website: www.schoolcraft.edu
Admissions email: N/A
Public
Application deadline (fall): N/A
Undergraduate student body: N/A full time, N/A part time
Expenses: 2020-2021: $5,020 in state, $6,940 out of state; room/board: N/A
Financial aid: N/A

Hillsdale College
Hillsdale MI
(517) 607-2327
U.S. News ranking: Nat. Lib. Arts, No. 46
Website: www.hillsdale.edu/
Admissions email: admissions@hillsdale.edu
Private; founded 1844
Affiliation: Undenominational
Freshman admissions: more selective; 2020-2021: 1,993 applied, 727 accepted. Neither SAT nor ACT required. ACT 25/75 percentile: 29-33. High school rank: N/A
Early decision deadline: 11/1, notification date: 12/1
Early action deadline: N/A, notification date: N/A
Application deadline (fall): 4/1
Undergraduate student body: 1,423 full time, 43 part time; 52% male, 48% female; 0% American Indian, 0% Asian, 0% black, 0% Hispanic, 0% multiracial, 0% Pacific Islander, 0% white, 0% international; 30% from in state; 70% live on campus; 22% of students in fraternities, 33% in sororities
Most popular majors: 12% Economics, General, 12% English Language and Literature, General, 10% History, General, 7% Political Science and Government, General, 6% Biology/Biological Sciences, General
Expenses: 2021-2022: $30,042; room/board: $12,140
Financial aid: (517) 607-2250; 51% of undergrads determined to have financial need; average aid package $22,441

Hope College
Holland MI
(616) 395-7850
U.S. News ranking: Nat. Lib. Arts, No. 111
Website: www.hope.edu
Admissions email: admissions@hope.edu
Private; founded 1866
Affiliation: Reformed Church in America
Freshman admissions: more selective; 2020-2021: 3,907 applied, 3,041 accepted. Neither SAT nor ACT required. SAT 25/75 percentile: 1090-1310. High school rank: 35% in top tenth, 64% in top quarter, 90% in top half
Early decision deadline: N/A, notification date: N/A
Early action deadline: 11/2, notification date: 11/26
Application deadline (fall): rolling
Undergraduate student body: 2,908 full time, 153 part time; 37% male, 63% female; 0% American Indian, 2% Asian, 3% black, 7% Hispanic, 3% multiracial, 0% Pacific Islander, 82% white, 2% international; 67% from in state; 78% live on campus; 17% of students in fraternities, 21% in sororities
Most popular majors: 16% Business, Management, Marketing, and Related Support Services, 11% Psychology, 10% Education, 8% Social Sciences, 7% Engineering

Expenses: 2021-2022: $36,650; room/board: $11,000
Financial aid: (616) 395-7765; 56% of undergrads determined to have financial need; average aid package $30,229

Jackson College[1]
Jackson MI
(517) 796-8622
U.S. News ranking: Reg. Coll. (Mid. W), unranked
Admissions email: N/A
Public
Application deadline (fall): N/A
Undergraduate student body: N/A full time, N/A part time
Expenses: 2020-2021: $9,318 in state, $11,933 out of state; room/board: $10,000
Financial aid: N/A

Kalamazoo College
Kalamazoo MI
(800) 253-3602
U.S. News ranking: Nat. Lib. Arts, No. 71
Website: www.kzoo.edu
Admissions email: admission@kzoo.edu
Private; founded 1833
Freshman admissions: more selective; 2020-2021: 3,456 applied, 2,569 accepted. Neither SAT nor ACT required. SAT 25/75 percentile: 1150-1360. High school rank: 42% in top tenth, 78% in top quarter, 97% in top half
Early decision deadline: 11/1, notification date: 12/1
Early action deadline: 11/1, notification date: 12/20
Application deadline (fall): 1/15
Undergraduate student body: 1,426 full time, 25 part time; 41% male, 59% female; 0% American Indian, 6% Asian, 6% black, 16% Hispanic, 6% multiracial, 0% Pacific Islander, 58% white, 5% international; 65% from in state; 0% live on campus; 0% of students in fraternities, 0% in sororities
Most popular majors: 16% Social Sciences, 12% Physical Sciences, 11% Biological and Biomedical Sciences, 11% Business, Management, Marketing, and Related Support Services, 11% Psychology
Expenses: 2021-2022: $54,372; room/board: $10,932
Financial aid: (269) 337-7192; 71% of undergrads determined to have financial need; average aid package $47,033

Kettering University
Flint MI
(800) 955-4464
U.S. News ranking: Reg. U. (Mid. W), No. 12
Website: www.kettering.edu
Admissions email: admissions@kettering.edu
Private; founded 1919
Freshman admissions: more selective; 2020-2021: 1,974 applied, 1,464 accepted. Neither SAT nor ACT required. SAT 25/75 percentile: 1180-1360.

High school rank: 42% in top tenth, 71% in top quarter, 96% in top half
Early decision deadline: N/A, notification date: N/A
Early action deadline: 11/15, notification date: 12/15
Application deadline (fall): rolling
Undergraduate student body: 1,597 full time, 62 part time; 78% male, 22% female; 0% American Indian, 6% Asian, 2% black, 5% Hispanic, 4% multiracial, 0% Pacific Islander, 78% white, 3% international; N/A from in state; 2% live on campus; 8% of students in fraternities, 6% in sororities
Most popular majors: 58% Mechanical Engineering, 13% Electrical and Electronics Engineering, 6% Chemical Engineering, 6% Computer Engineering, General, 5% Computer Science
Expenses: 2021-2022: $44,380; room/board: $8,400
Financial aid: (810) 762-7859; 69% of undergrads determined to have financial need; average aid package $25,056

Kuyper College[1]
Grand Rapids MI
(800) 511-3749
U.S. News ranking: Reg. Coll. (Mid. W), No. 55
Website: www.kuyper.edu
Admissions email: admissions@kuyper.edu
Private
Application deadline (fall): N/A
Undergraduate student body: N/A full time, N/A part time
Expenses: 2020-2021: $23,970; room/board: $7,930
Financial aid: (616) 988-3656

Lake Michigan College[1]
Benton Harbor MI
(269) 927-8100
U.S. News ranking: Reg. Coll. (Mid. W), unranked
Website: www.theamericancollege.edu
Admissions email: N/A
Public
Application deadline (fall): N/A
Undergraduate student body: N/A full time, N/A part time
Expenses: 2020-2021: $6,743 in state, $6,743 out of state; room/board: $9,980
Financial aid: N/A

Lake Superior State University
Sault Ste. Marie MI
(906) 635-2231
U.S. News ranking: Reg. Coll. (Mid. W), No. 45
Website: www.lssu.edu
Admissions email: admissions@lssu.edu
Public; founded 1946
Freshman admissions: selective; 2020-2021: 1,709 applied, 1,176 accepted. Neither SAT nor ACT required. SAT 25/75 percentile: 950-1180. High school rank: 11% in top tenth, 31% in

top quarter, 65% in top half
Early decision deadline: N/A, notification date: N/A
Early action deadline: N/A, notification date: N/A
Application deadline (fall): rolling
Undergraduate student body: 1,474 full time, 435 part time; 45% male, 55% female; 7% American Indian, 1% Asian, 1% black, 1% Hispanic, 0% multiracial, 0% Pacific Islander, 65% white, 3% international; 96% from in state; 45% live on campus; N/A of students in fraternities, N/A in sororities
Most popular majors: 18% Homeland Security, Law Enforcement, Firefighting and Related Protective Services, 15% Business, Management, Marketing, and Related Support Services, 12% Health Professions and Related Programs, 7% Engineering, 7% Natural Resources and Conservation
Expenses: 2021-2022: $13,312 in state, $13,312 out of state; room/board: $10,488
Financial aid: (906) 635-2678; 67% of undergrads determined to have financial need; average aid package $11,669

Lawrence Technological University
Southfield MI
(248) 204-3160
U.S. News ranking: Reg. U. (Mid. W), No. 37
Website: www.ltu.edu
Admissions email: admissions@ltu.edu
Private; founded 1932
Freshman admissions: selective; 2020-2021: 2,588 applied, 2,134 accepted. Neither SAT nor ACT required. SAT 25/75 percentile: 1020-1280. High school rank: 0% in top tenth, 22% in top quarter, 67% in top half
Early decision deadline: N/A, notification date: N/A
Early action deadline: N/A, notification date: N/A
Application deadline (fall): rolling
Undergraduate student body: 1,630 full time, 508 part time; 69% male, 31% female; 0% American Indian, 3% Asian, 10% black, 3% Hispanic, 3% multiracial, 0% Pacific Islander, 68% white, 9% international; 90% from in state; 38% live on campus; 7% of students in fraternities, 11% in sororities
Most popular majors: 46% Engineering, 16% Architecture and Related Services, 9% Computer and Information Sciences and Support Services, 8% Business, Management, Marketing, and Related Support Services, 7% Engineering Technologies and Engineering-Related Fields
Expenses: 2021-2022: $37,680; room/board: $11,055
Financial aid: (248) 204-2280; 66% of undergrads determined to have financial need; average aid package $27,517

Madonna University
Livonia MI
(734) 432-5339
U.S. News ranking: Reg. U. (Mid. W), No. 74
Website: www.madonna.edu
Admissions email: admissions@madonna.edu
Private; founded 1937
Affiliation: Roman Catholic
Freshman admissions: selective; 2020-2021: 1,132 applied, 774 accepted. Neither SAT nor ACT required. SAT 25/75 percentile: 920-1110. High school rank: 10% in top tenth, 28% in top quarter, 66% in top half
Early decision deadline: N/A, notification date: N/A
Early action deadline: N/A, notification date: N/A
Application deadline (fall): rolling
Undergraduate student body: 1,571 full time, 720 part time; 35% male, 65% female; 0% American Indian, 3% Asian, 11% black, 4% Hispanic, 4% multiracial, 0% Pacific Islander, 63% white, 11% international; 3% from in state; 17% live on campus; N/A of students in fraternities, N/A in sororities
Most popular majors: 33% Health Professions and Related Programs, 23% Business, Management, Marketing, and Related Support Services, 12% Homeland Security, Law Enforcement, Firefighting and Related Protective Services, 4% Biological and Biomedical Sciences, 4% Public Administration and Social Service Professions
Expenses: 2021-2022: $24,900; room/board: $11,890
Financial aid: (734) 432-5662; 76% of undergrads determined to have financial need; average aid package $14,831

Michigan State University
East Lansing MI
(517) 355-8332
U.S. News ranking: Nat. U., No. 83
Website: www.msu.edu/
Admissions email: admis@msu.edu
Public; founded 1855
Freshman admissions: more selective; 2020-2021: 45,426 applied, 34,663 accepted. Either SAT or ACT required. SAT 25/75 percentile: 1100-1300. High school rank: 27% in top tenth, 59% in top quarter, 92% in top half
Early decision deadline: N/A, notification date: N/A
Early action deadline: 11/1, notification date: 1/15
Application deadline (fall): rolling
Undergraduate student body: 34,588 full time, 3,903 part time; 49% male, 51% female; 1% American Indian, 7% Asian, 8% black, 6% Hispanic, 4% multiracial, 0% Pacific Islander, 68% white, 7% international; N/A from in state; 6% live on campus; 11% of students in fraternities, 2% in sororities
Most popular majors: 19% Business, Management, Marketing, and Related Support

Services, 11% Biological and Biomedical Sciences, 11% Communication, Journalism, and Related Programs, 10% Engineering, 9% Social Sciences
Expenses: 2021-2022: $14,460 in state, $39,766 out of state; room/board: $10,522
Financial aid: (517) 353-5940; 47% of undergrads determined to have financial need; average aid package $16,869

Michigan Technological University
Houghton MI
(906) 487-2335
U.S. News ranking: Nat. U., No. 148
Website: www.mtu.edu
Admissions email: mtu4u@mtu.edu
Public; founded 1885
Freshman admissions: more selective; 2020-2021: 7,476 applied, 5,260 accepted. Neither SAT nor ACT required. SAT 25/75 percentile: 1160-1350. High school rank: 32% in top tenth, 64% in top quarter, 92% in top half
Early decision deadline: N/A, notification date: N/A
Early action deadline: N/A, notification date: N/A
Application deadline (fall): rolling
Undergraduate student body: 5,294 full time, 348 part time; 71% male, 29% female; 0% American Indian, 2% Asian, 1% black, 3% Hispanic, 4% multiracial, 0% Pacific Islander, 87% white, 1% international; 78% from in state; 43% live on campus; 9% of students in fraternities, 10% in sororities
Most popular majors: 60% Engineering, 8% Business, Management, Marketing, and Related Support Services, 8% Computer and Information Sciences and Support Services, 6% Engineering Technologies and Engineering-Related Fields, 3% Natural Resources and Conservation
Expenses: 2021-2022: $16,966 in state, $38,112 out of state; room/board: $11,655
Financial aid: (906) 487-2622; 61% of undergrads determined to have financial need; average aid package $16,783

Northern Michigan University
Marquette MI
(906) 227-2650
U.S. News ranking: Reg. U. (Mid. W), No. 82
Website: nmu.edu/
Admissions email: admissions@nmu.edu
Public; founded 1899
Freshman admissions: less selective; 2020-2021: 6,233 applied, 4,169 accepted. Neither SAT nor ACT required. SAT 25/75 percentile: 950-1180. High school rank: N/A
Early decision deadline: N/A, notification date: N/A
Early action deadline: N/A,

notification date: N/A
Application deadline (fall): rolling
Undergraduate student body: 5,880 full time, 854 part time; 42% male, 58% female; 1% American Indian, 1% Asian, 2% black, 5% Hispanic, 4% multiracial, 0% Pacific Islander, 86% white, 1% international; 75% from in state; 43% live on campus; N/A of students in fraternities, N/A in sororities
Most popular majors: 14% Business, Management, Marketing, and Related Support Services, 13% Health Professions and Related Programs, 11% Biological and Biomedical Sciences, 8% Visual and Performing Arts, 6% Natural Resources and Conservation
Expenses: 2021-2022: $11,680 in state, $17,176 out of state; room/board: $11,572
Financial aid: (906) 227-2327; 66% of undergrads determined to have financial need; average aid package $11,847

Northwestern Michigan College[1]
Traverse City MI
(231) 995-1000
U.S. News ranking: Reg. Coll. (Mid. W), unranked
Admissions email: N/A
Public
Application deadline (fall): N/A
Undergraduate student body: N/A full time, N/A part time
Expenses: 2020-2021: $8,280 in state, $10,491 out of state; room/board: $8,275
Financial aid: N/A

Northwood University
Midland MI
(989) 837-4273
U.S. News ranking: Business, unranked
Website: www.northwood.edu
Admissions email: miadmit@northwood.edu
Private; founded 1959
Freshman admissions: selective; 2020-2021: 1,036 applied, 793 accepted. Neither SAT nor ACT required. SAT 25/75 percentile: 990-1180. High school rank: 9% in top tenth, 31% in top quarter, 72% in top half
Early decision deadline: N/A, notification date: N/A
Early action deadline: N/A, notification date: N/A
Application deadline (fall): rolling
Undergraduate student body: 1,013 full time, 44 part time; 67% male, 33% female; 0% American Indian, 1% Asian, 6% black, 5% Hispanic, 3% multiracial, 0% Pacific Islander, 74% white, 3% international; 90% from in state; 53% live on campus; 9% of students in fraternities, 11% in sororities
Most popular majors: 86% Business, Management, Marketing, and Related Support Services, 6% Parks, Recreation, Leisure, and Fitness Studies, 4% Communication, Journalism, and Related Programs, 2% Computer

and Information Sciences and Support Services, 2% Health Professions and Related Programs
Expenses: 2021-2022: $30,520; room/board: $11,440
Financial aid: (989) 837-4230; 62% of undergrads determined to have financial need; average aid package $24,330

Oakland University
Rochester MI
(248) 370-3360
U.S. News ranking: Nat. U., second tier
Website: www.oakland.edu
Admissions email: visit@oakland.edu
Public; founded 1957
Freshman admissions: selective; 2020-2021: 12,054 applied, 9,776 accepted. Neither SAT nor ACT required. SAT 25/75 percentile: 980-1210. High school rank: 20% in top tenth, 47% in top quarter, 80% in top half
Early decision deadline: N/A, notification date: N/A
Early action deadline: N/A, notification date: N/A
Application deadline (fall): rolling
Undergraduate student body: 12,057 full time, 3,043 part time; 43% male, 57% female; 0% American Indian, 5% Asian, 8% black, 4% Hispanic, 3% multiracial, 0% Pacific Islander, 72% white, 2% international; 96% from in state; 11% live on campus; 3% of students in fraternities, 2% in sororities
Most popular majors: 24% Health Professions and Related Programs, 19% Business, Management, Marketing, and Related Support Services, 11% Engineering, 5% Biological and Biomedical Sciences, 5% Communication, Journalism, and Related Programs
Expenses: 2021-2022: $13,934 in state, $24,708 out of state; room/board: $11,022
Financial aid: (248) 370-2550; 61% of undergrads determined to have financial need; average aid package $10,238

Olivet College[7]
Olivet MI
(800) 456-7189
U.S. News ranking: Reg. Coll. (Mid. W), No. 45
Website: www.olivetcollege.edu
Admissions email: admissions@olivetcollege.edu
Private; founded 1844
Affiliation: United Church of Christ
Freshman admissions: less selective; 2020-2021: N/A applied, N/A accepted. Either SAT or ACT required. SAT 25/75 percentile: N/A. High school rank: N/A
Early decision deadline: N/A, notification date: N/A
Early action deadline: N/A, notification date: N/A
Application deadline (fall): 8/31
Undergraduate student body: 887 full time, 81 part time
Most popular majors: Information not available
Expenses: 2021-2022: $31,104; room/board: $10,838

Financial aid: (269) 749-7645; 92% of undergrads determined to have financial need; average aid package $22,443

Rochester University
Rochester Hills MI
(248) 218-2222
U.S. News ranking: Reg. Coll. (Mid. W), No. 53
Website: www.RochesterU.edu
Admissions email: admissions@RochesterU.edu
Private; founded 1959
Affiliation: Churches of Christ
Freshman admissions: less selective; 2020-2021: 530 applied, 527 accepted. Either SAT or ACT required. SAT 25/75 percentile: 840-1060. High school rank: N/A
Early decision deadline: N/A, notification date: N/A
Early action deadline: N/A, notification date: N/A
Application deadline (fall): rolling
Undergraduate student body: 745 full time, 453 part time; 37% male, 63% female; 1% American Indian, 2% Asian, 22% black, 2% Hispanic, 3% multiracial, 0% Pacific Islander, 67% white, 2% international; 93% from in state; 23% live on campus; N/A of students in fraternities, N/A in sororities
Most popular majors: 25% Early Childhood Education and Teaching, 11% Psychology, General, 9% Mass Communication/Media Studies, 9% Organizational Leadership, 8% Business Administration and Management, General
Expenses: 2021-2022: $25,462; room/board: $9,106
Financial aid: (248) 218-2056

Saginaw Valley State University
University Center MI
(989) 964-4200
U.S. News ranking: Reg. U. (Mid. W), No. 112
Website: www.svsu.edu
Admissions email: admissions@svsu.edu
Public; founded 1963
Freshman admissions: selective; 2020-2021: 6,881 applied, 6,156 accepted. Neither SAT nor ACT required. SAT 25/75 percentile: 970-1190. High school rank: 17% in top tenth, 45% in top quarter, 78% in top half
Early decision deadline: N/A, notification date: N/A
Early action deadline: N/A, notification date: N/A
Application deadline (fall): rolling
Undergraduate student body: 6,018 full time, 1,188 part time; 36% male, 64% female; 0% American Indian, 1% Asian, 8% black, 5% Hispanic, 4% multiracial, 0% Pacific Islander, 77% white, 4% international; 98% from in state; 31% live on campus; 3% of students in fraternities, 3% in sororities
Most popular majors: 24% Health Professions and Related Programs, 19% Business, Management, Marketing, and Related Support

Services, 6% Biological and Biomedical Sciences, 6% Public Administration and Social Service Professions, 5% Engineering
Expenses: 2021-2022: $11,130 in state, $26,144 out of state; room/board: N/A
Financial aid: (989) 964-4900; 66% of undergrads determined to have financial need; average aid package $10,410

Schoolcraft College[1]
Livonia MI
(734) 462-4400
U.S. News ranking: Reg. Coll. (Mid. W), unranked
Website: www.ptcollege.edu
Admissions email: N/A
Public
Application deadline (fall): N/A
Undergraduate student body: N/A full time, N/A part time
Expenses: 2020-2021: $5,364 in state, $7,522 out of state; room/board: N/A
Financial aid: N/A

Siena Heights University[1]
Adrian MI
(517) 264-7180
U.S. News ranking: Reg. U. (Mid. W), second tier
Website: www.sienaheights.edu
Admissions email: admissions@sienaheights.edu
Private; founded 1919
Affiliation: Roman Catholic
Application deadline (fall): 8/1
Undergraduate student body: N/A full time, N/A part time
Expenses: 2020-2021: $27,642; room/board: $11,430
Financial aid: (517) 264-7110

Spring Arbor University
Spring Arbor MI
(800) 968-0011
U.S. News ranking: Reg. U. (Mid. W), No. 54
Website: www.arbor.edu/
Admissions email: admissions@arbor.edu
Private; founded 1873
Affiliation: Free Methodist
Freshman admissions: selective; 2020-2021: 1,504 applied, 952 accepted. Either SAT or ACT required. SAT 25/75 percentile: 983-1190. High school rank: 20% in top tenth, 48% in top quarter, 78% in top half
Early decision deadline: N/A, notification date: N/A
Early action deadline: N/A, notification date: N/A
Application deadline (fall): 8/1
Undergraduate student body: 968 full time, 382 part time; 32% male, 68% female; 0% American Indian, 1% Asian, 9% black, 5% Hispanic, 3% multiracial, 0% Pacific Islander, 75% white, 1% international; 85% from in state; 67% live on campus; 0% of students in fraternities, 0% in sororities
Most popular majors: 8% Business Administration and Management, General, 7% Registered Nursing,

Nursing Administration, Nursing Research and Clinical Nursing, Other, 6% Psychology, General, 5% English Language and Literature, General, 5% Health and Physical Education/Fitness, General
Expenses: 2021-2022: $31,080; room/board: $10,456
Financial aid: (517) 750-6463; 78% of undergrads determined to have financial need; average aid package $25,451

University of Detroit Mercy
Detroit MI
(313) 993-1245
U.S. News ranking: Nat. U., No. 187
Website: www.udmercy.edu
Admissions email: admissions@udmercy.edu
Private; founded 1877
Affiliation: Roman Catholic
Freshman admissions: selective; 2020-2021: 3,985 applied, 3,168 accepted. Neither SAT nor ACT required. SAT 25/75 percentile: 1050-1260. High school rank: 26% in top tenth, 56% in top quarter, 86% in top half
Early decision deadline: N/A, notification date: N/A
Early action deadline: 12/1, notification date: 12/1
Application deadline (fall): 3/1
Undergraduate student body: 2,214 full time, 419 part time; 38% male, 62% female; 0% American Indian, 7% Asian, 13% black, 6% Hispanic, 2% multiracial, 0% Pacific Islander, 59% white, 6% international; 88% from in state; 15% live on campus; 1% of students in fraternities, 2% in sororities
Most popular majors: 36% Registered Nursing/Registered Nurse, 15% Biology/Biological Sciences, General, 7% Business Administration and Management, General, 4% Dental Hygiene/Hygienist, 4% Engineering, General
Expenses: 2021-2022: $30,154; room/board: $10,240
Financial aid: (313) 993-3354; 61% of undergrads determined to have financial need; average aid package $23,682

University of Michigan–Ann Arbor
Ann Arbor MI
(734) 764-7433
U.S. News ranking: Nat. U., No. 23
Website: umich.edu
Admissions email: N/A
Public; founded 1817
Freshman admissions: most selective; 2020-2021: 65,021 applied, 16,974 accepted. Neither SAT nor ACT required. SAT 25/75 percentile: 1340-1560. High school rank: 77% in top tenth, 95% in top quarter, 99% in top half
Early decision deadline: N/A, notification date: N/A
Early action deadline: 11/15, notification date: 1/31

Application deadline (fall): 2/1
Undergraduate student body: 29,851 full time, 1,478 part time; 50% male, 50% female; 0% American Indian, 16% Asian, 4% black, 7% Hispanic, 5% multiracial, 0% Pacific Islander, 55% white, 7% international; 61% from in state; 21% live on campus; 8% of students in fraternities, 17% in sororities
Most popular majors: 11% Computer and Information Sciences, General, 8% Business Administration and Management, General, 6% Economics, General, 4% Experimental Psychology, 4% Physiological Psychology/Psychobiology
Expenses: 2021-2022: $16,178 in state, $53,232 out of state; room/board: $12,592
Financial aid: (734) 763-6600; 41% of undergrads determined to have financial need; average aid package $30,333

University of Michigan–Dearborn
Dearborn MI
(313) 593-5100
U.S. News ranking: Reg. U. (Mid. W), No. 31
Website: umdearborn.edu/
Admissions email: umd-admissions@umich.edu
Public; founded 1959
Freshman admissions: selective; 2020-2021: 7,300 applied, 4,928 accepted. Either SAT or ACT required. SAT 25/75 percentile: 1090-1320. High school rank: N/A
Early decision deadline: N/A, notification date: N/A
Early action deadline: N/A, notification date: N/A
Application deadline (fall): 9/4
Undergraduate student body: 5,012 full time, 1,713 part time; 54% male, 46% female; 0% American Indian, 9% Asian, 8% black, 6% Hispanic, 4% multiracial, 0% Pacific Islander, 68% white, 2% international; 4% from in state; N/A live on campus; N/A of students in fraternities, N/A in sororities
Most popular majors: 23% Engineering, 22% Business, Management, Marketing, and Related Support Services, 9% Psychology, 8% Biological and Biomedical Sciences, 7% Computer and Information Sciences and Support Services
Expenses: 2021-2022: $13,816 in state, $28,048 out of state; room/board: N/A
Financial aid: (313) 593-5300; 66% of undergrads determined to have financial need; average aid package $16,647

University of Michigan–Flint
Flint MI
(810) 762-3300
U.S. News ranking: Nat. U., second tier
Website: www.umflint.edu
Admissions email: admissions@umich.edu
Public; founded 1956

Freshman admissions: selective; 2020-2021: 4,017 applied, 3,110 accepted. Either SAT or ACT required. SAT 25/75 percentile: 970-1210. High school rank: 19% in top tenth, 44% in top quarter, 80% in top half
Early decision deadline: N/A, notification date: N/A
Early action deadline: N/A, notification date: N/A
Application deadline (fall): 8/22
Undergraduate student body: 3,300 full time, 2,124 part time; 37% male, 63% female; 1% American Indian, 2% Asian, 13% black, 6% Hispanic, 4% multiracial, 0% Pacific Islander, 71% white, 2% international; N/A from in state; 2% live on campus; 1% of students in fraternities, 2% in sororities
Most popular majors: 33% Health Professions and Related Programs, 22% Business, Management, Marketing, and Related Support Services, 8% Biological and Biomedical Sciences, 8% Psychology, 4% Visual and Performing Arts
Expenses: 2021-2022: $12,892 in state, $24,622 out of state; room/board: $9,092
Financial aid: (810) 762-3444; 73% of undergrads determined to have financial need; average aid package $13,143

Walsh College[1]
Troy MI
(248) 823-1600
U.S. News ranking: Business, unranked
Website: www.walshcollege.edu
Admissions email: admissions@walshcollege.edu
Private; founded 1922
Application deadline (fall): rolling
Undergraduate student body: N/A full time, N/A part time
Expenses: 2020-2021: $18,309; room/board: N/A
Financial aid: (248) 823-1665

Wayne State University
Detroit MI
(313) 577-2100
U.S. News ranking: Nat. U., No. 249
Website: wayne.edu/
Admissions email: studentservice@wayne.edu
Public; founded 1868
Freshman admissions: selective; 2020-2021: 17,231 applied, 11,794 accepted. Neither SAT nor ACT required. SAT 25/75 percentile: 1000-1200. High school rank: N/A
Early decision deadline: 12/15, notification date: 3/8
Early action deadline: N/A, notification date: N/A
Application deadline (fall): 8/1
Undergraduate student body: 13,407 full time, 4,106 part time; 41% male, 59% female; 0% American Indian, 12% Asian, 16% black, 6% Hispanic, 4% multiracial, 0% Pacific Islander, 57% white, 2% international; 2% from in state; 7% live on campus; N/A of students in fraternities, N/A

in sororities
Most popular majors: 8% Psychology, General, 5% International Business/Trade/Commerce, 4% Biology/Biological Sciences, General, 4% Computer and Information Sciences, General, 4% Public Health, General
Expenses: 2021-2022: $15,199 in state, $32,727 out of state; room/board: $11,743
Financial aid: (313) 577-2100; 72% of undergrads determined to have financial need; average aid package $12,409

Western Michigan University
Kalamazoo MI
(269) 387-2000
U.S. News ranking: Nat. U., No. 263
Website: wmich.edu/
Admissions email: ask-wmu@wmich.edu
Public; founded 1903
Freshman admissions: selective; 2020-2021: 16,582 applied, 14,085 accepted. Neither SAT nor ACT required. SAT 25/75 percentile: 1010-1220. High school rank: 14% in top tenth, 38% in top quarter, 72% in top half
Early decision deadline: N/A, notification date: N/A
Early action deadline: N/A, notification date: N/A
Application deadline (fall): rolling
Undergraduate student body: 13,296 full time, 3,258 part time; 50% male, 50% female; 0% American Indian, 2% Asian, 10% black, 8% Hispanic, 4% multiracial, 0% Pacific Islander, 68% white, 5% international; 84% from in state; 21% live on campus; N/A of students in fraternities, N/A in sororities
Most popular majors: 22% Business, Management, Marketing, and Related Support Services, 10% Health Professions and Related Programs, 8% Engineering, 7% Multi/Interdisciplinary Studies, 6% Visual and Performing Arts
Expenses: 2021-2022: $14,257 in state, $17,591 out of state; room/board: $10,884
Financial aid: (269) 387-6000; 55% of undergrads determined to have financial need; average aid package $11,682

MINNESOTA

Augsburg University
Minneapolis MN
(612) 330-1001
U.S. News ranking: Reg. U. (Mid. W), No. 24
Website: www.augsburg.edu
Admissions email: admissions@augsburg.edu
Private; founded 1869
Affiliation: Evangelical Lutheran Church
Freshman admissions: selective; 2020-2021: 2,746 applied, 2,008 accepted. Neither SAT nor ACT required. ACT 25/75

percentile: 17-23. High school rank: N/A
Early decision deadline: N/A, notification date: N/A
Early action deadline: N/A, notification date: N/A
Application deadline (fall): 8/1
Undergraduate student body: 2,202 full time, 310 part time; 43% male, 57% female; 1% American Indian, 11% Asian, 21% black, 13% Hispanic, 6% multiracial, 1% Pacific Islander, 42% white, 2% international; N/A from in state; 30% live on campus; N/A of students in fraternities, N/A in sororities
Most popular majors: 22% Business, Management, Marketing, and Related Support Services, 9% Health Professions and Related Programs, 9% Psychology, 9% Social Sciences, 7% Education
Expenses: 2020-2021: $41,086; room/board: $10,885
Financial aid: (612) 330-1046

Bemidji State University
Bemidji MN
(218) 755-2040
U.S. News ranking: Reg. U. (Mid. W), No. 88
Website: www.bemidjistate.edu
Admissions email: admissions@bemidjistate.edu
Public; founded 1919
Freshman admissions: selective; 2020-2021: 3,043 applied, 2,113 accepted. Either SAT or ACT required. ACT 25/75 percentile: 19-24. High school rank: 11% in top tenth, 36% in top quarter, 71% in top half
Early decision deadline: N/A, notification date: N/A
Early action deadline: N/A, notification date: N/A
Application deadline (fall): rolling
Undergraduate student body: 2,762 full time, 1,333 part time; 43% male, 57% female; 3% American Indian, 1% Asian, 3% black, 3% Hispanic, 5% multiracial, 0% Pacific Islander, 82% white, 2% international
Most popular majors: Information not available
Expenses: 2021-2022: $9,192 in state, $9,192 out of state; room/board: $8,920
Financial aid: (218) 755-2034; 72% of undergrads determined to have financial need; average aid package $9,905

Bethany Lutheran College
Mankato MN
(507) 344-7331
U.S. News ranking: Nat. Lib. Arts, second tier
Website: www.blc.edu
Admissions email: admiss@blc.edu
Private; founded 1927
Affiliation: Other
Freshman admissions: selective; 2020-2021: 665 applied, 429 accepted. Neither SAT nor ACT required. ACT 25/75 percentile: 20-26. High school rank: 15% in top tenth, 40% in top quarter, 66% in top half

Early decision deadline: N/A, notification date: N/A
Early action deadline: N/A, notification date: N/A
Application deadline (fall): 7/1
Undergraduate student body: 633 full time, 136 part time; 46% male, 54% female; 0% American Indian, 3% Asian, 3% black, 4% Hispanic, 4% multiracial, 0% Pacific Islander, 68% white, 16% international
Most popular majors: 17% Business Administration and Management, General, 10% Exercise Physiology, 8% Biology/Biological Sciences, General, 8% Communication and Media Studies, 8% Legal Professions and Studies
Expenses: 2021-2022: $28,660; room/board: $8,180
Financial aid: (507) 344-7328; 70% of undergrads determined to have financial need; average aid package $22,728

Bethel University
St. Paul MN
(800) 255-8706
U.S. News ranking: Nat. U., No. 202
Website: www.bethel.edu
Admissions email: undergrad-admissions@bethel.edu
Private; founded 1871
Affiliation: Baptist
Freshman admissions: more selective; 2020-2021: 1,646 applied, 1,426 accepted. Neither SAT nor ACT required. ACT 25/75 percentile: 21-28. High school rank: 26% in top tenth, 53% in top quarter, 88% in top half
Early decision deadline: N/A, notification date: N/A
Early action deadline: N/A, notification date: N/A
Application deadline (fall): rolling
Undergraduate student body: 2,313 full time, 397 part time; 38% male, 62% female; 0% American Indian, 5% Asian, 4% black, 5% Hispanic, 4% multiracial, 0% Pacific Islander, 80% white, 0% international; 82% from in state; 64% live on campus; 0% of students in fraternities, 0% in sororities
Most popular majors: 22% Business, Management, Marketing, and Related Support Services, 22% Health Professions and Related Programs, 8% Communication, Journalism, and Related Programs, 8% Education, 6% Biological and Biomedical Sciences
Expenses: 2021-2022: $40,080; room/board: $11,150
Financial aid: (651) 638-6241; 73% of undergrads determined to have financial need; average aid package $33,816

Carleton College
Northfield MN
(507) 222-4190
U.S. News ranking: Nat. Lib. Arts, No. 9
Website: www.carleton.edu
Admissions email: admissions@carleton.edu
Private; founded 1866

Freshman admissions: most selective; 2020-2021: 6,892 applied, 1,460 accepted. Neither SAT nor ACT required. ACT 25/75 percentile: 30-34. High school rank: 70% in top tenth, 93% in top quarter, 99% in top half
Early decision deadline: 11/15, notification date: 12/15
Early action deadline: N/A, notification date: N/A
Application deadline (fall): 1/15
Undergraduate student body: 1,918 full time, 22 part time; 48% male, 52% female; 0% American Indian, 10% Asian, 6% black, 9% Hispanic, 8% multiracial, 0% Pacific Islander, 56% white, 10% international; 18% from in state; 76% live on campus; 0% of students in fraternities, 0% in sororities
Most popular majors: 19% Social Sciences, 12% Computer and Information Sciences and Support Services, 11% Mathematics and Statistics
Expenses: 2021-2022: $60,225; room/board: $15,375
Financial aid: (507) 222-4138; 60% of undergrads determined to have financial need; average aid package $53,497

College of St. Benedict
St. Joseph MN
(320) 363-5060
U.S. News ranking: Nat. Lib. Arts, No. 92
Website: www.csbsju.edu
Admissions email: admissions@csbsju.edu
Private; founded 1913
Affiliation: Roman Catholic
Freshman admissions: more selective; 2020-2021: 1,845 applied, 1,550 accepted. Neither SAT nor ACT required. ACT 25/75 percentile: 21-28. High school rank: 30% in top tenth, 61% in top quarter, 90% in top half
Early decision deadline: N/A, notification date: N/A
Early action deadline: 12/15, notification date: 1/15
Application deadline (fall): rolling
Undergraduate student body: 1,655 full time, 13 part time; 0% male, 100% female; 1% American Indian, 4% Asian, 3% black, 9% Hispanic, 0% multiracial, 0% Pacific Islander, 80% white, 3% international; 84% from in state; 89% live on campus; 0% of students in fraternities, 0% in sororities
Most popular majors: 11% Biology/Biological Sciences, General, 11% Registered Nursing/Registered Nurse, 10% Business Administration and Management, General, 9% Psychology, General, 7% Speech Communication and Rhetoric
Expenses: 2021-2022: $50,126; room/board: $11,574
Financial aid: (320) 363-5388; 70% of undergrads determined to have financial need; average aid package $40,668

The College of St. Scholastica
Duluth MN
(218) 723-6046
U.S. News ranking: Nat. U., No. 239
Website: www.css.edu
Admissions email: admissions@css.edu
Private; founded 1912
Affiliation: Roman Catholic
Freshman admissions: selective; 2020-2021: 1,922 applied, 1,409 accepted. Neither SAT nor ACT required. ACT 25/75 percentile: 22-27. High school rank: 21% in top tenth, 54% in top quarter, 82% in top half
Early decision deadline: N/A, notification date: N/A
Early action deadline: N/A, notification date: N/A
Application deadline (fall): rolling
Undergraduate student body: 1,934 full time, 310 part time; 29% male, 71% female; 1% American Indian, 3% Asian, 4% black, 3% Hispanic, 4% multiracial, 0% Pacific Islander, 82% white, 2% international; 87% from in state; 39% live on campus; N/A of students in fraternities, N/A in sororities
Most popular majors: 43% Registered Nursing/Registered Nurse, 10% Social Work, 7% Psychology, General, 4% Biology/Biological Sciences, General, 4% Health Information/Medical Records Administration/Administrator
Expenses: 2021-2022: $39,410; room/board: $10,696
Financial aid: (218) 723-7027; 78% of undergrads determined to have financial need; average aid package $27,293

Concordia College at Moorhead
Moorhead MN
(800) 699-9897
U.S. News ranking: Nat. Lib. Arts, No. 141
Website: www.concordiacollege.edu
Admissions email: admissions@cord.edu
Private; founded 1891
Affiliation: Evangelical Lutheran Church
Freshman admissions: selective; 2020-2021: 4,024 applied, 2,337 accepted. Neither SAT nor ACT required. ACT 25/75 percentile: 20-27. High school rank: 20% in top tenth, 49% in top quarter, 85% in top half
Early decision deadline: N/A, notification date: N/A
Early action deadline: N/A, notification date: N/A
Application deadline (fall): 9/10
Undergraduate student body: 1,886 full time, 53 part time; 42% male, 58% female; 1% American Indian, 2% Asian, 3% black, 3% Hispanic, 1% multiracial, 0% Pacific Islander, 83% white, 4% international; 69% from in state; 53% live on campus; 0% of students in fraternities, 0% in sororities
Most popular majors: 19%

Business, Management, Marketing, and Related Support Services, 12% Education, 11% Biological and Biomedical Sciences, 8% Health Professions and Related Programs, 7% Communication, Journalism, and Related Programs
Expenses: 2021-2022: $28,016; room/board: $9,300
Financial aid: (218) 299-3010; 74% of undergrads determined to have financial need; average aid package $34,134

Concordia University–St. Paul
St. Paul MN
(651) 641-8230
U.S. News ranking: Reg. U. (Mid. W), No. 88
Website: www.csp.edu
Admissions email: admissions@csp.edu
Private; founded 1893
Affiliation: Lutheran Church - Missouri Synod
Freshman admissions: selective; 2020-2021: 2,554 applied, 1,752 accepted. Neither SAT nor ACT required. ACT 25/75 percentile: 17-24. High school rank: N/A
Early decision deadline: N/A, notification date: N/A
Early action deadline: N/A, notification date: N/A
Application deadline (fall): 8/1
Undergraduate student body: 2,387 full time, 1,156 part time; 36% male, 64% female; 0% American Indian, 11% Asian, 12% black, 8% Hispanic, 5% multiracial, 0% Pacific Islander, 59% white, 2% international; 63% from in state; 15% live on campus; N/A of students in fraternities, N/A in sororities
Most popular majors: 17% Business Administration and Management, General, 10% Kinesiology and Exercise Science, 9% Nursing Practice, 7% Psychology, General, 6% Child Development
Expenses: 2021-2022: $23,900; room/board: $9,900
Financial aid: (651) 603-6300; 76% of undergrads determined to have financial need; average aid package $14,954

Crown College[1]
St. Bonifacius MN
(952) 446-4142
U.S. News ranking: Reg. U. (Mid. W), second tier
Website: www.crown.edu
Admissions email: admissions@crown.edu
Private; founded 1916
Affiliation: Christ and Missionary Alliance Church
Application deadline (fall): 8/20
Undergraduate student body: N/A full time, N/A part time
Expenses: 2020-2021: $27,980; room/board: $9,200
Financial aid: (952) 446-4177

Dunwoody College of Technology

Minneapolis MN
(800) 292-4625
U.S. News ranking: Reg. Coll. (Mid. W), unranked
Website: www.dunwoody.edu
Admissions email: info@dunwoody.edu
Private; founded 1914
Freshman admissions: least selective; 2020-2021: 684 applied, 427 accepted. Neither SAT nor ACT required. SAT 25/75 percentile: N/A. High school rank: 8% in top tenth, 29% in top quarter, 67% in top half
Early decision deadline: N/A, notification date: N/A
Early action deadline: N/A, notification date: N/A
Application deadline (fall): rolling
Undergraduate student body: 1,058 full time, 223 part time; 82% male, 18% female; 0% American Indian, 5% Asian, 5% black, 3% Hispanic, 5% multiracial, 0% Pacific Islander, 78% white, 0% international; 97% from in state; 3% live on campus; 0% of students in fraternities, 0% in sororities
Most popular majors: 28% Manufacturing Engineering, 15% Architecture, 15% Construction Management, 14% Mechanical Engineering, 13% Interior Design
Expenses: 2021-2022: $23,247; room/board: N/A
Financial aid: (612) 381-3347; 71% of undergrads determined to have financial need; average aid package $11,750

Gustavus Adolphus College

St. Peter MN
(507) 933-7676
U.S. News ranking: Nat. Lib. Arts, No. 79
Website: gustavus.edu
Admissions email: admission@gustavus.edu
Private; founded 1862
Affiliation: Evangelical Lutheran Church
Freshman admissions: more selective; 2020-2021: 4,737 applied, 3,345 accepted. Neither SAT nor ACT required. ACT 25/75 percentile: 24-30. High school rank: 29% in top tenth, 63% in top quarter, 95% in top half
Early decision deadline: N/A, notification date: N/A
Early action deadline: 11/1, notification date: 11/15
Application deadline (fall): 5/1
Undergraduate student body: 2,218 full time, 27 part time; 41% male, 59% female; 0% American Indian, 5% Asian, 4% black, 6% Hispanic, 4% multiracial, 0% Pacific Islander, 78% white, 3% international; 83% from in state; 87% live on campus; 13% of students in fraternities, 14% in sororities
Most popular majors: 12% Social Sciences, 11% Business, Management, Marketing, and Related Support Services, 9% Biological and Biomedical Sciences, 9% Psychology, 8%

Parks, Recreation, Leisure, and Fitness Studies
Expenses: 2021-2022: $50,690; room/board: $10,700
Financial aid: (507) 933-7527; 64% of undergrads determined to have financial need; average aid package $46,561

Hamline University

St. Paul MN
(651) 523-2207
U.S. News ranking: Reg. U. (Mid. W), No. 12
Website: www.hamline.edu
Admissions email: admission@hamline.edu
Private; founded 1854
Affiliation: United Methodist
Freshman admissions: selective; 2020-2021: 4,441 applied, 3,062 accepted. Neither SAT nor ACT required. ACT 25/75 percentile: 20-26. High school rank: 14% in top tenth, 43% in top quarter, 79% in top half
Early decision deadline: 11/1, notification date: 11/15
Early action deadline: 12/1, notification date: N/A
Application deadline (fall): rolling
Undergraduate student body: 1,861 full time, 64 part time; 37% male, 63% female; 0% American Indian, 9% Asian, 10% black, 11% Hispanic, 7% multiracial, 0% Pacific Islander, 59% white, 1% international; N/A from in state; 30% live on campus; N/A of students in fraternities, N/A in sororities
Most popular majors: 18% Social Sciences, 17% Business, Management, Marketing, and Related Support Services, 10% Psychology, 7% Legal Professions and Studies, 6% Biological and Biomedical Sciences
Expenses: 2021-2022: $45,504; room/board: $10,980
Financial aid: (651) 523-2933; 85% of undergrads determined to have financial need; average aid package $34,615

Macalester College

St. Paul MN
(651) 696-6357
U.S. News ranking: Nat. Lib. Arts, No. 27
Website: www.macalester.edu
Admissions email: admissions@macalester.edu
Private; founded 1874
Freshman admissions: most selective; 2020-2021: 6,373 applied, 2,466 accepted. Neither SAT nor ACT required. SAT 25/75 percentile: 1280-1450. High school rank: 66% in top tenth, 91% in top quarter, 98% in top half
Early decision deadline: 11/1, notification date: 12/6
Early action deadline: 11/1, notification date: 12/20
Application deadline (fall): 1/15
Undergraduate student body: 2,012 full time, 37 part time; 41% male, 59% female; 0% American Indian, 9% Asian, 5% black, 11% Hispanic, 8% multiracial, 0% Pacific Islander, 53% white, 14% international; 19% from in

state; 62% live on campus; 0% of students in fraternities, 0% in sororities
Most popular majors: 22% Social Sciences, 12% Biological and Biomedical Sciences, 10% Mathematics and Statistics
Expenses: 2021-2022: $60,518; room/board: $13,542
Financial aid: (651) 696-6214; 67% of undergrads determined to have financial need; average aid package $53,873

Metropolitan State University[1]

St. Paul MN
(651) 772-7600
U.S. News ranking: Nat. U., second tier
Website: www.metrostate.edu
Admissions email: admissions@metrostate.edu
Public
Application deadline (fall): N/A
Undergraduate student body: N/A full time, N/A part time
Expenses: 2020-2021: $8,249 in state, $15,673 out of state; room/board: N/A
Financial aid: N/A

Minneapolis College of Art and Design

Minneapolis MN
(612) 874-3800
U.S. News ranking: Arts, unranked
Website: www.mcad.edu
Admissions email: admissions@mcad.edu
Private; founded 1886
Freshman admissions: selective; 2020-2021: 695 applied, 380 accepted. Neither SAT nor ACT required. ACT 25/75 percentile: 19-24. High school rank: N/A
Early decision deadline: N/A, notification date: N/A
Early action deadline: 12/1, notification date: 12/15
Application deadline (fall): 4/1
Undergraduate student body: 645 full time, 26 part time; 30% male, 70% female; 3% American Indian, 10% Asian, 7% black, 10% Hispanic, 2% multiracial, 0% Pacific Islander, 64% white, 2% international
Most popular majors: 68% Visual and Performing Arts, 21% Communications Technologies/ Technicians and Support Services, 5% Business, Management, Marketing, and Related Support Services, 3% Communication, Journalism, and Related Programs, 2% Precision Production
Expenses: 2020-2021: $41,794; room/board: N/A
Financial aid: (612) 874-3733

Minnesota State University–Mankato

Mankato MN
(507) 389-1822
U.S. News ranking: Reg. U. (Mid. W), No. 79
Website: mankato.mnsu.edu/
Admissions email: admissions@mnsu.edu
Public; founded 1868

Freshman admissions: selective; 2020-2021: 10,411 applied, 7,002 accepted. Neither SAT nor ACT required. ACT 25/75 percentile: 19-24. High school rank: 10% in top tenth, 29% in top quarter, 70% in top half
Early decision deadline: N/A, notification date: N/A
Early action deadline: N/A, notification date: N/A
Application deadline (fall): rolling
Undergraduate student body: 10,507 full time, 2,222 part time; 45% male, 55% female; 0% American Indian, 4% Asian, 6% black, 5% Hispanic, 4% multiracial, 0% Pacific Islander, 72% white, 8% international
Most popular majors: 6% Registered Nursing/Registered Nurse, 5% Psychology, General, 4% Biology/Biological Sciences, General, 4% Business Administration and Management, General, 4% Elementary Education and Teaching
Expenses: 2021-2022: $9,146 in state, $18,200 out of state; room/board: $10,198
Financial aid: (507) 389-1866; 49% of undergrads determined to have financial need; average aid package $10,401

Minnesota State University–Moorhead

Moorhead MN
(800) 593-7246
U.S. News ranking: Reg. U. (Mid. W), No. 88
Website: www.mnstate.edu
Admissions email: admissions@mnstate.edu
Public; founded 1887
Freshman admissions: selective; 2020-2021: 3,688 applied, 2,436 accepted. Neither SAT nor ACT required. ACT 25/75 percentile: 19-24. High school rank: 12% in top tenth, 35% in top quarter, 71% in top half
Early decision deadline: N/A, notification date: N/A
Early action deadline: N/A, notification date: N/A
Application deadline (fall): rolling
Undergraduate student body: 3,534 full time, 913 part time; 38% male, 62% female; 1% American Indian, 2% Asian, 5% black, 4% Hispanic, 4% multiracial, 0% Pacific Islander, 81% white, 4% international; 31% from in state; 23% live on campus; 1% of students in fraternities, 2% in sororities
Most popular majors: 20% Business, Management, Marketing, and Related Support Services, 16% Education, 12% Health Professions and Related Programs, 8% Visual and Performing Arts, 6% Public Administration and Social Service Professions
Expenses: 2021-2022: $9,468 in state, $17,564 out of state; room/board: $9,830
Financial aid: (218) 477-2251; 61% of undergrads determined to have financial need; average aid package $3,292

North Central University[1]

Minneapolis MN
(800) 289-6222
U.S. News ranking: Reg. Coll. (Mid. W), No. 49
Website: www.northcentral.edu
Admissions email: admissions@northcentral.edu
Private; founded 1930
Affiliation: Assemblies of God Church
Application deadline (fall): rolling
Undergraduate student body: N/A full time, N/A part time
Expenses: 2020-2021: $26,280; room/board: $8,180
Financial aid: (612) 343-4485

Southwest Minnesota State University[1]

Marshall MN
(507) 537-6286
U.S. News ranking: Reg. U. (Mid. W), second tier
Website: www.smsu.edu
Admissions email: smsu.admissions@smsu.edu
Public; founded 1963
Application deadline (fall): 9/1
Undergraduate student body: N/A full time, N/A part time
Expenses: 2021-2022: $9,485 in state, $9,485 out of state; room/board: $9,216
Financial aid: (507) 537-6281; 63% of undergrads determined to have financial need; average aid package $10,027

St. Catherine University

St. Paul MN
(800) 945-4599
U.S. News ranking: Nat. U., No. 227
Website: www.stkate.edu
Admissions email: admissions@stkate.edu
Private; founded 1905
Affiliation: Roman Catholic
Freshman admissions: selective; 2020-2021: 1,606 applied, 1,242 accepted. Neither SAT nor ACT required. ACT 25/75 percentile: 19-25. High school rank: 25% in top tenth, 60% in top quarter, 92% in top half
Early decision deadline: N/A, notification date: N/A
Early action deadline: N/A, notification date: N/A
Application deadline (fall): rolling
Undergraduate student body: 1,898 full time, 1,085 part time; 5% male, 95% female; 0% American Indian, 12% Asian, 11% black, 12% Hispanic, 4% multiracial, 0% Pacific Islander, 57% white, 1% international; 74% from in state; 23% live on campus; N/A of students in fraternities, N/A in sororities
Most popular majors: 43% Health Professions and Related Programs, 10% Business, Management, Marketing, and Related Support Services, 8% Psychology, 8% Public Administration and Social Service Professions, 4% Social Sciences
Expenses: 2021-2022: $46,494; room/board: $9,600

Financial aid: (651) 690-6061; 67% of undergrads determined to have financial need; average aid package $37,475

St. Cloud State University

St. Cloud MN
(320) 308-2244
U.S. News ranking: Reg. U. (Mid. W), No. 95
Website: www.stcloudstate.edu
Admissions email:
scsu4u@stcloudstate.edu
Public; founded 1869
Freshman admissions: selective; 2020-2021: 5,251 applied, 4,867 accepted. Neither SAT nor ACT required. ACT 25/75 percentile: 18-24. High school rank: 8% in top tenth, 20% in top quarter, 59% in top half
Early decision deadline: N/A, notification date: N/A
Early action deadline: N/A, notification date: N/A
Application deadline (fall): 8/15
Undergraduate student body: 5,939 full time, 3,685 part time; 46% male, 54% female; 0% American Indian, 7% Asian, 10% black, 5% Hispanic, 3% multiracial, 0% Pacific Islander, 64% white, 10% international; 88% from in state; 15% live on campus; 2% of students in fraternities, 2% in sororities
Most popular majors: 20% Business, Management, Marketing, and Related Support Services, 11% Health Professions and Related Programs, 10% Education, 6% Computer and Information Sciences and Support Services, 6% Psychology
Expenses: 2021-2022: $9,170 in state, $1,288 out of state; room/board: $9,444
Financial aid: (320) 308-2047; 55% of undergrads determined to have financial need; average aid package $13,212

St. John's University

Collegeville MN
(320) 363-5060
U.S. News ranking: Nat. Lib. Arts, No. 105
Website: www.csbsju.edu
Admissions email:
admissions@csbsju.edu
Private; founded 1857
Affiliation: Roman Catholic
Freshman admissions: selective; 2020-2021: 1,595 applied, 1,298 accepted. Neither SAT nor ACT required. ACT 25/75 percentile: 22-27. High school rank: 14% in top tenth, 39% in top quarter, 78% in top half
Early decision deadline: N/A, notification date: N/A
Early action deadline: 12/15, notification date: 1/15
Application deadline (fall): rolling
Undergraduate student body: 1,546 full time, 23 part time; 100% male, 0% female; 1% American Indian, 4% Asian, 5% black, 7% Hispanic, 0% multiracial, 0% Pacific Islander, 79% white, 4% international; 81% from in state; 86% live on campus; 0% of students in fraternities, 0% in

sororities
Most popular majors: 16% Business Administration and Management, General, 15% Accounting, 8% Biology/Biological Sciences, General, 8% Economics, General, 5% Computer Science
Expenses: 2021-2022: $49,842; room/board: $11,592
Financial aid: (320) 363-3664; 66% of undergrads determined to have financial need; average aid package $38,007

St. Mary's University of Minnesota

Winona MN
(507) 457-1700
U.S. News ranking: Reg. U. (Mid. W), No. 34
Website: www.smumn.edu/admission
Admissions email:
admissions@smumn.edu
Private; founded 1912
Affiliation: Roman Catholic
Freshman admissions: selective; 2020-2021: 1,459 applied, 1,355 accepted. Neither SAT nor ACT required. ACT 25/75 percentile: 20-26. High school rank: N/A
Early decision deadline: N/A, notification date: N/A
Early action deadline: N/A, notification date: N/A
Application deadline (fall): 5/1
Undergraduate student body: 1,052 full time, 277 part time; 43% male, 57% female; 0% American Indian, 3% Asian, 7% black, 10% Hispanic, 1% multiracial, 0% Pacific Islander, 71% white, 2% international; 40% from in state; 85% live on campus; 4% of students in fraternities, 3% in sororities
Most popular majors: 15% Business Administration and Management, General, 9% Health/Health Care Administration/Management, 6% Management Science, 6% Registered Nursing/Registered Nurse, 5% Information Science/Studies
Expenses: 2021-2022: $39,410; room/board: $9,920
Financial aid: (612) 238-4552; 74% of undergrads determined to have financial need; average aid package $31,759

St. Olaf College

Northfield MN
(507) 786-3025
U.S. News ranking: Nat. Lib. Arts, No. 62
Website: wp.stolaf.edu/
Admissions email:
admissions@stolaf.edu
Private; founded 1874
Affiliation: Evangelical Lutheran Church
Freshman admissions: more selective; 2020-2021: 5,231 applied, 2,658 accepted. Neither SAT nor ACT required. ACT 25/75 percentile: 25-32. High school rank: 39% in top tenth, 69% in top quarter, 97% in top half
Early decision deadline: 11/15, notification date: 12/15
Early action deadline: 11/1, notification date: 12/23

Application deadline (fall): 1/15
Undergraduate student body: 2,916 full time, 37 part time; 41% male, 59% female; 0% American Indian, 7% Asian, 3% black, 8% Hispanic, 4% multiracial, 0% Pacific Islander, 67% white, 10% international; N/A from in state; 91% live on campus; N/A of students in fraternities, N/A in sororities
Most popular majors: 19% Social Sciences, 12% Biological and Biomedical Sciences, 12% Visual and Performing Arts, 7% Foreign Languages, Literatures, and Linguistics, 7% Psychology
Expenses: 2021-2022: $52,680; room/board: $12,000
Financial aid: (507) 786-3521; 73% of undergrads determined to have financial need; average aid package $42,266

University of Minnesota–Crookston

Crookston MN
(800) 232-6466
U.S. News ranking: Reg. Coll. (Mid. W), No. 25
Website: www.crk.umn.edu
Admissions email:
UMCinfo@umn.edu
Public; founded 1966
Freshman admissions: selective; 2020-2021: 1,616 applied, 1,166 accepted. Neither SAT nor ACT required. ACT 25/75 percentile: 18-22. High school rank: 16% in top tenth, 43% in top quarter, 78% in top half
Early decision deadline: N/A, notification date: N/A
Early action deadline: N/A, notification date: N/A
Application deadline (fall): rolling
Undergraduate student body: 1,128 full time, 1,402 part time; 42% male, 58% female; 1% American Indian, 4% Asian, 4% black, 5% Hispanic, 3% multiracial, 0% Pacific Islander, 74% white, 4% international; 30% from in state; 22% live on campus; N/A of students in fraternities, N/A in sororities
Most popular majors: 41% Business, Management, Marketing, and Related Support Services, 14% Agriculture, Agriculture Operations, and Related Sciences, 11% Health Professions and Related Programs, 8% Multi/Interdisciplinary Studies, 6% Natural Resources and Conservation
Expenses: 2021-2022: $12,556 in state, $12,556 out of state; room/board: N/A
Financial aid: (218) 281-8564; 67% of undergrads determined to have financial need; average aid package $11,696

University of Minnesota–Duluth

Duluth MN
(218) 726-7171
U.S. News ranking: Reg. U. (Mid. W), No. 41
Website: www.d.umn.edu
Admissions email:
umdadmis@d.umn.edu
Public; founded 1947

Freshman admissions: selective; 2020-2021: 9,190 applied, 7,219 accepted. Neither SAT nor ACT required. ACT 25/75 percentile: 21-26. High school rank: 19% in top tenth, 47% in top quarter, 82% in top half
Early decision deadline: N/A, notification date: N/A
Early action deadline: N/A, notification date: N/A
Application deadline (fall): 8/1
Undergraduate student body: 7,943 full time, 1,358 part time; 51% male, 49% female; 1% American Indian, 4% Asian, 2% black, 3% Hispanic, 4% multiracial, 0% Pacific Islander, 84% white, 1% international; 85% from in state; 22% live on campus; N/A of students in fraternities, N/A in sororities
Most popular majors: 6% Marketing/Marketing Management, General, 6% Mechanical Engineering, 6% Psychology, General, 5% Biology/Biological Sciences, General, 4% Finance, General
Expenses: 2021-2022: $13,850 in state, $19,148 out of state; room/board: $8,796
Financial aid: (218) 726-8000; 52% of undergrads determined to have financial need; average aid package $12,881

University of Minnesota Morris

Morris MN
(888) 866-3382
U.S. News ranking: Nat. Lib. Arts, No. 141
Website: morris.umn.edu/
Admissions email:
admissions@morris.umn.edu
Public; founded 1959
Freshman admissions: more selective; 2020-2021: 4,190 applied, 2,709 accepted. Either SAT or ACT required. ACT 25/75 percentile: 21-28. High school rank: 26% in top tenth, 52% in top quarter, 86% in top half
Early decision deadline: N/A, notification date: N/A
Early action deadline: N/A, notification date: N/A
Application deadline (fall): 8/1
Undergraduate student body: 1,209 full time, 125 part time; 40% male, 60% female; 9% American Indian, 2% Asian, 3% black, 7% Hispanic, 17% multiracial, 0% Pacific Islander, 56% white, 5% international; 76% from in state; 46% live on campus; N/A of students in fraternities, N/A in sororities
Most popular majors: 17% Biology/Biological Sciences, General, 8% Psychology, General, 7% Computer Science, 6% Business Administration and Management, General, 6% English Language and Literature, General
Expenses: 2021-2022: $13,848 in state, $15,940 out of state; room/board: $9,064
Financial aid: (320) 589-6046; 66% of undergrads determined to have financial need; average aid package $12,597

University of Minnesota–Twin Cities

Minneapolis MN
(800) 752-1000
U.S. News ranking: Nat. U., No. 68
Website: twin-cities.umn.edu/
Admissions email:
N/A
Public; founded 1851
Freshman admissions: more selective; 2020-2021: 38,237 applied, 26,628 accepted. Neither SAT nor ACT required. ACT 25/75 percentile: 25-31. High school rank: 49% in top tenth, 81% in top quarter, 98% in top half
Early decision deadline: N/A, notification date: N/A
Early action deadline: 11/1, notification date: 1/31
Application deadline (fall): rolling
Undergraduate student body: 28,989 full time, 7,072 part time; 46% male, 54% female; 0% American Indian, 11% Asian, 6% black, 5% Hispanic, 4% multiracial, 0% Pacific Islander, 64% white, 7% international; 74% from in state; 13% live on campus; N/A of students in fraternities, N/A in sororities
Most popular majors: 12% Biological and Biomedical Sciences, 12% Social Sciences, 11% Engineering, 10% Business, Management, Marketing, and Related Support Services, 8% Computer and Information Sciences and Support Services
Expenses: 2021-2022: $15,253 in state, $33,843 out of state; room/board: $11,354
Financial aid: (800) 400-8636; 45% of undergrads determined to have financial need; average aid package $14,114

University of Northwestern–St. Paul

St. Paul MN
(800) 692-4020
U.S. News ranking: Reg. U. (Mid. W), No. 46
Website: www.unwsp.edu
Admissions email:
admissions@unwsp.edu
Private; founded 1902
Affiliation: Undenominational
Freshman admissions: more selective; 2020-2021: 1,080 applied, 996 accepted. Neither SAT nor ACT required. ACT 25/75 percentile: 21-27. High school rank: 29% in top tenth, 50% in top quarter, 80% in top half
Early decision deadline: N/A, notification date: N/A
Early action deadline: 11/15, notification date: 12/1
Application deadline (fall): 8/1
Undergraduate student body: 2,091 full time, 1,272 part time; 37% male, 63% female; 0% American Indian, 3% Asian, 4% black, 5% Hispanic, 4% multiracial, 0% Pacific Islander, 81% white, 1% international; 20% from in state; 57% live on campus; 0% of students in fraternities, 0% in sororities
Most popular majors: 14% Registered Nursing/Registered Nurse, 8% Psychology,

General, 6% Biology/Biological Sciences, General, 5% Business Administration and Management, General, 4% Theological and Ministerial Studies, Other
Expenses: 2021-2022: $34,180; room/board: $10,268
Financial aid: (651) 631-5321; 76% of undergrads determined to have financial need; average aid package $24,708

University of St. Thomas
St. Paul MN
(651) 962-6150
U.S. News ranking: Nat. U., No. 136
Website: www.stthomas.edu
Admissions email: admissions@stthomas.edu
Private; founded 1885
Affiliation: Roman Catholic
Freshman admissions: more selective; 2020-2021: 6,757 applied, 6,047 accepted. Neither SAT nor ACT required. ACT 25/75 percentile: 23-29. High school rank: 22% in top tenth, 56% in top quarter, 89% in top half
Early decision deadline: N/A, notification date: N/A
Early action deadline: N/A, notification date: N/A
Application deadline (fall): rolling
Undergraduate student body: 6,126 full time, 207 part time; 53% male, 47% female; 0% American Indian, 5% Asian, 4% black, 7% Hispanic, 4% multiracial, 0% Pacific Islander, 74% white, 3% international; N/A from in state; 34% live on campus; N/A of students in fraternities, N/A in sororities
Most popular majors: 40% Business, Management, Marketing, and Related Support Services, 9% Biological and Biomedical Sciences, 9% Engineering, 7% Social Sciences, 4% Philosophy and Religious Studies
Expenses: 2021-2022: $48,609; room/board: $11,812
Financial aid: (651) 962-6168; 54% of undergrads determined to have financial need; average aid package $34,828

Winona State University
Winona MN
(507) 457-5100
U.S. News ranking: Reg. U. (Mid. W), No. 41
Website: www.winona.edu
Admissions email: admissions@winona.edu
Public; founded 1858
Freshman admissions: selective; 2020-2021: 6,803 applied, 5,115 accepted. Neither SAT nor ACT required. ACT 25/75 percentile: 19-25. High school rank: 11% in top tenth, 33% in top quarter, 71% in top half
Early decision deadline: N/A, notification date: N/A
Early action deadline: N/A, notification date: N/A
Application deadline (fall): 7/16
Undergraduate student body: 5,476 full time, 932 part time; 34%

male, 66% female; 0% American Indian, 3% Asian, 3% black, 4% Hispanic, 3% multiracial, 0% Pacific Islander, 84% white, 2% international; N/A from in state; 23% live on campus; N/A of students in fraternities, N/A in sororities
Most popular majors: 20% Business, Management, Marketing, and Related Support Services, 18% Health Professions and Related Programs, 16% Education, 6% Parks, Recreation, Leisure, and Fitness Studies, 5% Biological and Biomedical Sciences
Expenses: 2020-2021: $9,780 in state, $15,971 out of state; room/board: $9,310
Financial aid: (507) 457-2800

MISSISSIPPI

Alcorn State University
Lorman MS
(601) 877-6147
U.S. News ranking: Reg. U. (S), No. 74
Website: www.alcorn.edu
Admissions email: ksampson@alcorn.edu
Public; founded 1871
Freshman admissions: selective; 2020-2021: 6,846 applied, 2,582 accepted. Either SAT or ACT required. ACT 25/75 percentile: 16-25. High school rank: 16% in top tenth, 24% in top quarter, 73% in top half
Early decision deadline: N/A, notification date: N/A
Early action deadline: N/A, notification date: N/A
Application deadline (fall): rolling
Undergraduate student body: 2,345 full time, 384 part time; 34% male, 66% female; 0% American Indian, 0% Asian, 90% black, 1% Hispanic, 2% multiracial, 0% Pacific Islander, 2% white, 5% international
Most popular majors: 20% Biological and Biomedical Sciences, 8% Liberal Arts and Sciences, General Studies and Humanities, 7% Business, Management, Marketing, and Related Support Services, 5% Agriculture, Agriculture Operations, and Related Sciences, 5% Psychology
Expenses: 2021-2022: $7,596 in state, $7,596 out of state; room/board: $10,787
Financial aid: (601) 877-6672; 97% of undergrads determined to have financial need; average aid package $8,907

Belhaven University[7]
Jackson MS
(601) 968-5940
U.S. News ranking: Reg. U. (S), No. 54
Website: www.belhaven.edu
Admissions email: admission@belhaven.edu
Private; founded 1883
Affiliation: Presbyterian
Freshman admissions: selective; 2020-2021: 2,172 applied,

1,157 accepted. Neither SAT nor ACT required. ACT 25/75 percentile: 19-23. High school rank: N/A
Early decision deadline: N/A, notification date: N/A
Early action deadline: N/A, notification date: N/A
Application deadline (fall): rolling
Undergraduate student body: 1,177 full time, 951 part time
Most popular majors: 43% Business Administration and Management, General, 7% Applied Psychology, 6% Health/ Health Care Administration/ Management, 5% Bible/Biblical Studies, 5% Registered Nursing/ Registered Nurse
Expenses: 2021-2022: $27,825; room/board: $8,950
Financial aid: (601) 968-5933; 78% of undergrads determined to have financial need; average aid package $15,342

Blue Mountain College
Blue Mountain MS
(662) 685-4161
U.S. News ranking: Reg. Coll. (S), No. 17
Website: bmc.edu/
Admissions email: admissions@bmc.edu
Private; founded 1873
Affiliation: Southern Baptist
Freshman admissions: selective; 2020-2021: 226 applied, 224 accepted. Either SAT or ACT required. ACT 25/75 percentile: 18-23. High school rank: 5% in top tenth, 27% in top quarter, 67% in top half
Early decision deadline: N/A, notification date: N/A
Early action deadline: N/A, notification date: N/A
Application deadline (fall): rolling
Undergraduate student body: 596 full time, 329 part time; 43% male, 57% female; 1% American Indian, 0% Asian, 15% black, 4% Hispanic, 3% multiracial, 0% Pacific Islander, 75% white, 2% international; 79% from in state; 52% live on campus; 0% of students in fraternities, 0% in sororities
Most popular majors: 21% Business Administration and Management, General, 15% Elementary Education and Teaching, 15% Psychology, General, 12% Bible/Biblical Studies, 6% Liberal Arts and Sciences, General Studies and Humanities, Other
Expenses: 2021-2022: $17,380; room/board: $8,120
Financial aid: (662) 685-4771; 79% of undergrads determined to have financial need; average aid package $13,568

Delta State University
Cleveland MS
(662) 846-4020
U.S. News ranking: Reg. U. (S), No. 74
Website: deltastate.edu
Admissions email: admissions@deltastate.edu
Public; founded 1924

Freshman admissions: selective; 2020-2021: 517 applied, 515 accepted. Either SAT or ACT required. ACT 25/75 percentile: 18-23. High school rank: 18% in top tenth, 41% in top quarter, 72% in top half
Early decision deadline: N/A, notification date: N/A
Early action deadline: N/A, notification date: N/A
Application deadline (fall): rolling
Undergraduate student body: 1,667 full time, 664 part time; 41% male, 59% female; 0% American Indian, 0% Asian, 33% black, 2% Hispanic, 2% multiracial, 0% Pacific Islander, 56% white, 5% international; 83% from in state; 34% live on campus; 12% of students in fraternities, 17% in sororities
Most popular majors: 12% Registered Nursing/Registered Nurse, 9% Elementary Education and Teaching, 9% Physical Education Teaching and Coaching, 5% Biology/Biological Sciences, General, 5% Social Work
Expenses: 2021-2022: $8,360 in state, $8,360 out of state; room/board: $8,114
Financial aid: (662) 846-4670; 65% of undergrads determined to have financial need; average aid package $10,464

Jackson State University
Jackson MS
(866) 843-3578
U.S. News ranking: Nat. U., second tier
Website: www.jsums.edu
Admissions email: futuretigers@jsums.edu
Public; founded 1877
Freshman admissions: less selective; 2020-2021: 9,551 applied, 8,594 accepted. Either SAT or ACT required. ACT 25/75 percentile: 17-20. High school rank: N/A
Early decision deadline: N/A, notification date: N/A
Early action deadline: N/A, notification date: N/A
Application deadline (fall): 9/19
Undergraduate student body: 4,171 full time, 497 part time; 34% male, 66% female; 0% American Indian, 0% Asian, 92% black, 1% Hispanic, 1% multiracial, 0% Pacific Islander, 3% white, 2% international
Most popular majors: 12% Biology/ Biological Sciences, General, 8% Multi-/Interdisciplinary Studies, Other, 8% Social Work, 7% Education, Other, 6% Health/ Health Care Administration/ Management
Expenses: 2020-2021: $8,445 in state, $9,445 out of state; room/board: $9,129
Financial aid: (601) 979-2227; 89% of undergrads determined to have financial need; average aid package $11,183

Millsaps College
Jackson MS
(601) 974-1050
U.S. News ranking: Nat. Lib. Arts, No. 114
Website: www.millsaps.edu
Admissions email: admissions@millsaps.edu
Private; founded 1890
Affiliation: United Methodist
Freshman admissions: selective; 2020-2021: 2,796 applied, 1,952 accepted. Either SAT or ACT required. ACT 25/75 percentile: 21-26. High school rank: N/A
Early decision deadline: N/A, notification date: N/A
Early action deadline: 11/15, notification date: 1/15
Application deadline (fall): 7/1
Undergraduate student body: 656 full time, 9 part time; 44% male, 56% female; 1% American Indian, 3% Asian, 24% black, 5% Hispanic, 0% multiracial, 0% Pacific Islander, 61% white, 3% international; 47% from in state; 75% live on campus; 51% of students in fraternities, 47% in sororities
Most popular majors: 26% Business Administration and Management, General, 11% Biology/Biological Sciences, General, 10% Accounting, 9% Psychology, General, 6% Political Science and Government, General
Expenses: 2021-2022: $42,960; room/board: $14,210
Financial aid: (601) 974-1220; 68% of undergrads determined to have financial need; average aid package $36,986

Mississippi College
Clinton MS
(601) 925-3800
U.S. News ranking: Nat. U., second tier
Website: www.mc.edu
Admissions email: admissions@mc.edu
Private; founded 1826
Affiliation: Southern Baptist
Freshman admissions: more selective; 2020-2021: 2,559 applied, 736 accepted. Either SAT or ACT required. ACT 25/75 percentile: 21-29. High school rank: 35% in top tenth, 53% in top quarter, 76% in top half
Early decision deadline: N/A, notification date: N/A
Early action deadline: N/A, notification date: N/A
Application deadline (fall): rolling
Undergraduate student body: 2,291 full time, 466 part time; 40% male, 60% female; 0% American Indian, 2% Asian, 18% black, 4% Hispanic, 2% multiracial, 0% Pacific Islander, 71% white, 3% international; 69% from in state; 55% live on campus; 24% of students in fraternities, 34% in sororities
Most popular majors: 20% Registered Nursing/Registered Nurse, 8% Kinesiology and Exercise Science, 7% Biomedical Sciences, General, 7% Business Administration and Management, General, 6% Psychology, General

Expenses: 2021-2022: $20,302; room/board: $11,400
Financial aid: (601) 925-3212; 39% of undergrads determined to have financial need; average aid package $19,387

Mississippi State University
Mississippi State MS
(662) 325-2224
U.S. News ranking: Nat. U., No. 196
Website: www.msstate.edu
Admissions email: admit@admissions.msstate.edu
Public; founded 1878
Freshman admissions: more selective; 2020-2021: 16,151 applied, 12,924 accepted. Either SAT or ACT required. ACT 25/75 percentile: 22-30. High school rank: 29% in top tenth, 55% in top quarter, 83% in top half
Early decision deadline: N/A, notification date: N/A
Early action deadline: N/A, notification date: N/A
Application deadline (fall): rolling
Undergraduate student body: 17,089 full time, 1,714 part time; 50% male, 50% female; 1% American Indian, 2% Asian, 17% black, 3% Hispanic, 2% multiracial, 0% Pacific Islander, 73% white, 1% international; 32% from in state; 26% live on campus; 15% of students in fraternities, 18% in sororities
Most popular majors: 20% Business, Management, Marketing, and Related Support Services, 16% Engineering, 7% Agriculture, 7% Multi/Interdisciplinary Studies, 6% Agriculture, Agriculture Operations, and Related Sciences
Expenses: 2021-2022: $9,220 in state, $24,900 out of state; room/board: $10,630
Financial aid: (662) 325-2450; 67% of undergrads determined to have financial need; average aid package $14,320

Mississippi University for Women
Columbus MS
(662) 329-7106
U.S. News ranking: Reg. U. (S), No. 44
Website: www.muw.edu
Admissions email: admissions@muw.edu
Public; founded 1884
Freshman admissions: selective; 2020-2021: 516 applied, 511 accepted. Either SAT or ACT required. ACT 25/75 percentile: 19-24. High school rank: 31% in top tenth, 63% in top quarter, 86% in top half
Early decision deadline: N/A, notification date: N/A
Early action deadline: N/A, notification date: N/A
Application deadline (fall): rolling
Undergraduate student body: 1,835 full time, 583 part time; 20% male, 80% female; 2% American Indian, 1% Asian, 41% black, 0% Hispanic, 0% multiracial, 0% Pacific Islander, 55% white, 1% international; 88% from in

state; 15% live on campus; 3% of students in fraternities, 9% in sororities
Most popular majors: 48% Registered Nursing/Registered Nurse, 14% Business Administration and Management, General, 5% Psychology, General, 5% Public Health Education and Promotion, 3% Elementary Education and Teaching
Expenses: 2021-2022: $7,756 in state, $7,756 out of state; room/board: $7,908
Financial aid: (662) 329-7114; 74% of undergrads determined to have financial need; average aid package $8,656

Mississippi Valley State University
Itta Bena MS
(662) 254-3344
U.S. News ranking: Reg. U. (S), second tier
Website: www.mvsu.edu
Admissions email: admsn@mvsu.edu
Public; founded 1950
Freshman admissions: less selective; 2020-2021: 3,351 applied, 2,772 accepted. Either SAT or ACT required. ACT 25/75 percentile: 14-18. High school rank: 15% in top tenth, 35% in top quarter, 50% in top half
Early decision deadline: N/A, notification date: N/A
Early action deadline: N/A, notification date: N/A
Application deadline (fall): 8/17
Undergraduate student body: 1,231 full time, 463 part time; 40% male, 60% female; 0% American Indian, 0% Asian, 94% black, 2% Hispanic, 1% multiracial, 0% Pacific Islander, 1% white, 0% international; 67% from in state; 45% live on campus; 0% of students in fraternities, 0% in sororities
Most popular majors: 12% Business, Management, Marketing, and Related Support Services, 11% Public Administration and Social Service Professions, 10% Biological and Biomedical Sciences, 9% Liberal Arts and Sciences, General Studies and Humanities, 9% Parks, Recreation, Leisure, and Fitness Studies
Expenses: 2020-2021: $6,746 in state, $6,746 out of state; room/board: $7,998
Financial aid: (662) 254-3335

Rust College[1]
Holly Springs MS
(662) 252-8000
U.S. News ranking: Nat. Lib. Arts, second tier
Website: www.rustcollege.edu
Admissions email: admissions@rustcollege.edu
Private; founded 1866
Affiliation: United Methodist
Application deadline (fall): rolling
Undergraduate student body: N/A full time, N/A part time
Expenses: 2020-2021: $9,900, room/board: $4,300
Financial aid: (662) 252-8000

Tougaloo College[1]
Tougaloo MS
(601) 977-7768
U.S. News ranking: Nat. Lib. Arts, second tier
Website: www.tougaloo.edu
Admissions email: admission@tougaloo.edu
Private; founded 1869
Affiliation: United Church of Christ
Application deadline (fall): 7/1
Undergraduate student body: N/A full time, N/A part time
Expenses: 2021-2022: $11,398; room/board: $6,720
Financial aid: (601) 977-7769; 85% of undergrads determined to have financial need; average aid package $12,500

University of Mississippi
University MS
(662) 915-7226
U.S. News ranking: Nat. U., No. 148
Website: www.olemiss.edu
Admissions email: admissions@olemiss.edu
Public; founded 1848
Freshman admissions: more selective; 2020-2021: 16,383 applied, 14,421 accepted. Neither SAT nor ACT required. ACT 25/75 percentile: 22-30. High school rank: 23% in top tenth, 46% in top quarter, 77% in top half
Early decision deadline: N/A, notification date: N/A
Early action deadline: N/A, notification date: N/A
Application deadline (fall): rolling
Undergraduate student body: 14,839 full time, 1,340 part time; 42% male, 58% female; 0% American Indian, 2% Asian, 12% black, 4% Hispanic, 2% multiracial, 0% Pacific Islander, 77% white, 1% international; 60% from in state; 23% live on campus; 35% of students in fraternities, 45% in sororities
Most popular majors: 9% Digital Communication and Media/Multimedia, 8% Accounting, 5% Multi/Interdisciplinary Studies, 4% Finance, General, 4% Psychology, General
Expenses: 2021-2022: $9,034 in state, $25,876 out of state; room/board: $11,142
Financial aid: (662) 915-5788; 49% of undergrads determined to have financial need; average aid package $12,246

University of Southern Mississippi
Hattiesburg MS
(601) 266-5000
U.S. News ranking: Nat. U., second tier
Website: www.usm.edu/admissions
Admissions email: admissions@usm.edu
Public; founded 1910
Freshman admissions: selective; 2020-2021: 9,683 applied, 9,328 accepted. Either SAT or ACT required. ACT 25/75 percentile: 19-26. High school rank: N/A
Early decision deadline: N/A,

notification date: N/A
Early action deadline: N/A, notification date: N/A
Application deadline (fall): rolling
Undergraduate student body: 9,644 full time, 1,807 part time; 36% male, 64% female; 0% American Indian, 1% Asian, 29% black, 4% Hispanic, 3% multiracial, 0% Pacific Islander, 61% white, 1% international; 32% from in state; 23% live on campus; 10% of students in fraternities, 14% in sororities
Most popular majors: 15% Business Administration and Management, General, 14% Registered Nursing/Registered Nurse, 11% Elementary Education and Teaching, 10% Biology/Biological Sciences, General, 10% Psychology, General
Expenses: 2020-2021: $9,160 in state, $11,160 out of state; room/board: $11,260
Financial aid: (601) 266-4774

William Carey University
Hattiesburg MS
(601) 318-6103
U.S. News ranking: Nat. U., second tier
Website: www.wmcarey.edu
Admissions email: admissions@wmcarey.edu
Private; founded 1892
Affiliation: Southern Baptist
Freshman admissions: more selective; 2020-2021: 758 applied, 419 accepted. Either SAT or ACT required. ACT 25/75 percentile: 20-28. High school rank: 27% in top tenth, 61% in top quarter, 85% in top half
Early decision deadline: N/A, notification date: N/A
Early action deadline: N/A, notification date: N/A
Application deadline (fall): rolling
Undergraduate student body: 1,974 full time, 1,290 part time; 33% male, 67% female; 0% American Indian, 1% Asian, 27% black, 2% Hispanic, 0% multiracial, 0% Pacific Islander, 62% white, 5% international; 79% from in state; 20% live on campus; 0% of students in fraternities, 2% in sororities
Most popular majors: 18% Registered Nursing/Registered Nurse, 11% Biology/Biological Sciences, General, 9% Business Administration and Management, General, 9% Elementary Education and Teaching, 9% Psychology, General
Expenses: 2021-2022: $14,100; room/board: $4,695
Financial aid: (601) 318-6153; 94% of undergrads determined to have financial need; average aid package $17,000

Avila University[1]
Kansas City MO
(816) 501-2400
U.S. News ranking: Reg. U. (Mid. W), second tier
Website: www.Avila.edu

Admissions email: admissions@mail.avila.edu
Private
Application deadline (fall): N/A
Undergraduate student body: N/A full time, N/A part time
Expenses: 2020-2021: $21,115; room/board: $8,815
Financial aid: N/A

Central Methodist University – College of Liberal Arts and Sciences
Fayette MO
(660) 248-6251
U.S. News ranking: Reg. Coll. (Mid. W), No. 40
Website: www.centralmethodist.edu
Admissions email: admissions@centralmethodist.edu
Private; founded 1854
Affiliation: United Methodist
Freshman admissions: selective; 2020-2021: 1,310 applied, 1,249 accepted. Neither SAT nor ACT required. ACT 25/75 percentile: 18-23. High school rank: 14% in top tenth, 23% in top quarter, 69% in top half
Early decision deadline: N/A, notification date: N/A
Early action deadline: N/A, notification date: N/A
Application deadline (fall): 8/15
Undergraduate student body: 1,130 full time, 11 part time; 50% male, 50% female; 0% American Indian, 1% Asian, 11% black, 10% Hispanic, 4% multiracial, 0% Pacific Islander, 66% white, 5% international; 68% from in state; 69% live on campus; 17% of students in fraternities, 24% in sororities
Most popular majors: 18% Health Professions and Related Programs, 14% Biological and Biomedical Sciences, 11% Business, Management, Marketing, and Related Support Services
Expenses: 2021-2022: $26,470; room/board: $8,650
Financial aid: (660) 248-6245

College of the Ozarks
Point Lookout MO
(800) 222-0525
U.S. News ranking: Reg. Coll. (Mid. W), No. 1
Website: www.cofo.edu
Admissions email: admissions@cofo.edu
Private; founded 1906
Affiliation: Interdenominational
Freshman admissions: more selective; 2020-2021: 2,437 applied, 348 accepted. Either SAT or ACT required. ACT 25/75 percentile: 21-25. High school rank: 26% in top tenth, 67% in top quarter, 92% in top half
Early decision deadline: N/A, notification date: N/A
Early action deadline: N/A, notification date: N/A
Application deadline (fall): rolling
Undergraduate student body: 1,476 full time, 13 part time; 45% male, 55% female; 1% American Indian, 1% Asian, 1% black, 4% Hispanic, 3% multiracial,

0% Pacific Islander, 86% white, 2% international; 65% from in state; 92% live on campus; 0% of students in fraternities, 0% in sororities
Most popular majors: 8% Business Administration and Management, General, 6% Elementary Education and Teaching, 6% Psychology, General, 5% Registered Nursing/Registered Nurse, 4% Criminal Justice/Safety Studies
Expenses: 2021-2022: $19,960; room/board: $7,900
Financial aid: (417) 690-3292; 90% of undergrads determined to have financial need; average aid package $19,500

Columbia College[1]
Columbia MO
(573) 875-7352
U.S. News ranking: Reg. U. (Mid. W), second tier
Website: www.ccis.edu
Admissions email: admissions@ccis.edu
Private; founded 1851
Application deadline (fall): rolling
Undergraduate student body: N/A full time, N/A part time
Expenses: 2020-2021: $24,320; room/board: $8,500
Financial aid: (573) 875-7390

Cottey College
Nevada MO
(888) 526-8839
U.S. News ranking: Reg. Coll. (Mid. W), No. 4
Website: www.cottey.edu
Admissions email: admit@cottey.edu
Private; founded 1884
Freshman admissions: selective; 2020-2021: 329 applied, 325 accepted. Neither SAT nor ACT required. ACT 25/75 percentile: 19-24. High school rank: 18% in top tenth, 36% in top quarter, 72% in top half
Early decision deadline: N/A, notification date: N/A
Early action deadline: N/A, notification date: N/A
Application deadline (fall): rolling
Undergraduate student body: 278 full time, 5 part time; 0% male, 100% female; 1% American Indian, 1% Asian, 5% black, 11% Hispanic, 2% multiracial, 0% Pacific Islander, 70% white, 10% international; 23% from in state; 69% live on campus; 0% of students in fraternities, 0% in sororities
Most popular majors: 28% Research and Experimental Psychology, Other, 23% Biology/Biological Sciences, General, 9% Business/Commerce, General, 9% Education, General, 9% English Language and Literature, General
Expenses: 2021-2022: $23,114; room/board: $7,918
Financial aid: (417) 667-8181; 79% of undergrads determined to have financial need; average aid package $22,958

Culver-Stockton College
Canton MO
(800) 537-1883
U.S. News ranking: Reg. Coll. (Mid. W), No. 34
Website: www.culver.edu
Admissions email: admission@culver.edu
Private; founded 1853
Affiliation: Christian Church (Disciples of Christ)
Freshman admissions: selective; 2020-2021: 1,618 applied, 1,591 accepted. Either SAT or ACT required. ACT 25/75 percentile: 18-22. High school rank: 8% in top tenth, 25% in top quarter, 61% in top half
Early decision deadline: N/A, notification date: N/A
Early action deadline: N/A, notification date: N/A
Application deadline (fall): rolling
Undergraduate student body: 860 full time, 94 part time; 55% male, 45% female; 1% American Indian, 1% Asian, 16% black, 7% Hispanic, 3% multiracial, 0% Pacific Islander, 68% white, 3% international; 44% from in state; 81% live on campus; 39% of students in fraternities, 47% in sororities
Most popular majors: 13% Business Administration and Management, General, 13% Psychology, General, 8% Criminal Justice/Law Enforcement Administration, 7% Health and Wellness, General, 7% Registered Nursing/Registered Nurse
Expenses: 2021-2022: $28,495; room/board: $9,045
Financial aid: (573) 288-6307; 82% of undergrads determined to have financial need; average aid package $21,322

Drury University
Springfield MO
(417) 873-7205
U.S. News ranking: Reg. U. (Mid. W), No. 12
Website: www.drury.edu
Admissions email: druryad@drury.edu
Private; founded 1873
Affiliation: Christian Church (Disciples of Christ)
Freshman admissions: more selective; 2020-2021: 1,602 applied, 1,133 accepted. Neither SAT nor ACT required. ACT 25/75 percentile: 21-28. High school rank: 26% in top tenth, 64% in top quarter, 94% in top half
Early decision deadline: N/A, notification date: N/A
Early action deadline: N/A, notification date: N/A
Application deadline (fall): 8/30
Undergraduate student body: 1,382 full time, 27 part time; 44% male, 56% female; 1% American Indian, 1% Asian, 4% black, 2% Hispanic, 3% multiracial, 0% Pacific Islander, 78% white, 7% international; 79% from in state; 64% live on campus; 16% of students in fraternities, 25% in sororities
Most popular majors: 23% Biological and Biomedical

Sciences, 17% Business, Management, Marketing, and Related Support Services, 8% Architecture and Related Services, 7% Communication, Journalism, and Related Programs, 7% Social Sciences
Expenses: 2021-2022: $32,415; room/board: $9,394
Financial aid: (417) 873-7312; 67% of undergrads determined to have financial need; average aid package $24,013

Evangel University[7]
Springfield MO
(800) 382-6435
U.S. News ranking: Reg. U. (Mid. W), second tier
Website: www.evangel.edu
Admissions email: admissions@evangel.edu
Private; founded 1955
Affiliation: Assemblies of God Church
Freshman admissions: selective; 2020-2021: N/A applied, N/A accepted. Neither SAT nor ACT required. ACT 25/75 percentile: 20-26. High school rank: N/A
Early decision deadline: N/A, notification date: N/A
Early action deadline: N/A, notification date: N/A
Application deadline (fall): rolling
Undergraduate student body: 1,264 full time, 115 part time
Most popular majors: 11% Business Administration and Management, General, 8% Elementary Education and Teaching, 6% Biology/Biological Sciences, General, 5% Biology/Biological Sciences, General, 5% Psychology, General
Expenses: 2021-2022: $25,648; room/board: $9,040
Financial aid: (417) 865-2811

Fontbonne University
St. Louis MO
(314) 889-1400
U.S. News ranking: Reg. U. (Mid. W), No. 51
Website: www.fontbonne.edu
Admissions email: admissions@fontbonne.edu
Private; founded 1923
Affiliation: Roman Catholic
Freshman admissions: selective; 2020-2021: 717 applied, 612 accepted. Neither SAT nor ACT required. ACT 25/75 percentile: 17-23. High school rank: N/A
Early decision deadline: N/A, notification date: N/A
Early action deadline: N/A, notification date: N/A
Application deadline (fall): rolling
Undergraduate student body: 728 full time, 88 part time; 38% male, 62% female; 0% American Indian, 2% Asian, 23% black, 2% Hispanic, 4% multiracial, 0% Pacific Islander, 62% white, 3% international; 85% from in state; 33% live on campus; N/A of students in fraternities, N/A in sororities
Most popular majors: 11% Business Administration and Management, General, 8% General Studies, 8% Special Education and Teaching, General,

7% Social Work, 6% Dietetics/Dietitian
Expenses: 2021-2022: $28,200; room/board: $10,700
Financial aid: (314) 889-1414; 82% of undergrads determined to have financial need; average aid package $12,766

Hannibal-LaGrange University[1]
Hannibal MO
(800) 454-1119
U.S. News ranking: Reg. Coll. (Mid. W), No. 55
Website: www.hlg.edu
Admissions email: admissions@hlg.edu
Private; founded 1858
Affiliation: Southern Baptist
Application deadline (fall): 8/27
Undergraduate student body: N/A full time, N/A part time
Expenses: 2020-2021: $24,000; room/board: $8,300
Financial aid: N/A

Harris-Stowe State University[1]
St. Louis MO
(314) 340-3300
U.S. News ranking: Reg. Coll. (Mid. W), second tier
Website: www.hssu.edu
Admissions email: admissions@hssu.edu
Public; founded 1857
Application deadline (fall): rolling
Undergraduate student body: N/A full time, N/A part time
Expenses: 2020-2021: $5,484 in state, $10,116 out of state; room/board: $9,491
Financial aid: (314) 340-3502

Kansas City Art Institute[1]
Kansas City MO
(816) 472-4852
U.S. News ranking: Arts, unranked
Website: www.kcai.edu
Admissions email: admiss@kcai.edu
Private; founded 1885
Application deadline (fall): N/A
Undergraduate student body: N/A full time, N/A part time
Expenses: 2020-2021: $40,100; room/board: $11,900
Financial aid: (816) 802-3448

Lincoln University
Jefferson City MO
(573) 681-5102
U.S. News ranking: Reg. Coll. (Mid. W), second tier
Website: www.lincolnu.edu
Admissions email: admissions@lincolnu.edu
Public; founded 1866
Freshman admissions: less selective; 2020-2021: 4,840 applied, 2,965 accepted. Either SAT or ACT required. ACT 25/75 percentile: 14-19. High school rank: 4% in top tenth, 12% in top quarter, 41% in top half
Early decision deadline: N/A, notification date: N/A

Early action deadline: N/A, notification date: N/A
Application deadline (fall): rolling
Undergraduate student body: 1,312 full time, 580 part time; 40% male, 60% female; 0% American Indian, 1% Asian, 57% black, 3% Hispanic, 4% multiracial, 0% Pacific Islander, 27% white, 4% international; 70% from in state; 47% live on campus; N/A of students in fraternities, N/A in sororities
Most popular majors: 14% Business Administration and Management, General, 13% Registered Nursing/Registered Nurse, 8% Criminal Justice/Law Enforcement Administration, 7% Biology/Biological Sciences, General, 7% Elementary Education and Teaching
Expenses: 2020-2021: $7,910 in state, $14,712 out of state; room/board: $7,282
Financial aid: (573) 681-5032

Lindenwood University
St. Charles MO
(636) 949-4949
U.S. News ranking: Nat. U., second tier
Website: www.lindenwood.edu
Admissions email: admissions@lindenwood.edu
Private; founded 1827
Freshman admissions: selective; 2020-2021: 2,695 applied, 2,483 accepted. Neither SAT nor ACT required. ACT 25/75 percentile: 19-25. High school rank: N/A
Early decision deadline: N/A, notification date: N/A
Early action deadline: N/A, notification date: N/A
Application deadline (fall): rolling
Undergraduate student body: 4,199 full time, 623 part time; 44% male, 56% female; 0% American Indian, 1% Asian, 14% black, 5% Hispanic, 3% multiracial, 1% Pacific Islander, 60% white, 9% international; 65% from in state; 42% live on campus; 2% of students in fraternities, 5% in sororities
Most popular majors: 18% Business/Commerce, General, 6% Kinesiology and Exercise Science, 5% Criminal Justice/Safety Studies, 4% Marketing/Marketing Management, General, 4% Psychology, General
Expenses: 2021-2022: $18,640; room/board: $10,200
Financial aid: (636) 949-4923; 62% of undergrads determined to have financial need; average aid package $16,896

Maryville University of St. Louis
St Louis MO
(800) 627-9855
U.S. News ranking: Nat. U., No. 202
Website: www.maryville.edu
Admissions email: admissions@maryville.edu
Private; founded 1872
Freshman admissions: selective; 2020-2021: 2,503 applied,

2,375 accepted. Neither SAT nor ACT required. ACT 25/75 percentile: 19-26. High school rank: 26% in top tenth, 58% in top quarter, 85% in top half
Early decision deadline: N/A, notification date: N/A
Early action deadline: N/A, notification date: N/A
Application deadline (fall): 8/28
Undergraduate student body: 3,249 full time, 2,255 part time; 33% male, 67% female; 1% American Indian, 3% Asian, 14% black, 8% Hispanic, 3% multiracial, 0% Pacific Islander, 64% white, 2% international; 53% from in state; 11% live on campus; 0% of students in fraternities, 0% in sororities
Most popular majors: 35% Health Professions and Related Programs, 18% Business, Management, Marketing, and Related Support Services, 10% Psychology, 8% Military Technologies and Applied Sciences, 7% Biological and Biomedical Sciences
Expenses: 2021-2022: $27,166; room/board: $12,000
Financial aid: (314) 529-2827; 66% of undergrads determined to have financial need; average aid package $19,790

Missouri Baptist University[1]
St. Louis MO
(314) 434-2290
U.S. News ranking: Reg. U. (Mid. W), second tier
Website: www.mobap.edu
Admissions email: admissions@mobap.edu
Private; founded 1964
Application deadline (fall): rolling
Undergraduate student body: N/A full time, N/A part time
Expenses: 2020-2021: $29,360; room/board: $10,730
Financial aid: (314) 744-7639

Missouri Southern State University[1]
Joplin MO
(417) 781-6778
U.S. News ranking: Reg. Coll. (Mid. W), second tier
Website: www.mssu.edu
Admissions email: admissions@mssu.edu
Public; founded 1937
Application deadline (fall): rolling
Undergraduate student body: N/A full time, N/A part time
Expenses: 2020-2021: $7,462 in state, $14,924 out of state; room/board: $7,137
Financial aid: (417) 659-5422

Missouri State University[1]
Springfield MO
(800) 492-7900
U.S. News ranking: Nat. U., second tier
Website: www.missouristate.edu
Admissions email: info@missouristate.edu
Public; founded 1906
Undergraduate student body: N/A full time, N/A part time

Expenses: 2020-2021: $7,938 in state, $16,608 out of state; room/board: $9,284
Financial aid: (417) 836-5262

Missouri University of Science and Technology
Rolla MO
(573) 341-4165
U.S. News ranking: Nat. U., No. 179
Website: www.mst.edu
Admissions email: admissions@mst.edu
Public; founded 1870
Freshman admissions: more selective; 2020-2021: 5,528 applied, 4,503 accepted. Neither SAT nor ACT required. ACT 25/75 percentile: 25-31. High school rank: 42% in top tenth, 74% in top quarter, 95% in top half
Early decision deadline: N/A, notification date: N/A
Early action deadline: N/A, notification date: N/A
Application deadline (fall): 7/1
Undergraduate student body: 5,412 full time, 674 part time; 77% male, 23% female; 0% American Indian, 4% Asian, 3% black, 5% Hispanic, 3% multiracial, 0% Pacific Islander, 81% white, 2% international; 88% from in state; 45% live on campus; 26% of students in fraternities, 28% in sororities
Most popular majors: 67% Engineering, 12% Computer and Information Sciences and Support Services, 6% Engineering Technologies and Engineering-Related Fields, 5% Physical Sciences, 4% Biological and Biomedical Sciences
Expenses: 2021-2022: $11,234 in state, $31,286 out of state; room/board: $11,028
Financial aid: (573) 341-4282; 56% of undergrads determined to have financial need; average aid package $15,654

Missouri Valley College
Marshall MO
(660) 831-4114
U.S. News ranking: Reg. Coll. (Mid. W), second tier
Website: www.moval.edu
Admissions email: admissions@moval.edu
Private; founded 1889
Affiliation: Presbyterian
Freshman admissions: less selective; 2020-2021: 2,898 applied, 1,802 accepted. Neither SAT nor ACT required. ACT 25/75 percentile: 15-20. High school rank: N/A
Early decision deadline: N/A, notification date: N/A
Early action deadline: N/A, notification date: N/A
Application deadline (fall): rolling
Undergraduate student body: 1,679 full time, 59 part time; 52% male, 48% female; 0% American Indian, 1% Asian, 17% black, 11% Hispanic, 5% multiracial, 3% Pacific Islander, 42% white, 19% international; N/A from in

state; 69% live on campus; 5% of students in fraternities, 5% in sororities
Most popular majors: 28% Business, Management, Marketing, and Related Support Services, 13% Parks, Recreation, Leisure, and Fitness Studies, 8% Health Professions and Related Programs, 7% Education, 7% Homeland Security, Law Enforcement, Firefighting and Related Protective Services
Expenses: 2021-2022: $22,000; room/board: $11,000
Financial aid: N/A

Missouri Western State University[1]
St. Joseph MO
(816) 271-4266
U.S. News ranking: Reg. U. (Mid. W), second tier
Website: www.missouriwestern.edu
Admissions email: admission@missouriwestern.edu
Public; founded 1969
Application deadline (fall): rolling
Undergraduate student body: N/A full time, N/A part time
Expenses: 2020-2021: $8,875 in state, $15,300 out of state; room/board: $10,030
Financial aid: (816) 271-4361

Northwest Missouri State University
Maryville MO
(800) 633-1175
U.S. News ranking: Reg. U. (Mid. W), No. 101
Website: www.nwmissouri.edu
Admissions email: admissions@nwmissouri.edu
Public; founded 1905
Freshman admissions: selective; 2020-2021: 8,144 applied, 5,816 accepted. Either SAT or ACT required. ACT 25/75 percentile: 19-24. High school rank: 17% in top tenth, 42% in top quarter, 78% in top half
Early decision deadline: N/A, notification date: N/A
Early action deadline: N/A, notification date: N/A
Application deadline (fall): rolling
Undergraduate student body: 4,813 full time, 669 part time; 41% male, 59% female; 0% American Indian, 1% Asian, 5% black, 4% Hispanic, 3% multiracial, 0% Pacific Islander, 83% white, 2% international; 69% from in state; 33% live on campus; 17% of students in fraternities, 16% in sororities
Most popular majors: 21% Health Professions and Related Programs, 20% Education, 11% Agriculture, Agriculture Operations, and Related Sciences, 9% Psychology, 6% Health Professions and Related Programs
Expenses: 2021-2022: $11,066 in state, $18,649 out of state; room/board: $10,696
Financial aid: (660) 562-1138; 67% of undergrads determined to have financial need; average aid package $10,864

Park University
Parkville MO
(877) 505-1059
U.S. News ranking: Reg. U. (Mid. W), second tier
Website: www.park.edu
Admissions email: enrollmentservices@park.edu
Private; founded 1875
Freshman admissions: less selective; 2020-2021: N/A applied, N/A accepted. Neither SAT nor ACT required. ACT 25/75 percentile: 17-23. High school rank: N/A
Early decision deadline: N/A, notification date: N/A
Early action deadline: N/A, notification date: N/A
Application deadline (fall): rolling
Undergraduate student body: 3,763 full time, 4,741 part time; 54% male, 46% female; 1% American Indian, 2% Asian, 19% black, 23% Hispanic, 6% multiracial, 1% Pacific Islander, 44% white, 2% international; 23% from in state; 3% live on campus; 0% of students in fraternities, 0% in sororities
Most popular majors: 27% Business Administration and Management, General, 13% Social Psychology, 9% Computer and Information Sciences, General, 8% Criminal Justice/Law Enforcement Administration, 8% Human Resources Management/Personnel Administration, General
Expenses: 2021-2022: $13,500; room/board: $8,084
Financial aid: (816) 584-6250; 71% of undergrads determined to have financial need; average aid package $8,690

Ranken Technical College[1]
Saint Louis MO
(314) 371-0236
U.S. News ranking: Reg. Coll. (Mid. W), second tier
Website: www.ranken.edu
Admissions email: N/A
Private
Application deadline (fall): N/A
Undergraduate student body: N/A full time, N/A part time
Expenses: 2020-2021: $15,947; room/board: $5,900
Financial aid: N/A

Rockhurst University
Kansas City MO
(816) 501-4100
U.S. News ranking: Reg. U. (Mid. W), No. 24
Website: www.rockhurst.edu
Admissions email: admission@rockhurst.edu
Private; founded 1910
Affiliation: Roman Catholic
Freshman admissions: more selective; 2020-2021: 3,629 applied, 2,645 accepted. Neither SAT nor ACT required. ACT 25/75 percentile: 21-27. High school rank: 24% in top tenth, 50% in top quarter, 83% in top half
Early decision deadline: N/A, notification date: N/A

Early action deadline: N/A, notification date: N/A
Application deadline (fall): rolling
Undergraduate student body: 1,845 full time, 901 part time; 35% male, 65% female; 1% American Indian, 4% Asian, 10% black, 13% Hispanic, 2% multiracial, 0% Pacific Islander, 64% white, 2% international; 37% from in state; 36% live on campus; 36% of students in fraternities, 40% in sororities
Most popular majors: 45% Health Professions and Related Programs, 14% Business, Management, Marketing, and Related Support Services, 8% Biological and Biomedical Sciences, 7% Psychology
Expenses: 2021-2022: $40,480; room/board: $10,030
Financial aid: (816) 501-4600; 69% of undergrads determined to have financial need; average aid package $30,267

Saint Louis University
St. Louis MO
(314) 977-2500
U.S. News ranking: Nat. U., No. 103
Website: www.slu.edu
Admissions email: admission@slu.edu
Private; founded 1818
Affiliation: Roman Catholic
Freshman admissions: more selective; 2020-2021: 16,580 applied, 9,208 accepted. Neither SAT nor ACT required. ACT 25/75 percentile: 25-31. High school rank: 39% in top tenth, 70% in top quarter, 91% in top half
Early decision deadline: N/A, notification date: N/A
Early action deadline: N/A, notification date: N/A
Application deadline (fall): rolling
Undergraduate student body: 6,856 full time, 501 part time; 39% male, 61% female; 0% American Indian, 12% Asian, 6% black, 7% Hispanic, 4% multiracial, 0% Pacific Islander, 65% white, 4% international; 38% from in state; 48% live on campus; 11% of students in fraternities, 25% in sororities
Most popular majors: 28% Health Professions and Related Programs, 19% Business, Management, Marketing, and Related Support Services, 8% Engineering, 7% Biological and Biomedical Sciences, 6% Parks, Recreation, Leisure, and Fitness Studies
Expenses: 2021-2022: $48,824; room/board: $13,310
Financial aid: (314) 977-2350; 60% of undergrads determined to have financial need; average aid package $37,807

Southeast Missouri State University
Cape Girardeau MO
(573) 651-2590
U.S. News ranking: Reg. U. (Mid. W), No. 74
Website: www.semo.edu
Admissions email: admissions@semo.edu
Public; founded 1873

Freshman admissions: selective; 2020-2021: 4,871 applied, 4,546 accepted. Neither SAT nor ACT required. ACT 25/75 percentile: 19-25. High school rank: 18% in top tenth, 46% in top quarter, 78% in top half
Early decision deadline: N/A, notification date: N/A
Early action deadline: N/A, notification date: N/A
Application deadline (fall): 7/1
Undergraduate student body: 6,823 full time, 2,106 part time; 39% male, 61% female; 0% American Indian, 1% Asian, 10% black, 3% Hispanic, 2% multiracial, 0% Pacific Islander, 79% white, 4% international; 79% from in state; 30% live on campus; 21% of students in fraternities, 18% in sororities
Most popular majors: 15% Business, Management, Marketing, and Related Support Services, 11% Education, 10% Health Professions and Related Programs, 9% Communication, Journalism, and Related Programs, 9% Liberal Arts and Sciences, General Studies and Humanities
Expenses: 2021-2022: $8,715 in state, $15,285 out of state; room/board: $9,834
Financial aid: (573) 651-2253; 63% of undergrads determined to have financial need; average aid package $10,006

Southwest Baptist University
Bolivar MO
(417) 328-1810
U.S. News ranking: Reg. U. (Mid. W), No. 117
Website: www.sbuniv.edu
Admissions email: admissions@sbuniv.edu
Private; founded 1878
Affiliation: Southern Baptist
Freshman admissions: selective; 2020-2021: 1,542 applied, 1,135 accepted. Either SAT or ACT required. ACT 25/75 percentile: 19-25. High school rank: 22% in top tenth, 47% in top quarter, 81% in top half
Early decision deadline: N/A, notification date: N/A
Early action deadline: N/A, notification date: N/A
Application deadline (fall): rolling
Undergraduate student body: 1,593 full time, 786 part time; 37% male, 63% female; 1% American Indian, 1% Asian, 5% black, 4% Hispanic, 2% multiracial, 0% Pacific Islander, 76% white, 2% international; 74% from in state; 43% live on campus; 0% of students in fraternities, 0% in sororities
Most popular majors: 18% Registered Nursing/Registered Nurse, 10% Elementary Education and Teaching, 9% Kinesiology and Exercise Science, 6% Business Administration and Management, General, 5% Psychology, General
Expenses: 2021-2022: $26,060; room/board: $8,150
Financial aid: (417) 328-1823; 81% of undergrads determined to have financial need; average aid package $23,632

Stephens College[1]
Columbia MO
(800) 876-7207
U.S. News ranking: Reg. U. (Mid. W), No. 108
Website: www.stephens.edu
Admissions email: apply@stephens.edu
Private; founded 1833
Application deadline (fall): rolling
Undergraduate student body: N/A full time, N/A part time
Expenses: 2020-2021: $23,385; room/board: $10,586
Financial aid: (573) 876-7106

Truman State University
Kirksville MO
(660) 785-4114
U.S. News ranking: Reg. U. (Mid. W), No. 6
Website: www.truman.edu
Admissions email: admissions@truman.edu
Public; founded 1867
Freshman admissions: more selective; 2020-2021: 3,839 applied, 2,768 accepted. Either SAT or ACT required. ACT 25/75 percentile: 24-30. High school rank: 53% in top tenth, 82% in top quarter, 97% in top half
Early decision deadline: N/A, notification date: N/A
Early action deadline: N/A, notification date: N/A
Application deadline (fall): rolling
Undergraduate student body: 3,687 full time, 702 part time; 41% male, 59% female; 0% American Indian, 3% Asian, 3% black, 4% Hispanic, 4% multiracial, 0% Pacific Islander, 78% white, 7% international; 85% from in state; 38% live on campus; 22% of students in fraternities, 21% in sororities
Most popular majors: 11% Business Administration and Management, General, 9% Biology/Biological Sciences, General, 9% Kinesiology and Exercise Science, 8% Psychology, General, 7% English Language and Literature, General
Expenses: 2021-2022: $8,689 in state, $16,410 out of state; room/board: $9,313
Financial aid: (660) 785-4130; 48% of undergrads determined to have financial need; average aid package $13,360

University of Central Missouri
Warrensburg MO
(660) 543-4290
U.S. News ranking: Reg. U. (Mid. W), No. 74
Website: www.ucmo.edu
Admissions email: admit@ucmo.edu
Public; founded 1871
Freshman admissions: selective; 2020-2021: 5,666 applied, 3,603 accepted. Neither SAT nor ACT required. ACT 25/75 percentile: 19-25. High school rank: 13% in top tenth, 37% in top quarter, 74% in top half
Early decision deadline: N/A, notification date: N/A

Early action deadline: N/A, notification date: N/A
Application deadline (fall): rolling
Undergraduate student body: 6,009 full time, 1,620 part time; 44% male, 56% female; 0% American Indian, 1% Asian, 9% black, 6% Hispanic, 5% multiracial, 0% Pacific Islander, 77% white, 1% international; 88% from in state; 20% live on campus; 10% of students in fraternities, 9% in sororities
Most popular majors: 14% Health Professions and Related Programs, 13% Business, Management, Marketing, and Related Support Services, 13% Education, 8% Engineering Technologies and Engineering-Related Fields, 8% Homeland Security, Law Enforcement, Firefighting and Related Protective Services
Expenses: 2021-2022: $9,068 in state, $16,815 out of state; room/board: $9,358
Financial aid: (660) 543-8266; 58% of undergrads determined to have financial need; average aid package $9,173

University of Missouri
Columbia MO
(573) 882-7786
U.S. News ranking: Nat. U., No. 122
Website: www.missouri.edu
Admissions email: mu4u@missouri.edu
Public; founded 1839
Freshman admissions: more selective; 2020-2021: 20,641 applied, 16,880 accepted. Either SAT or ACT required. ACT 25/75 percentile: 23-30. High school rank: 35% in top tenth, 65% in top quarter, 92% in top half
Early decision deadline: N/A, notification date: N/A
Early action deadline: N/A, notification date: N/A
Application deadline (fall): rolling
Undergraduate student body: 21,344 full time, 2,052 part time; 46% male, 54% female; 0% American Indian, 3% Asian, 7% black, 5% Hispanic, 4% multiracial, 0% Pacific Islander, 78% white, 1% international; 81% from in state; 30% live on campus; 24% of students in fraternities, 30% in sororities
Most popular majors: 18% Business, Management, Marketing, and Related Support Services, 15% Health Professions and Related Programs, 11% Communication, Journalism, and Related Programs, 8% Engineering, 6% Social Sciences
Expenses: 2021-2022: $11,475 in state, $30,450 out of state; room/board: $11,311
Financial aid: (573) 882-7506; 51% of undergrads determined to have financial need; average aid package $13,376

University of Missouri–Kansas City
Kansas City MO
(816) 235-8652
U.S. News ranking: Nat. U., No. 249
Website: www.umkc.edu
Admissions email: admissions@umkc.edu
Public; founded 1929
Freshman admissions: more selective; 2020-2021: 5,672 applied, 3,574 accepted. Neither SAT nor ACT required. ACT 25/75 percentile: 20-28. High school rank: 33% in top tenth, 58% in top quarter, 87% in top half
Early decision deadline: N/A, notification date: N/A
Early action deadline: N/A, notification date: N/A
Application deadline (fall): 6/15
Undergraduate student body: 6,071 full time, 4,965 part time; 42% male, 58% female; 0% American Indian, 9% Asian, 13% black, 10% Hispanic, 5% multiracial, 0% Pacific Islander, 54% white, 5% international; 80% from in state; 6% live on campus; 1% of students in fraternities, 3% in sororities
Most popular majors: 18% Business, Management, Marketing, and Related Support Services, 11% Health Professions and Related Programs, 8% Biological and Biomedical Sciences, 8% Engineering, 8% Liberal Arts and Sciences, General Studies and Humanities
Expenses: 2021-2022: $11,112 in state, $28,026 out of state; room/board: $11,005
Financial aid: (816) 235-1154; 63% of undergrads determined to have financial need; average aid package $11,184

University of Missouri–St. Louis
St. Louis MO
(314) 516-5451
U.S. News ranking: Nat. U., No. 239
Website: www.umsl.edu
Admissions email: admissions@umsl.edu
Public; founded 1963
Freshman admissions: more selective; 2020-2021: 3,511 applied, 2,022 accepted. Neither SAT nor ACT required. ACT 25/75 percentile: 21-27. High school rank: 38% in top tenth, 64% in top quarter, 90% in top half
Early decision deadline: N/A, notification date: N/A
Early action deadline: N/A, notification date: N/A
Application deadline (fall): 8/20
Undergraduate student body: 4,889 full time, 6,088 part time; 43% male, 57% female; 0% American Indian, 5% Asian, 16% black, 3% Hispanic, 4% multiracial, 0% Pacific Islander, 62% white, 2% international; 88% from in state; 8% live on campus; 0% of students in fraternities, 0% in sororities
Most popular majors: 28% Business, Management, Marketing, and Related Support

Services, 10% Health Professions and Related Programs, 9% Social Sciences, 8% Education, 7% Psychology
Expenses: 2021-2022: $11,390 in state, $30,570 out of state; room/board: $9,833
Financial aid: (314) 516-6608; 70% of undergrads determined to have financial need; average aid package $11,516

Washington University in St. Louis
St. Louis MO
(800) 638-0700
U.S. News ranking: Nat. U., No. 14
Website: www.wustl.edu
Admissions email: admissions@wustl.edu
Private; founded 1853
Freshman admissions: most selective; 2020-2021: 27,949 applied, 4,477 accepted. Neither SAT nor ACT required. ACT 25/75 percentile: 33-35. High school rank: 86% in top tenth, 99% in top quarter, 100% in top half
Early decision deadline: 11/1, notification date: 12/15
Early action deadline: N/A, notification date: N/A
Application deadline (fall): 1/3
Undergraduate student body: 7,077 full time, 576 part time; 47% male, 53% female; 0% American Indian, 18% Asian, 9% black, 11% Hispanic, 5% multiracial, 0% Pacific Islander, 48% white, 7% international; 11% from in state; 41% live on campus; 19% of students in fraternities, 10% in sororities
Most popular majors: 8% Computer Science, 6% Biology/Biological Sciences, General, 6% Experimental Psychology, 6% Mechanical Engineering, 5% Finance, General
Expenses: 2021-2022: $58,866; room/board: $17,900
Financial aid: (888) 547-6670; 42% of undergrads determined to have financial need; average aid package $55,407

Webster University
St. Louis MO
(314) 246-7800
U.S. News ranking: Reg. U. (Mid. W), No. 16
Website: www.webster.edu
Admissions email: admit@webster.edu
Private; founded 1915
Freshman admissions: more selective; 2020-2021: 2,249 applied, 1,506 accepted. Either SAT or ACT required. ACT 25/75 percentile: 20-27. High school rank: 20% in top tenth, 54% in top quarter, 77% in top half
Early decision deadline: N/A, notification date: N/A
Early action deadline: N/A, notification date: N/A
Application deadline (fall): 8/1
Undergraduate student body: 1,934 full time, 240 part time; 44% male, 56% female; 0% American Indian, 3% Asian, 11% black, 6% Hispanic, 5% multiracial, 0% Pacific Islander, 67% white, 0% international

Most popular majors: 25% Business Administration and Management, General, 7% Psychology, General, 6% International Relations and Affairs, 4% Computer Science, 4% Mass Communication/Media Studies
Expenses: 2021-2022: $28,700; room/board: $11,440
Financial aid: (800) 983-4623; 71% of undergrads determined to have financial need; average aid package $24,852

Westminster College[7]
Fulton MO
(800) 475-3361
U.S. News ranking: Nat. Lib. Arts, No. 158
Website: www.wcmo.edu/
Admissions email: admissions@westminster-mo.edu
Private; founded 1851
Affiliation: Presbyterian
Freshman admissions: selective; 2020-2021: 912 applied, 888 accepted. Neither SAT nor ACT required. ACT 25/75 percentile: 19-26. High school rank: 19% in top tenth, 37% in top quarter, 71% in top half
Early decision deadline: N/A, notification date: N/A
Early action deadline: N/A, notification date: N/A
Application deadline (fall): rolling
Undergraduate student body: 600 full time, 9 part time
Most popular majors: 29% Business, Management, Marketing, and Related Support Services, 15% Biological and Biomedical Sciences, 10% Parks, Recreation, Leisure, and Fitness Studies, 9% Social Sciences, 6% Education
Expenses: 2021-2022: $32,664; room/board: $11,414
Financial aid: (573) 592-5364; 83% of undergrads determined to have financial need; average aid package $27,827

William Jewell College
Liberty MO
(816) 415-7511
U.S. News ranking: Reg. Coll. (Mid. W), No. 8
Website: www.jewell.edu
Admissions email: admission@william.jewell.edu
Private; founded 1849
Freshman admissions: more selective; 2020-2021: 1,585 applied, 577 accepted. Neither SAT nor ACT required. ACT 25/75 percentile: 20-27. High school rank: 31% in top tenth, 56% in top quarter, 86% in top half
Early decision deadline: N/A, notification date: N/A
Early action deadline: N/A, notification date: N/A
Application deadline (fall): 8/1
Undergraduate student body: 730 full time, 8 part time; 48% male, 52% female; 0% American Indian, 2% Asian, 9% black, 7% Hispanic, 6% multiracial, 0% Pacific Islander, 72% white, 3% international; 62% from in state; 85% live on campus; 39% of students in fraternities, 55% in

sororities
Most popular majors: 33% Registered Nursing/Registered Nurse, 18% Business Administration and Management, General, 10% Biology/Biological Sciences, General, 7% Psychology, General, 6% Political Science and Government, General
Expenses: 2021-2022: $19,310; room/board: $9,860
Financial aid: (816) 415-5974; 69% of undergrads determined to have financial need; average aid package $31,295

William Woods University[1]
Fulton MO
(800) 995-3159
U.S. News ranking: Nat. U., second tier
Website: www.williamwoods.edu
Admissions email: admissions@williamwoods.edu
Private; founded 1870
Affiliation: Christian Church (Disciples of Christ)
Application deadline (fall): rolling
Undergraduate student body: N/A full time, N/A part time
Expenses: 2020-2021: $25,930; room/board: $9,990
Financial aid: (573) 592-1793

MONTANA

Carroll College
Helena MT
(406) 447-4384
U.S. News ranking: Reg. Coll. (W), No. 1
Website: www.carroll.edu
Admissions email: admission@carroll.edu
Private; founded 1909
Affiliation: Roman Catholic
Freshman admissions: more selective; 2020-2021: 1,449 applied, 1,058 accepted. Neither SAT nor ACT required. ACT 25/75 percentile: 22-27. High school rank: 37% in top tenth, 68% in top quarter, 93% in top half
Early decision deadline: N/A, notification date: N/A
Early action deadline: 12/1, notification date: 1/1
Application deadline (fall): 6/15
Undergraduate student body: 1,064 full time, 35 part time; 39% male, 61% female; 0% American Indian, 1% Asian, 0% black, 5% Hispanic, 4% multiracial, 0% Pacific Islander, 81% white, 1% international; 44% from in state; 83% live on campus; 0% of students in fraternities, 0% in sororities
Most popular majors: Information not available
Expenses: 2021-2022: $38,106; room/board: $10,416
Financial aid: (406) 447-5425; 63% of undergrads determined to have financial need; average aid package $30,602

Montana State University
Bozeman MT
(406) 994-2452
U.S. News ranking: Nat. U., No. 263
Website: www.montana.edu
Admissions email: admissions@montana.edu
Public; founded 1893
Freshman admissions: more selective; 2020-2021: 18,892 applied, 15,260 accepted. Neither SAT nor ACT required. ACT 25/75 percentile: 21-28. High school rank: 20% in top tenth, 47% in top quarter, 74% in top half
Early decision deadline: N/A, notification date: N/A
Early action deadline: N/A, notification date: N/A
Application deadline (fall): rolling
Undergraduate student body: 11,983 full time, 2,183 part time; 53% male, 47% female; 1% American Indian, 1% Asian, 0% black, 5% Hispanic, 5% multiracial, 0% Pacific Islander, 85% white, 1% international; N/A from in state; 25% live on campus; 2% of students in fraternities, 2% in sororities
Most popular majors: 11% Business/Commerce, General, 9% Registered Nursing/Registered Nurse, 6% Mechanical Engineering, 4% Chemical Engineering, 4% Psychology, General
Expenses: 2021-2022: $7,520 in state, $26,950 out of state; room/board: $10,400
Financial aid: (406) 994-2845; 42% of undergrads determined to have financial need; average aid package $11,777

Montana State University–Billings
Billings MT
(406) 657-2158
U.S. News ranking: Reg. U. (W), second tier
Website: www.msubillings.edu
Admissions email: admissions@msubillings.edu
Public; founded 1927
Freshman admissions: selective; 2020-2021: 1,474 applied, 1,470 accepted. Neither SAT nor ACT required. ACT 25/75 percentile: 17-24. High school rank: 14% in top tenth, 21% in top quarter, 69% in top half
Early decision deadline: N/A, notification date: N/A
Early action deadline: N/A, notification date: N/A
Application deadline (fall): rolling
Undergraduate student body: 1,985 full time, 1,617 part time; 34% male, 66% female; 5% American Indian, 1% Asian, 1% black, 7% Hispanic, 5% multiracial, 0% Pacific Islander, 78% white, 1% international; 90% from in state; 9% live on campus; N/A of students in fraternities, N/A in sororities
Most popular majors: 32% Business, Management, Marketing, and Related Support Services, 17% Education, 8% Health Professions and Related

Programs, 7% Liberal Arts and Sciences, General Studies and Humanities, 6% Psychology
Expenses: 2021-2022: $5,980 in state, $19,173 out of state; room/board: $7,420
Financial aid: (406) 657-2188; 59% of undergrads determined to have financial need; average aid package $9,922

Montana State University–Northern[1]
Havre MT
(406) 265-3704
U.S. News ranking: Reg. Coll. (W), second tier
Website: www.msun.edu
Admissions email: admissions@msun.edu
Public
Application deadline (fall): N/A
Undergraduate student body: N/A full time, N/A part time
Expenses: N/A
Financial aid: N/A

Montana Technological University
Butte MT
(406) 496-4256
U.S. News ranking: Reg. U. (W), No. 35
Website: www.mtech.edu/
Admissions email: admissions@mtech.edu
Public; founded 1893
Freshman admissions: selective; 2020-2021: 1,305 applied, 1,259 accepted. Neither SAT nor ACT required. ACT 25/75 percentile: 21-27. High school rank: 21% in top tenth, 58% in top quarter, 87% in top half
Early decision deadline: N/A, notification date: N/A
Early action deadline: N/A, notification date: N/A
Application deadline (fall): rolling
Undergraduate student body: 1,616 full time, 494 part time; 59% male, 41% female; 3% American Indian, 1% Asian, 1% black, 3% Hispanic, 0% multiracial, 0% Pacific Islander, 82% white, 3% international; 87% from in state; 16% live on campus; N/A of students in fraternities, N/A in sororities
Most popular majors: 16% Engineering, General, 13% Registered Nursing/Registered Nurse, 9% Mechanical Engineering, 9% Occupational Health and Industrial Hygiene, 8% Business/Commerce, General
Expenses: 2021-2022: $7,397 in state, $22,560 out of state; room/board: $10,170
Financial aid: (406) 496-4223; 51% of undergrads determined to have financial need; average aid package $11,409

Rocky Mountain College
Billings MT
(406) 657-1026
U.S. News ranking: Reg. U. (W), No. 55
Website: www.rocky.edu/

Admissions email: admissions@rocky.edu
Private; founded 1878
Affiliation: Presbyterian Church (USA)
Freshman admissions: selective; 2020-2021: 1,370 applied, 975 accepted. Either SAT or ACT required. ACT 25/75 percentile: 18-24. High school rank: 15% in top tenth, 43% in top quarter, 71% in top half
Early decision deadline: N/A, notification date: N/A
Early action deadline: N/A, notification date: N/A
Application deadline (fall): rolling
Undergraduate student body: 816 full time, 23 part time; 51% male, 49% female; 3% American Indian, 1% Asian, 3% black, 8% Hispanic, 7% multiracial, 0% Pacific Islander, 74% white, 4% international; 55% from in state; 51% live on campus; N/A of students in fraternities, N/A in sororities
Most popular majors: 15% Business, Management, Marketing, and Related Support Services, 13% Biological and Biomedical Sciences, 13% Transportation and Materials Moving, 10% Education, 10% Parks, Recreation, Leisure, and Fitness Studies
Expenses: 2021-2022: $31,335; room/board: $8,855
Financial aid: (406) 657-1031; 73% of undergrads determined to have financial need; average aid package $26,505

University of Montana
Missoula MT
(800) 462-8636
U.S. News ranking: Nat. U., No. 277
Website: www.umt.edu
Admissions email: admiss@umontana.edu
Public; founded 1893
Freshman admissions: selective; 2020-2021: 5,414 applied, 5,182 accepted. Either SAT or ACT required. ACT 25/75 percentile: 20-27. High school rank: 16% in top tenth, 37% in top quarter, 65% in top half
Early decision deadline: N/A, notification date: N/A
Early action deadline: N/A, notification date: N/A
Application deadline (fall): 7/31
Undergraduate student body: 5,654 full time, 1,321 part time; 43% male, 57% female; 5% American Indian, 1% Asian, 1% black, 6% Hispanic, 5% multiracial, 0% Pacific Islander, 76% white, 1% international; N/A from in state; 32% live on campus; 6% of students in fraternities, 6% in sororities
Most popular majors: 17% Business, Management, Marketing, and Related Support Services, 13% Biological and Biomedical Sciences, 11% Social Sciences, 10% Visual and Performing Arts, 9% Natural Resources and Conservation
Expenses: 2021-2022: $7,492 in state, $28,252 out of state; room/board: $11,054

Financial aid: (406) 243-5504; 57% of undergrads determined to have financial need; average aid package $11,631

University of Montana Western[1]

Dillon MT
(877) 683-7331
U.S. News ranking: Reg. Coll. (W), No. 22
Website: w.umwestern.edu/
Admissions email: admissions@umwestern.edu
Public; founded 1893
Application deadline (fall): rolling
Undergraduate student body: N/A full time, N/A part time
Expenses: 2021-2022: $5,726 in state, $17,116 out of state; room/board: $8,528
Financial aid: (406) 683-7893; 68% of undergrads determined to have financial need; average aid package $2,793

University of Providence[7]

Great Falls MT
(406) 791-5290
U.S. News ranking: Reg. Coll. (W), No. 23
Website: www.uprovidence.edu
Admissions email: admissions@uprovidence.edu
Private; founded 1932
Affiliation: Roman Catholic
Freshman admissions: less selective; 2020-2021: 272 applied, 268 accepted. Neither SAT nor ACT required. ACT 25/75 percentile: 16-23. High school rank: N/A
Early decision deadline: N/A, notification date: N/A
Early action deadline: N/A, notification date: N/A
Application deadline (fall): 8/15
Undergraduate student body: 528 full time, 262 part time
Most popular majors: 62% Health Professions and Related Programs, 12% Business, Management, Marketing, and Related Support Services, 6% Psychology, 5% Biological and Biomedical Sciences, 4% Homeland Security, Law Enforcement, Firefighting and Related Protective Services
Expenses: 2021-2022: $26,662; room/board: $10,170
Financial aid: (406) 791-5235

NEBRASKA

Bellevue University[1]

Bellevue NE
(402) 293-2000
U.S. News ranking: Reg. U. (Mid. W), second tier
Website: www.bellevue.edu
Admissions email: info@bellevue.edu
Private
Application deadline (fall): N/A
Undergraduate student body: N/A full time, N/A part time
Expenses: 2020-2021: $7,851; room/board: $9,090
Financial aid: (402) 557-7095

Chadron State College[1]

Chadron NE
(308) 432-6000
U.S. News ranking: Reg. U. (Mid. W), second tier
Website: www.csc.edu
Admissions email: inquire@csc.edu
Public; founded 1911
Application deadline (fall): N/A
Undergraduate student body: N/A full time, N/A part time
Expenses: 2020-2021: $7,634 in state, $7,664 out of state; room/board: $8,126
Financial aid: N/A

College of Saint Mary

Omaha NE
(402) 399-2407
U.S. News ranking: Reg. U. (Mid. W), No. 64
Website: www.csm.edu
Admissions email: enroll@csm.edu
Private; founded 1923
Affiliation: Roman Catholic
Freshman admissions: selective; 2020-2021: 453 applied, 232 accepted. Either SAT or ACT required. ACT 25/75 percentile: 19-23. High school rank: 2% in top tenth, 44% in top quarter, 71% in top half
Early decision deadline: N/A, notification date: N/A
Early action deadline: N/A, notification date: N/A
Application deadline (fall): rolling
Undergraduate student body: 659 full time, 21 part time; 0% male, 100% female; 0% American Indian, 2% Asian, 7% black, 14% Hispanic, 4% multiracial, 0% Pacific Islander, 66% white, 1% international; 79% from in state; 33% live on campus; N/A of students in fraternities, N/A in sororities
Most popular majors: 38% Registered Nursing/Registered Nurse, 28% Rehabilitation Science, 11% Human Biology, 8% General Studies, 3% Kinesiology and Exercise Science
Expenses: 2021-2022: $21,800; room/board: $8,000
Financial aid: (402) 399-2429; 75% of undergrads determined to have financial need; average aid package $17,310

Concordia University

Seward NE
(800) 535-5494
U.S. News ranking: Reg. U. (Mid. W), No. 37
Website: www.cune.edu
Admissions email: admiss@cune.edu
Private; founded 1894
Affiliation: Lutheran Church - Missouri Synod
Freshman admissions: selective; 2020-2021: 2,126 applied, 1,606 accepted. Neither SAT nor ACT required. ACT 25/75 percentile: 20-26. High school rank: 17% in top tenth, 39% in top quarter, 76% in top half
Early decision deadline: N/A, notification date: N/A

Early action deadline: N/A, notification date: N/A
Application deadline (fall): rolling
Undergraduate student body: 1,195 full time, 964 part time; 46% male, 54% female; 0% American Indian, 1% Asian, 2% black, 6% Hispanic, 3% multiracial, 0% Pacific Islander, 79% white, 2% international
Most popular majors: 36% Education, 10% Business, Management, Marketing, and Related Support Services, 9% Biological and Biomedical Sciences, 8% Theology and Religious Vocations, 6% Psychology
Expenses: 2021-2022: $36,200; room/board: $9,600
Financial aid: (402) 643-7270; 76% of undergrads determined to have financial need; average aid package $28,022

Creighton University

Omaha NE
(800) 282-5835
U.S. News ranking: Nat. U., No. 103
Website: www.creighton.edu
Admissions email: admissions@creighton.edu
Private; founded 1878
Affiliation: Roman Catholic
Freshman admissions: more selective; 2020-2021: 8,682 applied, 6,652 accepted. Neither SAT nor ACT required. ACT 25/75 percentile: 24-30. High school rank: 43% in top tenth, 73% in top quarter, 93% in top half
Early decision deadline: N/A, notification date: N/A
Early action deadline: 11/1, notification date: N/A
Application deadline (fall): rolling
Undergraduate student body: 4,330 full time, 128 part time; 41% male, 59% female; 0% American Indian, 8% Asian, 2% black, 9% Hispanic, 5% multiracial, 0% Pacific Islander, 72% white, 2% international; 77% from in state; 51% live on campus; 28% of students in fraternities, 43% in sororities
Most popular majors: 28% Business, Management, Marketing, and Related Support Services, 27% Health Professions and Related Programs, 15% Biological and Biomedical Sciences, 6% Construction Trades, 6% Psychology
Expenses: 2021-2022: $44,524; room/board: $11,670
Financial aid: (402) 280-2731; 49% of undergrads determined to have financial need; average aid package $31,346

Doane University

Crete NE
(402) 826-8222
U.S. News ranking: Nat. Lib. Arts, second tier
Website: www.doane.edu
Admissions email: admissions@doane.edu
Private; founded 1872
Freshman admissions: selective; 2020-2021: 1,955 applied, 1,345 accepted. Neither SAT

nor ACT required. ACT 25/75 percentile: 20-25. High school rank: 14% in top tenth, 43% in top quarter, 89% in top half
Early decision deadline: N/A, notification date: N/A
Early action deadline: N/A, notification date: N/A
Application deadline (fall): rolling
Undergraduate student body: 1,142 full time, 113 part time; 52% male, 48% female; 0% American Indian, 1% Asian, 4% black, 11% Hispanic, 3% multiracial, 0% Pacific Islander, 77% white, 2% international; 72% from in state; 72% live on campus; 22% of students in fraternities, 33% in sororities
Most popular majors: 15% Business Administration and Management, General, 12% Elementary Education and Teaching, 10% Biology/Biological Sciences, General, 4% Music, General, 4% Psychology, General
Expenses: 2021-2022: $38,080; room/board: $10,300
Financial aid: (402) 826-8260; 74% of undergrads determined to have financial need; average aid package $28,937

Hastings College

Hastings NE
(800) 532-7642
U.S. News ranking: Reg. Coll. (Mid. W), No. 17
Website: www.hastings.edu
Admissions email: hcadmissions@hastings.edu
Private; founded 1882
Affiliation: Presbyterian
Freshman admissions: selective; 2020-2021: 2,126 applied, 1,402 accepted. Neither SAT nor ACT required. ACT 25/75 percentile: 19-26. High school rank: N/A
Early decision deadline: N/A, notification date: N/A
Early action deadline: N/A, notification date: N/A
Application deadline (fall): 8/1
Undergraduate student body: 948 full time, 6 part time; 48% male, 52% female; 0% American Indian, 1% Asian, 6% black, 11% Hispanic, 3% multiracial, 0% Pacific Islander, 71% white, 3% international; N/A from in state; 64% live on campus; N/A of students in fraternities, N/A in sororities
Most popular majors: 22% Business, Management, Marketing, and Related Support Services, 19% Education, 8% Biological and Biomedical Sciences, 7% Social Sciences, 6% Multi/Interdisciplinary Studies
Expenses: 2021-2022: $33,590; room/board: $10,810
Financial aid: (402) 461-7431; 79% of undergrads determined to have financial need; average aid package $28,478

Midland University[1]

Fremont NE
(402) 941-6501
U.S. News ranking: Reg. U. (Mid. W), second tier
Website: www.midlandu.edu/

Admissions email: admissions@midlandu.edu
Private; founded 1883
Application deadline (fall): rolling
Undergraduate student body: N/A full time, N/A part time
Expenses: 2020-2021: $35,528; room/board: $9,226
Financial aid: N/A

Nebraska Wesleyan University

Lincoln NE
(402) 465-2218
U.S. News ranking: Reg. U. (Mid. W), No. 24
Website: www.nebrwesleyan.edu/
Admissions email: admissions@nebrwesleyan.edu
Private; founded 1887
Affiliation: United Methodist
Freshman admissions: more selective; 2020-2021: 2,435 applied, 1,693 accepted. Neither SAT nor ACT required. ACT 25/75 percentile: 22-29. High school rank: 20% in top tenth, 51% in top quarter, 86% in top half
Early decision deadline: N/A, notification date: N/A
Early action deadline: 10/15, notification date: N/A
Application deadline (fall): 8/15
Undergraduate student body: 1,665 full time, 108 part time; 42% male, 58% female; 0% American Indian, 2% Asian, 3% black, 7% Hispanic, 3% multiracial, 0% Pacific Islander, 81% white, 1% international; 84% from in state; 43% live on campus; 18% of students in fraternities, 22% in sororities
Most popular majors: 21% Business, Management, Marketing, and Related Support Services, 17% Health Professions and Related Programs, 9% Parks, Recreation, Leisure, and Fitness Studies, 8% Biological and Biomedical Sciences, 8% Education
Expenses: 2021-2022: $38,334; room/board: $11,657
Financial aid: (402) 465-2167; 74% of undergrads determined to have financial need; average aid package $26,720

Peru State College[1]

Peru NE
(402) 872-3815
U.S. News ranking: Reg. U. (Mid. W), second tier
Website: www.peru.edu
Admissions email: admissions@peru.edu
Public
Application deadline (fall): N/A
Undergraduate student body: N/A full time, N/A part time
Expenses: 2020-2021: $7,920 in state, $7,920 out of state; room/board: $8,680
Financial aid: N/A

Union College

Lincoln NE
(800) 228-4600
U.S. News ranking: Reg. Coll. (Mid. W), No. 31
Website: www.ucollege.edu
Admissions email:

enroll@ucollege.edu
Private; founded 1891
Affiliation: Seventh Day Adventist
Freshman admissions: selective;
2020-2021: 1,735 applied,
1,290 accepted. Neither SAT
nor ACT required. ACT 25/75
percentile: 18-24. High school
rank: N/A
Early decision deadline: N/A,
notification date: N/A
Early action deadline: N/A,
notification date: N/A
Application deadline (fall): 8/26
Undergraduate student body: 587
full time, 89 part time; 43%
male, 57% female; 0% American
Indian, 5% Asian, 9% black,
25% Hispanic, 4% multiracial,
1% Pacific Islander, 51% white,
5% international; N/A from in
state; 58% live on campus; 0%
of students in fraternities, 0% in
sororities
Most popular majors: 38% Health
Professions and Related Programs,
13% Business, Management,
Marketing, and Related Support
Services, 8% Biological and
Biomedical Sciences, 7%
Education, 7% Liberal Arts and
Sciences, General Studies and
Humanities
Expenses: 2021-2022: $26,060;
room/board: $7,210
Financial aid: (402) 486-2505;
75% of undergrads determined to
have financial need; average aid
package $17,776

University of Nebraska–Kearney
Kearney NE
(800) 532-7639
U.S. News ranking: Reg. U. (Mid.
W), No. 34
Website: www.unk.edu
Admissions email:
admissionsug@unk.edu
Public; founded 1903
Freshman admissions: selective;
2020-2021: 5,359 applied,
4,738 accepted. Either SAT
or ACT required. ACT 25/75
percentile: 19-26. High school
rank: 21% in top tenth, 46% in
top quarter, 77% in top half
Early decision deadline: N/A,
notification date: N/A
Early action deadline: N/A,
notification date: N/A
Application deadline (fall): 8/15
Undergraduate student body: 3,795
full time, 590 part time; 39%
male, 61% female; 0% American
Indian, 1% Asian, 2% black,
13% Hispanic, 3% multiracial,
0% Pacific Islander, 76% white,
5% international; 92% from in
state; 32% live on campus; 9%
of students in fraternities, 10%
in sororities
Most popular majors: 14%
Business Administration and
Management, General, 12%
Elementary Education and
Teaching, 7% Parks, Recreation
and Leisure Studies, 5% Family
and Consumer Economics and
Related Services, Other, 5%
General Studies
Expenses: 2021-2022: $7,940 in
state, $15,320 out of state; room/
board: $10,322

Financial aid: (308) 865-8520;
66% of undergrads determined to
have financial need; average aid
package $12,232

University of Nebraska–Lincoln
Lincoln NE
(800) 742-8800
U.S. News ranking: Nat. U.,
No. 136
Website: www.unl.edu
Admissions email:
Admissions@unl.edu
Public; founded 1869
Freshman admissions: more
selective; 2020-2021: 17,495
applied, 13,601 accepted. Neither
SAT nor ACT required. ACT 25/75
percentile: 22-28. High school
rank: 30% in top tenth, 59% in
top quarter, 89% in top half
Early decision deadline: N/A,
notification date: N/A
Early action deadline: N/A,
notification date: N/A
Application deadline (fall): 5/1
Undergraduate student body:
18,949 full time, 1,294 part
time; 52% male, 48% female;
0% American Indian, 3% Asian,
3% black, 8% Hispanic, 3%
multiracial, 0% Pacific Islander,
75% white, 6% international;
77% from in state; 37% live
on campus; 20% of students in
fraternities, 27% in sororities
Most popular majors: 23%
Business, Management,
Marketing, and Related Support
Services, 11% Engineering,
9% Agriculture, Agriculture
Operations, and Related Sciences,
8% Communication, Journalism,
and Related Programs, 7% Family
and Consumer Sciences/Human
Sciences
Expenses: 2021-2022: $9,872 in
state, $27,002 out of state; room/
board: $11,920
Financial aid: (402) 472-3484;
46% of undergrads determined to
have financial need; average aid
package $15,331

University of Nebraska–Omaha
Omaha NE
(402) 554-2393
U.S. News ranking: Nat. U.,
No. 263
Website: www.unomaha.edu/
Admissions email:
unoadmissions@unomaha.edu
Public; founded 1908
Freshman admissions: selective;
2020-2021: 8,864 applied,
7,294 accepted. Either SAT
or ACT required. ACT 25/75
percentile: 18-26. High school
rank: 20% in top tenth, 45% in
top quarter, 76% in top half
Early decision deadline: N/A,
notification date: N/A
Early action deadline: N/A,
notification date: N/A
Application deadline (fall): 8/1
Undergraduate student body:
10,362 full time, 2,406 part
time; 45% male, 55% female;
0% American Indian, 4% Asian,
7% black, 16% Hispanic, 5%
multiracial, 0% Pacific Islander,
62% white, 4% international;

90% from in state; 13% live
on campus; 2% of students in
fraternities, 2% in sororities
Most popular majors: 9% Criminal
Justice/Safety Studies, 6%
Biology/Biological Sciences,
General, 6% Psychology, General,
5% Elementary Education
and Teaching, 4% Business
Administration and Management,
General
Expenses: 2021-2022: $8,136 in
state, $21,718 out of state; room/
board: $10,195
Financial aid: (402) 554-3408;
57% of undergrads determined to
have financial need; average aid
package $10,268

Wayne State College
Wayne NE
(800) 228-9972
U.S. News ranking: Reg. U. (Mid.
W), No. 88
Website: www.wsc.edu/
Admissions email:
admit1@wsc.edu
Public; founded 1909
Freshman admissions: selective;
2020-2021: 2,715 applied,
2,715 accepted. Neither SAT
nor ACT required. ACT 25/75
percentile: 18-25. High school
rank: 14% in top tenth, 35% in
top quarter, 66% in top half
Early decision deadline: N/A,
notification date: N/A
Early action deadline: N/A,
notification date: N/A
Application deadline (fall): 8/24
Undergraduate student body: 2,822
full time, 618 part time; 42%
male, 58% female; 1% American
Indian, 1% Asian, 3% black,
8% Hispanic, 3% multiracial,
0% Pacific Islander, 81% white,
2% international; N/A from in
state; 45% live on campus; N/A
of students in fraternities, N/A in
sororities
Most popular majors: 26%
Education, 18% Business,
Management, Marketing, and
Related Support Services,
8% Homeland Security, Law
Enforcement, Firefighting and
Related Protective Services, 8%
Psychology, 6% English Language
and Literature/Letters
Expenses: 2021-2022: $7,428 in
state, $7,458 out of state; room/
board: $8,280
Financial aid: (402) 375-7430;
67% of undergrads determined to
have financial need; average aid
package $9,532

York College
York NE
(800) 950-9675
U.S. News ranking: Reg. Coll. (Mid.
W), No. 41
Website: www.york.edu
Admissions email: enroll@york.edu
Private; founded 1890
Affiliation: Churches of Christ
Freshman admissions: selective;
2020-2021: N/A applied, N/A
accepted. Either SAT or ACT
required. ACT 25/75 percentile:
17-21. High school rank: 7% in
top tenth, 43% in top quarter,
70% in top half

Early decision deadline: N/A,
notification date: N/A
Early action deadline: N/A,
notification date: N/A
Application deadline (fall): 8/31
Undergraduate student body: 438
full time, 28 part time; 52%
male, 48% female; 2% American
Indian, 0% Asian, 13% black,
20% Hispanic, 0% multiracial,
1% Pacific Islander, 51% white,
7% international
Most popular majors: Biology,
General, Business Administration
and Management, General,
Elementary Education and
Teaching, Psychology, Social
Sciences
Expenses: 2020-2021: $19,810;
room/board: $8,790
Financial aid: (402) 363-5624

NEVADA

College of Southern Nevada[1]
Las Vegas NV
(702) 651-5000
U.S. News ranking: Reg. Coll. (W),
unranked
Website: www.csn.edu
Admissions email:
N/A
Public; founded 1971
Application deadline (fall): N/A
Undergraduate student body: N/A
full time, N/A part time
Expenses: 2020-2021: $3,878 in
state, $11,355 out of state; room/
board: N/A
Financial aid: N/A

Great Basin College[1]
Elko NV
(775) 738-8493
U.S. News ranking: Reg. Coll. (W),
second tier
Website: www.gbcnv.edu
Admissions email:
admissions@gbcnv.edu
Public; founded 1967
Application deadline (fall): N/A
Undergraduate student body: N/A
full time, N/A part time
Expenses: 2020-2021: $3,248 in
state, $10,603 out of state; room/
board: $6,000
Financial aid: N/A

Nevada State College[1]
Henderson NV
(702) 992-2130
U.S. News ranking: Reg. Coll. (W),
second tier
Website: nsc.nevada.edu
Admissions email:
N/A
Public; founded 2002
Application deadline (fall): rolling
Undergraduate student body: N/A
full time, N/A part time
Expenses: 2020-2021: $6,075 in
state, $19,076 out of state; room/
board: N/A
Financial aid: N/A

Sierra Nevada University[1]
Incline Village NV
(866) 412-4636
U.S. News ranking: Reg. U. (W),
second tier
Website: www.sierranevada.edu
Admissions email:
admissions@sierranevada.edu
Private; founded 1969
Application deadline (fall): 8/26
Undergraduate student body: N/A
full time, N/A part time
Expenses: 2020-2021: $52,422;
room/board: $13,825
Financial aid: (775) 881-7428

University of Nevada–Las Vegas
Las Vegas NV
(702) 774-8658
U.S. News ranking: Nat. U.,
No. 249
Website: www.unlv.edu
Admissions email:
admissions@unlv.edu
Public; founded 1957
Freshman admissions: selective;
2020-2021: 13,262 applied,
10,786 accepted. Either SAT
or ACT required. ACT 25/75
percentile: 19-25. High school
rank: 22% in top tenth, 50% in
top quarter, 82% in top half
Early decision deadline: N/A,
notification date: N/A
Early action deadline: N/A,
notification date: N/A
Application deadline (fall): 6/1
Undergraduate student body:
19,843 full time, 6,019 part
time; 43% male, 57% female;
0% American Indian, 17% Asian,
8% black, 32% Hispanic, 11%
multiracial, 1% Pacific Islander,
28% white, 2% international;
12% from in state; 5% live
on campus; 4% of students in
fraternities, 4% in sororities
Most popular majors: 25%
Business, Management,
Marketing, and Related Support
Services, 8% Psychology, 6%
Health Professions and Related
Programs, 6% Homeland Security,
Law Enforcement, Firefighting and
Related Protective Services, 6%
Social Sciences
Expenses: 2021-2022: $9,886 in
state, $25,977 out of state; room/
board: $11,512
Financial aid: (833) 318-1228;
66% of undergrads determined to
have financial need; average aid
package $9,877

University of Nevada–Reno
Reno NV
(775) 784-4700
U.S. News ranking: Nat. U.,
No. 227
Website: www.unr.edu
Admissions email:
asknevada@unr.edu
Public; founded 1874
Freshman admissions: selective;
2020-2021: 9,644 applied,
8,419 accepted. Either SAT
or ACT required. ACT 25/75
percentile: 20-26. High school
rank: 25% in top tenth, 56% in
top quarter, 84% in top half

Early decision deadline: N/A, notification date: N/A
Early action deadline: 11/1, notification date: 11/15
Application deadline (fall): 4/7
Undergraduate student body: 14,323 full time, 2,529 part time; 46% male, 54% female; 1% American Indian, 8% Asian, 3% black, 23% Hispanic, 8% multiracial, 0% Pacific Islander, 55% white, 1% international; 75% from in state; 13% live on campus; 8% of students in fraternities, 7% in sororities
Most popular majors: 8% Health and Wellness, General, 6% Psychology, General, 5% Biology/Biological Sciences, General, 4% Business/Commerce, General, 4% Marketing/Marketing Management, General
Expenses: 2021-2022: $8,588 in state, $24,680 out of state; room/board: $12,216
Financial aid: (775) 784-4666; 55% of undergrads determined to have financial need; average aid package $9,500

Western Nevada College
Carson City NV
(775) 445-3277
U.S. News ranking: Reg. Coll. (W), unranked
Website: www.wnc.edu
Admissions email: admissions.records@wnc.edu
Public; founded 1971
Freshman admissions: least selective; 2020-2021: 1,028 applied, 1,028 accepted. Neither SAT nor ACT required. SAT 25/75 percentile: N/A. High school rank: N/A
Early decision deadline: N/A, notification date: N/A
Early action deadline: N/A, notification date: N/A
Application deadline (fall): rolling
Undergraduate student body: 1,175 full time, 2,320 part time; 43% male, 57% female; 2% American Indian, 3% Asian, 2% black, 25% Hispanic, 4% multiracial, 1% Pacific Islander, 57% white, 0% international; 96% from in state; 0% live on campus; 0% of students in fraternities, 0% in sororities
Most popular majors: 1% Building Construction Technology
Expenses: 2021-2022: $3,598 in state, $11,075 out of state; room/board: N/A
Financial aid: (775) 445-3264; 44% of undergrads determined to have financial need; average aid package $7,471

Colby-Sawyer College
New London NH
(800) 272-1015
U.S. News ranking: Reg. Coll. (N), No. 8
Website: colby-sawyer.edu/
Admissions email: admissions@colby-sawyer.edu
Private; founded 1837
Freshman admissions: selective;

2020-2021: 2,362 applied, 2,113 accepted. Neither SAT nor ACT required. SAT 25/75 percentile: 1010-1190. High school rank: N/A
Early decision deadline: N/A, notification date: N/A
Early action deadline: 12/1, notification date: 12/15
Application deadline (fall): rolling
Undergraduate student body: 811 full time, 65 part time; 26% male, 74% female; 1% American Indian, 3% Asian, 3% black, 2% Hispanic, 1% multiracial, 0% Pacific Islander, 80% white, 1% international; N/A from in state; 80% live on campus; N/A of students in fraternities, N/A in sororities
Most popular majors: 55% Health Professions and Related Programs, 30% Business, Management, Marketing, and Related Support Services, 14% Biological and Biomedical Sciences
Expenses: 2021-2022: $46,254; room/board: $15,891
Financial aid: (603) 526-3717; 83% of undergrads determined to have financial need; average aid package $39,004

Dartmouth College
Hanover NH
(603) 646-2875
U.S. News ranking: Nat. U., No. 13
Website: www.dartmouth.edu
Admissions email: apply@dartmouth.edu
Private; founded 1769
Freshman admissions: most selective; 2020-2021: 21,392 applied, 1,972 accepted. Neither SAT nor ACT required. SAT 25/75 percentile: 1440-1560. High school rank: 93% in top tenth, 99% in top quarter, 100% in top half
Early decision deadline: 11/1, notification date: 12/15
Early action deadline: N/A, notification date: N/A
Application deadline (fall): 1/2
Undergraduate student body: 4,169 full time, 1 part time; 51% male, 49% female; 1% American Indian, 15% Asian, 6% black, 10% Hispanic, 6% multiracial, 0% Pacific Islander, 49% white, 11% international; 3% from in state; 45% live on campus; 29% of students in fraternities, 33% in sororities
Most popular majors: 33% Social Sciences, 9% Engineering, 8% Biological and Biomedical Sciences, 8% Computer and Information Sciences and Support Services, 7% Mathematics and Statistics
Expenses: 2021-2022: $60,870; room/board: $17,586
Financial aid: (800) 443-3605; 52% of undergrads determined to have financial need; average aid package $51,197

Franklin Pierce University[1]
Rindge NH
(800) 437-0048
U.S. News ranking: Reg. U. (N), second tier
Website: www.franklinpierce.edu/
Admissions email: admissions@franklinpierce.edu
Private; founded 1962
Application deadline (fall): rolling
Undergraduate student body: N/A full time, N/A part time
Expenses: 2020-2021: $40,680; room/board: $14,454
Financial aid: (877) 372-7347

Granite State College[1]
Concord NH
(603) 513-1391
U.S. News ranking: Reg. U. (N), second tier
Website: www.granite.edu
Admissions email: gsc.admissions@granite.edu
Public; founded 1972
Application deadline (fall): rolling
Undergraduate student body: N/A full time, N/A part time
Expenses: 2021-2022: $7,791 in state, $9,015 out of state; room/board: N/A
Financial aid: (603) 513-1392; 70% of undergrads determined to have financial need; average aid package $7,035

Keene State College
Keene NH
(603) 358-2276
U.S. News ranking: Reg. Coll. (N), No. 9
Website: www.keene.edu
Admissions email: admissions@keene.edu
Public; founded 1909
Freshman admissions: less selective; 2020-2021: 5,343 applied, 4,844 accepted. Neither SAT nor ACT required. SAT 25/75 percentile: 980-1170. High school rank: 6% in top tenth, 25% in top quarter, 56% in top half
Early decision deadline: N/A, notification date: N/A
Early action deadline: N/A, notification date: N/A
Application deadline (fall): 4/1
Undergraduate student body: 2,985 full time, 114 part time; 45% male, 55% female; 0% American Indian, 1% Asian, 2% black, 5% Hispanic, 3% multiracial, 0% Pacific Islander, 82% white, 0% international; 47% from in state; 49% live on campus; 5% of students in fraternities, 4% in sororities
Most popular majors: 12% Engineering Technologies and Engineering-Related Fields, 10% Education, 10% Health Professions and Related Programs, 9% Social Sciences, 9% Visual and Performing Arts
Expenses: 2021-2022: $14,638 in state, $24,994 out of state; room/board: $13,204
Financial aid: (603) 358-2280; 69% of undergrads determined to have financial need; average aid package $14,550

New England College
Henniker NH
(603) 428-2223
U.S. News ranking: Reg. U. (N), second tier
Website: www.nec.edu
Admissions email: admission@nec.edu
Private; founded 1946
Freshman admissions: less selective; 2020-2021: 6,306 applied, 6,271 accepted. Neither SAT nor ACT required. SAT 25/75 percentile: 920-940. High school rank: N/A
Early decision deadline: N/A, notification date: N/A
Early action deadline: N/A, notification date: N/A
Application deadline (fall): rolling
Undergraduate student body: 1,641 full time, 135 part time; 42% male, 58% female; 1% American Indian, 1% Asian, 19% black, 10% Hispanic, 3% multiracial, 0% Pacific Islander, 49% white, 3% international; N/A from in state; 35% live on campus; N/A of students in fraternities, N/A in sororities
Most popular majors: 19% Business, Management, Marketing, and Related Support Services, 14% Visual and Performing Arts, 10% Psychology, 7% Health Professions and Related Programs, 6% Parks, Recreation, Leisure, and Fitness Studies
Expenses: 2021-2022: $39,648; room/board: $16,070
Financial aid: (603) 428-2436; 79% of undergrads determined to have financial need; average aid package $25,551

Plymouth State University
Plymouth NH
(603) 535-2237
U.S. News ranking: Reg. U. (N), No. 123
Website: www.plymouth.edu
Admissions email: admissions@plymouth.edu
Public; founded 1871
Freshman admissions: less selective; 2020-2021: 7,129 applied, 6,371 accepted. Neither SAT nor ACT required. SAT 25/75 percentile: 980-1130. High school rank: 5% in top tenth, 16% in top quarter, 43% in top half
Early decision deadline: N/A, notification date: N/A
Early action deadline: N/A, notification date: N/A
Application deadline (fall): 4/1
Undergraduate student body: 3,565 full time, 174 part time; 51% male, 49% female; 0% American Indian, 1% Asian, 3% black, 5% Hispanic, 3% multiracial, 0% Pacific Islander, 78% white, 1% international; 56% from in state; 58% live on campus; 1% of students in fraternities, 2% in sororities
Most popular majors: 10% Business/Commerce, General, 8% Criminal Justice/Safety Studies, 7% Elementary Education and Teaching, 6% Marketing/Marketing Management, General,

6% Psychology, General
Expenses: 2021-2022: $14,492 in state, $24,432 out of state; room/board: $11,580
Financial aid: (603) 535-2338; 67% of undergrads determined to have financial need; average aid package $13,439

Rivier University[1]
Nashua NH
(603) 888-1311
U.S. News ranking: Reg. U. (N), second tier
Website: rivier.edu
Admissions email: admissions@rivier.edu
Private
Application deadline (fall): rolling
Undergraduate student body: N/A full time, N/A part time
Expenses: 2020-2021: $34,510; room/board: $13,962
Financial aid: N/A

Saint Anselm College[1]
Manchester NH
(603) 641-7500
U.S. News ranking: Nat. Lib. Arts, No. 105
Website: www.anselm.edu
Admissions email: admission@anselm.edu
Private; founded 1889
Affiliation: Roman Catholic
Application deadline (fall): 2/1
Undergraduate student body: N/A full time, N/A part time
Expenses: 2020-2021: $43,140; room/board: $15,120
Financial aid: (603) 641-7110

Southern New Hampshire University
Manchester NH
(603) 645-9611
U.S. News ranking: Reg. U. (N), second tier
Website: www.snhu.edu
Admissions email: admission@snhu.edu
Private; founded 1932
Freshman admissions: less selective; 2020-2021: 5,309 applied, 4,634 accepted. Neither SAT nor ACT required. SAT 25/75 percentile: N/A. High school rank: 7% in top tenth, 26% in top quarter, 60% in top half
Early decision deadline: N/A, notification date: N/A
Early action deadline: N/A, notification date: N/A
Application deadline (fall): rolling
Undergraduate student body: 3,152 full time, 228 part time; 51% male, 49% female; 0% American Indian, 2% Asian, 3% black, 6% Hispanic, 2% multiracial, 0% Pacific Islander, 77% white, 2% international; 59% from in state; 1% live on campus; 2% of students in fraternities, 4% in sororities
Most popular majors: 42% Business, Management, Marketing, and Related Support Services, 12% Social Sciences, 9% Education, 8% Psychology, 6% Computer and Information Sciences and Support Services
Expenses: 2021-2022: $15,380; room/board: $11,800

Financial aid: (877) 455-7648; 46% of undergrads determined to have financial need; average aid package $24,137

Thomas More College of Liberal Arts[1]
Merrimack NH
(603) 880-8308
U.S. News ranking: Nat. Lib. Arts, second tier
Website: www.thomasmorecollege.edu
Admissions email: admissions@thomasmorecollege.edu
Private; founded 1978
Affiliation: Roman Catholic
Application deadline (fall): N/A
Undergraduate student body: N/A full time, N/A part time
Expenses: 2020-2021: $24,600; room/board: $8,700
Financial aid: (603) 880-8308

University of New Hampshire
Durham NH
(603) 862-1360
U.S. News ranking: Nat. U., No. 136
Website: www.unh.edu
Admissions email: admissions@unh.edu
Public; founded 1866
Freshman admissions: more selective; 2020-2021: 18,797 applied, 15,941 accepted. Neither SAT nor ACT required. SAT 25/75 percentile: 1090-1280. High school rank: 23% in top tenth, 51% in top quarter, 87% in top half
Early decision deadline: N/A, notification date: N/A
Early action deadline: 11/15, notification date: 1/15
Application deadline (fall): 2/1
Undergraduate student body: 11,371 full time, 379 part time; 44% male, 56% female; 0% American Indian, 3% Asian, 1% black, 4% Hispanic, 2% multiracial, 0% Pacific Islander, 84% white, 2% international; 48% from in state; 48% live on campus; 12% of students in fraternities, 16% in sororities
Most popular majors: 22% Business, Management, Marketing, and Related Support Services, 12% Engineering, 10% Biological and Biomedical Sciences, 7% Health Professions and Related Programs, 7% Social Sciences
Expenses: 2021-2022: $18,962 in state, $37,202 out of state; room/board: $12,366
Financial aid: (603) 862-3600; 65% of undergrads determined to have financial need; average aid package $21,917

Berkeley College
Woodland Park NJ
(800) 446-5400
U.S. News ranking: Reg. Coll. (N), No. 32
Website: berkeleycollege.edu/

Admissions email: admissions@berkeleycollege.edu
For-profit; founded 1931
Freshman admissions: least selective; 2020-2021: 1,032 applied, 952 accepted. Neither SAT nor ACT required. SAT 25/75 percentile: N/A. High school rank: N/A
Early decision deadline: N/A, notification date: N/A
Early action deadline: N/A, notification date: N/A
Application deadline (fall): 9/1
Undergraduate student body: 1,745 full time, 706 part time; 26% male, 74% female; 0% American Indian, 1% Asian, 14% black, 41% Hispanic, 1% multiracial, 0% Pacific Islander, 9% white, 1% international; 95% from in state; 0% live on campus; N/A of students in fraternities, N/A in sororities
Most popular majors: 26% Business Administration and Management, General, 18% Criminal Justice/Law Enforcement Administration, 13% Health/Health Care Administration/Management, 10% Accounting, 7% Fashion Merchandising
Expenses: 2021-2022: $27,600; room/board: N/A
Financial aid: (973) 200-1148; 95% of undergrads determined to have financial need; average aid package $10,372

Bloomfield College
Bloomfield NJ
(973) 748-9000
U.S. News ranking: Nat. Lib. Arts, second tier
Website: www.bloomfield.edu
Admissions email: admission@bloomfield.edu
Private; founded 1868
Affiliation: Presbyterian Church (USA)
Freshman admissions: least selective; 2020-2021: 4,195 applied, 3,551 accepted. Neither SAT nor ACT required. SAT 25/75 percentile: 800-970. High school rank: N/A
Early decision deadline: N/A, notification date: N/A
Early action deadline: 11/30, notification date: 12/20
Application deadline (fall): 7/29
Undergraduate student body: 1,402 full time, 131 part time; 37% male, 63% female; 1% American Indian, 2% Asian, 51% black, 31% Hispanic, 1% multiracial, 0% Pacific Islander, 8% white, 2% international
Most popular majors: 18% Sociology, 17% Visual and Performing Arts, General, 15% Registered Nursing/Registered Nurse, 14% Psychology, General, 12% Business Administration and Management, General
Expenses: 2021-2022: $30,680; room/board: $12,900
Financial aid: (973) 748-9000; 100% of undergrads determined to have financial need; average aid package $29,556

Caldwell University
Caldwell NJ
(973) 618-3600
U.S. News ranking: Reg. U. (N), No. 82
Website: www.caldwell.edu
Admissions email: admissions@caldwell.edu
Private; founded 1939
Affiliation: Roman Catholic
Freshman admissions: less selective; 2020-2021: 4,142 applied, 3,791 accepted. Neither SAT nor ACT required. SAT 25/75 percentile: 920-1110. High school rank: 15% in top tenth, 40% in top quarter, 66% in top half
Early decision deadline: N/A, notification date: N/A
Early action deadline: 12/1, notification date: 12/31
Application deadline (fall): 4/1
Undergraduate student body: 1,666 full time, 76 part time; 37% male, 63% female; 0% American Indian, 3% Asian, 16% black, 29% Hispanic, 2% multiracial, 0% Pacific Islander, 29% white, 10% international; N/A from in state; 18% live on campus; 2% of students in fraternities, 7% in sororities
Most popular majors: 13% Business Administration and Management, General, 12% Registered Nursing/Registered Nurse, 11% Psychology, General, 6% Biology/Biological Sciences, General, 6% Health Professions and Related Programs
Expenses: 2021-2022: $36,900; room/board: $12,760
Financial aid: (973) 618-3221; 81% of undergrads determined to have financial need; average aid package $33,182

Centenary University[1]
Hackettstown NJ
(800) 236-8679
U.S. News ranking: Reg. U. (N), No. 109
Website: www.centenaryuniversity.edu
Admissions email: CentUAdmissions@centenaryuniversity.edu
Private; founded 1867
Affiliation: United Methodist
Application deadline (fall): 8/15
Undergraduate student body: N/A full time, N/A part time
Expenses: 2020-2021: $34,498; room/board: $12,386
Financial aid: (908) 852-1400

The College of New Jersey
Ewing NJ
(609) 771-2131
U.S. News ranking: Reg. U. (N), No. 6
Website: www.tcnj.edu
Admissions email: admiss@tcnj.edu
Public; founded 1855
Freshman admissions: more selective; 2020-2021: 13,199 applied, 6,765 accepted. Neither SAT nor ACT required. SAT 25/75 percentile: 1140-1320. High school rank: 34% in top tenth, 67% in top quarter, 94%

in top half
Early decision deadline: 11/1, notification date: 12/1
Early action deadline: N/A, notification date: N/A
Application deadline (fall): 2/1
Undergraduate student body: 6,898 full time, 207 part time; 43% male, 57% female; 0% American Indian, 12% Asian, 6% black, 15% Hispanic, 2% multiracial, 0% Pacific Islander, 62% white, 1% international; 95% from in state; 11% live on campus; 21% of students in fraternities, 21% in sororities
Most popular majors: 18% Business Administration, Management and Operations, 7% Biology, General, 7% Teacher Education and Professional Development, Specific Levels and Methods, 6% Psychology, General, 6% Registered Nursing, Nursing Administration, Nursing Research and Clinical Nursing
Expenses: 2021-2022: $16,667 in state, $28,645 out of state; room/board: $13,416
Financial aid: (609) 771-2211; 50% of undergrads determined to have financial need; average aid package $11,459

Drew University
Madison NJ
(973) 408-3739
U.S. News ranking: Nat. Lib. Arts, No. 117
Website: www.drew.edu
Admissions email: cadm@drew.edu
Private; founded 1867
Affiliation: United Methodist
Freshman admissions: selective; 2020-2021: 3,989 applied, 2,918 accepted. Neither SAT nor ACT required. SAT 25/75 percentile: 1100-1300. High school rank: 26% in top tenth, 57% in top quarter, 93% in top half
Early decision deadline: 11/1, notification date: 12/15
Early action deadline: 12/15, notification date: 1/15
Application deadline (fall): 2/1
Undergraduate student body: 1,603 full time, 33 part time; 42% male, 58% female; 0% American Indian, 4% Asian, 9% black, 18% Hispanic, 3% multiracial, 0% Pacific Islander, 50% white, 13% international; 70% from in state; 8% live on campus; N/A of students in fraternities, N/A in sororities
Most popular majors: 19% Social Sciences, General, 16% Business Administration and Management, General, 11% Visual and Performing Arts, General, 10% Psychology, General, 6% English Language and Literature, General
Expenses: 2021-2022: $42,652; room/board: $15,868
Financial aid: (973) 408-3112; 66% of undergrads determined to have financial need; average aid package $34,857

Fairleigh Dickinson University
Teaneck NJ
(800) 338-8803
U.S. News ranking: Reg. U. (N), No. 44
Website: www.fdu.edu
Admissions email: admissions@fdu.edu
Private; founded 1942
Freshman admissions: selective; 2020-2021: 8,801 applied, 7,700 accepted. Neither SAT nor ACT required. SAT 25/75 percentile: 933-1140. High school rank: 15% in top tenth, 36% in top quarter, 71% in top half
Early decision deadline: N/A, notification date: N/A
Early action deadline: N/A, notification date: N/A
Application deadline (fall): rolling
Undergraduate student body: 4,642 full time, 3,722 part time; 42% male, 58% female; 0% American Indian, 5% Asian, 10% black, 31% Hispanic, 2% multiracial, 0% Pacific Islander, 39% white, 4% international; N/A from in state; 7% live on campus; 0% of students in fraternities, 0% in sororities
Most popular majors: 40% Liberal Arts and Sciences, General Studies and Humanities, 16% Business, Management, Marketing, and Related Support Services, 7% Biological and Biomedical Sciences, 6% Psychology, 5% Visual and Performing Arts
Expenses: 2021-2022: $33,082; room/board: $14,038
Financial aid: (973) 443-8700; 80% of undergrads determined to have financial need; average aid package $38,537

Felician University
Lodi NJ
(201) 355-1465
U.S. News ranking: Reg. U. (N), second tier
Website: www.felician.edu
Admissions email: admissions@felician.edu
Private; founded 1942
Affiliation: Roman Catholic
Freshman admissions: less selective; 2020-2021: 2,838 applied, 2,655 accepted. Neither SAT nor ACT required. SAT 25/75 percentile: 890-1050. High school rank: 13% in top tenth, 38% in top quarter, 75% in top half
Early decision deadline: N/A, notification date: N/A
Early action deadline: N/A, notification date: N/A
Application deadline (fall): 6/1
Undergraduate student body: 1,820 full time, 295 part time; 27% male, 73% female; 0% American Indian, 5% Asian, 20% black, 35% Hispanic, 1% multiracial, 0% Pacific Islander, 27% white, 3% international; 88% from in state; 19% live on campus; N/A of students in fraternities, N/A in sororities
Most popular majors: 35% Health Professions and Related Programs, 18% Business, Management, Marketing, and Related Support

Services, 10% Biological and Biomedical Sciences, 9% Psychology, 6% Homeland Security, Law Enforcement, Firefighting and Related Protective Services
Expenses: 2020-2021: $35,000; room/board: $13,140
Financial aid: (201) 559-6007; 89% of undergrads determined to have financial need; average aid package $27,835

Georgian Court University
Lakewood NJ
(800) 458-8422
U.S. News ranking: Reg. U. (N), No. 109
Website: georgian.edu
Admissions email: admissions@georgian.edu
Private; founded 1908
Affiliation: Roman Catholic
Freshman admissions: selective; 2020-2021: 1,843 applied, 1,491 accepted. Neither SAT nor ACT required. SAT 25/75 percentile: 940-1138. High school rank: 12% in top tenth, 36% in top quarter, 70% in top half
Early decision deadline: N/A, notification date: N/A
Early action deadline: N/A, notification date: N/A
Application deadline (fall): rolling
Undergraduate student body: 1,290 full time, 352 part time; 28% male, 72% female; 1% American Indian, 2% Asian, 11% black, 16% Hispanic, 1% multiracial, 0% Pacific Islander, 59% white, 2% international; 92% from in state; 19% live on campus; 0% of students in fraternities, 0% in sororities
Most popular majors: 20% Health Professions and Related Programs, 20% Psychology, 13% Business, Management, Marketing, and Related Support Services, 8% Public Administration and Social Service Professions, 7% Education
Expenses: 2021-2022: $34,481; room/board: $11,710
Financial aid: (732) 987-2258; 78% of undergrads determined to have financial need; average aid package $28,997

Kean University
Union NJ
(908) 737-7100
U.S. News ranking: Reg. U. (N), No. 126
Website: www.kean.edu
Admissions email: admitme@kean.edu
Public; founded 1855
Freshman admissions: less selective; 2020-2021: 10,138 applied, 7,913 accepted. Neither SAT nor ACT required. SAT 25/75 percentile: 920-1100. High school rank: N/A
Early decision deadline: N/A, notification date: N/A
Early action deadline: 12/1, notification date: 1/1
Application deadline (fall): 8/15
Undergraduate student body: 9,400 full time, 2,286 part time; 39% male, 61% female; 0% American Indian, 6% Asian, 20% black,

33% Hispanic, 2% multiracial, 0% Pacific Islander, 29% white, 2% international; N/A from in state; 7% live on campus; N/A of students in fraternities, N/A in sororities
Most popular majors: 16% Psychology, General, 11% Business Administration and Management, General, 7% Biology/Biological Sciences, General, 7% Speech Communication and Rhetoric, 6% Criminal Justice/Law Enforcement Administration
Expenses: 2021-2022: $12,595 in state, $19,771 out of state; room/board: N/A
Financial aid: (908) 737-3190; 72% of undergrads determined to have financial need; average aid package $11,346

Monmouth University
West Long Branch NJ
(800) 543-9671
U.S. News ranking: Reg. U. (N), No. 18
Website: www.monmouth.edu
Admissions email: admission@monmouth.edu
Private; founded 1933
Freshman admissions: selective; 2020-2021: 8,367 applied, 6,604 accepted. Neither SAT nor ACT required. SAT 25/75 percentile: 1040-1210. High school rank: 17% in top tenth, 44% in top quarter, 80% in top half
Early decision deadline: 11/15, notification date: 12/15
Early action deadline: 12/1, notification date: 1/15
Application deadline (fall): 3/1
Undergraduate student body: 4,093 full time, 170 part time; 39% male, 61% female; 0% American Indian, 2% Asian, 5% black, 15% Hispanic, 3% multiracial, 0% Pacific Islander, 69% white, 1% international; N/A from in state; 26% live on campus; 8% of students in fraternities, 23% in sororities
Most popular majors: 27% Business, Management, Marketing, and Related Support Services, 10% Health Professions and Related Programs, 9% Communication, Journalism, and Related Programs, 6% Biological and Biomedical Sciences, 6% Homeland Security, Law Enforcement, Firefighting and Related Protective Services
Expenses: 2021-2022: $41,680; room/board: $15,146
Financial aid: (732) 571-3463; 73% of undergrads determined to have financial need; average aid package $29,171

Montclair State University
Montclair NJ
(973) 655-4444
U.S. News ranking: Nat. U., No. 179
Website: www.montclair.edu
Admissions email: undergraduate.admissions@montclair.edu
Public; founded 1908

Freshman admissions: selective; 2020-2021: 11,888 applied, 9,827 accepted. Neither SAT nor ACT required. SAT 25/75 percentile: 980-1160. High school rank: 11% in top tenth, 35% in top quarter, 74% in top half
Early decision deadline: N/A, notification date: N/A
Early action deadline: 11/15, notification date: 12/15
Application deadline (fall): 3/1
Undergraduate student body: 14,543 full time, 1,831 part time; 38% male, 62% female; 0% American Indian, 7% Asian, 14% black, 32% Hispanic, 3% multiracial, 0% Pacific Islander, 40% white, 1% international; 96% from in state; 23% live on campus; N/A of students in fraternities, N/A in sororities
Most popular majors: 21% Business, Management, Marketing, and Related Support Services, 11% Visual and Performing Arts, 10% Family and Consumer Sciences/Human Sciences, 10% Psychology, 6% Communication, Journalism, and Related Programs
Expenses: 2021-2022: $13,298 in state, $21,417 out of state; room/board: $16,388
Financial aid: (973) 655-7020; 72% of undergrads determined to have financial need; average aid package $10,763

New Jersey City University
Jersey City NJ
(888) 441-6528
U.S. News ranking: Reg. U. (N), second tier
Website: www.njcu.edu/
Admissions email: admissions@njcu.edu
Public; founded 1927
Freshman admissions: less selective; 2020-2021: 6,545 applied, 6,305 accepted. Neither SAT nor ACT required. SAT 25/75 percentile: 880-1090. High school rank: 18% in top tenth, 44% in top quarter, 69% in top half
Early decision deadline: N/A, notification date: N/A
Early action deadline: N/A, notification date: N/A
Undergraduate student body: 4,921 full time, 923 part time; 42% male, 58% female; 0% American Indian, 8% Asian, 23% black, 43% Hispanic, 2% multiracial, 0% Pacific Islander, 18% white, 1% international; 1% from in state; 5% live on campus; N/A of students in fraternities, N/A in sororities
Most popular majors: Accounting, Biology/Biological Sciences, General, Corrections and Criminal Justice, Other, Psychology, General, Registered Nursing, Nursing Administration, Nursing Research and Clinical Nursing, Other
Expenses: 2021-2022: $13,168 in state, $23,460 out of state; room/board: N/A
Financial aid: (201) 200-3171; 87% of undergrads determined to have financial need; average aid package $12,003

New Jersey Institute of Technology
Newark NJ
(973) 596-3300
U.S. News ranking: Nat. U., No. 103
Website: www.njit.edu
Admissions email: admissions@njit.edu
Public; founded 1881
Freshman admissions: more selective; 2020-2021: 10,299 applied, 6,800 accepted. Neither SAT nor ACT required. SAT 25/75 percentile: 1200-1390. High school rank: 36% in top tenth, 64% in top quarter, 87% in top half
Early decision deadline: N/A, notification date: N/A
Early action deadline: 11/11, notification date: 12/16
Application deadline (fall): 3/1
Undergraduate student body: 7,389 full time, 1,695 part time; 74% male, 26% female; 0% American Indian, 23% Asian, 8% black, 21% Hispanic, 3% multiracial, 0% Pacific Islander, 34% white, 8% international; 96% from in state; 15% live on campus; 5% of students in fraternities, 5% in sororities
Most popular majors: 40% Engineering, 25% Computer and Information Sciences and Support Services, 13% Engineering Technologies and Engineering-Related Fields, 6% Biological and Biomedical Sciences, 5% Business, Management, Marketing, and Related Support Services
Expenses: 2021-2022: $17,674 in state, $33,386 out of state; room/board: $13,900
Financial aid: (973) 596-3476; 69% of undergrads determined to have financial need; average aid package $14,900

Princeton University
Princeton NJ
(609) 258-3060
U.S. News ranking: Nat. U., No. 1
Website: www.princeton.edu
Admissions email: uaoffice@princeton.edu
Private; founded 1746
Freshman admissions: most selective; 2020-2021: 32,835 applied, 1,848 accepted. Either SAT or ACT required. SAT 25/75 percentile: 1450-1570. High school rank: 89% in top tenth, 96% in top quarter, 99% in top half
Early decision deadline: N/A, notification date: N/A
Early action deadline: 11/1, notification date: 12/15
Application deadline (fall): 1/1
Undergraduate student body: 4,688 full time, 85 part time; 50% male, 50% female; 0% American Indian, 25% Asian, 9% black, 11% Hispanic, 6% multiracial, 0% Pacific Islander, 36% white, 12% international; 19% from in state; 0% live on campus; 0% of students in fraternities, 0% in sororities
Most popular majors: 20% Social Sciences, 15% Engineering,

12% Computer and Information Sciences and Support Services, 10% Biological and Biomedical Sciences, 9% Public Administration and Social Service Professions
Expenses: 2021-2022: $56,010; room/board: $18,180
Financial aid: (609) 258-3330; 62% of undergrads determined to have financial need; average aid package $52,681

Ramapo College of New Jersey
Mahwah NJ
(201) 684-7300
U.S. News ranking: Reg. U. (N), No. 34
Website: www.ramapo.edu
Admissions email: admissions@ramapo.edu
Public; founded 1969
Freshman admissions: selective; 2020-2021: 7,980 applied, 5,334 accepted. Either SAT or ACT required. SAT 25/75 percentile: 1030-1220. High school rank: 7% in top tenth, 43% in top quarter, 86% in top half
Early decision deadline: 11/1, notification date: 12/5
Early action deadline: 12/15, notification date: 2/1
Application deadline (fall): 2/1
Undergraduate student body: 4,720 full time, 692 part time; 42% male, 58% female; 0% American Indian, 9% Asian, 7% black, 20% Hispanic, 0% multiracial, 0% Pacific Islander, 58% white, 1% international; 96% from in state; 7% live on campus; 5% of students in fraternities, 8% in sororities
Most popular majors: 24% Business, Management, Marketing, and Related Support Services, 11% Health Professions and Related Programs, 10% Social Sciences, 8% Communication, Journalism, and Related Programs, 8% Psychology
Expenses: 2021-2022: $15,329 in state, $25,291 out of state; room/board: $12,792
Financial aid: (201) 684-7549; 52% of undergrads determined to have financial need; average aid package $11,464

Rider University
Lawrenceville NJ
(609) 896-9026
U.S. News ranking: Reg. U. (N), No. 27
Website: www.rider.edu
Admissions email: admissions@rider.edu
Private; founded 1865
Freshman admissions: selective; 2020-2021: 9,250 applied, 6,999 accepted. Neither SAT nor ACT required. SAT 25/75 percentile: 1020-1220. High school rank: 17% in top tenth, 46% in top quarter, 77% in top half
Early decision deadline: N/A, notification date: N/A
Early action deadline: 11/15, notification date: 12/15
Application deadline (fall): rolling
Undergraduate student body: 3,333

full time, 297 part time; 42% male, 58% female; 0% American Indian, 5% Asian, 14% black, 18% Hispanic, 4% multiracial, 0% Pacific Islander, 54% white, 2% international; 77% from in state; 25% live on campus; N/A of students in fraternities, N/A in sororities
Most popular majors: 34% Business, Management, Marketing, and Related Support Services, 21% Computer and Information Sciences and Support Services, 12% Education, 12% Visual and Performing Arts, 9% Psychology
Expenses: 2021-2022: $45,860; room/board: $15,500
Financial aid: (609) 896-5188; 78% of undergrads determined to have financial need; average aid package $35,460

Rowan University
Glassboro NJ
(856) 256-4200
U.S. News ranking: Nat. U., No. 179
Website: www.rowan.edu
Admissions email: admissions@rowan.edu
Public; founded 1923
Freshman admissions: selective; 2020-2021: 14,747 applied, 11,611 accepted. Neither SAT nor ACT required. SAT 25/75 percentile: 1020-1240. High school rank: N/A
Early decision deadline: N/A, notification date: N/A
Early action deadline: N/A, notification date: N/A
Application deadline (fall): 7/15
Undergraduate student body: 13,832 full time, 2,131 part time; 53% male, 47% female; 0% American Indian, 6% Asian, 10% black, 12% Hispanic, 4% multiracial, 0% Pacific Islander, 66% white, 1% international; 97% from in state; 24% live on campus; 4% of students in fraternities, 4% in sororities
Most popular majors: 10% Psychology, General, 8% Business Administration and Management, General, 7% Biology/Biological Sciences, General, 6% Criminal Justice/Police Science, 4% Finance, General
Expenses: 2021-2022: $14,377 in state, $23,409 out of state; room/board: $15,484
Financial aid: (856) 256-4281; 66% of undergrads determined to have financial need; average aid package $10,387

Rutgers School of Nursing[1]
NJ
Admissions email: N/A
Private
Application deadline (fall): N/A
Undergraduate student body: N/A full time, N/A part time
Expenses: N/A
Financial aid: N/A

Rutgers University–Camden
Camden NJ
(856) 225-6104
U.S. News ranking: Nat. U., No. 148
Website: www.camden.rutgers.edu/
Admissions email: admissions@camden.rutgers.edu
Public; founded 1926
Freshman admissions: selective; 2020-2021: 9,879 applied, 7,536 accepted. Neither SAT nor ACT required. SAT 25/75 percentile: 980-1170. High school rank: 18% in top tenth, 39% in top quarter, 77% in top half
Early decision deadline: N/A, notification date: N/A
Early action deadline: 11/1, notification date: 1/31
Application deadline (fall): rolling
Undergraduate student body: 4,608 full time, 894 part time; 38% male, 62% female; 0% American Indian, 11% Asian, 18% black, 19% Hispanic, 4% multiracial, 0% Pacific Islander, 43% white, 2% international
Most popular majors: 20% Registered Nursing/Registered Nurse, 15% Business Administration and Management, General, 9% Health Professions and Related Programs, 8% Psychology, General, 6% Criminal Justice/Safety Studies
Expenses: 2021-2022: $15,657 in state, $32,299 out of state; room/board: $12,652
Financial aid: (856) 225-6039; 79% of undergrads determined to have financial need; average aid package $15,244

Rutgers University–Newark
Newark NJ
(973) 353-5205
U.S. News ranking: Nat. U., No. 127
Website: www.newark.rutgers.edu/
Admissions email: newark@admissions.rutgers.edu
Public; founded 1908
Freshman admissions: selective; 2020-2021: 13,506 applied, 10,007 accepted. Neither SAT nor ACT required. SAT 25/75 percentile: 1010-1170. High school rank: 15% in top tenth, 40% in top quarter, 81% in top half
Early decision deadline: N/A, notification date: N/A
Early action deadline: 11/1, notification date: 1/31
Application deadline (fall): rolling
Undergraduate student body: 7,974 full time, 1,144 part time; 44% male, 56% female; 0% American Indian, 17% Asian, 19% black, 30% Hispanic, 3% multiracial, 0% Pacific Islander, 20% white, 8% international
Most popular majors: 13% Finance, General, 10% Accounting, 10% Criminal Justice/Safety Studies, 10% Logistics, Materials, and Supply Chain Management, 10% Psychology, General
Expenses: 2021-2022: $15,208 in state, $32,409 out of state; room/board: $13,930

Financial aid: (973) 353-5151; 76% of undergrads determined to have financial need; average aid package $14,477

Saint Elizabeth University
Morristown NJ
(973) 290-4700
U.S. News ranking: Reg. U. (N), No. 114
Website: www.steu.edu
Admissions email: apply@steu.edu
Private; founded 1899
Affiliation: Roman Catholic
Freshman admissions: least selective; 2020-2021: 1,515 applied, 1,142 accepted. Neither SAT nor ACT required. SAT 25/75 percentile: 803-1048. High school rank: N/A
Early decision deadline: N/A, notification date: N/A
Early action deadline: N/A, notification date: N/A
Application deadline (fall): rolling
Undergraduate student body: 632 full time, 154 part time; 31% male, 69% female; 0% American Indian, 3% Asian, 33% black, 27% Hispanic, 2% multiracial, 1% Pacific Islander, 23% white, 2% international; N/A from in state; 27% live on campus; 0% of students in fraternities, 0% in sororities
Most popular majors: 45% Health Professions and Related Programs, 11% Homeland Security, Law Enforcement, Firefighting and Related Protective Services, 11% Psychology, 8% Business, Management, Marketing, and Related Support Services, 7% Biological and Biomedical Sciences
Expenses: 2021-2022: $34,850; room/board: $12,744
Financial aid: (973) 290-4445

Saint Peter's University
Jersey City NJ
(201) 761-7100
U.S. News ranking: Reg. U. (N), No. 58
Website: www.saintpeters.edu
Admissions email: admissions@saintpeters.edu
Private; founded 1872
Affiliation: Roman Catholic
Freshman admissions: less selective; 2020-2021: 4,154 applied, 3,516 accepted. Neither SAT nor ACT required. SAT 25/75 percentile: 910-1090. High school rank: 12% in top tenth, 40% in top quarter, 70% in top half
Early decision deadline: N/A, notification date: N/A
Early action deadline: N/A, notification date: N/A
Application deadline (fall): rolling
Undergraduate student body: 2,038 full time, 317 part time; 41% male, 59% female; 0% American Indian, 8% Asian, 20% black, 49% Hispanic, 1% multiracial, 0% Pacific Islander, 14% white, 3% international; 92% from in state; 17% live on campus; N/A of students in fraternities, N/A in sororities

Most popular majors: 15% Biology/Biological Sciences, General, 11% Business Administration and Management, General, 10% Criminal Justice/Safety Studies, 6% Registered Nursing/Registered Nurse, 5% Computer and Information Sciences, General
Expenses: 2021-2022: $38,760; room/board: $16,300
Financial aid: (201) 761-6060; 88% of undergrads determined to have financial need; average aid package $34,621

Seton Hall University
South Orange NJ
(800) 843-4255
U.S. News ranking: Nat. U., No. 127
Website: www.shu.edu
Admissions email: thehall@shu.edu
Private; founded 1856
Affiliation: Roman Catholic
Freshman admissions: more selective; 2020-2021: 20,830 applied, 16,295 accepted. Neither SAT nor ACT required. SAT 25/75 percentile: 1150-1310. High school rank: 33% in top tenth, 60% in top quarter, 88% in top half
Early decision deadline: N/A, notification date: N/A
Early action deadline: 12/15, notification date: 1/31
Application deadline (fall): rolling
Undergraduate student body: 5,724 full time, 189 part time; 47% male, 53% female; 0% American Indian, 11% Asian, 8% black, 18% Hispanic, 4% multiracial, 0% Pacific Islander, 51% white, 3% international; 70% from in state; 23% live on campus; 15% of students in fraternities, 22% in sororities
Most popular majors: 10% Biology/Biological Sciences, General, 9% Finance, General, 8% Humanities/Humanistic Studies, 8% Registered Nursing/Registered Nurse, 6% Marketing/Marketing Management, General
Expenses: 2021-2022: $46,880; room/board: $15,834
Financial aid: (973) 761-9350

Stevens Institute of Technology
Hoboken NJ
(201) 216-5194
U.S. News ranking: Nat. U., No. 83
Website: www.stevens.edu
Admissions email: admissions@stevens.edu
Private; founded 1870
Freshman admissions: most selective; 2020-2021: 10,346 applied, 5,490 accepted. Neither SAT nor ACT required. SAT 25/75 percentile: 1320-1480. High school rank: 67% in top tenth, 94% in top quarter, 99% in top half
Early decision deadline: 11/15, notification date: 12/15
Early action deadline: N/A, notification date: N/A
Application deadline (fall): 1/15
Undergraduate student body: 3,632 full time, 29 part time; 71% male, 29% female; 0% American Indian, 18% Asian, 2% black,

13% Hispanic, 0% multiracial, 0% Pacific Islander, 59% white, 3% international; 63% from in state; 17% live on campus; 21% of students in fraternities, 31% in sororities
Most popular majors: 20% Mechanical Engineering, 12% Business Administration and Management, General, 10% Computer Science, 8% Chemical Engineering, 8% Computer Engineering, General
Expenses: 2021-2022: $56,920; room/board: $16,600
Financial aid: (201) 216-3400; 68% of undergrads determined to have financial need; average aid package $33,545

Stockton University
Galloway NJ
(609) 652-4261
U.S. News ranking: Reg. U. (N), No. 34
Website: www.stockton.edu
Admissions email: admissions@stockton.edu
Public; founded 1969
Freshman admissions: selective; 2020-2021: 7,262 applied, 5,614 accepted. Neither SAT nor ACT required. SAT 25/75 percentile: 1013-1190. High school rank: 14% in top tenth, 36% in top quarter, 72% in top half
Early decision deadline: N/A, notification date: N/A
Early action deadline: N/A, notification date: N/A
Application deadline (fall): 9/1
Undergraduate student body: 8,427 full time, 419 part time; 40% male, 60% female; 0% American Indian, 7% Asian, 9% black, 16% Hispanic, 3% multiracial, 0% Pacific Islander, 63% white, 1% international; 97% from in state; 23% live on campus; 9% of students in fraternities, 10% in sororities
Most popular majors: 21% Health Professions and Related Programs, 18% Business, Management, Marketing, and Related Support Services, 11% Social Sciences, 10% Biological and Biomedical Sciences, 8% Psychology
Expenses: 2021-2022: $14,885 in state, $22,467 out of state; room/board: $12,666
Financial aid: (609) 652-4203; 72% of undergrads determined to have financial need; average aid package $16,823

Thomas Edison State University[1]
Trenton NJ
(609) 777-5680
U.S. News ranking: Reg. U. (N), unranked
Admissions email: N/A
Public
Application deadline (fall): N/A
Undergraduate student body: N/A full time, N/A part time
Expenses: N/A
Financial aid: N/A

William Paterson University of New Jersey

Wayne NJ
(973) 720-2125
U.S. News ranking: Reg. U. (N), No. 90
Website: www.wpunj.edu/
Admissions email: admissions@wpunj.edu
Public; founded 1855
Freshman admissions: least selective; 2020-2021: 9,309 applied, 8,444 accepted. Neither SAT nor ACT required. SAT 25/75 percentile: N/A. High school rank: N/A
Early decision deadline: N/A, notification date: N/A
Early action deadline: N/A, notification date: N/A
Application deadline (fall): 6/1
Undergraduate student body: 6,480 full time, 1,491 part time; 42% male, 58% female; 0% American Indian, 7% Asian, 19% black, 34% Hispanic, 3% multiracial, 0% Pacific Islander, 34% white, 1% international; 98% from in state; 15% live on campus; 2% of students in fraternities, 3% in sororities
Most popular majors: 19% Business, Management, Marketing, and Related Support Services, 12% Health Professions and Related Programs, 12% Psychology, 8% Communication, Journalism, and Related Programs, 7% Homeland Security, Law Enforcement, Firefighting and Related Protective Services
Expenses: 2020-2021: $13,572 in state, $22,138 out of state; room/board: $14,040
Financial aid: (973) 720-3945; 74% of undergrads determined to have financial need; average aid package $12,017

NEW MEXICO

Eastern New Mexico University[1]

Portales NM
(575) 562-2178
U.S. News ranking: Reg. U. (W), second tier
Website: www.enmu.edu
Admissions email: admissions.office@enmu.edu
Public; founded 1934
Application deadline (fall): rolling
Undergraduate student body: N/A full time, N/A part time
Expenses: 2020-2021: $6,648 in state, $8,688 out of state; room/board: $7,526
Financial aid: (575) 562-2708

New Mexico Highlands University[1]

Las Vegas NM
(505) 454-3434
U.S. News ranking: Reg. U. (W), second tier
Website: www.nmhu.edu
Admissions email: admissions@nmhu.edu
Public; founded 1893
Application deadline (fall): rolling

Undergraduate student body: N/A full time, N/A part time
Expenses: 2020-2021: $6,558 in state, $10,998 out of state; room/board: $8,908
Financial aid: (505) 454-3430

New Mexico State University

Las Cruces NM
(575) 646-3121
U.S. News ranking: Nat. U., No. 227
Website: www.nmsu.edu
Admissions email: admissions@nmsu.edu
Public; founded 1888
Freshman admissions: selective; 2020-2021: 13,647 applied, 8,559 accepted. Either SAT or ACT required. ACT 25/75 percentile: 17-23. High school rank: 22% in top tenth, 49% in top quarter, 81% in top half
Early decision deadline: N/A, notification date: N/A
Early action deadline: N/A, notification date: N/A
Application deadline (fall): rolling
Undergraduate student body: 9,466 full time, 2,109 part time; 43% male, 57% female; 3% American Indian, 1% Asian, 2% black, 63% Hispanic, 2% multiracial, 0% Pacific Islander, 24% white, 3% international; 73% from in state; 16% live on campus; 2% of students in fraternities, 2% in sororities
Most popular majors: 16% Business/Commerce, General, 13% Engineering, General, 9% Chiropractic, 7% Liberal Arts and Sciences/Liberal Studies, 6% Criminal Justice/Safety Studies
Expenses: 2021-2022: $8,044 in state, $25,666 out of state; room/board: $11,407
Financial aid: (575) 646-4105; 68% of undergrads determined to have financial need; average aid package $16,468

New Mexico Tech

Socorro NM
(575) 835-5424
U.S. News ranking: Reg. U. (W), No. 20
Website: www.nmt.edu
Admissions email: Admission@nmt.edu
Public; founded 1889
Freshman admissions: more selective; 2020-2021: 1,754 applied, 1,694 accepted. Either SAT or ACT required. ACT 25/75 percentile: 23-30. High school rank: 35% in top tenth, 57% in top quarter, 88% in top half
Early decision deadline: N/A, notification date: N/A
Early action deadline: N/A, notification date: N/A
Application deadline (fall): 8/1
Undergraduate student body: 1,103 full time, 126 part time; 70% male, 30% female; 4% American Indian, 4% Asian, 1% black, 28% Hispanic, 4% multiracial, 0% Pacific Islander, 55% white, 1% international; 91% from in state; N/A live on campus; 0% of students in fraternities, 0% in sororities

Most popular majors: 26% Mechanical Engineering, 15% Computer and Information Sciences, General, 11% Electrical and Electronics Engineering, 7% Chemical Engineering, 6% Physics, General
Expenses: 2021-2022: $8,425 in state, $24,254 out of state; room/board: $8,518
Financial aid: (575) 835-5333; 54% of undergrads determined to have financial need; average aid package $14,075

Northern New Mexico College[1]

Espanola NM
(505) 747-2100
U.S. News ranking: Reg. Coll. (W), No. 34
Website: www.nnmc.edu
Admissions email: N/A
Public
Application deadline (fall): N/A
Undergraduate student body: N/A full time, N/A part time
Expenses: 2021-2022: $4,952 in state, $13,676 out of state; room/board: N/A
Financial aid: N/A

St. John's College)

Santa Fe NM
(505) 984-6060
U.S. News ranking: Nat. Lib. Arts, No. 75
Website: www.sjc.edu
Admissions email: santafe.admissions@sjc.edu
Private; founded 1696
Freshman admissions: more selective; 2020-2021: 476 applied, 328 accepted. Neither SAT nor ACT required. SAT 25/75 percentile: 1180-1430. High school rank: 47% in top tenth, 68% in top quarter, 79% in top half
Early decision deadline: 11/1, notification date: 12/1
Early action deadline: 11/15, notification date: 12/15
Application deadline (fall): rolling
Undergraduate student body: 258 full time, 11 part time; 54% male, 46% female; 0% American Indian, 3% Asian, 1% black, 10% Hispanic, 7% multiracial, 0% Pacific Islander, 57% white, 20% international; 18% from in state; 9% live on campus; 0% of students in fraternities, 0% in sororities
Most popular majors: 100% Liberal Arts and Sciences, General Studies and Humanities
Expenses: 2021-2022: $36,410; room/board: $14,278
Financial aid: (505) 984-6058; 72% of undergrads determined to have financial need; average aid package $29,979

University of New Mexico

Albuquerque NM
(505) 277-8900
U.S. News ranking: Nat. U., No. 196
Website: www.unm.edu
Admissions email: apply@unm.edu
Public; founded 1889
Freshman admissions: selective; 2020-2021: 13,880 applied, 7,483 accepted. Either SAT or ACT required. ACT 25/75 percentile: 17-25. High school rank: N/A
Early decision deadline: N/A, notification date: N/A
Early action deadline: N/A, notification date: N/A
Application deadline (fall): rolling
Undergraduate student body: 12,040 full time, 4,084 part time; 42% male, 58% female; 6% American Indian, 4% Asian, 3% black, 50% Hispanic, 4% multiracial, 0% Pacific Islander, 30% white, 2% international; 86% from in state; 7% live on campus; 3% of students in fraternities, 3% in sororities
Most popular majors: 16% Business, Management, Marketing, and Related Support Services, 16% Health Professions and Related Programs, 11% Psychology, 8% Biological and Biomedical Sciences, 6% Engineering
Expenses: 2020-2021: $8,863 in state, $24,924 out of state; room/board: $10,262
Financial aid: (505) 277-8900

University of the Southwest[1]

Hobbs NM
(575) 392-6563
U.S. News ranking: Reg. U. (W), second tier
Website: www.usw.edu
Admissions email: admissions@usw.edu
Private; founded 1962
Application deadline (fall): rolling
Undergraduate student body: N/A full time, N/A part time
Expenses: 2020-2021: $16,200; room/board: $9,930
Financial aid: N/A

Western New Mexico University

Silver City NM
(575) 538-6000
U.S. News ranking: Reg. U. (W), second tier
Website: www.wnmu.edu
Admissions email: admissions@wnmu.edu
Public; founded 1893
Freshman admissions: least selective; 2020-2021: N/A applied, N/A accepted. Neither SAT nor ACT required. SAT 25/75 percentile: N/A. High school rank: N/A
Early decision deadline: N/A, notification date: N/A
Early action deadline: N/A, notification date: N/A
Application deadline (fall): N/A
Undergraduate student body: 1,039 full time, 124 part time; 38%

male, 62% female; N/A American Indian, N/A Asian, N/A black, N/A Hispanic, N/A multiracial, N/A Pacific Islander, N/A white, N/A international
Most popular majors: 12% Criminal Justice/Safety Studies, 10% Registered Nursing/Registered Nurse, 10% Social Work, 8% Cell/Cellular and Molecular Biology, 8% Psychology, General
Expenses: 2021-2022: $7,377 in state, $15,233 out of state; room/board: $10,590
Financial aid: (575) 538-6172

NEW YORK

Adelphi University

Garden City NY
(800) 233-5744
U.S. News ranking: Nat. U., No. 172
Website: www.adelphi.edu
Admissions email: admissions@adelphi.edu
Private; founded 1896
Freshman admissions: selective; 2020-2021: 15,329 applied, 11,437 accepted. Neither SAT nor ACT required. SAT 25/75 percentile: 1060-1250. High school rank: 30% in top tenth, 59% in top quarter, 87% in top half
Early decision deadline: N/A, notification date: N/A
Early action deadline: 12/1, notification date: 12/31
Application deadline (fall): rolling
Undergraduate student body: 4,827 full time, 297 part time; 31% male, 69% female; 0% American Indian, 12% Asian, 9% black, 18% Hispanic, 3% multiracial, 0% Pacific Islander, 48% white, 4% international; 93% from in state; 90% live on campus; 9% of students in fraternities, 12% in sororities
Most popular majors: 34% Health Professions and Related Programs, 13% Business, Management, Marketing, and Related Support Services, 7% Psychology, 6% Biological and Biomedical Sciences, 6% Social Sciences
Expenses: 2021-2022: $42,475; room/board: $16,740
Financial aid: (516) 877-3080; 67% of undergrads determined to have financial need; average aid package $27,000

Alfred University

Alfred NY
(800) 541-9229
U.S. News ranking: Reg. U. (N), No. 44
Website: www.alfred.edu
Admissions email: admissions@alfred.edu
Private; founded 1836
Freshman admissions: selective; 2020-2021: 4,252 applied, 2,726 accepted. Neither SAT nor ACT required. SAT 25/75 percentile: 970-1200. High school rank: 18% in top tenth, 42% in top quarter, 76% in top half
Early decision deadline: 12/1, notification date: 12/15
Early action deadline: N/A, notification date: N/A

Application deadline (fall): rolling
Undergraduate student body: 1,521 full time, 73 part time; 50% male, 50% female; 0% American Indian, 2% Asian, 12% black, 9% Hispanic, 2% multiracial, 0% Pacific Islander, 60% white, 8% international; 70% from in state; 70% live on campus; 0% of students in fraternities, 0% in sororities
Most popular majors: 20% Fine/Studio Arts, General, 16% Mechanical Engineering, 8% Business Administration and Management, General, 6% Ceramic Sciences and Engineering, 6% Psychology, General
Expenses: 2021-2022: $36,276; room/board: $13,052
Financial aid: (607) 871-2150; 84% of undergrads determined to have financial need; average aid package $29,561

Bard College
Annandale on Hudson NY
(845) 758-7472
U.S. News ranking: Nat. Lib. Arts, No. 62
Website: www.bard.edu
Admissions email: admissions@bard.edu
Private; founded 1860
Affiliation: Episcopal Church, Reformed
Freshman admissions: more selective; 2020-2021: 4,961 applied, 2,946 accepted. Neither SAT nor ACT required. SAT 25/75 percentile: 1220-1418. High school rank: 34% in top tenth, 68% in top quarter, 90% in top half
Early decision deadline: 11/1, notification date: 1/1
Early action deadline: 11/1, notification date: 1/1
Application deadline (fall): 1/1
Undergraduate student body: 1,681 full time, 121 part time; 37% male, 63% female; 0% American Indian, 4% Asian, 6% black, 13% Hispanic, 5% multiracial, 0% Pacific Islander, 55% white, 11% international
Most popular majors: Information not available
Expenses: 2021-2022: $57,968; room/board: $16,760
Financial aid: (845) 758-7526; 76% of undergrads determined to have financial need; average aid package $53,354

Barnard College
New York NY
(212) 854-2014
U.S. News ranking: Nat. Lib. Arts, No. 17
Website: www.barnard.edu
Admissions email: admissions@barnard.edu
Private; founded 1889
Freshman admissions: most selective; 2020-2021: 9,411 applied, 1,280 accepted. Neither SAT nor ACT required. SAT 25/75 percentile: 1350-1518. High school rank: 90% in top tenth, 98% in top quarter, 100% in top half
Early decision deadline: 11/1,

notification date: 12/15
Early action deadline: N/A, notification date: N/A
Application deadline (fall): 1/1
Undergraduate student body: 2,651 full time, 93 part time; 0% male, 100% female; 0% American Indian, 18% Asian, 5% black, 12% Hispanic, 6% multiracial, 0% Pacific Islander, 45% white, 12% international; N/A from in state; 91% live on campus; N/A of students in fraternities, N/A in sororities
Most popular majors: 30% Social Sciences, 10% Psychology, 10% Visual and Performing Arts, 9% Biological and Biomedical Sciences, 7% English Language and Literature/Letters
Expenses: 2021-2022: $59,684; room/board: $18,486
Financial aid: (212) 854-2154; 35% of undergrads determined to have financial need; average aid package $46,011

Berkeley College
New York NY
(800) 446-5400
U.S. News ranking: Business, unranked
Website: www.berkeleycollege.edu
Admissions email: admissions@berkeleycollege.edu
For-profit; founded 1931
Freshman admissions: least selective; 2020-2021: 873 applied, 824 accepted. Neither SAT nor ACT required. SAT 25/75 percentile: N/A. High school rank: N/A
Early decision deadline: N/A, notification date: N/A
Early action deadline: N/A, notification date: N/A
Application deadline (fall): 9/1
Undergraduate student body: 1,703 full time, 673 part time; 35% male, 65% female; 0% American Indian, 2% Asian, 18% black, 25% Hispanic, 2% multiracial, 0% Pacific Islander, 4% white, 9% international; 81% from in state; 0% live on campus; N/A of students in fraternities, N/A in sororities
Most popular majors: 26% Business Administration and Management, General, 19% Criminal Justice/Law Enforcement Administration, 14% Health/Health Care Administration/Management, 9% Fashion Merchandising, 7% Legal Professions and Studies, Other
Expenses: 2021-2022: $27,600; room/board: $9,400
Financial aid: (973) 200-1148; 83% of undergrads determined to have financial need; average aid package $9,439

Binghamton University–SUNY
Binghamton NY
(607) 777-2171
U.S. News ranking: Nat. U., No. 83
Website: www.binghamton.edu
Admissions email: admit@binghamton.edu
Public; founded 1946
Freshman admissions: more selective; 2020-2021: 38,116

applied, 16,402 accepted. Either SAT or ACT required. SAT 25/75 percentile: 1290-1450. High school rank: 54% in top tenth, 85% in top quarter, 98% in top half
Early decision deadline: N/A, notification date: N/A
Early action deadline: 11/1, notification date: 1/15
Application deadline (fall): rolling
Undergraduate student body: 13,889 full time, 444 part time; 49% male, 51% female; 0% American Indian, 15% Asian, 5% black, 12% Hispanic, 3% multiracial, 0% Pacific Islander, 58% white, 5% international; 89% from in state; 40% live on campus; 16% of students in fraternities, 16% in sororities
Most popular majors: 6% Accounting, 6% Biology/Biological Sciences, General, 6% Psychology, General, 5% Business Administration and Management, General, 5% Computer Science
Expenses: 2021-2022: $10,319 in state, $27,909 out of state; room/board: $17,064
Financial aid: (607) 777-6358; 50% of undergrads determined to have financial need; average aid package $15,341

Boricua College[1]
New York NY
(212) 694-1000
U.S. News ranking: Reg. Coll. (N), second tier
Website: www.boricuacollege.edu/
Admissions email: isanchez@boricuacollege.edu
Private; founded 1973
Application deadline (fall): rolling
Undergraduate student body: N/A full time, N/A part time
Expenses: 2020-2021: $11,025; room/board: N/A
Financial aid: N/A

Canisius College
Buffalo NY
(800) 843-1517
U.S. News ranking: Reg. U. (N), No. 21
Website: www.canisius.edu
Admissions email: admissions@canisius.edu
Private; founded 1870
Affiliation: Roman Catholic
Freshman admissions: selective; 2020-2021: 3,453 applied, 2,625 accepted. Neither SAT nor ACT required. SAT 25/75 percentile: 1040-1240. High school rank: 23% in top tenth, 48% in top quarter, 83% in top half
Early decision deadline: N/A, notification date: N/A
Early action deadline: 11/1, notification date: 12/15
Application deadline (fall): rolling
Undergraduate student body: 1,915 full time, 65 part time; 51% male, 49% female; 0% American Indian, 3% Asian, 9% black, 7% Hispanic, 2% multiracial, 0% Pacific Islander, 71% white, 4% international; 88% from in state; 33% live on campus; 1% of students in fraternities, 1% in sororities

Most popular majors: 10% Animal Behavior and Ethology, 9% Research and Experimental Psychology, Other, 8% Accounting, 8% Biology/Biological Sciences, General, 7% Finance, General
Expenses: 2021-2022: $30,910; room/board: $11,994
Financial aid: (716) 888-2600; 70% of undergrads determined to have financial need; average aid package $23,328

Cazenovia College
Cazenovia NY
(800) 654-3210
U.S. News ranking: Reg. Coll. (N), No. 13
Website: www.cazenovia.edu
Admissions email: admission@cazenovia.edu
Private; founded 1824
Freshman admissions: less selective; 2020-2021: 2,243 applied, 1,619 accepted. Neither SAT nor ACT required. SAT 25/75 percentile: 893-1116. High school rank: 0% in top tenth, 11% in top quarter, 38% in top half
Early decision deadline: N/A, notification date: N/A
Early action deadline: N/A, notification date: N/A
Application deadline (fall): rolling
Undergraduate student body: 607 full time, 168 part time; 26% male, 74% female; 0% American Indian, 1% Asian, 12% black, 10% Hispanic, 3% multiracial, 0% Pacific Islander, 68% white, 0% international; 88% from in state; 73% live on campus; 0% of students in fraternities, 0% in sororities
Most popular majors: 24% Visual and Performing Arts, 21% Business, Management, Marketing, and Related Support Services, 20% Public Administration and Social Service Professions, 11% Homeland Security, Law Enforcement, Firefighting and Related Protective Services, 8% Psychology
Expenses: 2021-2022: $36,668; room/board: $14,734
Financial aid: (315) 655-7230; 73% of undergrads determined to have financial need; average aid package $35,873

Clarkson University
Potsdam NY
(800) 527-6577
U.S. News ranking: Nat. U., No. 127
Website: www.clarkson.edu/
Admissions email: admissions@clarkson.edu
Private; founded 1896
Freshman admissions: more selective; 2020-2021: 6,198 applied, 4,834 accepted. Neither SAT nor ACT required. SAT 25/75 percentile: 1150-1350. High school rank: 37% in top tenth, 71% in top quarter, 95% in top half
Early decision deadline: 12/1, notification date: 1/1
Early action deadline: N/A, notification date: N/A
Application deadline (fall): 1/15

Undergraduate student body: 2,845 full time, 60 part time; 69% male, 31% female; 0% American Indian, 4% Asian, 3% black, 5% Hispanic, 4% multiracial, 0% Pacific Islander, 79% white, 3% international; N/A from in state; 74% live on campus; 13% of students in fraternities, 9% in sororities
Most popular majors: 24% Mechanical Engineering, 10% Civil Engineering, General, 10% Engineering/Industrial Management, 7% Chemical Engineering, 6% Electrical and Electronics Engineering
Expenses: 2021-2022: $54,370; room/board: $17,615
Financial aid: (315) 268-6413; 80% of undergrads determined to have financial need; average aid package $47,436

Colgate University
Hamilton NY
(315) 228-7401
U.S. News ranking: Nat. Lib. Arts, No. 17
Website: www.colgate.edu
Admissions email: admission@colgate.edu
Private; founded 1819
Freshman admissions: more selective; 2020-2021: 8,583 applied, 2,358 accepted. Neither SAT nor ACT required. SAT 25/75 percentile: 1300-1470. High school rank: 65% in top tenth, 90% in top quarter, 99% in top half
Early decision deadline: 11/15, notification date: 12/15
Early action deadline: N/A, notification date: N/A
Application deadline (fall): 1/15
Undergraduate student body: 3,023 full time, 19 part time; 45% male, 55% female; 0% American Indian, 5% Asian, 4% black, 9% Hispanic, 4% multiracial, 0% Pacific Islander, 65% white, 9% international; 24% from in state; 92% live on campus; 21% of students in fraternities, 32% in sororities
Most popular majors: 9% Political Science and Government, General, 8% Econometrics and Quantitative Economics, 7% Economics, General, 6% Computer Science, 5% English Language and Literature, General
Expenses: 2021-2022: $61,966; room/board: $15,524
Financial aid: (315) 228-7431; 33% of undergrads determined to have financial need; average aid package $56,471

College of Mount St. Vincent
Bronx NY
(718) 405-3267
U.S. News ranking: Reg. U. (N), No. 90
Website: www.mountsaintvincent.edu
Admissions email: admissions.office@mountsaintvincent.edu
Private; founded 1847
Affiliation: Roman Catholic
Freshman admissions: less

selective; 2020-2021: 2,963 applied, 2,746 accepted. Neither SAT nor ACT required. SAT 25/75 percentile: 940-1060. High school rank: 8% in top tenth, 24% in top quarter, 43% in top half
Early decision deadline: N/A, notification date: N/A
Early action deadline: 11/15, notification date: 12/15
Application deadline (fall): rolling
Undergraduate student body: 2,199 full time, 81 part time; 24% male, 76% female; 0% American Indian, 6% Asian, 16% black, 34% Hispanic, 3% multiracial, 0% Pacific Islander, 26% white, 1% international; 89% from in state; 40% live on campus; 0% of students in fraternities, 0% in sororities
Most popular majors: 49% Registered Nursing/Registered Nurse, 13% Psychology, General, 11% Business Administration and Management, General, 8% Sociology, 6% Biology/Biological Sciences, General
Expenses: 2020-2021: $40,980; room/board: $11,000
Financial aid: (718) 405-3289

The College of Saint Rose

Albany NY
(518) 454-5150
U.S. News ranking: Reg. U. (N), No. 103
Website: www.strose.edu
Admissions email: admit@strose.edu
Private; founded 1920
Freshman admissions: less selective; 2020-2021: 6,373 applied, 5,218 accepted. Neither SAT nor ACT required. SAT 25/75 percentile: 1020-1190. High school rank: 12% in top tenth, 35% in top quarter, 75% in top half
Early decision deadline: N/A, notification date: N/A
Early action deadline: 12/1, notification date: 12/15
Application deadline (fall): 5/1
Undergraduate student body: 2,183 full time, 66 part time; 33% male, 67% female; 0% American Indian, 3% Asian, 16% black, 6% Hispanic, 15% multiracial, 0% Pacific Islander, 53% white, 3% international; 84% from in state; 42% live on campus; N/A of students in fraternities, N/A in sororities
Most popular majors: 21% Business, Management, Marketing, and Related Support Services, 19% Education, 10% Visual and Performing Arts, 9% Homeland Security, Law Enforcement, Firefighting and Related Protective Services, 9% Psychology
Expenses: 2021-2022: $35,370; room/board: $13,606
Financial aid: (518) 337-4915; 84% of undergrads determined to have financial need; average aid package $25,544

The College of Westchester[1]

White Plains NY
(914) 331-0853
U.S. News ranking: Reg. Coll. (N), No. 20
Admissions email: N/A
For-profit
Application deadline (fall): N/A
Undergraduate student body: N/A full time, N/A part time
Expenses: 2020-2021: $22,410; room/board: N/A
Financial aid: N/A

Columbia University

New York NY
(212) 854-2522
U.S. News ranking: Nat. U., No. 2
Website: www.columbia.edu
Admissions email: ugrad-ask@columbia.edu
Private; founded 1754
Freshman admissions: most selective; 2020-2021: 40,083 applied, 2,544 accepted. Either SAT or ACT required. SAT 25/75 percentile: 1470-1570. High school rank: 96% in top tenth, 99% in top quarter, 100% in top half
Early decision deadline: 11/1, notification date: 12/15
Early action deadline: N/A, notification date: N/A
Application deadline (fall): 1/1
Undergraduate student body: 6,170 full time, 0 part time; 49% male, 51% female; 1% American Indian, 21% Asian, 9% black, 15% Hispanic, 5% multiracial, 0% Pacific Islander, 31% white, 17% international; 21% from in state; N/A live on campus; 14% of students in fraternities, 12% in sororities
Most popular majors: 21% Social Sciences, 16% Engineering, 13% Computer and Information Sciences and Support Services, 6% Biological and Biomedical Sciences, 5% English Language and Literature/Letters
Expenses: 2021-2022: $63,530; room/board: $15,450
Financial aid: (212) 854-3711; 50% of undergrads determined to have financial need; average aid package $60,331

Cooper Union for the Advancement of Science and Art

New York NY
(212) 353-4120
U.S. News ranking: Reg. Coll. (N), No. 2
Website: cooper.edu
Admissions email: admissions@cooper.edu
Private; founded 1859
Freshman admissions: most selective; 2020-2021: 2,358 applied, 413 accepted. Neither SAT nor ACT required. SAT 25/75 percentile: 1330-1500. High school rank: 51% in top tenth, 73% in top quarter, 88% in top half
Early decision deadline: 11/1, notification date: 12/15

Early action deadline: N/A, notification date: N/A
Application deadline (fall): 1/5
Undergraduate student body: 802 full time, 4 part time; 56% male, 44% female; 0% American Indian, 28% Asian, 4% black, 12% Hispanic, 3% multiracial, 0% Pacific Islander, 32% white, 14% international; 62% from in state; 20% live on campus; 4% of students in fraternities, 0% in sororities
Most popular majors: 31% Fine/ Studio Arts, General, 19% Electrical and Electronics Engineering, 14% Civil Engineering, General, 14% Mechanical Engineering, 11% Chemical Engineering
Expenses: 2021-2022: $46,820; room/board: $17,812
Financial aid: N/A; 60% of undergrads determined to have financial need; average aid package $43,000

Cornell University

Ithaca NY
(607) 255-5241
U.S. News ranking: Nat. U., No. 17
Website: www.cornell.edu
Admissions email: admissions@cornell.edu
Private; founded 1865
Freshman admissions: most selective; 2020-2021: 51,500 applied, 5,514 accepted. Neither SAT nor ACT required. SAT 25/75 percentile: 1400-1540. High school rank: 84% in top tenth, 98% in top quarter, 100% in top half
Early decision deadline: 11/1, notification date: 12/15
Early action deadline: N/A, notification date: N/A
Application deadline (fall): 1/2
Undergraduate student body: 14,693 full time, 50 part time; 46% male, 54% female; 0% American Indian, 21% Asian, 7% black, 15% Hispanic, 5% multiracial, 0% Pacific Islander, 35% white, 10% international; 37% from in state; N/A live on campus; N/A of students in fraternities, N/A in sororities
Most popular majors: 15% Engineering, 13% Biological and Biomedical Sciences, 13% Business, Management, Marketing, and Related Support Services, 13% Computer and Information Sciences and Support Services, 12% Agriculture, Agriculture Operations, and Related Sciences
Expenses: 2021-2022: $61,015; room/board: $16,446
Financial aid: (607) 255-5145; 48% of undergrads determined to have financial need; average aid package $51,716

CUNY–Baruch College

New York NY
(646) 312-1400
U.S. News ranking: Reg. U. (N), No. 16
Website: www.baruch.cuny.edu
Admissions email: admissions@baruch.cuny.edu
Public; founded 1919

Freshman admissions: more selective; 2020-2021: 24,307 applied, 9,895 accepted. Either SAT or ACT required. SAT 25/75 percentile: 1150-1350. High school rank: 48% in top tenth, 77% in top quarter, 96% in top half
Early decision deadline: N/A, notification date: N/A
Early action deadline: N/A, notification date: N/A
Application deadline (fall): 2/1
Undergraduate student body: 12,421 full time, 3,353 part time; 52% male, 48% female; 0% American Indian, 34% Asian, 9% black, 25% Hispanic, 3% multiracial, 0% Pacific Islander, 20% white, 9% international; N/A from in state; 0% live on campus; N/A of students in fraternities, N/A in sororities
Most popular majors: 76% Business, Management, and Related Support Services, 7% Computer and Information Sciences and Support Services, 4% Psychology, 4% Social Sciences, 3% Communication, Journalism, and Related Programs
Expenses: 2021-2022: $8,071 in state, $19,971 out of state; room/ board: $15,795
Financial aid: (646) 312-1399; 68% of undergrads determined to have financial need; average aid package $9,909

CUNY–Brooklyn College

Brooklyn NY
(718) 951-5001
U.S. News ranking: Reg. U. (N), No. 70
Website: www.brooklyn.cuny.edu
Admissions email: adminqry@brooklyn.cuny.edu
Public; founded 1930
Freshman admissions: selective; 2020-2021: 29,464 applied, 14,655 accepted. Either SAT or ACT required. SAT 25/75 percentile: 1020-1180. High school rank: N/A
Early decision deadline: N/A, notification date: N/A
Early action deadline: N/A, notification date: N/A
Application deadline (fall): N/A
Undergraduate student body: 11,401 full time, 3,568 part time; 42% male, 58% female; 0% American Indian, 22% Asian, 20% black, 24% Hispanic, 3% multiracial, 0% Pacific Islander, 27% white, 3% international; N/A from in state; 0% live on campus; 1% of students in fraternities, 1% in sororities
Most popular majors: 28% Business, Management, Marketing, and Related Support Services, 17% Psychology, 9% Education
Expenses: 2021-2022: $7,440 in state, $19,110 out of state; room/ board: N/A
Financial aid: (718) 951-5051; 81% of undergrads determined to have financial need; average aid package $9,620

CUNY–City College

New York NY
(212) 650-7000
U.S. News ranking: Nat. U., No. 148
Website: www.ccny.cuny.edu/
Admissions email: admissions@ccny.cuny.edu
Public; founded 1847
Freshman admissions: selective; 2020-2021: 29,894 applied, 15,107 accepted. Neither SAT nor ACT required. SAT 25/75 percentile: 1050-1260. High school rank: N/A
Early decision deadline: N/A, notification date: N/A
Early action deadline: N/A, notification date: N/A
Application deadline (fall): rolling
Undergraduate student body: 9,847 full time, 2,740 part time; 47% male, 53% female; 0% American Indian, 26% Asian, 14% black, 38% Hispanic, 3% multiracial, 0% Pacific Islander, 13% white, 6% international; N/A from in state; N/A live on campus; 1% of students in fraternities, 1% in sororities
Most popular majors: 17% Engineering, 15% Psychology, 13% Social Sciences, 11% Biological and Biomedical Sciences, 10% Visual and Performing Arts
Expenses: 2021-2022: $7,340 in state, $19,010 out of state; room/ board: $17,427
Financial aid: (212) 650-5824; 81% of undergrads determined to have financial need; average aid package $5,141

CUNY–College of Staten Island

Staten Island NY
(718) 982-2010
U.S. News ranking: Reg. U. (N), second tier
Website: www.csi.cuny.edu
Admissions email: admissions@csi.cuny.edu
Public; founded 1976
Freshman admissions: selective; 2020-2021: 15,475 applied, 14,064 accepted. Neither SAT nor ACT required. SAT 25/75 percentile: 990-1160. High school rank: N/A
Early decision deadline: N/A, notification date: N/A
Early action deadline: N/A, notification date: N/A
Application deadline (fall): rolling
Undergraduate student body: 9,302 full time, 2,453 part time; 44% male, 56% female; 0% American Indian, 11% Asian, 15% black, 27% Hispanic, 3% multiracial, 0% Pacific Islander, 41% white, 3% international; 99% from in state; 2% live on campus; 0% of students in fraternities, 0% in sororities
Most popular majors: 21% Psychology, 18% Business, Management, Marketing, and Related Support Services, 10% Social Sciences, 6% English Language and Literature/Letters, 6% Health Professions and Related Programs

Expenses: 2021-2022: $7,489 in state, $19,159 out of state; room/board: $19,615
Financial aid: (718) 982-2030; 74% of undergrads determined to have financial need; average aid package $6,866

CUNY–Hunter College
New York NY
(212) 772-4490
U.S. News ranking: Reg. U. (N), No. 18
Website: www.hunter.cuny.edu
Admissions email: admissions@hunter.cuny.edu
Public; founded 1870
Freshman admissions: more selective; 2020-2021: 32,427 applied, 13,004 accepted. Neither SAT nor ACT required. SAT 25/75 percentile: 1150-1350. High school rank: N/A
Early decision deadline: N/A, notification date: N/A
Early action deadline: N/A, notification date: N/A
Application deadline (fall): 3/15
Undergraduate student body: 14,737 full time, 4,421 part time; 35% male, 65% female; 0% American Indian, 32% Asian, 12% black, 23% Hispanic, 0% multiracial, 0% Pacific Islander, 29% white, 5% international
Most popular majors: Information not available
Expenses: 2021-2022: $7,380 in state, $19,050 out of state; room/board: $12,123
Financial aid: (212) 772-4804; 80% of undergrads determined to have financial need; average aid package $10,342

CUNY–John Jay College of Criminal Justice
New York NY
(212) 237-8866
U.S. News ranking: Reg. U. (N), No. 44
Website: www.jjay.cuny.edu/
Admissions email: admissions@jjay.cuny.edu
Public; founded 1965
Freshman admissions: selective; 2020-2021: 21,009 applied, 7,850 accepted. Either SAT or ACT required. SAT 25/75 percentile: 1000-1150. High school rank: N/A
Early decision deadline: N/A, notification date: N/A
Early action deadline: N/A, notification date: N/A
Application deadline (fall): rolling
Undergraduate student body: 11,270 full time, 2,392 part time; 40% male, 60% female; 0% American Indian, 13% Asian, 20% black, 44% Hispanic, 0% multiracial, 0% Pacific Islander, 20% white, 3% international; N/A from in state; 1% live on campus; N/A of students in fraternities, N/A in sororities
Most popular majors: 52% Homeland Security, Law Enforcement, Firefighting and Related Protective Services, 15% Psychology, 14% Social Sciences, 5% Legal Professions and Studies, 4% Computer and Information

Sciences and Support Services
Expenses: 2020-2021: $3,465 in state, $18,000 out of state; room/board: N/A
Financial aid: (212) 237-8897

CUNY–Lehman College
Bronx NY
(718) 960-8700
U.S. News ranking: Reg. U. (N), No. 62
Website: www.lehman.cuny.edu
Admissions email: undergraduate.admissions@lehman.cuny.edu
Public; founded 1968
Freshman admissions: selective; 2020-2021: 27,653 applied, 11,591 accepted. Either SAT or ACT required. SAT 25/75 percentile: 960-1080. High school rank: N/A
Early decision deadline: N/A, notification date: N/A
Early action deadline: N/A, notification date: N/A
Application deadline (fall): 2/1
Undergraduate student body: 8,380 full time, 4,453 part time; 32% male, 68% female; 0% American Indian, 7% Asian, 33% black, 51% Hispanic, 0% multiracial, 0% Pacific Islander, 6% white, 3% international; 89% from in state; N/A live on campus; N/A of students in fraternities, N/A in sororities
Most popular majors: 11% Business Administration, Management and Operations, 10% Psychology, General, 9% Health and Medical Administrative Services, 9% Sociology, 6% Registered Nursing, Nursing Administration, Nursing Research and Clinical Nursing
Expenses: 2021-2022: $7,374 in state, $15,320 out of state; room/board: N/A
Financial aid: (718) 960-8545; 83% of undergrads determined to have financial need

CUNY–Medgar Evers College
Brooklyn NY
(718) 270-6024
U.S. News ranking: Reg. Coll. (N), second tier
Website: ares.mec.cuny.edu/admissions/admissions/
Admissions email: mecadmissions@mec.cuny.edu
Public; founded 1970
Freshman admissions: least selective; 2020-2021: 12,463 applied, 9,832 accepted. Neither SAT nor ACT required. SAT 25/75 percentile: 710-900. High school rank: N/A
Early decision deadline: N/A, notification date: N/A
Early action deadline: N/A, notification date: N/A
Application deadline (fall): rolling
Undergraduate student body: 3,886 full time, 1,381 part time; 27% male, 73% female; 0% American Indian, 3% Asian, 69% black, 17% Hispanic, 0% multiracial, 0% Pacific Islander, 2% white, 1% international; 1% from in state; 0% live on campus; 0%

of students in fraternities, 0% in sororities
Most popular majors: 28% Biology/Biological Sciences, General, 18% Psychology, General, 11% Business Administration and Management, General, 10% Social Work, 4% Public Administration
Expenses: 2021-2022: $7,250 in state, $18,920 out of state; room/board: N/A
Financial aid: (718) 270-6038; 93% of undergrads determined to have financial need; average aid package $9,548

CUNY–New York City College of Technology
Brooklyn NY
(718) 260-5500
U.S. News ranking: Reg. Coll. (N), No. 35
Website: www.citytech.cuny.edu
Admissions email: admissions@citytech.cuny.edu
Public; founded 1946
Freshman admissions: less selective; 2020-2021: 21,525 applied, 17,020 accepted. Neither SAT nor ACT required. SAT 25/75 percentile: N/A. High school rank: N/A
Early decision deadline: N/A, notification date: N/A
Early action deadline: N/A, notification date: N/A
Application deadline (fall): 9/1
Undergraduate student body: 9,846 full time, 5,667 part time; 53% male, 47% female; 0% American Indian, 21% Asian, 27% black, 34% Hispanic, 2% multiracial, 0% Pacific Islander, 10% white, 4% international
Most popular majors: 20% Engineering Technologies and Engineering-Related Fields, 19% Computer and Information Sciences and Support Services, 14% Health Professions and Related Programs, 12% Business, Management, Marketing, and Related Support Services, 11% Visual and Performing Arts
Expenses: 2021-2022: $7,320 in state, $15,270 out of state; room/board: N/A
Financial aid: N/A

CUNY–Queens College
Queens NY
(718) 997-5600
U.S. News ranking: Reg. U. (N), No. 50
Website: www.qc.cuny.edu/
Admissions email: admissions@qc.cuny.edu
Public; founded 1937
Freshman admissions: selective; 2020-2021: 25,621 applied, 13,704 accepted. Neither SAT nor ACT required. SAT 25/75 percentile: 1040-1190. High school rank: N/A
Early decision deadline: N/A, notification date: N/A
Early action deadline: N/A, notification date: N/A
Application deadline (fall): 2/1
Undergraduate student body: 12,479 full time, 4,223 part time; 45% male, 55% female; 0% American Indian, 29% Asian,

9% black, 30% Hispanic, 3% multiracial, 0% Pacific Islander, 23% white, 5% international; 99% from in state; 0% live on campus; 1% of students in fraternities, 1% in sororities
Most popular majors: 22% Social Sciences, 18% Psychology, 15% Business, Management, Marketing, and Related Support Services, 7% Computer and Information Sciences and Support Services, 7% Education
Expenses: 2021-2022: $7,538 in state, $19,208 out of state; room/board: $14,476
Financial aid: (718) 997-5102; 73% of undergrads determined to have financial need; average aid package $6,674

CUNY–York College
Jamaica NY
(718) 262-2165
U.S. News ranking: Reg. Coll. (N), No. 33
Website: www.york.cuny.edu/
Admissions email: admissions@york.cuny.edu
Public; founded 1966
Freshman admissions: less selective; 2020-2021: 15,522 applied, 8,190 accepted. Neither SAT nor ACT required. SAT 25/75 percentile: 870-1050. High school rank: N/A
Early decision deadline: N/A, notification date: N/A
Early action deadline: N/A, notification date: N/A
Application deadline (fall): 6/1
Undergraduate student body: 4,927 full time, 2,602 part time; 33% male, 67% female; 1% American Indian, 22% Asian, 37% black, 28% Hispanic, 4% multiracial, 0% Pacific Islander, 5% white, 4% international; 99% from in state; 0% live on campus; 0% of students in fraternities, 0% in sororities
Most popular majors: 24% Health Professions and Related Programs, 18% Business, Management, Marketing, and Related Support Services, 14% Psychology, 8% Social Sciences, 7% Computer and Information Sciences and Support Services
Expenses: 2021-2022: $7,358 in state, $19,028 out of state; room/board: N/A
Financial aid: (718) 262-2230; 83% of undergrads determined to have financial need; average aid package $5,137

Daemen College
Amherst NY
(716) 839-8225
U.S. News ranking: Nat. U., second tier
Website: www.daemen.edu/
Admissions email: admissions@daemen.edu
Private; founded 1947
Freshman admissions: selective; 2020-2021: 2,902 applied, 1,793 accepted. Neither SAT nor ACT required. SAT 25/75 percentile: 1060-1250. High school rank: 24% in top tenth, 53% in top quarter, 83% in top half

Early decision deadline: 11/1, notification date: N/A
Early action deadline: N/A, notification date: N/A
Application deadline (fall): rolling
Undergraduate student body: 1,465 full time, 173 part time; 30% male, 70% female; 0% American Indian, 3% Asian, 11% black, 7% Hispanic, 1% multiracial, 0% Pacific Islander, 74% white, 1% international; 92% from in state; 36% live on campus; N/A of students in fraternities, N/A in sororities
Most popular majors: 39% Registered Nursing/Registered Nurse, 25% Natural Sciences, 4% Health and Wellness, General, 4% Psychology, General, 4% Social Work
Expenses: 2021-2022: $31,250; room/board: $14,080
Financial aid: (716) 839-8254; 84% of undergrads determined to have financial need; average aid package $22,812

Dominican College
Orangeburg NY
(845) 848-7901
U.S. News ranking: Reg. U. (N), second tier
Website: www.dc.edu
Admissions email: admissions@dc.edu
Private; founded 1952
Freshman admissions: less selective; 2020-2021: 2,291 applied, 1,715 accepted. Neither SAT nor ACT required. SAT 25/75 percentile: 880-1080. High school rank: N/A
Early decision deadline: N/A, notification date: N/A
Early action deadline: N/A, notification date: N/A
Application deadline (fall): rolling
Undergraduate student body: 1,222 full time, 88 part time; 34% male, 66% female; 0% American Indian, 6% Asian, 18% black, 36% Hispanic, 2% multiracial, 0% Pacific Islander, 26% white, 3% international; 77% from in state; 40% live on campus; N/A of students in fraternities, N/A in sororities
Most popular majors: 31% Registered Nursing/Registered Nurse, 18% Social Sciences, General, 9% Occupational Therapy/Therapist, 6% Business Administration and Management, General, 6% Criminal Justice/Safety Studies
Expenses: 2021-2022: $31,460; room/board: $14,020
Financial aid: (845) 848-7818; 90% of undergrads determined to have financial need; average aid package $22,453

D'Youville College
Buffalo NY
(716) 829-7600
U.S. News ranking: Nat. U., second tier
Website: www.dyc.edu
Admissions email: admissions@dyc.edu
Private; founded 1908
Freshman admissions: selective; 2020-2021: 1,755 applied,

1,467 accepted. Either SAT or ACT required. SAT 25/75 percentile: 960-1150. High school rank: 10% in top tenth, 46% in top quarter, 70% in top half
Early decision deadline: N/A, notification date: N/A
Early action deadline: N/A, notification date: N/A
Application deadline (fall): rolling
Undergraduate student body: 1,114 full time, 361 part time; 24% male, 76% female; 1% American Indian, 8% Asian, 10% black, 5% Hispanic, 3% multiracial, 0% Pacific Islander, 65% white, 2% international; 9% from in state; 16% live on campus; 0% of students in fraternities, 0% in sororities
Most popular majors: 43% Registered Nursing/Registered Nurse, 9% Multi-/Interdisciplinary Studies, Other, 8% Physician Assistant, 7% Biology/Biological Sciences, General, 7% Dietetics/Dietitian
Expenses: 2021-2022: $29,998; room/board: $9,500
Financial aid: (716) 829-7500; 82% of undergrads determined to have financial need; average aid package $17,948

Elmira College
Elmira NY
(607) 735-1724
U.S. News ranking: Reg. Coll. (N), No. 9
Website: www.elmira.edu
Admissions email: admissions@elmira.edu
Private; founded 1855
Freshman admissions: selective; 2020-2021: 1,483 applied, 1,453 accepted. Neither SAT nor ACT required. SAT 25/75 percentile: 1020-1220. High school rank: N/A
Early decision deadline: N/A, notification date: N/A
Early action deadline: 10/15, notification date: 10/31
Application deadline (fall): rolling
Undergraduate student body: 682 full time, 31 part time; 32% male, 68% female; 0% American Indian, 2% Asian, 5% black, 6% Hispanic, 3% multiracial, 0% Pacific Islander, 76% white, 4% international
Most popular majors: 22% Registered Nursing/Registered Nurse, 15% Business Administration and Management, General, 9% Psychology, General, 8% Biology/Biological Sciences, General, 5% Elementary Education and Teaching
Expenses: 2021-2022: $36,228; room/board: $13,125
Financial aid: (607) 735-1728; 81% of undergrads determined to have financial need; average aid package $27,397

Farmingdale State College–SUNY
Farmingdale NY
(934) 420-2200
U.S. News ranking: Reg. Coll. (N), No. 15
Website: www.farmingdale.edu

Admissions email: admissions@farmingdale.edu
Public; founded 1912
Freshman admissions: selective; 2020-2021: 7,156 applied, 4,305 accepted. Either SAT or ACT required. SAT 25/75 percentile: 990-1150. High school rank: 12% in top tenth, 34% in top quarter, 65% in top half
Early decision deadline: N/A, notification date: N/A
Early action deadline: N/A, notification date: N/A
Application deadline (fall): 5/1
Undergraduate student body: 7,860 full time, 2,088 part time; 58% male, 42% female; 0% American Indian, 10% Asian, 10% black, 24% Hispanic, 3% multiracial, 0% Pacific Islander, 51% white, 2% international; 100% from in state; N/A live on campus; 2% of students in fraternities, 5% in sororities
Most popular majors: 24% High School/Secondary Diplomas and Certificates, 14% Multi-/Interdisciplinary Studies, 13% Engineering Technologies and Engineering-Related Fields, 13% Homeland Security, Law Enforcement, Firefighting and Related Protective Services, 8% Health Professions and Related Programs
Expenses: 2021-2022: $7,270 in state, $16,980 out of state; room/board: N/A
Financial aid: (934) 420-2578; 57% of undergrads determined to have financial need; average aid package $8,363

Fashion Institute of Technology
New York NY
(212) 217-3760
U.S. News ranking: Reg. U. (N), unranked
Website: www.fitnyc.edu
Admissions email: FITinfo@fitnyc.edu
Public; founded 1944
Freshman admissions: least selective; 2020-2021: 4,354 applied, 2,568 accepted. Neither SAT nor ACT required. SAT 25/75 percentile: N/A. High school rank: N/A
Early decision deadline: N/A, notification date: N/A
Early action deadline: N/A, notification date: N/A
Application deadline (fall): 1/1
Undergraduate student body: 6,966 full time, 993 part time; 17% male, 83% female; 0% American Indian, 13% Asian, 9% black, 23% Hispanic, 4% multiracial, 0% Pacific Islander, 41% white, 10% international; N/A from in state; 2% live on campus; N/A of students in fraternities, N/A in sororities
Most popular majors: 39% Business, Management, Marketing, and Related Support Services, 38% Visual and Performing Arts, 17% Communication, Journalism, and Related Programs

Expenses: 2020-2021: $5,913 in state, $16,493 out of state; room/board: $15,200
Financial aid: (212) 217-3560

Five Towns College[1]
Dix Hills NY
(631) 424-7000
U.S. News ranking: Reg. Coll. (N), No. 37
Website: www.ftc.edu
Admissions email: admissions@ftc.edu
For-profit; founded 1972
Application deadline (fall): rolling
Undergraduate student body: N/A full time, N/A part time
Expenses: 2021-2022: $25,070; room/board: $10,450
Financial aid: (631) 656-2164; 79% of undergrads determined to have financial need; average aid package $18,886

Fordham University
New York NY
(718) 817-4000
U.S. News ranking: Nat. U., No. 68
Website: www.fordham.edu
Admissions email: enroll@fordham.edu
Private; founded 1841
Affiliation: Roman Catholic
Freshman admissions: more selective; 2020-2021: 47,936 applied, 25,180 accepted. Neither SAT nor ACT required. SAT 25/75 percentile: 1230-1410. High school rank: 44% in top tenth, 71% in top quarter, 93% in top half
Early decision deadline: 11/1, notification date: 12/20
Early action deadline: 11/1, notification date: 12/20
Application deadline (fall): 1/1
Undergraduate student body: 8,887 full time, 512 part time; 43% male, 57% female; 0% American Indian, 12% Asian, 4% black, 16% Hispanic, 4% multiracial, 0% Pacific Islander, 55% white, 7% international
Most popular majors: 9% Business Administration and Management, General, 8% Finance, General, 6% Economics, General, 6% Psychology, General, 5% Political Science and Government, General
Expenses: 2021-2022: $55,776; room/board: $21,035
Financial aid: (718) 817-3800; 77% of undergrads determined to have financial need; average aid package $37,724

Hamilton College
Clinton NY
(800) 843-2655
U.S. News ranking: Nat. Lib. Arts, No. 13
Website: www.hamilton.edu
Admissions email: admission@hamilton.edu
Private; founded 1812
Freshman admissions: most selective; 2020-2021: 7,443 applied, 1,370 accepted. Neither SAT nor ACT required. SAT 25/75 percentile: 1380-1510. High school rank: 86% in top tenth, 99% in top quarter, 100% in top half

Early decision deadline: 11/15, notification date: 12/15
Early action deadline: N/A, notification date: N/A
Application deadline (fall): 1/1
Undergraduate student body: 1,897 full time, 3 part time; 46% male, 54% female; 0% American Indian, 7% Asian, 4% black, 10% Hispanic, 5% multiracial, 0% Pacific Islander, 65% white, 5% international; 23% from in state; 100% live on campus; 9% of students in fraternities, 8% in sororities
Most popular majors: 33% Social Sciences, 10% Biological and Biomedical Sciences, 7% English Language and Literature/Letters, 7% Foreign Languages, Literatures, and Linguistics, 6% Mathematics and Statistics
Expenses: 2021-2022: $59,970; room/board: $15,230
Financial aid: (800) 859-4413; 53% of undergrads determined to have financial need; average aid package $51,749

Hartwick College
Oneonta NY
(607) 431-4150
U.S. News ranking: Nat. Lib. Arts, No. 146
Website: www.hartwick.edu
Admissions email: admissions@hartwick.edu
Private; founded 1797
Freshman admissions: selective; 2020-2021: 3,603 applied, 3,354 accepted. Neither SAT nor ACT required. SAT 25/75 percentile: 1020-1180. High school rank: N/A
Early decision deadline: 11/1, notification date: 11/15
Early action deadline: N/A, notification date: N/A
Application deadline (fall): rolling
Undergraduate student body: 1,188 full time, 17 part time; 42% male, 58% female; 0% American Indian, 2% Asian, 11% black, 8% Hispanic, 3% multiracial, 0% Pacific Islander, 59% white, 2% international; N/A from in state; 87% live on campus; 7% of students in fraternities, 12% in sororities
Most popular majors: 25% Registered Nursing/Registered Nurse, 25% Sociology, 17% Business Administration and Management, General, 8% Music, General, 8% Psychology, General
Expenses: 2021-2022: $49,814; room/board: $13,615
Financial aid: (607) 431-4130; 82% of undergrads determined to have financial need; average aid package $42,916

Hilbert College[1]
Hamburg NY
(716) 649-7900
U.S. News ranking: Reg. Coll. (N), second tier
Website: www.hilbert.edu/
Admissions email: admissions@hilbert.edu
Private
Application deadline (fall): N/A

Undergraduate student body: N/A full time, N/A part time
Expenses: 2020-2021: $24,530; room/board: $10,294
Financial aid: N/A

Hobart and William Smith Colleges
Geneva NY
(315) 781-3622
U.S. News ranking: Nat. Lib. Arts, No. 75
Website: www.hws.edu
Admissions email: admissions@hws.edu
Private; founded 1822
Freshman admissions: more selective; 2020-2021: 3,940 applied, 2,437 accepted. Neither SAT nor ACT required. SAT 25/75 percentile: 1180-1360. High school rank: 36% in top tenth, 63% in top quarter, 92% in top half
Early decision deadline: 11/15, notification date: 12/15
Early action deadline: N/A, notification date: N/A
Application deadline (fall): 2/1
Undergraduate student body: 1,806 full time, 16 part time; 47% male, 53% female; 0% American Indian, 3% Asian, 7% black, 7% Hispanic, 3% multiracial, 0% Pacific Islander, 71% white, 5% international; 43% from in state; 90% live on campus; 18% of students in fraternities, 2% in sororities
Most popular majors: 14% Economics, 10% Communication and Media Studies, 8% Psychology, General, 7% English Language and Literature, General, 6% Biology, General
Expenses: 2021-2022: $60,275; room/board: $15,625
Financial aid: (315) 781-3315; 68% of undergrads determined to have financial need; average aid package $46,224

Hofstra University
Hempstead NY
(516) 463-6700
U.S. News ranking: Nat. U., No. 162
Website: www.hofstra.edu
Admissions email: admission@hofstra.edu
Private; founded 1935
Freshman admissions: more selective; 2020-2021: 24,062 applied, 16,630 accepted. Neither SAT nor ACT required. SAT 25/75 percentile: 1160-1330. High school rank: 32% in top tenth, 61% in top quarter, 90% in top half
Early decision deadline: N/A, notification date: N/A
Early action deadline: 11/15, notification date: 12/15
Application deadline (fall): rolling
Undergraduate student body: 5,806 full time, 314 part time; 45% male, 55% female; 0% American Indian, 12% Asian, 9% black, 14% Hispanic, 3% multiracial, 0% Pacific Islander, 55% white, 5% international; 35% from in state; 31% live on campus; 6% of students in fraternities, 12% in sororities

Most popular majors: 6% Finance, General, 6% Psychology, General, 5% Accounting, 4% Marketing/Marketing Management, General, 4% Radio, Television, and Digital Communication, Other
Expenses: 2021-2022: $51,360; room/board: $17,427
Financial aid: (516) 463-8000; 64% of undergrads determined to have financial need; average aid package $35,000

Houghton College
Houghton NY
(800) 777-2556
U.S. News ranking: Nat. Lib. Arts, No. 124
Website: www.houghton.edu
Admissions email: admission@houghton.edu
Private; founded 1883
Affiliation: Wesleyan
Freshman admissions: selective; 2020-2021: 861 applied, 804 accepted. Neither SAT nor ACT required. SAT 25/75 percentile: 1060-1300. High school rank: 18% in top tenth, 50% in top quarter, 76% in top half
Early decision deadline: N/A, notification date: N/A
Early action deadline: N/A, notification date: N/A
Application deadline (fall): rolling
Undergraduate student body: 806 full time, 89 part time; 40% male, 60% female; 0% American Indian, 2% Asian, 3% black, 1% Hispanic, 3% multiracial, 0% Pacific Islander, 58% white, 3% international
Most popular majors: 25% Business Administration and Management, General, 17% Biology/Biological Sciences, General, 15% Psychology, General, 13% Speech Communication and Rhetoric, 11% Elementary Education and Teaching
Expenses: 2021-2022: $16,446; room/board: $9,856
Financial aid: (585) 567-9328; 84% of undergrads determined to have financial need; average aid package $25,118

Iona College
New Rochelle NY
(914) 633-2502
U.S. News ranking: Reg. U. (N), No. 55
Website: www.iona.edu
Admissions email: admissions@iona.edu
Private; founded 1940
Affiliation: Roman Catholic
Freshman admissions: selective; 2020-2021: 10,319 applied, 8,869 accepted. Neither SAT nor ACT required. SAT 25/75 percentile: 1000-1190. High school rank: 12% in top tenth, 32% in top quarter, 67% in top half
Early decision deadline: 12/1, notification date: N/A
Early action deadline: 12/15, notification date: N/A
Application deadline (fall): 2/15
Undergraduate student body: 2,610 full time, 349 part time; 50% male, 50% female; 0% American Indian, 3% Asian, 13% black, 26% Hispanic, 2% multiracial,

0% Pacific Islander, 50% white, 3% international; 78% from in state; 30% live on campus; 5% of students in fraternities, 11% in sororities
Most popular majors: 40% Business, Management, Marketing, and Related Support Services, 10% Communication, Journalism, and Related Programs, 10% Homeland Security, Law Enforcement, Firefighting and Related Protective Services, 9% Psychology, 7% Social Sciences
Expenses: 2021-2022: $42,828; room/board: $17,222
Financial aid: (914) 633-2497; 87% of undergrads determined to have financial need; average aid package $28,286

Ithaca College
Ithaca NY
(800) 429-4274
U.S. News ranking: Reg. U. (N), No. 10
Website: www.ithaca.edu
Admissions email: admission@ithaca.edu
Private; founded 1892
Freshman admissions: more selective; 2020-2021: 12,906 applied, 9,767 accepted. Neither SAT nor ACT required. SAT 25/75 percentile: 1160-1320. High school rank: 23% in top tenth, 59% in top quarter, 87% in top half
Early decision deadline: 11/1, notification date: 12/15
Early action deadline: 12/1, notification date: 2/1
Application deadline (fall): 2/1
Undergraduate student body: 4,785 full time, 172 part time; 42% male, 58% female; 0% American Indian, 4% Asian, 6% black, 10% Hispanic, 4% multiracial, 0% Pacific Islander, 72% white, 2% international; 47% from in state; 3% live on campus; 0% of students in fraternities, 0% in sororities
Most popular majors: 9% Business Administration and Management, General, 7% Physical Therapy/Therapist, 7% Radio and Television, 6% Public Relations, Advertising, and Applied Communication, 5% Cinematography and Film/Video Production
Expenses: 2021-2022: $46,610; room/board: $15,844
Financial aid: (607) 274-3131; 69% of undergrads determined to have financial need; average aid package $40,963

Jamestown Business College[1]
Jamestown NY
(716) 664-5100
U.S. News ranking: Business, unranked
Admissions email: N/A
For-profit
Application deadline (fall): N/A
Undergraduate student body: N/A full time, N/A part time
Expenses: 2020-2021: $12,645; room/board: N/A
Financial aid: N/A

Juilliard School[1]
New York NY
(212) 799-5000
U.S. News ranking: Arts, unranked
Website: www.juilliard.edu
Admissions email: admissions@juilliard.edu
Private; founded 1905
Application deadline (fall): 12/1
Undergraduate student body: N/A full time, N/A part time
Expenses: 2021-2022: $51,480; room/board: $19,810
Financial aid: (212) 799-5000; 73% of undergrads determined to have financial need; average aid package $39,985

Keuka College
Keuka Park NY
(315) 279-5254
U.S. News ranking: Reg. U. (N), No. 126
Website: www.keuka.edu
Admissions email: admissions@keuka.edu
Private; founded 1890
Affiliation: American Baptist
Freshman admissions: selective; 2020-2021: 2,025 applied, 1,841 accepted. Neither SAT nor ACT required. SAT 25/75 percentile: 980-1150. High school rank: N/A
Early decision deadline: N/A, notification date: N/A
Early action deadline: N/A, notification date: N/A
Application deadline (fall): rolling
Undergraduate student body: 1,159 full time, 142 part time; 25% male, 75% female; 0% American Indian, 1% Asian, 5% black, 5% Hispanic, 4% multiracial, 0% Pacific Islander, 79% white, 0% international; 92% from in state; 62% live on campus; 0% of students in fraternities, 0% in sororities
Most popular majors: 25% Health Professions and Related Programs, 22% Public Administration and Social Service Professions, 19% Business, Management, Marketing, and Related Support Services, 8% Education, 6% Construction Trades
Expenses: 2021-2022: $35,030; room/board: $12,626
Financial aid: (315) 279-5232; 98% of undergrads determined to have financial need; average aid package $21,600

The King's College[1]
New York NY
(212) 659-3610
U.S. News ranking: Nat. Lib. Arts, second tier
Website: www.tkc.edu/
Admissions email: admissions@tkc.edu
Private; founded 1938
Affiliation: Undenominational
Application deadline (fall): rolling
Undergraduate student body: N/A full time, N/A part time
Expenses: 2021-2022: $37,690; room/board: $18,077
Financial aid: (646) 237-8902; 61% of undergrads determined to have financial need; average aid package $30,035

Le Moyne College
Syracuse NY
(315) 445-4300
U.S. News ranking: Reg. U. (N), No. 13
Website: www.lemoyne.edu
Admissions email: admission@lemoyne.edu
Private; founded 1946
Affiliation: Roman Catholic
Freshman admissions: selective; 2020-2021: 7,248 applied, 5,417 accepted. Neither SAT nor ACT required. SAT 25/75 percentile: 1060-1250. High school rank: 24% in top tenth, 55% in top quarter, 87% in top half
Early decision deadline: N/A, notification date: N/A
Early action deadline: 11/15, notification date: 12/15
Application deadline (fall): rolling
Undergraduate student body: 2,369 full time, 432 part time; 38% male, 62% female; 0% American Indian, 4% Asian, 6% black, 7% Hispanic, 3% multiracial, 0% Pacific Islander, 75% white, 1% international; 93% from in state; 46% live on campus; 0% of students in fraternities, 0% in sororities
Most popular majors: 35% Business, Management, Marketing, and Related Support Services, 15% Biological and Biomedical Sciences, 15% Psychology, 11% Health Professions and Related Programs, 8% Social Sciences
Expenses: 2021-2022: $36,610; room/board: $14,760
Financial aid: (315) 445-4400; 79% of undergrads determined to have financial need; average aid package $29,690

LIM College[7]
New York NY
(800) 677-1323
U.S. News ranking: Business, unranked
Website: www.limcollege.edu
Admissions email: admissions@limcollege.edu
For-profit; founded 1939
Freshman admissions: selective; 2020-2021: 1,355 applied, 1,139 accepted. Neither SAT nor ACT required. SAT 25/75 percentile: 940-1130. High school rank: N/A
Early decision deadline: N/A, notification date: N/A
Early action deadline: 11/15, notification date: 12/15
Application deadline (fall): rolling
Undergraduate student body: 1,266 full time, 82 part time
Most popular majors: Information not available
Expenses: 2020-2021: $28,756; room/board: $21,346
Financial aid: (212) 310-0689

Long Island University
Brookville NY
(516) 299-2900
U.S. News ranking: Nat. U., No. 288
Website: www.liu.edu
Admissions email: admissions@liu.edu

Private; founded 1926
Freshman admissions: selective; 2020-2021: 14,341 applied, 12,191 accepted. Either SAT or ACT required. SAT 25/75 percentile: 1080-1290. High school rank: 19% in top tenth, 35% in top quarter, 71% in top half
Early decision deadline: N/A, notification date: N/A
Early action deadline: 12/1, notification date: 12/15
Application deadline (fall): rolling
Undergraduate student body: 5,453 full time, 4,950 part time; 37% male, 63% female; 0% American Indian, 12% Asian, 14% black, 14% Hispanic, 2% multiracial, 0% Pacific Islander, 40% white, 3% international; 85% from in state; 20% live on campus; 15% of students in fraternities, 6% in sororities
Most popular majors: 26% Registered Nursing/Registered Nurse, 12% Pharmacy, Pharmaceutical Sciences, and Administration, Other, 7% Business Administration and Management, General, 7% Health Professions and Related Clinical Sciences, Other, 3% Psychology, General
Expenses: 2021-2022: $39,920; room/board: $15,258
Financial aid: (516) 299-4212; 78% of undergrads determined to have financial need; average aid package $28,378

Manhattan College
Riverdale NY
(718) 862-7200
U.S. News ranking: Reg. U. (N), No. 13
Website: manhattan.edu
Admissions email: admit@manhattan.edu
Private; founded 1853
Affiliation: Roman Catholic
Freshman admissions: selective; 2020-2021: 8,401 applied, 6,538 accepted. Neither SAT nor ACT required. SAT 25/75 percentile: 1030-1220. High school rank: N/A
Early decision deadline: 11/15, notification date: 12/15
Early action deadline: N/A, notification date: N/A
Application deadline (fall): rolling
Undergraduate student body: 3,178 full time, 174 part time; 58% male, 42% female; 0% American Indian, 4% Asian, 6% black, 26% Hispanic, 3% multiracial, 0% Pacific Islander, 50% white, 3% international; N/A from in state; 32% live on campus; N/A of students in fraternities, N/A in sororities
Most popular majors: 29% Engineering, 28% Business, Management, Marketing, and Related Support Services, 11% Education
Expenses: 2020-2021: $45,880; room/board: $17,380
Financial aid: (718) 862-7178

Manhattan School of Music[1]

New York NY
(917) 493-4436
U.S. News ranking: Arts, unranked
Website: msmnyc.edu/
Admissions email:
admission@msmnyc.edu
Private; founded 1917
Application deadline (fall): N/A
Undergraduate student body: N/A
full time, N/A part time
Expenses: 2020-2021: $49,270;
room/board: $16,305
Financial aid: (917) 493-4809

Manhattanville College

Purchase NY
(914) 323-5464
U.S. News ranking: Reg. U. (N),
No. 58
Website: www.mville.edu
Admissions email:
admissions@mville.edu
Private; founded 1841
Freshman admissions: selective;
2020-2021: 3,203 applied,
2,879 accepted. Neither SAT
nor ACT required. SAT 25/75
percentile: 1010-1160. High
school rank: 16% in top tenth,
18% in top quarter, 77% in
top half
Early decision deadline: N/A,
notification date: N/A
Early action deadline: 12/1,
notification date: 1/1
Application deadline (fall): rolling
Undergraduate student body: 1,333
full time, 76 part time; 41%
male, 59% female; 0% American
Indian, 2% Asian, 10% black,
29% Hispanic, 2% multiracial,
0% Pacific Islander, 51% white,
3% international; 76% from in
state; 38% live on campus; 0%
of students in fraternities, 0% in
sororities
Most popular majors: 23%
Business, Management,
Marketing, and Related Support
Services, 14% Communication,
Journalism, and Related Programs,
10% Visual and Performing
Arts, 9% Psychology, 9% Social
Sciences
Expenses: 2021-2022: $40,380;
room/board: $14,810
Financial aid: (914) 323-5357;
70% of undergrads determined to
have financial need; average aid
package $26,376

Marist College

Poughkeepsie NY
(845) 575-3226
U.S. News ranking: Reg. U. (N),
No. 10
Website: www.marist.edu
Admissions email:
admissions@marist.edu
Private; founded 1929
Freshman admissions: more
selective; 2020-2021: 11,715
applied, 6,449 accepted. Neither
SAT nor ACT required. SAT
25/75 percentile: 1130-1300.
High school rank: 22% in top
tenth, 53% in top quarter, 89%
in top half
Early decision deadline: 12/1,
notification date: 12/15

Early action deadline: 12/1,
notification date: 1/15
Application deadline (fall): 3/1
Undergraduate student body: 4,947
full time, 735 part time; 43%
male, 57% female; 0% American
Indian, 3% Asian, 5% black,
13% Hispanic, 3% multiracial,
0% Pacific Islander, 74% white,
2% international; 49% from in
state; 62% live on campus; 3%
of students in fraternities, 3% in
sororities
Most popular majors: 33%
Business, Management,
Marketing, and Related Support
Services, 14% Communication,
Journalism, and Related Programs,
12% Psychology, 8% Computer
and Information Sciences and
Support Services, 6% Visual and
Performing Arts
Expenses: 2021-2022: $42,995;
room/board: $17,560
Financial aid: (845) 575-3230;
55% of undergrads determined to
have financial need; average aid
package $27,481

Marymount Manhattan College

New York NY
(212) 517-0430
U.S. News ranking: Nat. Lib. Arts,
second tier
Website: www.mmm.edu
Admissions email:
admissions@mmm.edu
Private; founded 1936
Freshman admissions: selective;
2020-2021: 5,209 applied,
4,607 accepted. Neither SAT
nor ACT required. SAT 25/75
percentile: 960-1200. High
school rank: N/A
Early decision deadline: 11/1,
notification date: 12/1
Early action deadline: 12/1,
notification date: 12/22
Undergraduate student body: 1,485
full time, 236 part time; 18%
male, 82% female; 0% American
Indian, 3% Asian, 12% black,
19% Hispanic, 6% multiracial,
0% Pacific Islander, 55% white,
2% international; 36% from in
state; 20% live on campus; N/A
of students in fraternities, N/A in
sororities
Most popular majors: 57% Visual
and Performing Arts, 14%
Communication, Journalism, and
Related Programs, 13% Business,
Management, Marketing, and
Related Support Services, 4%
English Language and Literature/
Letters, 4% Multi/Interdisciplinary
Studies
Expenses: 2021-2022: $37,410;
room/board: $19,380
Financial aid: (212) 517-0500;
69% of undergrads determined to
have financial need; average aid
package $20,832

Medaille College[1]

Buffalo NY
(716) 880-2200
U.S. News ranking: Reg. U. (N),
second tier
Website: www.medaille.edu
Admissions email:
admissionsug@medaille.edu
Private; founded 1937

Application deadline (fall): rolling
Undergraduate student body: N/A
full time, N/A part time
Expenses: 2020-2021: $31,500;
room/board: $14,000
Financial aid: (716) 880-2256

Mercy College

Dobbs Ferry NY
(877) 637-2946
U.S. News ranking: Reg. U. (N),
second tier
Website: www.mercy.edu
Admissions email:
admissions@mercy.edu
Private; founded 1950
Freshman admissions: less
selective; 2020-2021: 7,246
applied, 5,939 accepted. Neither
SAT nor ACT required. SAT 25/75
percentile: 930-1110. High
school rank: N/A
Early decision deadline: N/A,
notification date: N/A
Early action deadline: N/A,
notification date: N/A
Application deadline (fall): rolling
Undergraduate student body: 5,699
full time, 1,381 part time; 29%
male, 71% female; 0% American
Indian, 4% Asian, 27% black,
43% Hispanic, 2% multiracial,
0% Pacific Islander, 17% white,
1% international; 93% from in
state; 7% live on campus; N/A
of students in fraternities, N/A in
sororities
Most popular majors: 30% Health
Professions and Related Programs,
17% Business, Management,
Marketing, and Related Support
Services, 13% Social Sciences,
9% Psychology, 7% Liberal Arts
and Sciences, General Studies and
Humanities
Expenses: 2021-2022: $20,734;
room/board: $13,800
Financial aid: (877) 637-2946;
88% of undergrads determined to
have financial need; average aid
package $14,351

Metropolitan College of New York[1]

New York NY
(212) 343-1234
U.S. News ranking: Reg. U. (N),
second tier
Website: www.mcny.edu
Admissions email:
admissions@mcny.edu
Private; founded 1964
Application deadline (fall): rolling
Undergraduate student body: N/A
full time, N/A part time
Expenses: 2020-2021: $20,188;
room/board: N/A
Financial aid: (212) 343-1234

Molloy College

Rockville Centre NY
(516) 323-4000
U.S. News ranking: Reg. U. (N),
No. 27
Website: www.molloy.edu
Admissions email:
admissions@molloy.edu
Private; founded 1955
Freshman admissions: selective;
2020-2021: 5,043 applied,
3,739 accepted. Neither SAT
nor ACT required. SAT 25/75
percentile: 1040-1230. High

school rank: 22% in top tenth,
66% in top quarter, 92% in
top half
Early decision deadline: N/A,
notification date: N/A
Early action deadline: 12/1,
notification date: 12/15
Application deadline (fall): rolling
Undergraduate student body: 2,746
full time, 764 part time; 27%
male, 73% female; 0% American
Indian, 8% Asian, 9% black,
20% Hispanic, 2% multiracial,
0% Pacific Islander, 58% white,
1% international; 95% from in
state; 5% live on campus; N/A
of students in fraternities, N/A in
sororities
Most popular majors: 53% Health
Professions and Related Programs,
13% Business, Management,
Marketing, and Related Support
Services, 7% Education, 4%
Biological and Biomedical
Sciences, 4% Homeland Security,
Law Enforcement, Firefighting and
Related Protective Services
Expenses: 2021-2022: $34,310;
room/board: $16,510
Financial aid: (516) 323-4200;
78% of undergrads determined to
have financial need; average aid
package $18,312

Monroe College

Bronx NY
(800) 556-6676
U.S. News ranking: Reg. U. (N),
No. 62
Website: www.monroecollege.edu
Admissions email:
admissions@monroecollege.edu
For-profit; founded 1933
Freshman admissions: selective;
2020-2021: 4,060 applied,
1,994 accepted. Neither SAT
nor ACT required. SAT 25/75
percentile: 1098-1113. High
school rank: N/A
Early decision deadline: N/A,
notification date: N/A
Early action deadline: 12/15,
notification date: 1/31
Application deadline (fall): rolling
Undergraduate student body: 4,162
full time, 1,577 part time; 33%
male, 67% female; 0% American
Indian, 2% Asian, 42% black,
44% Hispanic, 0% multiracial,
0% Pacific Islander, 3% white,
8% international; 89% from in
state; 7% live on campus; N/A
of students in fraternities, N/A in
sororities
Most popular majors: 16%
Business, Management,
Marketing, and Related Support
Services, 11% Health Professions
and Related Programs, 9%
Homeland Security, Law
Enforcement, Firefighting and
Related Protective Services,
6% Computer and Information
Sciences and Support Services,
4% Parks, Recreation, Leisure,
and Fitness Studies
Expenses: 2021-2022: $16,686;
room/board: $11,300
Financial aid: (718) 933-6700;
88% of undergrads determined to
have financial need; average aid
package $12,167

Mount St. Mary College

Newburgh NY
(845) 569-3488
U.S. News ranking: Reg. U. (N),
No. 94
Website: www.msmc.edu
Admissions email:
admissions@msmc.edu
Private; founded 1959
Freshman admissions: selective;
2020-2021: 2,178 applied,
1,964 accepted. Neither SAT
nor ACT required. SAT 25/75
percentile: 1000-1150. High
school rank: 11% in top tenth,
26% in top quarter, 64% in
top half
Early decision deadline: N/A,
notification date: N/A
Early action deadline: N/A,
notification date: N/A
Application deadline (fall): 8/15
Undergraduate student body: 1,479
full time, 302 part time; 27%
male, 73% female; 0% American
Indian, 2% Asian, 8% black,
19% Hispanic, 1% multiracial,
0% Pacific Islander, 57% white,
0% international; 89% from in
state; 40% live on campus; N/A
of students in fraternities, N/A in
sororities
Most popular majors: 37% Health
Professions and Related Programs,
17% Business, Management,
Marketing, and Related Support
Services, 7% History, 5% Social
Sciences
Expenses: 2021-2022: $36,132;
room/board: $17,490
Financial aid: (845) 569-3280;
77% of undergrads determined to
have financial need; average aid
package $23,834

Nazareth College

Rochester NY
(585) 389-2860
U.S. News ranking: Reg. U. (N),
No. 34
Website: www.naz.edu
Admissions email:
admissions@naz.edu
Private; founded 1924
Freshman admissions: more
selective; 2020-2021: 3,833
applied, 2,901 accepted. Neither
SAT nor ACT required. SAT
25/75 percentile: 1110-1280.
High school rank: 29% in top
tenth, 62% in top quarter, 90%
in top half
Early decision deadline: 11/5,
notification date: 12/15
Early action deadline: N/A,
notification date: N/A
Application deadline (fall): 2/1
Undergraduate student body: 2,063
full time, 84 part time; 27%
male, 73% female; 0% American
Indian, 3% Asian, 5% black,
6% Hispanic, 3% multiracial,
0% Pacific Islander, 78% white,
2% international; 87% from in
state; 52% live on campus; 0%
of students in fraternities, 0% in
sororities
Most popular majors: 29% Health
Professions and Related Programs,
11% Visual and Performing Arts,
9% Business, Management,
Marketing, and Related Support
Services, 7% Education, 7%

Psychology
Expenses: 2021-2022: $37,590;
room/board: $14,590
Financial aid: (585) 389-2310;
80% of undergrads determined to
have financial need; average aid
package $29,519

The New School
New York NY
(800) 292-3040
U.S. News ranking: Nat. U.,
No. 136
Website: www.newschool.edu
Admissions email:
admission@newschool.edu
Private; founded 1919
Freshman admissions: selective;
2020-2021: 8,829 applied,
6,027 accepted. Neither SAT
nor ACT required. SAT 25/75
percentile: 1140-1360. High
school rank: 17% in top tenth,
38% in top quarter, 79% in
top half
Early decision deadline: N/A,
notification date: N/A
Early action deadline: 11/1,
notification date: 12/20
Application deadline (fall): 8/1
Undergraduate student body: 5,684
full time, 746 part time; 25%
male, 75% female; 0% American
Indian, 11% Asian, 5% black,
12% Hispanic, 5% multiracial,
0% Pacific Islander, 33% white,
30% international; N/A from in
state; 22% live on campus; N/A
of students in fraternities, N/A in
sororities
Most popular majors: 58%
Visual and Performing Arts,
11% Computer and Information
Sciences and Support Services,
7% Communication, Journalism,
and Related Programs, 7% Liberal
Arts and Sciences, General
Studies and Humanities, 4%
English Language and Literature/
Letters
Expenses: 2021-2022: $52,979;
room/board: $17,800
Financial aid: (212) 229-8930;
38% of undergrads determined to
have financial need; average aid
package $27,212

New York Institute of Technology
Old Westbury NY
(800) 345-6948
U.S. News ranking: Reg. U. (N),
No. 34
Website: www.nyit.edu
Admissions email:
admissions@nyit.edu
Private; founded 1955
Freshman admissions: selective;
2020-2021: 11,007 applied,
8,220 accepted. Neither SAT
nor ACT required. SAT 25/75
percentile: 1060-1290. High
school rank: N/A
Early decision deadline: N/A,
notification date: N/A
Early action deadline: N/A,
notification date: N/A
Application deadline (fall): rolling
Undergraduate student body: 3,155
full time, 318 part time; 59%
male, 41% female; 0% American
Indian, 24% Asian, 10% black,
20% Hispanic, 5% multiracial,
0% Pacific Islander, 26% white,

10% international; 86% from in
state; 4% live on campus; N/A
of students in fraternities, N/A in
sororities
Most popular majors: 11%
Computer and Information
Sciences, General, 10%
Architectural and Building
Sciences/Technology, 9%
Electrical and Electronics
Engineering, 8% Biology/Biological
Sciences, General, 8% Finance,
General
Expenses: 2021-2022: $39,760;
room/board: $16,600
Financial aid: (516) 686-7680;
74% of undergrads determined to
have financial need; average aid
package $29,303

New York School of Interior Design[1]
New York NY
(212) 472-1500
U.S. News ranking: Arts, unranked
Website: www.nysid.edu
Admissions email:
N/A
Private
Application deadline (fall): N/A
Undergraduate student body: N/A
full time, N/A part time
Expenses: 2020-2021: $26,322;
room/board: $21,600
Financial aid: N/A

New York University
New York NY
(212) 998-4500
U.S. News ranking: Nat. U., No. 28
Website: www.nyu.edu
Admissions email:
admissions@nyu.edu
Private; founded 1831
Freshman admissions: most
selective; 2020-2021: 80,210
applied, 16,918 accepted. Neither
SAT nor ACT required. SAT 25/75
percentile: 1370-1540. High
school rank: 82% in top tenth,
100% in top quarter, 100% in
top half
Early decision deadline: 11/1,
notification date: 12/15
Early action deadline: N/A,
notification date: N/A
Application deadline (fall): 1/5
Undergraduate student body:
25,854 full time, 1,590 part
time; 43% male, 57% female;
0% American Indian, 19% Asian,
8% black, 17% Hispanic, 4%
multiracial, 0% Pacific Islander,
23% white, 24% international;
33% from in state; 22% live
on campus; 3% of students in
fraternities, 7% in sororities
Most popular majors: 17% Visual
and Performing Arts, 14%
Social Sciences, 13% Business,
Management, Marketing, and
Related Support Services, 9%
Liberal Arts and Sciences, General
Studies and Humanities, 8%
Health Professions and Related
Programs
Expenses: 2021-2022: $56,500;
room/board: $19,682
Financial aid: (212) 998-4444;
47% of undergrads determined to
have financial need; average aid
package $37,578

Niagara University
Niagara University NY
(716) 286-8700
U.S. News ranking: Reg. U. (N),
No. 21
Website: www.niagara.edu
Admissions email:
admissions@niagara.edu
Private; founded 1856
Affiliation: Roman Catholic
Freshman admissions: selective;
2020-2021: 3,740 applied,
3,456 accepted. Neither SAT
nor ACT required. SAT 25/75
percentile: 1015-1200. High
school rank: 18% in top tenth,
43% in top quarter, 77% in
top half
Early decision deadline: N/A,
notification date: N/A
Early action deadline: 12/15,
notification date: 1/3
Application deadline (fall): 8/30
Undergraduate student body: 2,654
full time, 72 part time; 36%
male, 64% female; 1% American
Indian, 2% Asian, 5% black,
5% Hispanic, 3% multiracial,
0% Pacific Islander, 66% white,
16% international; 90% from in
state; 40% live on campus; N/A
of students in fraternities, N/A in
sororities
Most popular majors: 25%
Education, 24% Business,
Management, Marketing, and
Related Support Services, 16%
Health Professions and Related
Programs, 7% Social Sciences,
4% Biological and Biomedical
Sciences
Expenses: 2021-2022: $35,980;
room/board: $12,400
Financial aid: (716) 286-8686;
70% of undergrads determined to
have financial need; average aid
package $28,406

Nyack College
New York NY
(646) 378-6101
U.S. News ranking: Reg. U. (N),
second tier
Website: www.nyack.edu
Admissions email:
admissions@nyack.edu
Private; founded 1882
Affiliation: Christ and Missionary
Alliance Church
Freshman admissions: less
selective; 2020-2021: 245
applied, 237 accepted. Neither
SAT nor ACT required. SAT 25/75
percentile: 845-1075. High
school rank: 8% in top tenth, 21%
in top quarter, 58% in top half
Early decision deadline: N/A,
notification date: N/A
Early action deadline: N/A,
notification date: N/A
Application deadline (fall): rolling
Undergraduate student body: 958
full time, 226 part time; 46%
male, 54% female; 1% American
Indian, 4% Asian, 26% black,
26% Hispanic, 2% multiracial,
0% Pacific Islander, 10% white,
29% international; N/A from in
state; 21% live on campus; N/A
of students in fraternities, N/A in
sororities
Most popular majors: 25%
Business, Management,
Marketing, and Related Support
Services, 16% Theology and

Religious Vocations, 12%
Psychology, 8% Education, 8%
Health Professions and Related
Programs
Expenses: 2020-2021: $25,500;
room/board: $15,000
Financial aid: (845) 675-4737

Pace University
New York NY
(800) 874-7223
U.S. News ranking: Nat. U.,
No. 213
Website: www.pace.edu
Admissions email:
undergradadmission@pace.edu
Private; founded 1906
Freshman admissions: selective;
2020-2021: 24,904 applied,
20,637 accepted. Neither SAT
nor ACT required. SAT 25/75
percentile: 1060-1240. High
school rank: 14% in top tenth,
43% in top quarter, 78% in
top half
Early decision deadline: 11/1,
notification date: 12/1
Early action deadline: 11/1,
notification date: 12/1
Application deadline (fall): 2/15
Undergraduate student body: 7,336
full time, 658 part time; 36%
male, 64% female; 0% American
Indian, 7% Asian, 10% black,
17% Hispanic, 5% multiracial,
0% Pacific Islander, 50% white,
8% international; 48% from in
state; 29% live on campus; 12%
of students in fraternities, 11%
in sororities
Most popular majors: 26%
Business, Management,
Marketing, and Related Support
Services, 17% Health Professions
and Related Programs, 14%
Visual and Performing Arts, 12%
Communication, Journalism, and
Related Programs, 7% Computer
and Information Sciences and
Support Services
Expenses: 2021-2022: $48,830;
room/board: $17,466
Financial aid: (877) 672-1830;
67% of undergrads determined to
have financial need; average aid
package $34,558

Paul Smith's College
Paul Smiths NY
(888) 873-6570
U.S. News ranking: Reg. Coll. (N),
No. 22
Website: www.paulsmiths.edu
Admissions email:
admissions@paulsmiths.edu
Private; founded 1946
Freshman admissions: less
selective; 2020-2021: 1,316
applied, 922 accepted. Neither
SAT nor ACT required. SAT 25/75
percentile: N/A. High school rank:
6% in top tenth, 22% in top
quarter, 66% in top half
Early decision deadline: N/A,
notification date: N/A
Early action deadline: N/A,
notification date: N/A
Application deadline (fall): 7/29
Undergraduate student body: 650
full time, 18 part time; 63%
male, 37% female; 1% American
Indian, 0% Asian, 6% black,
2% Hispanic, 1% multiracial,
0% Pacific Islander, 79% white,

1% international; 63% from in
state; 81% live on campus; 0%
of students in fraternities, 0% in
sororities
Most popular majors: 17%
Natural Resources Management
and Policy, 11% Wildlife, Fish
and Wildlands Science and
Management, 7% Environmental
Science, 7% Parks, Recreation
and Leisure Studies, 6% Fishing
and Fisheries Sciences and
Management
Expenses: 2020-2021: $30,194;
room/board: $14,720
Financial aid: (518) 327-6119

Plaza College[1]
Forest Hills NY
(718) 779-1430
U.S. News ranking: Reg. Coll. (N),
unranked
Website: www.plazacollege.edu
Admissions email:
N/A
For-profit; founded 1916
Application deadline (fall): N/A
Undergraduate student body: N/A
full time, N/A part time
Expenses: 2020-2021: $13,450;
room/board: N/A
Financial aid: N/A

Pratt Institute
Brooklyn NY
(718) 636-3514
U.S. News ranking: Arts, unranked
Website: www.pratt.edu
Admissions email:
admissions@pratt.edu
Private; founded 1887
Freshman admissions: more
selective; 2020-2021: 6,440
applied, 3,884 accepted. Neither
SAT nor ACT required. SAT 25/75
percentile: 1170-1360. High
school rank: N/A
Early decision deadline: N/A,
notification date: N/A
Early action deadline: 11/1,
notification date: 12/22
Application deadline (fall): 1/5
Undergraduate student body: 2,804
full time, 123 part time; 30%
male, 70% female; 0% American
Indian, 15% Asian, 4% black,
10% Hispanic, 3% multiracial,
0% Pacific Islander, 34% white,
33% international; 28% from in
state; 0% live on campus; N/A
of students in fraternities, N/A in
sororities
Most popular majors: 16%
Architectural and Building
Sciences/Technology, 10%
Graphic Design, 9% Industrial and
Product Design, 8% Illustration,
8% Interior Design
Expenses: 2021-2022: $55,072;
room/board: $14,668
Financial aid: (718) 636-3599;
40% of undergrads determined to
have financial need; average aid
package $33,772

Purchase College–SUNY
Purchase NY
(914) 251-6300
U.S. News ranking: Nat. Lib. Arts,
No. 155
Website: www.purchase.edu

Admissions email:
admissions@purchase.edu
Public; founded 1967
Freshman admissions: selective;
2020-2021: 4,594 applied,
3,386 accepted. Neither SAT
nor ACT required. SAT 25/75
percentile: 1100-1280. High
school rank: N/A
Early decision deadline: N/A,
notification date: N/A
Early action deadline: 11/15,
notification date: 1/1
Application deadline (fall): 7/1
Undergraduate student body: 3,284
full time, 326 part time; 40%
male, 60% female; 0% American
Indian, 4% Asian, 13% black,
26% Hispanic, 5% multiracial,
0% Pacific Islander, 49% white,
2% international; 83% from in
state; 21% live on campus; N/A
of students in fraternities, N/A in
sororities
Most popular majors: 10% Liberal
Arts and Sciences/Liberal Studies,
8% Psychology, General, 5%
Communication, Journalism, and
Related Programs, 5% Playwriting
and Screenwriting, 4% Fine and
Studio Arts Management
Expenses: 2021-2022: $8,566 in
state, $18,476 out of state; room/
board: $14,448
Financial aid: (914) 251-6354;
66% of undergrads determined to
have financial need; average aid
package $11,374

Rensselaer Polytechnic Institute
Troy NY
(518) 276-6216
U.S. News ranking: Nat. U., No. 55
Website: www.rpi.edu
Admissions email:
admissions@rpi.edu
Private; founded 1824
Freshman admissions: more
selective; 2020-2021: 16,661
applied, 9,539 accepted. Neither
SAT nor ACT required. SAT
25/75 percentile: 1300-1500.
High school rank: 55% in top
tenth, 87% in top quarter, 95%
in top half
Early decision deadline: 11/1,
notification date: 12/12
Early action deadline: 12/1,
notification date: 1/30
Application deadline (fall): 1/15
Undergraduate student body: 6,262
full time, 21 part time; 69%
male, 31% female; 0% American
Indian, 17% Asian, 5% black,
11% Hispanic, 5% multiracial,
0% Pacific Islander, 44% white,
16% international; 23% from in
state; 21% live on campus; 16%
of students in fraternities, 12%
in sororities
Most popular majors: 53%
Engineering, 18% Computer
and Information Sciences and
Support Services, 5% Business,
Management, Marketing, and
Related Support Services, 5%
Engineering Technologies and
Engineering-Related Fields, 4%
Mathematics and Statistics
Expenses: 2021-2022: $58,526;
room/board: $16,379

Financial aid: (518) 276-6813;
55% of undergrads determined to
have financial need; average aid
package $42,052

Roberts Wesleyan College
Rochester NY
(585) 594-6400
U.S. News ranking: Reg. U. (N),
No. 78
Website: www.roberts.edu
Admissions email:
admissions@roberts.edu
Private; founded 1866
Affiliation: Free Methodist
Freshman admissions: selective;
2020-2021: 1,538 applied,
1,166 accepted. Neither SAT
nor ACT required. SAT 25/75
percentile: 1020-1250. High
school rank: 24% in top tenth,
54% in top quarter, 84% in
top half
Early decision deadline: N/A,
notification date: N/A
Early action deadline: 11/15,
notification date: N/A
Application deadline (fall): 8/25
Undergraduate student body: 1,126
full time, 71 part time; 31%
male, 69% female; 0% American
Indian, 2% Asian, 10% black,
8% Hispanic, 4% multiracial,
0% Pacific Islander, 71% white,
4% international; 93% from in
state; 60% live on campus; N/A
of students in fraternities, N/A in
sororities
Most popular majors: 33% Health
Professions and Related Programs,
16% Education, 15% Business,
Management, Marketing, and
Related Support Services,
6% Homeland Security, Law
Enforcement, Firefighting and
Related Protective Services, 6%
Visual and Performing Arts
Expenses: 2021-2022: $34,390;
room/board: $11,302
Financial aid: (585) 594-6150;
57% of undergrads determined to
have financial need; average aid
package $26,992

Rochester Institute of Technology
Rochester NY
(585) 475-6631
U.S. News ranking: Nat. U.,
No. 117
Website: www.rit.edu
Admissions email:
admissions@rit.edu
Private; founded 1829
Freshman admissions: more
selective; 2020-2021: 21,672
applied, 15,958 accepted. Neither
SAT nor ACT required. SAT
25/75 percentile: 1220-1420.
High school rank: 39% in top
tenth, 74% in top quarter, 94%
in top half
Early decision deadline: 11/1,
notification date: 12/15
Early action deadline: N/A,
notification date: N/A
Application deadline (fall): rolling
Undergraduate student body:
12,122 full time, 1,290 part
time; 66% male, 34% female;
0% American Indian, 10% Asian,
5% black, 9% Hispanic, 4%
multiracial, 0% Pacific Islander,

65% white, 5% international
Most popular majors: 26%
Engineering, 18% Computer and
Information Sciences and Support
Services, 10% Engineering
Technologies and Engineering-
Related Fields, 10% Visual and
Performing Arts, 9% Business,
Management, Marketing, and
Related Support Services
Expenses: 2021-2022: $52,756;
room/board: $14,432
Financial aid: (585) 475-2186;
74% of undergrads determined to
have financial need; average aid
package $43,325

Russell Sage College
Troy NY
(518) 244-2217
U.S. News ranking: Nat. U.,
No. 227
Website: www.sage.edu
Admissions email:
admission@sage.edu
Private; founded 1916
Freshman admissions: less
selective; 2020-2021: 1,737
applied, 1,291 accepted. Neither
SAT nor ACT required. SAT 25/75
percentile: 910-1160. High
school rank: 1% in top tenth, 24%
in top quarter, 64% in top half
Early decision deadline: N/A,
notification date: N/A
Early action deadline: 12/1,
notification date: N/A
Application deadline (fall): rolling
Undergraduate student body: 1,183
full time, 104 part time; 22%
male, 78% female; 0% American
Indian, 5% Asian, 11% black,
9% Hispanic, 4% multiracial,
0% Pacific Islander, 58% white,
1% international; 92% from in
state; 42% live on campus; N/A
of students in fraternities, N/A in
sororities
Most popular majors: 42% Health
Professions and Related Programs,
12% Business, Management,
Marketing, and Related Support
Services, 11% Visual and
Performing Arts, 8% Psychology,
6% Social Sciences
Expenses: 2021-2022: $33,894;
room/board: $13,302
Financial aid: (518) 244-4525;
87% of undergrads determined to
have financial need

Sarah Lawrence College
Bronxville NY
(914) 395-2510
U.S. News ranking: Nat. Lib. Arts,
No. 71
Website: www.slc.edu
Admissions email:
slcadmit@sarahlawrence.edu
Private; founded 1926
Freshman admissions: more
selective; 2020-2021: 3,674
applied, 2,007 accepted. Neither
SAT nor ACT required. SAT
25/75 percentile: 1220-1410.
High school rank: 29% in top
tenth, 61% in top quarter, 87%
in top half
Early decision deadline: 11/1,
notification date: 12/15
Early action deadline: 11/1,
notification date: 12/15
Application deadline (fall): 1/15

Undergraduate student body: 1,275
full time, 17 part time; 24%
male, 76% female; 0% American
Indian, 4% Asian, 5% black,
10% Hispanic, 5% multiracial,
0% Pacific Islander, 58% white,
9% international; 21% from in
state; 30% live on campus; N/A
of students in fraternities, N/A in
sororities
Most popular majors: 100%
Liberal Arts and Sciences, General
Studies and Humanities
Expenses: 2021-2022: $59,470;
room/board: $16,358
Financial aid: (914) 395-2570;
59% of undergrads determined to
have financial need; average aid
package $39,377

School of Visual Arts[1]
New York NY
(212) 592-2100
U.S. News ranking: Arts, unranked
Website: www.sva.edu/admissions/
undergraduate
Admissions email:
admissions@sva.edu
For-profit; founded 1947
Application deadline (fall): N/A
Undergraduate student body: N/A
full time, N/A part time
Expenses: 2020-2021: $43,400;
room/board: $22,300
Financial aid: (212) 592-2043

Siena College
Loudonville NY
(518) 783-2423
U.S. News ranking: Reg. U. (N),
No. 13
Website: www.siena.edu
Admissions email:
admissions@siena.edu
Private; founded 1937
Affiliation: Roman Catholic
Freshman admissions: selective;
2020-2021: 8,326 applied,
6,716 accepted. Neither SAT
nor ACT required. SAT 25/75
percentile: 1060-1240. High
school rank: 18% in top tenth,
47% in top quarter, 81% in
top half
Early decision deadline: 12/1,
notification date: 1/1
Early action deadline: 10/15,
notification date: 1/7
Application deadline (fall): 2/15
Undergraduate student body: 3,123
full time, 177 part time; 44%
male, 56% female; 0% American
Indian, 5% Asian, 3% black,
9% Hispanic, 3% multiracial,
0% Pacific Islander, 77% white,
2% international; 82% from in
state; 69% live on campus; 0%
of students in fraternities, 0% in
sororities
Most popular majors: 11%
Accounting, 11% Psychology,
General, 9% Marketing/Marketing
Management, General, 8%
Finance, General, 7% Biology/
Biological Sciences, General
Expenses: 2021-2022: $40,225;
room/board: $16,095
Financial aid: (518) 783-2427;
74% of undergrads determined to
have financial need; average aid
package $32,583

Skidmore College
Saratoga Springs NY
(518) 580-5570
U.S. News ranking: Nat. Lib. Arts,
No. 38
Website: www.skidmore.edu
Admissions email:
admissions@skidmore.edu
Private; founded 1903
Freshman admissions: more
selective; 2020-2021: 10,433
applied, 3,356 accepted. Neither
SAT nor ACT required. SAT
25/75 percentile: 1220-1403.
High school rank: 33% in top
tenth, 70% in top quarter, 93%
in top half
Early decision deadline: 11/15,
notification date: 12/15
Early action deadline: N/A,
notification date: N/A
Application deadline (fall): 1/15
Undergraduate student body: 2,510
full time, 72 part time; 40%
male, 60% female; 0% American
Indian, 5% Asian, 6% black,
10% Hispanic, 5% multiracial,
0% Pacific Islander, 61% white,
10% international; 35% from in
state; 68% live on campus; 0%
of students in fraternities, 0% in
sororities
Most popular majors: 19% Social
Sciences, 14% Visual and
Performing Arts, 13% Business,
Management, Marketing, and
Related Support Services, 9%
Biological and Biomedical
Sciences, 9% Psychology
Expenses: 2021-2022: $60,152;
room/board: $16,068
Financial aid: (518) 580-5750;
51% of undergrads determined to
have financial need; average aid
package $51,750

St. Bonaventure University
St. Bonaventure NY
(800) 462-5050
U.S. News ranking: Reg. U. (N),
No. 18
Website: www.sbu.edu
Admissions email:
admissions@sbu.edu
Private; founded 1858
Affiliation: Roman Catholic
Freshman admissions: selective;
2020-2021: 3,015 applied,
2,300 accepted. Neither SAT
nor ACT required. SAT 25/75
percentile: 1030-1220. High
school rank: 17% in top tenth,
44% in top quarter, 73% in
top half
Early decision deadline: N/A,
notification date: N/A
Early action deadline: N/A,
notification date: N/A
Application deadline (fall): 7/30
Undergraduate student body: 1,787
full time, 52 part time; 53%
male, 47% female; 0% American
Indian, 4% Asian, 6% black,
7% Hispanic, 2% multiracial,
0% Pacific Islander, 76% white,
3% international; 77% from in
state; 84% live on campus; 0%
of students in fraternities, 0% in
sororities
Most popular majors: 11%
Marketing/Marketing Management,
General, 10% Finance, General,
8% Digital Communication

and Media/Multimedia, 8% Psychology, General, 6% Journalism
Expenses: 2021-2022: $37,640; room/board: $14,026
Financial aid: (716) 375-2020; 73% of undergrads determined to have financial need; average aid package $27,720

St. Francis College
Brooklyn Heights NY
(718) 489-5200
U.S. News ranking: Reg. Coll. (N), No. 15
Website: www.sfc.edu
Admissions email: admissions@sfc.edu
Private; founded 1859
Freshman admissions: less selective; 2020-2021: 5,492 applied, 4,642 accepted. Neither SAT nor ACT required. SAT 25/75 percentile: 890-1030. High school rank: N/A
Early decision deadline: N/A, notification date: N/A
Early action deadline: N/A, notification date: N/A
Application deadline (fall): rolling
Undergraduate student body: 2,517 full time, 129 part time; 37% male, 63% female; 1% American Indian, 4% Asian, 24% black, 29% Hispanic, 3% multiracial, 1% Pacific Islander, 25% white, 9% international; N/A from in state; 5% live on campus; 5% of students in fraternities, 5% in sororities
Most popular majors: 24% Health Professions and Related Programs, 20% Business, Management, Marketing, and Related Support Services, 10% Communication, Journalism, and Related Programs, 8% Biological and Biomedical Sciences, 8% Psychology
Expenses: 2021-2022: $27,298; room/board: $21,800
Financial aid: (718) 489-5259; 78% of undergrads determined to have financial need; average aid package $19,098

St. John Fisher College
Rochester NY
(585) 385-8064
U.S. News ranking: Nat. U., No. 187
Website: www.sjfc.edu
Admissions email: admissions@sjfc.edu
Private; founded 1948
Affiliation: Roman Catholic
Freshman admissions: selective; 2020-2021: 4,409 applied, 3,016 accepted. Neither SAT nor ACT required. SAT 25/75 percentile: 1060-1240. High school rank: 22% in top tenth, 58% in top quarter, 91% in top half
Early decision deadline: 12/1, notification date: 1/15
Early action deadline: N/A, notification date: N/A
Application deadline (fall): rolling
Undergraduate student body: 2,573 full time, 119 part time; 41% male, 59% female; 0% American Indian, 4% Asian, 5% black, 5% Hispanic, 2% multiracial,

0% Pacific Islander, 83% white, 0% international; 96% from in state; 52% live on campus; 0% of students in fraternities, 0% in sororities
Most popular majors: 31% Registered Nursing/Registered Nurse, 7% Biology/Biological Sciences, General, 6% Finance, General, 6% Psychology, General, 6% Sport and Fitness Administration/Management
Expenses: 2021-2022: $36,352; room/board: $13,020
Financial aid: (585) 385-8042; 76% of undergrads determined to have financial need; average aid package $24,577

St. John's University
Queens NY
(718) 990-2000
U.S. News ranking: Nat. U., No. 172
Website: www.stjohns.edu/
Admissions email: admhelp@stjohns.edu
Private; founded 1870
Affiliation: Roman Catholic
Freshman admissions: more selective; 2020-2021: 27,917 applied, 20,956 accepted. Neither SAT nor ACT required. SAT 25/75 percentile: 1080-1300. High school rank: 20% in top tenth, 46% in top quarter, 75% in top half
Early decision deadline: 11/15, notification date: 12/15
Early action deadline: 12/1, notification date: 1/1
Application deadline (fall): rolling
Undergraduate student body: 10,177 full time, 5,516 part time; 43% male, 57% female; 0% American Indian, 16% Asian, 14% black, 17% Hispanic, 5% multiracial, 0% Pacific Islander, 42% white, 4% international; 80% from in state; 13% live on campus; 5% of students in fraternities, 9% in sororities
Most popular majors: 26% Business, Management, Marketing, and Related Support Services, 10% Biological and Biomedical Sciences, 10% Health Professions and Related Programs, 9% Communication, Journalism, and Related Programs, 8% Homeland Security, Law Enforcement, Firefighting and Related Protective Services
Expenses: 2021-2022: $46,050; room/board: $18,250
Financial aid: (718) 990-2000; 70% of undergrads determined to have financial need; average aid package $31,772

St. Joseph's College
Brooklyn NY
(631) 687-4500
U.S. News ranking: Reg. U. (N), No. 78
Website: www.sjcny.edu/brooklyn
Admissions email: liadmissions@sjcny.edu
Private; founded 1916
Freshman admissions: selective; 2020-2021: 4,654 applied, 3,289 accepted. Neither SAT nor ACT required. SAT 25/75 percentile: 1020-1200. High

school rank: N/A
Early decision deadline: N/A, notification date: N/A
Early action deadline: N/A, notification date: N/A
Application deadline (fall): rolling
Undergraduate student body: 3,433 full time, 470 part time; 31% male, 69% female; 0% American Indian, 3% Asian, 9% black, 20% Hispanic, 2% multiracial, 0% Pacific Islander, 56% white, 1% international; 97% from in state; N/A live on campus; N/A of students in fraternities, N/A in sororities
Most popular majors: 16% Special Education and Teaching, General, 10% Business Administration and Management, General, 8% Registered Nursing/Registered Nurse, 7% Psychology, General, 5% Rhetoric and Composition
Expenses: 2021-2022: $30,576; room/board: N/A
Financial aid: (631) 687-2600; 77% of undergrads determined to have financial need; average aid package $16,167

St. Lawrence University
Canton NY
(315) 229-5261
U.S. News ranking: Nat. Lib. Arts, No. 57
Website: www.stlawu.edu
Admissions email: admissions@stlawu.edu
Private; founded 1856
Freshman admissions: more selective; 2020-2021: 5,952 applied, 2,813 accepted. Neither SAT nor ACT required. SAT 25/75 percentile: 1180-1360. High school rank: 40% in top tenth, 71% in top quarter, 94% in top half
Early decision deadline: 11/1, notification date: N/A
Early action deadline: N/A, notification date: N/A
Application deadline (fall): 2/1
Undergraduate student body: 2,249 full time, 31 part time; 45% male, 55% female; 0% American Indian, 2% Asian, 4% black, 6% Hispanic, 2% multiracial, 0% Pacific Islander, 76% white, 9% international; 37% from in state; 81% live on campus; 13% of students in fraternities, 17% in sororities
Most popular majors: 12% Business/Commerce, General, 12% Economics, General, 8% Biology/Biological Sciences, General, 7% Psychology, General, 7% Speech Communication and Rhetoric
Expenses: 2021-2022: $60,220; room/board: $15,530
Financial aid: (315) 229-5265; 62% of undergrads determined to have financial need; average aid package $51,447

Stony Brook University–SUNY
Stony Brook NY
(631) 632-6868
U.S. News ranking: Nat. U., No. 93
Website: www.stonybrook.edu

Admissions email: enroll@stonybrook.edu
Public; founded 1957
Freshman admissions: more selective; 2020-2021: 37,083 applied, 18,138 accepted. Either SAT or ACT required. SAT 25/75 percentile: 1230-1440. High school rank: 44% in top tenth, 77% in top quarter, 97% in top half
Early decision deadline: N/A, notification date: N/A
Early action deadline: N/A, notification date: N/A
Application deadline (fall): 1/15
Undergraduate student body: 16,586 full time, 1,424 part time; 50% male, 50% female; 0% American Indian, 30% Asian, 7% black, 14% Hispanic, 3% multiracial, 0% Pacific Islander, 30% white, 10% international; N/A from in state; 22% live on campus; 3% of students in fraternities, 3% in sororities
Most popular majors: 21% Health Professions and Related Programs, 10% Biological and Biomedical Sciences, 9% Business, Management, Marketing, and Related Support Services, 9% Engineering, 8% Computer and Information Sciences and Support Services
Expenses: 2021-2022: $10,410 in state, $28,080 out of state; room/board: $15,504
Financial aid: (631) 632-6840; 59% of undergrads determined to have financial need; average aid package $14,600

St. Thomas Aquinas College
Sparkill NY
(845) 398-4100
U.S. News ranking: Reg. U. (N), No. 114
Website: www.stac.edu
Admissions email: admissions@stac.edu
Private; founded 1952
Affiliation: Roman Catholic
Freshman admissions: less selective; 2020-2021: 1,793 applied, 1,557 accepted. Either SAT or ACT required. SAT 25/75 percentile: 900-1150. High school rank: 14% in top tenth, 31% in top quarter, 59% in top half
Early decision deadline: N/A, notification date: N/A
Early action deadline: N/A, notification date: N/A
Application deadline (fall): rolling
Undergraduate student body: 1,080 full time, 532 part time; 49% male, 51% female; 0% American Indian, 2% Asian, 12% black, 23% Hispanic, 1% multiracial, 0% Pacific Islander, 51% white, 6% international; 85% from in state; 19% live on campus; 0% of students in fraternities, 0% in sororities
Most popular majors: 24% Elementary Education and Teaching, 17% Business Administration and Management, General, 9% Criminal Justice/ Law Enforcement Administration, 7% Psychology, General, 4% Business, Management, Marketing, and Related Support

Services, Other
Expenses: 2021-2022: $35,200; room/board: $14,900
Financial aid: (845) 398-4097; 72% of undergrads determined to have financial need; average aid package $18,750

SUNY Brockport
Brockport NY
(585) 395-2751
U.S. News ranking: Reg. U. (N), No. 73
Website: www.brockport.edu/
Admissions email: admit@brockport.edu
Public; founded 1835
Freshman admissions: selective; 2020-2021: 9,202 applied, 5,348 accepted. Neither SAT nor ACT required. SAT 25/75 percentile: 1000-1160. High school rank: 10% in top tenth, 33% in top quarter, 70% in top half
Early decision deadline: N/A, notification date: N/A
Early action deadline: N/A, notification date: N/A
Application deadline (fall): 8/1
Undergraduate student body: 5,482 full time, 807 part time; 42% male, 58% female; 0% American Indian, 2% Asian, 12% black, 9% Hispanic, 3% multiracial, 0% Pacific Islander, 69% white, 1% international; 99% from in state; 29% live on campus; 1% of students in fraternities, 2% in sororities
Most popular majors: 22% Health Professions and Related Programs, 14% Business, Management, Marketing, and Related Support Services, 13% Parks, Recreation, Leisure, and Fitness Studies, 7% Psychology, 6% Homeland Security, Law Enforcement, Firefighting and Related Protective Services
Expenses: 2021-2022: $8,580 in state, $18,490 out of state; room/ board: $14,466
Financial aid: (585) 395-2501; 72% of undergrads determined to have financial need; average aid package $10,801

SUNY Buffalo State[7]
Buffalo NY
(716) 878-4017
U.S. News ranking: Reg. U. (N), No. 103
Website: www.buffalostate.edu
Admissions email: admissions@buffalostate.edu
Public; founded 1871
Freshman admissions: less selective; 2020-2021: 13,313 applied, 10,660 accepted. Either SAT or ACT required. SAT 25/75 percentile: 860-1060. High school rank: N/A
Early decision deadline: N/A, notification date: N/A
Early action deadline: N/A, notification date: N/A
Application deadline (fall): rolling
Undergraduate student body: 6,582 full time, 727 part time
Most popular majors: 14% Business, Management, Marketing, and Related Support Services, 11% Education,

10% Homeland Security, Law Enforcement, Firefighting and Related Protective Services, 8% Liberal Arts and Sciences, General Studies and Humanities, 8% Social Sciences
Expenses: 2021-2022: $8,486 in state, $18,396 out of state; room/board: $13,606
Financial aid: (716) 878-4902; 76% of undergrads determined to have financial need; average aid package $13,263

SUNY Cobleskill
Cobleskill NY
(518) 255-5525
U.S. News ranking: Reg. Coll. (N), No. 17
Website: www.cobleskill.edu
Admissions email: admissionsoffice@cobleskill.edu
Public; founded 1911
Freshman admissions: less selective; 2020-2021: 2,659 applied, 2,483 accepted. Neither SAT nor ACT required. SAT 25/75 percentile: 900-1110. High school rank: 6% in top tenth, 10% in top quarter, 39% in top half
Early decision deadline: N/A, notification date: N/A
Early action deadline: N/A, notification date: N/A
Application deadline (fall): rolling
Undergraduate student body: 1,917 full time, 170 part time; 43% male, 57% female; 0% American Indian, 2% Asian, 12% black, 13% Hispanic, 3% multiracial, 0% Pacific Islander, 67% white, 1% international; 90% from in state; 40% live on campus; 5% of students in fraternities, 5% in sororities
Most popular majors: 43% Animal Sciences, General, 26% Information Science/Studies, 5% Plant Sciences, General, 3% Culinary Arts/Chef Training, 3% Kindergarten/Preschool Education and Teaching
Expenses: 2021-2022: $8,956 in state, $19,176 out of state; room/board: $14,074
Financial aid: (518) 255-5637; 77% of undergrads determined to have financial need; average aid package $7,132

SUNY College–Cortland
Cortland NY
(607) 753-4711
U.S. News ranking: Reg. U. (N), No. 70
Website: www2.cortland.edu/home/
Admissions email: admissions@cortland.edu
Public; founded 1868
Freshman admissions: selective; 2020-2021: 12,392 applied, 6,469 accepted. Neither SAT nor ACT required. SAT 25/75 percentile: 1100-1220. High school rank: 12% in top tenth, 44% in top quarter, 89% in top half
Early decision deadline: N/A, notification date: N/A
Early action deadline: 11/15, notification date: 1/1
Application deadline (fall): rolling

Undergraduate student body: 6,093 full time, 163 part time; 44% male, 56% female; 0% American Indian, 1% Asian, 6% black, 14% Hispanic, 2% multiracial, 0% Pacific Islander, 73% white, 0% international
Most popular majors: 25% Education, 19% Parks, Recreation, Leisure, and Fitness Studies, 12% Social Sciences, 8% Business, Management, Marketing, and Related Support Services, 8% Health Professions and Related Programs
Expenses: 2021-2022: $8,896 in state, $18,806 out of state; room/board: $13,200
Financial aid: (607) 753-4717; 63% of undergrads determined to have financial need; average aid package $15,636

SUNY College of Environmental Science and Forestry
Syracuse NY
(315) 470-6600
U.S. News ranking: Nat. U., No. 117
Website: www.esf.edu
Admissions email: esfinfo@esf.edu
Public; founded 1911
Freshman admissions: more selective; 2020-2021: 1,927 applied, 1,163 accepted. Neither SAT nor ACT required. SAT 25/75 percentile: 1130-1300. High school rank: N/A
Early decision deadline: 12/1, notification date: 1/15
Early action deadline: N/A, notification date: N/A
Application deadline (fall): 2/1
Undergraduate student body: 1,632 full time, 99 part time; 53% male, 47% female; 0% American Indian, 4% Asian, 2% black, 6% Hispanic, 4% multiracial, 0% Pacific Islander, 77% white, 2% international; 77% from in state; 29% live on campus; N/A of students in fraternities, N/A in sororities
Most popular majors: 41% Environmental Biology, 24% Natural Resources Management and Policy, 20% Environmental/Environmental Health Engineering, 5% Environmental Chemistry, 5% Sustainability Studies
Expenses: 2021-2022: $9,216 in state, $19,976 out of state; room/board: $16,970
Financial aid: (315) 470-6670; 58% of undergrads determined to have financial need; average aid package $10,779

SUNY College of Technology at Alfred
Alfred NY
(800) 425-3733
U.S. News ranking: Reg. Coll. (N), No. 6
Website: www.alfredstate.edu
Admissions email: admissions@alfredstate.edu
Public; founded 1908
Freshman admissions: selective; 2020-2021: 5,982 applied, 4,290 accepted. Neither SAT nor ACT required. SAT 25/75

percentile: 940-1170. High school rank: N/A
Early decision deadline: N/A, notification date: N/A
Early action deadline: N/A, notification date: N/A
Application deadline (fall): rolling
Undergraduate student body: 3,356 full time, 311 part time; 62% male, 38% female; 0% American Indian, 2% Asian, 15% black, 10% Hispanic, 3% multiracial, 0% Pacific Islander, 71% white, 0% international; 96% from in state; 61% live on campus; 5% of students in fraternities, 9% in sororities
Most popular majors: 34% Business, Management, Marketing, and Related Support Services, 19% Engineering Technologies and Engineering-Related Fields, 16% Health Professions and Related Programs, 8% Computer and Information Sciences and Support Services, 6% Communications Technologies/Technicians and Support Services
Expenses: 2021-2022: $8,694 in state, $12,664 out of state; room/board: $13,180
Financial aid: (607) 587-4253; 82% of undergrads determined to have financial need; average aid package $11,444

SUNY College of Technology at Canton
Canton NY
(800) 388-7123
U.S. News ranking: Reg. Coll. (N), No. 12
Website: www.canton.edu/
Admissions email: admissions@canton.edu
Public; founded 1906
Freshman admissions: less selective; 2020-2021: 2,961 applied, 2,458 accepted. Neither SAT nor ACT required. SAT 25/75 percentile: 920-1130. High school rank: 6% in top tenth, 22% in top quarter, 56% in top half
Early decision deadline: N/A, notification date: N/A
Early action deadline: N/A, notification date: N/A
Application deadline (fall): rolling
Undergraduate student body: 2,624 full time, 498 part time; 43% male, 57% female; 1% American Indian, 2% Asian, 13% black, 11% Hispanic, 3% multiracial, 0% Pacific Islander, 66% white, 1% international; 96% from in state; 29% live on campus; 2% of students in fraternities, 2% in sororities
Most popular majors: 14% Health/Health Care Administration/Management, 10% Law Enforcement Investigation and Interviewing, 9% Business Administration and Management, General, 7% Registered Nursing/Registered Nurse
Expenses: 2021-2022: $8,689 in state, $18,599 out of state; room/board: $14,210
Financial aid: (315) 386-7616; 82% of undergrads determined to have financial need; average aid package $10,473

SUNY College of Technology–Delhi
Delhi NY
(607) 746-4550
U.S. News ranking: Reg. Coll. (N), No. 13
Website: www.delhi.edu/
Admissions email: enroll@delhi.edu
Public; founded 1913
Freshman admissions: less selective; 2020-2021: 4,167 applied, 2,939 accepted. Neither SAT nor ACT required. SAT 25/75 percentile: 920-1110. High school rank: 5% in top tenth, 20% in top quarter, 53% in top half
Early decision deadline: N/A, notification date: N/A
Early action deadline: 12/1, notification date: 12/15
Application deadline (fall): 8/15
Undergraduate student body: 2,389 full time, 598 part time; 45% male, 55% female; 0% American Indian, 2% Asian, 16% black, 18% Hispanic, 2% multiracial, 0% Pacific Islander, 57% white, 0% international; 97% from in state; 34% live on campus; 5% of students in fraternities, 4% in sororities
Most popular majors: 46% Registered Nursing/Registered Nurse, 9% Criminal Justice/Safety Studies, 8% Business Administration and Management, General, 8% Construction Management, 6% Hospitality Administration/Management, General
Expenses: 2020-2021: $8,830 in state, $12,600 out of state; room/board: $13,320
Financial aid: (607) 746-4570; 80% of undergrads determined to have financial need; average aid package $11,698

SUNY College–Old Westbury[1]
Old Westbury NY
(516) 876-3200
U.S. News ranking: Reg. U. (N), second tier
Website: www.oldwestbury.edu
Admissions email: enroll@oldwestbury.edu
Public; founded 1965
Application deadline (fall): rolling
Undergraduate student body: N/A full time, N/A part time
Expenses: 2020-2021: $8,122 in state, $18,032 out of state; room/board: $11,530
Financial aid: N/A

SUNY College–Oneonta[1]
Oneonta NY
(607) 436-2524
U.S. News ranking: Reg. U. (N), No. 73
Website: suny.oneonta.edu/
Admissions email: admissions@oneonta.edu
Public; founded 1889
Application deadline (fall): rolling
Undergraduate student body: N/A full time, N/A part time

Expenses: 2020-2021: $8,740 in state, $18,650 out of state; room/board: $14,120
Financial aid: N/A

SUNY College–Potsdam
Potsdam NY
(315) 267-2180
U.S. News ranking: Reg. U. (N), No. 78
Website: www.potsdam.edu
Admissions email: admissions@potsdam.edu
Public; founded 1816
Freshman admissions: selective; 2020-2021: 4,447 applied, 3,188 accepted. Neither SAT nor ACT required. SAT 25/75 percentile: 1068-1240. High school rank: N/A
Early decision deadline: N/A, notification date: N/A
Early action deadline: N/A, notification date: N/A
Application deadline (fall): rolling
Undergraduate student body: 2,705 full time, 137 part time; 37% male, 63% female; 2% American Indian, 2% Asian, 11% black, 13% Hispanic, 3% multiracial, 0% Pacific Islander, 66% white, 0% international; 97% from in state; 38% live on campus; 3% of students in fraternities, 7% in sororities
Most popular majors: 17% Education, 16% Visual and Performing Arts, 10% Business, Management, Marketing, and Related Support Services, 7% Psychology, 6% Social Sciences
Expenses: 2020-2021: $8,711 in state, $18,621 out of state; room/board: $13,900
Financial aid: (315) 267-2162; 74% of undergrads determined to have financial need; average aid package $14,296

SUNY Empire State College
Saratoga Springs NY
(518) 587-2100
U.S. News ranking: Reg. U. (N), second tier
Website: www.esc.edu
Admissions email: admissions@esc.edu
Public; founded 1971
Freshman admissions: less selective; 2020-2021: 471 applied, 279 accepted. Neither SAT nor ACT required. SAT 25/75 percentile: N/A. High school rank: N/A
Early decision deadline: N/A, notification date: N/A
Early action deadline: N/A, notification date: N/A
Application deadline (fall): rolling
Undergraduate student body: 3,653 full time, 5,492 part time; 36% male, 64% female; 0% American Indian, 3% Asian, 16% black, 14% Hispanic, 2% multiracial, 0% Pacific Islander, 55% white, 1% international
Most popular majors: 34% Business, Management, Marketing, and Related Support Services, 24% Public Administration and Social Service Professions, 9% Multi/

Interdisciplinary Studies
Expenses: 2021-2022: $7,630 in state, $17,540 out of state; room/board: N/A
Financial aid: N/A

SUNY–Fredonia

Fredonia NY
(800) 252-1212
U.S. News ranking: Reg. U. (N), No. 62
Website: www.fredonia.edu
Admissions email: admissions@fredonia.edu
Public; founded 1826
Freshman admissions: selective; 2020-2021: 5,754 applied, 4,157 accepted. Either SAT or ACT required. SAT 25/75 percentile: 1000-1210. High school rank: 13% in top tenth, 40% in top quarter, 73% in top half
Early decision deadline: N/A, notification date: N/A
Early action deadline: N/A, notification date: N/A
Application deadline (fall): rolling
Undergraduate student body: 3,732 full time, 124 part time; 42% male, 58% female; 1% American Indian, 2% Asian, 8% black, 10% Hispanic, 4% multiracial, 0% Pacific Islander, 73% white, 2% international; N/A from in state; 47% live on campus; 1% of students in fraternities, 1% in sororities
Most popular majors: 18% Visual and Performing Arts, 15% Education, 14% Business, Management, Marketing, and Related Support Services, 10% Communication, Journalism, and Related Programs, 7% Psychology
Expenses: 2021-2022: $9,245 in state, $18,625 out of state; room/board: $13,290
Financial aid: (716) 673-3253; 71% of undergrads determined to have financial need; average aid package $11,718

SUNY–Geneseo

Geneseo NY
(585) 245-5571
U.S. News ranking: Reg. U. (N), No. 16
Website: www.geneseo.edu
Admissions email: admissions@geneseo.edu
Public; founded 1871
Freshman admissions: more selective; 2020-2021: 10,250 applied, 6,289 accepted. Either SAT or ACT required. SAT 25/75 percentile: 1140-1310. High school rank: 36% in top tenth, 72% in top quarter, 95% in top half
Early decision deadline: 11/15, notification date: 12/15
Early action deadline: N/A, notification date: N/A
Application deadline (fall): 1/1
Undergraduate student body: 4,626 full time, 202 part time; 36% male, 64% female; 0% American Indian, 4% Asian, 3% black, 8% Hispanic, 2% multiracial, 0% Pacific Islander, 79% white, 1% international; 99% from in state; 43% live on campus; 18% of students in fraternities, 22% in

sororities
Most popular majors: 18% Social Sciences, 14% Biological and Biomedical Sciences, 14% Psychology, 12% Business, Management, Marketing, and Related Support Services, 11% Education
Expenses: 2020-2021: $8,731 in state, $18,641 out of state; room/board: $14,472
Financial aid: (585) 245-5731; 51% of undergrads determined to have financial need; average aid package $10,291

SUNY Maritime College

Throggs Neck NY
(718) 409-7221
U.S. News ranking: Reg. U. (N), No. 58
Website: www.sunymaritime.edu
Admissions email: admissions@sunymaritime.edu
Public; founded 1874
Freshman admissions: selective; 2020-2021: 1,455 applied, 1,058 accepted. Either SAT or ACT required. SAT 25/75 percentile: 1070-1230. High school rank: 17% in top tenth, 50% in top quarter, 83% in top half
Early decision deadline: 11/1, notification date: 12/15
Early action deadline: N/A, notification date: N/A
Application deadline (fall): 1/31
Undergraduate student body: 1,443 full time, 68 part time; 86% male, 14% female; 0% American Indian, 5% Asian, 5% black, 17% Hispanic, 3% multiracial, 0% Pacific Islander, 66% white, 2% international
Most popular majors: 36% Marine Science/Merchant Marine Officer, 16% Mechanical Engineering, 15% Business, Management, Marketing, and Related Support Services, Other, 12% Naval Architecture and Marine Engineering, 8% Industrial Engineering
Expenses: 2021-2022: $8,900 in state, $19,500 out of state; room/board: $14,000
Financial aid: (718) 409-7400; 55% of undergrads determined to have financial need; average aid package $4,836

SUNY Morrisville

Morrisville NY
(315) 684-6046
U.S. News ranking: Reg. Coll. (N), No. 22
Website: www.morrisville.edu
Admissions email: admissions@morrisville.edu
Public; founded 1908
Freshman admissions: less selective; 2020-2021: 4,528 applied, 3,474 accepted. Neither SAT nor ACT required. SAT 25/75 percentile: 860-1060. High school rank: 2% in top tenth, 14% in top quarter, 44% in top half
Early decision deadline: N/A, notification date: N/A
Early action deadline: N/A, notification date: N/A
Application deadline (fall): 8/17

Undergraduate student body: 2,065 full time, 421 part time; 46% male, 54% female; 0% American Indian, 1% Asian, 27% black, 9% Hispanic, 3% multiracial, 0% Pacific Islander, 59% white, 1% international
Most popular majors: 21% Registered Nursing/Registered Nurse, 7% Automobile/Automotive Mechanics Technology/Technician, 6% Business Administration and Management, General, 6% Corrections and Criminal Justice, Other, 6% Equestrian/Equine Studies
Expenses: 2021-2022: $8,670 in state, $12,920 out of state; room/board: $13,900
Financial aid: (315) 684-6289; 83% of undergrads determined to have financial need; average aid package $10,340

SUNY–New Paltz

New Paltz NY
(845) 257-3200
U.S. News ranking: Reg. U. (N), No. 31
Website: www.newpaltz.edu
Admissions email: admissions@newpaltz.edu
Public; founded 1828
Freshman admissions: selective; 2020-2021: 8,843 applied, 5,484 accepted. Either SAT or ACT required. SAT 25/75 percentile: 1070-1260. High school rank: N/A
Early decision deadline: N/A, notification date: N/A
Early action deadline: 11/15, notification date: 12/15
Application deadline (fall): 4/1
Undergraduate student body: 5,918 full time, 679 part time; 38% male, 62% female; 0% American Indian, 5% Asian, 7% black, 22% Hispanic, 3% multiracial, 0% Pacific Islander, 59% white, 2% international; 98% from in state; 25% live on campus; 5% of students in fraternities, 5% in sororities
Most popular majors: 14% Business, Management, Marketing, and Related Support Services, 14% Communication, Journalism, and Related Programs, 11% Education, 11% Psychology, 11% Social Sciences
Expenses: 2020-2021: $8,359 in state, $18,269 out of state; room/board: $14,294
Financial aid: (845) 257-3250; 60% of undergrads determined to have financial need; average aid package $11,562

SUNY–Oswego

Oswego NY
(315) 312-2250
U.S. News ranking: Reg. U. (N), No. 50
Website: www.oswego.edu
Admissions email: admiss@oswego.edu
Public; founded 1861
Freshman admissions: selective; 2020-2021: 12,277 applied, 8,459 accepted. Either SAT or ACT required. SAT 25/75 percentile: 1020-1190. High school rank: 15% in top tenth,

42% in top quarter, 75% in top half
Early decision deadline: N/A, notification date: N/A
Early action deadline: 11/30, notification date: 12/15
Application deadline (fall): rolling
Undergraduate student body: 6,211 full time, 462 part time; 48% male, 52% female; 0% American Indian, 3% Asian, 11% black, 13% Hispanic, 3% multiracial, 0% Pacific Islander, 68% white, 2% international; 4% from in state; 40% live on campus; 7% of students in fraternities, 6% in sororities
Most popular majors: 24% Business, Management, Marketing, and Related Support Services, 14% Communication, Journalism, and Related Programs, 10% Psychology, 8% Education, 7% Biological and Biomedical Sciences
Expenses: 2021-2022: $8,769 in state, $18,679 out of state; room/board: $14,103
Financial aid: (315) 312-2248; 61% of undergrads determined to have financial need; average aid package $11,115

SUNY–Plattsburgh

Plattsburgh NY
(888) 673-0012
U.S. News ranking: Reg. U. (N), No. 62
Website: www.plattsburgh.edu
Admissions email: admissions@plattsburgh.edu
Public; founded 1889
Freshman admissions: selective; 2020-2021: 7,358 applied, 4,360 accepted. Neither SAT nor ACT required. SAT 25/75 percentile: 910-1130. High school rank: 16% in top tenth, 38% in top quarter, 75% in top half
Early decision deadline: N/A, notification date: N/A
Early action deadline: N/A, notification date: N/A
Application deadline (fall): rolling
Undergraduate student body: 4,185 full time, 495 part time; 57% male, 43% female; 1% American Indian, 3% Asian, 11% black, 13% Hispanic, 2% multiracial, 0% Pacific Islander, 63% white, 5% international; 97% from in state; 35% live on campus; 15% of students in fraternities, 15% in sororities
Most popular majors: 28% Business, Management, Marketing, and Related Support Services, 11% Health Professions and Related Programs, 10% Communication, Journalism, and Related Programs, 7% Psychology, 6% Homeland Security, Law Enforcement, Firefighting and Related Protective Services
Expenses: 2021-2022: $9,005 in state, $18,915 out of state; room/board: $14,787
Financial aid: (518) 564-2072; 69% of undergrads determined to have financial need; average aid package $13,647

SUNY Polytechnic Institute – Utica/Albany

Utica NY
(315) 792-7500
U.S. News ranking: Reg. U. (N), No. 12
Website: www.sunypoly.edu
Admissions email: admissions@sunypoly.edu
Public; founded 1966
Freshman admissions: more selective; 2020-2021: 3,053 applied, 2,238 accepted. Neither SAT nor ACT required. SAT 25/75 percentile: 1000-1350. High school rank: 53% in top tenth, 73% in top quarter, 96% in top half
Early decision deadline: N/A, notification date: N/A
Early action deadline: 11/15, notification date: 12/15
Application deadline (fall): 8/1
Undergraduate student body: 1,912 full time, 335 part time; 65% male, 35% female; 0% American Indian, 8% Asian, 7% black, 9% Hispanic, 3% multiracial, 0% Pacific Islander, 70% white, 1% international; 99% from in state; 27% live on campus; N/A of students in fraternities, N/A in sororities
Most popular majors: 12% Computer and Information Sciences, General, 11% Business Administration and Management, General, 8% Registered Nursing/Registered Nurse, 5% Mechanical Engineering/Mechanical Technology/Technician, 5% Psychology, General
Expenses: 2021-2022: $8,561 in state, $18,471 out of state; room/board: $13,471
Financial aid: (315) 792-7210; 69% of undergrads determined to have financial need; average aid package $9,029

Syracuse University

Syracuse NY
(315) 443-3611
U.S. News ranking: Nat. U., No. 59
Website: www.syracuse.edu
Admissions email: orange@syr.edu
Private; founded 1870
Freshman admissions: more selective; 2020-2021: 32,005 applied, 21,994 accepted. Neither SAT nor ACT required. SAT 25/75 percentile: 1160-1370. High school rank: 33% in top tenth, 65% in top quarter, 90% in top half
Early decision deadline: 11/15, notification date: 12/15
Early action deadline: N/A, notification date: N/A
Application deadline (fall): 1/1
Undergraduate student body: 13,832 full time, 647 part time; 46% male, 54% female; 1% American Indian, 7% Asian, 7% black, 10% Hispanic, 4% multiracial, 0% Pacific Islander, 55% white, 14% international; 37% from in state; 53% live on campus; 23% of students in fraternities, 44% in sororities
Most popular majors: 15% Social Sciences, 14% Communication, Journalism, and Related Programs,

12% Business, Management, Marketing, and Related Support Services, 9% Visual and Performing Arts, 7% Computer and Information Sciences and Support Services
Expenses: 2021-2022: $57,591; room/board: $16,895
Financial aid: (315) 443-1513; 41% of undergrads determined to have financial need; average aid package $45,039

Touro College

New York NY
(212) 463-0400
U.S. News ranking: Nat. U., No. 213
Website: www.touro.edu
Admissions email: admissions.nyscas@touro.edu
Private; founded 1971
Freshman admissions: selective; 2020-2021: 1,778 applied, 1,351 accepted. Neither SAT nor ACT required. SAT 25/75 percentile: 1120-1360. High school rank: N/A
Early decision deadline: N/A, notification date: N/A
Early action deadline: N/A, notification date: N/A
Application deadline (fall): N/A
Undergraduate student body: 3,683 full time, 1,837 part time; 30% male, 70% female; 0% American Indian, 3% Asian, 13% black, 10% Hispanic, 1% multiracial, 0% Pacific Islander, 60% white, 2% international; 83% from in state; N/A live on campus; N/A of students in fraternities, N/A in sororities
Most popular majors: 20% Health Professions and Related Programs, 16% Psychology, 10% Business, Management, Marketing, and Related Support Services, 10% Multi/Interdisciplinary Studies, 9% Biological and Biomedical Sciences
Expenses: 2021-2022: $20,750; room/board: $11,550
Financial aid: (646) 565-6000; 73% of undergrads determined to have financial need; average aid package $10,354

Union College)

Schenectady NY
(518) 388-6112
U.S. News ranking: Nat. Lib. Arts, No. 50
Website: www.union.edu
Admissions email: admissions@union.edu
Private; founded 1795
Freshman admissions: more selective; 2020-2021: 7,622 applied, 3,145 accepted. Neither SAT nor ACT required. SAT 25/75 percentile: 1210-1400. High school rank: 58% in top tenth, 81% in top quarter, 95% in top half
Early decision deadline: 11/15, notification date: 12/15
Early action deadline: 11/1, notification date: 12/21
Application deadline (fall): 1/15
Undergraduate student body: 2,030 full time, 17 part time; 53% male, 47% female; 0% American Indian, 6% Asian, 5% black, 10%

Hispanic, 3% multiracial, 0% Pacific Islander, 68% white, 8% international; N/A from in state; 72% live on campus; 21% of students in fraternities, 37% in sororities
Most popular majors: 27% Social Sciences, 15% Biological and Biomedical Sciences, 14% Engineering, 8% Psychology, 6% Foreign Languages, Literatures, and Linguistics
Expenses: 2021-2022: $61,659; room/board: $15,198
Financial aid: (518) 388-6123; 55% of undergrads determined to have financial need; average aid package $48,910

United States Merchant Marine Academy

Kings Point NY
(866) 546-4778
U.S. News ranking: Reg. Coll. (N), No. 3
Website: www.usmma.edu
Admissions email: admissions@usmma.edu
Public; founded 1943
Freshman admissions: selective; 2020-2021: 1,763 applied, 281 accepted. Either SAT or ACT required. SAT 25/75 percentile: 1190-1330. High school rank: N/A
Early decision deadline: N/A, notification date: N/A
Early action deadline: N/A, notification date: N/A
Application deadline (fall): 2/1
Undergraduate student body: 1,028 full time, 0 part time; 79% male, 21% female; 0% American Indian, 6% Asian, 2% black, 5% Hispanic, 6% multiracial, 1% Pacific Islander, 80% white, 0% international
Most popular majors: 48% Marine Science/Merchant Marine Officer, 38% Naval Architecture and Marine Engineering, 14% Systems Engineering
Expenses: 2021-2022: $780 in state, $780 out of state; room/board: N/A
Financial aid: (516) 726-5638

United States Military Academy

West Point NY
(845) 938-4041
U.S. News ranking: Nat. Lib. Arts, No. 11
Website: westpoint.edu
Admissions email: admissions@westpoint.edu
Public; founded 1802
Freshman admissions: more selective; 2020-2021: 15,856 applied, 1,471 accepted. Either SAT or ACT required. SAT 25/75 percentile: 1210-1440. High school rank: 43% in top tenth, 70% in top quarter, 93% in top half
Early decision deadline: N/A, notification date: N/A
Early action deadline: N/A, notification date: N/A
Application deadline (fall): 1/31
Undergraduate student body: 4,536 full time, 0 part time; 76%

male, 24% female; 1% American Indian, 8% Asian, 13% black, 12% Hispanic, 3% multiracial, 0% Pacific Islander, 62% white, 1% international; N/A from in state; 100% live on campus; N/A of students in fraternities, N/A in sororities
Most popular majors: 24% Engineering, 19% Social Sciences, 6% Business, Management, Marketing, and Related Support Services, 6% Computer and Information Sciences and Support Services, 6% Foreign Languages, Literatures, and Linguistics
Expenses: 2021-2022: $0 in state, $0 out of state; room/board: N/A
Financial aid: N/A

University at Albany–SUNY

Albany NY
(518) 442-5435
U.S. News ranking: Nat. U., No. 172
Website: www.albany.edu
Admissions email: ugadmissions@albany.edu
Public; founded 1844
Freshman admissions: more selective; 2020-2021: 26,127 applied, 14,932 accepted. Neither SAT nor ACT required. SAT 25/75 percentile: 1080-1240. High school rank: 18% in top tenth, 49% in top quarter, 85% in top half
Early decision deadline: N/A, notification date: N/A
Early action deadline: 11/1, notification date: 1/15
Application deadline (fall): 3/1
Undergraduate student body: 12,203 full time, 979 part time; 48% male, 52% female; 0% American Indian, 8% Asian, 20% black, 18% Hispanic, 4% multiracial, 0% Pacific Islander, 44% white, 4% international; 96% from in state; 47% live on campus; 3% of students in fraternities, 3% in sororities
Most popular majors: 31% Social Sciences, 12% Business, Management, Marketing, and Related Support Services, 9% Psychology, 7% Communication, Journalism, and Related Programs, 7% Computer and Information Sciences and Support Services
Expenses: 2021-2022: $10,310 in state, $28,150 out of state; room/board: $15,053
Financial aid: (518) 442-3202; 68% of undergrads determined to have financial need; average aid package $10,852

University at Buffalo–SUNY

Buffalo NY
(716) 645-6900
U.S. News ranking: Nat. U., No. 93
Website: www.buffalo.edu
Admissions email: ub-admissions@buffalo.edu
Public; founded 1846
Freshman admissions: more selective; 2020-2021: 30,247 applied, 20,252 accepted. Either SAT or ACT required. SAT 25/75

percentile: 1140-1310. High school rank: 29% in top tenth, 61% in top quarter, 90% in top half
Early decision deadline: N/A, notification date: N/A
Early action deadline: 11/15, notification date: 11/1
Application deadline (fall): rolling
Undergraduate student body: 20,435 full time, 1,871 part time; 55% male, 45% female; 0% American Indian, 16% Asian, 8% black, 8% Hispanic, 3% multiracial, 0% Pacific Islander, 47% white, 14% international; 98% from in state; 21% live on campus; 1% of students in fraternities, 2% in sororities
Most popular majors: 17% Business, Management, Marketing, and Related Support Services, 16% Engineering, 15% Social Sciences, 12% Psychology, 8% Biological and Biomedical Sciences
Expenses: 2021-2022: $10,724 in state, $28,194 out of state; room/board: $14,136
Financial aid: (716) 645-8232; 57% of undergrads determined to have financial need; average aid package $10,229

University of Rochester

Rochester NY
(585) 275-3221
U.S. News ranking: Nat. U., No. 34
Website: www.rochester.edu
Admissions email: admit@admissions.rochester.edu
Private; founded 1850
Affiliation: Undenominational
Freshman admissions: most selective; 2020-2021: 19,607 applied, 6,947 accepted. Neither SAT nor ACT required. SAT 25/75 percentile: 1310-1500. High school rank: 71% in top tenth, 93% in top quarter, 100% in top half
Early decision deadline: 11/1, notification date: 12/15
Early action deadline: N/A, notification date: N/A
Application deadline (fall): 1/5
Undergraduate student body: 6,099 full time, 422 part time; 48% male, 52% female; 0% American Indian, 12% Asian, 5% black, 8% Hispanic, 4% multiracial, 0% Pacific Islander, 42% white, 27% international; 46% from in state; 57% live on campus; 15% of students in fraternities, 12% in sororities
Most popular majors: 14% Engineering, 12% Biological and Biomedical Sciences, 12% Health Professions and Related Programs, 11% Social Sciences, 9% Psychology
Expenses: 2021-2022: $59,344; room/board: $17,456
Financial aid: (585) 275-3226; 53% of undergrads determined to have financial need; average aid package $51,250

Utica College

Utica NY
(315) 792-3006
U.S. News ranking: Reg. U. (N), No. 90
Website: www.utica.edu
Admissions email: admiss@utica.edu
Private; founded 1946
Freshman admissions: selective; 2020-2021: 3,119 applied, 2,695 accepted. Neither SAT nor ACT required. SAT 25/75 percentile: 1015-1210. High school rank: 11% in top tenth, 38% in top quarter, 69% in top half
Early decision deadline: 11/15, notification date: 12/15
Early action deadline: 11/15, notification date: 12/15
Application deadline (fall): rolling
Undergraduate student body: 2,634 full time, 670 part time; 40% male, 60% female; 1% American Indian, 4% Asian, 10% black, 10% Hispanic, 2% multiracial, 0% Pacific Islander, 67% white, 1% international; 85% from in state; 37% live on campus; 2% of students in fraternities, 2% in sororities
Most popular majors: 47% Health Professions and Related Programs, 15% Homeland Security, Law Enforcement, Firefighting and Related Protective Services, 6% Business, Management, Marketing, and Related Support Services, 6% Psychology
Expenses: 2021-2022: $23,264; room/board: $12,572
Financial aid: (315) 792-3215; 80% of undergrads determined to have financial need; average aid package $15,697

Vassar College

Poughkeepsie NY
(845) 437-7300
U.S. News ranking: Nat. Lib. Arts, No. 22
Website: www.vassar.edu
Admissions email: admissions@vassar.edu
Private; founded 1861
Freshman admissions: most selective; 2020-2021: 8,663 applied, 2,126 accepted. Neither SAT nor ACT required. SAT 25/75 percentile: 1360-1520. High school rank: 73% in top tenth, 95% in top quarter, 99% in top half
Early decision deadline: 11/15, notification date: 12/15
Early action deadline: N/A, notification date: N/A
Application deadline (fall): 1/1
Undergraduate student body: 2,409 full time, 26 part time; 38% male, 62% female; 0% American Indian, 12% Asian, 4% black, 8% Hispanic, 9% multiracial, 0% Pacific Islander, 58% white, 8% international; N/A from in state; 82% live on campus; N/A of students in fraternities, N/A in sororities
Most popular majors: 22% Social Sciences, 15% Biological and Biomedical Sciences, 11% Visual and Performing Arts, 7% Multi/Interdisciplinary Studies, 6% Mathematics and Statistics

Expenses: 2021-2022: $62,870; room/board: $15,710
Financial aid: (845) 437-5320; 56% of undergrads determined to have financial need; average aid package $55,343

Vaughn College of Aeronautics and Technology[1]

Flushing NY
(718) 429-6600
U.S. News ranking: Reg. Coll. (N), No. 20
Website: www.vaughn.edu
Admissions email: admitme@vaughn.edu
Private; founded 1932
Application deadline (fall): rolling
Undergraduate student body: N/A full time, N/A part time
Expenses: 2020-2021: $26,150; room/board: $14,180
Financial aid: (718) 429-6600

Villa Maria College[1]

Buffalo NY
(716) 896-0700
U.S. News ranking: Reg. Coll. (N), second tier
Admissions email: N/A
Private
Application deadline (fall): N/A
Undergraduate student body: N/A full time, N/A part time
Expenses: 2020-2021: $25,400; room/board: N/A
Financial aid: (716) 961-1849

Wagner College

Staten Island NY
(718) 390-3411
U.S. News ranking: Reg. U. (N), No. 34
Website: www.wagner.edu
Admissions email: admissions@wagner.edu
Private; founded 1883
Freshman admissions: selective; 2020-2021: 2,604 applied, 1,834 accepted. Neither SAT nor ACT required. SAT 25/75 percentile: 1050-1250. High school rank: 20% in top tenth, 48% in top quarter, 76% in top half
Early decision deadline: N/A, notification date: N/A
Early action deadline: 12/1, notification date: 1/5
Application deadline (fall): 2/15
Undergraduate student body: 1,587 full time, 56 part time; 35% male, 65% female; 0% American Indian, 5% Asian, 8% black, 12% Hispanic, 3% multiracial, 0% Pacific Islander, 61% white, 5% international
Most popular majors: 32% Health Professions and Related Programs, 17% Business, Management, Marketing, and Related Support Services, 16% Visual and Performing Arts, 11% Social Sciences, 8% Psychology
Expenses: 2021-2022: $50,330; room/board: $15,022
Financial aid: (718) 390-3122; 55% of undergrads determined to have financial need; average aid package $33,378

Webb Institute

Glen Cove NY
(516) 671-8355
U.S. News ranking: Engineering, unranked
Website: www.webb.edu
Admissions email: admissions@webb.edu
Private; founded 1889
Freshman admissions: more selective; 2020-2021: 157 applied, 33 accepted. Neither SAT nor ACT required. SAT 25/75 percentile: 1420-1530. High school rank: 85% in top tenth, 100% in top quarter, 100% in top half
Early decision deadline: 10/15, notification date: 12/15
Early action deadline: N/A, notification date: N/A
Application deadline (fall): 1/15
Undergraduate student body: 101 full time, 0 part time; 76% male, 24% female; 0% American Indian, 5% Asian, 0% black, 5% Hispanic, 8% multiracial, 0% Pacific Islander, 80% white, 0% international; 29% from in state; N/A live on campus; N/A of students in fraternities, N/A in sororities
Most popular majors: 100% Naval Architecture and Marine Engineering
Expenses: 2021-2022: $56,455; room/board: $13,580
Financial aid: (516) 403-5928; 23% of undergrads determined to have financial need; average aid package $59,000

Wells College[1]

Aurora NY
(800) 952-9355
U.S. News ranking: Nat. Lib. Arts, No. 146
Website: www.wells.edu/
Admissions email: admissions@wells.edu
Private; founded 1868
Application deadline (fall): 3/1
Undergraduate student body: N/A full time, N/A part time
Expenses: 2021-2022: $32,450; room/board: $14,800
Financial aid: (315) 364-3289; 91% of undergrads determined to have financial need; average aid package $28,316

Yeshiva University

New York NY
(646) 592-4440
U.S. News ranking: Nat. U., No. 68
Website: www.yu.edu
Admissions email: yuadmit@ymail.yu.edu
Private; founded 1886
Freshman admissions: more selective; 2020-2021: 1,442 applied, 972 accepted. Neither SAT nor ACT required. ACT 25/75 percentile: 24-31. High school rank: 59% in top tenth, 81% in top quarter, 97% in top half
Early decision deadline: 11/1, notification date: 12/15
Early action deadline: N/A, notification date: N/A
Application deadline (fall): 2/1
Undergraduate student body: 1,956 full time, 61 part time; 53% male, 47% female; 0% American

Indian, 0% Asian, 0% black, 0% Hispanic, 0% multiracial, 0% Pacific Islander, 0% white, 8% international; 37% from in state; 40% live on campus; N/A of students in fraternities, N/A in sororities
Most popular majors: 33% Business, Management, Marketing, and Related Support Services, 15% Biological and Biomedical Sciences, 15% Psychology, 6% Multi/ Interdisciplinary Studies, 6% Social Sciences
Expenses: 2021-2022: $47,500; room/board: $13,000
Financial aid: (646) 592-6250; 50% of undergrads determined to have financial need; average aid package $47,224

NORTH CAROLINA

Appalachian State University

Boone NC
(828) 262-2120
U.S. News ranking: Reg. U. (S), No. 6
Website: www.appstate.edu
Admissions email: admissions@appstate.edu
Public; founded 1899
Freshman admissions: selective; 2020-2021: 18,178 applied, 14,453 accepted. Neither SAT nor ACT required. ACT 25/75 percentile: 22-27. High school rank: 16% in top tenth, 50% in top quarter, 87% in top half
Early decision deadline: N/A, notification date: N/A
Early action deadline: 11/1, notification date: 1/25
Application deadline (fall): 2/1
Undergraduate student body: 16,905 full time, 1,156 part time; 43% male, 57% female; 0% American Indian, 2% Asian, 4% black, 8% Hispanic, 4% multiracial, 0% Pacific Islander, 81% white, 0% international; N/A from in state; 30% live on campus; 8% of students in fraternities, 12% in sororities
Most popular majors: 21% Business, Management, Marketing, and Related Support Services, 10% Health Professions and Related Programs, 8% Communication, Journalism, and Related Programs, 8% Education, 8% Parks, Recreation, Leisure, and Fitness Studies
Expenses: 2021-2022: $7,950 in state, $23,557 out of state; room/board: $9,681
Financial aid: (828) 262-2190; 52% of undergrads determined to have financial need; average aid package $9,758

Barton College

Wilson NC
(800) 345-4973
U.S. News ranking: Reg. Coll. (S), No. 14
Website: www.barton.edu/
Admissions email: enroll@barton.edu
Private; founded 1902
Affiliation: Christian Church

(Disciples of Christ)
Freshman admissions: selective; 2020-2021: 3,890 applied, 1,651 accepted. Neither SAT nor ACT required. SAT 25/75 percentile: 930-1120. High school rank: 15% in top tenth, 36% in top quarter, 71% in top half
Early decision deadline: N/A, notification date: N/A
Early action deadline: N/A, notification date: N/A
Application deadline (fall): rolling
Undergraduate student body: 1,002 full time, 102 part time; 45% male, 55% female; 1% American Indian, 1% Asian, 24% black, 9% Hispanic, 4% multiracial, 0% Pacific Islander, 57% white, 4% international; 80% from in state; 51% live on campus; 7% of students in fraternities, 15% in sororities
Most popular majors: 18% Health Professions and Related Programs, 14% Parks, Recreation, Leisure, and Fitness Studies, 13% Business, Management, Marketing, and Related Support Services, 11% Public Administration and Social Service Professions
Expenses: 2021-2022: $33,430; room/board: $10,970
Financial aid: (252) 399-6371; 85% of undergrads determined to have financial need; average aid package $26,559

Belmont Abbey College

Belmont NC
(888) 222-0110
U.S. News ranking: Reg. Coll. (S), No. 19
Website: www. belmontabbeycollege.edu
Admissions email: admissions@bac.edu
Private; founded 1876
Affiliation: Roman Catholic
Freshman admissions: selective; 2020-2021: 2,292 applied, 1,836 accepted. Neither SAT nor ACT required. SAT 25/75 percentile: 970-1180. High school rank: 5% in top tenth, 24% in top quarter, 51% in top half
Early decision deadline: N/A, notification date: N/A
Early action deadline: 10/30, notification date: 11/5
Application deadline (fall): rolling
Undergraduate student body: 1,390 full time, 77 part time; 51% male, 49% female; 1% American Indian, 2% Asian, 12% black, 3% Hispanic, 0% multiracial, 0% Pacific Islander, 62% white, 2% international; N/A from in state; 61% live on campus; N/A of students in fraternities, N/A in sororities
Most popular majors: 37% Business, Management, Marketing, and Related Support Services, 17% Education, 9% Parks, Recreation, Leisure, and Fitness Studies, 8% Homeland Security, Law Enforcement, Firefighting and Related Protective Services, 6% Psychology
Expenses: 2021-2022: $18,500; room/board: $11,590

Financial aid: (704) 461-7006; 61% of undergrads determined to have financial need; average aid package $13,561

Bennett College[1]

Greensboro NC
(336) 370-8624
U.S. News ranking: Nat. Lib. Arts, second tier
Website: www.bennett.edu
Admissions email: admiss@bennett.edu
Private; founded 1873
Affiliation: United Methodist
Application deadline (fall): rolling
Undergraduate student body: N/A full time, N/A part time
Expenses: 2020-2021: $18,513; room/board: $8,114
Financial aid: (336) 517-2209

Brevard College

Brevard NC
(828) 641-0461
U.S. News ranking: Reg. Coll. (S), No. 21
Website: www.brevard.edu
Admissions email: admissions@brevard.edu
Private; founded 1853
Affiliation: United Methodist
Freshman admissions: selective; 2020-2021: 2,762 applied, 1,351 accepted. Neither SAT nor ACT required. ACT 25/75 percentile: 18-22. High school rank: 5% in top tenth, 19% in top quarter, 50% in top half
Early decision deadline: N/A, notification date: N/A
Early action deadline: N/A, notification date: N/A
Application deadline (fall): rolling
Undergraduate student body: 755 full time, 31 part time; 55% male, 45% female; 1% American Indian, 1% Asian, 14% black, 9% Hispanic, 5% multiracial, 0% Pacific Islander, 62% white, 2% international
Most popular majors: 18% Criminal Justice/Law Enforcement Administration, 14% Multi-/ Interdisciplinary Studies, Other, 13% Parks, Recreation and Leisure Studies, 7% Fine/ Studio Arts, General, 5% Health Professions and Related Programs
Expenses: 2021-2022: $30,250; room/board: $11,400
Financial aid: (828) 641-0113; 93% of undergrads determined to have financial need; average aid package $27,400

Campbell University

Buies Creek NC
(910) 893-1200
U.S. News ranking: Nat. U., No. 277
Website: www.campbell.edu
Admissions email: admissions@campbell.edu
Private; founded 1887
Affiliation: Baptist
Freshman admissions: selective; 2020-2021: 5,025 applied, 4,085 accepted. Neither SAT nor ACT required. SAT 25/75 percentile: 1010-1210. High school rank: 24% in top tenth, 53% in top quarter, 82% in top half

Early decision deadline: N/A, notification date: N/A
Early action deadline: N/A, notification date: N/A
Application deadline (fall): rolling
Undergraduate student body: 3,098 full time, 622 part time; 47% male, 53% female; 0% American Indian, 2% Asian, 15% black, 10% Hispanic, 5% multiracial, 0% Pacific Islander, 60% white, 2% international; 82% from in state; 57% live on campus; N/A of students in fraternities, N/A in sororities
Most popular majors: 11% Business Administration and Management, General, 8% Kinesiology and Exercise Science, 6% Psychology, General, 5% Biology/Biological Sciences, General, 5% Science Technologies/Technicians, Other
Expenses: 2021-2022: $38,160; room/board: $13,625
Financial aid: (910) 893-1310; 75% of undergrads determined to have financial need; average aid package $27,768

Catawba College
Salisbury NC
(800) 228-2922
U.S. News ranking: Reg. Coll. (S), No. 8
Website: www.catawba.edu
Admissions email: admission@catawba.edu
Private; founded 1851
Affiliation: United Church of Christ
Freshman admissions: selective; 2020-2021: 3,254 applied, 1,696 accepted. Neither SAT nor ACT required. SAT 25/75 percentile: 940-1130. High school rank: 12% in top tenth, 38% in top quarter, 72% in top half
Early decision deadline: N/A, notification date: N/A
Early action deadline: N/A, notification date: N/A
Undergraduate student body: 1,128 full time, 110 part time; 45% male, 55% female; 0% American Indian, 1% Asian, 19% black, 8% Hispanic, 4% multiracial, 0% Pacific Islander, 57% white, 5% international; 76% from in state; 55% live on campus; 0% of students in fraternities, 0% in sororities
Most popular majors: 22% Business, Management, Marketing, and Related Support Services, 13% Health Professions and Related Programs, 9% Education, 8% Natural Resources and Conservation, 8% Parks, Recreation, Leisure, and Fitness Studies
Expenses: 2021-2022: $32,380; room/board: $11,130
Financial aid: (704) 637-4416; 81% of undergrads determined to have financial need; average aid package $28,467

Chowan University
Murfreesboro NC
(252) 398-6230
U.S. News ranking: Nat. Lib. Arts, second tier
Website: chowan.edu/

Admissions email: admissions@chowan.edu
Private; founded 1848
Affiliation: Baptist
Freshman admissions: least selective; 2020-2021: 2,549 applied, 1,717 accepted. Neither SAT nor ACT required. SAT 25/75 percentile: 800-1020. High school rank: 5% in top tenth, 10% in top quarter, 34% in top half
Early decision deadline: N/A, notification date: N/A
Early action deadline: N/A, notification date: N/A
Application deadline (fall): rolling
Undergraduate student body: 1,081 full time, 19 part time; 55% male, 45% female; 1% American Indian, 0% Asian, 58% black, 3% Hispanic, 2% multiracial, 0% Pacific Islander, 18% white, 4% international
Most popular majors: Information not available
Expenses: 2020-2021: $25,880; room/board: $9,600
Financial aid: (252) 398-6269

Davidson College
Davidson NC
(800) 768-0380
U.S. News ranking: Nat. Lib. Arts, No. 13
Website: davidson.edu
Admissions email: admission@davidson.edu
Private; founded 1837
Affiliation: Presbyterian Church (USA)
Freshman admissions: most selective; 2020-2021: 5,621 applied, 1,124 accepted. Neither SAT nor ACT required. SAT 25/75 percentile: 1300-1460. High school rank: 76% in top tenth, 95% in top quarter, 99% in top half
Early decision deadline: 11/15, notification date: 12/15
Early action deadline: N/A, notification date: N/A
Application deadline (fall): 1/7
Undergraduate student body: 1,983 full time, 0 part time; 48% male, 52% female; 0% American Indian, 6% Asian, 6% black, 8% Hispanic, 4% multiracial, 0% Pacific Islander, 67% white, 7% international; 22% from in state; 74% live on campus; 29% of students in fraternities, 51% in sororities
Most popular majors: 15% Political Science and Government, General, 14% Biology/Biological Sciences, General, 14% Econometrics and Quantitative Economics, 10% Psychology, General, 7% Computer and Information Sciences, General
Expenses: 2021-2022: $55,000; room/board: $15,225
Financial aid: (704) 894-2232; 50% of undergrads determined to have financial need; average aid package $52,776

Duke University
Durham NC
(919) 684-3214
U.S. News ranking: Nat. U., No. 9
Website: www.duke.edu/

Admissions email: undergrad-admissions@duke.edu
Private; founded 1838
Freshman admissions: most selective; 2020-2021: 39,603 applied, 3,085 accepted. Either SAT or ACT required. ACT 25/75 percentile: 34-35. High school rank: 95% in top tenth, 99% in top quarter, 100% in top half
Early decision deadline: 11/1, notification date: 12/15
Early action deadline: N/A, notification date: N/A
Application deadline (fall): 1/3
Undergraduate student body: 6,572 full time, 145 part time; 49% male, 51% female; N/A American Indian, N/A Asian, N/A black, N/A Hispanic, N/A multiracial, N/A Pacific Islander, N/A white, N/A international
Most popular majors: 15% Computer Science, 10% Econometrics and Quantitative Economics, 10% Public Policy Analysis, General, 7% Biology/Biological Sciences, General, 6% Political Science and Government, General
Expenses: 2021-2022: $60,489; room/board: $17,484
Financial aid: (919) 684-6225; 42% of undergrads determined to have financial need; average aid package $58,612

East Carolina University
Greenville NC
(252) 328-6640
U.S. News ranking: Nat. U., No. 213
Website: www.ecu.edu
Admissions email: admissions@ecu.edu
Public; founded 1907
Freshman admissions: selective; 2020-2021: 20,306 applied, 17,856 accepted. Either SAT or ACT required. ACT 25/75 percentile: 19-24. High school rank: 13% in top tenth, 36% in top quarter, 71% in top half
Early decision deadline: N/A, notification date: N/A
Early action deadline: N/A, notification date: N/A
Application deadline (fall): 3/1
Undergraduate student body: 18,886 full time, 4,170 part time; 42% male, 58% female; 1% American Indian, 3% Asian, 16% black, 8% Hispanic, 4% multiracial, 0% Pacific Islander, 65% white, 0% international; 91% from in state; N/A live on campus; N/A of students in fraternities, N/A in sororities
Most popular majors: 18% Business, Management, Marketing, and Related Support Services, 17% Health Professions and Related Programs, 8% Engineering Technologies and Engineering-Related Fields, 6% Communication, Journalism, and Related Programs, 6% Education
Expenses: 2021-2022: $7,316 in state, $23,593 out of state; room/board: $10,136
Financial aid: (252) 328-6610; 59% of undergrads determined to have financial need; average aid package $11,212

Elizabeth City State University
Elizabeth City NC
(252) 335-3305
U.S. News ranking: Reg. Coll. (S), No. 33
Website: www.ecsu.edu
Admissions email: admissions@mail.ecsu.edu
Public; founded 1891
Freshman admissions: less selective; 2020-2021: 2,578 applied, 1,929 accepted. Either SAT or ACT required. SAT 25/75 percentile: 875-1059. High school rank: 2% in top tenth, 5% in top quarter, 33% in top half
Early decision deadline: N/A, notification date: N/A
Early action deadline: N/A, notification date: N/A
Application deadline (fall): 8/1
Undergraduate student body: 1,624 full time, 286 part time; 41% male, 59% female; 0% American Indian, 0% Asian, 70% black, 5% Hispanic, 5% multiracial, 0% Pacific Islander, 16% white, 1% international
Most popular majors: 10% Multi/Interdisciplinary Studies, 9% Biological and Biomedical Sciences, 9% Homeland Security, Law Enforcement, Firefighting and Related Protective Services, 8% Business, Management, Marketing, and Related Support Services, 7% Transportation and Materials Moving
Expenses: 2021-2022: $4,047 in state, $8,047 out of state; room/board: $8,462
Financial aid: (252) 335-4850

Elon University
Elon NC
(800) 334-8448
U.S. News ranking: Nat. U., No. 83
Website: www.elon.edu
Admissions email: admissions@elon.edu
Private; founded 1889
Freshman admissions: more selective; 2020-2021: 15,306 applied, 10,975 accepted. Neither SAT nor ACT required. SAT 25/75 percentile: 1140-1320. High school rank: 25% in top tenth, 52% in top quarter, 83% in top half
Early decision deadline: 11/1, notification date: 12/1
Early action deadline: 11/1, notification date: 12/20
Application deadline (fall): 1/10
Undergraduate student body: 6,073 full time, 218 part time; 40% male, 60% female; 0% American Indian, 2% Asian, 6% black, 6% Hispanic, 3% multiracial, 0% Pacific Islander, 80% white, 2% international; 20% from in state; 62% live on campus; 20% of students in fraternities, 39% in sororities
Most popular majors: 10% Finance, General, 10% Speech Communication and Rhetoric, 8% Marketing/Marketing Management, General, 5% Psychology, General, 4% Business Administration and Management, General
Expenses: 2021-2022: $38,725; room/board: $13,422

Financial aid: (336) 278-7640; 34% of undergrads determined to have financial need; average aid package $21,710

Fayetteville State University
Fayetteville NC
(910) 672-1371
U.S. News ranking: Reg. U. (S), No. 77
Website: www.uncfsu.edu/ fsu-admissions/undergraduate-admissions
Admissions email: admissions@uncfsu.edu
Public; founded 1867
Freshman admissions: less selective; 2020-2021: 4,611 applied, 3,660 accepted. Neither SAT nor ACT required. SAT 25/75 percentile: 840-1000. High school rank: 7% in top tenth, 23% in top quarter, 62% in top half
Early decision deadline: N/A, notification date: N/A
Early action deadline: N/A, notification date: N/A
Application deadline (fall): 6/30
Undergraduate student body: 3,959 full time, 1,702 part time; 29% male, 71% female; 2% American Indian, 2% Asian, 60% black, 9% Hispanic, 5% multiracial, 0% Pacific Islander, 19% white, 0% international; 94% from in state; 19% live on campus; 1% of students in fraternities, 1% in sororities
Most popular majors: 19% Registered Nursing/Registered Nurse, 11% Business Administration and Management, General, 11% Psychology, General, 10% Criminal Justice/Safety Studies, 6% Liberal Arts and Sciences/Liberal Studies
Expenses: 2021-2022: $5,398 in state, $17,006 out of state; room/board: $8,615
Financial aid: (910) 672-1325; 84% of undergrads determined to have financial need; average aid package $10,786

Gardner-Webb University[1]
Boiling Springs NC
(800) 253-6472
U.S. News ranking: Nat. U., No. 277
Website: www.gardner-webb.edu
Admissions email: admissions@gardner-webb.edu
Private; founded 1905
Affiliation: Baptist
Application deadline (fall): rolling
Undergraduate student body: N/A full time, N/A part time
Expenses: 2021-2022: $31,960; room/board: $10,540
Financial aid: (704) 406-4247; 78% of undergrads determined to have financial need; average aid package $28,475

Greensboro College
Greensboro NC
(336) 272-7102
U.S. News ranking: Reg. Coll. (S), No. 25
Website: www.greensboro.edu

Admissions email:
admissions@greensboro.edu
Private; founded 1838
Affiliation: United Methodist
Freshman admissions: selective;
2020-2021: 1,968 applied, 790
accepted. Neither SAT nor ACT
required. ACT 25/75 percentile:
16-21. High school rank: N/A
Early decision deadline: N/A,
notification date: N/A
Early action deadline: N/A,
notification date: N/A
Application deadline (fall): rolling
Undergraduate student body: 630
full time, 162 part time; 52%
male, 48% female; 1% American
Indian, 1% Asian, 25% black,
5% Hispanic, 6% multiracial,
0% Pacific Islander, 46% white,
0% international; 76% from in
state; 40% live on campus; 0%
of students in fraternities, 0% in
sororities
Most popular majors: 18%
Kinesiology and Exercise Science,
14% Business/Managerial
Economics, 8% Criminal Justice/
Law Enforcement Administration,
8% Psychology, General, 6%
Liberal Arts and Sciences/Liberal
Studies
Expenses: 2021-2022: $18,960;
room/board: $11,224
Financial aid: (336) 272-7102;
80% of undergrads determined to
have financial need; average aid
package $17,470

Guilford College

Greensboro NC
(800) 992-7759
U.S. News ranking: Nat. Lib. Arts,
second tier
Website: www.guilford.edu
Admissions email:
admission@guilford.edu
Private; founded 1837
Affiliation: Friends
Freshman admissions: selective;
2020-2021: 3,660 applied,
2,855 accepted. Neither SAT
nor ACT required. SAT 25/75
percentile: 930-1170. High school
rank: 12% in top tenth, 33% in
top quarter, 65% in top half
Early decision deadline: N/A,
notification date: N/A
Early action deadline: 12/1,
notification date: 12/15
Application deadline (fall): 8/10
Undergraduate student body: 1,290
full time, 130 part time; 47%
male, 53% female; 0% American
Indian, 3% Asian, 27% black,
14% Hispanic, 4% multiracial,
0% Pacific Islander, 49% white,
1% international
Most popular majors: Information
not available
Expenses: 2020-2021: $40,120;
room/board: $12,200
Financial aid: (336) 316-2354

High Point University

High Point NC
(800) 345-6993
U.S. News ranking: Reg. Coll. (S),
No. 1
Website: www.highpoint.edu
Admissions email:
admiss@highpoint.edu
Private; founded 1924
Affiliation: United Methodist

Freshman admissions: selective;
2020-2021: 11,266 applied,
8,680 accepted. Neither SAT
nor ACT required. SAT 25/75
percentile: 1070-1240. High
school rank: 19% in top tenth,
49% in top quarter, 80% in
top half
Early decision deadline: 11/1,
notification date: 11/22
Early action deadline: 11/15,
notification date: 12/15
Application deadline (fall): 3/1
Undergraduate student body: 4,575
full time, 53 part time; 44%
male, 56% female; 0% American
Indian, 2% Asian, 6% black, 6%
Hispanic, 4% multiracial, 0%
Pacific Islander, 77% white, 1%
international; 27% from in state;
94% live on campus; 16% of
students in fraternities, 43% in
sororities
Most popular majors: 36%
Business, Management,
Marketing, and Related Support
Services, 17% Communication,
Journalism, and Related Programs,
7% Parks, Recreation, Leisure,
and Fitness Studies, 6% Biological
and Biomedical Sciences, 6%
Visual and Performing Arts
Expenses: 2021-2022: $39,752;
room/board: $15,906
Financial aid: (336) 841-9124;
43% of undergrads determined to
have financial need; average aid
package $21,752

Johnson C. Smith University

Charlotte NC
(704) 378-1010
U.S. News ranking: Nat. Lib. Arts,
second tier
Website: www.jcsu.edu
Admissions email:
admissions@jcsu.edu
Private; founded 1867
Freshman admissions: least
selective; 2020-2021: 7,160
applied, 3,523 accepted. Either
SAT or ACT required. SAT 25/75
percentile: 800-980. High school
rank: N/A
Early decision deadline: N/A,
notification date: N/A
Early action deadline: N/A,
notification date: N/A
Application deadline (fall): rolling
Undergraduate student body: 1,191
full time, 62 part time; 38%
male, 62% female; 1% American
Indian, 0% Asian, 73% black,
1% Hispanic, 0% multiracial,
0% Pacific Islander, 1% white,
1% international; 44% from in
state; N/A live on campus; N/A
of students in fraternities, N/A in
sororities
Most popular majors: 22%
Business, Management,
Marketing, and Related Support
Services, 13% Biological and
Biomedical Sciences, 11% Public
Administration and Social Service
Professions, 11% Social Sciences,
10% Parks, Recreation, Leisure,
and Fitness Studies
Expenses: 2021-2022: $18,944;
room/board: $7,100
Financial aid: (704) 378-1498;
94% of undergrads determined to
have financial need; average aid
package $15,437

Lees-McRae College

Banner Elk NC
(828) 898-5241
U.S. News ranking: Reg. Coll. (S),
No. 28
Website: www.lmc.edu
Admissions email:
admissions@lmc.edu
Private; founded 1900
Affiliation: Presbyterian Church
(USA)
Freshman admissions: selective;
2020-2021: 1,430 applied,
1,048 accepted. Neither SAT
nor ACT required. SAT 25/75
percentile: 963-1140. High
school rank: N/A
Early decision deadline: N/A,
notification date: N/A
Early action deadline: 12/15,
notification date: 1/15
Application deadline (fall): rolling
Undergraduate student body: 788
full time, 48 part time; 33%
male, 67% female; 0% American
Indian, 1% Asian, 8% black,
6% Hispanic, 2% multiracial,
0% Pacific Islander, 73% white,
3% international; 69% from in
state; 66% live on campus; 0%
of students in fraternities, 0% in
sororities
Most popular majors: 18%
Biological and Biomedical
Sciences, 17% Health Professions
and Related Programs, 15%
Education, 14% Homeland
Security, Law Enforcement,
Firefighting and Related
Protective Services, 10% Public
Administration and Social Service
Professions
Expenses: 2021-2022: $28,290;
room/board: $11,550
Financial aid: (828) 898-3446

Lenoir-Rhyne University

Hickory NC
(828) 328-7300
U.S. News ranking: Reg. U. (S),
No. 40
Website: www.lr.edu
Admissions email:
admission@lr.edu
Private; founded 1891
Affiliation: Evangelical Lutheran
Church
Freshman admissions: selective;
2020-2021: 6,194 applied,
4,746 accepted. Neither SAT
nor ACT required. ACT 25/75
percentile: 18-23. High school
rank: N/A
Early decision deadline: N/A,
notification date: N/A
Early action deadline: 11/13,
notification date: 11/13
Application deadline (fall): rolling
Undergraduate student body: 1,566
full time, 217 part time; 41%
male, 59% female; 0% American
Indian, 2% Asian, 12% black,
9% Hispanic, 5% multiracial,
0% Pacific Islander, 65% white,
4% international; 81% from in
state; 51% live on campus; 7%
of students in fraternities, 9% in
sororities
Most popular majors: 24%
Business, Management,
Marketing, and Related Support
Services, 19% Health Professions
and Related Programs, 12%

Parks, Recreation, Leisure, and
Fitness Studies, 8% Education,
6% Psychology
Expenses: 2021-2022: $41,500;
room/board: $12,800
Financial aid: (828) 328-7300;
84% of undergrads determined to
have financial need; average aid
package $32,818

Livingstone College

Salisbury NC
(704) 216-6001
U.S. News ranking: Reg. Coll. (S),
second tier
Website: www.livingstone.edu/
Admissions email:
admissions@livingstone.edu
Private; founded 1879
Affiliation: African Methodist
Episcopal Zion Church
Freshman admissions: least
selective; 2020-2021: 5,378
applied, 3,720 accepted. Either
SAT or ACT required. SAT 25/75
percentile: 765-930. High school
rank: 3% in top tenth, 11% in top
quarter, 31% in top half
Early decision deadline: N/A,
notification date: N/A
Early action deadline: N/A,
notification date: N/A
Application deadline (fall): rolling
Undergraduate student body:
838 full time, 7 part time; 51%
male, 49% female; 1% American
Indian, 0% Asian, 89% black,
0% Hispanic, 4% multiracial,
0% Pacific Islander, 2% white,
0% international; 62% from in
state; 78% live on campus; 3%
of students in fraternities, 3% in
sororities
Most popular majors: 18%
Business Administration and
Management, General, 13%
Criminal Justice/Safety Studies,
13% Liberal Arts and Sciences/
Liberal Studies, 11% Sport
and Fitness Administration/
Management, 9% Biology/
Biological Sciences, General
Expenses: 2021-2022: $18,293;
room/board: $6,794
Financial aid: (704) 216-6069;
97% of undergrads determined to
have financial need; average aid
package $16,338

Mars Hill University

Mars Hill NC
(866) 642-4968
U.S. News ranking: Reg. Coll. (S),
No. 29
Website: www.mhu.edu
Admissions email:
admissions@mhu.edu
Private; founded 1856
Freshman admissions: selective;
2020-2021: 1,718 applied,
1,156 accepted. Neither SAT
nor ACT required. ACT 25/75
percentile: 17-21. High school
rank: 6% in top tenth, 27% in top
quarter, 62% in top half
Early decision deadline: N/A,
notification date: N/A
Early action deadline: N/A,
notification date: N/A
Application deadline (fall): rolling
Undergraduate student body: 963
full time, 56 part time; 47%
male, 53% female; 1% American
Indian, 1% Asian, 20% black,

6% Hispanic, 3% multiracial,
0% Pacific Islander, 64% white,
4% international; 74% from in
state; 54% live on campus; N/A
of students in fraternities, N/A in
sororities
Most popular majors: 17%
Business, Management,
Marketing, and Related Support
Services, 13% Health Professions
and Related Programs, 10%
Biological and Biomedical
Sciences, 10% Public
Administration and Social Service
Professions, 9% Homeland
Security, Law Enforcement,
Firefighting and Related Protective
Services
Expenses: N/A
Financial aid: (828) 689-1103

Meredith College

Raleigh NC
(919) 760-8581
U.S. News ranking: Nat. Lib. Arts,
No. 136
Website: www.meredith.edu
Admissions email:
admissions@meredith.edu
Private; founded 1891
Freshman admissions: selective;
2020-2021: 1,670 applied,
1,196 accepted. Neither SAT
nor ACT required. SAT 25/75
percentile: 1008-1200. High
school rank: 17% in top tenth,
39% in top quarter, 79% in
top half
Early decision deadline: 10/30,
notification date: 11/15
Early action deadline: 12/1,
notification date: 12/15
Application deadline (fall): 2/15
Undergraduate student body: 1,468
full time, 53 part time; 0% male,
100% female; 0% American
Indian, 4% Asian, 9% black,
11% Hispanic, 3% multiracial,
0% Pacific Islander, 66% white,
1% international; N/A from in
state; 40% live on campus; N/A
of students in fraternities, N/A in
sororities
Most popular majors: 17%
Business, Management,
Marketing, and Related Support
Services, 12% Psychology, 12%
Visual and Performing Arts, 10%
Social Sciences
Expenses: 2021-2022: $41,224;
room/board: $12,120
Financial aid: (919) 760-8565;
72% of undergrads determined to
have financial need; average aid
package $36,036

Methodist University[1]

Fayetteville NC
(910) 630-7027
U.S. News ranking: Reg. U. (S),
No. 102
Website: www.methodist.edu
Admissions email:
admissions@methodist.edu
Private; founded 1956
Affiliation: United Methodist
Application deadline (fall): rolling
Undergraduate student body: N/A
full time, N/A part time
Expenses: 2020-2021: $36,076;
room/board: $12,828
Financial aid: (910) 630-7000

Montreat College[1]

Montreat NC
(800) 622-6968
U.S. News ranking: Reg. U. (S), second tier
Website: www.montreat.edu
Admissions email: admissions@montreat.edu
Private; founded 1916
Application deadline (fall): rolling
Undergraduate student body: N/A full time, N/A part time
Expenses: 2021-2022: $29,462; room/board: $10,202
Financial aid: (800) 545-4656; 79% of undergrads determined to have financial need; average aid package $22,845

North Carolina Agricultural and Technical State University

Greensboro NC
(336) 334-7946
U.S. News ranking: Nat. U., No. 277
Website: www.ncat.edu
Admissions email: uadmit@ncat.edu
Public; founded 1891
Freshman admissions: selective; 2020-2021: 16,369 applied, 9,281 accepted. Either SAT or ACT required. SAT 25/75 percentile: 960-1130. High school rank: 14% in top tenth, 40% in top quarter, 79% in top half
Early decision deadline: N/A, notification date: N/A
Early action deadline: 10/15, notification date: 12/15
Application deadline (fall): 6/1
Undergraduate student body: 9,933 full time, 1,197 part time; 41% male, 59% female; 0% American Indian, 1% Asian, 83% black, 4% Hispanic, 4% multiracial, 0% Pacific Islander, 5% white, 1% international; 74% from in state; 20% live on campus; N/A of students in fraternities, N/A in sororities
Most popular majors: 13% Engineering, 11% Business, Management, Marketing, and Related Support Services, 9% Liberal Arts and Sciences, General Studies and Humanities, 8% Communication, Journalism, and Related Programs, 7% Parks, Recreation, Leisure, and Fitness Studies
Expenses: 2021-2022: $6,733 in state, $20,243 out of state; room/board: $8,290
Financial aid: (336) 334-7973; 83% of undergrads determined to have financial need; average aid package $12,609

North Carolina Central University

Durham NC
(919) 530-6298
U.S. News ranking: Reg. U. (S), No. 48
Website: www.nccu.edu
Admissions email: admissions@nccu.edu
Public; founded 1910
Freshman admissions: less selective; 2020-2021: 7,663

applied, 6,678 accepted. Either SAT or ACT required. SAT 25/75 percentile: 850-1010. High school rank: 8% in top tenth, 21% in top quarter, 61% in top half
Early decision deadline: N/A, notification date: N/A
Early action deadline: N/A, notification date: N/A
Application deadline (fall): rolling
Undergraduate student body: 4,962 full time, 1,105 part time; 30% male, 70% female; 0% American Indian, 1% Asian, 80% black, 6% Hispanic, 6% multiracial, 0% Pacific Islander, 5% white, 0% international
Most popular majors: 15% Business, Management, Marketing, and Related Support Services, 12% Social Sciences, 11% Homeland Security, Law Enforcement, Firefighting and Related Protective Services, 10% Health Professions and Related Programs, 8% Psychology
Expenses: 2021-2022: $6,584 in state, $19,291 out of state; room/board: $9,703
Financial aid: (919) 530-6180; 86% of undergrads determined to have financial need; average aid package $11,550

North Carolina State University

Raleigh NC
(919) 515-2434
U.S. News ranking: Nat. U., No. 79
Website: admissions.ncsu.edu
Admissions email: undergrad-admissions@ncsu.edu
Public; founded 1887
Freshman admissions: more selective; 2020-2021: 31,362 applied, 14,419 accepted. Neither SAT nor ACT required. ACT 25/75 percentile: 27-32. High school rank: 47% in top tenth, 83% in top quarter, 98% in top half
Early decision deadline: N/A, notification date: N/A
Early action deadline: 11/1, notification date: 1/30
Application deadline (fall): 1/15
Undergraduate student body: 22,929 full time, 3,221 part time; 52% male, 48% female; 0% American Indian, 8% Asian, 6% black, 7% Hispanic, 4% multiracial, 0% Pacific Islander, 68% white, 3% international; 88% from in state; 37% live on campus; 11% of students in fraternities, 15% in sororities
Most popular majors: 26% Engineering, 15% Business, Management, Marketing, and Related Support Services, 10% Biological and Biomedical Sciences, 7% Agriculture, Agriculture Operations, and Related Sciences, 4% Social Sciences
Expenses: 2021-2022: $9,131 in state, $29,916 out of state; room/board: $11,957
Financial aid: (919) 515-2421; 45% of undergrads determined to have financial need; average aid package $13,580

North Carolina Wesleyan College

Rocky Mount NC
(800) 488-6292
U.S. News ranking: Reg. Coll. (S), No. 44
Website: www.ncwc.edu
Admissions email: adm@ncwc.edu
Private; founded 1956
Affiliation: United Methodist
Freshman admissions: less selective; 2020-2021: 3,358 applied, 1,598 accepted. Neither SAT nor ACT required. ACT 25/75 percentile: 15-20. High school rank: 1% in top tenth, 9% in top quarter, 48% in top half
Early decision deadline: N/A, notification date: N/A
Early action deadline: N/A, notification date: N/A
Application deadline (fall): rolling
Undergraduate student body: 1,375 full time, 228 part time; 44% male, 56% female; 1% American Indian, 0% Asian, 42% black, 3% Hispanic, 4% multiracial, 0% Pacific Islander, 29% white, 8% international; 81% from in state; 60% live on campus; 1% of students in fraternities, 2% in sororities
Most popular majors: 22% Business Administration and Management, General, 19% Organizational Leadership, 15% Criminal Justice/Law Enforcement Administration, 14% Psychology, General, 6% Accounting
Expenses: 2021-2022: $33,746; room/board: $11,918
Financial aid: (252) 985-5290; 80% of undergrads determined to have financial need; average aid package $25,614

Pfeiffer University[1]

Misenheimer NC
(800) 338-2060
U.S. News ranking: Reg. U. (S), second tier
Website: www.pfeiffer.edu
Admissions email: admissions@pfeiffer.edu
Private; founded 1885
Affiliation: United Methodist
Application deadline (fall): rolling
Undergraduate student body: N/A full time, N/A part time
Expenses: 2020-2021: $31,840; room/board: $11,950
Financial aid: (704) 463-3060

Queens University of Charlotte

Charlotte NC
(800) 849-0202
U.S. News ranking: Reg. U. (S), No. 15
Website: www.queens.edu
Admissions email: admissions@queens.edu
Private; founded 1857
Affiliation: Presbyterian
Freshman admissions: selective; 2020-2021: 3,437 applied, 2,352 accepted. Neither SAT nor ACT required. SAT 25/75 percentile: 1040-1230. High school rank: 17% in top tenth, 39% in top quarter, 77% in top half

Early decision deadline: 11/1, notification date: 12/1
Early action deadline: 12/2, notification date: 12/31
Application deadline (fall): 9/5
Undergraduate student body: 1,535 full time, 135 part time; 33% male, 67% female; 0% American Indian, 3% Asian, 15% black, 14% Hispanic, 0% multiracial, 0% Pacific Islander, 55% white, 7% international; 59% from in state; N/A live on campus; N/A of students in fraternities, N/A in sororities
Most popular majors: 34% Health Professions and Related Programs, 16% Business, Management, Marketing, and Related Support Services, 11% Biological and Biomedical Sciences, 8% Visual and Performing Arts, 6% Communication, Journalism, and Related Programs
Expenses: 2021-2022: $38,726; room/board: $13,262
Financial aid: (704) 337-2339; 67% of undergrads determined to have financial need; average aid package $27,416

Saint Augustine's University

Raleigh NC
(919) 516-4012
U.S. News ranking: Reg. Coll. (S), second tier
Website: www.st-aug.edu
Admissions email: admissions@st-aug.edu
Private; founded 1867
Affiliation: Episcopal Church, Reformed
Freshman admissions: least selective; 2020-2021: 5,887 applied, 3,964 accepted. Either SAT or ACT required. SAT 25/75 percentile: 780-940. High school rank: N/A
Early decision deadline: N/A, notification date: N/A
Early action deadline: N/A, notification date: N/A
Application deadline (fall): rolling
Undergraduate student body: 922 full time, 188 part time; 51% male, 49% female; 0% American Indian, 0% Asian, 81% black, 0% Hispanic, 0% multiracial, 0% Pacific Islander, 0% white, 3% international
Most popular majors: 16% Criminal Justice/Safety Studies, 14% Business Administration and Management, General, 8% Biology/Biological Sciences, General, 8% Kinesiology and Exercise Science, 8% Sociology
Expenses: 2021-2022: $16,893; room/board: $8,942
Financial aid: (919) 516-4309

Salem College

Winston-Salem NC
(336) 721-2621
U.S. News ranking: Nat. Lib. Arts, No. 136
Website: www.salem.edu
Admissions email: admissions@salem.edu
Private; founded 1772
Affiliation: Moravian Church
Freshman admissions: selective; 2020-2021: 864 applied, 737

accepted. Either SAT or ACT required. ACT 25/75 percentile: 17-23. High school rank: 12% in top tenth, 37% in top quarter, 71% in top half
Early decision deadline: N/A, notification date: N/A
Early action deadline: N/A, notification date: N/A
Application deadline (fall): rolling
Undergraduate student body: 378 full time, 114 part time; 2% male, 98% female; 0% American Indian, 2% Asian, 15% black, 18% Hispanic, 7% multiracial, 0% Pacific Islander, 53% white, 0% international; 386% from in state; 85% live on campus; 0% of students in fraternities, 0% in sororities
Most popular majors: 14% Business Administration and Management, General, 10% Biology/Biological Sciences, General, 9% Education, General, 7% Criminal Justice/Safety Studies, 7% Psychology, General
Expenses: 2021-2022: $31,016; room/board: $12,300
Financial aid: (336) 721-2808; 83% of undergrads determined to have financial need; average aid package $25,638

Shaw University[1]

Raleigh NC
(800) 214-6683
U.S. News ranking: Reg. Coll. (S), second tier
Website: www.shawu.edu
Admissions email: admissions@shawu.edu
Private; founded 1865
Affiliation: Baptist
Application deadline (fall): 7/30
Undergraduate student body: N/A full time, N/A part time
Expenses: 2020-2021: $16,480; room/board: $8,514
Financial aid: (919) 546-8565

Southeastern Baptist Theological Seminary[1]

Wake Forest NC
(919) 761-2246
U.S. News ranking: Reg. U. (S), No. 77
Website: www.sebts.edu/
Admissions email: admissions@sebts.edu
Private; founded 1950
Affiliation: Southern Baptist
Application deadline (fall): 8/1
Undergraduate student body: N/A full time, N/A part time
Expenses: 2020-2021: $9,562; room/board: $6,756
Financial aid: N/A

UNC Greensboro

Greensboro NC
(336) 334-5243
U.S. News ranking: Nat. U., No. 239
Website: www.uncg.edu/
Admissions email: admissions@uncg.edu
Public; founded 1891
Freshman admissions: selective; 2020-2021: 9,872 applied, 8,641 accepted. Either SAT or ACT required. SAT 25/75

percentile: 980-1160. High school rank: 15% in top tenth, 42% in top quarter, 76% in top half
Early decision deadline: N/A, notification date: N/A
Early action deadline: 12/1, notification date: N/A
Application deadline (fall): rolling
Undergraduate student body: 13,391 full time, 2,604 part time; 33% male, 67% female; 0% American Indian, 5% Asian, 30% black, 13% Hispanic, 5% multiracial, 0% Pacific Islander, 43% white, 1% international; 97% from in state; 25% live on campus; 2% of students in fraternities, 1% in sororities
Most popular majors: 20% Business, Management, Marketing, and Related Support Services, 8% Health Professions and Related Programs, 8% Visual and Performing Arts, 7% Social Sciences, 6% Parks, Recreation, Leisure, and Fitness Studies
Expenses: 2021-2022: $7,404 in state, $22,564 out of state; room/board: $9,482
Financial aid: (336) 334-5702; 73% of undergrads determined to have financial need; average aid package $12,355

University of Mount Olive
Mount Olive NC
(919) 658-2502
U.S. News ranking: Reg. U. (S), No. 62
Website: www.umo.edu/
Admissions email: admissions@umo.edu
Private; founded 1951
Affiliation: Original Free Will Baptist
Freshman admissions: selective; 2020-2021: 2,237 applied, 1,385 accepted. Neither SAT nor ACT required. ACT 25/75 percentile: 16-22. High school rank: 7% in top tenth, 25% in top quarter, 64% in top half
Early decision deadline: N/A, notification date: N/A
Early action deadline: N/A, notification date: N/A
Application deadline (fall): rolling
Undergraduate student body: 1,348 full time, 1,001 part time; 34% male, 66% female; 0% American Indian, 1% Asian, 26% black, 9% Hispanic, 4% multiracial, 0% Pacific Islander, 55% white, 3% international
Most popular majors: Information not available
Expenses: 2020-2021: $22,194; room/board: $8,998
Financial aid: (919) 658-2502

University of North Carolina Asheville
Asheville NC
(828) 251-6481
U.S. News ranking: Nat. Lib. Arts, No. 146
Website: www.unca.edu
Admissions email: admissions@unca.edu
Public; founded 1927
Freshman admissions: selective; 2020-2021: 3,115 applied, 2,474 accepted. Neither SAT

nor ACT required. SAT 25/75 percentile: 1060-1270. High school rank: 15% in top tenth, 39% in top quarter, 78% in top half
Early decision deadline: 11/1, notification date: 12/15
Early action deadline: N/A, notification date: N/A
Application deadline (fall): 8/1
Undergraduate student body: 2,870 full time, 488 part time; 43% male, 57% female; 0% American Indian, 2% Asian, 5% black, 9% Hispanic, 5% multiracial, 0% Pacific Islander, 72% white, 1% international; 89% from in state; 41% live on campus; 1% of students in fraternities, 2% in sororities
Most popular majors: 12% Psychology, General, 8% Business Administration and Management, General, 7% Environmental Studies, 6% Biology/Biological Sciences, General, 6% Digital Arts
Expenses: 2021-2022: $7,244 in state, $24,592 out of state; room/board: $9,950
Financial aid: (828) 251-6535; 58% of undergrads determined to have financial need; average aid package $13,936

University of North Carolina–Chapel Hill
Chapel Hill NC
(919) 966-2211
U.S. News ranking: Nat. U., No. 28
Website: www.unc.edu
Admissions email: unchelp@admissions.unc.edu
Public; founded 1789
Freshman admissions: most selective; 2020-2021: 44,382 applied, 10,446 accepted. Either SAT or ACT required. ACT 25/75 percentile: 27-33. High school rank: 74% in top tenth, 95% in top quarter, 99% in top half
Early decision deadline: N/A, notification date: N/A
Early action deadline: 10/15, notification date: 1/31
Application deadline (fall): 1/15
Undergraduate student body: 18,509 full time, 890 part time; 40% male, 60% female; 0% American Indian, 12% Asian, 8% black, 9% Hispanic, 5% multiracial, 0% Pacific Islander, 57% white, 4% international; 87% from in state; 23% live on campus; 15% of students in fraternities, 17% in sororities
Most popular majors: 15% Social Sciences, 10% Biological and Biomedical Sciences, 10% Communication, Journalism, and Related Programs, 8% Psychology, 7% Computer and Information Sciences and Support Services
Expenses: 2021-2022: $8,992 in state, $36,776 out of state; room/board: $11,882
Financial aid: (919) 962-8396; 42% of undergrads determined to have financial need; average aid package $17,091

University of North Carolina–Charlotte
Charlotte NC
(704) 687-5507
U.S. News ranking: Nat. U., No. 227
Website: www.uncc.edu/
Admissions email: admissions@uncc.edu
Public; founded 1946
Freshman admissions: more selective; 2020-2021: 19,946 applied, 15,863 accepted. Neither SAT nor ACT required. SAT 25/75 percentile: 1100-1280. High school rank: 17% in top tenth, 46% in top quarter, 80% in top half
Early decision deadline: N/A, notification date: N/A
Early action deadline: 11/1, notification date: 1/30
Application deadline (fall): 6/1
Undergraduate student body: 21,104 full time, 3,071 part time; 53% male, 47% female; 0% American Indian, 9% Asian, 16% black, 12% Hispanic, 5% multiracial, 0% Pacific Islander, 55% white, 2% international; 95% from in state; 15% live on campus; 7% of students in fraternities, 9% in sororities
Most popular majors: 18% Business, Management, Marketing, and Related Support Services, 11% Health Professions and Related Programs, 10% Computer and Information Sciences and Support Services, 8% Engineering, 7% Social Sciences
Expenses: 2021-2022: $6,994 in state, $20,542 out of state; room/board: $12,896
Financial aid: (704) 687-5504; 60% of undergrads determined to have financial need; average aid package $9,639

University of North Carolina–Pembroke
Pembroke NC
(910) 521-6262
U.S. News ranking: Reg. U. (S), No. 65
Website: www.uncp.edu
Admissions email: admissions@uncp.edu
Public; founded 1887
Freshman admissions: less selective; 2020-2021: 5,021 applied, 4,588 accepted. Neither SAT nor ACT required. ACT 25/75 percentile: 17-21. High school rank: 12% in top tenth, 34% in top quarter, 72% in top half
Early decision deadline: N/A, notification date: N/A
Early action deadline: N/A, notification date: N/A
Application deadline (fall): 5/1
Undergraduate student body: 4,945 full time, 1,491 part time; 37% male, 63% female; 14% American Indian, 1% Asian, 30% black, 8% Hispanic, 6% multiracial, 0% Pacific Islander, 37% white, 1% international; 94% from in state; 29% live on campus; 1% of students in fraternities, 2% in sororities
Most popular majors: 12% Homeland Security, Law

Enforcement, Firefighting and Related Protective Services, 12% Social Sciences, 11% Business, Management, Marketing, and Related Support Services, 10% Biological and Biomedical Sciences, 9% Parks, Recreation, Leisure, and Fitness Studies
Expenses: 2021-2022: $1,000 in state, $5,000 out of state; room/board: N/A
Financial aid: (910) 521-6255; 76% of undergrads determined to have financial need; average aid package $9,093

University of North Carolina School of the Arts[1]
Winston-Salem NC
(336) 770-3291
U.S. News ranking: Arts, unranked
Website: www.uncsa.edu
Admissions email: admissions@uncsa.edu
Public; founded 1963
Application deadline (fall): 3/15
Undergraduate student body: N/A full time, N/A part time
Expenses: 2020-2021: $9,358 in state, $26,095 out of state; room/board: $9,456
Financial aid: (336) 770-3297

University of North Carolina–Wilmington
Wilmington NC
(910) 962-3243
U.S. News ranking: Nat. U., No. 187
Website: uncw.edu/admissions/
Admissions email: admissions@uncw.edu
Public; founded 1947
Freshman admissions: more selective; 2020-2021: 13,633 applied, 9,266 accepted. Either SAT or ACT required. ACT 25/75 percentile: 23-27. High school rank: 22% in top tenth, 46% in top quarter, 91% in top half
Early decision deadline: N/A, notification date: N/A
Early action deadline: 11/1, notification date: 1/20
Application deadline (fall): 2/1
Undergraduate student body: 11,989 full time, 2,661 part time; 36% male, 64% female; 0% American Indian, 2% Asian, 4% black, 8% Hispanic, 4% multiracial, 0% Pacific Islander, 78% white, 1% international; 89% from in state; 26% live on campus; 11% of students in fraternities, 9% in sororities
Most popular majors: 19% Business Administration and Management, General, 18% Registered Nursing/Registered Nurse, 6% Psychology, General, 6% Speech Communication and Rhetoric, 5% Biology/Biological Sciences, General
Expenses: 2021-2022: $7,238 in state, $21,303 out of state; room/board: $11,346
Financial aid: (910) 962-3177; 55% of undergrads determined to have financial need; average aid package $9,602

Wake Forest University
Winston-Salem NC
(336) 758-5201
U.S. News ranking: Nat. U., No. 28
Website: www.wfu.edu
Admissions email: admissions@wfu.edu
Private; founded 1834
Freshman admissions: most selective; 2020-2021: 11,959 applied, 3,825 accepted. Neither SAT nor ACT required. SAT 25/75 percentile: 1290-1470. High school rank: 73% in top tenth, 92% in top quarter, 98% in top half
Early decision deadline: 11/15, notification date: N/A
Early action deadline: N/A, notification date: N/A
Application deadline (fall): 1/1
Undergraduate student body: 5,367 full time, 74 part time; 46% male, 54% female; 0% American Indian, 4% Asian, 6% black, 8% Hispanic, 4% multiracial, 0% Pacific Islander, 69% white, 9% international; N/A from in state; 68% live on campus; 28% of students in fraternities, 57% in sororities
Most popular majors: 25% Social Sciences, 20% Business, Management, Marketing, and Related Support Services, 8% Biological and Biomedical Sciences, 8% Communication, Journalism, and Related Programs, 7% Psychology
Expenses: 2021-2022: $59,770; room/board: $18,014
Financial aid: (336) 758-5154; 27% of undergrads determined to have financial need; average aid package $55,536

Warren Wilson College
Asheville NC
(800) 934-3536
U.S. News ranking: Nat. Lib. Arts, second tier
Website: www.warren-wilson.edu/
Admissions email: admit@warren-wilson.edu
Private; founded 1894
Freshman admissions: selective; 2020-2021: 1,332 applied, 1,130 accepted. Neither SAT nor ACT required. ACT 25/75 percentile: 21-29. High school rank: 10% in top tenth, 25% in top quarter, 66% in top half
Early decision deadline: 11/1, notification date: 12/1
Early action deadline: 11/15, notification date: 12/1
Application deadline (fall): 7/3
Undergraduate student body: 618 full time, 6 part time; 32% male, 68% female; 1% American Indian, 1% Asian, 6% black, 6% Hispanic, 4% multiracial, 0% Pacific Islander, 77% white, 3% international; N/A from in state; N/A live on campus; 0% of students in fraternities, 0% in sororities
Most popular majors: 19% Psychology, General, 18% Environmental Studies, 9% Sociology, 8% Biology/Biological Sciences, General, 8% History, General

Expenses: 2021-2022: $38,400; room/board: $11,750
Financial aid: (828) 771-2082; 80% of undergrads determined to have financial need; average aid package $32,294

Western Carolina University
Cullowhee NC
(828) 227-7317
U.S. News ranking: Reg. U. (S), No. 21
Website: www.wcu.edu
Admissions email: admiss@email.wcu.edu
Public; founded 1889
Freshman admissions: selective; 2020-2021: 15,034 applied, 7,282 accepted. Either SAT or ACT required. ACT 25/75 percentile: 20-25. High school rank: 16% in top tenth, 41% in top quarter, 78% in top half
Early decision deadline: N/A, notification date: N/A
Early action deadline: 11/15, notification date: 12/15
Application deadline (fall): 3/1
Undergraduate student body: 8,760 full time, 1,757 part time; 45% male, 55% female; 1% American Indian, 1% Asian, 5% black, 8% Hispanic, 3% multiracial, 0% Pacific Islander, 78% white, 2% international; 88% from in state; N/A live on campus; N/A of students in fraternities, N/A in sororities
Most popular majors: 22% Business, Management, Marketing, and Related Support Services, 15% Health Professions and Related Programs, 8% Education, 7% Psychology, 6% Homeland Security, Law Enforcement, Firefighting and Related Protective Services
Expenses: 2021-2022: $1,000 in state, $5,000 out of state; room/board: N/A
Financial aid: (828) 227-7290

William Peace University
Raleigh NC
(919) 508-2214
U.S. News ranking: Reg. Coll. (S), No. 30
Website: www.peace.edu
Admissions email: admissions@peace.edu
Private; founded 1857
Affiliation: Presbyterian Church (USA)
Freshman admissions: selective; 2020-2021: 1,277 applied, 784 accepted. Neither SAT nor ACT required. ACT 25/75 percentile: 18-23. High school rank: N/A
Early decision deadline: N/A, notification date: N/A
Early action deadline: N/A, notification date: N/A
Application deadline (fall): rolling
Undergraduate student body: 733 full time, 97 part time; 46% male, 54% female; 1% American Indian, 2% Asian, 23% black, 13% Hispanic, 6% multiracial, 0% Pacific Islander, 53% white, 1% international; 87% from in state; 70% live on campus; N/A of students in fraternities, N/A in sororities

Most popular majors: 28% Business, Management, Marketing, and Related Support Services, 12% Psychology, 11% Social Sciences, 10% Communication, Journalism, and Related Programs, 10% Visual and Performing Arts
Expenses: 2021-2022: $32,450; room/board: $12,040
Financial aid: (919) 508-2284; 60% of undergrads determined to have financial need; average aid package $27,320

Wingate University
Wingate NC
(800) 755-5550
U.S. News ranking: Nat. U., second tier
Website: www.wingate.edu/
Admissions email: admit@wingate.edu
Private; founded 1896
Freshman admissions: selective; 2020-2021: 13,949 applied, 12,314 accepted. Either SAT or ACT required. SAT 25/75 percentile: 930-1140. High school rank: 11% in top tenth, 33% in top quarter, 71% in top half
Early decision deadline: N/A, notification date: N/A
Early action deadline: N/A, notification date: N/A
Application deadline (fall): rolling
Undergraduate student body: 2,602 full time, 81 part time; 40% male, 60% female; 0% American Indian, 2% Asian, 23% black, 7% Hispanic, 8% multiracial, 0% Pacific Islander, 51% white, 4% international; 69% from in state; 70% live on campus; 4% of students in fraternities, 12% in sororities
Most popular majors: 19% Business, Management, Marketing, and Related Support Services, 16% Biological and Biomedical Sciences, 15% Parks, Recreation, Leisure, and Fitness Studies, 9% Psychology, 7% Communication, Journalism, and Related Programs
Expenses: 2021-2022: $40,170; room/board: $10,270
Financial aid: (704) 233-8010; 80% of undergrads determined to have financial need; average aid package $32,293

Winston-Salem State University[1]
Winston-Salem NC
(336) 750-2070
U.S. News ranking: Reg. U. (S), No. 48
Website: www.wssu.edu
Admissions email: admissions@wssu.edu
Public; founded 1892
Application deadline (fall): 3/15
Undergraduate student body: N/A full time, N/A part time
Expenses: 2020-2021: $5,941 in state, $16,188 out of state; room/board: $10,888
Financial aid: N/A

NORTH DAKOTA

Bismarck State College[1]
Bismarck ND
(701) 224-2459
U.S. News ranking: Reg. Coll. (Mid. W), unranked
Website: bismarckstate.edu/
Admissions email: bsc.admissions@bismarckstate.edu
Public; founded 1939
Application deadline (fall): rolling
Undergraduate student body: N/A full time, N/A part time
Expenses: 2020-2021: $5,694 in state, $8,102 out of state; room/board: $7,103
Financial aid: (701) 224-5441

Dickinson State University
Dickinson ND
(701) 483-2175
U.S. News ranking: Reg. Coll. (Mid. W), No. 48
Website: www.dickinsonstate.edu/
Admissions email: dsu.hawks@dsu.nodak.edu
Public; founded 1918
Freshman admissions: selective; 2020-2021: 506 applied, 499 accepted. Neither SAT nor ACT required. ACT 25/75 percentile: 17-22. High school rank: N/A
Early decision deadline: N/A, notification date: N/A
Early action deadline: N/A, notification date: N/A
Application deadline (fall): rolling
Undergraduate student body: 966 full time, 415 part time; 40% male, 60% female; 1% American Indian, 1% Asian, 6% black, 7% Hispanic, 3% multiracial, 0% Pacific Islander, 79% white, 1% international; 63% from in state; 24% live on campus; N/A of students in fraternities, N/A in sororities
Most popular majors: 19% Business Administration and Management, General, 11% Accounting, 8% Human Resources Management/Personnel Administration, General, 8% Registered Nursing/Registered Nurse, 7% Elementary Education and Teaching
Expenses: 2021-2022: $9,118 in state, $11,218 out of state; room/board: $7,500
Financial aid: (701) 483-2371; 53% of undergrads determined to have financial need; average aid package $11,846

Mayville State University[1]
Mayville ND
(701) 788-4667
U.S. News ranking: Reg. Coll. (Mid. W), second tier
Website: www.mayvillestate.edu
Admissions email: masuadmissions@mayvillestate.edu
Public; founded 1889
Application deadline (fall): rolling
Undergraduate student body: N/A full time, N/A part time
Expenses: 2020-2021: $8,888 in state, $10,394 out of state; room/board: $6,945
Financial aid: (701) 788-4767

Minot State University
Minot ND
(701) 858-3350
U.S. News ranking: Reg. U. (Mid. W), No. 104
Website: www.minotstateu.edu
Admissions email: askmsu@minotstateu.edu
Public; founded 1913
Freshman admissions: selective; 2020-2021: 752 applied, 580 accepted. Either SAT or ACT required. ACT 25/75 percentile: 18-24. High school rank: 11% in top tenth, 34% in top quarter, 64% in top half
Early decision deadline: N/A, notification date: N/A
Early action deadline: N/A, notification date: N/A
Application deadline (fall): rolling
Undergraduate student body: 1,836 full time, 820 part time; 38% male, 62% female; 2% American Indian, 1% Asian, 3% black, 8% Hispanic, 6% multiracial, 0% Pacific Islander, 67% white, 11% international
Most popular majors: 25% Business, Management, Marketing, and Related Support Services, 16% Health Professions and Related Programs, 11% Public Administration and Social Service Professions, 7% Homeland Security, Law Enforcement, Firefighting and Related Protective Services, 5% Liberal Arts and Sciences, General Studies and Humanities
Expenses: 2021-2022: $8,164 in state, $8,164 out of state; room/board: $6,892
Financial aid: (701) 858-3375; 47% of undergrads determined to have financial need; average aid package $10,672

North Dakota State University
Fargo ND
(701) 231-8643
U.S. News ranking: Nat. U., No. 277
Website: www.ndsu.edu
Admissions email: NDSU.Admission@ndsu.edu
Public; founded 1890
Freshman admissions: selective; 2020-2021: 7,880 applied, 7,415 accepted. Neither SAT nor ACT required. ACT 25/75 percentile: 20-26. High school rank: 16% in top tenth, 42% in top quarter, 76% in top half
Early decision deadline: N/A, notification date: N/A
Early action deadline: N/A, notification date: N/A
Application deadline (fall): 8/1
Undergraduate student body: 9,339 full time, 1,216 part time; 51% male, 49% female; 1% American Indian, 2% Asian, 3% black, 3% Hispanic, 4% multiracial, 0% Pacific Islander, 87% white, 1% international; 42% from in state; 36% live on campus; 9% of students in fraternities, 8% in sororities
Most popular majors: 16% Health Professions and Related Programs, 15% Business, Management, Marketing, and Related Support

Services, 14% Engineering, 10% Agriculture, Agriculture Operations, and Related Sciences, 6% Biological and Biomedical Sciences
Expenses: 2020-2021: $10,168 in state, $14,471 out of state; room/board: $8,878
Financial aid: (701) 231-6221

University of Jamestown
Jamestown ND
(701) 252-3467
U.S. News ranking: Reg. Coll. (Mid. W), No. 35
Website: www.uj.edu
Admissions email: admissions@uj.edu
Private; founded 1883
Affiliation: Presbyterian Church (USA)
Freshman admissions: selective; 2020-2021: 1,356 applied, 975 accepted. Neither SAT nor ACT required. ACT 25/75 percentile: 19-24. High school rank: 11% in top tenth, 35% in top quarter, 60% in top half
Early decision deadline: N/A, notification date: N/A
Early action deadline: N/A, notification date: N/A
Application deadline (fall): 9/2
Undergraduate student body: 874 full time, 38 part time; 57% male, 43% female; 1% American Indian, 1% Asian, 5% black, 10% Hispanic, 3% multiracial, 0% Pacific Islander, 73% white, 6% international; 40% from in state; 67% live on campus; 0% of students in fraternities, 0% in sororities
Most popular majors: 21% Business, Management, Marketing, and Related Support Services, 16% Parks, Recreation, Leisure, and Fitness Studies, 14% Health Professions and Related Programs, 11% Education, 8% Biological and Biomedical Sciences
Expenses: 2021-2022: $23,498; room/board: $8,316
Financial aid: (701) 252-3467; 69% of undergrads determined to have financial need; average aid package $18,050

University of Mary
Bismarck ND
(701) 355-8030
U.S. News ranking: Nat. U., second tier
Website: www.umary.edu
Admissions email: marauder@umary.edu
Private; founded 1959
Affiliation: Roman Catholic
Freshman admissions: selective; 2020-2021: 1,412 applied, 1,369 accepted. Either SAT or ACT required. ACT 25/75 percentile: 20-26. High school rank: N/A
Early decision deadline: N/A, notification date: N/A
Early action deadline: N/A, notification date: N/A
Application deadline (fall): rolling

Undergraduate student body: 1,812 full time, 725 part time; 41% male, 59% female; 2% American Indian, 1% Asian, 2% black, 5% Hispanic, 2% multiracial, 0% Pacific Islander, 79% white, 0% international; 46% from in state; N/A live on campus; N/A of students in fraternities, N/A in sororities
Most popular majors: 18% Registered Nursing/Registered Nurse, 10% Business Administration and Management, General, 7% Psychology, General, 4% Elementary Education and Teaching, 4% General Studies
Expenses: 2021-2022: $20,628; room/board: $7,990
Financial aid: (701) 355-8226; 64% of undergrads determined to have financial need; average aid package $15,358

University of North Dakota
Grand Forks ND
(800) 225-5863
U.S. News ranking: Nat. U., No. 249
Website: und.edu
Admissions email: admissions@und.edu
Public; founded 1883
Freshman admissions: selective; 2020-2021: 5,662 applied, 4,912 accepted. Neither SAT nor ACT required. ACT 25/75 percentile: 21-26. High school rank: 23% in top tenth, 48% in top quarter, 78% in top half
Early decision deadline: N/A, notification date: N/A
Early action deadline: N/A, notification date: N/A
Application deadline (fall): 8/16
Undergraduate student body: 7,173 full time, 2,623 part time; 57% male, 43% female; 1% American Indian, 2% Asian, 2% black, 5% Hispanic, 5% multiracial, 0% Pacific Islander, 79% white, 4% international; 39% from in state; 22% live on campus; 12% of students in fraternities, 12% in sororities
Most popular majors: 6% Aeronautics/Aviation/Aerospace Science and Technology, General, 6% Psychology, General, 6% Registered Nursing/Registered Nurse, 5% General Studies, 5% Mechanical Engineering
Expenses: 2021-2022: $10,626 in state, $15,067 out of state; room/board: $10,276
Financial aid: (701) 777-3121; 48% of undergrads determined to have financial need; average aid package $15,347

Valley City State University
Valley City ND
(800) 532-8641
U.S. News ranking: Reg. Coll. (Mid. W), No. 44
Website: www.vcsu.edu
Admissions email: enrollment.services@vcsu.edu
Public; founded 1890
Freshman admissions: selective; 2020-2021: 458 applied, 370 accepted. Neither SAT nor ACT

required. ACT 25/75 percentile: 17-22. High school rank: N/A
Early decision deadline: N/A, notification date: N/A
Early action deadline: N/A, notification date: N/A
Application deadline (fall): rolling
Undergraduate student body: 894 full time, 647 part time; 41% male, 59% female; 1% American Indian, 1% Asian, 4% black, 6% Hispanic, 4% multiracial, 0% Pacific Islander, 82% white, 2% international; 68% from in state; 31% live on campus; 1% of students in fraternities, 1% in sororities
Most popular majors: 43% Elementary Education and Teaching, 9% Management Information Systems, General, 6% Wildlife, Fish and Wildlands Science and Management, 5% Music, General, 3% Health and Physical Education/Fitness, General
Expenses: 2021-2022: $8,187 in state, $12,961 out of state; room/board: $6,919
Financial aid: (701) 845-7541; 52% of undergrads determined to have financial need; average aid package $11,890

NORTHERN MARIANA ISLANDS

Northern Marianas College[1]
Saipan MP
(670) 237-6700
U.S. News ranking: Reg. Coll. (W), second tier
Website: www.hiwassee.edu
Admissions email: N/A
Public
Application deadline (fall): N/A
Undergraduate student body: N/A full time, N/A part time
Expenses: 2020-2021: $4,038 in state, $5,520 out of state; room/board: N/A
Financial aid: N/A

OHIO

Antioch College[7]
Yellow Springs OH
(937) 319-6082
U.S. News ranking: Nat. Lib. Arts, unranked
Website: antiochcollege.edu
Admissions email: admissions@antiochcollege.edu
Private; founded 1853
Freshman admissions: less selective; 2020-2021: 188 applied, 159 accepted. ACT 25/75 percentile: 17-25. High school rank: N/A
Early decision deadline: 11/15, notification date: N/A
Early action deadline: N/A, notification date: N/A
Application deadline (fall): rolling
Undergraduate student body: 114 full time, 2 part time
Most popular majors: 38% Liberal Arts and Sciences, General Studies and Humanities, Other

Expenses: 2020-2021: $35,568; room/board: $7,640
Financial aid: N/A

Art Academy of Cincinnati
Cincinnati OH
(513) 562-6262
U.S. News ranking: Arts, unranked
Website: www.artacademy.edu
Admissions email: admissions@artacademy.edu
Private; founded 1869
Freshman admissions: least selective; 2020-2021: 1,308 applied, 403 accepted. Neither SAT nor ACT required. SAT 25/75 percentile: N/A. High school rank: N/A
Early decision deadline: N/A, notification date: N/A
Early action deadline: 1/1, notification date: 2/15
Application deadline (fall): 8/1
Undergraduate student body: 202 full time, 9 part time; 30% male, 70% female; 0% American Indian, 2% Asian, 18% black, 6% Hispanic, 7% multiracial, 0% Pacific Islander, 65% white, 0% international; 72% from in state; 41% live on campus; 0% of students in fraternities, 0% in sororities
Most popular majors: 36% Illustration, 14% Painting, 12% Photography, 12% Sculpture, 7% Design and Visual Communications, General
Expenses: 2021-2022: $35,290; room/board: $8,000
Financial aid: (513) 562-8757; 78% of undergrads determined to have financial need; average aid package $1,700

Ashland University
Ashland OH
(419) 289-5052
U.S. News ranking: Reg. U. (Mid. W), No. 54
Website: www.ashland.edu/admissions
Admissions email: enrollme@ashland.edu
Private; founded 1878
Freshman admissions: selective; 2020-2021: 3,608 applied, 2,665 accepted. Either SAT or ACT required. ACT 25/75 percentile: 19-24. High school rank: 14% in top tenth, 38% in top quarter, 73% in top half
Early decision deadline: N/A, notification date: N/A
Early action deadline: N/A, notification date: N/A
Application deadline (fall): rolling
Undergraduate student body: 3,202 full time, 3,464 part time; 60% male, 40% female; 1% American Indian, 1% Asian, 20% black, 6% Hispanic, 1% multiracial, 0% Pacific Islander, 65% white, 1% international; 92% from in state; 19% live on campus; 13% of students in fraternities, 28% in sororities
Most popular majors: 26% Health Professions and Related Programs, 18% Business, Management, Marketing, and Related Support Services, 16% Communication, Journalism, and Related Programs,

9% Education, 6% Biological and Biomedical Sciences
Expenses: 2021-2022: $23,000; room/board: $10,940
Financial aid: (419) 289-5002; 78% of undergrads determined to have financial need; average aid package $15,933

Baldwin Wallace University
Berea OH
(440) 826-2222
U.S. News ranking: Reg. U. (Mid. W), No. 9
Website: www.bw.edu
Admissions email: admission@bw.edu
Private; founded 1845
Freshman admissions: selective; 2020-2021: 3,864 applied, 2,698 accepted. Neither SAT nor ACT required. ACT 25/75 percentile: 21-27. High school rank: 18% in top tenth, 46% in top quarter, 82% in top half
Early decision deadline: N/A, notification date: N/A
Early action deadline: N/A, notification date: N/A
Application deadline (fall): rolling
Undergraduate student body: 2,712 full time, 148 part time; 45% male, 55% female; 0% American Indian, 2% Asian, 8% black, 6% Hispanic, 6% multiracial, 0% Pacific Islander, 77% white, 0% international; 75% from in state; 52% live on campus; 12% of students in fraternities, 16% in sororities
Most popular majors: 21% Business, Management, Marketing, and Related Support Services, 13% Visual and Performing Arts, 12% Health Professions and Related Programs, 7% Biological and Biomedical Sciences, 7% Education
Expenses: 2021-2022: $35,366; room/board: $12,424
Financial aid: (440) 826-2108; 72% of undergrads determined to have financial need; average aid package $30,572

Bluffton University
Bluffton OH
(800) 488-3257
U.S. News ranking: Reg. Coll. (Mid. W), No. 31
Website: www.bluffton.edu
Admissions email: admissions@bluffton.edu
Private; founded 1899
Affiliation: Mennonite Church
Freshman admissions: selective; 2020-2021: 1,504 applied, 910 accepted. Neither SAT nor ACT required. ACT 25/75 percentile: 16-23. High school rank: 9% in top tenth, 26% in top quarter, 57% in top half
Early decision deadline: N/A, notification date: N/A
Early action deadline: N/A, notification date: N/A
Application deadline (fall): rolling
Undergraduate student body: 647 full time, 44 part time; 54% male, 46% female; 0% American Indian, 0% Asian, 12% black, 3% Hispanic, 4% multiracial, 0% Pacific Islander, 72% white,

3% international; 86% from in state; 84% live on campus; 0% of students in fraternities, 0% in sororities
Most popular majors: 33% Business, Management, Marketing, and Related Support Services, 13% Parks, Recreation, Leisure, and Fitness Studies, 10% Education
Expenses: 2021-2022: $34,502; room/board: $11,346
Financial aid: (419) 358-3266; 86% of undergrads determined to have financial need; average aid package $31,161

Bowling Green State University
Bowling Green OH
(419) 372-2478
U.S. News ranking: Nat. U., No. 249
Website: www.bgsu.edu/
Admissions email: choosebgsu@bgsu.edu
Public; founded 1910
Freshman admissions: selective; 2020-2021: 17,341 applied, 13,057 accepted. Either SAT or ACT required. ACT 25/75 percentile: 20-26. High school rank: 19% in top tenth, 43% in top quarter, 76% in top half
Early decision deadline: N/A, notification date: N/A
Early action deadline: N/A, notification date: N/A
Application deadline (fall): 7/15
Undergraduate student body: 12,483 full time, 2,505 part time; 44% male, 56% female; 0% American Indian, 1% Asian, 8% black, 4% Hispanic, 3% multiracial, 0% Pacific Islander, 80% white, 1% international; 88% from in state; 27% live on campus; 11% of students in fraternities, 6% in sororities
Most popular majors: 6% Education/Teaching of Individuals in Early Childhood Special Education Programs, 5% Education, Other, 4% Biology/Biological Sciences, General, 4% Criminal Justice/Safety Studies, 4% Psychology, General
Expenses: 2020-2021: $11,011 in state, $19,000 out of state; room/board: $9,662
Financial aid: (419) 372-2651; 61% of undergrads determined to have financial need; average aid package $14,086

Capital University
Columbus OH
(866) 544-6175
U.S. News ranking: Reg. U. (Mid. W), No. 37
Website: www.capital.edu
Admissions email: admission@capital.edu
Private; founded 1830
Affiliation: Evangelical Lutheran Church
Freshman admissions: selective; 2020-2021: 4,017 applied, 2,975 accepted. Neither SAT nor ACT required. ACT 25/75 percentile: 21-26. High school rank: 21% in top tenth, 50% in top quarter, 81% in top half

Early decision deadline: N/A, notification date: N/A
Early action deadline: N/A, notification date: N/A
Application deadline (fall): rolling
Undergraduate student body: 2,152 full time, 130 part time; 39% male, 61% female; 0% American Indian, 3% Asian, 9% black, 4% Hispanic, 6% multiracial, 0% Pacific Islander, 75% white, 1% international; 94% from in state; 44% live on campus; 1% of students in fraternities, 2% in sororities
Most popular majors: 18% Health Professions and Related Programs, 15% Business, Management, Marketing, and Related Support Services, 11% Education, 9% Visual and Performing Arts, 8% Biological and Biomedical Sciences
Expenses: 2021-2022: $39,338; room/board: $12,018
Financial aid: (614) 236-6771; 80% of undergrads determined to have financial need; average aid package $32,667

Case Western Reserve University
Cleveland OH
(216) 368-4450
U.S. News ranking: Nat. U., No. 42
Website: www.case.edu
Admissions email: admission@case.edu
Private; founded 1826
Freshman admissions: most selective; 2020-2021: 29,084 applied, 8,804 accepted. Neither SAT nor ACT required. SAT 25/75 percentile: 1340-1520. High school rank: 70% in top tenth, 95% in top quarter, 100% in top half
Early decision deadline: 11/1, notification date: 12/5
Early action deadline: 11/1, notification date: 12/19
Application deadline (fall): 1/15
Undergraduate student body: 5,289 full time, 144 part time; 54% male, 46% female; 0% American Indian, 23% Asian, 4% black, 10% Hispanic, 5% multiracial, 0% Pacific Islander, 42% white, 14% international; 26% from in state; 33% live on campus; 18% of students in fraternities, 24% in sororities
Most popular majors: 30% Engineering, 11% Biological and Biomedical Sciences, 10% Business, Management, Marketing, and Related Support Services, 10% Computer and Information Sciences and Support Services, 8% Social Sciences
Expenses: 2021-2022: $54,020; room/board: N/A
Financial aid: (216) 368-4530; 47% of undergrads determined to have financial need; average aid package $48,434

Cedarville University
Cedarville OH
(800) 233-2784
U.S. News ranking: Reg. U. (Mid. W), No. 17
Website: www.cedarville.edu

Admissions email: admissions@cedarville.edu
Private; founded 1887
Affiliation: Baptist
Freshman admissions: more selective; 2020-2021: 5,008 applied, 2,971 accepted. Neither SAT nor ACT required. ACT 25/75 percentile: 23-30. High school rank: 34% in top tenth, 62% in top quarter, 86% in top half
Early decision deadline: N/A, notification date: N/A
Early action deadline: N/A, notification date: N/A
Application deadline (fall): 8/1
Undergraduate student body: 3,540 full time, 484 part time; 45% male, 55% female; 0% American Indian, 3% Asian, 2% black, 1% Hispanic, 3% multiracial, 0% Pacific Islander, 88% white, 2% international; 43% from in state; 71% live on campus; 0% of students in fraternities, 0% in sororities
Most popular majors: 20% Health Professions and Related Programs, 16% Business, Management, Marketing, and Related Support Services, 10% Education, 10% Engineering, 7% Visual and Performing Arts
Expenses: 2021-2022: $33,374; room/board: $8,120
Financial aid: (937) 766-7866; 68% of undergrads determined to have financial need; average aid package $24,804

Central State University
Wilberforce OH
(937) 376-6348
U.S. News ranking: Reg. Coll. (Mid. W), second tier
Website: www.centralstate.edu
Admissions email: admissions@centralstate.edu
Public; founded 1887
Freshman admissions: least selective; 2020-2021: 10,191 applied, 5,915 accepted. Neither SAT nor ACT required. ACT 25/75 percentile: 14-17. High school rank: N/A
Early decision deadline: N/A, notification date: N/A
Early action deadline: N/A, notification date: N/A
Application deadline (fall): rolling
Undergraduate student body: 2,142 full time, 1,879 part time; 31% male, 69% female; 1% American Indian, 2% Asian, 52% black, 13% Hispanic, 1% multiracial, 0% Pacific Islander, 27% white, 3% international; 27% from in state; 26% live on campus; 1% of students in fraternities, 1% in sororities
Most popular majors: 23% Business/Commerce, General, 13% Psychology, General, 9% Biology/Biological Sciences, General, 9% Criminal Justice/Safety Studies, 8% Broadcast Journalism
Expenses: 2021-2022: $8,450 in state, $10,450 out of state; room/board: $9,718
Financial aid: (937) 376-6111; 95% of undergrads determined to have financial need; average aid package $9,500

Cleveland Institute of Art[1]
Cleveland OH
(216) 421-7418
U.S. News ranking: Arts, unranked
Website: www.cia.edu
Admissions email: admissions@cia.edu
Private; founded 1882
Application deadline (fall): rolling
Undergraduate student body: N/A full time, N/A part time
Expenses: 2020-2021: $44,385; room/board: $11,590
Financial aid: (216) 421-7425

Cleveland Institute of Music[1]
Cleveland OH
(216) 795-3107
U.S. News ranking: Arts, unranked
Website: www.cim.edu/
Admissions email: admission@cim.edu
Private; founded 1920
Application deadline (fall): 12/1
Undergraduate student body: N/A full time, N/A part time
Expenses: 2020-2021: $44,774; room/board: $12,500
Financial aid: (216) 795-3192

Cleveland State University
Cleveland OH
(216) 687-5411
U.S. News ranking: Nat. U., second tier
Website: www.csuohio.edu
Admissions email: admissions@csuohio.edu
Public; founded 1964
Freshman admissions: selective; 2020-2021: 7,830 applied, 7,815 accepted. Either SAT or ACT required. ACT 25/75 percentile: 18-24. High school rank: N/A
Early decision deadline: N/A, notification date: N/A
Early action deadline: 5/1, notification date: N/A
Application deadline (fall): 8/16
Undergraduate student body: 8,804 full time, 2,441 part time; 44% male, 56% female; 0% American Indian, 3% Asian, 15% black, 8% Hispanic, 4% multiracial, 0% Pacific Islander, 64% white, 4% international; 92% from in state; 6% live on campus; 1% of students in fraternities, 1% in sororities
Most popular majors: 8% Psychology, General, 6% Clinical/Medical Laboratory Science and Allied Professions, Other, 6% Registered Nursing/Registered Nurse, 5% Mechanical Engineering, 3% Biology/Biological Sciences, General
Expenses: 2021-2022: $11,426 in state, $16,480 out of state; room/board: $11,834
Financial aid: (216) 687-5594; 70% of undergrads determined to have financial need; average aid package $9,842

College of Wooster
Wooster OH
(330) 263-2322
U.S. News ranking: Nat. Lib. Arts, No. 71
Website: www.wooster.edu/
Admissions email: admissions@wooster.edu
Private; founded 1866
Freshman admissions: more selective; 2020-2021: 5,582 applied, 3,645 accepted. Neither SAT nor ACT required. ACT 25/75 percentile: 24-31. High school rank: 46% in top tenth, 68% in top quarter, 92% in top half
Early decision deadline: 11/1, notification date: 11/15
Early action deadline: 11/15, notification date: 12/31
Application deadline (fall): 2/15
Undergraduate student body: 1,921 full time, 3 part time; 46% male, 54% female; 0% American Indian, 3% Asian, 9% black, 7% Hispanic, 4% multiracial, 0% Pacific Islander, 60% white, 15% international; 38% from in state; 99% live on campus; 13% of students in fraternities, 20% in sororities
Most popular majors: 20% Biological and Biomedical Sciences, 18% Social Sciences, 7% Physical Sciences, 7% Psychology, 6% Mathematics and Statistics
Expenses: 2021-2022: $55,500; room/board: $13,100
Financial aid: (330) 263-2317; 68% of undergrads determined to have financial need; average aid package $46,457

Columbus College of Art and Design[1]
Columbus OH
(614) 222-3261
U.S. News ranking: Arts, unranked
Website: www.ccad.edu
Admissions email: admissions@ccad.edu
Private; founded 1879
Application deadline (fall): 8/1
Undergraduate student body: N/A full time, N/A part time
Expenses: 2020-2021: $37,370; room/board: $9,790
Financial aid: (614) 222-3274

Defiance College
Defiance OH
(419) 783-2359
U.S. News ranking: Reg. Coll. (Mid. W), No. 50
Website: www.defiance.edu
Admissions email: admissions@defiance.edu
Private; founded 1850
Affiliation: United Church of Christ
Freshman admissions: less selective; 2020-2021: 1,698 applied, 1,629 accepted. Neither SAT nor ACT required. ACT 25/75 percentile: 16-22. High school rank: 11% in top tenth, 17% in top quarter, 44% in top half
Early decision deadline: N/A, notification date: N/A
Early action deadline: N/A, notification date: N/A
Application deadline (fall): rolling
Undergraduate student body: 515 full time, 47 part time; 59% male, 41% female; 1% American Indian, 0% Asian, 23% black, 9% Hispanic, 2% multiracial, 0% Pacific Islander, 62% white, 0% international; 58% from in state; 85% live on campus; 0% of students in fraternities, 0% in sororities
Most popular majors: 14% Business/Commerce, General, 12% Kinesiology and Exercise Science, 12% Social Work, 11% Criminal Justice/Police Science, 11% Early Childhood Education and Teaching
Expenses: 2020-2021: $33,910; room/board: $10,614
Financial aid: (419) 783-2376

Denison University
Granville OH
(740) 587-6276
U.S. News ranking: Nat. Lib. Arts, No. 42
Website: www.denison.edu
Admissions email: admission@denison.edu
Private; founded 1831
Freshman admissions: most selective; 2020-2021: 9,079 applied, 2,558 accepted. Neither SAT nor ACT required. SAT 25/75 percentile: 1220-1430. High school rank: 71% in top tenth, 85% in top quarter, 100% in top half
Early decision deadline: 11/15, notification date: 12/15
Early action deadline: N/A, notification date: N/A
Application deadline (fall): 1/15
Undergraduate student body: 2,252 full time, 6 part time; 47% male, 53% female; 0% American Indian, 3% Asian, 6% black, 8% Hispanic, 4% multiracial, 0% Pacific Islander, 60% white, 16% international; 21% from in state; 99% live on campus; 26% of students in fraternities, 42% in sororities
Most popular majors: 11% Biology/Biological Sciences, General, 11% Communication and Media Studies, 9% International Business/Trade/Commerce, 8% Psychology, General, 5% Finance and Financial Management Services, Other
Expenses: 2021-2022: $57,500; room/board: $13,900
Financial aid: (740) 587-6276; 50% of undergrads determined to have financial need; average aid package $49,630

Franciscan University of Steubenville
Steubenville OH
(740) 283-6226
U.S. News ranking: Reg. U. (Mid. W), No. 19
Website: www.franciscan.edu
Admissions email: admissions@franciscan.edu
Private; founded 1946
Affiliation: Roman Catholic
Freshman admissions: more selective; 2020-2021: 2,074 applied, 1,514 accepted. Either SAT or ACT required. SAT 25/75 percentile: 1070-1290. High school rank: N/A

Early decision deadline: N/A, notification date: N/A
Early action deadline: N/A, notification date: N/A
Application deadline (fall): rolling
Undergraduate student body: 2,220 full time, 285 part time; 42% male, 58% female; 0% American Indian, 3% Asian, 1% black, 15% Hispanic, 2% multiracial, 0% Pacific Islander, 77% white, 1% international; 76% from in state; 60% live on campus; 0% of students in fraternities, 0% in sororities
Most popular majors: 17% Theology/Theological Studies, 11% Business Administration and Management, General, 10% Registered Nursing/Registered Nurse, 9% Elementary Education and Teaching, 7% Psychology, General
Expenses: 2021-2022: $30,180; room/board: $9,240
Financial aid: (740) 284-5216; 62% of undergrads determined to have financial need; average aid package $20,626

Franklin University[1]
Columbus OH
(888) 341-6237
U.S. News ranking: Business, unranked
Website: www.franklin.edu
Admissions email: info@franklin.edu
Private; founded 1902
Application deadline (fall): N/A
Undergraduate student body: N/A full time, N/A part time
Expenses: 2020-2021: $9,577; room/board: N/A
Financial aid: N/A

Heidelberg University
Tiffin OH
(419) 448-2330
U.S. News ranking: Reg. Coll. (Mid. W), No. 23
Website: www.heidelberg.edu
Admissions email: adminfo@heidelberg.edu
Private; founded 1850
Affiliation: United Church of Christ
Freshman admissions: selective; 2020-2021: 1,882 applied, 1,524 accepted. Either SAT or ACT required. ACT 25/75 percentile: 19-24. High school rank: N/A
Early decision deadline: N/A, notification date: N/A
Early action deadline: N/A, notification date: N/A
Application deadline (fall): 8/1
Undergraduate student body: 1,014 full time, 9 part time; 51% male, 49% female; 0% American Indian, 0% Asian, 8% black, 4% Hispanic, 4% multiracial, 0% Pacific Islander, 80% white, 1% international
Most popular majors: Information not available
Expenses: 2021-2022: $33,600; room/board: $11,070
Financial aid: (419) 448-2293; 86% of undergrads determined to have financial need; average aid package $27,982

Hiram College
Hiram OH
(330) 569-5169
U.S. News ranking: Reg. Coll. (Mid. W), No. 15
Website: www.hiram.edu
Admissions email: admission@hiram.edu
Private; founded 1850
Freshman admissions: selective; 2020-2021: 1,535 applied, 1,424 accepted. Neither SAT nor ACT required. ACT 25/75 percentile: 16-24. High school rank: 14% in top tenth, 40% in top quarter, 71% in top half
Early decision deadline: N/A, notification date: N/A
Early action deadline: N/A, notification date: N/A
Application deadline (fall): rolling
Undergraduate student body: 810 full time, 281 part time; 44% male, 56% female; 0% American Indian, 1% Asian, 16% black, 8% Hispanic, 3% multiracial, 0% Pacific Islander, 52% white, 1% international; 77% from in state; 70% live on campus; 0% of students in fraternities, 0% in sororities
Most popular majors: 34% Business, Management, Marketing, and Related Support Services, 16% Health Professions and Related Programs, 12% Education, 8% Biological and Biomedical Sciences, 7% Social Sciences
Expenses: 2021-2022: $25,000; room/board: $10,500
Financial aid: (330) 569-5441; 88% of undergrads determined to have financial need; average aid package $17,660

John Carroll University
University Heights OH
(888) 335-6800
U.S. News ranking: Reg. U. (Mid. W), No. 2
Website: jcu.edu/
Admissions email: admission@jcu.edu
Private; founded 1886
Affiliation: Roman Catholic
Freshman admissions: more selective; 2020-2021: 3,610 applied, 3,171 accepted. Neither SAT nor ACT required. ACT 25/75 percentile: 22-28. High school rank: 23% in top tenth, 50% in top quarter, 85% in top half
Early decision deadline: N/A, notification date: N/A
Early action deadline: 12/1, notification date: 12/15
Application deadline (fall): rolling
Undergraduate student body: 2,714 full time, 57 part time; 53% male, 47% female; 0% American Indian, 2% Asian, 3% black, 4% Hispanic, 2% multiracial, 0% Pacific Islander, 87% white, 1% international; 67% from in state; N/A live on campus; 9% of students in fraternities, 21% in sororities
Most popular majors: 36% Business, Management, Marketing, and Related Support Services, 10% Biological and Biomedical Sciences, 8%

Communication, Journalism, and Related Programs, 8% Psychology, 8% Social Sciences
Expenses: 2021-2022: $45,514; room/board: $12,876
Financial aid: (888) 335-6800; 70% of undergrads determined to have financial need; average aid package $37,055

Kent State University
Kent OH
(330) 672-2444
U.S. News ranking: Nat. U., No. 213
Website: www.kent.edu
Admissions email: admissions@kent.edu
Public; founded 1910
Freshman admissions: selective; 2020-2021: 18,085 applied, 15,269 accepted. Neither SAT nor ACT required. ACT 25/75 percentile: 20-26. High school rank: 17% in top tenth, 45% in top quarter, 79% in top half
Early decision deadline: N/A, notification date: N/A
Early action deadline: N/A, notification date: N/A
Application deadline (fall): 5/1
Undergraduate student body: 18,921 full time, 2,700 part time; 38% male, 62% female; 0% American Indian, 2% Asian, 9% black, 4% Hispanic, 4% multiracial, 0% Pacific Islander, 75% white, 3% international; 82% from in state; 18% live on campus; N/A of students in fraternities, N/A in sororities
Most popular majors: 23% Business, Management, Marketing, and Related Support Services, 15% Health Professions and Related Programs, 8% Education, 7% Visual and Performing Arts, 6% Psychology
Expenses: 2021-2022: $11,924 in state, $20,800 out of state; room/board: $12,412
Financial aid: (330) 672-2972; 59% of undergrads determined to have financial need; average aid package $11,183

Kenyon College
Gambier OH
(740) 427-5776
U.S. News ranking: Nat. Lib. Arts, No. 30
Website: www.kenyon.edu
Admissions email: admissions@kenyon.edu
Private; founded 1824
Freshman admissions: more selective; 2020-2021: 6,614 applied, 2,440 accepted. Neither SAT nor ACT required. SAT 25/75 percentile: 1280-1460. High school rank: 55% in top tenth, 80% in top quarter, 100% in top half
Early decision deadline: 11/15, notification date: 12/18
Early action deadline: N/A, notification date: N/A
Application deadline (fall): 1/15
Undergraduate student body: 1,608 full time, 9 part time; 43% male, 57% female; 0% American Indian, 5% Asian, 4% black, 7% Hispanic, 5% multiracial, 0% Pacific Islander, 68% white,

9% international; 12% from in state; 57% live on campus; 10% of students in fraternities, 8% in sororities
Most popular majors: 16% English Language and Literature, General, 11% Political Science and Government, General, 7% Psychology, General, 7% Sociology and Anthropology, 5% History, General
Expenses: 2021-2022: $63,310; room/board: $13,310
Financial aid: (740) 427-5430; 48% of undergrads determined to have financial need; average aid package $46,971

Lake Erie College
Painesville OH
(855) 467-8676
U.S. News ranking: Reg. U. (Mid. W), second tier
Website: www.lec.edu
Admissions email: admissions@lec.edu
Private; founded 1856
Freshman admissions: least selective; 2020-2021: 700 applied, 672 accepted. Neither SAT nor ACT required. SAT 25/75 percentile: N/A. High school rank: N/A
Early decision deadline: N/A, notification date: N/A
Early action deadline: 12/1, notification date: 12/15
Application deadline (fall): 8/1
Undergraduate student body: 660 full time, 32 part time; 53% male, 47% female; 1% American Indian, 1% Asian, 15% black, 5% Hispanic, 5% multiracial, 1% Pacific Islander, 61% white, 4% international; 67% from in state; 85% live on campus; 0% of students in fraternities, 0% in sororities
Most popular majors: 26% Business, Management, Marketing, and Related Support Services, 16% Education, 10% Agriculture, Agriculture Operations, and Related Sciences, 10% Biological and Biomedical Sciences, 10% Psychology
Expenses: 2021-2022: $34,046; room/board: $10,394
Financial aid: (440) 375-7100; 81% of undergrads determined to have financial need; average aid package $26,452

Lourdes University[1]
Sylvania OH
(419) 885-5291
U.S. News ranking: Reg. U. (Mid. W), second tier
Website: www.lourdes.edu
Admissions email: luadmits@lourdes.edu
Private; founded 1958
Affiliation: Roman Catholic
Application deadline (fall): rolling
Undergraduate student body: N/A full time, N/A part time
Expenses: 2020-2021: $25,644; room/board: $10,960
Financial aid: (419) 824-3504

Malone University
Canton OH
(330) 471-8145
U.S. News ranking: Reg. U. (Mid. W), No. 82
Website: www.malone.edu
Admissions email: admissions@malone.edu
Private; founded 1892
Affiliation: Friends
Freshman admissions: selective; 2020-2021: 1,306 applied, 970 accepted. Neither SAT nor ACT required. ACT 25/75 percentile: 19-25. High school rank: N/A
Early decision deadline: N/A, notification date: N/A
Early action deadline: N/A, notification date: N/A
Application deadline (fall): rolling
Undergraduate student body: 859 full time, 264 part time; 40% male, 60% female; 0% American Indian, 1% Asian, 8% black, 3% Hispanic, 5% multiracial, 0% Pacific Islander, 75% white, 2% international; N/A from in state; 56% live on campus; 0% of students in fraternities, 0% in sororities
Most popular majors: 13% Registered Nursing/Registered Nurse, 11% Business Administration and Management, General, 11% Business Administration, Management and Operations, Other, 5% Kinesiology and Exercise Science, 4% Sport and Fitness Administration/ Management
Expenses: 2021-2022: $33,400; room/board: $10,400
Financial aid: (330) 471-8161; 85% of undergrads determined to have financial need; average aid package $25,892

Marietta College
Marietta OH
(800) 331-7896
U.S. News ranking: Reg. Coll. (Mid. W), No. 6
Website: www.marietta.edu
Admissions email: admit@marietta.edu
Private; founded 1835
Freshman admissions: selective; 2020-2021: 2,435 applied, 1,799 accepted. Neither SAT nor ACT required. ACT 25/75 percentile: 20-25. High school rank: N/A
Early decision deadline: N/A, notification date: N/A
Early action deadline: N/A, notification date: N/A
Application deadline (fall): rolling
Undergraduate student body: 1,110 full time, 58 part time; 53% male, 47% female; 0% American Indian, 1% Asian, 4% black, 3% Hispanic, 4% multiracial, 0% Pacific Islander, 81% white, 4% international; 71% from in state; 73% live on campus; 5% of students in fraternities, 7% in sororities
Most popular majors: 25% Petroleum Engineering, 7% Marketing/Marketing Management, General, 6% Finance, General, 6% Health and Wellness, General, 4% Athletic Training/Trainer
Expenses: 2021-2022: $37,460; room/board: $11,768

Financial aid: (740) 376-4712; 82% of undergrads determined to have financial need; average aid package $37,404

Miami University–Oxford

Oxford OH
(513) 529-2531
U.S. News ranking: Nat. U., No. 103
Website: www.MiamiOH.edu
Admissions email: admission@MiamiOH.edu
Public; founded 1809
Freshman admissions: more selective; 2020-2021: 26,844 applied, 24,684 accepted. Either SAT or ACT required. ACT 25/75 percentile: 24-30. High school rank: 33% in top tenth, 61% in top quarter, 89% in top half
Early decision deadline: 11/15, notification date: 12/15
Early action deadline: 12/1, notification date: 2/1
Application deadline (fall): 2/1
Undergraduate student body: 16,079 full time, 443 part time; 49% male, 51% female; 0% American Indian, 3% Asian, 4% black, 5% Hispanic, 4% multiracial, 0% Pacific Islander, 75% white, 9% international; 64% from in state; 27% live on campus; 10% of students in fraternities, 16% in sororities
Most popular majors: 8% Finance, General, 6% Marketing/Marketing Management, General, 5% Psychology, General, 4% Digital Communication and Media/Multimedia, 4% Political Science and Government, General
Expenses: 2021-2022: $16,705 in state, $37,379 out of state; room/board: $15,080
Financial aid: (513) 529-8734; 34% of undergrads determined to have financial need; average aid package $16,883

Mount St. Joseph University

Cincinnati OH
(513) 244-4531
U.S. News ranking: Reg. U. (Mid. W), No. 79
Website: www.msj.edu/
Admissions email: admission@msj.edu
Private; founded 1920
Freshman admissions: selective; 2020-2021: 1,286 applied, 775 accepted. Either SAT or ACT required. ACT 25/75 percentile: 20-24. High school rank: 13% in top tenth, 39% in top quarter, 70% in top half
Early decision deadline: N/A, notification date: N/A
Early action deadline: N/A, notification date: N/A
Application deadline (fall): 8/17
Undergraduate student body: 1,002 full time, 471 part time; 43% male, 57% female; 0% American Indian, 1% Asian, 11% black, 3% Hispanic, 4% multiracial, 0% Pacific Islander, 80% white, 0% international
Most popular majors: Information not available

Expenses: 2021-2022: $33,250; room/board: $9,750
Financial aid: (513) 244-4418; 76% of undergrads determined to have financial need; average aid package $24,263

Mount Vernon Nazarene University

Mount Vernon OH
(866) 462-6868
U.S. News ranking: Reg. U. (Mid. W), No. 74
Website: www.mvnu.edu/
Admissions email: admissions@mvnu.edu
Private; founded 1968
Affiliation: Church of the Nazarene
Freshman admissions: selective; 2020-2021: 1,339 applied, 969 accepted. Either SAT or ACT required. ACT 25/75 percentile: 20-25. High school rank: N/A
Early decision deadline: N/A, notification date: N/A
Early action deadline: N/A, notification date: N/A
Application deadline (fall): rolling
Undergraduate student body: 1,504 full time, 268 part time; 40% male, 60% female; 0% American Indian, 1% Asian, 3% black, 3% Hispanic, 3% multiracial, 0% Pacific Islander, 87% white, 1% international; N/A from in state; 78% live on campus; 0% of students in fraternities, 0% in sororities
Most popular majors: 23% Business, Management, Marketing, and Related Support Services, 12% Health Professions and Related Programs, 10% Education, 10% Public Administration and Social Service Professions, 6% Visual and Performing Arts
Expenses: 2020-2021: $31,610; room/board: $8,890
Financial aid: (740) 397-9000

Muskingum University

New Concord OH
(740) 826-8137
U.S. News ranking: Reg. U. (Mid. W), No. 36
Website: www.muskingum.edu
Admissions email: adminfo@muskingum.edu
Private; founded 1837
Affiliation: Presbyterian Church (USA)
Freshman admissions: selective; 2020-2021: 2,237 applied, 1,782 accepted. Neither SAT nor ACT required. ACT 25/75 percentile: 18-23. High school rank: 16% in top tenth, 39% in top quarter, 70% in top half
Early decision deadline: N/A, notification date: N/A
Early action deadline: N/A, notification date: N/A
Application deadline (fall): rolling
Undergraduate student body: 1,348 full time, 200 part time; 45% male, 55% female; 0% American Indian, 1% Asian, 6% black, 3% Hispanic, 4% multiracial, 0% Pacific Islander, 81% white, 2% international
Most popular majors: 17% Health Professions and Related Programs, 9% Registered Nursing/

Registered Nurse, 8% Business Administration and Management, General, 6% Accounting, 6% History, General
Expenses: 2021-2022: $30,340; room/board: $12,050
Financial aid: (740) 826-8139; 95% of undergrads determined to have financial need; average aid package $23,292

Notre Dame College of Ohio[1]

Cleveland OH
(216) 373-5355
U.S. News ranking: Reg. U. (Mid. W), second tier
Website: www.notredamecollege.edu
Admissions email: admissions@ndc.edu
Private; founded 1922
Application deadline (fall): rolling
Undergraduate student body: N/A full time, N/A part time
Expenses: 2020-2021: $30,750; room/board: $10,250
Financial aid: (216) 373-5263

Oberlin College and Conservatory

Oberlin OH
(440) 775-8411
U.S. News ranking: Nat. Lib. Arts, No. 37
Website: www.oberlin.edu
Admissions email: college.admissions@oberlin.edu
Private; founded 1833
Freshman admissions: more selective; 2020-2021: 9,309 applied, 3,292 accepted. Neither SAT nor ACT required. SAT 25/75 percentile: 1270-1450. High school rank: 51% in top tenth, 82% in top quarter, 96% in top half
Early decision deadline: 12/15, notification date: 1/5
Early action deadline: N/A, notification date: N/A
Application deadline (fall): 1/15
Undergraduate student body: 2,614 full time, 33 part time; 41% male, 59% female; 0% American Indian, 5% Asian, 6% black, 8% Hispanic, 9% multiracial, 0% Pacific Islander, 59% white, 12% international; 8% from in state; 87% live on campus; 0% of students in fraternities, 0% in sororities
Most popular majors: 15% Music Performance, General, 8% Political Science and Government, General, 7% Biology/Biological Sciences, General, 7% History, General, 7% Psychology, General
Expenses: 2021-2022: $60,243; room/board: $17,854
Financial aid: (440) 775-8142; 54% of undergrads determined to have financial need; average aid package $46,532

Ohio Christian University

Circleville OH
(877) 762-8669
U.S. News ranking: Reg. U. (Mid. W), second tier
Website: www.ohiochristian.edu/

Admissions email: enroll@ohiochristian.edu
Private; founded 1948
Affiliation: Churches of Christ
Freshman admissions: less selective; 2020-2021: N/A applied, N/A accepted. Neither SAT nor ACT required. SAT 25/75 percentile: N/A. High school rank: N/A
Early decision deadline: N/A, notification date: N/A
Early action deadline: N/A, notification date: N/A
Application deadline (fall): N/A
Undergraduate student body: 1,034 full time, 927 part time; 41% male, 59% female; 1% American Indian, 1% Asian, 24% black, 4% Hispanic, 3% multiracial, 0% Pacific Islander, 67% white, 0% international
Most popular majors: 26% Business Administration and Management, General, 14% Bible/Biblical Studies, 14% Psychology, General, 5% Education, General
Expenses: 2021-2022: $21,906; room/board: $8,784
Financial aid: N/A

Ohio Dominican University

Columbus OH
(614) 251-4500
U.S. News ranking: Reg. U. (Mid. W), No. 64
Website: www.ohiodominican.edu
Admissions email: admissions@ohiodominican.edu
Private; founded 1911
Affiliation: Roman Catholic
Freshman admissions: selective; 2020-2021: 2,190 applied, 1,084 accepted. Neither SAT nor ACT required. ACT 25/75 percentile: 19-26. High school rank: 16% in top tenth, 40% in top quarter, 66% in top half
Early decision deadline: N/A, notification date: N/A
Early action deadline: N/A, notification date: N/A
Application deadline (fall): rolling
Undergraduate student body: 857 full time, 92 part time; 47% male, 53% female; 1% American Indian, 2% Asian, 25% black, 6% Hispanic, 5% multiracial, 0% Pacific Islander, 54% white, 3% international
Most popular majors: Information not available
Expenses: 2021-2022: $33,380; room/board: $11,450
Financial aid: (614) 251-4778; 80% of undergrads determined to have financial need; average aid package $26,657

Ohio Northern University

Ada OH
(888) 408-4668
U.S. News ranking: Reg. Coll. (Mid. W), No. 3
Website: www.onu.edu
Admissions email: admissions-ug@onu.edu
Private; founded 1871
Affiliation: United Methodist
Freshman admissions: more selective; 2020-2021: 4,218 applied, 2,749 accepted. Neither

SAT nor ACT required. ACT 25/75 percentile: 22-28. High school rank: N/A
Early decision deadline: N/A, notification date: N/A
Early action deadline: N/A, notification date: N/A
Application deadline (fall): 8/15
Undergraduate student body: 2,034 full time, 93 part time; 55% male, 45% female; 0% American Indian, 1% Asian, 3% black, 1% Hispanic, 4% multiracial, 0% Pacific Islander, 79% white, 1% international; 84% from in state; 69% live on campus; N/A of students in fraternities, N/A in sororities
Most popular majors: 20% Business, Management, Marketing, and Related Support Services, 20% Engineering, 11% Health Professions and Related Programs, 9% Visual and Performing Arts, 6% Parks, Recreation, Leisure, and Fitness Studies
Expenses: 2021-2022: $35,380; room/board: $12,650
Financial aid: (419) 772-2271; 79% of undergrads determined to have financial need; average aid package $30,288

Ohio State University–Columbus

Columbus OH
(614) 292-3980
U.S. News ranking: Nat. U., No. 49
Website: www.osu.edu
Admissions email: askabuckeye@osu.edu
Public; founded 1870
Freshman admissions: more selective; 2020-2021: 49,087 applied, 33,619 accepted. Neither SAT nor ACT required. ACT 25/75 percentile: 26-32. High school rank: 55% in top tenth, 90% in top quarter, 99% in top half
Early decision deadline: N/A, notification date: N/A
Early action deadline: 11/1, notification date: 1/31
Application deadline (fall): 2/1
Undergraduate student body: 42,734 full time, 4,250 part time; 50% male, 50% female; 0% American Indian, 8% Asian, 7% black, 5% Hispanic, 4% multiracial, 0% Pacific Islander, 66% white, 7% international; 76% from in state; 24% live on campus; 6% of students in fraternities, 10% in sororities
Most popular majors: 6% Finance, General, 5% Psychology, General, 4% Biology/Biological Sciences, General, 4% Marketing/Marketing Management, General, 4% Speech Communication and Rhetoric
Expenses: 2021-2022: $11,936 in state, $35,019 out of state; room/board: $13,352
Financial aid: (614) 292-0300; 45% of undergrads determined to have financial need; average aid package $15,880

Ohio University

Athens OH
(740) 593-4100
U.S. News ranking: Nat. U., No. 179
Website: www.ohio.edu
Admissions email: admissions@ohio.edu
Public; founded 1804
Freshman admissions: selective; 2020-2021: 22,518 applied, 19,700 accepted. Neither SAT nor ACT required. ACT 25/75 percentile: 21-26. High school rank: 20% in top tenth, 49% in top quarter, 82% in top half
Early decision deadline: N/A, notification date: N/A
Early action deadline: 11/15, notification date: N/A
Application deadline (fall): 2/1
Undergraduate student body: 14,661 full time, 4,252 part time; 39% male, 61% female; 0% American Indian, 2% Asian, 6% black, 4% Hispanic, 4% multiracial, 0% Pacific Islander, 81% white, 2% international; 82% from in state; 43% live on campus; 4% of students in fraternities, 7% in sororities
Most popular majors: 35% Registered Nursing/Registered Nurse, 5% Business Administration and Management, General, 3% Liberal Arts and Sciences, General Studies and Humanities, Other, 3% Marketing/Marketing Management, General, 3% Speech Communication and Rhetoric
Expenses: 2021-2022: $12,660 in state, $22,810 out of state; room/board: $12,172
Financial aid: (740) 593-4141; 56% of undergrads determined to have financial need; average aid package $9,461

Ohio Wesleyan University

Delaware OH
(800) 922-8953
U.S. News ranking: Nat. Lib. Arts, No. 98
Website: www.owu.edu
Admissions email: owuadmit@owu.edu
Private; founded 1842
Affiliation: United Methodist
Freshman admissions: more selective; 2020-2021: 3,961 applied, 2,710 accepted. Neither SAT nor ACT required. ACT 25/75 percentile: 23-29. High school rank: 28% in top tenth, 56% in top quarter, 86% in top half
Early decision deadline: 11/15, notification date: 11/30
Early action deadline: 12/1, notification date: 12/15
Application deadline (fall): 3/1
Undergraduate student body: 1,418 full time, 8 part time; 45% male, 55% female; 0% American Indian, 3% Asian, 7% black, 6% Hispanic, 5% multiracial, 0% Pacific Islander, 71% white, 6% international; 60% from in state; 100% live on campus; 30% of students in fraternities, 27% in sororities
Most popular majors: 19% Business, Management,

Marketing, and Related Support Services, 15% Biological and Biomedical Sciences, 11% Social Sciences, 8% Parks, Recreation, Leisure, and Fitness Studies, 6% Psychology
Expenses: 2021-2022: $48,832; room/board: $13,288
Financial aid: (740) 368-3050; 71% of undergrads determined to have financial need; average aid package $38,834

Otterbein University

Westerville OH
(614) 823-1500
U.S. News ranking: Reg. U. (Mid. W), No. 12
Website: www.otterbein.edu
Admissions email: UOtterB@Otterbein.edu
Private; founded 1847
Affiliation: United Methodist
Freshman admissions: selective; 2020-2021: 2,849 applied, 2,167 accepted. Either SAT or ACT required. ACT 25/75 percentile: 20-27. High school rank: 25% in top tenth, 54% in top quarter, 85% in top half
Early decision deadline: N/A, notification date: N/A
Early action deadline: N/A, notification date: N/A
Application deadline (fall): rolling
Undergraduate student body: 2,136 full time, 177 part time; 38% male, 62% female; 0% American Indian, 3% Asian, 8% black, 6% Hispanic, 5% multiracial, 0% Pacific Islander, 76% white, 0% international; 89% from in state; 48% live on campus; 27% of students in fraternities, 26% in sororities
Most popular majors: 14% Health Professions and Related Programs, 10% Biological and Biomedical Sciences, 9% Visual and Performing Arts, 7% Education
Expenses: 2021-2022: $33,674; room/board: $11,692
Financial aid: (614) 823-1502; 72% of undergrads determined to have financial need; average aid package $24,996

Shawnee State University

Portsmouth OH
(740) 351-4778
U.S. News ranking: Reg. U. (Mid. W), second tier
Website: www.shawnee.edu
Admissions email: admissions@shawnee.edu
Public; founded 1986
Freshman admissions: selective; 2020-2021: 3,612 applied, 2,595 accepted. Neither SAT nor ACT required. ACT 25/75 percentile: 18-24. High school rank: 19% in top tenth, 44% in top quarter, 75% in top half
Early decision deadline: N/A, notification date: N/A
Early action deadline: N/A, notification date: N/A
Application deadline (fall): 7/1
Undergraduate student body: 2,521 full time, 778 part time; 44% male, 56% female; 1% American Indian, 1% Asian, 4% black, 0% Hispanic, 2% multiracial, 0%

Pacific Islander, 85% white, 1% international
Most popular majors: 11% Health/Health Care Administration/Management, 8% Health and Medical Administrative Services, Other, 6% Registered Nursing/Registered Nurse, 5% Business Administration and Management, General, 5% Plastics and Polymer Engineering Technology/Technician
Expenses: 2021-2022: $8,930 in state, $14,973 out of state; room/board: $11,003
Financial aid: (740) 351-4243; 61% of undergrads determined to have financial need; average aid package $15,637

Tiffin University[7]

Tiffin OH
(419) 448-3423
U.S. News ranking: Reg. U. (Mid. W), second tier
Website: www.tiffin.edu
Admissions email: admiss@tiffin.edu
Private; founded 1888
Freshman admissions: selective; 2020-2021: 4,738 applied, 2,960 accepted. Neither SAT nor ACT required. ACT 25/75 percentile: 17-22. High school rank: N/A
Early decision deadline: N/A, notification date: N/A
Early action deadline: N/A, notification date: N/A
Application deadline (fall): rolling
Undergraduate student body: 1,626 full time, 568 part time
Most popular majors: 34% Business, Management, Marketing, and Related Support Services, 31% Homeland Security, Law Enforcement, Firefighting and Related Protective Services, 14% Psychology, 5% Computer and Information Sciences and Support Services, 4% Parks, Recreation, Leisure, and Fitness Studies
Expenses: 2021-2022: $28,480; room/board: $11,700
Financial aid: (419) 448-3279; 82% of undergrads determined to have financial need; average aid package $20,325

Union Institute and University[1]

Cincinnati OH
(800) 861-6400
U.S. News ranking: Nat. U., second tier
Website: www.myunion.edu
Admissions email: admissions@myunion.edu
Private; founded 1964
Affiliation: Other
Application deadline (fall): rolling
Undergraduate student body: N/A full time, N/A part time
Expenses: 2020-2021: $15,686; room/board: N/A
Financial aid: (513) 487-1126

University of Akron

Akron OH
(330) 972-7077
U.S. News ranking: Nat. U., second tier
Website: www.uakron.edu

Admissions email: admissions@uakron.edu
Public; founded 1870
Freshman admissions: selective; 2020-2021: 13,321 applied, 10,292 accepted. Either SAT or ACT required. ACT 25/75 percentile: 19-26. High school rank: 19% in top tenth, 45% in top quarter, 76% in top half
Early decision deadline: N/A, notification date: N/A
Early action deadline: N/A, notification date: N/A
Application deadline (fall): 8/1
Undergraduate student body: 10,791 full time, 2,860 part time; 52% male, 48% female; 0% American Indian, 3% Asian, 11% black, 3% Hispanic, 4% multiracial, 0% Pacific Islander, 75% white, 2% international; 94% from in state; 13% live on campus; N/A of students in fraternities, N/A in sororities
Most popular majors: 8% Registered Nursing/Registered Nurse, 7% Mechanical Engineering, 5% Organizational Leadership, 4% Accounting, 3% Psychology, General
Expenses: 2021-2022: $11,880 in state, $15,410 out of state; room/board: $13,788
Financial aid: (330) 972-5860; 63% of undergrads determined to have financial need; average aid package $9,437

University of Cincinnati

Cincinnati OH
(513) 556-1100
U.S. News ranking: Nat. U., No. 148
Website: www.uc.edu
Admissions email: admissions@uc.edu
Public; founded 1819
Freshman admissions: more selective; 2020-2021: 23,960 applied, 18,306 accepted. Neither SAT nor ACT required. ACT 25/75 percentile: 23-29. High school rank: 25% in top tenth, 52% in top quarter, 85% in top half
Early decision deadline: N/A, notification date: N/A
Early action deadline: N/A, notification date: N/A
Application deadline (fall): 3/1
Undergraduate student body: 24,301 full time, 4,356 part time; 50% male, 50% female; 0% American Indian, 5% Asian, 7% black, 4% Hispanic, 4% multiracial, 0% Pacific Islander, 74% white, 4% international; 82% from in state; 17% live on campus; 10% of students in fraternities, 8% in sororities
Most popular majors: 21% Business, Management, Marketing, and Related Support Services, 16% Health Professions and Related Programs, 13% Engineering, 6% Biological and Biomedical Sciences, 6% Visual and Performing Arts
Expenses: 2021-2022: $12,138 in state, $27,472 out of state; room/board: $12,288
Financial aid: (513) 556-6982; 43% of undergrads determined to have financial need; average aid package $8,634

University of Cincinnati–UC Blue Ash College[1]

Cincinnati OH
(513) 745-5600
U.S. News ranking: Reg. Coll. (Mid. W), unranked
Website: www.rwc.uc.edu/
Admissions email: N/A
Public
Application deadline (fall): N/A
Undergraduate student body: N/A full time, N/A part time
Expenses: 2020-2021: $6,256 in state, $15,054 out of state; room/board: $11,874
Financial aid: N/A

University of Dayton

Dayton OH
(800) 837-7433
U.S. News ranking: Nat. U., No. 127
Website: www.udayton.edu
Admissions email: admission@udayton.edu
Private; founded 1850
Affiliation: Roman Catholic
Freshman admissions: selective; 2020-2021: 16,456 applied, 13,401 accepted. Neither SAT nor ACT required. ACT 25/75 percentile: 23-29. High school rank: 27% in top tenth, 55% in top quarter, 86% in top half
Early decision deadline: N/A, notification date: N/A
Early action deadline: 11/1, notification date: 11/1
Application deadline (fall): 3/1
Undergraduate student body: 8,314 full time, 330 part time; 51% male, 49% female; 0% American Indian, 2% Asian, 4% black, 7% Hispanic, 3% multiracial, 0% Pacific Islander, 80% white, 4% international; 50% from in state; 69% live on campus; 12% of students in fraternities, 22% in sororities
Most popular majors: Information not available
Expenses: 2021-2022: $44,890; room/board: $14,870
Financial aid: (800) 427-5029; 59% of undergrads determined to have financial need; average aid package $36,535

University of Findlay

Findlay OH
(419) 434-4732
U.S. News ranking: Nat. U., No. 263
Website: www.findlay.edu
Admissions email: admissions@findlay.edu
Private; founded 1882
Affiliation: Church of God
Freshman admissions: selective; 2020-2021: 3,320 applied, 2,639 accepted. Either SAT or ACT required. ACT 25/75 percentile: 20-26. High school rank: N/A
Early decision deadline: N/A, notification date: N/A
Early action deadline: N/A, notification date: N/A
Application deadline (fall): rolling
Undergraduate student body: 2,161 full time, 1,571 part time; 36%

male, 64% female; 0% American Indian, 2% Asian, 5% black, 4% Hispanic, 2% multiracial, 0% Pacific Islander, 70% white, 4% international
Most popular majors: 30% Agriculture, Agriculture Operations, and Related Sciences, 19% Business, Management, Marketing, and Related Support Services, 18% Health Professions and Related Programs, 5% Education, 5% Psychology
Expenses: 2021-2022: $36,720; room/board: $10,488
Financial aid: (419) 434-4791

University of Mount Union

Alliance OH
(330) 823-2590
U.S. News ranking: Reg. Coll. (Mid. W), No. 10
Website: www.mountunion.edu/
Admissions email: admission@mountunion.edu
Private; founded 1846
Freshman admissions: selective; 2020-2021: 3,422 applied, 2,649 accepted. Either SAT or ACT required. ACT 25/75 percentile: 19-25. High school rank: 22% in top tenth, 53% in top quarter, 85% in top half
Early decision deadline: N/A, notification date: N/A
Early action deadline: N/A, notification date: N/A
Application deadline (fall): rolling
Undergraduate student body: 1,925 full time, 33 part time; 52% male, 48% female; 0% American Indian, 1% Asian, 8% black, 4% Hispanic, 4% multiracial, 0% Pacific Islander, 78% white, 2% international; 81% from in state; 60% live on campus; 14% of students in fraternities, 26% in sororities
Most popular majors: 8% Kinesiology and Exercise Science, 8% Marketing/Marketing Management, General, 6% Biology/Biological Sciences, General, 6% Early Childhood Education and Teaching, 5% Computer Engineering, General
Expenses: 2021-2022: $33,400; room/board: $10,900
Financial aid: (330) 823-2674; 77% of undergrads determined to have financial need; average aid package $24,683

University of Northwestern Ohio[1]

Lima OH
(419) 998-3120
U.S. News ranking: Reg. Coll. (Mid. W), second tier
Website: www.unoh.edu/
Admissions email: info@unoh.edu
Private
Application deadline (fall): N/A
Undergraduate student body: N/A full time, N/A part time
Expenses: 2020-2021: $11,550; room/board: $6,900
Financial aid: N/A

University of Rio Grande[1]

Rio Grande OH
(740) 245-7208
U.S. News ranking: Reg. Coll. (Mid. W), second tier
Website: www.rio.edu
Admissions email: admissions@rio.edu
Private; founded 1876
Application deadline (fall): rolling
Undergraduate student body: N/A full time, N/A part time
Expenses: 2020-2021: $21,186; room/board: $8,342
Financial aid: (740) 245-7285

University of Toledo

Toledo OH
(419) 530-8888
U.S. News ranking: Nat. U., second tier
Website: www.utoledo.edu
Admissions email: enroll@utoledo.edu
Public; founded 1872
Freshman admissions: selective; 2020-2021: 9,673 applied, 9,158 accepted. Neither SAT nor ACT required. ACT 25/75 percentile: 20-26. High school rank: 23% in top tenth, 49% in top quarter, 79% in top half
Early decision deadline: N/A, notification date: N/A
Early action deadline: N/A, notification date: N/A
Application deadline (fall): rolling
Undergraduate student body: 11,447 full time, 2,959 part time; 49% male, 51% female; 0% American Indian, 2% Asian, 10% black, 5% Hispanic, 4% multiracial, 0% Pacific Islander, 69% white, 5% international; N/A from in state; 20% live on campus; N/A of students in fraternities, N/A in sororities
Most popular majors: 27% Business, Management, Marketing, and Related Support Services, 16% Engineering, 16% Health Professions and Related Programs, 5% Education, 4% Multi/Interdisciplinary Studies
Expenses: 2021-2022: $11,458 in state, $20,818 out of state; room/board: $12,908
Financial aid: (419) 530-8700; 59% of undergrads determined to have financial need; average aid package $11,280

Ursuline College

Pepper Pike OH
(440) 449-4203
U.S. News ranking: Reg. U. (Mid. W), No. 64
Website: www.ursuline.edu
Admissions email: admission@ursuline.edu
Private; founded 1871
Affiliation: Roman Catholic
Freshman admissions: selective; 2020-2021: 667 applied, 472 accepted. Neither SAT nor ACT required. ACT 25/75 percentile: 18-24. High school rank: 7% in top tenth, 39% in top quarter, 86% in top half
Early decision deadline: N/A, notification date: N/A
Early action deadline: N/A,

notification date: N/A
Application deadline (fall): rolling
Undergraduate student body: 519 full time, 155 part time; 8% male, 92% female; 0% American Indian, 3% Asian, 24% black, 1% Hispanic, 6% multiracial, 0% Pacific Islander, 61% white, 2% international; 87% from in state; 23% live on campus; N/A of students in fraternities, N/A in sororities
Most popular majors: 60% Registered Nursing/Registered Nurse, 7% Psychology, General, 6% Social Work, 4% Art Therapy/Therapist, 3% Biology/Biological Sciences, General
Expenses: 2021-2022: $35,660; room/board: $11,580
Financial aid: (440) 646-8309; 82% of undergrads determined to have financial need; average aid package $24,014

Walsh University

North Canton OH
(800) 362-9846
U.S. News ranking: Reg. U. (Mid. W), No. 54
Website: www.walsh.edu
Admissions email: admissions@walsh.edu
Private; founded 1958
Affiliation: Roman Catholic
Freshman admissions: selective; 2020-2021: 2,112 applied, 1,617 accepted. Neither SAT nor ACT required. ACT 25/75 percentile: 19-26. High school rank: N/A
Early decision deadline: N/A, notification date: N/A
Early action deadline: N/A, notification date: N/A
Application deadline (fall): rolling
Undergraduate student body: 1,531 full time, 319 part time; 44% male, 56% female; 0% American Indian, 1% Asian, 6% black, 3% Hispanic, 3% multiracial, 0% Pacific Islander, 47% white, 8% international; N/A from in state; 46% live on campus; N/A of students in fraternities, N/A in sororities
Most popular majors: 21% Health Professions and Related Programs, 19% Business, Management, Marketing, and Related Support Services, 14% Education, 11% Biological and Biomedical Sciences, 6% Psychology
Expenses: 2021-2022: $32,100; room/board: $11,390
Financial aid: (330) 490-7146; 66% of undergrads determined to have financial need; average aid package $25,432

Wilberforce University[1]

Wilberforce OH
(800) 367-8568
U.S. News ranking: Reg. Coll. (Mid. W), second tier
Website: www.wilberforce.edu
Admissions email: admissions@wilberforce.edu
Private
Application deadline (fall): N/A
Undergraduate student body: N/A full time, N/A part time

Expenses: 2020-2021: $13,250; room/board: $7,000
Financial aid: N/A

Wilmington College

Wilmington OH
(937) 481-2260
U.S. News ranking: Reg. Coll. (Mid. W), No. 35
Website: www.wilmington.edu/
Admissions email: admission@wilmington.edu
Private; founded 1870
Affiliation: Friends
Freshman admissions: selective; 2020-2021: 1,558 applied, 1,133 accepted. Either SAT or ACT required. ACT 25/75 percentile: 18-24. High school rank: N/A
Early decision deadline: N/A, notification date: N/A
Early action deadline: N/A, notification date: N/A
Application deadline (fall): 8/1
Undergraduate student body: 1,115 full time, 50 part time; 45% male, 55% female; 1% American Indian, 1% Asian, 9% black, 3% Hispanic, 4% multiracial, 0% Pacific Islander, 77% white, 1% international; 90% from in state; 61% live on campus; 20% of students in fraternities, 24% in sororities
Most popular majors: 25% Business Administration and Management, General, 19% Agricultural Business and Management, General, 9% Education, General, 7% Accounting, 6% Sport and Fitness Administration/Management
Expenses: 2021-2022: $28,770; room/board: $10,600
Financial aid: (937) 481-2337; 85% of undergrads determined to have financial need; average aid package $29,193

Wittenberg University

Springfield OH
(937) 327-6314
U.S. News ranking: Nat. Lib. Arts, No. 155
Website: www.wittenberg.edu/
Admissions email: admission@wittenberg.edu
Private; founded 1845
Affiliation: Evangelical Lutheran Church
Freshman admissions: selective; 2020-2021: 2,807 applied, 2,735 accepted. Neither SAT nor ACT required. ACT 25/75 percentile: 18-26. High school rank: 17% in top tenth, 40% in top quarter, 73% in top half
Early decision deadline: 11/15, notification date: 12/1
Early action deadline: 12/1, notification date: 1/1
Application deadline (fall): rolling
Undergraduate student body: 1,388 full time, 57 part time; 47% male, 53% female; 0% American Indian, 1% Asian, 10% black, 5% Hispanic, 5% multiracial, 0% Pacific Islander, 77% white, 0% international; 78% from in state; 80% live on campus; 27% of students in fraternities, 30% in sororities

Most popular majors: 24% Business, Management, Marketing, and Related Support Services, 10% Biological and Biomedical Sciences, 10% Education, 10% Social Sciences, 8% Parks, Recreation, Leisure, and Fitness Studies
Expenses: 2021-2022: $42,268; room/board: $11,046
Financial aid: (937) 327-7318; 78% of undergrads determined to have financial need; average aid package $35,435

Wright State University

Dayton OH
(937) 775-5700
U.S. News ranking: Nat. U., second tier
Website: www.wright.edu
Admissions email: admissions@wright.edu
Public; founded 1967
Freshman admissions: selective; 2020-2021: 5,226 applied, 4,998 accepted. Neither SAT nor ACT required. ACT 25/75 percentile: 18-25. High school rank: 21% in top tenth, 41% in top quarter, 71% in top half
Early decision deadline: N/A, notification date: N/A
Early action deadline: N/A, notification date: N/A
Application deadline (fall): 8/23
Undergraduate student body: 6,356 full time, 1,976 part time; 45% male, 55% female; 0% American Indian, 3% Asian, 11% black, 4% Hispanic, 5% multiracial, 0% Pacific Islander, 74% white, 2% international; 98% from in state; 12% live on campus; N/A of students in fraternities, N/A in sororities
Most popular majors: 26% Business, Management, Marketing, and Related Support Services, 14% Health Professions and Related Programs, 13% Engineering, 7% Education, 7% Psychology
Expenses: 2021-2022: $9,679 in state, $19,097 out of state; room/board: $9,014
Financial aid: (937) 775-4000; 61% of undergrads determined to have financial need; average aid package $11,860

Xavier University

Cincinnati OH
(877) 982-3648
U.S. News ranking: Reg. U. (Mid. W), No. 5
Website: www.xavier.edu
Admissions email: xuadmit@xavier.edu
Private; founded 1831
Affiliation: Roman Catholic
Freshman admissions: selective; 2020-2021: 14,805 applied, 12,024 accepted. Neither SAT nor ACT required. ACT 25/75 percentile: 22-28. High school rank: 23% in top tenth, 55% in top quarter, 87% in top half
Early decision deadline: N/A, notification date: N/A
Early action deadline: N/A, notification date: N/A
Application deadline (fall): rolling

Undergraduate student body: 5,055 full time, 249 part time; 43% male, 57% female; 0% American Indian, 3% Asian, 10% black, 6% Hispanic, 4% multiracial, 0% Pacific Islander, 75% white, 1% international; 45% from in state; 42% live on campus; 0% of students in fraternities, 0% in sororities
Most popular majors: 24% Registered Nursing/Registered Nurse, 7% Marketing/Marketing Management, General, 6% Liberal Arts and Sciences/Liberal Studies, 5% Biology/Biological Sciences, General, 5% Finance, General
Expenses: 2021-2022: $42,460; room/board: $13,580
Financial aid: (513) 745-3142; 57% of undergrads determined to have financial need; average aid package $26,343

Youngstown State University
Youngstown OH
(877) 468-6978
U.S. News ranking: Reg. U. (Mid. W), second tier
Website: www.ysu.edu
Admissions email: enroll@ysu.edu
Public; founded 1908
Freshman admissions: selective; 2020-2021: 8,615 applied, 6,018 accepted. Neither SAT nor ACT required. ACT 25/75 percentile: 18-24. High school rank: 14% in top tenth, 40% in top quarter, 73% in top half
Early decision deadline: N/A, notification date: N/A
Early action deadline: N/A, notification date: N/A
Application deadline (fall): 8/1
Undergraduate student body: 8,231 full time, 2,237 part time; 45% male, 55% female; 0% American Indian, 1% Asian, 8% black, 4% Hispanic, 4% multiracial, 0% Pacific Islander, 76% white, 3% international; 84% from in state; 12% live on campus; 3% of students in fraternities, 4% in sororities
Most popular majors: 7% General Studies, 7% Registered Nursing/Registered Nurse, 6% Criminal Justice/Safety Studies, 5% Biology/Biological Sciences, General, 5% Social Work
Expenses: 2021-2022: $10,214 in state, $15,854 out of state; room/board: $9,775
Financial aid: (330) 941-2031; 65% of undergrads determined to have financial need; average aid package $10,233

OKLAHOMA

Bacone College[1]
Muskogee OK
(888) 682-5514
U.S. News ranking: Reg. Coll. (W), second tier
Website: www.bacone.edu/
Admissions email: admissions@bacone.edu
Private
Application deadline (fall): rolling
Undergraduate student body: N/A full time, N/A part time

Expenses: 2020-2021: $14,700; room/board: $8,600
Financial aid: N/A

Cameron University
Lawton OK
(580) 581-2289
U.S. News ranking: Reg. U. (W), second tier
Website: www.cameron.edu/
Admissions email: admissions@cameron.edu
Public; founded 1908
Freshman admissions: selective; 2020-2021: 868 applied, 868 accepted. Neither SAT nor ACT required. ACT 25/75 percentile: 16-21. High school rank: 4% in top tenth, 13% in top quarter, 36% in top half
Early decision deadline: N/A, notification date: N/A
Early action deadline: N/A, notification date: N/A
Application deadline (fall): rolling
Undergraduate student body: 2,304 full time, 1,155 part time; 36% male, 64% female; 6% American Indian, 2% Asian, 12% black, 15% Hispanic, 11% multiracial, 0% Pacific Islander, 47% white, 2% international; 89% from in state; 11% live on campus; 3% of students in fraternities, 2% in sororities
Most popular majors: 12% Business Administration and Management, General, 10% Health and Physical Education/Fitness, General, 8% Corrections and Criminal Justice, Other, 8% Psychology, General, 7% Elementary Education and Teaching
Expenses: 2021-2022: $4,740 in state, $14,160 out of state; room/board: $5,810
Financial aid: (580) 581-2293; 71% of undergrads determined to have financial need; average aid package $9,658

East Central University
Ada OK
(580) 559-5628
U.S. News ranking: Reg. U. (W), second tier
Website: www.ecok.edu
Admissions email: admissions@ecok.edu
Public; founded 1909
Freshman admissions: selective; 2020-2021: 874 applied, 843 accepted. ACT required. ACT 25/75 percentile: 17-23. High school rank: N/A
Early decision deadline: N/A, notification date: N/A
Early action deadline: N/A, notification date: N/A
Application deadline (fall): rolling
Undergraduate student body: 2,456 full time, 483 part time; 42% male, 58% female; N/A American Indian, N/A Asian, N/A black, N/A Hispanic, N/A multiracial, N/A Pacific Islander, N/A white, N/A international; 17% from in state; 35% live on campus; 3% of students in fraternities, 3% in sororities
Most popular majors: Information not available

Expenses: 2021-2022: $7,052 in state, $16,412 out of state; room/board: $7,538
Financial aid: (580) 559-5243

Langston University[1]
Langston OK
(405) 466-3231
U.S. News ranking: Reg. U. (W), second tier
Website: www.langston.edu/
Admissions email: admissions@langston.edu
Public; founded 1897
Application deadline (fall): rolling
Undergraduate student body: N/A full time, N/A part time
Expenses: 2020-2021: $6,509 in state, $13,889 out of state; room/board: $10,513
Financial aid: (405) 466-3357

Mid-America Christian University[1]
Oklahoma City OK
(405) 691-3800
U.S. News ranking: Reg. U. (W), second tier
Website: www.macu.edu
Admissions email: info@macu.edu
Private
Application deadline (fall): N/A
Undergraduate student body: N/A full time, N/A part time
Expenses: 2020-2021: $18,838; room/board: $8,392
Financial aid: N/A

Northeastern State University
Tahlequah OK
(918) 444-2200
U.S. News ranking: Reg. U. (W), second tier
Website: www.nsuok.edu
Admissions email: nsuinfo@nsuok.edu
Public; founded 1846
Freshman admissions: selective; 2020-2021: 1,253 applied, 1,247 accepted. ACT required. ACT 25/75 percentile: 17-23. High school rank: 27% in top tenth, 52% in top quarter, 82% in top half
Early decision deadline: N/A, notification date: N/A
Early action deadline: N/A, notification date: N/A
Application deadline (fall): rolling
Undergraduate student body: 4,178 full time, 1,812 part time; 36% male, 64% female; 20% American Indian, 2% Asian, 5% black, 7% Hispanic, 16% multiracial, 0% Pacific Islander, 48% white, 2% international; 95% from in state; 17% live on campus; 9% of students in fraternities, 6% in sororities
Most popular majors: 9% Registered Nursing/Registered Nurse, 8% Criminal Justice/Law Enforcement Administration, 8% Research and Experimental Psychology, Other, 6% General Studies, 5% Kinesiology and Exercise Science
Expenses: 2021-2022: $6,915 in state, $15,315 out of state; room/board: $8,074

Financial aid: (918) 444-3410; 68% of undergrads determined to have financial need; average aid package $13,900

Northwestern Oklahoma State University
Alva OK
(580) 327-8545
U.S. News ranking: Reg. U. (W), second tier
Website: www.nwosu.edu
Admissions email: recruit@nwosu.edu
Public; founded 1897
Freshman admissions: selective; 2020-2021: 1,012 applied, 711 accepted. Either SAT or ACT required. ACT 25/75 percentile: 17-22. High school rank: 13% in top tenth, 32% in top quarter, 63% in top half
Early decision deadline: N/A, notification date: N/A
Early action deadline: N/A, notification date: N/A
Application deadline (fall): rolling
Undergraduate student body: 1,291 full time, 351 part time; 41% male, 59% female; 8% American Indian, 0% Asian, 7% black, 13% Hispanic, 1% multiracial, 0% Pacific Islander, 60% white, 1% international
Most popular majors: 13% Registered Nursing/Registered Nurse, 10% Business Administration and Management, General, 10% Parks, Recreation, Leisure, and Fitness Studies, Other, 9% Agribusiness/Agricultural Business Operations, 9% General Studies
Expenses: 2020-2021: $8,173 in state, $15,286 out of state; room/board: $5,200
Financial aid: N/A

Oklahoma Baptist University
Shawnee OK
(405) 585-5000
U.S. News ranking: Reg. Coll. (W), No. 6
Website: www.okbu.edu
Admissions email: admissions@okbu.edu
Private; founded 1910
Affiliation: Southern Baptist
Freshman admissions: selective; 2020-2021: 3,239 applied, 1,891 accepted. Either SAT or ACT required. ACT 25/75 percentile: 20-26. High school rank: 29% in top tenth, 58% in top quarter, 87% in top half
Early decision deadline: N/A, notification date: N/A
Early action deadline: N/A, notification date: N/A
Application deadline (fall): 8/1
Undergraduate student body: 1,590 full time, 57 part time; 41% male, 59% female; N/A American Indian, N/A Asian, N/A black, N/A Hispanic, N/A multiracial, N/A Pacific Islander, N/A white, N/A international
Most popular majors: Information not available
Expenses: 2021-2022: $32,050; room/board: $7,940

Financial aid: (405) 585-5020; 75% of undergrads determined to have financial need; average aid package $23,496

Oklahoma Christian University
Oklahoma City OK
(405) 425-5050
U.S. News ranking: Reg. U. (W), No. 46
Website: www.oc.edu/
Admissions email: admissions@oc.edu
Private; founded 1950
Affiliation: Churches of Christ
Freshman admissions: more selective; 2020-2021: 2,186 applied, 1,338 accepted. Either SAT or ACT required. ACT 25/75 percentile: 20-27. High school rank: N/A
Early decision deadline: N/A, notification date: N/A
Early action deadline: N/A, notification date: N/A
Application deadline (fall): rolling
Undergraduate student body: 1,547 full time, 151 part time; 48% male, 52% female; 2% American Indian, 1% Asian, 6% black, 7% Hispanic, 8% multiracial, 0% Pacific Islander, 71% white, 5% international; 46% from in state; 76% live on campus; 25% of students in fraternities, 36% in sororities
Most popular majors: 14% Health Professions and Related Programs, 12% Business, Management, Marketing, and Related Support Services, 11% Engineering, 8% Liberal Arts and Sciences, General Studies and Humanities, 7% Computer and Information Sciences and Support Services
Expenses: 2021-2022: $24,990; room/board: $7,900
Financial aid: (405) 425-5190; 69% of undergrads determined to have financial need; average aid package $27,653

Oklahoma City University[7]
Oklahoma City OK
(405) 208-5050
U.S. News ranking: Nat. U., No. 239
Website: www.okcu.edu
Admissions email: uadmissions@okcu.edu
Private; founded 1904
Affiliation: United Methodist
Freshman admissions: selective; 2020-2021: 1,788 applied, 1,295 accepted. Either SAT or ACT required. ACT 25/75 percentile: 22-29. High school rank: N/A
Early decision deadline: N/A, notification date: N/A
Early action deadline: N/A, notification date: N/A
Application deadline (fall): rolling
Undergraduate student body: 1,478 full time, 48 part time
Most popular majors: 20% Liberal Arts and Sciences, General Studies and Humanities, 16% Business, Management, Marketing, and Related Support Services

Expenses: 2021-2022: $32,744; room/board: $11,136
Financial aid: (405) 208-5210; 61% of undergrads determined to have financial need; average aid package $23,838

Oklahoma Panhandle State University

Goodwell OK
(580) 349-1373
U.S. News ranking: Reg. Coll. (W), No. 24
Website: www.opsu.edu
Admissions email: academicrecords@opsu.edu
Public; founded 1909
Freshman admissions: less selective; 2020-2021: 1,445 applied, 1,344 accepted. Neither SAT nor ACT required. ACT 25/75 percentile: 14-23. High school rank: 8% in top tenth, 28% in top quarter, 60% in top half
Early decision deadline: N/A, notification date: N/A
Early action deadline: N/A, notification date: N/A
Application deadline (fall): rolling
Undergraduate student body: 1,011 full time, 326 part time; 45% male, 55% female; 7% American Indian, 1% Asian, 10% black, 26% Hispanic, 2% multiracial, 0% Pacific Islander, 49% white, 4% international; 57% from in state; N/A live on campus; N/A of students in fraternities, N/A in sororities
Most popular majors: Information not available
Expenses: 2021-2022: $7,665 in state, $7,665 out of state; room/board: $5,972
Financial aid: (580) 349-1580; 49% of undergrads determined to have financial need

Oklahoma State University

Stillwater OK
(405) 744-5358
U.S. News ranking: Nat. U., No. 187
Website: go.okstate.edu
Admissions email: admissions@okstate.edu
Public; founded 1890
Freshman admissions: more selective; 2020-2021: 17,164 applied, 11,515 accepted. Neither SAT nor ACT required. ACT 25/75 percentile: 21-27. High school rank: 29% in top tenth, 57% in top quarter, 85% in top half
Early decision deadline: N/A, notification date: N/A
Early action deadline: N/A, notification date: N/A
Application deadline (fall): rolling
Undergraduate student body: 17,583 full time, 2,724 part time; 49% male, 51% female; 4% American Indian, 2% Asian, 4% black, 9% Hispanic, 10% multiracial, 0% Pacific Islander, 68% white, 3% international; 72% from in state; 25% live on campus; 20% of students in fraternities, 25% in sororities
Most popular majors: 25% Business, Management, Marketing, and Related Support Services, 13% Engineering,

10% Agriculture, Agriculture Operations, and Related Sciences, 7% Biological and Biomedical Sciences, 5% Liberal Arts and Sciences, General Studies and Humanities
Expenses: 2021-2022: $9,019 in state, $24,539 out of state; room/board: $9,106
Financial aid: (405) 744-6604; 53% of undergrads determined to have financial need; average aid package $15,922

Oklahoma State University Institute of Technology–Okmulgee

Okmulgee OK
(918) 293-4680
U.S. News ranking: Reg. Coll. (W), No. 31
Website: osuit.edu/admissions
Admissions email: osuit.admissions@okstate.edu
Public; founded 1946
Freshman admissions: less selective; 2020-2021: 2,049 applied, 911 accepted. Neither SAT nor ACT required. ACT 25/75 percentile: 15-20. High school rank: 8% in top tenth, 25% in top quarter, 58% in top half
Early decision deadline: N/A, notification date: N/A
Early action deadline: N/A, notification date: N/A
Application deadline (fall): rolling
Undergraduate student body: 1,447 full time, 884 part time; 66% male, 34% female; 13% American Indian, 1% Asian, 4% black, 8% Hispanic, 14% multiracial, 0% Pacific Islander, 55% white, 1% international; 94% from in state; 26% live on campus; 0% of students in fraternities, 0% in sororities
Most popular majors: 62% Information Technology, 38% Instrumentation Technology/Technician
Expenses: 2021-2022: $5,774 in state, $11,384 out of state; room/board: $7,100
Financial aid: (918) 293-5222; 71% of undergrads determined to have financial need; average aid package $10,618

Oklahoma State University–Oklahoma City[1]

Oklahoma City OK
(405) 945-3224
U.S. News ranking: Reg. Coll. (W), unranked
Website: www.osuokc.edu/
Admissions email: admissions@osuokc.edu
Public; founded 1961
Application deadline (fall): rolling
Undergraduate student body: N/A full time, N/A part time
Expenses: 2020-2021: $5,070 in state, $10,908 out of state; room/board: N/A
Financial aid: (405) 945-3211

Oklahoma Wesleyan University[1]

Bartlesville OK
(866) 222-8226
U.S. News ranking: Reg. U. (W), second tier
Website: www.okwu.edu
Admissions email: admissions@okwu.edu
Private; founded 1972
Affiliation: Wesleyan
Application deadline (fall): rolling
Undergraduate student body: N/A full time, N/A part time
Expenses: 2020-2021: $28,924; room/board: $8,596
Financial aid: (918) 335-6282

Oral Roberts University

Tulsa OK
(800) 678-8876
U.S. News ranking: Reg. Coll. (W), No. 7
Website: www.oru.edu
Admissions email: admissions@oru.edu
Private; founded 1963
Affiliation: Interdenominational
Freshman admissions: selective; 2020-2021: 3,959 applied, 3,103 accepted. Either SAT or ACT required. ACT 25/75 percentile: 18-27. High school rank: 22% in top tenth, 43% in top quarter, 74% in top half
Early decision deadline: N/A, notification date: N/A
Early action deadline: N/A, notification date: N/A
Application deadline (fall): rolling
Undergraduate student body: 2,670 full time, 999 part time; 39% male, 61% female; 2% American Indian, 2% Asian, 13% black, 11% Hispanic, 3% multiracial, 0% Pacific Islander, 44% white, 10% international; 59% from in state; 54% live on campus; 0% of students in fraternities, 0% in sororities
Most popular majors: 25% Business, Management, Marketing, and Related Support Services, 16% Theology and Religious Vocations, 8% Visual and Performing Arts, 7% Communication, Journalism, and Related Programs, 7% Health Professions and Related Programs
Expenses: 2021-2022: $31,558; room/board: $8,850
Financial aid: (918) 495-6510; 68% of undergrads determined to have financial need; average aid package $28,270

Rogers State University

Claremore OK
(918) 343-7546
U.S. News ranking: Reg. Coll. (W), No. 25
Website: www.rsu.edu/
Admissions email: admissions@rsu.edu
Public; founded 1909
Freshman admissions: less selective; 2020-2021: 1,226 applied, 1,056 accepted. Either SAT or ACT required. ACT 25/75 percentile: 17-20. High school rank: 16% in top tenth, 19% in

top quarter, 64% in top half
Early decision deadline: N/A, notification date: N/A
Early action deadline: N/A, notification date: N/A
Application deadline (fall): rolling
Undergraduate student body: 2,190 full time, 1,181 part time; 37% male, 63% female; 13% American Indian, 1% Asian, 4% black, 7% Hispanic, 17% multiracial, 0% Pacific Islander, 55% white, 2% international; N/A from in state; 18% live on campus; N/A of students in fraternities, N/A in sororities
Most popular majors: 22% Business Administration and Management, General, 12% Biology/Biological Sciences, General, 10% Registered Nursing/Registered Nurse, 9% Sport and Fitness Administration/Management, 8% Social Sciences, General
Expenses: 2021-2022: $7,470 in state, $15,810 out of state; room/board: $8,975
Financial aid: (918) 343-7553; 74% of undergrads determined to have financial need; average aid package $9,560

Southeastern Oklahoma State University[1]

Durant OK
(580) 745-2060
U.S. News ranking: Reg. U. (W), second tier
Website: www.se.edu
Admissions email: admissions@se.edu
Public; founded 1909
Affiliation: Other
Application deadline (fall): rolling
Undergraduate student body: N/A full time, N/A part time
Expenses: 2020-2021: $6,750 in state, $15,390 out of state; room/board: $6,800
Financial aid: (580) 745-2186

Southern Nazarene University

Bethany OK
(405) 491-6324
U.S. News ranking: Reg. U. (W), No. 64
Website: www.snu.edu
Admissions email: admissions@snu.edu
Private; founded 1899
Affiliation: Church of the Nazarene
Freshman admissions: selective; 2020-2021: 688 applied, 278 accepted. Either SAT or ACT required. ACT 25/75 percentile: 18-23. High school rank: 16% in top tenth, 34% in top quarter, 73% in top half
Early decision deadline: N/A, notification date: N/A
Early action deadline: N/A, notification date: N/A
Application deadline (fall): N/A
Undergraduate student body: 1,287 full time, 242 part time; 47% male, 53% female; 3% American Indian, 2% Asian, 16% black, 16% Hispanic, 7% multiracial, 0% Pacific Islander, 55% white, 2% international; 73% from in

state; 37% live on campus; N/A of students in fraternities, N/A in sororities
Most popular majors: 22% Business Administration and Management, General, 22% Organizational Behavior Studies, 9% Human Development and Family Studies, General, 8% General Studies, 6% Registered Nursing/Registered Nurse
Expenses: 2021-2022: $27,000; room/board: $8,400
Financial aid: (405) 491-6310; 73% of undergrads determined to have financial need; average aid package $18,547

Southwestern Christian University

Bethany OK
(405) 789-7661
U.S. News ranking: Reg. Coll. (W), No. 33
Website: www.swcu.edu/
Admissions email: admissions@swcu.edu
Private; founded 1946
Affiliation: Pentecostal Holiness Church
Freshman admissions: selective; 2020-2021: 422 applied, 136 accepted. Either SAT or ACT required. ACT 25/75 percentile: 16-20. High school rank: N/A
Early decision deadline: N/A, notification date: N/A
Early action deadline: N/A, notification date: N/A
Application deadline (fall): rolling
Undergraduate student body: 407 full time, 50 part time; 54% male, 46% female; 6% American Indian, 0% Asian, 20% black, 11% Hispanic, 6% multiracial, 2% Pacific Islander, 42% white, 12% international; 67% from in state; N/A live on campus; 0% of students in fraternities, 2% in sororities
Most popular majors: 20% Sport and Fitness Administration/Management, 14% Business Administration and Management, General, 14% Kinesiology and Exercise Science, 8% Public Administration and Social Service Professions, 7% Bible/Biblical Studies
Expenses: 2021-2022: $22,108; room/board: $8,900
Financial aid: (405) 789-7661; 71% of undergrads determined to have financial need; average aid package $5,500

Southwestern Oklahoma State University

Weatherford OK
(580) 774-3782
U.S. News ranking: Reg. U. (W), No. 82
Website: www.swosu.edu
Admissions email: admissions@swosu.edu
Public; founded 1901
Freshman admissions: selective; 2020-2021: 2,132 applied, 1,987 accepted. Neither SAT nor ACT required. ACT 25/75 percentile: 18-23. High school rank: 22% in top tenth, 43% in

top quarter, 74% in top half
Early decision deadline: N/A,
notification date: N/A,
Early action deadline: N/A,
notification date: N/A
Application deadline (fall): rolling
Undergraduate student body: 3,234
full time, 787 part time; 40%
male, 60% female; 4% American
Indian, 2% Asian, 5% black,
12% Hispanic, 10% multiracial,
0% Pacific Islander, 63% white,
3% international; 92% from in
state; 29% live on campus; 1%
of students in fraternities, 2% in
sororities
Most popular majors: 24%
Registered Nursing/Registered
Nurse, 12% Business
Administration and Management,
General, 10% Pharmaceutical
Sciences, 4% Elementary
Education and Teaching, 4%
Parks, Recreation and Leisure
Facilities Management, General
Expenses: 2020-2021: $7,913 in
state, $15,023 out of state; room/
board: $6,230
Financial aid: (580) 774-3786

University of Central Oklahoma
Edmond OK
(405) 974-2727
U.S. News ranking: Reg. U. (W),
No. 71
Website: www.uco.edu/
Admissions email:
onestop@uco.edu
Public; founded 1890
Freshman admissions: selective;
2020-2021: 4,540 applied,
3,685 accepted. Either SAT
or ACT required. ACT 25/75
percentile: 19-24. High school
rank: 18% in top tenth, 41% in
top quarter, 74% in top half
Early decision deadline: N/A,
notification date: N/A
Early action deadline: N/A,
notification date: N/A
Application deadline (fall): rolling
Undergraduate student body: 9,205
full time, 3,456 part time; 38%
male, 62% female; 3% American
Indian, 4% Asian, 9% black, 13%
Hispanic, 11% multiracial, 0%
Pacific Islander, 53% white, 3%
international
Most popular majors: 8% General
Studies, 6% Forensic Science
and Technology, 6% Psychology,
General, 5% Registered Nursing/
Registered Nurse, 4% Finance,
General
Expenses: 2021-2022: $8,030 in
state, $18,917 out of state; room/
board: N/A
Financial aid: (405) 974-2727;
63% of undergrads determined to
have financial need; average aid
package $8,965

University of Oklahoma
Norman OK
(405) 325-2251
U.S. News ranking: Nat. U.,
No. 127
Website: www.ou.edu
Admissions email:
admissions@ou.edu
Public; founded 1890

Freshman admissions: more
selective; 2020-2021: 15,451
applied, 12,883 accepted. Neither
SAT nor ACT required. ACT 25/75
percentile: 23-29. High school
rank: 31% in top tenth, 62% in
top quarter, 91% in top half
Early decision deadline: N/A,
notification date: N/A
Early action deadline: 11/1,
notification date: N/A
Application deadline (fall): 2/1
Undergraduate student body:
18,534 full time, 2,849 part
time; 49% male, 51% female;
3% American Indian, 7% Asian,
5% black, 11% Hispanic, 9%
multiracial, 0% Pacific Islander,
60% white, 3% international;
61% from in state; 29% live
on campus; 30% of students in
fraternities, 37% in sororities
Most popular majors: 24%
Business, Management,
Marketing, and Related Support
Services, 13% Engineering, 9%
Communication, Journalism, and
Related Programs, 7% Liberal Arts
and Sciences, General Studies and
Humanities, 6% Social Sciences
Expenses: 2021-2022: $9,312 in
state, $25,116 out of state; room/
board: $11,700
Financial aid: (405) 325-9000;
47% of undergrads determined to
have financial need; average aid
package $15,275

University of Science and Arts of Oklahoma
Chickasha OK
(405) 574-1357
U.S. News ranking: Nat. Lib. Arts,
second tier
Website: www.usao.edu
Admissions email:
usao-admissions@usao.edu
Public; founded 1908
Freshman admissions: selective;
2020-2021: 1,021 applied, 134
accepted. Neither SAT nor ACT
required. ACT 25/75 percentile:
19-24. High school rank: N/A
Early decision deadline: N/A,
notification date: N/A
Early action deadline: N/A,
notification date: N/A
Application deadline (fall): 8/30
Undergraduate student body: 661
full time, 55 part time; 35%
male, 65% female; N/A American
Indian, N/A Asian, N/A black, N/A
Hispanic, N/A multiracial, N/A
Pacific Islander, N/A white, N/A
international
Most popular majors: Information
not available
Expenses: 2021-2022: $8,040 in
state, $18,900 out of state; room/
board: $6,360
Financial aid: (405) 574-1350;
67% of undergrads determined to
have financial need; average aid
package $13,129

University of Tulsa
Tulsa OK
(918) 631-2307
U.S. News ranking: Nat. U.,
No. 136
Website: utulsa.edu
Admissions email:
admission@utulsa.edu
Private; founded 1894

Affiliation: Presbyterian Church
(USA)
Freshman admissions: more
selective; 2020-2021: 5,815
applied, 4,025 accepted. Neither
SAT nor ACT required. ACT 25/75
percentile: 23-31. High school
rank: 48% in top tenth, 77% in
top quarter, 93% in top half
Early decision deadline: N/A,
notification date: N/A
Early action deadline: N/A,
notification date: N/A
Application deadline (fall): rolling
Undergraduate student body: 2,819
full time, 110 part time; 52%
male, 48% female; 3% American
Indian, 6% Asian, 7% black, 9%
Hispanic, 10% multiracial, 0%
Pacific Islander, 53% white, 9%
international; 57% from in state;
62% live on campus; 19% of
students in fraternities, 21% in
sororities
Most popular majors: 9%
Mechanical Engineering, 6%
Computer Science, 6% Petroleum
Engineering, 5% Kinesiology and
Exercise Science, 4% Psychology,
General
Expenses: 2021-2022: $44,838;
room/board: $12,422
Financial aid: (918) 631-2670;
57% of undergrads determined to
have financial need; average aid
package $40,390

OREGON

Bushnell University
Eugene OR
(541) 684-7201
U.S. News ranking: Reg. U. (W),
No. 84
Website: www.bushnell.edu/
Admissions email:
admissions@bushnell.edu
Private; founded 1895
Affiliation: Christian Church
(Disciples of Christ)
Freshman admissions: selective;
2020-2021: 415 applied, 283
accepted. Neither SAT nor ACT
required. SAT 25/75 percentile:
1023-1186. High school rank:
N/A
Early decision deadline: N/A,
notification date: N/A
Early action deadline: N/A,
notification date: N/A
Application deadline (fall): rolling
Undergraduate student body: 426
full time, 113 part time; 39%
male, 61% female; 3% American
Indian, 4% Asian, 4% black,
5% Hispanic, 9% multiracial,
2% Pacific Islander, 68% white,
3% international; 38% from in
state; 56% live on campus; N/A
of students in fraternities, N/A in
sororities
Most popular majors: 16%
Business/Commerce, General,
15% Nursing Administration,
12% Elementary Education
and Teaching, 12% Multi-/
Interdisciplinary Studies, Other,
8% Psychology, General
Expenses: 2021-2022: $32,320;
room/board: $10,190
Financial aid: (541) 684-7201;
80% of undergrads determined to
have financial need; average aid
package $24,152

Corban University
Salem OR
(800) 845-3005
U.S. News ranking: Reg. Coll. (W),
No. 12
Website: www.corban.edu
Admissions email:
admissions@corban.edu
Private; founded 1935
Affiliation: Evangelical Christian
Freshman admissions: selective;
2020-2021: 1,924 applied, 930
accepted. Neither SAT nor ACT
required. SAT 25/75 percentile:
975-1185. High school rank:
23% in top tenth, 35% in top
quarter, 83% in top half
Early decision deadline: N/A,
notification date: N/A
Early action deadline: N/A,
notification date: N/A
Application deadline (fall): 8/1
Undergraduate student body: 881
full time, 69 part time; 42%
male, 58% female; 1% American
Indian, 2% Asian, 3% black, 10%
Hispanic, 6% multiracial, 1%
Pacific Islander, 68% white, 2%
international
Most popular majors: 22%
Business, Management,
Marketing, and Related Support
Services, 12% Education, 12%
Psychology, 8% English Language
and Literature/Letters, 8% Multi/
Interdisciplinary Studies
Expenses: 2020-2021: $34,188;
room/board: $10,463
Financial aid: (503) 375-7106

Eastern Oregon University
La Grande OR
(541) 962-3393
U.S. News ranking: Reg. U. (W),
No. 92
Website: www.eou.edu
Admissions email:
admissions@eou.edu
Public; founded 1929
Freshman admissions: selective;
2020-2021: 644 applied, 607
accepted. Neither SAT nor ACT
required. SAT 25/75 percentile:
930-1145. High school rank:
16% in top tenth, 40% in top
quarter, 73% in top half
Early decision deadline: N/A,
notification date: N/A
Early action deadline: 2/1,
notification date: N/A
Application deadline (fall): 9/1
Undergraduate student body: 1,517
full time, 1,028 part time; 40%
male, 60% female; 2% American
Indian, 1% Asian, 2% black, 14%
Hispanic, 5% multiracial, 3%
Pacific Islander, 67% white, 1%
international
Most popular majors: 29%
Business, Management,
Marketing, and Related Support
Services, 14% Education, 8%
Multi/Interdisciplinary Studies, 8%
Social Sciences, 6% Homeland
Security, Law Enforcement,
Firefighting and Related Protective
Services
Expenses: 2021-2022: $9,696 in
state, $22,386 out of state; room/
board: $10,600
Financial aid: (541) 962-3550;
71% of undergrads determined to
have financial need; average aid
package $10,786

George Fox University
Newberg OR
(800) 765-4369
U.S. News ranking: Nat. U.,
No. 213
Website: www.georgefox.edu
Admissions email:
admissions@georgefox.edu
Private; founded 1891
Affiliation: Friends
Freshman admissions: selective;
2020-2021: 2,684 applied,
2,440 accepted. Neither SAT
nor ACT required. SAT 25/75
percentile: 1020-1240. High
school rank: 32% in top tenth,
61% in top quarter, 85% in
top half
Early decision deadline: N/A,
notification date: N/A
Early action deadline: 11/1,
notification date: 12/9
Application deadline (fall): rolling
Undergraduate student body: 2,260
full time, 213 part time; 40%
male, 60% female; 0% American
Indian, 5% Asian, 1% black,
14% Hispanic, 8% multiracial,
1% Pacific Islander, 70% white,
1% international; 60% from in
state; 49% live on campus; 0%
of students in fraternities, 0% in
sororities
Most popular majors: 16%
Registered Nursing, Nursing
Administration, Nursing
Research and Clinical Nursing,
10% Business Administration,
Management and Operations, 7%
Engineering, General, 7% Teacher
Education and Professional
Development, Specific Levels and
Methods, 6% Psychology, General
Expenses: 2021-2022: $38,520;
room/board: $12,700
Financial aid: (503) 554-2302;
72% of undergrads determined to
have financial need; average aid
package $24,624

Lewis & Clark College
Portland OR
(800) 444-4111
U.S. News ranking: Nat. Lib. Arts,
No. 82
Website: www.lclark.edu
Admissions email:
admissions@lclark.edu
Private; founded 1867
Freshman admissions: more
selective; 2020-2021: 5,402
applied, 4,353 accepted. Neither
SAT nor ACT required. SAT
25/75 percentile: 1198-1380.
High school rank: 29% in top
tenth, 60% in top quarter, 91%
in top half
Early decision deadline: 11/1,
notification date: 12/15
Early action deadline: 11/1,
notification date: 12/31
Application deadline (fall): 1/15
Undergraduate student body: 1,811
full time, 19 part time; 38%
male, 62% female; 0% American
Indian, 4% Asian, 2% black,
13% Hispanic, 9% multiracial,
0% Pacific Islander, 65% white,
4% international; 11% from in
state; 55% live on campus; 0%
of students in fraternities, 0% in
sororities
Most popular majors: 26% Social
Sciences, 14% Psychology,
11% Biological and Biomedical

Sciences, 8% Visual and
Performing Arts, 6% English
Language and Literature/Letters
Expenses: 2021-2022: $57,404;
room/board: $13,946
Financial aid: (503) 768-7090;
59% of undergrads determined to
have financial need; average aid
package $47,584

Linfield University
McMinnville OR
(800) 640-2287
U.S. News ranking: Nat. Lib. Arts,
No. 117
Website: www.linfield.edu
Admissions email:
admission@linfield.edu
Private; founded 1858
Affiliation: American Baptist
Freshman admissions: selective;
2020-2021: 2,250 applied,
1,804 accepted. Neither SAT
nor ACT required. SAT 25/75
percentile: 1050-1210. High
school rank: N/A
Early decision deadline: N/A,
notification date: N/A
Early action deadline: 11/1,
notification date: 1/15
Application deadline (fall): rolling
Undergraduate student body: 1,365
full time, 27 part time; 38%
male, 62% female; 1% American
Indian, 6% Asian, 2% black,
20% Hispanic, 8% multiracial,
1% Pacific Islander, 61% white,
1% international; 62% from in
state; 74% live on campus; 27%
of students in fraternities, 30%
in sororities
Most popular majors: 46% Health
Professions and Related Programs,
16% Business, Management,
Marketing, and Related Support
Services, 5% Education, 5%
Social Sciences, 4% Biological
and Biomedical Sciences
Expenses: 2021-2022: $45,962;
room/board: $13,200
Financial aid: (503) 883-2225;
77% of undergrads determined to
have financial need; average aid
package $37,798

Oregon State University
Corvallis OR
(541) 737-4411
U.S. News ranking: Nat. U.,
No. 162
Website: oregonstate.edu
Admissions email:
osuadmit@oregonstate.edu
Public; founded 1868
Freshman admissions: more
selective; 2020-2021: 17,500
applied, 14,631 accepted. Neither
SAT nor ACT required. SAT
25/75 percentile: 1080-1310.
High school rank: 28% in top
tenth, 55% in top quarter, 87%
in top half
Early decision deadline: N/A,
notification date: N/A
Early action deadline: 11/1,
notification date: 12/15
Application deadline (fall): 9/1
Undergraduate student body:
18,084 full time, 8,560 part
time; 52% male, 48% female;
1% American Indian, 8% Asian,
2% black, 12% Hispanic, 7%
multiracial, 0% Pacific Islander,

62% white, 6% international
Most popular majors: Information
not available
Expenses: 2021-2022: $12,188
in state, $32,288 out of state;
room/board: $14,760
Financial aid: (541) 737-2241;
50% of undergrads determined to
have financial need; average aid
package $12,042

Oregon Tech[1]
Klamath Falls OR
(541) 885-1150
U.S. News ranking: Reg. Coll. (W),
No. 10
Website: www.oit.edu
Admissions email: oit@oit.edu
Public; founded 1947
Application deadline (fall): 9/4
Undergraduate student body: N/A
full time, N/A part time
Expenses: 2020-2021: $11,265
in state, $31,377 out of state;
room/board: $9,936
Financial aid: (541) 885-1280

Pacific Northwest College of Art[1]
Portland OR
(503) 226-4391
U.S. News ranking: Arts, unranked
Website: www.pnca.edu
Admissions email:
admissions@pnca.edu
Private
Application deadline (fall): N/A
Undergraduate student body: N/A
full time, N/A part time
Expenses: 2020-2021: $41,750;
room/board: $15,365
Financial aid: N/A

Pacific University
Forest Grove OR
(503) 352-2218
U.S. News ranking: Nat. U.,
No. 187
Website: www.pacificu.edu
Admissions email:
admissions@pacificu.edu
Private; founded 1849
Freshman admissions: selective;
2020-2021: 2,458 applied,
2,195 accepted. Neither SAT
nor ACT required. SAT 25/75
percentile: 1050-1230. High
school rank: N/A
Early decision deadline: N/A,
notification date: N/A
Early action deadline: N/A,
notification date: N/A
Application deadline (fall): 8/15
Undergraduate student body: 1,687
full time, 71 part time; 36%
male, 64% female; 1% American
Indian, 12% Asian, 2% black,
15% Hispanic, 13% multiracial,
2% Pacific Islander, 46% white,
1% international; N/A from in
state; 53% live on campus; 2%
of students in fraternities, 8% in
sororities
Most popular majors: 16% Health
Professions and Related Programs,
12% Biological and Biomedical
Sciences, 12% Education,
11% Business, Management,
Marketing, and Related Support
Services, 9% Social Sciences
Expenses: 2021-2022: $50,070;
room/board: $13,892

Financial aid: (503) 352-2871;
80% of undergrads determined to
have financial need; average aid
package $43,383

Portland State University
Portland OR
(800) 547-8887
U.S. News ranking: Nat. U.,
No. 288
Website: www.pdx.edu
Admissions email:
admissions@pdx.edu
Public; founded 1946
Freshman admissions: selective;
2020-2021: 6,701 applied,
6,379 accepted. Neither SAT
nor ACT required. SAT 25/75
percentile: 1000-1190. High
school rank: 16% in top tenth,
42% in top quarter, 84% in
top half
Early decision deadline: N/A,
notification date: N/A
Early action deadline: N/A,
notification date: N/A
Application deadline (fall): rolling
Undergraduate student body:
12,753 full time, 6,206 part
time; 44% male, 56% female;
1% American Indian, 10% Asian,
4% black, 19% Hispanic, 7%
multiracial, 1% Pacific Islander,
51% white, 4% international;
15% from in state; 9% live
on campus; 1% of students in
fraternities, 1% in sororities
Most popular majors: 22%
Business, Management,
Marketing, and Related Support
Services, 12% Social Sciences,
7% Health Professions and
Related Programs, 7% Multi/
Interdisciplinary Studies, 7%
Psychology
Expenses: 2021-2022: $8,649 in
state, $23,769 out of state; room/
board: $12,108
Financial aid: (503) 725-3461;
70% of undergrads determined to
have financial need; average aid
package $10,727

Reed College[1]
Portland OR
(503) 777-7511
U.S. News ranking: Nat. Lib. Arts,
No. 62
Website: www.reed.edu/
Admissions email:
admission@reed.edu
Private
Application deadline (fall): N/A
Undergraduate student body: N/A
full time, N/A part time
Expenses: 2020-2021: $60,620;
room/board: $14,980
Financial aid: N/A

Southern Oregon University
Ashland OR
(541) 552-6411
U.S. News ranking: Reg. U. (W),
No. 67
Website: www.sou.edu
Admissions email:
admissions@sou.edu
Public; founded 1926
Freshman admissions: selective;
2020-2021: 2,317 applied,
2,093 accepted. Either SAT

or ACT required. SAT 25/75
percentile: 980-1200. High
school rank: N/A
Early decision deadline: N/A,
notification date: N/A
Early action deadline: N/A,
notification date: N/A
Application deadline (fall): rolling
Undergraduate student body: 2,810
full time, 1,639 part time; 39%
male, 61% female; 2% American
Indian, 1% Asian, 2% black,
11% Hispanic, 9% multiracial,
1% Pacific Islander, 63% white,
1% international; 63% from in
state; 15% live on campus; N/A
of students in fraternities, N/A in
sororities
Most popular majors: 18%
Accounting and Business/
Management, 13% Psychology,
General, 10% Education, General,
7% Drama and Dramatics/
Theatre Arts, General, 7% Speech
Communication and Rhetoric
Expenses: 2020-2021: $10,710
in state, $27,990 out of state;
room/board: $14,629
Financial aid: N/A

University of Oregon
Eugene OR
(800) 232-3825
U.S. News ranking: Nat. U., No. 99
Website: www.uoregon.edu
Admissions email:
uoadmit@uoregon.edu
Public; founded 1876
Freshman admissions: selective;
2020-2021: 28,720 applied,
23,963 accepted. Neither SAT
nor ACT required. SAT 25/75
percentile: 1090-1290. High
school rank: N/A
Early decision deadline: N/A,
notification date: N/A
Early action deadline: 11/1,
notification date: 12/15
Application deadline (fall): 1/15
Undergraduate student body:
16,400 full time, 1,645 part
time; 45% male, 55% female;
1% American Indian, 7% Asian,
3% black, 14% Hispanic, 9%
multiracial, 0% Pacific Islander;
60% white, 5% international;
44% from in state; 17% live
on campus; 15% of students in
fraternities, 17% in sororities
Most popular majors: 11%
Business/Commerce, General,
8% Social Sciences, General,
7% Psychology, General, 6%
Advertising, 6% Economics,
General
Expenses: 2021-2022: $13,856
in state, $39,308 out of state;
room/board: $13,509
Financial aid: (541) 346-3221;
46% of undergrads determined to
have financial need; average aid
package $11,430

University of Portland
Portland OR
(888) 627-5601
U.S. News ranking: Reg. U. (W),
No. 3
Website: www.up.edu
Admissions email:
admissions@up.edu
Private; founded 1901
Affiliation: Roman Catholic

Freshman admissions: selective;
2020-2021: 12,633 applied,
9,700 accepted. Neither SAT
nor ACT required. SAT 25/75
percentile: 1130-1320. High
school rank: N/A
Early decision deadline: N/A,
notification date: N/A
Early action deadline: N/A,
notification date: N/A
Application deadline (fall): 1/15
Undergraduate student body: 3,456
full time, 103 part time; 39%
male, 61% female; 0% American
Indian, 18% Asian, 2% black,
14% Hispanic, 8% multiracial,
1% Pacific Islander, 52% white,
2% international; N/A from in
state; 6% live on campus; N/A
of students in fraternities, N/A in
sororities
Most popular majors: 21% Health
Professions and Related Programs,
13% Biological and Biomedical
Sciences, 12% Engineering,
11% Business, Management,
Marketing, and Related
Support Services, 6% Science
Technologies/Technicians
Expenses: 2021-2022: $49,864;
room/board: $14,608
Financial aid: (503) 943-7311;
55% of undergrads determined to
have financial need; average aid
package $35,791

Warner Pacific University[1]
Portland OR
(503) 517-1020
U.S. News ranking: Reg. Coll. (W),
No. 9
Website: www.warnerpacific.edu
Admissions email:
admissions@warnerpacific.edu
Private; founded 1937
Affiliation: Church of God
Application deadline (fall): rolling
Undergraduate student body: N/A
full time, N/A part time
Expenses: 2021-2022: $19,860;
room/board: $9,432
Financial aid: (503) 517-1091;
84% of undergrads determined to
have financial need; average aid
package $16,022

Western Oregon University
Monmouth OR
(503) 838-8211
U.S. News ranking: Reg. U. (W),
No. 55
Website: www.wou.edu
Admissions email:
wolfgram@wou.edu
Public; founded 1856
Freshman admissions: selective;
2020-2021: 3,566 applied,
2,822 accepted. Neither SAT
nor ACT required. SAT 25/75
percentile: 950-1200. High school
rank: 23% in top tenth, 42% in
top quarter, 66% in top half
Early decision deadline: N/A,
notification date: N/A
Early action deadline: N/A,
notification date: N/A
Application deadline (fall): rolling
Undergraduate student body: 3,449
full time, 621 part time; 36%
male, 64% female; 1% American
Indian, 3% Asian, 3% black,
21% Hispanic, 5% multiracial,

2% Pacific Islander, 59% white, 3% international; 81% from in state; 25% live on campus; 1% of students in fraternities, 1% in sororities
Most popular majors: 16% Education, 12% Multi/Interdisciplinary Studies, 10% Business, Management, Marketing, and Related Support Services, 10% Psychology, 8% Homeland Security, Law Enforcement, Firefighting and Related Protective Services
Expenses: 2020-2021: $10,194 in state, $29,004 out of state; room/board: $10,802
Financial aid: (503) 838-8679; 74% of undergrads determined to have financial need; average aid package $10,774

Willamette University
Salem OR
(503) 370-6303
U.S. News ranking: Nat. Lib. Arts, No. 71
Website: www.willamette.edu
Admissions email: bearcat@willamette.edu
Private; founded 1842
Affiliation: United Methodist
Freshman admissions: more selective; 2020-2021: 4,010 applied, 3,215 accepted. Neither SAT nor ACT required. SAT 25/75 percentile: 1130-1360. High school rank: 46% in top tenth, 81% in top quarter, 97% in top half
Early decision deadline: 11/15, notification date: 12/30
Early action deadline: 11/15, notification date: 12/30
Application deadline (fall): 1/15
Undergraduate student body: 1,264 full time, 39 part time; 43% male, 57% female; 1% American Indian, 6% Asian, 2% black, 16% Hispanic, 8% multiracial, 0% Pacific Islander, 62% white, 1% international; 31% from in state; 54% live on campus; 21% of students in fraternities, 16% in sororities
Most popular majors: 9% Economics, General, 8% Environmental Science, 8% Psychology, General, 7% Biology/Biological Sciences, General, 7% Communication and Media Studies, Other
Expenses: 2021-2022: $44,306; room/board: $13,700
Financial aid: (503) 370-6273; 66% of undergrads determined to have financial need; average aid package $34,908

PENNSYLVANIA

Albright College
Reading PA
(800) 252-1856
U.S. News ranking: Nat. Lib. Arts, second tier
Website: www.albright.edu/
Admissions email: admission@albright.edu
Private; founded 1856
Affiliation: United Methodist
Freshman admissions: selective; 2020-2021: 5,373 applied, 4,412 accepted. Neither SAT

nor ACT required. SAT 25/75 percentile: 1000-1190. High school rank: 15% in top tenth, 38% in top quarter, 65% in top half
Early decision deadline: N/A, notification date: N/A
Early action deadline: N/A, notification date: N/A
Application deadline (fall): rolling
Undergraduate student body: 1,464 full time, 73 part time; 42% male, 58% female; 0% American Indian, 2% Asian, 26% black, 17% Hispanic, 4% multiracial, 0% Pacific Islander, 48% white, 1% international; N/A from in state; 73% live on campus; 17% of students in fraternities, 15% in sororities
Most popular majors: 31% Business, Management, Marketing, and Related Support Services, 14% Visual and Performing Arts, 13% Psychology, 11% Social Sciences, 7% Biological and Biomedical Sciences
Expenses: 2021-2022: $27,678; room/board: $13,176
Financial aid: (610) 921-7515; 86% of undergrads determined to have financial need; average aid package $23,309

Allegheny College
Meadville PA
(800) 521-5293
U.S. News ranking: Nat. Lib. Arts, No. 85
Website: allegheny.edu
Admissions email: admissions@allegheny.edu
Private; founded 1815
Affiliation: United Methodist
Freshman admissions: more selective; 2020-2021: 4,380 applied, 3,204 accepted. Neither SAT nor ACT required. SAT 25/75 percentile: 1140-1350. High school rank: 31% in top tenth, 62% in top quarter, 85% in top half
Early decision deadline: 11/1, notification date: 11/15
Early action deadline: 12/1, notification date: 1/1
Application deadline (fall): 2/15
Undergraduate student body: 1,598 full time, 65 part time; 44% male, 56% female; 0% American Indian, 4% Asian, 9% black, 9% Hispanic, 4% multiracial, 0% Pacific Islander, 69% white, 3% international; 52% from in state; 81% live on campus; 21% of students in fraternities, 22% in sororities
Most popular majors: 11% Economics, General, 10% Biology/Biological Sciences, General, 10% Environmental Science, 10% Psychology, General, 8% Speech Communication and Rhetoric
Expenses: 2021-2022: $52,530; room/board: $13,420
Financial aid: (800) 835-7780; 75% of undergrads determined to have financial need; average aid package $45,575

Alvernia University
Reading PA
(610) 796-8269
U.S. News ranking: Reg. U. (N), No. 97
Website: www.alvernia.edu/
Admissions email: admissions@alvernia.edu
Private; founded 1958
Affiliation: Roman Catholic
Freshman admissions: selective; 2020-2021: 3,683 applied, 2,579 accepted. Neither SAT nor ACT required. SAT 25/75 percentile: 940-1130. High school rank: N/A
Early decision deadline: N/A, notification date: N/A
Early action deadline: N/A, notification date: N/A
Application deadline (fall): rolling
Undergraduate student body: 1,655 full time, 390 part time; 32% male, 68% female; 0% American Indian, 2% Asian, 11% black, 13% Hispanic, 3% multiracial, 0% Pacific Islander, 65% white, 2% international; 70% from in state; 57% live on campus; 0% of students in fraternities, 0% in sororities
Most popular majors: 17% Health Professions and Related Clinical Sciences, Other, 16% Registered Nursing/Registered Nurse, 9% Health Professions and Related Programs, 8% Criminal Justice/Law Enforcement Administration, 8% Substance Abuse/Addiction Counseling
Expenses: 2020-2021: $38,030; room/board: $13,280
Financial aid: (610) 796-8356

Arcadia University
Glenside PA
(215) 572-2910
U.S. News ranking: Reg. U. (N), No. 44
Website: www.arcadia.edu
Admissions email: admiss@arcadia.edu
Private; founded 1853
Freshman admissions: selective; 2020-2021: 8,884 applied, 6,541 accepted. Neither SAT nor ACT required. SAT 25/75 percentile: 1030-1230. High school rank: 22% in top tenth, 48% in top quarter, 82% in top half
Early decision deadline: N/A, notification date: N/A
Early action deadline: N/A, notification date: N/A
Application deadline (fall): rolling
Undergraduate student body: 1,769 full time, 245 part time; 32% male, 68% female; 0% American Indian, 6% Asian, 10% black, 11% Hispanic, 5% multiracial, 0% Pacific Islander, 62% white, 2% international
Most popular majors: Information not available
Expenses: 2020-2021: $45,340; room/board: $14,050
Financial aid: (215) 572-2980

Bloomsburg University of Pennsylvania
Bloomsburg PA
(570) 389-4316
U.S. News ranking: Reg. U. (N), No. 119
Website: www.bloomu.edu
Admissions email: buadmiss@bloomu.edu
Public; founded 1839
Freshman admissions: selective; 2020-2021: 7,292 applied, 6,492 accepted. Neither SAT nor ACT required. SAT 25/75 percentile: 960-1150. High school rank: 10% in top tenth, 32% in top quarter, 64% in top half
Early decision deadline: N/A, notification date: N/A
Early action deadline: N/A, notification date: 5/1
Application deadline (fall): rolling
Undergraduate student body: 6,939 full time, 801 part time; 40% male, 60% female; 0% American Indian, 1% Asian, 7% black, 8% Hispanic, 2% multiracial, 0% Pacific Islander, 76% white, 0% international; 91% from in state; 18% live on campus; N/A of students in fraternities, N/A in sororities
Most popular majors: 23% Business, Management, Marketing, and Related Support Services, 13% Health Professions and Related Programs, 10% Homeland Security, Law Enforcement, Firefighting and Related Protective Services, 8% Communication, Journalism, and Related Programs, 8% Education
Expenses: 2021-2022: $10,958 in state, $22,532 out of state; room/board: $10,528
Financial aid: (570) 389-4297; 64% of undergrads determined to have financial need; average aid package $9,580

Bryn Athyn College of the New Church[7]
Bryn Athyn PA
(267) 502-6000
U.S. News ranking: Nat. Lib. Arts, second tier
Website: www.brynathyn.edu
Admissions email: admissions@brynathyn.edu
Private; founded 1877
Affiliation: Other
Freshman admissions: less selective; 2020-2021: 350 applied, 272 accepted. Either SAT or ACT required. SAT 25/75 percentile: 930-1198. High school rank: N/A
Early decision deadline: N/A, notification date: N/A
Early action deadline: N/A, notification date: N/A
Application deadline (fall): rolling
Undergraduate student body: 257 full time, 15 part time
Most popular majors: 30% Biological and Biomedical Sciences, 23% Business, Management, Marketing, and Related Support Services, 23% Psychology, 11% Education, 7% Social Sciences

Expenses: 2021-2022: $26,214; room/board: $12,984
Financial aid: (267) 502-6000

Bryn Mawr College
Bryn Mawr PA
(610) 526-5152
U.S. News ranking: Nat. Lib. Arts, No. 30
Website: www.brynmawr.edu
Admissions email: admissions@brynmawr.edu
Private; founded 1885
Freshman admissions: most selective; 2020-2021: 3,311 applied, 1,270 accepted. Neither SAT nor ACT required. SAT 25/75 percentile: 1240-1500. High school rank: 66% in top tenth, 93% in top quarter, 99% in top half
Early decision deadline: 11/15, notification date: 12/20
Early action deadline: N/A, notification date: N/A
Application deadline (fall): 1/15
Undergraduate student body: 1,297 full time, 3 part time; 0% male, 100% female; 0% American Indian, 12% Asian, 5% black, 10% Hispanic, 5% multiracial, 0% Pacific Islander, 46% white, 19% international
Most popular majors: 26% Social Sciences, 10% Foreign Languages, Literatures, and Linguistics, 10% Mathematics and Statistics, 9% Psychology, 8% Multi/Interdisciplinary Studies
Expenses: 2021-2022: $56,320; room/board: $17,370
Financial aid: (610) 526-5245; 49% of undergrads determined to have financial need; average aid package $53,032

Bucknell University
Lewisburg PA
(570) 577-3000
U.S. News ranking: Nat. Lib. Arts, No. 38
Website: www.bucknell.edu
Admissions email: admissions@bucknell.edu
Private; founded 1846
Freshman admissions: more selective; 2020-2021: 9,890 applied, 3,712 accepted. Neither SAT nor ACT required. SAT 25/75 percentile: 1220-1400. High school rank: 54% in top tenth, 90% in top quarter, 98% in top half
Early decision deadline: 11/15, notification date: 12/15
Early action deadline: N/A, notification date: N/A
Application deadline (fall): 1/15
Undergraduate student body: 3,686 full time, 9 part time; 48% male, 52% female; 0% American Indian, 5% Asian, 4% black, 7% Hispanic, 4% multiracial, 0% Pacific Islander, 75% white, 5% international; 23% from in state; 91% live on campus; 34% of students in fraternities, 38% in sororities
Most popular majors: 9% Political Science and Government, General, 7% Accounting and Finance, 7% Biology/Biological Sciences, General, 7% Economics, General, 5% Mechanical Engineering

Expenses: 2021-2022: $59,802; room/board: $14,874
Financial aid: (570) 577-1331; 40% of undergrads determined to have financial need; average aid package $39,000

Cabrini University[1]
Radnor PA
(610) 902-8552
U.S. News ranking: Reg. U. (N), second tier
Website: www.cabrini.edu
Admissions email: admit@cabrini.edu
Private; founded 1957
Affiliation: Roman Catholic
Application deadline (fall): 9/5
Undergraduate student body: N/A full time, N/A part time
Expenses: 2020-2021: $33,845; room/board: $12,965
Financial aid: (610) 902-8424

Cairn University[1]
Langhorne PA
(215) 702-4235
U.S. News ranking: Reg. U. (N), second tier
Website: cairn.edu/
Admissions email: admissions@cairn.edu
Private; founded 1913
Affiliation: Undenominational
Application deadline (fall): rolling
Undergraduate student body: N/A full time, N/A part time
Expenses: 2020-2021: $29,853; room/board: $11,187
Financial aid: (215) 702-4243

California University of Pennsylvania
California PA
(724) 938-4404
U.S. News ranking: Reg. U. (N), second tier
Website: www.calu.edu/
Admissions email: admissions@calu.edu
Public; founded 1852
Affiliation: Episcopal Church, Reformed
Freshman admissions: less selective; 2020-2021: 3,805 applied, 3,589 accepted. Neither SAT nor ACT required. SAT 25/75 percentile: 920-1120. High school rank: 7% in top tenth, 26% in top quarter, 60% in top half
Early decision deadline: N/A, notification date: N/A
Early action deadline: N/A, notification date: N/A
Application deadline (fall): 8/21
Undergraduate student body: 3,863 full time, 922 part time; 44% male, 56% female; 0% American Indian, 1% Asian, 12% black, 4% Hispanic, 4% multiracial, 0% Pacific Islander, 76% white, 1% international; 89% from in state; 7% live on campus; 4% of students in fraternities, 7% in sororities
Most popular majors: 18% Health Professions and Related Programs, 11% Business, Management, Marketing, and Related Support Services, 10% Parks, Recreation, Leisure, and Fitness Studies, 8% Homeland Security, Law Enforcement, Firefighting and

Related Protective Services, 6% Social Sciences
Expenses: 2021-2022: $11,108 in state, $14,966 out of state; room/board: $10,416
Financial aid: (724) 938-4415; 79% of undergrads determined to have financial need; average aid package $10,928

Carlow University
Pittsburgh PA
(412) 578-6059
U.S. News ranking: Reg. U. (N), No. 70
Website: www.carlow.edu
Admissions email: admissions@carlow.edu
Private; founded 1929
Affiliation: Roman Catholic
Freshman admissions: selective; 2020-2021: 635 applied, 599 accepted. Either SAT or ACT required. SAT 25/75 percentile: 980-1140. High school rank: 16% in top tenth, 32% in top quarter, 60% in top half
Early decision deadline: N/A, notification date: N/A
Early action deadline: N/A, notification date: N/A
Application deadline (fall): rolling
Undergraduate student body: 1,009 full time, 268 part time; 56% male, 44% female; 0% American Indian, 3% Asian, 16% black, 3% Hispanic, 4% multiracial, 0% Pacific Islander, 71% white, 0% international; 94% from in state; 20% live on campus; 0% of students in fraternities, N/A in sororities
Most popular majors: 49% Health Professions and Related Programs, 11% Biological and Biomedical Sciences, 8% Business, Management, Marketing, and Related Support Services, 8% Psychology, 5% Education
Expenses: 2020-2021: $31,446; room/board: $12,260
Financial aid: (412) 578-6171

Carnegie Mellon University
Pittsburgh PA
(412) 268-2082
U.S. News ranking: Nat. U., No. 25
Website: www.cmu.edu
Admissions email: admission@andrew.cmu.edu
Private; founded 1900
Freshman admissions: most selective; 2020-2021: 26,189 applied, 4,524 accepted. Neither SAT nor ACT required. SAT 25/75 percentile: 1460-1560. High school rank: 89% in top tenth, 100% in top quarter, 100% in top half
Early decision deadline: 11/1, notification date: 12/15
Early action deadline: N/A, notification date: N/A
Application deadline (fall): 1/1
Undergraduate student body: 6,764 full time, 309 part time; 50% male, 50% female; 0% American Indian, 33% Asian, 4% black, 9% Hispanic, 4% multiracial, 0% Pacific Islander, 23% white, 21% international; 13% from in state; 14% live on campus; 16% of students in fraternities, 15%

in sororities
Most popular majors: 13% Computer Science, 9% Business Administration and Management, General, 9% Electrical and Electronics Engineering, 9% Systems Science and Theory, 8% Mechanical Engineering
Expenses: 2021-2022: $58,924; room/board: $16,150
Financial aid: (412) 268-8981; 40% of undergrads determined to have financial need; average aid package $49,988

Cedar Crest College
Allentown PA
(800) 360-1222
U.S. News ranking: Reg. U. (N), No. 85
Website: www.cedarcrest.edu
Admissions email: admissions@cedarcrest.edu
Private; founded 1867
Freshman admissions: selective; 2020-2021: 1,392 applied, 971 accepted. Either SAT or ACT required. SAT 25/75 percentile: 970-1170. High school rank: 15% in top tenth, 48% in top quarter, 80% in top half
Early decision deadline: N/A, notification date: N/A
Early action deadline: N/A, notification date: N/A
Application deadline (fall): rolling
Undergraduate student body: 815 full time, 273 part time; 7% male, 93% female; 0% American Indian, 3% Asian, 9% black, 14% Hispanic, 3% multiracial, 0% Pacific Islander, 59% white, 5% international; 81% from in state; 36% live on campus; N/A of students in fraternities, N/A in sororities
Most popular majors: 28% Registered Nursing/Registered Nurse, 13% Business Administration and Management, General, 7% Psychology, General, 6% Accounting, 6% Health Communication
Expenses: 2021-2022: $42,591; room/board: $12,519
Financial aid: (610) 606-4666; 92% of undergrads determined to have financial need; average aid package $31,292

Central Penn College[1]
Summerdale PA
(717) 728-2401
U.S. News ranking: Reg. Coll. (N), second tier
Website: www.centralpenn.edu
Admissions email: admissions@centralpenn.edu
For-profit; founded 1881
Application deadline (fall): rolling
Undergraduate student body: N/A full time, N/A part time
Expenses: 2020-2021: $18,714; room/board: $7,416
Financial aid: (717) 728-2261

Chatham University
Pittsburgh PA
(800) 837-1290
U.S. News ranking: Nat. U., No. 172
Website: www.chatham.edu

Admissions email: admissions@chatham.edu
Private; founded 1869
Freshman admissions: more selective; 2020-2021: 2,505 applied, 1,658 accepted. Neither SAT nor ACT required. SAT 25/75 percentile: 1050-1250. High school rank: 29% in top tenth, 55% in top quarter, 83% in top half
Early decision deadline: N/A, notification date: N/A
Early action deadline: N/A, notification date: N/A
Application deadline (fall): 8/1
Undergraduate student body: 1,070 full time, 287 part time; 27% male, 73% female; 0% American Indian, 3% Asian, 5% black, 5% Hispanic, 2% multiracial, 0% Pacific Islander, 77% white, 3% international; 76% from in state; 53% live on campus; N/A of students in fraternities, N/A in sororities
Most popular majors: 16% Biological and Biomedical Sciences, 13% Health Professions and Related Programs, 12% Psychology, 10% Business, Management, Marketing, and Related Support Services, 9% Multi/Interdisciplinary Studies
Expenses: 2021-2022: $40,877; room/board: $13,305
Financial aid: (412) 365-1849; 79% of undergrads determined to have financial need; average aid package $30,420

Chestnut Hill College
Philadelphia PA
(215) 248-7001
U.S. News ranking: Reg. U. (N), No. 119
Website: www.chc.edu
Admissions email: admissions@chc.edu
Private; founded 1924
Affiliation: Roman Catholic
Freshman admissions: less selective; 2020-2021: 1,697 applied, 1,649 accepted. Either SAT or ACT required. SAT 25/75 percentile: 900-1090. High school rank: 8% in top tenth, 24% in top quarter, 60% in top half
Early decision deadline: N/A, notification date: N/A
Early action deadline: N/A, notification date: N/A
Application deadline (fall): rolling
Undergraduate student body: 939 full time, 155 part time; 54% male, 46% female; 0% American Indian, 1% Asian, 31% black, 13% Hispanic, 4% multiracial, 0% Pacific Islander, 36% white, 2% international; 73% from in state; 0% live on campus; 0% of students in fraternities, 0% in sororities
Most popular majors: 22% Business, Management, Marketing, and Related Support Services, 17% Public Administration and Social Service Professions, 15% Homeland Security, Law Enforcement, Firefighting and Related Protective Services, 9% Biological and Biomedical Sciences, 8% Psychology

Expenses: 2021-2022: $38,360; room/board: $11,800
Financial aid: (215) 248-7182; 84% of undergrads determined to have financial need; average aid package $29,065

Cheyney University of Pennsylvania[1]
Cheyney PA
(610) 399-2275
U.S. News ranking: Nat. Lib. Arts, second tier
Website: www.cheyney.edu
Admissions email: admissions@cheyney.edu
Public; founded 1837
Application deadline (fall): N/A
Undergraduate student body: N/A full time, N/A part time
Expenses: N/A
Financial aid: N/A

Clarion University of Pennsylvania
Clarion PA
(814) 393-2306
U.S. News ranking: Reg. U. (N), No. 114
Website: www.clarion.edu
Admissions email: admissions@clarion.edu
Public; founded 1867
Freshman admissions: selective; 2020-2021: 2,675 applied, 2,520 accepted. Neither SAT nor ACT required. SAT 25/75 percentile: 950-1120. High school rank: 12% in top tenth, 32% in top quarter, 66% in top half
Early decision deadline: N/A, notification date: N/A
Early action deadline: N/A, notification date: N/A
Application deadline (fall): rolling
Undergraduate student body: 2,889 full time, 698 part time; 31% male, 69% female; 0% American Indian, 1% Asian, 8% black, 3% Hispanic, 2% multiracial, 0% Pacific Islander, 82% white, 0% international; 92% from in state; 15% live on campus; 2% of students in fraternities, 4% in sororities
Most popular majors: 26% Health Professions and Related Programs, 16% Business, Management, Marketing, and Related Support Services, 16% Liberal Arts and Sciences, General Studies and Humanities, 6% Education, 4% Psychology
Expenses: 2021-2022: $11,173 in state, $15,031 out of state; room/board: $12,930
Financial aid: (814) 393-2315; 77% of undergrads determined to have financial need; average aid package $12,011

Curtis Institute of Music[1]
Philadelphia PA
(215) 893-5252
U.S. News ranking: Arts, unranked
Website: www.curtis.edu
Admissions email: admissions@curtis.edu
Private; founded 1924
Application deadline (fall): N/A

Undergraduate student body: N/A full time, N/A part time
Expenses: 2020-2021: $3,015; room/board: $14,842
Financial aid: (215) 717-3188

Delaware Valley University
Doylestown PA
(215) 489-2211
U.S. News ranking: Reg. U. (N), No. 126
Website: www.delval.edu
Admissions email: admitme@delval.edu
Private; founded 1896
Freshman admissions: selective; 2020-2021: 2,091 applied, 1,915 accepted. Neither SAT nor ACT required. SAT 25/75 percentile: 940-1155. High school rank: 7% in top tenth, 29% in top quarter, 59% in top half
Early decision deadline: N/A, notification date: N/A
Early action deadline: N/A, notification date: N/A
Application deadline (fall): rolling
Undergraduate student body: 1,591 full time, 250 part time; 40% male, 60% female; 0% American Indian, 1% Asian, 10% black, 8% Hispanic, 3% multiracial, 0% Pacific Islander, 69% white, 0% international; 40% from in state; 53% live on campus; 0% of students in fraternities, 1% in sororities
Most popular majors: 35% Agriculture, Agriculture Operations, and Related Sciences, 18% Business, Management, Marketing, and Related Support Services, 14% Biological and Biomedical Sciences, 12% Natural Resources and Conservation, 6% Homeland Security, Law Enforcement, Firefighting and Related Protective Services
Expenses: 2021-2022: $40,670; room/board: $14,850
Financial aid: (215) 489-2975; 82% of undergrads determined to have financial need; average aid package $32,274

DeSales University
Center Valley PA
(610) 282-1100
U.S. News ranking: Reg. U. (N), No. 73
Website: www.desales.edu
Admissions email: admiss@desales.edu
Private; founded 1964
Affiliation: Roman Catholic
Freshman admissions: selective; 2020-2021: 3,192 applied, 2,610 accepted. Neither SAT nor ACT required. SAT 25/75 percentile: 1010-1240. High school rank: N/A
Early decision deadline: N/A, notification date: N/A
Early action deadline: N/A, notification date: N/A
Application deadline (fall): 8/1
Undergraduate student body: 1,930 full time, 468 part time; 37% male, 63% female; 0% American Indian, 3% Asian, 6% black, 12% Hispanic, 3% multiracial, 0% Pacific Islander, 70% white,

0% international; 73% from in state; 42% live on campus; N/A of students in fraternities, N/A in sororities
Most popular majors: 19% Registered Nursing/Registered Nurse, 9% Business Administration and Management, General, 7% Psychology, General, 6% Accounting, 6% Health Professions and Related Clinical Sciences, Other
Expenses: 2021-2022: $41,000; room/board: $13,300
Financial aid: (610) 282-1100; 75% of undergrads determined to have financial need; average aid package $28,552

Dickinson College
Carlisle PA
(800) 644-1773
U.S. News ranking: Nat. Lib. Arts, No. 50
Website: www.dickinson.edu
Admissions email: admissions@dickinson.edu
Private; founded 1783
Freshman admissions: more selective; 2020-2021: 5,375 applied, 2,776 accepted. Neither SAT nor ACT required. SAT 25/75 percentile: 1220-1380. High school rank: 49% in top tenth, 76% in top quarter, 98% in top half
Early decision deadline: 11/15, notification date: 12/15
Early action deadline: N/A, notification date: N/A
Application deadline (fall): 1/15
Undergraduate student body: 1,837 full time, 95 part time; 41% male, 59% female; 0% American Indian, 5% Asian, 6% black, 9% Hispanic, 4% multiracial, 0% Pacific Islander, 63% white, 12% international; 27% from in state; 100% live on campus; 5% of students in fraternities, 23% in sororities
Most popular majors: 13% International Business/Trade/Commerce, 10% Political Science and Government, General, 8% Psychology, General, 7% Economics, General, 6% Mathematics, General
Expenses: 2021-2022: $58,708; room/board: $15,252
Financial aid: (717) 245-1308; 68% of undergrads determined to have financial need; average aid package $48,617

Drexel University
Philadelphia PA
(800) 237-3935
U.S. News ranking: Nat. U., No. 103
Website: www.drexel.edu
Admissions email: enroll@drexel.edu
Private; founded 1891
Freshman admissions: more selective; 2020-2021: 31,237 applied, 24,112 accepted. Neither SAT nor ACT required. SAT 25/75 percentile: 1180-1380. High school rank: 40% in top tenth, 71% in top quarter, 94% in top half
Early decision deadline: 11/1, notification date: 12/15

Early action deadline: 11/1, notification date: 12/15
Application deadline (fall): 1/15
Undergraduate student body: 13,156 full time, 1,396 part time; 52% male, 48% female; 0% American Indian, 21% Asian, 7% black, 7% Hispanic, 4% multiracial, 0% Pacific Islander, 49% white, 9% international; 49% from in state; 11% of students in fraternities, 9% in sororities
Most popular majors: 23% Business, Management, Marketing, and Related Support Services, 19% Engineering, 19% Health Professions and Related Programs, 10% Visual and Performing Arts, 6% Computer and Information Sciences and Support Services
Expenses: 2021-2022: $57,136; room/board: $16,488
Financial aid: (215) 895-1600; 61% of undergrads determined to have financial need; average aid package $38,686

Duquesne University
Pittsburgh PA
(412) 396-6222
U.S. News ranking: Nat. U., No. 148
Website: www.duq.edu
Admissions email: admissions@duq.edu
Private; founded 1878
Affiliation: Roman Catholic
Freshman admissions: more selective; 2020-2021: 8,335 applied, 6,434 accepted. Neither SAT nor ACT required. SAT 25/75 percentile: 1120-1270. High school rank: 17% in top tenth, 48% in top quarter, 81% in top half
Early decision deadline: N/A, notification date: N/A
Early action deadline: N/A, notification date: N/A
Application deadline (fall): 8/15
Undergraduate student body: 5,292 full time, 91 part time; 36% male, 64% female; 0% American Indian, 4% Asian, 5% black, 5% Hispanic, 3% multiracial, 0% Pacific Islander, 80% white, 2% international; 71% from in state; 61% live on campus; 16% of students in fraternities, 25% in sororities
Most popular majors: 17% Nursing Science, 7% Biology/Biological Sciences, General, 5% Finance, General, 5% Marketing/Marketing Management, General, 4% Psychology, General
Expenses: 2021-2022: $43,526; room/board: $14,144
Financial aid: (412) 396-6607; 65% of undergrads determined to have financial need; average aid package $27,998

Eastern University
St. Davids PA
(800) 452-0996
U.S. News ranking: Reg. U. (N), No. 103
Website: www.eastern.edu
Admissions email: admissions@eastern.edu
Private; founded 1952

Affiliation: American Baptist
Freshman admissions: selective; 2020-2021: 2,095 applied, 1,346 accepted. Neither SAT nor ACT required. SAT 25/75 percentile: 1010-1190. High school rank: N/A
Early decision deadline: N/A, notification date: N/A
Early action deadline: N/A, notification date: N/A
Application deadline (fall): 8/31
Undergraduate student body: 1,299 full time, 580 part time; 32% male, 68% female; 0% American Indian, 2% Asian, 21% black, 16% Hispanic, 3% multiracial, 0% Pacific Islander, 44% white, 3% international; 71% from in state; 43% live on campus; N/A of students in fraternities, N/A in sororities
Most popular majors: 15% Early Childhood Education and Teaching, 8% Business Administration and Management, General, 8% Registered Nursing/Registered Nurse, 6% Criminology, 6% Psychology, General
Expenses: 2021-2022: $35,590; room/board: $12,120
Financial aid: (610) 225-5102; 83% of undergrads determined to have financial need; average aid package $28,083

East Stroudsburg University
East Stroudsburg PA
(570) 422-3542
U.S. News ranking: Reg. U. (N), second tier
Website: www.esu.edu/admissions/index.cfm
Admissions email: admission@esu.edu
Public; founded 1893
Freshman admissions: less selective; 2020-2021: 5,253 applied, 4,207 accepted. Neither SAT nor ACT required. SAT 25/75 percentile: 900-1110. High school rank: 2% in top tenth, 12% in top quarter, 42% in top half
Early decision deadline: N/A, notification date: N/A
Early action deadline: N/A, notification date: N/A
Application deadline (fall): 5/1
Undergraduate student body: 4,499 full time, 496 part time; 42% male, 58% female; 0% American Indian, 2% Asian, 20% black, 15% Hispanic, 4% multiracial, 0% Pacific Islander, 54% white, 0% international; 81% from in state; 0% live on campus; 3% of students in fraternities, 4% in sororities
Most popular majors: 12% Business Administration and Management, General, 7% Criminal Justice/Safety Studies, 7% Kinesiology and Exercise Science, 7% Psychology, General, 5% Biology/Biological Sciences, General
Expenses: 2021-2022: $11,199 in state, $23,691 out of state; room/board: $11,400
Financial aid: (570) 422-2800; 58% of undergrads determined to have financial need; average aid package $10,488

Edinboro University of Pennsylvania
Edinboro PA
(888) 846-2676
U.S. News ranking: Reg. U. (N), second tier
Website: www.edinboro.edu
Admissions email: admissions@edinboro.edu
Public; founded 1857
Freshman admissions: selective; 2020-2021: 3,266 applied, 2,776 accepted. Either SAT or ACT required. SAT 25/75 percentile: 960-1160. High school rank: 13% in top tenth, 34% in top quarter, 68% in top half
Early decision deadline: N/A, notification date: N/A
Early action deadline: N/A, notification date: N/A
Application deadline (fall): rolling
Undergraduate student body: 2,749 full time, 397 part time; 40% male, 60% female; 0% American Indian, 1% Asian, 6% black, 4% Hispanic, 4% multiracial, 0% Pacific Islander, 82% white, 1% international; 87% from in state; 37% live on campus; N/A of students in fraternities, N/A in sororities
Most popular majors: 15% Visual and Performing Arts, 11% Health Professions and Related Programs, 10% Business, Management, Marketing, and Related Support Services, 8% Education, 7% Parks, Recreation, Leisure, and Fitness Studies
Expenses: 2021-2022: $10,543 in state, $14,401 out of state; room/board: $10,120
Financial aid: (814) 732-3500; 76% of undergrads determined to have financial need; average aid package $11,105

Elizabethtown College
Elizabethtown PA
(717) 361-1400
U.S. News ranking: Nat. Lib. Arts, No. 117
Website: www.etown.edu
Admissions email: admissions@etown.edu
Private; founded 1899
Freshman admissions: selective; 2020-2021: 1,696 applied, 1,454 accepted. Neither SAT nor ACT required. SAT 25/75 percentile: 1080-1280. High school rank: 28% in top tenth, 58% in top quarter, 85% in top half
Early decision deadline: N/A, notification date: N/A
Early action deadline: N/A, notification date: N/A
Application deadline (fall): rolling
Undergraduate student body: 1,486 full time, 202 part time; 39% male, 61% female; 0% American Indian, 3% Asian, 3% black, 5% Hispanic, 1% multiracial, 0% Pacific Islander, 86% white, 1% international; 73% from in state; 71% live on campus; 0% of students in fraternities, 0% in sororities
Most popular majors: 24% Business, Management, Marketing, and Related Support Services, 15% Health Professions

and Related Programs, 10% Biological and Biomedical Sciences, 7% Education, 6% Engineering
Expenses: 2021-2022: $34,600; room/board: $12,330
Financial aid: (717) 361-1404; 71% of undergrads determined to have financial need; average aid package $21,795

Franklin & Marshall College
Lancaster PA
(717) 358-3953
U.S. News ranking: Nat. Lib. Arts, No. 42
Website: www.fandm.edu
Admissions email: admission@fandm.edu
Private; founded 1787
Freshman admissions: more selective; 2020-2021: 9,062 applied, 3,308 accepted. Neither SAT nor ACT required. SAT 25/75 percentile: 1210-1440. High school rank: 61% in top tenth, 86% in top quarter, 98% in top half
Early decision deadline: 11/15, notification date: 12/15
Early action deadline: N/A, notification date: N/A
Application deadline (fall): 1/15
Undergraduate student body: 2,236 full time, 18 part time; 43% male, 57% female; 0% American Indian, 4% Asian, 7% black, 11% Hispanic, 3% multiracial, 0% Pacific Islander, 56% white, 17% international; 69% from in state; 99% live on campus; 12% of students in fraternities, 22% in sororities
Most popular majors: 16% Multi-/Interdisciplinary Studies, Other, 9% Economics, General, 8% Business Administration and Management, General, 7% Political Science and Government, General, 6% Computer Science
Expenses: 2021-2022: $63,401; room/board: $14,740
Financial aid: (717) 358-3991; 57% of undergrads determined to have financial need; average aid package $55,996

Gannon University
Erie PA
(814) 871-7240
U.S. News ranking: Nat. U., No. 227
Website: www.gannon.edu
Admissions email: admissions@gannon.edu
Private; founded 1925
Affiliation: Roman Catholic
Freshman admissions: selective; 2020-2021: 4,442 applied, 3,520 accepted. Neither SAT nor ACT required. SAT 25/75 percentile: 990-1210. High school rank: N/A
Early decision deadline: N/A, notification date: N/A
Early action deadline: N/A, notification date: N/A
Application deadline (fall): rolling
Undergraduate student body: 2,721 full time, 487 part time; 39% male, 61% female; 0% American Indian, 1% Asian, 5% black, 4% Hispanic, 4% multiracial, 0%

Pacific Islander, 73% white, 9% international
Most popular majors: Information not available
Expenses: 2021-2022: $34,526; room/board: $14,600
Financial aid: (814) 871-7337; 77% of undergrads determined to have financial need; average aid package $28,447

Geneva College
Beaver Falls PA
(724) 847-6500
U.S. News ranking: Reg. U. (N), No. 73
Website: www.geneva.edu
Admissions email: admissions@geneva.edu
Private; founded 1848
Affiliation: Reformed Presbyterian Church
Freshman admissions: selective; 2020-2021: 1,642 applied, 1,201 accepted. Neither SAT nor ACT required. SAT 25/75 percentile: 980-1240. High school rank: 20% in top tenth, 43% in top quarter, 75% in top half
Early decision deadline: N/A, notification date: N/A
Early action deadline: N/A, notification date: N/A
Application deadline (fall): rolling
Undergraduate student body: 1,055 full time, 146 part time; 52% male, 48% female; 0% American Indian, 2% Asian, 7% black, 3% Hispanic, 3% multiracial, 0% Pacific Islander, 79% white, 2% international; 72% from in state; 61% live on campus; 0% of students in fraternities, 0% in sororities
Most popular majors: 22% Engineering, General, 8% Business Administration and Management, General, 6% Teacher Education, Multiple Levels, 5% Computer and Information Sciences, General, 4% Accounting
Expenses: 2021-2022: $29,970; room/board: $10,850
Financial aid: (724) 847-6532; 84% of undergrads determined to have financial need; average aid package $23,112

Gettysburg College
Gettysburg PA
(800) 431-0803
U.S. News ranking: Nat. Lib. Arts, No. 54
Website: www.gettysburg.edu/
Admissions email: admiss@gettysburg.edu
Private; founded 1832
Freshman admissions: more selective; 2020-2021: 6,468 applied, 3,120 accepted. Neither SAT nor ACT required. SAT 25/75 percentile: 1270-1410. High school rank: 60% in top tenth, 83% in top quarter, 99% in top half
Early decision deadline: 11/15, notification date: 12/15
Early action deadline: N/A, notification date: N/A
Application deadline (fall): 1/15
Undergraduate student body: 2,495 full time, 10 part time; 48% male, 52% female; 0% American

Indian, 3% Asian, 4% black, 10% Hispanic, 2% multiracial, 0% Pacific Islander, 74% white, 4% international; 28% from in state; N/A live on campus; 27% of students in fraternities, 34% in sororities
Most popular majors: 11% Political Science and Government, General, 10% Business Administration and Management, General, 8% Economics, General, 7% English Language and Literature, General, 7% Exercise Physiology
Expenses: 2021-2022: $59,960; room/board: $14,370
Financial aid: (717) 337-6611; 62% of undergrads determined to have financial need; average aid package $50,166

Grove City College[1]
Grove City PA
(724) 458-2100
U.S. News ranking: Nat. Lib. Arts, No. 105
Website: www.gcc.edu
Admissions email: admissions@gcc.edu
Private; founded 1876
Affiliation: Undenominational
Application deadline (fall): 3/20
Undergraduate student body: N/A full time, N/A part time
Expenses: 2021-2022: $19,310; room/board: $10,680
Financial aid: (724) 458-3300; 46% of undergrads determined to have financial need; average aid package $9,373

Gwynedd Mercy University
Gwynedd Valley PA
(215) 641-5510
U.S. News ranking: Reg. U. (N), No. 119
Website: www.gmercyu.edu/
Admissions email: admissions@gmercyu.edu
Private; founded 1948
Affiliation: Roman Catholic
Freshman admissions: selective; 2020-2021: 904 applied, 889 accepted. Neither SAT nor ACT required. SAT 25/75 percentile: 950-1140. High school rank: 7% in top tenth, 30% in top quarter, 60% in top half
Early decision deadline: N/A, notification date: N/A
Early action deadline: N/A, notification date: N/A
Application deadline (fall): 8/20
Undergraduate student body: 1,553 full time, 437 part time; 26% male, 74% female; 1% American Indian, 4% Asian, 18% black, 3% Hispanic, 2% multiracial, 0% Pacific Islander, 60% white, 0% international; 88% from in state; 8% live on campus; 0% of students in fraternities, 0% in sororities
Most popular majors: 71% Health Professions and Related Programs, 12% Business, Management, Marketing, and Related Support Services, 5% Education, 4% Psychology, 2% Homeland Security, Law Enforcement, Firefighting and Related Protective Services

Expenses: 2021-2022: $36,244; room/board: $12,270
Financial aid: (215) 646-7300; 83% of undergrads determined to have financial need; average aid package $22,614

Harrisburg University of Science and Technology[1]
Harrisburg PA
(717) 901-5150
U.S. News ranking: Reg. U. (N), second tier
Website: www.harrisburgu.edu
Admissions email: admissions@harrisburgu.edu
Private; founded 2001
Application deadline (fall): rolling
Undergraduate student body: N/A full time, N/A part time
Expenses: 2020-2021: $23,900; room/board: N/A
Financial aid: (717) 901-5115

Haverford College
Haverford PA
(610) 896-1350
U.S. News ranking: Nat. Lib. Arts, No. 16
Website: www.haverford.edu
Admissions email: admission@haverford.edu
Private; founded 1833
Freshman admissions: most selective; 2020-2021: 4,530 applied, 826 accepted. Neither SAT nor ACT required. SAT 25/75 percentile: 1360-1520. High school rank: 94% in top tenth, 99% in top quarter, 100% in top half
Early decision deadline: 11/15, notification date: 12/15
Early action deadline: N/A, notification date: N/A
Application deadline (fall): 1/15
Undergraduate student body: 1,298 full time, 9 part time; 46% male, 54% female; 0% American Indian, 11% Asian, 6% black, 13% Hispanic, 6% multiracial, 0% Pacific Islander, 51% white, 12% international; 12% from in state; 98% live on campus; 0% of students in fraternities, 0% in sororities
Most popular majors: 31% Social Sciences, General, 15% Physical Sciences, 10% Biology/Biological Sciences, General, 8% Computer and Information Sciences, General, 8% Psychology, General
Expenses: 2021-2022: $60,940; room/board: $17,300
Financial aid: (610) 896-1350; 45% of undergrads determined to have financial need; average aid package $54,713

Holy Family University[1]
Philadelphia PA
(215) 637-3050
U.S. News ranking: Reg. U. (N), second tier
Website: www.holyfamily.edu
Admissions email: admissions@holyfamily.edu
Private; founded 1954
Affiliation: Roman Catholic
Application deadline (fall): rolling

Undergraduate student body: N/A full time, N/A part time
Expenses: 2020-2021: $31,640; room/board: $14,500
Financial aid: (267) 341-3233

Immaculata University
Immaculata PA
(610) 647-4400
U.S. News ranking: Nat. U., No. 227
Website: www.immaculata.edu
Admissions email: admiss@immaculata.edu
Private; founded 1920
Affiliation: Roman Catholic
Freshman admissions: selective; 2020-2021: 1,942 applied, 1,603 accepted. Neither SAT nor ACT required. SAT 25/75 percentile: 993-1170. High school rank: 14% in top tenth, 35% in top quarter, 64% in top half
Early decision deadline: N/A, notification date: N/A
Early action deadline: N/A, notification date: N/A
Application deadline (fall): rolling
Undergraduate student body: 942 full time, 672 part time; 30% male, 70% female; 0% American Indian, 3% Asian, 15% black, 10% Hispanic, 2% multiracial, 0% Pacific Islander, 69% white, 1% international
Most popular majors: Information not available
Expenses: 2021-2022: $27,750; room/board: $12,620
Financial aid: (610) 647-4400; 74% of undergrads determined to have financial need; average aid package $18,001

Indiana University of Pennsylvania
Indiana PA
(724) 357-2230
U.S. News ranking: Nat. U., second tier
Website: www.iup.edu
Admissions email: admissions-inquiry@iup.edu
Public; founded 1875
Freshman admissions: less selective; 2020-2021: 9,030 applied, 8,407 accepted. Neither SAT nor ACT required. SAT 25/75 percentile: 930-1130. High school rank: 11% in top tenth, 30% in top quarter, 64% in top half
Early decision deadline: N/A, notification date: N/A
Early action deadline: N/A, notification date: N/A
Application deadline (fall): rolling
Undergraduate student body: 7,060 full time, 950 part time; 40% male, 60% female; 0% American Indian, 1% Asian, 11% black, 5% Hispanic, 5% multiracial, 0% Pacific Islander, 75% white, 2% international; 94% from in state; 25% live on campus; 8% of students in fraternities, 8% in sororities
Most popular majors: 8% Criminology, 7% Registered Nursing/Registered Nurse, 5% Business Administration and Management, General, 5% Health and Physical Education/Fitness, General, 5% Speech Communication and Rhetoric

Expenses: 2021-2022: $13,144 in state, $17,464 out of state; room/board: $12,570
Financial aid: (724) 357-2218; 72% of undergrads determined to have financial need; average aid package $13,998

Juniata College[1]
Huntingdon PA
(877) 586-4282
U.S. News ranking: Nat. Lib. Arts, No. 75
Website: www.juniata.edu
Admissions email: admissions@juniata.edu
Private; founded 1876
Application deadline (fall): 3/15
Undergraduate student body: N/A full time, N/A part time
Expenses: 2020-2021: $49,175; room/board: $13,050
Financial aid: (814) 641-3144

Keystone College
La Plume PA
(570) 945-8111
U.S. News ranking: Reg. Coll. (N), No. 28
Website: www.keystone.edu
Admissions email: admissions@keystone.edu
Private; founded 1868
Freshman admissions: less selective; 2020-2021: 1,698 applied, 1,337 accepted. Neither SAT nor ACT required. SAT 25/75 percentile: 880-1090. High school rank: N/A
Early decision deadline: N/A, notification date: N/A
Early action deadline: N/A, notification date: N/A
Application deadline (fall): rolling
Undergraduate student body: 1,012 full time, 312 part time; 42% male, 58% female; 1% American Indian, 1% Asian, 13% black, 9% Hispanic, 3% multiracial, 0% Pacific Islander, 64% white, 0% international; 81% from in state; 31% live on campus; 0% of students in fraternities, 0% in sororities
Most popular majors: 22% Business Administration and Management, General, 12% Applied Psychology, 12% Education, General, 11% Sport and Fitness Administration/Management
Expenses: 2021-2022: $17,300; room/board: $11,900
Financial aid: N/A

King's College
Wilkes-Barre PA
(888) 546-4772
U.S. News ranking: Reg. U. (N), No. 62
Website: www.kings.edu
Admissions email: admissions@kings.edu
Private; founded 1946
Affiliation: Roman Catholic
Freshman admissions: selective; 2020-2021: 3,467 applied, 2,798 accepted. Neither SAT nor ACT required. SAT 25/75 percentile: 1010-1210. High school rank: 17% in top tenth, 38% in top quarter, 70% in top half

Early decision deadline: 12/1, notification date: 12/15
Early action deadline: 12/1, notification date: 12/15
Application deadline (fall): rolling
Undergraduate student body: 1,901 full time, 158 part time; 51% male, 49% female; 0% American Indian, 3% Asian, 5% black, 10% Hispanic, 3% multiracial, 0% Pacific Islander, 70% white, 6% international; 28% from in state; 46% live on campus; 0% of students in fraternities, 0% in sororities
Most popular majors: 17% Health Professions and Related Clinical Sciences, Other, 10% Accounting, 8% Criminal Justice/Safety Studies, 7% Business Administration and Management, General, 6% Marketing/Marketing Management, General
Expenses: 2021-2022: $40,882; room/board: $14,285
Financial aid: (570) 208-5900; 78% of undergrads determined to have financial need; average aid package $29,778

Kutztown University of Pennsylvania
Kutztown PA
(610) 683-4060
U.S. News ranking: Reg. U. (N), No. 123
Website: www.kutztown.edu
Admissions email: admissions@kutztown.edu
Public; founded 1866
Freshman admissions: selective; 2020-2021: 6,870 applied, 6,370 accepted. Either SAT or ACT required. SAT 25/75 percentile: 950-1120. High school rank: 8% in top tenth, 26% in top quarter, 61% in top half
Early decision deadline: N/A, notification date: N/A
Early action deadline: N/A, notification date: N/A
Application deadline (fall): rolling
Undergraduate student body: 6,286 full time, 659 part time; 43% male, 57% female; 0% American Indian, 2% Asian, 8% black, 10% Hispanic, 3% multiracial, 0% Pacific Islander, 73% white, 1% international; 88% from in state; 35% live on campus; 6% of students in fraternities, 8% in sororities
Most popular majors: 18% Business Administration and Management, General, 9% Psychology, General, 6% Criminal Justice/Safety Studies, 4% Elementary Education and Teaching, 4% Special Education and Teaching, General
Expenses: 2020-2021: $11,298 in state, $15,156 out of state; room/board: $10,660
Financial aid: (610) 683-4077; 71% of undergrads determined to have financial need; average aid package $9,899

Lackawanna College[1]
Scranton PA
(570) 961-7898
U.S. News ranking: Reg. Coll. (N), unranked
Website: www.lackawanna.edu

Admissions email: admissions@lackawanna.edu
Private
Application deadline (fall): rolling
Undergraduate student body: N/A full time, N/A part time
Expenses: 2020-2021: $16,130; room/board: $10,300
Financial aid: N/A

Lafayette College
Easton PA
(610) 330-5100
U.S. News ranking: Nat. Lib. Arts, No. 38
Website: www.lafayette.edu/
Admissions email: admissions@lafayette.edu
Private; founded 1826
Freshman admissions: more selective; 2020-2021: 8,215 applied, 2,922 accepted. Neither SAT nor ACT required. SAT 25/75 percentile: 1250-1440. High school rank: 61% in top tenth, 85% in top quarter, 99% in top half
Early decision deadline: 11/15, notification date: 12/15
Early action deadline: N/A, notification date: N/A
Application deadline (fall): 1/15
Undergraduate student body: 2,457 full time, 57 part time; 49% male, 51% female; 0% American Indian, 4% Asian, 5% black, 8% Hispanic, 4% multiracial, 0% Pacific Islander, 67% white, 9% international; 19% from in state; 16% live on campus; 17% of students in fraternities, 26% in sororities
Most popular majors: 37% Social Sciences, 20% Engineering, 10% Biological and Biomedical Sciences, 6% Psychology, 5% Visual and Performing Arts
Expenses: 2021-2022: $56,364; room/board: $16,670
Financial aid: (610) 330-5055; 33% of undergrads determined to have financial need; average aid package $40,842

Lancaster Bible College
Lancaster PA
(717) 560-8271
U.S. News ranking: Reg. U. (N), second tier
Website: www.lbc.edu/
Admissions email: admissions@lbc.edu
Private; founded 1933
Affiliation: Undenominational
Freshman admissions: less selective; 2020-2021: 373 applied, 362 accepted. Neither SAT nor ACT required. SAT 25/75 percentile: 980-1210. High school rank: N/A
Early decision deadline: N/A, notification date: N/A
Early action deadline: N/A, notification date: N/A
Application deadline (fall): rolling
Undergraduate student body: 792 full time, 818 part time; 46% male, 54% female; 0% American Indian, 1% Asian, 21% black, 5% Hispanic, 17% multiracial, 0% Pacific Islander, 48% white, 0% international; 71% from in state; 59% live on campus; 0%

of students in fraternities, 0% in sororities
Most popular majors: 40% Bible/Biblical Studies, 14% Business Administration, Management and Operations, Other, 8% Social Work, 6% Communication and Media Studies, Other, 6% Elementary Education and Teaching
Expenses: 2021-2022: $27,390; room/board: $10,100
Financial aid: (717) 560-8254; 77% of undergrads determined to have financial need; average aid package $23,878

La Roche University[1]
Pittsburgh PA
(800) 838-4572
U.S. News ranking: Reg. U. (N), second tier
Website: www.laroche.edu
Admissions email: admissions@laroche.edu
Private; founded 1963
Affiliation: Roman Catholic
Application deadline (fall): rolling
Undergraduate student body: N/A full time, N/A part time
Expenses: 2021-2022: $31,570; room/board: $12,634
Financial aid: (412) 536-1125; 72% of undergrads determined to have financial need; average aid package $31,008

La Salle University
Philadelphia PA
(215) 951-1500
U.S. News ranking: Reg. U. (N), No. 43
Website: www.lasalle.edu
Admissions email: admiss@lasalle.edu
Private; founded 1863
Affiliation: Roman Catholic
Freshman admissions: selective; 2020-2021: 6,151 applied, 4,696 accepted. Neither SAT nor ACT required. SAT 25/75 percentile: 980-1180. High school rank: N/A
Early decision deadline: N/A, notification date: N/A
Early action deadline: 11/1, notification date: 12/1
Application deadline (fall): rolling
Undergraduate student body: 2,822 full time, 468 part time; 36% male, 64% female; 0% American Indian, 5% Asian, 18% black, 17% Hispanic, 3% multiracial, 0% Pacific Islander, 52% white, 3% international; 71% from in state; N/A live on campus; N/A of students in fraternities, N/A in sororities
Most popular majors: 11% Marketing/Marketing Management, General, 10% Registered Nursing/Registered Nurse, 7% Accounting, 7% Finance, General, 6% Psychology, General
Expenses: 2020-2021: $32,450; room/board: $15,222
Financial aid: (215) 951-1070

Lebanon Valley College[1]
Annville PA
(717) 867-6181
U.S. News ranking: Reg. U. (N), No. 73
Website: www.lvc.edu
Admissions email: admission@lvc.edu
Private; founded 1866
Affiliation: United Methodist
Application deadline (fall): rolling
Undergraduate student body: N/A full time, N/A part time
Expenses: 2020-2021: $46,030; room/board: $12,500
Financial aid: (717) 867-6126

Lehigh University
Bethlehem PA
(610) 758-3100
U.S. News ranking: Nat. U., No. 49
Website: www1.lehigh.edu
Admissions email: admissions@lehigh.edu
Private; founded 1865
Freshman admissions: more selective; 2020-2021: 12,389 applied, 6,138 accepted. Neither SAT nor ACT required. SAT 25/75 percentile: 1260-1433. High school rank: 66% in top tenth, 89% in top quarter, 98% in top half
Early decision deadline: 11/1, notification date: 12/15
Early action deadline: N/A, notification date: N/A
Application deadline (fall): 1/15
Undergraduate student body: 5,070 full time, 133 part time; 54% male, 46% female; 0% American Indian, 8% Asian, 5% black, 10% Hispanic, 4% multiracial, 0% Pacific Islander, 61% white, 9% international; 26% from in state; 24% live on campus; 25% of students in fraternities, 34% in sororities
Most popular majors: 14% Finance, General, 7% Mechanical Engineering, 5% Accounting, 5% Industrial Engineering, 5% Marketing/Marketing Management, General
Expenses: 2021-2022: $57,470; room/board: $15,330
Financial aid: (610) 758-3181; 42% of undergrads determined to have financial need; average aid package $49,917

Lincoln University
Lincoln University PA
(800) 790-0191
U.S. News ranking: Reg. U. (N), second tier
Website: www.lincoln.edu
Admissions email: admissions@lincoln.edu
Public; founded 1854
Freshman admissions: less selective; 2020-2021: 3,871 applied, 3,497 accepted. Neither SAT nor ACT required. SAT 25/75 percentile: 860-1028. High school rank: 5% in top tenth, 20% in top quarter, 55% in top half
Early decision deadline: N/A, notification date: N/A
Early action deadline: N/A, notification date: N/A

Application deadline (fall): 5/1
Undergraduate student body: 1,680 full time, 215 part time; 31% male, 69% female; 0% American Indian, 0% Asian, 84% black, 6% Hispanic, 3% multiracial, 0% Pacific Islander, 1% white, 3% international; 48% from in state; 28% live on campus; 6% of students in fraternities, 3% in sororities
Most popular majors: 18% Health Professions and Related Programs, 17% Public Administration and Social Service Professions, 13% Communication, Journalism, and Related Programs, 10% Business, Management, Marketing, and Related Support Services, 8% Homeland Security, Law Enforcement, Firefighting and Related Protective Services
Expenses: 2021-2022: $11,556 in state, $17,060 out of state; room/board: $10,076
Financial aid: (800) 561-2606; 88% of undergrads determined to have financial need; average aid package $12,981

Lock Haven University of Pennsylvania
Lock Haven PA
(570) 484-2011
U.S. News ranking: Reg. U. (N), No. 109
Website: www.lockhaven.edu
Admissions email: admissions@lockhaven.edu
Public; founded 1870
Freshman admissions: selective; 2020-2021: 2,413 applied, 2,246 accepted. Neither SAT nor ACT required. SAT 25/75 percentile: 930-1130. High school rank: 10% in top tenth, 34% in top quarter, 68% in top half
Early decision deadline: N/A, notification date: N/A
Early action deadline: N/A, notification date: N/A
Application deadline (fall): rolling
Undergraduate student body: 2,311 full time, 416 part time; 38% male, 62% female; 1% American Indian, 1% Asian, 7% black, 3% Hispanic, 1% multiracial, 0% Pacific Islander, 85% white, 0% international; 96% from in state; 11% live on campus; 3% of students in fraternities, 4% in sororities
Most popular majors: 21% Health Professions and Related Programs, 18% Parks, Recreation, Leisure, and Fitness Studies, 15% Business, Management, Marketing, and Related Support Services, 9% Homeland Security, Law Enforcement, Firefighting and Related Protective Services, 6% Education
Expenses: 2021-2022: $10,878 in state, $20,452 out of state; room/board: $10,368
Financial aid: (570) 484-2452; 77% of undergrads determined to have financial need; average aid package $9,269

Lycoming College
Williamsport PA
(800) 345-3920
U.S. News ranking: Nat. Lib. Arts, No. 124
Website: www.lycoming.edu/
Admissions email: admissions@lycoming.edu
Private; founded 1812
Affiliation: United Methodist
Freshman admissions: selective; 2020-2021: 2,917 applied, 1,910 accepted. Neither SAT nor ACT required. SAT 25/75 percentile: 1010-1210. High school rank: 23% in top tenth, 52% in top quarter, 80% in top half
Early decision deadline: 11/15, notification date: 12/1
Early action deadline: 12/1, notification date: 12/15
Application deadline (fall): rolling
Undergraduate student body: 1,059 full time, 8 part time; 46% male, 54% female; 0% American Indian, 2% Asian, 15% black, 13% Hispanic, 4% multiracial, 0% Pacific Islander, 59% white, 3% international; 57% from in state; 85% live on campus; 11% of students in fraternities, 17% in sororities
Most popular majors: 26% Business, Management, Marketing, and Related Support Services, 23% Social Sciences, 15% Psychology, 10% Visual and Performing Arts, 7% Biological and Biomedical Sciences
Expenses: 2021-2022: $43,962; room/board: $13,772
Financial aid: (570) 321-4140; 89% of undergrads determined to have financial need; average aid package $42,943

Mansfield University of Pennsylvania
Mansfield PA
(800) 577-6826
U.S. News ranking: Nat. Lib. Arts, second tier
Website: www.mansfield.edu
Admissions email: admissns@mansfield.edu
Public; founded 1857
Freshman admissions: selective; 2020-2021: 2,136 applied, 2,051 accepted. Neither SAT nor ACT required. SAT 25/75 percentile: 960-1130. High school rank: 11% in top tenth, 33% in top quarter, 75% in top half
Early decision deadline: N/A, notification date: N/A
Early action deadline: N/A, notification date: N/A
Application deadline (fall): rolling
Undergraduate student body: 1,489 full time, 291 part time; 36% male, 64% female; 0% American Indian, 0% Asian, 12% black, 5% Hispanic, 3% multiracial, 0% Pacific Islander, 76% white, 1% international
Most popular majors: Information not available
Expenses: 2021-2022: $10,846 in state, $13,162 out of state; room/board: $10,168

Financial aid: N/A; 57% of undergrads determined to have financial need; average aid package $13,404

Marywood University
Scranton PA
(866) 279-9663
U.S. News ranking: Reg. U. (N), No. 44
Website: www.marywood.edu
Admissions email: YourFuture@marywood.edu
Private; founded 1915
Affiliation: Roman Catholic
Freshman admissions: selective; 2020-2021: 2,231 applied, 1,830 accepted. Neither SAT nor ACT required. SAT 25/75 percentile: 1000-1180. High school rank: 15% in top tenth, 49% in top quarter, 82% in top half
Early decision deadline: N/A, notification date: N/A
Early action deadline: N/A, notification date: N/A
Application deadline (fall): rolling
Undergraduate student body: 1,680 full time, 128 part time; 33% male, 67% female; 0% American Indian, 3% Asian, 3% black, 9% Hispanic, 2% multiracial, 0% Pacific Islander, 75% white, 1% international; 75% from in state; 27% live on campus; 0% of students in fraternities, 5% in sororities
Most popular majors: 37% Health Professions and Related Programs, 10% Business, Management, Marketing, and Related Support Services, 9% Architecture and Related Services, 8% Education, 7% Biological and Biomedical Sciences
Expenses: 2021-2022: $37,284; room/board: $14,338
Financial aid: (570) 348-6225; 81% of undergrads determined to have financial need; average aid package $29,453

Mercyhurst University
Erie PA
(814) 824-2202
U.S. News ranking: Reg. U. (N), No. 50
Website: www.mercyhurst.edu
Admissions email: admug@mercyhurst.edu
Private; founded 1926
Affiliation: Roman Catholic
Freshman admissions: selective; 2020-2021: 3,444 applied, 3,031 accepted. Neither SAT nor ACT required. SAT 25/75 percentile: 1030-1220. High school rank: N/A
Early decision deadline: N/A, notification date: N/A
Early action deadline: N/A, notification date: N/A
Application deadline (fall): rolling
Undergraduate student body: 2,355 full time, 76 part time; 43% male, 57% female; 1% American Indian, 1% Asian, 5% black, 5% Hispanic, 1% multiracial, 0% Pacific Islander, 80% white, 4% international; 50% from in state; 80% live on campus; 0% of students in fraternities, 0% in sororities

Most popular majors: 27% Business, Management, Marketing, and Related Support Services, 13% Military Technologies and Applied Sciences, 9% Health Professions and Related Programs, 8% Biological and Biomedical Sciences, 6% Visual and Performing Arts
Expenses: 2021-2022: $42,680; room/board: $13,594
Financial aid: (814) 824-2288; 78% of undergrads determined to have financial need; average aid package $34,231

Messiah University
Mechanicsburg PA
(717) 691-6000
U.S. News ranking: Reg. U. (N), No. 23
Website: www.messiah.edu
Admissions email: admissions@messiah.edu
Private; founded 1909
Affiliation: Interdenominational
Freshman admissions: more selective; 2020-2021: 2,549 applied, 1,976 accepted. Neither SAT nor ACT required. SAT 25/75 percentile: 1080-1310. High school rank: 31% in top tenth, 62% in top quarter, 91% in top half
Early decision deadline: N/A, notification date: N/A
Early action deadline: N/A, notification date: N/A
Application deadline (fall): rolling
Undergraduate student body: 2,424 full time, 190 part time; 40% male, 60% female; 0% American Indian, 3% Asian, 3% black, 6% Hispanic, 3% multiracial, 0% Pacific Islander, 81% white, 3% international; 65% from in state; 89% live on campus; N/A of students in fraternities, N/A in sororities
Most popular majors: 10% Engineering, General, 8% Registered Nursing/Registered Nurse, 5% Health Professions and Related Programs, 5% Psychology, General, 4% Social Work
Expenses: 2021-2022: $38,370; room/board: $11,220
Financial aid: (717) 691-6007; 72% of undergrads determined to have financial need; average aid package $27,879

Millersville University of Pennsylvania
Millersville PA
(717) 871-4625
U.S. News ranking: Reg. U. (N), No. 97
Website: www.millersville.edu
Admissions email: Admissions@millersville.edu
Public; founded 1855
Freshman admissions: selective; 2020-2021: 6,381 applied, 5,395 accepted. Neither SAT nor ACT required. SAT 25/75 percentile: 980-1170. High school rank: 13% in top tenth, 37% in top quarter, 66% in top half
Early decision deadline: N/A, notification date: N/A
Early action deadline: N/A, notification date: N/A

Application deadline (fall): rolling
Undergraduate student body: 5,096 full time, 1,397 part time; 41% male, 59% female; 0% American Indian, 3% Asian, 9% black, 11% Hispanic, 1% multiracial, 0% Pacific Islander, 74% white, 1% international; 92% from in state; 10% live on campus; 4% of students in fraternities, 4% in sororities
Most popular majors: 12% Education, 10% Health Professions and Related Programs, 9% Business, Management, Marketing, and Related Support Services, 9% Social Sciences, 7% Communication, Journalism, and Related Programs
Expenses: 2021-2022: $12,256 in state, $21,976 out of state; room/board: $13,350
Financial aid: (717) 871-5100; 60% of undergrads determined to have financial need; average aid package $8,758

Misericordia University
Dallas PA
(570) 674-6264
U.S. News ranking: Nat. U., No. 202
Website: www.misericordia.edu/
Admissions email: admiss@misericordia.edu
Private; founded 1924
Affiliation: Roman Catholic
Freshman admissions: selective; 2020-2021: 1,897 applied, 1,580 accepted. Neither SAT nor ACT required. SAT 25/75 percentile: 1040-1215. High school rank: 19% in top tenth, 51% in top quarter, 82% in top half
Early decision deadline: N/A, notification date: N/A
Early action deadline: N/A, notification date: N/A
Application deadline (fall): rolling
Undergraduate student body: 1,473 full time, 372 part time; 33% male, 67% female; 0% American Indian, 2% Asian, 3% black, 3% Hispanic, 4% multiracial, 0% Pacific Islander, 85% white, 0% international; 72% from in state; 38% live on campus; 0% of students in fraternities, 0% in sororities
Most popular majors: 19% Health Professions and Related Programs, 13% Business/Commerce, General, 11% Registered Nursing/Registered Nurse, 6% Psychology, General, 5% Medical Radiologic Technology/Science - Radiation Therapist
Expenses: 2021-2022: $35,940; room/board: $14,520
Financial aid: (570) 674-6222; 80% of undergrads determined to have financial need; average aid package $26,838

Moore College of Art & Design[1]
Philadelphia PA
(215) 965-4015
U.S. News ranking: Arts, unranked
Website: www.moore.edu
Admissions email: admiss@moore.edu

Private; founded 1848
Application deadline (fall): rolling
Undergraduate student body: N/A
full time, N/A part time
Expenses: 2020-2021: $44,806;
room/board: $16,836
Financial aid: N/A

Moravian University
Bethlehem PA
(610) 861-1320
U.S. News ranking: Nat. Lib. Arts,
No. 141
Website: www.moravian.edu
Admissions email:
admission@moravian.edu
Private; founded 1742
Affiliation: Moravian Church
Freshman admissions: selective;
2020-2021: 2,386 applied,
1,880 accepted. Neither SAT
nor ACT required. SAT 25/75
percentile: 1030-1190. High
school rank: 19% in top tenth,
48% in top quarter, 84% in
top half
Early decision deadline: N/A,
notification date: N/A
Early action deadline: N/A,
notification date: N/A
Application deadline (fall): rolling
Undergraduate student body: 1,859
full time, 138 part time; 39%
male, 61% female; 0% American
Indian, 2% Asian, 3% black,
12% Hispanic, 2% multiracial,
0% Pacific Islander, 72% white,
3% international; 76% from in
state; 49% live on campus; 14%
of students in fraternities, 21%
in sororities
Most popular majors: 24%
Registered Nursing/Registered
Nurse, 11% Business
Administration and Management,
General, 8% Psychology, General,
5% Sociology, 4% Accounting
Expenses: 2021-2022: $48,730;
room/board: $14,471
Financial aid: (610) 861-1330;
85% of undergrads determined to
have financial need; average aid
package $30,023

Mount Aloysius College
Cresson PA
(814) 886-6383
U.S. News ranking: Reg. Coll. (N),
No. 35
Website: www.mtaloy.edu
Admissions email:
admissions@mtaloy.edu
Private; founded 1853
Freshman admissions: least
selective; 2020-2021: 1,428
applied, 1,360 accepted. Neither
SAT nor ACT required. SAT 25/75
percentile: N/A. High school
rank: N/A
Early decision deadline: N/A,
notification date: N/A
Early action deadline: N/A,
notification date: N/A
Application deadline (fall): rolling
Undergraduate student body: 958
full time, 1,812 part time; 34%
male, 66% female; 0% American
Indian, 1% Asian, 4% black,
1% Hispanic, 0% multiracial,
0% Pacific Islander, 80% white,
5% international; N/A from in
state; 40% live on campus; N/A
of students in fraternities, N/A in

sororities
Most popular majors: 32% Health
Professions and Related Programs,
23% Business, Management,
Marketing, and Related Support
Services, 14% Biological and
Biomedical Sciences, 9%
Computer and Information
Sciences and Support Services,
5% Homeland Security, Law
Enforcement, Firefighting and
Related Protective Services
Expenses: 2021-2022: $24,890;
room/board: $11,634
Financial aid: (814) 886-6357;
89% of undergrads determined to
have financial need; average aid
package $17,102

Muhlenberg College
Allentown PA
(484) 664-3200
U.S. News ranking: Nat. Lib. Arts,
No. 67
Website: www.muhlenberg.edu
Admissions email:
admissions@muhlenberg.edu
Private; founded 1848
Affiliation: Lutheran Church in
America
Freshman admissions: more
selective; 2020-2021: 4,543
applied, 2,825 accepted. Neither
SAT nor ACT required. SAT
25/75 percentile: 1170-1350.
High school rank: 40% in top
tenth, 72% in top quarter, 91%
in top half
Early decision deadline: 11/15,
notification date: 12/15
Early action deadline: N/A,
notification date: N/A
Application deadline (fall): 2/1
Undergraduate student body: 1,974
full time, 89 part time; 40%
male, 60% female; 0% American
Indian, 4% Asian, 4% black,
9% Hispanic, 3% multiracial,
0% Pacific Islander, 72% white,
2% international; 33% from in
state; 30% live on campus; 10%
of students in fraternities, 6% in
sororities
Most popular majors: 24%
Business/Commerce, General,
20% Visual and Performing
Arts, General, 10% Biology/
Biological Sciences, General, 9%
Social Sciences, General, 8%
Psychology, General
Expenses: 2021-2022: $55,830;
room/board: $12,935
Financial aid: (484) 664-3175;
67% of undergrads determined to
have financial need; average aid
package $39,452

Neumann University
Aston PA
(610) 558-5616
U.S. News ranking: Reg. U. (N),
second tier
Website: www.neumann.edu
Admissions email:
neumann@neumann.edu
Private; founded 1965
Affiliation: Roman Catholic
Freshman admissions: less
selective; 2020-2021: 3,341
applied, 2,684 accepted. Neither
SAT nor ACT required. SAT 25/75
percentile: 900-1080. High
school rank: N/A

Early decision deadline: N/A,
notification date: N/A
Early action deadline: 12/1,
notification date: 12/24
Application deadline (fall): 8/15
Undergraduate student body: 1,441
full time, 491 part time; 36%
male, 64% female; 0% American
Indian, 2% Asian, 29% black,
7% Hispanic, 3% multiracial,
0% Pacific Islander, 55% white,
1% international; 33% from in
state; 31% live on campus; N/A
of students in fraternities, N/A in
sororities
Most popular majors: 22%
Registered Nursing, Nursing
Administration, Nursing Research
and Clinical Nursing, Other, 19%
Liberal Arts and Sciences/Liberal
Studies, 11% Homeland Security,
Law Enforcement, Firefighting and
Related Protective Services, Other,
6% Business Administration
and Management, General, 4%
Education/Teaching of Individuals
in Elementary Special Education
Programs
Expenses: 2021-2022: $34,460;
room/board: $15,100
Financial aid: (610) 558-5521;
83% of undergrads determined to
have financial need; average aid
package $24,281

Peirce College
Philadelphia PA
(888) 467-3472
U.S. News ranking: Reg. Coll. (N),
unranked
Website: www.peirce.edu
Admissions email: info@peirce.edu
Private; founded 1865
Freshman admissions: least
selective; 2020-2021: N/A
applied, N/A accepted. Neither
SAT nor ACT required. SAT 25/75
percentile: N/A. High school
rank: N/A
Early decision deadline: N/A,
notification date: N/A
Early action deadline: N/A,
notification date: N/A
Application deadline (fall): rolling
Undergraduate student body: 225
full time, 722 part time; 27%
male, 73% female; 1% American
Indian, 3% Asian, 54% black,
10% Hispanic, 2% multiracial,
0% Pacific Islander, 20% white,
1% international
Most popular majors: 41%
Business, Management,
Marketing, and Related Support
Services, 20% Health Professions
and Related Programs, 14%
Legal Professions and Studies,
12% Computer and Information
Sciences and Support Services,
11% Homeland Security, Law
Enforcement, Firefighting and
Related Protective Services
Expenses: 2020-2021: $15,060;
room/board: N/A
Financial aid: N/A

Pennsylvania Academy of the Fine Arts[1]
Philadelphia PA
(215) 972-7625
U.S. News ranking: Arts, unranked
Website: www.pafa.edu

Admissions email:
admissions@pafa.edu
Private; founded 1805
Application deadline (fall): 8/29
Undergraduate student body: N/A
full time, N/A part time
Expenses: 2020-2021: $42,000;
room/board: $13,420
Financial aid: N/A

Pennsylvania College of Art & Design
Lancaster PA
(800) 689-0379
U.S. News ranking: Arts, unranked
Website: pcad.edu
Admissions email:
admissions@pcad.edu
Private; founded 1982
Freshman admissions: least
selective; 2020-2021: 378
applied, 178 accepted. Neither
SAT nor ACT required. SAT 25/75
percentile: N/A. High school
rank: N/A
Early decision deadline: N/A,
notification date: N/A
Early action deadline: N/A,
notification date: N/A
Application deadline (fall): rolling
Undergraduate student body:
237 full time, 3 part time; 30%
male, 70% female; 0% American
Indian, 3% Asian, 12% black,
5% Hispanic, 7% multiracial, 0%
Pacific Islander, 70% white, 0%
international
Most popular majors: 32%
Illustration, 22% Graphic Design,
18% Fine/Studio Arts, General,
17% Game and Interactive Media
Design, 11% Photography
Expenses: 2020-2021: $27,650;
room/board: $10,638
Financial aid: N/A

Pennsylvania College of Technology
Williamsport PA
(570) 327-4761
U.S. News ranking: Reg. Coll. (N),
No. 9
Website: www.pct.edu
Admissions email:
admissions@pct.edu
Public; founded 1914
Freshman admissions: less
selective; 2020-2021: 4,246
applied, 3,118 accepted. Neither
SAT nor ACT required. SAT 25/75
percentile: 980-1160. High
school rank: 4% in top tenth, 21%
in top quarter, 49% in top half
Early decision deadline: N/A,
notification date: N/A
Early action deadline: N/A,
notification date: N/A
Application deadline (fall): 7/1
Undergraduate student body: 3,690
full time, 856 part time; 61%
male, 39% female; 0% American
Indian, 1% Asian, 3% black,
4% Hispanic, 3% multiracial,
0% Pacific Islander, 87% white,
0% international; 90% from in
state; 29% live on campus; N/A
of students in fraternities, N/A in
sororities
Most popular majors: 27% Health
Professions and Related Programs,
18% Engineering Technologies
and Engineering-Related Fields,
13% Mechanic and Repair
Technologies/Technicians, 9%

Construction Trades, 8% Business,
Management, Marketing, and
Related Support Services
Expenses: 2021-2022: $17,910
in state, $25,620 out of state;
room/board: $11,004
Financial aid: (570) 327-4766;
75% of undergrads determined to
have financial need

Pennsylvania State University–University Park
University Park PA
(814) 865-5471
U.S. News ranking: Nat. U., No. 63
Website: www.psu.edu
Admissions email:
admissions@psu.edu
Public; founded 1855
Freshman admissions: more
selective; 2020-2021: 73,861
applied, 40,031 accepted. Neither
SAT nor ACT required. SAT 25/75
percentile: 1150-1340. High
school rank: N/A
Early decision deadline: N/A,
notification date: N/A
Early action deadline: 11/1,
notification date: 12/24
Application deadline (fall): rolling
Undergraduate student body:
38,309 full time, 1,500 part
time; 53% male, 47% female;
0% American Indian, 6% Asian,
4% black, 7% Hispanic, 4%
multiracial, 0% Pacific Islander,
65% white, 12% international;
N/A from in state; 26% live
on campus; N/A of students in
fraternities, N/A in sororities
Most popular majors: 16%
Engineering, 15% Business,
Management, Marketing, and
Related Support Services, 10%
Computer and Information
Sciences and Support Services,
9% Social Sciences, 8%
Communication, Journalism, and
Related Programs
Expenses: 2021-2022: $18,898
in state, $36,476 out of state;
room/board: $10,958
Financial aid: (814) 865-6301;
46% of undergrads determined to
have financial need; average aid
package $11,390

Pittsburgh Technical College[1]
Oakdale PA
(412) 809-5100
U.S. News ranking: Reg. Coll. (N),
unranked
Website: www.ptcollege.edu
Admissions email:
james@ptcollege.edu
Private; founded 1946
Affiliation: Undenominational
Application deadline (fall): rolling
Undergraduate student body: N/A
full time, N/A part time
Expenses: 2020-2021: $16,485;
room/board: $10,602
Financial aid: (412) 809-5100

Point Park University
Pittsburgh PA
(800) 321-0129
U.S. News ranking: Reg. U. (N),
No. 82
Website: www.pointpark.edu

Admissions email: enroll@pointpark.edu
Private; founded 1960
Freshman admissions: selective; 2020-2021: 5,411 applied, 3,761 accepted. Either SAT or ACT required. SAT 25/75 percentile: 953-1180. High school rank: 11% in top tenth, 31% in top quarter, 65% in top half
Early decision deadline: N/A, notification date: N/A
Early action deadline: N/A, notification date: N/A
Application deadline (fall): rolling
Undergraduate student body: 2,410 full time, 381 part time; 39% male, 61% female; 0% American Indian, 2% Asian, 13% black, 6% Hispanic, 4% multiracial, 0% Pacific Islander, 71% white, 3% international; 72% from in state; 28% live on campus; N/A of students in fraternities, N/A in sororities
Most popular majors: 12% Dance, General, 9% Business Administration and Management, General, 9% Business, Management, Marketing, and Related Support Services, Other, 5% Cinematography and Film/Video Production, 4% Criminal Justice/Safety Studies
Expenses: 2021-2022: $35,610; room/board: $12,940
Financial aid: (412) 392-3930; 92% of undergrads determined to have financial need; average aid package $28,146

Robert Morris University
Moon Township PA
(412) 397-5200
U.S. News ranking: Nat. U., No. 187
Website: www.rmu.edu
Admissions email: admissions@rmu.edu
Private; founded 1921
Freshman admissions: selective; 2020-2021: 4,468 applied, 3,827 accepted. Neither SAT nor ACT required. SAT 25/75 percentile: 1040-1230. High school rank: 24% in top tenth, 48% in top quarter, 79% in top half
Early decision deadline: N/A, notification date: N/A
Early action deadline: N/A, notification date: N/A
Application deadline (fall): rolling
Undergraduate student body: 3,070 full time, 242 part time; 55% male, 45% female; 0% American Indian, 1% Asian, 5% black, 4% Hispanic, 6% multiracial, 0% Pacific Islander, 75% white, 6% international; 84% from in state; 45% live on campus; 14% of students in fraternities, 17% in sororities
Most popular majors: 34% Business, Management, Marketing, and Related Support Services, 14% Health Professions and Related Programs, 13% Engineering, 8% Homeland Security, Law Enforcement, Firefighting and Related Protective Services, 5% Computer and Information Sciences and Support Services

Expenses: 2021-2022: $32,770; room/board: $12,320
Financial aid: (412) 397-6250; 79% of undergrads determined to have financial need; average aid package $25,799

Rosemont College[1]
Rosemont PA
(610) 526-2966
U.S. News ranking: Reg. U. (N), second tier
Website: www.rosemont.edu
Admissions email: admissions@rosemont.edu
Private; founded 1921
Affiliation: Roman Catholic
Application deadline (fall): rolling
Undergraduate student body: N/A full time, N/A part time
Expenses: 2020-2021: $20,650; room/board: $13,130
Financial aid: (610) 527-0200

Saint Joseph's University
Philadelphia PA
(610) 660-1300
U.S. News ranking: Reg. U. (N), No. 8
Website: www.sju.edu
Admissions email: admit@sju.edu
Private; founded 1851
Affiliation: Roman Catholic
Freshman admissions: more selective; 2020-2021: 7,633 applied, 6,111 accepted. Neither SAT nor ACT required. SAT 25/75 percentile: 1100-1290. High school rank: 25% in top tenth, 51% in top quarter, 80% in top half
Early decision deadline: 11/1, notification date: 12/20
Early action deadline: 11/1, notification date: 12/20
Application deadline (fall): rolling
Undergraduate student body: 3,945 full time, 354 part time; 47% male, 53% female; 0% American Indian, 3% Asian, 6% black, 8% Hispanic, 3% multiracial, 0% Pacific Islander, 77% white, 1% international; 46% from in state; 53% live on campus; 5% of students in fraternities, 25% in sororities
Most popular majors: 10% Finance, General, 8% Marketing/Marketing Management, General, 7% Accounting, 7% Management Science, 6% Special Products Marketing Operations
Expenses: 2021-2022: $47,940; room/board: $14,840
Financial aid: (610) 660-1346; 61% of undergrads determined to have financial need; average aid package $34,865

Saint Vincent College
Latrobe PA
(800) 782-5549
U.S. News ranking: Nat. Lib. Arts, No. 146
Website: www.stvincent.edu
Admissions email: admission@stvincent.edu
Private; founded 1846
Affiliation: Roman Catholic
Freshman admissions: selective; 2020-2021: 2,310 applied,

1,666 accepted. Neither SAT nor ACT required. SAT 25/75 percentile: 960-1190. High school rank: 20% in top tenth, 47% in top quarter, 76% in top half
Early decision deadline: N/A, notification date: N/A
Early action deadline: N/A, notification date: N/A
Application deadline (fall): 5/1
Undergraduate student body: 1,415 full time, 47 part time; 55% male, 45% female; 0% American Indian, 1% Asian, 6% black, 5% Hispanic, 3% multiracial, 0% Pacific Islander, 81% white, 1% international; N/A from in state; 66% live on campus; N/A of students in fraternities, N/A in sororities
Most popular majors: 24% Business, Management, Marketing, and Related Support Services, 12% Biological and Biomedical Sciences, 10% Psychology, 9% Social Sciences, 6% Communication, Journalism, and Related Programs
Expenses: 2021-2022: $39,162; room/board: $12,520
Financial aid: (724) 805-2555; 78% of undergrads determined to have financial need; average aid package $33,945

Seton Hill University
Greensburg PA
(724) 838-4281
U.S. News ranking: Reg. U. (N), No. 34
Website: www.setonhill.edu
Admissions email: admit@setonhill.edu
Private; founded 1883
Affiliation: Roman Catholic
Freshman admissions: selective; 2020-2021: 2,572 applied, 2,023 accepted. Neither SAT nor ACT required. SAT 25/75 percentile: 1000-1200. High school rank: 26% in top tenth, 50% in top quarter, 77% in top half
Early decision deadline: N/A, notification date: N/A
Early action deadline: N/A, notification date: N/A
Application deadline (fall): 8/15
Undergraduate student body: 1,605 full time, 142 part time; 34% male, 66% female; 0% American Indian, 2% Asian, 8% black, 4% Hispanic, 3% multiracial, 0% Pacific Islander, 80% white, 1% international; N/A from in state; 48% live on campus; N/A of students in fraternities, N/A in sororities
Most popular majors: 20% Business, Management, Marketing, and Related Support Services, 17% Health Professions and Related Programs, 10% Visual and Performing Arts, 9% Parks, Recreation, Leisure, and Fitness Studies, 8% Education
Expenses: 2021-2022: $39,068; room/board: $12,960
Financial aid: (724) 830-1010; 76% of undergrads determined to have financial need; average aid package $29,064

Shippensburg University of Pennsylvania
Shippensburg PA
(717) 477-1231
U.S. News ranking: Reg. U. (N), No. 94
Website: www.ship.edu
Admissions email: admiss@ship.edu
Public; founded 1871
Freshman admissions: selective; 2020-2021: 6,759 applied, 6,347 accepted. Either SAT or ACT required. SAT 25/75 percentile: 940-1150. High school rank: 11% in top tenth, 28% in top quarter, 62% in top half
Early decision deadline: N/A, notification date: N/A
Early action deadline: N/A, notification date: N/A
Application deadline (fall): rolling
Undergraduate student body: 4,733 full time, 591 part time; 47% male, 53% female; 0% American Indian, 1% Asian, 15% black, 7% Hispanic, 5% multiracial, 0% Pacific Islander, 71% white, 1% international; N/A from in state; 32% live on campus; 10% of students in fraternities, 9% in sororities
Most popular majors: 35% Business, Management, Marketing, and Related Support Services, 9% Psychology, 8% Education, 5% Biological and Biomedical Sciences, 5% Homeland Security, Law Enforcement, Firefighting and Related Protective Services
Expenses: 2020-2021: $13,394 in state, $13,872 out of state; room/board: $12,006
Financial aid: (717) 477-1131; 71% of undergrads determined to have financial need; average aid package $10,063

Slippery Rock University of Pennsylvania
Slippery Rock PA
(800) 929-4778
U.S. News ranking: Reg. U. (N), No. 78
Website: www.sru.edu/admissions
Admissions email: asktherock@sru.edu
Public; founded 1889
Freshman admissions: selective; 2020-2021: 5,480 applied, 4,047 accepted. Either SAT or ACT required. SAT 25/75 percentile: 980-1150. High school rank: 15% in top tenth, 39% in top quarter, 75% in top half
Early decision deadline: N/A, notification date: N/A
Early action deadline: N/A, notification date: N/A
Application deadline (fall): rolling
Undergraduate student body: 6,860 full time, 555 part time; 44% male, 56% female; 0% American Indian, 1% Asian, 5% black, 3% Hispanic, 4% multiracial, 0% Pacific Islander, 84% white, 2% international; 91% from in state; 10% live on campus; 5% of students in fraternities, 8% in sororities

Most popular majors: 23% Visual and Performing Arts, 11% Business, Management, Marketing, and Related Support Services, 10% Engineering Technologies and Engineering-Related Fields, 7% Education, 6% Communication, Journalism, and Related Programs
Expenses: 2021-2022: $10,507 in state, $18,223 out of state; room/board: $11,210
Financial aid: (724) 738-2044; 65% of undergrads determined to have financial need; average aid package $9,498

St. Francis University
Loretto PA
(814) 472-3100
U.S. News ranking: Reg. U. (N), No. 23
Website: www.francis.edu/Admissions/
Admissions email: admissions@francis.edu
Private; founded 1847
Affiliation: Roman Catholic
Freshman admissions: selective; 2020-2021: 1,965 applied, 1,480 accepted. Neither SAT nor ACT required. SAT 25/75 percentile: 1010-1220. High school rank: 22% in top tenth, 58% in top quarter, 79% in top half
Early decision deadline: N/A, notification date: N/A
Early action deadline: N/A, notification date: N/A
Application deadline (fall): rolling
Undergraduate student body: 1,476 full time, 869 part time; 38% male, 62% female; 0% American Indian, 2% Asian, 7% black, 2% Hispanic, 2% multiracial, 0% Pacific Islander, 81% white, 1% international; 73% from in state; 65% live on campus; 13% of students in fraternities, 22% in sororities
Most popular majors: 14% Physician Assistant, 11% Occupational Therapy/Therapist, 6% Accounting, 6% Biology/Biological Sciences, General, 6% Registered Nursing/Registered Nurse
Expenses: 2020-2021: $39,278; room/board: $13,084
Financial aid: (814) 472-3010

Susquehanna University
Selinsgrove PA
(800) 326-9672
U.S. News ranking: Nat. Lib. Arts, No. 117
Website: www.susqu.edu
Admissions email: suadmiss@susqu.edu
Private; founded 1858
Affiliation: Evangelical Lutheran Church
Freshman admissions: selective; 2020-2021: 4,594 applied, 4,013 accepted. Neither SAT nor ACT required. SAT 25/75 percentile: 1070-1240. High school rank: 23% in top tenth, 53% in top quarter, 84% in top half
Early decision deadline: 11/15, notification date: 12/1

Early action deadline: 11/1, notification date: 12/1
Application deadline (fall): rolling
Undergraduate student body: 2,211 full time, 112 part time; 43% male, 57% female; 0% American Indian, 2% Asian, 6% black, 7% Hispanic, 3% multiracial, 0% Pacific Islander, 79% white, 1% international; N/A from in state; 89% live on campus; 19% of students in fraternities, 17% in sororities
Most popular majors: 22% Business, Management, Marketing, and Related Support Services, 15% Communication, Journalism, and Related Programs, 12% Biological and Biomedical Sciences, 8% English Language and Literature/Letters, 7% Social Sciences
Expenses: 2021-2022: $53,060; room/board: $14,350
Financial aid: (570) 372-4450; 79% of undergrads determined to have financial need; average aid package $40,633

Swarthmore College
Swarthmore PA
(610) 328-8300
U.S. News ranking: Nat. Lib. Arts, No. 3
Website: www.swarthmore.edu
Admissions email: admissions@swarthmore.edu
Private; founded 1864
Freshman admissions: most selective; 2020-2021: 11,630 applied, 1,054 accepted. Neither SAT nor ACT required. SAT 25/75 percentile: 1395-1540. High school rank: 93% in top tenth, 100% in top quarter, 100% in top half
Early decision deadline: 11/15, notification date: 12/15
Early action deadline: N/A, notification date: N/A
Application deadline (fall): 1/4
Undergraduate student body: 1,437 full time, 0 part time; 49% male, 51% female; 0% American Indian, 18% Asian, 8% black, 13% Hispanic, 9% multiracial, 0% Pacific Islander, 33% white, 15% international
Most popular majors: 25% Social Sciences, 11% Computer and Information Sciences and Support Services, 10% Biological and Biomedical Sciences, 6% Mathematics and Statistics, 6% Visual and Performing Arts
Expenses: 2021-2022: $56,056; room/board: $17,150
Financial aid: (610) 328-8358; 56% of undergrads determined to have financial need; average aid package $51,382

Temple University
Philadelphia PA
(215) 204-7200
U.S. News ranking: Nat. U., No. 103
Website: www.temple.edu
Admissions email: askanowl@temple.edu
Public; founded 1884
Freshman admissions: more selective; 2020-2021: 33,805 applied, 24,144 accepted. Neither

SAT nor ACT required. SAT 25/75 percentile: 1090-1280. High school rank: N/A
Early decision deadline: N/A, notification date: N/A
Early action deadline: 11/1, notification date: 1/10
Application deadline (fall): 2/1
Undergraduate student body: 24,884 full time, 2,331 part time; 45% male, 55% female; 0% American Indian, 13% Asian, 14% black, 8% Hispanic, 4% multiracial, 0% Pacific Islander, 55% white, 4% international; 78% from in state; 12% live on campus; 4% of students in fraternities, 7% in sororities
Most popular majors: 25% Business, Management, Marketing, and Related Support Services, 11% Communication, Journalism, and Related Programs, 8% Health Professions and Related Programs, 7% Visual and Performing Arts, 6% Biological and Biomedical Sciences
Expenses: 2021-2022: $20,291 in state, $34,801 out of state; room/board: $13,144
Financial aid: (215) 204-2244; 66% of undergrads determined to have financial need; average aid package $13,126

Thiel College
Greenville PA
(800) 248-4435
U.S. News ranking: Reg. Coll. (N), No. 18
Website: www.thiel.edu
Admissions email: admission@thiel.edu
Private; founded 1866
Affiliation: Evangelical Lutheran Church
Freshman admissions: less selective; 2020-2021: 1,679 applied, 1,402 accepted. Neither SAT nor ACT required. SAT 25/75 percentile: 890-1150. High school rank: 11% in top tenth, 30% in top quarter, 71% in top half
Early decision deadline: N/A, notification date: N/A
Early action deadline: N/A, notification date: N/A
Application deadline (fall): rolling
Undergraduate student body: 727 full time, 5 part time; 50% male, 50% female; N/A American Indian, N/A Asian, N/A black, N/A Hispanic, N/A multiracial, N/A Pacific Islander, N/A white, N/A international
Most popular majors: Information not available
Expenses: 2021-2022: $34,470; room/board: $13,968
Financial aid: (724) 589-2178

Thomas Jefferson University
Philadelphia PA
(800) 951-7287
U.S. News ranking: Nat. U., No. 148
Website: www.jefferson.edu/
Admissions email: enroll@jefferson.edu
Private; founded 1824
Freshman admissions: more selective; 2020-2021: 4,469 applied, 3,121 accepted. Neither

SAT nor ACT required. SAT 25/75 percentile: 1090-1270. High school rank: 27% in top tenth, 56% in top quarter, 88% in top half
Early decision deadline: N/A, notification date: N/A
Early action deadline: 11/1, notification date: 12/4
Application deadline (fall): 7/31
Undergraduate student body: 3,216 full time, 567 part time; 27% male, 73% female; 0% American Indian, 8% Asian, 13% black, 12% Hispanic, 8% multiracial, 0% Pacific Islander, 54% white, 2% international; 62% from in state; 23% live on campus; 2% of students in fraternities, 2% in sororities
Most popular majors: Information not available
Expenses: 2020-2021: $41,715; room/board: $13,881
Financial aid: (215) 951-2940

University of Pennsylvania
Philadelphia PA
(215) 898-7507
U.S. News ranking: Nat. U., No. 8
Website: www.upenn.edu
Admissions email: info@admissions.upenn.edu
Private; founded 1740
Freshman admissions: most selective; 2020-2021: 42,205 applied, 3,789 accepted. Neither SAT nor ACT required. SAT 25/75 percentile: 1460-1570. High school rank: 96% in top tenth, 99% in top quarter, 100% in top half
Early decision deadline: 11/1, notification date: 12/14
Early action deadline: N/A, notification date: N/A
Application deadline (fall): 1/5
Undergraduate student body: 9,692 full time, 180 part time; 46% male, 54% female; 0% American Indian, 25% Asian, 8% black, 10% Hispanic, 5% multiracial, 0% Pacific Islander, 36% white, 13% international; 19% from in state; N/A live on campus; 30% of students in fraternities, 28% in sororities
Most popular majors: 21% Business, Management, Marketing, and Related Support Services, 15% Social Sciences, 10% Biological and Biomedical Sciences, 9% Engineering, 7% Computer and Information Sciences and Support Services
Expenses: 2021-2022: $61,710; room/board: $17,304
Financial aid: (215) 898-1988; 45% of undergrads determined to have financial need; average aid package $57,025

University of Pittsburgh at Bradford[1]
Bradford PA
(800) 872-1787
U.S. News ranking: Reg. Coll. (N), No. 18
Website: www.upb.pitt.edu
Admissions email: admissions@pitt.edu

Public; founded 1963
Application deadline (fall): rolling
Undergraduate student body: N/A full time, N/A part time
Expenses: 2021-2022: $14,354 in state, $25,994 out of state; room/board: $9,612
Financial aid: (814) 362-7550; 85% of undergrads determined to have financial need; average aid package $16,922

University of Pittsburgh–Greensburg[1]
Greensburg PA
(724) 837-7040
U.S. News ranking: Nat. Lib. Arts, second tier
Admissions email: N/A
Public
Application deadline (fall): N/A
Undergraduate student body: N/A full time, N/A part time
Expenses: 2020-2021: $14,114 in state, $25,582 out of state; room/board: $10,870
Financial aid: N/A

University of Pittsburgh–Johnstown[1]
Johnstown PA
(814) 269-7000
U.S. News ranking: Reg. Coll. (N), No. 28
Admissions email: N/A
Public
Application deadline (fall): N/A
Undergraduate student body: N/A full time, N/A part time
Expenses: 2020-2021: $14,090 in state, $25,558 out of state; room/board: $10,060
Financial aid: N/A

University of Pittsburgh–Pittsburgh Campus
Pittsburgh PA
(412) 624-7488
U.S. News ranking: Nat. U., No. 59
Website: www.pitt.edu/
Admissions email: pitt.admissions@pitt.edu
Public; founded 1787
Freshman admissions: more selective; 2020-2021: 32,549 applied, 20,791 accepted. Either SAT or ACT required. SAT 25/75 percentile: 1243-1420. High school rank: 54% in top tenth, 86% in top quarter, 99% in top half
Early decision deadline: N/A, notification date: N/A
Early action deadline: N/A, notification date: N/A
Application deadline (fall): rolling
Undergraduate student body: 18,274 full time, 923 part time; 46% male, 54% female; 0% American Indian, 12% Asian, 5% black, 6% Hispanic, 5% multiracial, 0% Pacific Islander, 67% white, 4% international; 65% from in state; 35% live on campus; 9% of students in fraternities, 13% in sororities
Most popular majors: 14%

Business, Management, Marketing, and Related Support Services, 12% Engineering, 12% Health Professions and Related Programs, 11% Biological and Biomedical Sciences, 10% Social Sciences
Expenses: 2021-2022: $19,092 in state, $34,124 out of state; room/board: N/A
Financial aid: (412) 624-7488; 50% of undergrads determined to have financial need; average aid package $15,223

University of Scranton
Scranton PA
(570) 941-7540
U.S. News ranking: Reg. U. (N), No. 5
Website: www.scranton.edu
Admissions email: admissions@scranton.edu
Private; founded 1888
Affiliation: Roman Catholic
Freshman admissions: more selective; 2020-2021: 9,111 applied, 7,315 accepted. Either SAT or ACT required. SAT 25/75 percentile: 1100-1280. High school rank: 35% in top tenth, 63% in top quarter, 88% in top half
Early decision deadline: N/A, notification date: N/A
Early action deadline: 11/15, notification date: 12/15
Application deadline (fall): 3/1
Undergraduate student body: 3,499 full time, 159 part time; 41% male, 59% female; 0% American Indian, 3% Asian, 2% black, 11% Hispanic, 2% multiracial, 0% Pacific Islander, 77% white, 1% international; 57% from in state; 59% live on campus; N/A of students in fraternities, N/A in sororities
Most popular majors: 23% Business, Management, Marketing, and Related Support Services, 19% Health Professions and Related Programs, 13% Biological and Biomedical Sciences, 7% Parks, Recreation, Leisure, and Fitness Studies
Expenses: 2021-2022: $48,462; room/board: $15,990
Financial aid: (570) 941-7701; 70% of undergrads determined to have financial need; average aid package $34,283

University of the Arts[1]
Philadelphia PA
(215) 717-6049
U.S. News ranking: Arts, unranked
Website: www.uarts.edu
Admissions email: admissions@uarts.edu
Private; founded 1876
Application deadline (fall): rolling
Undergraduate student body: N/A full time, N/A part time
Expenses: 2020-2021: $46,680; room/board: $17,630
Financial aid: (215) 717-6170

University of Valley Forge

Phoenixville PA
(800) 432-8322
U.S. News ranking: Reg. Coll. (N), No. 25
Website: www.valleyforge.edu/
Admissions email: admissions@valleyforge.edu
Private; founded 1939
Affiliation: Assemblies of God Church
Freshman admissions: less selective; 2020-2021: 522 applied, 329 accepted. Neither SAT nor ACT required. SAT 25/75 percentile: 900-1088. High school rank: 6% in top tenth, 27% in top quarter, 61% in top half
Early decision deadline: N/A, notification date: N/A
Early action deadline: N/A, notification date: N/A
Application deadline (fall): 8/1
Undergraduate student body: 396 full time, 99 part time; 47% male, 53% female; 0% American Indian, 3% Asian, 16% black, 22% Hispanic, 6% multiracial, 0% Pacific Islander, 48% white, 1% international; 42% from in state; 72% live on campus; 0% of students in fraternities, 0% in sororities
Most popular majors: 39% Theology and Religious Vocations, 19% Communication, Journalism, and Related Programs, 9% Education, 8% Psychology, 7% Business, Management, Marketing, and Related Support Services
Expenses: 2021-2022: $23,070; room/board: $9,544
Financial aid: (610) 917-1475; 87% of undergrads determined to have financial need; average aid package $18,091

Ursinus College

Collegeville PA
(610) 409-3200
U.S. News ranking: Nat. Lib. Arts, No. 85
Website: www.ursinus.edu
Admissions email: admission@ursinus.edu
Private; founded 1869
Freshman admissions: more selective; 2020-2021: 3,834 applied, 3,084 accepted. Neither SAT nor ACT required. SAT 25/75 percentile: 1150-1330. High school rank: 24% in top tenth, 54% in top quarter, 82% in top half
Early decision deadline: 12/1, notification date: 12/15
Early action deadline: 11/1, notification date: 12/15
Application deadline (fall): 2/1
Undergraduate student body: 1,484 full time, 9 part time; 51% male, 49% female; 0% American Indian, 4% Asian, 7% black, 7% Hispanic, 4% multiracial, 0% Pacific Islander, 74% white, 1% international; 63% from in state; 76% live on campus; 6% of students in fraternities, 13% in sororities
Most popular majors: 31% Biological and Biomedical Sciences, 20% Social Sciences,

9% Communication, Journalism, and Related Programs, 8% Psychology, 5% Physical Sciences
Expenses: 2021-2022: $56,600; room/board: $14,060
Financial aid: (610) 409-3600; 73% of undergrads determined to have financial need; average aid package $43,338

Villanova University

Villanova PA
(610) 519-4000
U.S. News ranking: Nat. U., No. 49
Website: www.villanova.edu
Admissions email: gotovu@villanova.edu
Private; founded 1842
Affiliation: Roman Catholic
Freshman admissions: most selective; 2020-2021: 22,083 applied, 6,770 accepted. Neither SAT nor ACT required. SAT 25/75 percentile: 1320-1460. High school rank: 72% in top tenth, 95% in top quarter, 99% in top half
Early decision deadline: 11/1, notification date: 12/20
Early action deadline: 11/1, notification date: 1/15
Application deadline (fall): 1/15
Undergraduate student body: 6,793 full time, 244 part time; 47% male, 53% female; 0% American Indian, 6% Asian, 5% black, 9% Hispanic, 3% multiracial, 0% Pacific Islander, 72% white, 2% international; 21% from in state; 69% live on campus; 21% of students in fraternities, 26% in sororities
Most popular majors: 24% Business, Management, Marketing, and Related Support Services, 14% Health Professions and Related Programs, 13% Engineering, 13% Social Sciences, 7% Communication, Journalism, and Related Programs
Expenses: 2021-2022: $59,900; room/board: $15,386
Financial aid: (610) 519-4010; 46% of undergrads determined to have financial need; average aid package $47,136

Washington and Jefferson College

Washington PA
(724) 223-6025
U.S. News ranking: Nat. Lib. Arts, No. 92
Website: www.washjeff.edu
Admissions email: admission@washjeff.edu
Private; founded 1781
Freshman admissions: selective; 2020-2021: 2,504 applied, 2,251 accepted. Neither SAT nor ACT required. SAT 25/75 percentile: 1040-1270. High school rank: 25% in top tenth, 49% in top quarter, 80% in top half
Early decision deadline: 12/1, notification date: 12/15
Early action deadline: 1/15, notification date: 2/15
Application deadline (fall): 3/1
Undergraduate student body: 1,158 full time, 8 part time; 50% male, 50% female; 0% American Indian, 2% Asian, 8% black, 6%

Hispanic, 4% multiracial, 0% Pacific Islander, 75% white, 1% international; 75% from in state; 44% live on campus; 29% of students in fraternities, 33% in sororities
Most popular majors: 14% Business/Commerce, General, 11% Psychology, General, 8% Political Science and Government, General, 6% Accounting, 6% Chemistry, General
Expenses: 2021-2022: $50,169; room/board: $13,272
Financial aid: (724) 223-6019; 79% of undergrads determined to have financial need; average aid package $42,727

Waynesburg University

Waynesburg PA
(800) 225-7393
U.S. News ranking: Reg. U. (N), No. 58
Website: www.waynesburg.edu/
Admissions email: admissions@waynesburg.edu
Private; founded 1849
Affiliation: Presbyterian Church (USA)
Freshman admissions: selective; 2020-2021: 1,584 applied, 1,425 accepted. Neither SAT nor ACT required. SAT 25/75 percentile: 980-1170. High school rank: 22% in top tenth, 49% in top quarter, 80% in top half
Early decision deadline: N/A, notification date: N/A
Early action deadline: N/A, notification date: N/A
Application deadline (fall): rolling
Undergraduate student body: 1,208 full time, 49 part time; 42% male, 58% female; 0% American Indian, 1% Asian, 4% black, 3% Hispanic, 3% multiracial, 0% Pacific Islander, 85% white, 0% international; 77% from in state; N/A live on campus; N/A of students in fraternities, N/A in sororities
Most popular majors: 24% Registered Nursing/Registered Nurse, 11% Criminal Justice/Law Enforcement Administration, 6% Speech Communication and Rhetoric, 5% Business Administration and Management, General
Expenses: 2021-2022: $27,450; room/board: $11,380
Financial aid: (724) 852-3208; 80% of undergrads determined to have financial need; average aid package $21,883

West Chester University of Pennsylvania

West Chester PA
(610) 436-3414
U.S. News ranking: Reg. U. (N), No. 50
Website: www.wcupa.edu/
Admissions email: ugadmiss@wcupa.edu
Public; founded 1871
Freshman admissions: selective; 2020-2021: 14,240 applied, 12,277 accepted. Neither SAT nor ACT required. SAT 25/75

percentile: 1010-1180. High school rank: 14% in top tenth, 36% in top quarter, 73% in top half
Early decision deadline: N/A, notification date: N/A
Early action deadline: N/A, notification date: N/A
Application deadline (fall): rolling
Undergraduate student body: 13,056 full time, 1,656 part time; 40% male, 60% female; 0% American Indian, 3% Asian, 11% black, 6% Hispanic, 4% multiracial, 0% Pacific Islander, 74% white, 0% international; 90% from in state; 3% live on campus; 13% of students in fraternities, 13% in sororities
Most popular majors: 25% Business, Management, Marketing, and Related Support Services, 15% Health Professions and Related Programs, 10% Education, 8% English Language and Literature/Letters, 7% Psychology
Expenses: 2021-2022: $9,993 in state, $21,567 out of state; room/board: $9,494
Financial aid: (610) 436-2627; 54% of undergrads determined to have financial need; average aid package $9,318

Westminster College

New Wilmington PA
(724) 946-7100
U.S. News ranking: Nat. Lib. Arts, No. 117
Website: www.westminster.edu
Admissions email: admis@westminster.edu
Private; founded 1852
Affiliation: Presbyterian Church (USA)
Freshman admissions: selective; 2020-2021: 2,221 applied, 2,102 accepted. Neither SAT nor ACT required. SAT 25/75 percentile: 990-1200. High school rank: 22% in top tenth, 23% in top quarter, 35% in top half
Early decision deadline: N/A, notification date: N/A
Early action deadline: 11/15, notification date: 12/1
Application deadline (fall): 5/1
Undergraduate student body: 1,094 full time, 62 part time; 44% male, 56% female; 1% American Indian, 0% Asian, 5% black, 1% Hispanic, 1% multiracial, 0% Pacific Islander, 78% white, 0% international; N/A from in state; 76% live on campus; 27% of students in fraternities, 42% in sororities
Most popular majors: 28% Business, Management, Marketing, and Related Support Services, 16% Foreign Languages, Literatures, and Linguistics, 8% Social Sciences, 7% Education, 7% Psychology
Expenses: 2021-2022: $38,230; room/board: $11,670
Financial aid: (724) 946-7102; 84% of undergrads determined to have financial need; average aid package $32,460

Widener University

Chester PA
(610) 499-4126
U.S. News ranking: Nat. U., No. 213
Website: www.widener.edu
Admissions email: admissions.office@widener.edu
Private; founded 1821
Freshman admissions: selective; 2020-2021: 5,739 applied, 4,280 accepted. Neither SAT nor ACT required. SAT 25/75 percentile: 1035-1210. High school rank: N/A
Early decision deadline: N/A, notification date: N/A
Early action deadline: N/A, notification date: N/A
Application deadline (fall): rolling
Undergraduate student body: 2,633 full time, 279 part time; 43% male, 57% female; 0% American Indian, 3% Asian, 13% black, 6% Hispanic, 3% multiracial, 0% Pacific Islander, 71% white, 1% international; 60% from in state; N/A live on campus; 14% of students in fraternities, 19% in sororities
Most popular majors: Information not available
Expenses: 2021-2022: $49,706; room/board: $14,808
Financial aid: (610) 499-4161; 77% of undergrads determined to have financial need; average aid package $34,940

Wilkes University

Wilkes-Barre PA
(570) 408-4400
U.S. News ranking: Nat. U., No. 213
Website: www.wilkes.edu
Admissions email: admissions@wilkes.edu
Private; founded 1933
Freshman admissions: selective; 2020-2021: 3,633 applied, 3,334 accepted. Either SAT or ACT required. SAT 25/75 percentile: 1040-1230. High school rank: 18% in top tenth, 46% in top quarter, 79% in top half
Early decision deadline: N/A, notification date: N/A
Early action deadline: N/A, notification date: N/A
Application deadline (fall): rolling
Undergraduate student body: 1,996 full time, 247 part time; 48% male, 52% female; 0% American Indian, 2% Asian, 5% black, 8% Hispanic, 3% multiracial, 0% Pacific Islander, 73% white, 6% international; 76% from in state; 41% live on campus; 0% of students in fraternities, 0% in sororities
Most popular majors: 18% Business, Management, Marketing, and Related Support Services, 18% Health Professions and Related Programs, 16% Engineering, 7% Biological and Biomedical Sciences, 5% Social Sciences
Expenses: 2021-2022: $39,914; room/board: $15,698
Financial aid: (570) 408-4512; 79% of undergrads determined to have financial need; average aid package $28,902

Wilson College[1]
Chambersburg PA
(800) 421-8402
U.S. News ranking: Reg. U. (N),
No. 126
Website: www.wilson.edu
Admissions email:
admissions@wilson.edu
Private; founded 1869
Affiliation: Presbyterian Church
(USA)
Application deadline (fall): rolling
Undergraduate student body: N/A
full time, N/A part time
Expenses: 2021-2022: $26,200;
room/board: $11,840
Financial aid: (717) 262-2016;
79% of undergrads determined to
have financial need; average aid
package $20,076

York College of Pennsylvania
York PA
(717) 849-1600
U.S. News ranking: Reg. U. (N),
No. 85
Website: www.ycp.edu
Admissions email:
admissions@ycp.edu
Private; founded 1787
Freshman admissions: selective;
2020-2021: 5,787 applied,
4,092 accepted. Either SAT
or ACT required. SAT 25/75
percentile: 990-1180. High school
rank: 10% in top tenth, 35% in
top quarter, 71% in top half
Early decision deadline: 12/15,
notification date: 10/1
Early action deadline: N/A,
notification date: N/A
Application deadline (fall): 8/23
Undergraduate student body: 3,438
full time, 310 part time; 44%
male, 56% female; 0% American
Indian, 2% Asian, 6% black,
8% Hispanic, 4% multiracial,
0% Pacific Islander, 78% white,
1% international; 65% from in
state; 54% live on campus; 6%
of students in fraternities, 11%
in sororities
Most popular majors: 20%
Business, Management,
Marketing, and Related Support
Services, 18% Health Professions
and Related Programs, 8%
Education, 7% Engineering,
7% Homeland Security, Law
Enforcement, Firefighting and
Related Protective Services
Expenses: 2021-2022: $22,350;
room/board: $12,050
Financial aid: (717) 815-6539;
65% of undergrads determined to
have financial need; average aid
package $14,850

PUERTO RICO

American University of Puerto Rico–Manati[1]
Bayamon PR
(787) 620-2040
U.S. News ranking: Reg. Coll. (S),
second tier
Website: www.aupr.edu/
Admissions email:
N/A
Private

Application deadline (fall): N/A
Undergraduate student body: N/A
full time, N/A part time
Expenses: 2020-2021: $6,555;
room/board: N/A
Financial aid: N/A

Bayamon Central University[1]
Bayamon PR
(787) 786-3030
U.S. News ranking: Reg. U. (S),
second tier
Website: www.ucb.edu.pr/
Admissions email:
N/A
Private
Application deadline (fall): N/A
Undergraduate student body: N/A
full time, N/A part time
Expenses: 2020-2021: $5,462;
room/board: $2,700
Financial aid: N/A

Caribbean University[1]
Bayamon PR
(787) 780-0070
U.S. News ranking: Reg. U. (S),
second tier
Website: www.caribbean.edu/
Admissions email:
N/A
Private
Application deadline (fall): N/A
Undergraduate student body: N/A
full time, N/A part time
Expenses: 2020-2021: $5,496;
room/board: N/A
Financial aid: N/A

Colegio Universitario de San Juan[1]
San Juan PR
(787) 480-2400
U.S. News ranking: Reg. Coll. (S),
second tier
Website: www.pierce.ctc.edu
Admissions email:
N/A
Public
Application deadline (fall): N/A
Undergraduate student body: N/A
full time, N/A part time
Expenses: 2020-2021: $2,340 in
state, $2,340 out of state; room/
board: N/A
Financial aid: N/A

EDP University of Puerto Rico Inc–San Juan[1]
San Juan PR
787-765-3560
U.S. News ranking: Reg. U. (S),
No. 80
Website: www.greenriver.edu/
Admissions email:
N/A
Private
Application deadline (fall): N/A
Undergraduate student body: N/A
full time, N/A part time
Expenses: 2020-2021: $6,200;
room/board: N/A
Financial aid: N/A

Escuela de Artes Plasticas de Puerto Rico[1]
San Juan PR
(787) 725-8120
U.S. News ranking: Arts, unranked
Website: www.eap.edu
Admissions email:
N/A
Public
Application deadline (fall): N/A
Undergraduate student body: N/A
full time, N/A part time
Expenses: 2020-2021: $3,942 in
state, $6,582 out of state; room/
board: N/A
Financial aid: N/A

Inter American University of Puerto Rico–Aguadilla
Aguadilla PR
(787) 891-0925
U.S. News ranking: Reg. U. (S),
second tier
Website: aguadilla.inter.edu
Admissions email:
dperez@aguadilla.inter.edu
Private; founded 1957
Freshman admissions: less
selective; 2020-2021: 1,496
applied, 639 accepted. Either
SAT or ACT required. SAT 25/75
percentile: N/A. High school
rank: N/A
Early decision deadline: N/A,
notification date: N/A
Early action deadline: N/A,
notification date: N/A
Application deadline (fall): 8/16
Undergraduate student body: 2,690
full time, 620 part time; 40%
male, 60% female; 0% American
Indian, 0% Asian, 0% black,
100% Hispanic, 0% multiracial,
0% Pacific Islander, 0% white,
0% international
Most popular majors: 12% Criminal
Justice/Safety Studies, 10%
Biology/Biological Sciences,
General, 10% Registered Nursing/
Registered Nurse
Expenses: 2020-2021: $5,974;
room/board: N/A
Financial aid: (787) 891-0925

Inter American University of Puerto Rico–Arecibo[1]
Arecibo PR
(787) 878-5195
U.S. News ranking: Reg. U. (S),
second tier
Website: www.arecibo.inter.edu
Admissions email:
N/A
Private; founded 1957
Application deadline (fall): rolling
Undergraduate student body: 2,546
full time, 455 part time
Expenses: 2020-2021: $5,986;
room/board: N/A
Financial aid: (787) 878-5475

Inter American University of Puerto Rico–Barranquitas
Barranquitas PR
(787) 857-3600
U.S. News ranking: Reg. Coll. (S),
No. 62
Website: www.br.inter.edu/

Admissions email:
aicolon@br.inter.edu
Private; founded 1957
Affiliation: Other
Freshman admissions: less
selective; 2020-2021: 916
applied, 374 accepted. Neither
SAT nor ACT required. SAT 25/75
percentile: N/A. High school
rank: N/A
Early decision deadline: N/A,
notification date: N/A
Early action deadline: N/A,
notification date: N/A
Application deadline (fall): rolling
Undergraduate student body: 998
full time, 176 part time; 33%
male, 67% female; 0% American
Indian, 0% Asian, 0% black,
100% Hispanic, 0% multiracial,
0% Pacific Islander, 0% white,
0% international
Most popular majors: 44%
Registered Nursing/Registered
Nurse, 12% Biotechnology,
9% Radiologic Technology/
Science - Radiographer, 7% Office
Management and Supervision,
5% Biology/Biological Sciences,
General
Expenses: 2021-2022: $5,974;
room/board: N/A
Financial aid: (787) 857-3600;
99% of undergrads determined to
have financial need; average aid
package $819

Inter American University of Puerto Rico–Bayamon
Bayamon PR
(787) 279-1912
U.S. News ranking: Reg. Coll. (S),
second tier
Website: interbayamon3.
azurewebsites.net/
Admissions email:
admisiones@bayamon.inter.edu
Private; founded 1912
Freshman admissions: less
selective; 2020-2021: 1,788
applied, 859 accepted. Neither
SAT nor ACT required. SAT 25/75
percentile: N/A. High school
rank: N/A
Early decision deadline: N/A,
notification date: N/A
Early action deadline: N/A,
notification date: N/A
Application deadline (fall): N/A
Undergraduate student body: 3,500
full time, 540 part time; 55%
male, 45% female; 0% American
Indian, 0% Asian, 0% black, 99%
Hispanic, 0% multiracial, 0%
Pacific Islander, 0% white, 0%
international
Most popular majors: 13%
Homeland Security, Law
Enforcement, Firefighting and
Related Protective Services,
8% Biological and Biomedical
Sciences, 8% Health Professions
and Related Programs, 6%
Business, Management,
Marketing, and Related Support
Services, 6% Communications
Technologies/Technicians and
Support Services
Expenses: 2021-2022: $6,012;
room/board: $8,232
Financial aid: (787) 279-1912;
98% of undergrads determined to
have financial need; average aid
package $564

Inter American University of Puerto Rico–Fajardo[1]
Fajardo PR
(787) 860-3100
U.S. News ranking: Reg. U. (S),
second tier
Website: www.fajardo.inter.edu
Admissions email:
ada.caraballo@fajardo.inter.edu
Private; founded 1912
Application deadline (fall): 5/15
Undergraduate student body: N/A
full time, N/A part time
Expenses: 2020-2021: $6,012;
room/board: N/A
Financial aid: (787) 863-2390

Inter American University of Puerto Rico–Guayama[7]
Guayama PR
(787) 864-7059
U.S. News ranking: Reg. Coll. (S),
second tier
Website: www.guayama.inter.edu/
Admissions email:
laura.ferrer@guayama.inter.edu
Private; founded 1958
Freshman admissions: less
selective; 2020-2021: 578
applied, 243 accepted. Neither
SAT nor ACT required. SAT 25/75
percentile: N/A. High school
rank: N/A
Early decision deadline: N/A,
notification date: N/A
Early action deadline: N/A,
notification date: N/A
Application deadline (fall): rolling
Undergraduate student body: 1,238
full time, 312 part time
Most popular majors: 54%
Registered Nursing/Registered
Nurse, 8% Accounting, 6%
Biology/Biological Sciences,
General, 5% Biotechnology, 5%
Criminal Justice/Safety Studies
Expenses: 2020-2021: $5,974;
room/board: N/A
Financial aid: (787) 864-2222

Inter American University of Puerto Rico–Metropolitan Campus[1]
San Juan PR
(787) 250-1912
U.S. News ranking: Nat. U.,
second tier
Website: www.metro.inter.edu/
Admissions email:
rrobles@metro.inter.edu
Private; founded 1962
Application deadline (fall): N/A
Undergraduate student body: N/A
full time, N/A part time
Expenses: 2021-2022: $7,584;
room/board: N/A
Financial aid: (787) 250-1912;
92% of undergrads determined to
have financial need; average aid
package $954

Inter American University of Puerto Rico–Ponce[1]
Mercedita PR
(787) 841-0110
U.S. News ranking: Reg. U. (S),
second tier

Website: www.ponce.inter.edu
Admissions email:
admisiones@ponce.inter.edu
Private; founded 1962
Application deadline (fall): N/A
Undergraduate student body: 2,756
full time, 647 part time
Expenses: 2021-2022: $5,182;
room/board: N/A
Financial aid: (787) 284-1912;
98% of undergrads determined to
have financial need; average aid
package $732

Inter American University of Puerto Rico–San German[1]

San German PR
(787) 264-1912
U.S. News ranking: Nat. U.,
No. 263
Website: www.sg.inter.edu/
Admissions email:
milcama@sg.inter.edu
Private; founded 1912
Freshman admissions: less
selective; 2020-2021: 1,420
applied, 633 accepted. Neither
SAT nor ACT required. SAT 25/75
percentile: N/A. High school
rank: N/A
Early decision deadline: N/A,
notification date: N/A
Early action deadline: N/A,
notification date: N/A
Application deadline (fall): rolling
Undergraduate student body: 2,642
full time, 501 part time; 44%
male, 56% female; 0% American
Indian, 0% Asian, 0% black,
100% Hispanic, 0% multiracial,
0% Pacific Islander, 0% white,
0% international
Most popular majors: 25% Biology/
Biological Sciences, General,
10% Registered Nursing/
Registered Nurse, 8% Psychology,
General, 7% Sport and Fitness
Administration/Management, 5%
Computer Science
Expenses: 2020-2021: $6,012;
room/board: $5,664
Financial aid: N/A

Pontifical Catholic University of Puerto Rico–Arecibo[1]

Arecibo PR
(787) 881-1212
U.S. News ranking: Reg. U. (S),
second tier
Website: www.edcc.edu
Admissions email:
N/A
Private
Undergraduate student body: N/A
full time, N/A part time
Expenses: 2020-2021: $5,408;
room/board: N/A
Financial aid: N/A

Pontifical Catholic University of Puerto Rico–Ponce[1]

Ponce PR
(787) 841-2000
U.S. News ranking: Nat. U.,
second tier
Website: www.pucpr.edu
Admissions email:
admisiones@pucpr.edu
Private; founded 1948

Affiliation: Roman Catholic
Application deadline (fall): 8/19
Undergraduate student body: N/A
full time, N/A part time
Expenses: 2020-2021: $5,510;
room/board: $5,150
Financial aid: (787) 841-2000

Puerto Rico Conservatory of Music[1]

San Juan PR
(787) 751-0160
U.S. News ranking: Arts, unranked
Website: www.cmpr.edu
Admissions email:
http://cmpr.edu/admisiones
Public
Application deadline (fall): N/A
Undergraduate student body: N/A
full time, N/A part time
Expenses: 2020-2021: $3,370 in
state, $3,850 out of state; room/
board: N/A
Financial aid: N/A

Universidad Adventista de las Antillas[1]

Mayaguez PR
(787) 834-9595
U.S. News ranking: Reg. Coll. (S),
No. 66
Website: www.uaa.edu/esp/
Admissions email:
N/A
Private
Application deadline (fall): N/A
Undergraduate student body: N/A
full time, N/A part time
Expenses: 2021-2022: $6,270;
room/board: N/A
Financial aid: N/A

Universidad Ana G. Mendez–Carolina Campus[1]

Carolina PR

U.S. News ranking: Reg. U. (S),
second tier
Website: www.suagm.edu/une/
Admissions email:
N/A
Private; founded 1949
Application deadline (fall): rolling
Undergraduate student body: N/A
full time, N/A part time
Expenses: 2020-2021: $5,820;
room/board: N/A
Financial aid: N/A

Universidad Ana G. Mendez–Cupey Campus[1]

Rio Piedras PR
(787) 766-1717
U.S. News ranking: Reg. U. (S),
second tier
Website: www.suagm.edu/
Admissions email:
N/A
Private
Application deadline (fall): rolling
Undergraduate student body: N/A
full time, N/A part time
Expenses: 2020-2021: $5,820;
room/board: N/A
Financial aid: N/A

Universidad Ana G. Mendez–Gurabo Campus[1]

Gurabo PR
(787) 743-7979
U.S. News ranking: Nat. U.,
second tier
Website: www.ut.suagm.edu
Admissions email:
admisiones-ut@suagm.edu
Private; founded 1972
Application deadline (fall): rolling
Undergraduate student body: N/A
full time, N/A part time
Expenses: 2020-2021: $5,820;
room/board: N/A
Financial aid: N/A

Universidad del Sagrado Corazon

Santurce PR
(787) 728-1515
U.S. News ranking: Reg. U. (S),
second tier
Website: www.sagrado.edu/
Admissions email:
admision@sagrado.edu
Private; founded 1935
Affiliation: Roman Catholic
Freshman admissions: less
selective; 2020-2021: 3,981
applied, 1,724 accepted. Neither
SAT nor ACT required. SAT 25/75
percentile: N/A. High school
rank: N/A
Early decision deadline: N/A,
notification date: N/A
Early action deadline: N/A,
notification date: N/A
Application deadline (fall): rolling
Undergraduate student body: 3,597
full time, 500 part time; 37%
male, 63% female; 0% American
Indian, 0% Asian, 0% black,
100% Hispanic, 0% multiracial,
0% Pacific Islander, 0% white,
0% international; 0% from in
state; 0% live on campus; 0%
of students in fraternities, 0% in
sororities
Most popular majors: 36%
Registered Nursing/Registered
Nurse, 6% Radio, Television, and
Digital Communication, Other, 5%
Journalism, 4% Public Relations,
Advertising, and Applied
Communication, 3% Advertising
Expenses: 2021-2022: $6,120;
room/board: $9,320
Financial aid: (787) 728-1515

Universidad Politecnica de Puerto Rico

Hato Rey PR
(787) 622-8000
U.S. News ranking: Engineering,
unranked
Website: www.pupr.edu
Admissions email:
admisiones@pupr.edu
Private; founded 1966
Freshman admissions: least
selective; 2020-2021: 763
applied, 728 accepted. Neither
SAT nor ACT required. SAT 25/75
percentile: N/A. High school
rank: N/A
Early decision deadline: N/A,
notification date: N/A
Early action deadline: N/A,
notification date: N/A

Application deadline (fall): rolling
Undergraduate student body: 1,777
full time, 1,941 part time; 74%
male, 26% female; 0% American
Indian, 0% Asian, 0% black,
99% Hispanic, 0% multiracial,
0% Pacific Islander, 0% white,
0% international; N/A from in
state; 1% live on campus; N/A
of students in fraternities, N/A in
sororities
Most popular majors: 17%
Engineering Mechanics, 16%
Industrial Engineering, 13%
Electrical and Electronics
Engineering, 12% Computer
Engineering, General, 7%
Biomedical/Medical Engineering
Expenses: 2020-2021: $8,640;
room/board: $11,928
Financial aid: N/A

University of Puerto Rico–Aguadilla[1]

Aguadilla PR
(787) 890-2681
U.S. News ranking: Reg. Coll. (S),
No. 57
Website: www.uprag.edu/
Admissions email:
melba.serrano@upr.edu
Public; founded 1972
Application deadline (fall): 5/31
Undergraduate student body: N/A
full time, N/A part time
Expenses: 2020-2021: $4,768 in
state, $6,665 out of state; room/
board: N/A
Financial aid: (787) 890-2681

University of Puerto Rico–Arecibo

Arecibo PR
(787) 815-0000
U.S. News ranking: Reg. Coll. (S),
No. 52
Website: www.upra.edu/
Admissions email:
admisiones.arecibo@upr.edu
Public; founded 1967
Freshman admissions: less
selective; 2020-2021: 1,655
applied, 1,154 accepted. Neither
SAT nor ACT required. SAT 25/75
percentile: N/A. High school
rank: N/A
Early decision deadline: N/A,
notification date: N/A
Early action deadline: N/A,
notification date: N/A
Application deadline (fall): 1/31
Undergraduate student body: 3,197
full time, 217 part time; 39%
male, 61% female; 0% American
Indian, 0% Asian, 0% black,
100% Hispanic, 0% multiracial,
0% Pacific Islander, 0% white,
0% international
Most popular majors: 17%
Microbiology, General, 17%
Registered Nursing/Registered
Nurse, 14% Radio and Television
Broadcasting Technology/
Technician, 12% Industrial
and Organizational Psychology,
8% Industrial Production
Technologies/Technicians, Other
Expenses: 2020-2021: $4,178 in
state, $4,178 out of state; room/
board: N/A
Financial aid: (787) 815-0000

University of Puerto Rico–Bayamon[1]

Bayamon PR
(787) 993-8952
U.S. News ranking: Reg. Coll. (S),
No. 62
Website: www.uprb.edu/
Admissions email:
N/A
Public; founded 1971
Application deadline (fall): 2/15
Undergraduate student body: N/A
full time, N/A part time
Expenses: 2020-2021: $4,198 in
state, $4,198 out of state; room/
board: N/A
Financial aid: (787) 993-8953

University of Puerto Rico–Cayey[1]

Cayey PR
(787) 738-2161
U.S. News ranking: Nat. Lib. Arts,
second tier
Website: cayey.upr.edu/oficina-de-
admisiones
Admissions email:
admisiones.cayey@upr.edu
Public; founded 1967
Application deadline (fall): N/A
Undergraduate student body: N/A
full time, N/A part time
Expenses: 2020-2021: $4,208 in
state, $6,192 out of state; room/
board: N/A
Financial aid: (787) 738-2161

University of Puerto Rico–Humacao[1]

Humacao PR
(787) 850-9301
U.S. News ranking: Reg. Coll. (S),
No. 47
Website: www.uprh.edu/~admision/
Admissions email:
carmen.rivera19@upr.edu
Public; founded 1962
Application deadline (fall): 1/31
Undergraduate student body: N/A
full time, N/A part time
Expenses: 2020-2021: $4,208 in
state, $4,208 out of state; room/
board: N/A
Financial aid: N/A

University of Puerto Rico–Mayaguez[1]

Mayaguez PR
(787) 832-4040
U.S. News ranking: Reg. U. (S),
No. 62
Website: www.uprm.edu
Admissions email:
admisiones@uprm.edu
Public; founded 1911
Affiliation: Undenominational
Application deadline (fall): 6/11
Undergraduate student body: N/A
full time, N/A part time
Expenses: 2020-2021: $4,168 in
state, $6,162 out of state; room/
board: N/A
Financial aid: (787) 265-3863

University of Puerto Rico–Ponce[1]
Ponce PR
(787) 844-8181
U.S. News ranking: Nat. Lib. Arts, No. 158
Website: www.uprp.edu
Admissions email: admi.ponce@upr.edu
Public; founded 1970
Application deadline (fall): 1/31
Undergraduate student body: N/A full time, N/A part time
Expenses: 2020-2021: $4,198 in state, $4,198 out of state; room/board: N/A
Financial aid: (787) 844-8181

University of Puerto Rico–Rio Piedras[1]
Rio Piedras PR
(787) 764-3680
U.S. News ranking: Nat. U., No. 288
Website: www.uprrp.edu/
Admissions email: N/A
Public; founded 1903
Application deadline (fall): 1/31
Undergraduate student body: N/A full time, N/A part time
Expenses: 2020-2021: $4,198 in state, $4,198 out of state; room/board: N/A
Financial aid: (787) 552-1324

University of Puerto Rico–Utuado[1]
Utuado PR
(787) 894-2316
U.S. News ranking: Reg. Coll. (S), second tier
Website: www.uprutuado.edu
Admissions email: admisiones.utuado@upr.edu
Public; founded 1978
Application deadline (fall): 1/31
Undergraduate student body: N/A full time, N/A part time
Expenses: 2020-2021: $4,168 in state, $6,152 out of state; room/board: N/A
Financial aid: (787) 894-3810

Brown University
Providence RI
(401) 863-2378
U.S. News ranking: Nat. U., No. 14
Website: www.brown.edu/admission/undergraduate/
Admissions email: admission@brown.edu
Private; founded 1764
Freshman admissions: most selective; 2020-2021: 36,793 applied, 2,822 accepted. Neither SAT nor ACT required. SAT 25/75 percentile: 1440-1560. High school rank: 95% in top tenth, 99% in top quarter, 100% in top half
Early decision deadline: 11/1, notification date: 12/15
Early action deadline: N/A, notification date: N/A
Application deadline (fall): 1/5
Undergraduate student body: 6,605 full time, 187 part time; 47% male, 53% female; 0% American Indian, 19% Asian, 7% black, 11% Hispanic, 6% multiracial, 0% Pacific Islander, 42% white, 11% international; 6% from in state; 72% live on campus; 11% of students in fraternities, 12% in sororities
Most popular majors: 13% Computer Science, 11% Econometrics and Quantitative Economics, 5% Applied Mathematics, General, 5% Biology/Biological Sciences, General, 5% History, General
Expenses: 2021-2022: $62,404; room/board: $16,346
Financial aid: (401) 863-2721; 45% of undergrads determined to have financial need; average aid package $56,301

Bryant University
Smithfield RI
(800) 622-7001
U.S. News ranking: Reg. U. (N), No. 7
Website: www.bryant.edu
Admissions email: admission@bryant.edu
Private; founded 1863
Freshman admissions: more selective; 2020-2021: 7,521 applied, 5,700 accepted. Neither SAT nor ACT required. SAT 25/75 percentile: 1120-1280. High school rank: 20% in top tenth, 52% in top quarter, 88% in top half
Early decision deadline: 11/1, notification date: 12/1
Early action deadline: 11/15, notification date: 1/15
Application deadline (fall): 2/1
Undergraduate student body: 3,254 full time, 26 part time; 62% male, 38% female; 0% American Indian, 4% Asian, 3% black, 7% Hispanic, 2% multiracial, 0% Pacific Islander, 77% white, 6% international; N/A from in state; 79% live on campus; 7% of students in fraternities, 12% in sororities
Most popular majors: 79% Business, Management, Marketing, and Related Support Services, 5% Mathematics and Statistics, 4% Communication, Journalism, and Related Programs, 4% Social Sciences, 2% Psychology
Expenses: 2021-2022: $47,782; room/board: $16,528
Financial aid: (401) 232-6020; 57% of undergrads determined to have financial need; average aid package $27,163

Johnson & Wales University
Providence RI
(800) 342-5598
U.S. News ranking: Reg. U. (N), No. 94
Website: www.jwu.edu/
Admissions email: providence@admissions.jwu.edu
Private; founded 1914
Freshman admissions: selective; 2020-2021: 10,145 applied, 8,776 accepted. Neither SAT nor ACT required. SAT 25/75 percentile: 980-1170. High school rank: 10% in top tenth, 29% in top quarter, 59% in top half
Early decision deadline: N/A, notification date: N/A
Early action deadline: 11/1, notification date: 11/15
Application deadline (fall): rolling
Undergraduate student body: 4,604 full time, 516 part time; 39% male, 61% female; 1% American Indian, 3% Asian, 14% black, 14% Hispanic, 2% multiracial, 0% Pacific Islander, 57% white, 4% international
Most popular majors: 15% Foodservice Systems Administration/Management, 8% Business Administration and Management, General, 7% Parks, Recreation and Leisure Facilities Management, General, 6% Criminal Justice/Law Enforcement Administration, 6% Culinary Arts/Chef Training
Expenses: 2021-2022: $35,950; room/board: $17,601
Financial aid: (401) 598-1857; 77% of undergrads determined to have financial need; average aid package $26,418

New England Institute of Technology
East Greenwich RI
(800) 736-7744
U.S. News ranking: Reg. Coll. (N), unranked
Website: www.neit.edu/
Admissions email: admissions@neit.edu
Private; founded 1940
Freshman admissions: less selective; 2020-2021: 1,996 applied, 1,399 accepted. Neither SAT nor ACT required. SAT 25/75 percentile: 950-1140. High school rank: N/A
Early decision deadline: N/A, notification date: N/A
Early action deadline: N/A, notification date: N/A
Application deadline (fall): rolling
Undergraduate student body: 1,579 full time, 264 part time; 62% male, 38% female; 0% American Indian, 0% Asian, 1% black, 11% Hispanic, 3% multiracial, 0% Pacific Islander, 8% white, 1% international; 53% from in state; 15% live on campus; 0% of students in fraternities, 0% in sororities
Most popular majors: 16% Registered Nursing/Registered Nurse, 14% Cyber/Electronic Operations and Warfare, 9% Communications Technology/Technician, 9% Mechanical Engineering/Mechanical Technology/Technician, 8% Computer Software Engineering
Expenses: 2021-2022: $32,445; room/board: $14,505
Financial aid: (401) 780-4108

Providence College
Providence RI
(401) 865-2535
U.S. News ranking: Reg. U. (N), No. 1
Website: www.providence.edu
Admissions email: pcadmiss@providence.edu
Private; founded 1917
Affiliation: Roman Catholic
Freshman admissions: more selective; 2020-2021: 10,817 applied, 5,826 accepted. Neither SAT nor ACT required. SAT 25/75 percentile: 1135-1310. High school rank: 43% in top tenth, 73% in top quarter, 94% in top half
Early decision deadline: 11/1, notification date: 12/1
Early action deadline: 11/15, notification date: 1/1
Application deadline (fall): 1/15
Undergraduate student body: 4,098 full time, 200 part time; 45% male, 55% female; 0% American Indian, 2% Asian, 3% black, 10% Hispanic, 2% multiracial, 0% Pacific Islander, 77% white, 2% international; 12% from in state; 67% live on campus; 0% of students in fraternities, 0% in sororities
Most popular majors: 42% Business, Management, Marketing, and Related Support Services, 12% Social Sciences, 8% Biological and Biomedical Sciences, 6% Education, 6% Psychology
Expenses: 2021-2022: $55,988; room/board: $16,060
Financial aid: (401) 865-2286; 48% of undergrads determined to have financial need; average aid package $40,800

Rhode Island College
Providence RI
(800) 669-5760
U.S. News ranking: Reg. U. (N), No. 119
Website: www.ric.edu
Admissions email: admissions@ric.edu
Public; founded 1854
Freshman admissions: less selective; 2020-2021: 4,709 applied, 3,827 accepted. Either SAT or ACT required. SAT 25/75 percentile: 870-1100. High school rank: 14% in top tenth, 36% in top quarter, 75% in top half
Early decision deadline: N/A, notification date: N/A
Early action deadline: N/A, notification date: N/A
Application deadline (fall): 3/15
Undergraduate student body: 4,608 full time, 1,384 part time; 30% male, 70% female; 0% American Indian, 3% Asian, 10% black, 25% Hispanic, 2% multiracial, 0% Pacific Islander, 53% white, 0% international; 87% from in state; 6% live on campus; 2% of students in fraternities, 3% in sororities
Most popular majors: 21% Health Professions and Related Programs, 16% Business, Management, Marketing, and Related Support Services, 10% Education, 9% Psychology, 8% Public Administration and Social Service Professions
Expenses: 2021-2022: $10,702 in state, $15,140 out of state; room/board: $13,077
Financial aid: (401) 456-8033; 71% of undergrads determined to have financial need; average aid package $8,725

Rhode Island School of Design
Providence RI
(401) 454-6300
U.S. News ranking: Arts, unranked
Website: www.risd.edu
Admissions email: admissions@risd.edu
Private; founded 1877
Freshman admissions: more selective; 2020-2021: 4,001 applied, 1,085 accepted. Neither SAT nor ACT required. SAT 25/75 percentile: 1250-1470. High school rank: N/A
Early decision deadline: 11/1, notification date: 12/12
Early action deadline: N/A, notification date: N/A
Application deadline (fall): 2/1
Undergraduate student body: 1,736 full time, 0 part time; 34% male, 66% female; 0% American Indian, 22% Asian, 4% black, 9% Hispanic, 6% multiracial, 0% Pacific Islander, 26% white, 30% international; 4% from in state; 53% live on campus; N/A of students in fraternities, N/A in sororities
Most popular majors: 20% Illustration, 14% Systems Science and Theory, 10% Graphic Design, 9% Architectural and Building Sciences/Technology, 8% Film/Video and Photographic Arts, Other
Expenses: 2021-2022: $56,290; room/board: $14,790
Financial aid: (401) 454-6661; 40% of undergrads determined to have financial need; average aid package $37,320

Roger Williams University
Bristol RI
(800) 458-7144
U.S. News ranking: Reg. U. (N), No. 27
Website: www.rwu.edu
Admissions email: admit@rwu.edu
Private; founded 1956
Freshman admissions: selective; 2020-2021: 8,775 applied, 7,547 accepted. Neither SAT nor ACT required. SAT 25/75 percentile: 1070-1240. High school rank: 14% in top tenth, 40% in top quarter, 74% in top half
Early decision deadline: N/A, notification date: N/A
Early action deadline: 11/15, notification date: 12/1
Application deadline (fall): 2/1
Undergraduate student body: 3,828 full time, 518 part time; 49% male, 51% female; 0% American Indian, 2% Asian, 3% black, 9% Hispanic, 2% multiracial, 0% Pacific Islander, 76% white, 1% international; 21% from in state; 66% live on campus; 0% of students in fraternities, 0% in sororities
Most popular majors: 25% Business, Management, Marketing, and Related Support Services, 12% Homeland Security, Law Enforcement, Firefighting and Related Protective Services, 10% Architecture and Related Services, 7% Biological and Biomedical

Sciences, 7% Psychology
Expenses: 2021-2022: $39,594; room/board: $16,012
Financial aid: (401) 254-3100; 66% of undergrads determined to have financial need; average aid package $26,004

Salve Regina University
Newport RI
(888) 467-2583
U.S. News ranking: Reg. U. (N), No. 23
Website: www.salve.edu
Admissions email: admissions@salve.edu
Private; founded 1934
Affiliation: Roman Catholic
Freshman admissions: selective; 2020-2021: 4,972 applied, 3,710 accepted. Neither SAT nor ACT required. SAT 25/75 percentile: 1100-1240. High school rank: 14% in top tenth, 43% in top quarter, 79% in top half
Early decision deadline: N/A, notification date: N/A
Early action deadline: 11/1, notification date: 12/25
Application deadline (fall): rolling
Undergraduate student body: 2,084 full time, 66 part time; 34% male, 66% female; 0% American Indian, 1% Asian, 1% black, 8% Hispanic, 3% multiracial, 0% Pacific Islander, 81% white, 2% international; 17% from in state; 51% live on campus; N/A of students in fraternities, N/A in sororities
Most popular majors: 21% Business, Management, Marketing, and Related Support Services, 17% Health Professions and Related Programs, 13% Education, 12% Homeland Security, Law Enforcement, Firefighting and Related Protective Services, 8% Psychology
Expenses: 2021-2022: $44,200; room/board: $15,870
Financial aid: (401) 341-2901; 75% of undergrads determined to have financial need; average aid package $29,369

University of Rhode Island
Kingston RI
(401) 874-7100
U.S. News ranking: Nat. U., No. 162
Website: www.uri.edu
Admissions email: admission@uri.edu
Public; founded 1892
Freshman admissions: selective; 2020-2021: 23,856 applied, 18,013 accepted. Neither SAT nor ACT required. SAT 25/75 percentile: 1090-1260. High school rank: 19% in top tenth, 51% in top quarter, 87% in top half
Early decision deadline: N/A, notification date: N/A
Early action deadline: 12/1, notification date: 1/31
Application deadline (fall): 2/1
Undergraduate student body: 12,711 full time, 1,362 part time; 44% male, 56% female;

0% American Indian, 3% Asian, 5% black, 11% Hispanic, 3% multiracial, 0% Pacific Islander, 74% white, 1% international; 50% from in state; 29% live on campus; 16% of students in fraternities, 16% in sororities
Most popular majors: 16% Health Professions and Related Programs, 12% Business, Management, Marketing, and Related Support Services, 10% Engineering, 8% Communication, Journalism, and Related Programs
Expenses: 2021-2022: $15,332 in state, $33,354 out of state; room/board: $13,268
Financial aid: (401) 874-9500; 82% of undergrads determined to have financial need; average aid package $17,679

SOUTH CAROLINA

Allen University
Columbia SC
(877) 625-5368
U.S. News ranking: Nat. Lib. Arts, second tier
Website: www.allenuniversity.edu
Admissions email: admissions@allenuniversity.edu
Private; founded 1870
Affiliation: African Methodist Episcopal
Freshman admissions: least selective; 2020-2021: 3,383 applied, 2,074 accepted. Neither SAT nor ACT required. SAT 25/75 percentile: 699-821. High school rank: 1% in top tenth, 7% in top quarter, 30% in top half
Early decision deadline: N/A, notification date: N/A
Early action deadline: N/A, notification date: N/A
Application deadline (fall): rolling
Undergraduate student body: 577 full time, 79 part time; 55% male, 45% female; N/A American Indian, N/A Asian, N/A black, N/A Hispanic, N/A multiracial, N/A Pacific Islander, N/A white, N/A international; N/A from in state; N/A live on campus; 10% of students in fraternities, 20% in sororities
Most popular majors: 26% Health and Physical Education/ Fitness, Other, 26% Social Sciences, General, 16% Business Administration and Management, General
Expenses: 2021-2022: $13,340; room/board: $7,894
Financial aid: (803) 376-5791; 95% of undergrads determined to have financial need; average aid package $14,545

Anderson University
Anderson SC
(864) 231-5607
U.S. News ranking: Reg. U. (S), No. 44
Website: www.andersonuniversity.edu
Admissions email: admission@andersonuniversity.edu
Private; founded 1911
Affiliation: Southern Baptist
Freshman admissions: more selective; 2020-2021: 3,805 applied, 2,254 accepted. Neither

SAT nor ACT required. SAT 25/75 percentile: 1040-1230. High school rank: 40% in top tenth, 64% in top quarter, 86% in top half
Early decision deadline: N/A, notification date: N/A
Early action deadline: N/A, notification date: N/A
Application deadline (fall): rolling
Undergraduate student body: 2,683 full time, 402 part time; 32% male, 68% female; 0% American Indian, 1% Asian, 5% black, 5% Hispanic, 2% multiracial, 0% Pacific Islander, 83% white, 1% international; 80% from in state; 48% live on campus; N/A of students in fraternities, N/A in sororities
Most popular majors: 21% Registered Nursing/Registered Nurse, 5% Accounting, 5% Corrections and Criminal Justice, Other, 5% Teacher Education, Multiple Levels, 4% Marketing/ Marketing Management, General
Expenses: 2021-2022: $30,720; room/board: $10,900
Financial aid: (864) 231-2181; 76% of undergrads determined to have financial need; average aid package $21,576

Benedict College
Columbia SC
(803) 705-4910
U.S. News ranking: Reg. Coll. (S), second tier
Website: www.benedict.edu
Admissions email: admissions@benedict.edu
Private; founded 1870
Affiliation: Baptist
Freshman admissions: less selective; 2020-2021: 8,114 applied, 5,887 accepted. Neither SAT nor ACT required. SAT 25/75 percentile: 800-1010. High school rank: 13% in top tenth, 31% in top quarter, 61% in top half
Early decision deadline: N/A, notification date: N/A
Early action deadline: N/A, notification date: N/A
Application deadline (fall): rolling
Undergraduate student body: 1,703 full time, 24 part time; 41% male, 59% female; 1% American Indian, 0% Asian, 84% black, 3% Hispanic, 0% multiracial, 0% Pacific Islander, 1% white, 8% international
Most popular majors: Biology/ Biological Sciences, General, Business Administration and Management, General, Human Development and Family Studies, General, Social Work, Sport and Fitness Administration/ Management
Expenses: 2021-2022: $17,492; room/board: $6,386
Financial aid: (803) 705-4418; 100% of undergrads determined to have financial need; average aid package $20,221

Bob Jones University
Greenville SC
(800) 252-6363
U.S. News ranking: Reg. U. (S), No. 31
Website: www.bju.edu/admission

Admissions email: admission@bju.edu
Private; founded 1927
Affiliation: Evangelical Christian
Freshman admissions: selective; 2020-2021: 1,153 applied, 970 accepted. Either SAT or ACT required. ACT 25/75 percentile: 21-28. High school rank: 6% in top tenth, 14% in top quarter, 40% in top half
Early decision deadline: N/A, notification date: N/A
Early action deadline: N/A, notification date: N/A
Application deadline (fall): rolling
Undergraduate student body: 2,287 full time, 326 part time; 45% male, 55% female; 1% American Indian, 3% Asian, 3% black, 8% Hispanic, 2% multiracial, 0% Pacific Islander, 75% white, 5% international; 40% from in state; 73% live on campus; N/A of students in fraternities, N/A in sororities
Most popular majors: 10% Business Administration and Management, General, 5% Accounting, 5% Bible/Biblical Studies, 5% Counseling Psychology, 4% Registered Nursing/Registered Nurse
Expenses: 2021-2022: $20,900; room/board: $8,580
Financial aid: (864) 242-5100; 73% of undergrads determined to have financial need; average aid package $14,945

Charleston Southern University
Charleston SC
(843) 863-7050
U.S. News ranking: Reg. U. (S), No. 57
Website: www.charlestonsouthern. edu/
Admissions email: enroll@csuniv.edu
Private; founded 1964
Affiliation: Baptist
Freshman admissions: selective; 2020-2021: 3,363 applied, 2,664 accepted. Either SAT or ACT required. SAT 25/75 percentile: 990-1170. High school rank: 20% in top tenth, 54% in top quarter, 78% in top half
Early decision deadline: N/A, notification date: N/A
Early action deadline: N/A, notification date: N/A
Application deadline (fall): rolling
Undergraduate student body: 2,491 full time, 229 part time; 36% male, 64% female; 0% American Indian, 1% Asian, 17% black, 6% Hispanic, 3% multiracial, 0% Pacific Islander, 61% white, 1% international; 83% from in state; N/A live on campus; 0% of students in fraternities, 0% in sororities
Most popular majors: 16% Registered Nursing/Registered Nurse, 7% Biology/Biological Sciences, General, 6% Business Administration and Management, General, 6% Criminal Justice/Law Enforcement Administration, 6% Kinesiology and Exercise Science
Expenses: 2020-2021: $27,800; room/board: $10,400
Financial aid: (843) 863-7050

The Citadel, The Military College of South Carolina
Charleston SC
(843) 953-5230
U.S. News ranking: Reg. U. (S), No. 2
Website: www.citadel.edu
Admissions email: admissions@citadel.edu
Public; founded 1842
Affiliation: Undenominational
Freshman admissions: selective; 2020-2021: 2,524 applied, 2,018 accepted. Neither SAT nor ACT required. SAT 25/75 percentile: 1030-1210. High school rank: 10% in top tenth, 32% in top quarter, 63% in top half
Early decision deadline: N/A, notification date: N/A
Early action deadline: N/A, notification date: N/A
Application deadline (fall): rolling
Undergraduate student body: 2,654 full time, 204 part time; 86% male, 14% female; 0% American Indian, 2% Asian, 7% black, 7% Hispanic, 5% multiracial, 0% Pacific Islander, 76% white, 1% international; 68% from in state; 100% live on campus; 0% of students in fraternities, 0% in sororities
Most popular majors: 29% Business, Management, Marketing, and Related Support Services, 23% Engineering, 10% Homeland Security, Law Enforcement, Firefighting and Related Protective Services, 7% Social Sciences, 6% Parks, Recreation, Leisure, and Fitness Studies
Expenses: 2021-2022: $14,808 in state, $38,064 out of state; room/board: $7,968
Financial aid: (843) 953-5187; 53% of undergrads determined to have financial need; average aid package $19,607

Claflin University
Orangeburg SC
(800) 922-1276
U.S. News ranking: Reg. Coll. (S), No. 7
Website: www.claflin.edu
Admissions email: admissions@claflin.edu
Private; founded 1869
Affiliation: United Methodist
Freshman admissions: less selective; 2020-2021: 9,261 applied, 6,032 accepted. Either SAT or ACT required. SAT 25/75 percentile: 840-1040. High school rank: 13% in top tenth, 36% in top quarter, 75% in top half
Early decision deadline: N/A, notification date: N/A
Early action deadline: N/A, notification date: N/A
Application deadline (fall): 8/1
Undergraduate student body: 1,806 full time, 163 part time; 29% male, 71% female; 1% American Indian, 0% Asian, 92% black, 1% Hispanic, 0% multiracial, 0% Pacific Islander, 1% white, 2% international

Most popular majors: 11% Psychology, General, 10% Sport and Fitness Administration/Management, 7% Biology/Biological Sciences, General, 7% Business Administration and Management, General, 6% Criminal Justice/Law Enforcement Administration
Expenses: 2020-2021: $17,046; room/board: $9,480
Financial aid: (803) 535-5720

Clemson University
Clemson SC
(864) 656-2287
U.S. News ranking: Nat. U., No. 75
Website: www.clemson.edu
Admissions email: cuadmissions@clemson.edu
Public; founded 1889
Freshman admissions: more selective; 2020-2021: 28,600 applied, 17,715 accepted. Either SAT or ACT required. SAT 25/75 percentile: 1210-1390. High school rank: 53% in top tenth, 85% in top quarter, 98% in top half
Early decision deadline: N/A, notification date: N/A
Early action deadline: N/A, notification date: N/A
Application deadline (fall): 5/1
Undergraduate student body: 20,021 full time, 847 part time; 51% male, 49% female; 0% American Indian, 3% Asian, 6% black, 6% Hispanic, 4% multiracial, 0% Pacific Islander, 80% white, 1% international; 64% from in state; 33% live on campus; 8% of students in fraternities, 17% in sororities
Most popular majors: 8% Business Administration and Management, General, 6% Biology/Biological Sciences, General, 6% Psychology, General, 5% Marketing, Other, 5% Mechanical Engineering
Expenses: 2020-2021: $15,120 in state, $37,712 out of state; room/board: $11,414
Financial aid: (864) 656-2280; 43% of undergrads determined to have financial need; average aid package $11,779

Coastal Carolina University
Conway SC
(843) 349-2170
U.S. News ranking: Reg. U. (S), No. 48
Website: www.coastal.edu
Admissions email: admissions@coastal.edu
Public; founded 1954
Freshman admissions: selective; 2020-2021: 14,152 applied, 9,970 accepted. Neither SAT nor ACT required. SAT 25/75 percentile: 1020-1180. High school rank: 12% in top tenth, 37% in top quarter, 71% in top half
Early decision deadline: N/A, notification date: N/A
Early action deadline: N/A, notification date: N/A
Application deadline (fall): rolling
Undergraduate student body: 8,529 full time, 971 part time; 44%

male, 56% female; 0% American Indian, 1% Asian, 18% black, 6% Hispanic, 4% multiracial, 0% Pacific Islander, 66% white, 1% international; 49% from in state; 40% live on campus; 2% of students in fraternities, 5% in sororities
Most popular majors: 9% Business Administration and Management, General, 8% Speech Communication and Rhetoric, 7% Marine Biology and Biological Oceanography, 7% Marketing/Marketing Management, General, 6% Kinesiology and Exercise Science
Expenses: 2021-2022: $11,640 in state, $27,394 out of state; room/board: $9,368
Financial aid: (843) 349-2313; 65% of undergrads determined to have financial need; average aid package $12,417

Coker College[1]
Hartsville SC
(843) 383-8050
U.S. News ranking: Reg. U. (S), second tier
Website: www.coker.edu
Admissions email: admissions@coker.edu
Private; founded 1908
Undergraduate student body: N/A full time, N/A part time
Expenses: 2020-2021: $31,524; room/board: $9,892
Financial aid: (843) 383-8050

College of Charleston
Charleston SC
(843) 953-5670
U.S. News ranking: Reg. U. (S), No. 9
Website: www.cofc.edu
Admissions email: admissions@cofc.edu
Public; founded 1770
Freshman admissions: selective; 2020-2021: 15,214 applied, 11,307 accepted. Neither SAT nor ACT required. SAT 25/75 percentile: 1070-1240. High school rank: 23% in top tenth, 51% in top quarter, 84% in top half
Early decision deadline: 10/15, notification date: 12/1
Early action deadline: 11/1, notification date: 12/15
Application deadline (fall): 4/1
Undergraduate student body: 8,466 full time, 834 part time; 34% male, 66% female; 0% American Indian, 2% Asian, 7% black, 7% Hispanic, 4% multiracial, 0% Pacific Islander, 78% white, 1% international; 37% from in state; 22% live on campus; 21% of students in fraternities, 30% in sororities
Most popular majors: 8% Business Administration and Management, General, 7% Biology/Biological Sciences, General, 7% Speech Communication and Rhetoric, 6% Public Health Education and Promotion, 5% Psychology, General
Expenses: 2021-2022: $12,978 in state, $34,438 out of state; room/board: $13,185

Financial aid: (843) 953-5540; 47% of undergrads determined to have financial need; average aid package $14,933

Columbia College
Columbia SC
(800) 277-1301
U.S. News ranking: Reg. U. (S), No. 40
Website: www.columbiasc.edu
Admissions email: admissions@columbiasc.edu
Private; founded 1854
Affiliation: United Methodist
Freshman admissions: least selective; 2020-2021: 786 applied, 763 accepted. Neither SAT nor ACT required. SAT 25/75 percentile: 820-1050. High school rank: 5% in top tenth, 23% in top quarter, 61% in top half
Early decision deadline: N/A, notification date: N/A
Early action deadline: N/A, notification date: N/A
Application deadline (fall): rolling
Undergraduate student body: 641 full time, 338 part time; 13% male, 87% female; 0% American Indian, 1% Asian, 40% black, 7% Hispanic, 3% multiracial, 0% Pacific Islander, 36% white, 0% international; 90% from in state; 30% live on campus; N/A of students in fraternities, 5% in sororities
Most popular majors: 23% Criminal Justice/Safety Studies, 7% Crisis/Emergency/Disaster Management, 6% Biology/Biological Sciences, General, 6% Business Administration and Management, General, 5% Speech-Language Pathology/Pathologist
Expenses: 2021-2022: $20,880; room/board: $8,320
Financial aid: (803) 786-3612; 88% of undergrads determined to have financial need; average aid package $15,784

Columbia International University
Columbia SC
(800) 777-2227
U.S. News ranking: Reg. U. (S), No. 38
Website: www.ciu.edu
Admissions email: yesciu@ciu.edu
Private; founded 1923
Affiliation: Multiple Protestant Denomination
Freshman admissions: selective; 2020-2021: 448 applied, 227 accepted. Either SAT or ACT required. SAT 25/75 percentile: 940-1150. High school rank: 8% in top tenth, 31% in top quarter, 62% in top half
Early decision deadline: N/A, notification date: N/A
Early action deadline: N/A, notification date: N/A
Application deadline (fall): 8/1
Undergraduate student body: 589 full time, 268 part time; 50% male, 50% female; 0% American Indian, 1% Asian, 22% black, 5% Hispanic, 1% multiracial, 0% Pacific Islander, 55% white, 4% international

Most popular majors: 36% Bible/Biblical Studies, 13% Missions/Missionary Studies and Missiology, 10% Curriculum and Instruction, 7% Divinity/Ministry, 5% Counseling Psychology
Expenses: 2021-2022: $25,590; room/board: $8,950
Financial aid: (803) 807-5037; 80% of undergrads determined to have financial need; average aid package $19,930

Converse College[1]
Spartanburg SC
(864) 596-9040
U.S. News ranking: Reg. U. (S), No. 40
Website: www.converse.edu
Admissions email: admissions@converse.edu
Private; founded 1889
Application deadline (fall): 8/1
Undergraduate student body: N/A full time, N/A part time
Expenses: 2020-2021: $19,860; room/board: $11,600
Financial aid: (864) 596-9019

Erskine College
Due West SC
(864) 379-8838
U.S. News ranking: Reg. Coll. (S), No. 11
Website: www.erskine.edu
Admissions email: admissions@erskine.edu
Private; founded 1839
Affiliation: Presbyterian
Freshman admissions: selective; 2020-2021: 1,225 applied, 820 accepted. Neither SAT nor ACT required. SAT 25/75 percentile: 919-1137. High school rank: 13% in top tenth, 29% in top quarter, 69% in top half
Early decision deadline: N/A, notification date: N/A
Early action deadline: N/A, notification date: N/A
Application deadline (fall): rolling
Undergraduate student body: 733 full time, 76 part time; 66% male, 34% female; 1% American Indian, 1% Asian, 17% black, 5% Hispanic, 0% multiracial, 0% Pacific Islander, 42% white, 0% international; 70% from in state; 77% live on campus; N/A of students in fraternities, N/A in sororities
Most popular majors: 28% Business/Commerce, General, 14% Psychology, General, 13% Biology/Biological Sciences, General, 7% Health and Physical Education/Fitness, General, 5% Sport and Fitness Administration/Management
Expenses: 2021-2022: $36,510; room/board: $11,465
Financial aid: (864) 379-8886

Francis Marion University
Florence SC
(843) 661-1231
U.S. News ranking: Reg. U. (S), No. 60
Website: www.fmarion.edu
Admissions email: admissions@fmarion.edu
Public; founded 1970

Freshman admissions: less selective; 2020-2021: 4,266 applied, 3,210 accepted. Either SAT or ACT required. ACT 25/75 percentile: 15-21. High school rank: 14% in top tenth, 39% in top quarter, 73% in top half
Early decision deadline: N/A, notification date: N/A
Early action deadline: N/A, notification date: N/A
Application deadline (fall): rolling
Undergraduate student body: 2,852 full time, 780 part time; 32% male, 68% female; 1% American Indian, 1% Asian, 40% black, 4% Hispanic, 3% multiracial, 0% Pacific Islander, 49% white, 1% international; 96% from in state; 36% live on campus; 6% of students in fraternities, 7% in sororities
Most popular majors: 23% Health Professions and Related Programs, 19% Business, Management, Marketing, and Related Support Services, 11% Biological and Biomedical Sciences, 10% Psychology, 9% Education
Expenses: 2021-2022: $11,160 in state, $21,544 out of state; room/board: $8,230
Financial aid: (843) 661-1190; 76% of undergrads determined to have financial need; average aid package $11,315

Furman University
Greenville SC
(864) 294-2034
U.S. News ranking: Nat. Lib. Arts, No. 46
Website: www.furman.edu/
Admissions email: admissions@furman.edu
Private; founded 1826
Freshman admissions: more selective; 2020-2021: 5,194 applied, 3,389 accepted. Neither SAT nor ACT required. ACT 25/75 percentile: 28-32. High school rank: 44% in top tenth, 77% in top quarter, 96% in top half
Early decision deadline: 11/15, notification date: 12/1
Early action deadline: 11/1, notification date: 12/20
Application deadline (fall): 1/15
Undergraduate student body: 2,294 full time, 51 part time; 39% male, 61% female; 0% American Indian, 3% Asian, 7% black, 6% Hispanic, 4% multiracial, 0% Pacific Islander, 77% white, 3% international; 69% from in state; 97% live on campus; 30% of students in fraternities, 58% in sororities
Most popular majors: 16% Social Sciences, 12% Communication, Journalism, and Related Programs, 11% Health Professions and Related Programs, 9% Business, Management, Marketing, and Related Support Services, 7% Biological and Biomedical Sciences
Expenses: 2021-2022: $53,372; room/board: $13,698
Financial aid: (864) 294-2351; 45% of undergrads determined to have financial need; average aid package $43,146

Lander University

Greenwood SC
(864) 388-8307
U.S. News ranking: Reg. Coll. (S), No. 39
Website: www.lander.edu
Admissions email: admissions@lander.edu
Public; founded 1872
Freshman admissions: selective; 2020-2021: 5,627 applied, 3,209 accepted. Neither SAT nor ACT required. SAT 25/75 percentile: 920-1110. High school rank: 11% in top tenth, 34% in top quarter, 73% in top half
Early decision deadline: N/A, notification date: N/A
Early action deadline: N/A, notification date: N/A
Application deadline (fall): rolling
Undergraduate student body: 3,159 full time, 232 part time; 32% male, 68% female; 0% American Indian, 1% Asian, 25% black, 2% Hispanic, 5% multiracial, 0% Pacific Islander, 64% white, 0% international
Most popular majors: 25% Business Administration and Management, General, 9% Psychology, General, 8% Registered Nursing/Registered Nurse, 5% Biology/Biological Sciences, General, 5% Kinesiology and Exercise Science
Expenses: 2020-2021: $11,700 in state, $21,300 out of state; room/board: $9,970
Financial aid: (864) 388-8340

Limestone University

Gaffney SC
(864) 488-4554
U.S. News ranking: Reg. Coll. (S), No. 53
Website: www.limestone.edu
Admissions email: admiss@limestone.edu
Private; founded 1845
Affiliation: Undenominational
Freshman admissions: selective; 2020-2021: 2,171 applied, 1,477 accepted. Neither SAT nor ACT required. SAT 25/75 percentile: 930-1140. High school rank: 9% in top tenth, 26% in top quarter, 55% in top half
Early decision deadline: N/A, notification date: N/A
Early action deadline: N/A, notification date: N/A
Application deadline (fall): 8/22
Undergraduate student body: 1,399 full time, 419 part time; 46% male, 54% female; 0% American Indian, 0% Asian, 35% black, 3% Hispanic, 2% multiracial, 0% Pacific Islander, 37% white, 3% international; 74% from in state; 34% live on campus; 0% of students in fraternities, 2% in sororities
Most popular majors: 39% Business, Management, Marketing, and Related Support Services, 17% Public Administration and Social Service Professions, 8% Liberal Arts and Sciences, General Studies and Humanities, 6% Computer and Information Sciences and Support Services, 6% Health Professions and Related Programs

Expenses: 2021-2022: $26,300; room/board: $10,645
Financial aid: (864) 488-8251; 74% of undergrads determined to have financial need; average aid package $17,851

Morris College[1]

Sumter SC
(803) 934-3225
U.S. News ranking: Reg. Coll. (S), second tier
Website: www.morris.edu
Admissions email: admissions@morris.edu
Private; founded 1908
Affiliation: Baptist
Application deadline (fall): rolling
Undergraduate student body: N/A full time, N/A part time
Expenses: 2020-2021: $14,980; room/board: $6,672
Financial aid: N/A

Newberry College

Newberry SC
(800) 845-4955
U.S. News ranking: Reg. Coll. (S), No. 11
Website: www.newberry.edu/
Admissions email: admission@newberry.edu
Private; founded 1856
Affiliation: Lutheran Church in America
Freshman admissions: less selective; 2020-2021: 2,163 applied, 1,224 accepted. Neither SAT nor ACT required. SAT 25/75 percentile: 890-1100. High school rank: 7% in top tenth, 20% in top quarter, 58% in top half
Early decision deadline: N/A, notification date: N/A
Early action deadline: N/A, notification date: N/A
Application deadline (fall): rolling
Undergraduate student body: 1,231 full time, 25 part time; 57% male, 43% female; 0% American Indian, 0% Asian, 32% black, 3% Hispanic, 4% multiracial, 0% Pacific Islander, 49% white, 6% international; 78% from in state; 76% live on campus; 7% of students in fraternities, 20% in sororities
Most popular majors: 13% Business Administration and Management, General, 11% Registered Nursing/Registered Nurse, 11% Sport and Fitness Administration/Management, 10% Biology/Biological Sciences, General, 6% Respiratory Therapy Technician/Assistant
Expenses: 2021-2022: $28,250; room/board: $11,700
Financial aid: (803) 321-5127; 85% of undergrads determined to have financial need; average aid package $25,031

North Greenville University

Tigerville SC
(864) 977-7001
U.S. News ranking: Reg. U. (S), No. 70
Website: www.ngu.edu
Admissions email: admissions@ngu.edu
Private; founded 1892

Affiliation: Southern Baptist
Freshman admissions: selective; 2020-2021: 2,484 applied, 1,688 accepted. Either SAT or ACT required. SAT 25/75 percentile: 950-1190. High school rank: 14% in top tenth, 33% in top quarter, 65% in top half
Early decision deadline: N/A, notification date: N/A
Early action deadline: N/A, notification date: N/A
Application deadline (fall): 8/22
Undergraduate student body: 1,658 full time, 335 part time; 46% male, 54% female; 0% American Indian, 1% Asian, 8% black, 4% Hispanic, 3% multiracial, 0% Pacific Islander, 66% white, 1% international; N/A from in state; 55% live on campus; N/A of students in fraternities, N/A in sororities
Most popular majors: 20% Business, Management, Marketing, and Related Support Services, 17% Education, 12% Liberal Arts and Sciences, General Studies and Humanities, 9% Theology and Religious Vocations, 7% Parks, Recreation, Leisure, and Fitness Studies
Expenses: 2021-2022: $22,470; room/board: $10,640
Financial aid: (864) 977-7057; 100% of undergrads determined to have financial need

Presbyterian College

Clinton SC
(800) 476-7272
U.S. News ranking: Nat. Lib. Arts, No. 128
Website: www.presby.edu
Admissions email: mfox@presby.edu
Private; founded 1880
Affiliation: Presbyterian Church (USA)
Freshman admissions: selective; 2020-2021: 2,016 applied, 1,428 accepted. Neither SAT nor ACT required. SAT 25/75 percentile: 1030-1200. High school rank: 25% in top tenth, 55% in top quarter, 86% in top half
Early decision deadline: N/A, notification date: N/A
Early action deadline: 11/15, notification date: 12/15
Application deadline (fall): 6/30
Undergraduate student body: 976 full time, 72 part time; 46% male, 54% female; 0% American Indian, 1% Asian, 16% black, 6% Hispanic, 4% multiracial, 0% Pacific Islander, 69% white, 3% international; 69% from in state; 95% live on campus; 33% of students in fraternities, 38% in sororities
Most popular majors: 26% Business, Management, Marketing, and Related Support Services, 16% History, 13% Psychology, 11% Biological and Biomedical Sciences, 10% Biological and Biomedical Sciences
Expenses: 2021-2022: $41,060; room/board: $11,100

Financial aid: (864) 833-8287; 78% of undergrads determined to have financial need; average aid package $39,115

South Carolina State University[7]

Orangeburg SC
(803) 536-7185
U.S. News ranking: Reg. U. (S), No. 88
Website: www.scsu.edu
Admissions email: admissions@scsu.edu
Public; founded 1896
Freshman admissions: least selective; 2020-2021: 3,128 applied, 2,943 accepted. Either SAT or ACT required. ACT 25/75 percentile: 14-18. High school rank: 13% in top tenth, 30% in top quarter, 51% in top half
Early decision deadline: N/A, notification date: N/A
Early action deadline: N/A, notification date: N/A
Application deadline (fall): 7/31
Undergraduate student body: 1,781 full time, 239 part time
Most popular majors: 15% Biology/Biological Sciences, General, 12% Family and Consumer Sciences/Human Sciences, General, 9% Criminal Justice/Law Enforcement Administration, 6% Business Administration and Management, General, 6% Mass Communication/Media Studies
Expenses: 2021-2022: $11,060 in state, $21,750 out of state; room/board: $9,890
Financial aid: (803) 536-7067

Southern Wesleyan University[1]

Central SC
(864) 644-5550
U.S. News ranking: Reg. U. (S), No. 84
Website: www.swu.edu
Admissions email: admissions@swu.edu
Private
Application deadline (fall): N/A
Undergraduate student body: N/A full time, N/A part time
Expenses: 2020-2021: $25,676; room/board: $9,370
Financial aid: N/A

University of South Carolina

Columbia SC
(803) 777-7700
U.S. News ranking: Nat. U., No. 117
Website: www.sc.edu
Admissions email: admissions-ugrad@sc.edu
Public; founded 1801
Freshman admissions: more selective; 2020-2021: 34,957 applied, 23,894 accepted. Neither SAT nor ACT required. SAT 25/75 percentile: 1140-1340. High school rank: 28% in top tenth, 58% in top quarter, 88% in top half
Early decision deadline: N/A, notification date: N/A
Early action deadline: 10/15, notification date: 12/20

Application deadline (fall): 12/1
Undergraduate student body: 26,174 full time, 1,096 part time; 46% male, 54% female; 0% American Indian, 4% Asian, 9% black, 5% Hispanic, 4% multiracial, 0% Pacific Islander, 75% white, 2% international; 61% from in state; 27% live on campus; 23% of students in fraternities, 32% in sororities
Most popular majors: 6% Finance and Financial Management Services, 6% Public Health, 5% Research and Experimental Psychology, 4% Biology, General, 4% Public Relations, Advertising, and Applied Communication
Expenses: 2021-2022: $12,688 in state, $33,928 out of state; room/board: $10,990
Financial aid: (803) 777-8134; 50% of undergrads determined to have financial need; average aid package $10,202

University of South Carolina–Aiken

Aiken SC
(803) 641-3366
U.S. News ranking: Reg. Coll. (S), No. 17
Website: www.usca.edu
Admissions email: admit@usca.edu
Public; founded 1961
Freshman admissions: selective; 2020-2021: 3,055 applied, 1,707 accepted. Either SAT or ACT required. SAT 25/75 percentile: 970-1150. High school rank: 14% in top tenth, 44% in top quarter, 80% in top half
Early decision deadline: N/A, notification date: N/A
Early action deadline: N/A, notification date: N/A
Application deadline (fall): 7/1
Undergraduate student body: 2,600 full time, 684 part time; 34% male, 66% female; 0% American Indian, 1% Asian, 25% black, 6% Hispanic, 5% multiracial, 0% Pacific Islander, 59% white, 2% international; 87% from in state; 22% live on campus; 8% of students in fraternities, 8% in sororities
Most popular majors: 26% Business, Management, Marketing, and Related Support Services, 16% Health Professions and Related Programs, 11% Parks, Recreation, Leisure, and Fitness Studies, 10% Education, 8% Biological and Biomedical Sciences
Expenses: 2021-2022: $10,760 in state, $21,218 out of state; room/board: $8,202
Financial aid: (803) 641-3476; 64% of undergrads determined to have financial need; average aid package $12,161

University of South Carolina–Beaufort

Bluffton SC
(843) 208-8000
U.S. News ranking: Nat. Lib. Arts, second tier
Website: www.uscb.edu
Admissions email: admissions@uscb.edu
Public; founded 1959

Freshman admissions: selective; 2020-2021: 2,096 applied, 1,403 accepted. Either SAT or ACT required. SAT 25/75 percentile: 940-1110. High school rank: 7% in top tenth, 37% in top quarter, 71% in top half **Early decision deadline:** N/A, notification date: N/A **Early action deadline:** N/A, notification date: N/A **Application deadline (fall):** 7/1 **Undergraduate student body:** 1,670 full time, 329 part time; 32% male, 68% female; 0% American Indian, 1% Asian, 21% black, 9% Hispanic, 4% multiracial, 0% Pacific Islander, 61% white, 1% international; 12% from in state; 37% live on campus; N/A of students in fraternities, N/A in sororities **Most popular majors:** Information not available **Expenses:** 2021-2022: $10,344 in state, $21,390 out of state; room/board: N/A **Financial aid:** (843) 521-4117

University of South Carolina–Upstate

Spartanburg SC
(864) 503-5246
U.S. News ranking: Reg. Coll. (S), No. 15
Website: www.uscupstate.edu/
Admissions email: admissions@uscupstate.edu
Public; founded 1967
Freshman admissions: selective; 2020-2021: 3,862 applied, 2,028 accepted. Either SAT or ACT required. SAT 25/75 percentile: 900-1090. High school rank: 12% in top tenth, 36% in top quarter, 72% in top half **Early decision deadline:** N/A, notification date: N/A **Early action deadline:** N/A, notification date: N/A **Application deadline (fall):** rolling **Undergraduate student body:** 4,374 full time, 1,146 part time; 33% male, 67% female; 0% American Indian, 3% Asian, 34% black, 7% Hispanic, 5% multiracial, 0% Pacific Islander, 48% white, 2% international; 94% from in state; 11% live on campus; N/A of students in fraternities, N/A in sororities **Most popular majors:** 25% Registered Nursing/Registered Nurse, 14% Business Administration and Management, General, 8% Liberal Arts and Sciences/Liberal Studies, 7% Criminal Justice/Law Enforcement Administration, 6% Psychology, General **Expenses:** 2020-2021: $11,925 in state, $23,427 out of state; room/board: $8,598 **Financial aid:** (864) 503-5340; 64% of undergrads determined to have financial need; average aid package $10,077

Voorhees College

Denmark SC
(803) 780-1030
U.S. News ranking: Reg. Coll. (S), No. 48
Website: www.voorhees.edu
Admissions email: admissions@voorhees.edu
Private; founded 1897
Affiliation: Protestant Episcopal
Freshman admissions: least selective; 2020-2021: N/A applied, N/A accepted. Neither SAT nor ACT required. ACT 25/75 percentile: 12-17. High school rank: N/A **Early decision deadline:** N/A, notification date: N/A **Early action deadline:** N/A, notification date: N/A **Application deadline (fall):** 8/31 **Undergraduate student body:** 339 full time, 29 part time; 39% male, 61% female; 0% American Indian, 0% Asian, 97% black, 0% Hispanic, 0% multiracial, 0% Pacific Islander, 1% white, 2% international **Most popular majors:** 19% Criminal Justice/Law Enforcement Administration, 13% Sport and Fitness Administration/Management, 10% Biology/Biological Sciences, General, 10% Business Administration and Management, General, 8% Computer and Information Sciences, General **Expenses:** 2021-2022: $12,630; room/board: $7,346 **Financial aid:** (803) 780-1154; 92% of undergrads determined to have financial need; average aid package $15,248

Winthrop University

Rock Hill SC
(803) 323-2191
U.S. News ranking: Reg. U. (S), No. 17
Website: www.winthrop.edu
Admissions email: admissions@winthrop.edu
Public; founded 1886
Affiliation: Other
Freshman admissions: selective; 2020-2021: 6,705 applied, 4,287 accepted. Neither SAT nor ACT required. SAT 25/75 percentile: 940-1150. High school rank: 16% in top tenth, 41% in top quarter, 76% in top half **Early decision deadline:** N/A, notification date: N/A **Early action deadline:** N/A, notification date: N/A **Application deadline (fall):** rolling **Undergraduate student body:** 3,992 full time, 414 part time; 32% male, 68% female; 0% American Indian, 2% Asian, 32% black, 6% Hispanic, 5% multiracial, 0% Pacific Islander, 54% white, 1% international; 10% from in state; 35% live on campus; N/A of students in fraternities, 2% in sororities **Most popular majors:** 19% Business, Management, Marketing, and Related Support Services, 12% Education, 11% Visual and Performing Arts, 9% Biological and Biomedical Sciences, 8% Parks, Recreation, Leisure, and Fitness Studies

Expenses: 2021-2022: $15,836 in state, $30,166 out of state; room/board: $9,774 **Financial aid:** (803) 323-2189; 75% of undergrads determined to have financial need; average aid package $14,309

Wofford College

Spartanburg SC
(864) 597-4130
U.S. News ranking: Nat. Lib. Arts, No. 67
Website: www.wofford.edu
Admissions email: admissions@wofford.edu
Private; founded 1854
Affiliation: United Methodist
Freshman admissions: more selective; 2020-2021: 4,102 applied, 2,174 accepted. Neither SAT nor ACT required. SAT 25/75 percentile: 1160-1328. High school rank: 34% in top tenth, 66% in top quarter, 92% in top half **Early decision deadline:** 11/1, notification date: 12/1 **Early action deadline:** 11/15, notification date: 2/1 **Application deadline (fall):** 1/15 **Undergraduate student body:** 1,750 full time, 22 part time; 46% male, 54% female; 0% American Indian, 2% Asian, 8% black, 5% Hispanic, 3% multiracial, 0% Pacific Islander, 81% white, 1% international; 58% from in state; 88% live on campus; 46% of students in fraternities, 42% in sororities **Most popular majors:** 16% Biology/Biological Sciences, General, 11% Finance, General, 7% Accounting, 7% Business/Managerial Economics, 6% Psychology, General **Expenses:** 2021-2022: $49,550; room/board: $14,345 **Financial aid:** (864) 597-4160; 60% of undergrads determined to have financial need; average aid package $41,965

SOUTH DAKOTA

Augustana University

Sioux Falls SD
(605) 274-5516
U.S. News ranking: Reg. U. (Mid. W), No. 10
Website: www.augie.edu
Admissions email: admission@augie.edu
Private; founded 1860
Affiliation: Evangelical Lutheran Church
Freshman admissions: more selective; 2020-2021: 2,037 applied, 1,454 accepted. Neither SAT nor ACT required. ACT 25/75 percentile: 22-28. High school rank: 31% in top tenth, 65% in top quarter, 88% in top half **Early decision deadline:** N/A, notification date: N/A **Early action deadline:** N/A, notification date: N/A **Application deadline (fall):** rolling **Undergraduate student body:** 1,567 full time, 95 part time; 38% male, 62% female; 1% American Indian, 2% Asian, 3% black, 3% Hispanic, 2% multiracial,

0% Pacific Islander, 84% white, 4% international; 51% from in state; 58% live on campus; 0% of students in fraternities, 0% in sororities **Most popular majors:** 17% Health Professions and Related Programs, 15% Business, Management, Marketing, and Related Support Services, 11% Biological and Biomedical Sciences, 10% Education, 8% Social Sciences **Expenses:** 2021-2022: $35,914; room/board: $8,858 **Financial aid:** (605) 274-5216; 62% of undergrads determined to have financial need; average aid package $28,707

Black Hills State University

Spearfish SD
(605) 642-6131
U.S. News ranking: Reg. U. (Mid. W), second tier
Website: www.bhsu.edu/
Admissions email: Admissions@bhsu.edu
Public; founded 1887
Freshman admissions: selective; 2020-2021: 1,826 applied, 1,515 accepted. Neither SAT nor ACT required. ACT 25/75 percentile: 18-24. High school rank: N/A **Early decision deadline:** N/A, notification date: N/A **Early action deadline:** N/A, notification date: N/A **Application deadline (fall):** rolling **Undergraduate student body:** 1,794 full time, 1,598 part time; 38% male, 63% female; 3% American Indian, 1% Asian, 1% black, 6% Hispanic, 4% multiracial, 0% Pacific Islander, 83% white, 2% international **Most popular majors:** Information not available **Expenses:** 2021-2022: $8,764 in state, $11,866 out of state; room/board: $7,302 **Financial aid:** (605) 642-6145

Dakota State University

Madison SD
(605) 256-5139
U.S. News ranking: Reg. U. (Mid. W), No. 82
Website: www.dsu.edu
Admissions email: admissions@dsu.edu
Public; founded 1881
Freshman admissions: selective; 2020-2021: 706 applied, 589 accepted. Neither SAT nor ACT required. ACT 25/75 percentile: 19-26. High school rank: 10% in top tenth, 30% in top quarter, 60% in top half **Early decision deadline:** N/A, notification date: N/A **Early action deadline:** N/A, notification date: N/A **Application deadline (fall):** rolling **Undergraduate student body:** 1,495 full time, 1,245 part time; 62% male, 38% female; 1% American Indian, 2% Asian, 3% black, 4% Hispanic, 4% multiracial, 0% Pacific Islander, 81% white, 2% international; 59% from in state; 37% live on campus; 0%

of students in fraternities, 0% in sororities **Most popular majors:** 58% Computer and Information Sciences and Support Services, 15% Education, 11% Business, Management, Marketing, and Related Support Services **Expenses:** 2021-2022: $9,633 in state, $12,735 out of state; room/board: $7,424 **Financial aid:** (605) 256-5152; 58% of undergrads determined to have financial need; average aid package $8,836

Dakota Wesleyan University

Mitchell SD
(800) 333-8506
U.S. News ranking: Reg. Coll. (Mid. W), No. 22
Website: www.dwu.edu
Admissions email: admissions@dwu.edu
Private; founded 1885
Affiliation: United Methodist
Freshman admissions: selective; 2020-2021: 1,218 applied, 782 accepted. Neither SAT nor ACT required. ACT 25/75 percentile: 18-23. High school rank: 12% in top tenth, 36% in top quarter, 72% in top half **Early decision deadline:** N/A, notification date: N/A **Early action deadline:** N/A, notification date: N/A **Application deadline (fall):** rolling **Undergraduate student body:** 622 full time, 158 part time; 43% male, 57% female; 2% American Indian, 1% Asian, 2% black, 8% Hispanic, 4% multiracial, 0% Pacific Islander, 83% white, 0% international; N/A from in state; N/A live on campus; 0% of students in fraternities, 0% in sororities **Most popular majors:** 36% Registered Nursing/Registered Nurse, 10% Business Administration and Management, General, 8% Elementary Education and Teaching, 7% Kinesiology and Exercise Science, 6% Criminal Justice/Safety Studies **Expenses:** 2021-2022: $30,870; room/board: $7,100 **Financial aid:** (605) 995-2663; 83% of undergrads determined to have financial need; average aid package $19,166

Mount Marty University

Yankton SD
(855) 686-2789
U.S. News ranking: Reg. U. (Mid. W), No. 108
Website: www.mountmarty.edu
Admissions email: admissions@mountmarty.edu
Private; founded 1936
Freshman admissions: selective; 2020-2021: 737 applied, 578 accepted. Either SAT or ACT required. ACT 25/75 percentile: 17-22. High school rank: N/A **Early decision deadline:** N/A, notification date: N/A **Early action deadline:** N/A, notification date: N/A

Application deadline (fall): 8/30
Undergraduate student body: 573 full time, 405 part time; 48% male, 52% female; 3% American Indian, 1% Asian, 9% black, 10% Hispanic, 1% multiracial, 0% Pacific Islander, 68% white, 6% international; 43% from in state; 72% live on campus; 0% of students in fraternities, 0% in sororities
Most popular majors: 22% Education, General, 14% Business Administration and Management, General, 10% Registered Nursing/Registered Nurse, 8% Social Sciences, General, 6% Health and Physical Education/Fitness, Other
Expenses: 2021-2022: $29,980; room/board: $8,554
Financial aid: (605) 668-1589; 77% of undergrads determined to have financial need; average aid package $31,324

Northern State University
Aberdeen SD
(800) 678-5330
U.S. News ranking: Reg. U. (Mid. W), No. 79
Website: www.northern.edu
Admissions email: admissions@northern.edu
Public; founded 1901
Freshman admissions: selective; 2020-2021: 1,038 applied, 817 accepted. Either SAT or ACT required. ACT 25/75 percentile: 19-25. High school rank: 14% in top tenth, 34% in top quarter, 65% in top half
Early decision deadline: N/A, notification date: N/A
Early action deadline: N/A, notification date: N/A
Application deadline (fall): rolling
Undergraduate student body: 1,149 full time, 1,819 part time; 40% male, 60% female; 2% American Indian, 2% Asian, 3% black, 4% Hispanic, 5% multiracial, 0% Pacific Islander, 81% white, 3% international; 71% from in state; 38% live on campus; 0% of students in fraternities, 0% in sororities
Most popular majors: 29% Business, Management, Marketing, and Related Support Services, 21% Education, 11% Biological and Biomedical Sciences, 9% Parks, Recreation, Leisure, and Fitness Studies, 5% English Language and Literature/Letters
Expenses: 2021-2022: $8,845 in state, $11,947 out of state; room/board: $9,150
Financial aid: (605) 626-2640; 61% of undergrads determined to have financial need; average aid package $11,597

South Dakota School of Mines and Technology
Rapid City SD
(605) 394-5209
U.S. News ranking: Engineering, unranked
Website: www.sdsmt.edu

Admissions email: admissions@sdsmt.edu
Public; founded 1885
Freshman admissions: more selective; 2020-2021: 1,329 applied, 1,137 accepted. Either SAT or ACT required. ACT 25/75 percentile: 24-30. High school rank: 25% in top tenth, 55% in top quarter, 85% in top half
Early decision deadline: N/A, notification date: N/A
Early action deadline: N/A, notification date: N/A
Application deadline (fall): rolling
Undergraduate student body: 1,675 full time, 444 part time; 75% male, 25% female; 1% American Indian, 2% Asian, 1% black, 5% Hispanic, 4% multiracial, 0% Pacific Islander, 84% white, 2% international
Most popular majors: 20% Mechanical Engineering, 12% Civil Engineering, General, 11% Chemical Engineering, 9% Computer and Information Sciences, General, 8% Industrial Engineering
Expenses: 2021-2022: $12,110 in state, $16,530 out of state; room/board: $9,420
Financial aid: (605) 394-2274

South Dakota State University
Brookings SD
(800) 952-3541
U.S. News ranking: Nat. U., No. 288
Website: www.sdstate.edu/
Admissions email: SDSU.Admissions@sdstate.edu
Public; founded 1881
Freshman admissions: selective; 2020-2021: 5,290 applied, 4,705 accepted. Neither SAT nor ACT required. ACT 25/75 percentile: 20-26. High school rank: 18% in top tenth, 43% in top quarter, 75% in top half
Early decision deadline: N/A, notification date: N/A
Early action deadline: N/A, notification date: N/A
Application deadline (fall): 9/1
Undergraduate student body: 7,788 full time, 2,188 part time; 46% male, 54% female; 1% American Indian, 1% Asian, 2% black, 2% Hispanic, 2% multiracial, 0% Pacific Islander, 88% white, 3% international; 52% from in state; N/A live on campus; N/A of students in fraternities, N/A in sororities
Most popular majors: 16% Registered Nursing/Registered Nurse, 5% Mechanical Engineering, 4% Animal Sciences, General, 4% Pharmaceutics and Drug Design, 3% Human Development and Family Studies, General
Expenses: 2021-2022: $9,299 in state, $12,809 out of state; room/board: $8,054
Financial aid: (605) 688-4695; 50% of undergrads determined to have financial need; average aid package $8,625

University of Sioux Falls
Sioux Falls SD
(605) 331-6600
U.S. News ranking: Reg. U. (Mid. W), No. 82
Website: www.usiouxfalls.edu
Admissions email: admissions@usiouxfalls.edu
Private; founded 1883
Affiliation: American Baptist
Freshman admissions: selective; 2020-2021: 1,646 applied, 1,520 accepted. Neither SAT nor ACT required. ACT 25/75 percentile: 20-25. High school rank: 18% in top tenth, 39% in top quarter, 73% in top half
Early decision deadline: N/A, notification date: N/A
Early action deadline: N/A, notification date: N/A
Application deadline (fall): rolling
Undergraduate student body: 1,182 full time, 172 part time; 36% male, 64% female; 1% American Indian, 1% Asian, 4% black, 2% Hispanic, 7% multiracial, 0% Pacific Islander, 83% white, 0% international; 57% from in state; 46% live on campus; N/A of students in fraternities, N/A in sororities
Most popular majors: 21% Business, Management, Marketing, and Related Support Services, 20% Health Professions and Related Programs, 9% Education, 8% Psychology, 7% Social Sciences
Expenses: 2021-2022: $19,900; room/board: $7,930
Financial aid: (605) 331-6623; 61% of undergrads determined to have financial need; average aid package $12,913

University of South Dakota
Vermillion SD
(877) 269-6837
U.S. News ranking: Nat. U., No. 239
Website: www.usd.edu
Admissions email: admissions@usd.edu
Public; founded 1862
Freshman admissions: selective; 2020-2021: 3,392 applied, 3,085 accepted. Neither SAT nor ACT required. ACT 25/75 percentile: 20-25. High school rank: 15% in top tenth, 40% in top quarter, 71% in top half
Early decision deadline: N/A, notification date: N/A
Early action deadline: N/A, notification date: N/A
Application deadline (fall): N/A
Undergraduate student body: 4,741 full time, 2,362 part time; 35% male, 65% female; N/A American Indian, N/A Asian, N/A black, N/A Hispanic, N/A multiracial, N/A Pacific Islander, N/A white, N/A international
Most popular majors: Information not available
Expenses: 2021-2022: $9,432 in state, $12,942 out of state; room/board: $8,600
Financial aid: (605) 658-6250

TENNESSEE

Austin Peay State University
Clarksville TN
(931) 221-7661
U.S. News ranking: Reg. U. (S), No. 44
Website: www.apsu.edu
Admissions email: admissions@apsu.edu
Public; founded 1927
Freshman admissions: selective; 2020-2021: 7,346 applied, 6,696 accepted. Neither SAT nor ACT required. ACT 25/75 percentile: 19-24. High school rank: 13% in top tenth, 36% in top quarter, 74% in top half
Early decision deadline: N/A, notification date: N/A
Early action deadline: N/A, notification date: N/A
Application deadline (fall): 8/4
Undergraduate student body: 6,161 full time, 2,926 part time; 39% male, 61% female; 0% American Indian, 2% Asian, 22% black, 9% Hispanic, 7% multiracial, 0% Pacific Islander, 57% white, 1% international; 57% from in state; 11% live on campus; 4% of students in fraternities, 6% in sororities
Most popular majors: Information not available
Expenses: 2021-2022: $8,761 in state, $14,305 out of state; room/board: $10,350
Financial aid: (931) 221-7907; 83% of undergrads determined to have financial need; average aid package $5,822

Belmont University
Nashville TN
(615) 460-6785
U.S. News ranking: Nat. U., No. 162
Website: www.Belmont.edu
Admissions email: buadmission@belmont.edu
Private; founded 1890
Affiliation: Interdenominational
Freshman admissions: more selective; 2020-2021: 8,926 applied, 7,429 accepted. Neither SAT nor ACT required. ACT 25/75 percentile: 23-30. High school rank: 29% in top tenth, 61% in top quarter, 88% in top half
Early decision deadline: N/A, notification date: N/A
Early action deadline: N/A, notification date: N/A
Application deadline (fall): 8/1
Undergraduate student body: 6,330 full time, 296 part time; 34% male, 66% female; 0% American Indian, 2% Asian, 5% black, 7% Hispanic, 4% multiracial, 0% Pacific Islander, 79% white, 1% international; 31% from in state; N/A live on campus; N/A of students in fraternities, N/A in sororities
Most popular majors: 44% Visual and Performing Arts, 13% Business, Management, Marketing, and Related Support Services, 13% Health Professions and Related Programs, 5% Communication, Journalism, and Related Programs, 4%

Communications Technologies/Technicians and Support Services
Expenses: 2021-2022: $38,430; room/board: $13,240
Financial aid: (615) 460-6403; 53% of undergrads determined to have financial need; average aid package $24,098

Bethel University[1]
McKenzie TN
(731) 352-4030
U.S. News ranking: Reg. U. (S), second tier
Website: www.bethelu.edu
Admissions email: admissions@bethelu.edu
Private; founded 1842
Affiliation: Cumberland Presbyterian
Application deadline (fall): 8/16
Undergraduate student body: N/A full time, N/A part time
Expenses: 2021-2022: $17,520; room/board: $9,648
Financial aid: (731) 352-4000; 78% of undergrads determined to have financial need; average aid package $10,056

Bryan College
Dayton TN
(800) 277-9522
U.S. News ranking: Reg. U. (S), No. 65
Website: www.bryan.edu
Admissions email: admissions@bryan.edu
Private; founded 1930
Affiliation: Evangelical Christian
Freshman admissions: selective; 2020-2021: 985 applied, 542 accepted. Neither SAT nor ACT required. ACT 25/75 percentile: 18-25. High school rank: 11% in top tenth, 41% in top quarter, 74% in top half
Early decision deadline: N/A, notification date: N/A
Early action deadline: N/A, notification date: N/A
Application deadline (fall): rolling
Undergraduate student body: 642 full time, 599 part time; 45% male, 55% female; 0% American Indian, 0% Asian, 6% black, 5% Hispanic, 3% multiracial, 0% Pacific Islander, 83% white, 2% international; 71% from in state; 82% live on campus; N/A of students in fraternities, N/A in sororities
Most popular majors: 47% Business, Management, Marketing, and Related Support Services, 9% Psychology, 4% Theology and Religious Vocations, 3% Biological and Biomedical Sciences, 3% Visual and Performing Arts
Expenses: 2021-2022: $17,360; room/board: $8,050
Financial aid: (423) 775-7339; 74% of undergrads determined to have financial need; average aid package $15,151

Carson-Newman University

Jefferson City TN
(800) 678-9061
U.S. News ranking: Nat. U.,
second tier
Website: www.cn.edu
Admissions email:
admitme@cn.edu
Private; founded 1851
Affiliation: Baptist
Freshman admissions: selective;
2020-2021: 3,022 applied,
2,397 accepted. Either SAT
or ACT required. ACT 25/75
percentile: 19-25. High school
rank: N/A
Early decision deadline: N/A,
notification date: N/A
Early action deadline: N/A,
notification date: N/A
Application deadline (fall): rolling
Undergraduate student body: 1,592
full time, 130 part time; 41%
male, 59% female; 0% American
Indian, 1% Asian, 9% black,
5% Hispanic, 3% multiracial,
0% Pacific Islander, 76% white,
3% international; 19% from in
state; 49% live on campus; 0%
of students in fraternities, 0% in
sororities
Most popular majors: 14%
Business Administration
and Management, General,
12% Registered Nursing/
Registered Nurse, 6% Biology/
Biological Sciences, General,
5% Psychology, General, 4%
Accounting
Expenses: 2021-2022: $31,320;
room/board: $9,474
Financial aid: (865) 471-3247;
81% of undergrads determined to
have financial need; average aid
package $25,278

Christian Brothers University

Memphis TN
(901) 321-3205
U.S. News ranking: Reg. U. (S),
No. 24
Website: www.cbu.edu
Admissions email:
admissions@cbu.edu
Private; founded 1871
Affiliation: Roman Catholic
Freshman admissions: more
selective; 2020-2021: 4,325
applied, 2,160 accepted. Neither
SAT nor ACT required. ACT 25/75
percentile: 22-27. High school
rank: 27% in top tenth, 57% in
top quarter, 84% in top half
Early decision deadline: N/A,
notification date: N/A
Early action deadline: N/A,
notification date: N/A
Application deadline (fall): rolling
Undergraduate student body: 1,311
full time, 237 part time; 45%
male, 55% female; 1% American
Indian, 4% Asian, 21% black,
8% Hispanic, 8% multiracial, 0%
Pacific Islander, 31% white, 4%
international
Most popular majors: 20%
Business Administration and
Management, General, 10%
Business/Commerce, General,
10% Natural Sciences, 7%
Psychology, General, 6%
Accounting

Expenses: 2021-2022: $34,820;
room/board: $8,350
Financial aid: (901) 321-3305;
65% of undergrads determined to
have financial need; average aid
package $27,508

Cumberland University

Lebanon TN
(615) 444-2562
U.S. News ranking: Reg. U. (S),
No. 93
Website: www.cumberland.edu
Admissions email:
admissions@cumberland.edu
Private; founded 1842
Freshman admissions: selective;
2020-2021: 2,872 applied,
1,554 accepted. Neither SAT
nor ACT required. ACT 25/75
percentile: 18-23. High school
rank: N/A
Early decision deadline: N/A,
notification date: N/A
Early action deadline: N/A,
notification date: N/A
Application deadline (fall): rolling
Undergraduate student body: 1,886
full time, 511 part time; 41%
male, 59% female; 1% American
Indian, 2% Asian, 11% black,
6% Hispanic, 0% multiracial, 0%
Pacific Islander, 59% white, 3%
international
Most popular majors: Information
not available
Expenses: 2021-2022: $25,412;
room/board: $9,000
Financial aid: (615) 547-1399;
84% of undergrads determined to
have financial need; average aid
package $18,596

East Tennessee State University

Johnson City TN
(423) 439-4213
U.S. News ranking: Nat. U.,
No. 288
Website: www.etsu.edu
Admissions email:
go2etsu@etsu.edu
Public; founded 1911
Freshman admissions: selective;
2020-2021: 8,685 applied,
6,812 accepted. Neither SAT
nor ACT required. ACT 25/75
percentile: 20-27. High school
rank: 34% in top tenth, 42% in
top quarter, 53% in top half
Early decision deadline: N/A,
notification date: N/A
Early action deadline: N/A,
notification date: N/A
Application deadline (fall): 8/15
Undergraduate student body: 8,812
full time, 1,893 part time; 40%
male, 60% female; 0% American
Indian, 1% Asian, 7% black, 4%
Hispanic, 4% multiracial, 0%
Pacific Islander, 79% white, 1%
international
Most popular majors: Information
not available
Expenses: 2020-2021: $9,259 in
state, $27,406 out of state; room/
board: $8,938
Financial aid: (423) 439-4300

Fisk University

Nashville TN
(888) 702-0022
U.S. News ranking: Nat. Lib. Arts,
No. 146
Website: www.fisk.edu
Admissions email:
admissions@fisk.edu
Private; founded 1866
Freshman admissions: selective;
2020-2021: 6,345 applied,
4,217 accepted. Either SAT
or ACT required. SAT 25/75
percentile: 990-1210. High school
rank: 32% in top tenth, 50% in
top quarter, 79% in top half
Early decision deadline: N/A,
notification date: N/A
Early action deadline: 11/1,
notification date: 12/31
Application deadline (fall): rolling
Undergraduate student body: 851
full time, 28 part time; 33%
male, 67% female; 0% American
Indian, 0% Asian, 80% black,
1% Hispanic, 1% multiracial, 0%
Pacific Islander, 0% white, 10%
international
Most popular majors: 22% Biology/
Biological Sciences, General,
22% Business Administration
and Management, General, 12%
Psychology, General, 10% English
Language and Literature, General,
10% Physics, General
Expenses: 2020-2021: $22,132;
room/board: $11,112
Financial aid: (615) 329-8585

Freed-Hardeman University

Henderson TN
(731) 348-3481
U.S. News ranking: Reg. U. (S),
No. 31
Website: www.fhu.edu
Admissions email:
admissions@fhu.edu
Private; founded 1869
Affiliation: Churches of Christ
Freshman admissions: more
selective; 2020-2021: 1,405
applied, 1,136 accepted. Either
SAT or ACT required. ACT 25/75
percentile: 21-27. High school
rank: 28% in top tenth, 63% in
top quarter, 85% in top half
Early decision deadline: N/A,
notification date: N/A
Early action deadline: N/A,
notification date: N/A
Application deadline (fall): rolling
Undergraduate student body: 1,312
full time, 415 part time; 43%
male, 57% female; 1% American
Indian, 1% Asian, 4% black,
0% Hispanic, 1% multiracial,
0% Pacific Islander, 87% white,
1% international; N/A from in
state; 83% live on campus; N/A
of students in fraternities, N/A in
sororities
Most popular majors: 18%
Business, Management,
Marketing, and Related Support
Services, 15% Health Professions
and Related Programs, 11%
Education, 7% Philosophy and
Religious Studies, 7% Psychology
Expenses: 2021-2022: $23,300;
room/board: $7,950

Financial aid: (731) 989-6662;
72% of undergrads determined to
have financial need; average aid
package $20,534

King University

Bristol TN
(423) 652-4861
U.S. News ranking: Reg. U. (S),
No. 52
Website: www.king.edu
Admissions email:
admissions@king.edu
Private; founded 1867
Affiliation: Presbyterian
Freshman admissions: selective;
2020-2021: 781 applied, 470
accepted. Neither SAT nor ACT
required. ACT 25/75 percentile:
19-25. High school rank: 14%
in top tenth, 39% in top quarter,
73% in top half
Early decision deadline: N/A,
notification date: N/A
Early action deadline: N/A,
notification date: N/A
Application deadline (fall): rolling
Undergraduate student body: 1,252
full time, 183 part time; 36%
male, 64% female; 1% American
Indian, 1% Asian, 4% black,
0% Hispanic, 2% multiracial,
0% Pacific Islander, 84% white,
2% international; N/A from in
state; 17% live on campus; N/A
of students in fraternities, N/A in
sororities
Most popular majors: 30%
Business, Management,
Marketing, and Related Support
Services, 30% Health Professions
and Related Programs, 6%
Computer and Information
Sciences and Support Services,
5% Education, 5% Homeland
Security, Law Enforcement,
Firefighting and Related Protective
Services
Expenses: 2020-2021: $18,513;
room/board: $9,386
Financial aid: (423) 652-4728;
83% of undergrads determined to
have financial need; average aid
package $17,498

Lane College[7]

Jackson TN
(731) 426-7533
U.S. News ranking: Nat. Lib. Arts,
second tier
Website: www.lanecollege.edu
Admissions email:
admissions@lanecollege.edu
Private; founded 1882
Affiliation: Christian Methodist
Episcopal
Freshman admissions: least
selective; 2020-2021: 7,134
applied, 4,333 accepted. Neither
SAT nor ACT required. ACT 25/75
percentile: 14-16. High school
rank: N/A
Early decision deadline: N/A,
notification date: N/A
Early action deadline: N/A,
notification date: N/A
Application deadline (fall): 7/1
Undergraduate student body: 1,048
full time, 47 part time
Most popular majors: 26%
Business Administration and
Management, General, 15%
Biology/Biological Sciences,
General, 13% Sociology, 11%

Criminal Justice/Safety Studies,
11% Mass Communication/Media
Studies
Expenses: 2020-2021: $11,790;
room/board: $7,610
Financial aid: N/A

Lee University

Cleveland TN
(423) 614-8500
U.S. News ranking: Reg. U. (S),
No. 27
Website: www.leeuniversity.edu
Admissions email:
admissions@leeuniversity.edu
Private; founded 1918
Affiliation: Church of God
Freshman admissions: selective;
2020-2021: 2,236 applied,
1,856 accepted. Either SAT
or ACT required. ACT 25/75
percentile: 21-27. High school
rank: 27% in top tenth, 53% in
top quarter, 77% in top half
Early decision deadline: N/A,
notification date: N/A
Early action deadline: N/A,
notification date: N/A
Application deadline (fall): rolling
Undergraduate student body: 3,459
full time, 1,211 part time; 38%
male, 62% female; 0% American
Indian, 1% Asian, 5% black,
1% Hispanic, 4% multiracial,
0% Pacific Islander, 82% white,
3% international; 48% from in
state; 44% live on campus; 11%
of students in fraternities, 9% in
sororities
Most popular majors: 15%
Theology and Religious Vocations,
14% Communication, Journalism,
and Related Programs, 12%
Education, 11% Business,
Management, Marketing, and
Related Support Services, 11%
Health Professions and Related
Programs
Expenses: 2021-2022: $20,500;
room/board: $8,510
Financial aid: (423) 614-8300;
71% of undergrads determined to
have financial need; average aid
package $14,176

LeMoyne-Owen College[1]

Memphis TN
(901) 435-1500
U.S. News ranking: Reg. Coll. (S),
second tier
Website: www.loc.edu/
Admissions email:
admission@loc.edu
Private; founded 1862
Affiliation: United Church of Christ
Application deadline (fall): N/A
Undergraduate student body: N/A
full time, N/A part time
Expenses: 2020-2021: $12,076;
room/board: $6,100
Financial aid: (901) 435-1550

Lincoln Memorial University

Harrogate TN
(423) 869-6280
U.S. News ranking: Nat. U.,
No. 249
Website: www.lmunet.edu/
Admissions email:
admissions@lmunet.edu
Private; founded 1897

Freshman admissions: selective; 2020-2021: 1,632 applied, 1,120 accepted. Neither SAT nor ACT required. ACT 25/75 percentile: 19-25. High school rank: 23% in top tenth, 45% in top quarter, 78% in top half **Early decision deadline:** N/A, notification date: N/A **Early action deadline:** N/A, notification date: N/A **Application deadline (fall):** rolling **Undergraduate student body:** 1,305 full time, 512 part time; 28% male, 72% female; 1% American Indian, 1% Asian, 6% black, 0% Hispanic, 0% multiracial, 0% Pacific Islander, 85% white, 4% international; 61% from in state; 35% live on campus; 3% of students in fraternities, 4% in sororities **Most popular majors:** 24% Health Professions and Related Programs, 6% Business, Management, Marketing, and Related Support Services, 5% Biological and Biomedical Sciences, 4% Parks, Recreation, Leisure, and Fitness Studies, 2% Agriculture, Agriculture Operations, and Related Sciences **Expenses:** 2021-2022: $24,210; room/board: $10,674 **Financial aid:** (423) 869-6465; 100% of undergrads determined to have financial need; average aid package $21,497

Lipscomb University
Nashville TN
(615) 966-1776
U.S. News ranking: Nat. U., No. 213
Website: www.lipscomb.edu
Admissions email: admissions@lipscomb.edu
Private; founded 1891
Affiliation: Churches of Christ
Freshman admissions: more selective; 2020-2021: 3,621 applied, 2,227 accepted. Neither SAT nor ACT required. ACT 25/75 percentile: 22-29. High school rank: 29% in top tenth, 63% in top quarter, 88% in top half **Early decision deadline:** N/A, notification date: N/A **Early action deadline:** N/A, notification date: N/A **Application deadline (fall):** rolling **Undergraduate student body:** 2,798 full time, 199 part time; 39% male, 61% female; 0% American Indian, 3% Asian, 7% black, 9% Hispanic, 3% multiracial, 0% Pacific Islander, 72% white, 3% international; 65% from in state; 47% live on campus; 23% of students in fraternities, 24% in sororities **Most popular majors:** 23% Business, Management, Marketing, and Related Support Services, 14% Biological and Biomedical Sciences, 9% Health Professions and Related Programs, 8% Visual and Performing Arts, 7% Education **Expenses:** 2021-2022: $35,752; room/board: $13,976 **Financial aid:** (615) 966-6205; 62% of undergrads determined to have financial need; average aid package $24,408

Maryville College
Maryville TN
(865) 981-8092
U.S. News ranking: Reg. Coll. (S), No. 5
Website: www.maryvillecollege.edu
Admissions email: admissions@maryvillecollege.edu
Private; founded 1819
Affiliation: Presbyterian Church (USA)
Freshman admissions: selective; 2020-2021: 2,321 applied, 1,442 accepted. Either SAT or ACT required. ACT 25/75 percentile: 20-28. High school rank: 31% in top tenth, 45% in top quarter, 70% in top half **Early decision deadline:** 11/1, notification date: 11/15 **Early action deadline:** N/A, notification date: N/A **Application deadline (fall):** rolling **Undergraduate student body:** 985 full time, 87 part time; 43% male, 57% female; 1% American Indian, 1% Asian, 9% black, 6% Hispanic, 4% multiracial, 0% Pacific Islander, 75% white, 3% international; 78% from in state; 62% live on campus; 0% of students in fraternities, 0% in sororities **Most popular majors:** 20% Business, Management, and Related Support Services, 15% Psychology, 13% Biological and Biomedical Sciences, 9% Education, 8% Visual and Performing Arts **Expenses:** 2021-2022: $37,016; room/board: $12,306 **Financial aid:** (865) 981-8100; 81% of undergrads determined to have financial need; average aid package $32,746

Middle Tennessee State University
Murfreesboro TN
(615) 898-2233
U.S. News ranking: Nat. U., No. 288
Website: www.mtsu.edu
Admissions email: admissions@mtsu.edu
Public; founded 1911
Freshman admissions: selective; 2020-2021: 9,096 applied, 8,568 accepted. Either SAT or ACT required. ACT 25/75 percentile: 20-26. High school rank: N/A **Early decision deadline:** N/A, notification date: N/A **Early action deadline:** N/A, notification date: N/A **Application deadline (fall):** rolling **Undergraduate student body:** 15,520 full time, 3,668 part time; 46% male, 54% female; 0% American Indian, 4% Asian, 18% black, 7% Hispanic, 4% multiracial, 0% Pacific Islander, 64% white, 2% international; 92% from in state; 10% live on campus; N/A of students in fraternities, N/A in sororities **Most popular majors:** 6% Multi-/Interdisciplinary Studies, Other, 5% Business Administration and Management, General, 5% Music Management, 5% Psychology, General, 4% Aeronautics/Aviation/Aerospace Science and Technology, General **Expenses:** 2021-2022: $9,592 in state, $29,584 out of state; room/board: $8,414 **Financial aid:** (615) 898-5454; 65% of undergrads determined to have financial need; average aid package $10,361

Milligan University
Milligan TN
(423) 461-8730
U.S. News ranking: Reg. U. (S), No. 10
Website: www.milligan.edu
Admissions email: admissions@milligan.edu
Private; founded 1866
Affiliation: Christian Churches and Churches of Christ
Freshman admissions: selective; 2020-2021: 518 applied, 514 accepted. Either SAT or ACT required. ACT 25/75 percentile: 21-26. High school rank: 26% in top tenth, 52% in top quarter, 84% in top half **Early decision deadline:** N/A, notification date: N/A **Early action deadline:** N/A, notification date: N/A **Application deadline (fall):** 8/28 **Undergraduate student body:** 786 full time, 155 part time; 48% male, 52% female; 0% American Indian, 1% Asian, 5% black, 6% Hispanic, 1% multiracial, 0% Pacific Islander, 78% white, 7% international; 62% from in state; 75% live on campus; 0% of students in fraternities, 0% in sororities **Most popular majors:** 23% Business/Commerce, General, 14% Health and Physical Education/Fitness, General, 11% Registered Nursing/Registered Nurse, 7% Engineering, General, 7% Psychology, General **Expenses:** 2021-2022: $36,140; room/board: $7,500 **Financial aid:** (423) 975-8049; 75% of undergrads determined to have financial need; average aid package $26,324

Rhodes College
Memphis TN
(901) 843-3700
U.S. News ranking: Nat. Lib. Arts, No. 54
Website: www.rhodes.edu
Admissions email: adminfo@rhodes.edu
Private; founded 1848
Affiliation: Presbyterian
Freshman admissions: more selective; 2020-2021: 5,074 applied, 2,606 accepted. Neither SAT nor ACT required. ACT 25/75 percentile: 27-32. High school rank: 53% in top tenth, 86% in top quarter, 99% in top half **Early decision deadline:** 11/1, notification date: 12/1 **Early action deadline:** 11/15, notification date: 1/15 **Application deadline (fall):** 1/15 **Undergraduate student body:** 1,790 full time, 50 part time; 40% male, 60% female; 0% American Indian, 7% Asian, 10% black, 6% Hispanic, 6% multiracial, 0% Pacific Islander, 64% white, 6% international; 30% from in state; 2% live on campus; 26% of students in fraternities, 38% in sororities **Most popular majors:** 20% Social Sciences, 17% Business, Management, Marketing, and Related Support Services, 17% Liberal Arts and Sciences, General Studies and Humanities, 6% History, 6% Physical Sciences **Expenses:** 2021-2022: $50,910; room/board: $12,656 **Financial aid:** (901) 843-3808; 53% of undergrads determined to have financial need; average aid package $43,430

Southern Adventist University
Collegedale TN
(423) 236-2835
U.S. News ranking: Reg. U. (S), No. 65
Website: www.southern.edu
Admissions email: admissions@southern.edu
Private; founded 1892
Affiliation: Seventh Day Adventist
Freshman admissions: selective; 2020-2021: 2,281 applied, 1,687 accepted. Either SAT or ACT required. ACT 25/75 percentile: 19-27. High school rank: N/A **Early decision deadline:** N/A, notification date: N/A **Early action deadline:** N/A, notification date: N/A **Application deadline (fall):** rolling **Undergraduate student body:** 2,103 full time, 281 part time; 44% male, 56% female; 0% American Indian, 12% Asian, 8% black, 25% Hispanic, 7% multiracial, 1% Pacific Islander, 43% white, 5% international; 33% from in state; N/A live on campus; 0% of students in fraternities, 0% in sororities **Most popular majors:** 22% Registered Nursing/Registered Nurse, 6% Biology/Biological Sciences, General, 6% Biomedical Sciences, General, 6% Kinesiology and Exercise Science, 5% Elementary Education and Teaching **Expenses:** 2021-2022: $23,210; room/board: $7,440 **Financial aid:** (423) 236-2535; 66% of undergrads determined to have financial need; average aid package $18,116

Tennessee State University
Nashville TN
(615) 963-5101
U.S. News ranking: Nat. U., second tier
Website: www.tnstate.edu
Admissions email: admissions@tnstate.edu
Public; founded 1912
Freshman admissions: less selective; 2020-2021: 10,648 applied, 6,115 accepted. Either SAT or ACT required. ACT 25/75 percentile: 16-20. High school rank: N/A **Early decision deadline:** N/A, notification date: N/A

Tennessee Techn University
Cookeville TN
(800) 255-8881
U.S. News ranking: Nat. U., No. 277
Website: www.tntech.edu
Admissions email: admissions@tntech.edu
Public; founded 1915
Freshman admissions: more selective; 2020-2021: 6,781 applied, 5,400 accepted. Neither SAT nor ACT required. ACT 25/75 percentile: 21-28. High school rank: 31% in top tenth, 59% in top quarter, 83% in top half **Early decision deadline:** N/A, notification date: N/A **Early action deadline:** N/A, notification date: N/A **Application deadline (fall):** rolling **Undergraduate student body:** 7,834 full time, 944 part time; 54% male, 46% female; 0% American Indian, 2% Asian, 4% black, 4% Hispanic, 4% multiracial, 0% Pacific Islander, 83% white, 2% international; 96% from in state; 25% live on campus; 8% of students in fraternities, 9% in sororities **Most popular majors:** 18% Engineering, 16% Business, Management, Marketing, and Related Support Services, 11% Education, 6% Health Professions and Related Programs, 6% Multi-/Interdisciplinary Studies **Expenses:** 2021-2022: $10,522 in state, $16,027 out of state; room/board: $8,850 **Financial aid:** (931) 372-3503; 74% of undergrads determined to have financial need; average aid package $12,352

Tennessee Wesleyan University
Athens TN
(423) 746-5286
U.S. News ranking: Reg. Coll. (S), No. 19
Website: www.tnwesleyan.edu

Early action deadline: N/A, notification date: N/A **Application deadline (fall):** 7/1 **Undergraduate student body:** 4,816 full time, 1,184 part time; 36% male, 64% female; 0% American Indian, 1% Asian, 83% black, 2% Hispanic, 2% multiracial, 0% Pacific Islander, 10% white, 2% international; 52% from in state; N/A live on campus; N/A of students in fraternities, N/A in sororities **Most popular majors:** 10% Business Administration and Management, General, 7% Criminal Justice/Law Enforcement Administration, 6% Communication and Media Studies, 6% Psychology, General, 5% Teacher Education, Multiple Levels **Expenses:** 2021-2022: $9,208 in state, $21,910 out of state; room/board: $8,166 **Financial aid:** (615) 963-5701; 79% of undergrads determined to have financial need; average aid package $14,062

Admissions email: admissions@tnwesleyan.edu
Private; founded 1857
Affiliation: United Methodist
Freshman admissions: selective; 2020-2021: 1,039 applied, 633 accepted. Neither SAT nor ACT required. ACT 25/75 percentile: 19-25. High school rank: N/A
Early decision deadline: N/A, notification date: N/A
Early action deadline: N/A, notification date: N/A
Application deadline (fall): rolling
Undergraduate student body: 947 full time, 109 part time; 37% male, 63% female; 0% American Indian, 1% Asian, 10% black, 5% Hispanic, 3% multiracial, 0% Pacific Islander, 72% white, 5% international; 88% from in state; 35% live on campus; 2% of students in fraternities, 4% in sororities
Most popular majors: 32% Business Administration and Management, General, 30% Registered Nursing/Registered Nurse, 10% Elementary Education and Teaching, 9% Health and Physical Education/Fitness, General, 4% Psychology, General
Expenses: 2021-2022: $26,590; room/board: $8,400
Financial aid: (423) 746-5209; 76% of undergrads determined to have financial need; average aid package $21,593

Trevecca Nazarene University
Nashville TN
(615) 248-1320
U.S. News ranking: Nat. U., second tier
Website: www.trevecca.edu
Admissions email: admissions_und@trevecca.edu
Private; founded 1901
Affiliation: Church of the Nazarene
Freshman admissions: selective; 2020-2021: 1,461 applied, 918 accepted. Either SAT or ACT required. ACT 25/75 percentile: 20-25. High school rank: 18% in top tenth, 46% in top quarter, 78% in top half
Early decision deadline: N/A, notification date: N/A
Early action deadline: N/A, notification date: N/A
Application deadline (fall): 8/1
Undergraduate student body: 1,326 full time, 769 part time; 39% male, 61% female; 0% American Indian, 1% Asian, 13% black, 11% Hispanic, 4% multiracial, 0% Pacific Islander, 60% white, 10% international; 67% from in state; 78% live on campus; 0% of students in fraternities, 0% in sororities
Most popular majors: 39% Business, Management, Marketing, and Related Support Services, 11% Health·Professions and Related Programs, 8% Psychology, 8% Theology and Religious Vocations, 5% Computer and Information Sciences and Support Services
Expenses: 2020-2021: $26,898; room/board: $9,100
Financial aid: (615) 248-1253

Tusculum University
Greeneville TN
(423) 636-7312
U.S. News ranking: Reg. U. (S), No. 88
Website: www.tusculum.edu
Admissions email: admission@tusculum.edu
Private; founded 1794
Affiliation: Presbyterian
Freshman admissions: selective; 2020-2021: 2,443 applied, 1,644 accepted. Neither SAT nor ACT required. ACT 25/75 percentile: 18-24. High school rank: N/A
Early decision deadline: N/A, notification date: N/A
Early action deadline: N/A, notification date: N/A
Application deadline (fall): rolling
Undergraduate student body: 1,090 full time, 263 part time; 42% male, 58% female; 1% American Indian, 0% Asian, 11% black, 3% Hispanic, 2% multiracial, 0% Pacific Islander, 63% white, 5% international
Most popular majors: Information not available
Expenses: 2021-2022: $26,060; room/board: $9,600
Financial aid: (423) 636-5377; 84% of undergrads determined to have financial need; average aid package $22,527

Union University
Jackson TN
(800) 338-6466
U.S. News ranking: Nat. U., No. 187
Website: www.uu.edu
Admissions email: admissions@uu.edu
Private; founded 1823
Affiliation: Southern Baptist
Freshman admissions: more selective; 2020-2021: 2,503 applied, 1,440 accepted. Either SAT or ACT required. ACT 25/75 percentile: 22-30. High school rank: 36% in top tenth, 61% in top quarter, 88% in top half
Early decision deadline: N/A, notification date: N/A
Early action deadline: N/A, notification date: N/A
Application deadline (fall): rolling
Undergraduate student body: 1,711 full time, 385 part time; 34% male, 66% female; 1% American Indian, 2% Asian, 17% black, 1% Hispanic, 0% multiracial, 0% Pacific Islander, 70% white, 2% international; 66% from in state; 77% live on campus; 11% of students in fraternities, 22% in sororities
Most popular majors: 35% Registered Nursing/Registered Nurse, 13% Organizational Leadership, 6% Social Work, 4% Marketing/Marketing Management, General, 2% Psychology, General
Expenses: 2021-2022: $35,660; room/board: $10,360
Financial aid: (731) 661-5015; 88% of undergrads determined to have financial need; average aid package $25,583

University of Memphis
Memphis TN
(901) 678-2111
U.S. News ranking: Nat. U., No. 249
Website: www.memphis.edu
Admissions email: recruitment@memphis.edu
Public; founded 1912
Freshman admissions: selective; 2020-2021: 13,317 applied, 11,346 accepted. Either SAT or ACT required. ACT 25/75 percentile: 19-26. High school rank: 19% in top tenth, 42% in top quarter, 72% in top half
Early decision deadline: N/A, notification date: N/A
Early action deadline: N/A, notification date: N/A
Application deadline (fall): 7/1
Undergraduate student body: 12,063 full time, 5,320 part time; 39% male, 61% female; 0% American Indian, 4% Asian, 37% black, 7% Hispanic, 4% multiracial, 0% Pacific Islander, 45% white, 1% international; N/A from in state; 16% live on campus; N/A of students in fraternities, N/A in sororities
Most popular majors: 19% Business Administration and Management, General, 12% Kinesiology and Exercise Science, 8% Multi-/Interdisciplinary Studies, Other, 8% Public Health, General, 6% Psychology, General
Expenses: 2021-2022: $9,912 in state, $16,764 out of state; room/board: $9,732
Financial aid: (901) 678-4995; 77% of undergrads determined to have financial need; average aid package $12,564

University of Tennessee
Knoxville TN
(865) 974-1111
U.S. News ranking: Nat. U., No. 103
Website: utk.edu
Admissions email: admissions@utk.edu
Public; founded 1794
Freshman admissions: more selective; 2020-2021: 25,423 applied, 19,867 accepted. Neither SAT nor ACT required. ACT 25/75 percentile: 25-31. High school rank: 41% in top tenth, 69% in top quarter, 91% in top half
Early decision deadline: N/A, notification date: N/A
Early action deadline: 11/1, notification date: 12/15
Application deadline (fall): rolling
Undergraduate student body: 22,914 full time, 1,340 part time; 47% male, 53% female; 0% American Indian, 4% Asian, 6% black, 5% Hispanic, 4% multiracial, 0% Pacific Islander, 79% white, 1% international; 79% from in state; 27% live on campus; 5% of students in fraternities, 14% in sororities
Most popular majors: 24% Business, Management, Marketing, and Related Support Services, 12% Engineering, 8% Parks, Recreation, Leisure, and Fitness Studies, 7% Social

Sciences, 6% Health Professions and Related Programs
Expenses: 2021-2022: $13,244 in state, $31,434 out of state; room/board: $12,150
Financial aid: (865) 974-1111; 53% of undergrads determined to have financial need; average aid package $14,395

University of Tennessee–Chattanooga
Chattanooga TN
(423) 425-4662
U.S. News ranking: Nat. U., second tier
Website: www.utc.edu
Admissions email: utcmocs@utc.edu
Public; founded 1886
Freshman admissions: selective; 2020-2021: 7,938 applied, 6,597 accepted. Either SAT or ACT required. ACT 25/75 percentile: 21-26. High school rank: N/A
Early decision deadline: N/A, notification date: N/A
Early action deadline: N/A, notification date: N/A
Application deadline (fall): 5/1
Undergraduate student body: 9,234 full time, 1,107 part time; 42% male, 58% female; 0% American Indian, 3% Asian, 10% black, 6% Hispanic, 2% multiracial, 0% Pacific Islander, 75% white, 1% international; 92% from in state; 29% live on campus; 12% of students in fraternities, 17% in sororities
Most popular majors: 22% Business, Management, Marketing, and Related Support Services, 9% Engineering, 9% Parks, Recreation, Leisure, and Fitness Studies, 8% Psychology, 6% Education
Expenses: 2021-2022: $9,848 in state, $25,966 out of state; room/board: $10,462
Financial aid: (423) 425-4677; 59% of undergrads determined to have financial need; average aid package $11,327

University of Tennessee–Martin
Martin TN
(800) 829-8861
U.S. News ranking: Reg. U. (S), No. 31
Website: www.utm.edu
Admissions email: admitme@utm.edu
Public; founded 1900
Freshman admissions: selective; 2020-2021: 9,001 applied, 5,846 accepted. ACT required. ACT 25/75 percentile: 21-26. High school rank: 18% in top tenth, 44% in top quarter, 79% in top half
Early decision deadline: N/A, notification date: N/A
Early action deadline: N/A, notification date: N/A
Application deadline (fall): rolling
Undergraduate student body: 4,669 full time, 1,728 part time; 39% male, 61% female; 0% American Indian, 1% Asian, 13% black,

4% Hispanic, 3% multiracial, 0% Pacific Islander, 78% white, 1% international; 90% from in state; 30% live on campus; 13% of students in fraternities, 15% in sororities
Most popular majors: 19% Agriculture, Agriculture Operations, and Related Sciences, 16% Business, Management, Marketing, and Related Support Services, 13% Multi/Interdisciplinary Studies, 9% Parks, Recreation, Leisure, and Fitness Studies, 7% Education
Expenses: 2021-2022: $9,912 in state, $15,952 out of state; room/board: $6,750
Financial aid: (731) 881-7040; 73% of undergrads determined to have financial need; average aid package $12,169

The University of Tennessee Southern
Pulaski TN
(931) 363-9800
U.S. News ranking: Reg. Coll. (S), No. 35
Website: www.utsouthern.edu
Admissions email: N/A
Private; founded 1870
Freshman admissions: selective; 2020-2021: 664 applied, 653 accepted. Either SAT or ACT required. ACT 25/75 percentile: 17-23. High school rank: N/A
Early decision deadline: N/A, notification date: N/A
Early action deadline: N/A, notification date: N/A
Application deadline (fall): rolling
Undergraduate student body: 682 full time, 109 part time; 41% male, 59% female; 1% American Indian, 0% Asian, 10% black, 6% Hispanic, 4% multiracial, 0% Pacific Islander, 72% white, 4% international; 74% from in state; N/A live on campus; N/A of students in fraternities, N/A in sororities
Most popular majors: 35% Business Administration and Management, General, 12% Health and Physical Education/Fitness, General, 11% Registered Nursing/Registered Nurse, 10% Behavioral Sciences, 10% Biology/Biological Sciences, General
Expenses: 2020-2021: $25,850; room/board: $8,600
Financial aid: (931) 424-7366

The University of the South
Sewanee TN
(800) 522-2234
U.S. News ranking: Nat. Lib. Arts, No. 50
Website: www.sewanee.edu
Admissions email: admiss@sewanee.edu
Private; founded 1857
Affiliation: Protestant Episcopal
Freshman admissions: more selective; 2020-2021: 4,191 applied, 2,350 accepted. Neither SAT nor ACT required. ACT 25/75 percentile: 25-30. High school rank: 31% in top tenth, 66% in top quarter, 89% in top half

Early decision deadline: 11/15, notification date: 12/15
Early action deadline: 12/1, notification date: 1/31
Application deadline (fall): 2/1
Undergraduate student body: 1,689 full time, 27 part time; 47% male, 53% female; 0% American Indian, 1% Asian, 5% black, 6% Hispanic, 3% multiracial, 0% Pacific Islander, 81% white, 4% international; 22% from in state; 88% live on campus; 57% of students in fraternities, 72% in sororities
Most popular majors: 15% Economics, General, 12% English Language and Literature, General, 10% Psychology, General, 9% International/Global Studies, 9% Political Science and Government, General
Expenses: 2021-2022: $49,418; room/board: $14,112
Financial aid: (931) 598-1312; 46% of undergrads determined to have financial need; average aid package $41,512

Vanderbilt University

Nashville TN
(800) 288-0432
U.S. News ranking: Nat. U., No. 14
Website: www.vanderbilt.edu
Admissions email: admissions@vanderbilt.edu
Private; founded 1873
Freshman admissions: most selective; 2020-2021: 36,646 applied, 4,259 accepted. Neither SAT nor ACT required. ACT 25/75 percentile: 33-35. High school rank: 90% in top tenth, 97% in top quarter, 99% in top half
Early decision deadline: 11/1, notification date: 12/15
Early action deadline: N/A, notification date: N/A
Application deadline (fall): 1/1
Undergraduate student body: 6,983 full time, 74 part time; 49% male, 51% female; 0% American Indian, 16% Asian, 11% black, 10% Hispanic, 6% multiracial, 0% Pacific Islander, 42% white, 9% international; 11% from in state; 50% live on campus; 27% of students in fraternities, 43% in sororities
Most popular majors: 11% Economics, General, 10% Multi-/Interdisciplinary Studies, Other, 9% Social Sciences, General, 7% Computer Science, 6% Mathematics, General
Expenses: 2021-2022: $56,966; room/board: $18,376
Financial aid: (615) 322-3591; 49% of undergrads determined to have financial need; average aid package $55,258

Watkins College of Art, Design & Film[1]

Nashville TN
(615) 383-4848
U.S. News ranking: Arts, unranked
Website: www.watkins.edu
Admissions email: admission@watkins.edu
Private
Application deadline (fall): N/A
Undergraduate student body: N/A full time, N/A part time
Expenses: N/A
Financial aid: N/A

Welch College

Gallatin TN
(615) 675-5359
U.S. News ranking: Reg. Coll. (S), No. 8
Website: www.welch.edu
Admissions email: recruit@welch.edu
Private; founded 1942
Affiliation: Free Will Baptist Church
Freshman admissions: selective; 2020-2021: 164 applied, 129 accepted. Either SAT or ACT required. ACT 25/75 percentile: 20-26. High school rank: 0% in top tenth, 0% in top quarter, 77% in top half
Early decision deadline: N/A, notification date: N/A
Early action deadline: N/A, notification date: N/A
Application deadline (fall): rolling
Undergraduate student body: 256 full time, 90 part time; 45% male, 55% female; 0% American Indian, 1% Asian, 9% black, 5% Hispanic, 4% multiracial, 0% Pacific Islander, 78% white, 2% international; 32% from in state; 43% live on campus; N/A of students in fraternities, N/A in sororities
Most popular majors: 24% Business Administration and Management, General, 14% Bible/Biblical Studies, 14% Pastoral Studies/Counseling, 14% Secondary Education and Teaching, 11% Psychology, General
Expenses: 2021-2022: $19,582; room/board: $7,932
Financial aid: (615) 675-5278; 76% of undergrads determined to have financial need; average aid package $13,986

TEXAS

Abilene Christian University

Abilene TX
(800) 460-6228
U.S. News ranking: Reg. U. (W), No. 16
Website: www.acu.edu
Admissions email: info@admissions.acu.edu
Private; founded 1906
Affiliation: Churches of Christ
Freshman admissions: selective; 2020-2021: 10,534 applied, 6,679 accepted. Neither SAT nor ACT required. SAT 25/75 percentile: 1010-1220. High school rank: 25% in top tenth, 54% in top quarter, 81% in top half
Early decision deadline: N/A, notification date: N/A
Early action deadline: 11/1, notification date: 11/15
Application deadline (fall): 2/15
Undergraduate student body: 3,297 full time, 197 part time; 38% male, 62% female; 0% American Indian, 1% Asian, 9% black, 20% Hispanic, 4% multiracial, 0% Pacific Islander, 61% white, 3% international; 85% from in state; 50% live on campus; 11% of students in fraternities, 20% in sororities

Most popular majors: 9% Registered Nursing/Registered Nurse, 9% Sport and Fitness Administration/Management, 6% Business Administration and Management, General, 6% Finance, General, 6% Psychology, General
Expenses: 2021-2022: $39,350; room/board: $11,628
Financial aid: (325) 674-2300; 68% of undergrads determined to have financial need; average aid package $25,930

Angelo State University

San Angelo TX
(325) 942-2041
U.S. News ranking: Reg. U. (W), No. 92
Website: www.angelo.edu
Admissions email: admissions@angelo.edu
Public; founded 1928
Freshman admissions: selective; 2020-2021: 3,795 applied, 2,894 accepted. Neither SAT nor ACT required. SAT 25/75 percentile: 950-1130. High school rank: 17% in top tenth, 41% in top quarter, 76% in top half
Early decision deadline: N/A, notification date: N/A
Early action deadline: N/A, notification date: N/A
Application deadline (fall): rolling
Undergraduate student body: 5,243 full time, 3,947 part time; 40% male, 60% female; 0% American Indian, 1% Asian, 7% black, 40% Hispanic, 3% multiracial, 0% Pacific Islander, 47% white, 2% international; 94% from in state; 29% live on campus; 2% of students in fraternities, 2% in sororities
Most popular majors: 19% Business, Management, Marketing, and Related Support Services, 12% Multi/Interdisciplinary Studies, 10% Health Professions and Related Programs, 8% Parks, Recreation, Leisure, and Fitness Studies, 6% Agriculture, Agriculture Operations, and Related Sciences
Expenses: 2021-2022: $9,610 in state, $21,550 out of state; room/board: $9,030
Financial aid: (325) 942-2246; 67% of undergrads determined to have financial need; average aid package $10,458

Art Institute of Houston[1]

Houston TX
(713) 623-2040
U.S. News ranking: Arts, unranked
Website: www.artinstitute.edu/houston/
Admissions email: N/A
For-profit
Application deadline (fall): N/A
Undergraduate student body: N/A full time, N/A part time
Expenses: 2020-2021: $19,354; room/board: N/A
Financial aid: N/A

Austin College

Sherman TX
(800) 526-4276
U.S. News ranking: Nat. Lib. Arts, No. 111
Website: www.austincollege.edu
Admissions email: admission@austincollege.edu
Private; founded 1849
Affiliation: Presbyterian
Freshman admissions: more selective; 2020-2021: 4,288 applied, 2,113 accepted. Neither SAT nor ACT required. SAT 25/75 percentile: 1110-1310. High school rank: 26% in top tenth, 57% in top quarter, 86% in top half
Early decision deadline: 12/1, notification date: 1/15
Early action deadline: 12/1, notification date: 1/15
Application deadline (fall): 3/1
Undergraduate student body: 1,281 full time, 4 part time; 47% male, 53% female; 1% American Indian, 13% Asian, 9% black, 24% Hispanic, 3% multiracial, 0% Pacific Islander, 49% white, 2% international; N/A from in state; 71% live on campus; 29% of students in fraternities, 32% in sororities
Most popular majors: 13% Business, Management, Marketing, and Related Support Services, 12% Biological and Biomedical Sciences, 12% Social Sciences, 10% Psychology, 8% Health Professions and Related Programs
Expenses: 2021-2022: $43,525; room/board: $12,230
Financial aid: (903) 813-2900; 67% of undergrads determined to have financial need; average aid package $40,492

Baylor University

Waco TX
(800) 229-5678
U.S. News ranking: Nat. U., No. 75
Website: www.baylor.edu
Admissions email: Admissions@Baylor.edu
Private; founded 1845
Affiliation: Baptist
Freshman admissions: more selective; 2020-2021: 33,680 applied, 23,061 accepted. Neither SAT nor ACT required. ACT 25/75 percentile: 26-31. High school rank: 50% in top tenth, 79% in top quarter, 96% in top half
Early decision deadline: 11/1, notification date: 12/15
Early action deadline: 11/1, notification date: 1/15
Application deadline (fall): 2/1
Undergraduate student body: 14,145 full time, 254 part time; 40% male, 60% female; 0% American Indian, 8% Asian, 5% black, 16% Hispanic, 5% multiracial, 0% Pacific Islander, 61% white, 4% international; 34% from in state; 33% live on campus; N/A of students in fraternities, N/A in sororities
Most popular majors: 8% Registered Nursing/Registered Nurse, 7% Biology/Biological Sciences, General, 5% Accounting, 5% Speech Communication and Rhetoric, 4%

Marketing/Marketing Management, General
Expenses: 2021-2022: $50,232; room/board: $14,324
Financial aid: (254) 710-2611; 54% of undergrads determined to have financial need; average aid package $32,214

Brazosport College[1]

Lake Jackson TX
(979) 230-3000
U.S. News ranking: Reg. Coll. (W), unranked
Website: www.brazosport.edu
Admissions email: N/A
Public
Application deadline (fall): N/A
Undergraduate student body: N/A full time, N/A part time
Expenses: 2020-2021: $3,304 in state, $4,738 out of state; room/board: N/A
Financial aid: N/A

Concordia University Texas[1]

Austin TX
(800) 865-4282
U.S. News ranking: Reg. U. (W), second tier
Website: www.concordia.edu
Admissions email: admissions@concordia.edu
Private; founded 1926
Application deadline (fall): 8/1
Undergraduate student body: N/A full time, N/A part time
Expenses: 2020-2021: $33,800; room/board: $11,920
Financial aid: (512) 313-4672

Dallas Baptist University

Dallas TX
(214) 333-5360
U.S. News ranking: Nat. U., No. 288
Website: www.dbu.edu
Admissions email: admiss@dbu.edu
Private; founded 1898
Affiliation: Baptist
Freshman admissions: selective; 2020-2021: 4,704 applied, 4,637 accepted. Either SAT or ACT required. SAT 25/75 percentile: 980-1200. High school rank: 18% in top tenth, 40% in top quarter, 72% in top half
Early decision deadline: N/A, notification date: N/A
Early action deadline: N/A, notification date: N/A
Application deadline (fall): rolling
Undergraduate student body: 2,283 full time, 591 part time; 42% male, 58% female; 0% American Indian, 2% Asian, 9% black, 18% Hispanic, 2% multiracial, 0% Pacific Islander, 58% white, 6% international; 91% from in state; 67% live on campus; 15% of students in fraternities, 24% in sororities
Most popular majors: 12% Multi-/Interdisciplinary Studies, Other, 11% Business Administration and Management, General, 10% Psychology, General, 6% Finance, General, 6% Speech Communication and Rhetoric

Expenses: 2021-2022: $33,620; room/board: $8,528
Financial aid: (214) 333-5363; 66% of undergrads determined to have financial need; average aid package $20,574

East Texas Baptist University
Marshall TX
(800) 804-3828
U.S. News ranking: Reg. Coll. (W), No. 15
Website: www.etbu.edu
Admissions email: admissions@etbu.edu
Private; founded 1912
Affiliation: Baptist
Freshman admissions: selective; 2020-2021: 1,597 applied, 1,149 accepted. Neither SAT nor ACT required. ACT 25/75 percentile: 17-22. High school rank: 10% in top tenth, 33% in top quarter, 66% in top half
Early decision deadline: N/A, notification date: N/A
Early action deadline: N/A, notification date: N/A
Application deadline (fall): 8/24
Undergraduate student body: 1,266 full time, 299 part time; 46% male, 54% female; 1% American Indian, 1% Asian, 21% black, 13% Hispanic, 2% multiracial, 0% Pacific Islander, 60% white, 1% international; 88% from in state; 81% live on campus; 0% of students in fraternities, 0% in sororities
Most popular majors: 14% Multi-/Interdisciplinary Studies, Other, 11% Registered Nursing/Registered Nurse, 8% Business Administration and Management, General, 7% Elementary Education and Teaching, 6% Biology/Biological Sciences, General
Expenses: 2021-2022: $27,980; room/board: $9,894
Financial aid: (903) 923-2137; 82% of undergrads determined to have financial need; average aid package $20,936

Hardin-Simmons University
Abilene TX
(325) 670-1206
U.S. News ranking: Reg. U. (W), No. 41
Website: www.hsutx.edu/
Admissions email: admissions@hsutx.edu
Private; founded 1891
Affiliation: Baptist
Freshman admissions: selective; 2020-2021: 2,308 applied, 2,089 accepted. Neither SAT nor ACT required. SAT 25/75 percentile: 960-1150. High school rank: 33% in top tenth, 48% in top quarter, 75% in top half
Early decision deadline: N/A, notification date: N/A
Early action deadline: N/A, notification date: N/A
Application deadline (fall): rolling
Undergraduate student body: 1,522 full time, 96 part time; 48% male, 52% female; 1% American Indian, 1% Asian, 12% black, 23% Hispanic, 4% multiracial,

0% Pacific Islander, 55% white, 3% international; 3% from in state; 57% live on campus; 6% of students in fraternities, 10% in sororities
Most popular majors: 25% Business, Management, Marketing, and Related Support Services, 10% Biological and Biomedical Sciences, 10% Education, 10% Parks, Recreation, Leisure, and Fitness Studies, 7% Health Professions and Related Programs
Expenses: 2021-2022: $31,686; room/board: $9,940
Financial aid: (325) 670-1595; 77% of undergrads determined to have financial need; average aid package $32,443

Houston Baptist University
Houston TX
(281) 649-3211
U.S. News ranking: Reg. U. (W), No. 61
Website: www.hbu.edu
Admissions email: admissions@hbu.edu
Private; founded 1960
Affiliation: Baptist
Freshman admissions: selective; 2020-2021: 8,518 applied, 6,162 accepted. Neither SAT nor ACT required. SAT 25/75 percentile: 1000-1180. High school rank: 25% in top tenth, 58% in top quarter, 83% in top half
Early decision deadline: N/A, notification date: N/A
Early action deadline: N/A, notification date: N/A
Application deadline (fall): rolling
Undergraduate student body: 2,146 full time, 587 part time; 33% male, 67% female; 0% American Indian, 9% Asian, 20% black, 37% Hispanic, 4% multiracial, 0% Pacific Islander, 22% white, 5% international; 95% from in state; 28% live on campus; 1% of students in fraternities, 5% in sororities
Most popular majors: 29% Health Professions and Related Programs, 16% Business, Management, Marketing, and Related Support Services, 9% Parks, Recreation, Leisure, and Fitness Studies, 8% Biological and Biomedical Sciences, 8% Psychology
Expenses: 2021-2022: $35,500; room/board: $9,286
Financial aid: (281) 649-3186; 77% of undergrads determined to have financial need; average aid package $29,801

Howard Payne University
Brownwood TX
(325) 649-8020
U.S. News ranking: Reg. Coll. (W), No. 20
Website: www.hputx.edu
Admissions email: enroll@hputx.edu
Private; founded 1889
Affiliation: Baptist
Freshman admissions: selective; 2020-2021: 1,638 applied, 795 accepted. Neither SAT nor ACT

required. SAT 25/75 percentile: 920-1090. High school rank: 12% in top tenth, 35% in top quarter, 70% in top half
Early decision deadline: N/A, notification date: N/A
Early action deadline: N/A, notification date: N/A
Application deadline (fall): rolling
Undergraduate student body: 699 full time, 282 part time; 51% male, 49% female; 1% American Indian, 0% Asian, 11% black, 27% Hispanic, 5% multiracial, 0% Pacific Islander, 52% white, 0% international
Most popular majors: 16% Business Administration and Management, General, 8% Criminology, 8% Health and Physical Education/Fitness, General, 4% General Studies, 4% Psychology, General
Expenses: 2021-2022: $30,358; room/board: $9,148
Financial aid: (325) 649-8015; 92% of undergrads determined to have financial need; average aid package $23,137

Huston-Tillotson University[1]
Austin TX
(512) 505-3029
U.S. News ranking: Reg. Coll. (W), No. 34
Website: htu.edu/
Admissions email: admission@htu.edu
Private
Application deadline (fall): 5/1
Undergraduate student body: N/A full time, N/A part time
Expenses: 2020-2021: $14,703; room/board: $8,449
Financial aid: N/A

Jarvis Christian College[1]
Hawkins TX
(903) 730-4890
U.S. News ranking: Reg. Coll. (W), second tier
Website: www.jarvis.edu
Admissions email: Recruitment@jarvis.edu
Private; founded 1912
Affiliation: Christian Church (Disciples of Christ)
Application deadline (fall): 8/1
Undergraduate student body: N/A full time, N/A part time
Expenses: 2020-2021: $11,720; room/board: $9,880
Financial aid: (903) 730-4890

Lamar University
Beaumont TX
(409) 880-8888
U.S. News ranking: Nat. U., second tier
Website: www.lamar.edu
Admissions email: admissions@lamar.edu
Public; founded 1923
Freshman admissions: selective; 2020-2021: 5,948 applied, 5,015 accepted. Either SAT or ACT required. SAT 25/75 percentile: 940-1120. High school rank: 12% in top tenth, 39% in top quarter, 76% in top half

Early decision deadline: N/A, notification date: N/A
Early action deadline: N/A, notification date: N/A
Undergraduate student body: 4,657 full time, 3,898 part time; 40% male, 60% female; 0% American Indian, 5% Asian, 25% black, 22% Hispanic, 3% multiracial, 0% Pacific Islander, 41% white, 1% international; 97% from in state; 27% live on campus; N/A of students in fraternities, N/A in sororities
Most popular majors: Information not available
Expenses: 2021-2022: $10,586 in state, $22,826 out of state; room/board: $9,590
Financial aid: (409) 880-7011; 67% of undergrads determined to have financial need; average aid package $6,671

LeTourneau University
Longview TX
(903) 233-4300
U.S. News ranking: Reg. U. (W), No. 30
Website: www.letu.edu
Admissions email: admissions@letu.edu
Private; founded 1946
Freshman admissions: selective; 2020-2021: 2,201 applied, 1,235 accepted. Neither SAT nor ACT required. SAT 25/75 percentile: 1110-1330. High school rank: 30% in top tenth, 54% in top quarter, 85% in top half
Early decision deadline: N/A, notification date: N/A
Early action deadline: N/A, notification date: N/A
Application deadline (fall): rolling
Undergraduate student body: 1,373 full time, 1,480 part time; 55% male, 45% female; 1% American Indian, 1% Asian, 9% black, 6% Hispanic, 5% multiracial, 0% Pacific Islander, 66% white, 3% international; 72% from in state; 67% live on campus; N/A of students in fraternities, N/A in sororities
Most popular majors: 21% Engineering, 19% Business, Management, Marketing, and Related Support Services, 9% Transportation and Materials Moving, 8% Education, 7% Health Professions and Related Programs
Expenses: 2021-2022: $33,490; room/board: $10,170
Financial aid: (903) 233-4350; 67% of undergrads determined to have financial need; average aid package $24,239

Lubbock Christian University
Lubbock TX
(806) 720-7151
U.S. News ranking: Reg. U. (W), No. 71
Website: lcu.edu
Admissions email: admissions@lcu.edu
Private; founded 1957
Affiliation: Churches of Christ
Freshman admissions: selective; 2020-2021: 373 applied, 360 accepted. Either SAT or ACT

required. ACT 25/75 percentile: 19-25. High school rank: 20% in top tenth, 46% in top quarter, 76% in top half
Early decision deadline: 10/31, notification date: 12/15
Early action deadline: 6/15, notification date: 7/15
Application deadline (fall): 6/15
Undergraduate student body: 1,156 full time, 226 part time; 38% male, 62% female; 1% American Indian, 1% Asian, 4% black, 22% Hispanic, 1% multiracial, 0% Pacific Islander, 65% white, 2% international; 93% from in state; 35% live on campus; 22% of students in fraternities, 19% in sororities
Most popular majors: 24% Health Professions and Related Programs, 13% Business, Management, Marketing, and Related Support Services, 10% Education, 7% Parks, Recreation, Leisure, and Fitness Studies, 6% Biological and Biomedical Sciences
Expenses: 2020-2021: $24,260; room/board: $8,070
Financial aid: (806) 720-7176

McMurry University
Abilene TX
(325) 793-4700
U.S. News ranking: Reg. Coll. (W), No. 11
Website: mcm.edu/
Admissions email: admissions@mcm.edu
Private; founded 1923
Affiliation: United Methodist
Freshman admissions: selective; 2020-2021: 1,798 applied, 852 accepted. Neither SAT nor ACT required. SAT 25/75 percentile: 940-1130. High school rank: 15% in top tenth, 32% in top quarter, 71% in top half
Early decision deadline: N/A, notification date: N/A
Early action deadline: 12/18, notification date: N/A
Application deadline (fall): 8/15
Undergraduate student body: 953 full time, 134 part time; 50% male, 50% female; 1% American Indian, 0% Asian, 16% black, 30% Hispanic, 3% multiracial, 0% Pacific Islander, 47% white, 2% international; 95% from in state; 48% live on campus; 14% of students in fraternities, 15% in sororities
Most popular majors: 28% Business, Management, Marketing, and Related Support Services, 22% Education, 8% Parks, Recreation, Leisure, and Fitness Studies, 8% Social Sciences, 8% Visual and Performing Arts
Expenses: 2021-2022: $29,190; room/board: $9,050
Financial aid: (325) 793-4978; 85% of undergrads determined to have financial need; average aid package $23,654

Midland College[1]
Midland TX
(432) 685-4500
U.S. News ranking: Reg. Coll. (W), unranked
Website: www.midland.edu/

Admissions email:
pebensberger@midland.edu
Public
Application deadline (fall): N/A
Undergraduate student body: N/A
full time, N/A part time
Expenses: 2020-2021: $4,350 in
state, $5,610 out of state; room/
board: $5,250
Financial aid: N/A

Midwestern State University
Wichita Falls TX
(940) 397-4334
U.S. News ranking: Reg. U. (W),
No. 77
Website: msutexas.edu/
Admissions email:
admissions@msutexas.edu
Public; founded 1922
Freshman admissions: less
selective; 2020-2021: 4,023
applied, 3,617 accepted. Neither
SAT nor ACT required. SAT 25/75
percentile: 910-1100. High school
rank: 12% in top tenth, 37% in
top quarter, 72% in top half
Early decision deadline: N/A,
notification date: N/A
Early action deadline: N/A,
notification date: N/A
Application deadline (fall): 8/8
Undergraduate student body: 3,851
full time, 1,290 part time; 37%
male, 63% female; 1% American
Indian, 3% Asian, 15% black,
22% Hispanic, 4% multiracial,
0% Pacific Islander, 47% white,
7% international; N/A from in
state; N/A live on campus; 5%
of students in fraternities, 6% in
sororities
Most popular majors: Information
not available
Expenses: 2021-2022: $9,776 in
state, $11,726 out of state; room/
board: $9,780
Financial aid: (940) 397-4214;
62% of undergrads determined to
have financial need; average aid
package $10,854

Our Lady of the Lake University
San Antonio TX
(210) 431-3961
U.S. News ranking: Nat. U.,
second tier
Website: www.ollusa.edu
Admissions email:
admission@ollusa.edu
Private; founded 1895
Affiliation: Roman Catholic
Freshman admissions: less
selective; 2020-2021: 4,182
applied, 4,090 accepted. Neither
SAT nor ACT required. SAT 25/75
percentile: 890-1060. High school
rank: 13% in top tenth, 39% in
top quarter, 72% in top half
Early decision deadline: N/A,
notification date: N/A
Early action deadline: N/A,
notification date: N/A
Application deadline (fall): 8/20
Undergraduate student body: 1,177
full time, 117 part time; 31%
male, 69% female; 0% American
Indian, 0% Asian, 6% black,
80% Hispanic, 0% multiracial,
0% Pacific Islander, 8% white,
2% international; 2% from in
state; 37% live on campus; 1%

of students in fraternities, 1% in
sororities
Most popular majors: 17% Public
Administration and Social Service
Professions, 15% Psychology,
14% Business, Management,
Marketing, and Related Support
Services, 10% Health Professions
and Related Programs, 10%
Homeland Security, Law
Enforcement, Firefighting and
Related Protective Services
Expenses: 2021-2022: $29,926;
room/board: $10,242
Financial aid: (210) 434-6711;
87% of undergrads determined to
have financial need; average aid
package $24,516

Paul Quinn College[1]
Dallas TX
(214) 379-5546
U.S. News ranking: Reg. Coll. (W),
second tier
Website: www.rtc.edu
Admissions email:
N/A
Private
Application deadline (fall): N/A
Undergraduate student body: N/A
full time, N/A part time
Expenses: 2020-2021: $9,992;
room/board: $9,450
Financial aid: N/A

Prairie View A&M University[1]
Prairie View TX
(936) 261-1000
U.S. News ranking: Reg. U. (W),
second tier
Website: www.pvamu.edu
Admissions email:
admission@pvamu.edu
Public; founded 1876
Application deadline (fall): 6/1
Undergraduate student body: N/A
full time, N/A part time
Expenses: 2020-2021: $11,099
in state, $26,127 out of state;
room/board: $8,979
Financial aid: (936) 261-1000

Rice University
Houston TX
(713) 348-7423
U.S. News ranking: Nat. U., No. 17
Website: www.rice.edu
Admissions email:
admission@rice.edu
Private; founded 1912
Freshman admissions: most
selective; 2020-2021: 23,455
applied, 2,555 accepted. Neither
SAT nor ACT required. SAT 25/75
percentile: 1460-1570. High
school rank: 92% in top tenth,
98% in top quarter, 100% in
top half
Early decision deadline: 11/1,
notification date: 12/15
Early action deadline: N/A,
notification date: N/A
Application deadline (fall): 1/1
Undergraduate student body: 3,960
full time, 116 part time; 52%
male, 48% female; 0% American
Indian, 28% Asian, 8% black,
16% Hispanic, 5% multiracial,
0% Pacific Islander, 31% white,
12% international; 40% from in
state; 38% live on campus; 0%
of students in fraternities, 0% in

sororities
Most popular majors: 10%
Computer and Information
Sciences, General, 6%
Biochemistry, 5% Economics,
General, 4% Kinesiology and
Exercise Science, 4% Psychology,
General
Expenses: 2021-2022: $52,895;
room/board: $14,800
Financial aid: (713) 348-4958;
45% of undergrads determined to
have financial need; average aid
package $54,051

Sam Houston State University
Huntsville TX
(936) 294-1828
U.S. News ranking: Nat. U., No.
249
Website: www.shsu.edu
Admissions email:
admissions@shsu.edu
Public; founded 1879
Freshman admissions: selective;
2020-2021: 12,025 applied,
11,123 accepted. Neither SAT
nor ACT required. SAT 25/75
percentile: 970-1120. High school
rank: 33% in top tenth, 53% in
top quarter, 81% in top half
Early decision deadline: N/A,
notification date: N/A
Early action deadline: N/A,
notification date: N/A
Application deadline (fall): 8/1
Undergraduate student body:
15,011 full time, 3,779 part
time; 37% male, 63% female;
1% American Indian, 2% Asian,
18% black, 26% Hispanic, 3%
multiracial, 0% Pacific Islander,
48% white, 1% international;
98% from in state; 17% live
on campus; 6% of students in
fraternities, 5% in sororities
Most popular majors: 20%
Business, Management,
Marketing, and Related Support
Services, 20% Homeland Security,
Law Enforcement, Firefighting
and Related Protective Services,
10% Health Professions and
Related Programs, 10% Multi/
Interdisciplinary Studies,
5% Agriculture, Agriculture
Operations, and Related Sciences
Expenses: 2021-2022: $11,034
in state, $23,274 out of state;
room/board: $9,670
Financial aid: (936) 294-1774;
64% of undergrads determined to
have financial need; average aid
package $11,751

Schreiner University
Kerrville TX
(830) 792-7217
U.S. News ranking: Reg. Coll. (W),
No. 8
Website: www.schreiner.edu
Admissions email:
admissions@schreiner.edu
Private; founded 1923
Affiliation: Presbyterian Church
(USA)
Freshman admissions: selective;
2020-2021: 1,398 applied,
1,344 accepted. Neither SAT
nor ACT required. SAT 25/75
percentile: 920-1160. High school
rank: 10% in top tenth, 29% in
top quarter, 64% in top half

Early decision deadline: N/A,
notification date: N/A
Early action deadline: N/A,
notification date: N/A
Application deadline (fall): 8/1
Undergraduate student body: 994
full time, 151 part time; 46%
male, 54% female; 1% American
Indian, 1% Asian, 5% black, 35%
Hispanic, 3% multiracial, 0%
Pacific Islander, 54% white, 1%
international
Most popular majors: Information
not available
Expenses: 2021-2022: $33,927;
room/board: $10,719
Financial aid: (830) 792-7303;
76% of undergrads determined to
have financial need; average aid
package $25,807

SMU
Dallas TX
(800) 323-0672
U.S. News ranking: Nat. U., No. 68
Website: www.smu.edu
Admissions email:
ugadmission@smu.edu
Private; founded 1911
Affiliation: United Methodist
Freshman admissions: more
selective; 2020-2021: 14,010
applied, 7,379 accepted. Either
SAT or ACT required. ACT 25/75
percentile: 29-33. High school
rank: 47% in top tenth, 79% in
top quarter, 94% in top half
Early decision deadline: 11/1,
notification date: 12/31
Early action deadline: 11/1,
notification date: 12/31
Application deadline (fall): 1/15
Undergraduate student body: 6,616
full time, 211 part time; 51%
male, 49% female; 0% American
Indian, 8% Asian, 5% black, 13%
Hispanic, 4% multiracial, 0%
Pacific Islander, 64% white, 6%
international; N/A from in state;
45% live on campus; 26% of
students in fraternities, 35% in
sororities
Most popular majors: 26%
Business, Management,
Marketing, and Related
Support Services, 12% Social
Sciences, 9% Engineering, 8%
Communication, Journalism,
and Related Programs, 8%
Mathematics and Statistics
Expenses: 2021-2022: $60,236;
room/board: $17,438
Financial aid: (214) 768-3417;
30% of undergrads determined to
have financial need; average aid
package $48,082

South Texas College[1]
McAllen TX
(956) 872-8311
U.S. News ranking: Reg. Coll. (W),
second tier
Website: www.southtexascollege.
edu/
Admissions email:
N/A
Public
Application deadline (fall): N/A
Undergraduate student body: N/A
full time, N/A part time
Expenses: 2020-2021: $4,530 in
state, $7,920 out of state; room/
board: N/A
Financial aid: N/A

Southwestern Adventist University[1]
Keene TX
(817) 202-6749
U.S. News ranking: Reg. Coll. (W),
No. 32
Website: www.swau.edu
Admissions email:
admission@swau.edu
Private; founded 1893
Affiliation: Seventh Day Adventist
Application deadline (fall): 8/1
Undergraduate student body: N/A
full time, N/A part time
Expenses: 2020-2021: $22,836;
room/board: $7,900
Financial aid: (817) 202-6262

Southwestern Assemblies of God University[1]
Waxahachie TX
(888) 937-7248
U.S. News ranking: Reg. U. (W),
second tier
Website: www.sagu.edu/
Admissions email:
admissions@sagu.edu
Private; founded 1927
Application deadline (fall): rolling
Undergraduate student body: N/A
full time, N/A part time
Expenses: 2020-2021: $19,834;
room/board: $7,582
Financial aid: (972) 825-4730

Southwestern Christian College[1]
Terrell TX
(972) 524-3341
U.S. News ranking: Reg. Coll. (W),
unranked
Website: www.swcc.edu
Admissions email:
N/A
Private
Application deadline (fall): N/A
Undergraduate student body: N/A
full time, N/A part time
Expenses: 2020-2021: $8,132;
room/board: $6,270
Financial aid: N/A

Southwestern University
Georgetown TX
(512) 863-1200
U.S. News ranking: Nat. Lib. Arts,
No. 98
Website: www.southwestern.edu
Admissions email:
admission@southwestern.edu
Private; founded 1840
Affiliation: United Methodist
Freshman admissions: more
selective; 2020-2021: 4,578
applied, 2,260 accepted. Neither
SAT nor ACT required. SAT
25/75 percentile: 1110-1300.
High school rank: 27% in top
tenth, 63% in top quarter, 92%
in top half
Early decision deadline: 11/1,
notification date: 12/1
Early action deadline: 12/1,
notification date: 3/1
Application deadline (fall): 2/1
Undergraduate student body: 1,488
full time, 17 part time; 45%
male, 55% female; 0% American
Indian, 4% Asian, 5% black,
25% Hispanic, 4% multiracial,

0% Pacific Islander, 59% white, 1% international; 88% from in state; 56% live on campus; 21% of students in fraternities, 22% in sororities
Most popular majors: 22% Business/Commerce, General, 9% Psychology, General, 8% Speech Communication and Rhetoric, 7% Biology/Biological Sciences, General, 7% Political Science and Government, General
Expenses: 2021-2022: $46,800; room/board: $12,000
Financial aid: (512) 863-1259; 60% of undergrads determined to have financial need; average aid package $39,370

St. Edward's University
Austin TX
(512) 448-8500
U.S. News ranking: Reg. U. (W), No. 9
Website: www.stedwards.edu
Admissions email: seu.admit@stedwards.edu
Private; founded 1885
Affiliation: Roman Catholic
Freshman admissions: selective; 2020-2021: 5,203 applied, 4,751 accepted. Neither SAT nor ACT required. SAT 25/75 percentile: 1030-1225. High school rank: 17% in top tenth, 49% in top quarter, 78% in top half
Early decision deadline: N/A, notification date: N/A
Early action deadline: N/A, notification date: N/A
Application deadline (fall): 5/1
Undergraduate student body: 2,820 full time, 194 part time; 37% male, 63% female; 0% American Indian, 3% Asian, 4% black, 49% Hispanic, 3% multiracial, 0% Pacific Islander, 34% white, 5% international; 81% from in state; 25% live on campus; N/A of students in fraternities, N/A in sororities
Most popular majors: 9% Psychology, General, 7% Biology/Biological Sciences, General, 7% Business Administration and Management, General, 5% Finance, General, 5% Speech Communication and Rhetoric
Expenses: 2021-2022: $49,996; room/board: $13,942
Financial aid: (512) 448-8516; 73% of undergrads determined to have financial need; average aid package $41,516

Stephen F. Austin State University[1]
Nacogdoches TX
(936) 468-2504
U.S. News ranking: Nat. U., second tier
Website: www.sfasu.edu
Admissions email: admissions@sfasu.edu
Public; founded 1923
Application deadline (fall): rolling
Undergraduate student body: N/A full time, N/A part time
Expenses: 2020-2021: $10,600 in state, $21,616 out of state; room/board: $9,642
Financial aid: (936) 468-2230

St. Mary's University of San Antonio
San Antonio TX
(210) 436-3126
U.S. News ranking: Reg. U. (W), No. 10
Website: www.stmarytx.edu
Admissions email: uadm@stmarytx.edu
Private; founded 1852
Affiliation: Roman Catholic
Freshman admissions: selective; 2020-2021: 5,210 applied, 4,408 accepted. Neither SAT nor ACT required. SAT 25/75 percentile: 1020-1220. High school rank: 24% in top tenth, 53% in top quarter, 78% in top half
Early decision deadline: N/A, notification date: N/A
Early action deadline: N/A, notification date: N/A
Application deadline (fall): 1/15
Undergraduate student body: 2,037 full time, 102 part time; 57% male, 43% female; 0% American Indian, 3% Asian, 3% black, 69% Hispanic, 1% multiracial, 0% Pacific Islander, 15% white, 5% international; 94% from in state; 29% live on campus; N/A of students in fraternities, N/A in sororities
Most popular majors: 22% Business, Management, Marketing, and Related Support Services, 13% Social Sciences, 10% Biological and Biomedical Sciences, 10% Engineering, 9% Psychology
Expenses: 2021-2022: $34,564; room/board: $11,156
Financial aid: (210) 436-3141; 73% of undergrads determined to have financial need; average aid package $28,929

Sul Ross State University
Alpine TX
(432) 837-8055
U.S. News ranking: Reg. U. (W), second tier
Website: www.sulross.edu
Admissions email: admissions@sulross.edu
Public; founded 1917
Freshman admissions: less selective; 2020-2021: 1,012 applied, 1,012 accepted. Neither SAT nor ACT required. SAT 25/75 percentile: 848-1040. High school rank: 4% in top tenth, 15% in top quarter, 45% in top half
Early decision deadline: N/A, notification date: N/A
Early action deadline: N/A, notification date: N/A
Application deadline (fall): rolling
Undergraduate student body: 1,154 full time, 635 part time; 38% male, 62% female; 1% American Indian, 0% Asian, 5% black, 69% Hispanic, 3% multiracial, 0% Pacific Islander, 21% white, 0% international; 99% from in state; 53% live on campus; 0% of students in fraternities, 0% in sororities
Most popular majors: 17% Business Administration and Management, General, 17% Multi-/Interdisciplinary Studies,

Other, 12% Homeland Security, 10% Kinesiology and Exercise Science, 9% Psychology, General
Expenses: 2021-2022: $9,004 in state, $21,244 out of state; room/board: $8,724
Financial aid: (432) 837-8059; 78% of undergrads determined to have financial need; average aid package $12,768

Tarleton State University
Stephenville TX
(800) 687-8236
U.S. News ranking: Reg. U. (W), No. 77
Website: www.tarleton.edu
Admissions email: uadm@tarleton.edu
Public; founded 1899
Freshman admissions: selective; 2020-2021: 9,879 applied, 5,694 accepted. Either SAT or ACT required. SAT 25/75 percentile: 950-1130. High school rank: 12% in top tenth, 27% in top quarter, 80% in top half
Early decision deadline: N/A, notification date: N/A
Early action deadline: 12/1, notification date: N/A
Application deadline (fall): 8/1
Undergraduate student body: 8,554 full time, 3,339 part time; 37% male, 63% female; 0% American Indian, 1% Asian, 8% black, 22% Hispanic, 4% multiracial, 0% Pacific Islander, 63% white, 1% international; 3% from in state; 31% live on campus; N/A of students in fraternities, N/A in sororities
Most popular majors: 8% Kinesiology and Exercise Science, 8% Registered Nursing/Registered Nurse, 7% Business/Commerce, General, 6% Psychology, General, 5% Multi-/Interdisciplinary Studies, Other
Expenses: 2021-2022: $9,728 in state, $21,998 out of state; room/board: $10,206
Financial aid: (254) 968-9070; 65% of undergrads determined to have financial need; average aid package $11,381

Texas A&M International University
Laredo TX
(956) 326-2200
U.S. News ranking: Reg. U. (W), No. 64
Website: www.tamiu.edu
Admissions email: enroll@tamiu.edu
Public; founded 1970
Freshman admissions: selective; 2020-2021: 7,079 applied, 4,172 accepted. Either SAT or ACT required. SAT 25/75 percentile: 920-1100. High school rank: 21% in top tenth, 52% in top quarter, 86% in top half
Early decision deadline: N/A, notification date: N/A
Early action deadline: N/A, notification date: N/A
Application deadline (fall): 8/1
Undergraduate student body: 5,512 full time, 1,572 part time; 39%

male, 61% female; 0% American Indian, 0% Asian, 1% black, 95% Hispanic, 0% multiracial, 0% Pacific Islander, 2% white, 1% international; 98% from in state; 7% live on campus; 1% of students in fraternities, 1% in sororities
Most popular majors: 15% Business Administration and Management, General, 13% Criminal Justice/Law Enforcement Administration, 12% Psychology, General, 11% Biology/Biological Sciences, General, 7% Multi/ Interdisciplinary Studies
Expenses: 2021-2022: $9,149 in state, $21,719 out of state; room/board: $9,002
Financial aid: (956) 326-2225; 85% of undergrads determined to have financial need; average aid package $11,022

Texas A&M University
College Station TX
(979) 845-1060
U.S. News ranking: Nat. U., No. 68
Website: www.tamu.edu
Admissions email: admissions@tamu.edu
Public; founded 1876
Freshman admissions: more selective; 2020-2021: 43,307 applied, 27,287 accepted. Neither SAT nor ACT required. SAT 25/75 percentile: 1160-1380. High school rank: 66% in top tenth, 92% in top quarter, 99% in top half
Early decision deadline: N/A, notification date: N/A
Early action deadline: 10/15, notification date: N/A
Application deadline (fall): 12/1
Undergraduate student body: 49,442 full time, 6,126 part time; 53% male, 47% female; 0% American Indian, 9% Asian, 2% black, 25% Hispanic, 3% multiracial, 0% Pacific Islander, 58% white, 1% international; N/A from in state; 20% live on campus; N/A of students in fraternities, N/A in sororities
Most popular majors: 16% Business, Management, Marketing, and Related Support Services, 16% Engineering, 12% Multi/Interdisciplinary Studies, 8% Agriculture, Agriculture Operations, and Related Sciences, 8% Biological and Biomedical Sciences
Expenses: 2021-2022: $13,178 in state, $40,087 out of state; room/board: $11,400
Financial aid: (979) 845-3236; 45% of undergrads determined to have financial need; average aid package $16,611

Texas A&M University–Commerce
Commerce TX
(903) 886-5000
U.S. News ranking: Nat. U., second tier
Website: www.tamuc.edu/
Admissions email: admissions@tamuc.edu
Public; founded 1889
Freshman admissions: selective; 2020-2021: 9,652 applied,

3,056 accepted. Neither SAT nor ACT required. SAT 25/75 percentile: 955-1150. High school rank: 19% in top tenth, 46% in top quarter, 80% in top half
Early decision deadline: N/A, notification date: N/A
Early action deadline: N/A, notification date: N/A
Application deadline (fall): 8/15
Undergraduate student body: 5,590 full time, 2,472 part time; 40% male, 60% female; 1% American Indian, 2% Asian, 20% black, 22% Hispanic, 7% multiracial, 0% Pacific Islander, 41% white, 6% international; 94% from in state; 23% live on campus; 1% of students in fraternities, 2% in sororities
Most popular majors: 32% Multi/Interdisciplinary Studies, 13% Business, Management, Marketing, and Related Support Services, 7% Liberal Arts and Sciences, General Studies and Humanities, 4% Agriculture, Agriculture Operations, and Related Sciences, 4% Homeland Security, Law Enforcement, Firefighting and Related Protective Services
Expenses: 2021-2022: $10,026 in state, $22,266 out of state; room/board: $10,066
Financial aid: (903) 886-5096; 67% of undergrads determined to have financial need; average aid package $9,762

Texas A&M University–Corpus Christi
Corpus Christi TX
(361) 825-2624
U.S. News ranking: Nat. U., second tier
Website: www.tamucc.edu/
Admissions email: adiss@tamucc.edu
Public; founded 1947
Freshman admissions: selective; 2020-2021: 8,540 applied, 7,697 accepted. Either SAT or ACT required. SAT 25/75 percentile: 1000-1180. High school rank: 16% in top tenth, 50% in top quarter, 80% in top half
Early decision deadline: N/A, notification date: N/A
Early action deadline: N/A, notification date: N/A
Application deadline (fall): 7/1
Undergraduate student body: 6,284 full time, 2,199 part time; 39% male, 61% female; 0% American Indian, 3% Asian, 4% black, 52% Hispanic, 2% multiracial, 0% Pacific Islander, 36% white, 2% international; 95% from in state; 20% live on campus; 0% of students in fraternities, 1% in sororities
Most popular majors: 21% Health Professions and Related Programs, 17% Business, Management, Marketing, and Related Support Services, 9% Biological and Biomedical Sciences, 9% Multi/ Interdisciplinary Studies, 6% Psychology
Expenses: 2021-2022: $21,066 in state, $46,735 out of state; room/board: $11,927

Financial aid: (361) 825-2332; 65% of undergrads determined to have financial need; average aid package $13,325

Texas A&M University–Kingsville
Kingsville TX
(361) 593-2315
U.S. News ranking: Nat. U., second tier
Website: www.tamuk.edu
Admissions email: admissions@tamuk.edu
Public; founded 1925
Freshman admissions: selective; 2020-2021: 6,308 applied, 5,546 accepted. Neither SAT nor ACT required. SAT 25/75 percentile: 920-1090. High school rank: 16% in top tenth, 43% in top quarter, 73% in top half
Early decision deadline: N/A, notification date: N/A
Early action deadline: N/A, notification date: N/A
Application deadline (fall): 8/1
Undergraduate student body: 4,379 full time, 1,295 part time; 49% male, 51% female; 0% American Indian, 1% Asian, 5% black, 74% Hispanic, 1% multiracial, 0% Pacific Islander, 15% white, 3% international; 97% from in state; 19% live on campus; N/A of students in fraternities, N/A in sororities
Most popular majors: 27% Engineering, 9% Agriculture, Agriculture Operations, and Related Sciences, 8% Biological and Biomedical Sciences, 8% Business, Management, Marketing, and Related Support Services, 8% Parks, Recreation, Leisure, and Fitness Studies
Expenses: 2020-2021: $9,688 in state, $23,106 out of state; room/board: $8,848
Financial aid: (361) 593-3911

Texas A&M University–San Antonio[1]
San Antonio TX
(210) 784-1000
U.S. News ranking: Reg. U. (W), unranked
Admissions email: N/A
Public
Application deadline (fall): N/A
Undergraduate student body: N/A full time, N/A part time
Expenses: N/A
Financial aid: N/A

Texas A&M University–Texarkana[1]
Texarkana TX
(903) 223-3069
U.S. News ranking: Reg. U. (W), No. 71
Website: www.tamut.edu
Admissions email: admissions@tamut.edu
Public; founded 1971
Application deadline (fall): rolling
Undergraduate student body: N/A full time, N/A part time

Expenses: 2020-2021: $7,458 in state, $8,358 out of state; room/board: $8,621
Financial aid: (903) 334-6601

Texas Christian University
Fort Worth TX
(800) 828-3764
U.S. News ranking: Nat. U., No. 83
Website: www.tcu.edu
Admissions email: frogmail@tcu.edu
Private; founded 1873
Affiliation: Christian Church (Disciples of Christ)
Freshman admissions: more selective; 2020-2021: 21,145 applied, 10,155 accepted. Neither SAT nor ACT required. ACT 25/75 percentile: 25-31. High school rank: 39% in top tenth, 71% in top quarter, 93% in top half
Early decision deadline: 11/1, notification date: 12/1
Early action deadline: 11/1, notification date: 12/15
Application deadline (fall): 2/1
Undergraduate student body: 9,448 full time, 256 part time; 41% male, 59% female; 0% American Indian, 3% Asian, 5% black, 16% Hispanic, 3% multiracial, 0% Pacific Islander, 67% white, 4% international; 51% from in state; 48% live on campus; 42% of students in fraternities, 53% in sororities
Most popular majors: 24% Business, Management, Marketing, and Related Support Services, 14% Communication, Journalism, and Related Programs, 12% Health Professions and Related Programs, 10% Social Sciences, 5% Visual and Performing Arts
Expenses: 2021-2022: $51,660; room/board: $14,040
Financial aid: (817) 257-7858; 40% of undergrads determined to have financial need; average aid package $35,694

Texas College[1]
Tyler TX
(903) 593-8311
U.S. News ranking: Reg. Coll. (W), second tier
Website: www.texascollege.edu
Admissions email: cmarshall-biggins@texascollege.edu
Private
Application deadline (fall): N/A
Undergraduate student body: N/A full time, N/A part time
Expenses: 2020-2021: $10,000; room/board: $8,400
Financial aid: N/A

Texas Lutheran University
Seguin TX
(800) 771-8521
U.S. News ranking: Reg. Coll. (W), No. 5
Website: www.tlu.edu
Admissions email: admissions@tlu.edu
Private; founded 1891
Affiliation: Evangelical Lutheran Church

Freshman admissions: selective; 2020-2021: 2,683 applied, 1,591 accepted. Neither SAT nor ACT required. SAT 25/75 percentile: 1020-1170. High school rank: 16% in top tenth, 46% in top quarter, 78% in top half
Early decision deadline: N/A, notification date: N/A
Early action deadline: N/A, notification date: N/A
Application deadline (fall): 2/1
Undergraduate student body: 1,410 full time, 45 part time; 45% male, 55% female; 0% American Indian, 1% Asian, 8% black, 40% Hispanic, 3% multiracial, 0% Pacific Islander, 46% white, 0% international; 99% from in state; 35% live on campus; N/A of students in fraternities, N/A in sororities
Most popular majors: 26% Business, Management, Marketing, and Related Support Services, 13% Education, 13% Parks, Recreation, Leisure, and Fitness Studies, 9% Health Professions and Related Programs, 7% Biological and Biomedical Sciences
Expenses: 2021-2022: $32,970; room/board: $11,000
Financial aid: (830) 372-8010; 82% of undergrads determined to have financial need; average aid package $26,307

Texas Southern University
Houston TX
(713) 313-7071
U.S. News ranking: Nat. U., second tier
Website: www.tsu.edu
Admissions email: admissions@tsu.edu
Public; founded 1927
Freshman admissions: less selective; 2020-2021: 6,687 applied, 4,438 accepted. Either SAT or ACT required. SAT 25/75 percentile: 890-1030. High school rank: 9% in top tenth, 27% in top quarter, 60% in top half
Early decision deadline: 12/1, notification date: N/A
Early action deadline: N/A, notification date: N/A
Application deadline (fall): 8/1
Undergraduate student body: 4,204 full time, 1,094 part time; 36% male, 64% female; 0% American Indian, 2% Asian, 83% black, 8% Hispanic, 3% multiracial, 0% Pacific Islander, 1% white, 3% international; 85% from in state; 21% live on campus; N/A of students in fraternities, N/A in sororities
Most popular majors: Information not available
Expenses: 2020-2021: $9,173 in state, $21,443 out of state; room/board: $9,280
Financial aid: (713) 313-7071

Texas State University
San Marcos TX
(512) 245-2364
U.S. News ranking: Nat. U., second tier
Website: www.txstate.edu

Admissions email: admissions@txstate.edu
Public; founded 1899
Freshman admissions: selective; 2020-2021: 25,461 applied, 21,524 accepted. Either SAT or ACT required. SAT 25/75 percentile: 1010-1180. High school rank: 11% in top tenth, 41% in top quarter, 84% in top half
Early decision deadline: N/A, notification date: N/A
Early action deadline: N/A, notification date: N/A
Application deadline (fall): 5/1
Undergraduate student body: 26,536 full time, 6,657 part time; 41% male, 59% female; 0% American Indian, 3% Asian, 10% black, 41% Hispanic, 4% multiracial, 0% Pacific Islander, 42% white, 0% international; 98% from in state; 17% live on campus; 5% of students in fraternities, 5% in sororities
Most popular majors: 7% Multi-/Interdisciplinary Studies, Other, 6% Business Administration and Management, General, 6% Psychology, General, 5% Kinesiology and Exercise Science, 5% Marketing/Marketing Management, General
Expenses: 2021-2022: $11,851 in state, $24,091 out of state; room/board: $10,977
Financial aid: (512) 245-2315; 61% of undergrads determined to have financial need; average aid package $10,263

Texas Tech University
Lubbock TX
(806) 742-1480
U.S. News ranking: Nat. U., No. 213
Website: www.ttu.edu
Admissions email: admissions@ttu.edu
Public; founded 1923
Freshman admissions: selective; 2020-2021: 29,131 applied, 20,400 accepted. Neither SAT nor ACT required. SAT 25/75 percentile: 1070-1240. High school rank: 18% in top tenth, 51% in top quarter, 88% in top half
Early decision deadline: N/A, notification date: N/A
Early action deadline: N/A, notification date: N/A
Application deadline (fall): 8/1
Undergraduate student body: 29,010 full time, 4,259 part time; 51% male, 49% female; 0% American Indian, 3% Asian, 6% black, 29% Hispanic, 4% multiracial, 0% Pacific Islander, 54% white, 2% international; 92% from in state; 23% live on campus; 13% of students in fraternities, 19% in sororities
Most popular majors: 16% Business, Management, Marketing, and Related Support Services, 14% Engineering, 8% Family and Consumer Sciences/Human Sciences, 7% Communication, Journalism, and Related Programs, 7% Multi/Interdisciplinary Studies
Expenses: 2021-2022: $11,852 in state, $24,092 out of state;

room/board: $10,346
Financial aid: (806) 834-1780; 47% of undergrads determined to have financial need; average aid package $10,722

Texas Wesleyan University
Fort Worth TX
(817) 531-4422
U.S. News ranking: Nat. U., second tier
Website: www.txwes.edu
Admissions email: admission@txwes.edu
Private; founded 1890
Affiliation: United Methodist
Freshman admissions: selective; 2020-2021: N/A applied, N/A accepted. Either SAT or ACT required. SAT 25/75 percentile: 1008-1160. High school rank: N/A
Early decision deadline: N/A, notification date: N/A
Early action deadline: N/A, notification date: N/A
Application deadline (fall): rolling
Undergraduate student body: 1,268 full time, 212 part time; 45% male, 55% female; 0% American Indian, 1% Asian, 19% black, 35% Hispanic, 5% multiracial, 0% Pacific Islander, 26% white, 11% international
Most popular majors: 21% Nurse Anesthetist, 13% Business Administration and Management, General, 6% Multi-/Interdisciplinary Studies, Other, 5% Psychology, General, 4% Bilingual and Multilingual Education
Expenses: 2020-2021: $33,408; room/board: $9,730
Financial aid: (817) 531-4420

Texas Woman's University
Denton TX
(940) 898-3188
U.S. News ranking: Nat. U., second tier
Website: www.twu.edu
Admissions email: admissions@twu.edu
Public; founded 1901
Freshman admissions: selective; 2020-2021: 5,824 applied, 5,456 accepted. Neither SAT nor ACT required. SAT 25/75 percentile: 940-1140. High school rank: 18% in top tenth, 44% in top quarter, 78% in top half
Early decision deadline: N/A, notification date: N/A
Early action deadline: N/A, notification date: N/A
Application deadline (fall): 8/20
Undergraduate student body: 6,863 full time, 3,793 part time; 13% male, 87% female; 0% American Indian, 9% Asian, 19% black, 33% Hispanic, 4% multiracial, 0% Pacific Islander, 32% white, 3% international; 82% from in state; 17% live on campus; 1% of students in fraternities, 2% in sororities
Most popular majors: 30% Health Professions and Related Programs, 11% Business, Management, Marketing, and Related Support Services, 11% Liberal Arts

and Sciences, General Studies and Humanities, 9% Multi/Interdisciplinary Studies, 6% Parks, Recreation, Leisure, and Fitness Studies
Expenses: 2021-2022: $10,234 in state, $22,474 out of state; room/board: $10,500
Financial aid: (940) 898-3064; 66% of undergrads determined to have financial need; average aid package $12,979

Trinity University
San Antonio TX
(800) 874-6489
U.S. News ranking: Reg. U. (W), No. 1
Website: www.trinity.edu
Admissions email: admissions@trinity.edu
Private; founded 1869
Affiliation: Presbyterian
Freshman admissions: more selective; 2020-2021: 9,394 applied, 3,158 accepted. Neither SAT nor ACT required. SAT 25/75 percentile: 1260-1430. High school rank: 51% in top tenth, 84% in top quarter, 98% in top half
Early decision deadline: 11/1, notification date: 12/15
Early action deadline: 11/1, notification date: 12/15
Application deadline (fall): 1/15
Undergraduate student body: 2,457 full time, 47 part time; 48% male, 52% female; 0% American Indian, 8% Asian, 4% black, 21% Hispanic, 5% multiracial, 0% Pacific Islander, 56% white, 4% international; N/A from in state; 33% live on campus; 7% of students in fraternities, 13% in sororities
Most popular majors: 22% Business, Management, Marketing, and Related Support Services, 14% Social Sciences, 9% Biological and Biomedical Sciences, 6% English Language and Literature/Letters, 6% Foreign Languages, Literatures, and Linguistics
Expenses: 2021-2022: $47,392; room/board: $13,892
Financial aid: (210) 999-8005; 46% of undergrads determined to have financial need; average aid package $42,991

Tyler Junior College[1]
Tyler TX
(903) 510-2200
U.S. News ranking: Reg. Coll. (W), unranked
Admissions email: N/A
Public
Application deadline (fall): rolling
Undergraduate student body: N/A full time, N/A part time
Expenses: 2020-2021: $4,762 in state, $5,482 out of state; room/board: $8,640
Financial aid: N/A

University of Dallas
Irving TX
(800) 628-6999
U.S. News ranking: Reg. U. (W), No. 6
Website: www.udallas.edu
Admissions email: ugadmis@udallas.edu
Private; founded 1956
Affiliation: Roman Catholic
Freshman admissions: more selective; 2020-2021: 4,645 applied, 2,498 accepted. Neither SAT nor ACT required. SAT 25/75 percentile: 1130-1350. High school rank: 38% in top tenth, 76% in top quarter, 94% in top half
Early decision deadline: N/A, notification date: N/A
Early action deadline: 12/1, notification date: 1/15
Application deadline (fall): 8/1
Undergraduate student body: 1,424 full time, 23 part time; 45% male, 55% female; 0% American Indian, 6% Asian, 2% black, 25% Hispanic, 3% multiracial, 0% Pacific Islander, 59% white, 3% international; 67% from in state; 61% live on campus; 0% of students in fraternities, 0% in sororities
Most popular majors: 20% Business, Management, Marketing, and Related Support Services, 13% Social Sciences, 12% Biological and Biomedical Sciences, 11% English Language and Literature/Letters, 11% Theology and Religious Vocations
Expenses: 2021-2022: $46,602; room/board: $13,472
Financial aid: (972) 721-5266; 65% of undergrads determined to have financial need; average aid package $37,742

University of Houston
Houston TX
(713) 743-1010
U.S. News ranking: Nat. U., No. 179
Website: www.uh.edu
Admissions email: admissions@uh.edu
Public; founded 1927
Freshman admissions: more selective; 2020-2021: 28,645 applied, 17,986 accepted. Neither SAT nor ACT required. SAT 25/75 percentile: 1120-1310. High school rank: 33% in top tenth, 67% in top quarter, 90% in top half
Early decision deadline: N/A, notification date: N/A
Early action deadline: N/A, notification date: N/A
Application deadline (fall): 5/31
Undergraduate student body: 28,966 full time, 10,199 part time; 49% male, 51% female; 0% American Indian, 23% Asian, 10% black, 37% Hispanic, 3% multiracial, 0% Pacific Islander, 21% white, 4% international; 98% from in state; 8% live on campus; 2% of students in fraternities, 4% in sororities
Most popular majors: 27% Business, Management, Marketing, and Related Support Services, 8% Engineering, 7% Psychology, 6% Biological

and Biomedical Sciences, 6% Computer and Information Sciences and Support Services
Expenses: 2021-2022: $11,870 in state, $27,110 out of state; room/board: $9,962
Financial aid: (713) 743-1010; 63% of undergrads determined to have financial need; average aid package $12,741

University of Houston–Clear Lake
Houston TX
(281) 283-2500
U.S. News ranking: Reg. U. (W), unranked
Website: www.uhcl.edu
Admissions email: admissions@uhcl.edu
Public; founded 1974
Freshman admissions: selective; 2020-2021: 1,604 applied, 1,341 accepted. Either SAT or ACT required. SAT 25/75 percentile: 1000-1180. High school rank: 14% in top tenth, 38% in top quarter, 73% in top half
Early decision deadline: N/A, notification date: N/A
Early action deadline: N/A, notification date: N/A
Application deadline (fall): 6/1
Undergraduate student body: 3,436 full time, 3,130 part time; 37% male, 63% female; 4% American Indian, 8% Asian, 7% black, 45% Hispanic, 3% multiracial, 0% Pacific Islander, 35% white, 1% international
Most popular majors: 16% Natural Resources and Conservation, Other, 8% Accounting, 8% Psychology, General, 5% Biology/Biological Sciences, General, 5% Business Administration and Management, General
Expenses: 2021-2022: $9,054 in state, $25,704 out of state; room/board: $6,454
Financial aid: (281) 283-2482; 69% of undergrads determined to have financial need; average aid package $12,110

University of Houston–Downtown
Houston TX
(713) 221-8522
U.S. News ranking: Reg. U. (W), No. 88
Website: www.uhd.edu
Admissions email: uhdadmit@uhd.edu
Public; founded 1974
Freshman admissions: less selective; 2020-2021: 5,973 applied, 5,554 accepted. Neither SAT nor ACT required. SAT 25/75 percentile: 900-1080. High school rank: 4% in top tenth, 26% in top quarter, 63% in top half
Early decision deadline: N/A, notification date: N/A
Early action deadline: N/A, notification date: N/A
Application deadline (fall): 6/1
Undergraduate student body: 6,865 full time, 6,798 part time; 37% male, 63% female; 0% American Indian, 9% Asian, 18% black, 55% Hispanic, 2% multiracial, 0% Pacific Islander, 13% white,

2% international; N/A from in state; 0% live on campus; 1% of students in fraternities, 1% in sororities
Most popular majors: 30% Business, Management, Marketing, and Related Support Services, 29% Multi/Interdisciplinary Studies, 8% Homeland Security, Law Enforcement, Firefighting and Related Protective Services, 7% Psychology, 4% Computer and Information Sciences and Support Services
Expenses: 2021-2022: $8,889 in state, $21,129 out of state; room/board: N/A
Financial aid: (713) 221-8041; 76% of undergrads determined to have financial need; average aid package $7,924

University of Houston–Victoria[1]
Victoria TX
(877) 970-4848
U.S. News ranking: Reg. U. (W), second tier
Website: www.uhv.edu/
Admissions email: admissions@uhv.edu
Public; founded 1973
Application deadline (fall): 8/1
Undergraduate student body: N/A full time, N/A part time
Expenses: 2020-2021: $7,313 in state, $17,129 out of state; room/board: $9,860
Financial aid: N/A

University of Mary Hardin-Baylor
Belton TX
(254) 295-4520
U.S. News ranking: Reg. U. (W), No. 41
Website: www.umhb.edu
Admissions email: admission@umhb.edu
Private; founded 1845
Affiliation: Baptist
Freshman admissions: selective; 2020-2021: 11,243 applied, 10,152 accepted. Either SAT or ACT required. SAT 25/75 percentile: 1010-1190. High school rank: 16% in top tenth, 45% in top quarter, 82% in top half
Early decision deadline: N/A, notification date: N/A
Early action deadline: N/A, notification date: N/A
Application deadline (fall): rolling
Undergraduate student body: 3,085 full time, 294 part time; 33% male, 67% female; 0% American Indian, 2% Asian, 13% black, 24% Hispanic, 3% multiracial, 0% Pacific Islander, 54% white, 1% international; 97% from in state; 52% live on campus; N/A of students in fraternities, N/A in sororities
Most popular majors: 29% Health Professions and Related Programs, 17% Business, Management, Marketing, and Related Support Services, 10% Education, 8% Psychology, 7% Parks, Recreation, Leisure, and Fitness Studies
Expenses: 2021-2022: $31,600; room/board: $9,500

Financial aid: (254) 295-4517; 83% of undergrads determined to have financial need; average aid package $18,041

University of North Texas
Denton TX
(940) 565-2681
U.S. News ranking: Nat. U., No. 277
Website: www.unt.edu
Admissions email: unt.freshmen@unt.edu
Public; founded 1890
Freshman admissions: selective; 2020-2021: 21,325 applied, 17,985 accepted. Neither SAT nor ACT required. SAT 25/75 percentile: 1050-1240. High school rank: 20% in top tenth, 53% in top quarter, 89% in top half
Early decision deadline: N/A, notification date: N/A
Early action deadline: N/A, notification date: N/A
Application deadline (fall): 8/1
Undergraduate student body: 26,302 full time, 6,392 part time; 47% male, 53% female; 0% American Indian, 7% Asian, 14% black, 28% Hispanic, 4% multiracial, 0% Pacific Islander, 41% white, 4% international; N/A from in state; 15% live on campus; 1% of students in fraternities, 4% in sororities
Most popular majors: 19% Business, Management, Marketing, and Related Support Services, 12% Multi/Interdisciplinary Studies, 8% Liberal Arts and Sciences, General Studies and Humanities, 8% Visual and Performing Arts, 7% Communication, Journalism, and Related Programs
Expenses: 2021-2022: $11,994 in state, $24,234 out of state; room/board: $10,158
Financial aid: (940) 565-3901; 61% of undergrads determined to have financial need; average aid package $13,285

University of North Texas at Dallas[1]
Dallas TX
(972) 780-3642
U.S. News ranking: Reg. U. (W), No. 82
Website: www.untdallas.edu
Admissions email: admissions@untdallas.edu
Public; founded 2010
Application deadline (fall): 8/10
Undergraduate student body: N/A full time, N/A part time
Expenses: N/A
Financial aid: N/A

University of St. Thomas
Houston TX
(713) 525-3500
U.S. News ranking: Reg. U. (W), No. 20
Website: www.stthom.edu
Admissions email: admissions@stthom.edu
Private; founded 1947

Affiliation: Roman Catholic
Freshman admissions: selective; 2020-2021: 1,074 applied, 1,032 accepted. Neither SAT nor ACT required. SAT 25/75 percentile: 1005-1170. High school rank: 22% in top tenth, 50% in top quarter, 83% in top half
Early decision deadline: N/A, notification date: N/A
Early action deadline: N/A, notification date: N/A
Application deadline (fall): 8/15
Undergraduate student body: 1,969 full time, 494 part time; 38% male, 62% female; 0% American Indian, 12% Asian, 9% black, 50% Hispanic, 2% multiracial, 0% Pacific Islander, 19% white, 6% international; 3% from in state; 18% live on campus; N/A of students in fraternities, N/A in sororities
Most popular majors: 20% Business, Management, Marketing, and Related Support Services, 17% Liberal Arts and Sciences, General Studies and Humanities, 13% Health Professions and Related Programs, 12% Social Sciences, 10% Biological and Biomedical Sciences
Expenses: 2021-2022: $31,560; room/board: $9,470
Financial aid: (713) 525-2170; 70% of undergrads determined to have financial need; average aid package $23,507

University of Texas at Arlington

Arlington TX
(817) 272-6287
U.S. News ranking: Nat. U., No. 288
Website: www.uta.edu
Admissions email: admissions@uta.edu
Public; founded 1895
Freshman admissions: selective; 2020-2021: 14,620 applied, 12,829 accepted. Neither SAT nor ACT required. SAT 25/75 percentile: 1050-1250. High school rank: 28% in top tenth, 63% in top quarter, 87% in top half
Early decision deadline: N/A, notification date: N/A
Early action deadline: N/A, notification date: N/A
Application deadline (fall): 8/20
Undergraduate student body: 19,770 full time, 15,294 part time; 38% male, 62% female; 0% American Indian, 13% Asian, 15% black, 31% Hispanic, 4% multiracial, 0% Pacific Islander, 31% white, 4% international; 87% from in state; 7% live on campus; 0% of students in fraternities, 1% in sororities
Most popular majors: 42% Health Professions and Related Programs, 14% Business, Management, Marketing, and Related Support Services, 7% Engineering, 4% Biological and Biomedical Sciences, 4% Computer and Information Sciences and Support Services

Expenses: 2021-2022: $11,727 in state, $29,299 out of state; room/board: $10,516
Financial aid: (817) 272-3568; 69% of undergrads determined to have financial need; average aid package $11,754

University of Texas at Austin

Austin TX
(512) 475-7399
U.S. News ranking: Nat. U., No. 38
Website: www.utexas.edu
Admissions email: admissions@austin.utexas.edu
Public; founded 1883
Freshman admissions: most selective; 2020-2021: 57,241 applied, 18,291 accepted. Neither SAT nor ACT required. SAT 25/75 percentile: 1210-1470. High school rank: 87% in top tenth, 96% in top quarter, 99% in top half
Early decision deadline: N/A, notification date: N/A
Early action deadline: N/A, notification date: N/A
Application deadline (fall): 12/1
Undergraduate student body: 37,404 full time, 2,644 part time; 44% male, 56% female; 0% American Indian, 23% Asian, 4% black, 26% Hispanic, 4% multiracial, 0% Pacific Islander, 37% white, 4% international; 92% from in state; 8% live on campus; 12% of students in fraternities, 16% in sororities
Most popular majors: 13% Engineering, 12% Business, Management, Marketing, and Related Support Services, 12% Communication, Journalism, and Related Programs, 10% Biological and Biomedical Sciences, 10% Social Sciences
Expenses: 2021-2022: $11,448 in state, $40,032 out of state; room/board: $12,286
Financial aid: (512) 475-6282; 40% of undergrads determined to have financial need; average aid package $12,193

University of Texas at Dallas

Richardson TX
(972) 883-2270
U.S. News ranking: Nat. U., No. 136
Website: www.utdallas.edu
Admissions email: interest@utdallas.edu
Public; founded 1969
Freshman admissions: more selective; 2020-2021: 15,411 applied, 12,230 accepted. Neither SAT nor ACT required. SAT 25/75 percentile: 1220-1450. High school rank: 42% in top tenth, 70% in top quarter, 94% in top half
Early decision deadline: N/A, notification date: N/A
Early action deadline: N/A, notification date: N/A
Application deadline (fall): 5/1
Undergraduate student body: 17,979 full time, 3,208 part time; 56% male, 44% female; 0% American Indian, 38% Asian, 5% black, 18% Hispanic, 4%

multiracial, 0% Pacific Islander, 28% white, 4% international; 91% from in state; 12% live on campus; 2% of students in fraternities, 5% in sororities
Most popular majors: 10% Computer and Information Sciences, General, 6% Accounting, 6% Biology/ Biological Sciences, General, 5% Information Technology, 5% Psychology, General
Expenses: 2021-2022: $14,564 in state, $39,776 out of state; room/board: $12,142
Financial aid: (972) 883-4020; 50% of undergrads determined to have financial need; average aid package $14,499

University of Texas at San Antonio

San Antonio TX
(210) 458-8000
U.S. News ranking: Nat. U., second tier
Website: www.utsa.edu
Admissions email: prospects@utsa.edu
Public; founded 1969
Freshman admissions: selective; 2020-2021: 21,597 applied, 18,043 accepted. Either SAT or ACT required. SAT 25/75 percentile: 1020-1210. High school rank: 18% in top tenth, 58% in top quarter, 88% in top half
Early decision deadline: N/A, notification date: N/A
Early action deadline: N/A, notification date: N/A
Application deadline (fall): 6/1
Undergraduate student body: 23,018 full time, 6,941 part time; 49% male, 51% female; 0% American Indian, 6% Asian, 8% black, 59% Hispanic, 4% multiracial, 0% Pacific Islander, 21% white, 1% international; N/A from in state; 4% live on campus; 3% of students in fraternities, 4% in sororities
Most popular majors: 19% Business, Management, Marketing, and Related Support Services, 8% Engineering, 8% Health Professions and Related Programs, 8% Psychology, 7% Computer and Information Sciences and Support Services
Expenses: 2021-2022: $10,535 in state, $25,920 out of state; room/board: $10,600
Financial aid: (210) 458-8000

University of Texas at Tyler

Tyler TX
(903) 566-7203
U.S. News ranking: Nat. U., second tier
Website: www.uttyler.edu
Admissions email: admissions@uttyler.edu
Public; founded 1971
Freshman admissions: selective; 2020-2021: 3,344 applied, 3,064 accepted. Either SAT or ACT required. SAT 25/75 percentile: 1030-1220. High school rank: 14% in top tenth, 41% in top quarter, 75% in top half

Early decision deadline: N/A, notification date: N/A
Early action deadline: N/A, notification date: N/A
Application deadline (fall): 8/24
Undergraduate student body: 4,834 full time, 2,403 part time; 40% male, 60% female; 0% American Indian, 4% Asian, 10% black, 24% Hispanic, 4% multiracial, 0% Pacific Islander, 54% white, 3% international; 97% from in state; 23% live on campus; 5% of students in fraternities, 8% in sororities
Most popular majors: 30% Health Professions and Related Programs, 17% Business, Management, Marketing, and Related Support Services, 12% Engineering, 11% Multi/Interdisciplinary Studies, 5% Parks, Recreation, Leisure, and Fitness Studies
Expenses: 2021-2022: $9,596 in state, $25,016 out of state; room/board: $9,907
Financial aid: (903) 566-7180; 78% of undergrads determined to have financial need; average aid package $9,394

University of Texas–El Paso

El Paso TX
(915) 747-5890
U.S. News ranking: Nat. U., second tier
Website: www.utep.edu
Admissions email: futureminer@utep.edu
Public; founded 1914
Freshman admissions: less selective; 2020-2021: 13,121 applied, 13,117 accepted. Neither SAT nor ACT required. SAT 25/75 percentile: 900-1100. High school rank: 18% in top tenth, 39% in top quarter, 67% in top half
Early decision deadline: N/A, notification date: N/A
Early action deadline: N/A, notification date: N/A
Application deadline (fall): 9/5
Undergraduate student body: 14,632 full time, 6,485 part time; 44% male, 56% female; 0% American Indian, 1% Asian, 2% black, 86% Hispanic, 1% multiracial, 0% Pacific Islander, 5% white, 4% international; 91% from in state; N/A live on campus; N/A of students in fraternities, N/A in sororities
Most popular majors: 15% Business, Management, Marketing, and Related Support Services, 14% Engineering, 12% Health Professions and Related Programs, 12% Multi/Interdisciplinary Studies, 9% Biological and Biomedical Sciences
Expenses: 2021-2022: $9,544 in state, $24,952 out of state; room/board: N/A
Financial aid: (915) 747-5204; 79% of undergrads determined to have financial need; average aid package $11,789

University of Texas of the Permian Basin

Odessa TX
(432) 552-2605
U.S. News ranking: Reg. U. (W), No. 64
Website: www.utpb.edu
Admissions email: admissions@utpb.edu
Public; founded 1973
Freshman admissions: selective; 2020-2021: 1,389 applied, 1,221 accepted. Either SAT or ACT required. SAT 25/75 percentile: 940-1130. High school rank: 20% in top tenth, 40% in top quarter, 82% in top half
Early decision deadline: N/A, notification date: N/A
Early action deadline: N/A, notification date: N/A
Application deadline (fall): 8/26
Undergraduate student body: 2,030 full time, 2,724 part time; 40% male, 60% female; 0% American Indian, 2% Asian, 7% black, 52% Hispanic, 3% multiracial, 0% Pacific Islander, 33% white, 3% international
Most popular majors: Information not available
Expenses: 2021-2022: $30,169 in state, $30,169 out of state; room/board: $10,002
Financial aid: (432) 552-2620; 61% of undergrads determined to have financial need; average aid package $11,235

University of Texas–Rio Grande Valley

Edinburg TX
(888) 882-4026
U.S. News ranking: Nat. U., second tier
Website: www.utrgv.edu/en-us/index.htm
Admissions email: admissions@utrgv.edu
Public; founded 2013
Freshman admissions: selective; 2020-2021: 12,097 applied, 9,727 accepted. Either SAT or ACT required. ACT 25/75 percentile: 17-22. High school rank: 22% in top tenth, 53% in top quarter, 82% in top half
Early decision deadline: N/A, notification date: N/A
Early action deadline: N/A, notification date: N/A
Application deadline (fall): 7/1
Undergraduate student body: 21,292 full time, 5,470 part time; 41% male, 59% female; 0% American Indian, 1% Asian, 0% black, 93% Hispanic, 0% multiracial, 0% Pacific Islander, 2% white, 2% international; N/A from in state; 2% live on campus; N/A of students in fraternities, N/A in sororities
Most popular majors: 12% Biological and Biomedical Sciences, 12% Business, Management, Marketing, and Related Support Services, 10% Homeland Security, Law Enforcement, Firefighting and Related Protective Services, 10% Psychology, 9% Multi/Interdisciplinary Studies

Expenses: 2020-2021: $8,917 in state, $18,733 out of state; room/board: $8,126
Financial aid: N/A

University of the Incarnate Word

San Antonio TX
(210) 829-6005
U.S. News ranking: Nat. U., No. 263
Website: www.uiw.edu
Admissions email: admis@uiwtx.edu
Private; founded 1881
Affiliation: Roman Catholic
Freshman admissions: selective; 2020-2021: 6,879 applied, 6,645 accepted. Neither SAT nor ACT required. SAT 25/75 percentile: 950-1140. High school rank: 18% in top tenth, 42% in top quarter, 73% in top half
Early decision deadline: N/A, notification date: N/A
Early action deadline: N/A, notification date: N/A
Application deadline (fall): rolling
Undergraduate student body: 3,916 full time, 1,165 part time; 38% male, 62% female; 0% American Indian, 2% Asian, 8% black, 60% Hispanic, 2% multiracial, 0% Pacific Islander, 18% white, 3% international; 93% from in state; 13% live on campus; N/A of students in fraternities, N/A in sororities
Most popular majors: 10% Business Administration and Management, General, 8% Registered Nursing/Registered Nurse, 7% Biology/Biological Sciences, General, 7% Psychology, General, 5% Business Administration, Management and Operations, Other
Expenses: 2021-2022: $33,100; room/board: $13,122
Financial aid: (210) 829-6008; 78% of undergrads determined to have financial need; average aid package $20,548

Wade College[1]

Dallas TX
(214) 637-3530
U.S. News ranking: Reg. Coll. (W), unranked
Admissions email: N/A
For-profit
Application deadline (fall): N/A
Undergraduate student body: N/A full time, N/A part time
Expenses: 2020-2021: $14,955; room/board: N/A
Financial aid: N/A

Wayland Baptist University

Plainview TX
(806) 291-3500
U.S. News ranking: Reg. U. (W), second tier
Website: www.wbu.edu
Admissions email: admitme@wbu.edu
Private; founded 1908
Affiliation: Baptist
Freshman admissions: selective; 2020-2021: 899 applied, 753 accepted. Neither SAT nor ACT

required. SAT 25/75 percentile: 900-1090. High school rank: 10% in top tenth, 23% in top quarter, 53% in top half
Early decision deadline: N/A, notification date: N/A
Early action deadline: N/A, notification date: N/A
Application deadline (fall): rolling
Undergraduate student body: 1,590 full time, 1,425 part time; 48% male, 52% female; 1% American Indian, 3% Asian, 17% black, 34% Hispanic, 5% multiracial, 4% Pacific Islander, 33% white, 2% international; 83% from in state; 56% live on campus; 0% of students in fraternities, 0% in sororities
Most popular majors: 41% Business Administration and Management, General, 26% Liberal Arts and Sciences, General Studies and Humanities, Other, 9% Public Administration and Social Service Professions, 8% Criminal Justice/Law Enforcement Administration, 5% Registered Nursing/Registered Nurse
Expenses: 2021-2022: $22,004; room/board: $8,416
Financial aid: (806) 291-3520; 67% of undergrads determined to have financial need; average aid package $13,703

West Texas A&M University

Canyon TX
(806) 651-2020
U.S. News ranking: Reg. U. (W), No. 71
Website: www.wtamu.edu
Admissions email: admissions@wtamu.edu
Public; founded 1910
Freshman admissions: selective; 2020-2021: 5,426 applied, 4,451 accepted. Either SAT or ACT required. ACT 25/75 percentile: 18-23. High school rank: 18% in top tenth, 44% in top quarter, 75% in top half
Early decision deadline: N/A, notification date: N/A
Early action deadline: N/A, notification date: N/A
Application deadline (fall): 8/1
Undergraduate student body: 5,621 full time, 1,719 part time; 42% male, 58% female; 0% American Indian, 2% Asian, 5% black, 32% Hispanic, 3% multiracial, 0% Pacific Islander, 55% white, 1% international; 87% from in state; 18% live on campus; 5% of students in fraternities, 17% in sororities
Most popular majors: 19% Business, Management, Marketing, and Related Support Services, 14% Health Professions and Related Programs, 12% Liberal Arts and Sciences, General Studies and Humanities, 10% Multi/Interdisciplinary Studies, 6% Communications Technologies/Technicians and Support Services
Expenses: 2021-2022: $9,204 in state, $10,834 out of state; room/board: $8,576
Financial aid: (806) 651-2055; 63% of undergrads determined to have financial need; average aid package $9,728

Wiley College

Marshall TX
(903) 927-3311
U.S. News ranking: Reg. Coll. (W), No. 36
Website: www.wileyc.edu
Admissions email: admissions@wileyc.edu
Private; founded 1873
Affiliation: United Methodist
Freshman admissions: least selective; 2020-2021: 2,820 applied, 436 accepted. Neither SAT nor ACT required. ACT 25/75 percentile: 13-15. High school rank: N/A
Early decision deadline: N/A, notification date: N/A
Early action deadline: N/A, notification date: N/A
Application deadline (fall): 8/18
Undergraduate student body: 555 full time, 60 part time; 43% male, 57% female; 0% American Indian, 0% Asian, 90% black, 2% Hispanic, 0% multiracial, 0% Pacific Islander, 4% white, 3% international; 45% from in state; 56% live on campus; 1% of students in fraternities, 1% in sororities
Most popular majors: 31% Non-Profit/Public/Organizational Management, 18% Criminal Justice/Police Science, 10% Sociology
Expenses: 2021-2022: $12,500; room/board: $5,000
Financial aid: (903) 927-3252; 89% of undergrads determined to have financial need; average aid package $5,666

UTAH

Dixie State University[1]

Saint George UT
(435) 652-7702
U.S. News ranking: Reg. Coll. (W), second tier
Website: www.dixie.edu
Admissions email: admissions@dixie.edu
Public; founded 1911
Application deadline (fall): 8/15
Undergraduate student body: N/A full time, N/A part time
Expenses: 2020-2021: $5,662 in state, $16,260 out of state; room/board: $6,968
Financial aid: (435) 652-7575

Snow College[1]

Ephraim UT
(435) 283-7159
U.S. News ranking: Reg. Coll. (W), No. 28
Website: www.snow.edu/admissions/
Admissions email: admissions@snow.edu
Public; founded 1888
Application deadline (fall): rolling
Undergraduate student body: N/A full time, N/A part time
Expenses: 2020-2021: $3,912 in state, $13,156 out of state; room/board: $3,900
Financial aid: N/A

Southern Utah University

Cedar City UT
(435) 586-7740
U.S. News ranking: Reg. U. (W), No. 67
Website: www.suu.edu
Admissions email: admissions@suu.edu
Public; founded 1897
Freshman admissions: selective; 2020-2021: 16,694 applied, 12,614 accepted. Neither SAT nor ACT required. ACT 25/75 percentile: 21-27. High school rank: 22% in top tenth, 47% in top quarter, 77% in top half
Early decision deadline: N/A, notification date: N/A
Early action deadline: N/A, notification date: N/A
Application deadline (fall): rolling
Undergraduate student body: 7,652 full time, 3,597 part time; 40% male, 60% female; 1% American Indian, 1% Asian, 2% black, 8% Hispanic, 2% multiracial, 1% Pacific Islander, 74% white, 4% international; N/A from in state; 10% live on campus; N/A of students in fraternities, N/A in sororities
Most popular majors: 13% Business, Management, Marketing, and Related Support Services, 8% Education, 8% Psychology, 7% Biological and Biomedical Sciences, 6% Parks, Recreation, Leisure, and Fitness Studies
Expenses: 2021-2022: $6,726 in state, $20,542 out of state; room/board: $7,500
Financial aid: (435) 586-7735; 63% of undergrads determined to have financial need; average aid package $9,176

University of Utah

Salt Lake City UT
(801) 581-8761
U.S. News ranking: Nat. U., No. 99
Website: www.utah.edu/
Admissions email: admissions@utah.edu
Public; founded 1850
Freshman admissions: more selective; 2020-2021: 18,419 applied, 14,624 accepted. Neither SAT nor ACT required. ACT 25/75 percentile: 22-29. High school rank: N/A
Early decision deadline: N/A, notification date: N/A
Early action deadline: 12/1, notification date: 1/15
Application deadline (fall): 4/1
Undergraduate student body: 18,749 full time, 5,894 part time; 52% male, 48% female; 0% American Indian, 6% Asian, 1% black, 14% Hispanic, 6% multiracial, 0% Pacific Islander, 66% white, 5% international; 74% from in state; 12% live on campus; 6% of students in fraternities, 8% in sororities
Most popular majors: 7% Research and Experimental Psychology, Other, 7% Speech Communication and Rhetoric, 4% Biology/Biological Sciences, General, 4% Kinesiology and Exercise Science, 4% Registered Nursing/Registered Nurse
Expenses: 2021-2022: $9,816 in state, $31,389 out of state; room/board: $10,662
Financial aid: (801) 581-6211; 43% of undergrads determined to have financial need; average aid package $21,702

Utah State University

Logan UT
(435) 797-1079
U.S. News ranking: Nat. U., No. 249
Website: www.usu.edu
Admissions email: admit@usu.edu
Public; founded 1888
Freshman admissions: more selective; 2020-2021: 15,949 applied, 14,520 accepted. Either SAT or ACT required. ACT 25/75 percentile: 21-29. High school rank: 22% in top tenth, 48% in top quarter, 77% in top half
Early decision deadline: N/A, notification date: N/A
Early action deadline: N/A, notification date: N/A
Application deadline (fall): rolling
Undergraduate student body: 17,118 full time, 7,529 part time; 45% male, 55% female; 2% American Indian, 1% Asian, 1% black, 6% Hispanic, 2% multiracial, 0% Pacific Islander, 83% white, 1% international; N/A from in state; N/A live on campus; 1% of students in fraternities, 1% in sororities
Most popular majors: 8% Communication Sciences and Disorders, General, 8% Economics, General, 4% Human Development and Family Studies, General, 4% Multi-/Interdisciplinary Studies, Other, 4% Psychology, General
Expenses: 2021-2022: $8,055 in state, $23,434 out of state; room/board: $6,040
Financial aid: (435) 797-0173; 51% of undergrads determined to have financial need; average aid package $11,677

Utah Valley University[1]

Orem UT
(801) 863-8706
U.S. News ranking: Reg. U. (W), second tier
Website: www.uvu.edu/
Admissions email: admissions@uvu.edu
Public; founded 1941
Application deadline (fall): 8/1
Undergraduate student body: N/A full time, N/A part time
Expenses: 2020-2021: $5,906 in state, $16,806 out of state; room/board: N/A
Financial aid: (801) 863-6746

Weber State University

Ogden UT
(801) 626-6743
U.S. News ranking: Reg. U. (W), No. 77
Website: weber.edu
Admissions email: admissions@weber.edu
Public; founded 1889

Nurse

Freshman admissions: selective; 2020-2021: 7,985 applied, 7,985 accepted. Neither SAT nor ACT required. ACT 25/75 percentile: 18-24. High school rank: 12% in top tenth, 32% in top quarter, 65% in top half
Early decision deadline: N/A, notification date: N/A
Early action deadline: N/A, notification date: N/A
Application deadline (fall): 8/31
Undergraduate student body: 12,042 full time, 16,643 part time; 43% male, 57% female; 1% American Indian, 2% Asian, 2% black, 12% Hispanic, 4% multiracial, 1% Pacific Islander, 74% white, 1% international; N/A from in state; 4% live on campus; 3% of students in fraternities, 4% in sororities
Most popular majors: 15% Registered Nursing/Registered Nurse, 5% Computer Science, 4% Clinical/Medical Laboratory Technician, 4% Selling Skills and Sales Operations, 4% Speech Communication and Rhetoric
Expenses: 2021-2022: $5,956 in state, $16,138 out of state; room/board: $8,400
Financial aid: (801) 626-7569; 58% of undergrads determined to have financial need; average aid package $6,959

Westminster College
Salt Lake City UT
(801) 832-2200
U.S. News ranking: Reg. U. (W), No. 18
Website: www.westminstercollege.edu
Admissions email: admission@westminstercollege.edu
Private; founded 1875
Affiliation: Undenominational
Freshman admissions: more selective; 2020-2021: 1,921 applied, 1,680 accepted. Neither SAT nor ACT required. ACT 25/75 percentile: 21-28. High school rank: 21% in top tenth, 54% in top quarter, 82% in top half
Early decision deadline: N/A, notification date: N/A
Early action deadline: N/A, notification date: N/A
Application deadline (fall): rolling
Undergraduate student body: 1,345 full time, 82 part time; 39% male, 61% female; 0% American Indian, 2% Asian, 3% black, 12% Hispanic, 5% multiracial, 0% Pacific Islander, 70% white, 4% international; 38% from in state; 28% live on campus; N/A of students in fraternities, N/A in sororities
Most popular majors: 23% Health Professions and Related Programs, 21% Business, Management, Marketing, and Related Support Services, 7% Biological and Biomedical Sciences, 6% Visual and Performing Arts, 5% Social Sciences
Expenses: 2021-2022: $38,680; room/board: $11,681
Financial aid: (801) 832-2500; 64% of undergrads determined to have financial need; average aid package $32,040

VERMONT

Bennington College
Bennington VT
(800) 833-6845
U.S. News ranking: Nat. Lib. Arts, No. 79
Website: www.bennington.edu
Admissions email: admissions@bennington.edu
Private; founded 1932
Freshman admissions: more selective; 2020-2021: 1,382 applied, 829 accepted. Neither SAT nor ACT required. SAT 25/75 percentile: 1240-1400. High school rank: 39% in top tenth, 61% in top quarter, 85% in top half
Early decision deadline: 11/15, notification date: 12/11
Early action deadline: 12/1, notification date: 1/31
Application deadline (fall): 1/15
Undergraduate student body: 606 full time, 91 part time; 34% male, 66% female; 0% American Indian, 1% Asian, 3% black, 12% Hispanic, 3% multiracial, 0% Pacific Islander, 59% white, 19% international; 4% from in state; 80% live on campus; N/A of students in fraternities, N/A in sororities
Most popular majors: 44% Visual and Performing Arts, 13% English Language and Literature/Letters, 13% Social Sciences, 6% Public Administration and Social Service Professions, 5% Foreign Languages, Literatures, and Linguistics
Expenses: 2021-2022: $59,638; room/board: $17,210
Financial aid: (802) 440-4325; 80% of undergrads determined to have financial need; average aid package $39,707

Castleton University[1]
Castleton VT
(800) 639-8521
U.S. News ranking: Reg. Coll. (N), No. 26
Website: www.castleton.edu
Admissions email: info@castleton.edu
Public; founded 1787
Application deadline (fall): rolling
Undergraduate student body: N/A full time, N/A part time
Expenses: 2020-2021: $13,044 in state, $30,012 out of state; room/board: $11,694
Financial aid: N/A

Champlain College
Burlington VT
(800) 570-5858
U.S. News ranking: Reg. U. (N), No. 62
Website: www.champlain.edu
Admissions email: admission@champlain.edu
Private; founded 1878
Freshman admissions: selective; 2020-2021: 3,273 applied, 2,787 accepted. Neither SAT nor ACT required. SAT 25/75 percentile: 1110-1300. High school rank: 11% in top tenth, 32% in top quarter, 66% in top half

Early decision deadline: 11/15, notification date: N/A
Early action deadline: N/A, notification date: N/A
Application deadline (fall): 1/15
Undergraduate student body: 1,796 full time, 95 part time; 63% male, 37% female; 0% American Indian, 4% Asian, 3% black, 7% Hispanic, 4% multiracial, 0% Pacific Islander, 76% white, 1% international; 24% from in state; 72% live on campus; N/A of students in fraternities, N/A in sororities
Most popular majors: 9% Computer and Information Systems Security/Information Assurance, 8% Game and Interactive Media Design, 7% Computer Science, 6% Business Administration and Management, General, 6% Computer Graphics
Expenses: 2021-2022: $42,984; room/board: $15,854
Financial aid: (802) 865-5435; 65% of undergrads determined to have financial need; average aid package $31,254

Goddard College[1]
Plainfield VT
(800) 906-8312
U.S. News ranking: Reg. U. (N), unranked
Website: www.goddard.edu
Admissions email: admissions@goddard.edu
Private; founded 1863
Application deadline (fall): N/A
Undergraduate student body: N/A full time, N/A part time
Expenses: 2020-2021: $18,210; room/board: N/A
Financial aid: (800) 468-4888

Landmark College
Putney VT
(802) 387-6718
U.S. News ranking: Reg. Coll. (N), unranked
Website: www.landmark.edu/admissions/virtualtour
Admissions email: admissions@landmark.edu
Private; founded 1985
Freshman admissions: least selective; 2020-2021: 363 applied, 199 accepted. Neither SAT nor ACT required. SAT 25/75 percentile: N/A. High school rank: N/A
Early decision deadline: N/A, notification date: N/A
Early action deadline: N/A, notification date: N/A
Application deadline (fall): N/A
Undergraduate student body: 322 full time, 173 part time; 68% male, 32% female; 1% American Indian, 2% Asian, 5% black, 8% Hispanic, 3% multiracial, 0% Pacific Islander, 67% white, 2% international; 96% from in state; 87% live on campus; 0% of students in fraternities, 0% in sororities
Most popular majors: 53% Liberal Arts and Sciences, General Studies and Humanities, Other, 27% Fine/Studio Arts, General, 13% Computer Science, 7% Speech Communication and Rhetoric

Expenses: 2021-2022: $61,490; room/board: $13,690
Financial aid: (802) 781-6178; 53% of undergrads determined to have financial need; average aid package $31,269

Marlboro College[1]
Marlboro VT
(800) 343-0049
U.S. News ranking: Nat. Lib. Arts, second tier
Website: www.marlboro.edu
Admissions email: admissions@marlboro.edu
Private; founded 1946
Application deadline (fall): rolling
Undergraduate student body: N/A full time, N/A part time
Expenses: N/A
Financial aid: (802) 258-9237

Middlebury College
Middlebury VT
(802) 443-3000
U.S. News ranking: Nat. Lib. Arts, No. 9
Website: www.middlebury.edu
Admissions email: admissions@middlebury.edu
Private; founded 1800
Freshman admissions: most selective; 2020-2021: 9,174 applied, 2,022 accepted. Neither SAT nor ACT required. SAT 25/75 percentile: 1340-1520. High school rank: 80% in top tenth, 98% in top quarter, 100% in top half
Early decision deadline: 11/15, notification date: 12/15
Early action deadline: N/A, notification date: N/A
Application deadline (fall): 1/4
Undergraduate student body: 2,552 full time, 28 part time; 47% male, 53% female; 0% American Indian, 8% Asian, 4% black, 11% Hispanic, 6% multiracial, 0% Pacific Islander, 60% white, 10% international
Most popular majors: 15% Econometrics and Quantitative Economics, 8% Computer Science, 6% Environmental Studies, 6% Political Science and Government, General, 4% Neuroscience
Expenses: 2021-2022: $59,770; room/board: $17,050
Financial aid: (802) 443-5228; 48% of undergrads determined to have financial need; average aid package $55,460

Northern Vermont University[1]
Johnson VT
(800) 635-2356
U.S. News ranking: Reg. U. (N), second tier
Website: www.jsc.edu
Admissions email: JSCAdmissions@jsc.edu
Public; founded 1828
Application deadline (fall): rolling
Undergraduate student body: N/A full time, N/A part time
Expenses: 2020-2021: $12,804 in state, $26,892 out of state; room/board: $11,694
Financial aid: N/A

Norwich University
Northfield VT
(800) 468-6679
U.S. News ranking: Reg. U. (N), No. 55
Website: www.norwich.edu
Admissions email: admissions@norwich.edu
Private; founded 1819
Freshman admissions: selective; 2020-2021: 4,088 applied, 3,014 accepted. Neither SAT nor ACT required. SAT 25/75 percentile: 1040-1230. High school rank: N/A
Early decision deadline: N/A, notification date: N/A
Early action deadline: N/A, notification date: N/A
Application deadline (fall): rolling
Undergraduate student body: 2,522 full time, 714 part time; 74% male, 26% female; 1% American Indian, 3% Asian, 5% black, 10% Hispanic, 4% multiracial, 0% Pacific Islander, 69% white, 3% international; 13% from in state; 59% live on campus; 0% of students in fraternities, 0% in sororities
Most popular majors: 21% Intelligence, General, 17% Criminal Justice/Law Enforcement Administration, 13% Business Administration and Management, General, 9% Computer Science, 8% Mechanical Engineering
Expenses: 2021-2022: $44,020; room/board: $15,226
Financial aid: (802) 485-3015; 74% of undergrads determined to have financial need; average aid package $35,106

Saint Michael's College
Colchester VT
(800) 762-8000
U.S. News ranking: Nat. Lib. Arts, No. 126
Website: www.smcvt.edu
Admissions email: admission@smcvt.edu
Private; founded 1904
Affiliation: Roman Catholic
Freshman admissions: more selective; 2020-2021: 3,184 applied, 2,796 accepted. Neither SAT nor ACT required. SAT 25/75 percentile: 1130-1280. High school rank: 26% in top tenth, 55% in top quarter, 79% in top half
Early decision deadline: N/A, notification date: N/A
Early action deadline: 11/1, notification date: 12/21
Application deadline (fall): 2/1
Undergraduate student body: 1,492 full time, 45 part time; 47% male, 53% female; 0% American Indian, 2% Asian, 2% black, 6% Hispanic, 2% multiracial, 0% Pacific Islander, 82% white, 3% international; 19% from in state; 90% live on campus; N/A of students in fraternities, N/A in sororities
Most popular majors: 13% Business Administration and Management, General, 10% Psychology, General, 9% Biology/Biological Sciences, General, 5% Elementary Education and

Teaching, 4% Environmental
Studies
Expenses: 2021-2022: $48,690;
room/board: $14,280
Financial aid: (802) 654-3243;
67% of undergrads determined to
have financial need; average aid
package $37,118

Sterling College[1]
Craftsbury Common VT
(802) 586-7711
U.S. News ranking: Nat. Lib. Arts,
second tier
Website: www.sterlingcollege.edu
Admissions email:
admissions@sterlingcollege.edu
Private; founded 1958
Application deadline (fall): N/A
Undergraduate student body: N/A
full time, N/A part time
Expenses: 2020-2021: $39,200;
room/board: $10,400
Financial aid: N/A

University of Vermont
Burlington VT
(802) 656-3370
U.S. News ranking: Nat. U.,
No. 117
Website: www.uvm.edu
Admissions email:
admissions@uvm.edu
Public; founded 1791
Freshman admissions: more
selective; 2020-2021: 18,564
applied, 13,240 accepted. Neither
SAT nor ACT required. SAT
25/75 percentile: 1160-1350.
High school rank: 33% in top
tenth, 74% in top quarter, 95%
in top half
Early decision deadline: N/A,
notification date: N/A
Early action deadline: 11/1,
notification date: 12/15
Application deadline (fall): 1/15
Undergraduate student body:
10,235 full time, 901 part time;
39% male, 61% female; 0%
American Indian, 3% Asian,
1% black, 5% Hispanic, 3%
multiracial, 0% Pacific Islander,
82% white, 3% international;
29% from in state; 42% live
on campus; 5% of students in
fraternities, 5% in sororities
Most popular majors: 11% Natural
Resources and Conservation, 11%
Social Sciences, 10% Biological
and Biomedical Sciences,
10% Business, Management,
Marketing, and Related Support
Services, 9% Health Professions
and Related Programs
Expenses: 2021-2022: $19,002
in state, $43,890 out of state;
room/board: $13,324
Financial aid: (802) 656-5700;
53% of undergrads determined to
have financial need, average aid
package $27,906

Vermont Technical
College
Randolph Center VT
(802) 728-1244
U.S. News ranking: Reg. Coll. (N),
No. 26
Website: www.vtc.edu
Admissions email:
admissions@vtc.edu
Public; founded 1866

Freshman admissions: selective;
2020-2021: 908 applied, 549
accepted. Neither SAT nor ACT
required. SAT 25/75 percentile:
988-1170. High school rank: N/A
Early decision deadline: N/A,
notification date: N/A
Early action deadline: N/A,
notification date: N/A
Application deadline (fall): rolling
Undergraduate student body: 865
full time, 617 part time; 50%
male, 50% female; 0% American
Indian, 1% Asian, 3% black,
3% Hispanic, 4% multiracial,
2% Pacific Islander, 85% white,
0% international; 11% from in
state; 9% live on campus; N/A
of students in fraternities, N/A in
sororities
Most popular majors: 31%
Engineering Technologies and
Engineering-Related Fields,
29% Health Professions and
Related Programs, 21% Business,
Management, Marketing, and
Related Support Services,
6% Construction Trades, 4%
Architecture and Related Services
Expenses: 2021-2022: $16,522
in state, $29,938 out of state;
room/board: $12,044
Financial aid: (802) 728-1248;
81% of undergrads determined to
have financial need; average aid
package $14,270

VIRGIN ISLANDS

University of the
Virgin Islands
St. Thomas VI
(340) 693-1150
U.S. News ranking: Reg. Coll. (S),
No. 35
Website: www.uvi.edu
Admissions email: admit@uvi.edu
Public; founded 1962
Freshman admissions: less
selective; 2020-2021: 640
applied, 638 accepted. Neither
SAT nor ACT required. SAT 25/75
percentile: 813-1020. High school
rank: 17% in top tenth, 49% in
top quarter, 80% in top half
Early decision deadline: N/A,
notification date: N/A
Early action deadline: N/A,
notification date: N/A
Application deadline (fall): 4/30
Undergraduate student body: 1,034
full time, 553 part time; 30%
male, 70% female; 0% American
Indian, 1% Asian, 73% black,
12% Hispanic, 1% multiracial,
0% Pacific Islander, 3% white,
6% international
Most popular majors: 17%
Registered Nursing/Registered
Nurse, 14% Business
Administration and Management,
General, 9% Accounting, 9%
Biology/Biological Sciences,
General, 9% Criminal Justice/
Police Science
Expenses: 2021-2022: $5,235 in
state, $14,496 out of state; room/
board: $8,554
Financial aid: (340) 692-4192;
74% of undergrads determined to
have financial need; average aid
package $9,950

VIRGINIA

Averett University
Danville VA
(434) 791-5600
U.S. News ranking: Reg. Coll. (S),
No. 21
Website: www.averett.edu
Admissions email:
admit@averett.edu
Private; founded 1859
Affiliation: Other
Freshman admissions: less
selective; 2020-2021: 1,853
applied, 1,849 accepted. Either
SAT or ACT required. SAT 25/75
percentile: 880-1090. High
school rank: 7% in top tenth, 21%
in top quarter, 54% in top half
Early decision deadline: N/A,
notification date: N/A
Early action deadline: N/A,
notification date: N/A
Application deadline (fall): rolling
Undergraduate student body: 867
full time, 26 part time; 56%
male, 44% female; 1% American
Indian, 1% Asian, 28% black,
4% Hispanic, 5% multiracial,
0% Pacific Islander, 54% white,
7% international; N/A from in
state; 54% live on campus; N/A
of students in fraternities, N/A in
sororities
Most popular majors: 22%
Business, Management,
Marketing, and Related Support
Services, 16% Parks, Recreation,
Leisure, and Fitness Studies,
14% Health Professions and
Related Programs, 9% Education,
6% Homeland Security, Law
Enforcement, Firefighting and
Related Protective Services
Expenses: 2021-2022: $37,050;
room/board: $11,140
Financial aid: (434) 791-5646;
84% of undergrads determined to
have financial need; average aid
package $29,703

Bluefield College[1]
Bluefield VA
(276) 326-4231
U.S. News ranking: Reg. Coll. (S),
second tier
Website: www.bluefield.edu
Admissions email:
admissions@bluefield.edu
Private; founded 1922
Affiliation: Baptist
Application deadline (fall): rolling
Undergraduate student body: N/A
full time, N/A part time
Expenses: 2021-2022: $28,870;
room/board: $10,677
Financial aid: (276) 326-4215;
90% of undergrads determined to
have financial need; average aid
package $19,594

Bridgewater College
Bridgewater VA
(800) 759-8328
U.S. News ranking: Nat. Lib. Arts,
second tier
Website: www.bridgewater.edu
Admissions email:
admissions@bridgewater.edu
Private; founded 1880
Affiliation: Church of Brethren
Freshman admissions: selective;
2020-2021: 3,684 applied,

2,805 accepted. Neither SAT
nor ACT required. SAT 25/75
percentile: 980-1170. High school
rank: 15% in top tenth, 41% in
top quarter, 71% in top half
Early decision deadline: N/A,
notification date: N/A
Early action deadline: 11/15,
notification date: 12/1
Application deadline (fall): 5/1
Undergraduate student body: 1,539
full time, 13 part time; 45%
male, 55% female; 0% American
Indian, 1% Asian, 15% black,
8% Hispanic, 7% multiracial,
0% Pacific Islander, 64% white,
2% international; 77% from in
state; 57% live on campus; 0%
of students in fraternities, 0% in
sororities
Most popular majors: 17%
Business Administration and
Management, General, 12%
Health and Physical Education/
Fitness, General, 8% Biology/
Biological Sciences, General,
8% Mass Communication/Media
Studies, 7% Psychology, General
Expenses: 2021-2022: $38,460;
room/board: $13,360
Financial aid: (540) 828-5376;
83% of undergrads determined to
have financial need; average aid
package $34,656

Christopher Newport
University
Newport News VA
(757) 594-7015
U.S. News ranking: Reg. U. (S),
No. 6
Website: cnu.edu/
Admissions email: admit@cnu.edu
Public; founded 1960
Freshman admissions: selective;
2020-2021: 7,311 applied,
5,587 accepted. Neither SAT
nor ACT required. SAT 25/75
percentile: 1090-1270. High
school rank: 17% in top tenth,
47% in top quarter, 82% in
top half
Early decision deadline: 11/15,
notification date: 12/15
Early action deadline: 12/1,
notification date: 1/15
Application deadline (fall): 2/1
Undergraduate student body: 4,653
full time, 105 part time; 45%
male, 55% female; 0% American
Indian, 4% Asian, 7% black, 7%
Hispanic, 6% multiracial, 0%
Pacific Islander, 76% white, 0%
international; 93% from in state;
71% live on campus; 23% of
students in fraternities, 27% in
sororities
Most popular majors: 15%
Business Administration and
Management, General, 14%
Biology/Biological Sciences,
General, 14% Psychology,
General, 9% Speech
Communication and Rhetoric, 6%
Political Science and Government,
General
Expenses: 2021-2022: $14,924
in state, $27,390 out of state;
room/board: $11,760
Financial aid: (757) 594-7170;
40% of undergrads determined to
have financial need; average aid
package $11,554

Eastern Mennonite
University
Harrisonburg VA
(800) 368-2665
U.S. News ranking: Reg. U. (S),
No. 35
Website: www.emu.edu
Admissions email:
admiss@emu.edu
Private; founded 1917
Affiliation: Mennonite Church
Freshman admissions: selective;
2020-2021: 1,398 applied,
1,004 accepted. Neither SAT
nor ACT required. SAT 25/75
percentile: 980-1230. High
school rank: N/A
Early decision deadline: N/A,
notification date: N/A
Early action deadline: N/A,
notification date: N/A
Application deadline (fall): rolling
Undergraduate student body: 807
full time, 84 part time; 40%
male, 60% female; 0% American
Indian, 2% Asian, 8% black, 8%
Hispanic, 6% multiracial, 0%
Pacific Islander, 67% white, 3%
international
Most popular majors: 41%
Registered Nursing/Registered
Nurse, 8% Organizational Behavior
Studies, 6% Liberal Arts and
Sciences/Liberal Studies, 5%
Psychology, General, 5% Social
Work
Expenses: 2021-2022: $39,990;
room/board: $11,900
Financial aid: (540) 432-4137;
75% of undergrads determined to
have financial need; average aid
package $34,423

ECPI University
Virginia Beach VA
(866) 499-0336
U.S. News ranking: Reg. U. (S),
second tier
Website: www.ecpi.edu/
Admissions email:
request@ecpi.edu
For-profit; founded 1966
Freshman admissions: less
selective; 2020-2021: 5,542
applied, 4,453 accepted. Neither
SAT nor ACT required. SAT 25/75
percentile: N/A. High school
rank: N/A
Early decision deadline: N/A,
notification date: N/A
Early action deadline: N/A,
notification date: N/A
Application deadline (fall): rolling
Undergraduate student body:
13,869 full time, 61 part time;
38% male, 62% female; 1%
American Indian, 3% Asian,
40% black, 11% Hispanic, 4%
multiracial, 0% Pacific Islander,
38% white, 0% international
Most popular majors: 20%
Licensed Practical/Vocational
Nurse Training, 16% Registered
Nursing/Registered Nurse, 12%
Medical/Clinical Assistant,
9% Computer and Information
Systems Security/Information
Assurance, 9% Network
and System Administration/
Administrator
Expenses: 2021-2022: $16,639;
room/board: N/A
Financial aid: (888) 658-7597

Emory and Henry College

Emory VA
(800) 848-5493
U.S. News ranking: Nat. Lib. Arts, No. 158
Website: www.ehc.edu
Admissions email: ehadmiss@ehc.edu
Private; founded 1836
Affiliation: United Methodist
Freshman admissions: selective; 2020-2021: 1,704 applied, 1,368 accepted. Neither SAT nor ACT required. SAT 25/75 percentile: 960-1150. High school rank: 16% in top tenth, 40% in top quarter, 72% in top half
Early decision deadline: 11/15, notification date: 12/15
Early action deadline: N/A, notification date: N/A
Application deadline (fall): rolling
Undergraduate student body: 905 full time, 51 part time; 48% male, 52% female; 0% American Indian, 0% Asian, 10% black, 4% Hispanic, 4% multiracial, 0% Pacific Islander, 78% white, 0% international; 64% from in state; N/A live on campus; N/A of students in fraternities, N/A in sororities
Most popular majors: 13% Social Sciences, 12% Education, 12% Parks, Recreation, Leisure, and Fitness Studies, 9% Business, Management, Marketing, and Related Support Services, 8% Psychology
Expenses: 2021-2022: $35,350; room/board: $13,550
Financial aid: (276) 944-6105; 91% of undergrads determined to have financial need; average aid package $31,079

Ferrum College

Ferrum VA
(800) 868-9797
U.S. News ranking: Reg. Coll. (S), No. 55
Website: www.ferrum.edu
Admissions email: admissions@ferrum.edu
Private; founded 1913
Freshman admissions: less selective; 2020-2021: 3,206 applied, 2,431 accepted. Neither SAT nor ACT required. SAT 25/75 percentile: 910-1060. High school rank: N/A
Early decision deadline: N/A, notification date: N/A
Early action deadline: N/A, notification date: N/A
Application deadline (fall): rolling
Undergraduate student body: 940 full time, 20 part time; 58% male, 42% female; 0% American Indian, 1% Asian, 31% black, 7% Hispanic, 7% multiracial, 0% Pacific Islander, 50% white, 1% international; 77% from in state; 85% live on campus; 3% of students in fraternities, 9% in sororities
Most popular majors: 16% Criminal Justice/Safety Studies, 13% Physical Education Teaching and Coaching, 12% Business Administration and Management, General, 8% Health/Medical Preparatory Programs, Other,

7% Agricultural Business and Management, General
Expenses: 2020-2021: $36,695; room/board: $12,400
Financial aid: N/A

George Mason University

Fairfax VA
(703) 993-2400
U.S. News ranking: Nat. U., No. 148
Website: www2.gmu.edu
Admissions email: admissions@gmu.edu
Public; founded 1972
Freshman admissions: selective; 2020-2021: 21,198 applied, 18,909 accepted. Neither SAT nor ACT required. SAT 25/75 percentile: 1100-1300. High school rank: 16% in top tenth, 41% in top quarter, 77% in top half
Early decision deadline: N/A, notification date: N/A
Early action deadline: 11/1, notification date: 12/15
Application deadline (fall): 1/15
Undergraduate student body: 21,604 full time, 5,501 part time; 51% male, 49% female; 0% American Indian, 22% Asian, 11% black, 16% Hispanic, 5% multiracial, 0% Pacific Islander, 37% white, 5% international; 87% from in state; 10% live on campus; 4% of students in fraternities, 5% in sororities
Most popular majors: 19% Business, Management, Marketing, and Related Support Services, 11% Computer and Information Sciences and Support Services, 9% Health Professions and Related Programs, 9% Social Sciences, 8% Homeland Security, Law Enforcement, Firefighting and Related Protective Services
Expenses: 2021-2022: $13,119 in state, $36,579 out of state; room/board: $12,630
Financial aid: (703) 993-2353; 56% of undergrads determined to have financial need; average aid package $14,238

Hampden-Sydney College

Hampden-Sydney VA
(800) 755-0733
U.S. News ranking: Nat. Lib. Arts, No. 98
Website: www.hsc.edu
Admissions email: admissions@hsc.edu
Private; founded 1775
Affiliation: Presbyterian
Freshman admissions: selective; 2020-2021: 1,906 applied, 896 accepted. Neither SAT nor ACT required. SAT 25/75 percentile: 1040-1220. High school rank: 15% in top tenth, 39% in top quarter, 71% in top half
Early decision deadline: N/A, notification date: N/A
Early action deadline: 1/15, notification date: 2/15
Application deadline (fall): 3/1
Undergraduate student body: 879 full time, 2 part time; 100% male, 0% female; 0% American Indian, 0% Asian, 7% black, 5%

Hispanic, 3% multiracial, 0% Pacific Islander, 82% white, 0% international; 72% from in state; 95% live on campus; 33% of students in fraternities, N/A in sororities
Most popular majors: 31% Business/Managerial Economics, 15% History, General, 10% Biology/Biological Sciences, General, 9% Political Science and Government, General, 8% Economics, General
Expenses: 2021-2022: $49,504; room/board: $14,278
Financial aid: (434) 223-6265; 70% of undergrads determined to have financial need; average aid package $36,523

Hampton University

Hampton VA
(757) 727-5328
U.S. News ranking: Nat. U., No. 202
Website: www.hamptonu.edu
Admissions email: admissions@hamptonu.edu
Private; founded 1868
Freshman admissions: selective; 2020-2021: 10,811 applied, 3,892 accepted. Neither SAT nor ACT required. SAT 25/75 percentile: 980-1160. High school rank: 13% in top tenth, 20% in top quarter, 71% in top half
Early decision deadline: N/A, notification date: N/A
Early action deadline: 11/1, notification date: 12/31
Application deadline (fall): 3/1
Undergraduate student body: 2,814 full time, 249 part time; 34% male, 66% female; 0% American Indian, 0% Asian, 95% black, 1% Hispanic, 0% multiracial, 0% Pacific Islander, 1% white, 1% international; 24% from in state; 0% live on campus; 0% of students in fraternities, 0% in sororities
Most popular majors: 12% Psychology, General, 10% Biology/Biological Sciences, General, 8% Business Administration and Management, General, 7% Kinesiology and Exercise Science, 6% Business Administration, Management and Operations, Other
Expenses: 2021-2022: $29,287; room/board: $12,986
Financial aid: (757) 727-5635; 48% of undergrads determined to have financial need; average aid package $5,303

Hollins University

Roanoke VA
(800) 456-9595
U.S. News ranking: Nat. Lib. Arts, No. 105
Website: www.hollins.edu
Admissions email: huadm@hollins.edu
Private; founded 1842
Freshman admissions: selective; 2020-2021: 3,056 applied, 2,469 accepted. Either SAT or ACT required. SAT 25/75 percentile: 1050-1260. High school rank: 20% in top tenth, 54% in top quarter, 85% in top half

Early decision deadline: 11/1, notification date: N/A
Early action deadline: 11/15, notification date: 12/1
Application deadline (fall): rolling
Undergraduate student body: 677 full time, 10 part time; 0% male, 100% female; 0% American Indian, 2% Asian, 11% black, 7% Hispanic, 8% multiracial, 0% Pacific Islander, 60% white, 9% international; 53% from in state; 64% live on campus; N/A of students in fraternities, N/A in sororities
Most popular majors: 19% English Language and Literature/Letters, 18% Visual and Performing Arts, 12% Social Sciences, 9% Business, Management, Marketing, and Related Support Services, 9% Psychology
Expenses: 2021-2022: $40,170; room/board: $14,660
Financial aid: (540) 362-6332; 75% of undergrads determined to have financial need; average aid package $38,293

James Madison University

Harrisonburg VA
(540) 568-5681
U.S. News ranking: Reg. U. (S), No. 3
Website: www.jmu.edu
Admissions email: admissions@jmu.edu
Public; founded 1908
Freshman admissions: selective; 2020-2021: 23,922 applied, 19,255 accepted. Neither SAT nor ACT required. SAT 25/75 percentile: 1120-1280. High school rank: 17% in top tenth, 48% in top quarter, 89% in top half
Early decision deadline: N/A, notification date: N/A
Early action deadline: 11/1, notification date: 1/15
Application deadline (fall): 1/15
Undergraduate student body: 18,420 full time, 1,307 part time; 42% male, 58% female; 0% American Indian, 5% Asian, 5% black, 7% Hispanic, 5% multiracial, 0% Pacific Islander, 75% white, 1% international; 79% from in state; 30% live on campus; 3% of students in fraternities, 7% in sororities
Most popular majors: 19% Health Professions and Related Programs, 16% Business, Management, Marketing, and Related Support Services, 9% Communication, Journalism, and Related Programs, 7% Social Sciences, 6% Liberal Arts and Sciences, General Studies and Humanities
Expenses: 2021-2022: $11,720 in state, $28,646 out of state; room/board: $11,550
Financial aid: (540) 568-7820; 38% of undergrads determined to have financial need; average aid package $10,103

Liberty University

Lynchburg VA
(800) 543-5317
U.S. News ranking: Nat. U., second tier
Website: www.liberty.edu
Admissions email: admissions@liberty.edu
Private; founded 1971
Affiliation: Evangelical Christian
Freshman admissions: selective; 2020-2021: 61,640 applied, 30,896 accepted. Either SAT or ACT required. SAT 25/75 percentile: 1040-1250. High school rank: 38% in top tenth, 77% in top quarter, 92% in top half
Early decision deadline: N/A, notification date: N/A
Early action deadline: N/A, notification date: N/A
Application deadline (fall): rolling
Undergraduate student body: 30,168 full time, 17,820 part time; 43% male, 57% female; 0% American Indian, 2% Asian, 10% black, 7% Hispanic, 3% multiracial, 0% Pacific Islander, 56% white, 1% international; N/A from in state; 16% live on campus; N/A of students in fraternities, N/A in sororities
Most popular majors: 20% Business, Management, Marketing, and Related Support Services, 15% Multi/Interdisciplinary Studies, 12% Psychology, 7% Education, 7% Philosophy and Religious Studies
Expenses: 2021-2022: $24,910; room/board: $11,200
Financial aid: (434) 582-2270; 69% of undergrads determined to have financial need; average aid package $15,634

Longwood University

Farmville VA
(434) 395-2060
U.S. News ranking: Reg. U. (S), No. 19
Website: www.longwood.edu/
Admissions email: admissions@longwood.edu
Public; founded 1839
Freshman admissions: selective; 2020-2021: 6,724 applied, 5,873 accepted. Neither SAT nor ACT required. SAT 25/75 percentile: 960-1140. High school rank: 1% in top tenth, 6% in top quarter, 36% in top half
Early decision deadline: 11/2, notification date: 12/15
Early action deadline: 12/1, notification date: 1/15
Application deadline (fall): rolling
Undergraduate student body: 3,319 full time, 621 part time; 31% male, 69% female; 0% American Indian, 1% Asian, 11% black, 6% Hispanic, 5% multiracial, 0% Pacific Islander, 74% white, 1% international; 97% from in state; 60% live on campus; 15% of students in fraternities, 17% in sororities
Most popular majors: 14% Business, Management, Marketing, and Related Support Services, 14% Liberal Arts and Sciences, General Studies and Humanities, 11% Health Professions and Related Programs,

8% Social Sciences, 7% Psychology
Expenses: 2021-2022: $14,400 in state, $25,980 out of state; room/board: $13,744
Financial aid: (434) 395-2077; 62% of undergrads determined to have financial need; average aid package $12,437

Mary Baldwin University
Staunton VA
(800) 468-2262
U.S. News ranking: Nat. U., second tier
Website: www.marybaldwin.edu
Admissions email: admit@marybaldwin.edu
Private; founded 1842
Freshman admissions: selective; 2020-2021: 7,188 applied, 6,261 accepted. Neither SAT nor ACT required. SAT 25/75 percentile: 940-1120. High school rank: N/A
Early decision deadline: N/A, notification date: N/A
Early action deadline: N/A, notification date: N/A
Application deadline (fall): rolling
Undergraduate student body: 1,131 full time, 346 part time; 20% male, 80% female; 0% American Indian, 3% Asian, 32% black, 7% Hispanic, 6% multiracial, 0% Pacific Islander, 43% white, 1% international
Most popular majors: 17% Business Administration, Management and Operations, 15% Liberal Arts and Sciences, General Studies and Humanities, 9% Social Work, 8% Health and Medical Administrative Services, 8% Registered Nursing, Nursing Administration, Nursing Research and Clinical Nursing
Expenses: 2021-2022: $31,085; room/board: $9,730
Financial aid: (540) 887-7022; 85% of undergrads determined to have financial need; average aid package $25,569

Marymount University
Arlington VA
(703) 284-1500
U.S. News ranking: Reg. U. (S), No. 38
Website: www.marymount.edu
Admissions email: admissions@marymount.edu
Private; founded 1950
Affiliation: Roman Catholic
Freshman admissions: selective; 2020-2021: 3,048 applied, 2,598 accepted. Neither SAT nor ACT required. SAT 25/75 percentile: 983-1188. High school rank: 5% in top tenth, 14% in top quarter, 47% in top half
Early decision deadline: N/A, notification date: N/A
Early action deadline: 11/15, notification date: 12/14
Application deadline (fall): rolling
Undergraduate student body: 1,861 full time, 180 part time; 35% male, 65% female; 0% American Indian, 7% Asian, 16% black, 25% Hispanic, 5% multiracial, 0% Pacific Islander, 30% white, 14% international; 64% from in

state; 27% live on campus; N/A of students in fraternities, N/A in sororities
Most popular majors: 19% Registered Nursing/Registered Nurse, 15% Business Administration and Management, General, 12% Information Technology, 9% Health Professions and Related Programs, 8% Psychology, General
Expenses: 2021-2022: $35,250; room/board: $14,500
Financial aid: (703) 284-1530; 60% of undergrads determined to have financial need; average aid package $23,425

Norfolk State University
Norfolk VA
(757) 823-8396
U.S. News ranking: Reg. U. (S), No. 70
Website: www.nsu.edu
Admissions email: admissions@nsu.edu
Public; founded 1935
Freshman admissions: least selective; 2020-2021: 6,944 applied, 6,324 accepted. Either SAT or ACT required. SAT 25/75 percentile: 840-1020. High school rank: 4% in top tenth, 15% in top quarter, 55% in top half
Early decision deadline: N/A, notification date: N/A
Early action deadline: N/A, notification date: N/A
Undergraduate student body: 4,529 full time, 463 part time; 32% male, 68% female; 0% American Indian, 0% Asian, 84% black, 4% Hispanic, 2% multiracial, 0% Pacific Islander, 3% white, 0% international; 74% from in state; 39% live on campus; N/A of students in fraternities, N/A in sororities
Most popular majors: 12% Business/Commerce, General, 11% Sociology, 9% Psychology, General, 8% Communication, Journalism, and Related Programs, Other, 8% Social Work
Expenses: 2021-2022: $9,622 in state, $20,790 out of state; room/board: N/A
Financial aid: (757) 823-8381

Old Dominion University
Norfolk VA
(757) 683-3685
U.S. News ranking: Nat. U., No. 263
Website: www.odu.edu
Admissions email: admissions@odu.edu
Public; founded 1930
Freshman admissions: selective; 2020-2021: 13,651 applied, 13,024 accepted. Neither SAT nor ACT required. SAT 25/75 percentile: 960-1170. High school rank: 10% in top tenth, 31% in top quarter, 68% in top half
Early decision deadline: N/A, notification date: N/A
Early action deadline: 12/1, notification date: 1/15
Application deadline (fall): 2/1
Undergraduate student body: 14,740 full time, 4,882 part

time; 44% male, 56% female; 0% American Indian, 5% Asian, 32% black, 9% Hispanic, 6% multiracial, 0% Pacific Islander, 44% white, 1% international; 92% from in state; 16% live on campus; 5% of students in fraternities, 4% in sororities
Most popular majors: 8% Psychology, General, 6% Criminology, 6% Multi-/Interdisciplinary Studies, Other, 6% Rhetoric and Composition, 5% Mental and Social Health Services and Allied Professions, Other
Expenses: 2021-2022: $11,520 in state, $31,680 out of state; room/board: $13,088
Financial aid: (757) 683-3683; 67% of undergrads determined to have financial need; average aid package $11,193

Radford University
Radford VA
(540) 831-5371
U.S. News ranking: Reg. U. (S), No. 29
Website: www.radford.edu
Admissions email: admissions@radford.edu
Public; founded 1910
Freshman admissions: less selective; 2020-2021: 14,994 applied, 11,798 accepted. Neither SAT nor ACT required. SAT 25/75 percentile: 920-1110. High school rank: 7% in top tenth, 23% in top quarter, 57% in top half
Early decision deadline: N/A, notification date: N/A
Early action deadline: 12/1, notification date: 1/15
Application deadline (fall): rolling
Undergraduate student body: 6,788 full time, 519 part time; 38% male, 62% female; 0% American Indian, 2% Asian, 18% black, 8% Hispanic, 6% multiracial, 0% Pacific Islander, 63% white, 1% international; 93% from in state; 45% live on campus; 8% of students in fraternities, 9% in sororities
Most popular majors: 16% Health Professions and Related Programs, 15% Business, Management, Marketing, and Related Support Services, 9% Multi/Interdisciplinary Studies, 8% Education, 8% Psychology
Expenses: 2021-2022: $11,542 in state, $23,177 out of state; room/board: $10,036
Financial aid: (540) 831-5408; 68% of undergrads determined to have financial need; average aid package $11,109

Randolph College
Lynchburg VA
(800) 745-7692
U.S. News ranking: Nat. Lib. Arts, No. 141
Website: www.randolphcollege.edu/
Admissions email: admissions@randolphcollege.edu
Private; founded 1891
Freshman admissions: selective; 2020-2021: 1,335 applied, 1,197 accepted. Neither SAT nor ACT required. SAT 25/75 percentile: 950-1160. High school

rank: 23% in top tenth, 49% in top quarter, 83% in top half
Early decision deadline: N/A, notification date: N/A
Early action deadline: 11/15, notification date: N/A
Application deadline (fall): rolling
Undergraduate student body: 492 full time, 16 part time; 39% male, 61% female; 0% American Indian, 2% Asian, 19% black, 10% Hispanic, 7% multiracial, 0% Pacific Islander, 58% white, 3% international; 77% from in state; 78% live on campus; 0% of students in fraternities, 0% in sororities
Most popular majors: 13% Social Sciences, 12% Biological and Biomedical Sciences, 11% Business, Management, Marketing, and Related Support Services, 9% Physical Sciences, 9% Psychology
Expenses: 2021-2022: $26,890; room/board: $11,000
Financial aid: (434) 947-8128; 76% of undergrads determined to have financial need; average aid package $20,364

Randolph-Macon College
Ashland VA
(800) 888-1762
U.S. News ranking: Nat. Lib. Arts, No. 111
Website: www.rmc.edu
Admissions email: admissions@rmc.edu
Private; founded 1830
Affiliation: United Methodist
Freshman admissions: selective; 2020-2021: 2,684 applied, 1,914 accepted. Neither SAT nor ACT required. SAT 25/75 percentile: 1030-1218. High school rank: 21% in top tenth, 48% in top quarter, 82% in top half
Early decision deadline: N/A, notification date: N/A
Early action deadline: 11/15, notification date: 1/1
Application deadline (fall): 3/1
Undergraduate student body: 1,531 full time, 23 part time; 45% male, 55% female; 0% American Indian, 1% Asian, 9% black, 6% Hispanic, 5% multiracial, 0% Pacific Islander, 76% white, 2% international; 20% from in state; N/A live on campus; 17% of students in fraternities, 28% in sororities
Most popular majors: 16% Business/Commerce, General, 13% Biology/Biological Sciences, General, 10% Communication and Media Studies
Expenses: 2021-2022: $45,150; room/board: $13,130
Financial aid: (804) 752-7259; 68% of undergrads determined to have financial need; average aid package $31,802

Regent University
Virginia Beach VA
(800) 373-5504
U.S. News ranking: Nat. U., No. 277
Website: www.regent.edu/
Admissions email:

admissions@regent.edu
Private; founded 1978
Affiliation: Undenominational
Freshman admissions: selective; 2020-2021: 4,120 applied, 2,078 accepted. Either SAT or ACT required. SAT 25/75 percentile: 940-1220. High school rank: 15% in top tenth, 33% in top quarter, 58% in top half
Early decision deadline: N/A, notification date: N/A
Early action deadline: N/A, notification date: N/A
Application deadline (fall): 8/1
Undergraduate student body: 2,376 full time, 2,163 part time; 38% male, 62% female; 1% American Indian, 2% Asian, 27% black, 10% Hispanic, 5% multiracial, 0% Pacific Islander, 50% white, 1% international; 42% from in state; 14% live on campus; N/A of students in fraternities, N/A in sororities
Most popular majors: 13% Speech Communication and Rhetoric, 12% Psychology, General, 9% Business Administration and Management, General, 8% Bible/Biblical Studies, 6% English Language and Literature, General
Expenses: 2021-2022: $18,820; room/board: $7,004
Financial aid: (757) 352-4385; 80% of undergrads determined to have financial need; average aid package $11,180

Roanoke College
Salem VA
(540) 375-2270
U.S. News ranking: Nat. Lib. Arts, No. 128
Website: www.roanoke.edu
Admissions email: admissions@roanoke.edu
Private; founded 1842
Affiliation: Evangelical Lutheran Church
Freshman admissions: selective; 2020-2021: 5,296 applied, 4,138 accepted. Neither SAT nor ACT required. SAT 25/75 percentile: 1040-1240. High school rank: 16% in top tenth, 38% in top quarter, 77% in top half
Early decision deadline: 11/18, notification date: 12/15
Early action deadline: N/A, notification date: N/A
Application deadline (fall): rolling
Undergraduate student body: 1,883 full time, 38 part time; 43% male, 57% female; 0% American Indian, 2% Asian, 5% black, 5% Hispanic, 4% multiracial, 0% Pacific Islander, 82% white, 2% international; 55% from in state; 78% live on campus; 18% of students in fraternities, 16% in sororities
Most popular majors: 19% Business Administration and Management, General, 9% Psychology, General, 7% Biology/Biological Sciences, General, 7% Communication and Media Studies, 6% Sociology
Expenses: 2021-2022: $48,180; room/board: $14,990
Financial aid: (540) 375-2235; 75% of undergrads determined to have financial need; average aid package $38,600

Shenandoah University
Winchester VA
(540) 665-4581
U.S. News ranking: Nat. U., No. 263
Website: www.su.edu
Admissions email: admit@su.edu
Private; founded 1875
Affiliation: United Methodist
Freshman admissions: selective; 2020-2021: 2,646 applied, 1,968 accepted. Neither SAT nor ACT required. SAT 25/75 percentile: 990-1220. High school rank: 15% in top tenth, 41% in top quarter, 68% in top half
Early decision deadline: N/A, notification date: N/A
Early action deadline: N/A, notification date: N/A
Application deadline (fall): 8/1
Undergraduate student body: 2,097 full time, 170 part time; 40% male, 60% female; 2% American Indian, 3% Asian, 11% black, 8% Hispanic, 0% multiracial, 0% Pacific Islander, 60% white, 1% international; 60% from in state; 47% live on campus; 0% of students in fraternities, 0% in sororities
Most popular majors: 28% Health Professions and Related Programs, 14% Biological and Biomedical Sciences, 13% Visual and Performing Arts, 10% Business, Management, Marketing, and Related Support Services, 8% Psychology
Expenses: 2021-2022: $34,490; room/board: $11,020
Financial aid: (540) 665-4538; 75% of undergrads determined to have financial need; average aid package $23,236

Southern Virginia University[1]
Buena Vista VA
(540) 261-8400
U.S. News ranking: Nat. Lib. Arts, second tier
Admissions email: N/A
Private
Application deadline (fall): N/A
Undergraduate student body: N/A full time, N/A part time
Expenses: 2020-2021: $17,696; room/board: $8,774
Financial aid: (540) 261-8463

Sweet Briar College
Sweet Briar VA
(800) 381-6142
U.S. News ranking: Nat. Lib. Arts, No. 165
Website: www.sbc.edu
Admissions email: admissions@sbc.edu
Private; founded 1901
Freshman admissions: selective; 2020-2021: 872 applied, 664 accepted. Neither SAT nor ACT required. SAT 25/75 percentile: 1010-1210. High school rank: N/A
Early decision deadline: 11/1, notification date: N/A
Early action deadline: 11/1, notification date: 11/16
Application deadline (fall): rolling

Undergraduate student body: 353 full time, 3 part time; 0% male, 100% female; 2% American Indian, 3% Asian, 10% black, 4% Hispanic, 1% multiracial, 0% Pacific Islander, 72% white, 4% international; 52% from in state; 88% live on campus; 0% of students in fraternities, 0% in sororities
Most popular majors: 15% Business/Commerce, General, 12% Biology/Biological Sciences, General, 10% Creative Writing, 10% Engineering Science, 10% Psychology, General
Expenses: 2021-2022: $23,080; room/board: $13,880
Financial aid: (434) 381-6156; 77% of undergrads determined to have financial need; average aid package $20,252

University of Lynchburg
Lynchburg VA
(434) 544-8300
U.S. News ranking: Reg. U. (S), No. 21
Website: www.lynchburg.edu
Admissions email: admissions@lynchburg.edu
Private; founded 1903
Affiliation: Christian Church (Disciples of Christ)
Freshman admissions: selective; 2020-2021: 3,694 applied, 3,593 accepted. Neither SAT nor ACT required. SAT 25/75 percentile: 960-1160. High school rank: 11% in top tenth, 25% in top quarter, 50% in top half
Early decision deadline: 11/15, notification date: 12/15
Early action deadline: N/A, notification date: N/A
Application deadline (fall): 9/1
Undergraduate student body: 1,764 full time, 58 part time; 39% male, 61% female; 0% American Indian, 1% Asian, 11% black, 7% Hispanic, 3% multiracial, 0% Pacific Islander, 75% white, 1% international; 73% from in state; 72% live on campus; 12% of students in fraternities, 12% in sororities
Most popular majors: 17% Health Professions and Related Programs, 16% Biological and Biomedical Sciences, 14% Social Sciences, 11% Business, Management, Marketing, and Related Support Services, 7% Education
Expenses: 2021-2022: $33,500; room/board: $12,490
Financial aid: (800) 426-8101; 76% of undergrads determined to have financial need; average aid package $32,514

University of Mary Washington
Fredericksburg VA
(540) 654-2000
U.S. News ranking: Reg. U. (S), No. 19
Website: www.umw.edu
Admissions email: admit@umw.edu
Public; founded 1908
Freshman admissions: selective; 2020-2021: 6,154 applied, 4,564 accepted. Neither SAT nor ACT required. SAT 25/75

percentile: 1090-1270. High school rank: 6% in top tenth, 50% in top quarter, 79% in top half
Early decision deadline: 11/1, notification date: 12/10
Early action deadline: 11/15, notification date: 12/15
Application deadline (fall): rolling
Undergraduate student body: 3,439 full time, 554 part time; 35% male, 65% female; 0% American Indian, 4% Asian, 8% black, 11% Hispanic, 5% multiracial, 0% Pacific Islander, 68% white, 1% international; 91% from in state; 42% live on campus; 0% of students in fraternities, 0% in sororities
Most popular majors: 16% Business Administration and Management, General, 10% Psychology, General, 8% Biology/Biological Sciences, General, 7% Liberal Arts and Sciences/Liberal Studies, 6% Computer and Information Sciences, General
Expenses: 2020-2021: $13,845 in state, $30,502 out of state; room/board: $11,734
Financial aid: (540) 654-2468

University of Richmond
Univ. of Richmond VA
(804) 289-8640
U.S. News ranking: Nat. Lib. Arts, No. 22
Website: www.richmond.edu
Admissions email: admission@richmond.edu
Private; founded 1830
Freshman admissions: more selective; 2020-2021: 12,060 applied, 3,727 accepted. Either SAT or ACT required. SAT 25/75 percentile: 1280-1460. High school rank: 50% in top tenth, 82% in top quarter, 98% in top half
Early decision deadline: 11/1, notification date: 12/15
Early action deadline: 11/1, notification date: 1/20
Application deadline (fall): 1/1
Undergraduate student body: 3,107 full time, 184 part time; 47% male, 53% female; 0% American Indian, 7% Asian, 7% black, 11% Hispanic, 5% multiracial, 0% Pacific Islander, 60% white, 7% international; 20% from in state; 71% live on campus; 20% of students in fraternities, 18% in sororities
Most popular majors: 35% Business, Management, Marketing, and Related Support Services, 12% Social Sciences, 9% Multi/Interdisciplinary Studies, 8% Biological and Biomedical Sciences, 5% Computer and Information Sciences and Support Services
Expenses: 2021-2022: $58,570; room/board: $13,950
Financial aid: (804) 289-8438; 39% of undergrads determined to have financial need; average aid package $53,919

University of Virginia
Charlottesville VA
(434) 982-3200
U.S. News ranking: Nat. U., No. 25
Website: www.virginia.edu
Admissions email: undergradadmission@virginia.edu
Public; founded 1819
Freshman admissions: most selective; 2020-2021: 40,878 applied, 9,230 accepted. Neither SAT nor ACT required. SAT 25/75 percentile: 1320-1510. High school rank: 90% in top tenth, 98% in top quarter, 99% in top half
Early decision deadline: 11/1, notification date: 1/31
Early action deadline: 11/1, notification date: 1/31
Application deadline (fall): 1/1
Undergraduate student body: 16,312 full time, 999 part time; 44% male, 56% female; 0% American Indian, 16% Asian, 7% black, 7% Hispanic, 5% multiracial, 0% Pacific Islander, 56% white, 4% international; N/A from in state; 26% live on campus; N/A of students in fraternities, N/A in sororities
Most popular majors: 20% Liberal Arts and Sciences, General Studies and Humanities, 17% Social Sciences, 12% Engineering, 8% Business, Management, Marketing, and Related Support Services, 6% Biological and Biomedical Sciences
Expenses: 2021-2022: $19,698 in state, $53,666 out of state; room/board: $12,660
Financial aid: (434) 982-6000; 36% of undergrads determined to have financial need; average aid package $31,188

University of Virginia–Wise
Wise VA
(888) 282-9324
U.S. News ranking: Nat. Lib. Arts, No. 158
Website: www.uvawise.edu
Admissions email: admissions@uvawise.edu
Public; founded 1954
Freshman admissions: selective; 2020-2021: 1,017 applied, 838 accepted. Either SAT or ACT required. SAT 25/75 percentile: 980-1170. High school rank: 20% in top tenth, 43% in top quarter, 75% in top half
Early decision deadline: N/A, notification date: N/A
Early action deadline: 12/1, notification date: 12/15
Application deadline (fall): 8/15
Undergraduate student body: 1,116 full time, 789 part time; 38% male, 62% female; 0% American Indian, 2% Asian, 10% black, 1% Hispanic, 1% multiracial, 0% Pacific Islander, 77% white, 0% international
Most popular majors: 13% Psychology, General, 11% Education, General, 9% Business Administration and Management, General, 8% Registered Nursing, Nursing Administration, Nursing Research and Clinical Nursing

Expenses: 2021-2022: $11,162 in state, $29,977 out of state; room/board: $11,593
Financial aid: (276) 328-0139; 82% of undergrads determined to have financial need; average aid package $14,399

Virginia Commonwealth University
Richmond VA
(800) 841-3638
U.S. News ranking: Nat. U., No. 172
Website: www.vcu.edu
Admissions email: ugrad@vcu.edu
Public; founded 1838
Freshman admissions: selective; 2020-2021: 17,368 applied, 15,739 accepted. Neither SAT nor ACT required. SAT 25/75 percentile: 1060-1250. High school rank: 18% in top tenth, 47% in top quarter, 80% in top half
Early decision deadline: N/A, notification date: N/A
Early action deadline: N/A, notification date: N/A
Undergraduate student body: 18,734 full time, 3,209 part time; 38% male, 62% female; 0% American Indian, 14% Asian, 20% black, 11% Hispanic, 8% multiracial, 0% Pacific Islander, 42% white, 2% international; 95% from in state; 20% live on campus; 6% of students in fraternities, 5% in sororities
Most popular majors: 12% Business, Management, Marketing, and Related Support Services, 11% Visual and Performing Arts, 9% Psychology, 8% Biological and Biomedical Sciences, 8% Education
Expenses: 2021-2022: $15,028 in state, $35,676 out of state; room/board: $11,615
Financial aid: (804) 828-6669; 61% of undergrads determined to have financial need; average aid package $14,604

Virginia Military Institute
Lexington VA
(800) 767-4207
U.S. News ranking: Nat. Lib. Arts, No. 67
Website: www.vmi.edu
Admissions email: admissions@vmi.edu
Public; founded 1839
Freshman admissions: selective; 2020-2021: 1,543 applied, 924 accepted. Either SAT or ACT required. SAT 25/75 percentile: 1070-1260. High school rank: 12% in top tenth, 40% in top quarter, 76% in top half
Early decision deadline: 11/15, notification date: 12/15
Early action deadline: N/A, notification date: N/A
Application deadline (fall): 2/1
Undergraduate student body: 1,698 full time, 0 part time; 87% male, 13% female; 0% American Indian, 5% Asian, 6% black, 8% Hispanic, 3% multiracial, 1% Pacific Islander, 75% white,

2% international; 65% from in state; 100% live on campus; 0% of students in fraternities, 0% in sororities
Most popular majors: 13% Civil Engineering, General, 13% Economics, General, 13% International Relations and Affairs, 11% History, General, 10% Psychology, General
Expenses: 2020-2021: $19,210 in state, $47,220 out of state; room/board: $10,060
Financial aid: (540) 464-7208

Virginia State University[1]
Petersburg VA
(804) 524-5902
U.S. News ranking: Reg. U. (S), No. 84
Website: www.vsu.edu
Admissions email: admiss@vsu.edu
Public; founded 1882
Application deadline (fall): 5/1
Undergraduate student body: N/A full time, N/A part time
Expenses: 2021-2022: $9,056 in state, $19,576 out of state; room/board: $11,208
Financial aid: (800) 823-7214; 92% of undergrads determined to have financial need; average aid package $12,858

Virginia Tech
Blacksburg VA
(540) 231-6267
U.S. News ranking: Nat. U., No. 75
Website: www.vt.edu
Admissions email: admissions@vt.edu
Public; founded 1872
Freshman admissions: more selective; 2020-2021: 30,571 applied, 20,456 accepted. Neither SAT nor ACT required. SAT 25/75 percentile: 1170-1370. High school rank: N/A
Early decision deadline: 11/1, notification date: N/A
Early action deadline: 12/1, notification date: 2/22
Application deadline (fall): 1/15
Undergraduate student body: 29,112 full time, 908 part time; 57% male, 43% female; 0% American Indian, 11% Asian, 5% black, 8% Hispanic, 5% multiracial, 0% Pacific Islander, 63% white, 6% international; 25% from in state; 28% live on campus; N/A of students in fraternities, N/A in sororities
Most popular majors: 23% Engineering, 20% Business, Management, Marketing, and Related Support Services, 9% Biological and Biomedical Sciences, 9% Social Sciences, 8% Family and Consumer Sciences/Human Sciences
Expenses: 2021-2022: $14,174 in state, $33,253 out of state; room/board: $10,110
Financial aid: (540) 231-5179; 39% of undergrads determined to have financial need; average aid package $11,217

Virginia Union University
Richmond VA
(804) 257-5600
U.S. News ranking: Nat. Lib. Arts, second tier
Website: www.vuu.edu/
Admissions email: admissions@vuu.edu
Private; founded 1865
Affiliation: Baptist
Freshman admissions: least selective; 2020-2021: 6,208 applied, 4,678 accepted. Neither SAT nor ACT required. SAT 25/75 percentile: 780-920. High school rank: 3% in top tenth, 22% in top quarter, 37% in top half
Early decision deadline: N/A, notification date: N/A
Early action deadline: N/A, notification date: N/A
Application deadline (fall): 6/30
Undergraduate student body: 1,069 full time, 140 part time; 47% male, 53% female; 1% American Indian, 0% Asian, 92% black, 2% Hispanic, 1% multiracial, 0% Pacific Islander, 1% white, 1% international; 53% from in state; 28% live on campus; N/A of students in fraternities, N/A in sororities
Most popular majors: 23% Divinity/Ministry, 12% Criminology, 9% Biology/Biological Sciences, General, 7% Business Administration and Management, General, 7% Teacher Education, Multiple Levels
Expenses: 2021-2022: $14,030; room/board: $8,978
Financial aid: (804) 257-5882; 76% of undergrads determined to have financial need; average aid package $13,872

Virginia Wesleyan University
Virginia Beach VA
(757) 455-3208
U.S. News ranking: Nat. Lib. Arts, second tier
Website: www.vwu.edu
Admissions email: enrollment@vwu.edu
Private; founded 1961
Affiliation: United Methodist
Freshman admissions: selective; 2020-2021: 2,195 applied, 1,624 accepted. Neither SAT nor ACT required. SAT 25/75 percentile: 960-1190. High school rank: 14% in top tenth, 39% in top quarter, 72% in top half
Early decision deadline: N/A, notification date: N/A
Early action deadline: N/A, notification date: N/A
Application deadline (fall): rolling
Undergraduate student body: 1,188 full time, 86 part time; 41% male, 59% female; 1% American Indian, 2% Asian, 24% black, 10% Hispanic, 6% multiracial, 0% Pacific Islander, 54% white, 1% international; 77% from in state; 66% live on campus; 10% of students in fraternities, 10% in sororities
Most popular majors: 16% Business, Management, Marketing, and Related Support Services, 11% Social Sciences,

8% Biological and Biomedical Sciences, 8% Homeland Security, Law Enforcement, Firefighting and Related Protective Services, 7% Psychology
Expenses: 2021-2022: $36,910; room/board: $10,700
Financial aid: (757) 455-3345; 75% of undergrads determined to have financial need; average aid package $27,398

Washington and Lee University
Lexington VA
(540) 458-8710
U.S. News ranking: Nat. Lib. Arts, No. 11
Website: www.wlu.edu
Admissions email: admissions@wlu.edu
Private; founded 1749
Freshman admissions: most selective; 2020-2021: 4,996 applied, 1,223 accepted. Neither SAT nor ACT required. SAT 25/75 percentile: 1350-1500. High school rank: 80% in top tenth, 98% in top quarter, 100% in top half
Early decision deadline: 11/1, notification date: 12/15
Early action deadline: N/A, notification date: N/A
Application deadline (fall): 1/1
Undergraduate student body: 1,821 full time, 1 part time; 49% male, 51% female; 0% American Indian, 4% Asian, 3% black, 6% Hispanic, 4% multiracial, 0% Pacific Islander, 77% white, 4% international; 17% from in state; 73% live on campus; 79% of students in fraternities, 70% in sororities
Most popular majors: 21% Business Administration and Management, General, 13% Accounting, 13% Economics, General, 12% Political Science and Government, General, 6% History, General
Expenses: 2021-2022: $59,380; room/board: $16,270
Financial aid: (540) 458-8717; 45% of undergrads determined to have financial need; average aid package $60,561

William & Mary
Williamsburg VA
(757) 221-4223
U.S. News ranking: Nat. U., No. 38
Website: www.wm.edu
Admissions email: admission@wm.edu
Public; founded 1693
Freshman admissions: most selective; 2020-2021: 14,201 applied, 5,987 accepted. Neither SAT nor ACT required. SAT 25/75 percentile: 1300-1490. High school rank: 77% in top tenth, 95% in top quarter, 99% in top half
Early decision deadline: 11/1, notification date: N/A
Early action deadline: N/A, notification date: N/A
Application deadline (fall): 1/1
Undergraduate student body: 6,131 full time, 105 part time; 41% male, 59% female; 0% American Indian, 9% Asian, 7% black, 9%

Hispanic, 6% multiracial, 0% Pacific Islander, 59% white, 5% international; 70% from in state; 54% live on campus; 20% of students in fraternities, 28% in sororities
Most popular majors: 24% Social Sciences, 10% Biological and Biomedical Sciences, 10% Business, Management, Marketing, and Related Support Services, 8% Multi/Interdisciplinary Studies, 7% Psychology
Expenses: 2021-2022: $23,812 in state, $46,467 out of state; room/board: $13,332
Financial aid: (757) 221-2420; 37% of undergrads determined to have financial need; average aid package $25,653

WASHINGTON

Bellevue College[1]
Bellevue WA
(425) 564-1000
U.S. News ranking: Reg. Coll. (W), unranked
Website: www.bellevuecollege.edu
Admissions email: N/A
Public
Application deadline (fall): N/A
Undergraduate student body: N/A full time, N/A part time
Expenses: 2020-2021: $3,958 in state, $9,349 out of state; room/board: $13,530
Financial aid: N/A

Bellingham Technical College[1]
Bellingham WA
(360) 752-7000
U.S. News ranking: Reg. Coll. (W), unranked
Website: www.spokanefalls.edu
Admissions email: N/A
Public
Application deadline (fall): N/A
Undergraduate student body: N/A full time, N/A part time
Expenses: N/A
Financial aid: N/A

Cascadia College[1]
Bothell WA
(425) 352-8000
U.S. News ranking: Reg. Coll. (W), unranked
Website: www.national.edu/locations/campuses/austin/
Admissions email: admissions@cascadia.edu
Public; founded 2000
Application deadline (fall): rolling
Undergraduate student body: N/A full time, N/A part time
Expenses: 2020-2021: $4,226 in state, $4,788 out of state; room/board: N/A
Financial aid: N/A

Centralia College[1]
Centralia WA
(360) 736-9391
U.S. News ranking: Reg. Coll. (W), unranked
Admissions email: N/A

Public
Application deadline (fall): N/A
Undergraduate student body: N/A full time, N/A part time
Expenses: 2020-2021: $4,652 in state, $5,113 out of state; room/board: $11,118
Financial aid: N/A

Central Washington University
Ellensburg WA
(509) 963-1211
U.S. News ranking: Reg. U. (W), No. 46
Website: www.cwu.edu
Admissions email: admissions@cwu.edu
Public; founded 1891
Freshman admissions: less selective; 2020-2021: 12,226 applied, 10,421 accepted. Neither SAT nor ACT required. SAT 25/75 percentile: 910-1110. High school rank: N/A
Early decision deadline: N/A, notification date: N/A
Early action deadline: N/A, notification date: N/A
Application deadline (fall): rolling
Undergraduate student body: 9,135 full time, 1,182 part time; 46% male, 54% female; 1% American Indian, 5% Asian, 4% black, 18% Hispanic, 9% multiracial, 1% Pacific Islander, 51% white, 3% international; 93% from in state; 15% live on campus; N/A of students in fraternities, N/A in sororities
Most popular majors: 19% Business, Management, Marketing, and Related Support Services, 13% Engineering, 9% Computer and Information Sciences and Support Services, 9% Social Sciences, 7% Psychology
Expenses: 2021-2022: $7,733 in state, $23,809 out of state; room/board: $13,787
Financial aid: (509) 963-1611; 58% of undergrads determined to have financial need; average aid package $11,385

City University of Seattle[1]
Seattle WA
(888) 422-4898
U.S. News ranking: Reg. U. (W), unranked
Website: www.cityu.edu
Admissions email: info@cityu.edu
Private; founded 1973
Application deadline (fall): N/A
Undergraduate student body: N/A full time, N/A part time
Expenses: N/A
Financial aid: N/A

Clark College[1]
Vancouver WA
(360) 992-2000
U.S. News ranking: Reg. Coll. (W), unranked
Website: www.tacomacc.edu
Admissions email: N/A
Public
Application deadline (fall): N/A
Undergraduate student body: N/A full time, N/A part time

Expenses: 2020-2021: $3,957 in state, $9,718 out of state; room/board: N/A
Financial aid: N/A

Clover Park Technical College[1]
Lakewood WA
(253) 589-5800
U.S. News ranking: Reg. Coll. (W), unranked
Website: www.cptc.edu
Admissions email: admissions@cptc.edu
Public
Application deadline (fall): N/A
Undergraduate student body: N/A full time, N/A part time
Expenses: 2020-2021: $5,740 in state, $5,740 out of state; room/board: N/A
Financial aid: N/A

Columbia Basin College[1]
Pasco WA
(509) 547-0511
U.S. News ranking: Reg. Coll. (W), unranked
Admissions email: N/A
Public
Application deadline (fall): N/A
Undergraduate student body: N/A full time, N/A part time
Expenses: 2020-2021: $5,755 in state, $7,484 out of state; room/board: $9,920
Financial aid: N/A

Cornish College of the Arts[1]
Seattle WA
(800) 726-2787
U.S. News ranking: Arts, unranked
Website: www.cornish.edu
Admissions email: admission@cornish.edu
Private; founded 1914
Application deadline (fall): N/A
Undergraduate student body: N/A full time, N/A part time
Expenses: 2020-2021: $34,398; room/board: $13,036
Financial aid: (206) 726-5063

Eastern Washington University
Cheney WA
(509) 359-2397
U.S. News ranking: Reg. U. (W), No. 60
Website: www.ewu.edu
Admissions email: admissions@ewu.edu
Public; founded 1882
Freshman admissions: less selective; 2020-2021: 6,023 applied, 4,840 accepted. Neither SAT nor ACT required. SAT 25/75 percentile: 880-1100. High school rank: N/A
Early decision deadline: N/A, notification date: N/A
Early action deadline: N/A, notification date: N/A
Application deadline (fall): 5/15
Undergraduate student body: 8,685 full time, 1,608 part time; 43% male, 57% female; N/A American Indian, N/A Asian, N/A black,

N/A Hispanic, N/A multiracial, N/A Pacific Islander, N/A white, N/A international; N/A from in state; 6% live on campus; N/A of students in fraternities, N/A in sororities
Most popular majors: 20% Business, Management, Marketing, and Related Support Services, 9% Biological and Biomedical Sciences, 9% Education, 8% Psychology, 8% Social Sciences
Expenses: 2021-2022: $7,908 in state, $26,328 out of state; room/board: $13,027
Financial aid: (509) 359-2314; 54% of undergrads determined to have financial need; average aid package $11,480

Edmonds Community College[1]
Lynnwood WA
(425) 640-1459
U.S. News ranking: Reg. Coll. (W), unranked
Website: www.wvc.edu
Admissions email: N/A
Public
Application deadline (fall): N/A
Undergraduate student body: N/A full time, N/A part time
Expenses: 2020-2021: $4,107 in state, $9,498 out of state; room/board: $11,118
Financial aid: N/A

The Evergreen State College[1]
Olympia WA
(360) 867-6170
U.S. News ranking: Reg. U. (W), No. 50
Website: www.evergreen.edu
Admissions email: admissions@evergreen.edu
Public; founded 1967
Application deadline (fall): rolling
Undergraduate student body: N/A full time, N/A part time
Expenses: 2020-2021: $8,325 in state, $28,515 out of state; room/board: $12,735
Financial aid: (360) 867-6205

Gonzaga University
Spokane WA
(800) 322-2584
U.S. News ranking: Nat. U., No. 79
Website: www.gonzaga.edu
Admissions email: admissions@gonzaga.edu
Private; founded 1887
Affiliation: Roman Catholic
Freshman admissions: more selective; 2020-2021: 8,409 applied, 6,129 accepted. Neither SAT nor ACT required. SAT 25/75 percentile: 1160-1350. High school rank: 39% in top tenth, 75% in top quarter, 96% in top half
Early decision deadline: N/A, notification date: N/A
Early action deadline: N/A, notification date: N/A
Application deadline (fall): 2/1
Undergraduate student body: 4,751 full time, 101 part time; 47% male, 53% female; 0% American Indian, 6% Asian, 1% black,

11% Hispanic, 7% multiracial, 0% Pacific Islander, 70% white, 1% international; 50% from in state; 40% live on campus; 0% of students in fraternities, 0% in sororities
Most popular majors: 27% Business, Management, Marketing, and Related Support Services, 13% Social Sciences, 11% Biological and Biomedical Sciences, 10% Engineering, 7% Communication, Journalism, and Related Programs
Expenses: 2021-2022: $48,470; room/board: $13,192
Financial aid: (509) 313-6562; 49% of undergrads determined to have financial need; average aid package $39,930

Grays Harbor College[1]
Aberdeen WA
(360) 532-9020
U.S. News ranking: Reg. Coll. (W), unranked
Website: www.yvcc.edu
Admissions email: N/A
Public
Application deadline (fall): N/A
Undergraduate student body: N/A full time, N/A part time
Expenses: 2020-2021: $4,296 in state, $9,687 out of state; room/board: N/A
Financial aid: N/A

Green River College[1]
Auburn WA
(253) 833-9111
U.S. News ranking: Reg. Coll. (W), unranked
Website: uwc.edu
Admissions email: N/A
Public
Application deadline (fall): N/A
Undergraduate student body: N/A full time, N/A part time
Expenses: 2020-2021: $4,233 in state, $4,694 out of state; room/board: N/A
Financial aid: N/A

Heritage University[1]
Toppenish WA
(509) 865-8500
U.S. News ranking: Reg. U. (W), second tier
Website: www.heritage.edu
Admissions email: admissions@heritage.edu
Private
Application deadline (fall): N/A
Undergraduate student body: N/A full time, N/A part time
Expenses: 2020-2021: $18,332; room/board: N/A
Financial aid: N/A

Highline College[1]
Des Moines WA
(206) 878-3710
U.S. News ranking: Reg. Coll. (W), unranked
Website: www.marianas.edu/
Admissions email: N/A
Public
Application deadline (fall): N/A

Undergraduate student body: N/A full time, N/A part time
Expenses: N/A
Financial aid: N/A

Lake Washington Institute of Technology[1]
Kirkland WA
(425) 739-8104
U.S. News ranking: Reg. Coll. (W), unranked
Website: www.lwtech.edu/
Admissions email: admissions@lwtech.edu
Public; founded 1949
Application deadline (fall): rolling
Undergraduate student body: N/A full time, N/A part time
Expenses: N/A
Financial aid: (425) 739-8106

North Seattle College[1]
Seattle WA
(206) 934-3600
U.S. News ranking: Reg. Coll. (W), unranked
Admissions email: N/A
Public
Application deadline (fall): N/A
Undergraduate student body: N/A full time, N/A part time
Expenses: 2020-2021: $4,123 in state, $4,123 out of state; room/board: N/A
Financial aid: N/A

Northwest University
Kirkland WA
(425) 889-5231
U.S. News ranking: Reg. U. (W), No. 55
Website: www.northwestu.edu
Admissions email: admissions@northwestu.edu
Private; founded 1934
Affiliation: Assemblies of God Church
Freshman admissions: selective; 2020-2021: 496 applied, 460 accepted. Neither SAT nor ACT required. SAT 25/75 percentile: 1010-1205. High school rank: N/A
Early decision deadline: N/A, notification date: N/A
Early action deadline: N/A, notification date: N/A
Application deadline (fall): 8/1
Undergraduate student body: 815 full time, 23 part time; 32% male, 68% female; 1% American Indian, 4% Asian, 3% black, 9% Hispanic, 7% multiracial, 1% Pacific Islander, 56% white, 4% international; 77% from in state; 65% live on campus; 0% of students in fraternities, 0% in sororities
Most popular majors: 17% Registered Nursing/Registered Nurse, 12% Theological and Ministerial Studies, Other, 11% Communication and Media Studies, Other, 11% Psychology, General, 10% Business Administration and Management, General
Expenses: 2021-2022: $33,980; room/board: $9,700

Undergraduate student body: N/A full time, N/A part time
Expenses: N/A
Financial aid: N/A

Lake Washington Institute of Technology[1]
Financial aid: (425) 889-5336; 77% of undergrads determined to have financial need; average aid package $26,052

Olympic College[1]
Bremerton WA
(360) 792-6050
U.S. News ranking: Reg. Coll. (W), unranked
Website: www.olympic.edu
Admissions email: N/A
Public
Application deadline (fall): N/A
Undergraduate student body: N/A full time, N/A part time
Expenses: 2020-2021: $3,971 in state, $9,362 out of state; room/board: $10,385
Financial aid: N/A

Pacific Lutheran University
Tacoma WA
(800) 274-6758
U.S. News ranking: Reg. U. (W), No. 14
Website: www.plu.edu
Admissions email: admission@plu.edu
Private; founded 1890
Affiliation: Lutheran Church in America
Freshman admissions: more selective; 2020-2021: 3,306 applied, 2,853 accepted. Neither SAT nor ACT required. SAT 25/75 percentile: 1100-1300. High school rank: 36% in top tenth, 69% in top quarter, 96% in top half
Early decision deadline: N/A, notification date: N/A
Early action deadline: N/A, notification date: N/A
Application deadline (fall): 8/15
Undergraduate student body: 2,486 full time, 58 part time; 36% male, 64% female; 0% American Indian, 11% Asian, 4% black, 14% Hispanic, 11% multiracial, 1% Pacific Islander, 56% white, 1% international; 78% from in state; 34% live on campus; 0% of students in fraternities, 0% in sororities
Most popular majors: 13% Business Administration and Management, General, 11% Registered Nursing/Registered Nurse, 7% Kinesiology and Exercise Science, 6% Multi-/Interdisciplinary Studies, Other, 6% Psychology, General
Expenses: 2021-2022: $47,976; room/board: $11,482
Financial aid: (253) 535-7161; 75% of undergrads determined to have financial need; average aid package $41,342

Peninsula College[1]
Port Angeles WA
(360) 452-9277
U.S. News ranking: Reg. Coll. (W), unranked
Website: www.pencol.edu
Admissions email: N/A
Public
Application deadline (fall): N/A

Undergraduate student body: N/A full time, N/A part time
Expenses: 2020-2021: $4,218 in state, $4,671 out of state; room/board: N/A
Financial aid: N/A

Renton Technical College[1]

Renton WA
(425) 235-2352
U.S. News ranking: Reg. Coll. (W), unranked
Website: aupr.edu
Admissions email: N/A
Public
Application deadline (fall): N/A
Undergraduate student body: N/A full time, N/A part time
Expenses: 2020-2021: $5,671 in state, $6,131 out of state; room/board: N/A
Financial aid: N/A

Saint Martin's University

Lacey WA
(800) 368-8803
U.S. News ranking: Reg. U. (W), No. 35
Website: www.stmartin.edu
Admissions email: admissions@stmartin.edu
Private; founded 1895
Affiliation: Roman Catholic
Freshman admissions: selective; 2020-2021: 1,698 applied, 1,593 accepted. Neither SAT nor ACT required. SAT 25/75 percentile: 950-1145. High school rank: N/A
Early decision deadline: N/A, notification date: N/A
Early action deadline: N/A, notification date: N/A
Application deadline (fall): 7/31
Undergraduate student body: 1,254 full time, 140 part time; 44% male, 56% female; 1% American Indian, 9% Asian, 7% black, 19% Hispanic, 12% multiracial, 5% Pacific Islander, 43% white, 3% international; 77% from in state; 37% live on campus; N/A of students in fraternities, N/A in sororities
Most popular majors: 22% Business, Management, Marketing, and Related Support Services, 20% Engineering, 11% Psychology, 9% Biological and Biomedical Sciences, 5% Social Sciences
Expenses: 2021-2022: $40,690; room/board: $12,850
Financial aid: (360) 486-8868; 77% of undergrads determined to have financial need; average aid package $31,744

Seattle Central College[1]

Seattle WA
(206) 934-5450
U.S. News ranking: Reg. Coll. (W), unranked
Website: www.seattlecentral.edu/
Admissions email: Admissions.Central@seattlecolleges.edu
Public; founded 1966

Application deadline (fall): rolling
Undergraduate student body: N/A full time, N/A part time
Expenses: 2020-2021: $4,053 in state, $4,053 out of state; room/board: N/A
Financial aid: N/A

Seattle Pacific University

Seattle WA
(800) 366-3344
U.S. News ranking: Nat. U., No. 227
Website: www.spu.edu
Admissions email: admissions@spu.edu
Private; founded 1891
Affiliation: Free Methodist
Freshman admissions: selective; 2020-2021: 3,923 applied, 3,555 accepted. Either SAT or ACT required. SAT 25/75 percentile: 1010-1160. High school rank: N/A
Early decision deadline: N/A, notification date: N/A
Early action deadline: 11/15, notification date: 1/5
Application deadline (fall): 2/1
Undergraduate student body: 2,606 full time, 96 part time; 33% male, 67% female; 0% American Indian, 14% Asian, 7% black, 16% Hispanic, 9% multiracial, 1% Pacific Islander, 46% white, 5% international; N/A from in state; 35% live on campus; N/A of students in fraternities, N/A in sororities
Most popular majors: 13% Business, Management, Marketing, and Related Support Services, 9% Biological and Biomedical Sciences, 9% Psychology, 9% Visual and Performing Arts, 8% Social Sciences
Expenses: 2021-2022: $35,646; room/board: $13,404
Financial aid: (206) 281-2061; 73% of undergrads determined to have financial need; average aid package $41,500

Seattle University

Seattle WA
(206) 296-2000
U.S. News ranking: Nat. U., No. 127
Website: www.seattleu.edu
Admissions email: admissions@seattleu.edu
Private; founded 1891
Affiliation: Roman Catholic
Freshman admissions: more selective; 2020-2021: 7,914 applied, 6,587 accepted. Neither SAT nor ACT required. SAT 25/75 percentile: 1130-1330. High school rank: 24% in top tenth, 55% in top quarter, 91% in top half
Early decision deadline: N/A, notification date: N/A
Early action deadline: 11/15, notification date: 12/23
Application deadline (fall): rolling
Undergraduate student body: 4,092 full time, 207 part time; 40% male, 60% female; 0% American Indian, 21% Asian, 3% black, 13% Hispanic, 9% multiracial, 1% Pacific Islander, 39% white,

10% international; 44% from in state; 27% live on campus; 0% of students in fraternities, 0% in sororities
Most popular majors: Information not available
Expenses: 2021-2022: $49,335; room/board: $13,035
Financial aid: (206) 296-5852; 55% of undergrads determined to have financial need; average aid package $40,525

Skagit Valley College[1]

Mount Vernon WA
(360) 416-7600
U.S. News ranking: Reg. Coll. (W), unranked
Website: www.pucpr.edu/arecibo
Admissions email: N/A
Public
Application deadline (fall): N/A
Undergraduate student body: N/A full time, N/A part time
Expenses: 2020-2021: $4,000 in state, $6,884 out of state; room/board: $9,600
Financial aid: N/A

South Seattle College[1]

Seattle WA
(206) 764-5300
U.S. News ranking: Reg. Coll. (W), unranked
Website: www.southseattle.edu
Admissions email: N/A
Public
Application deadline (fall): N/A
Undergraduate student body: N/A full time, N/A part time
Expenses: 2020-2021: $4,214 in state, $4,214 out of state; room/board: N/A
Financial aid: N/A

Spokane Community College[1]

Spokane WA
(509) 533-7000
U.S. News ranking: Reg. Coll. (W), unranked
Website: www.cunisanjuan.edu
Admissions email: N/A
Public
Application deadline (fall): N/A
Undergraduate student body: N/A full time, N/A part time
Expenses: N/A
Financial aid: N/A

Spokane Falls Community College[1]

Spokane WA
(509) 533-3500
U.S. News ranking: Reg. Coll. (W), unranked
Website: www.psm.edu
Admissions email: N/A
Public
Application deadline (fall): N/A
Undergraduate student body: N/A full time, N/A part time
Expenses: N/A
Financial aid: N/A

Tacoma Community College[1]

Tacoma WA
(253) 566-5000
U.S. News ranking: Reg. Coll. (W), unranked
Website: www.edpuniversity.edu
Admissions email: N/A
Public
Application deadline (fall): N/A
Undergraduate student body: N/A full time, N/A part time
Expenses: 2020-2021: $4,560 in state, $10,016 out of state; room/board: N/A
Financial aid: N/A

University of Puget Sound

Tacoma WA
(253) 879-3211
U.S. News ranking: Nat. Lib. Arts, No. 85
Website: www.pugetsound.edu
Admissions email: admission@pugetsound.edu
Private; founded 1888
Freshman admissions: more selective; 2020-2021: 5,230 applied, 4,518 accepted. Neither SAT nor ACT required. SAT 25/75 percentile: 1130-1342. High school rank: 28% in top tenth, 62% in top quarter, 91% in top half
Early decision deadline: 11/1, notification date: 1/1
Early action deadline: 11/1, notification date: 1/15
Application deadline (fall): 1/15
Undergraduate student body: 1,830 full time, 68 part time; 41% male, 59% female; 0% American Indian, 8% Asian, 2% black, 10% Hispanic, 9% multiracial, 1% Pacific Islander, 66% white, 1% international; N/A from in state; 9% live on campus; 25% of students in fraternities, 23% in sororities
Most popular majors: 12% Business Administration and Management, General, 11% Psychology, General, 7% Biology/Biological Sciences, General, 6% Computer Science, 6% Economics, General
Expenses: 2021-2022: $55,670; room/board: $13,950
Financial aid: (253) 879-3214; 53% of undergrads determined to have financial need; average aid package $41,222

University of Washington

Seattle WA
(206) 543-9686
U.S. News ranking: Nat. U., No. 59
Website: www.washington.edu
Admissions email: pseegert@uw.edu
Public; founded 1861
Freshman admissions: more selective; 2020-2021: 43,778 applied, 24,467 accepted. Neither SAT nor ACT required. SAT 25/75 percentile: 1200-1457. High school rank: 56% in top tenth, 86% in top quarter, 98% in top half

Early decision deadline: N/A, notification date: N/A
Early action deadline: N/A, notification date: N/A
Application deadline (fall): 11/15
Undergraduate student body: 29,329 full time, 6,253 part time; 45% male, 55% female; 0% American Indian, 26% Asian, 3% black, 9% Hispanic, 8% multiracial, 0% Pacific Islander, 36% white, 15% international; N/A from in state; 12% live on campus; 13% of students in fraternities, 15% in sororities
Most popular majors: 12% Social Sciences, 11% Biological and Biomedical Sciences, 10% Computer and Information Sciences and Support Services, 10% Engineering, 8% Business, Management, Marketing, and Related Support Services
Expenses: 2021-2022: $12,076 in state, $39,906 out of state; room/board: $14,871
Financial aid: (206) 543-6101; 40% of undergrads determined to have financial need; average aid package $18,380

University of Washington–Bothell[1]

Bothell WA
(425) 352-5000
U.S. News ranking: Reg. U. (W), No. 27
Admissions email: N/A
Public
Application deadline (fall): N/A
Undergraduate student body: N/A full time, N/A part time
Expenses: 2020-2021: $11,649 in state, $39,018 out of state; room/board: $13,191
Financial aid: N/A

University of Washington–Tacoma[1]

Tacoma WA
(253) 692-4000
U.S. News ranking: Reg. U. (W), No. 30
Admissions email: N/A
Public
Application deadline (fall): N/A
Undergraduate student body: N/A full time, N/A part time
Expenses: 2020-2021: $11,889 in state, $39,258 out of state; room/board: $12,258
Financial aid: N/A

Walla Walla University

College Place WA
(509) 527-2327
U.S. News ranking: Reg. U. (W), No. 77
Website: www.wallawalla.edu
Admissions email: info@wallawalla.edu
Private; founded 1892
Affiliation: Seventh Day Adventist
Freshman admissions: less selective; 2020-2021: 1,606 applied, 1,135 accepted. Neither SAT nor ACT required. SAT 25/75 percentile: N/A. High school rank: N/A

Early decision deadline: N/A, notification date: N/A
Early action deadline: N/A, notification date: N/A
Application deadline (fall): rolling
Undergraduate student body: 1,305 full time, 240 part time; 51% male, 49% female; N/A American Indian, N/A Asian, N/A black, N/A Hispanic, N/A multiracial, N/A Pacific Islander, N/A white, N/A international
Most popular majors: 22% Health Professions and Related Programs, 16% Engineering, 12% Business, Management, Marketing, and Related Support Services, 6% Biological and Biomedical Sciences, 5% Education
Expenses: 2021-2022: $30,531; room/board: $9,441
Financial aid: (509) 527-2815; 64% of undergrads determined to have financial need; average aid package $24,045

Washington State University
Pullman WA
(888) 468-6978
U.S. News ranking: Nat. U., No. 179
Website: www.wsu.edu
Admissions email: admissions@wsu.edu
Public; founded 1890
Freshman admissions: selective; 2020-2021: 21,198 applied, 16,947 accepted. Neither SAT nor ACT required. SAT 25/75 percentile: 1020-1210. High school rank: N/A
Early decision deadline: N/A, notification date: N/A
Early action deadline: N/A, notification date: N/A
Application deadline (fall): rolling
Undergraduate student body: 22,315 full time, 3,155 part time; 45% male, 55% female; 0% American Indian, 6% Asian, 3% black, 17% Hispanic, 7% multiracial, 0% Pacific Islander, 61% white, 4% international; 85% from in state; 5% live on campus; 21% of students in fraternities, 26% in sororities
Most popular majors: 19% Business, Management, Marketing, and Related Support Services, 11% Engineering, 10% Social Sciences, 8% Communication, Journalism, and Related Programs, 7% Biological and Biomedical Sciences
Expenses: 2021-2022: $12,417 in state, $27,733 out of state; room/board: $11,750
Financial aid: (509) 335-9711; 55% of undergrads determined to have financial need; average aid package $14,237

Wenatchee Valley College[1]
Wenatchee WA
(509) 682-6800
U.S. News ranking: Reg. Coll. (W), unranked
Website: www.cascadia.edu
Admissions email: N/A
Public
Application deadline (fall): N/A

Undergraduate student body: N/A full time, N/A part time
Expenses: 2020-2021: $4,320 in state, $4,734 out of state; room/board: $7,500
Financial aid: N/A

Western Washington University
Bellingham WA
(360) 650-3440
U.S. News ranking: Reg. U. (W), No. 16
Website: www.wwu.edu
Admissions email: admissions@wwu.edu
Public; founded 1893
Freshman admissions: selective; 2020-2021: 10,220 applied, 9,556 accepted. Neither SAT nor ACT required. SAT 25/75 percentile: 1080-1270. High school rank: N/A
Early decision deadline: N/A, notification date: N/A
Early action deadline: 11/1, notification date: 12/31
Application deadline (fall): 1/31
Undergraduate student body: 12,622 full time, 1,572 part time; 43% male, 57% female; 0% American Indian, 6% Asian, 2% black, 11% Hispanic, 9% multiracial, 0% Pacific Islander, 69% white, 1% international; N/A from in state; 7% live on campus; N/A of students in fraternities, N/A in sororities
Most popular majors: 14% Business, Management, Marketing, and Related Support Services, 11% Social Sciences, 8% Multi/Interdisciplinary Studies, 7% Natural Resources and Conservation, 6% Visual and Performing Arts
Expenses: 2021-2022: $8,703 in state, $25,930 out of state; room/board: $13,079
Financial aid: (360) 650-3470; 45% of undergrads determined to have financial need; average aid package $18,494

Whatcom Community College[1]
Bellingham WA
(360) 383-3000
U.S. News ranking: Reg. Coll. (W), unranked
Website: www.marlboro.edu/academics/graduate
Admissions email: N/A
Public
Application deadline (fall): N/A
Undergraduate student body: N/A full time, N/A part time
Expenses: 2020-2021: $4,764 in state, $10,209 out of state; room/board: $8,460
Financial aid: N/A

Whitman College
Walla Walla WA
(509) 527-5176
U.S. News ranking: Nat. Lib. Arts, No. 38
Website: www.whitman.edu
Admissions email: admission@whitman.edu
Private; founded 1883
Freshman admissions: more

selective; 2020-2021: 4,964 applied, 2,687 accepted. Neither SAT nor ACT required. SAT 25/75 percentile: 1230-1430. High school rank: 49% in top tenth, 83% in top quarter, 99% in top half
Early decision deadline: 11/15, notification date: 12/20
Early action deadline: N/A, notification date: N/A
Application deadline (fall): 1/15
Undergraduate student body: 1,288 full time, 72 part time; 41% male, 59% female; 0% American Indian, 7% Asian, 3% black, 9% Hispanic, 7% multiracial, 0% Pacific Islander, 60% white, 10% international; 35% from in state; 11% live on campus; 19% of students in fraternities, 16% in sororities
Most popular majors: 24% Social Sciences, 16% Biological and Biomedical Sciences, 11% Visual and Performing Arts, 9% Psychology, 6% Physical Sciences
Expenses: 2021-2022: $55,982; room/board: $13,800
Financial aid: (509) 527-5178; 49% of undergrads determined to have financial need; average aid package $49,511

Whitworth University
Spokane WA
(509) 777-4786
U.S. News ranking: Reg. U. (W), No. 4
Website: www.whitworth.edu
Admissions email: admissions@whitworth.edu
Private; founded 1890
Affiliation: Presbyterian
Freshman admissions: selective; 2020-2021: 3,914 applied, 3,562 accepted. Neither SAT nor ACT required. SAT 25/75 percentile: 1050-1270. High school rank: 33% in top tenth, 64% in top quarter, 88% in top half
Early decision deadline: N/A, notification date: N/A
Early action deadline: 1/15, notification date: 2/15
Application deadline (fall): 8/1
Undergraduate student body: 2,307 full time, 61 part time; 40% male, 60% female; 1% American Indian, 5% Asian, 3% black, 13% Hispanic, 9% multiracial, 2% Pacific Islander, 64% white, 4% international; 70% from in state; 47% live on campus; N/A of students in fraternities, N/A in sororities
Most popular majors: 15% Health Professions and Related Programs, 13% Business, Management, Marketing, and Related Support Services, 9% Psychology, 8% Education, 8% Physical Sciences
Expenses: 2021-2022: $47,590; room/board: $12,500
Financial aid: (509) 777-3215; 74% of undergrads determined to have financial need; average aid package $42,134

Yakima Valley College[1]
Yakima WA
(509) 574-4600
U.S. News ranking: Reg. Coll. (W), unranked
Website: usfsm.edu/
Admissions email: N/A
Public
Application deadline (fall): N/A
Undergraduate student body: N/A full time, N/A part time
Expenses: 2020-2021: $4,770 in state, $5,231 out of state; room/board: $8,364
Financial aid: N/A

WEST VIRGINIA

Alderson Broaddus University
Philippi WV
(800) 263-1549
U.S. News ranking: Reg. Coll. (S), No. 51
Website: www.ab.edu
Admissions email: admissions@ab.edu
Private; founded 1871
Affiliation: American Baptist
Freshman admissions: less selective; 2020-2021: 2,189 applied, 1,155 accepted. Either SAT or ACT required. SAT 25/75 percentile: 850-1050. High school rank: 6% in top tenth, 22% in top quarter, 49% in top half
Early decision deadline: N/A, notification date: N/A
Early action deadline: N/A, notification date: N/A
Application deadline (fall): 8/25
Undergraduate student body: 713 full time, 53 part time; 56% male, 44% female; 1% American Indian, 1% Asian, 32% black, 8% Hispanic, 1% multiracial, 0% Pacific Islander, 53% white, 4% international; 34% from in state; 82% live on campus; 4% of students in fraternities, 5% in sororities
Most popular majors: 18% Registered Nursing/Registered Nurse, 13% Business Administration and Management, General, 10% Kinesiology and Exercise Science, 10% Sport and Fitness Administration/Management, 8% Psychology, General
Expenses: 2021-2022: $30,020; room/board: $9,860
Financial aid: (304) 457-6354; 88% of undergrads determined to have financial need; average aid package $20,650

Bluefield State College
Bluefield WV
(304) 327-4065
U.S. News ranking: Reg. Coll. (S), No. 48
Website: bluefieldstate.edu/
Admissions email: bscadmit@bluefieldstate.edu
Public; founded 1895
Freshman admissions: less selective; 2020-2021: 802 applied, 720 accepted. Either

SAT or ACT required. SAT 25/75 percentile: 850-1070. High school rank: 21% in top tenth, 46% in top quarter, 73% in top half
Early decision deadline: N/A, notification date: N/A
Early action deadline: N/A, notification date: N/A
Application deadline (fall): 8/1
Undergraduate student body: 949 full time, 294 part time; 35% male, 65% female; 0% American Indian, 0% Asian, 9% black, 1% Hispanic, 3% multiracial, 0% Pacific Islander, 84% white, 2% international
Most popular majors: 21% Health Professions and Related Programs, 20% Engineering Technologies and Engineering-Related Fields, 20% Liberal Arts and Sciences, General Studies and Humanities
Expenses: 2021-2022: $8,084 in state, $15,282 out of state; room/board: $9,400
Financial aid: (304) 327-4426; 83% of undergrads determined to have financial need; average aid package $3,357

Concord University
Athens WV
(888) 384-5249
U.S. News ranking: Reg. U. (S), No. 91
Website: www.concord.edu
Admissions email: admissions@concord.edu
Public; founded 1872
Freshman admissions: selective; 2020-2021: 1,625 applied, 1,488 accepted. Either SAT or ACT required. SAT 25/75 percentile: 880-1090. High school rank: 18% in top tenth, 42% in top quarter, 76% in top half
Early decision deadline: N/A, notification date: N/A
Early action deadline: N/A, notification date: N/A
Application deadline (fall): N/A
Undergraduate student body: 1,388 full time, 75 part time; 41% male, 59% female; 0% American Indian, 1% Asian, 6% black, 1% Hispanic, 5% multiracial, 0% Pacific Islander, 79% white, 5% international; 19% from in state; 45% live on campus; N/A of students in fraternities, N/A in sororities
Most popular majors: 20% Liberal Arts and Sciences, General Studies and Humanities, 16% Business, Management, Marketing, and Related Support Services, 13% Education, 9% Biological and Biomedical Sciences, 9% Social Sciences
Expenses: 2021-2022: $8,465 in state, $18,215 out of state; room/board: $9,444
Financial aid: (304) 384-5358; 75% of undergrads determined to have financial need; average aid package $8,831

Davis and Elkins College
Elkins WV
(304) 637-1230
U.S. News ranking: Reg. Coll. (S), No. 27
Website: www.dewv.edu/

Admissions email: admission@dewv.edu
Private; founded 1904
Affiliation: Presbyterian Church (USA)
Freshman admissions: less selective; 2020-2021: 995 applied, 691 accepted. Either SAT or ACT required. SAT 25/75 percentile: 860-1060. High school rank: N/A
Early decision deadline: N/A, notification date: N/A
Early action deadline: N/A, notification date: N/A
Application deadline (fall): rolling
Undergraduate student body: 691 full time, 47 part time; 41% male, 59% female; 0% American Indian, 1% Asian, 3% black, 2% Hispanic, 0% multiracial, 0% Pacific Islander, 29% white, 4% international; 52% from in state; 69% live on campus; 11% of students in fraternities, 11% in sororities
Most popular majors: Information not available
Expenses: 2021-2022: $29,960; room/board: $9,800
Financial aid: (304) 637-1366; 80% of undergrads determined to have financial need; average aid package $27,428

Fairmont State University
Fairmont WV
(304) 367-4010
U.S. News ranking: Reg. U. (S), No. 91
Website: www.fairmontstate.edu
Admissions email: admit@fairmontstate.edu
Public; founded 1865
Freshman admissions: selective; 2020-2021: 2,439 applied, 2,301 accepted. Either SAT or ACT required. SAT 25/75 percentile: 890-1110. High school rank: 17% in top tenth, 39% in top quarter, 70% in top half
Early decision deadline: N/A, notification date: N/A
Early action deadline: N/A, notification date: N/A
Application deadline (fall): 8/1
Undergraduate student body: 2,861 full time, 712 part time; 41% male, 59% female; 0% American Indian, 0% Asian, 4% black, 2% Hispanic, 3% multiracial, 0% Pacific Islander, 88% white, 2% international; 88% from in state; 25% live on campus; 1% of students in fraternities, 2% in sororities
Most popular majors: 24% Registered Nursing/Registered Nurse, 10% Business Administration and Management, General, 7% Criminal Justice/Safety Studies, 5% Education, General, 5% Political Science and Government, General
Expenses: 2021-2022: $7,970 in state, $17,497 out of state; room/board: $10,022
Financial aid: (304) 367-4826; 67% of undergrads determined to have financial need; average aid package $9,116

Glenville State College
Glenville WV
(304) 462-4128
U.S. News ranking: Reg. Coll. (S), No. 43
Website: www.glenville.edu
Admissions email: admissions@glenville.edu
Public; founded 1872
Freshman admissions: less selective; 2020-2021: 1,966 applied, 1,917 accepted. Either SAT or ACT required. SAT 25/75 percentile: 840-1040. High school rank: N/A
Early decision deadline: N/A, notification date: N/A
Early action deadline: N/A, notification date: N/A
Application deadline (fall): rolling
Undergraduate student body: 1,096 full time, 487 part time; 53% male, 47% female; 1% American Indian, 1% Asian, 16% black, 2% Hispanic, 0% multiracial, 0% Pacific Islander, 75% white, 1% international; 84% from in state; 38% live on campus; N/A of students in fraternities, N/A in sororities
Most popular majors: Information not available
Expenses: 2021-2022: $8,386 in state, $10,014 out of state; room/board: $10,382
Financial aid: (304) 462-6171; 84% of undergrads determined to have financial need; average aid package $13,208

Marshall University
Huntington WV
(800) 642-3499
U.S. News ranking: Nat. U., No. 288
Website: www.marshall.edu
Admissions email: admissions@marshall.edu
Public; founded 1837
Freshman admissions: selective; 2020-2021: 6,719 applied, 5,997 accepted. Either SAT or ACT required. SAT 25/75 percentile: 940-1150. High school rank: N/A
Early decision deadline: N/A, notification date: N/A
Early action deadline: N/A, notification date: N/A
Application deadline (fall): 8/9
Undergraduate student body: 7,001 full time, 1,770 part time; 42% male, 58% female; 0% American Indian, 1% Asian, 6% black, 3% Hispanic, 3% multiracial, 0% Pacific Islander, 85% white, 1% international
Most popular majors: Information not available
Expenses: 2021-2022: $8,552 in state, $19,606 out of state; room/board: $10,054
Financial aid: (304) 696-3162; 69% of undergrads determined to have financial need; average aid package $11,440

Ohio Valley University
Vienna WV
(877) 446-8668
U.S. News ranking: Reg. Coll. (S), second tier
Website: www.ovu.edu
Admissions email: admissions@ovu.edu
Private; founded 1958
Affiliation: Churches of Christ
Freshman admissions: less selective; 2020-2021: 289 applied, 274 accepted. Either SAT or ACT required. ACT 25/75 percentile: 18-23. High school rank: N/A
Early decision deadline: N/A, notification date: N/A
Early action deadline: N/A, notification date: N/A
Application deadline (fall): 8/14
Undergraduate student body: 229 full time, 24 part time; 56% male, 44% female; 1% American Indian, 1% Asian, 5% black, 8% Hispanic, 2% multiracial, 0% Pacific Islander, 49% white, 22% international
Most popular majors: 46% Business/Commerce, General, 8% Bible/Biblical Studies, 8% Psychology, General, 5% Mathematics Teacher Education, 2% Biochemistry
Expenses: 2021-2022: $22,550; room/board: $8,790
Financial aid: (304) 865-6076; 64% of undergrads determined to have financial need; average aid package $17,721

Salem University[1]
Salem WV
(304) 326-1109
U.S. News ranking: Reg. U. (S), second tier
Website: www.salemu.edu
Admissions email: admissions@salemu.edu
For-profit
Application deadline (fall): N/A
Undergraduate student body: N/A full time, N/A part time
Expenses: 2020-2021: $16,900; room/board: $8,400
Financial aid: N/A

Shepherd University
Shepherdstown WV
(304) 876-5212
U.S. News ranking: Nat. Lib. Arts, second tier
Website: www.shepherd.edu
Admissions email: admission@shepherd.edu
Public; founded 1871
Freshman admissions: selective; 2020-2021: 1,651 applied, 1,613 accepted. Either SAT or ACT required. SAT 25/75 percentile: 940-1150. High school rank: N/A
Early decision deadline: N/A, notification date: N/A
Early action deadline: 11/15, notification date: 12/1
Application deadline (fall): rolling
Undergraduate student body: 2,255 full time, 461 part time; 41% male, 59% female; 0% American Indian, 2% Asian, 8% black, 7% Hispanic, 5% multiracial, 0% Pacific Islander, 74% white, 1% international; 69% from in state; 32% live on campus; 2% of students in fraternities, 3% in sororities
Most popular majors: 15% Health Professions and Related Programs, 14% Liberal Arts and Sciences, General Studies and Humanities, 12% Business, Management, Marketing, and Related Support Services, 11% Education, 6% Parks, Recreation, Leisure, and Fitness Studies
Expenses: 2021-2022: $7,784 in state, $18,224 out of state; room/board: $12,462
Financial aid: (304) 876-5470; 60% of undergrads determined to have financial need; average aid package $12,565

University of Charleston
Charleston WV
(800) 995-4682
U.S. News ranking: Nat. U., second tier
Website: www.ucwv.edu
Admissions email: admissions@ucwv.edu
Private; founded 1888
Freshman admissions: selective; 2020-2021: 2,793 applied, 1,716 accepted. Neither SAT nor ACT required. ACT 25/75 percentile: 19-23. High school rank: N/A
Early decision deadline: N/A, notification date: N/A
Early action deadline: N/A, notification date: N/A
Application deadline (fall): rolling
Undergraduate student body: 1,189 full time, 926 part time; 58% male, 42% female; 2% American Indian, 1% Asian, 9% black, 4% Hispanic, 0% multiracial, 0% Pacific Islander, 53% white, 6% international
Most popular majors: 51% Organizational Leadership, 8% Business Administration and Management, General, 8% Registered Nursing/Registered Nurse, 7% Biology/Biological Sciences, General, 4% Accounting
Expenses: 2020-2021: $31,400; room/board: $9,510
Financial aid: (304) 357-4944

West Liberty University
West Liberty WV
(304) 336-8076
U.S. News ranking: Reg. U. (S), No. 59
Website: www.westliberty.edu
Admissions email: admissions@westliberty.edu
Public; founded 1837
Freshman admissions: selective; 2020-2021: 1,857 applied, 1,271 accepted. Either SAT or ACT required. ACT 25/75 percentile: 17-23. High school rank: 16% in top tenth, 43% in top quarter, 76% in top half
Early decision deadline: N/A, notification date: N/A
Early action deadline: N/A, notification date: N/A
Application deadline (fall): rolling
Undergraduate student body: 1,767 full time, 358 part time; 36% male, 64% female; 0% American Indian, 1% Asian, 4% black, 1% Hispanic, 1% multiracial, 0% Pacific Islander, 77% white, 3% international
Most popular majors: 16% Business Administration and Management, General, 11% General Studies, 10% Dental Hygiene/Hygienist, 8% Registered Nursing/Registered Nurse, 7% Elementary Education and Teaching
Expenses: 2020-2021: $8,150 in state, $16,090 out of state; room/board: $9,806
Financial aid: (304) 336-8016

West Virginia State University[1]
Institute WV
(304) 766-4345
U.S. News ranking: Reg. Coll. (S), No. 62
Website: www.wvstateu.edu
Admissions email: admissions@wvstateu.edu
Public; founded 1891
Application deadline (fall): 8/17
Undergraduate student body: N/A full time, N/A part time
Expenses: 2020-2021: $8,437 in state, $14,125 out of state; room/board: $12,886
Financial aid: (304) 204-4361

West Virginia University[1]
Morgantown WV
(304) 442-3146
U.S. News ranking: Nat. U., No. 249
Website: www.wvu.edu
Admissions email: go2wvu@mail.wvu.edu
Public; founded 1867
Application deadline (fall): 8/1
Undergraduate student body: N/A full time, N/A part time
Expenses: 2020-2021: $8,976 in state, $25,320 out of state; room/board: $10,948
Financial aid: (304) 293-8571

West Virginia University Institute of Technology[1]
Beckley WV
(304) 442-3146
U.S. News ranking: Reg. Coll. (S), No. 66
Website: www.wvutech.edu
Admissions email: tech-admissions@mail.wvu.edu
Public; founded 1895
Application deadline (fall): rolling
Undergraduate student body: N/A full time, N/A part time
Expenses: 2020-2021: $7,560 in state, $18,912 out of state; room/board: $11,314
Financial aid: (304) 293-8571

West Virginia University–Parkersburg[1]
Parkersburg WV
(304) 424-8000
U.S. News ranking: Reg. Coll. (S), second tier
Website: www.wvup.edu
Admissions email: info@mail.wvup.edu

BEST COLLEGES

Public
Application deadline (fall): N/A
Undergraduate student body: N/A
full time, N/A part time
Expenses: 2020-2021: $3,890 in
state, $8,642 out of state; room/
board: N/A
Financial aid: N/A

West Virginia Wesleyan College
Buckhannon WV
(800) 722-9933
U.S. News ranking: Reg. U. (S),
No. 60
Website: www.wvwc.edu
Admissions email:
admissions@wvwc.edu
Private; founded 1890
Affiliation: United Methodist
Freshman admissions: selective;
2020-2021: 2,175 applied,
1,433 accepted. Neither SAT
nor ACT required. SAT 25/75
percentile: 880-1100. High school
rank: 18% in top tenth, 30% in
top quarter, 69% in top half
Early decision deadline: N/A,
notification date: N/A
Early action deadline: N/A,
notification date: N/A
Application deadline (fall): 8/15
Undergraduate student body:
971 full time, 8 part time; 46%
male, 54% female; 0% American
Indian, 1% Asian, 12% black,
5% Hispanic, 4% multiracial,
0% Pacific Islander, 73% white,
5% international; 43% from in
state; N/A live on campus; 25%
of students in fraternities, 25%
in sororities
Most popular majors: 14%
Business, Management,
Marketing, and Related Support
Services, 12% Education, 9%
Parks, Recreation, Leisure, and
Fitness Studies, 8% Social
Sciences, 7% Biological and
Biomedical Sciences
Expenses: 2021-2022: $32,612;
room/board: $10,054
Financial aid: (304) 473-8080;
79% of undergrads determined to
have financial need; average aid
package $32,675

Wheeling University
Wheeling WV
(304) 243-2359
U.S. News ranking: Reg. U. (S),
No. 80
Website: www.wheeling.edu
Admissions email:
admiss@wheeling.edu
Private; founded 1954
Affiliation: Roman Catholic
Freshman admissions: less
selective; 2020-2021: 1,032
applied, 812 accepted. Neither
SAT nor ACT required. SAT 25/75
percentile: 890-1090. High
school rank: N/A
Early decision deadline: N/A,
notification date: N/A
Early action deadline: N/A,
notification date: N/A
Application deadline (fall): rolling
Undergraduate student body:
582 full time, 0 part time; 58%
male, 42% female; 1% American
Indian, 2% Asian, 26% black,
7% Hispanic, 0% multiracial,
0% Pacific Islander, 50% white,

5% international; 18% from in
state; 89% live on campus; 0%
of students in fraternities, 0% in
sororities
Most popular majors: 28%
Business Administration and
Management, General, 27%
Registered Nursing/Registered
Nurse, 13% Education, General,
10% Criminal Justice/Safety
Studies, 8% Kinesiology and
Exercise Science
Expenses: 2020-2021: $29,290;
room/board: $10,620
Financial aid: (304) 243-2304

WISCONSIN

Alverno College
Milwaukee WI
(414) 382-6100
U.S. News ranking: Reg. U. (Mid.
W), No. 69
Website: www.alverno.edu
Admissions email:
admissions@alverno.edu
Private; founded 1887
Affiliation: Roman Catholic
Freshman admissions: selective;
2020-2021: 758 applied, 593
accepted. Either SAT or ACT
required. ACT 25/75 percentile:
17-20. High school rank: N/A
Early decision deadline: N/A,
notification date: N/A
Early action deadline: N/A,
notification date: N/A
Application deadline (fall): rolling
Undergraduate student body: 864
full time, 229 part time; 3%
male, 97% female; 0% American
Indian, 5% Asian, 13% black,
35% Hispanic, 4% multiracial,
0% Pacific Islander, 41% white,
0% international; 90% from in
state; 14% live on campus; N/A
of students in fraternities, 0% in
sororities
Most popular majors: 33% Health
Professions and Related Programs,
18% Education, 13% Liberal Arts
and Sciences, General Studies
and Humanities, 12% Business,
Management, Marketing, and
Related Support Services, 6%
Psychology
Expenses: 2021-2022: $31,258;
room/board: $8,620
Financial aid: (414) 382-6040;
88% of undergrads determined to
have financial need; average aid
package $27,291

Beloit College
Beloit WI
(608) 363-2500
U.S. News ranking: Nat. Lib. Arts,
No. 75
Website: www.beloit.edu
Admissions email:
admissions@beloit.edu
Private; founded 1846
Freshman admissions: more
selective; 2020-2021: 3,140
applied, 1,832 accepted. Neither
SAT nor ACT required. ACT 25/75
percentile: 21-29. High school
rank: 28% in top tenth, 59% in
top quarter, 92% in top half
Early decision deadline: 11/1,
notification date: 12/1
Early action deadline: 12/1,
notification date: 1/1
Application deadline (fall): 7/1

Undergraduate student body: 924
full time, 54 part time; 46%
male, 54% female; 0% American
Indian, 3% Asian, 9% black,
17% Hispanic, 3% multiracial,
0% Pacific Islander, 49% white,
15% international; 21% from in
state; 74% live on campus; 14%
of students in fraternities, 18%
in sororities
Most popular majors: 22%
Social Sciences, 10% Physical
Sciences, 10% Psychology, 7%
English Language and Literature/
Letters, 7% Foreign Languages,
Literatures, and Linguistics
Expenses: 2021-2022: $54,680;
room/board: $10,028
Financial aid: (608) 363-2696;
67% of undergrads determined to
have financial need; average aid
package $51,934

Cardinal Stritch University
Milwaukee WI
(414) 410-4040
U.S. News ranking: Nat. U.,
second tier
Website: www.stritch.edu
Admissions email:
admissions@stritch.edu
Private; founded 1937
Affiliation: Roman Catholic
Freshman admissions: selective;
2020-2021: 736 applied, 566
accepted. Neither SAT nor ACT
required. ACT 25/75 percentile:
17-23. High school rank: 21%
in top tenth, 45% in top quarter,
76% in top half
Early decision deadline: N/A,
notification date: N/A
Early action deadline: N/A,
notification date: N/A
Application deadline (fall): rolling
Undergraduate student body: 576
full time, 492 part time; 30%
male, 70% female; 1% American
Indian, 2% Asian, 18% black,
19% Hispanic, 3% multiracial,
0% Pacific Islander, 35% white,
21% international
Most popular majors: 25%
Registered Nursing/Registered
Nurse, 12% Organizational
Leadership, 7% Business
Administration and Management,
General, 5% Business/Commerce,
General, 5% Elementary
Education and Teaching
Expenses: 2021-2022: $34,762;
room/board: $9,766
Financial aid: (414) 410-4016;
63% of undergrads determined to
have financial need; average aid
package $26,935

Carroll University
Waukesha WI
(262) 524-7220
U.S. News ranking: Reg. U. (Mid.
W), No. 31
Website: www.carrollu.edu/
Admissions email:
admission@carrollu.edu
Private; founded 1846
Affiliation: Presbyterian
Freshman admissions: selective;
2020-2021: N/A applied, N/A
accepted. Neither SAT nor ACT
required. ACT 25/75 percentile:
21-26. High school rank: 22%
in top tenth, 54% in top quarter,

86% in top half
Early decision deadline: N/A,
notification date: N/A
Early action deadline: N/A,
notification date: N/A
Application deadline (fall): rolling
Undergraduate student body: 2,783
full time, 174 part time; 31%
male, 69% female; 0% American
Indian, 4% Asian, 2% black, 9%
Hispanic, 3% multiracial, 0%
Pacific Islander, 79% white, 1%
international
Most popular majors: 17%
Registered Nursing/Registered
Nurse, 14% Kinesiology and
Exercise Science, 9% Psychology,
General, 7% Biology/Biological
Sciences, General, 6% Health/
Health Care Administration/
Management
Expenses: 2021-2022: $35,140;
room/board: $10,340
Financial aid: (262) 524-7296;
76% of undergrads determined to
have financial need; average aid
package $26,862

Carthage College
Kenosha WI
(262) 551-6000
U.S. News ranking: Reg. Coll. (Mid.
W), No. 14
Website: www.carthage.edu
Admissions email:
admissions@carthage.edu
Private; founded 1847
Affiliation: Evangelical Lutheran
Church
Freshman admissions: selective;
2020-2021: 7,099 applied,
5,440 accepted. Neither SAT
nor ACT required. ACT 25/75
percentile: 20-26. High school
rank: 17% in top tenth, 45% in
top quarter, 79% in top half
Early decision deadline: N/A,
notification date: N/A
Early action deadline: 11/15,
notification date: 11/22
Application deadline (fall): rolling
Undergraduate student body: 2,554
full time, 87 part time; 44%
male, 56% female; 0% American
Indian, 2% Asian, 5% black,
15% Hispanic, 4% multiracial,
0% Pacific Islander, 69% white,
1% international; 38% from in
state; 61% live on campus; 1%
of students in fraternities, 1% in
sororities
Most popular majors: 28%
Business, Management,
Marketing, and Related Support
Services, 9% Biological and
Biomedical Sciences, 9%
Education, 9% Visual and
Performing Arts, 7% Health
Professions and Related Programs
Expenses: 2021-2022: $33,000;
room/board: $12,400
Financial aid: (262) 551-6001;
75% of undergrads determined to
have financial need; average aid
package $22,646

Concordia University Wisconsin
Mequon WI
(262) 243-4300
U.S. News ranking: Nat. U.,
No. 277
Website: www.cuw.edu

Admissions email:
admissions@cuw.edu
Private; founded 1881
Affiliation: Lutheran Church -
Missouri Synod
Freshman admissions: more
selective; 2020-2021: 3,509
applied, 2,475 accepted. Neither
SAT nor ACT required. ACT 25/75
percentile: 20-26. High school
rank: 32% in top tenth, 58% in
top quarter, 86% in top half
Early decision deadline: N/A,
notification date: N/A
Early action deadline: N/A,
notification date: N/A
Application deadline (fall): N/A
Undergraduate student body: 2,236
full time, 859 part time; 37%
male, 63% female; 1% American
Indian, 2% Asian, 8% black, 6%
Hispanic, 3% multiracial, 0%
Pacific Islander, 71% white, 4%
international
Most popular majors: Information
not available
Expenses: 2021-2022: $31,952;
room/board: $11,750
Financial aid: (262) 243-2025

Edgewood College[1]
Madison WI
(608) 663-2294
U.S. News ranking: Nat. U.,
No. 239
Website: www.edgewood.edu
Admissions email:
admissions@edgewood.edu
Private; founded 1927
Affiliation: Roman Catholic
Application deadline (fall): 8/1
Undergraduate student body: N/A
full time, N/A part time
Expenses: 2020-2021: $31,700;
room/board: $11,700
Financial aid: (608) 663-4300

Herzing University[1]
Madison WI
(800) 596-0724
U.S. News ranking: Reg. U. (Mid.
W), second tier
Website: www.herzing.edu/
Admissions email:
info@msn.herzing.edu
Private; founded 1965
Affiliation: Other
Application deadline (fall): N/A
Undergraduate student body: N/A
full time, N/A part time
Expenses: 2020-2021: $14,200;
room/board: N/A
Financial aid: N/A

Holy Family College[1]
Manitowoc WI
(920) 686-6175
U.S. News ranking: Reg. U. (Mid.
W), second tier
Website: www.sl.edu
Admissions email:
admissions@sl.edu
Private; founded 1935
Affiliation: Roman Catholic
Application deadline (fall): rolling
Undergraduate student body: N/A
full time, N/A part time
Expenses: N/A
Financial aid: (920) 686-6175

Lakeland University[1]
Plymouth WI
(920) 565-1226
U.S. News ranking: Reg. U. (Mid. W), second tier
Website: www.lakeland.edu
Admissions email: admissions@lakeland.edu
Private; founded 1862
Application deadline (fall): rolling
Undergraduate student body: N/A full time, N/A part time
Expenses: 2020-2021: $30,777; room/board: $9,634
Financial aid: N/A

Lawrence University
Appleton WI
(800) 227-0982
U.S. News ranking: Nat. Lib. Arts, No. 62
Website: www.lawrence.edu
Admissions email: admissions@lawrence.edu
Private; founded 1847
Freshman admissions: more selective; 2020-2021: 3,028 applied, 2,087 accepted. Neither SAT nor ACT required. ACT 25/75 percentile: 26-32. High school rank: 40% in top tenth, 69% in top quarter, 97% in top half
Early decision deadline: 11/1, notification date: 12/1
Early action deadline: 11/1, notification date: 12/15
Application deadline (fall): 1/15
Undergraduate student body: 1,393 full time, 39 part time; 45% male, 55% female; 0% American Indian, 6% Asian, 6% black, 11% Hispanic, 4% multiracial, 0% Pacific Islander, 59% white, 12% international; 24% from in state; 62% live on campus; 8% of students in fraternities, 8% in sororities
Most popular majors: 20% Visual and Performing Arts, 15% Social Sciences, 14% Biological and Biomedical Sciences, 9% Psychology, 7% Physical Sciences
Expenses: 2021-2022: $52,401; room/board: $11,184
Financial aid: (920) 832-6584; 64% of undergrads determined to have financial need; average aid package $45,529

Maranatha Baptist University
Watertown WI
(920) 206-2327
U.S. News ranking: Reg. Coll. (Mid. W), No. 25
Website: www.mbu.edu
Admissions email: admissions@mbu.edu
Private; founded 1968
Affiliation: Baptist
Freshman admissions: more selective; 2020-2021: 282 applied, 227 accepted. Either SAT or ACT required. ACT 25/75 percentile: 20-28. High school rank: 44% in top tenth, 52% in top quarter, 65% in top half
Early decision deadline: N/A, notification date: N/A
Early action deadline: N/A, notification date: N/A
Application deadline (fall): rolling
Undergraduate student body: 519

full time, 229 part time; 41% male, 59% female; 0% American Indian, 2% Asian, 1% black, 5% Hispanic, 4% multiracial, 0% Pacific Islander, 84% white, 1% international; 22% from in state; 69% live on campus; N/A of students in fraternities, N/A in sororities
Most popular majors: 10% Business Administration and Management, General, 9% Humanities/Humanistic Studies, 9% Registered Nursing/Registered Nurse, 8% Pastoral Studies/Counseling, 7% Early Childhood Education and Teaching
Expenses: 2021-2022: $18,050; room/board: $7,980
Financial aid: (920) 206-2318

Marian University
Fond du Lac WI
(920) 923-7650
U.S. News ranking: Reg. U. (Mid. W), No. 112
Website: www.marianuniversity.edu/
Admissions email: admissions@marianuniversity.edu
Private; founded 1936
Affiliation: Roman Catholic
Freshman admissions: less selective; 2020-2021: 1,551 applied, 1,052 accepted. Either SAT or ACT required. ACT 25/75 percentile: 17-22. High school rank: 1% in top tenth, 30% in top quarter, 60% in top half
Early decision deadline: N/A, notification date: N/A
Early action deadline: N/A, notification date: N/A
Application deadline (fall): rolling
Undergraduate student body: 1,119 full time, 171 part time; 31% male, 69% female; 1% American Indian, 1% Asian, 6% black, 9% Hispanic, 2% multiracial, 0% Pacific Islander, 73% white, 4% international
Most popular majors: 15% Registered Nursing/Registered Nurse, 8% Family Practice Nurse/Nursing, 6% Teacher Education and Professional Development, Specific Levels and Methods, Other, 5% Psychology, General, 5% Radiologic Technology/Science - Radiographer
Expenses: 2021-2022: $29,130; room/board: $7,970
Financial aid: (920) 923-7614; 87% of undergrads determined to have financial need; average aid package $21,490

Marquette University
Milwaukee WI
(800) 222-6544
U.S. News ranking: Nat. U., No. 83
Website: www.marquette.edu
Admissions email: admissions@marquette.edu
Private; founded 1881
Affiliation: Roman Catholic
Freshman admissions: more selective; 2020-2021: 15,324 applied, 12,641 accepted. Neither SAT nor ACT required. ACT 25/75 percentile: 25-30. High school rank: 39% in top tenth, 75% in top quarter, 96% in top half

Early decision deadline: N/A, notification date: N/A
Early action deadline: N/A, notification date: N/A
Application deadline (fall): 12/1
Undergraduate student body: 7,715 full time, 309 part time; 45% male, 55% female; 0% American Indian, 6% Asian, 4% black, 15% Hispanic, 3% multiracial, 0% Pacific Islander, 69% white, 2% international; 33% from in state; 45% live on campus; N/A of students in fraternities, N/A in sororities
Most popular majors: 23% Business, Management, Marketing, and Related Support Services, 13% Biological and Biomedical Sciences, 11% Engineering, 11% Social Sciences, 9% Health Professions and Related Programs
Expenses: 2021-2022: $45,766; room/board: $14,140
Financial aid: (414) 288-4000; 59% of undergrads determined to have financial need; average aid package $34,034

Milwaukee Institute of Art and Design[1]
Milwaukee WI
(414) 291-8070
U.S. News ranking: Arts, unranked
Website: www.miad.edu
Admissions email: admissions@miad.edu
Private; founded 1974
Application deadline (fall): 8/15
Undergraduate student body: N/A full time, N/A part time
Expenses: 2020-2021: $39,560; room/board: $9,490
Financial aid: (414) 847-3270

Milwaukee School of Engineering
Milwaukee WI
(800) 332-6763
U.S. News ranking: Reg. U. (Mid. W), No. 8
Website: www.msoe.edu
Admissions email: explore@msoe.edu
Private; founded 1903
Freshman admissions: more selective; 2020-2021: 4,059 applied, 2,439 accepted. Neither SAT nor ACT required. ACT 25/75 percentile: 25-30. High school rank: N/A
Early decision deadline: N/A, notification date: N/A
Early action deadline: N/A, notification date: N/A
Application deadline (fall): N/A
Undergraduate student body: 2,412 full time, 98 part time; 72% male, 28% female; 0% American Indian, 5% Asian, 2% black, 8% Hispanic, 3% multiracial, 0% Pacific Islander, 72% white, 3% international; 63% from in state; 31% live on campus; N/A of students in fraternities, N/A in sororities
Most popular majors: 22% Mechanical Engineering, 15% Electrical and Electronics Engineering, 12% Registered Nursing/Registered Nurse, 8% Bioengineering and Biomedical Engineering, 7% Computer

Software Engineering
Expenses: 2021-2022: $45,099; room/board: $10,827
Financial aid: (414) 277-7224; 80% of undergrads determined to have financial need; average aid package $31,046

Mount Mary University
Milwaukee WI
(414) 930-3024
U.S. News ranking: Reg. U. (Mid. W), No. 51
Website: www.mtmary.edu
Admissions email: mmu-admiss@mtmary.edu
Private; founded 1913
Affiliation: Roman Catholic
Freshman admissions: selective; 2020-2021: 1,296 applied, 687 accepted. Neither SAT nor ACT required. ACT 25/75 percentile: 16-20. High school rank: 17% in top tenth, 41% in top quarter, 73% in top half
Early decision deadline: N/A, notification date: N/A
Early action deadline: N/A, notification date: N/A
Undergraduate student body: 577 full time, 59 part time; 0% male, 100% female; 0% American Indian, 8% Asian, 18% black, 27% Hispanic, 3% multiracial, 0% Pacific Islander, 35% white, 1% international; 93% from in state; 21% live on campus; N/A of students in fraternities, N/A in sororities
Most popular majors: 24% Health Professions and Related Programs, 16% Business, Management, Marketing, and Related Support Services, 12% Psychology, 11% Visual and Performing Arts, 7% Biological and Biomedical Sciences
Expenses: 2021-2022: $32,760; room/board: $9,640
Financial aid: (414) 930-3431; 92% of undergrads determined to have financial need; average aid package $26,879

Northland College
Ashland WI
(715) 682-1224
U.S. News ranking: Reg. Coll. (Mid. W), No. 19
Website: www.northland.edu
Admissions email: admit@northland.edu
Private; founded 1892
Freshman admissions: selective; 2020-2021: 1,706 applied, 1,097 accepted. Neither SAT nor ACT required. ACT 25/75 percentile: 22-23. High school rank: 22% in top tenth, 51% in top quarter, 89% in top half
Early decision deadline: N/A, notification date: N/A
Early action deadline: N/A, notification date: N/A
Application deadline (fall): rolling
Undergraduate student body: 545 full time, 25 part time; 46% male, 54% female; 3% American Indian, 2% Asian, 4% black, 7% Hispanic, 5% multiracial, 0% Pacific Islander, 69% white, 7% international; 42% from in state; 67% live on campus; 0%

of students in fraternities, 0% in sororities
Most popular majors: 13% Business Administration and Management, General, 10% Biology/Biological Sciences, General, 9% Natural Resources Conservation and Research, Other, 8% Sociology, 6% Forestry, Other
Expenses: 2021-2022: $39,895; room/board: $9,688
Financial aid: (715) 682-1255; 80% of undergrads determined to have financial need; average aid package $33,297

Ripon College
Ripon WI
(920) 748-8709
U.S. News ranking: Nat. Lib. Arts, No. 128
Website: www.ripon.edu
Admissions email: adminfo@ripon.edu
Private; founded 1851
Freshman admissions: selective; 2020-2021: 2,614 applied, 1,936 accepted. Neither SAT nor ACT required. ACT 25/75 percentile: 18-25. High school rank: 12% in top tenth, 46% in top quarter, 83% in top half
Early decision deadline: N/A, notification date: N/A
Early action deadline: N/A, notification date: N/A
Application deadline (fall): rolling
Undergraduate student body: 801 full time, 15 part time; 47% male, 53% female; 0% American Indian, 2% Asian, 3% black, 10% Hispanic, 3% multiracial, 0% Pacific Islander, 79% white, 2% international; 70% from in state; 98% live on campus; 31% of students in fraternities, 27% in sororities
Most popular majors: 16% Business/Commerce, General, 12% Biology/Biological Sciences, General, 9% History, General, 8% Political Science and Government, General, 8% Psychology, General
Expenses: 2021-2022: $48,100; room/board: $9,090
Financial aid: (920) 748-8101; 89% of undergrads determined to have financial need; average aid package $40,800

St. Norbert College
De Pere WI
(800) 236-4878
U.S. News ranking: Nat. Lib. Arts, No. 117
Website: www.snc.edu
Admissions email: admit@snc.edu
Private; founded 1898
Affiliation: Roman Catholic
Freshman admissions: more selective; 2020-2021: 3,358 applied, 2,829 accepted. Neither SAT nor ACT required. ACT 25/75 percentile: 22-28. High school rank: 27% in top tenth, 60% in top quarter, 90% in top half
Early decision deadline: N/A, notification date: N/A
Early action deadline: N/A, notification date: N/A
Application deadline (fall): rolling
Undergraduate student body: 1,851 full time, 16 part time; 41% male, 59% female; 1% American

Indian, 1% Asian, 1% black, 5% Hispanic, 2% multiracial, 0% Pacific Islander, 88% white, 1% international; 78% from in state; 86% live on campus; 10% of students in fraternities, 10% in sororities
Most popular majors: 27% Business, Management, Marketing, and Related Support Services, 12% Education, 11% Communication, Journalism, and Related Programs, 10% Biological and Biomedical Sciences, 10% Social Sciences
Expenses: 2021-2022: $41,887; room/board: $11,158
Financial aid: (920) 403-3071; 68% of undergrads determined to have financial need; average aid package $28,755

University of Wisconsin–Eau Claire
Eau Claire WI
(715) 836-5415
U.S. News ranking: Reg. U. (Mid. W), No. 41
Website: www.uwec.edu
Admissions email: admissions@uwec.edu
Public; founded 1916
Freshman admissions: selective; 2020-2021: 5,577 applied, 5,002 accepted. Neither SAT nor ACT required. ACT 25/75 percentile: 21-26. High school rank: 19% in top tenth, 48% in top quarter, 89% in top half
Early decision deadline: N/A, notification date: N/A
Early action deadline: N/A, notification date: N/A
Application deadline (fall): 8/20
Undergraduate student body: 9,131 full time, 672 part time; 38% male, 62% female; 0% American Indian, 3% Asian, 1% black, 4% Hispanic, 3% multiracial, 0% Pacific Islander, 87% white, 2% international; 68% from in state; 22% live on campus; N/A of students in fraternities, N/A in sororities
Most popular majors: 24% Business, Management, Marketing, and Related Support Services, 14% Health Professions and Related Programs, 8% Education, 6% Biological and Biomedical Sciences, 6% Psychology
Expenses: 2021-2022: $8,874 in state, $17,150 out of state; room/board: $8,572
Financial aid: (715) 836-3000; 45% of undergrads determined to have financial need; average aid package $10,591

University of Wisconsin–Green Bay[1]
Green Bay WI
(920) 465-2111
U.S. News ranking: Reg. U. (Mid. W), No. 104
Website: www.uwgb.edu
Admissions email: uwgb@uwgb.edu
Public; founded 1965
Application deadline (fall): rolling
Undergraduate student body: N/A full time, N/A part time

Expenses: 2020-2021: $7,873 in state, $16,091 out of state; room/board: $7,280
Financial aid: (920) 465-2111

University of Wisconsin–La Crosse
La Crosse WI
(608) 785-8939
U.S. News ranking: Reg. U. (Mid. W), No. 37
Website: www.uwlax.edu
Admissions email: admissions@uwlax.edu
Public; founded 1909
Freshman admissions: more selective; 2020-2021: 5,563 applied, 4,550 accepted. Neither SAT nor ACT required. ACT 25/75 percentile: 22-26. High school rank: 23% in top tenth, 60% in top quarter, 96% in top half
Early decision deadline: N/A, notification date: N/A
Early action deadline: N/A, notification date: N/A
Application deadline (fall): N/A
Undergraduate student body: 8,797 full time, 682 part time; 43% male, 57% female; 0% American Indian, 2% Asian, 1% black, 4% Hispanic, 3% multiracial, 0% Pacific Islander, 89% white, 0% international; N/A from in state; 29% live on campus; N/A of students in fraternities, N/A in sororities
Most popular majors: 24% Business, Management, Marketing, and Related Support Services, 14% Biological and Biomedical Sciences, 10% Psychology
Expenses: 2020-2021: $9,109 in state, $17,928 out of state; room/board: $6,637
Financial aid: (608) 785-8604; 42% of undergrads determined to have financial need; average aid package $7,823

University of Wisconsin–Madison
Madison WI
(608) 262-3961
U.S. News ranking: Nat. U., No. 42
Website: www.wisc.edu
Admissions email: onwisconsin@admissions.wisc.edu
Public; founded 1848
Freshman admissions: more selective; 2020-2021: 45,941 applied, 26,289 accepted. Neither SAT nor ACT required. ACT 25/75 percentile: 27-32. High school rank: 51% in top tenth, 88% in top quarter, 99% in top half
Early decision deadline: N/A, notification date: N/A
Early action deadline: 11/1, notification date: 12/31
Application deadline (fall): 2/1
Undergraduate student body: 30,089 full time, 3,496 part time; 48% male, 52% female; 0% American Indian, 8% Asian, 2% black, 6% Hispanic, 4% multiracial, 0% Pacific Islander, 68% white, 9% international; 61% from in state; 22% live on campus; 9% of students in fraternities, 8% in sororities
Most popular majors: 8% Computer and Information Sciences,

General, 8% Economics, General, 6% Psychology, General, 5% Biology/Biological Sciences, General, 5% Political Science and Government, General
Expenses: 2021-2022: $10,720 in state, $38,608 out of state; room/board: $12,548
Financial aid: (608) 262-3060; 35% of undergrads determined to have financial need; average aid package $18,976

University of Wisconsin–Milwaukee
Milwaukee WI
(414) 229-2222
U.S. News ranking: Nat. U., second tier
Website: www.uwm.edu
Admissions email: undergraduateadmissions@uwm.edu
Public; founded 1956
Freshman admissions: selective; 2020-2021: 8,583 applied, 8,312 accepted. Neither SAT nor ACT required. ACT 25/75 percentile: 19-24. High school rank: 12% in top tenth, 20% in top quarter, 66% in top half
Early decision deadline: N/A, notification date: N/A
Early action deadline: N/A, notification date: N/A
Application deadline (fall): 9/1
Undergraduate student body: 16,618 full time, 3,595 part time; 46% male, 54% female; 0% American Indian, 7% Asian, 7% black, 13% Hispanic, 4% multiracial, 0% Pacific Islander, 66% white, 2% international; 88% from in state; 10% live on campus; N/A of students in fraternities, N/A in sororities
Most popular majors: 20% History, 11% Business, Management, Marketing, and Related Support Services, 8% Homeland Security, Law Enforcement, Firefighting and Related Protective Services, 7% Communication, Journalism, and Related Programs, 6% Foreign Languages, Literatures, and Linguistics
Expenses: 2020-2021: $9,254 in state, $21,119 out of state; room/board: $10,692
Financial aid: N/A

University of Wisconsin–Oshkosh[1]
Oshkosh WI
(920) 424-3164
U.S. News ranking: Reg. U. (Mid. W), No. 101
Website: www.uwosh.edu
Admissions email: admissions@uwosh.edu
Public; founded 1871
Application deadline (fall): rolling
Undergraduate student body: N/A full time, N/A part time
Expenses: 2020-2021: $7,717 in state, $15,290 out of state; room/board: $8,506
Financial aid: (920) 424-3377

University of Wisconsin–Parkside[7]
Kenosha WI
(262) 595-2355
U.S. News ranking: Nat. Lib. Arts, second tier
Website: www.uwp.edu/
Admissions email: admissions@uwp.edu
Public; founded 1968
Freshman admissions: selective; 2020-2021: 2,048 applied, 1,358 accepted. Neither SAT nor ACT required. ACT 25/75 percentile: 17-23. High school rank: 15% in top tenth, 37% in top quarter, 76% in top half
Early decision deadline: N/A, notification date: N/A
Early action deadline: N/A, notification date: N/A
Application deadline (fall): rolling
Undergraduate student body: 2,947 full time, 857 part time
Most popular majors: 28% Business, Management, and Related Support Services, 10% Psychology, 8% Homeland Security, Law Enforcement, Firefighting and Related Protective Services, 7% Biological and Biomedical Sciences, 6% Visual and Performing Arts
Expenses: 2021-2022: $7,444 in state, $15,714 out of state; room/board: $8,408
Financial aid: (262) 595-2574; 62% of undergrads determined to have financial need; average aid package $9,277

University of Wisconsin–Platteville[1]
Platteville WI
(608) 342-1125
U.S. News ranking: Reg. U. (Mid. W), No. 82
Website: www.uwplatt.edu
Admissions email: admit@uwplatt.edu
Public; founded 1866
Application deadline (fall): rolling
Undergraduate student body: N/A full time, N/A part time
Expenses: 2020-2021: $7,873 in state, $16,148 out of state; room/board: $7,770
Financial aid: (608) 342-6188

University of Wisconsin–River Falls
River Falls WI
(715) 425-3500
U.S. News ranking: Reg. U. (Mid. W), No. 95
Website: www.uwrf.edu
Admissions email: admissions@uwrf.edu
Public; founded 1874
Freshman admissions: selective; 2020-2021: 2,782 applied, 2,138 accepted. Either SAT or ACT required. ACT 25/75 percentile: 19-25. High school rank: 12% in top tenth, 24% in top quarter, 73% in top half
Early decision deadline: N/A, notification date: N/A
Early action deadline: N/A, notification date: N/A
Application deadline (fall): rolling

Undergraduate student body: 4,800 full time, 628 part time; 35% male, 65% female; 0% American Indian, 3% Asian, 1% black, 4% Hispanic, 3% multiracial, 0% Pacific Islander, 89% white, 1% international; 52% from in state; 32% live on campus; N/A of students in fraternities, N/A in sororities
Most popular majors: 19% Agriculture, Agriculture Operations, and Related Sciences, 17% Business, Management, Marketing, and Related Support Services, 13% Education
Expenses: 2021-2022: $8,063 in state, $15,636 out of state; room/board: $6,870
Financial aid: (715) 425-3141; 53% of undergrads determined to have financial need; average aid package $7,038

University of Wisconsin–Stevens Point
Stevens Point WI
(715) 346-2441
U.S. News ranking: Reg. U. (Mid. W), No. 64
Website: www.uwsp.edu
Admissions email: admiss@uwsp.edu
Public; founded 1894
Freshman admissions: selective; 2020-2021: 5,929 applied, 5,091 accepted. Neither SAT nor ACT required. ACT 25/75 percentile: 19-24. High school rank: 9% in top tenth, 30% in top quarter, 67% in top half
Early decision deadline: N/A, notification date: N/A
Early action deadline: N/A, notification date: N/A
Application deadline (fall): rolling
Undergraduate student body: 6,415 full time, 1,223 part time; 44% male, 56% female; 0% American Indian, 3% Asian, 2% black, 5% Hispanic, 3% multiracial, 0% Pacific Islander, 85% white, 1% international; 89% from in state; 28% live on campus; 4% of students in fraternities, 5% in sororities
Most popular majors: 9% Business Administration and Management, General, 5% Biology/Biological Sciences, General, 5% Communication and Media Studies, 5% Psychology, General, 5% Sociology
Expenses: 2021-2022: $8,354 in state, $17,058 out of state; room/board: $7,640
Financial aid: (715) 346-4771; 55% of undergrads determined to have financial need; average aid package $10,096

University of Wisconsin–Stout
Menomonie WI
(715) 232-1232
U.S. News ranking: Reg. U. (Mid. W), No. 69
Website: www.uwstout.edu
Admissions email: admissions@uwstout.edu
Public; founded 1891

Freshman admissions: selective; 2020-2021: 3,416 applied, 3,040 accepted. Either SAT or ACT required. ACT 25/75 percentile: 20-25. High school rank: 10% in top tenth, 32% in top quarter, 68% in top half
Early decision deadline: N/A, notification date: N/A
Early action deadline: N/A, notification date: N/A
Application deadline (fall): rolling
Undergraduate student body: 5,589 full time, 1,300 part time; 58% male, 42% female; 0% American Indian, 4% Asian, 2% black, 1% Hispanic, 6% multiracial, 0% Pacific Islander, 87% white, 1% international; N/A from in state; 39% live on campus; 2% of students in fraternities, 3% in sororities
Most popular majors: 31% Business, Management, Marketing, and Related Support Services, 12% Visual and Performing Arts, 11% Computer and Information Sciences and Support Services, 8% Education, 7% Engineering
Expenses: 2020-2021: $9,488 in state, $17,455 out of state; room/board: $7,398
Financial aid: (715) 232-1363; 49% of undergrads determined to have financial need; average aid package $10,854

University of Wisconsin–Superior[1]

Superior WI
(715) 394-8230
U.S. News ranking: Nat. Lib. Arts, second tier
Website: www.uwsuper.edu
Admissions email: admissions@uwsuper.edu
Public; founded 1893
Application deadline (fall): 8/1
Undergraduate student body: N/A full time, N/A part time

Expenses: 2020-2021: $8,142 in state, $15,712 out of state; room/board: $7,200
Financial aid: (715) 394-8200

University of Wisconsin–Whitewater

Whitewater WI
(262) 472-1440
U.S. News ranking: Reg. U. (Mid. W), No. 49
Website: www.uww.edu
Admissions email: uwwadmit@uww.edu
Public; founded 1868
Freshman admissions: selective; 2020-2021: 5,139 applied, 4,832 accepted. Neither SAT nor ACT required. ACT 25/75 percentile: 19-24. High school rank: 8% in top tenth, 27% in top quarter, 69% in top half
Early decision deadline: N/A, notification date: N/A
Early action deadline: N/A, notification date: N/A
Application deadline (fall): rolling
Undergraduate student body: 8,939 full time, 1,489 part time; 51% male, 49% female; 0% American Indian, 2% Asian, 4% black, 8% Hispanic, 3% multiracial, 0% Pacific Islander, 82% white, 1% international; 84% from in state; 34% live on campus; 5% of students in fraternities, 6% in sororities
Most popular majors: 40% Business, Management, Marketing, and Related Support Services, 13% Education, 8% Communication, Journalism, and Related Programs, 8% Social Sciences, 5% Visual and Performing Arts
Expenses: 2021-2022: $7,729 in state, $16,601 out of state; room/board: $7,184

Financial aid: (262) 472-1130; 54% of undergrads determined to have financial need; average aid package $8,875

Viterbo University

La Crosse WI
(608) 796-3010
U.S. News ranking: Reg. U. (Mid. W), No. 61
Website: www.viterbo.edu
Admissions email: admission@viterbo.edu
Private; founded 1890
Affiliation: Roman Catholic
Freshman admissions: selective; 2020-2021: 1,325 applied, 1,050 accepted. Neither SAT nor ACT required. ACT 25/75 percentile: 20-25. High school rank: 19% in top tenth, 43% in top quarter, 77% in top half
Early decision deadline: N/A, notification date: N/A
Early action deadline: N/A, notification date: N/A
Application deadline (fall): rolling
Undergraduate student body: 1,443 full time, 293 part time; 25% male, 75% female; 0% American Indian, 2% Asian, 7% black, 5% Hispanic, 3% multiracial, 0% Pacific Islander, 79% white, 2% international; 26% from in state; 38% live on campus; 0% of students in fraternities, 0% in sororities
Most popular majors: 53% Health Professions and Related Programs, 20% Business, Management, Marketing, and Related Support Services, 5% Education, 5% Public Administration and Social Service Professions, 5% Visual and Performing Arts
Expenses: 2021-2022: $30,610; room/board: $9,865
Financial aid: (608) 796-3900

Wisconsin Lutheran College

Milwaukee WI
(414) 443-8811
U.S. News ranking: Reg. Coll. (Mid. W), No. 19
Website: www.wlc.edu/
Admissions email: admissions@wlc.edu
Private; founded 1973
Affiliation: Wisconsin Evangelical Lutheran Synod
Freshman admissions: selective; 2020-2021: 981 applied, 938 accepted. Neither SAT nor ACT required. ACT 25/75 percentile: 21-27. High school rank: 21% in top tenth, 47% in top quarter, 87% in top half
Early decision deadline: N/A, notification date: N/A
Early action deadline: N/A, notification date: N/A
Application deadline (fall): rolling
Undergraduate student body: 938 full time, 96 part time; 45% male, 55% female; 0% American Indian, 1% Asian, 5% black, 8% Hispanic, 3% multiracial, 0% Pacific Islander, 80% white, 1% international; 74% from in state; 65% live on campus; 0% of students in fraternities, 0% in sororities
Most popular majors: 19% Business Administration, Management and Operations, Other, 14% Business Administration and Management, General, 10% Registered Nursing/Registered Nurse, 6% Biology/Biological Sciences, General, 6% Kinesiology and Exercise Science
Expenses: 2021-2022: $32,766; room/board: $11,050
Financial aid: (414) 443-8856; 81% of undergrads determined to have financial need; average aid package $23,953

University of Wyoming

Laramie WY
(307) 766-5160
U.S. News ranking: Nat. U., No. 196
Website: www.uwyo.edu
Admissions email: admissions@uwyo.edu
Public; founded 1886
Freshman admissions: selective; 2020-2021: 4,919 applied, 4,635 accepted. Neither SAT nor ACT required. ACT 25/75 percentile: 21-28. High school rank: 23% in top tenth, 52% in top quarter, 82% in top half
Early decision deadline: N/A, notification date: N/A
Early action deadline: N/A, notification date: N/A
Application deadline (fall): 8/10
Undergraduate student body: 7,783 full time, 1,559 part time; 48% male, 52% female; 1% American Indian, 1% Asian, 1% black, 6% Hispanic, 4% multiracial, 0% Pacific Islander, 76% white, 2% international; 66% from in state; 13% live on campus; 6% of students in fraternities, 7% in sororities
Most popular majors: 6% Registered Nursing/Registered Nurse, 5% Elementary Education and Teaching, 5% Psychology, General, 4% Management Science, 3% Kinesiology and Exercise Science
Expenses: 2021-2022: $6,097 in state, $20,647 out of state; room/board: $11,144
Financial aid: (307) 766-2116; 47% of undergrads determined to have financial need; average aid package $10,803

More @ usnews.com/bestcolleges